PLUTARCH

PLOTINU[S]

P9-DHD-697

TACITUS

AUGUSTINE

EPICTETUS

Hadrian's wall
constructed

Birth and death
of Jesus Christ

NICOMACHUS

PTOLEMY

LUCRETIUS

MARCUS AURELIUS

Books replace scrolls

VIRGIL

GALEN

Julius Caesar
assassinated

DESCARTES

MONTESQUIEU

MILTON

VOLTAIRE

MOLIÈRE

HUME

French
Revolution

PASCAL

ROUSSEAU

HUYGENS

DIDEROT

ADAM SMITH

Church bans Galileo's
teaching of Copernican
doctrine

KANT

GIBBON

MONTAIGNE

LOCKE

BOSWELL

GILBERT

SPINOZA

JEFFERSON

CERVANTES

RACINE

LAVOISIER

BACON

NEWTON

JOHN JAY

GALILEO

SWIFT

GOETHE

BERKELEY

SHAKESPEARE

MADISON

KEPLER

HAMILTON

HARVEY

Industrial Revolution
begins

HOBBES

GREAT BOOKS
OF THE
WESTERN WORLD

MORTIMER J. ADLER
Editor in Chief

15

PTOLEMY
COPERNICUS
KEPLER

PTOLEMY: The Almagest

NICOLAUS COPERNICUS:
On the Revolutions of the Heavenly Spheres

JOHANNES KEPLER:
Epitome of Copernican Astronomy: IV–V
The Harmonies of the World: V

ROBERT P. GWINN,
Publisher,
Chairman, Board of Directors

PETER B. NORTON, *President*

PHILIP W. GOETZ, *Editor in Chief*

ENCYCLOPÆDIA BRITANNICA, INC.
CHICAGO

AUCKLAND GENEVA LONDON MADRID MANILA PARIS
ROME SEOUL SYDNEY TOKYO TORONTO

Ptolemy: *The Almagest: I–V* translated by R. Catesby Taliaferro. Copyright, 1938, 1939, 1948, by Encyclopædia Britannica, Inc.

Nicolaus Copernicus: *On the Revolutions of the Heavenly Spheres* translated by Charles Glenn Wallis. Copyright, 1939, by Encyclopædia Britannica, Inc.

Johannes Kepler: *Epitome of Copernican Astronomy: IV and V* translated by Charles Glenn Wallis. Copyright, 1939, by Encyclopædia Britannica, Inc.

THE UNIVERSITY OF CHICAGO

*The Great Books is published with the editorial advice
of the faculties of The University of Chicago*

First Edition © 1952
Second Edition © 1990

Encyclopædia Britannica, Inc.
All Rights Reserved

Library of Congress Catalog Card Number: 90-80213
International Standard Book Number: 0-85229-531-6

Manufactured in the United States of America

GENERAL CONTENTS

*

THE ALMAGEST, p. 1
By Ptolemy (Claudius Ptolemaeus)
Translated by R. Catesby Taliaferro

*

Introduction, Symbols, and Abbreviations, and a Short Bibliography to Copernicus and Kepler, p. 481

*

ON THE REVOLUTIONS OF THE HEAVENLY SPHERES, p. 505
By Nicolaus Copernicus
Translated by Charles Glenn Wallis

*

EPITOME OF COPERNICAN ASTRONOMY: IV and V, p. 845
THE HARMONIES OF THE WORLD: V, p. 1009
By Johannes Kepler
Translated by Charles Glenn Wallis

*

GENERAL CONTENTS

Ptolemy

THE ALMAGEST

BIOGRAPHICAL NOTE

PTOLEMY, A.D. c.100-c.178

THE life of Claudius Ptolemaeus is almost entirely unknown despite his fame as an astronomer and geographer. What little can be said of his personal history has to be pieced together from indications in his writings, two ancient scholia, and brief notices by much later writers, some of them Arabian. From these it appears that Ptolemy was born at Ptolemais Hermii, a Grecian city of the Egyptian Thebaid; even this is not certain, since another early source gives his birth-place as Pelusium. His work is traditionally associated with Alexandria, but according to one scholium, he devoted his life to astromony and lived for forty years at Canopus, about fifteen miles east of the capital. Ptolemy himself notes that he made his observations "in the parallel of Alexandria." The dates of his birth and death are also uncertain. His observations recorded in the *Almagest* extend from A.D. 127 to 151; the Arabic writers claim that he lived to the age of seventy-eight; from this evidence it is inferred that Ptolemy's life covered the first three quarters of the second century and the reigns of Trajan, Hadrian, Antoninus Pius, and Marcus Aurelius. There seems to be no basis for the claim once made that he was related to the royal house of the Ptolemies.

From his writings it is evident that Ptolemy knew well the work of his predecessors, and most of what is now known about ancient astronomy owes its preservation to him. He was particularly indebted to Hipparchus (c. 130 B.C.), "that enthusiastic worker and lover of truth," whom Ptolemy considered his master. From his own observation he was able to add to the records compiled by prior astronomers; he increased by several hundred stars the list drawn up by Hipparchus. His discoveries are said to have been inscribed on pillars erected in the temple of Serapis at Canopus.

Ptolemy's fame as an astronomer rests chiefly upon the *Almagest*. This work was originally known as *The Mathematical Composition*, but after it had come to be used as a text in astronomy, it was called *The Great Astronomer* to distinguish it from a collection known as *The Little Astronomer*. The Arabs called it "The Greatest," prefixing the article *al* to the Greek *megiste*, and ever since it has been known as the *Almagest*.

In addition to his great work, Ptolemy composed many shorter books dealing with the heavens. In his *Hypothesis on the Planets* he provided a summary of part of the *Almagest* and a brief statement of the principal theories explaining the motion of the heavenly bodies. He drew up a list of annual sidereal phenomena and also a chronological table of Assyrian, Persian, Greek, and Roman kings for use in reckoning the lapse of time between an event and a given fixed date. The two astrological writings, the *Tetrabiblon* (or *Quadripartitum*) and the *Centiloquium*, are usually attributed to Ptolemy, although their authenticity has sometimes been doubted. Of his other mathematical works, the most important are the *Harmonica*, a treatise on music, and the *Optics*, which is apparently the first recorded attempt at a theory of refraction of luminous rays through media of different densities.

After the *Almagest*, Ptolemy's most important work is his *Guide to Geography*, the most comprehensive and scientific work of antiquity on the subject. It consists largely of a tabulation of places with their latitude and longitude, but it also contains an estimate of the size and extent of the "inhabited world" and a discussion of map-making. The *Guide* came to be for geography what the *Almagest* was for astronomy, and until well into the Renaissance, Ptolemy was hardly less celebrated as a geographer than as an astronomer.

CONTENTS

CONTENTS

APPENDIX A

APPENDIX B

APPENDIX C

INTRODUCTION

The Mathematical Composition of Claudius Ptolemy in thirteen books, called also by an Arabic transliteration of ἡ μεϑίστη [συντάξις] *The Almagest,* is the only completely comprehensive treatise of Greek astronomy to come down to us, if we except Aristarchus' *On the Sizes and Distances of the Sun and Moon,* a complete and remarkable mathematical treatment of a very limited astronomical subject. The works of the greatest Greek astronomers—Eudoxus, Heraclides of Pontus, Aristarchus of Samos, Apollonius of Perga, and Hipparchus—are lost for the most part, and we only know their contents from this treatise and other very meagre sources. For detail, completeness, and perfection, the *Composition of Ptolemy* might be said to contain all those which preceded it; its prediction of the phenomena is on the whole as adequate as the instruments used— they were surprisingly accurate—could possibly allow for. But its perfection is such that it often covers up the modes of discovery, and its geocentric theory is propounded with only the barest references to its heliocentric opponents.

The *Composition* more or less dates itself. In Book XI, chapter 5, Ptolemy says he observed Saturn, 7 Pachom, year 11 of Hadrian; and although he does not directly attribute to himself the observation, it is almost certain he made the observation of the eclipse of the moon mentioned in IV, 9, which took place 17 Pachom, Hadrian 9. This last is the earliest he mentions of those which could have been made by himself. The latest is given in X, where Ptolemy says he observed Venus, 11 Thoth, Antonine 14. All the observations, therefore, mentioned in this book and attributable to Ptolemy himself fall between 17 Pachom, Hadrian 9 and 11 Thoth, Antonine 14, and were made in Alexandria. It is also stated in III, 4, that the spring equinox fell on 7 Pachom, Antonine 3. These dates are in terms of Egyptian years and *The Table of the Kings* which are explained in Appendix A. In terms of the Christian Era and Julian years, historians give Hadrian's accession as 11 Aug., A.D. 117 and his death as July, A.D. 138. Using the rules given in Appendix A, one concludes that the observations made by Ptolemy and mentioned in *The Composition* lie between A.D. 127 and 151.

Book I deals first with the general assumptions of the science such as the sphericity of the earth, the earth's size relative to the sphere of the fixed stars, and the geocentric hypothesis. The arguments in favour of this last are all drawn from Aristotelian physics, and this is almost the only place where physical arguments are used since the point of view is usually purely mathematical and fairly sophisticated about the futility of dealing otherwise with sensible appearances.

The geocentric theory of Ptolemy was not the only theory known to the Greeks nor even at times the most accepted. The Pythagoreans, prior to Plato, had theories involving a motion of the earth, and we know that Aristarchus of Samos after Plato had a heliocentric theory which in all essentials was that of

1

Copernicus. We also know that Heraclides of Pontus, a contemporary of Plato and a member of the Platonic Academy, placed Venus and Mercury on epicycles about the sun and supposed the earth to turn on its axis; and it is even likely that he had either the system of Copernicus with the sun as centre and the planets including the earth revolving about, or the system of Tycho Brahe with the planets revolving about the sun and the sun about the earth, or both systems. There is much dispute over Plato's astronomical descriptions, but it is very possible that the *Timaeus* gives the outline of a heliocentric theory like that of Copernicus.[1]

Then follows a vigorous development of those theorems in plane and spherical trigonometry necessary for the astronomical theories which follow. And Book I ends with a determination of the inclination of the ecliptic and equator.

Book II works out the co-ascensions of arcs on the ecliptic and equator for the oblique sphere, that is, for the horizons in different latitudes, the shadows of gnomons in the different latitudes, and the inclinations of different circles with each other in the latitudes. The reader who is out to get the larger aspects of the lunar and planetary theories can well afford to skip most of this Book and only read it when referred to later on.

Book III presents the theory of the sun and its one anomaly. It is here that the great principle of all Greek planetary theory is laid down: *all planetary appearances must be accounted for by the uniform motion of the planet in a circle with or without the uniform motion of this circle's centre on another circle called its deferent, and so on to any required complication.* In this Book, however, Ptolemy states this principle in its restricted form, the one used by Copernicus:—all planetary appearances must be accounted for by the uniform motion of the planet on a circle *where the motion is uniform with respect to the centre of that circle* with or without the uniform motion of this circle's centre on another circle *where the motion of the first circle's centre is uniform with respect to the centre of the second circle,* and so on to any required complication.

The principle in its restricted form is used by Ptolemy only for the sun. In Books V, IX, and X, for the moon and other planets, he uses without preliminary warning the more general form of the principle which allows the centre of a circle to move uniformly about a point *not* the centre of the deferent circle. Such a point is called the centre of the equant.

This principle, which might be called the law of inertia of Greek celestial mechanics, was probably first suggested by Plato in a much less dogmatic form. All that is seemingly implied in the dialogues is that irregular appearances of the planets must be supposed capable of rational explanation, and that the circle and uniform motion are the most likely tools for this. The system of Eudoxus, devised at this time, is perhaps the most rigorous application of the principle of uniform motion in a circle. For here the planet's motion is composed of the motions of concentric spheres moving uniformly about one point, the earth their common centre. From the point of view of mathematical ingenuity this was the most brilliant application of the principle, but required too much to save the more complicated appearances; it was not flexible enough. Aristotle took the principle literally and therefore was led, by his theory of being and substance which preclude a purely mathematical physics of the Platonic kind, to make a radical distinction between celestial mechanics and terrestrial me-

[1]See Appendix C.

chanics. In considering all heavenly bodies impassible (except for the fact they could be seen), Aristotle gave a physical and metaphysical sanction to the purely mathematical principle of uniform motion in a circle. He did, however, using Eudoxus' system, extend his theory of the transmission of motion by contact to these bodies so that he assumed the movement of the outer sphere of the fixed stars is transmitted to the inner spheres moving the planets by mechanical contact. Since this transmission from one planetary sphere to another would involve also transmission of movements particular to the planet, counteracting spheres had to be introduced to differentiate out the right motion.

Although this same physical sanction is not explicitly mentioned by Ptolemy in the *Composition*, yet it is stated in the most direct and meaningful way by Ptolemy in Book II of his *Hypothesis on the Planets*. The heavenly bodies suffer no influence from without; they have no relation to each other; the particular motions of each particular planet follow from the essence of that planet and are like the will and understanding in men. One might almost say that the law of universal gravitation is expressly denied, and reserved only in a very particular form for bodies on the earth's surface in such treatises as Archimedes' *On Floating Bodies* and *On the Centers of Gravity of Planes*. For it is assumed that the earth or rather the earth's centre attracts only bodies below the lunar sphere. It is, of course, Kepler who, probably under the influence of Gilbert's work on magnetism, assumes for the first time in *The Commentaries on Mars* that all bodies attract each other. It was reserved for Newton to state the classical law of inertia in the light of Kepler's assumption: all bodies continue in the same straight line and at uniform speed unless disturbed.

It is also in Book III that the first principles of the epicycle and eccentric are worked out.

Book IV begins the study of the moon and its first or epicyclic anomaly.

Book V continues the study of the moon with its solar or eccentric anomaly, equant anomaly, and a fourth anomaly called the inclination of the moon's epicycle. There is also a discussion of the moon's parallaxes and of the distances of the moon and sun from the earth in terms of the earth's radius and a discussion of the relative magnitudes of these bodies.

Book VI continues the study of the moon with respect to its phases and eclipses.

Books VII and VIII are devoted to the sphere of the fixed stars and to the precession of the equinoxes.

Book IX begins the study of the planets Mercury, Venus, Mars, Jupiter, and Saturn. The order of these planets is given. The Ptolemaic geocentric theory furnishes no very sound principles for their ordering; only a heliocentric theory or a geocentric theory like Brahe's could give one. But the ordering turns out pretty much as the heliocentric theory would require except that Venus and Mercury are placed between the earth and the sun instead of around it. A general introduction is given to their movements, and Mercury is treated in detail. Mercury is the most complicated of the five: it requires not only an epicycle, eccentric, and equant as the others do, but it requires that the centre of the eccentric move about another circle. Mercury remains just as complicated in the system of Copernicus. It is well known that it was never completely explained by the principles of Newton's mechanics and that it is only taken care of in the general theory of relativity.

Book x contains the detailed discussions of Venus and Mars, and Book xi of Jupiter and Saturn.

Book xii is the most interesting perhaps from the kinematic point of view. It contains the statement of an eccentric theory of the planets Mars, Jupiter, and Saturn, equivalent to the epicyclic one used by Ptolemy and which very evidently forms the bridge from Ptolemy's and Hipparchus' geocentric theory to Aristarchus' heliocentric theory. The theorems on station points and regressions, probably due to Apollonius of Perga, are remarkable. These solve the problem: given the angular speed of a star on its epicycle and the angular speed of the epicycle on its deferent and the ratio of the radii of the epicycle and deferent, to find the necessary and sufficient conditions that the star will appear to stop and regress for an observer at the centre of the deferent and at what points.

Book xiii contains the theory of the planets' lateral deviations from the ecliptic.

The translator wishes to thank Dr. George Comenetz, Mr. John Kieffer, Dr. Jacob Klein, Prof. Alexandre Koyré, and Mr. John Weber for their suggestions and criticisms. They are in no way to blame for any immoderate statements.

R. C. T.

Portsmouth, Rhode Island, 1946.

ABBREVIATIONS USED IN THE TRANSLATION

ecc. rad. = eccentric's radius
epic. rad. = epicycle's radius
hypt. = hypotenuse
1. betw. c. = line between centers
rect. AB, BC = rectangle contained by AB and BC
sect. = sector or section
sq. = square
trgl. = triangle

BIBLIOGRAPHY OF PTOLEMY'S ASTRONOMICAL WORKS

Editio princeps of the *Syntaxis*, Basle, 1538, with the commentaries of Pappus and Theon.

Composition mathématique, 2 vols., edit. Halma, Paris, 1813-16. Greek text and French translation. Reprinted.

Syntaxis mathematica, 2 vols., edit. Heiberg, Leipzig, 1898-1903.

Opera astronomica minora, edit. Heiberg, Leipzig, 1907.

There is a German translation of the Heiberg edition by Manitius, 1912-1913. This English translation is from the text of Heiberg; any deviation is noted.

BOOK ONE

1. PREFACE

THOSE who have been true philosophers, Syrus, seem to me to have very wisely separated the theoretical part of philosophy from the practical. For even if it happens the practical turns out to be theoretical prior to its being practical, nevertheless a great difference would be found in them; not only because some of the moral virtues can belong to the everyday ignorant man and it is impossible to come by the theory of whole sciences without learning, but also because in practical matters the greatest advantage is to be had from a continued and repeated operation upon the things themselves, while in theoretical knowledge it is to be had by a progress onward. We accordingly thought it up to us so to train our actions even in the application of the imagination as not to forget in whatever things we happen upon the consideration of their beautiful and well-ordered disposition, and to indulge in meditation mostly for the exposition of many beautiful theorems and especially of those specifically called mathematical.

For indeed Aristotle quite properly divides also the theoretical into three immediate genera: the physical, the mathematical, and the theological. For given that all beings have their existence from matter and form and motion, and that none of these can be seen, but only thought, in its subject separately from the others, if one should seek out in its simplicity the first cause of the first movement of the universe, he would find God invisible and unchanging. And the kind of science which seeks after Him is the theological; for such an act [ἐνέργεια] can only be thought as high above somewhere near the loftiest things of the universe and is absolutely apart from sensible things. But the kind of science which traces through the material and ever moving quality, and has to do with the white, the hot, the sweet, the soft, and such things, would be called physical; and such an essence [οὐσία], since it is only generally what it is, is to be found in corruptible things and below the lunar sphere. And the kind of science which shows up quality with respect to forms and local motions, seeking figure, number, and magnitude, and also place, time, and similar things, would be defined as mathematical. For such an essence falls, as it were, between the other two, not only because it can be conceived both through the senses and without the senses, but also because it is an accident in absolutely all beings both mortal and immortal, changing with those things that ever change, according to their inseparable form, and preserving unchangeable the changelessness of form in things eternal and of an ethereal nature.

And therefore meditating that the other two genera of the theoretical would be expounded in terms of conjecture rather than in terms of scientific understanding: the theological because it is in no way phenomenal and attainable, but the physical because its matter is unstable and obscure, so that for this reason philosophers could never hope to agree on them; and meditating that only the mathematical, if approached enquiringly, would give its practitioners certain

5

and trustworthy knowledge with demonstration both arithmetic and geometric resulting from indisputable procedures, we were led to cultivate most particularly as far as lay in our power this theoretical discipline [θεωρία]. And especially were we led to cultivate that discipline developed in respect to divine and heavenly things as being the only one concerned with the study of things which are always what they are, and therefore able itself to be always what it is—which is indeed the proper mark of a science—because of its own clear and ordered understanding, and yet to cooperate with the other disciplines no less than they themselves. For that special mathematical theory would most readily prepare the way to the theological, since it alone could take good aim at that unchangeable and separate act, so close to that act are the properties having to do with translations and arrangements of movements, belonging to those heavenly beings which are sensible and both moving and moved, but eternal and impassible. Again as concerns the physical there would not be just chance correspondances. For the general property of the material essence is pretty well evident from the peculiar fashion of its local motion—for example, the corruptible and incorruptible from straight and circular movements, and the heavy and light or passive and active from movement to the center and movement from the center. And indeed this same discipline would more than any other prepare understanding persons with respect to nobleness of actions and character by means of the sameness, good order, due proportion, and simple directness contemplated in divine things, making its followers lovers of that divine beauty, and making habitual in them, and as it were natural, a like condition of the soul.

And so we ourselves try to increase continuously our love of the discipline of things which are always what they are, by learning what has already been discovered in such sciences by those really applying themselves to them, and also by making a small original contribution such as the period of time from them to us could well make possible. And therefore we shall try and set forth as briefly as possible as many theorems as we recognize to have come to light up to the present, and in such a way that those who have already been initiated somewhat may follow, arranging in proper order for the completeness of the treatise all matters useful to the theory of heavenly things. And in order not to make the treatise too long we shall only report what was rigorously proved by the ancients, perfecting as far as we can what was not fully proved or not proved as well as possible.

2. On the Order of the Theorems

A view, therefore, of the general relation of the whole earth to the whole of the heavens will begin this composition of ours. And next, of things in particular, there will first be an account of the ecliptic's position and of the places of that part of the earth inhabited by us, and again of the difference, in order, between each of them according to the inclinations of their horizons. For the theory of these, once understood, facilitates the examination of the rest. And, secondly, there will be an account of the solar and lunar movements and of their incidents. For without a prior understanding of these one could not profitably consider what concerns the stars. The last part, in view of this plan, will be an account of the stars. Those things having to do with the sphere of what are called the fixed stars would reasonably come first, and then those having to do with what are called the five planets. And we shall try and show each of these things using as beginnings and foundations for what we wish to find, the evident and certain appearances from the observations of the ancients and our own, and applying the consequences of these conceptions by means of geometrical demonstrations.

And so, in general, we have to state that the heavens are spherical and move spherically; that the earth, in figure, is sensibly spherical also when taken as a whole; in position, lies right in the middle of the heavens, like a geometrical centre; in magnitude and distance, has the ratio of a point with respect to the sphere of the fixed stars, having itself no local motion at all. And we shall go through each of these points briefly to bring them to mind.

3. That the Heavens Move Spherically

It is probable the first notions of these things came to the ancients from some such observation as this. For they kept seeing the sun and moon and other stars always moving from rising to setting in parallel circles, beginning to move upward from below as if out of the earth itself, rising little by little to the top, and then coming around again and going down in the same way until at last they would disappear as if falling into the earth. And then again they would see them, after remaining some time invisible, rising and setting as if from another beginning; and they saw that the times and also the places of rising and setting generally corresponded in an ordered and regular way.

But most of all the observed circular orbit of those stars which are always visible, and their revolution about one and the same centre, led them to this spherical notion. For necessarily this point became the pole of the heavenly sphere; and the stars nearer to it were those that spun around in smaller circles, and those farther away made greater circles in their revolutions in proportion to the distance, until a sufficient distance brought one to the disappearing stars. And then they saw that those near the always-visible stars disappeared for a short time, and those farther away for a longer time proportionately. And for these reasons alone it was sufficient for them to assume this notion as a principle, and forthwith to think through also the other things consequent upon these same appearances, in accordance with the development of the science. For absolutely all the appearances contradict the other opinions.

If, for example, one should assume the movement of the stars to be in a straight line to infinity, as some have opined, how could it be explained that each star will be observed daily moving from the same starting point? For how could the stars turn back while rushing on to infinity? Or how could they turn back without appearing to do so? Or how is it they do not disappear with their size gradually diminishing, but on the contrary seem larger when they are about to disappear, being covered little by little as if cut off by the earth's surface? But certainly to suppose that they light up from the earth and then again go out in it would appear most absurd. For if anyone should agree that such an order in their magnitudes and number, and again in the distances, places, and times is accomplished in this way at random and by chance, and that one whole part of the earth has an incandescent nature and another a nature capable of extinguishing, or rather that the same part lights the stars up for some people and puts them out for others, and that the same stars happen to appear to some people either lit up or put out and to others not yet so—even if anyone, I say, should accept all such absurdities, what could we say about the always-visible stars which neither rise nor set? Or why don't the stars which light up and go out rise and set for every part of the earth, and why aren't those which are not affected in this way always above the earth for every part of the earth? For in this hypothesis the same stars will not always light up and go out for some people, and never for others. But it is evident to everyone that the same stars rise and set for some parts, and do neither of these things for others.

In a word, whatever figure other than the spherical be assumed for the movement of the heavens, there must be unequal linear distances from the earth to parts of the heavens, wherever or however the earth be situated, so that the magnitudes and angular distances of the stars with respect to each other would appear unequal to the same people within each revolution, now larger now smaller. But this is not observed to happen. For it is not a shorter linear distance which makes them appear larger at the horizon, but the steaming up of the moisture surrounding the earth between them and our eyes, just as things put under water appear larger the farther down they are placed.

The following considerations also lead to the spherical notion: the fact that instruments for measuring time cannot agree with any hypothesis save the spherical one; that, since the movement of the heavenly bodies ought to be the least impeded and most facile, the circle among plane figures offers the easiest path of motion, and the sphere among solids; likewise that, since of different figures having equal perimeters those having the more angles are the greater, the circle is the greatest of plane figures and the sphere of solid figures, and the heavens are greater than any other body.

Moreover, certain physical considerations lead to such a conjecture. For example, the fact that of all bodies the ether has the finest and most homogeneous parts [ὁμοιομερέστερος]; but the surfaces of homogeneous parts must have homogeneous parts, and only the circle is such among plane figures and the sphere among solids. And since the ether is not plane but solid, it can only be spherical. Likewise the fact that nature has built all earthly and corruptible bodies wholly out of rounded figures but with heterogeneous parts, and all divine bodies in the ether out of spherical figures with homogeneous parts, since if they were plane or disc-like they would not appear circular to all those who see them from different parts of the earth at the same time. Therefore it would seem reasonable that the ether surrounding them and of a like nature be also spherical, and that because of the homogeneity of its parts it moves circularly and regularly.

4. That also the Earth, Taken as a Whole, Is Sensibly Spherical

Now, that also the earth taken as a whole is sensibly spherical, we could most likely think out in this way. For again it is possible to see that the sun and moon and the other stars do not rise and set at the same time for every observer on the earth, but always earlier for those living towards the orient and later for those living towards the occident. For we find that the phenomena of eclipses taking place at the same time, especially those of the moon, are not recorded at the same hours for everyone—that is, relatively to equal intervals of time from noon; but we always find later hours recorded for observers towards the orient than for those towards the occident. And since the differences in the hours is found to be proportional to the distances between the places, one would reasonably suppose the surface of the earth spherical, with the result that the general uniformity of curvature would assure every part's covering those following it proportionately. But this would not happen if the figure were any other, as can be seen from the following considerations.

For, if it were concave, the rising stars would appear first to people towards the occident; and if it were flat, the stars would rise and set for all people together and at the same time; and if it were a pyramid, a cube, or any other polygonal figure, they would again appear at the same time for all observers on the same straight line. But none of these things appears to happen. It is further clear that it could not be cylindrical with the curved surface turned to the risings and settings and the plane bases to the poles of the universe, which some think more plausible. For then never would any of the stars be always visible to any of the inhabitants of the curved surface, but either all the stars would both rise and set for observers or the same stars for an equal distance from either of the poles would always be invisible to all observers. Yet the more we advance towards the north pole, the more the southern stars are hidden and the northern stars appear. So it is clear that here the curvature of the earth covering parts uniformly in oblique directions proves its spherical form on every side. Again, whenever we sail towards mountains or any high places from whatever angle and in whatever direction, we see their bulk little by little increasing as if they were arising from the sea, whereas before they seemed submerged because of the curvature of the water's surface.

5. That the Earth Is in the Middle of the Heavens

Now with this done, if one should next take up the question of the earth's position, the observed appearances with respect to it could only be understood if we put it in the middle of the heavens as the centre of the sphere. If this were not so, then the earth would either have to be off the axis but equidistant from the poles, or on the axis but farther advanced towards one of the poles, or neither on the axis nor equidistant from the poles.

The following considerations are opposed to the first of these three positions—namely, that if the earth were conceived as placed off the axis either above or below in respect to certain parts of the earth, those parts, in the right sphere, would never have any equinox since the section above the earth and the section below the earth would always be cut unequally by the horizon. Again, if the sphere were inclined with respect to these parts, either they would have no equinox or else the equinox would not take place midway between the summer and winter solstices. The distances would be unequal because the equator which is the greatest of those parallel circles described about the poles would not be cut in half by the horizon; but one of the circles parallel to it, either to the north or to the south, would be so cut in half. It is absolutely agreed by all, however, that these distances are everywhere equal because the increase from the equinox to the longest day at the summer tropic are equal to the decreases to the least days at the winter tropic. And if the deviation for certain parts of the earth were supposed either towards the orient or the occident, it would result that for these parts neither the sizes and angular distances of the stars would appear equal and the same at the eastern and western horizons, nor would the time from rising to the meridian be equal to the time from the meridian to setting. But these things evidently are altogether contrary to the appearances.

As to the second position where the earth would be on the axis but farther advanced towards one of the poles, one could again object that, if this were so,

the plane of the horizon in each latitude would always cut into uneven parts the
sections of the heavens below the earth and above, different with respect to each
other and to themselves for each different deviation. And the horizon could cut
into two even parts only in the right sphere. But in the case of the inclined
sphere with the nearer pole ever visible, the horizon would always make the part
above the earth less and the part below the earth greater with the result that
also the great circle through the centre of the signs of the zodiac [ecliptic] would
be cut unequally by the plane of the horizon. But this has never been seen, for
six of the twelve parts are always and everywhere visible above the earth, and
the other six invisible; and again when all these last six are all at once visible,
the others are at the same time invisible. And so—from the fact that the same
semicircles are cut off entirely, now above the earth, now below—it is evident
that the sections of the zodiac are cut in half by the horizon.

And, in general, if the earth did not have its position under the equator but
lay either to the north or south nearer one of the poles, the result would be that,
during the equinoxes, the shadows of the gnomons at sunrise would never perceptibly be on a straight line with those at sunset in planes parallel to the horizon. But the contrary is everywhere seen to occur. And it is immediately clear
that it is not possible to advance the third position since each of the obstacles
to the first two would be present here also.

In brief, all the observed order of the increases and decreases of day and night
would be thrown into utter confusion if the earth were not in the middle. And
there would be added the fact that the eclipses of the moon could not take place
for all parts of the heavens by a diametrical opposition to the sun, for the earth
would often not be interposed between them in their diametrical oppositions,
but at distances less than a semicircle.

6. That the Earth Has the Ratio of a Point to the Heavens

Now, that the earth has sensibly the ratio of a point to its distance from the
sphere of the so-called fixed stars gets great support from the fact that in all
parts of the earth the sizes and angular distances of the stars at the same times
appear everywhere equal and alike, for the observations of the same stars in the
different latitudes are not found to differ in the least.

Moreover, this must be added: that sundials placed in any part of the earth
and the centres of armillary spheres can play the role of the earth's true centre
for the sightings and the rotations of the shadows, as much in conformity with
the hypotheses of the appearances as if they were at the true midpoint of the
earth.

And the earth is clearly a point also from this fact: that everywhere the planes
drawn through the eye, which we call horizons, always exactly cut in half the
whole sphere of the heavens. And this would not happen if the magnitude of the
earth with respect to its distance from the heavens were perceptible; but only
the plane drawn through the point at the earth's centre would exactly cut the
sphere in half, and those drawn through any other part of the earth's surface
would make the sections below the earth greater than those above.

7. That the Earth Does Not in any Way Move Locally

By the same arguments as the preceding it can be shown that the earth can
neither move in any one of the aforesaid oblique directions, nor ever change at

all from its place at the centre. For the same things would result as if it had another position than at the centre. And so it also seems to me superfluous to look for the causes of the motion to the centre when it is once for all clear from the very appearances that the earth is in the middle of the world and all weights move towards it. And the easiest and only way to understand this is to see that, once the earth has been proved spherical considered as a whole and in the middle of the universe as we have said, then the tendencies and movements of heavy bodies (I mean their proper movements)[1] are everywhere and always at right angles to the tangent plane drawn through the falling body's point of contact with the earth's surface. For because of this it is clear that, if they were not stopped by the earth's surface, they too would go all the way to the centre itself, since the straight line drawn to the centre of a sphere is always perpendicular to the plane tangent to the sphere's surface at the intersection of that line.

All those who think it paradoxical that so great a weight as the earth should not waver or move anywhere seem to me to go astray by making their judgment with an eye to their own affects and not to the property of the whole. For it would not still appear so extraordinary to them, I believe, if they stopped to think that the earth's magnitude compared to the whole body surrounding it is in the ratio of a point to it. For thus it seems possible for that which is relatively least to be supported and pressed against from all sides equally and at the same angle by that which is absolutely greatest and homogeneous. For there is no "above" and "below" in the universe with respect to the earth, just as none could be conceived of in a sphere. And of the compound bodies in the universe, to the extent of their proper and natural motion, the light and subtle ones are scattered in flames to the outside and to the circumference, and they seem to rush in the upward direction relative to each one because we too call "up" from above our heads to the enveloping surface of the universe; but the heavy and coarse bodies move to the middle and centre and they seem to fall downwards because again we all call "down" the direction from our feet to the earth's centre. And they properly subside about the middle under the everywhere-equal and like resistance and impact against each other. Therefore the solid body of the earth is reasonably considered as being the largest relative to those moving against it and as remaining unmoved in any direction by the force of the very small weights, and as it were absorbing their fall. And if it had some one common movement, the same as that of the other weights, it would clearly leave them all behind because of its much greater magnitude. And the animals and other weights would be left hanging in the air, and the earth would very quickly fall out of the heavens. Merely to conceive such things makes them appear ridiculous.

[1]All local motions or movements according to place are divided by Aristotle into natural and violent local motions. In the case of compound bodies (that is, those bodies subject to generation and corruption and consisting of all those, and only those, bodies lying below the lunar sphere), the natural local motions are those of unimpeded and unpropelled fall; the violent local motions are any propelled or interrupted motions. In the case of simple bodies (that is, the heavenly bodies within and above the lunar sphere), there are only natural local motions: the regular or uniform circular motions. Ptolemy here calls the natural local motions of compound bodies their proper motions. This distinction between natural and violent motions is preserved by Galileo. For in his *Two New Sciences,* natural motion is treated in the "Third Day" and violent motion in the "Fourth Day." In the Newtonian system, the distinction is dissolved in a general mathematical treatment, a treatment more in line with the Platonic myth of the *Timaeus,* and so it loses all meaning.

Now some people, although they have nothing to oppose to these arguments, agree on something, as they think, more plausible. And it seems to them there is nothing against their supposing, for instance, the heavens immobile and the earth as turning on the same axis from west to east very nearly one revolution a day; or that they both should move to some extent, but only on the same axis as we said, and conformably to the overtaking of the one by the other.

But it has escaped their notice that, indeed, as far as the appearances of the stars are concerned, nothing would perhaps keep things from being in accordance with this simpler conjecture, but that in the light of what happens around us in the air such a notion would seem altogether absurd. For in order for us to grant them what is unnatural in itself, that the lightest and subtlest bodies either do not move at all or no differently from those of contrary nature, while those less light and less subtle bodies in the air are clearly more rapid than all the more terrestrial ones; and to grant that the heaviest and most compact bodies have their proper swift and regular motion, while again these terrestrial bodies are certainly at times not easily moved by anything else—for us to grant these things, they would have to admit that the earth's turning is the swiftest of absolutely all the movements about it because of its making so great a revolution in a short time, so that all those things that were not at rest on the earth would seem to have a movement contrary to it, and never would a cloud be seen to move toward the east nor anything else that flew or was thrown into the air. For the earth would always outstrip them in its eastward motion, so that all other bodies would seem to be left behind and to move towards the west.

For if they should say that the air is also carried around with the earth in the same direction and at the same speed, none the less the bodies contained in it would always seem to be outstripped by the movement of both. Or if they should be carried around as if one with the air, neither the one nor the other would appear as outstripping, or being outstripped by, the other. But these bodies would always remain in the same relative position and there would be no movement or change either in the case of flying bodies or projectiles. And yet we shall clearly see all such things taking place as if their slowness or swiftness did not follow at all from the earth's movement.

8. That There Are Two Different Prime Movements in the Heavens

It will be sufficient for these hypotheses, which have to be assumed for the detailed expositions following them, to have been outlined here in such a summary way since they will finally be established and confirmed by the agreement of the consequent proofs with the appearances. In addition to those already mentioned, this general assumption would also be rightly made that there are two different prime movements in the heavens. One is that by which everything moves from east to west, always in the same way and at the same speed with revolutions in circles parallel to each other and clearly described about the poles of the regularly revolving sphere. Of these circles the greatest is called the equator, because it alone is always cut exactly in half by the horizon which is a great circle of the sphere, and because everywhere the sun's revolution about it is sensibly equinoctial. The other movement is that according to which the spheres of the stars make certain local motions in the direction opposite to that of the movement just described and around other poles than those of that first revolution. And we assume that it is so because, while, from each day's observation, all the heavenly bodies are seen to move generally in paths sensibly similar and parallel to the equator and to rise, culminate, and set (for such is the property of the first movement), yet from subsequent and more continuous observation, even if all the other stars appear to preserve their angular distances with respect to each other and their properties as regards their places within the first movement, still the sun and moon and planets make certain complex movements unequal to each other, but all contrary to the general movement, towards the east opposite to the movement of the fixed stars which preserve their respective angular distances and are moved as if by one sphere.

If, then, this movement of the planets also took place in circles parallel to the equator—that is, around the same poles as those of the first revolution—it would be sufficient to assume for them all one and the same revolving movement in conformity with the first. For it would then be plausible to suppose that their movement was the result of a lag and not of a contrary movement. But they always seem, at the same time they move towards the east, to deviate towards the north and south poles without any uniform magnitude's being observed in this deviation, so that this seems to befall them through impulsions. But although this deviation is irregular on the hypothesis of one prime movement, it is regular when effected by a circle oblique to the equator. And so such a circle is conceived one and the same for, and proper to, the planets, quite exactly expressed and as it were described by the motion of the sun, but traveled also by the moon and planets which ever turn about it with every deviation from it on the part of any planet either way, a deviation within a prescribed distance and governed by rule. And since this is seen to be a great circle also because of the sun's equal oscillation to the north and south of the equator, and since the eastward movements of all the planets (as we said) take place on one and the same circle, it was necessary to suppose a second movement different from the general one, a movement about the poles of this oblique circle or ecliptic in the direction opposite to that of the first movement.

Then if we think of a great circle described through the poles of both the circles just mentioned, which necessarily cuts each of them—that is, the equator and the circle inclined to it—exactly in half and at right angles, there will be four points on the oblique circle or ecliptic: the two made by the equator diametrically opposite each other and called the equinoxes of which the one guarding the northern approach is called spring, and the opposite one autumn. And the two made by the circle drawn through both sets of poles, also clearly diametrically opposite each other, are called the tropics, of which the one to the south of the equator is called winter, and the one to the north summer.

The one first movement which contains all the others will be thought of then as described and as if defined by the great circle, through both sets of poles, which is carried around and carries with it all the rest from east to west about the poles of the equator. And these poles are as if they were on what is called the meridian, which differs from the circle through both sets of poles in this alone: that it is not always drawn through the poles of the ecliptic, but is conceived as continuously at right angles to the horizon and therefore called the meridian, since such a position cutting in half as it does each of the two hemispheres, that below the earth and that above, provides midday and midnight. But the second movement, consisting of many parts and contained by the first, and embracing itself all the planetary spheres,[1] is carried by the first as we said, and revolves about the poles of the ecliptic in the opposite direction. And these poles of the ecliptic being on the circle effecting the first revolution—that is, on the circle drawn through all four poles together—are carried around with it as one would expect; and, moving therefore with a motion opposite to the second prime movement, in this way keep the position of the great circle which is the ecliptic ever the same with respect to the equator.

9. On the Particular Notions

A summary and general preliminary explanation would contain some such exposition as the foregoing of the things to be presupposed. But now we are going to begin the detailed proofs. And we think the first of these is that by means of which is calculated the length of the arc between the poles of the equator and the ecliptic, lying on the great circle drawn through these poles. To this end we must first see expounded the method of computing the size of chords inscribed in a circle, and we are now going to demonstrate this geometrically for each case, once for all.

10. On the Size of Chords in a Circle

With an eye to immediate use, we shall now make a tabular exposition of the size of these chords by dividing the circumference into 360 parts and setting side by side the chords as the arcs subtended by them increase by a half part. That is, the diameter of the circle will be cut into 120 parts for ease in calculation; [and we shall take the arcs, considering them with respect to the number they contain of the circumference's 360 parts, and compare them with the subtending chords by finding out the number the chords contain of the diameter's 120 parts.] But first we shall show how, with as few theorems as possible and the same ones, we make a methodical and rapid calculation of their sizes so that we may not only have the magnitudes of the chords set out without knowing the why and wherefore but so that we may also easily manage a proof by means of a systematic geometrical construction. In general we shall use the sexagesimal system because of the difficulty of fractions, and we shall follow out the multiplications and divisions, aiming always at such an approximation as will leave no error worth considering as far as the accuracy of the senses is concerned.

Then first let there be the semicircle ABC on the diameter ADC and around centre D, and let straight line DB be erected on AC at right angles. Let DC be bisected at E, and EB be joined; and let EF be laid out equal to EB, and let FB be joined.

I say that the straight line FD is the side of a regular inscribed decagon, and BF that of a pentagon.

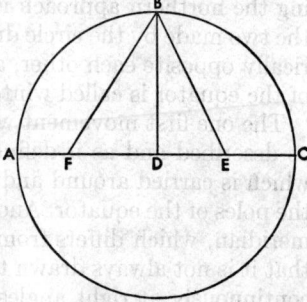

For since the straight line DC is bisected at E and a straight line DF is added to it,

rect. $CF,FD+$ sq. $ED=$ sq. EF,   [Eucl. ii, 6]

since $=$ sq. BE,

$$BE=EF.$$

But
$$\text{sq. } ED + \text{sq. } DB = \text{sq. } BE. \qquad \text{[Eucl. I, 47]}$$
Therefore
$$\text{rect. } CF, FD + \text{sq. } ED = \text{sq. } ED + \text{sq. } DB.$$
And, subtracting the common square on ED,
$$\text{rect. } CF, FD = \text{sq. } DB$$
$$= \text{sq. } DC.$$
Therefore CF is cut at D in extreme and mean ratio [Eucl. VI, def. 3]. Since, then, the side of the hexagon and the side of the decagon which are inscribed in the same circle, when they are in the same straight line, cut that line in extreme and mean ratio [Eucl. XIII, 9], and since the radius DC is equal to the side of the hexagon [Eucl. IV, 15 coroll.], therefore FD is equal to the side of the decagon.

And likewise, since the square on the side of the pentagon is equal to the square on the side of the hexagon together with the square on the side of the decagon, all inscribed in the same circle [Eucl. XIII, 10], and since in the right triangle BDF
$$\text{sq. } BF = \text{sq. } DB + \text{sq. } FD$$
where DB is the side of the hexagon and FD the side of the decagon, the straight line BF is equal to the side of the pentagon.

Since, then, as I said, we suppose the diameter divided into 120 parts, therefore by what we have just established, being half the circle's radius,
$$ED = 30 \text{ such parts,}$$
and
$$\text{sq. } ED = 900;$$
and
$$\text{rad. } DB = 60 \text{ such parts,}$$
and
$$\text{sq. } DB = 3600;$$
and
$$\text{sq. } BE = \text{sq. } EF = 4500.$$
Then
$$EF = 67^p 4' 55''^1$$
in length, and by subtraction
$$FD = 37^p 4' 55''.$$
Therefore the side of the decagon, subtending an arc of 36° of the whole circumference's 360°, will have $37^p 4' 55''$ of the diameter's 120^p.

Since again
$$FD = 37^p 4' 55'',$$
$$\text{sq. } FD = 1375^p 4' 14'',$$
$$\text{sq. } DB = 3600^p,$$
and
$$\text{sq. } FD + \text{sq. } DB = \text{sq. } BF,$$
therefore, in length,

---

[1]From now on, we shall indicate "parts such as the diameter's 120" by a p-superscript. Thus $67^p4'55''$ means "$67 + \frac{4}{60} + \frac{55}{3600}$ parts such as the diameter's 120." And we shall indicate "parts such as the circumference's 360" by the ordinary notation for angular degrees. For the measures of arcs and angles exactly correspond. Thus $47°42'40''$ means "$47 + \frac{42}{60} + \frac{40}{3600}$ parts such as the circumference's 360" or "parts such as 4 right angles' 360."

$$BF \doteq 70^{\text{p}}32'3''.$$

And therefore the side of the pentagon, subtending an arc of 72°, is 70ᵖ32′3″.

It is immediately clear that the side of the hexagon, subtending an arc of 60° and being equal to the radius, is itself 60ᵖ. And likewise, since the side of the inscribed square, subtending an arc of 90°, is, when squared, double the square on the radius, and since the side of the inscribed equilateral triangle is, when squared, triple the square on the radius, and since the square on the radius is 3,600ᵖ, the square on the side of the square will add up to 7,200ᵖ, and the square on the side of the equilateral triangle to 10,800ᵖ. And so in length

$$\text{chord of arc } 90° \doteq 84^{\text{p}}51'10'',$$

and

$$\text{chord of arc } 120° \doteq 103^{\text{p}}55'23''.$$

And so these chords are easily gotten by themselves. Thence it is evident that, with these chords given, it will be easy to get the chords which subtend the supplements, since the squares on them added together are equal to the square on the diameter. For example, since it was shown

$$\text{chord of arc } 36° = 37^{\text{p}}4'55'',$$
$$\text{sq. chord of arc } 36° = 1375^{\text{p}}4'15'',$$

and

$$\text{sq. diameter} = 14,400^{\text{p}},$$

therefore, for the supplement,

$$\text{sq. chord of arc } 144° = 13,024^{\text{p}}55'45'',$$

and, in length,

$$\text{chord of arc } 144° \doteq 114^{\text{p}}7'37'';$$

and the others in like manner.

And we shall next show, by expounding a lemma very useful for this present business, how the rest of the chords can be derived successively from those we already have.

For let there be a circle with any sort of inscribed quadrilateral $ABCD$, and let AC and BD be joined.

It is to be proved that

rect. AC, BD = rect. AB, DC + rect. AD, BC.

For let it be laid out such that

angle ABE = angle DBC.

If then we add the common angle EBD,

angle ABD = angle EBC.

But also

angle BDA = angle BCE.   [Eucl. III, 21],

for they subtend the same arc. Then triangle ABD is equiangular with triangle BCE. Hence

$$BC : CE :: BD : AD \quad \text{[Eucl. VI, 4]}.$$

Therefore

rect. BC, AD = rect. BD, CE.   [Eucl. VI, 16].

Again since

angle ABE = angle CBD

and also

angle BAE = angle BDC,

therefore triangle ABE is equiangular with triangle BCD. Hence

$$AB : AE :: BD : CD.$$

Therefore

$$\text{rect. } AB, CD = \text{rect. } BD, AE.$$

But it was also proved

$$\text{rect. } BC, AD = \text{rect. } BD, CE.$$

Therefore also

$$\text{rect. } AC, BD = \text{rect. } AB, CD + \text{rect. } BC, AD. \qquad \text{[Eucl. II, 1].}$$

Which was to be proved.

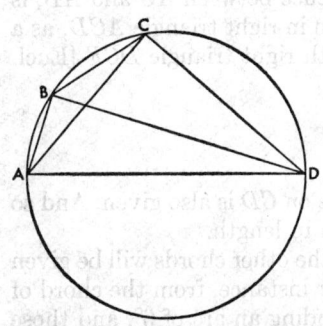

Now that this has been expounded, let there be the semicircle $ABCD$ on diameter AD, and from the point A let there be drawn the two straight lines AB, AC, and let the length of each of them have been given in terms of such parts as the given diameter's 120; and let BC be joined.

I say that BC is also given.

For let BD and CD be joined. Then clearly they are also given because they subtend the supplements. Since, then, the quadrilateral $ABCD$ is inscribed in a circle, therefore

$$\text{rect. } AB, CD + \text{rect. } AD, BC = \text{rect. } AC, BD$$

[p. 16]

And rectangle AC, BD is given, and also rectangle AB, CD. Therefore the remaining rectangle AD, BC is also given. And AD is the diameter. Hence the straight line BC is also given. And it is now clear to us that, if two arcs are given and the two chords subtending them, then also the chord subtending the difference between the two arcs will be given. And it is evident that by means of this theorem we can inscribe many other chords in arcs which are the differences between arcs directly given; for instance, the chord subtending an arc of 12°, since we have the chords of 60° and 72°.

Again, given any chord in a circle, let it be proposed to find the chord of half the arc of the given chord.

And let there be the semicircle ABC on diameter AC, and let CB be the given chord. And let the arc be bisected at D, and let AB, AD, BD, and DC be joined. And let DF be drawn from D perpendicular to AC.

I say that

$$CF = \text{half } (AC - AB).$$

For let AE be laid out such that

$$AE = AB,$$

and let DB be joined. Since

$$AB = AE,$$

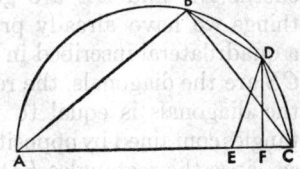

and AD is common, therefore the two sides AB and AD are equal to the two sides AE and AD respectively. And

$$\text{angle } BAD = \text{angle } EAD; \qquad \text{[Eucl. III, 27]}$$

therefore also

$$\text{base } BD = \text{base } DE.$$

But

$$\text{chord } BD = \text{chord } CD,$$

and therefore

chord $CD = DE$.

Since then, in the isosceles triangle DEC, DF has been dropped from the vertex perpendicular to the base, therefore

$$EF = CF.$$ [Eucl. I, 26]

But $$CE = AC - AB;$$

therefore

$$CF = \text{half } (AC - AB).$$

And so, since, given the chord of arc BC, chord AE of its supplement is also given [p. 16], therefore CF, which is half the difference between AC and AB, is given too. But when the perpendicular DF is drawn in right triangle ACD, as a consequence right triangle ACD is equiangular with right triangle DCF [Eucl. VI, 8], and

$$AC : CD :: CD : CF.$$

Therefore

$$\text{rect. } AC, CF = \text{sq. } CD.$$

But rectangle AC, CF is given, therefore the square on CD is also given. And so the chord CD of half the arc BC will also be given in length.

And so again, by means of this theorem, most of the other chords will be given as subtending the halves of arcs already found. For instance, from the chord of an arc of 12°, there can be gotten the chord subtending an arc of 6°, and those subtending arcs of 3°, 1½°, and ¾° respectively. And we shall find from calculation that

$$\text{chord of arc } 1\tfrac{1}{2}° \doteqdot 1^{\text{p}}34'15'',$$

and

$$\text{chord of arc } \tfrac{3}{4}° \doteqdot 0^{\text{p}}47'8''.$$

Again let there be the circle $ABCD$ on diameter AD with center at F. And from A let there be cut off consecutively two given arcs, AB and BC; and let the given chords subtending them, AB and BC, be joined.

I say that, if we join AC, then AC will be given also.

For let the circle's diameter BFE be drawn through B, and let BD, DC, CE, and DE be joined. Then from this it is clear that, by means of BC, chord CE is given; and, by means of AB, chords BD and DE are given [p. 16]. And by things we have already proved, since $BCDE$ is a quadrilateral inscribed in a circle, and BD and CE are the diagonals, the rectangle contained by the diagonals is equal to the sum of the rectangles contained by opposite sides [p. 16, 17]. And so, since the rectangles BD, CE and BC, DE are

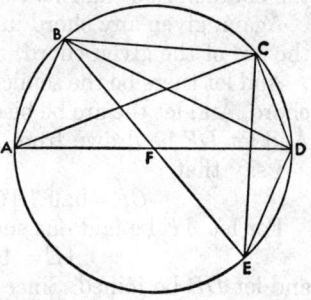

given, therefore the rectangle BE, CD is given also. But the diameter BE is given too, and the remaining side CD will be given. Therefore the chord AC of the supplement will be given also. And so, if two arcs and their chords are given, then by means of this theorem the chord of both these arcs together will be given.

And it is evident that, by continually combining the chord of an arc 1½° with those so far set out and calculating the sums, we shall inscribe all those chords which, when doubled, are divisible by three; and only those chords will still be skipped which fall within 1½° intervals. For there will be two such chords skipped in each interval, since we are carrying out this inscribing of chords by successive additions of ½°. And so if we could compute the chord subtending an arc of ½°, then this chord, by addition to, and subtraction from, the chords which are separated by 1½° intervals and have already been given, will fill in all the rest of the intermediate chords. But since, given any chord such as that subtending an arc of 1½°, the chord of a third of the arc is in no way geometrically given (and if it were possible, we could then compute the chord of an arc of ½°), therefore we shall first look for the chord of an arc of 1° by means of chords subtending arcs of 1½° and ¾°. We shall do this by presenting a little lemma which, even if it may not suffice for determining their sizes in general, can yet in the case of these very small chords keep them indistinguishable from chords rigorously determined.

For I say that, if two unequal chords are inscribed in a circle, the greater has to the less a ratio less than the arc on the greater has to the arc on the less.

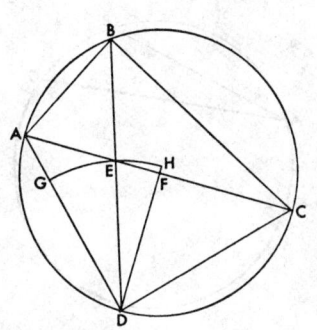

For let there be the circle *ABCD*; and let unequal chords be inscribed in it, *AB* the less and *BC* the greater.

I say that
    chord *BC* : chord *AB* < arc *BC* : arc *AB*.

For let angle *ABC* be bisected by *BD*, and let *AEC*, *AD*, and *CD* be joined. And since angle *ABC* has been bisected by the straight line *DEB*,

    chord *CD* = chord *AD*,
                                    [Eucl. III, 26, 29]
and

            CE > *AE*.   [Eucl. VI. 3]

Then let *DF* be dropped from *D* perpendicular to *AEC*. Now since

            AD > *DE*,
            DE > *DF*,[1]

therefore the circle described with centre *D* and radius *DE* cuts *AD* and falls beyond *DF*. Then let the circle *GEH* be drawn and the straight line *DFH* be produced. And since

            sect. *DEH* > trgl. *DEF*,
and
            trgl. *DEA* > sect. *DEG*,
therefore
            trgl. *DEF* : trgl. *DEA* < sect. *DEH* : sect. *DEG*.   [Eucl. v, 8]
But
            trgl. *DEF* : trgl. *DEA* : : *EF* : *AE*,   [Eucl. VI, 1]
and
        sect. *DEH* : sect. *DEG* : : angle *FDE* : angle *EDA*.
Therefore

---

[1]For *DF* produced will bisect arc *ABC* [Eucl. III, 3, 26]; hence it will fall on the side of *B* towards *C*. Therefore

            DE > *DF*,   [Eucl. I, 21]
            AD > *DE*.

$$EF : AE < \text{angle } FDE : \text{angle } EDA.$$

Then *componendo*

$$AF : AE < \text{angle } FDA : \text{angle } EDA.$$

And doubling the antecedents

$$CA : AE < \text{angle } CDA : \text{angle } EDA.$$

And *separando*

$$CE : AE < \text{angle } CDB : \text{angle } BDA.$$

But

$$CE : AE :: BC : AB, \qquad\qquad\qquad \text{[Eucl. vi, 3]}$$

and

$$\text{angle } CDB : \text{angle } BDA :: \text{arc } BC : \text{arc } AB. \qquad \text{[Eucl. vi, 33]}$$

Therefore

$$\text{chord } BC : \text{chord } AB < \text{arc } BC : \text{arc } AB.$$

Now, then, with this laid down, let there be the circle ABC, and let the two chords AB and AC be inscribed in it. And first let AB be given as subtending an arc of $\frac{3}{4}°$, and AC an arc of $1°$.

Since

$$\text{chord } AC : \text{chord } AB < \text{arc } AC : \text{arc } AB,$$

and

$$\text{arc } AC = 1\frac{1}{3} \ (\text{arc } AB),$$

therefore

$$\text{chord } AC < 1\frac{1}{3} \ (\text{chord } AB).$$

But it was proved [p. 18]

$$\text{chord } AB = 0^{\text{p}}47'8''.$$

Therefore

$$\text{chord } AC < 1^{\text{p}}2'50'',$$

for

$$1^{\text{p}}2'50'' \doteq 1\frac{1}{3} \ (0^{\text{p}}47'8'').$$

Again, with the same figure, let chord AB be given as subtending an arc of $1°$, and chord AC an arc of $1\frac{1}{2}°$.

Likewise then, since

$$\text{arc } AC = 1\frac{1}{2} \ (\text{arc } AB),$$
$$\text{chord } AC < 1\frac{1}{2} \ (\text{chord } AB).$$

But we proved [p. 18]

$$\text{chord } AC = 1^{\text{p}}34'15''.$$

Therefore

$$\text{chord } AB > 1^{\text{p}}2'50'',$$

for

$$1^{\text{p}}34'15'' \doteq 1\frac{1}{2} \ (1^{\text{p}}2'50'').$$

And so, since it has been proved that the chord of an arc of $1°$ is both greater and less than the same number of parts, clearly we shall have

$$\text{chord of arc } 1° \doteq 1^{\text{p}}2'50'';$$

and by means of earlier proofs we saw

$$\text{chord of arc } \frac{1}{2}° \doteq 0^{\text{p}}31'25''.$$

And the remaining intervals will be filled in as we have just said. For example, in the first interval we find the chord subtending an arc of $2°$ by adding $\frac{1}{2}°$ and $1\frac{1}{2}°$, and the chord subtending an arc of $2\frac{1}{2}°$ by subtracting $\frac{1}{2}°$ from $3°$, and so on for the rest.

So the business of chords in a circle can be easily handled in this way, I think.

And as I said, in order to have the magnitudes set out immediately to hand, we shall draw up tables of 45 rows each, for symmetry's sake. And the first column will contain the magnitudes of the arcs increasing by $\frac{1}{2}°$, and the second column will contain the magnitudes of the chords subtending them in terms of the diameter's assumed 120 parts. The third column will contain the thirtieth of the increase of the chord as the corresponding arc increases by $\frac{1}{2}°$, so that we may have a mean addition, accurate for the senses, for each increase of $\frac{1}{60}°$ in the corresponding arcs, and so be able to calculate readily the chords falling within the $\frac{1}{2}°$ intervals. And it is to be remarked that by means of these same theorems, if we should suspect some typographical error in connection with any of the chords computed here, we can easily check and correct it either by means of the chord of an arc double the arc of the chord which is being examined, or by means of the difference of certain other given chords, or by means of the chord subtending the supplement. And here is the table:

11. TABLE OF CHORDS

Arcs	Chords			Sixtieths[1]				Arcs	Chords			Sixtieths			
$\frac{1}{2}$	0	31	25	0	1	2	50	$16\frac{1}{2}$	17	13	9	0	1	2	10
1	1	2	50	0	1	2	50	17	17	44	14	0	1	2	7
$1\frac{1}{2}$	1	34	15	0	1	2	50	$17\frac{1}{2}$	18	15	17	0	1	2	5
2	2	5	40	0	1	2	50	18	18	46	19	0	1	2	2
$2\frac{1}{2}$	2	37	4	0	1	2	48	$18\frac{1}{2}$	19	17	21	0	1	2	0
3	3	8	28	0	1	2	48	19	19	48	21	0	1	1	57
$3\frac{1}{2}$	3	39	52	0	1	2	48	$19\frac{1}{2}$	20	19	19	0	1	1	54
4	4	11	16	0	1	2	47	20	20	50	16	0	1	1	51
$4\frac{1}{2}$	4	42	40	0	1	2	47	$20\frac{1}{2}$	21	21	11	0	1	1	48
5	5	14	4	0	1	2	46	21	21	52	6	0	1	1	45
$5\frac{1}{2}$	5	45	27	0	1	2	45	$21\frac{1}{2}$	22	22	58	0	1	1	42
6	6	16	49	0	1	2	44	22	22	53	49	0	1	1	39
$6\frac{1}{2}$	6	48	11	0	1	2	43	$22\frac{1}{2}$	23	24	39	0	1	1	36
7	7	19	33	0	1	2	42	23	23	55	27	0	1	1	33
$7\frac{1}{2}$	7	50	54	0	1	2	41	$23\frac{1}{2}$	24	26	13	0	1	1	30
8	8	22	15	0	1	2	40	24	24	56	58	0	1	1	26
$8\frac{1}{2}$	8	53	35	0	1	2	39	$24\frac{1}{2}$	25	27	41	0	1	1	22
9	9	24	54	0	1	2	38	25	25	58	22	0	1	1	19
$9\frac{1}{2}$	9	56	13	0	1	2	37	$25\frac{1}{2}$	26	29	1	0	1	1	15
10	10	27	32	0	1	2	35	26	26	59	38	0	1	1	11
$10\frac{1}{2}$	10	58	49	0	1	2	33	$26\frac{1}{2}$	27	30	14	0	1	1	8
11	11	30	5	0	1	2	32	27	28	0	48	0	1	1	4
$11\frac{1}{2}$	12	1	21	0	1	2	30	$27\frac{1}{2}$	28	31	20	0	1	1	0
12	12	32	36	0	1	2	28	28	29	1	50	0	1	0	56
$12\frac{1}{2}$	13	3	50	0	1	2	27	$28\frac{1}{2}$	29	32	18	0	1	0	52
13	13	35	4	0	1	2	25	29	30	2	44	0	1	0	48
$13\frac{1}{2}$	14	6	16	0	1	2	23	$29\frac{1}{2}$	30	33	8	0	1	0	44
14	14	37	27	0	1	2	21	30	31	3	30	0	1	0	40
$14\frac{1}{2}$	15	8	38	0	1	2	19	$30\frac{1}{2}$	31	33	50	0	1	0	35
15	15	39	47	0	1	2	17	31	32	4	7	0	1	0	31
$15\frac{1}{2}$	16	10	56	0	1	2	15	$31\frac{1}{2}$	32	34	22	0	1	0	27
16	16	42	3	0	1	2	13	32	33	4	35	0	1	0	22

[1]The sexagesimal system is carried out one place further in this column. Thus 0°1′2″50′ ″ represents $\frac{1}{60}+\frac{2}{3600}+\frac{50}{216000}$ which is $\frac{1}{30}$ of the increase of the second chord over the first.

Arcs	Chords			Sixtieths				Arcs	Chords			Sixtieths			
32½	33	34	46	0	1	0	17	58½	58	38	5	0	0	54	45
33	34	4	55	0	1	0	12	59	59	5	27	0	0	54	37
33½	34	35	1	0	1	0	8	59½	59	32	45	0	0	54	29
34	35	5	5	0	1	0	3	60	60	0	0	0	0	54	21
34½	35	35	6	0	0	59	57	60½	60	27	11	0	0	54	12
35	36	5	5	0	0	59	52	61	60	54	17	0	0	54	4
35½	36	35	1	0	0	59	48	61½	61	21	19	0	0	53	56
36	37	4	55	0	0	59	43	62	61	48	17	0	0	53	47
36½	37	34	47	0	0	59	38	62½	62	15	10	0	0	53	39
37	38	4	36	0	0	59	32	63	62	42	0	0	0	53	30
37½	38	34	22	0	0	59	27	63½	63	8	45	0	0	53	22
38	39	4	5	0	0	59	22	64	63	35	25	0	0	53	13
38½	39	33	46	0	0	59	16	64½	64	2	2	0	0	53	4
39	40	3	25	0	0	59	11	65	64	28	34	0	0	52	55
39½	40	33	0	0	0	59	5	65½	64	55	1	0	0	52	46
40	41	2	33	0	0	59	0	66	65	21	24	0	0	52	37
40½	41	32	3	0	0	58	54	66½	65	47	43	0	0	52	28
41	42	1	30	0	0	58	48	67	66	13	57	0	0	52	19
41½	42	30	54	0	0	58	42	67½	66	40	7	0	0	52	10
42	43	0	15	0	0	58	36	68	67	6	12	0	0	52	1
42½	43	29	33	0	0	58	31	68½	67	32	12	0	0	51	52
43	43	58	49	0	0	58	25	69	67	58	8	0	0	51	43
43½	44	28	1	0	0	58	18	69½	68	23	59	0	0	51	33
44	44	57	10	0	0	58	12	70	68	49	45	0	0	51	23
44½	45	26	16	0	0	58	6	70½	69	15	27	0	0	51	14
45	45	55	19	0	0	58	0	71	69	41	4	0	0	51	4
45½	46	24	19	0	0	57	54	71½	70	6	36	0	0	50	55
46	46	53	16	0	0	57	47	72	70	32	4	0	0	50	45
46½	47	22	9	0	0	57	41	72½	70	57	26	0	0	50	35
47	47	51	0	0	0	57	34	73	71	22	44	0	0	50	26
47½	48	19	47	0	0	57	27	73½	71	47	56	0	0	50	16
48	48	48	30	0	0	57	21	74	72	13	4	0	0	50	6
48½	49	17	11	0	0	57	14	74½	72	38	7	0	0	49	56
49	49	45	48	0	0	57	7	75	73	3	5	0	0	49	46
49½	50	14	21	0	0	57	0	75½	73	27	58	0	0	49	36
50	50	42	51	0	0	56	53	76	73	52	46	0	0	49	26
50½	51	11	18	0	0	56	46	76½	74	17	29	0	0	49	16
51	51	39	41	0	0	56	39	77	74	42	7	0	0	49	6
51½	52	8	0	0	0	56	32	77½	75	6	39	0	0	48	55
52	52	36	16	0	0	56	25	78	75	31	7	0	0	48	45
52½	53	4	29	0	0	56	18	78½	75	55	29	0	0	48	34
53	53	32	38	0	0	56	10	79	76	19	46	0	0	48	24
53½	54	0	43	0	0	56	3	79½	76	43	58	0	0	48	13
54	54	28	44	0	0	55	55	80	77	8	5	0	0	48	3
54½	54	56	42	0	0	55	48	80½	77	32	6	0	0	47	52
55	55	24	36	0	0	55	40	81	77	56	2	0	0	47	41
55½	55	52	26	0	0	55	33	81½	78	19	52	0	0	47	31
56	56	20	12	0	0	55	25	82	78	43	38	0	0	47	20
56½	56	47	54	0	0	55	17	82½	79	7	18	0	0	47	9
57	57	15	33	0	0	55	9	83	79	30	52	0	0	46	58
57½	57	43	7	0	0	55	1	83½	79	54	21	0	0	46	47
58	58	10	38	0	0	54	53	84	80	17	45	0	0	46	36

Arcs	Chords			Sixtieths				Arcs	Chords			Sixtieths			
84½	80	41	3	0	0	46	25	110½	98	35	52	0	0	35	42
85	81	4	15	0	0	46	14	111	98	53	43	0	0	35	29
85½	81	27	22	0	0	46	3	111½	99	11	27	0	0	35	15
86	81	50	24	0	0	45	52	112	99	29	5	0	0	35	1
86½	82	13	19	0	0	45	40	112½	99	46	35	0	0	34	48
87	82	36	9	0	0	45	29	113	100	3	59	0	0	34	34
87½	82	58	54	0	0	45	18	113½	100	21	16	0	0	34	20
88	83	21	33	0	0	45	6	114	100	38	26	0	0	34	6
88½	83	44	6	0	0	44	55	114½	100	55	28	0	0	33	53
89	84	6	33	0	0	44	43	115	101	12	25	0	0	33	39
89½	84	28	54	0	0	44	31	115½	101	29	15	0	0	33	25
90	84	51	10	0	0	44	20	116	101	45	57	0	0	33	11
90½	85	13	20	0	0	44	8	116½	102	2	33	0	0	32	57
91	85	35	24	0	0	43	57	117	102	19	1	0	0	32	43
91½	85	57	23	0	0	43	45	117½	102	35	22	0	0	32	29
92	86	19	15	0	0	43	33	118	102	51	37	0	0	32	15
92½	86	41	2	0	0	43	21	118½	103	7	44	0	0	32	0
93	87	2	42	0	0	43	9	119	103	23	44	0	0	31	46
93½	87	24	17	0	0	42	57	119½	103	39	37	0	0	31	32
94	87	45	45	0	0	42	45	120	103	55	23	0	0	31	18
94½	88	7	7	0	0	42	33	120½	104	11	2	0	0	31	4
95	88	28	24	0	0	42	21	121	104	26	34	0	0	30	49
95½	88	49	34	0	0	42	9	121½	104	41	59	0	0	30	35
96	89	10	39	0	0	41	57	122	104	57	16	0	0	30	21
96½	89	31	37	0	0	41	45	122½	105	12	26	0	0	30	7
97	89	52	29	0	0	41	33	123	105	27	30	0	0	29	52
97½	90	13	15	0	0	41	21	123½	105	42	26	0	0	29	37
98	90	33	55	0	0	41	8	124	105	57	14	0	0	29	23
98½	90	54	29	0	0	40	55	124½	106	11	55	0	0	29	8
99	91	14	56	0	0	40	42	125	106	26	29	0	0	28	54
99½	91	35	17	0	0	40	30	125½	106	40	56	0	0	28	39
100	91	55	32	0	0	40	17	126	106	55	15	0	0	28	24
100½	92	15	40	0	0	40	4	126½	107	9	27	0	0	28	10
101	92	35	42	0	0	39	52	127	107	23	32	0	0	27	56
101½	92	55	38	0	0	39	39	127½	107	37	30	0	0	27	40
102	93	15	27	0	0	39	26	128	107	51	20	0	0	27	25
102½	93	35	11	0	0	39	13	128½	108	5	2	0	0	27	10
103	93	54	47	0	0	39	0	129	108	18	37	0	0	26	56
103½	94	14	17	0	0	38	47	129½	108	32	5	0	0	26	41
104	94	33	41	0	0	38	34	130	108	45	25	0	0	26	26
104½	94	52	58	0	0	38	21	130½	108	58	38	0	0	26	11
105	95	12	9	0	0	38	8	131	109	11	44	0	0	25	56
105½	95	31	13	0	0	37	55	131½	109	24	42	0	0	25	41
106	95	50	11	0	0	37	42	132	109	37	32	0	0	25	26
106½	96	9	2	0	0	37	29	132½	109	50	15	0	0	25	11
107	96	27	47	0	0	37	16	133	110	2	50	0	0	24	56
107½	96	46	24	0	0	37	3	133½	110	15	18	0	0	24	41
108	97	4	56	0	0	36	50	134	110	27	39	0	0	24	26
108½	97	23	20	0	0	36	36	134½	110	39	52	0	0	24	10
109	97	41	38	0	0	36	23	135	110	51	57	0	0	23	55
109½	97	59	49	0	0	36	9	135½	111	3	54	0	0	23	40
110	98	17	54	0	0	35	56	136	111	15	44	0	0	23	25

Arcs	Chords			Sixtieths			
136½	111	27	26	0	0	23	9
137	111	39	1	0	0	22	54
137½	111	50	28	0	0	22	39
138	112	1	47	0	0	22	24
138½	112	12	59	0	0	22	8
139	112	24	3	0	0	21	53
139½	112	35	0	0	0	21	37
140	112	45	48	0	0	21	22
140½	112	56	29	0	0	21	7
141	113	7	2	0	0	20	51
141½	113	17	26	0	0	20	36
142	113	27	44	0	0	20	20
142½	113	37	54	0	0	20	4
143	113	47	56	0	0	19	49
143½	113	57	50	0	0	19	33
144	114	7	37	0	0	19	17
144½	114	17	15	0	0	19	2
145	114	26	46	0	0	18	46
145½	114	36	9	0	0	18	30
146	114	45	24	0	0	18	14
146½	114	54	31	0	0	17	59
147	115	3	30	0	0	17	43
147½	115	12	22	0	0	17	27
148	115	21	6	0	0	17	11
148½	115	29	41	0	0	16	55
149	115	38	9	0	0	16	40
149½	115	46	29	0	0	16	24
150	115	54	40	0	0	16	8
150½	116	2	44	0	0	15	52
151	116	10	40	0	0	15	36
151½	116	18	28	0	0	15	20
152	116	26	8	0	0	15	4
152½	116	33	40	0	0	14	48
153	116	41	4	0	0	14	32
153½	116	48	20	0	0	14	16
154	116	55	28	0	0	14	0
154½	117	2	28	0	0	13	44
155	117	9	20	0	0	13	28
155½	117	16	4	0	0	13	12
156	117	22	40	0	0	12	56
156½	117	29	8	0	0	12	40
157	117	35	28	0	0	12	24
157½	117	41	40	0	0	12	7
158	117	47	43	0	0	11	51
158½	117	53	39	0	0	11	35
159	117	59	27	0	0	11	19
159½	118	5	7	0	0	10	3
160	118	10	37	0	0	10	47
160½	118	16	1	0	0	10	31
161	118	21	16	0	0	10	14
161½	118	26	23	0	0	9	58
162	118	31	22	0	0	9	42
162½	118	36	13	0	0	9	25
163	118	40	55	0	0	9	9
163½	118	45	30	0	0	8	53
164	118	49	56	0	0	8	37
164½	118	54	15	0	0	8	20
165	118	58	25	0	0	8	4
165½	119	2	26	0	0	7	48
166	119	6	20	0	0	7	31
166½	119	10	6	0	0	7	15
167	119	13	44	0	0	6	59
167½	119	17	13	0	0	6	42
168	119	20	34	0	0	6	26
168½	119	23	47	0	0	6	10
169	119	26	52	0	0	5	53
169½	119	29	49	0	0	5	37
170	119	32	37	0	0	5	20
170½	119	35	17	0	0	5	4
171	119	37	49	0	0	4	48
171½	119	40	13	0	0	4	31
172	119	42	28	0	0	4	14
172½	119	44	35	0	0	3	58
173	119	46	35	0	0	3	42
173½	119	48	26	0	0	3	26
174	119	50	8	0	0	3	9
174½	119	51	43	0	0	2	53
175	119	53	10	0	0	2	36
175½	119	54	27	0	0	2	20
176	119	55	38	0	0	2	3
176½	119	56	39	0	0	1	47
177	119	57	32	0	0	1	30
177½	119	58	18	0	0	1	14
178	119	58	55	0	0	0	57
178½	119	59	24	0	0	0	41
179	119	59	44	0	0	0	25
179½	119	59	56	0	0	0	9
180	120	0	0	0	0	0	0

12. On the Arc Between the Tropics

Now that the question of the value of chords in a circle has been treated, our first task will be, as we have said, to show how much the oblique circle through the middle of the zodiac [the ecliptic] is inclined to the equator—that is, what ratio the great circle which passes through both sets of poles has to the arc intercepted on it by these poles. This arc is evidently equal to the arc from either of the tropic points to the equator, along this same circle. And we can immediately get the measure of this arc instrumentally, with some such simple construction as the following.

We shall make a brass circle, suitable in size, accurately turned, with its surfaces standing square. And we shall use it as a meridian, dividing it into the 360 parts supposed for the great circle, and each of these into as many parts as there is room for. Then, fitting into this circle another little circle, thinner than it, in such a way that their sides remain in the same plane and the smaller circle can turn without hindrance within the greater circle to the north and south, always in the same plane, we shall place, on one of the smaller circle's two sides at two diametrically opposite points, small prisms of the same size pointing in exactly the same straight line with each other and with the centre of the circles. And in the middle of the prisms' width we shall place fine pointers touching the side of the greater circle and its divisions. And then we shall fit that circle securely on a small and convenient column for its several uses, and stand the base of the column on a pavement in the open air exactly parallel to the plane of the horizon. And we shall take care that the plane of the circles is perpendicular to that of the horizon and parallel to that of the meridian. The first condition is satisfied by means of a plumb line which is suspended from the highest point of the circles and which is watched until, by correction of the underpinning, it is directed to the diametrically opposite point below. And the second condition is satisfied by very visibly drawing a meridian line in the plane below the column and turning the circles from side to side until their plane is sighted parallel to the line. And after a placement of this kind had been made, we would observe the sun's advance to the north and south, moving the inside circle at middays until the lower prism was completely shadowed by the whole of the upper prism. And when this was done, the needle points would show us each time how many degrees from the zenith the sun's center stood on the meridian line.

And we used to make this observation still more readily by constructing, instead of circles, a steady square block of rock or wood having one of its faces regular and accurately shaped. And using as a centre the vertex of one of its angles, we drew a quadrant, drawing out from the centre point to the circumference those straight lines which contain the right angle of the quadrant, and likewise dividing the circumference into 90 parts, and dividing these again. And after this, on one of the straight lines, the one which was to be perpendicular to the plane of the horizon and to face south, we laid two small right cylinders in every way equal and similarly fashioned, one on the centre exactly at the midpoint of the indicated circle and the other at the lower extremity of the straight line. Then, standing the marked side of the block along the meridian line drawn in the supporting plane of the horizon so that it would also be parallel to the plane of the meridian, again making adjustments with fine splints in accord with a plumb line right across the cylinders perpendicular to the plane of the horizon, we would observe as before the midday shadow from the centre cylinder, putting something at the graduated circumference to show more clearly its position. And marking the middle of the shadow we would note down the division of the quadrant, and this would clearly indicate the latitude of the sun's path on the meridian.

Now from such observations and especially from those made by us over several periods while the sun was near the tropics, seeing the marker count off from the zenith always an equal number of divisions on the meridian and the same ones both for the winter tropics and for the summer tropics, we found the arc from the northernmost to the southernmost limit, which is the arc between the tropic points, to be always more than 47°40′ but less than 47°45′. And with this there results nearly the same ratio as that of Eratosthenes and as that which Hipparchus used. For the arc between the tropics turns out to be very nearly 11 out of the meridian's 83 parts.

And immediately from this observation it is easy to deduce the latitudes of the places where we make the observations, once we have taken the midpoint of the two limits, which is on the equator, and the arc between this point and the zenith. For the arc between the poles and the plane of the horizon is clearly equal to this arc.

13. PRELIMINARIES TO THE SPHERICAL PROOFS

And since it is next in order to demonstrate the respective values of the arcs on great circles drawn through the poles of the equator and cut off between the equator and the ecliptic, we shall explain very short and easy lemmas by means of which we shall effect nearly all the proofs of theorems dealing with spheres.

Now let the two straight lines BE and CD, drawn to two straight lines AB and AC, cut each other at F.

I say that $AC : AE$ comp. $CD : DF, BF : BE$.

For let EG be drawn through E parallel to CD. Since the straight lines CD and EG are parallel, $AC : AE : : CD : EG$ [Eucl. VI, 4].

Then if we supply the straight line DF,

$$CD : EG \text{ comp. } CD : DF, DF : EG.$$

And

$$DF : EG : : BF : BE, \quad \text{[Eucl. VI, 4].}$$

again because EG and DF are parallel. Therefore

$$AC : AE \text{ comp. } CD : DF, BF : BE.$$

Which it was proposed to prove.

And in the same way it can be shown, by drawing a straight line through A parallel to EF and producing CDG to meet it, that

$$CE : AE \text{ comp. } CF : DF, BD : AB.$$

For again since AG is parallel to EF

$$CF : FG : : CE : AE \quad \text{[Eucl. VI, 2].}$$

But if we supply DF,

$$CF : FG \text{ comp. } CF : DF, DF : FG.$$

But

$$DF : FG : : BD : AB$$

because AB and FG are drawn through to the parallels AG and BF. Therefore

$$CF : FG \text{ comp. } CF : DF, BD : AB.$$

But

$$CE : AE : : CF : FG.$$

And therefore

$$CE : AE \text{ comp. } CF : DF, BD : AB.$$

Which was to be proved.

Again, let there be the circle ABC with centre D; and let there be taken on its circumference three points A, B, and C in such a way that each of the arcs AB and BC is less than a semicircle (and let the same thing be understood of the arcs taken hereafter). And let the straight lines AC and DEB be joined.

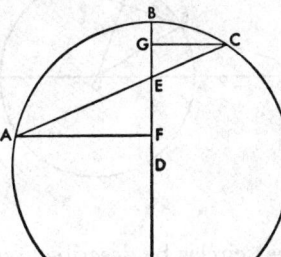

I say that chord 2 arc AB : chord 2 arc BC : : $AE : CE$.

For let the straight lines AF and CG be drawn from the points A and C perpendicular to BD. Since AF is parallel to CG and AEC crosses them, therefore

$$AF : CG : : AE : CE \quad \text{[Eucl. vi, 4]}.$$

But

$$AF : CG : : \text{chord 2 arc } AB : \text{chord 2 arc } BC.$$

For the ones are the halves of the others respectively. And therefore

$$AE : CE : : \text{chord 2 arc } AB : \text{chord 2 arc } BC.$$

Which was to be proved.

And it follows from this that, if the whole arc AC is given and also the ratio of the chord of twice arc AB to the chord of twice arc BC, then each of the arcs AB and BC is given.

For with the same figure laid out, let AD be joined, and from D let DF be drawn perpendicular to AEC. It is clear then that, given arc AC, angle ADF which subtends the half of it is given, and also the whole triangle ADF. Now with the whole line AC given, since

$$AE : CE : : \text{chord 2 arc } AB : \text{chord 2 arc } BC,$$

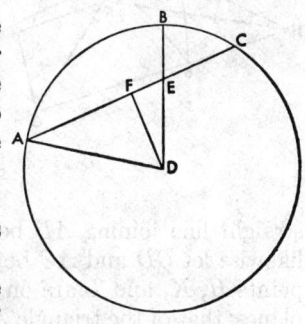

therefore AE is given[1], and the remainder EF is given. And for this reason and since DF is given, both angle EDF of the right triangle EDF and the whole angle ADB are given. And so both arcs AB and BC are given. Which was to be proved.

Again, let there be the circle ABC with centre D, and on its circumference let there be taken three points A, B, and C in such a way that each of the arcs AB and AC is less than a semicircle (and let this same condition be understood for the arcs to be taken hereafter). And let AD and BC be joined and the resulting straight lines be produced to meet at E.

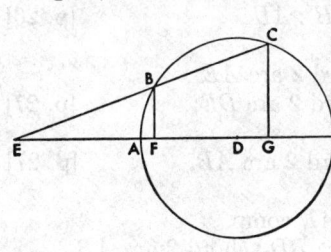

I say that

$$CE : BE : : \text{chord 2 arc } AC : \text{chord 2 arc } AB.$$

For, as in the previous lemma, if from the points B and C we drop BF and CG perpendicular to AD, then, since they are parallel,

$$CG : BF : : CE : BE.$$

And so also

$$CE : BE : : \text{chord 2 arc } AC : \text{chord 2 arc } AB.$$

[1]For *componendo*
$AC : CE : : \text{chord 2 arc } AB + \text{chord 2 arc } BC : \text{chord 2 arc } BC.$

Which was to be proved.

And then from this it follows that, even if the arc BC alone be given along with the ratio of the chord of twice arc AC to the chord of twice arc AB, then arc AB is given.

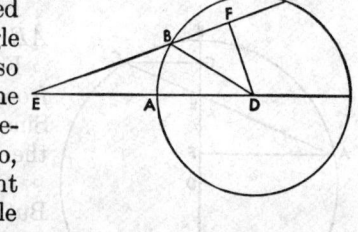

For again in a similar figure, with BD joined and DF dropped perpendicular to BC, angle BDF subtending half arc BC is given, and also the whole right triangle BDF. And since also the ratio of CE to BE is given and chord BC, therefore BE is given and the whole line EBF. And so, since DF is given, angle EDF of the same right triangle is also given, and by subtraction angle EDB. Hence arc AB is also given.

And with these conclusions in mind, let arcs of great circles be described on a spherical surface in such a way that two arcs BE and CD, drawn to two arcs AB and AC, intersect each other at the point F. And let each of these arcs be less than a semicircle (and let the same condition be understood in all the figures).

Then I say that

chord 2 arc CE : chord 2 arc AE comp.

chord 2 arc CF : chord 2 arc DF,

chord 2 arc BD : chord 2 arc AB.

For let the centre of the sphere be taken, and let it be $G;$ and from the point G let the straight lines BG, FG, and EG be drawn to the intersections of the circles at B, F, and E. And let the straight line joining AD be produced to meet BG produced at point H. And likewise let CD and AC be joined and cut FG and EG at K and L. Then the points H, K, and L are on one straight line, because they are at once in two planes: that of the triangle ACD, and that of the circle BFE. When these points are joined, we have two straight lines HL and CD intersecting at point K and cutting two other straight lines AH and AC. Therefore

$$CL : AL \text{ comp. } CK : DK, DH : AH.$$ [p. 26]

But

$$CL : AL :: \text{chord 2 arc } CE : \text{chord 2 arc } AE,$$

$$CK : KD :: \text{chord 2 arc } CF : \text{chord 2 arc } DF;$$ [p. 27]

and

$$DH : AH :: \text{chord 2 arc } BD : \text{chord 2 arc } AB.$$ [p. 27]

And therefore

chord 2 arc CE : chord 2 arc AE comp.

chord 2 arc CF : chord 2 arc DF, chord 2 arc BD : chord 2 arc AB.

In the same way, by straight lines constructed in a plane, it is also proved that

chord 2 arc AC : chord 2 arc AE comp.

chord 2 arc CD : chord 2 arc DF, chord 2 arc BF : chord 2 arc BE.[1]

Which things it was required to prove.

[1]This analogous theorem is proved thus: With the same arcs as in the preceding figure, produce the straight lines CE, CF, and EF of the four intersecting great circles of a sphere whose

14. On the Arcs Between the Equator and the Ecliptic

Now that this theorem has been expounded, we shall make the first application of the arcs as worked out above, in the following way:

For let the circle $ABCD$ be the circle through the poles of the equator and

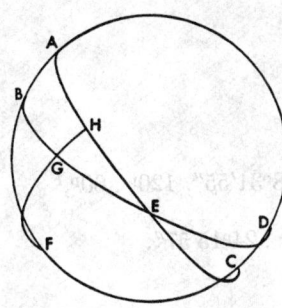

the poles of the ecliptic; and let AEC be the semicircle of the equator, and BED the semicircle of the ecliptic, and the point E their intersection at the spring equinox so that point B is the winter tropic and D the summer tropic. And let the pole of the equator AEC be taken on arc ABC, and let it be the point F. And let the arc EG be taken on the ecliptic, and suppose it to be 30°, and through the points F and G let the arc FGH of a great circle be drawn.

And let it be proposed to find the arc GH.

Let it be understood now and generally in all such proofs, so we shall not have to repeat the same thing for each one, that, whenever we say of how many parts or divisions the magnitudes of arcs or straight lines consist, we mean, in the case of arcs, of such divisions as the circumference of the great circle has 360; and, in the case of straight lines, of such as the same circle's diameter has 120.

Since, then, in the construction of the great circles, the two arcs FH and BE have been drawn to the arcs AF and AE, intersecting at the point G, therefore

chord 2 arc AF : chord 2 arc AB comp.

chord 2 arc FH : chord 2 arc GH, chord 2 arc EG : chord 2 arc BE. [p. 28 Fn]

But

$$2 \text{ arc } AF = 180°,$$
$$\text{chord 2 arc } AF = 120^{\text{p}}.$$

---

centre is G. Let CE and AG meet at H, CF and DG at L, and EF and BG at K. Then the points H, L, and K lie in the same straight line since they all lie on the intersection of the same two planes: that of circle BAG, and that of triangle FEC.

Then

$$CH : EH \text{ comp. } CL : FL, FK : EK \qquad \text{[p. 26]}$$

But

$$CH : EH :: \text{chord 2 arc } AC : \text{chord 2 arc } AE,$$
$$CL : FL :: \text{chord 2 arc } CD : \text{chord 2 arc } DF,$$

and

$$FK : EK :: \text{chord 2 arc } BF : \text{chord 2 arc } BE. \qquad \text{[p. 27]}$$

Substituting in the first expression, we have shown what was required.

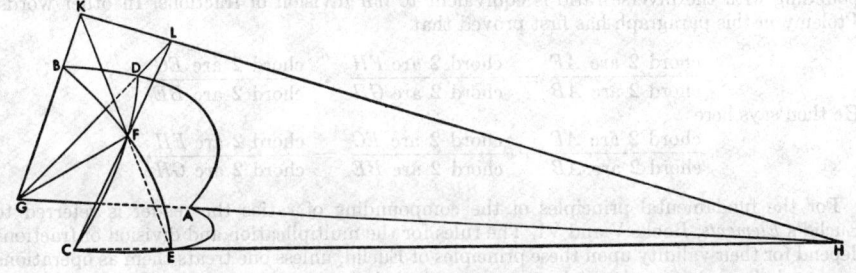

And according to the ratio of 83 parts to 11, agreed to by us [p. 26],

$$2 \text{ arc } AB = 47°42'40'',$$

and therefore

$$\text{chord } 2 \text{ arc } AB = 48^\text{p}31'55''.$$

And again

$$2 \text{ arc } EG = 60°,$$
$$\text{chord } 2 \text{ arc } EG = 60^\text{p};$$

and

$$2 \text{ arc } BE = 180°,$$
$$\text{chord } 2 \text{ arc } BE = 120^\text{p}.$$

Therefore

chord 2 arc FH : chord 2 arc GH comp. 120^p : $48^\text{p}31'55''$, 120^p : 60^p,[1]

or

$$\text{chord } 2 \text{ arc } FH : \text{chord } 2 \text{ arc } GH : : 120^\text{p} : 24^\text{p}15'57''.$$

And

$$2 \text{ arc } FH = 180°,$$
$$\text{chord } 2 \text{ arc } FH = 120^\text{p};$$

and therefore

$$\text{chord } 2 \text{ arc } GH = 24^\text{p}15'57''.$$

And so

$$2 \text{ arc } GH = 23°19'59'',$$
$$\text{arc } GH \doteqdot 11°40'.$$

And again let

$$\text{arc } EG = 60°,$$

so that, the others remaining the same,

$$2 \text{ arc } EG = 120°$$
$$\text{chord } 2 \text{ arc } EG = 103^\text{p}55'23''.$$

Then again

$$\text{chord } 2 \text{ arc } FH : \text{chord } 2 \text{ arc } GH : : 120^\text{p} : 42^\text{p}1'48''.$$

And

$$\text{chord } 2 \text{ arc } FH = 120^\text{p}$$

And so also

$$\text{chord } 2 \text{ arc } GH = 42^\text{p}1'48''.$$

And therefore

$$2 \text{ arc } GH = 41°0'18''$$
$$\text{arc } GH = 20°30'9''.$$

Which things were to be proved.

[1]Since the compounding of ratios is equivalent to our multiplication of fractions, compounding with the inverse ratio is equivalent to our division of fractions. In other words, Ptolemy in this paragraph has first proved that

$$\frac{\text{chord } 2 \text{ arc } AF}{\text{chord } 2 \text{ arc } AB} = \frac{\text{chord } 2 \text{ arc } FH}{\text{chord } 2 \text{ arc } GH} \cdot \frac{\text{chord } 2 \text{ arc } EG}{\text{chord } 2 \text{ arc } BE}$$

He then says here

$$\frac{\text{chord } 2 \text{ arc } AF}{\text{chord } 2 \text{ arc } AB} \div \frac{\text{chord } 2 \text{ arc } EG}{\text{chord } 2 \text{ arc } BE} = \frac{\text{chord } 2 \text{ arc } FH}{\text{chord } 2 \text{ arc } GH}.$$

For the fundamental principles of the compounding of ratios the reader is referred to Euclid's *Elements*, Books V and VI. The rules for the multiplication and division of fractions depend for their validity upon these principles of Euclid, unless one treats them as operations in a symbolic system, as in modern mathematical theory.

And now in the same way, by calculating the values for successive arcs, we shall lay out a table for the 90° of a quadrant, containing the values of arcs like those already proved. And here is the table:

15. TABLE OF OBLIQUITY .

Arcs of the Ecliptic	Arcs of the Meridian			Arcs of the Ecliptic	Arcs of the Meridian			Arcs of the Ecliptic	Arcs of the Meridian			Arcs of the Ecliptic	Arcs of the Meridian		
1	0	24	16	25	9	50	29	46	16	54	47	70	22	20	11
2	0	48	31	26	10	12	46	47	17	12	16	71	22	28	57
3	1	12	46	27	10	34	57	48	17	29	27	72	22	37	17
4	1	37	0	28	10	56	44	49	17	46	20	73	22	45	11
5	2	1	12	29	11	18	25	50	18	2	53	74	22	52	39
6	2	25	22	30	11	39	59	51	18	19	15	75	22	59	41
7	2	49	30	31	12	1	20	52	18	35	5	76	23	6	17
8	3	13	35	32	12	22	30	53	18	50	41	77	23	12	27
9	3	37	37	33	12	43	28	54	19	5	57	78	23	18	11
10	4	1	38	34	13	4	14	55	19	20	56	79	23	23	28
11	4	25	32	35	13	24	47	56	19	35	28	80	23	28	16
12	4	49	24	36	13	45	6	57	19	49	42	81	23	32	30
13	5	13	11	37	14	5	11	58	20	3	31	82	23	36	35
14	5	36	53	38	14	25	2	59	20	17	4	83	23	40	2
15	6	0	31	39	14	44	39	60	20	30	9	84	23	43	2
16	6	24	1	40	15	4	4	61	20	42	58	85	23	45	34
17	6	47	26	41	15	23	10	62	20	55	24	86	23	47	39
18	7	10	45	42	15	42	2	63	21	7	21	87	23	49	16
19	7	33	57	43	16	0	38	64	21	18	58	88	23	50	25
20	7	57	3	44	16	18	58	65	21	30	11	89	23	51	6
21	8	20	0	45	16	37	20	66	21	41	0	90	23	51	20
22	8	42	50					67	21	51	25				
23	9	5	32					68	22	1	25				
24	9	28	5					69	22	11	11				

16. ON ASCENSIONS IN THE RIGHT SPHERE

And next it would be proper to demonstrate all together the values of the arcs on the equator determined by circles drawn through the poles of the equator and given divisions of the ecliptic. For in this way we shall know corresponding to how many equatorial time-degrees the divisions of the ecliptic cross the meridian for any place and the horizon in the right sphere, because it is only in the right sphere that the horizon passes through the poles of the equator.

Then let the last figure be constructed again. And again given the arc EG of the ecliptic, first as 30°, let it be required to find the arc EH on the equator.

Then in the same way as before

chord 2 arc BF : chord 2 arc AB comp.

chord 2 arc FG : chord 2 arc GH,

chord 2 arc EH : chord 2 arc AE. [p. 28]

But

$$2 \text{ arc } BF = 132°17'20'',$$
$$\text{chord } 2 \text{ arc } BF = 109^{\text{p}}44'53''.$$

And

$$2 \text{ arc } AB = 47°42'40'',$$
$$\text{chord } 2 \text{ arc } AB = 48^{\text{p}}31'55''.$$

And again

$$2 \text{ arc } FG = 156°40'1'',$$
$$\text{chord } 2 \text{ arc } FG = 117^{\text{p}}31'15'';$$

and

$$2 \text{ arc } GH = 23°19'59'' \qquad\qquad \text{[table, §14]}$$
$$\text{chord } 2 \text{ arc } GH = 24^{\text{p}}15'57''.$$

Therefore

$$\text{chord } 2 \text{ arc } EH : \text{chord } 2 \text{ arc } AE \text{ comp.}$$
$$109^{\text{p}}44'53'' : 48^{\text{p}}31'55'', \ 24^{\text{p}}15'57'' : 117^{\text{p}}31'15'';$$

or

$$\text{chord } 2 \text{ arc } EH : \text{chord } 2 \text{ arc } AE :: 54^{\text{p}}52'26'' : 117^{\text{p}}31'15''$$

And

$$54^{\text{p}}52'26'' : 117^{\text{p}}31'15'' :: 56^{\text{p}}1'25'' : 120^{\text{p}}.$$

And

$$2 \text{ arc } AE = 180°,$$
$$\text{chord } 2 \text{ arc } AE = 120^{\text{p}}.$$

Therefore

$$\text{chord } 2 \text{ arc } EH = 56^{\text{p}}1'25'';$$

and so

$$2 \text{ arc } EH \doteqdot 55°40',$$
$$\text{arc } EH \doteqdot 27°50'.$$

Again let

$$\text{arc } EG = 60°.$$

And so, the others remaining the same,
$$2 \text{ arc } FG = 138°59'42''$$
$$\text{chord } 2 \text{ arc } FG = 112^{\text{p}}23'56'';$$

and

$$2 \text{ arc } GH = 41°0'16'',$$
$$\text{chord } 2 \text{ arc } GH = 42^{\text{p}}1'48''.$$

Therefore

$$\text{chord } 2 \text{ arc } EH : \text{chord } 2 \text{ arc } AE \text{ comp.}$$
$$109^{\text{p}}44'53'' : 48^{\text{p}}31'55'', \ 42^{\text{p}}1'48'' : 112^{\text{p}}23'56'';$$

or

$$\text{chord } 2 \text{ arc } EH : \text{chord } 2 \text{ arc } AE :: 95^{\text{p}}2'40'' : 112^{\text{p}}23'56''.$$

And

$$95^{\text{p}}2'40'' : 112^{\text{p}}23'56'' :: 101^{\text{p}}28'20'' : 120^{\text{p}}.$$

But

$$\text{chord } 2 \text{ arc } AE = 120^{\text{p}};$$

and so

$$\text{chord } 2 \text{ arc } EH = 101^{\text{p}}28'20''.$$

And therefore

$$2 \text{ arc } EH \doteqdot 115°28',$$
$$\text{arc } EH \doteqdot 57°44'.$$

It has been shown that the first 30° from the equinoctial point on the ecliptic corresponds to 27°50' in time on the equator; and the second 30° on the ecliptic to 29°54' on the equator, since they both together were proved to be 57°44'. And it is evident that the third 30° on the ecliptic will correspond in time to the remainder of the equator's quadrant, that is to 32°16', since the ecliptic's quadrant corresponds in time to the equator's quadrant, both being cut off by the same circles through the poles of the equator.

In the same way, following this same method, we calculated the arcs of the equator corresponding in time to each 10° of the ecliptic because arcs smaller than these have practically equal differences as they increase. We shall set them out also, in order to have at hand, as we said, the amount of time it takes each arc to cross the meridian for any place and the horizon in the right sphere. And we take as our starting place the point 10° from the equinox.

The first arc of 10° on the ecliptic takes 9°10' equatorial time; the second, 9°15'; the third, 9°25'; so that the first 30° on the ecliptic totals 27°50' equatorial time. The fourth arc takes 9°40'; the fifth, 9°58'; the sixth, 10°16'; so that the second 30° on the ecliptic totals 29°54' equatorial time. The seventh arc takes 10°34'; the eighth, 10°47'; the ninth, 10°55'; so that the third 30° on the ecliptic totals 32°16' equatorial time, and the whole quadrant 90°.

And from this it is evident that the order is the same for the other quadrants, everything being the same in each of them, because the sphere is given as right; that is, the equator is not oblique to the horizon.

BOOK TWO

1. On the General Position of the Inhabited World

Now that, in the first book of the Composition, we have gone through those things concerning the system of the universe which had first to be understood in summary form, and as many other things concerning the right sphere as would be considered useful to an understanding of questions treated here, we shall try in the following book to present again, in the handiest possible way, the more important of those things having to do with the oblique sphere.

And now this we must first understand in a general way that, if the earth is supposed cut into four equal parts by the equator and one circle through its poles, the extent of the part inhabited by us is very nearly enclosed in one or the other of the northern quadrants. And this would certainly be evident in the case of latitude—that is, of the passage from south to north—because everywhere the noon shadows of gnomons at the equinox fall to the north and never to the south. And also in the case of longitude—that is, of the passage from east to west—because the same eclipses, and especially the lunar ones, observed at the same time by those inhabiting the extreme eastern sections of that part of the earth inhabited by us and by those inhabiting the extreme western sections, neither precede nor lag behind by more than twelve equatorial hours. But the quarter part of the sphere in longitude embraces a twelve-hour interval since it is bounded by one of the semicircular arcs of the equator.

Of the particular things which must be understood for the business at hand, one should especially consider the arrangement, one by one, of the circles north of the equator and parallel to it, according to the particularities of the places situated under them. That is, how far the poles of the equator are from the horizon; or how far the zenith is from the equator along the meridian circle; and in what places the sun reaches the zenith, and when and how many times that happens; what are the ratios of the equinoctial and tropical shadows cast at noon to their gnomons; and what are the differences of the longest and shortest days with respect to the equinoxes; and as many other things as are observed relative to the increase and decrease of solar days, with the correspondances in the risings and settings of the equator and ecliptic, and with the properties and magnitudes of the angles formed by the principal great circles.

2. Given the Magnitude of the Longest Day, How the Arcs on the Horizon Intercepted by the Equator and the Ecliptic are Given

As a general example, let the circle drawn through Rhodes parallel to the equator be considered, where the height of the pole is 36° and the longest day is 14½ equatorial hours.[1] And let the circle $ABCD$ be the meridian; and BED the

---

[1] An equatorial hour is $\frac{1}{24}$ of the 360° of the equator or 15°. In other words an equatorial hour is $\frac{1}{24}$ of a stellar day, a stellar day being the time it takes a fixed star to pass from a meridian back again to that same meridan, that is one complete revolution of the equator. For the purposes of Book II, Ptolemy considers the sun such a fixed star, although it will be

34

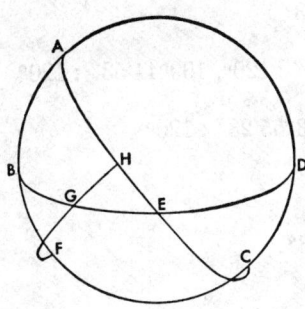

eastern semicircle of the horizon; and likewise *AEC* the semicircle of the equator, and *F* its southern pole. And let the ecliptic's winter-tropic point rise through *G*; and let *FGH* be drawn as the quadrant of the great circle through *F* and *G*.

And first let the magnitude of the longest day be given; and let it be required to find the arc *EG* of the horizon.

Now, since the turning of the sphere takes place around the poles of the equator, it is evident that the points *G* and *H* will be at the meridian *ABCD* at the same time. And the time from the rising of *G* to its culmination at the upper meridian is contained by arc *HA* of the equator, and from its crossing the lower meridian to its rising by arc *CH*. It follows that the length of time of the day is double that contained by arc *HA*, and the length of time of the night is double that contained by arc *CH*. For the sections above and below the earth of the circles parallel to the equator are exactly cut in half by the meridian.

Therefore, since the arc *EH* is half the difference between the shortest or longest day and the equinoctial day, it is 1¼ hours on the given parallel or 18°45′ in time, and the remainder of the quadrant, arc *HA*, is 71°15′ in time. Since then, in the same way as in the previous proofs, the arcs *EB* and *FH* of great circles cutting each other at *G* have been drawn to the two arcs *AE* and *AF* of great circles,

chord 2 arc *HA* : chord 2 arc *AE* comp. chord 2 arc *FH* : chord 2 arc *FG*,
chord 2 arc *BG* : chord 2 arc *EB*   [p. 28]

But

$$2 \text{ arc } HA = 142°30′,$$
$$\text{chord } 2 \text{ arc } HA = 113^{\text{p}}37′54″;$$

and

$$2 \text{ arc } AE = 180°,$$
$$\text{chord } 2 \text{ arc } AE = 120^{\text{p}};$$

and

$$2 \text{ arc } FH = 180°,$$
$$\text{chord } 2 \text{ arc } FH = 120^{\text{p}};$$

and

$$2 \text{ arc } FG^1 = 132°17′20″$$

[1]The arc *FG* is 66°8′40″, since the arc *GH* which marks the obliquity of the ecliptic is 23°51′20″.

pointed out in detail in Book III that this is not the case, just as it has already been stated in general in Book I. Therefore all the calculations relative to the sun in Book II are in error by the small amount such neglect entails.

In Book III, there is introduced the notion of a solar day, a solar day being the time it takes the sun to pass from a meridian back to that same meridian. The solar day, it will be seen, is very nearly 59′ [of arc] longer than the stellar day. Now in Book III an hour is defined as ½₄ of the solar day; and this hour is used interchangeably with the equatorial hour, although it is very nearly 2½′ longer than it. But the total error could never come to as much as 59′, which is less than 4 minutes in time; and Ptolemy declares that his instruments cannot be accurate within less than 15 minutes in time. Therefore this ambiguity will have no effect on the accuracy of the calculations.

The degrees on the equator are often referred to as "degrees in time" or "time-degrees" in referring to their time-measuring aspect.

$$\text{chord } 2 \text{ arc } FG = 109^{\text{p}}44'53''$$

Then

$$\text{chord } 2 \text{ arc } BG : \text{chord } 2 \text{ arc } EB \text{ comp. } 113^{\text{p}}37'54'' : 120^{\text{p}}, \; 109^{\text{p}}44'53'' : 120^{\text{p}}$$

or

$$\text{chord } 2 \text{ arc } BG : \text{chord } 2 \text{ arc } EB : : 103^{\text{p}}55'23'' : 120^{\text{p}}$$

And since it is a quadrant,

$$\text{chord } 2 \text{ arc } EB = 120^{\text{p}},$$

and therefore

$$\text{chord } 2 \text{ arc } BG = 103^{\text{p}}55'23''.$$

And so

$$2 \text{ arc } BG = 120°,$$
$$\text{arc } BG = 60°$$

And therefore as remainder

$$\text{arc } EG = 30°.$$

Which was to be shown.

3. How, with the Same Things Given, the Height of the Pole is Given, and Conversely

Now again, with this given, let it be required to find the height of the pole; that is, arc BF of the meridian. Then, in the same figure

$$\text{chord } 2 \text{ arc } EH : \text{chord } 2 \text{ arc } HA \text{ comp. chord } 2 \text{ arc } EG : \text{chord } 2 \text{ arc } BG,$$
$$\text{chord } 2 \text{ arc } BF : \text{chord } 2 \text{ arc } AF. \qquad \text{[p. 28]}$$

But

$$2 \text{ arc } EH = 37°30',$$
$$\text{chord } 2 \text{ arc } EH = 38^{\text{p}}34'22'';$$

and

$$2 \text{ arc } HA = 142°30',$$
$$\text{chord } 2 \text{ arc } HA = 113^{\text{p}}37'54'';$$

and again

$$2 \text{ arc } EG = 60°,$$
$$\text{chord } 2 \text{ arc } EG = 60^{\text{p}}.$$

Then

$$\text{chord } 2 \text{ arc } BF : \text{chord } 2 \text{ arc } AF \text{ comp. } 38^{\text{p}}34'22'' : 113^{\text{p}}37'54'',$$
$$103^{\text{p}}55'23'' : 60^{\text{p}}$$

or very nearly

$$\text{chord } 2 \text{ arc } BF : \text{chord } 2 \text{ arc } AF : : 70^{\text{p}}33' : 120^{\text{p}}.$$

And again

$$\text{chord } 2 \text{ arc } AF = 120^{\text{p}},$$

and therefore

$$\text{chord } 2 \text{ arc } BF = 70^{\text{p}}33'.$$

And so

$$2 \text{ arc } BF = 72°1',$$
$$\text{arc } BF = 36°.$$

Again, conversely, let arc BF, the height of the pole, be given by observation as 36°; and let it be required to find the difference between the longest or shortest day and the equinoctial day, that is twice arc EH. Then

$$\text{chord } 2 \text{ arc } BF : \text{chord } 2 \text{ arc } AB \text{ comp. chord } 2 \text{ arc } FG : \text{chord } 2 \text{ arc } GH,$$
$$\text{chord } 2 \text{ arc } EH : \text{chord } 2 \text{ arc } AE.$$

But

2 arc $BF = 72°$,

chord 2 arc $BF = 70^p32'3''$;

and

2 arc $AB = 108°$,

chord 2 arc $AB = 97^p4'56''$;

and again

2 arc $FG = 132°17'20''$

chord 2 arc $FG = 109^p44'53''$;

and

2 arc $GH = 47°42'40''$,

chord 2 arc $GH = 48^p31'55''$.

Then

chord 2 arc EH : chord 2 arc AE comp. $70^p32'3''$: $97^p4'56''$,

$48^p31'55''$: $109^p44'53''$,

or

chord 2 arc EH : chord 2 arc AE :: $31^p11'23''$: $97^p4'56''$.

And since, very nearly,

$31^p11'23''$: $97^p4'56''$ :: $38^p34'$: 120^p,

and

chord 2 arc $AE = 120^p$,

therefore it is inferred

chord 2 arc $EH = 38^p34'$.

And so

2 arc $EH = 37°30'$

or $2\frac{1}{2}$ equatorial hours. Which was to be shown.

Likewise the arc EG of the horizon will be given because the given ratio of the chord of 2 arc AF to the chord of 2 arc AB is compounded of the given ratio of the chord of 2 arc FH to the chord of 2 arc GH and the ratio of the chord of 2 arc EG to the chord of 2 arc BE. And so, since BE is given, the magnitude of arc EG is left.

It is evident that—even if we did not suppose the point G to be the winter tropic, but some point at one of the other divisions of the ecliptic—each of the arcs EH and EG would still be given in the same way. For we have set up, by means of the Table of Obliquity, the arcs on the meridian cut off by each division of the ecliptic and by the equator—that is, the arcs like GH.

From this it follows that the divisions of the ecliptic made by the same parallels—that is, those equidistant from the same tropic point—make sections on the horizon the same and on the same side of the equator, and the magnitudes of the days and nights equal to each other, like to like.

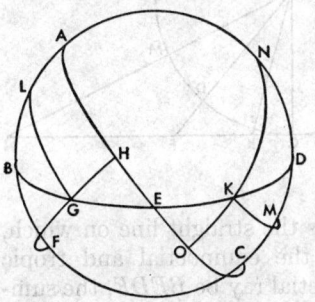

At the same time it is proved that the points produced by equal parallels—that is, those equidistant from the same equinoctial point—make equal arcs on the horizon from either side of the equator, and make the magnitudes of the days and nights equal contrariwise, unlike to unlike. For if, in the figure already set out, we take also the point *K* as the point where the circle equal and parallel to that through *G* cuts the semicircle of the horizon *BED*, and if we fill in the sections *GL* and *KM* of the parallels, which are clearly contrariwise and equal, and if we draw the quadrant *NKO* through *K* and the north pole, then the arcs *AH* and *OC* will be equal. For *GL* and *KM* are equal as like to like; and the remainder *EH* will be equal to the remainder *EO*. And the two sides of the similar three-sided figures *EGH* and *EKO* will be equal to each other, *EH* to *EO* and *GH* to *KO*, and each of the angles at *H* and *O* are right, so that base *EG* is equal to base *EK*.

4. How One is to Calculate at What Places, When, and How Many Times, the Sun Comes to the Zenith

Now it is easy, once given these things, to calculate when and how many times the sun comes to the zenith. For since it is at once evident that the sun does not come to the zenith at all in those places under parallels farther away from the equator than the approximate 23°51′20″ of the distance of the summer tropic point, and that it does so once, at the summer tropic itself, for those places under parallels at an equal distance from the equator, therefore it is also clear it comes to the zenith twice in those places at a distance less than that just given. And the setup of the Table of Obliquity makes the answer to the question, "When?" an easy one. For taking to the second column the number of degrees by which the parallel in question is distant from the equator—that is, in the case of those parallels within the summer tropic—we shall have, in the first column, the corresponding number of degrees of the quarter of the ecliptic. And at the distance from either equinoctial point given by this number of degrees, the sun comes to the zenith for the places under this parallel on the side of the summer tropic.

5. How, from Things Explained, the Ratios of the Gnomons to their Equinoctial and Tropic Shadows at Noon are Found

Now it will be made clear in the following manner that also the proposed ratios of the shadows to the gnomons are obtained more simply, if the arc between the tropics and the arc between the horizon and the poles are given.

For let the circle *ABCD* be the meridian around center *E*; and with *A* as zenith let the diameter *AEC* be drawn; and let *CKFN*, in the plane of the meridian, be perpendicular to it. *CKFN* is clearly parallel to the intersection of the meridian-plane and the horizon-plane. And since the earth as a whole is sensibly in the ratio of a point and centre to the solar sphere so that the centre *E* does not differ from the top of the gnomon, therefore

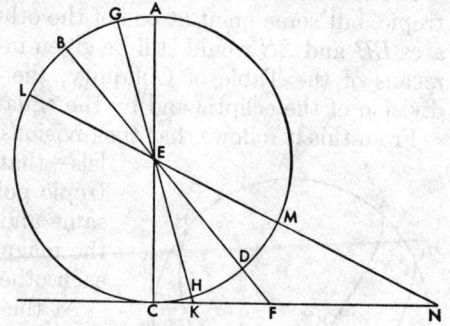

let *CE* be thought of as the gnomon, and *CKFN* as the straight line on which, at noon, the ends of the shadows fall. And let the equinoctial and tropic noontide rays be drawn through *E*. Let the equinoctial ray be *BEDF*, the summer tropic ray be *GEHK*, and the winter one *LEMN;* so that *CK* is the summer shadow, *CF* is the equinoctial shadow, and *CN* the winter shadow.

Therefore, since the arc *CD*, which is equal to the height of the pole above the horizon, is, in the given latitude, 36°, and the meridian *ABC* 360°, and each of the arcs *HD* and *DM* approximately 23°51′20″, it is evident that, as remainder,

$$\text{arc } CH = 12°8′40″,$$

and, by addition,

$$\text{arc } CM = 59°51′20″.$$

And so, of the angles subtending these arcs,

$$\text{angle } KEC = 12°8′40″,$$
$$\text{angle } FEC = 36°,$$
$$\text{angle } NEC = 59°51′20″.$$

And

$$\text{angle } KEC = 24°17′20″ \text{ to 2 rt.,}$$
$$\text{angle } FEC = 72° \text{ to 2 rt.,}$$
$$\text{angle } NEC = 119°42′40″ \text{ to 2 rt.}$$

And then, on the circles about the right triangles *KEC*, *FEC*, and *NEC*,

$$\text{arc } CK = 24°17′20″,$$
$$\text{arc } CE = 155°42′40″$$

as remainder of the semicircle; and

$$\text{arc } CF = 72°,$$
$$\text{arc } CE = 108°$$

likewise; and

$$\text{arc } CN = 119°42′40″,$$
$$\text{arc } CE = 60°17′20″$$

again as remainder of the semicircle. And so, of these chords,

$$\text{chord } CE = 117^{\text{p}}18′51″$$

where

$$\text{chord } CK = 25^{\text{p}}14′43″;$$

and

$$\text{chord } CE = 97^{\text{p}}4′56″$$

where

$$\text{chord } CF = 70^{\text{p}}32′4″;$$

and

$$\text{chord } CE = 60^{\text{p}}15′42″$$

where

$$\text{chord } CN = 103^{\text{p}}46′16″.$$

And therefore, where *CE* equals 60^{p}, *CK* the summer shadow equals 12^{p}55′, *CF* the equinoctial shadow 43^{p}36′, and *CN* the winter shadow very nearly 103^{p}20′.

It is therefore clear that, conversely, if any two ratios alone of these three of the gnomon *CE* to its shadows are given, then the height of the pole and the arc between the tropics are given, since, if any two of the angles at *E* are given, the other is also given. For the arcs *HD* and *DM* are equal. But for the sake of accuracy in observations, the height of the pole and the arc between the tropics should certainly be taken in the way we have already shown. For the ratios of these shadows to their gnomons do not always agree, because the time of the equinoctial shadows is somehow in itself undetermined, and the ends of the winter shadows are hard to distinguish.

6. Exposition of the Properties of Each Parallel

In this same way we shall consider the most important of the properties we have expounded for the other parallels also. And taking parallels at intervals of inclination of ¼ equatorial hour, which is sufficient, we shall make a general exposition of their incidents before making a detailed one.

i. We shall begin with the parallel under the equator which very nearly bounds the southern part of the whole quarter of the earth inhabited by us and which alone has all days and nights equal to each other. For only there are all the sphere's parallels to the equator cut in half by the horizon, so that all their sections above the earth are similar to each other and equal to the corresponding sections under the earth. And this is not the case with any of the inclinations of the sphere. Again, only the equator is everywhere cut in half by the horizon and makes the days along it sensibly equal to the nights, since it is also a great circle. But the others are divided unequally; and, in the latitudes inhabited by us, the parallels south of the equator have their sections above earth less than their sections below earth and their days shorter than their nights, but conversely the parallels north of the equator have their sections above earth greater and their days longer.

And this parallel is also amphiscian, since for those living under it the sun is twice at the zenith, at the intersections of the equator and the ecliptic, so that at those times only are the gnomons shadowless at noon. And when the sun passes through the northern hemisphere the gnomons' shadows fall to the south, and when it passes through the southern, to the north. Thereupon, the summer and winter shadows are very nearly 26½ to the gnomon's 60.

We say "the shadows at noon," speaking generally and as making no appreciable difference, because the equinoxes and tropics are by no means usually completed exactly at noon.

And all those stars which revolve along the equator pass through the zenith for those under this parallel. And they are all seen to rise and set, since the poles of the sphere are on the horizon, none of the parallels makes a circle which is always visible or invisible, and no meridians are cut short. People say they believe there are human habitations under the equator; for, according to them, it is very temperate because the sun does not tarry about the zenith, such is the speed of its passage through the divisions of the equator; and, therefore, the summer heat would be temperate. Nor is the sun in the tropics very far from the zenith, so that the winter would not be severe. But we could not say with any conviction what sort of habitations they are; for up until now they have remained inaccessible to people from the part of the earth inhabited by us, and what is said about them should be considered conjecture rather than true information. Therefore, briefly, the properties of the parallel under the equator would be such as we have given.

Concerning the other parallels, between which some think the inhabited portions of the earth are contained, we shall present them in what is common in order not to repeat ourselves in each instance. Thus, for each of the parallels that follow, those stars which are distant from the equator by an arc on the circle through its poles equal to the distance of the given parallel from it, all such stars will pass through the zenith. The always-visible circle is that drawn with the north pole as a pole at the angular distance of the height of the pole, and the stars contained by it are always visible. And the always-invisible circle is that drawn with the south pole as pole at the same distance, and the stars within it are always invisible.

ii. The second parallel is that whose longest day is $12\frac{1}{4}$ equatorial hours. And it is $4\frac{1}{4}°$ from the equator, and is drawn through the island of Taprobane [Ceylon]. And it is one of the amphiscian parallels, since the sun is twice at the zenith for those living under it and twice makes the gnomons shadowless at noon when it is $79\frac{1}{2}°$ from the summer tropic on either side. And so for $159°$ of its passage the shadows of the gnomons fall to the south, and for the other $201°$ to the north. Thereupon the equinoctial shadow is $4+\frac{1}{3}+\frac{1}{12}$, the summer shadow $21\frac{1}{3}$, and the winter 32, to the gnomon's 60.

iii. The third parallel is that whose longest day is $12\frac{1}{2}$ equatorial hours. And it is $8°25'$ from the equator and it is drawn through the Aualitic Gulf [Gulf of Aden]. And it is amphiscian since the sun is twice at the zenith for those living under it, and twice makes the gnomons shadowless at noon, when it is $69°$ from the summer tropic on either side. And so for $138°$ of its passage the shadows of the gnomons fall to the south, and for the other $222°$ to the north. There the equinoctial shadow is $8+\frac{1}{2}+\frac{1}{3}$, the summer shadow $16+\frac{1}{2}+\frac{1}{3}$, and the winter $37+\frac{1}{2}+\frac{1}{3}+\frac{1}{15}$, to the gnomon's 60.

iv. The fourth parallel is that whose longest day is $12\frac{3}{4}$ equatorial hours. And it is $12\frac{1}{2}°$ from the equator and is drawn through the Adulitic Gulf [Annesley Bay]. And it is amphiscian, since the sun is twice at the zenith for those living under it and twice makes the gnomons shadowless at noon, when it is $57\frac{2}{3}°$ from the summer tropic on either side. And so for $115\frac{1}{3}°$ of its passage the shadows of the gnomons fall to the south, and for the other $244\frac{2}{3}°$ to the north. Thereupon the equinoctial shadow is $13\frac{1}{3}$, the summer shadow 12, and the winter $44\frac{1}{6}$, to the gnomon's 60.

v. The fifth parallel is that whose longest day is 13 equatorial hours. And it is $16°27'$ from the equator and is drawn through the island of Meroë. And it is also amphiscian since the sun is twice at the zenith for those who live under it and twice makes the gnomons shadowless at noon, when it is $45°$ from the summer tropic on either side. And so for $90°$ of its passage the shadows of the gnomons fall to the south, and for the other $270°$ to the north. Thereupon the equinoctial shadow is $17+\frac{1}{2}+\frac{1}{4}$, the summer shadow $7+\frac{1}{2}+\frac{1}{4}$, and the winter 51, to the gnomon's 60.

vi. The sixth parallel is that whose longest day is $13\frac{1}{4}$ equatorial hours. And it is $20°14'$ from the equator and is drawn through the country of the Napatians. And it is also amphiscian since the sun is twice at the zenith for those living under it and twice makes the gnomons shadowless at noon, when it is $31°$ from the summer tropic on either side. And so for $62°$ of its passage the shadows of the gnomons fall to the south, and for the other $298°$ to the north. Thereupon the equinoctial shadow is $22\frac{1}{6}$, the summer shadow $3+\frac{1}{2}+\frac{1}{4}$, and the winter $58\frac{1}{6}$, to the gnomon's 60.

vii. The seventh parallel is that whose longest day is $13\frac{1}{2}$ equatorial hours. And it is $23°51'$ from the equator and is drawn through Soëne [Aswan]. And it is the first parallel of those called heteroscian, because for those living under it the shadows of the gnomons never fall to the south; but the sun is at the zenith at the summer tropic only, and only then are the gnomons observed to be shadowless. For their distance from the equator is that of the summer tropic point. And the rest of the time the shadows of the gnomons fall to the north. Thereupon the equinoctial shadow is 26½, the winter shadow 65+¼+⅓, to the gnomon's 60, and the summer shadowless. And all the parallels to the north of this one, as far as the one bounding our inhabited world, are heteroscian. For the gnomons at these parallels are never shadowless at noon and they never throw their shadows to the south but always to the north, because the sun is never at the zenith for these people.

viii. The eighth parallel is that whose longest day is 13¾ equatorial hours. And it is 27°12′ from the equator and is drawn through Ptolemais in the Thebais, also called Hermeias. Thereupon the summer shadow is 3½, the equinoctial shadow 36+½+⅓, and the winter 74⅙, to the gnomon's 60.

ix. The ninth parallel is that whose longest day is 14 equatorial hours. And it is 30°22′ from the equator and is drawn through the low countries of Egypt. Thereupon the summer shadow is 6+½+⅓, the equinoctial shadow 35$\frac{1}{12}$, and the winter 83$\frac{1}{12}$, to the gnomon's 60.

x. The tenth parallel is that whose longest day is 14¼ equatorial hours. And it is 33°18′ from the equator and is drawn through the middle of Phoenicia. Thereupon the summer shadow is 10, the equinoctial shadow 39½, and the winter 93$\frac{1}{12}$, to the gnomon's 60.

xi. The eleventh parallel is that whose longest day is 14½ equatorial hours. And it is 36° from the equator and is drawn through Rhodes. Thereupon the summer shadow is 12+½+⅓+$\frac{1}{12}$, the equinoctial shadow 43+½+⅓, and the winter 103⅓.

xii. The twelfth parallel is that whose longest day is 14¾ equatorial hours. And it is 38°35′ from the equator and is drawn through Smyrna. Thereupon the summer shadow is 15⅔, the equinoctial shadow 47+½+⅓, and the winter 114+½+⅓+$\frac{1}{12}$, to the gnomon's 60.

xiii. The thirteenth parallel is that whose longest day is 15 equatorial hours. And it is 40°56′ from the equator and is drawn through the Hellespont. Thereupon the summer shadow is 18½, the equinoctial shadow 52⅙, and the winter 127+½+⅓, to the gnomon's 60.

xiv. The fourteenth parallel is that whose longest day is 15¼ equatorial hours. And it is 43°4′ from the equator and is drawn through Marseilles. Thereupon the summer shadow is 20+½+⅓, the equinoctial shadow 55+½+⅓+$\frac{1}{12}$, and the winter 144, to the gnomon's 60.

xv. The fifteenth parallel is that whose longest day is 15½ equatorial hours. And it is 45°1′ from the equator and is drawn through the middle of Pontus. Thereupon the summer shadow is 23¼, the equinoctial shadow 60, and the winter 155$\frac{1}{12}$, to the gnomon's 60.

xvi. The sixteenth parallel is that whose longest day is 15¾ equatorial hours. And it is 46°51′ from the equator and is drawn through the source of the river Ister [Danube]. Thereupon the summer shadow is 25½, the equinoctial shadow 63+½+⅓+$\frac{1}{12}$, and the winter 171⅙, to the gnomon's 60.

xvii. The seventeenth parallel is that whose longest day is 16 equatorial hours. And it is 48°32′ from the equator and is drawn through the mouth of the Borysthenes [Dnieper]. Thereupon the summer shadow is 27½, the equinoctial shadow 67+½+⅓, and the winter 188+½+$\frac{1}{12}$.

xviii. The eighteenth parallel is that whose longest day is 16¼ equatorial hours. And it is 50°4′ from the equator and is drawn through the middle of

Palus Maeotis [the Sea of Azof]. Thereupon the summer shadow is $29+\frac{1}{2}+\frac{1}{3}$ $+\frac{1}{12}$, the equinoctial shadow $71\frac{2}{3}$, and the winter $208\frac{1}{3}$, to the gnomon's 60.

xix. The nineteenth parallel is that whose longest day is $16\frac{1}{2}$ equatorial hours. And it is $51°40'$ from the equator and is drawn through the southernmost parts of Britain. Thereupon the summer shadow is $31+\frac{1}{3}+\frac{1}{12}$, the equinoctial shadow $75+\frac{1}{3}+\frac{1}{12}$, and the winter $229\frac{1}{3}$, to the gnomon's 60.

xx. The twentieth parallel is that whose longest day is $16\frac{3}{4}$ equatorial hours. And it is $52°50'$ from the equator and is drawn through the mouth of the Rhine. Thereupon the summer shadow is $33\frac{1}{3}$, the equinoctial shadow $79\frac{1}{12}$, and the winter $253\frac{1}{6}$, to the gnomon's 60.

xxi. The twenty-first parallel is that whose longest day is 17 equatorial hours. And it is $54°30'$ from the equator and is drawn through the mouth of the Tanais [Don]. Thereupon the summer shadow is $34+\frac{1}{2}+\frac{1}{3}+\frac{1}{12}$, the equinoctial shadow $82+\frac{1}{2}+\frac{1}{12}$, and the winter $278+\frac{1}{2}+\frac{1}{4}$, to the gnomon's 60.

xxii. The twenty-second parallel is that whose longest day is $17\frac{1}{4}$ equatorial hours. And it is $55°$ from the equator and is drawn through Brigantium [York] of Great Britain. Thereupon the summer shadow is $36\frac{1}{4}$, the equinoctial shadow $85\frac{2}{3}$, and the winter $304\frac{1}{2}$.

xxiii. The twenty-third parallel is that whose longest day is $17\frac{1}{2}$ equatorial hours. And it is $56°$ from the equator and is drawn through the middle of Great Britain. Thereupon the summer shadow is $37\frac{2}{3}$, the equinoctial $88+\frac{1}{2}+\frac{1}{3}$, and the winter $335\frac{1}{4}$, to the gnomon's 60.

xxiv. The twenty-fourth parallel is that whose longest day is $17\frac{3}{4}$ equatorial hours. And it is $57°$ from the equator and is drawn through Caturactonium of Britain. Thereupon the summer shadow is $39\frac{1}{3}$, the equinoctial shadow $92+\frac{1}{3}+\frac{1}{12}$, and the winter $372\frac{1}{12}$, to the gnomon's 60.

xxv. The twenty-fifth parallel is that whose longest day is 18 equatorial hours. And it is $58°$ from the equator and is drawn through the southern parts of Little Britain. Thereupon the summer shadow is $40\frac{2}{3}$, the equinoctial shadow 96, and the winter $419\frac{1}{12}$, to the gnomon's 60.

xxvi. The twenty-sixth parallel is that whose longest day is $18\frac{1}{2}$ equatorial hours. And it is $59\frac{1}{2}°$ from the equator and is drawn through the middle of Little Britain.

We have not here used an increase of a quarter hour, because the parallels are now very close and the difference between the heights of the pole does not come to a full degree, and because it does not seem called for to finish out completely, in like fashion, the still more northern parallels. And for this reason we have thought it superfluous also to set out the ratios of the shadows to the gnomons as in the case of those places already defined.

xxvii. And further where the longest day is 19 equatorial hours, there the parallel is $61°$ from the equator and is drawn through the northern parts of Little Britain.

xxviii. And where the longest day is $19\frac{1}{2}$ equatorial hours, there the parallel is $62°$ from the equator and is drawn through what are called the Ebrides Islands [Hebrides].

xxix. And where the longest day is 20 equatorial hours, there the parallel is $63°$ from the equator and is drawn through the Island of Thule.

xxx. And where the longest day is 21 equatorial hours, there the parallel is $64\frac{1}{2}°$ from the equator and is drawn through unknown Scythian nations.

xxxi. And where the longest day is 22 equatorial hours, there the parallel is 65½° from the equator.

xxxii. And where the longest day is 23 equatorial hours, there the parallel is 66° from the equator.

xxxiii. And where the longest day is 24 equatorial hours, there the parallel is 66°8′40″ from the equator. And this is the first of the periscian parallels. For since the sun at the summer tropic does not set for that parallel, the shadows of the gnomons fall to every side of the horizon. And the parallel through the summer tropic is there always visible, and through the winter tropic always invisible, because they both touch the horizon from different directions. And the ecliptic coincides with the horizon whenever the point of the spring equinox is just rising from it.

xxxiv. And if anyone for the sake of knowledge generally should want some of the broader incidents of the still more northern latitudes, he would find, where the height of the north pole is very nearly 67°, there 15° along the ecliptic on either side of the summer tropic do not set; so that the longest day and the turning of the shadows to all parts of the horizon last for nearly a month. For these things can be easily understood from the Table of Obliquity, already given. For by as many degrees as we find the parallel distant from the equator—as for instance that parallel which cuts off 15° of the ecliptic on either side of the summer tropic and which is then either always invisible or always visible along the intercepted section of the ecliptic—by just so many degrees does the height of the north pole lack being a quadrant or 90°.

xxxv. And then where the height of the pole is 69½°, there it would be found that 30° on either side of the summer tropic do not set; so that the longest day and the periscian gnomons last nearly two months.

xxxvi. And where the height of the pole is 73⅓°, there it would be found that 45° on either side of the summer tropic do not set; so that the longest day and the periscian gnomons last nearly three months.

xxxvii. And where the height of the pole is 78⅓°, there it would be found that 60° on either side of the summer tropic do not set; so that the longest day and the wheeling of the shadows are accomplished in nearly 4 months.

xxxviii. And where the height of the pole is 84°, there it would be found that 75° on either side of the summer tropic do not set; so that again the longest day would last for nearly 5 months and the periscian gnomons the same length of time.

xxxix. And where the north pole is raised from the horizon the 90° of the whole quadrant, there the whole semicircle of the ecliptic north of the equator is never below the earth, and the whole southern semicircle is never above the earth; so that there is one day and one night in each year, each nearly six months long, and the gnomons are always periscian. And the properties of this latitude are that the north pole is always at the zenith, the equator occupies the position of the always visible and at the same time invisible circle and also of the horizon, putting the whole hemisphere north of itself above the earth and that south of it below the earth.

7. ON THE CO-ASCENSIONS OF THE ECLIPTIC AND THE EQUATOR IN THE OBLIQUE SPHERE

Now that the general matters observed concerning the latitudes have been explained, the next thing would be to show how the co-ascending time-arcs of the equator and the ecliptic can be gotten for each latitude. And from these all the other particularities will be deduced. We shall use the names of the zodiacal signs for the dodecatemories of the ecliptic as if they began from the equinoctial and tropic points, calling the first dodecatemory from the spring equinox in the direction opposite the movement of the universe the Ram, the second the Bull, and so on according to the order of the twelve signs handed down to us.

And first we shall show that arcs on the ecliptic equidistant from the same equinoctial point always ascend with equal arcs on the equator.

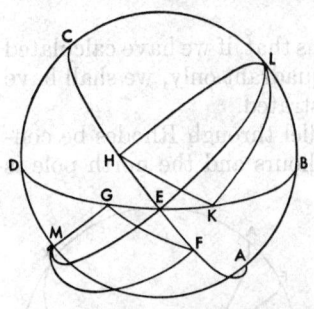

For let the circle *ABCD* be the meridian, and *BED* the semicircle of the horizon, and *AEC* the semicircle of the equator. And let *FG* and *HK* be two sections of the ecliptic, so that each of the points *F* and *H* is assumed to be the point of the spring equinox, and so that the ends of the equal arcs *FG* and *HK*, taken on either side of it, ascend through the points *K* and *G*.

I say that the arcs of the equator ascending with either of them, that is *EF* and *EH*, are equal.

For let the points *L* and *M* be taken as the poles of the equator, and let the sections of great circles, *LEM*, *HL*, *KL*, *FM*, and *GM* be drawn through them. Then since

$$\text{arc } FG = \text{arc } HK,$$

and the parallels through *K* and *G* are equidistant from the equator on either side so that

$$\text{arc } LK = \text{arc } MG$$

and

$$\text{arc } EK = \text{arc } EG, \qquad\qquad\qquad \text{[p. 37, 38]}$$

therefore *LKH* and *MGF* have their sides equal respectively, and so also do *LEK* and *MEG*. Therefore

$$\text{angle } KLE = \text{angle } GME,$$
$$\text{angle } KLH = \text{angle } GMF,$$

so that, by subtraction,

$$\text{angle } ELH = \text{angle } EMF.$$

And therefore

$$\text{base } EH = \text{base } EF.$$

Which was to be proved.

And again we shall prove that the arcs on the equator, ascending with equal arcs of the ecliptic equidistant from the same tropic point, are both together equal to the sum of the corresponding two in the right sphere.

For let the meridian *ABCD* be set out, and the semicircle of the horizon *BED*, and the semicircle of the equator *AEC*. And let two equal arcs on the ecliptic equidistant from the winter tropic point be drawn, the arc *FG* with *F* as the autumn

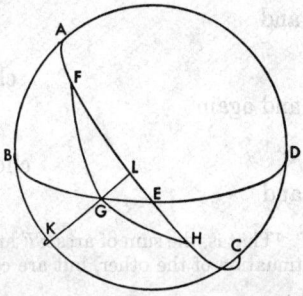

equinox and the arc GH with H as the spring equinox, so that the point G is the rising point of both on the horizon (because the arcs FG and GH are cut off by the same circle parallel to the equator), and so that clearly arcs EH and GH co-ascend and also EF and FG.

It is immediately evident, then, that the whole arc HEF[1] is equal to the ascensions in the right sphere of the arcs FG and GH. For if we suppose the south pole of the equator to be the point K, and draw through K and the point G the quadrant of a great circle KGL which represents the horizon in the right sphere, then arc HL ascends with arc GH in the right sphere, and likewise arc LF with arc GF. And so the two together, arcs HL and LF, are equal to the other two together, arcs HE and EF, and are contained by the same arc HF. Which was to be proved.

And for these reasons it has now become clear to us that, if we have calculated the particular co-ascensions in each latitude for a quadrant only, we shall have those of the other three quadrants already demonstrated.

Then with these things established, let the parallel through Rhodes be considered, where the longest day is 14½ equatorial hours and the north pole is raised 36° above the horizon. And let the circle $ABCD$ be the meridian; and likewise BED the semicircle of the horizon, AEC the semicircle of the equator, and FGH the semicircle of the ecliptic, so that G is assumed to be the spring equinox. And with the north pole at the point K, let the quadrant of a great circle, arc KLM, be drawn through it and L, the intersection of the ecliptic and the horizon.

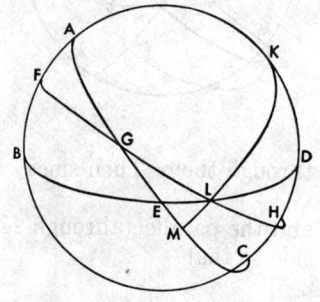

And given the arc GL, let it be required to find the arc on the equator ascending with it, that is GE. And let GL first embrace the dodecatemory corresponding to the Ram.

Now, since again in this construction the arcs DE and KM of great circles, cutting each other at L, have been drawn to the two arcs CE and CK of great circles, therefore

chord 2 arc DK : chord 2 arc CD comp. chord 2 arc KL : chord 2 arc LM,
    chord 2 arc EM : chord 2 arc CE.

But
$$2 \text{ arc } DK = 72°,$$
$$\text{chord 2 arc } DK = 70^{\text{p}}32'4'';$$

and
$$2 \text{ arc } CD = 108°,$$
$$\text{chord 2 arc } CD = 97^{\text{p}}4'56'';$$

and again
$$2 \text{ arc } KL = 156°41',$$
$$\text{chord 2 arc } KL = 117^{\text{p}}31'15'';$$

and

---

[1]That is, the sum of arcs EF and EH; for they are not, of course, naturally the one the continuation of the other, but are considered so for the purposes of proof.

$$2 \text{ arc } LM^1 = 23°19'59'',$$
$$\text{chord } 2 \text{ arc } LM = 24^p15'57''.$$

Then

$$\text{chord } 2 \text{ arc } EM : \text{chord } 2 \text{ arc } CE \text{ comp. } 70^p32'4'' : 97^p4'56'',$$
$$24^p15'57'' : 117^p31'15'',$$

or

$$\text{chord } 2 \text{ arc } EM : \text{chord } 2 \text{ arc } CE : : 18^p0'5'' : 120^p.$$

And

$$\text{chord } 2 \text{ arc } CE = 120^p,$$

therefore

$$\text{chord } 2 \text{ arc } EM = 18^p0'5''.$$

And so

$$2 \text{ arc } EM \coloneqq 17°16',$$
$$\text{arc } EM = 8°38'$$

But since the whole arc GM ascends with arc GL in the right sphere, therefore [p. 32]

$$\text{arc } GM = 27°50',$$

and therefore, by subtraction,

$$\text{arc } EG = 19°12'.$$

And it is proved therewith that the dodecatemory which is the Fishes ascends in the same time, $19°12'$; and that of the Virgin and that of the Balance is, each, what is left when this is subtracted from double the ascension in the right sphere [twice arc GM], that is $36°28'$ in time [p. 45].[2] Which was to be proved.

Again, let the arc GL embrace the $60°$ of the two dodecatemories of the ecliptic, the signs of the Ram and the Bull. Then, because of this assumption, the other things remaining the same,

$$2 \text{ arc } KL = 138°59'42'',$$
$$\text{chord } 2 \text{ arc } KL = 112^p23'56'';$$

and

$$2 \text{ arc } LM = 41°0'18'',$$
$$\text{chord arc } LM = 42^p1'48''.$$

Then again

$$\text{chord } 2 \text{ arc } EM : \text{chord } 2 \text{ arc } CE \text{ comp. } 70^p32'4'' : 97^p4'56'',$$
$$42^p1'48'' : 112^p23'56'',$$

or

$$\text{chord } 2 \text{ arc } EM : \text{chord } 2 \text{ arc } CE : : 32^p36'4'' : 120^p.$$

And

$$\text{chord } 2 \text{ arc } CE = 120^p,$$

therefore

$$\text{chord } 2 \text{ arc } EM = 32^p36'4''.$$

And so

$$2 \text{ arc } EM \coloneqq 31°32',$$

[1]GL is given as $30°$; hence LM is given in the Table of Obliquity, and KL is the difference between LM and $90°$.

[2]In other words, the ascensions on either side of the autumn equinox are gotten by doubling arc GM and subtracting arc EG. For the arc EG and the arc to be found are arcs on the equator ascending with equal arcs on the ecliptic equidistant from the winter tropic, and are therefore both together equal to the two equatorial arcs ascending in the right sphere—that is, twice arc GM.

arc $EM = 15°46'$.

But, for the same reasons [p. 32], it has already been proved

arc $GM = 57°44'$;

and therefore, by subtraction,

arc $EG = 41°58'$.

Therefore the Ram and the Bull together ascend in 41°58' in time, with 19°12' of which the Ram has just been proved to ascend. And therefore the dodecatemory which is the Bull ascends with 22°46' in time.

And again, for the same reasons as before, the dodecatemory which is the Water Bearer will ascend with an equal 22°46' in time; and the Lion and the Scorpion, each, with what is left when this is subtracted from double the ascension in the right sphere; that is, 37°2' in time.

And since the longest day is 14½ equatorial hours and the shortest day 9½ hours, it is evident that the semicircle from the Crab (Cancer) to the Archer will ascend with 217°30' in equatorial time, and the semicircle from the Goat (Capricorn) to the Twins with 142°30'. And so each of the quadrants on either side of the spring equinox will ascend with 71°15' in time, and each of the quadrants on either side of the autumn equinox with 108°45' in time. And therefore there remain the dodecatemories, the Twins and Goat (Capricorn), each of which will ascend with the 29°17' in time left over from the 71°15' in time of the quadrant; and there remain the dodecatemories, the Crab (Cancer) and the Archer, each of which will ascend with the 35°15' in time left over from the 108°45' in time of the quadrant.

It is clear that in this same way we could also get the coascensions of the ecliptic for smaller divisions.

But we could also calculate them in an easier and more systematic way, thus:

For first let the circle $ABCD$ be the meridian, BED the semicircle of the horizon, AEC that of the equator, and FEG that of the ecliptic, assuming the intersection E to be the spring equinox. And let the arc EH on the ecliptic be taken at random, and let the section HK of the parallel to the equator through H be drawn. And taking L as the pole of the equator, let there be drawn through it the quadrants of great circles LHM, LKN, and LE.

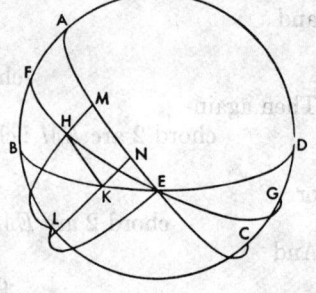

It is thus immediately evident that the section EH of the ecliptic ascends with arc EM of the equator in the right sphere, but in the oblique sphere with the arc equal to MN, since the parallel's arc HK, with which section EH ascends, is similar to arc MN of the equator and the similar arcs of parallels have everywhere their ascensions in equal times. Therefore the ascension of section EH in the oblique sphere is less than that in the right sphere by arc EN. And it has also now been proved in general that, if certain arcs of great circles like LKN are thus drawn, the section EN will contain the difference between the ascensions in the right and oblique spheres of arcs on the ecliptic cut off by E and the parallel drawn through K. Which was to be proved.

Now, with this first considered, let the figure be laid out with only the meridian and the semicircles of the horizon and the equator. And through F, the south

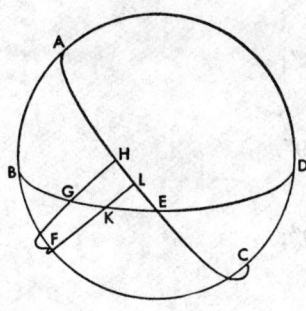

pole of the equator, let the quadrants of two great circles be drawn, *FGH* and *FKL*. And let *G* be assumed to be the intersection of the horizon and the parallel drawn through the winter tropic; and *K* the intersection of the horizon and the parallel drawn through the beginning of the Fishes, for example, or any other of the divisions of the given quadrant.

Now again the arcs of great circles, *FKL* and *EKG*, intersecting at *K*, have been drawn to the arcs of great circles *FH* and *EH*. And

chord 2 arc *GH* : chord 2 arc *FG* comp.

chord 2 arc *EH* : chord 2 arc *EL*,

chord 2 arc *KL* : chord 2 arc *FK*.

But 2 arc *GH* is given the same in all latitudes, for it is the distance between the tropics. And for this reason the remainder, 2 arc *FG*, is also given. And likewise, for the same sections of the ecliptic, 2 arc *KL* is the same for all latitudes and is given by the Table of Obliquity; and for this same reason 2 arc *FK* is given. And so the ratio

chord 2 arc *EH* : chord 2 arc *EL*

is left also as the same in all latitudes for the same divisions of the quadrant.

If, then, these things being true, we take the increasing values of arc *KL* for each increase of 10° on the quadrant from the spring equinox to the winter tropic (for a division into arcs of this length will be sufficient for our use), we always have

2 arc *GH* = 47°42′40″,
chord 2 arc *GH* = 48ᴾ31′55″,

and

2 arc *FG* = 132°17′20″
chord 2 arc *FG* = 109ᴾ44′53″.

And when *K* is 10° from the spring equinox in the direction of the winter tropic, we likewise also have

2 arc *KL* = 8°3′16″,
chord 2 arc *KL* = 8ᴾ25′39″;

and

2 arc *FK* = 171°56′44″,
chord 2 arc *FK* = 119ᴾ42′14″.

And likewise, when it is 20° away, we have

2 arc *KL* = 15°54′6″,
chord 2 arc *KL* = 16ᴾ35′56″;

and

2 arc *FK* = 164°5′54″,
chord 2 arc *FK* = 118ᴾ50′47″.

And when it is 30° away, we have

2 arc *KL* = 23°19′58″,
chord 2 arc *KL* = 24ᴾ15′56″;

and

2 arc *FK* = 156°40′2″,
chord 2 arc *FK* = 117ᴾ31′15″.

And when it is 40° away, we have
$$2 \text{ arc } KL = 30°8'8'',$$
$$\text{chord } 2 \text{ arc } KL = 31^\text{p}11'43'';$$
and
$$2 \text{ arc } FK = 149°51'52'',$$
$$\text{chord } 2 \text{ arc } FK = 115^\text{p}52'19''.$$
And when it is 50° away, we have
$$2 \text{ arc } KL = 36°5'46'',$$
$$\text{chord } 2 \text{ arc } KL = 37^\text{p}10'39'';$$
and
$$2 \text{ arc } FK = 143°54'14'',$$
$$\text{chord } 2 \text{ arc } FK = 114^\text{p}5'44''.$$
And when it is 60° away, we have
$$2 \text{ arc } KL = 41°0'18'',$$
$$\text{chord } 2 \text{ arc } KL = 42^\text{p}1'48''$$
and
$$2 \text{ arc } FK = 138°59'42'',$$
$$\text{chord } 2 \text{ arc } FK = 112^\text{p}23'57''.$$
And when it is 70° away, we have
$$2 \text{ arc } KL = 44°40'22''$$
$$\text{chord } 2 \text{ arc } KL = 45^\text{p}36'18'';$$
and
$$2 \text{ arc } FK = 135°19'38'',$$
$$\text{chord } 2 \text{ arc } FK = 110^\text{p}59'47''.$$
And when it is 80° away, we have
$$2 \text{ arc } KL = 46°56'32'',$$
$$\text{chord } 2 \text{ arc } KL = 47^\text{p}47'40'';$$
and
$$2 \text{ arc } FK = 133°3'28'',$$
$$\text{chord } 2 \text{ arc } FK = 110^\text{p}4'16''.$$
And therefore, if we compound the ratio
$$\text{chord } 2 \text{ arc } GH : \text{chord } 2 \text{ arc } FG$$
or
$$48^\text{p}31'55'' : 109^\text{p}44'53''$$
with the inverse of
$$\text{chord } 2 \text{ arc } KL : \text{chord } 2 \text{ arc } FK$$
for each 10° as just laid out, the result is the ratio
$$\text{chord } 2 \text{ arc } EH : \text{chord } 2 \text{ arc } EL.$$
And this is the same for all latitudes:—as 60ᵖ to 9ᵖ33', when K is 10° from the equinox; to 18ᵖ57', when 20° away; to 28ᵖ1', when 30° away; to 36ᵖ33', when 40° away; to 44ᵖ12', when 50° away; to 50ᵖ44', when 60° away; to 55ᵖ45', when 70° away; to 58ᵖ55', when 80° away.

Therefore it is evident that, being given 2 arc EH for each latitude since it is equal to the difference between the equinoctial day and the shortest day in time, and being given its chord and the ratio of this chord to that of 2 arc EL, we also have given 2 arc EL. And if we subtract the half of it—that is, arc EL itself containing the difference we have spoken of before [p. 48]—from the ascensions in the right sphere of the given arc of the ecliptic, we shall find the ascension of the same arc in the given latitude.

For let the latitude of the parallel of Rhodes be taken for an example, where

$$2 \text{ arc } EH = 37°30,$$
$$\text{chord } 2 \text{ arc } EH = 38^{\text{p}}34'.$$

Then since

$$60^{\text{p}} : 38^{\text{p}}34' : : 9^{\text{p}}33' : 6^{\text{p}}8'$$
$$: : 18^{\text{p}}57' : 12^{\text{p}}11'$$
$$: : 28^{\text{p}}1' : 18^{\text{p}}$$
$$: : 36^{\text{p}}33' : 23^{\text{p}}29'$$
$$: : 44^{\text{p}}12' : 28^{\text{p}}25'$$
$$: : 50^{\text{p}}44' : 32^{\text{p}}37'$$
$$: : 55^{\text{p}}45' : 35^{\text{p}}52'$$
$$: : 58^{\text{p}}55' : 37^{\text{p}}52',$$

therefore the chord of 2 arc EL is also available for each of the sections as they increase in the usual manner by 10°. And the half of the arc subtending this chord (that is, EL itself) is 2°56' at the first 10°; 5°50' at the second; 8°38' at the third; 11°17' at the fourth; 13°42' at the fifth; 15°46' at the sixth; 17°24' at the seventh; 18°24' at the eighth; and clearly 18°45' at the ninth.[1] And so, since in the right sphere the arc through the first 10° on the ecliptic ascends with 9°10' in time; through the second, with 18°25'; through the third, with 27°50'; through the fourth, with 37°30'; through the fifth, with 47°28'; through the sixth, with 57°44'; through the seventh, with 68°18'; through the eighth, with 79°5'; and through the ninth, with the 90° in time of the whole quadrant; therefore it is evident that, if we subtract from each of the ascensions in the right sphere just mentioned the corresponding difference or arc EL, we shall have the ascensions of those same arcs in the given latitude. And so the arc through the first 10° of the ecliptic will ascend with 6°14' in time; through the second 10° of the ecliptic, with 12°35' in time; through the third 10°, with 19°12'; through the fourth, with 26°13'; through the fifth, with 33°46'; through the sixth, with 41°58'; through the seventh, with 50°54'; through the eighth, with 60°41'; and through the ninth or the whole quadrant, with the 71°15' taken from the half of the day. And therefore the first 10° of the ecliptic with 6°14' in time; the second with 6°21'; the third with 6°37'; the fourth with 7°1'; the fifth with 7°33'; the sixth with 8°12'; the seventh with 8°56'; the eighth with 9°47'; and the ninth with 10°34'.

And now with these things demonstrated, the ascensions of the other quadrants are in consequence also demonstrated immediately. And having calculated in the same way the ascensions of the other parallels for each 10°, which is as far as it is possible to anticipate their use in every case, we shall set them out in a table for use in the rest of this treatise, beginning with the parallel under the equator and going as far as that whose longest day is 17 hours, and advancing by half-hour increases because of the almost uniform increases of the periods within the half-hours. Then, placing first the 36 divisions of 10° each, we next set beside each one the time of its own ascension and then the successive additions of them, in the following manner:

[1]For when K is at 90° it coincides with H. Hence EL coincides with EH.

8. Table of Ascensions by 10°

| Signs | Tens | Right Sphere | | Through the Atlantic Gulf | | Through Meroë | |
		12 hours time	Lat. 0°0' total time	12½ hours time	Lat. 8°25' total time	13 hours time	Lat. 16°27' total time
Ram	10	9° 10'	9° 10'	8° 35'	8° 35'	7° 58'	7° 58'
	20	9° 15'	18° 25'	8° 39'	17° 14'	8° 5'	16° 3'
	30	9° 25'	27° 50'	8° 52'	26° 6'	8° 17'	24° 20'
Bull	10	9° 40'	37° 30'	9° 8'	35° 14'	8° 36'	32° 56'
	20	9° 58'	47° 28'	9° 29'	44° 43'	9° 1'	41° 57'
	30	10° 16'	57° 44'	9° 51'	54° 34'	9° 27'	51° 24'
Twins	10	10° 34'	68° 18'	10° 15'	64° 49'	9° 56'	61° 20'
	20	10° 47'	79° 5'	10° 35'	75° 24'	10° 23'	71° 43'
	30	10° 55'	90° 0'	10° 51'	86° 15'	10° 47'	82° 30'
Crab (Cancer)	10	10° 55'	100° 55'	10° 59'	97° 14'	11° 3'	93° 33'
	20	10° 47'	111° 42'	10° 59'	108° 13'	11° 11'	104° 44'
	30	10° 34'	122° 16'	10° 53'	119° 6'	11° 12'	115° 56'
Lion	10	10° 16'	132° 32'	10° 41'	129° 47'	11° 5'	127° 1'
	20	9° 58'	142° 30'	10° 27'	140° 14'	10° 55'	137° 56'
	30	9° 40'	152° 10'	10° 12'	150° 26'	10° 44'	148° 40'
Virgin	10	9° 25'	161° 35'	9° 58'	160° 24'	10° 33'	159° 13'
	20	9° 15'	170° 50'	9° 51'	170° 15'	10° 25'	169° 38'
	30	9° 10'	180° 0'	9° 45'	180° 0'	10° 22'	180° 0'
Balance	10	9° 10'	189° 10'	9° 45'	189° 45'	10° 22'	190° 22'
	20	9° 15'	198° 25'	9° 51'	199° 36'	10° 25'	200° 47'
	30	9° 25'	207° 50'	9° 58'	209° 34'	10° 33'	211° 20'
Scorpion	10	9° 40'	217° 30'	10° 12'	219° 46'	10° 44'	222° 4'
	20	9° 58'	227° 28'	10° 27'	230° 13'	10° 55'	232° 59'
	30	10° 16'	237° 44'	10° 41'	240° 54'	11° 5'	244° 4'
Archer	10	10° 34'	248° 18'	10° 53'	251° 47'	11° 12'	255° 16'
	20	10° 47'	259° 5'	10° 59'	262° 46'	11° 11'	266° 27'
	30	10° 55'	270° 0'	10° 59'	273° 45'	11° 3'	277° 30'
Goat (Capricorn)	10	10° 55'	280° 55'	10° 51'	284° 36'	10° 47'	288° 17'
	20	10° 47'	291° 42'	10° 35'	295° 11'	10° 23'	298° 40'
	30	10° 34'	302° 16'	10° 15'	305° 26'	9° 56'	308° 36'
Water Bearer	10	10° 16'	312° 32'	9° 51'	315° 17'	9° 27'	318° 3'
	20	9° 58'	322° 30'	9° 29'	324° 46'	9° 1'	327° 4'
	30	9° 40'	332° 10'	9° 8'	333° 54'	8° 36'	335° 40'
Fishes	10	9° 25'	341° 35'	8° 52'	342° 46'	8° 17'	343° 57'
	20	9° 15'	350° 50'	8° 39'	351° 25'	8° 5'	352° 2'
	30	9° 10'	360° 0'	8° 35'	360° 0'	7° 58'	360° 0'

8. TABLE OF ASCENSIONS BY 10°—Continued

Signs	Tens	Through Soëne 13½ hours time	Lat. 23°51′ total time	Through the low countries of Egypt 14 hours time	Lat. 30°22′ total time	Through Rhodes 14½ hours time	Lat. 36° total time
Ram	10	7° 23′	7° 23′	6° 48′	6° 48′	6° 14′	6° 14′
	20	7° 29′	14° 52′	6° 55′	13° 43′	6° 21′	12° 35′
	30	7° 45′	22° 37′	7° 10′	20° 53′	6° 37′	19° 12′
Bull	10	8° 4′	30° 41′	7° 33′	28° 26′	7° 1′	26° 13′
	20	8° 31′	39° 12′	8° 2′	36° 28′	7° 33′	33° 46′
	30	9° 3′	48° 15′	8° 37′	45° 5′	8 12′	41° 58′
Twins	10	9° 36′	57° 51′	9° 17′	54° 22′	8° 56′	50° 54′
	20	10° 11′	68° 2′	10° 0′	64° 22′	9° 47′	60° 41′
	30	10° 43′	78° 45′	10° 38′	75° 0′	10° 34′	71° 15′
Crab (Cancer)	10	11° 7′	89° 52′	11° 12′	86° 12′	11° 16′	82° 31′
	20	11° 23′	101° 15′	11° 34′	97° 46′	11° 47′	94° 18′
	30	11° 32′	112° 47′	11° 51′	109° 37′	12° 12′	106° 30′
Lion	10	11° 29′	124° 16′	11° 55′	121° 32′	12° 20′	118° 50′
	20	11° 25′	135° 41′	11° 54′	133° 26′	12° 23′	131° 13′
	30	11° 16′	146° 57′	11° 47′	145° 13′	12° 19′	143° 32′
Virgin	10	11° 5′	158° 2′	11° 40′	156° 53′	12° 13′	155° 45′
	20	11° 1′	169° 3′	11° 35′	168° 28′	12° 9′	167° 54′
	30	10° 57′	180° 0′	11° 32′	180° 0′	12° 6′	180° 0′
Balance	10	10° 57′	190° 57′	11° 32′	191° 32′	12° 6′	192° 6′
	20	11° 1′	201° 58′	11° 35′	203° 7′	12° 9′	204° 15′
	30	11° 5′	213° 3′	11° 40′	214° 47′	12° 13′	216° 28′
Scorpion	10	11° 16′	224° 19′	11° 47′	226° 34′	12° 19′	228° 47′
	20	11° 25′	235° 44′	11° 54′	238° 28′	12° 23′	241° 10′
	30	11° 29′	247° 13′	11° 55′	250° 23′	12° 20′	253° 30′
Archer	10	11° 32′	258° 45′	11° 51′	262° 14′	12° 12′	265° 42′
	20	11° 23′	270° 8′	11° 34′	273° 48′	11° 47′	277° 29′
	30	11° 7′	281° 15′	11° 12′	285° 0′	11° 16′	288° 45′
Goat (Capricorn)	10	10° 43′	291° 58′	10° 38′	295° 38′	10° 34′	299° 19′
	20	10° 11′	302° 9′	10° 0′	305° 38′	9° 47′	309° 6′
	30	9° 36′	311° 45′	9° 17′	314° 55′	8° 56′	318° 2′
Water Bearer	10	9° 3′	320° 48′	8° 37′	323° 32′	8° 12′	326° 14′
	20	8° 31′	329° 19′	8° 2′	331° 34′	7° 33′	333° 47′
	30	8° 4′	337° 23′	7° 33′	339° 7′	7° 1′	340° 48′
Fishes	10	7° 45′	345° 8′	7° 10′	346° 17′	6° 37′	347° 25′
	20	7° 29′	352° 37′	6° 55′	353° 12′	6° 21′	353° 46′
	30	7° 23′	360° 0′	6° 48′	360° 0′	6° 14′	360° 0′

8. TABLE OF ASCENSIONS BY 10°—Continued

Signs	Tens	Through the Hellespont		Through the middle of Pontus		Through the mouth of the Borysthenes	
		15 hours time	Lat. 40°56' total time	15½ hours time	Lat. 45°1' total time	16 hours time	Lat. 48° total time
Ram	10	5° 40'	5° 40'	5° 8'	5° 8'	4° 36'	4° 36'
	20	5° 47'	11° 27'	5° 14'	10° 22'	4° 43'	9° 19'
	30	6° 5'	17° 32'	5° 33'	15° 55'	5° 1'	14° 20'
Bull	10	6° 29'	24° 1'	5° 58'	21° 53'	5° 26'	19° 46'
	20	7° 4'	31° 5'	6° 34'	28° 27'	6° 5'	25° 51'
	30	7° 46'	38° 51'	7° 20'	35° 47'	6° 52'	32° 43'
Twins	10	8° 38'	47° 29'	8° 15'	44° 2'	7° 53'	40° 36'
	20	9° 32'	57° 1'	9° 19'	53° 21'	9° 5'	49° 41'
	30	10° 29'	67° 30'	10° 24'	63° 45'	10° 19'	60° 0'
Crab (Cancer)	10	11° 21'	78° 51'	11° 26'	75° 11'	11° 31'	71° 31'
	20	12° 2'	90° 53'	12° 15'	87° 26'	12° 29'	84° 0'
	30	12° 30'	103° 23'	12° 53'	100° 19'	13° 15'	97° 15'
Lion	10	12° 46'	116° 9'	13° 12'	113° 31'	13° 40'	110° 55'
	20	12° 52'	129° 1'	13° 22'	126° 53'	13° 51'	124° 46'
	30	12° 51'	141° 52'	13° 22'	140° 15'	13° 54'	138° 40'
Virgin	10	12° 45'	154° 37'	13° 17'	153° 32'	13° 49'	152° 29'
	20	12° 43'	167° 20'	13° 16'	166° 48'	13° 47'	166° 16'
	30	12° 40'	180° 0'	13° 12'	180° 0'	13° 44'	180° 0'
Balance	10	12° 40'	192° 40'	13° 12'	193° 12'	13° 44'	193° 44'
	20	12° 43'	205° 23'	13° 16'	206° 28'	13° 47'	207° 31'
	30	12° 45'	218° 8'	13° 17'	219° 45'	13° 49'	221° 20'
Scorpion	10	12° 51'	230° 59'	13° 22'	233° 7'	13° 54'	235° 14'
	20	12° 52'	243° 51'	13° 22'	246° 29'	13° 51'	249° 5'
	30	12° 46'	256° 37'	13° 12'	259° 41'	13° 40'	262° 45'
Archer	10	12° 30'	269° 7'	12° 53'	272° 34'	13° 15'	276° 0'
	20	12° 2'	281° 9'	12° 15'	284° 49'	12° 29'	288° 29'
	30	11° 21'	292° 30'	11° 26'	296° 15'	11° 31°	300° 0'
Goat (Capricorn)	10	10° 29'	302° 59'	10° 24'	306° 39'	10° 19'	310° 19'
	20	9° 32'	312° 31'	9° 19'	315° 58'	9° 5'	319° 24'
	30	8° 38'	321° 9'	8° 15'	324° 13'	7° 53'	327° 17'
Water Bearer	10	7° 46'	328° 55'	7° 20'	331° 33'	6° 52'	334° 9'
	20	7° 4'	335° 59'	6° 34'	338° 7'	6° 5'	340° 14'
	30	6° 29'	342° 28'	5° 58'	344° 5'	5° 26'	345° 40'
Fishes	10	6° 5'	348° 33'	5° 33'	349° 38'	5° 1'	350° 41'
	20	5° 47'	354° 20'	5° 14'	354° 52'	4° 43'	355° 24'
	30	5° 40'	360° 0'	5° 8'	360° 0'	4° 36'	360° 0'

8. TABLE OF ASCENSIONS BY 10°—Continued

| Signs | Tens | Through the southernmost parts of Britain | | Through the mouth of the Tanais | |
		16½ hours time	Lat. 51°30′ total time	17 hours time	Lat. 54°1′ total time
Ram	10	4° 5′	4° 5′	3° 36′	3° 36′
	20	4° 12′	8° 17′	3° 43′	7° 19′
	30	4° 31′	12° 48′	4° 0′	11° 19′
Bull	10	4° 56′	17° 44′	4° 26′	15° 45′
	20	5° 34′	23° 18′	5° 4′	20° 49′
	30	6° 25′	29° 43′	5° 56′	26° 45′
Twins	10	7° 29′	37° 12′	7° 5′	33° 50′
	20	8° 49′	46° 1′	8° 33′	42° 23′
	30	10° 14′	56° 15′	10° 7′	52° 30′
Crab (Cancer)	10	11° 36′	67° 51′	11° 43′	64° 13′
	20	12° 45′	80° 36′	13° 1′	77° 14′
	30	13° 39′	94° 15′	14° 3′	91° 17′
Lion	10	14° 7′	108° 22′	14° 36′	105° 53′
	20	14° 22′	122° 44′	14° 52′	120° 45′
	30	14° 24′	137° 8′	14° 54′	135° 39′
Virgin	10	14° 19′	151° 27′	14° 50′	150° 29′
	20	14° 18′	165° 45′	14° 47′	165° 16′
	30	14° 15′	180° 0′	14° 44′	180° 0′
Balance	10	14° 15′	194° 15′	14° 44′	194° 44′
	20	14° 18′	208° 33′	14° 47′	209° 31′
	30	14° 19′	222° 52′	14° 50′	224° 21′
Scorpion	10	14° 24′	237° 16′	14° 54′	239° 15′
	20	14° 22′	251° 38′	14° 52′	254° 7′
	30	14° 7′	265° 45′	14° 36′	268° 43′
Archer	10	13° 39′	279° 24′	14° 3′	282° 46′
	20	12° 45′	292° 9′	13° 1′	295° 47′
	30	11° 36′	303° 45′	11° 43′	307° 30′
Goat (Capricorn)	10	10° 14′	313° 59′	10° 7′	317° 37′
	20	8° 49′	322° 48′	8° 33′	326° 10′
	30	7° 29′	330° 17′	7° 5′	333° 15′
Water Bearer	10	6° 25′	336° 42′	5° 56′	339° 11′
	20	5° 34′	342° 16′	5° 4′	344° 15′
	30	4° 56′	347° 12′	4° 26′	348° 41′
Fishes	10	4° 31′	351° 43′	4° 0′	352° 41′
	20	4° 12′	355° 55′	3° 43′	356° 24′
	30	4° 5′	360° 0′	3° 36′	360° 0′

9. On Particular Consequences of the Ascensions

It will be evident through the systematic means given below that, once the times of the ascensions have been set out by us in the foregoing manner, all the rest of those things which concern the particular will be easily available, and we shall neither need proofs with figures for each of them, nor more tables.

For the first the length of the given day or night is gotten by calculating the degrees in time of the particular latitude: (1) in the case of the day by adding up the degrees in equatorial time from the point of the sun eastward to the point exactly opposite on the ecliptic, (2) in the case of the night, from the point opposite to the sun. For if we take a fifteenth of the total time, we shall get how many equatorial hours the given distance is; but if we take a twelfth, we shall get how many degrees in time the seasonal hour of the same distance is.

And the magnitude of the hour is also more easily found if, out of the foregoing table, the difference is taken laterally between the totals of successive additions of time in the parallel under the equator and that of the given latitude: (1) in the case of the day at the point of the sun; (2) in the case of the night, at the point directly opposite on the ecliptic. For taking ⅙ of the difference so found and adding it to the 15° in time of the equatorial hour when the sun is in the northern hemisphere, and subtracting it when it is in the southern, we shall get the number of degrees in time of the given seasonal hour.[1]

And consequently we reduce the given seasonal hours to equatorial hours by multiplying the number of such hours in the day by the number of time-degrees in the hour for that day in that latitude, and the number in the night by the number of degrees in the hour for that night. For by taking ⅟₁₅ of the total we shall have the number of equatorial hours. Conversely we reduce the given equatorial hours to seasonal hours by multiplying by 15 and dividing by the given number of time-degrees for the hour of that particular interval.

Again, given the time and any seasonal hour, we shall get the degree of the ecliptic which is rising at that time by multiplying the number of hours from the rising of the sun for the day, from the setting of the sun for the night, by the proper number of time-degrees for that hour. For we compare the resulting number with the ascensions of the given latitude: in the case of the day beginning with the sun and going eastward; in the case of the night, from the opposite point on the ecliptic. And to whatever degree the number corresponds we shall say that degree rises at that moment.

And if we wish to get the degree culminating, we multiply the seasonal hours, counted always from midday to the given hour, by the proper number of time-degrees for that hour. Beginning from the sun eastward, with the ascensions in the right sphere, we compare the resulting number, and on whatever degree the number falls, that degree will be culminating at that moment.

Likewise from the degree given as rising we shall get the degree culminating by locating the number resulting from the successive additions corresponding to the degree given as rising, in the table of the proper latitude. For by always subtracting from it the 90° in time of the quadrant, we shall find the degree culminating as that corresponding to the number resulting from this subtraction found in the column of successive additions of the right sphere. And con-

---

[1]For this difference, according to the construction of the Table [p. 52], is arc *EL* which is half the difference between the given and the equinoctial day [p. 50].

versely, from the degree given as culminating, we shall again get the degree
which is rising by considering the number resulting from the successive additions corresponding to the degree given as rising, in the table of the right sphere.
For after always adding the 90° in time, we shall look for the degree, corresponding to the resulting number, in the column of successive additions of the given
latitude. And then we shall have the degree rising at that moment.

And it is also evident that for those living under the same meridian the sun
is the same number of equatorial hours from noon or midnight; but for those
not living under the same meridian, it will differ by as many equatorial hours
as one meridian differs from the other.

10. On the Angles Formed by the Ecliptic and the Meridian

Since we still have to treat of the angles, to complete this theory—I mean
those angles made by the ecliptic—it must first be understood that we say a
right angle is contained by great circles if, when a circle is drawn with the intersection of the given great circles as pole and any distance, the arc intercepted
on this circle by the sections of the great circles containing the angle is a quadrant. And in general we say that whatever ratio the intercepted arc has to the
circle drawn in the manner we described, that same ratio does the angle contained by the inclination of the planes have to four right angles. And so, since
we suppose the perimeter to be 360°, whatever number of degrees the intercepted arc is found to be, that same number will the angle subtending it be.
For instance, one right angle is 90°.

Of the angles made by the ecliptic the most useful with respect to this theory
are: (1) those contained by its intersection with the meridian, (2) those contained by its intersection with the horizon for each position, and likewise (3)
those contained by its intersection with the great circle drawn through the
horizon's poles. And along with the exposition of these last angles will be given
also an exposition of the arcs intercepted on this great circle by the intersection
and the horizon's pole—that is, the zenith. For every one of the aforementioned things, when demonstrated, has a very considerable place in the theory
and contributes most especially to researches concerning the parallaxes of the
moon, since such work cannot advance without the prior understanding of these.

But since there are four angles contained by the intersection of the two
circles (that is, by the ecliptic and one of those intersecting it), and since we are
going to speak of just one of them always similar in position, it is first necessary
to determine that in general, of the two angles on either side of that arc of the
ecliptic east of the intersection of the circles, the one
on the north is to be considered, so that the incidents and quantities which will be demonstrated belong to such angles. And since the demonstration of
the angles of the ecliptic considered with respect to
the meridian is simpler, we shall begin with it, and
we shall first prove that points on the ecliptic equidistant from the same equinoctial point make the
resulting angles equal to each other.

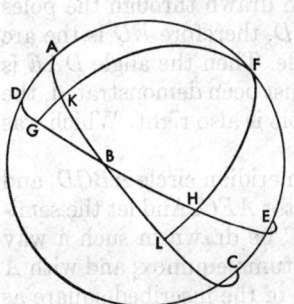

For let ABC be the arc of the equator, and DBE
the arc of the ecliptic, and point F the pole of the
equator. And with arcs BG and BH cut off equal on

either side of the equinoctial point B, let there be drawn through the pole F and
the points G and H the arcs of meridian circles FKG and FHL.

I say that

$$\text{angle } KGB = \text{angle } FHE.$$

For the three-sided figure BGK is equiangular with the three-sided figure
BHL, since it has its three sides equal to the three sides of the other respectively,
GB to BH, GK to HL, and BK to BL. For all these things have been proved before [Book I, Chaps. 14, 15]. And therefore

$$\text{angle } KGB = \text{angle } BHL = \text{angle } FHE.$$

Which was to be proved.

Again it must be proved that, given two points on the ecliptic equidistant
from the same tropic point, the angles there formed with the meridian are together equal to two right angles.

For let ABC be an arc of the ecliptic with B given as the tropic point. And
with the equal arcs BD and BE intercepted on either
side of it, let the arcs of meridian circles FD and FE
be drawn through the points D and E and the pole
F of the equator.

I say that

angle FDB+angle $FEC = 2$ rt. angles.

And this is immediately evident. For since the
points D and E are equidistant from the same tropic
point,

$$\text{arc } DF = \text{arc } EF.$$

And therefore

$$\text{angle } FDB = \text{angle } FEB$$

But

$$\text{angle } FEB + \text{angle } FEC = 2 \text{ rt. angles.}$$

And therefore

$$\text{angle } FDB + \text{angle } FEC = 2 \text{ rt. angles.}$$

Which was to be proved.

And with these things understood first, let there be the meridian circle $ABCD$,
and the semicircle of the ecliptic AEC with the point A taken as the winter
tropic. And with A as pole and with a side of the inscribed square as distance

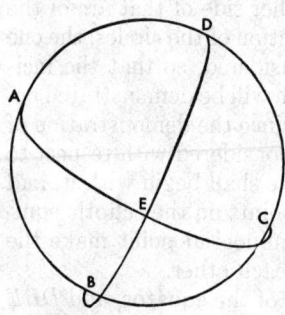

let the semicircle BED be drawn. Since then the
meridian $ABCD$ has been drawn through the poles
of AEC and those of BED, therefore ED is the arc
of the quadrant of a circle. Then the angle DAE is
right. And, by what has just been demonstrated, the
angle at the summer tropic is also right. Which was
to be proved.

Again let there be the meridian circle $ABCD$, and
the semicircle of the equator AEC. And let the semicircle of the ecliptic AFC be drawn in such a way
that the point A is the autumn equinox; and with A
as pole and with the side of the inscribed square as
distance, let the semicircle $BFED$ be drawn.

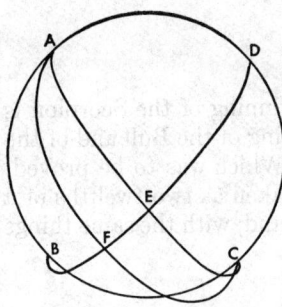

For the same reasons, then, since $ABCD$ has been drawn through the poles of AEC and BED, therefore AF and ED are quadrants. And so the point F is the winter tropic, and as already proved

arc $EF = 23°51'$.

And therefore, by addition,

arc $FED = 113°51'$,
angle $DAF = 113°51'$.

And therefore, as already proved, the angle at the point of the spring equinox is what remains of two right angles or 66°9'.

Again let there be the meridian circle $ABCD$, and the semicircle of the equator AEC, and that of the ecliptic BFD, so that the point F is taken as the autumn equinox, the arc BF first as one twelfth of the circle, that of the Virgin, and the point B clearly as the beginning of the Virgin. And again with B as pole and with the side of the inscribed square as distance let the semicircle $GHEK$ be drawn.

And let it be required to find angle KBH.

Since, then, the meridian $ABCD$ has been drawn through the poles of AEC and GEK, each of the arcs BG, BH, and EG is a quadrant. Because of the construction,

chord 2 arc AB : chord 2 arc AG comp.
chord 2 arc BF : chord 2 arc FH,
chord 2 arc EH : chord 2 arc EG.

But from things already proved

2 arc $AB = 23°20'$,
chord 2 arc $AB = 24^{p}16'$;

and

2 arc $AG = 156°40'$,
chord 2 arc $AG = 117^{p}31'$;

and again

2 arc $BF = 60°$,
chord 2 arc $BF = 60^{p}$;

and

2 arc $FH = 120°$,
chord 2 arc $FH = 103^{p}55'23''$.

Then again

chord 2 arc EH : chord 2 arc EG comp. $24^{p}16'$: $117^{p}31'$, $103^{p}55'23''$: 60^{p}

or, very nearly,

chord 2 arc EH : chord 2 arc EG : : $42^{p}58'$: 120^{p}

And

chord 2 arc $EG = 120^{p}$;

and therefore

chord 2 arc $EH = 42^{p}58'$.

And so

2 arc $EH = 42°$,
arc $EH = 21°$.

And therefore, by addition,

$$\text{arc } HEK = 111°,$$
$$\text{angle } KBH = 111°;$$

and, by previous proofs, the angle formed at the beginning of the Scorpion is also 111°, and each of the angles formed at the beginning of the Bull and of the Fishes is the 69° which remain from two right angles. Which was to be proved.

Again, with the same construction, let arc BF be taken as two twelfths of a circle, so that the point B is the beginning of the Lion and, with the same things being assumed, so that

$$2 \text{ arc } AB = 41°,$$
$$\text{chord } 2 \text{ arc } AB = 42^\text{p}2';$$

and

$$2 \text{ arc } AG = 139°,$$
$$\text{chord } 2 \text{ arc } AG = 112^\text{p}24';$$

and again

$$2 \text{ arc } BF = 120°,$$
$$\text{chord } 2 \text{ arc } BF = 103^\text{p}55'23'';$$

and

$$2 \text{ arc } FH = 60°$$
$$\text{chord } 2 \text{ arc } FH = 60^\text{p}.$$

Then

$$\text{chord } 2 \text{ arc } EH : \text{chord } 2 \text{ arc } EG \text{ comp. } 42^\text{p}2' : 112^\text{p}24', 60^\text{p} : 103^\text{p}55'23''$$

or

$$\text{chord } 2 \text{ arc } EH : \text{chord } 2 \text{ arc } EG : : 25^\text{p}53' : 120^\text{p}.$$

Therefore

$$\text{chord } 2 \text{ arc } EH = 25^\text{p}53',$$

And so

$$2 \text{ arc } EH = 25°,$$
$$\text{arc } EH = 12\frac{1}{2}°.$$

Therefore, by addition,

$$\text{arc } HEK = 102\frac{1}{2}°,$$
$$\text{angle } KBH = 102\frac{1}{2}°.$$

And for this reason the angle formed at the beginning of the Archer is also $102\frac{1}{2}°$, and each of the angles formed at the beginning of the Twins and of the Water Bearer is what remains of two right angles, or $77\frac{1}{2}°$.

And we have proved what was required; and the method will be the same for still smaller sections of the ecliptic. But the exposition of the twelve signs is sufficient for the needs of this treatise.

11. On the Angles Formed by the Ecliptic and the Horizon

And next we shall show how we can also get, for a given latitude, the angles formed by the ecliptic and the horizon; for they have a simpler system than the others that are left to do. Now it is clear that those formed with the meridian are the same as those formed with the horizon in the right sphere. But to get those in the oblique sphere it is first necessary to prove that points on the ecliptic equidistant from the same equinoctial point make with the horizon, angles equal to each other.

For let there be the meridian circle $ABCD$, and the semicircle of the equator

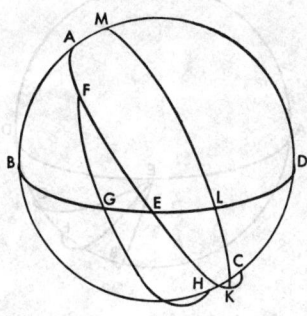

AEC, and that of the horizon *BED*. And let two
sections of the ecliptic, *FGH* and *KLM*, be drawn
in such a way that each of the points *F* and *K* is
taken to be the autumn equinox, and

$$\text{arc } FG = \text{arc } KL.$$

I say that also

$$\text{angle } EGH = \text{angle } DLK.$$

And this is immediately evident. For the three-
sided figure *EFG* is equiangular with the three-
sided figure *EKL*, since, by previous proofs, it
has its three sides equal respectively to the three
sides of the other; *FG* to *KL*, the section of the
horizon *GE* to *EL*, and the ascension arc *EF* to
EK. Therefore also

$$\text{angle } EGF = \text{angle } ELK,$$

and the supplements

$$\text{angle } EGH = \text{angle } DLK.$$

Which was to be proved.

And I say also that the two angles formed at two points directly opposite,
one at the east and the other at the west, together make two right angles.

For if we draw circle *ABCD* as the horizon and *AECF* as the ecliptic, cutting
each other at the points *A* and *C*,

$$\text{angle } FAD + \text{angle } DAE = 2 \text{ rt. angles.}$$

But

$$\text{angle } FAD = \text{angle } FCD$$

so that

$$\text{angle } FCD + \text{angle } DAE = 2 \text{ rt. angles.}$$

Which was to be proved.

And now that these things are so—since angles
formed by the ecliptic and the same horizon, at
points on the ecliptic equidistant from the same
equinoctial point, have been proved equal—it
will also follow that the angle at the east and the
angle at the west, for points equidistant from the

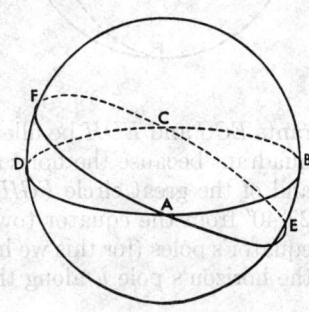

same tropic and formed by the ecliptic and the horizon, will together equal two
right angles. And so, for this reason, if we find the rising angles from the Ram to
the Balance, the rising angles of the other semicircle will be made known at the
same time, and also the setting angles of both. And we shall briefly expound how
this is demonstrated, using again as an example the same parallel—that is, the
one where the north pole is 36° above the horizon.

Now, the angles formed by the ecliptic and the horizon at the equinoctial
points can be easily found. For if we draw the circle *ABCD* as the meridian and
AED as the eastern semicircle of the horizon, and *EF* as a quadrant of the equator, and if we draw the two arcs of the ecliptic *BE* and *CE* in such a way that
the point *E* is conceived as the fall equinox with respect to the quadrant *BE* and
as the spring equinox with respect to *CE*, and *B* in the first instance becomes the
winter tropic and *C* in the second becomes the summer tropic, then it is inferred
that, since it is supposed

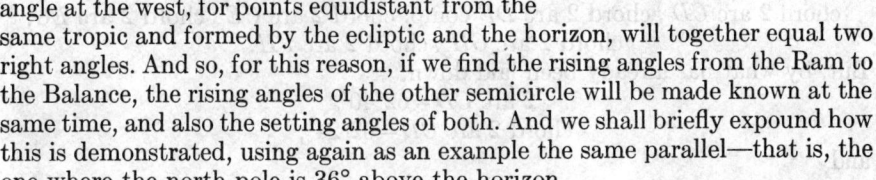

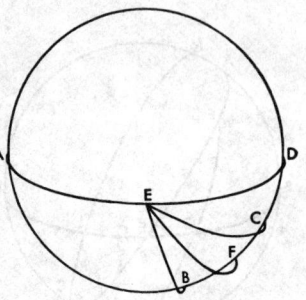

arc $DF = 54°$,

and

arc BF = arc $CG = 23°51'$,

therefore

arc $CD = 30°9'$,
arc $BD = 77°51'$.

And so, since the point E is a pole of the meridian ABC, therefore the angle DEC formed at the beginning of the Ram will be 30°9', and angle DEB formed at the beginning of the Balance will be 77°51'.

To show clearly the method for getting the others, let it be required, for example, to find the rising angle formed at the beginning of the Bull by the eclip-

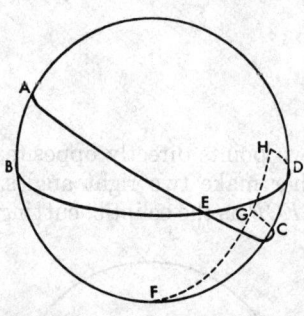

tic and the horizon. And let there be the meridian circle $ABCD$ and the eastern semicircle of the given horizon RED. And let the semicircle of the ecliptic AEC be drawn so that the point E is the beginning of the Bull. And since in this same latitude, when the beginning of the Bull is just rising, the point 17°41' within the Crab is at the meridian under the earth (for we showed [p. 56] how to get such results easily from our Table of Ascensions). Therefore the arc CE is less than a quadrant. Then let the section HGF of a great circle be drawn with E as pole and the side of the inscribed square as distance; and let the quadrants ECG and EDH be filled out. But each of the arcs DCF and FGH is also a quadrant because the horizon BEH is through the poles of the meridian FCD and of the great circle FGH. Again, since the point 17°41' within the Crab is 22°40' from the equator towards the north along the great circle through the equator's poles (for this we have also proved), and since the equator is 36° from the horizon's pole F along the same arc FCD, therefore it is inferred

arc $CF = 58°40'$.

Now with this given, because of the construction,

chord 2 arc CD : chord 2 arc DF comp. chord 2 arc CE : chord 2 arc EG,
chord 2 arc GH : chord 2 arc FH.

But, by what has already been laid down,

2 arc $CD = 62°40'$,
chord 2 arc $CD = 62^p24'$;

and

2 arc $DF = 180°$,
chord 2 arc $DF = 120^p$;

and again

2 arc $CE = 155°22'$,
chord 2 arc $CE = 117^p14'$;

and

2 arc $EG = 180°$,
chord 2 arc $EG = 120^p$.

Then
$$\text{chord } 2 \text{ arc } GH : \text{chord } 2 \text{ arc } FH \text{ comp. } 62^\text{p}24' : 120^\text{p}, 120^\text{p} : 117^\text{p}14'$$
or
$$\text{chord } 2 \text{ arc } GH : \text{chord } 2 \text{ arc } FH :: 63^\text{p}52' : 120^\text{p}.$$
And
$$\text{chord } 2 \text{ arc } FH = 120^\text{p};$$
therefore
$$\text{chord } 2 \text{ arc } GH = 63^\text{p}52'.$$
And so
$$2 \text{ arc } GH = 64°20',$$
$$\text{arc } GH = 32°10',$$
$$\text{angle } GEH = 32°10'.$$
Which was to be proved.

Not to draw out this treatise by repeating for each case, the same method will be understood as used for the other signs and latitudes.

12. On the Angles and Arcs Made by the Ecliptic with, and on, the Circle through the Poles of the Horizon

Now there remains the method by which we can get the angles formed by the ecliptic and the circle through the poles of the horizon for each latitude and position. And, as we said, there will result, at the same time and in each case, a demonstration of the arc on the circle through the poles of the horizon intercepted by the zenith and the intersection with the ecliptic. And again we shall set out the fundamental things for this particular situation; and we shall prove first that, if two points on the ecliptic equidistant from the same tropic intercept an equal number of time degrees on either side of the meridian (the one to the east, the other to the west), then the arcs on great circles from the zenith to each of these points are equal to each other, and the angles formed at these points in the way we have stipulated are equal to two right angles.

For let there be a section of the meridian, ABC, and take the zenith B on it,

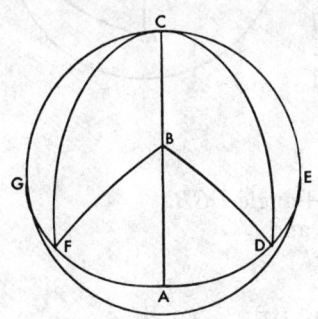

and the pole of the equator C. And let two sections of the ecliptic, ADE and AFG, be drawn in such a way that the points D and F are equidistant from the same tropic and intercept equal arcs on the parallel through them from either side of the meridian ABC. And let the arcs of great circles, CD and CF, be drawn through the points D and F from the equator's pole C; and from the zenith B the arcs of great circles BD and BF.

I say that
$$\text{arc } BD = \text{arc } BF,$$
and
$$\text{angle } BDE + \text{angle } BFA = 2 \text{ rt. angles.}$$

For since the points D and F are equidistant from the meridian ABC by equal arcs on the parallel through them,
$$\text{angle } BCD = \text{angle } BCF.$$
Then we have the two three-sided figures BCD and BCF having two sides equal to two sides respectively, CD to CF and BC common, and the angles

contained by the equal sides equal—that is, angle BCD to angle BCF. And therefore

$$\text{base } BD = \text{base } BF,$$
$$\text{angle } BFC = \text{angle } BCD.$$

But since it has just been proved that the angles at points equidistant from the same tropic and formed by the ecliptic and circles through the equator's poles are together equal to two right angles, therefore

$$\text{angle } CDE + \text{angle } CFA = 2 \text{ rt. angles.}$$

But it was proved also

$$\text{angle } BDC = \text{angle } BFC.$$

And therefore

$$\text{angle } BDE + \text{angle } BFA = 2 \text{ rt. angles.}$$

Which was to be proved.

Again, it must be proved that, when the same points on the ecliptic are equidistant in time from either side of the meridian, the arcs of great circles from the zenith to these points are equal to each other; and the angles formed by these arcs with the ecliptic (the one in the east and the other in the west) are together equal to the two angles at the same point formed by the ecliptic and the meridian at that point, whenever the culminations of the points in either position are either both to the north or both to the south of the zenith.

First let them be taken both to the south, and let there be the section of the meridian $ABCD$, and on it the zenith C, and the pole of the equator D. And let two sections of the ecliptic, AEF and BGH, be drawn so that points E and G, taken as the same, are equally distant from the meridian $ABCD$ on either side by an arc of the parallel through the point. And again let the sections of great circles, CE and CG, be drawn through these points from C; and DE and DG, from D.

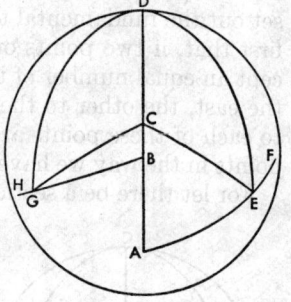

By the same reasoning as before, since the points E and G, on the same parallel, make on that parallel equal arcs on either side from the meridian, therefore the three-sided figure CDE is equiangular and equilateral with the figure CDG, so that

$$\text{arc } CE = \text{arc } CG.$$

I say then that

$$\text{angle } CEF + \text{angle } CGB = \text{angle } DEF + \text{angle } DGB.$$

For since angle DEF is the same as angle DGB, and

$$\text{angle } CED = \text{angle } DGC,$$

therefore

$$\text{angle } CED + \text{angle } CGB = \text{angle } DEF.$$

And so also

$$\text{angle } CEF + \text{angle } CGB = \text{angle } DEF + \text{angle } DGB.$$

Which was to be proved.

Let the same sections of the aforementioned circles be again constructed so that this time the points A and B are north of the point C.

I say that the same thing will follow, that is

$$\text{angle } KEF + \text{angle } LGB = \text{angle } DEF + \text{angle } DGB.$$

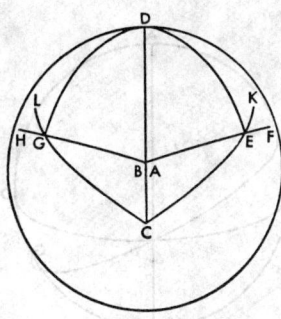

For since the angle *DEF* is the same as angle *DGB* and

angle *DEK* = angle *DGL*,

therefore, by addition,

angle *LGB* = angle *DEF* + angle *DEK*.

And so

angle *KEF* + angle *LGB* = angle *DEF* + angle *DGB*.

Now, again, let a similar figure be set out so that this time the point of the ecliptic's eastern section when culminating, that is *A*, is south of the zenith *C*, and the point of the western section when culminating, that is *B*, is north of it.

I say that

angle *CEF* + angle *LGB* = angle *DEF*
    + angle *DGB* + 2 rt. angles

For since

angle *DGC* = angle *DEC*,

and

angle *DGC* + angle *DGL* = 2 rt. angles,

therefore also

angle *DEC* + angle *DGL* = 2 rt. angles.

But angle *DEF* is the same as angle *DBG*. And so

angle *CEF* + angle *LGB* = angle *DEF* +
    angle *DGB* + angle *DEC* + angle *DGL*

or

angle *CEF* + angle *LGB* = 2 angle *DEF* + 2 rt. angles.

Which was to be proved.

And let the final combination be set out in a similar figure: the point *A* of the ecliptic's eastern section culminating north of the point *C*, and the point *B* of the western section culminating south of it.

I say that

angle *KEF* + angle *CGB* + 2 rt. angles = 2 angle *DEF*.

For, by the same reasoning, again

angle *KEF* + angle *CGB* + angle *DEK* +
    angle *DGC* = angle *DEF* + angle *DGB*

or

angle *KEF* + angle *CGB* + angle *DEK* +
    angle *DGC* = 2 angle *DEF*.

But

angle *DEK* + angle *DGC* = 2 rt. angles,

because

angle *DEK* + angle *DEC* = 2 rt. angles

and

angle *DEC* = angle *DGC*.

Which was to be proved.

And it will be immediately clear that, from the angles and arcs formed by the ecliptic with the great circle through the zenith in the way we have described, those formed on the meridian and the horizon can be easily gotten. For if we draw the meridian circle *ABCD*, and the semicircle of the horizon *BED*, and that of the ecliptic *FEG* in any manner whatsoever, then, whenever we conceive the great circle drawn through the zenith *A* as passing through the culminating point *F*, it will coincide with the meridian *ABCD*. And the angle *DFE* is immediately given us because the point *F* and the angle formed at it by the meridian [Book II, Chap. 10] are given. And the arc *AF* is given because we know how far on the meridian the point *F* is from the equator, and how far the equator is from the zenith *A*. And whenever we

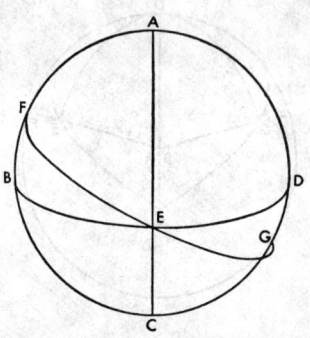

conceive the great circle drawn through *A* as passing through the rising point *E* (for example, the semicircle *AEC*) then it is immediately clear that the arc *AE* will always be a quadrant; because the point *A* is the pole of the horizon *BED*. And since for the same cause the angle *AED* is always right, and the angle formed by the ecliptic and the horizon (that is, angle *DEG*) is given. Therefore the whole angle *AEG* is also given. Which was to be proved.

And so it is clear that, since things are thus, if, in each latitude, we calculate only the angles and arcs preceding the meridian and only those from the beginning of the Crab to the beginning of the Goat, we shall have calculated at the same time [p. 63; p. 64] the angles and arcs which follow the meridian, and for the rest of the signs both those preceding and those following.

To make the method here clear for each position, again as an example, we shall set out what will be a general demonstration through one theorem, supposing that, in the same latitude (that is, where the north pole is 36° above the horizon), the beginning of the Crab for instance is one equatorial hour to the east of the meridian. And in this position, for this parallel, the point 16°12' within the Twins is culminating and the point 17°37' within the Virgin is rising.

Then let there be the meridian circle *ABCD*; and the semicircle of the horizon *BED*; and that of the ecliptic *FGH* in such a way that the point *G* is the beginning of the Crab, the point *F* 16°12' within the Twins, and *H* 17°37' within the Virgin. And let section *AGEC* of the great circle through the zenith *A* and through *G*, the beginning of the Crab, be drawn.

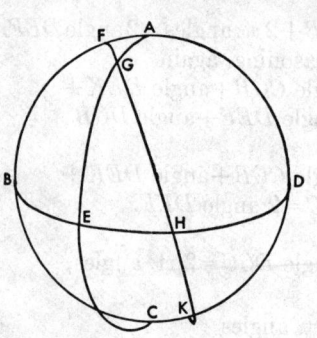

And let it be required first to find arc *AG*.
Then it is evident that

arc *FH* = 91°25',
arc *GH* = 77°37'.

And likewise since the point 16°12' within the Twins intercepts 23°7' on the meridian from the equator northward and the equator is 36° from the zenith *A*, therefore

arc *AF* = 12°53',

and, by subtraction from the quadrant,

arc *BF* = 77°7'.

With these things given, it again follows from the construction that chord 2 arc BF : chord 2 arc AB comp. chord 2 arc FH : chord 2 arc GH,

chord 2 arc EG : chord 2 arc AE.

But
$$2 \text{ arc } BF = 154°14',$$
$$\text{chord } 2 \text{ arc } BF = 116^{\text{p}}59';$$

and
$$2 \text{ arc } AB = 180°,$$
$$\text{chord } 2 \text{ arc } AB = 120^{\text{p}};$$

and again
$$2 \text{ arc } FH = 182°50',$$
$$\text{chord } 2 \text{ arc } FH = 119^{\text{p}}58';$$

and
$$2 \text{ arc } GH = 155°14',$$
$$\text{chord } 2 \text{ arc } GH = 117^{\text{p}}12'.$$

Therefore

chord 2 arc EG : chord 2 arc AE comp. $116^{\text{p}}59'$: 120^{p}, $117^{\text{p}}12'$: $119^{\text{p}}58'$

or

chord 2 arc EG : chord 2 arc AE : : $114^{\text{p}}16'$: 120^{p}.

And
$$\text{chord } 2 \text{ arc } AE = 120^{\text{p}};$$

and therefore
$$\text{chord } 2 \text{ arc } EG = 114^{\text{p}}16'.$$

And so
$$2 \text{ arc } EG = 114°26',$$
$$\text{arc } EG = 72°13'.$$

And therefore, by subtraction from the quadrant,
$$\text{arc } AG = 17°47'.$$

Which was to be proved.

And next we shall also find the angle AGH in this way: let the same figure be

set out, and with G as pole and with the side of the inscribed square as distance let the section KLM of a great circle be drawn so that, since circle AGE has been drawn through the poles of EHM and KLM, each of the arcs EM and KM is a quadrant. Then again, because of the construction,

chord 2 arc EG : chord 2 arc EK comp.

chord 2 arc GH : chord 2 arc HL,

chord 2 arc LM : chord 2 arc KM.

But
$$2 \text{ arc } EG = 144°26',$$
$$\text{chord } 2 \text{ arc } EG = 114^{\text{p}}16';$$

and
$$2 \text{ arc } EK = 35°34',$$
$$\text{chord } 2 \text{ arc } EK = 36^{\text{p}}38';$$

and
$$2 \text{ arc } GH = 155°14',$$
$$\text{chord } 2 \text{ arc } GH = 117^{\text{p}}12';$$

and
$$2 \text{ arc } HL = 24°46'$$
$$\text{chord } 2 \text{ arc } HL = 25^{\text{p}}44'.$$

And so

chord 2 arc LM : chord 2 arc KM comp. $114^{\text{p}}16'$: $36^{\text{p}}38'$, $25^{\text{p}}44'$: $117^{\text{p}}12'$
or very nearly
$$\text{chord } 2 \text{ arc } LM : \text{chord } 2 \text{ arc } KM :: 82^{\text{p}}11' : 120^{\text{p}}.$$

And
$$\text{chord } 2 \text{ arc } KM = 120^{\text{p}};$$
therefore
$$\text{chord } 2 \text{ arc } LM = 82^{\text{p}}11'.$$

And so
$$2 \text{ arc } LM = 86°28',$$
$$\text{arc } LM = 43°14'.$$

And therefore, by subtraction,
$$\text{arc } KL = 46°46'$$
$$\text{angle } LGK = 46°46'.$$

And so, by subtraction from two right angles,
$$\text{angle } AGH = 133°14'.$$

Which was to be proved.

Now, the method of finding these arcs and angles is inferred to be the same also for the rest. But to have them set out, ready to hand, we have calculated as many of the other arcs and angles as seemed likely to be useful for the detailed researches. And we have begun geometrically with the parallel through Meroë where the longest day is 13 equatorial hours and have gone to the parallel drawn above Pontus through the mouth of the Borysthenes. And we have used again, as in the case of the ascensions, an increase each time of a half hour for the latitudes, of a twelfth of a circle for the sections of the ecliptic, and of one equatorial hour for the positions either east or west of the meridian. And we set them out in tables, one for each latitude and sign, putting in the first column for each position the number of its equatorial hours' distance from either side of the meridian; in the second column the lengths of the arcs running, as we said, from the zenith to the beginning of the sign in question; and in the third and fourth columns the sizes of the angles formed at the intersections and situated in the way we defined, with the positions east of the meridian in the third column and those west in the fourth. And it is necessary to remember, as we stipulated in the beginning, that, of the two angles contained by the section of the ecliptic east of the intersection, we have always taken the one to the north of it, comparing the size of each of them with the 90° of a right angle. And here are the tables.[1]

[1]Since, for latitudes between the tropic of the Crab (Cancer) and the tropic of the Goat (Capricorn), the zeniths lie on the meridian between the points where the two tropics culminate, therefore, as the tropic of the Crab, for instance, is considered at the meridian and then farther and farther eastward, the arc of the great circle through the zenith and the tropic, first south of the ecliptic, comes nearer and nearer to coinciding with the ecliptic. Finally it does coincide, and then passes to the northern side of the ecliptic. The angle in question starts as a right angle, becomes smaller and smaller, does not exist or is equal to two right angles, and then starting again as if from two right angles gets smaller and smaller. This is repeated, *mutatis mutandi*, for all the signs. The letter N or S placed after an angle in the tables indicates that the point of the ecliptic culminating is north or south of the zenith for that angle and all below it until a change is indicated.

13. EXPOSITION OF THE ANGLES AND ARCS BY PARALLELS OR LATITUDES.

Of the Parallel through Meroë 13 hours lat. 16° 27'.

Crab

Hours	Arcs	Eastern Angles	Western Angles
Noon	7° 24'	90° 0'	154°(n) 44'
1°	15° 55'	25° 16'	170° 45'
2°	29° 3'	9° 15'	178° 22'
3°	42° 42'	1° 38'	4°(s) 53'
4°	56° 25'	175° 7'	9° 42'
5°	70° 2'	170° 18'	15° 19'
6° 30'	83° 27'	164° 41'	18° 3'
	90° 0'	161° 57'	

Lion

Hours	Arcs	Eastern Angles	Western Angles
Noon	4° 3'	102°(n) 30'	178°(n) 57'
1°	14° 20'	26° 3'	9°(s) 32'
2°	28° 42'	15° 28'	14° 55'
3°	42° 43'	10° 5'	18° 41'
4°	56° 49'	6° 19'	22° 27'
5°	70° 38'	2° 33'	28° 0'
6° 25'	84° 17'	177°(s) 0'	30° 9'
	90° 0'	174° 51'	

Virgin

Hours	Arcs	Eastern Angles	Western Angles
Noon	4° 47'	111°(s) 0'	0°(s) 0'
1°	15° 20'	0°(n) 0'	42° 0'
2°	29° 28'	8° 0'	34° 0'
3°	43° 40'	9° 15'	32° 45'
4°	58° 13'	8° 39'	33° 21'
5°	72° 36'	6° 53'	35° 7'
6° 14'	86° 41'	5° 37'	36° 23'
	90° 0'	4° 9'	37° 51'

Balance

Hours	Arcs	Eastern Angles	Western Angles
Noon	16° 27'	113°(s) 51'	72°(s) 49'
1°	22° 8'	154° 53'	54° 25'
2°	33° 50'	173° 17'	46° 19'
3°	47° 20'	1°(n) 23'	42° 34'
4°	61° 22'	5° 8'	40° 33'
5°	75° 39'	7° 7'	40° 18'
6°	90° 0'	7° 24'	

Scorpion

Hours	Arcs	Eastern Angles	Western Angles
Noon	28° 7'	111°(s) 0'	83°(s) 0'
1°	31° 46'	139° 59'	64° 1'
2°	40° 52'	157°	52° 37'
3°	52° 30'	169° 23'	45° 19'
4°	65° 40'	176° 41'	40° 19'
5° 46'	79° 18'	1°(n) 41'	37° 51'
	90° 0'	4° 9'	

Archer

Hours	Arcs	Eastern Angles	Western Angles
Noon	36° 57'	102°(s) 30'	79°(s) 48'
1°	39° 46'	125° 12'	61° 55'
2°	47° 15'	143° 5'	48° 57'
3°	57° 33'	156° 3'	40° 12'
4°	69° 30'	164° 48'	33° 17'
5° 35'	82° 18'	171° 43'	30° 9'
	90° 0'	174° 51'	

Ram

Hours	Arcs	Eastern Angles	Western Angles
Noon	16° 27'	66°(s) 27'	25°(s) 7'
1°	22° 8'	107° 11'	6° 43'
2°	33° 50'	125° 35'	178°(n) 37'
3°	47° 20'	133° 41'	174° 52'
4°	61° 22'	137° 26'	172° 51'
5°	75° 39'	139° 27'	172° 36'
6°	90° 0'	139° 42'	

Bull

Hours	Arcs	Eastern Angles	Western Angles
Noon	4° 47'	69°(s) 0'	180°(n) 0'
1°	15° 20'	138° 0'	172° 0'
2°	29° 28'	146° 0'	170° 45'
3°	43° 40'	147° 15'	171° 21'
4°	58° 13'	146° 39'	173° 7'
5°	72° 36'	144° 53'	174° 23'
6° 14'	86° 41'	143° 37'	175° 51'
	90° 0'	142° 9'	

Twins

Hours	Arcs	Eastern Angles	Western Angles
Noon	4° 3'	77°(n) 30'	57° 57'
1°	14° 20'	1° 3'	32'
2°	28° 42'	170°(s) 28'	169° 55'
3°	42° 43'	165° 5'	173° 41'
4°	56° 49'	161° 19'	177° 27'
5°	70° 38'	157° 33'	3°(s) 0'
6°	84° 17'	152° 17'	5° 9'
6° 25'	90° 0'	149° 0'	

Goat

Hours	Arcs	Eastern Angles	Western Angles
Noon	40° 18'	90°(s) 0'	68°(s) 36'
1°	42° 54'	111° 24'	51° 9'
2°	49° 58'	128° 51'	38° 11'
3°	59° 35'	141° 49'	28° 35'
4°	71° 4'	151° 25'	21° 12'
5°	83° 31'	158° 48'	18° 3'
5° 30'	90° 0'	161° 57'	

Water Bearer

Hours	Arcs	Eastern Angles	Western Angles
Noon	36° 57'	77°(s) 30'	54°(s) 48'
1°	39° 46'	100° 12'	36° 55'
2°	47° 15'	118° 0'	23° 57'
3°	57° 33'	131° 3'	15° 12'
4°	69° 30'	139° 48'	8° 17'
5°	82° 18'	146° 43'	5° 9'
5° 35'	90° 0'	149° 51'	

Fishes

Hours	Arcs	Eastern Angles	Western Angles
Noon	28° 7'	69°(s) 0'	41°(s) 0'
1°	31° 46'	97° 59'	22° 1'
2°	40° 52'	115° 23'	10° 37'
3°	52° 30'	127° 41'	3° 19'
4°	65° 40'	134° 41'	178°(n) 19'
5°	79° 18'	139° 41'	175° 51'
5° 46'	90° 0'	142° 9'	

13. Exposition of the Angles and Arcs by Parallels or Latitudes.—Continued

Of the Parallel through Soëne 13½ hours lat. 23°51'.

Crab

Hours	Arcs	Eastern Angles	Western Angles
Noon	0° 0'	90° 0'	0° 0'
1°	13° 43'	176° 15'	3° 45'
2°	27° 23'	173° 51'	6° 9'
3°	41° 20'	168° 15'	11° 45'
4°	54° 27'	166° 51'	13° 9'
5°	67° 42'	162° 42'	17° 18'
6°	80° 36'	157° 59'	22° 1'
6° 45'	90° 0'	153° 46'	26° 14'

Lion

Hours	Arcs	Eastern Angles	Western Angles
Noon	3° 21'	102° 30'	28° 56'
1°	14° 18'	176° 4'	25° 0'
2°	27° 56'	180° 0'	25° 57'
3°	41° 44'	179° 3'	27° 42'
4°	55° 14'	177° 18'	31° 20'
5°	68° 43'	173° 40'	36° 4'
6°	81° 52'	168° 56'	38° 7'
6° 38'	90° 0'	166° 53'	

Virgin

Hours	Arcs	Eastern Angles	Western Angles
Noon	12° 11'	111° 0'	63° 20'
1°	18° 42'	158° 40'	48° 16'
2°	30° 57'	173° 44'	43° 57'
3°	44° 22'	178° 3'	42° 0'
4°	58° 1'	180° 0'	42° 45'
5°	71° 43'	179° 15'	44° 21'
6°	85° 20'	177° 39'	45° 19'
6° 21'	90° 0'	176° 41'	

Balance

Hours	Arcs	Eastern Angles	Western Angles
Noon	23° 51'	113° 51'	83° 32'
1°	27° 56'	144° 10'	65° 29'
2°	37° 36'	162° 13'	
3°	49° 42'	171° 45'	55° 57'
4°	62° 47'	176° 59'	50° 43'
5°	76° 20'	179° 3'	48° 39'
6°	90° 0'	180° 0'	47° 42'

Scorpion

Hours	Arcs	Eastern Angles	Western Angles
Noon	35° 31'	111° 0'	88° 45'
1°	38° 25'	133° 15'	71° 42'
2°	46° 2'	150° 18'	60° 19'
3°	56° 30'	161° 41'	52° 55'
4°	68° 31'	169° 5'	47° 30'
5°	81° 22'	174° 30'	45° 19'
5° 39'	90° 0'	176° 41'	

Archer

Hours	Arcs	Eastern Angles	Western Angles
Noon	44° 21'	102° 30'	83° 30'
1°	46° 40'	121° 30'	67° 44'
2°	53° 4'	137° 16'	55° 35'
3°	62° 18'	149° 25'	47° 2'
4°	73° 20'	157° 58'	40° 14'
5°	85° 23'	164° 46'	38° 7'
5° 22'	90° 0'	166° 53'	

Goat

Hours	Arcs	Eastern Angles	Western Angles
Noon	47° 42'	90° 0'	
1°	49° 52'	108° 3'	71° 57'
2°	55° 52'	123° 31'	56° 29'
3°	64° 37'	135° 37'	44° 23'
4°	75° 12'	144° 57'	35° 3'
5°	86° 54'	152° 0'	28° 0'
5° 15'	90° 0'	153° 46'	26° 14'

Water Bearer

Hours	Arcs	Eastern Angles	Western Angles
Noon	44° 21'	77° 30'	58° 30'
1°	46° 40'	96° 30'	42° 44'
2°	53° 4'	112° 16'	30° 25'
3°	62° 18'	124° 25'	22° 2'
4°	73° 20'	132° 58'	15° 14'
5°	85° 23'	139° 46'	13° 7'
5° 22'	90° 0'	141° 53'	

Fishes

Hours	Arcs	Eastern Angles	Western Angles
Noon	35° 31'	69° 0'	46° 45'
1°	38° 25'	91° 15'	29° 42'
2°	46° 2'	108° 18'	18° 19'
3°	56° 30'	119° 41'	10° 55'
4°	68° 31'	127° 5'	5° 30'
5°	81° 22'	132° 30'	3° 19'
5° 39'	90° 0'	134° 41'	

Ram

Hours	Arcs	Eastern Angles	Western Angles
Noon	23° 51'	66° 9'	35° 50'
1°	27° 56'	96° 28'	17° 47'
2°	37° 36'	114° 31'	8° 15'
3°	49° 42'	124° 3'	3° 1'
4°	62° 47'	129° 17'	0° 57'
5°	76° 20'	131° 21'	0° 0'
6°	90° 0'	132° 18'	

Bull

Hours	Arcs	Eastern Angles	Western Angles
Noon	12° 11'	69° 0'	21° 20'
1°	18° 42'	116° 40'	6° 16'
2°	30° 57'	131° 44'	1° 57'
3°	44° 22'	136° 22'	0° 0'
4°	58° 1'	138° 0'	0° 45'
5°	71° 43'	137° 15'	2° 21'
6°	85° 20'	135° 39'	3° 19'
6° 21'	90° 0'	134° 41'	

Twins

Hours	Arcs	Eastern Angles	Western Angles
Noon	3° 21'	77° 30'	3° 56'
1°	14° 18'	151° 0'	0° 0'
2°	27° 56'	155° 0'	0° 57'
3°	41° 44'	154° 3'	2° 42'
4°	55° 14'	152° 18'	6° 20'
5°	68° 43'	148° 40'	11° 4'
6°	81° 52'	143° 56'	13° 7'
6° 38'	90° 0'	141° 53'	

13. Exposition of the Angles and Arcs by Parallels or Latitudes.—Continued

Of the Parallel through the Low Countries of Egypt 14 hours lat. 30°22'.

Ram

Hours	Arcs	Eastern Angles	Western Angles
Noon	30° 22'	66° 9'	42° 28'
1°	33° 35'	89° 50'	25° 41'
2°	41° 39'	106° 37'	
3°	52° 25'	116° 28'	15° 50'
4°	64° 28'	122° 5'	10° 5'
5°	77° 6'	124° 39'	7° 39'
6°	90° 0'	125° 47'	6° 31'

Bull

Hours	Arcs	Eastern Angles	Western Angles
Noon	18° 42'	69° 0'	34° 42'
1°	23° 18'	103° 18'	17° 35'
2°	33° 30'	120° 25'	
3°	45° 36'	127° 34'	10° 26'
4°	58° 21'	130° 10'	7° 50'
5°	71° 15'	130° 28'	7° 32'
6°	84° 7'	129° 5'	8° 55'
6° 28'	90° 0'	127° 55'	10° 5'

Twins

Hours	Arcs	Eastern Angles	Western Angles
Noon	9° 52'	77° 30'	26° 47'
1°	16° 45'	128° 13'	13° 38'
2°	28° 44'	141° 22'	
3°	41° 31'	144° 26'	10° 34'
4°	54° 27'	144° 8'	10° 52'
5°	67° 17'	142° 17'	12° 59'
6°	79° 48'	138° 46'	16° 14'
6° 51'	90° 0'	134° 49'	20° 11'

Goat

Hours	Arcs	Eastern Angles	Western Angles
Noon	54° 13'	90° 0'	74° 26'
1°	56° 6'	105° 34'	60° 37'
2°	61° 22'	119° 23'	
3°	69° 17'	130° 46'	49° 14'
4°	78° 59'	139° 28'	40° 30'
5°	90° 0'	146° 28'	33° 32'

Water Bearer

Hours	Arcs	Eastern Angles	Western Angles
Noon	50° 52'	77° 30'	61° 21'
1°	52° 53'	93° 39'	47° 9'
2°	58° 27'	107° 51'	
3°	66° 44'	119° 1'	35° 59'
4°	76° 51'	127° 37'	27° 23'
5°	88° 9'	133° 43'	21° 17'
5° 9'	90° 0'	134° 49'	20° 11'

Fishes

Hours	Arcs	Eastern Angles	Western Angles
Noon	42° 2'	69° 0'	50° 28'
1°	44° 26'	87° 32'	35° 22'
2°	50° 58'	102° 38'	
3°	60° 19'	113° 33'	24° 27'
4°	71° 20'	120° 56'	17° 6'
5°	83° 19'	125° 54'	12° 59'
5° 32'	90° 0'	127° 55'	10° 5'

Balance

Hours	Arcs	Eastern Angles	Western Angles
Noon	30° 22'	113° 51'	90° 10'
1°	33° 35'	137° 32'	73° 23'
2°	41° 39'	154° 19'	
3°	52° 25'	164° 10'	63° 32'
4°	64° 28'	169° 47'	57° 55'
5°	77° 6'	172° 21'	55° 21'
6°	90° 0'	173° 29'	54° 13'

Scorpion

Hours	Arcs	Eastern Angles	Western Angles
Noon	42° 2'	111° 0'	92° 28'
1°	44° 26'	129° 32'	77° 22'
2°	50° 58'	144° 38'	
3°	60° 19'	155° 33'	66° 27'
4°	71° 20'	162° 56'	59° 4'
5°	83° 19'	167° 54'	54° 6'
5° 32'	90° 0'	169° 55'	52° 5'

Archer

Hours	Arcs	Eastern Angles	Western Angles
Noon	50° 52'	102° 30'	86° 21'
1°	52° 53'	118° 39'	72° 9'
2°	58° 27'	132° 51'	
3°	66° 44'	144° 1'	60° 59'
4°	76° 51'	152° 37'	52° 23'
5°	88° 9'	158° 43'	46° 54'
5° 9'	90° 0'	159° 49'	45° 11'

Crab

Hours	Arcs	Eastern Angles	Western Angles
Noon	6° 31'	90° 0'	30° 0'
1°	14° 56'	150° 0'	20° 22'
2°	27° 23'	159° 38'	
3°	40° 19'	160° 30'	19° 30'
4°	53° 54'	158° 51'	21° 51'
5°	65° 55'	156° 0'	24° 0'
6°	78° 15'	151° 49'	28° 11'
7°	90° 0'	146° 28'	33° 32'

Lion

Hours	Arcs	Eastern Angles	Western Angles
Noon	9° 52'	102° 30'	51° 47'
1°	16° 45'	153° 13'	38° 38'
2°	28° 44'	166° 22'	
3°	41° 31'	169° 26'	35° 34'
4°	54° 27'	169° 8'	35° 52'
5°	67° 17'	167° 1'	37° 59'
6°	79° 48'	163° 46'	41° 14'
6° 51'	90° 0'	159° 49'	45° 11'

Virgin

Hours	Arcs	Eastern Angles	Western Angles
Noon	18° 42'	111° 0'	76° 42'
1°	23° 18'	145° 18'	59° 35'
2°	33° 30'	162° 25'	
3°	45° 36'	169° 34'	52° 26'
4°	58° 21'	172° 10'	49° 50'
5°	71° 15'	172° 28'	49° 32'
6°	84° 7'	171° 5'	50° 55'
6° 28'	90° 0'	169° 55'	45° 5'

13. Exposition of the Angles and Arcs by Parallels or Latitudes.—Continued

Of the Parallel through Rhodes 14½ hours lat. 36°.

Ram

Hours	Arcs	Eastern Angles	Western Angles
Noon	36° 0'	66° 9'	46° 37'
1°	38° 37'	85° 41'	31° 31'
2°	45° 31'	100° 47'	
3°	55° 6'	110° 27'	21° 51'
4°	66° 9'	116° 16'	16° 2'
5°	77° 56'	118° 54'	13° 24'
6°	90° 0'	120° 9'	12° 9'

Bull

Hours	Arcs	Eastern Angles	Western Angles
Noon	24° 20'	69° 0'	42° 22'
1°	27° 51'	95° 38'	26° 1'
2°	36° 24'	111° 59'	
3°	47° 14'	120° 10'	17° 50'
4°	59° 0'	123° 40'	14° 20'
5°	71° 5'	124° 34'	13° 26'
6°	83° 9'	123° 30'	14° 30'
6° 35'	90° 0'	122° 7'	15° 53'

Twins

Hours	Arcs	Eastern Angles	Western Angles
Noon	15° 30'	77° 30'	40° 28'
1°	20° 20'	114° 32'	24° 41'
2°	30° 28'	130° 19'	
3°	42° 6'	135° 37'	19° 23'
4°	54° 12'	137° 11'	19° 49'
5°	66° 17'	136° 5'	18° 55'
6°	78° 7'	133° 10'	21° 50'
7°	89° 27'	128° 39'	26° 21'
7° 4'	90° 0'	128° 36'	26° 24'

Crab

Hours	Arcs	Eastern Angles	Western Angles
Noon	12° 9'	90° 0'	46° 46'
1°	17° 47'	133° 14'	32° 15'
2°	28° 22'	147° 45'	
3°	40° 27'	151° 46'	28° 14'
4°	52° 36'	151° 52'	28° 8'
5°	64° 36'	149° 54'	30° 6'
6°	76° 16'	146° 25'	33° 35'
7°	87° 23'	141° 30'	38° 30'
7° 15'	90° 0'	140° 1'	39° 59'

Lion

Hours	Arcs	Eastern Angles	Western Angles
Noon	15° 30'	102° 30'	65° 28'
1°	20° 20'	139° 32'	49° 41'
2°	30° 28'	155° 19'	
3°	42° 6'	160° 37'	44° 23'
4°	54° 12'	162° 11'	42° 49'
5°	66° 17'	161° 5'	43° 55'
6°	78° 7'	158° 10'	46° 50'
7°	89° 27'	153° 39'	51° 21'
7° 4'	90° 0'	153° 36'	51° 24'

Virgin

Hours	Arcs	Eastern Angles	Western Angles
Noon	24° 20'	111° 0'	84° 22'
1°	27° 51'	137° 38'	68° 1'
2°	36° 24'	153° 59'	
3°	47° 14'	162° 10'	59° 50'
4°	59° 0'	165° 40'	56° 20'
5°	71° 5'	166° 34'	55° 26'
6°	83° 9'	165° 30'	56° 30'
6° 35'	90° 0'	164° 7'	57° 53'

Balance

Hours	Arcs	Eastern Angles	Western Angles
Noon	36° 0'	113° 51'	94° 19'
1°	38° 37'	133° 23'	79° 19'
2°	45° 31'	148° 23'	
3°	55° 6'	158° 9'	69° 33'
4°	66° 9'	163° 58'	63° 44'
5°	77° 56'	166° 36'	61° 6'
6°	90° 0'	167° 51'	59° 51'

Scorpion

Hours	Arcs	Eastern Angles	Western Angles
Noon	47° 40'	111° 0'	95° 10'
1°	49° 42'	126° 50'	81° 40'
2°	55° 26'	140° 20'	
3°	63° 48'	150° 34'	71° 26'
4°	73° 55'	157° 51'	64° 9'
5°	85° 5'	162° 28'	59° 32'
5° 25'	90° 0'	164° 7'	57° 53'

Archer

Hours	Arcs	Eastern Angles	Western Angles
Noon	56° 30'	102° 30'	88° 21'
1°	58° 14'	116° 39'	75° 37'
2°	63° 13'	129° 23'	
3°	70° 41'	139° 47'	65° 13'
4°	80° 2'	147° 47'	57° 13'
4° 56'	90° 0'	153° 36'	51° 24'

Goat

Hours	Arcs	Eastern Angles	Western Angles
Noon	59° 51'	90° 0'	76° 15'
1°	61° 30'	103° 45'	63° 50'
2°	66° 12'	116° 10'	
3°	73° 22'	126° 36'	53° 24'
4°	82° 24'	134° 56'	45° 4'
4° 45'	90° 0'	140° 1'	39° 59'

Water Bearer

Hours	Arcs	Eastern Angles	Western Angles
Noon	56° 30'	77° 30'	63° 21'
1°	58° 14'	91° 39'	50° 37'
2°	63° 13'	104° 23'	
3°	70° 41'	114° 47'	40° 13'
4°	80° 2'	122° 47'	32° 13'
4° 56'	90° 0'	128° 36'	26° 24'

Fishes

Hours	Arcs	Eastern Angles	Western Angles
Noon	47° 40'	69° 0'	53° 10'
1°	49° 42'	84° 50'	39° 40'
2°	55° 26'	98° 20'	
3°	63° 48'	108° 34'	29° 26'
4°	73° 55'	115° 51'	22° 9'
5°	85° 5'	120° 28'	17° 32'
5° 25'	90° 0'	122° 7'	15° 53'

13. EXPOSITION OF THE ANGLES AND ARCS BY PARALLELS OR LATITUDES.—Continued.

Of the Parallel through the Hellespont 15 hours lat. 40°56'.

Ram

Hours	Arcs	Eastern Angles	Western Angles
Noon	40° 56'	66° 9'	50° 3'
1°	43° 8'	82° 15'	36° 22'
2°	49° 7'	95° 56'	
3°	57° 42'	105° 26'	26° 52'
4°	67° 50'	111° 5'	21° 13'
5°	78° 45'	114° 17'	18° 1'
6°	90° 0'	115° 13'	17° 5'

Bull

Hours	Arcs	Eastern Angles	Western Angles
Noon	29° 16'	69° 0'	47° 30'
1°	32° 5'	90° 30'	32° 0'
2°	39° 22'	105° 30'	
3°	49° 3'	114° 0'	24° 0'
4°	59° 50'	118° 7'	19° 53'
5°	71° 5'	119° 24'	18° 36'
6°	82° 22'	118° 40'	19° 20'
6° 42'	90° 0'	116° 59'	21° 1'

Twins

Hours	Arcs	Eastern Angles	Western Angles
Noon	20° 26'	77° 30'	54° 0'
1°	24° 5'	106° 6'	48° 6'
2°	32° 37'	122° 0'	33° 0'
3°	43° 8'	128° 50'	26° 10'
4°	54° 19'	131° 5'	23° 55'
5°	65° 36'	130° 8'	24° 52'
6°	76° 46'	128° 24'	26° 36'
7°	87° 24'	124° 6'	30° 54'
7° 16'	90° 0'	123° 0'	31° 54'

Goat

Hours	Arcs	Eastern Angles	Western Angles
Noon	64° 47'	90° 0'	77° 33'
1°	66° 15'	102° 27'	66° 25'
2°	70° 30'	113° 35'	
3°	77° 4'	122° 55'	57° 5'
4°	85° 18'	130° 58'	49° 2'
4° 30'	90° 0'	134° 16'	45° 44'

Water Bearer

Hours	Arcs	Eastern Angles	Western Angles
Noon	61° 26'	77° 30'	64° 55'
1°	63° 24'	90° 5'	53° 31'
2°	67° 24'	101° 29'	
3°	74° 13'	111° 10'	43° 50'
4°	82° 48'	118° 45'	36° 15'
4° 44'	90° 0'	123° 6'	31° 54'

Fishes

Hours	Arcs	Eastern Angles	Western Angles
Noon	52° 36'	69° 0'	55° 14'
1°	54° 23'	82° 46'	43° 5'
2°	59° 25'	94° 55'	
3°	66° 58'	104° 24'	33° 36'
4°	76° 15'	111° 10'	26° 50'
5°	86° 38'	115° 45'	22° 15'
5° 18'	90° 0'	116° 59'	21° 1'

Balance

Hours	Arcs	Eastern Angles	Western Angles
Noon	40° 56'	113° 51'	97° 45'
1°	43° 8'	129° 57'	84° 4'
2°	49° 7'	143° 38'	
3°	57° 42'	153° 8'	74° 34'
4°	67° 50'	158° 47'	68° 55'
5°	78° 45'	161° 59'	65° 43'
6°	90° 0'	162° 55'	64° 47'

Scorpion

Hours	Arcs	Eastern Angles	Western Angles
Noon	52° 36'	111° 0'	97° 14'
1°	54° 23'	124° 46'	85° 5'
2°	59° 25'	136° 55'	
3°	66° 58'	146° 24'	75° 36'
4°	76° 15'	153° 10'	68° 50'
5°	86° 38'	157° 45'	64° 15'
5° 18'	90° 0'	158° 59'	63° 1'

Archer

Hours	Arcs	Eastern Angles	Western Angles
Noon	61° 26'	102° 30'	89° 55'
1°	63° 0'	115° 5'	78° 31'
2°	67° 24'	126° 29'	
3°	74° 13'	136° 10'	68° 50'
4°	82° 48'	143° 45'	61° 15'
4° 44'	90° 0'	148° 6'	56° 54'

Crab

Hours	Arcs	Eastern Angles	Western Angles
Noon	17° 5'	90° 0'	57° 28'
1°	21° 18'	122° 32'	41° 31'
2°	30° 17'	138° 29'	
3°	41° 37'	144° 18'	35° 42'
4°	52° 25'	145° 38'	34° 22'
5°	63° 47'	144° 28'	35° 32'
6°	74° 48'	141° 30'	38° 30'
7°	85° 9'	137° 5'	42° 55'
7° 30'	90° 0'	134° 16'	45° 44'

Lion

Hours	Arcs	Eastern Angles	Western Angles
Noon	20° 26'	102° 30'	73° 54'
1°	24° 5'	131° 6'	58° 0'
2°	32° 37'	147° 0'	
3°	43° 8'	153° 50'	51° 10'
4°	54° 19'	156° 5'	48° 55'
5°	65° 36'	155° 8'	49° 52'
6°	76° 46'	153° 24'	51° 36'
7°	87° 24'	149° 6'	55° 54'
7° 16'	90° 0'	148° 6'	56° 54'

Virgin

Hours	Arcs	Eastern Angles	Western Angles
Noon	29° 16'	111° 0'	89° 30'
1°	32° 5'	132° 30'	74° 30'
2°	39° 22'	147° 30'	
3°	49° 3'	156° 0'	66° 0'
4°	59° 50'	160° 7'	61° 53'
5°	71° 5'	161° 24'	60° 36'
6°	82° 22'	160° 40'	61° 20'
6° 42'	90° 0'	158° 59'	63° 1'

13. EXPOSITION OF THE ANGLES AND ARCS BY PARALLELS OR LATITUDES.—Continued

Of the Parallel through the Middle of Pontus 15½ hours lat. 45°1'.

Ram

Hours	Arcs	Eastern Angles	Western Angles
Noon	45° 1'	66° 9'	51° 41'
1°	46° 55'	80° 37'	
2°	52° 17'	92° 44'	39° 34'
3°	60° 1'	101° 22'	30° 56'
4°	69° 19'	107° 6'	25° 12'
5°	79° 28'	110° 13'	22° 5'
6°	90° 0'	111° 8'	21° 10'

Bull

Hours	Arcs	Eastern Angles	Western Angles
Noon	33° 21'	69° 0'	50° 45'
1°	35° 43'	87° 15'	37° 10'
2°	42° 4'	100° 50'	
3°	50° 46'	109° 9'	28° 51'
4°	60° 44'	113° 31'	24° 29'
5°	71° 12'	115° 3'	22° 57'
6°	81° 46'	114° 31'	23° 29'
6° 48'	90° 0'	112° 43'	25° 17'

Twins

Hours	Arcs	Eastern Angles	Western Angles
Noon	24° 31'	77° 30'	55° 11'
1°	27° 29'	99° 49'	39° 13'
2°	34° 48'	115° 47'	
3°	44° 20'	123° 5'	31° 55'
4°	54° 37'	126° 5'	28° 55'
5°	65° 15'	126° 7'	28° 53'
6°	75° 39'	124° 20'	30° 40'
7°	85° 39'	120° 39'	34° 21'
7° 28'	90° 0'	118° 25'	36° 35'

Goat

Hours	Arcs	Eastern Angles	Western Angles
Noon	68° 52'	90° 0'	
1°	70° 14'	101° 11'	78° 49'
2°	74° 5'	111° 30'	68° 30'
3°	80° 6'	120° 29'	59° 31'
4°	87° 42'	128° 13'	51° 47'
4° 15'	90° 0'	129° 21'	50° 39'

Water Bearer

Hours	Arcs	Eastern Angles	Western Angles
Noon	65° 31'	77° 30'	66° 10'
1°	66° 55'	88° 50'	55° 39'
2°	70° 58'	99° 21'	
3°	77° 14'	108° 19'	46° 41'
4°	85° 10'	115° 20'	39° 40'
4° 32'	90° 0'	118° 25'	36° 35'

Fishes

Hours	Arcs	Eastern Angles	Western Angles
Noon	56° 41'	69° 0'	56° 29'
1°	58° 19'	81° 31'	45° 44'
2°	62° 49'	92° 16'	
3°	69° 42'	101° 12'	36° 48'
4°	78° 16'	107° 31'	30° 29'
5°	87° 56'	112° 6'	25° 54'
5° 12'	90° 0'	112° 43'	25° 17'

Balance

Hours	Arcs	Eastern Angles	Western Angles
Noon	45° 1'	113° 51'	99° 23'
1°	46° 55'	128° 19'	
2°	52° 17'	140° 26'	87° 16'
3°	60° 1'	149° 4'	78° 38'
4°	69° 19'	154° 48'	72° 54'
5°	79° 28'	157° 55'	69° 47'
6°	90° 0'	158° 50'	68° 59'

Scorpion

Hours	Arcs	Eastern Angles	Western Angles
Noon	56° 41'	111° 0'	98° 29'
1°	58° 19'	123° 31'	87° 44'
2°	62° 49'	134° 16'	
3°	69° 42'	143° 12'	78° 48'
4°	78° 16'	149° 31'	72° 29'
5°	87° 56'	154° 6'	67° 54'
5° 12'	90° 0'	154° 43'	67° 17'

Archer

Hours	Arcs	Eastern Angles	Western Angles
Noon	65° 31'	102° 30'	91° 10'
1°	66° 55'	113° 50'	80° 39'
2°	70° 58'	124° 21'	
3°	77° 14'	133° 19'	71° 41'
4°	85° 10'	140° 20'	64° 40'
4° 32'	90° 0'	143° 25'	61° 35'

Crab

Hours	Arcs	Eastern Angles	Western Angles
Noon	21° 10'	90° 0'	63° 55'
1°	24° 32'	116° 5'	48° 30'
2°	32° 12'	131° 30'	
3°	42° 1'	138° 17'	41° 43'
4°	52° 29'	140° 40'	39° 39'
5°	63° 4'	140° 2'	39° 58'
6°	73° 24'	137° 32'	42° 28'
7°	83° 17'	133° 39'	46° 34'
7° 45'	90° 0'	129° 25'	50° 39'

Lion

Hours	Arcs	Eastern Angles	Western Angles
Noon	24° 31'	102° 30'	80° 45'
1°	27° 29'	124° 49'	64° 10'
2°	34° 48'	140° 47'	
3°	44° 20'	148° 5'	56° 55'
4°	54° 37'	151° 5'	53° 55'
5°	65° 15'	151° 7'	53° 53'
6°	75° 39'	149° 20'	55° 40'
7°	85° 39'	145° 39'	59° 21'
7° 28'	90° 0'	143° 25'	61° 35'

Virgin

Hours	Arcs	Eastern Angles	Western Angles
Noon	33° 21'	111° 0'	92° 45'
1°	35° 43'	129° 15'	79° 10'
2°	42° 4'	142° 50'	
3°	50° 46'	151° 9'	70° 51'
4°	60° 44'	155° 31'	66° 29'
5°	71° 12'	157° 3'	64° 57'
6°	81° 46'	156° 31'	65° 29'
6° 48'	90° 0'	154° 43'	67° 17'

13. EXPOSITION OF THE ANGLES AND ARCS BY PARALLELS OR LATITUDES.—Continued

Of the Parallel through the Borysthenes 16 hours lat. 48°32′.

Ram

Hours	Arcs	Eastern Angles	Western Angles
Noon	48°32′	66°9′	53°30′
1°	50°21′	78°48′	42°20′
2°	54°59′	89°58′	
3°	62°5′	98°4′	34°14′
4°	70°41′	103°36′	28°42′
5°	80°8′	106°41′	25°37′
6°	90°0′	107°37′	24°41′

Bull

Hours	Arcs	Eastern Angles	Western Angles
Noon	36°52′	69°0′	53°15′
1°	38°56′	84°45′	40°53′
2°	44°31′	97°7′	
3°	52°25′	105°9′	32°51′
4°	61°35′	109°36′	28°24′
5°	71°22′	111°23′	26°37′
6°	81°17′	110°58′	27°2′
6°54′	90°0′	109°22′	28°38′

Twins

Hours	Arcs	Eastern Angles	Western Angles
Noon	28°2′	77°30′	57°51′
1°	30°32′	97°9′	44°6′
2°	36°55′	110°54′	
3°	45°30′	118°28′	36°32′
4°	55°3′	121°50′	33°10′
5°	64°59′	122°19′	32°41′
6°	74°47′	120°46′	34°14′
7°	84°10′	117°27′	37°33′
7°40′	90°0′	114°20′	40°40′

Goat

Hours	Arcs	Eastern Angles	Western Angles
Noon	72°23′	90°0′	79°45′
1°	73°38′	100°15′	70°13′
2°	77°10′	109°47′	
3°	82°44′	118°3′	61°57′
4°	90°0′	124°58′	55°2′

Water Bearer

Hours	Arcs	Eastern Angles	Western Angles
Noon	69°2′	77°30′	67°11′
1°	70°20′	87°49′	57°29′
2°	74°2′	97°31′	
3°	79°48′	105°49′	49°11′
4°	87°14′	112°25′	42°35′
4°20′	90°0′	114°20′	40°40′

Fishes

Hours	Arcs	Eastern Angles	Western Angles
Noon	60°12′	69°12′	57°55′
1°	61°38′	80°5′	47°44′
2°	65°36′	90°16′	
3°	72°5′	98°26′	39°34′
4°	80°3′	104°28′	33°32′
5°	89°3′	109°2′	28°58′
5°6′	90°0′	109°22′	28°38′

Balance

Hours	Arcs	Eastern Angles	Western Angles
Noon	48°32′	113°51′	101°12′
1°	50°21′	126°30′	90°2′
2°	54°59′	137°40′	
3°	62°5′	145°46′	81°56′
4°	70°41′	151°18′	76°24′
5°	80°8′	154°23′	73°19′
6°	90°0′	155°19′	72°23′

Scorpion

Hours	Arcs	Eastern Angles	Western Angles
Noon	60°12′	111°0′	99°55′
1°	61°38′	122°5′	89°50′
2°	65°36′	132°10′	
3°	72°5′	140°26′	81°34′
4°	80°3′	146°28′	75°32′
5°	89°3′	151°2′	70°58′
5°6′	90°0′	151°22′	70°38′

Archer

Hours	Arcs	Eastern Angles	Western Angles
Noon	69°2′	102°30′	92°11′
1°	70°20′	112°49′	82°29′
2°	74°2′	122°31′	
3°	79°48′	130°49′	74°11′
4°	87°14′	137°25′	67°35′
4°20′	90°0′	139°20′	65°40′

Crab

Hours	Arcs	Eastern Angles	Western Angles
Noon	24°41′	90°0′	68°16′
1°	27°30′	111°44′	53°53′
2°	34°9′	126°7′	
3°	43°2′	133°18′	46°42′
4°	52°44′	136°6′	43°54′
5°	62°40′	136°4′	43°56′
6°	72°24′	134°0′	46°0′
7°	81°38′	130°16′	49°44′
8°	90°0′	124°58′	55°2′

Lion

Hours	Arcs	Eastern Angles	Western Angles
Noon	28°2′	102°30′	82°51′
1°	30°32′	122°9′	69°6′
2°	36°55′	135°54′	
3°	45°30′	143°28′	61°32′
4°	55°3′	146°50′	58°10′
5°	64°59′	147°19′	57°41′
6°	74°47′	145°46′	59°14′
7°	84°10′	142°27′	62°33′
7°40′	90°0′	139°20′	65°40′

Virgin

Hours	Arcs	Eastern Angles	Western Angles
Noon	36°52′	111°0′	95°15′
1°	38°56′	126°45′	82°53′
2°	44°31′	139°7′	
3°	52°25′	147°9′	74°51′
4°	61°35′	151°36′	70°24′
5°	71°22′	153°23′	68°37′
6°	81°17′	152°58′	69°2′
6°54′	90°0′	151°22′	70°38′

And now, although the business of the angles has been worked out and there is left to add to these things now established a research into the positions of the principal cities of each province according to their longitudes and latitudes for the calculations of the appearance observed in them, we shall do this exposition as a special geographical treatise by itself; and we shall follow the writings of those who have especially worked in this kind of thing, finding out how many degrees each city is from the equator along the meridian drawn through that city, and how many degrees east or west of the meridian of Alexandria each city is. For we arrange the times of the other places with reference to this meridian.

Now we have thought it pertinent to add this much about these positions: whenever we wish to know, at a given hour in one of these places, what hour it is in some other if their meridians are different, we must take the number of degrees they differ from each other along the equator, and, according as the one sought is east or west of the one given, increase or decrease the given hour by that number of degrees to get the hour defined at the same time in the place sought.

BOOK THREE

Now that we have methodically gone through, in all that has been put together up until now, those things which have first to be completely grasped mathematically concerning the heavens and the earth, and also concerning the obliquity of the sun's path through the middle of the zodiac [along the ecliptic] and its particular incidents in the right sphere and the oblique sphere for each latitude, we consider it proper after all this to treat of the sun and moon and to take account of the incidents concerning their movements, since without a prior understanding of them none of the appearances having to do with the stars can be discovered. And we find the treatise on the sun's movement advanced first, for again, without this, matters concerning the moon could not be grasped in detail.

1. On the Year's Magnitude

SINCE finding the year's time-length is the first of all the things demonstrated concerning the sun, we shall first learn from the treatises of the ancients the disagreements and difficulties concerning their statement on this, and especially from that of Hipparchus, a diligent and truth-loving man. For he is brought to a difficulty of this kind especially by the fact that, for the apparent returns of the sun with respect to the tropics and equinoxes, the length of the year is found to be less than 365¼ days, but for its returns observed with respect to the fixed stars it is found to be more. And from that he conjectures that the sphere of the fixed stars also has a very slow movement, and like that of the planets is in the direction contrary to that of the prime movement which revolves the circle that passes through the poles of the equator and the ecliptic. And we shall show this is so and how it comes about, in the chapters on the fixed stars. For matters concerning them could not be seen in their entirety without a prior understanding of the sun and moon.

But for the present research we believe that we must consider the length of the year looking only to the sun's return with respect to itself—that is, with respect to the oblique circle made by it [the ecliptic]—and that we must define the length of the year as the time in which the sun proceeds continuously from some fixed point of this circle back to the same point, supposing as we do that the only proper principles of this return are the points of this circle determined by the tropics and equinoxes. For, if we tell the story mathematically, we shall not find a more proper return than that which carries the sun through the same configuration both in space and time, whether it be considered with respect to the horizons or the meridian or the magnitude of the solar days; and we shall find no other principles of the ecliptic except those accidentally defined by the tropic and equinoctial points. And if one examines the subject more physically, he will not find a more reasonable return than that which brings the sun from a like to a like weather-condition and from the same season to the same season; nor will he find other principles than those by which the seasons are the most completely distinguished. And the return of the sun considered with respect to the fixed stars seems quite inept for this reason particularly that their sphere is observed to make an ordered movement contrary to that of the heavens. For, with things this way, nothing will keep one from saying that the length of the sun's year is the time it takes the sun to overtake Saturn, for instance, or some other star. And so there would be many different years.

And so we think it proper to consider such a period of time the sun's year which is found, by as many observations as possible taken over a rather long interval, from one tropic or equinox back to the same.

But since a suspected inequality in the periods of even this return, suspected through continuous and successive observations, more or less worried Hipparchus, we shall try briefly to show how this is not at all disturbing, since we are sure by the continuous instrumental observations we have made of the tropics and equinoxes that these periods are not unequal. For we find them differing by no appreciable amount from the additional quarter day, but at times by about as much as could be attributed to the error due to the construction or position of the instruments. For we guess from what Hipparchus reports that the error with regards to inequality belongs rather to the observations. For after he has first set out, in his treatise *On the Precession of the Tropic and Equinoctial Points*, the summer and winter tropics seeming to him to have been accurately observed and in order, he himself agrees that there is not such a difference between them as to recognize for this reason an inequality in the year. For he adds this: "Then it is clear from these observations that the differences in the years have been altogether small. But in the case of the tropics I do not despair of Archimedes' and my having made an error of as much as a quarter day both in observation and calculation. But the irregularity of the years can be accurately perceived from observations made on the bronze ring situated in what is called the Square Hall in Alexandria which is supposed to indicate the equinoctial day as that on which its concave surface begins to be lighted up from the opposite side."[1]

Then he lists, first, the dates of those autumn equinoxes which have been very accurately observed. One fell in the year 17 of the Third Callippic Period, Mesore 30, at the setting of the sun; and another three years after, year 20, on the first of the intercalated days in the morning, which should have been noon, so that there was a disagreement of a quarter day. And another a year after, year 21, at the sixth hour, which agreed with the preceding observation. And another

---

[1]The inequality of the year is here being judged in terms of the number of solar days. This might seem arbitrary, since the days might be unequal. And indeed it will be seen later on in this Book that the solar days are considered to be unequal. But the theory of their irregularity will be such that their inequality is exactly symmetrical within each year. But, of course, to judge that the inequality is symmetrical, it is necessary to fall back on something else supposed equal. The Greeks usually supposed it to be the stellar day, the time it takes a fixed star to go from a meridian back to the same meridian again. This is practically true for Ptolemy, but not absolutely so, because of the precession of the equinoxes. For, as we shall see in Book VII, the fixed stars move from west to east about the poles of the ecliptic nearly a half a degree in a hundred years. This introduces an irregularity in the length of the stellar day exactly parallel to one of the irregularities in the length of the solar day described in Chapter 9 of this Book, but one so small in magnitude that it could not be perceived from day to day, or even from year to year.

eleven years after, year 32, on the third of the intercalated days at midnight before the fourth. And it should have been in the morning, so that there was again a disagreement of a quarter day. And another a year after, year 33, on the fourth of the intercalated days in the morning, which agreed with the preceding observation. And another three years after, year 36, on the fourth of the intercalated days in the evening. And it should have been at midnight so that there was again a disagreement of a quarter day.

And next he lists those spring equinoxes likewise accurately observed. One fell in the year 32 of the Third Callippic Period, Mechir 27, in the morning. But he adds: "The ring in Alexandria was also lighted up equally on both sides at the fifth hour, so that the same equinox differently observed differed by nearnearly five hours." And he says the equinoxes following, up to the year 37, agreed with the addition of a quarter day. And eleven years after, year 43, Mechir 29-30, just after midnight, he says, there was a spring equinox, which also agreed with the observation in the year 32; and also, he says, with the observations in the following years up to the year 50. For in that year it fell on Phamenoth 1 at sunset, within very nearly $1\frac{3}{4}$ days of that of the year 43, which is also proportional to the 7 intervening years. And so in these observations there was no perceptible difference although it is possible for there to be an error of as much as a quarter day, not only as regards the tropic observations, but also the equinoctial. For even if the position or discrimination of the instruments is inaccurate by only $\frac{1}{3600}$ of the circle through the poles of the equator, at the equinoctial intersections the sun makes up for this advance in latitude by shifting $\frac{1}{4}°$ in longitude along the ecliptic, so that there could be an inconsistency of very nearly a quarter day. And there could be a greater error still in the case of instruments not placed permanently and not then corrected for each observation, but which have been attached for some time to the pavement with a view to keeping a steady position for a good while, where yet some long unnoticed shift has been made in them. And anyone can see an example of this in the bronze rings in the palestra of our city, which are supposed to be in the plane of the equator. For in making observations we find such a distortion in their placement, and especially in the case of the largest and oldest, that at times their concave surfaces twice suffer a shift in lighting at the same equinoxes.

But certainly from such things Hipparchus himself does not think there is anything solid to support a suspicion of inequality in the lengths of years. But he says he finds by calculating from certain eclipses of the moon that the irregularity of the years, on the average, does not embrace a difference greater than three quarters of a day. And this would merit some attention if it were so and not evidently belied by the reasons he offers. For he calculates, by the lunar eclipses observed near certain fixed stars, by how much in each case the star Spica precedes the autumn equinox. And in this way he thinks he finds that once it was at its greatest distance of $6\frac{1}{2}°$, for the time he observed, and once at its least distance of $5\frac{1}{4}°$. And he infers from this fact that, since it is not possible for Spica to move so far in such a short time, it is likely that the sun, from which Hipparchus examines the positions of the fixed stars, does not always make its return in an equal time.

But he has overlooked the point that, since this calculation cannot proceed without laying down the sun's position at the eclipse, he, taking for this purpose in each case the tropics and equinoxes accurately observed by himself in those very years, thereby immediately makes clear that in comparing the years there is no difference beyond the addition of the quarter day.

For example, from the observation of the eclipse in the year 32 of the Third Callippic Period he thinks he finds Spica preceding the autumn equinox by $6\frac{1}{2}°$; but from the eclipse in the year 43 of the same period, by $5\frac{1}{4}°$. And likewise setting beside these calculations the spring equinoxes accurately observed in those same years—so that by means of these he may get the sun's positions at the middle of the eclipses, and from these the moon's positions, and from the moon's those of the stars—he says that the spring equinox of the year 32 fell on Mechir 27 in the morning, and that of the year 43 on Mechir 29-30 after midnight, nearly $2\frac{3}{4}$ days later than that of the year 32, which is just equal to the quarter day added for each of the 11 intervening years. If, then, the sun has made its return to these equinoxes in neither more nor less time than the additional quarter day, and if it is not possible for the star Spica to have moved $1\frac{1}{4}°$ in so few years, how could it be otherwise than absurd to take the results calculated from the principles assumed as an accusation against the very principles combined to produce them, as if one were unable to saddle anything else with the cause of this excessive movement of Spica except the equinoxes assumed at the same time to have been accurately and inaccurately observed, although there were many things which could have introduced such an error?[1] For it would seem much more possible that the distances of the moon at the eclipses with respect to the nearest fixed stars had been estimated rather roughly; or that the calculations either of the moon's parallaxes for the sighting of its apparent positions or of the sun's movement from the equinoxes to the middle of the eclipses had been effected neither truly nor accurately.

And I think Hipparchus himself recognized there is nothing convincing in such things as far as imposing a second anomaly on the sun, but I think he only wishes for the love of the truth not to keep back anything which could in anyway bring one to suspect. And so he himself used hypotheses concerning the sun and moon with just one anomaly belonging to the sun, an anomaly which is redeemed in the year considered with respect to the tropics and equinoxes. And in supposing these revolutions to be equal in time we do not observe the appearances at the eclipses differing in any perceptible way from the calculations based on these hypotheses. For it would be quite perceptible if a correction for the inequality of the year were not made at the same time, even if it were only a difference of one degree or very nearly two standard hours.

From all these things, and from the times of the returns which we ourselves have gotten from the consecutive passages of the sun observed by us, we do not find the magnitude of the year unequal if it is considered with respect to some one thing and not one time with respect to the tropic and equinoctial points and another with respect to the fixed stars. Nor do we find any more proper period of return than that which carries the sun from one tropic or equinoctial point, or any other point on the ecliptic, back to that same point. And we do think it entirely proper to explain the appearances by the simplest hypotheses

---

[1]Hipparchus' logic, contrary to what Ptolemy says, seems impeccable insofar as he is saying that assumptions which lead to their contradictories are false. But the reasoning must be right, and Ptolemy is also suggesting that there were many steps in between which might have been false.

possible, so long as nothing perceptible appears contrary to this deduction.

And therefore it has become clear to us from what Hipparchus has shown that the length of the year observed with respect to the tropics and equinoxes is less than $365\frac{1}{4}$ days, but it would not be possible to find out with very great certainty by how much it is less since the increase of a quarter day remains perceptibly unchanged for many years because of the very small difference. And so the extra amount can be perceived only when it is found added up together over a longer period of time. And it must be divided among the intervening years of the interval and it must be observed for a greater and a smaller number of years than this same interval. And the period of return will be gotten the more accurately the longer the time between the observations compared. And this is the case not only with this period of return, but with all of them. For the error resulting from the weakness of the observations themselves, even if they are managed accurately, is small and very nearly the same as far as the senses are concerned both for appearances considered over a long time and for those considered over a short time. And this error of observation, when it is distributed over fewer years, makes the error in the length of the year greater and also in multiples of it over a longer period of time; and it makes the error in the length of the year smaller when distributed over a greater number of years.

And therefore it is properly thought sufficient if, when we consider how much the time between us and the old yet accurate observations can help in the approximation of the supposed periods of revolution, we try to introduce them with the others and do not willingly forego the proper verification, and if we suppose the establishing of dates for a whole long age or for some great multiple of time between observations is the work for another's love of wisdom and truth. Because of their age, then, the summer tropics observed by the pupils of Meton and Euctemon and those observed after them by the pupils of Aristarchus should be compared with those observed by us. But because the observations of the tropics are generally hard to determine and, moreover, because the observations handed down by these people were taken more or less in the rough, as Hipparchus also seems to have thought, we pass them over. We have used for this comparison the observation of the equinoxes, and, because of their accuracy, especially those given Hipparchus' approval as having been most certainly taken by him, and those most carefully observed by ourselves with the instruments for such purposes described at the beginning of this treatise. And from these we find that, in very nearly 300 years, the tropics and equinoxes fall one day sooner than the quarter-day addition to 365 days allows.

For in the year 32 of the Third Callippic Period Hipparchus singles out especially the autumn equinox as most accurately observed, and he says he calculates it to have fallen at midnight between the third and fourth of the intercalated days. And this is the year 178 after the death of Alexander. And 285 years after in the year 3 of Antonine (which is 463 years after the death of Alexander) we observed, again most correctly, the autumn equinox as having fallen on Athyr 9 about one hour after sunrise. Therefore the return added on in all the 285 Egyptian years, that is those of 365 days each, all told $70 + \frac{1}{4} + \frac{1}{20}$ days instead of the $71\frac{1}{4}$ days due these years by the regular quarter-day addition. And so the return fell sooner by very nearly 1 day less $\frac{1}{20}$ than the regular quarter-day addition allowed.

And likewise Hipparchus again says the spring equinox in the same year 32 of the Third Callippic Period was very accurately observed to have fallen on Mechir 27 in the morning. And this is 178 years after the death of Alexander. And likewise 285 years later (463 years after the death of Alexander) we find the spring equinox has fallen on Pactom 7 very nearly one hour after noon, so that the period reached the aforesaid $70+\frac{1}{4}+\frac{1}{20}$ days very nearly, instead of the regular quarter-day addition to the 285 years of $71\frac{1}{4}$ days. Therefore the return of the spring equinox fell sooner by 1 day less $\frac{1}{20}$ than the regular quarter-day addition allowed. And so, since 300 years to 285 years, and 1 day to 1 day less $\frac{1}{20}$, are the same ratio, it is inferred that in very nearly 300 years the sun's return with respect to the equinoctial points is sooner by 1 day than the regular quarter-day addition allows.

Even if, because of its antiquity, we compare the summer tropic more or less roughly recorded by the pupils of Meton and Euctemon with that calculated by us, we shall find the same thing. For it is recorded to have taken place Athenianwise in the Magistracy of Apseudes, Egyptianwise Phamenoth 21 in the morning, and we, in the same 463rd year after the death of Alexander, very carefully calculated it to have fallen on Mesore 11-12 two hours after midnight. And from the summer tropic recorded under Apseudes to that observed by the pupils of Aristarchus in the year 50 of the First Callippic Period, as Hipparchus also says, is 152 years. And from this year 50 (which was the 44th year after the death of Alexander) to the 463rd year [after the death of Alexander], the year of our observation, is 419 years. Therefore, in the intervening 571 years of the whole interval, if the summer tropic observed by the pupils of Euctemon fell at the beginning of Phamenoth 21, very nearly $140+\frac{1}{2}+\frac{1}{3}$ days have been added to the complete Egyptian years instead of the regular quarter-day addition to the 571 years of $142+\frac{1}{2}+\frac{1}{4}$ days; so that this return fell sooner by 2 days less $\frac{1}{12}$ than the regular quarter-day addition allowed. It is therefore evident that in 600 complete Egyptian years, the lengths of the solar years anticipate the regular quarter-day addition by nearly 2 whole days.

And with many other observations we find this same thing happening, and we see Hipparchus several times agreeing to this. For in his treatise *On the Length of the Year*, when he compares the summer tropic observed by Aristarchus at the end of the year 50 of the First Callippic Period with the one taken again very accurately by himself at the end of the year 43 of the Third Callippic Period, he says as follows: "It is evident, therefore, that in 145 years the tropic has fallen sooner by half a day and night together than the regular quarter-day addition allows." And again in his treatise *On Intercalated Months and Days*, saying first that the year, for the pupils of Meton and Euctemon, contains $365+\frac{1}{4}+\frac{1}{76}$ days and according to Callippus only $365\frac{1}{4}$ days, he adds this: "And we have found as many whole months in the 19 years as they, but we have found that the year comes to $\frac{1}{300}$ day less than the regularly added quarter day, so that in 300 Egyptian years the sum of the solar years is 5 days less than Meton's and only 1 day less than Callippus'." And also in summarizing his views by citing his own works, he says as follows: "And I have also treated the question of the length of the year in a book in which I show that the solar year (that is, the time in which the sun goes from a tropic back to the same tropic or from an equinox back to the same equinox) contains 365 days and less than $\frac{1}{4}$ day by $\frac{1}{300}$ of a day and night, and not as the mathematicians think $365\frac{1}{4}$ days."

I think, then, it has been made clear that the appearances observed up to this time concerning the magnitude of the year agree with the size just assigned the return of the tropic and equinoctial points by a concurrence of present appearances with earlier ones. And since all this is so, if we distribute the one day over the 300 years, there falls to each year 12″ of a day. And if we subtract this from the 365 days 15′ where the quarter day has been added, we shall have the length of the year we are looking for—that is, 365 days 14′ 48″. And this number of days can be taken by us as the nearest approximation possible from the observations we have at present.

And as regards the scrutiny of the movements of the sun and the other planets in their particularities which is best furnished ready to hand and all set out by the orderly construction of tables, we believe it is the necessary purpose and aim of the mathematician to show forth all the appearances of the heavens as products of regular and circular motions. And it is incumbent upon him to construct such tables as, proper and consequent upon this purpose, separate out the particular regular[1] motions from the anomaly which seems to result from the hypotheses of circles, and show forth their apparent movements as a combination and union of all together. In order, then, that we may get this sort of thing in more serviceable form for the demonstration under consideration, we shall set out the regular movements of the sun in their particularities in this way.

For since a return has been proved to be 365 days 14′48″, if we divide these into the 360° of one circle, we shall have the sun's mean daily movement along the ecliptic as approximately $0°59^{i}8^{ii}17^{iii}13^{iv}12^{v}31^{vi}$;[2] for it will suffice to carry out the fractions to this power of sixtieths. And again, taking $\frac{1}{24}$ of the daily movement along the ecliptic, we shall have for the hourly movement approximately $0°2^{i}27^{ii}50^{iii}43^{iv}3^{v}1^{vi}$. Likewise multiplying the daily movement by the 30 days of a month, we shall have the mean monthly movement of $29°34^{i}8^{ii}36^{iii}36^{iv}15^{v}30^{vi}$; and multiplying by the 365 days of an Egyptian year we shall have the mean yearly movement of $359°45^{i}24^{ii}45^{iii}21^{iv}8^{v}35^{vi}$. Again multiplying the mean yearly movement by 18 years, because of the symmetry which will appear in the construction of the tables, and subtracting the whole circles, we shall have the surplus for the 18-year period, that is $355°37^{i}25^{ii}36^{iii}20^{iv}34^{v}30^{vi}$.

We have accordingly drawn up three tables of the regular movement of the sun, one in forty-five rows and the others in two parts. The first table contains the mean movements for the 18-year periods; the second table contains first the movements for the Egyptian years, and then for hours; the third, first the movements for months and, under that, for days. The numbers designating the time are set out in the first columns, and in the next columns the degrees, minutes, etc., are put beside them according to the proper combinations of each. And the tables are as follows:

[1]The word "regular" is here used as a translation of the Greek word ὁμαλός. On the other hand ἀνομαλία, its privative, is translated by the technical "anomaly" instead of by the more obvious "irregularity." There will be times, however, when "irregularity" is used. The Greek word ὁμαλός has three meanings, all significant in an astronomical context: (1) regular, (2) uniform, (3) mean or average. It is evident that "regular" and "uniform" are here synonymous. But also the regular movement of the sun is computed as the average or mean movement of the sun for the interval of a solar year.

[2]The superscripts indicate the powers of the sixtieths in the denominator. Thus in ordinary fractions this would be written $\frac{59}{60} + \frac{8}{60^2} + \frac{17}{60^3} + \frac{13}{60^4}$, etc.

2. TABLE OF THE SUN'S REGULAR MOVEMENT

Distance from the apogee 265°15'; mean epoch 0°45' within the Fishes

18-year period	De-grees	I	II	III	IV	V	VI	18-year period	De-grees	I	II	III	IV	V	VI
18	355	37	25	36	20	34	30	450	250	35	40	8	34	22	30
36	351	14	51	12	41	9	0	468	246	13	5	44	54	57	0
54	346	52	16	49	1	43	30	486	241	50	31	21	15	31	30
72	342	29	42	25	22	18	0	504	237	27	56	57	36	6	0
90	338	7	8	1	42	52	30	522	233	5	22	33	56	40	30
108	333	44	33	38	3	27	0	540	228	42	48	10	17	15	0
126	329	21	59	14	24	1	30	558	224	20	13	46	37	49	30
144	324	59	24	50	44	36	0	576	219	57	39	22	58	24	0
162	320	36	50	27	5	10	30	594	215	35	4	59	18	58	30
180	316	14	16	3	25	45	0	612	211	12	30	35	39	33	0
198	311	51	41	39	46	19	30	630	206	49	56	12	0	7	30
216	307	29	7	16	6	54	0	648	202	27	21	48	20	42	0
234	303	6	32	52	27	28	30	666	198	4	47	24	41	16	30
252	298	43	58	28	48	3	0	684	193	42	13	1	1	51	0
270	294	21	24	5	8	37	30	702	189	19	38	37	22	25	30
288	289	58	49	41	29	12	0	720	184	57	4	13	43	0	0
306	285	36	15	17	49	46	30	738	180	34	29	50	3	34	30
324	281	13	40	54	10	21	0	756	176	11	55	26	24	9	0
342	276	51	6	30	30	55	30	774	171	49	21	2	44	43	30
360	272	28	32	6	51	30	0	792	167	26	46	39	5	18	0
378	268	5	57	43	12	4	30	810	163	4	12	15	25	52	30
396	263	43	23	19	32	39	0								
414	259	20	48	55	53	13	30								
432	254	58	14	32	13	48	0								

2. TABLE OF THE SUN'S REGULAR MOVEMENT—Continued

Distance from the apogee 265°15'; mean epoch 0°45' within the Fishes

Single years	Degrees	I	II	III	IV	V	VI	Single years	Degrees	I	II	III	IV	V	VI
1	359	45	24	45	21	8	35	10	357	34	7	33	31	25	50
2	359	30	49	30	42	17	10	11	357	19	32	18	52	34	25
3	359	16	14	16	3	25	45	12	357	4	57	4	13	43	0
4	359	1	39	1	24	34	20	13	356	50	21	49	34	51	35
5	358	47	3	46	45	42	55	14	356	35	46	34	56	0	10
6	358	32	28	32	6	51	30	15	356	21	11	20	17	8	45
7	358	17	53	17	28	0	5	16	356	6	36	5	38	17	20
8	358	3	18	2	49	8	40	17	355	52	0	50	59	25	55
9	357	48	42	48	10	17	15	18	355	37	25	36	20	34	30

Hours	Degrees	I	II	III	IV	V	VI	Hours	Degrees	I	II	III	IV	V	VI
1	0	2	27	50	43	3	1	13	0	32	1	59	19	39	16
2	0	4	55	41	26	6	2	14	0	34	29	50	2	42	18
3	0	7	23	32	9	9	3	15	0	36	57	40	45	45	19
4	0	9	51	22	52	12	5	16	0	39	25	31	28	48	20
5	0	12	19	13	35	15	6	17	0	41	53	22	11	51	21
6	0	14	47	4	18	18	7	18	0	44	21	12	54	54	23
7	0	17	14	55	1	21	9	19	0	46	49	3	37	57	24
8	0	19	42	45	44	24	10	20	0	49	16	54	21	0	25
9	0	22	10	36	27	27	11	21	0	51	44	45	4	3	27
10	0	24	38	27	10	30	12	22	0	54	12	35	47	6	28
11	0	27	6	17	53	33	14	23	0	56	40	26	30	9	29
12	0	29	34	8	36	36	15	24	0	59	8	17	13	12	31

The surplus of the distance from the apogee of the sun 5°30' within the Twins to its mean epoch in the year I of Nabonassar 0°45' within the Fishes is 265°15'.

2. Table of the Sun's Regular Movement—Continued

Distance from the apogee 265°15'; mean epoch 0°45' within the Fishes

Egyptian mo'ths	De-grees	I	II	III	IV	V	VI	Egyptian mo'ths	De-grees	I	II	III	IV	V	VI
30	29	34	8	36	36	15	30	210	206	59	0	16	13	48	30
60	59	8	17	13	12	31	0	240	236	33	8	52	50	4	0
90	88	42	25	49	48	46	30	270	266	7	17	29	26	19	30
120	118	16	34	26	25	2	0	300	295	41	26	6	2	35	0
150	147	50	43	3	1	17	30	330	325	15	34	42	38	50	30
180	177	24	51	39	37	33	0	360	354	49	43	19	15	6	0

Days	De-grees	I	II	III	IV	V	VI	Days	De-grees	I	II	III	IV	V	VI
1	0	59	8	17	13	12	31	16	15	46	12	35	31	20	16
2	1	58	16	34	26	25	2	17	16	45	20	52	44	32	47
3	2	57	24	51	39	37	33	18	17	44	29	9	57	45	18
4	3	56	33	8	52	50	4	19	18	43	37	27	10	57	49
5	4	55	41	26	6	2	35	20	19	42	45	44	24	10	20
6	5	54	49	43	19	15	6	21	20	41	54	1	37	22	51
7	6	53	58	0	32	27	37	22	21	41	2	18	50	35	22
8	7	53	6	17	45	40	8	23	22	40	10	35	3	47	53
9	8	52	14	34	58	52	39	24	23	39	18	53	17	0	24
10	9	51	22	52	12	5	10	25	24	38	27	10	30	12	55
11	10	50	31	9	25	17	41	26	25	37	35	27	43	25	26
12	11	49	39	26	38	30	12	27	26	36	43	44	56	37	57
13	12	48	47	43	51	42	43	28	27	35	52	2	9	50	28
14	13	47	56	1	4	55	14	29	28	35	0	19	23	2	59
15	14	47	4	18	18	7	45	30	29	34	8	36	36	15	30

3. On the Hypotheses concerning Regular and Circular Movement

Since the next thing is to explain the apparent irregularity of the sun, it is first necessary to assume in general that the motions of the planets in the direction contrary to the movement of the heavens are all regular and circular by nature, like the movement of the universe in the other direction. That is, the straight lines, conceived as revolving the stars or their circles, cut off in equal times on absolutely all circumferences equal angles at the centres of each;[1] and their apparent irregularities result from the positions and arrangements of the circles on their spheres through which they produce these movements, but no departure from their unchangeableness has really occurred in their nature in regard to the supposed disorder of their appearances.

But the cause of this irregular appearance can be accounted for by as many as two primary simple hypotheses. For if their movement is considered with respect to a circle in the plane of the ecliptic concentric with the cosmos so that our eye is the centre, then it is necessary to suppose that they make their regular

[1]This principle of celestial mechanics will be considerably broadened in the case of the moon and the other five planets as treated in Books V, IX, and X.

movements either along circles not concentric with the cosmos, or along concentric circles; not with these simply, but with other circles borne upon them called epicycles. For according to either hypothesis it will appear possible for the planets seemingly to pass, in equal periods of time, through unequal arcs of the ecliptic circle which is concentric with the cosmos.

For if, in the case of the hypothesis of eccentricity, we conceive the eccentric

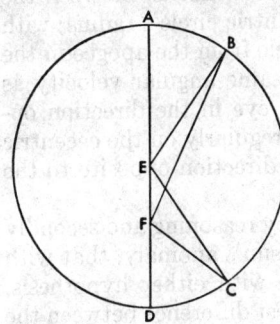

circle *ABCD* on which the star moves regularly, with *E* as center and with diameter *AED*, and the point *F* on it as your eye so that the point *A* becomes the apogee and the point *D* the perigee; and if, cutting off equal arcs *AB* and *DC*, we join *BE*, *BF*, *CE*, and *CF*, then it will be evident that the star moving through each of the arcs *AB* and *CD* in an equal period of time will seem to have passed through unequal arcs on the circle described around *F* as a centre. For since

angle *BEA* = angle *CED*,

therefore angle *BFA* is less than either of them, and angle *CFD* greater [Eucl. I, 16].

And if in the hypothesis of the epicycle we conceive the circle *ABCD* concentric with the ecliptic with centre *E* and diameter *AEC*, and the epicycle *FGHK* borne on it on which the star moves, with its centre at *A*, then it will be immediately evident also that as the epicycle passes regularly along the circle *ABCD*, from *A* to *B* for example, and the star along the epicycle, the star will appear indifferently to be at *A* the centre of the epicycle when it is at *F* or *H*; but when it is at other points, it will not. But having come to *G*, for instance, it will seem to have produced a movement greater than the regular movement by the arc *AG*; and having come to *K*, likewise less by the arc *AK*.

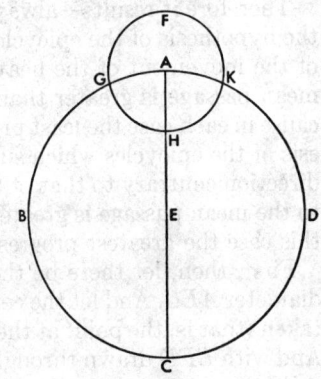

Then with the hypothesis of eccentricity it is always the case that the least movement belongs to the apogee and the greatest movement to the perigee, since angle *AFB* is always less than angle *DFC*. But both cases can come about with the hypothesis of the epicycle. For when the epicycle moves contrary to the heavens [from west to east], for example from *A* to *B*, if the star so moves on the epicycle that it goes from the apogee again contrary to the heavens (that is, from *F* in the direction of *G*), there will result at the apogee the greatest advance, because the epicycle and the star are moving the same way. But if the movement of the star on the epicycle is in the direction of that of the heavens [from east to west], that is, from *F* towards *K*, conversely the least advance will be effected at the apogee because the star is then moving contrary to the movement of the epicycle.

With these things established, it must next be understood that, in the case of those planets which effect two anomalies, it is possible to combine both of these hypotheses, as we shall show in the chapters concerning them. But, in the case of those planets subject to only one anomaly, one of the hypotheses will suffice. And it must be understood that all the appearances can be cared for interchangeably according to either hypothesis, when the same ratios are involved in each. In other words, the hypotheses are interchangeable when, in the case of the hypothesis of the epicycle, the ratio of the epicycle's radius to the radius of the circle carrying it[1] is the same as, in the case of the hypothesis of eccentricity, the ratio of the line between the centres (that is, between the eye and the centre of the eccentric circle), to the eccentric circle's radius; with the added conditions that the star move on the epicycle from the apogee in the direction of the movement of the heavens with the same angular velocity as the epicycle moves on the circle concentric with the eye in the direction opposite to that of the heavens, and that the star move regularly on the eccentric circle with the same angular velocity also and in the direction opposite to the movement of the heavens.

And we shall briefly show in a systematic way, first by reasoning and secondly by the numbers discovered in the appearances of the sun's anomaly, that with the above assumptions the same appearances agree with either hypothesis.

I say first, then, that on either hypothesis the greatest difference between the regular movement and the apparent irregular movement (difference by which the mean passage of the stars is apprehended) occurs when the apparent angular distance cuts off a quadrant from the apogee; and that the time from the apogee to this mean passage is greater than from this mean passage to the perigee.

Therefore it results—always on the hypothesis of the eccentric circles, and on the hypothesis of the epicycle whenever their movements occur in the direction of the movement of the heavens—that the time from the least passage to the mean passage is greater than that from the mean to the greatest passage, because in each case the least progress is effected at the apogee. But on the hypothesis of the epicycles which supposes the revolutions of the stars on them in the direction contrary to that of the heavens, conversely the time from the greatest to the mean passage is greater than that from the mean to the least, because in this case the greatest progress is effected at the apogee.

First, then, let there be the star's eccentric circle $ABCD$ with centre E and diameter AEC. And let the centre of the ecliptic be taken (that is, the point at the eye), and let it be F. And with BFD drawn through F at right angles to AEC, let the star be supposed at points B and D, so that the apparent angular distance on either side from the apogee A is clearly a quadrant.

It must be proved that the greatest difference between the regular and irregular movements occurs at the points B and D.

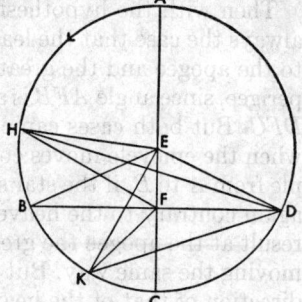

For let EB and ED be joined. Then it is immediately evident that the arc of the anomalistic difference has to the whole circle the same ratio that angle EBF has to 4 right angles, since the angle AEB subtends the arc of the regular movement and angle AFB that of the apparent irregular movement, and angle EBF is the difference between them.

[1]The circle carrying the epicycle is often called the deferent.

I say, then, that no other angle can be constructed on the circumference of the circle $ABCD$ and on the straight line EF greater than these two at B and D.

For let the angles EHF and EKF be constructed at the points H and K, and let HD and KD be joined. Since then in every triangle the greater side subtends the greater angle, and

$$HF > FD, \qquad\qquad\qquad \text{[Eucl. III, 7,3]}$$

also   angle $HDF >$ angle DHF

But   angle $EDH =$ angle EHD

since $EH = ED.$

And therefore   angle $EDF >$ angle EHF,

                            angle $EBD >$ angle EHF.

Again since $DF > KF,$

                            angle $FKD >$ angle FDK.

But   angle $EKD =$ angle EDK,

since again $EK = ED.$

And therefore, by subtraction,

angle $EDF >$ angle EKF,

angle $EBF >$ angle EKF.

Therefore it is not possible to construct other angles in the way we have described greater than those at points B and D.[1]

And at the same time it is proved that arc AB, which embraces the time from the least to the mean movement, is greater than arc BC which embraces the time from the mean to the greatest movement, by twice the arc containing the anomalistic difference. For

angle $AEB =$ angle $EFB +$ angle EBF,

$=$ rt. angle $+$ angle EBF,

and

angle $BEC +$ angle $EBF =$ rt. angle.

Again, to prove the same thing occurs in the other hypothesis, let there be the circle ABC concentric with the cosmos, with center D and diameter ABD; and let there be in the same plane the epicycle EFG with centre A, carried on it. And let the star be supposed at G where it appears to be a quadrant's distance from the apogee point. And let AG and DGC be joined.

[1]The Greeks, in general, avoided the notion of a body's speed at a given point, and Ptolemy here handles the problem in the classic way, in terms of boundary points. Thus by proving that the greatest difference between the angle of the regular movement and that of the apparent irregular movement is at a point an apparent quadrant's distance from the apogee, it then follows that this point is a boundary point such that for all arcs between it and the apogee the star will appear to move more slowly than its regular or average movement, and for all arcs between it and the perigee the star will appear to move faster than its regular or average movement. Ptolemy therefore calls the point itself the point of the star's mean passage. It is not very different from saying in modern terms that the speed of the star at this point is its regular speed.

That the point of greatest anomalistic difference is such a boundary point is simply stated by Ptolemy and not explained. The explanation is this: From the apogee to the point of greatest difference the apparent angular speed of the star is always slower than its regular speed, for otherwise the difference between the two angles traveled would not be getting greater and greater. Likewise from the point of greatest difference to the perigee the apparent angular speed is greater than the regular speed, for otherwise the difference between the two angles traveled would not be getting less and less.

I say that the straight line *DGC* is tangent to the epicycle. For at that time there occurs the greatest difference between the regular and irregular movements.

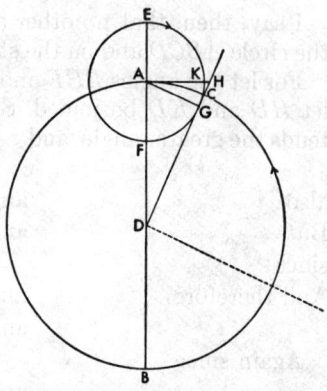

For since the regular movement from the apogee is contained by the angle *EAG* (for the star traverses the epicycle, and the epicycle the circle *ABC*, with the same angular velocity), and the difference between the regular and apparent movements is contained by the angle *ADG*, therefore it is evident that also the difference between angle *EAG* and angle *ADG* (that is, angle *AGD*) contains the apparent angular distance of the star from the apogee. And so, since it is assumed to be the angle of a quadrant, angle *AGD* will also be a right angle, and therefore the straight line *DGC* will be tangent to the epicycle *EFG* [Eucl. III, 16, Por.]. Therefore the arc *AC* between the centre *A* and the tangent is the greatest anomalistic difference.

And in the same way arc *EG*, which, according to the motion assumed for the epicycle, embraces the time from the least to the mean movement, is greater than arc *GF*, which embraces the time from the mean to the greatest movement. And it is greater by twice arc *AC*. For if we produce the straight line *DGH* and draw *AKH* at right angles to *EF*, then

$$\text{angle } KAG = \text{angle } ADC, \qquad \text{[Eucl. VI, 8]}$$

and arc *KG* is similar to arc *AC*. Therefore arc *EKG* is greater than a quadrant by arc *AC*, and arc *FG* is less than a quadrant by arc *AC*. Which it was required to prove.[1]

And next it will be clearly seen that, even in the other particular movements,

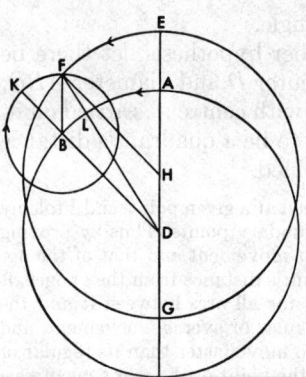

in the case of both hypotheses, for equal times, all the same things will occur with respect to the regular and apparent movements and the differences between them—that is, the anomalistic difference.

For let there be the circle *ABC* with centre *D*, concentric with the ecliptic; and the eccentric *EFG* with center *H*, equal to the concentric circle *ABC*; and the diameter *EAHD* common to both, through the centres *D* and *H* and the apogee *E*. And with arc *AB* taken at random length on the concentric circle, let the epicycle *KF* with centre *B* and radius *DH* be described, and let *KBD* be joined.

I say that the star will be borne by either movement to *F*, the intersection of the eccentric

[1]In the case where the star moves on the epicycle in the same direction that the epicycle moves on the concentric circle, the mean passage and greatest anomalistic difference do not occur an apparent quadrant's distance from the apogee—that is, if the angular velocity of the star on the epicycle is the same as that of the epicycle's centre on the concentric circle. But it is greater than a quadrant's distance from the apogee. This is immediately evident if we refer to the previous figure and suppose *DGH* drawn tangent on the opposite side of the epicycle.

circle and the epicycle, in the same amount of time. That is, the three arcs, EF on the eccentric, AB on the concentric, and KF on the epicycle are similar to each other; and the difference between the regular and irregular movements, and the apparent passage of the star, will be similar and the same under either hypothesis.

For let FH, BF, and DF be joined. Since the opposite sides of the quadrilateral $BDHF$ are equal to each other, FH to BD, and BF to DH, the quadrilateral $BDFH$ is a parallelogram. Therefore the three angles EHF, ADB, and FBK are equal. And so, since they are angles at the centres, the arcs subtended by them—EF on the eccentric, AB on the concentric, and KF on the epicycle—are similar to one another. Therefore by either motion, the star will be brought to the same point F in an equal period of time, and will appear to have passed from the apogee along the same arc of the ecliptic, AL. And accordingly the anomalistic difference will be the same according to either hypothesis, since we have already proved that the difference contained by angle DFH on the hypothesis of eccentricity is of the same kind as that contained by angle BDF on the hypothesis of the epicycle, and since these angles are here also alternate and equal, with FH proved parallel to BD.

And it is clear that for all distances these same results will follow, $HDFB$ being always a parallelogram and the eccentric circle being described by the movement of the star on the epicycle whenever the relations under either hypothesis are both similar and equal.

But it will also become clear in the following way that, even if they are only similar but unequal in magnitude, the same appearances will again result. For in the same way, let there be the circle ABC with centre D, concentric with the cosmos; and its diameter ADC passing through the star's apogee and perigee; and the epicycle about B at the random distance of arc AB from the apogee A. And let the star have moved through arc EF similar to AB since the returns of the circles take place in the same time. And let the straight lines DBE, BF, and DF be joined.

It is immediately clear that, on this hypothesis, angle ADE and angle FBE are always equal, and that the star will appear on the straight line DF.

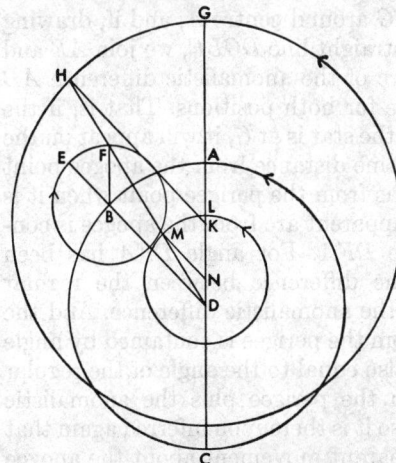

I say also that, on the hypothesis of eccentricity, both if the eccentric circle is greater than the concentric circle and if it is less, with only the similarity of the relations and the isochronism of the returns assumed, the star will again appear on the same straight line DF.

For let the eccentric circle GH be drawn greater, as we said, with its centre at K on AC; and likewise LM less, with centre N. And producing $DMFH$ and $DLAG$, let HK and MN be joined. Since

$$DB : BF :: HK : KD :: MN : ND,$$

and since

$$\text{angle } BFD = \text{angle } MDN$$

because of the parallels DA and BF, therefore the three triangles are equiangular [Eucl. vi, 7], and the angles BDF, DHK, and DMN, subtending the corresponding sides, are equal. Therefore the straight lines BD, HK, and MN are parallel, so that also angles ADB, AKH, and ANM are equal. And since they are angles at the centres of the circles, therefore the arcs subtended by them, AB, GH, and LM, will be similar. Therefore, in the same length of time, not only has the epicycle traversed arc AB, and the star arc EF, but also on the eccentric circles the star will have traversed arcs GH and LM; and in each case, therefore, it will be observed on the same straight line $DMFH$, being at the point F in the case of the epicycle, at H for the greater eccentric, at M for the smaller eccentric, and likewise for all positions.

And furthermore it results that, when the star appears to have traversed equal arcs both from the apogee and the perigee, the anomalistic difference in either position will be equal.

For, on the hypothesis of eccentricity, if we describe the eccentric circle $ABCD$ about centre E with diameter AEC through the apogee A, with the eye supposed on it at F, and if, drawing through F the straight line BFD at random, we join EB and ED, then the apparent courses will be equal and opposite; that is, angle AFB of the course from the apogee and angle CFD of that from the perigee. And the anomalistic difference will be the same because BE is equal to DE and angle EBF to angle EDF. And so the arc from the apogee A and the arc from the perigee C (that is, the arcs contained by angles AFB and CFD, respectively) are, the one greater and the other less, than the regular movement by the same difference of the apparent arc; because AEB is greater than angle AFB and angle CED less than angle CFD.

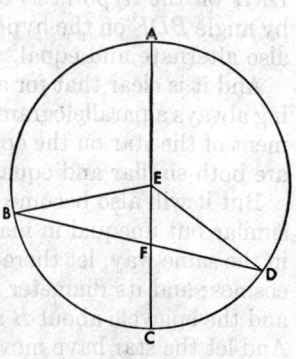

And, on the hypothesis of the epicycle, if we describe likewise the concentric circle around centre D and with diameter ADC, and the epicycle EFG around centre A, and if, drawing at random the straight line $DGBF$, we join AF and AG, then the arc of the anomalistic difference AB will be the same for both positions. That is, if the star is at F or if the star is at G, it will appear on the ecliptic at the same distance from the apogee point when it is at F as from the perigee point when it is at G, since the apparent arc from the apogee is contained by angle DFA. For angle DFA has been shown to be the difference between the regular movement and the anomalistic difference. And the apparent arc from the perigee is contained by angle FGA. For it is also equal to the angle of the regular movement from the perigee plus the anomalistic difference. And so it is thereupon inferred again that the mean movement is greater than the apparent movement about the apogee (that is, angle EAF than angle AFD) and the mean movement is less than the

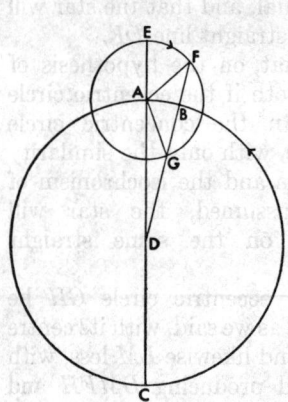

apparent about the perigee (that is, angle GAD than angle AGF), both by the same difference, by angle ADG. Which was to be proved.

4. On the Apparent Irregularity or Anomaly of the Sun

With these things explained, it is now necessary to take up the apparent irregularity or anomaly of the sun; because there is one only, and it is such that the time from the least movement to the mean is greater than the time from the mean to the greatest movement. For we find this agrees with the appearances. And this can be accomplished by either hypothesis:—(1) by that of the epicycle when the movement of the sun is in the direction of the movement of the heavens on its arc at the apogee. But (2) it would be more reasonable to stick to the hypothesis of eccentricity which is simpler and completely effected by one and not two movements.

Now, the first question is that of finding the ratio of eccentricity of the sun's circle—that is, what ratio the line between the eccentric circle's centre and the ecliptic's centre at the eye has to the radius of the eccentric circle; and next at what section of the ecliptic the apogee of the eccentric circle is to be found. And these things have been shown in a serious way by Hipparchus. For having supposed the time from the spring equinox to the summer tropic to be $94\frac{1}{2}$ days, and the time from the summer tropic to the autumn equinox to be $92\frac{1}{2}$ days, he proves from these appearances alone that the straight line between the aforesaid centres is very nearly $\frac{1}{24}$ the radius of the eccentric circle; and that its apogee precedes the summer tropic by very nearly $24\frac{1}{2}°$ of the ecliptic's $360°$.

And we too find that the time-periods of these quarters and these ratios are very nearly the same even now, so that in this way it is clear to us that the sun's eccentric circle always preserves the same position with respect to the tropic and equinoctial points. And not to establish this position on hearsay only, but to expound the theory systematically with our own numbers, we shall prove these things ourselves, using these same appearances as regards the eccentric circle— that is, as we said, $94\frac{1}{2}$ days from the spring equinox to the summer tropic and $92\frac{1}{2}$ days from the summer tropic to the autumn equinox. For with the very accurate observations made by us in the year 463 after the death of Alexander we find a complete agreement in the number of days between the summer tropic and the equinoxes. For as we said [pp. 81-82], the autumn equinox fell on Athyr 9 after sunrise, the spring equinox on Pachom 7 after midday, which makes an interval of $178\frac{1}{4}$ days, and the summer tropic on Mesore 11-12 after midnight, which makes the interval from the spring equinox to the summer tropic $94\frac{1}{2}$ days, and leaves very nearly $92\frac{1}{2}$ days for the interval from the summer tropic to the following autumn equinox.

Then let there be the ecliptic circle $ABCD$ with centre E, and let the two diameters AC and BD be drawn in it perpendicular to each other through the tropic and equinoctial points. And let A be supposed the spring point, B the summer, and the rest accordingly.

Now, that the centre of the eccentric circle will fall between the straight lines EA and EB, is clear on the one hand from the fact that the semicircle ABC embraces more time than half a year and therefore cuts off a section of the eccentric greater than a semicircle, and on the other hand from the fact that the quadrant AB itself also embraces more time and cuts off a greater arc of the eccentric than quadrant BC.

This being so, let the point F be supposed the centre of the eccentric circle, and let the diameter EFG be drawn through both centres and the apogee. And with centre F and any radius, let the eccentric circle of the sun $HKLM$ be drawn, and through F the line NQO parallel to AC and the line PRS parallel to BD. And again let HTU, the perpendicular from H to NQO, and KWX, the perpendicular from K to PRS, be drawn.

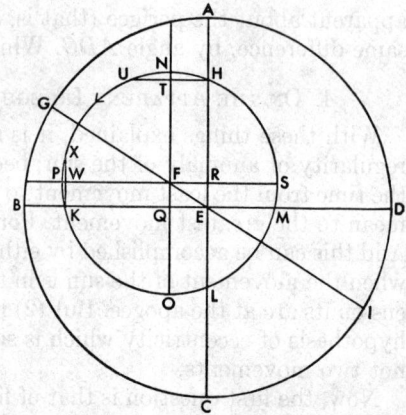

Since, then, the sun, moving regularly on the circle $HKLM$, traverses arc HK in $94\frac{1}{2}$ days and arc KL in $92\frac{1}{2}$ days, and since it covers regularly in $94\frac{1}{2}$ days very nearly $93°9'$, and in $92\frac{1}{2}$ days $91°11'$ [Chap. II, Table of Sun's Regular Movement], therefore

$$\text{arc } HKL = 184°20',$$

and

$$\text{arc } NH + \text{arc } LO = 4°20'$$

by subtraction of the semicircle NPO. And

$$\text{arc } HNU = 2 \text{ arc } HN = 4°20'.$$

And so

$$\text{chord } HU = 4^{\text{p}}32'$$

where

$$\text{ecc. diam.} = 120^{\text{p}}$$

And, the half of chord HU,

$$HT = EQ = 2^{\text{p}}16'.$$

Again, since

$$\text{arc } HNPK = 93°9'$$

and

$$\text{arc } HN = 2°10'$$

and

$$\text{quadrant } NP = 90°,$$

therefore, by subtraction,

$$\text{arc } PK = 0°59'$$

and

$$\text{arc } KPX = 2 \text{ arc } PK = 1°58'.$$

And so

$$\text{chord } KWX = 2^{\text{p}}4'$$

and, the half of it,

$$KW = FQ = 1^{\text{p}}2'.$$

But, it was proved

$$EQ = 2^{\text{p}}16'.$$

And since

$$\text{sq. } FQ + \text{sq. } EQ = \text{sq. } EF,$$

therefore, in length,

$$EF \doteq 2^p29'30''$$

where

$$\text{rad. ecc.} = 60^p.$$

Therefore the radius of the eccentric circle is very nearly twenty-four times the line between its centre and that of the ecliptic.

Again since

$$FQ = 1^p2'$$

where it was proved

$$EF = 2^p29'30'',$$

therefore

$$FQ \doteq 49^p46'$$

where

$$\text{hypt. } EF = 120^p,$$

and, on the circle about right triangle EFQ,

$$\text{arc } FQ = 49°.$$

And therefore

$$\text{angle } FEQ = 49° \text{ to 2 rt.}$$
$$= 24°30'.$$

And so, since the angle is at the centre of the ecliptic, arc BG by which the apogee G precedes the summer tropic point B, is also 24°30'.

Finally, since the quadrants OS and SN are each 90°, and

$$\text{arc } OL = \text{arc } HN = 2°10',$$

and

$$\text{arc } MS = 0°59',$$

therefore

$$\text{arc } LM = 86°51'$$

and

$$\text{arc } MH = 88°49'.$$

But the sun moves regularly through 86°51' in 88⅛ days, and through 88° 49' in very nearly 90⅛ days [Chap. 2, Table of Sun's Regular Movement]. And so the sun will appear to traverse arc CD, which is the arc from the autumn equinox to the winter tropic in 88⅛ days; and arc DA, which is the arc from the winter tropic to the spring equinox, in very nearly 90⅛ days. And these things have been found by us in accord with what Hipparchus says.

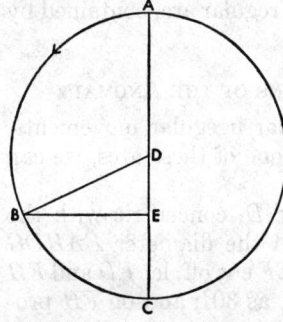

Now with these quantities, let us find out first how much is the greatest difference between the regular and irregular movements, and at what point this occurs.

Then let there be the eccentric circle ABC with centre D and diameter ADC through the apogee A; and on it let there be the centre of the ecliptic E. And let EB be drawn perpendicular to AC, and DB be joined. Since

$$1. \text{ betw. c. } DE = 2^p30'$$

where

$$\text{rad. } BD = 60^p$$

according to the ratio of 1 to 24, therefore
$$DE = 5^p$$
where
$$\text{hypt. } BD = 120^p,$$
and, on the circle about right triangle BDE,
$$\text{arc } DE = 4°46'.$$
And so angle DBE which contains the greatest anomalistic difference will be 4°46′ to 2 right angles′ and 2°23′ to 4 right angles′ 360°. And
$$\text{rt. angle } BED = 90°$$
and
$$\text{angle } BDA = \text{angle } BED + \text{angle } DBE = 92°23'.$$
And since angle BDA is at the centre of the eccentric circle and angle BED of the ecliptic, we shall have the greatest anomalistic difference as 2°23′. And as for the arcs at which this occurs, that of the eccentric which is regular is 92°23′ from the apogee, and that of the ecliptic which is apparent and irregular is a quadrant or 90°, as we have already proved. And it is clear from what has been set out that in the opposite section the apparent mean passage and the greatest anomalistic difference will be at 270°, and the regular mean passage at 267°37′ on the eccentric.

In order to show with numbers also that the same quantities can be inferred on the hypothesis of the epicycle when there are the same ratios in the way we described, let there be the circle ABC with centre D and diameter ADC, concentric with the ecliptic, and the epicycle EFG with centre A. And let the straight line DFB be drawn from D tangent to the epicycle, and let AF be joined. Then likewise
$$AD = 24\ AF,$$
so that again also
$$AF = 5^p$$
where

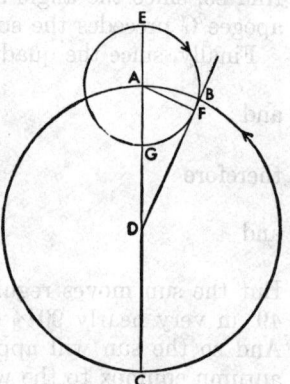

$$\text{hypt. } AD = 120^p,$$
and, on the circle about right triangle ADF,
$$\text{arc } AF = 4°46' \text{ to 2 rt.}$$
$$= 2°23'$$
Therefore, the greatest anomalistic difference (that is, arc AB) is thereupon found rightly to be 2°23′; and the irregular arc, since it is contained by the right angle AFD, to be 90° and the regular arc, contained by angle EAF, again to be 92°23′.

5. On the Examination of Particular Sections of the Anomaly

And to be able to distinguish at any time particular irregular movements, we shall again show for either hypothesis how, given one of these arcs, we can get the others also.

Then first let there be the circle ABC with centre D, concentric with the ecliptic; and the eccentric circle with centre H; and the diameter $EAHDG$ through both centres and the apogee E. And with arc EF cut off, let FD and FH be joined. And first let arc EF be given, for instance, as 30°; and on FH produced let fall the perpendicular DK from D.

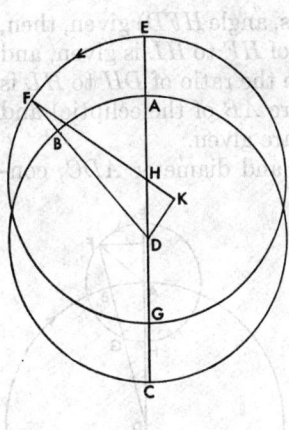

Since then it is assumed

$$\text{arc } EF = 30°,$$

therefore

$$\text{angle } EHF = \text{angle } DHK = 30°$$
$$= 60° \text{ to 2 rt.}$$

And therefore, on the circle about right triangle *DHK*,

$$\text{arc } DK = 60°,$$

and, the rest of the semicircle,

$$\text{arc } HK = 120°. \qquad \text{[Eucl. III, 31]}$$

And therefore

$$DK = 60^p$$

and

$$KH = 103^p55'$$

where

$$\text{hypt. } DH = 120^p.$$

And so

$$DK = 1^p15',$$
$$HK = 2^p10',$$
$$KHF = 62^p10'$$

where

$$DH = 2^p30',$$
$$\text{rad. } FH = 60^p.$$

And since

$$\text{sq. } DK + \text{sq. } FHK = \text{sq. } FD,$$
$$\text{hypt. } FD = 62^p11'.$$

And therefore

$$DK = 2^p25'$$

where

$$FD = 120^p,$$

and, on the circle about right triangle *FDK*,

$$\text{arc } DK = 2°18'.$$

And so

$$\text{angle } DFK = 2°18' \text{ to 2 rt.}$$
$$= 1°9'.$$

Therefore the anomalistic difference at that time is 1°9′. But angle *EHF* was 30°, and therefore the remaining angle *ADB* (that is, arc *AB* on the ecliptic) is 28°51′.

And with the same construction, if *HL* is dropped from *H* perpendicular to *FD*, it will be immediately clear that also, if any other angle is given, the rest are given. For if we suppose the arc *AB* on the ecliptic given (that is, angle *HDL*), then the ratio of *DH* to *HL* is given. And if the ratio *DH* to *HF* is given, the ratio of *HF* to *HL* is also given; and therefore we shall have angle *HFL* given (that is, the anomalistic difference) and angle *EHF* (that is, arc *EF* of the eccentric circle).

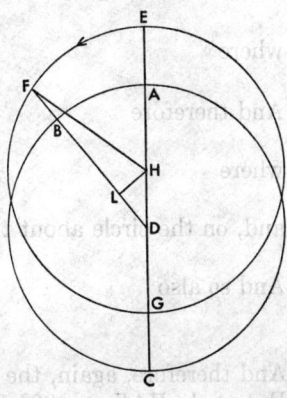

And if we suppose the anomalistic difference (that is, angle HFD) given, then, conversely, the same things will occur. For the ratio of HF to HL is given, and given from the first is the ratio of HF to HD. And so the ratio of DH to HL is also given; and therefore also angle HDL (that is, arc AB of the ecliptic) and angle EHF (that is, arc EF on the eccentric circle) are given.

Again let there be the circle ABC with centre D and diameter ADC, concentric with the ecliptic, and the epicycle $EFGH$ with centre A, in the same ratio. And let arc EF be cut off, and FBD and FA joined. Again let arc EF be supposed 30°, and let the line KF be drawn from F perpendicular to AE.
Since

$$\text{arc } EF = 30°,$$
$$\text{angle } EAF = 30°$$
$$= 60° \text{ to 2 rt.}$$

And so, on the circle about right triangle AFK,
$$\text{arc } FK = 60°,$$
and, the remainder of the semicircle,
$$\text{arc } AK = 120°.$$
And therefore
$$\text{chord } FK = 60^{\text{p}},$$
$$\text{chord } AK = 103^{\text{p}}55'$$
where
$$\text{diam. } AF = 120^{\text{p}}.$$
And so
$$FK = 1^{\text{p}}15',$$
$$AK = 2^{\text{p}}10',$$
$$KAD = 62^{\text{p}}10'$$
where
$$\text{hypt. } AF = 2^{\text{p}}30',$$
$$\text{rad. } AD = 60^{\text{p}}.$$
And since
$$\text{sq. } FK + \text{sq. } KAD = \text{sq. } FBD,$$
therefore, in length,
$$FD = 62^{\text{p}}11'$$
where
$$FK = 1^{\text{p}}15'.$$
And therefore
$$FK = 2^{\text{p}}25'$$
where
$$\text{hypt. } DF = 120^{\text{p}},$$
and, on the circle about the right triangle DFK,
$$\text{arc } FK = 2°18'.$$
And so also
$$\text{angle } FDK = 2°18' \text{ to 2 rt.}$$
$$= 1°9'.$$
And therefore, again, the anomalistic difference, which is arc AB, is also 1°9'. But angle EAF was 30°. Therefore the remaining angle AFD (that is, the ap-

parent arc of the ecliptic) is 28°51′, which agrees with the magnitudes proved on the hypothesis of eccentricity.

Likewise in this case too, even if any other angle is given, the others will also

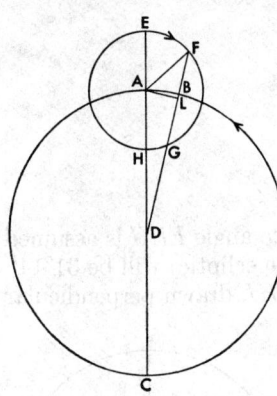

be given if, with the same construction, AL is drawn from A perpendicular to FD. For if, conversely, we give the apparent arc of the ecliptic (that is, angle AFD) then the ratio of AF to AL is also given. And since the ratio of AF to AD was given from the beginning, the ratio of AD to AL is also given. And therefore angle ADB (that is, arc AB which is the anomalistic difference) is given; and also angle EAF (that is, arc EF) of the epicycle.

And if we suppose the anomalistic difference given (that is, angle ADB) then, conversely, the ratio of AD to AL will likewise be given. But since the ratio of AD to AF was given from the beginning, the ratio of AF to AL is also given, and therefore angle AFD is given (that is, the apparent arc of the ecliptic) and angle EAF (that is, arc EF of the epicycle).

Again, with the previous construction of the eccentric circle, let the arc FG be cut off from the perigee G on the eccentric circle and be assumed to be 30°. And let DFB and FH be joined, and let DK be dropped from D perpendicular to HF.

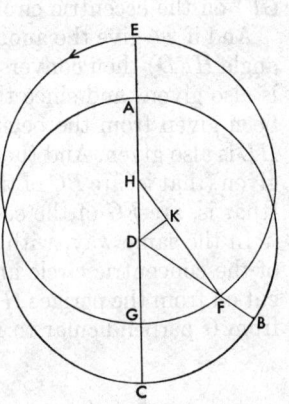

Since

$$\text{arc } FG = 30°,$$
$$\text{angle } FHG = 30°$$
$$= 60° \text{ to } 2 \text{ rt.}$$

And so, on the circle about right triangle DHK,

$$\text{arc } DK = 60°$$

and, the remainder of the semicircle,

$$\text{arc } KH = 120°.$$

And therefore

$$\text{chord } DK = 60^p,$$
$$\text{chord } KH = 103^p55′$$

where

$$\text{diam. } DH = 120^p.$$

And therefore

$$DK = 1^p15′,$$
$$HK = 2^p10′,$$
$$KF = 57^p50′,$$

where

$$\text{hypt. } DH = 2^p30′,$$
$$\text{rad. } HF = 60^p.$$

And since

$$\text{sq. } DK + \text{sq. } KF = \text{sq. } DF,$$

therefore, in length,

$$DF = 57^p51′$$

where
$$DK = 1^\text{p}15'.$$
And therefore
$$DK = 2^\text{p}34'36''$$
where
$$\text{hypt. } DF = 120^\text{p},$$
and, on the circle about right triangle DFK,
$$\text{arc } DK = 2°27'.$$
And so
$$\text{angle } DFK = 2°27' \text{ to 2 rt.}$$
$$\fallingdotseq 1°14'.$$
Therefore the anomalistic difference is 1°14′. And since angle FHG is assumed to be 30°, the whole angle BDC (that is, arc BC of the ecliptic) will be 31°14′.

And in the same way now, with BD produced and HL drawn perpendicular to it, if we give arc BC of the ecliptic (that is, angle HDL), then the ratio of DH to HL is also given; and since the ratio of HD to HF was given from the beginning, the ratio of FH to HL is also given. And therefore we have angle HFD given, that is, the anomalistic difference; and angle FHD (that is, arc GF) on the eccentric circle.

And if we give the anomalistic difference (that is, angle HFD) then conversely the ratio of FH to HL is also given; and since the ratio of FH to DH has been given from the beginning, the ratio of DH to HL is also given. And therefore we have angle HDL given (that is, arc BC of the ecliptic) and angle FHG (that is, arc FG of the eccentric circle).

In the same way, with the previous construction of the concentric circle and epicycle, let arc HG be cut off from the perigee H at 30°. And let AG and DGB be joined, and GK drawn from G perpendicular to AD.

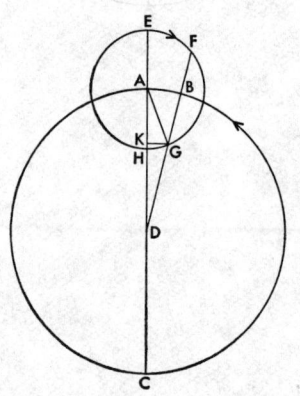

Then since again
$$\text{arc } GH = 30°,$$
$$\text{angle } HAG = 30°$$
$$= 60° \text{ to 2 rt.}$$
And so, on the circle about right triangle GKA,
$$\text{arc } GK = 60°$$
and, the remainder of the semicircle,
$$\text{arc } AK = 120°.$$
And therefore
$$\text{chord } GK = 60^\text{p},$$
$$\text{chord } AK = 103^\text{p}55'$$
where
$$\text{hypt. } AG = 120^\text{p}.$$
And therefore
$$GK = 1^\text{p}15',$$
$$AK = 2^\text{p}10',$$
$$KD = 57^\text{p}50'$$

where
$$AG = 2^p 30',$$
$$\text{rad. } AD = 60^p.$$

And since
$$\text{sq. } GK + \text{sq. } KD = \text{sq. } DG,$$
therefore, in length,
$$DG \doteqdot 57^p 51'$$
where
$$GK = 1^p 15'.$$

And therefore
$$GK = 2^p 34' 36''$$
where
$$DG = 120^p;$$
and, on the circle about right triangle DGK,
$$\text{arc } GK = 2°27'.$$

And so also
$$\text{angle } GDK = 2°27' \text{ to } 2 \text{ rt.}$$
$$\doteqdot 1°14'.$$

Therefore the anomalistic difference (that is, arc AB) is here also very nearly $1°14'$. And since angle KAG is assumed to be $30°$, the whole angle BGA which contains the apparent arc of the ecliptic will be $31°14'$, agreeing with the magnitudes found for the eccentric circle.

And likewise here also, with AL drawn perpendicular to DB, if we give the

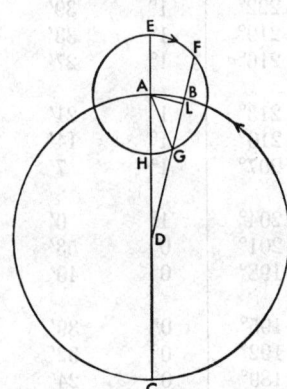

arc of the ecliptic (that is, angle AGL), then the ratio of AG to AL is given; and since the ratio of AG to AD has been given from the beginning, the ratio of AD to AL is also given. And therefore we have angle ADB given (that is, arc AB which is the anomalistic difference) and angle HAG (that is, arc HG of the epicycle).

And, again, if we give arc AB of the anomalistic difference (that is, angle ADB) then, conversely, the ratio of AD to AL is likewise given; and since the ratio of AD to AG has been given from the beginning, the ratio of AG to AL is also given. And therefore we shall have angle AGL given (that is, the arc of the ecliptic) and angle HAG (that is, arc HG of the epicycle). And we have shown what was proposed.

Now, although, by means of these theorems, various tables of the sections containing the anomalistic distinctions of the apparent courses can be constructed, yet that one containing the anomalistic differences arranged side by side with the regular arcs will better serve us for getting easily the magnitudes of the particular corrections, both because of its conformity with the hypotheses themselves and because of the simplicity and facility in the calculation for each section. Therefore we followed the first of the theorems set out with numbers for the particular sections, and calculated geometrically just as before the anomalistic differences corresponding to each of the regular arcs. And in general, both in the case of the sun and of the other planets, we divide the quadrants at the apogees into 15 sections, so that the comparison is at intervals of 6°; and the quadrants at the perigees into 30 sections so that the comparison in this case is at intervals of 3°. This is done because the differences in excess at the perigees are greater than those corresponding to equal sections at the apogee.

And so we shall arrange the table of the sun's anomaly into forty-five rows and three columns. And of these columns the first two contain the numbers of the 360° of regular movement, while the first fifteen rows embrace the two quadrants at the apogee, and the other thirty those at the perigee. And the third column contains the degrees of anomalistic difference to be added or subtracted, corresponding to each of the regular numbers. And here is the table:

6. TABLE OF THE SUN'S ANOMALY

1. Common numbers (Degrees of Regular Movement)		3. Additive—subtractive differences		1. Common numbers (Degrees of Regular Movement)		3. Additive—subtractive differences	
6°	354°	0°	14′	120°	240°	2°	6′
12°	348°	0°	28′	123°	237°	2°	2′
18°	342°	0°	42′	126°	234°	1°	58′
24°	336°	0°	56′	129°	231°	1°	54′
30°	330°	1°	9′	132°	228°	1°	49′
36°	324°	1°	21′	135°	225°	1°	44′
42°	318°	1°	32′	138°	222°	1°	39′
48°	312°	1°	43′	141°	219°	1°	33′
54°	306°	1°	53′	144°	216°	1°	27′
60°	300°	2°	1′	147°	213°	1°	21′
66°	294°	2°	8′	150°	210°	1°	14′
72°	288°	2°	14′	153°	207°	1°	7′
78°	282°	2°	18′	156°	204°	1°	0′
84°	276°	2°	21′	159°	201°	0°	53′
90°	270°	2°	23′	162°	198°	0°	46′
93°	267°	2°	23′	165°	195°	0°	39′
96°	264°	2°	23′	168°	192°	0°	32′
99°	261°	2°	22′	171°	189°	0°	24′
102°	258°	2°	21′	174°	186°	0°	16′
105°	255°	2°	20′	177°	183°	0°	8′
108°	252°	2°	18′	180°	180°	0°	0′
111°	249°	2°	16′				
114°	246°	2°	13′				
117°	243°	2°	10′				

7. On the Epoch of the Sun's Mean Course

Since there remains to be established the epoch of the sun's regular movement for finding out its particular course at any time, we shall make the following exposition, using again in general, both in the case of the sun and of the other planets, the passages most accurately observed by ourselves, and taking the establishing of the epochs back to the beginning of the reign of Nabonassar by means of the mean movements already demonstrated. For we have ancient observations completely preserved from that period to the present.

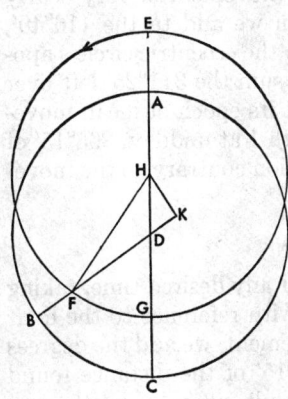

Then let there be the circle with centre D concentric with the ecliptic; and the eccentric circle of the sun EFG with centre H; and the diameter $EAGC$ through both centres and the apogee E. And let B be supposed the fall equinox point on the ecliptic; and let BFD and FH be joined; and let HK be dropped from H perpendicular to FD.

Since the point B, the autumn equinox, is at the beginning of the sign of the Balance, and the perigee C $5\frac{1}{2}°$ within the sign of the Archer, therefore
$$\text{arc } BC = 65°30'.$$

And therefore
$$\text{angle } BDC = \text{angle } HDK = 65°30'$$
$$= 131° \text{ to 2 rt.}$$
And so, on the circle about right triangle DHK,
$$\text{arc } HK = 131°,$$
and
$$\text{chord } HK = 109^{\text{p}}12'$$

where
$$\text{diam. } DH = 120^{\text{p}}.$$
Therefore
$$HK = 4^{\text{p}}33'$$
where
$$DH = 5^{\text{p}},$$
$$\text{hypt. } FH = 120^{\text{p}}.$$
And, on the circle about right triangle FHK,
$$\text{arc } HK = 4°20'.$$
And so
$$\text{angle } HFK = 4°20' \text{ to 2 rt.}$$
$$= 2°10'.$$
But it was proved
$$\text{angle } BDC = 65°30',$$
and therefore the remaining angle FHG (that is, arc FG on the eccentric circle) is 63°20′. Therefore, when the sun is at the autumn equinox, it precedes the perigee (that is, the point $5\frac{1}{2}°$ within the Archer) by 63°20′ mean movement; and it is 116°40′ in mean movement from the apogee (that is, $5\frac{1}{2}°$ within the Twins) in the direction contrary to the movement of the heavens.

Now that this is understood—since, of the first equinoxes observed by us, one of the most accurate occured as the autumn equinox in the year 17 of Hadrian, Egyptianwise Athyr 7, very nearly 2 hours after midday—it is clear that at that time the sun was 116°40′ in mean movement on the eccentric circle, away from the apogee in the direction contrary to the movement of the heavens. But from the reign of Nabonassar to the death of Alexander amounts to 424 Egyptian years; and from the death of Alexander to the reign of Augustus, 294 years; and from the year 1 of Augustus, Egyptianwise Thoth 1, midday (for we establish the epochs from midday) to the year 17 of Hadrian, Athyr 7, 2 hours after midday, amounts to 161 years, 66 days, and 2 equatorial hours. And therefore from the year 1 of Nabonassar, Egyptianwise Thoth 1, midday, to the time of the autumn equinox just mentioned amounts to 879 Egyptian years, 66 days, and 2 equatorial hours.

But in that amount of time the sun makes a mean movement of very nearly 211°25′ over and above the complete circles. If then we add to the 116°40′, representing the distance of this autumn equinox from the eccentric circle's apogee, the 360° of a whole circle and subtract from the sum the 311°25′ left over from the time between, then we shall have the sun at its epoch of mean movement in the year 1 of Nabonassar, Egyptianwise Thoth 1 at midday, 265°15′ of mean movement distant from the apogee in the direction contrary to the movement of the heavens, and 0°45′ within the Fishes.

8. On Calculating the Sun

Whenever we wish to know the course of the sun for any desired time, taking the total time from the epoch to the proposed date with reference to the hour in Alexandria and taking it to the tables of mean movement, we add the degrees corresponding to the particular numbers to the 265°15′ of the distance found above; and striking the complete circles out of the result, we subtract the rest from the 5°30′ within the Twins backwards in the order of the signs [from west to east]. And wherever the number falls, there we find the mean course of the sun. Next we take the same number (that is, the number of degrees from the apogee to the mean course) to the Table of Anomaly. And, if the number falls in the first column (that is, if it is not greater than 180°), then we subtract the corresponding degrees in the third column from the position of the mean course; but, if it falls in the second column (that is, if it is greater than 180°), then we add it to the mean course. And thus we find the true and apparent sun.

9. On the Inequality of Solar Days

Now this is pretty nearly all of the theory of the sun considered by itself. But it would be well to add briefly to this something concerning the inequality of the solar days, a matter which ought to be cleared up before what follows. For each of the simple mean movements we have given receives a uniform increase, as if the solar days were equal in time; but this is contrary to true theory. Now, given that the revolution of the universe is effected regularly about the poles of the equator, if the cyclical return is taken either with respect to the horizon or the meridian (whichever point is the more easily distinguishable), it is clear that one complete turn of the cosmos is the return of the same equatorial point from some section either of the horizon or the meridian back to that same section, and the solar day considered simply is the return of the sun from some section either of the horizon or of the meridian back again to the same section. The regular [or mean] solar day is, therefore, that embracing a course of 360° equatorial time proper to one revolution of the equator plus very nearly 59′ equatorial time for the sun's contrary mean movement along the ecliptic. And the irregular solar day is that embracing a course of 360° equatorial time proper to one revolution of the equator plus the extra arc, either at the horizon or at the meridian, corresponding to the sun's contrary irregular movement.

And so this section of the equator which is traversed over and above the 360° equatorial time must be an unequal one because of the sun's apparent irregularity, and because equal sections of the ecliptic do not traverse the horizon or the meridian in equal periods of time. Each of these extra sections makes the difference between the regular and irregular return, in the case of one solar day, a difference indistinguishable by the senses; but a total of many solar days makes a very sensible difference.

Now, the sun's greatest anomalistic difference occurs at intervals of one mean movement of the sun to the other. For in this way the total of solar days will differ from the total of regular [or mean] solar days by very nearly $4\frac{3}{4}°$ equatorial time; and the total in one interval will differ from the total in the other by twice as much, that is by $9\frac{1}{2}°$ equatorial time. And this is so because the apparent course of the sun is less, in the semicircle of the apogee, than the regular course by $4\frac{3}{4}°$, but greater, in the semicircle of the perigee, by the same amount.[1]

And the greatest difference of irregularity in the corresponding risings or settings occurs in the semicircles bounded by the tropic points. For then the ascensions in each of these semicircles will differ from the 180° equatorial time of those considered regularly by the difference between the shortest or longest day and the equinoctial day; and they will differ from each other by the difference between the longest day or night and the shortest day or night. But the greatest difference of inequality in the case of simultaneous culminations occurs in the intervals containing two signs, one sign on each side of the tropic or equinoctial point. For those at the tropics taken together will differ from the regular by very nearly $4\frac{1}{2}°$ equatorial time, but from those at the equinoctial points taken together by 9° equatorial time. For the latter are less than the mean movement, and the former are greater by nearly an equal amount.[2] And thence we establish the beginnings of the solar days at the positions of the sun as it passes the meridian, and not from the sun's risings or settings; because the difference considered with respect to horizons can amount to many hours and is not the same everywhere, but changes with the excess of the longest over the shortest day in each latitude of the sphere. But the difference at the meridian is the same everywhere and does not exceed the total time of the sun's anomalistic difference.

And the difference in the intervals to be added or subtracted is constructed out of the combination of both of the aforesaid differences: that of the sun's

[1]For the greatest anomalistic differences, it has already been proved, occur at the apparent distance of a quadrant from the apogee, which are also the points of mean movement. Now, it has been shown that the difference between the angles of the regular and irregular movements from the mean to the apogee is 2°23′ and from the apogee to the other mean again 2°23′, the regular exceeding in both cases. The same thing occurs from the mean through the perigee to the other mean, the irregular exceeding in both cases.

[2]This difference is demonstrated in the Table of Ascensions for the Right Sphere, Book II. The difference in the co-ascensions of the ecliptic and equator is additive for the ecliptic in the Twins and the Crab, and the Archer and the Goat. It is subtractive for the ecliptic in the Fishes and the Ram, and the Virgin and the Balance. The other signs are all mixed. The equator here, of course, represents the regular movement of the sun for the mean solar days; and the ecliptic represents the irregular movement of the sun for the irregular true solar days.

anomaly and that of the culminations. And the interval from the middle of the Water Bearer to the Balance is subtractive for either difference; and the interval from the Scorpion to the middle of the Water Bearer is additive. For each of these sections either adds or subtracts with respect to the solar anomaly at most very nearly $3\frac{2}{3}°$ equatorial time, and with respect to the culminations very nearly $4\frac{2}{3}°$ equatorial time. And so, at most, the difference in the solar day, gotten from the combination of the two, amounts, for either interval, to $8\frac{1}{3}°$ equatorial time over and above the regular difference—that is, $\frac{1}{2}+\frac{1}{18}$ [equatorial] hour. And with respect to each other it amounts to $16\frac{2}{3}°$ equatorial time —that is, $1\frac{1}{9}$ [equatorial] hours. Now, if this difference is neglected in the case of the sun, it perhaps would not hurt the study of its appearances to any appreciable extent; but in the case of the moon, because of the rapidity of its movement, it would produce a considerable difference even for $3\frac{1}{5}°$.

In order to reduce the solar days given over any interval of time (and by solar days I mean from midday or midnight to midday or midnight) to regular solar days, we find out for the beginning and end of the given interval at what part of the ecliptic the sun is to be found both in its regular and irregular movements. Then, taking the surplus over and above complete revolutions accumulated in the irregular interval (that is, from apparent position to apparent position) to the Table of Ascensions in the Right Sphere, we find out with how many degrees equatorial time the degrees of the irregular interval, as we said, culminate. Then we take the difference between the amount of time thus found and the degrees of the regular interval and calculate the part of the corresponding equatorial hour. And if the amount of time found in the Table of Ascensions in the Right Sphere is greater than that of the regular interval, we add this difference to the given number of solar days; if less, we subtract. And finally, in this way, we have the time expressed in mean solar days. We shall use this correction especially in the successive additions of the mean movements in the moon's tables. And it is immediately seen that, given the regular [or mean] solar days, the simply considered seasonal solar days are gotten by an addition or subtraction in the converse order.[1]

[1]If the sun moved regularly along the equator instead of moving irregularly along the ecliptic, the solar days would all be regular. Their irregularity, then, is due to two things: (1) the irregularity of the sun's movement, and (2) the fact that the sun moves on a circle oblique to the equator.

Now, as far as the solar days are concerned, it is not the arc of the ecliptic that is directly involved, but the corresponding or co-ascending arc of the equator. For the culminations which define solar days take place at the meridian, and the meridian is through the pole of the equator. Therefore we first find the arc on the equator co-ascending with the apparent arc traversed by the sun along the ecliptic.

Now if the arc of the sun's regular movement is less than the equatorial arc co-ascending with the apparent arc, then the number of actual solar days is less than the number of regular ones. But if the arc of the sun's regular movement is greater, then the number of actual solar days is greater than the number of regular ones. For when the sun moves faster than the regular, then the actual solar day is longer than the mean solar day and there are fewer of them in a given time; but, when it moves slower, then the actual solar day is shorter.

And in each case the difference between the number of actual solar days and the number of corresponding regular solar days is expressed by the difference between the equatorial arc corresponding to the apparent arc on the ecliptic and the arc of regular movement. For (1) if the regular arc is less than the equator's arc, then the apparent arc is reaching the meridian that many time-degrees later; and so just so many time-degrees have been lost to the number of regular solar days. For the same number of regular solar days as actual solar days would only take the sun the length of the arc of regular movement, if we consider it as moving on the

Now, according to the epoch we have chosen (that is, the year 1 of Nabonassar, Egyptianwise Thoth 1 at midday), the sun's mean position, as we have just shown [p. 104], was 0°45' within the Fishes. But, considered with its anomaly, its position was very nearly 3°8' within the Fishes.

---

equator. It would perhaps be clearer if we imagined that the regular arc were less by a revolution than the equator's arc representing the apparent arc on the ecliptic. Then the number of actual solar days would be one day less than the number of regular solar days. For the sun would have moved back one whole circle, and thus would have come to the meridian one time less over the period assigned than if it had moved back according to the regular movement. And by the same argument (2) if the regular arc is greater, just so many time-degrees have been added to the number of regular solar days. Therefore, in the first case, we add the difference to the number of actual solar days to get the number of regular solar days; and, in the second case, we subtract.

BOOK FOUR

1. From What Kind of Observations an Inquiry into the Moon Must be Conducted

Having now organized in the preceding book all the incidents one could observe with respect to the sun's movement, we begin next in order with the treatise on the moon. First we think it is not proper to proceed simply and haphazardly in the use of observations for this purpose; but for the general understanding of the moon it is best to attend especially to those demonstrations which not only cover a longer period of time but also are gotten from the observations of lunar eclipses. For it is only by means of these that the positions of the moon can be found in an accurate way, since the other kinds of observations which depend either on its courses with respect to the fixed stars, or on instruments, or on the solar eclipses, can, because of the moon's parallaxes, be very deceptive. But with respect to the particular incidents the inquiry can be carried on from the other observations also.

For since the distance from the earth's centre to the lunar sphere is not as that to the ecliptic circle which is so great that the magnitude of the earth is in the ratio of a point to it, therefore the straight line drawn from the moon's centre to sections of the ecliptic, according to which the true courses of all the stars are conceived, necessarily does not everywhere sensibly coincide with the straight line according to which its apparent course is observed—that is, the straight line drawn from some part of the earth's surface or rather from the observer's eye to the moon's centre. But when the moon is directly above the observer, then only are the straight lines drawn from the earth's centre and the observer's eye to the moon's centre and the ecliptic one and the same straight line. And when it is in any way whatsoever removed from the zenith, a difference of inclination in these straight lines follows; and therefore the apparent course differs from the true one for different positions of the eye as it moves downward. For the positions of the moon seen from the earth's centre are determined proportionately to the magnitudes of the angles resulting from the inclination.

Therefore, when solar eclipses take place through the intervention and interposition of the moon, and when their occurrence shapes its passing shadow into a cone from our eye to the sun, the result is that these things are not fulfilled everywhere in the same way either in magnitudes or times, nor to all alike for the causes we have assigned; nor does the moon appear to shadow the same parts of the sun. But in the case of lunar eclipses no such difference follows from the parallaxes, since the eclipse of the moon does not involve the eye of the observer as an incidental cause. For the moon always receives its light from the sun; and, when the moon is opposite it, the whole of it appears to us lighted up, because the whole of the bright hemisphere is also at that time turned towards us. But when it is opposite the sun in such a way that it falls into the cone of the earth's shadow which is always revolving opposite the sun, then the moon be-

108

comes darkened proportionately to the extent it enters the cone, since the earth screens the rays of the sun. Therefore it appears to be eclipsed similarly for all parts of the earth both as to magnitudes and as to the times of the intervals.

Therefore, insofar as we are concerned with a general examination of the true positions of the moon but not of apparent ones[1] (the true ones to be ascertained because the ordered and similar thing should be necessarily preferred to disordered and dissimilar things), we say we must not use the other observations where the positions depend on the eye of the observers, but only the observations of the moon's eclipses, since there the eye is in no way involved in getting the positions. For whatever section of the ecliptic the sun is found to occupy at the midtime of the eclipse when the moon's centre is directly opposite in true longitude to the sun's centre, the section opposite that section the moon's centre will also truly occupy at the same midtime of the eclipse.

2. On the Moon's Periods of Time

Let this be our brief exposition as to what observations are to be used for general considerations of the moon. We shall try and give an account of how the ancients proceeded in their demonstrations, and how we can make a more useful differentiation of the hypotheses which conform to the appearances.

Now, since the moon appears to move irregularly both in longitude and latitude,[2] and not to cross the ecliptic nor to have a cyclical return in its latitudinal course at equal intervals of time; and since, without the discovery of the interval in which this irregularity is redeemed, necessarily the periods of the others could not be gotten; and since, from particular observations, the moon appears to have its mean, greatest, and least movements in all parts of the zodiac, and to be at its northernmost point, southernmost point, and on the ecliptic itself at all parts of the zodiac, very reasonably therefore the ancient mathematicians sought a certain time in which the moon would always move the same distance in longitude, for this alone could redeem the irregularity. Comparing, then, for the causes we have assigned, the observations of the lunar eclipses, they tried to find what multitude of lunar months would always be isochronous with other equal multitudes and would embrace an equal number of circles in longitude, either whole or in parts. Now the even more ancient ones in a more or less rough

---

[1]In the case of the sun, there were the mean positions and the true (ἀκριβής) positions. And the true positions were taken as coinciding with the apparent ones. For the true positions are the projections of the sun on the ecliptic by a straight line through the earth's centre and the sun's centre; the apparent ones are the projections on the ecliptic by a straight line through the observer's eye and the sun's centre. In the case of the moon, they are all three distinct by reason of the parallaxes.

[2]The moon's latitudinal movement is its movement along a great circle inclined to the ecliptic. It is not, as might be thought, its movement along an arc at right angles to the ecliptic. This inclined circle is the moon's oblique circle which is not to be confused with the ecliptic itself, the sun's oblique circle. The moon's longitudinal movement is its movement considered with reference to the ecliptic, just as the sun's is its movement with respect to the equator. The sun's movement with respect to the equator is distinguished from its movement along the ecliptic because of the great obliquity of the one to the other. In the case of the moon, the inclination of its oblique circle with respect to the ecliptic is so small as to be negligible for such considerations. But the moon's returns in latitude do not appear to correspond to its returns in longitude—that is, its successive returns to the same parallel to the ecliptic take place at different great circles through the ecliptic's poles. Hence it is necessary to suppose that the nodes of its oblique circle move with respect to the ecliptic, and therefore it is necessary to distinguish its latitudinal movement from its longitudinal.

way assumed that period of time to be 6,585⅓ days. For in this period they saw accomplished very nearly 223 lunar months, 239 restitutions of anomaly, 242 latitudinal cycles, and 241 longitudinal cycles plus the 10⅔° which the sun also adds to its 18 complete revolutions in that time, their restitutions being observed with respect to the fixed stars. And they called this interval of time "periodic" as being the least to collect approximately the differences of the movements into one complete cyclical restitution. In order to arrange it in terms of whole days, they tripled the 6,585⅓ days and got the number 19,756 which they called an evolution [ἐξελιγμός]. And likewise tripling the others, they had 669 lunar months, 717 restitutions of anomaly, 726 latitudinal cycles, and 723 longitudinal cycles plus the 32° which the sun also adds to its 54 complete revolutions.

And again Hipparchus proved by calculations from his own and Chaldean observations that these numbers were not accurate. For he shows by the observations he lays down that the least number of days in which the moment of eclipse recurs, after an equal number of months and an equal number of movements, is 126,007 days and 1 equatorial hour. And in this amount of time he finds fulfilled 4,267 lunar months, 4,573 complete restitutions of anomaly, 4,612 zodiacal revolutions less the 7½° (very nearly) which the sun also lacks of completing 345 circles, these restitutions again being observed with respect to the fixed stars. And so he finds, when the given number of days is distributed over the 4,267 lunar months, that the mean time of the lunar month amounts to very nearly 29 days 31^{i}50^{ii}8^{iii}20^{iv}. Then he shows that in this period of time the corresponding intervals from lunar eclipse to lunar eclipse are equal, so that the restitution of irregularity becomes evident from the fact that always in this amount of time there are contained just so many lunar months, and that to the 4,611 revolutions, equal in longitude, are added 352½° in accordance with the sun's syzygies.

But if one should seek, not the number of months from lunar eclipse to lunar eclipse, but only from a conjunction or full moon to the corresponding syzygy, he would find a still smaller number for the restitution of anomaly and for the lunar months by taking their only common measure 17, which brings the result to 251 lunar months and 269 restitutions of anomaly. But this period of time was found no longer to complete the latitudinal restitution. For the return of the eclipses appeared to save the equalities only with respect to the intervals of time and of the longitudinal revolutions, but not with respect to the magnitudes and similarities of the shadows cast, from which the latitude is known.

Now, having already found the time of the return of anomaly, Hipparchus again compares the intervals of lunar months bounded by eclipses in every way similar both in the magnitude and length of time of the shadows cast and in which was no anomalistic difference, so that the latitudinal course for that reason appears to make a cyclical return. And he shows that such a revolution is completed in 5,458 lunar months and 5,923 latitudinal cycles.

Now this was somewhat the way in which our predecessors dealt with these researches. But we would consider it neither a simple nor easy way, but one demanding much methodical diligence. For, first, it would be no use for us to grant that the durations of the intervals are accurately found to be equal to each other, unless the sun effected either the same anomalistic difference or none for each of the intervals. For if this should not be so, and there should be, as I said, some anomalistic difference of the sun, then neither will the sun, nor evidently the moon, have made equal revolutions in equal periods of time. If, for instance, each of the distances compared in addition to the complete and equal solar years takes on another half year, and if in this amount of time the sun happens to have moved in the first interval from its mean movement in the Fishes, and in the second interval from its mean movement in the Virgin, then in the first interval it will have added on less than the semicircle by nearly $4\frac{3}{4}°$; and in the second interval, more than the semicircle by the same amount. And so in the same time the moon has a surplus, over and above complete circles, of $175\frac{1}{4}°$ in the first interval; and $184\frac{3}{4}°$ in the second.

Hence we say it is first necessary that this sort of accident be characteristic of the intervals in their relationship to the sun: either (1) that it embrace whole circles; or (2) that for one interval it add on a semicircle from the apogee and for the other a semicircle from the perigee; or (3) that for both it begin from the same section; or (4) that it be equidistant on each side of either the apogee or the perigee, for the first eclipse in one interval and for the second eclipse in the other. For only in this way would its anomalistic difference be either equal or absent in each interval, so that the extra arcs would be equal either to each other, or to each other and arcs of regular movement.

And, secondly, we think that like attention should be paid to the courses of the moon. For if no distinctions are made here, it will again appear possible for the moon to be able to add on equal longitudinal arcs in equal periods of time without any restitution of its anomaly. And this will happen (1) if for each of the intervals it begins from the same course which is to be added or subtracted and does not stop at the same; or (2) if in one interval it begins from the greatest movement and stops at the least, while in the other it starts from the least and ends at the greatest; or (3) if the first course of one interval and the last course of the other are equidistant on each side of either the course of greatest movement or the course of least movement. For each of these cases, if it come about, will either again produce no anomalistic difference or the same, and therefore make the longitudinal surpluses equal, but will effect no restitution of anomaly. Therefore the intervals considered must fall under none of these cases if they are to embrace a restitution of anomaly.

But on the contrary, if complete restitutions of anomaly are not embraced by the intervals, we should choose those which can most thoroughly manifest the inequality; that is, we should choose them when they begin not only from different courses but also from ones very different either in magnitude or power; (a) in magnitude as when in one interval it begins from the least course and does not end with the greatest and when in the other interval it begins from the greatest and does not end with the least, for in this way the difference of longitudinal surplus will be greatest if whole cycles of anomaly are not completed, especially when one quadrant or three quadrants of one anomaly are left over, the intervals then being unequal by twice the anomalistic difference; and (b) in power as when in each of the intervals it begins from the mean course, and not from the same mean, but in one interval from the mean additively and in the other subtractively; for in this way, if the anomaly is not restored, the longitudinal surpluses will differ from each other the most—by twice the anomalistic difference if the surpluses are again a quadrant or three quadrants of an anomalistic cycle, or four times the difference if a half cycle.

And, therefore, we see that Hipparchus was most attentive, as he judged, in his choice of the intervals gotten for this research. And we see he used the case where the moon, in one interval, started from the greatest course and did not stop with the least, and, in the other interval, started from the least and did not stop with the greatest; and redeemed the resulting anomalistic difference of the sun, although it is short a bit because the sun's return fails of complete circles by very nearly one quarter of a sign which is not the same sign and does not produce an equal anomalistic difference in each of the intervals.

And we say these things, not to belittle this method of getting at the periods of return, but to bring to mind that, when it is done with the proper care and consequent calculation, it can rectify the difference; but that, if any at all of the incidents explained are neglected, it will completely falsify the solution sought; and that a rectification which accurately takes into account all the incidents of the observations is very difficult for those who are making a discerning choice of these observations.

Now, of the periodic returns given according to the calculations made by Hipparchus, that of the lunar month, as we said, appears to have been calculated as soundly as possible and not to differ by any sensible amount from the true one. But the periodic return in latitude and the restitution of anomaly appear to be off by an appreciable amount. So much so that we have immediately seen the flaw from the simpler and easier means employed by us in view of the same discrimination. And we shall immediately demonstrate these methods along with the quantity of the moon's anomaly. But first we set out, for greater service in what follows, the particular mean movements in latitude, longitude, and anomaly, in accordance with the proposed times of return of the periodic movements modified by that correction which will be demonstrated later.

3. On the Moon's Regular Movements in Detail

If now we multiply the sun's mean daily movement, proved to be very nearly $0°59^i8^{ii}17^{iii}13^{iv}12^v31^{vi}$, by the 29 days $31^i50^{ii}8^{iii}20^{iv}$ of one lunar month, and add to the result the $360°$ of one circle, then we shall have the longitudinal course of the moon's mean movement in one lunar month—that is, very nearly $389°6^i23^{ii}1^{iii}24^{iv}2^v30^{vi}57^{vii}$. Distributing these over the days of the lunar month we shall have the moon's daily movement in longitude—that is, very nearly $13°10^i34^{ii}58^{iii}33^{iv}30^v30^{vi}$.

Again, multiplying the 269 circles of the anomaly by the $360°$ of one circle, we shall have the number $96,840°$. Distributing these over the 7,412 days $10^i44^{ii}51^{iii}40^{iv}$ of the 251 lunar months, we shall have a daily mean movement of anomaly of $13°3^i53^{ii}56^{iii}29^{iv}38^v38^{vi}$.

Likewise multiplying the 5,923 returns in latitude by the $360°$ of one circle, we shall have the number $2,132,280°$. Distributing these over the 161,277 days $58^i58^{ii}3^{iii}20^{iv}$ of the 5,458 lunar months, we shall have the daily mean latitudinal movement of $13°13^i45^{ii}39^{iii}40^{iv}17^v19^{vi}$.

Again, subtracting the sun's daily mean movement from the moon's daily mean movement in longitude, we shall have the daily mean elongation of $12°11^i26^{ii}41^{iii}20^{iv}17^v59^{vi}$.

Through the methods we shall employ later on, as we have already said, we find that the daily mean movement in longitude remains practically unchanged and that, of course, the movement of elongation remains about the same, too;

but that the daily mean movement of anomaly is less by $11^{iv}46^{v}39^{vi}$, so that it becomes $13°3^{i}53^{ii}56^{iii}17^{iv}51^{v}59^{vi}$, and that the daily mean movement in latitude is more by $8^{iv}39^{v}18^{vi}$, so that it becomes $13°13^{i}45^{ii}39^{iii}48^{iv}56^{v}37^{vi}$.

If, in accordance with these daily movements, we take one twenty-fourth of each, we shall have the hourly mean movement in longitude of $0°32^{i}56^{ii}27^{iii}26^{iv}23^{v}46^{vi}15^{vii}$; the hourly mean movement of anomaly of $0°32^{i}39^{ii}44^{iii}50^{iv}44^{v}39^{v}57^{vii}30^{viii}$; in latitude of $0°33^{i}4^{ii}24^{iii}9^{iv}32^{v}21^{v}32^{vii}30^{viii}$; and of elongation of $0°30^{i}28^{ii}36^{iii}43^{iv}20^{v}44^{vi}57^{vii}30^{viii}$. And if we multiply the daily movements by thirty and subtract the complete circles, we shall have the monthly mean surplus in longitude of $35°17^{i}29^{ii}16^{iii}45^{iv}15^{v}$; the monthly mean surplus of anomaly of $31°56^{i}58^{ii}8^{iii}55^{iv}59^{v}30^{vi}$; in latitude of $36°52^{i}49^{ii}54^{iii}28^{iv}18^{v}31^{vi}$; and of elongation of $5°43^{i}20^{ii}40^{iii}8^{iv}59^{v}30^{vi}$.

Again, multiplying the daily mean movements by the 365 days of an Egyptian year and subtracting the complete circles, we shall have the yearly mean surplus in longitude of $129°22^{i}46^{ii}13^{iii}50^{iv}32^{v}30^{vi}$; the yearly mean surplus of anomaly of $88°43^{i}7^{ii}28^{iii}41^{iv}13^{v}55^{vi}$; in latitude of $148°42^{i}47^{ii}12^{iii}44^{iv}25^{v}5^{vi}$; and of elongation of $129°37^{i}21^{ii}28^{iii}29^{iv}23^{v}55^{vi}$.

Next, multiplying the yearly movements by eighteen for greater facility as we said, in using the table, and subtracting the complete circles, we shall have an eighteen-year mean surplus in longitude of $168°49^{i}52^{ii}9^{iii}9^{iv}45^{v}$; an eighteen-year mean surplus of anomaly of $156°56^{i}14^{ii}36^{iii}22^{iv}10^{v}30^{vi}$; in latitude of $156°50^{i}9^{ii}49^{iii}19^{iv}31^{v}30^{vi}$; and of elongation of $173°12^{i}26^{ii}32^{iii}49^{iv}10^{v}30^{vi}$.

Then we shall construct, as in the case of the sun, 3 tables, again of 45 rows and 5 columns each. Now the first column will contain the particular times: in the first table, the eighteen-year periods; in the second table, the years and then again the hours; in the third table, the months and then again the days. And the other four columns contain the particular comparisons in degrees: the second column those in longitude, the third those of anomaly, the fourth those in latitude, and the fifth those of elongation. See tables on following pages.

4. Tables of the Mean Movements of the Moon, Table I

Col. 1 Years	Col. 2 Degrees	Longitudinal Surplus 11°22' within the Bull[1]						Col. 3 Degrees	Surplus of Anomaly 268°49'					
		I	II	III	IV	V	VI		I	II	III	IV	V	VI
18	168	49	52	9	9	45	0	156	56	14	36	22	10	30
36	337	39	44	18	19	30	0	313	52	29	12	44	21	0
54	146	29	36	27	29	15	0	110	48	43	49	6	31	30
72	315	19	28	36	39	0	0	267	44	58	25	28	42	0
90	124	9	20	45	48	45	0	64	41	13	1	50	52	30
108	292	59	12	54	58	30	0	221	37	27	38	13	3	0
126	101	49	5	4	8	15	0	18	33	42	14	35	13	30
144	270	38	57	13	18	0	0	175	29	56	50	57	24	0
162	79	28	49	22	27	45	0	332	26	11	27	19	34	30
180	248	18	41	31	37	30	0	129	22	26	3	41	45	0
198	57	8	33	40	47	15	0	286	18	40	40	3	55	30
216	225	58	25	49	57	0	0	83	14	55	16	26	6	0
234	34	48	17	59	6	45	0	240	11	9	52	48	16	30
252	203	38	10	8	16	30	0	37	7	24	29	10	27	0
270	12	28	2	17	26	15	0	194	3	39	5	32	37	30
288	181	17	54	26	36	0	0	350	59	53	41	54	48	0
306	350	7	46	35	45	45	0	147	56	8	18	16	58	30
324	158	57	38	44	55	30	0	304	52	22	54	39	9	0
342	327	47	30	54	5	15	0	101	48	37	31	1	19	30
360	136	37	23	3	15	0	0	258	44	52	7	23	30	0
378	305	27	15	12	24	45	0	55	41	6	43	45	40	30
396	114	17	7	21	34	30	0	212	37	21	20	7	51	0
414	283	6	59	30	44	15	0	9	33	35	56	30	1	30
432	91	56	51	39	54	0	0	166	29	50	32	52	12	0
450	260	46	43	49	3	45	0	323	26	5	9	14	22	30
468	69	36	35	58	13	30	0	120	22	19	45	36	33	0
486	238	26	28	7	23	15	0	277	18	34	21	58	43	30
504	47	16	20	16	33	0	0	74	14	48	58	20	54	0
522	216	6	12	25	42	45	0	231	11	3	34	43	4	30
540	24	56	4	34	52	30	0	28	7	18	11	5	15	0
558	193	45	56	44	2	15	0	185	3	32	47	27	25	30
576	2	35	48	53	12	0	0	341	59	47	23	49	36	0
594	171	25	41	2	21	45	0	138	56	2	0	11	46	30
612	340	15	33	11	31	30	0	295	52	16	36	33	57	0
630	149	5	25	20	41	15	0	92	48	31	12	56	7	30
648	317	55	17	29	51	0	0	249	44	45	49	18	18	0
666	126	45	9	39	0	45	0	46	41	0	25	40	28	30
684	295	35	1	48	10	30	0	203	37	15	2	2	39	0
702	104	24	53	57	20	15	0	0	33	29	38	24	49	30
720	273	14	46	6	30	0	0	157	29	44	14	47	0	0
738	82	4	38	15	39	45	0	314	25	58	51	9	10	30
756	250	54	30	24	49	30	0	111	22	13	27	31	21	0
774	59	44	22	33	59	15	0	268	18	28	3	53	31	30
792	228	34	14	43	9	0	0	65	14	42	40	15	42	0
810	37	24	6	52	18	45	0	222	10	57	16	37	52	30

[1]These numbers under the headings refer, of course, to the surpluses at the epochs in the year 1 of Nabonassar.

4. TABLES OF THE MEAN MOVEMENTS OF THE MOON, TABLE I—Continued

Col. 1 Years	Col. 4 Degrees	Latitudinal Surplus 354°15'						Col. 5 Degrees	Surplus of Elongation 70°37'					
		I	II	III	IV	V	VI		I	II	III	IV	V	VI
18	156	50	9	49	19	31	30	173	12	26	32	49	10	30
36	313	40	19	38	39	3	0	346	24	53	5	38	21	0
54	110	30	29	27	58	34	30	159	37	19	38	27	31	30
72	267	20	39	17	18	6	0	332	49	46	11	16	42	0
90	64	10	49	6	37	37	30	146	2	12	44	5	52	30
108	221	0	58	55	57	9	0	319	14	39	16	55	3	0
126	17	51	8	45	16	40	30	132	27	5	49	44	13	30
144	174	41	18	34	36	12	0	305	39	32	22	33	24	0
162	331	31	28	23	55	43	30	118	51	58	55	22	34	30
180	128	21	38	13	15	15	0	292	4	25	28	11	45	0
198	285	11	48	2	34	46	30	105	16	52	1	0	55	30
216	82	1	57	51	54	18	0	278	29	18	33	50	6	0
234	238	52	7	41	13	49	30	91	41	45	6	39	16	30
252	35	42	17	30	33	21	0	264	54	11	39	28	27	0
270	192	32	27	19	52	52	30	78	6	38	12	17	37	30
288	349	22	37	9	12	24	0	251	19	4	45	6	48	0
306	146	12	46	58	31	55	30	64	31	31	17	55	58	30
324	303	2	56	47	51	27	0	237	43	57	50	45	9	0
342	99	53	6	37	10	58	30	50	56	24	23	34	19	30
360	256	43	16	26	30	30	0	224	8	50	56	23	30	0
378	53	33	26	15	50	1	30	37	21	17	29	12	40	30
396	210	23	36	5	9	33	0	210	33	44	2	1	51	0
414	7	13	45	54	29	4	30	23	46	10	34	51	1	30
432	164	3	55	43	48	36	0	196	58	37	7	40	12	0
450	320	54	5	33	8	7	30	10	11	3	40	29	22	30
468	117	44	15	22	27	39	0	183	23	30	13	18	33	0
486	274	34	25	11	47	10	30	356	35	56	46	7	43	30
504	71	24	35	1	6	42	0	169	48	23	18	56	54	0
522	228	14	44	50	26	13	30	343	0	49	51	46	4	30
540	25	4	54	39	45	45	0	156	13	16	24	35	15	0
558	181	55	4	29	5	16	30	329	25	42	57	24	25	30
576	338	45	14	18	24	48	0	142	38	9	30	13	36	0
594	135	35	24	7	44	19	30	315	50	36	3	2	46	30
612	292	25	33	57	3	51	0	129	3	2	35	51	57	0
630	89	15	43	46	23	22	30	302	15	29	8	41	7	30
648	246	5	53	35	42	54	0	115	27	55	41	30	18	0
666	42	56	3	25	2	25	30	288	40	22	14	19	28	30
684	199	46	13	14	21	57	0	101	52	48	47	8	39	0
702	356	36	23	3	41	28	30	275	5	15	19	57	49	30
720	153	26	32	53	1	0	0	88	17	41	52	47	0	0
738	310	16	42	42	20	31	30	261	30	8	25	36	10	30
756	107	6	52	31	40	3	0	74	42	34	58	25	21	0
774	263	57	2	20	59	34	30	247	55	1	31	14	31	30
792	60	47	12	10	19	6	0	61	7	28	4	3	42	0
810	217	37	21	59	38	37	30	234	19	54	36	52	52	30

4. Tables of the Mean Movements of the Moon, Table II

Col. 1 Years	Col. 2 Degrees	Longitudinal Surplus						Col. 3 Degrees	Surplus of Anomaly					
		I	II	III	IV	V	VI		I	II	III	IV	V	VI
1	129	22	46	13	50	32	30	88	43	7	28	41	13	55
2	258	45	32	27	41	5	0	177	26	14	57	22	27	50
3	28	8	18	41	31	37	30	266	9	22	26	3	41	45
4	157	31	4	55	22	10	0	354	52	29	54	44	55	40
5	286	53	51	9	12	42	30	83	35	37	23	26	9	35
6	56	16	37	23	3	15	0	172	18	44	52	7	23	30
7	185	39	23	36	53	47	30	261	1	52	20	48	37	25
8	315	2	9	50	44	20	0	349	44	59	49	29	51	20
9	84	24	56	4	34	52	30	78	28	7	18	11	5	15
10	213	47	42	18	25	25	0	167	11	14	46	52	19	10
11	343	10	28	32	15	57	30	255	54	22	15	33	33	5
12	112	33	14	46	6	30	0	344	37	29	44	14	47	0
13	241	56	0	59	57	2	30	73	20	37	12	56	0	55
14	11	18	47	13	47	35	0	162	3	44	41	37	14	50
15	140	41	33	27	38	7	30	250	46	52	10	18	28	45
16	270	4	19	41	28	40	0	339	29	59	38	59	42	40
17	39	27	5	55	19	12	30	68	13	7	7	40	56	35
18	168	49	52	9	9	45	0	156	56	14	36	22	10	30

Hours	Longitudinal Surplus							Surplus of Anomaly						
1	0	32	56	27	26	23	46	0	32	39	44	50	44	40
2	1	5	52	54	52	47	32	1	5	19	29	41	29	20
3	1	38	49	22	19	11	18	1	37	59	14	32	14	0
4	2	11	45	49	45	35	5	2	10	38	59	22	58	40
5	2	44	42	17	11	58	51	2	43	18	44	13	43	20
6	3	17	38	44	38	22	37	3	15	58	29	4	28	0
7	3	50	35	12	4	46	23	3	48	38	13	55	12	40
8	4	23	31	39	31	10	10	4	21	17	58	45	57	20
9	4	56	28	6	57	33	56	4	53	57	43	36	42	0
10	5	29	24	34	23	57	42	5	26	37	28	27	26	40
11	6	2	21	1	50	21	28	5	59	17	13	18	11	20
12	6	35	17	29	16	45	15	6	31	56	58	8	56	0
13	7	8	13	56	43	9	1	7	4	36	42	59	40	39
14	7	41	10	24	9	32	47	7	37	16	27	50	25	19
15	8	14	6	51	35	56	33	8	9	56	12	41	9	59
16	8	47	3	19	2	20	20	8	42	35	57	31	54	39
17	9	19	59	46	28	44	6	9	15	15	42	22	39	19
18	9	52	56	13	55	7	52	9	47	55	27	13	23	59
19	10	25	52	41	21	31	38	10	20	35	12	4	8	39
20	10	58	49	8	47	55	25	10	53	14	56	54	53	19
21	11	31	45	36	14	19	11	11	25	54	41	45	37	59
22	12	4	42	3	40	42	57	11	58	34	26	36	22	39
23	12	37	38	31	7	6	43	12	31	14	11	27	7	19
24	13	10	34	58	33	30	30	13	3	53	56	17	51	59

4. Tables of the Mean Movements of the Moon, Table II—Continued

Col. 1 Single Years	Col. 4 Degrees	Latitudinal Surplus						Col. 5 Degrees	Surplus of Elongation					
		I	II	III	IV	V	VI		I	II	III	IV	V	VI
1	148	42	47	12	44	25	5	129	37	21	28	29	23	55
2	297	25	34	25	28	50	10	259	14	42	56	58	47	50
3	86	8	21	38	13	15	15	28	52	4	25	28	11	45
4	234	51	8	50	57	40	20	158	29	25	53	57	35	40
5	23	33	56	3	42	5	25	288	6	47	22	26	59	35
6	172	16	43	16	26	30	30	57	44	8	50	56	23	30
7	320	59	30	29	10	55	35	187	21	30	19	25	47	25
8	109	42	17	41	55	20	40	316	58	51	47	55	11	20
9	258	25	4	54	39	45	45	86	36	13	16	24	35	15
10	47	7	52	7	24	10	50	216	13	34	44	53	59	10
11	195	50	39	20	8	35	55	345	50	56	13	23	23	5
12	344	33	26	32	53	1	0	115	28	17	41	52	47	0
13	133	16	13	45	37	26	5	245	5	39	10	22	10	55
14	281	59	0	58	21	51	10	14	43	0	38	51	34	50
15	70	41	48	11	6	16	15	144	20	22	7	20	58	45
16	219	24	35	23	50	41	20	273	57	43	35	50	22	40
17	8	7	22	36	35	6	25	43	35	5	4	19	46	35
18	156	50	9	49	19	31	30	173	12	26	32	49	10	30

Hours		Latitudinal Surplus							Surplus of Elongation					
1	0	33	4	24	9	32	22	0	30	28	36	43	20	45
2	1	6	8	48	19	4	43	1	0	57	13	26	41	30
3	1	39	13	12	28	37	5	1	31	25	50	10	2	15
4	2	12	17	36	38	9	26	2	1	54	26	53	23	0
5	2	45	22	0	47	41	48	2	32	23	3	36	43	45
6	3	18	26	24	57	14	9	3	2	51	40	20	4	30
7	3	51	30	49	6	46	31	3	33	20	17	3	25	15
8	4	24	35	13	16	18	52	4	3	48	53	46	46	0
9	4	57	39	37	25	51	14	4	34	17	30	30	6	45
10	5	30	44	1	35	23	35	5	4	46	7	13	27	30
11	6	3	48	25	44	55	57	5	35	14	43	56	48	15
12	6	36	52	49	54	28	19	6	5	43	20	40	9	0
13	7	9	57	14	4	0	40	6	36	11	57	23	29	44
14	7	43	1	38	13	33	2	7	6	40	34	6	50	29
15	8	16	6	2	23	5	23	7	37	9	10	50	11	14
16	8	49	10	26	32	37	45	8	7	37	47	33	31	59
17	9	22	14	50	42	10	6	8	38	6	24	16	52	44
18	9	55	19	14	51	42	28	9	8	35	1	0	13	29
19	10	28	23	39	1	14	49	9	39	3	37	43	34	14
20	11	1	28	3	10	47	11	10	9	32	14	26	54	59
21	11	34	32	27	20	19	32	10	40	0	51	10	15	44
22	12	7	36	51	29	51	54	11	10	29	27	53	36	29
23	12	40	41	15	39	24	15	11	40	58	4	36	57	14
24	13	13	45	39	48	56	37	12	11	26	41	20	17	59

4. Tables of the Mean Movements of the Moon, Table III

Col. 1 Months	Col. 2 Degrees	Longitudinal Surplus						Col. 3 Degrees	Surplus of Anomaly					
		I	II	III	IV	V	VI		I	II	III	IV	V	VI
30	35	17	29	16	45	15	0	31	56	58	8	55	59	30
60	70	34	58	33	30	30	0	63	53	56	17	51	59	0
90	105	52	27	50	15	45	0	95	50	54	26	47	58	30
120	141	9	57	7	1	0	0	127	47	52	35	43	58	0
150	176	27	26	23	46	15	0	159	44	50	44	39	57	30
180	211	44	55	40	31	30	0	191	41	48	53	35	57	0
210	247	2	24	57	16	45	0	223	38	47	2	31	56	30
240	282	19	54	14	2	0	0	255	35	45	11	27	56	0
270	317	37	23	30	47	15	0	287	32	43	20	23	55	30
300	352	54	52	47	32	30	0	319	29	41	29	19	55	0
330	28	12	22	4	17	45	0	351	26	39	38	15	54	30
360	63	29	51	21	3	0	0	23	23	37	47	11	54	0

Days		Longitudinal Surplus							Surplus of Anomaly					
1	13	10	34	58	33	30	30	13	3	53	56	17	51	59
2	26	21	9	57	7	1	0	26	7	47	52	35	43	58
3	39	31	44	55	40	31	30	39	11	41	48	53	35	57
4	52	42	19	54	14	2	0	52	15	35	45	11	27	56
5	65	52	54	52	47	32	30	65	19	29	41	29	19	55
6	79	3	29	51	21	3	0	78	23	23	37	47	11	54
7	92	14	4	49	54	33	30	91	27	17	34	5	3	53
8	105	24	39	48	28	4	0	104	31	11	30	22	55	52
9	118	35	14	47	1	34	30	117	35	5	26	40	47	51
10	131	45	49	45	35	5	0	130	38	59	22	58	39	50
11	144	56	24	44	8	35	30	143	42	53	19	16	31	49
12	158	6	59	42	42	6	0	156	46	47	15	34	23	48
13	171	17	34	41	15	36	30	169	50	41	11	52	15	47
14	184	28	9	39	49	7	0	182	54	35	8	10	7	46
15	197	38	44	38	22	37	30	195	58	29	4	27	59	45
16	210	49	19	36	56	8	0	209	2	23	0	45	51	44
17	223	59	54	35	29	38	30	222	6	16	57	3	43	43
18	237	10	29	34	3	9	0	235	10	10	53	21	35	42
19	250	21	4	32	36	39	30	248	14	4	49	39	27	41
20	263	31	39	31	10	10	0	261	17	58	45	57	19	40
21	276	42	14	29	43	40	30	274	21	52	42	15	11	39
22	289	52	49	28	17	11	0	287	25	46	38	33	3	38
23	303	3	24	26	50	41	30	300	29	40	34	50	55	37
24	316	13	59	25	24	12	0	313	33	34	31	8	47	36
25	329	24	34	23	57	42	30	326	37	28	27	26	39	35
26	342	35	9	22	31	13	0	339	41	22	23	44	31	34
27	355	45	44	21	4	43	30	352	45	16	20	2	23	33
28	8	56	19	19	38	14	0	5	49	10	16	20	15	32
29	22	6	54	18	11	44	30	18	53	4	12	38	7	31
30	35	17	29	16	45	15	0	31	56	58	8	55	59	30

4. Tables of the Mean Movements of the Moon, Table III—Continued

Col. 1 Months	Col. 4 Degrees	Latitudinal Surplus I	II	III	IV	V	VI	Col. 5 Degrees	Surplus of Elongation I	II	III	IV	V	VI
30	36	52	49	54	28	18	30	5	43	20	40	8	59	30
60	73	45	39	48	56	37	0	11	26	41	20	17	59	0
90	110	38	29	43	24	55	30	17	10	2	0	26	58	30
120	147	31	19	37	53	14	0	22	53	22	40	35	58	0
150	184	24	9	32	21	32	30	28	36	43	20	44	57	30
180	221	16	59	26	49	51	0	34	20	4	0	53	57	0
210	258	9	49	21	18	9	30	40	3	24	41	2	56	30
240	295	2	39	15	46	28	0	45	46	45	21	11	56	0
270	331	55	29	10	14	46	30	51	30	6	1	20	55	30
300	8	48	19	4	43	5	0	57	13	26	41	29	55	0
330	45	41	8	59	11	23	30	62	56	47	21	38	54	30
360	82	33	58	53	39	42	0	68	40	8	1	47	54	0

Days		Latitudinal Surplus							Surplus of Elongation					
1	13	13	45	39	48	56	37	12	11	26	41	20	17	59
2	26	27	31	19	37	53	14	24	22	53	22	40	35	58
3	39	41	16	59	26	49	51	36	34	20	4	0	53	57
4	52	55	2	39	15	46	28	48	45	46	45	21	11	56
5	66	8	48	19	4	43	5	60	57	13	26	41	29	55
6	79	22	33	58	53	39	42	73	8	40	8	1	47	54
7	92	36	19	38	42	36	19	85	20	6	49	22	5	53
8	105	50	5	18	31	32	56	97	31	33	30	42	23	52
9	119	3	50	58	20	29	33	109	43	0	12	2	41	51
10	132	17	36	38	9	26	10	121	54	26	53	22	59	50
11	145	31	22	17	58	22	47	134	5	53	34	43	17	49
12	158	45	7	57	47	19	24	146	17	20	16	3	35	48
13	171	58	53	37	36	16	1	158	28	46	57	23	53	47
14	185	12	39	17	25	12	38	170	40	13	38	44	11	46
15	198	26	24	57	14	9	15	182	51	40	20	4	29	45
16	211	40	10	37	3	5	52	195	3	7	1	24	47	44
17	224	53	56	16	52	2	29	207	14	33	42	45	5	43
18	238	7	41	56	40	59	6	219	26	0	24	5	23	42
19	251	21	27	36	29	55	43	231	37	27	5	25	41	41
20	264	35	13	16	18	52	20	243	48	53	46	45	59	40
21	277	48	58	56	7	48	57	256	0	20	28	6	17	39
22	291	2	44	35	56	45	34	268	11	47	9	26	35	38
23	304	16	30	15	45	42	11	280	23	13	50	46	53	37
24	317	30	15	55	34	38	48	292	34	40	32	7	11	36
25	330	44	1	35	23	35	25	304	46	7	13	27	29	35
26	343	57	47	15	12	32	2	316	57	33	54	47	47	34
27	357	11	32	55	1	28	39	329	9	0	36	8	5	33
28	10	25	18	34	50	25	16	341	20	27	17	28	23	32
29	23	39	4	14	39	21	53	353	31	53	58	48	41	31
30	36	52	49	54	28	18	30	5	43	20	40	8	59	30

5. That, in the Case of the Simple Hypothesis of the Moon, both the Hypothesis of Eccentricity and of the Epicycle Produce the Same Appearances

And after these things there follows an explication of the manner and size of the moon's anomaly. At present we shall develop the explication as if there were that one anomaly belonging to it to which alone nearly all our predecessors appear to have turned their attention; I mean to that anomaly completed in the period of return already mentioned. Afterwards we shall show that the moon effects a second anomaly in its elongations from the sun,[1] an anomaly which becomes greatest at the two quarters and is twice redeemed in the month's time, at conjunctions and full moons.

We shall use this order of demonstration because the second can never be found without the first's being implied by it. But the first can be found without the second since it is derived from lunar eclipses where there is no sensible difference due to the anomaly relative to the sun. And in the first proof we shall follow the methods we see Hipparchus used. For considering three lunar eclipses, we shall demonstrate the size of the greatest difference at the point of mean movement and the position of the apogee; we shall show that considered in itself this first anomaly can be effected both by the hypothesis of the epicycle and the hypothesis of eccentricity and the appearances will be the same; but that this last hypothesis would be more properly applied to the second anomaly relative to the sun in the combination of both anomalies.

And so, in making this research, we shall see that again in the case of the simple anomaly of the moon the appearances are the same in either of these hypotheses even if the time-periods of the two returns—(1) that relative to the anomaly and (2) that relative to the ecliptic—are not equal to each other as in the case of the sun, but are unequal as in the case of the moon, with only the ratios being again supposed the same. Since, then, the moon effects its return with respect to the ecliptic more rapidly than its return with respect to this anomaly, therefore it is evident that, on the hypothesis of the epicycle, in equal times the epicycle will move on the circle concentric with the ecliptic through an arc greater than the one similar to that traversed by the moon on the epicycle itself; but that, on the hypothesis of eccentricity, the moon will traverse an arc on the eccentric circle similar to that traversed on the epicycle, and the eccentric will turn about the ecliptic's centre, in the same direction as the moon,[2] through an arc equal to the excess of the longitudinal course over the anomalistic course—that is, the excess of the concentric circle's arc over the epicycle's. For in this way not only the sameness of the ratios but also the equality of the times of each of the movements will be saved in both hypotheses.

Now, these things being supposed as necessary and immediate consequences,

---

[1]This second anomaly of the moon with respect to the sun is the first of those appearances which tie the planets to the sun instead of the earth. As we shall see later, each of the five planets has an anomaly with respect to the sun besides its other anomalies. And thus even on the geocentric hypothesis of Ptolemy, there are manifested inevitably heliocentric appearances. And so it is no wonder the Greeks had heliocentric theories. Nor is the appearance of the Copernican theory anything very extraordinary; Copernicus had only to look at Ptolemy. Ptolemy himself sees all this when he says, in Book I, that the heliocentric theory would be simpler as far as the planets are concerned.

[2]That is, both movements of the eccentric hypothesis—(1) that of the moon on the ec-

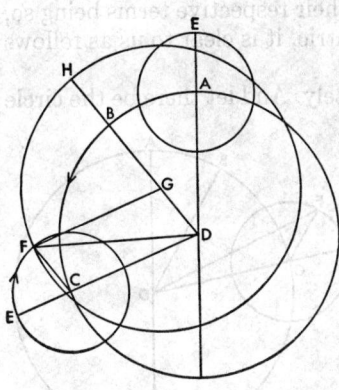

let there be the circle ABC concentric with the ecliptic, with centre D and radius AD; and the epicycle EF with centre C. And let it be assumed that, when the epicycle was at A, the moon was at E, the epicycle's apogee; and that in the same time the epicycle has traversed the arc AC and the moon the arc EF. And let DE and CF be joined. And since the arc AC is greater than the arc similar to EF, let BC be taken similar to EF and let BD be joined. It is clear, then, that in the same time the eccentric circle has moved through angle ADB, the excess of one of the courses over the other, and that its centre and apogee have come to be along the straight line BD. This being so, let DG be laid off equal to CF, and let FG be joined. And with centre G and radius FG, let the eccentric circle FH be drawn.

I say that

$$FG : DG :: CD : CF;$$

and that, according to this last hypothesis also, the moon will be at point F—that is, arc FH will also be similar to arc EF.

For since

$$\text{angle } BDC = \text{angle } ECF,$$

CF is parallel to DG. And

$$CF = DG;$$

and therefore

$$FG = CD,$$

and is parallel to it. And

$$FG : DG :: CD : CF.$$

Again, since CD is parallel to FG,

$$\text{angle } BDC = \text{angle } FGH.$$

But it was supposed

$$\text{angle } BDC = \text{angle } ECF.$$

And so also arc FH is similar to arc EF. Therefore, in the same time according to either hypothesis, the moon has arrived at the point F, since it has moved through the epicycle's arc EF and the eccentric's arc FH, which have been proved similar, and since the epicycle's centre has moved through arc AC and the eccentric's centre through arc AB, the excess of arc AC over arc EF. Which was to be proved.

---

centric, and (2) that of the eccentric about the ecliptic's centre or the earth—are from west to east in the general direction of the moon's movement on the ecliptic or of the epicycle's centre on the concentric circle.

The equivalent epicyclic hypothesis is, of course, the case where the epicycle's centre moves counter-clockwise while the epicycle itself turns clockwise. In the case of the moon, Ptolemy does not explicitly state, as he does with the other five planets, why it is necessary to take one epicyclic hypothesis and not the other. The reason is obvious. By the tables of observations it was known that the time from the moon's mean movement in longitude through its greatest movement back to the mean is always less than the time from its mean movement through its least movement back to the mean.

And, even if only the ratios are equal without their respective terms being so, and the eccentric circle is not equal to the concentric, it is clear to us as follows that the result will be the same.

For let each of the hypotheses be drawn separately. And let there be the circle
ABC concentric with the ecliptic, with centre *D* and radius *AD;* and the epicycle *EF* with centre *C*. And let the moon be at *F*. And again let there be the eccentric circle *GHK* with centre *L* and diameter *HLM*. And on this diameter let there be the ecliptic's centre *M;* and let the point *K* be the moon. And in the first figure let *DCE, CF, DF* be joined; and in the second figure *GM, KM, KL*.

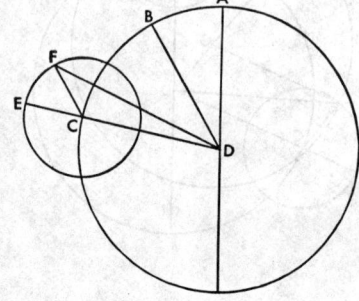

And let

$$CD : CE :: HL : LM.$$

And let the epicycle have moved through angle *ADC* and the moon through angle *ECF* in the same time. And let the eccentric circle have moved through angle *GMH*

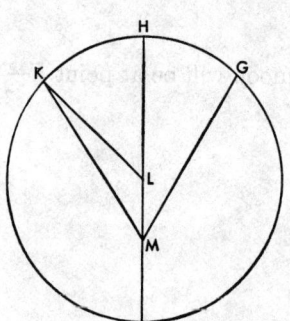

and the moon in turn through angle *HLK* in the same time. Then, because of the relations assumed to hold between the movements,

$$\text{angle } ECF = \text{angle } HLK$$

and

$$\text{angle } ADC = \text{angle } GMH + \text{angle } HLK.$$

This being so, I say that, again on either hypothesis, in the same time the moon will appear to have traversed equal arcs; that is,

$$\text{angle } ADF = \text{angle } GMK.$$

For the moon at the beginning of the interval is at the apogees, and appears along the straight lines *AD* and *GM;* and at the end of the interval is at the points *F* and *K*, and appears along the straight lines *DF* and *KM*.

For again let arc *BC* be laid out similar to each of the arcs *HK* and *EF*, and let *BD* be joined. Then, since

$$CD : CF :: KL : LM,$$

and since the sides about the equal angles at *C* and *L* are for that reason proportional, therefore the triangle *CDF* is equiangular with the triangle *KLM* and the angles opposite the proportional sides are equal. Therefore

$$\text{angle } CFD = \text{angle } KML.$$

But also

$$\text{angle } BDF = \text{angle } CFD$$

since it is supposed

$$\text{angle } ECF = \text{angle } BDC$$

and since, therefore, *CF* and *BD* are parallel. Therefore

$$\text{angle } BDF = \text{angle } KML.$$

But angle *ADB*, the excess of one movement over the other, is assumed equal to angle *GMH*, the passage of the eccentric. And therefore, by addition,

$$\text{angle } ADF = \text{angle } GMK.$$

Which was to be proved.

6. Demonstration of the Moon's First and Simple Anomaly

Now that we have understood this much, we shall demonstrate this lunar anomaly on the hypothesis of the epicycle for the reason we assigned, first using three of the oldest eclipses we have which seem to have been faithfully recorded, and then again three from the present very accurately observed by ourselves. In this way our inspection will extend over the longest time possible; and especially it will be evident that the anomalistic difference comes to be very nearly the same in both cases, and that the surplus of the mean movements is always found to agree with that computed from the periods of time already given with our corrections. With respect, then, to the demonstration of the first anomaly considered in itself, let the hypothesis of the epicycle, the one we have chosen, be applied as follows:

Let the concentric circle be conceived on the lunar sphere and lying in the same plane with the ecliptic. And let another circle be conceived inclined to this one proportionately to the quantity of the moon's latitudinal course, and borne from east to west around the ecliptic's centre at a regular speed equal to the excess of the latitudinal movement over the longitudinal. Then on this oblique circle we suppose the epicycle to be moving regularly but from west to east according to the latitudinal return, which (considered with respect to the ecliptic) produces, of course, the longitudinal movement. And on the epicycle we suppose the moon to be passing through the arc of the apogee from east to west, according to the anomalistic return. Yet in this demonstration we shall not be concerned with the latitudinal advance nor with the obliquity of the lunar circle since no appreciable difference results in the longitudinal movement from an inclination of this amount.

I.—Then of the three ancient eclipses observed in Babylon, of which we spoke, the first is recorded as having taken place in the year 1 of Mardokempad, Egyptianwise Thoth 29-30. And the eclipse began, it is stated, more than one hour after the rise of the moon, and the eclipse was total. Now, since the sun was very nearly at the end of the Fishes, and the night was very nearly 12 equatorial hours, evidently the beginning of the eclipse was $4\frac{1}{2}$ equatorial hours before midnight, and the middle of the eclipse, since it was complete, was $2\frac{1}{2}$ hours before midnight. Therefore, in Alexandria, the midtime of this eclipse occurred $3\frac{1}{3}$ equatorial hours before midnight. For we establish hour-positions with respect to its meridian, and the meridian through Alexandria is west of that through Babylon by $\frac{1}{2}+\frac{1}{3}$ equatorial hour. And at that hour the sun's true position was very nearly $24\frac{1}{2}°$ within the Fishes.

The second of the eclipses is recorded as having occurred in the year 2 of Mardokempad, Egyptianwise Thoth 18-19. And there was an eclipse, it says, of 3 digits[1] from the southern end at midnight. Since, then, the middle of the eclipse appears to have occurred in Babylon at midnight, it must have occurred in Alexandria $\frac{1}{2}+\frac{1}{3}$ of an hour before midnight. And at that hour the sun's true position was $13\frac{3}{4}°$ within the Fishes.

The third of the eclipses is recorded as having taken place in the same year 2 of Mardokempad, Egyptianwise Phamenoth 15-16. And the eclipse began, it says, after the rise of the moon, and there was an eclipse of more than half from the northern end. Now, since the sun was near the beginning of Virgin, the night

[1] A digit is 1/12 of the moon's apparent diameter.

in Babylon was very nearly 11 equatorial hours, and half the night 5½ hours. Therefore the beginning of the eclipse occurred, at most, 5 equatorial hours before midnight since it began after the moon's rise; and the middle of the eclipse 3½ hours before midnight, since the whole time of an eclipse of this magnitude must have been very nearly 3 hours. Therefore in Alexandria, in turn, the middle of the eclipse was effected 4⅓ equatorial hours before midnight. And at this hour the sun's true position was very nearly 3¼° within the Virgin.

It is thus clear that, from the middle of the first eclipse to that of the second, the sun had moved, and the moon too, 349°15′ over and above the complete circles; and from the middle of the second eclipse to that of the third 169°30′. But the interval of time between the first and second contains 354 days and 2½ equatorial hours for those considering them simply, but relative to the calculation of regular solar days 2+½+¹⁄₁₅ hours; and between the second and third 176 days and again 20½ equatorial hours simply considered, but 20⅕ hours accurately considered. And the moon moves regularly (for in this amount of time there will be no sensible difference even if one follow revolutions very close upon the true ones)[1] in 354 days and 2+½+¹⁄₁₅ equatorial hours, 306°25′ of its cycle of anomaly over and above the complete circles, and 345°51′ in longitude. And in 176 days and 20⅕ equatorial hours, 150°26′ of its cycle of anomaly, and very nearly 170°7′ in longitude. It is clear, then, that the 306°25′ of the epicycle's first interval have added 3°24′ to the moon's mean movement; and that the 150°26′ of the second interval have subtracted 37′ from the mean movement.

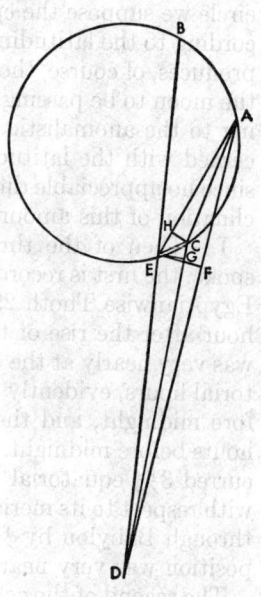

These things being assumed, let there be the moon's epicycle ABC. And let point A be the moon's position in the middle of the first eclipse, and B its position in the middle of the second, and C its position in the middle of the third. Let the moon's movement on the epicycle be thought as taking place from B to A and from A to C in such a way that the arc ACB of 306°25′, which it has traveled from the first eclipse to the second, adds 3°24′ to the mean movement; and that the arc BAC of 150°26′, which it has traveled from the second eclipse to the third, subtracts 37′ from the mean movement. And therefore in such a way that the passage from B to A of 53°35′ subtracts the 3°24′ from the mean movement, and the passage from A to C of 96°51′ adds 2°47′ to the mean movement.[2]

[1]In establishing the mean positions for the moon in each of the two series of eclipses, the lengths of the time-intervals are so small that there is no sensible difference if one use the averages of Hipparchus or the corrected ones given by Ptolemy in the tables. This remark is necessary because it is from a comparison of the second eclipse in the old series and in the new series, in Chapter 7 of this Book, an interval of some 854 Egyptian years, that the corrections are gotten—very small, indeed, but appreciable. Otherwise Ptolemy would be pulling himself up by his boot-straps.

[2]Whatever A to B adds, B to A must subtract, since A to A being a complete cycle neither adds nor subtracts. Likewise if B to C subtracts 37′ and B to A 3°24′, then A to C must add the difference between 37′ and 3°24′, or 2°47′.

Now, that it is impossible for the epicycle's perigee to be on the arc BAC is clear from the fact that this arc is subtractive and less than a semicircle. But the greatest movement is assumed to be at the perigee. Since, then, it must be on the arc BEC, let the centre of the ecliptic and of the circle carrying the epicycle's centre be taken, and let it be D. And let the straight lines DA, DEB, DC, from the center of the three points of eclipse, be joined.

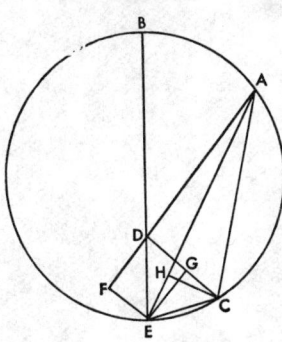

Then, generally—in order that we may easily apply this theorem in similar demonstrations, both in case we prove them by the hypothesis of the epicycle as here, and by the hypothesis of eccentricity when the centre D is taken within the circle—let one of the three straight lines we just joined be produced to the opposite arc, as here we have DEB drawn from the point B of the second eclipse to E. And let a straight line, in this case AC, join the other two points of eclipse. And from the intersection made by the line produced, E for instance, let straight lines be joined to the other two points, in this case the lines EA and EC. And let perpendiculars be dropped on the straight lines from these other two points to the centre of the ecliptic, that is EF on AD and EG on CD. From one of these two points, in this case C, let the perpendicular be drawn to the line joining the other point, in this case A, to the principal intersection made by the line produced, here E—that is, CH on AE. And from whatever intersection we extend the construction, we shall always find the same ratios resulting for the numbers of the demonstration; and the choice is made only with a view to facility.

Since, then, arc AB was proved to subtend $3°24'$ of the ecliptic, therefore, considered as an angle at the ecliptic's centre,

$$\text{angle } ADB = 3°24'$$
$$= 6°48' \text{ to 2 rt.}$$

And so also, on the circle about right triangle DEF,

$$\text{arc } EF = 6°48',$$
$$\text{chord } EF = 7^{\text{p}}7'$$

where

$$\text{hypt. } DE = 120^{\text{p}}.$$

Likewise, since

$$\text{arc } AB = 53°35',$$

therefore, being on the circumference, also

$$\text{angle } BEA = 53°35' \text{ to 2 rt.}$$

But it was seen

$$\text{angle } ADB = 6°48' \text{ to 2 rt.}$$

and therefore, by subtraction,

$$\text{angle } EAF = 46°47' \text{ to 2 rt.}$$

And so, on the circle about right triangle AEF,

$$\text{arc } EF = 46°47',$$
$$\text{chord } EF = 47^{\text{p}}38'30''$$

where

$$\text{hypt. } AE = 120^{\text{p}}.$$

And
$$AE = 17^p55'32''$$
where
$$EF = 7^p7',$$
and
$$DE = 120^p.$$

Again, since arc BAC subtends 37' of the ecliptic, considered as an angle at the centre of the ecliptic,
$$\text{angle } BDC = 37'$$
$$= 1°14' \text{ to 2 rt.}$$
And so, on the circle about right triangle DEG,
$$\text{arc } EG = 1°14',$$
$$\text{chord } EG = 1^p17'30''$$
where
$$\text{hypt. } DE = 120^p.$$

Likewise, since
$$\text{arc } BAC = 150°26',$$
being on the circumference,
$$\text{angle } BEC = 150°26' \text{ to 2 rt.}$$
But it was seen
$$\text{angle } BDC = 1°14' \text{ to 2 rt.}$$
and therefore, by subtraction,
$$\text{angle } DCE = 149°12' \text{ to 2 rt.}$$
And so, on the circle about right triangle CEG,
$$\text{arc } EG = 149°12',$$
$$\text{chord } EG = 115^p41'21''$$
where
$$\text{hypt. } CE = 120.^p$$

And therefore
$$CE = 1^p20'23''$$
where
$$EG = 1^p17'30'',$$
and
$$DE = 120^p,$$
and where it was proved
$$AE = 17^p55'32''.$$

Again, since it was proved
$$\text{arc } AC = 96°51',$$
therefore, being on the circumference,
$$\text{angle } AEC = 96°51' \text{ to 2 rt.}$$
And so, on the circle about right triangle CEH,
$$\text{arc } CH = 96°51',$$
and, as remainder of the semicircle,
$$\text{arc } EH = 83°9'.$$
And therefore
$$\text{chord } CH = 89^p46'14'',$$
$$\text{chord } EH = 79^p37'55''$$
where
$$\text{hypt. } CE = 120^p.$$

And therefore
$$CH = 1^p0'8'',$$
$$EH = 0^p53'21''$$
where
$$CE = 1^p20'23'',$$
and where it was proved
$$AE = 17^p55'32'';$$
and therefore, by subtraction,
$$AH = 17^p2'11''$$
where
$$CH = 1^p0'8''.$$
And
$$\text{sq. } AH = 290^p14'19'',$$
$$\text{sq. } CH = 1^p0'17''$$
which added together give
$$\text{sq. } AC = 291^p14'36''.$$
Therefore, in length,
$$AC = 17^p3'57'',$$
$$CE = 1^p20'23''$$
where
$$DE = 120^p.$$
And
$$\text{chord } AC = 89^p46'14''$$
where
$$\text{epic. diam.} = 120^p;$$
for it subtends arc AC and
$$\text{arc } AC = 96°51'.$$
And therefore
$$DE = 631^p13'48'',$$
$$CE = 7^p2'50''$$
where
$$AC = 89^p46'14''$$
and
$$\text{epic. diam.} = 120^p.$$
And so
$$\text{arc } CE = 6°44'1''.$$
But it is assumed
$$\text{arc } BAC = 150°26',$$
and therefore, by addition,
$$\text{arc } BCE = 157°10'1'',$$
$$\text{chord } BE = 117^p37'32''$$
where
$$\text{epic. diam.} = 120^p,$$
$$DE = 631^p13'48''.$$

If, then, this line BE were equal to the epicycle's diameter, the epicycle's centre would fall on it, and the ratio of the diameters would be immediately evident. But since it is less than the diameter, and arc BCE is less than a semicircle, it is clear that the epicycle's centre will fall outside the sector $BACE$.

Then let the point K be taken as centre, and let the straight line $DMKL$ be drawn from D, the centre of the ecliptic, through K in such a way that point L becomes the epicycle's apogee, and M the perigee.

Since then

rect. $BD, DE =$ rect. LD, DM, [Eucl. III, 36]

and since we have proved

$$BE = 117^p37'32'',$$
$$DE = 631^p13'49'',$$

and, by addition,

$$BD = 748^p51'20''$$

where, as the epicycle's diameter,

$$LKM = 120^p,$$

therefore

rect $BD, DE =$ rect. $LD, DM = 472,700^p5'32''$.

And again since

rect. $LD, DM +$ sq. $KM =$ sq. $DK,$ [Eucl. II, 6]

and since, as radius of the epicycle,

$$KM = 60^p,$$

therefore

$$\text{sq. } DK = 472,700^p5'32'' + 3,600^p$$
$$= 476,300^p5'32''.$$

And therefore, as the radius of the circle concentric with the ecliptic and carrying the epicycle,

$$DK = 690^p8'42''$$

where, as the epicycle's radius,

$$KM = 60^p.$$

And so

epic. rad. $= 5^p13'$

where the radius of the circle carrying the epicycle and concentric with the eye is 60^p.

And in a similar figure let fall KNX from the centre K perpendicular to line BE, and let BK be joined.

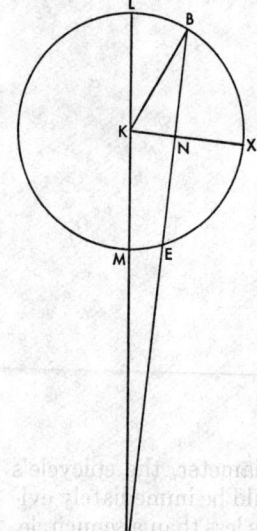

Since then

$$DE = 631^p13'48'',$$
$$EN = \text{half } BE$$
$$= 58^p48'46'',$$

where

$$DK = 690^p8'42''$$

so that, by addition,

$$DEN = 690^p2'34'',$$

therefore

$$DN = 119^p58'57''$$

where

$$DK = 120^p.$$

And, on the circle about right triangle DNK,

arc $DN = 178°2'$.

And so also

angle $DKN = 178°2'$ to 2 rt.
$= 89°1'$.

And therefore, on the epicycle

$$\text{arc } MX = 89°1',$$

and, as remainder of the semicircle,

$$\text{arc } LBX = 90°59'.$$

And

$$\text{arc } BX = \text{half arc } BXE = 78°35',$$

since it was proved

$$\text{arc } BXE = 157°10'.$$

And therefore, by subtraction, the arc BL of the epicycle, which is the moon's distance from the apogee at the middle of the second eclipse, is 12°24'.

And likewise, since it was proved

$$\text{angle } DKN = 89°1',$$

therefore, by subtraction, angle KDN, which subtends the arc subtracted from the mean longitudinal course and resulting from the anomaly due to the epicycle's arc BL, is its complement 59'. Therefore the moon's mean longitudinal position at the middle of the second eclipse was 14°44' within the Virgin, since indeed its true position was 13°45' within the Virgin, with the sun 13°45' within the Fishes.

II.—Again, of the three eclipses we have chosen from those most carefully observed by us in Alexandria, the first occurred in the year 17 of Hadrian, Egyptianwise Paÿni 20-21; and we accurately calculated the middle of it to have occurred ¾ equatorial hour before midnight. And the eclipse was total. At this hour the sun's true position was very nearly 13¼° within the Bull.

The second occurred in the year 19 of Hadrian, Egyptianwise Choïac 2-3; and we calculated the middle of it to have occurred 1 equatorial hour before midnight. And there was an eclipse to the extent of ½+⅓ of the diameter from the northern side. And at this hour the sun's true position was very nearly 25⅙° within the Balance.

The third of the eclipses occurred in the year 20 of Hadrian, Egyptianwise Pharmouthi 19-20; and we calculated the middle of it to have occurred 4 equatorial hours after midnight. And there was an eclipse to the extent of ½ of the diameter from the northern side. And at that hour the sun's true position was very nearly 14°12' within the Fishes.

Now, it is clear that the moon and also the sun have moved, from the middle of the first eclipse to the middle of the second, 161°55' over and above the complete circles; and from the middle of the second to the middle of the third, 138° 55'. The time of the first interval is 1 Egyptian year 166 days and 23¾ equatorial hours simply considered, but 23⅝ hours accurately considered. And the time of the second interval is again 1 Egyptian year 137 days and 5 equatorial hours simply considered, but 5½ hours accurately considered.

Now in 1 year, 166 days, and 23⅝ equatorial hours, the moon makes a mean movement of 110°21' of its anomalistic cycle over and above the complete circles, and very nearly 169°37' in longitude; and in 1 year, 137 days, and 5½ equatorial hours, 81°36' of its anomalistic cycle, and very nearly 137°34' in longitude. It is clear, then, that the 110°21' on the epicycle of the first interval subtract 7°42' from the mean longitudinal course, and that the 81°36' of the second interval add 1°21' to the mean longitudinal course.

Now, these things being assumed, let there again be the moon's epicycle ABC.

And let the point A be taken as the moon's position in the middle of the first eclipse; B that of the second eclipse; and C that of the third. And let the movement of the moon be conceived as passing from A to B and then to C in such a way that arc AB of 110°21' subtracts, as we said, 7°42' from the mean longitudinal course; and that arc BC of 81°36' adds 1°21' to the mean longitudinal course; and that the remaining arc CA of 168°3' adds 6°21'.

That the apogee must be on the arc AB is clear from the fact that it can neither be on arc BC nor arc CA, since each of them is additive and less than a semicircle. And yet, as if this were not assumed, let the centre of the ecliptic and of the circle on which the epicycle is borne be taken, and let it be D. Let the straight lines DEA, DB, DC be joined from the centre to the three points of eclipse. And with BC joined, let the straight lines EB and EC be drawn from E to B and C; and EF and EG perpendicular to BD and DC; and again from C let CH be drawn perpendicular to BE.

Since then arc AB subtends 7°42' of the ecliptic, therefore, being at the centre of the ecliptic,

$$\text{angle } ADB = 7°42'$$
$$= 15°24' \text{ to 2 rt.}$$

And so also, on the circle about right triangle DEF,

$$\text{arc } EF = 15°24',$$
$$\text{chord } EF = 16^{\text{p}}4'42''$$

where

$$\text{hypt. } DE = 120^{\text{p}}.$$

Likewise, since

$$\text{arc } AB = 110°21',$$

therefore, being on the circumference,

$$\text{angle } AEB = 110°21' \text{ to 2 rt.}$$

But

$$\text{angle } ADB = 15°24' \text{ to 2 rt.}$$

Therefore, by subtraction,

$$\text{angle } EBD = 94°57' \text{ to 2 rt.}$$

And so, on the circle about right triangle BEF,

$$\text{arc } EF = 94°57',$$
$$\text{chord } EF = 88^{\text{p}}26'17''$$

where

$$\text{hypt. } BE = 120^{\text{p}}.$$

And therefore

$$BE = 21^{\text{p}}48'59''$$

where

$$EF = 16^{\text{p}}4'42'',$$
$$DE = 120^{\text{p}}$$

Again, since arc AEC was shown to embrace 6°21' of the ecliptic, therefore being at the centre of the ecliptic

$$\text{angle } ADC = 6°21'$$
$$= 12°42' \text{ to 2 rt.}$$

And so, on the circle about right triangle DEG,
$$\text{arc } EG = 12°42',$$
$$\text{chord } EG = 13^{\mathrm{p}}16'19''$$
where
$$\text{hypt. } DE = 120^{\mathrm{p}}.$$

Likewise, since, by addition,
$$\text{arc } ABC = 191°57',$$
therefore, being on the circumference,
$$\text{angle } AEC = 191°57' \text{ to 2 rt.}$$
But
$$\text{angle } ADC = 12°42' \text{ to 2 rt.}$$
Therefore, by subtraction,
$$\text{angle } ECD = 179°15' \text{ to 2 rt.}$$
And so also, on the circle about right triangle CEG,
$$\text{arc } EG = 179°15',$$
$$\text{chord } EG = 119^{\mathrm{p}}59'50''$$
where
$$\text{hypt. } CE = 120^{\mathrm{p}}.$$

And therefore
$$CE = 13^{\mathrm{p}}16'20''$$
where
$$EG = 13^{\mathrm{p}}16'19'',$$
and
$$DE = 120^{\mathrm{p}},$$
and where it was proved
$$BE = 21^{\mathrm{p}}48'59''.$$

Again, since
$$\text{arc } BC = 81°36',$$
therefore, being on the circumference,
$$\text{angle } BEC = 81°36' \text{ to 2 rt.}$$
And so, on the circle about right triangle CEH,
$$\text{arc } CH = 81°36',$$
and, as remainder of the semicircle,
$$\text{arc } EH = 98°24'.$$
And therefore
$$\text{chord } CH = 78^{\mathrm{p}}24'37'',$$
$$\text{chord } EH = 90^{\mathrm{p}}50'22''$$
where
$$\text{hypt. } CE = 120^{\mathrm{p}}.$$

And therefore
$$CH = 8^{\mathrm{p}}40'20'',$$
$$EH = 10^{\mathrm{p}}2'49''$$
where
$$CE = 13^{\mathrm{p}}16'20''$$
and
$$BE = 21^{\mathrm{p}}48'59''.$$
Therefore, by subtraction,
$$BH = 11^{\mathrm{p}}46'10''$$

where
$$CH = 8^\text{p}40'20''.$$
And
$$\text{sq. } BH = 138^\text{p}31'11'',$$
$$\text{sq. } CH = 75^\text{p}12'27'';$$
and
$$\text{sq. } BC = 138^\text{p}31'11'' + 75^\text{p}12'27''$$
$$= 213^\text{p}43'38''.$$

Therefore, in length,
$$BC = 14^\text{p}37'10''$$
where
$$DE = 120^\text{p},$$
$$CE = 13^\text{p}16'20''.$$

But also
$$BC = 78^\text{p}24'37''$$
where
$$\text{epic. diam.} = 120^\text{p},$$
for it subtends arc BC which is $81°36'$. And therefore
$$DE = 643^\text{p}36'39'',$$
$$CE = 71^\text{p}11'4''$$
where
$$BC = 78^\text{p}24'37'',$$
$$\text{epic. diam.} = 120^\text{p}.$$
And so, on the epicycle,
$$\text{arc } CE = 72°46'10''.$$
And it is assumed
$$\text{arc } CEA = 168°3'.$$
Therefore, by subtraction,
$$\text{arc } AE = 95°16'50'';$$
and
$$\text{chord } AE = 88^\text{p}40'17''$$
where
$$\text{epic. diam.} = 120^\text{p},$$
$$DE = 643^\text{p}36'39''.$$

Now again, since arc AE was shown to be less than a semicircle, it is clear that the epicycle's centre will fall outside the segment AE. Then let it be taken and let it be K; and let $DMKL$ be joined so that again point L becomes the apogee and M the perigee. Now since
$$\text{rect. } AD, DE = \text{rect. } LD, DM,$$
and since we have shown that
$$AE = 88^\text{p}40'17'',$$
$$DE = 643^\text{p}36'39'',$$
and, by addition,
$$AD = 732^\text{p}16'56''$$
where, as epicycle's diameter,
$$LKM = 120^\text{p},$$
therefore
$$\text{rect. } LD, DM = 471,304^\text{p}46'17''.$$

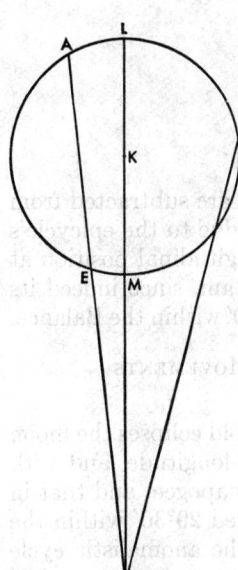

And again, since
$$\text{rect. } LD, DM + \text{sq. } KM = \text{sq. } DK,$$
and since KM, the epicycle's radius, when squared, is
3,600ᴾ, therefore
$$\text{sq. } DK = 471,304^{\text{p}}46'17'' + 3600^{\text{p}}$$
$$= 474,904^{\text{p}}46'17''.$$
And therefore, as the radius of the circle bearing the
epicycle and concentric with the ecliptic,
$$DK = 689^{\text{p}}8'$$
where, as the epicycle's radius,
$$KM = 60^{\text{p}}.$$
And so
$$\text{epic. rad.} = 5^{\text{p}}14'$$
where the straight line between the epicycle's centre
and the ecliptic's centre is 60ᴾ. And this is very nearly
the same ratio as that demonstrated a little while
ago with the other eclipses.

Again with the same figure, let the straight line
KNX be drawn perpendicular to DEA from the centre K, and let AK be joined.

Now since
$$DE = 643^{\text{p}}36'39'',$$
and
$$EN = \text{half } AE = 44^{\text{p}}20'8''$$
so that, by addition,
$$DEN = 687^{\text{p}}56'47''$$
where
$$DK = 689^{\text{p}}8',$$
therefore also
$$DN = 119^{\text{p}}47'36''$$
where
$$\text{hypt. } DK = 120^{\text{p}};$$
and, on the circle about right triangle DKN,
$$\text{arc } DN = 173°17'.$$
And so
$$\text{angle } DKN = 173°17' \text{ to 2 rt.}$$
$$= 86°38'30''.$$
And therefore, on the epicycle,
$$\text{arc } MEX = 86°38'30''$$
and, as remainder of the semicircle,
$$\text{arc } LAX = 93°21'30''.$$
And
$$\text{arc } AX = \text{half arc } AE = 47°38'30'',$$
and therefore, by subtraction,
$$\text{arc } AL = 45°43',$$
But it was assumed
$$\text{arc } AB = 110°21'.$$
And therefore the remainder arc BL, the distance of the moon from the apogee
at the middle of the second eclipse, is 64°38'.

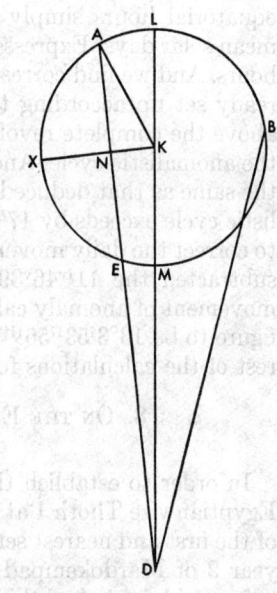

Likewise, since it was proved

$$\text{angle } DKN \doteq 86°38'$$

and, as its complement,

$$\text{angle } KDN = 3°22',$$

and since it was assumed

$$\text{angle } ADB = 7°42',$$

therefore, by subtraction, angle LDB, which subtends the arc subtracted from the mean longitudinal course resulting from the anomaly due to the epicycle's arc BL, will be 4°20′. And therefore the moon's mean longitudinal position at the middle of the second eclipse was 29°30′ within the Ram, since indeed its true position was 25°10′ within the Ram with the sun 25°10′ within the Balance.

7. On the Correction of the Moon's Mean Movements of Longitude and Anomaly

Since we showed that in the middle of the second of the old eclipses the moon was situated 14°44′ within the Virgin according to mean longitude, and with respect to the anomalistic cycle 12°24′ from the epicycle's apogee; and that in the middle of the second of our own eclipses it was situated 29°30′ within the Ram according to mean longitude, and with respect to the anomalistic cycle 64°38′ from the epicycle's apogee, therefore it is clear that, in the interval of time between the two eclipses, the moon has run in mean movement over and above complete revolutions 224°46′ in longitude and 52°14′ of its anomalistic cycle. But the interval of time from the year 2 of Mardokempad, Thoth 18-19, ½+⅓ equatorial hours before midnight to the year 19 of Hadrian, Choïac 2-3, 1 equatorial hour before midnight is 854 Egyptian years, 73 days, and 23½+⅓ equatorial hours simply calculated, but 23⅓ hours accurately calculated in mean solar days. Expressed entirely in days this is 311,783 days 23⅓ equatorial hours. And we find corresponding to them, for the daily movements we have already set up according to the hypotheses preceding the correction, over and above the complete revolutions surpluses of 224°46′ in longitude and 52°31′ in the anomalistic cycle. And so the longitudinal surplus, as we said, is found to be the same as that deduced from our observations, but the surplus in the anomalistic cycle exceeds by 17′. And therefore, before setting out the tables, in order to correct the daily movements, we distributed the 17′ over the number of days, subtracted the $11^{iv}46^{v}39^{vi}$ corresponding to each day from the daily mean movement of anomaly calculated before the correction, and found the corrected figure to be $13°3^{i}53^{ii}56^{iii}17^{iv}51^{v}59^{vi}$. And in accordance with this we made the rest of the calculations for the tables.

8. On the Epoch of the Moon's Mean Movements of Longitude and Anomaly

In order to establish the epochs of two cycles in the year 1 of Nabonassar, Egyptianwise Thoth 1 at midday, we take the time from this date to the second of the first and nearest series of three eclipses, which, as we said, occurred in the year 2 of Mardokempad, Egyptianwise Thoth 18-19, ½+⅓ equatorial hour before midnight. And this makes a total of 27 Egyptian years, 17 days, and very nearly 11⅙ hours considered both simply and accurately. And corresponding to this interval of time there is a surplus, over and above the complete revolutions, of 123°22′ in longitude and a surplus of 103°35′ of the anomalistic cycle. If we subtract each of these numbers from each of the corresponding numbers proper to the positions of the second eclipse, then, in the year 1 of Nabonassar, Egyptianwise Thoth 1 at midday, we shall have the moon's mean position 11°22' within the Bull and 268°49' from the epicycle's apogee in the anomalistic cycle. And its elongation from the sun will be clearly 70°37', since the sun's position at that time has been demonstrated to be 0°45' within the Fishes.

9. On the Correction of the Moon's Mean Latitudinal Movements and their Epochs

Now this is the way we have established the cycles of longitude and anomaly and their epochs. But in the case of the latitudinal cycles we were quite wrong earlier in using Hipparchus' assumption that the moon measures its own circle of revolution very nearly 650 times, and the circle of [the earth's] shadow 2½ times when the moon is at its mean distance at the syzygies.[1] For with these assumptions and the inclination of the moon's oblique circle, the limits of its particular eclipses are given. Then, taking the intervals of eclipse and calculating from the size of the shadows cast in mid-eclipse the true latitudinal courses on the oblique circle from either node, and distinguishing by means of the anomalistic difference already demonstrated the periodic from the true courses,[2] we find in this way the positions of the latitudinal cycle at mid-eclipse and the surplus over and above the complete revolutions which accrues in the time between. But by using more elegant methods which need none of the former hypotheses for getting what is desired, we have found that the latitudinal course is quite faulty. And from the course obtained now without them we have proved that these hypotheses concerning magnitudes and distances were not right, and we have made corrections.

We have done likewise in the case of the hypotheses concerning Saturn and Mercury, changing certain things not altogether accurately determined before us by having fallen later upon surer observations. For it behooves those going forward with this theory inquiringly and for the love of truth to use the new and surest methods found, not only for the correction of the old hypotheses but also of their own if they need it; and not to think it disgraceful (for it is a great and divine profession) even if they happen upon a correction for greater accuracy due to others and not only to themselves.

Later in this treatise we shall explain in the proper places how we prove each of these things. At present, for the sake of sequence, we shall turn to the demonstration of the latitudinal course. And here is the method.

Now, in the correction of the mean course we first looked for lunar eclipses from among those accurately recorded, as far apart in time as possible, in which

[1]By the moon's mean distance at the syzygies is here meant the linear distance from the earth of the centre of the moon's epicycle at the syzygies. This is speaking strictly; practically it is the distance from the earth to the moon when it is at the point of mean movement on its epicycle at the syzygies. For it will be seen later, in Book V, that the moon's epicycle is borne on a moving eccentric in such a way that the epicycle's centre is always at the apogee of the eccentric at the syzygies. Hence the mean distance at the syzygies is strictly the distance from the earth to the apogee of the moon's eccentric circle. These distances are calculated in detail in Chapter 13 of Book V.

[2]The true latitudinal return is the latitudinal return with respect to the moon; and the periodic latitudinal return is the latitudinal return with respect to the centre of the moon's epicycle. Hence, as we shall see, when the anomalistic difference is known it is possible to find the latitudinal position of the epicycle's centre.

the magnitudes of the shadows were equal, near the same node with both shadows either on the southern or northern side, and in which, moreover, the moon was at the same distance from the earth. All this being so, it necessarily follows that the moon's centre in each of the eclipses is equidistant on the same side of the same node; and, therefore, that the true course of the moon embraces complete latitudinal cycles in the time between the observations.

We then took, first, the eclipse observed in Babylon in the year 31 of Darius, Egyptianwise Tybi 3-4 at the middle of the sixth hour; and the moon was eclipsed to a breadth of 2 digits from the southern side.

Second, we took that observed in Alexandria in the year 9 of Hadrian, Egyptianwise Pachom 17-18 at $3\frac{3}{5}$ equatorial hours before midnight; and the moon was eclipsed likewise to the extent of $\frac{1}{6}$ of its diameter from the southern side.

And the latitudinal course of the moon was in each eclipse near the descending node. For this is taken from more general hypotheses. And the distance was very nearly equal and a little towards the perigee from the mean. For this becomes clear from the previous demonstrations of the anomaly. Now since, whenever the moon is eclipsed from the southern side, its centre is north of the ecliptic, it is clear the moon, in each of the eclipses, precedes the descending node by an equal amount.

But at the first eclipse the moon was 100°19' from the epicycle's apogee, for the middle of this eclipse occurred in Babylon $\frac{1}{2}$ hour before midnight, and in Alexandria $1\frac{1}{3}$ hours before midnight. And the time from its epoch in the reign of Nabonassar totals 256 years, 122 days, and $10\frac{2}{3}$ equatorial hours simply considered, but $10\frac{1}{4}$ hours with respect to mean solar days. Therefore, the true course was less than the periodic course by 5°[1]. In the second eclipse the moon was 251°53' from the epicycle's apogee. Here the time from the epoch to the middle of the eclipse totals 871 years, 256 days, and $8\frac{2}{5}$ equatorial hours considered simply, but $8\frac{1}{12}$ accurately considered. Therefore, the true course was more than the mean course by 4°53'. Consequently, in the interval of time between the two eclipses, which contains 615 Egyptian years, 133 days, and $21 + \frac{1}{2} + \frac{1}{3}$ equatorial hours, the true latitudinal course of the moon consists of complete cycles; but the periodic falls short of complete cycles by a total of 9°53' from the two anomalistic differences. But calculated from the mean courses set out according to Hipparchus' hypotheses, the periodic course falls short of complete restitutions by very nearly 10°2'. Therefore the mean latitudinal course is 9' greater than his hypotheses allow.

Now, distributing these over the given number of days which is very nearly 224,609, and adding the resulting $8^{iv}39^{v}18^{vi}$ to the daily mean movement already demonstrated according to those hypotheses, we found the corrected daily mean movement to be $13°13^{i}45^{ii}39^{iii}48^{iv}56^{v}37^{vi}$. And again, in accordance with this result, we made out the rest of the additions in the tables.

Once the periodic latitudinal movement had been demonstrated in this way, in order to establish its position we again looked for an interval between two well-observed eclipses having the same incidents as the former—that is, where the distances of the moon were very nearly equal, and the shadows cast were equal, being in both cases either on the northern side or on the southern side,

---

[1]This is taken from the Table of the Moon's First and Simple Anomaly which is Chapter 10 of this Book. This table is only for the anomalies at the syzygies because of the later use of an eccentric deferent.

but where the nodes were no longer the same but opposite.

The first of these eclipses is the one we used in connection with the demonstration of the anomaly, which occurred in the year 2 of Mardokempad, Egyptianwise Thoth 18-19, at midnight in Babylon, and ½+⅓ equatorial hour before midnight in Alexandria. And the moon was observed to be eclipsed 3 digits' breadth from the south.

The second is the one Hipparchus used, occurring in the year 20 of Darius, successor of Cambyses, Egyptianwise Epiphi 28-29, 6⅓ equatorial hours after nightfall. And here likewise the moon was eclipsed to the extent of a quarter of its diameter from the southern side. The middle of the eclipse in Babylon was at ⅖ equatorial hour before midnight, since a half-night at that time was very nearly 6+½+¼ equatorial hours, and in Alexandria 1¼ equatorial hours before midnight.

Each of these eclipses occurred when the moon was near the apogee, but the first at the ascending node and the second at the descending node, so that the moon's centre was an equal distance north of the ecliptic in these eclipses also.

Then let there be the oblique circle of the moon *ABC* with diameter *AC*; and

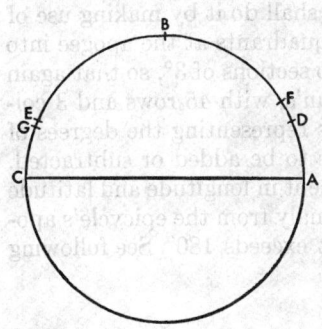

let point *A* be supposed the ascending node, *C* the descending node, and *B* the northernmost limit. And let equal arcs *AD* and *CE* be cut off from each of the nodes *A* and *C*, in the direction of the northern limit *B*, so that in the first eclipse the moon's centre is at *D*, and in the second at *E*.

But the time from the epoch to the first eclipse is 27 Egyptian years, 17 days, and 11⅙ equatorial hours considered both simply and accurately. And, therefore, the moon was 12°24′ from the epicycle's apogee and the periodic course was 59′ greater than the true one, and the time from the epoch to the second eclipse is likewise 245 Egyptian years, 327 days, and 10+½+¼ equatorial hours simply considered and 10¼ accurately considered. The moon hence was 2°44′ from the epicycle's apogee, and the periodic course was 13′ greater than the true one. The time between the observations (amounting as it does to 218 Egyptian years, 309 days, and 23½ equatorial hours) gives, according to the mean latitudinal movement just demonstrated, a surplus of 160°4′.

Now, with these things in mind let the mean course of the moon's centre be in the first eclipse at *F*, and in the second at *G*. And since

$$\text{arc } FBG = 160°4',$$
$$\text{arc } DF = 59',$$
$$\text{arc } EG = 13',$$

therefore

$$\text{arc } ED = 160°50'.$$

And therefore

$$\text{arc } AD + \text{arc } CE = 19°10'$$

the rest of the semicircle. And since

$$\text{arc } AD = \text{arc } CE,$$

therefore

$$\text{arc } AD = \text{arc } CE = 9°35'.$$

This is the amount by which the moon's true course, in the first eclipse, lay east of the ascending node, and, in the second eclipse, lay west of the descending node. Therefore, by addition and subtraction,

$$\text{arc } AF = 10°34',$$
$$\text{arc } CG = 9°22'.$$

And so the moon's periodic course, in the first eclipse, lay east of the ascending node 10°34', and was 280°34' from the northern limit B; and, in the second eclipse, lay west of the descending node 9°22', and was 80°38' from the same northern limit.

Finally, since the time from the epoch to the middle of the first eclipse embraces a latitudinal surplus of 286°19', therefore, if we subtract this surplus from a circle plus the 280°34' representing the position of the first eclipse, we shall have the epoch of the latitudinal cycle in the year 1 of Nabonassar, Egyptianwise Thoth 1 at midday; and it will be 354°15' from the northern limit.

As for the determinations of the calculations for the conjunctions and full moons—since for these passages we need take no heed of the second anomaly to be demonstrated later—we shall set out the table of the particular sections geometrically again as in the case of the sun. And we shall do it by making use of the ratio of 60 to 5¼, and dividing as before the quadrants at the apogee into sections of 6° and the quadrants at the perigee into sections of 3°, so that again the scheme of the table is similar to that of the sun's, with 45 rows and 3 columns. The first two columns contain the numbers representing the degrees of anomaly, and the third the corresponding degrees to be added or subtracted. They are to be subtracted in computing the movement in longitude and latitude when the total number representing the arc of anomaly from the epicycle's apogee is less than 180°, and are to be added when it exceeds 180°. See following table:

10. TABLE OF THE MOON'S FIRST AND SIMPLE ANOMALY

Common numbers		Additive— subtractive		Common numbers		Additive— subtractive	
1	2	3		1	2	3	
6	354	0	29	120	240	4	31
12	348	0	57	123	237	4	24
18	342	1	25	126	234	4	16
24	336	1	53	129	231	4	7
30	330	2	19	132	228	3	57
36	324	2	44	135	225	3	46
42	318	3	8	138	222	3	35
48	312	3	31	141	219	3	23
54	306	3	51	144	216	3	10
60	300	4	8	147	213	2	57
66	294	4	24	150	210	2	43
72	288	4	38	153	207	2	28
78	282	4	49	156	204	2	13
84	276	4	56	159	201	1	57
90	270	4	59	162	198	1	41
93	267	5	0	165	195	1	25
96	264	5	1	168	192	1	9
99	261	5	0	171	189	0	52
102	258	4	59	174	186	0	35
105	255	4	57	177	183	0	18
108	252	4	53	180	180	0	0
111	249	4	49				
114	246	4	44				
117	243	4	38				

11. THAT THE QUANTITY OF THE MOON'S ANOMALY AS GIVEN BY HIPPARCHUS DID NOT DIFFER BECAUSE OF THE DISSIMILARITY IN HYPOTHESES, BUT BECAUSE OF THE CALCULATIONS

These things having been demonstrated in this way, it would be reasonable to try and find out why, in the case of the lunar eclipses compared by Hipparchus in his research on this anomaly, the ratio does not tally with that demonstrated by us; and why the first ratio, demonstrated according to the hypothesis of eccentricity, does not agree with the second calculated according to the hypothesis of the epicycle. For according to the first demonstration, he finds the ratio of the eccentric's radius to the line between its centre and the ecliptic's centre to be very nearly 3,144 to 327⅔, which is the same as the ratio of 60ᵖ to 6ᵖ15′. And according to the second demonstration, he finds the ratio of the line from the ecliptic's centre to the epicycle's centre to the epicycle's radius to be 3,122½ to 247½, which is the same as the ratio of 60^p to $4^p46'$. And the ratio of 60 to 6¼ makes the greatest anomalistic difference 5°49'; and the ratio of 60^p to $4^p46'$ makes the greatest difference $4^p34'$. But in our calculations the ratio of 60 to 5¼ makes the greatest difference very nearly 5°.

Now, it became evident to us a little way back, from the fact that the same appearances would result interchangeably from either hypothesis, that this discrepancy does not follow, as some think, from the difference of the hypotheses; and that if we should make our calculations with numbers we would find the same ratio resulting from either hypothesis if one should follow the same appearances for each, and not different ones like Hipparchus. For in this way, with different eclipses supposed, it is possible for the error to have occurred, either because of the observations themselves or because of the calculations of the intervals.

In these eclipses we find the syzygies well observed and we find that they occurred according to the hypotheses of regular and irregular movements we have just demonstrated. But we find that the calculations of the intervals by which the ratio is demonstrated were not made with the greatest care possible. And beginning with the first three eclipses we shall go through each one of these calculations.

Now he says these three eclipses were given out by those crossing over from Babylon as having been observed there, that the first of them occurred in the Athenian magistracy of Phanostratus in the month of Poseideon, and that the moon was eclipsed to the extent of a small bit of its circle on the side of the summer rising point, the night failing a half hour of being finished. And he says it was still eclipsed when setting. Now, this date is the year 366 of Nabonassar, Egyptianwise, as he himself says, Thoth 26-27, 5½ seasonal hours after midnight, since there remained a half hour of night. But when the sun is at the end of the Archer in Babylon, the night hour is 18° equatorial time. For then the night is 14⅖ equatorial hours. Therefore the 5½ seasonal hours come to 6⅗ equatorial hours. The beginning of the eclipse hence occurred 18⅗ equatorial hours after midday of Thoth 26. But since a small part was shadowed, the whole time of the eclipse must have been very nearly 1½ hours. Therefore in Alexandria the middle of the eclipse must have occurred 18½ equatorial hours after midday of Thoth 26. And the time from the epoch in the year 1 of Nabonassar to the eclipse in question is 365 Egyptian years, 25 days, and 18½ equatorial hours considered simply, but 18¼ hours considered accurately. And calculating according to our hypotheses we find the sun's true position at this time to be 28°18' within the Archer; and find the moon's mean position to be 24°20' within the Twins, but true position to be 28°17', since according to its anomalistic cycle it is 227°43' from the epicycle's apogee.

Again, he says, the next eclipse occurred in the Athenian magistracy of Phanostratus in the month of Scirophorion, but Egyptianwise Phamenoth 24-25. And the moon was eclipsed, he says, on the side of the summer rising point at the end of the first hour of the night. Now, this date is the year 366 of Nabonassar, Phamenoth 24-25, at most 5½ seasonal hours before midnight. But when the sun is at the extremity of the Twins, the night-hour in Babylon is 12° equatorial time. Therefore 5½ seasonal hours make 4⅖ equatorial hours, and the beginning of the eclipse occurred 7⅗ equatorial hours after midday of Phamenoth 24. But since the whole eclipse is recorded as having lasted 3 hours, the middle of the eclipse evidently occurred $9\frac{1}{10}$ equatorial hours after midday. In Alexandria, therefore, it must have occurred very nearly $8\frac{1}{4}$ equatorial hours after midday. And again the time from the epochs to the middle of the eclipse is 365 Egyptian years, 203 days, and $8\frac{1}{4}$ equatorial hours simply considered, but $7+\frac{1}{2}+\frac{1}{3}$ hours accurately considered. And we find the sun's true position at this time to be 21°46′ within the Twins; and the moon's mean position to be 23°58′ within the Archer, but true position 21°48′, since according to its anomalistic cycle it is 27°37′ from the epicycle's apogee. And the interval from the first to the second eclipse comes to 177 days and $13\frac{3}{5}$ equatorial hours, and 173°28′ of the sun's movement, while Hipparchus proceeded as if the interval were 177 days and $13+\frac{1}{2}+\frac{1}{4}$ equatorial hours, and $172\frac{7}{8}°$ of the sun's movement.

And he says the third eclipse occurred in the Athenian magistracy of Evandrus on the first day of the month of Poseideon, Egyptianwise Thoth 16-17. And the eclipse, he says, was total, beginning from the direction of the summer rising point at the end of the fourth hour of the night. Now, this date is the year 367 of Nabonassar, Thoth 16-17, at most $2\frac{1}{2}$ hours before midnight. But when the sun is about two-thirds the way within the Archer, the night-hour in Babylon is nearly 18° equatorial time. Therefore $2\frac{1}{2}$ seasonal hours make 3 equatorial hours. And so the beginning of the eclipse occurred 9 equatorial hours after midday of Thoth 16. But since the eclipse was total, the whole time of the eclipse was very nearly 4 equatorial hours, and the middle of it was evidently 11 hours after midday. In Alexandria, therefore, the middle of the eclipse must have occurred $10\frac{1}{6}$ equatorial hours after midday of Thoth 16. And the time from the epochs to the middle of this eclipse is 366 Egyptian years, 15 days, and again $10\frac{1}{6}$ equatorial hours simply considered, but $9+\frac{1}{2}+\frac{1}{3}$ hours accurately considered. At this time we find the sun's true position to be 17°30′ within the Archer; and the moon's mean position 17°21′ within the Twins, but its true position 17°28′ because, according to its anomalistic cycle, it is 181°12′ from the epicycle's apogee. And the interval from the second to the third eclipse comes to 177 days and 2 equatorial hours, and 175°44′ of the sun's movement, while Hipparchus again assumes the interval to be 177 days and $1\frac{2}{3}$ hours, and 175°8′ of the sun's movement.

Now, in his calculations of the intervals he appears to have made an error, in the case of the days, of $\frac{1}{6}$ equatorial hour and $\frac{1}{3}$ equatorial hour; and, in the degrees of the sun's movement, to have made an error of very nearly $\frac{3}{5}°$ in each of them. And this is enough to exclude just a chance disagreement in the quantity of the ratio.

And next we shall pass to the three later eclipses set out by him, which he says were observed in Alexandria. He says the first of these occurred in the year 54 of the Second Callippic Period, Egyptianwise Mesore 16, in which the moon began to be eclipsed $\frac{1}{2}$ hour before rising and returned to its full size in the middle of the third hour. Therefore the mid-eclipse occurred at the beginning of the second hour or 5 seasonal hours before midnight, and about as many equatorial hours since the sun was near the end of the Virgin. And so the middle of the eclipse occurred in Alexandria 7 equatorial hours after midday of Mesore 16. The time from the epochs in the year 1 of Nabonassar is 546 Egyptian years, 345 days, and 7 equatorial hours simply considered, but $6\frac{1}{2}$ hours accurately considered.

And again we find that at this time the sun's true position is 26°6′ within the Virgin; and the moon's mean position 22° within the Fishes, and its true position 26°7′ because, according to its anomalistic cycle, it is 300°13′ from the epicycle's apogee.

The next eclipse occurred, he says, in the year 55 of the same period, Egyptianwise Mechir 9; and it began after the night had run 5⅓ hours, and the eclipse was total. Therefore the beginning of the eclipse occurred 11⅓ equatorial hours after midday of Mechir 9, since the sun was now near the end of the Fishes. And the middle of the eclipse was 13⅓ equatorial hours after midday since the eclipse of the moon was total. The time from the epochs to the middle of the eclipse is 547 Egyptian years, 158 days, and very nearly 13⅓ equatorial hours both simply and accurately computed. Likewise we find that at this time the sun's true position is 26°17′ within the Fishes; and the moon's mean position 1°7′ within the Balance, and its true position 26°16′ within the Virgin, since according to its anomalistic cycle it is 109°28′ from the apogee. And the interval from the first to the second eclipse comes to 178 days and 6+½+⅓ equatorial hours, and 180°11′ of the sun's movement, while Hipparchus proceeded as if the interval were 178 days and 6 equatorial hours, and 180°20′ of the sun's movement.

And he says the third eclipse occurred in the same year 55 of this Second Period, Egyptianwise Mesore 5; and it began after the night had run 6⅔ hours, and the eclipse was total. The middle of the eclipse, he says, occurred at about 8⅓ hours in the night, that is 2⅓ seasonal hours after midnight. But when the sun is about the middle of the Virgin, the night-hour in Alexandria is 14⅖° equatorial time. Therefore the 2⅓ seasonal hours make very nearly 2¼ equatorial hours. And so the middle of the eclipse occurred 14¼ equatorial hours after midday of Mesore 5. Again the time from the epochs to the middle of this eclipse is 547 Egyptian years, 334 days, and 14¼ equatorial hours simply considered, but 13+½+¼ accurately considered. And we find that the sun's true position at this time is 15°12′ within the Virgin; and the moon's mean position 10°24′ within the Fishes, but true position 15°13′, since according to its anomalistic cycle it is 249°9′ from the epicycle's apogee. And the interval from the second to the third eclipse comes to 176 days and ⅖ equatorial hour, and 168°55′ of the sun's movement, while Hipparchus again assumes this interval to be 176 days and 1⅓ equatorial hours, and 168°33′ of the sun's movement.

Therefore it here appears that in the degrees of the sun's movement he has made an error of very nearly (⅙+⅕)°, and an error in days of very nearly ½+⅓+1/10 equatorial hour. These errors can work an appreciable difference in the ratio of the hypothesis.

Now we have seen the cause of this disagreement. We have also seen that with still more confidence we can use the ratio of anomaly demonstrated by us for the moon's syzygies, for their eclipses are found likewise to agree most completely with our hypotheses.

BOOK FIVE

1. On the Construction of the Astrolabe

We now find that the hypothesis set up with reference to the first and simple anomaly is sufficient for the moon's syzygies with respect to the sun, both the synodical and the plenilunar, as well as for the eclipses which accompany them, even if we take this anomaly by itself. But, as regards the particular passages of the moon's other positions relative to the sun, it would not be found sufficient. For, as we said, a second anomaly of the moon is discovered relative to its elongations from the sun, an anomaly which is reduced to the first at the syzygies, and is greatest at the first and third quarters. We were brought to this examination and opinion by the courses of the moon observed and recorded by Hipparchus, and by those we ourselves obtained with an instrument we constructed for this purpose. And here is the kind of thing it is.

We take two circles accurately turned with four perpendicular surfaces each, similar in magnitude, and in every way equal and similar to each other. And we fit them at right angles to each other with a common diameter, so that one of them is conceived to be the ecliptic and the other becomes the meridian through the poles of the ecliptic and of the equator [solstitial colure]. On this circle we take, with the side of the inscribed square, the points defining the poles of the ecliptic, and we place at both of them pivots projecting from the inside and outside surfaces. And on the outside pivots we place another circle having its concave surface exactly touching everywhere the convex surface of the circles already fitted together, and able to revolve in longitude about these poles of the ecliptic. Likewise on the inside pivots we place another circle having its convex surface everywhere exactly touching the concave surface of the two circles and likewise revolving in longitude about the same poles as the outside circle. Now, dividing this inside circle and the one used for the ecliptic each into the usual 360 parts and these in turn into as many parts as practicable, we fit in under the inner circle another little circle with diametrically opposite projecting sights. And we fit it in so that it can move in the same plane with this inner circle with respect to each of the poles, for latitudinal observations. With this done, on the circle we supposed through both sets of poles, we lay off, from each of the ecliptic's poles, the arc we computed to lie between the ecliptic's poles and the equator's. We place the limits of these arcs diametrically opposite each other on the meridian like that exhibited in the beginning of this treatise relative to the observations of the meridian arc between the tropics, so that, when this meridian has been placed in the same position (in other words when it has been placed perpendicular to the plane of the horizon and in accordance with the height of the pole of the place in question and parallel to the plane of the natural meridian) then the inner circles may move about the equator's poles from east to west in accord with the prime movement of the universe.

143

Now, arranging the instrument in this way, whenever the sun and moon could appear together above the earth, we placed the outside circle of the astrolabe as nearly as possible at the sun's degree at that hour. And we revolved the colure until, with the intersection of the circles at the sun's degree turned precisely to the sun itself, the two circles, the ecliptic and the circle through its poles, obscured each other; or, if it were a star being sighted, until, with one eye placed at one side of the outside circle, already correctly arranged just under the proper section of the ecliptic, the star as if stuck to both surfaces is sighted on the opposite side in the plane through both circles. We moved the other and inside circle of the astrolabe towards the moon or any other star being examined until, simultaneously with the sun or star in question, the moon or other star to be examined is lined up with both sights of the little circle fitted within the inside circle.

In this way, we find out, from the inside circle's intersection at a division of the circle corresponding to the ecliptic, what longitudinal section of the ecliptic they occupy and how many degrees distant they are either north or south on the circle through the ecliptic's poles. And this last reading is made, by means of the division of the inner circle, from the interval between the middle of the upper sight of the little circle fitted under it and the ecliptic.

2. On the Hypothesis of the Moon's Double Anomaly

Now, with this kind of observation, the moon's distances with respect to the sun, both those recorded by Hipparchus and those observed by us, were found at times to agree with the calculations made according to the hypothesis already advanced, and at other times to disagree and differ, sometimes a little, sometimes a great deal. With a continuously greater and more meticulous checking of our own, we learned concerning the order of this irregularity that always at conjunctions and full moons there was either little or no appreciable discrepancy and only such as the moon's parallaxes could account for; and that, in and about the first and third quarters, there is very little or no discrepancy when the moon is at the epicycle's apogee or perigee, but the most when the moon in its mean courses effects the greatest difference of first anomaly. We found that in whichever of the two semicircles the first anomaly is subtractive, the moon's position is found to be advanced even less than the result of this first subtraction allows; but, when it is additive, it is likewise found to be more advanced. And this occurs in proportion to the magnitude of the first addition-subtraction. So by this order we see at a glance that it is necessary to suppose the moon's epicycle is borne on an eccentric circle with its apogee at the conjunctions and full moons, and its perigee at the first and third quarters. And this would be the result if the first hypothesis is given this correction.

For let the circle concentric with the ecliptic and situated in the moon's oblique plane be conceived as before, to take care of latitude, as moving from east to west about the poles of the ecliptic at a speed equal to the excess of the latitudinal movement over the longitudinal. And let the moon, in turn, be conceived as revolving about the epicycle, moving at its apogee from east to west in accordance with the restitution of the first anomaly. Then in this oblique plane we suppose two regular movements opposite to each other, both about the centre of the ecliptic: one revolving the epicycle's centre from west to east according to the latitudinal movement; and one revolving the centre and apogee of the eccentric circle, which is taken in this same plane always bearing the epicycle's centre, and turning it from east to west at a speed equal to the excess of twice the moon's elongation from the sun over the latitudinal movement—that is, the excess of the moon's mean longitudinal movement over the sun's.

And so, for example, in one day the epicycle's centre appears to move very nearly 13°14′ in latitude from west to east, traversing 13°11′ in longitude because of the oblique circle's retrogression of the 3′ excess from east to west. And in turn the eccentric's apogee is rotated in that same opposite direction from east to west 11°9′, by which amount 24°23′ (double the moon's elongation) exceeds 13°14′. Thus, because of the two movements' retrogression in the opposite direction about the ecliptic's centre, as we said, the movement made by the epicycle's centre will differ from that of the eccentric's by the arc composed of 13°14′ plus 11°9′, which is very nearly double the 12°11½′ of the elongation. Therefore the epicycle will traverse the eccentric circle's circumference twice in a mean month's time, and its return to the eccentric's apogee is assumed to take place at mean conjunctions and full moons.[1]

But to see the details of the hypothesis more thoroughly, again let there be conceived the circle $ABCD$ concentric with the ecliptic and lying in the moon's oblique plane, about E as centre and AEC as diameter. At the same time suppose the point A to be the eccentric's apogee, the epicycle's centre, the northern limit, the beginning of the Ram, and the mean sun.

Then, I say, in one day's course the whole plane moves from east to west, or from A to D, very nearly 3′ about centre E, so that the northern limit A comes to be 29°57′ within the Fishes. In the case of the two contrary regular movements effected by a straight line similar to EA again about E, the ecliptic's centre, I say that, likewise in a day's course, the straight line similar to EA through the eccentric's centre and revolving westward at a regular speed to ED carries the eccentric's apogee to D, describes the eccentric circle DG about centre F, and makes an arc AD of 11°9′; but that the straight line through the epicycle's centre revolving about E, this time eastward, at a regular speed to EB[2] carries the epicycle's centre to G and makes an arc AB of 13°14′. And so G, the epicycle's centre, appears to be 13°14′ in latitudinal movement distant from the northern

---

[1] The mean conjunctions and full moons or mean syzygies are the conjunctions and oppositions of the centre of the moon's epicycle and the mean sun.

[2] The great principle of celestial mechanics enunciated in Chapter 3 of Book II—namely, that the stars must move on circles regularly about the centres of those circles (which is taken also to mean that the centres of epicycles must move regularly about the centres of their deferents)—is here modified or broadened to the principle that a star or the centre of an epicycle must move on a circle and must move regularly about some one point which need not be the centre of the circle it moves on. Thus, here the centre of the moon's epicycle G moves regularly about E and not about F, the centre of its deferent. E is said to be the centre of its equant. As we shall see later, all the planets have such a centre and fall under this broader principle.

It is this broader principle and its application here that Copernicus attacks in Chapter 2 of Book IV, *On the Revolutions of the Heavenly Spheres*. There are other inadequacies which he points out in that chapter, as we shall see in the course of this Book.

limit A; but 13°11′ within the Ram in longitude, because the northern limit A is 29°57′ within the Fishes; and to be 24°23′, the sum of arcs AD and AB, from D the eccentric's apogee, which is double the daily movement of elongation.

In this way, since the two movements together through B and through D make a complete return to each other in half a mean month's time, it is evident that in a quarter or three quarters of a mean month's time they will always be directly opposite each other—that is, at the first and third quarters in terms of mean movement—and that, when the epicycle's centre along EB is directly opposite the eccentric's apogee along ED it will be at the eccentric's perigee.

It is clear that, with things thus disposed, as regards the eccentric circle or the dissimilarity of arcs DB and DG there is no difference in the regular movement since the straight line EB, because of its rotation about E instead of F the eccentric's centre, traverses at a regular speed, not arc DG of the eccentric circle, but arc DB of the ecliptic. But only as regards the difference due to the epicycle itself will there be a change. For the epicycle when nearer the earth will always increase the anomalistic difference, the additive equally with the subtractive, the angle at the eye intercepting it being made greater in positions about the perigee.

There will be no general difference, then, for the first hypothesis is when the epicycle's centre is at the apogee A. This happens at mean conjunctions and full moons.

For if we draw the epicycle MN about A, the ratio of AE to AM is the same as that demonstrated by means of eclipses. And the difference will be greatest when the epicycle is passing G, the eccentric's perigee—as, for example, the one drawn through the points X and O. This occurs at the first and third quarters considered in terms of mean movement. For the ratio of XG to GE is greater than all those constructed at the other positions, since XG, the epicycle's radius, is always equal and the same, and the line EG from the earth's centre is less than all the others drawn to the eccentric circle.

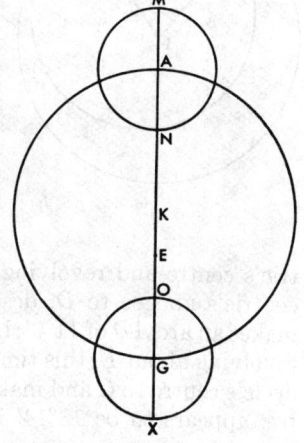

3. On the Size of the Moon's Solar Anomaly

To see, then, how much the greatest anomalistic difference comes to when the epicycle happens to be borne at the eccentric's perigee, we observed those of the moon's elongations sighted with the sun in which the moon's courses approached the mean (for then the anomalistic difference becomes greatest); in which its elongation from the sun taken in terms of mean movement was very nearly a quadrant or when the epicycle was near the eccentric's perigee; and in which, given these conditions, the moon did not display a parallax in longitude. Given these circumstances, and given as the true one, the longitudinal distance apparent in its sighting, the second anomaly's difference could be gotten with certainty. In making an examination of such observations, we find that, when the epicycle is at the perigee, the greatest anomalistic difference with respect to the mean movement is very nearly 7⅔°, and with respect to the first anomaly is 2⅔°.

For example, to have our own judgment in the case of one or two observations, we sighted the sun and moon in the year 2 of Antonine, Egyptianwise Phamenoth 25, after sunrise, or 5¼ equatorial hours before noon. With the sun sighted $(18+\frac{1}{2}+\frac{1}{3})°$ within the Water Bearer and the point ¼° within the Archer culminating, the moon's apparent position was 9⅔° within the Scorpion, and its true position was the same, since in Alexandria, when the moon is in the first part of the Scorpion very nearly 1½ hours west of the meridian, it does not display an appreciable parallax in longitude. The time from the epochs in the year 1 of Nabonassar to this observation is 885 Egyptian years, 203 days, and $18+\frac{1}{2}+\frac{1}{4}$ equatorial hours, both simply and accurately considered. And corresponding to this amount of time we find the sun's mean position to be 16°27' within the Water Bearer, and its true position 18°50' which agrees with the sighting of the astrolabe. From the first hypothesis, the moon at that hour is found to be 17°20' within the Scorpion in mean longitude, so that its mean elongation from the sun is very nearly a quadrant, and in anomaly it is 87°19' from the epicycle's apogee, near which the greatest anomalistic difference occurs. Therefore, the true course was less than the regular one by 7⅔° instead of the first anomaly's 5°.

Again, in order to have before us the difference in like cases from among those observed by Hipparchus, we shall first set out one which he says he observed in the year 50 of the Third Callippic Period, Egyptianwise Epiphi 16, ⅔ of the first hour having passed. Now the course, he says, was mean.[1] And with the sun sighted $(8+\frac{1}{2}+\frac{1}{12})°$ within the Lion, the moon's apparent position was 12⅓° within the Bull, and its true position was very nearly the same. Therefore the moon's true elongation from the sun was 86°15'. But when the sun is in the first part of the Lion, in Rhodes where the observation occurred, the day-hour is 17⅓° in time. Therefore the 5⅓ seasonal hours before noon make 6⅙ equatorial hours, so that the observation occurred 6⅙ equatorial hours before noon of Epiphi 16 with the point 9° within the Bull culminating. Consequently the time from the epochs to this observation totals 619 Egyptian years, 314 days, and $17+\frac{1}{2}+\frac{1}{3}$ equatorial hours simply considered, but $17+\frac{1}{2}+\frac{1}{4}$ accurately considered. And according to our hypotheses (since the meridian through Rhodes is the same as that through Alexandria), for this amount of time we find the sun's mean position to be 10°27' within the Lion, but its true position to be 8°20'. And we find the moon's mean longitudinal position to be 4°25' within the Bull so that its mean elongation from the sun is again nearly a quadrant, and in anomaly is 257°47' from the epicycle's apogee, very near which the greatest difference of epicyclic anomaly occurs. Therefore, the distance from the moon's mean position to the sun's true position totals 93°55'. But the moon's true elongation from the sun was observed to be 86°15'. The moon's true position was hence 7⅔° ahead of the regular course, instead of being 5° ahead as the first hypothesis allows.

It is now evident that, of the two observations made at the first and third quarters, ours was found to be less by 2⅔° than the amount determined according to the first anomaly, that of Hipparchus exceeding by the same amount; for ours was subtractive and Hipparchus' additive. From other observations of this kind we find the greatest anomalistic difference to be 7⅔°, whenever the epicycle is in the section belonging to the eccentric's perigee.

---

[1]The correction of Halma has been accepted here. The manuscripts and the Basel Edition read "241" for "mean." Heiberg corrects to "two hundred and forty-first."

4. On the Lunar Circle's Ratio of Eccentricity

Now this being so, let there be the moon's eccentric circle *ABC* about *D* as centre and *ADC* as diameter. And on this diameter let *E* be taken as the ecliptic's centre so that *A* is the eccentric's apogee and *C* its perigee. And let there be drawn the moon's epicycle *FGH* with centre *C*, and let the tangent *EHB* be drawn to it, and let *CH* be joined.

Then, since the greatest anomalistic difference is produced on this tangent of the moon's epicycle (this being shown to total 7⅔°), therefore, being at the ecliptic's centre,

$$\text{angle } CEH = 7°40'$$
$$= 15°20' \text{ to 2 rt.}$$

And therefore, on the circle about right triangle *CEH*,

$$\text{arc } CH = 15°20',$$
$$\text{chord } CH \doteq 16^{\text{p}}$$

where

$$\text{hypt. } CE = 120^{\text{p}}.$$

And so *CE*, the line from the ecliptic's centre to the eccentric's perigee, will also be 39ᵖ22′ to the already-demonstrated 5ᵖ15′ of the epicycle's radius and the 60ᵖ of *AE*, the line from the ecliptic's centre to the eccentric's apogee. And, therefore, the whole diameter *AC* will be 99ᵖ22′, the eccentric's radius *AD* 49ᵖ41′, and *DE* the line between the centres of the ecliptic and eccentric 10ᵖ19′. So we have shown the ratio contained by the eccentricity.[1]

5. On the Inclination of the Moon's Epicycle

Now this number of circles would be added to the hypotheses for an explanation of the appearances at the syzygies and again at the first and third quarters. But from a consideration of the particular courses where it is either crescent or gibbous and when its epicycle is between the eccentric's apogee and perigee, in the case of the moon we find a peculiar incident concerning the epicycle's inclination. For in general it is necessary to suppose one and the same point on epicycles with respect to which the returns of the movements on them are accomplished. We call this the regular apogee from which we begin the numbers of the epicyclic movement, as the point *F* in the preceding figure; and this point is determined by the line of centres, such as *DEC*, when the epicycle is at the apogees and perigees of the eccentric circles. Now, for all the other hypotheses, we see absolutely nothing in the appearances contrary to this supposition: that the diameter through the epicycle's apogee (*FCG*, for instance) always and in

[1]From this theory of eccentricity it follows that the moon's distance from the earth varies by as much as 34 to 65, or nearly 1 to 2. And since, for small angles, the tangents are nearly proportional to the angles, the size of the moon's diameter (as Copernicus points out in Chapter 2 of Book IV, *On the Revolutions of the Heavenly Spheres*) will vary as 1 to 2. But ,by observation, this is not true. The diameter varies very nearly as 55 to 65, just as the epicyclic theory without the eccentric theory allows. Hence at this point the Ptolemaic theory, in saving the appearances of the angular distances, is unable to save the appearances of the diameter's variations.

the other courses of the epicycles keeps the same direction as the line which revolves the epicycle's centre at a regular speed (in this case EC); and that, consequently, it always points to the centre of revolution at which in equal times are intercepted the equal angles of the regular movement.

But in the case of the moon, the appearances are opposed to the epicyclic diameter, FG's being inclined towards E the centre of revolution and keeping the same direction as EC in the passages between A and C. True enough, we find it, always pointing to one and the same point on the diameter AC; not to the ecliptic's center E nor to the eccentric's center D, however, but to the point the same distance from E on the same side of the eccentric's perigee as DE, the line between the centres.[1]

Again we shall show this is so by choosing from several observations two which can bring this to light most efficiently—that is, two observations where the epicycle was in the mean distances, and the moon either at the epicycle's perigee or apogee. For it is in such passages that the greatest difference in these inclinations occurs.

Hipparchus writes that he observed the sun and moon with instruments in Rhodes, in the year 197 after Alexander's death, Egyptianwise Pharmouthi 11, at the beginning of the second hour. And he says that, with the sun sighted $(7+\frac{1}{2}+\frac{1}{4})°$ within the Bull, the apparent position of the moon's centre was $21\frac{2}{3}°$ within the Fishes, and its true position $(21+\frac{1}{3}+\frac{1}{8})°$ within the Fishes. Therefore, at that time, the true moon's eastern elongation from the true sun was very nearly $313°42'$. But since the observation occurred at the beginning of the second hour or very nearly 5 seasonal hours before noon of Pharmouthi 11, and since in Rhodes at that time the seasonal hours were equivalent to very nearly $5\frac{2}{3}$ equatorial hours, therefore the time from our epoch to this observation totals 620 Egyptian years, 219 days, and $18\frac{1}{3}$ equatorial hours simply considered, but only 18 hours accurately considered. Corresponding to this time, we find the regular sun's position to be $6°41'$ within the Bull, but the true sun's position to be $7°45'$; and the regular moon's longitudinal position to be $22°13'$ within the Fishes, and in anomaly the moon to be $185°30'$ from the epicycle's mean apogee.[2] And so the regular moon's elongation from the true sun totals $314°28'$.

Now all this being granted, let ABC be the moon's eccentric circle with centre

[1]Again in Chapter 2 of Book IV, *On the Revolutions of the Heavenly Spheres*, Copernicus sharply criticises this third lunar anomaly where the regular movement of the moon on the epicycle is no longer tied to the regular movement of the epicycle on its deferent. For the result of this contriving of movements is that the moon moves irregularly about the epicycle's centre. Copernicus says that the initial violation of the strict principle of celestial mechanics, with respect to the epicycle's movement on its deferent, necessitates this further irregularity.

But Ptolemy might well reply that even if these movements, so contrived, turn out to move the stars on their epicycles irregularly with respect to the centres of the epicycles, and the epicycles irregularly with respect to the centres of their deferents, yet these irregular movements are such as can be computed and mastered by means of circles and regular movements, and this is all that is necessary.

[2]The apparent apogee and apparent perigee are those defined in the normal way, by a straight line through the epicycle's centre and the ecliptic's centre, or the earth. The mean apogee and mean perigee are those defined in another regular way to fit the particular appearances. As Ptolemy says, in the case of the moon, they are defined by a line through the epicycle's centre and a point on the line of apsides other than the earth. It is evident that the apparent and mean apogees coincide at the quarters and syzygies. Furthermore, the apparent and regular apogees always coincide in the case of the moon.

D and diameter ADC, on which let
there be the ecliptic's centre E.
And with B as centre let the moon's
epicycle FGH be drawn. Let the
epicycle be revolved eastward as
from B to A, and let the moon be
revolved on the epicycle from F to
G and H, letting DB and $EHBF$ be
joined.

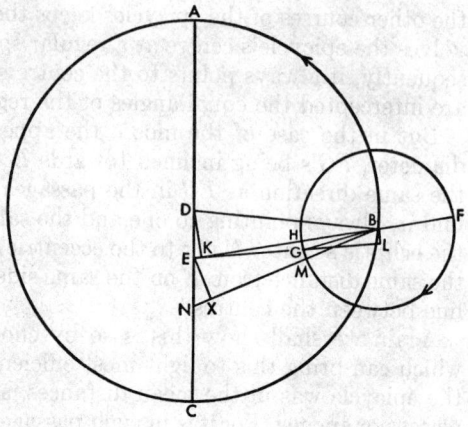

Now, since a mean lunar month's
time embraces two returns of the
epicycle with respect to the eccentric, and since in the foregoing position the mean moon was 315°32′
from the mean sun, it follows that
if we double this amount and subtract a complete circle we shall
have, for that time, the epicycle's distance of 271°4′ eastward from the eccentric's apogee. And so, by subtraction,

$$\text{angle } AEB = 88°56'.$$

Then let DK be drawn from D perpendicular to BE.

Now, since

$$\text{angle } DEB = 88°56'$$
$$= 177°52' \text{ to 2 rt.,}$$

therefore also, on the circle about right triangle DEK,

$$\text{arc } DK = 177°52',$$

and, by subtraction from the semicircle,

$$\text{arc } EK = 2°8'.$$

And therefore

$$\text{chord } DK = 119^\mathrm{p}59',$$
$$\text{chord } EK = 2^\mathrm{p}14'$$

where

$$\text{diam. } DE = 120^\mathrm{p}.$$

And therefore

$$DK = 10^\mathrm{p}19',$$
$$EK = 0^\mathrm{p}12'$$

where again

$$\text{1. betw. c. } DE = 10^\mathrm{p}19'$$

and

$$\text{ecc. rad. } BD = 49^\mathrm{p}41'.$$

And since

$$\text{sq. } BD - \text{sq. } DK = \text{sq. } BK,$$

therefore

$$BK = 48^\mathrm{p}36',$$

and, by addition,

$$BE = 48^\mathrm{p}48'.$$

Again, since the mean moon's elongation from the true sun was 314°28′, and
in the observation the true moon's elongation from the true sun was 313°42′ so
that the moon's anomalistic difference subtracts 46′, and since the moon's regu-

lar course is sighted along the line EB, therefore let the moon be supposed at the point G, for it was near the epicycle's perigee. And with EG and BG joined, let BL be drawn from B perpendicular to EG produced.

Since it contains the moon's anomalistic difference,
$$\text{angle } BEL = 0°46'$$
$$= 1°32' \text{ to 2 rt.}$$
And so also, on the circle about right triangle BEL,
$$\text{arc } BL = 1°32',$$
$$\text{chord } BL = 1^{\mathrm{p}}36'$$
where
$$\text{hypt. } BE = 120^{\mathrm{p}}.$$

And so
$$BL = 0^{\mathrm{p}}39'$$
where
$$BE = 48^{\mathrm{p}}48'$$
and
$$\text{epic. rad. } BG = 5^{\mathrm{p}}15'.$$

And therefore
$$BL = 14^{\mathrm{p}}52'$$
where
$$\text{epic. rad. } BG = 120^{\mathrm{p}}.$$
And, on the circle about right triangle BGL,
$$\text{arc } BL = 14°14'.$$

And so
$$\text{angle } BGL = 14°14' \text{ to 2 rt.,}$$
and, by subtraction,
$$\text{angle } EBG = 12°42' \text{ to 2 rt.}$$
$$= 6°21'.$$
Therefore, on the epicycle,
$$\text{arc } GH = 6°21'$$
which is the distance from the moon to the true perigee.

But since the moon, at the time of the observation, was $185°30'$ distant from the epicycle's mean apogee, it is evident that the mean perigee precedes the moon or point G. Let it be M, and let BMN be drawn and EX from E perpendicular to it.

Then, since it was shown
$$\text{arc } GH = 6°21'$$
and it is assumed
$$\text{arc } GM = 5°30'$$
from the perigee so that, by addition,
$$\text{arc } HM = 11°51',$$
therefore
$$\text{angle } EBX = 11°51'$$
$$= 23°42' \text{ to 2 rt.}$$
And so also, on the circle about right triangle BEX,
$$\text{arc } EX = 23°42';$$

$$\text{chord } EX = 24^{\text{p}}39'$$

where

$$\text{hypt. } BE = 120^{\text{p}}.$$

And therefore

$$EX = 10^{\text{p}}2'$$

where

$$BE = 48^{\text{p}}48'.$$

Again, since

$$\text{angle } AEB = 177°52' \text{ to 2 rt.}$$

and

$$\text{angle } EBN = 23°42' \text{ to 2 rt.,}$$

therefore, by subtraction,

$$\text{angle } ENB = 154°10' \text{ to 2 rt.}$$

And so also, on the circle about right triangle ENX,

$$\text{arc } EX = 154°10';$$
$$\text{chord } EX = 116^{\text{p}}58'$$

where

$$\text{hypt. } EN = 120^{\text{p}}.$$

And therefore

$$EN = 10^{\text{p}}18'$$

where

$$EX = 10^{\text{p}}2'$$

and

$$1. \text{ betw. c. } DE = 10^{\text{p}}19'.$$

Therefore, the inclination of the straight line BM through the mean perigee to N cuts off EN very nearly equal to DE.

Likewise—to show that the same thing occurs also for the opposite parts of the eccentric and epicycle—we have again taken from among the intervals observed by Hipparchus in Rhodes, as we said, the one sighted in the same year 197 after Alexander's death, Egyptianwise Paÿni 17, at 9⅓ hours. At that time, he says, with the sun sighted 10⁹⁄₁₀° within the Crab, the moon's apparent position was about 29° within the Lion. And this was its true position also, since in Rhodes towards the end of the Lion, at very nearly one hour after noon, the moon does not display a parallax in longitude. Therefore, at that time, the true moon's eastern elongation from the true sun was 48°6'. But since the observation occurred 3⅓ seasonal hours after noon of Paÿni 17, and in Rhodes at that date these came to very nearly 4 equatorial hours, the time from this observation to our epoch is 620 Egyptian years, 286 days, and 4 equatorial hours simply considered, but 3⅔ hours accurately considered. Likewise corresponding to this time we find the regular sun's position to be 12°5' within the Crab, but the true sun's position 10°40'; and the regular moon's position in longitude to be 27°20' within the Lion so that the regular moon's elongation from the true sun totals 46°40', in anomaly the moon being 333°12' from the epicycle's mean apogee.

Now, with these things granted, again let there be the moon's eccentric circle ABC with centre D and diameter ADC on which let E be taken as the ecliptic's centre. And let the moon's epicycle FGH be described about the point B, and let DB and $EHBF$ be joined

Since, then, double the moon's mean elongation from the sun contains 90°30',

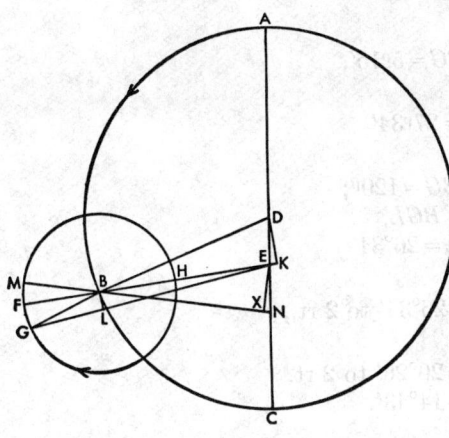

therefore for reasons already given

angle $AEB = 90°30'$
$= 181°$ to 2 rt.

Therefore if we extend the line BE and drop DK from D perpendicular to it, then, as supplement,

angle $DEK = 179°$ to 2 rt.

And so also, on the circle about right triangle DEK,

arc $DK = 179°$

and, as remainder of the semicircle,

arc $EK = 1°$.

And therefore

chord $DK = 119^{p}59'$,
chord $EK = 1^{p}3'$,

where

hypt. $DE = 120^{p}$.

And so

$$DK = 10^{p}19',$$
$$EK = 0^{p}5'$$

where

1. betw. c. $DE = 10^{p}19'$,
ecc. rad. $BD = 49^{p}41'$.

And since

sq. $BD -$ sq. $DK =$ sq. BK,

we shall have

$$BK = 48^{p}36'$$

and, by subtraction,

$$BE = 48^{p}31'.$$

Again, since the regular moon's elongation from the true sun was 46°40', but the true moon's elongation was 48°6' (so that the anomalistic difference has added 1°26'), let the moon, since it was near the epicycle's apogee, be supposed at point G. And with EG and BG joined, let BL be drawn from B perpendicular to EG.

Since, then,

angle $BEL = 1°26'$
$= 2°52'$ to 2 rt.

therefore also, on the circle about right triangle BEL

arc $BL = 2°52'$;
chord $BL = 2^{p}59'$

where

hypt. $BE = 120^{p}$.

And therefore

$$BL = 1^{p}12'$$

where

$$BE = 48^{p}31'$$

and

$$\text{epic. rad. } BG = 5^{\text{p}}15'.$$

And so

$$BL = 27^{\text{p}}34'$$

where

$$\text{hypt. } BG = 120^{\text{p}};$$
and, on the circle about right triangle BGL,
$$\text{arc } BL = 26°34'$$
And therefore
$$\text{angle } BGL = 26°34' \text{ to 2 rt.},$$
and, by addition,
$$\text{angle } FBG = 29°26' \text{ to 2 rt.}$$
$$= 14°43'.$$
Therefore, on the epicycle,
$$\text{arc } FG = 14°43',$$
which is the moon's distance to the true apogee.

But since at the time of the observation the moon was $333°12'$ from the mean apogee, if we suppose the mean apogee at M and, joining MBN, drop EX from E perpendicular to it, then
$$\text{arc } GFM = 26°48'$$
the rest of the circle, and, by subtraction,
$$\text{arc } FM = 12°5'.$$
And so
$$\text{angle } MBF = \text{angle } EBX = 12°5'$$
$$= 24°10' \text{ to 2 rt.}$$
And also, on the circle about right triangle BEX,
$$\text{arc } EX = 24°10';$$
$$\text{chord } EX = 25^{\text{p}}7'$$
where
$$\text{hypt. } BE = 120^{\text{p}}.$$
And therefore
$$EX = 10^{\text{p}}8'$$
where
$$BE = 48^{\text{p}}31'$$
and
$$1. \text{ betw. c. } DE = 10^{\text{p}}19'.$$
Again, since it is assumed
$$\text{angle } AEB = 181° \text{ to 2 rt.},$$
and it was proved
$$\text{angle } EBN = 24°10' \text{ to 2 rt.}$$
so that by subtraction
$$\text{angle } ENB = 156°50' \text{ to 2 rt.},$$
therefore also, on the circle about right triangle ENX,
$$\text{arc } EX = 156°50';$$
$$\text{chord } EX = 117^{\text{p}}33'$$
where
$$\text{hypt. } EN = 120^{\text{p}}.$$

And therefore
$$EN = 10^{\mathrm{p}}20'$$
where
$$EX = 10^{\mathrm{p}}8'$$
and
$$\text{1. betw. c. } DE = 10^{\mathrm{p}}19'.$$

Therefore the inclination of the straight line MB through the mean apogee M to N has again cut off EN very nearly equal to DE, the line between the centres.

From several other observations we find that very nearly the same ratios result, so that in this way the property of the epicycle's inclination in the moon's hypothesis is established. For on the one hand the revolution of the epicycle's centre takes place about the ecliptic's centre E; on the other hand the epicycle's diameter which defines the epicycle's mean-apogee point no longer points to E, the centre of regular rotation, as for the other stars, but always points to N on the other side of E from D at a distance equal to DE, the line between the centres.

6. How the Moon's True Course is Gotten Geometrically from its Periodic Movements

With these things demonstrated, it would be proper next to add how, for particular courses of the moon, by taking the epochs of the mean movements we could find, from the elongation-number and the moon's epicyclic number, the addition or subtraction to the mean longitudinal course due to the anomalistic difference. This determination is gotten geometrically from theorems like those we have already expounded.

For example, in the case of the last figure we gave, let us suppose the same periodic movements of elongation and anomaly—that is, for double the elongation, 90°30′, and for anomaly 333°12′ from the epicycle's apogee. Let us draw NX perpendicular, instead of EX, and GL instead of BL. And by the same means, with the angles at the centre E given and the hypotenuses DE and NE given equal, it can be shown that

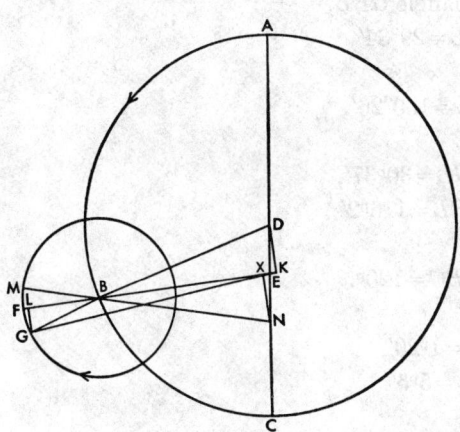

$$DK \doteqdot 10^{\mathrm{p}}19',$$
$$NX \doteqdot 10^{\mathrm{p}}19'$$

where
$$\text{ecc. rad. } BD = 49^{\mathrm{p}}41',$$
$$\text{epic. rad. } BG = 5^{\mathrm{p}}15',$$
and
$$EK = EX = 0^{\mathrm{p}}5.'$$

And, therefore, as we showed before,
$$BK = 48^{\mathrm{p}}36',$$
$$BE = 48^{\mathrm{p}}31',$$
and, by subtraction,
$$BX = 48^{\mathrm{p}}26'.$$

And so, since

$$\text{sq. } BX + \text{sq. } NX = \text{sq. } BN,$$

we shall have in length

$$BN = 49^\text{p}31'$$

where

$$NX = 10^\text{p}19'.$$

And therefore

$$NX \fallingdotseq 25^\text{p}$$

where

$$\text{hypt. } BN = 120^\text{p};$$

and, on the circle about right triangle BNX,

$$\text{arc } NX = 24°3'.$$

And so also

$$\text{angle } NBX = \text{angle } FBM = 24°3' \text{ to 2 rt.},$$
$$\fallingdotseq 12°1'.$$

And therefore, on the epicycle, also

$$\text{arc } FM = 12°1'.$$

But since the point G, the moon, is the remainder of the circle or $26°48'$ distant from the mean apogee M, therefore we shall have, by subtraction,

$$\text{arc } FG = 14°47'.$$

And so also

$$\text{angle } FBG = 14°47'$$
$$= 29°34' \text{ to 2 rt.}$$

And also, on the circle about right triangle GBL,

$$\text{arc } GL = 29°34',$$

and, as remainder of the semicircle,

$$\text{arc } BL = 150°26'.$$

And therefore

$$\text{chord } GL = 30^\text{p}37',$$
$$\text{chord } BL = 116^\text{p}2'$$

where

$$\text{hypt. } BG = 120^\text{p}.$$

And so

$$GL = 1^\text{p}20',$$
$$BL = 5^\text{p}5'$$

where

$$\text{epic. rad.} = 5^\text{p}15'$$

and where it was proved

$$BE = 48^\text{p}31'.$$

And therefore, by addition,

$$EBL = 53^\text{p}36'$$

where

$$GL = 1^\text{p}20'.$$

And again since

$$\text{sq. } EBL + \text{sq. } GL = \text{sq. } EG,$$

therefore, we shall have in length

$$EG \doteq 53^\text{p}37'.$$

And so

$$GL = 2^\text{p}59'$$

where

$$\text{hypt. } EG = 120^\text{p};$$

and, on the circle about right triangle EGL,

$$\text{arc } GL = 2°52'.$$

And therefore, as the anomalistic difference,

$$\text{angle } GEL = 2°52' \text{ to 2 rt.}$$
$$= 1°26'.$$

Which it was required to show.

7. Construction of the Table of General Lunar Anomaly

To have a methodical determination of the particular addition-subtractions set out in a table, we have again used the same geometrical figures and filled out the table we constructed according to the simple hypothesis, with columns which readily correct for the second anomaly. For after the first two columns containing the numbers, we have added a third column containing the addition-subtractions corresponding to the anomalistic number for reducing this number, calculated by the mean passages from the mean apogee or M, to the true apogee or F. In the foregoing case of a distance between the moon and the eccentric's apogee of 90°30′, we showed the arc FM to be 12°1′ so that, although the moon's distance from the mean apogee was only 333°12′, its distance from the true apogee was 345°13′. It is with respect to this last number that the epicyclic addition-subtraction for mean longitudinal movement must be taken. In brief, therefore, we have gotten the quantities of addition-subtraction, at convenient intervals of arc-length, for the other numbers of the moon's distance, and we have put them in the third column beside the proper number.

The fourth column contains the anomalistic differences due to the epicycle and already set out; here the greatest addition-subtraction comes to very nearly 5°1′ according to the ratio of 60ᵖ to 5ᵖ15′. The fifth column contains the excess amounts of the differences resulting from the second anomaly over those from the first, the greatest addition-subtraction from the second totaling $7\frac{2}{3}°$, according to the ratio of 60 to 8. And so the fourth column provides for the epicycle's position at the eccentric's apogee near the syzygies; but the fifth column consists of the excess amounts gotten from the anomaly produced at the eccentric's perigee near the first and third quarters.

To find proportionately the parts of these excess amounts corresponding to the passages between these two positions on the eccentric, we have added a sixth column containing the sixtieth part of that difference for each number of elongation; and this must be added to the first anomaly's addition-subtraction laid out in the fourth column. And we have gotten them in this way:

Let there be the moon's eccentric circle *ABC* with centre *D* and diameter
ADC on which let the ecliptic's centre *E*
be taken. And with arc *AB* cut off and
with the epicycle *FGHK* described about
B, let *EBF* be drawn. By way of example, let the moon's elongation be given as
60° so that, for the same reasons already
demonstrated, angle *AEB* is double the
elongation of 120°. And let *DL* be drawn
from *D* perpendicular to *BE* produced,
and let *GBKD* be drawn through; let the
straight line (in this case *EMN*) from
the centre *E* to the moon be supposed
tangent to the epicycle so as to have the
greatest anomalistic difference; and let
BM be joined.

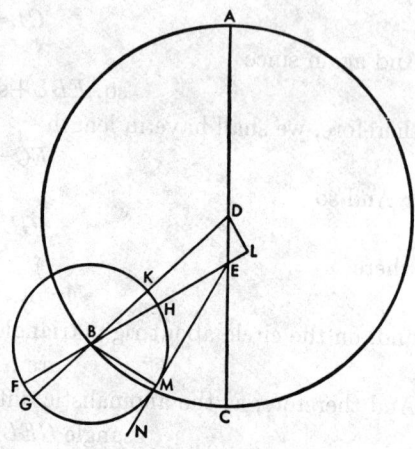

Now, since it is assumed

$$\text{angle } AEB = 120°$$
$$= 240° \text{ to 2 rt.,}$$

therefore, as supplement,

$$\text{angle } DEL = 120° \text{ to 2 rt.}$$

And so, on the circle about right triangle *DEL*,

$$\text{arc } DL = 120°,$$

and, as remainder of the semicircle,

$$\text{arc } EL = 60°.$$

And therefore

$$\text{chord } EL = 60^p,$$
$$\text{chord } DL = 103^p55'$$

where

$$\text{hypt. } DE = 120^p.$$

And therefore

$$EL = 5^p10',$$
$$DL = 8^p56'$$

where

$$DE = 10^p19',$$
$$BD = 49^p41'.$$

And

$$\text{sq. } BD - \text{sq. } DL = \text{sq. } BL;$$

therefore, in length,

$$BEL = 48^p53',$$

and, by subtraction,

$$BE = 43^p43'$$

where

$$\text{epic. rad. } BM = 5^p15'.$$

And therefore

$$BM = 14^p25'$$

where

$$\text{hypt. } BE = 120^p;$$

and, on the circle about right triangle BEM,

$$\text{arc } BM = 13°48'.$$

Therefore, as the angle which contains the greatest anomalistic difference,

$$\text{angle } BEM = 13°48' \text{ to 2 rt.}$$
$$= 6°54'.$$

The anomalistic difference for this distance of elongation thus differs from the 5°1' produced at the apogee by 1°53'. But the complete difference up to the perigee is 2°39'. And therefore the difference of 1°53' will be 42°48' to the greatest difference's 60°. We shall put this 42°38' in the sixth column in the row with the number 120° which here indicates the distance of the epicycle from the eccentric's apogee.

Likewise for the other sections we have calculated by the same means the parts so taken of the excess of one anomaly over the other, placing beside the proper numbers the sixtieth part of this excess corresponding to each one. And, of course, the whole 60 such parts have been put in a row with double the number 90°, the elongation, for the resulting 180° is at the eccentric's perigee.

We have added a seventh column containing the latitudinal passages of the moon on a circle through the ecliptic's poles corresponding to each part of the ecliptic; or, in other words, the arcs intercepted on the circle through the ecliptic's poles between the ecliptic and the moon's oblique circle. And for this we have used the same proof as that by which we calculated the arcs on the circle through the equator's poles, and which lie between the ecliptic and the equator. But in this case the arc on the great circle through the poles of the ecliptic and of the moon's oblique circle, lying between the ecliptic and the northern or southern limit of the oblique circle, is very nearly 5°. For, according to both Hipparchus and ourselves in calculating the appearances pertaining to the northernmost and southernmost courses, the moon's greatest passage was found to be just about that much on either side of the ecliptic. Nearly all things pertaining to lunar observation, considered with respect to the stars and by means of instruments, agree with greatest latitudinal courses of this size. And things to be demonstrated later will agree also. And the following is the table of general lunar anomaly.[1]

---

[1]This table is fairly complicated and condensed, and Ptolemy's explanation is not too clear. We shall here give a clearer and more analytical summary.

In the first place, the first two columns are called "common numbers" because these numbers play different roles for the different columns that follow.

With respect to column 3, columns 1 and 2 contain the numbers of arcs on the eccentric indicating the distance of the epicycle's centre from the eccentric's apogee. And column 3 contains the corresponding addition-subtractions to be made in the moon's distances from the epicycle's mean apogee, in order to determine its distance from the epicycle's true apogee.

With respect to column 4, columns 1 and 2 contain the numbers of arcs on the epicycle indicating the moon's distance from the epicycle's true apogee. And column 4 contains the corresponding addition-subtractions in longitude and latitude which correct for the anomaly when the epicycle is at the eccentric's apogee. These last numbers correspond to the addition-subtractions in the table of the first lunar anomaly, but they are here given their proper place within the general scheme of lunar anomaly.

With respect to column 5, columns 1 and 2 again contain the numbers of arcs on the epicycle indicating the moon's distances from the epicycle's true apogee. And column 5 contains the corresponding additions-subtractions in longitude due to the second lunar anomaly when the epicycle is at the eccentric's perigee, and which are over and above those due to the first anomaly. In other words, these are the differences between the first and general anomalies.

With respect to column 6, columns 1 and 2 contain the numbers of arcs on the eccentric

8. Table of the General Lunar Anomaly

1	2	3		4		5		6		7		
Common Numbers		Addition— subtractions for distances from eccentric's apogee		Addition— subtractions in longitude and latitude for epicycle		Epicyclic difference		Difference in sixtieths		Latitude		
6	354	0	53	0	29	0	14	0	12	4	58	*Northern limit*
12	348	1	46	0	57	0	28	0	24	4	54	
18	342	2	39	1	25	0	42	1	20	4	45	
24	336	3	31	1	53	0	56	2	16	4	34	
30	330	4	23	2	19	1	10	3	24	4	20	
36	324	5	15	2	44	1	23	4	32	4	3	
42	318	6	7	3	8	1	35	6	25	3	43	
48	312	6	58	3	31	1	45	8	18	3	20	
54	306	7	48	3	51	1	54	10	22	2	56	
60	300	8	36	4	8	2	3	12	26	2	30	
66	294	9	22	4	24	2	11	15	5	2	2	
72	288	10	6	4	38	2	18	17	44	1	33	
78	282	10	48	4	49	2	25	20	34	1	3	
84	276	11	27	4	56	2	31	23	24	0	32	
90	270	12	0	4	59	2	35	26	36	0	0	
93	267	12	15	5	0	2	37	28	12	0	16	
96	264	12	28	5	1	2	38	29	49	0	32	
99	261	12	39	5	0	2	39	31	25	0	48	
102	258	12	48	4	59	2	39	33	1	1	3	
105	255	12	56	4	57	2	39	34	37	1	17	
108	252	13	3	4	53	2	38	36	14	1	33	
111	249	13	6	4	49	2	38	37	50	1	48	
114	246	13	9	4	44	2	37	39	26	2	2	
117	243	13	7	4	38	2	35	41	2	2	16	
120	240	13	4	4	32	2	32	42	38	2	30	
123	237	12	59	4	25	2	28	44	3	2	43	
126	234	12	50	4	16	2	24	45	28	2	56	
129	231	12	36	4	7	2	20	46	53	3	8	
132	228	12	16	3	57	2	16	48	18	3	20	
135	225	11	54	3	46	2	11	49	32	3	32	
138	222	11	29	3	35	2	5	50	45	3	43	
141	219	11	2	3	23	1	58	51	59	3	53	
144	216	10	33	3	10	1	51	53	12	4	3	
147	213	10	0	2	57	1	43	54	3	4	11	
150	210	9	22	2	43	1	35	54	54	4	20	
155	207	8	38	2	28	1	27	55	45	4	27	
156	204	7	48	2	13	1	19	56	36	4	34	
159	201	6	56	1	57	1	11	57	15	4	40	
162	198	6	3	1	41	1	2	57	55	4	45	
165	195	5	8	1	25	0	52	58	35	4	50	
168	192	4	11	1	9	0	42	59	4	4	54	
171	189	3	12	0	52	0	31	59	26	4	56	
174	186	2	11	0	35	0	21	59	37	4	58	
177	183	1	7	0	18	0	10	59	49	4	59	*Southern limit*
180	180	0	0	0	0	0	0	60	0	5	0	

9. On General Calculations of the Moon

Now whenever we wish, by means of this tabular set up, to calculate the lunar anomaly we take the moon's mean movements, for the date in question in Alexandria, and we take them in longitude, elongation, anomaly, and latitude in the way we have shown. Always doubling the first number of elongation calculated, and subtracting a whole circle from the product if we can, we carry the result to this Table of Anomaly. We then add the degrees in the third column corresponding to it to the mean degrees of anomaly, if the number doubled runs up to 180°; but, if it exceeds 180°, we subtract it. Again we carry the resulting true number of anomaly to this same table, and we note down the addition-subtraction corresponding to it in the fourth column, and also the corresponding difference in the fifth column.

After this we again carry the double of the number indicating the mean elongation to the same first two columns; and, as many sixtieths in the sixth column as correspond to it, just so many do we take of the difference from the fifth column which we have already noted down. We always add the result to the addition-subtraction we found in the fourth column. If the true anomalistic number is not above 180°, we subtract this sum from the mean longitude and latitude; but, if it is above 180°, we add it. Of the two resulting numbers we take the one in longitude and add it to the mean position calculated at the epoch; and whatever it comes out to, we shall say the moon is truly at that place.

We carry the latitudinal number, computed from the northern limit, to this indicating the distances of the epicycle's centre from the eccentric's apogee. And column 6 contains the corresponding differences between the first anomaly and the general anomaly when the moon lies on the tangent from the earth to

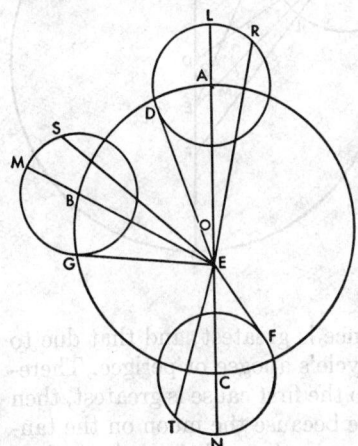

the epicycle or when the epicyclic addition-subtraction is greatest. But these differences are here expressed in terms of the greatest difference among them, which is taken as 60. It is then assumed that, for all practical purposes, the ratio of a difference for a given position of the epicycle to the greatest difference when the epicycle is at the eccentric's perigee is the same for all positions on the epicycle. In other words, taking the eccentric about O and the centre of the ecliptic E, and drawing equal epicycles at the apogee and perigee, A and C, and another equal epicycle at a chance position B, let the tangents from E to the three epicycles be drawn, and let equal arcs LR, MS, and NT be taken from their apogees. Then Ptolemy is assuming that, for all practical purposes, we can use the following proportion:

angle CEF — angle AED :
angle BEG — angle AED : :
angle NET — angle LER :
angle SEM — angle LER.

Now, column 6 gives us the first ratio for different positions of B. And therefore, knowing the differences between angle NET and angle LER, for different lengths of LR and TN, from column 5, we can find the differences between angle SEM and angle LER.

With respect to column 7, columns 1 and 2 contain the numbers of the arcs of the moon's oblique circle, beginning at the northern limit and ending at the southern. And column 7 contains the corresponding numbers of arcs intercepted on circles through the poles of the ecliptic, between the ecliptic and the moon's oblique circle.

same table. And whatever number of degrees in latitude in the seventh column correspond to it, by just so many is the moon's centre distant from the ecliptic along the great circle drawn through the ecliptic's poles. If the number carried is in the first 15 rows, this distance is to the north of the ecliptic; but if it is in the rows below, the distance is to the south of the ecliptic. The first column of numbers embraces the movement from north to south, and the second column the movement from south to north.

10. That no Appreciable Difference is Produced at the Syzygies by the Moon's Eccentric Circle

Now, it is reasonable for some to suspect that at times an appreciable difference occurs at the conjunctions, full moons, and eclipses accompanying them, because of the moon's eccentric circle. For the epicycle's centre does not always fall exactly on the eccentric's apogee at these periods, but can miss it to the extent that the return of the epicycle's centre to the eccentric's apogee is effected at the mean syzygies, but true conjunctions and full moons are taken with the anomaly of each of the two luminaries. Therefore we shall try and show that this difference can produce no error worth mentioning in the appearances at the syzygies, even if the difference due to the circle's eccentricity is neglected.

For let *ABC* be the moon's eccentric circle with centre *D* and diameter *ADC* on which let the point *E* be taken as the ecliptic's centre and *F* on the side opposite *D* as the centre of epicyclic inclination. And with arc *AB* cut off from the apogee *A*, let the epicycle *GHL* be described about *B*, and let *BD* and *GBE* and also *BLF* be joined.

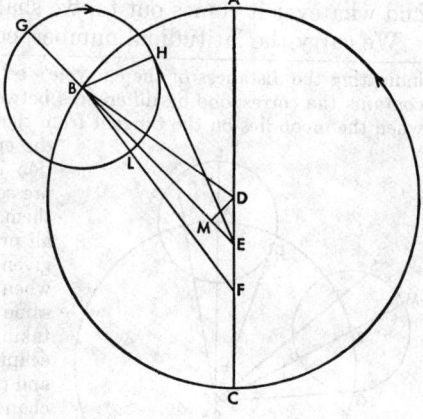

Now, the magnitude of the anomaly can differ in two ways from that proper to the epicycle's position at the apogee *A*: (1) by cutting off a greater angle at *E* because of its position towards the perigee, and (2) by having the diameter through the mean apogee and perigee not directed to the center *E* but to the point *F*.

The difference due to the first cause is greatest when the moon's anomalistic difference is greatest; and that due to the second cause, when the moon is at the epicycle's apogee or perigee. Therefore it is evident that, when the difference due to the first cause is greatest, then that due to the second will be entirely negligible because the moon on the tangents to the epicycle makes very little difference in the addition-subtraction; and it is evident that the true syzygy will possibly differ from the mean by as much as the anomalistic differences of both luminaries put together, either by addition or by subtraction. But when (according to the second cause) the difference in inclination is the greatest, then the difference from the first cause is negligible because the entire anomaly is either nothing or very little when the moon is at the epicycle's apogee or perigee; and the true syzygy will differ from the mean syzygy by the difference of solar anomaly alone.

(1) Then let the sun be assumed to effect the greatest addition of 2°23′, and also the moon itself to effect first the greatest subtraction of 5°1′ so that angle AEB contains 14°48′, the double of the 7°24′ of the two together. And let the tangent EH from E to the epicycle be drawn, and the perpendicular BH be joined; and also let DM be drawn from D perpendicular to BE.

Since, then,

$$\text{angle } AEB = 14°48′$$
$$= 29°36′ \text{ to 2 rt.,}$$

therefore also, on the circle about right triangle DEM,

$$\text{arc } DM = 29°36′,$$

and, as remainder of the semicircle,

$$\text{arc } EM = 150°24′.$$

And

$$\text{chord } DM = 30^{\text{p}}39′,$$
$$\text{chord } EM = 116^{\text{p}}1′$$

where

$$\text{hypt. } DE = 120^{\text{p}}.$$

And so

$$DM = 2^{\text{p}}38′,$$
$$EM = 9^{\text{p}}59′$$

where

$$\text{1. betw. c. } DE = 10^{\text{p}}19′$$

and

$$\text{ecc. rad. } BD = 49^{\text{p}}41′.$$

And since

$$\text{sq. } BD - \text{sq. } DM = \text{sq. } BM,$$

therefore, in length,

$$BM = 49^{\text{p}}37′,$$

and, by addition,

$$BME = 59^{\text{p}}36′$$

where

$$\text{epic. rad. } BH = 5^{\text{p}}15′.$$

And therefore

$$BH = 10^{\text{p}}34′$$

where

$$\text{hypt. } BE = 120^{\text{p}};$$

and, on the circle about right triangle BEH,

$$\text{arc } BH = 10°6′.$$

And therefore, as the angle of greatest anomalistic difference,

$$\text{angle } BEH = 10°6′ \text{ to 2 rt.}$$
$$= 5°3′$$

instead of the 5°1′ produced when the epicycle is at the apogee A. Therefore from this cause the anomalistic difference diverges by 2′, which is an error of less than $\frac{1}{16}$ of an hour.

(2) Again let the moon be supposed at
L the mean perigee, so that angle AEB
clearly contains very nearly the double
of the sun's anomaly alone, that is 4°46'.
And with EL joined in a figure similar to
the last, let the perpendiculars LN, DM,
and FX be dropped from L, D, and F to
BE produced. And, just as before, since

angle at $E = 4°46'$
$= 9°32'$ to 2 rt.,

therefore, on the circles about right triangles EDM and EFX,

arc $DM = $ arc $FX = 9°32'$.

And, as remainders of semicircles,

arc $EM = $ arc $EX = 170°28'$.

And therefore

chord $DM = $ chord $FX = 9^{\mathrm{p}}58'$,
chord $EM = $ chord $EX = 119^{\mathrm{p}}35'$

where

hypt. $DE = $ hypt. $EF = 120^{\mathrm{p}}$.

And so

$DM = FX = 0^{\mathrm{p}}51'$,
$EM = EX = 10^{\mathrm{p}}17'$

where

$DE = EF = 10^{\mathrm{p}}19'$

and

ecc. rad. $DB = 49^{\mathrm{p}}41'$.

And since

sq. $BD - $ sq. $DM = $ sq. BM,

therefore, in length,

$BM \fallingdotseq 49^{\mathrm{p}}41'$.

And so

$BE = 59^{\mathrm{p}}58'$

and, by addition,

$BX = 70^{\mathrm{p}}15'$

where

$FX = 0^{\mathrm{p}}51'$.

And, in the same way also,

hypt. $BF \fallingdotseq 70^{\mathrm{p}}15'$.

And

$BF : FX :: BL : LN$
$BF : BX :: BL : BN$.

And so

$LN = 0^{\mathrm{p}}4'$,
$BN \fallingdotseq 5^{\mathrm{p}}15'$,

and, by subtraction,

$EN = 54^{\mathrm{p}}43'$

where

epic. rad. $BL = 5^{\mathrm{p}}15'$

and it was proved
$$BE = 59^{\mathrm{p}}58'.$$
And since, therefore, the hypotenuse EL differs inappreciably from $54^{\mathrm{p}}43'$, it is inferred that
$$LN \doteq 0^{\mathrm{p}}8'$$
where
$$\text{hypt. } EL = 120^{\mathrm{p}};$$
and that, on the circle about right triangle ELN,
$$\text{arc } LN = 0°8'.$$
And, therefore, angle BEL, by which the moon differs because of the inclination to F, will also be $0°8'$ to 2 right angles' $360°$, or $0°4'$.

So in this case the moon's anomalistic difference has diverged by $4'$, which produces no appreciable error in the appearances at the syzygies, and hardly amounts to $\frac{1}{8}$ of an hour. And it is not extraordinary for such an error to occur often in the observations themselves.

We have added all this, not because it is impossible to calculate these differences along with the examination of the syzygies, but because there is no appreciable error for us in the proofs by means of the lunar eclipses we have set out, even if we have not used the hypothesis of eccentricity in the developed form we give it in what follows.

11. On the Moon's Parallaxes

Now, the means used in getting the true passages of the moon would be generally speaking these: Since in the case of the moon it turns out that the apparent passage is not sensibly the same as the true passage (because, as we said, the earth does not have the ratio of a point to the radius of the moon's sphere) it would be necessary, and consequent, both for other appearances and especially for those observed about the solar eclipses, to get the measure of the parallaxes from which one will be able to determine the passages considered from the observer's eye—that is, from some part of the earth's surface—by means of the true passages conceived with respect to the centre of the earth and ecliptic; and, conversely, to determine the true passages by means of the apparent.

Since it is a necessary condition of this research that the particular magnitudes of the parallaxes cannot be worked out without one's having as given the ratio of the linear distance nor the ratio of the linear distance without some parallax's being given, it is clear that in the case of those stars having no sensible parallax (that is, those with respect to which the earth is in the ratio of a point) getting the ratio of the distance would be impossible. But only in the case of those which display a parallax, as the moon, would it be possible to find the ratio of the distance by means of some first-given parallax, because a parallactic observation can be gotten in itself, but not the size of the distance.

Now, Hipparchus made this examination chiefly from the sun. Since, from certain other incidents of the sun and moon about which we shall give an account later on, it follows that when the linear distance for one of the luminaries is given the distance for the other is also given, he tries by conjecturing the sun's distance to demonstrate the moon's. He first supposes the sun to display only the least sensible parallax in order to get its distance. And then by means of the solar eclipse recorded by him, from calculations with the sun—first as if displaying no sensible parallax and secondly as if displaying a sufficient parallax—

he arrives at the ratios of the lunar distance, different for each of these hypotheses, although not only is the magnitude of the sun's parallax altogether in doubt but also whether it displays any parallax at all.

12. On the Construction of an Instrument for Determining Parallaxes

To record nothing unclear in this research, we built an instrument by which we could observe as accurately as possible how much and by how great a distance from the zenith on the great circle through the moon and the horizon's poles the moon displays a parallax.

We made two four-sided rods, not less than four cubits in length in order to divide them into a great many parts, and proportionate in compass so as not to be bent by their length, but to be extended very true and in a straight line on each of their sides. Then we drew straight lines on each of them in the middle of the wider side. At each end of one of the rods on the centre line we put small square right prisms equal and parallel, each having a hole placed exactly in the middle—the one for the eye having a small hole, the one for the moon a larger hole—so that, when an eye is placed at the prism with the smaller hole, the whole moon can appear through the other hole in a straight line with it.

Then we bored evenly each of the rods on the centre line near one of their extremities; in the case of the rod with the prisms, near the extremity bearing the prism with the larger hole. Through them both we fitted an axle so the sides of the rods with the lines would be bound together as if by a centre; the rod with the prisms could thus be turned in any direction without wobbling. The other rod, the one without prisms, we fixed on a base. On the centre line of each rod we took points equidistant from the lower extremities and as far as possible from the axle-centre, dividing the line so defined on the fixed rod into 60 parts and each of these into as many as possible. And on the back of this same rod, near its extremities, we placed small prisms having their sides in the same direction in a straight line with each other and everywhere equidistant from that same centre line, so that the rod could be stood straight and without inclination to the horizon's plane by hanging a plumb-line through them.

Having the meridian line already established in a plane parallel to the horizon's, we stood the instrument upright in a shadowless place so that the faces of the rods, where they were joined together by the axle, were turned to the south parallel to the meridian line, and so that the rod with the base stood straight without inclination and fixed without deviation, while the other rod could be revolved around the axle in the plane of the meridian, subject to tightening. We added also another small thin rod, fitted on straight for revolving on a short pin at the lower end of the graduated line. And we anticipated the greatest sweep of the equidistant end of the other rod's line so that the third rod, on being revolved with it, could show the distance between the two extremities in terms of a chord.

Then, in the following manner, we make observations of the moon at its passages on the meridian about the tropic points of the ecliptic, since in these positions the great circles through the poles of the horizon and the centre of the moon are very nearly the same as those drawn through the poles of the ecliptic with respect to which the moon's latitudinal passages are observed; the true distance from the zenith can, therefore, be gotten immediately and easily. Turning the rod with the prisms towards the moon in its passages at the meridian until its centre was sighted through both holes at the centre of the larger one, and marking on the fine small rod the distance between the ends of the straight lines on the other rods and applying it to the line of the upright rod which had been cut into 60 parts, we found out how many parts the chord of this distance has to the 60 of the radius of the circle described by the revolution in the meridian plane. And getting the arc subtended by a chord of such length, we thus had the arc by which the moon's apparent centre was distant from the zenith along the great circle drawn through the poles of the horizon and this apparent centre—a great circle which at that time was the same as the meridian through the poles of the equator and of the ecliptic.

For observing the moon's greatest latitudinal passage, we used to sight it especially when it was at the summer tropic point and again at the northernmost limit of the moon's oblique circle. This was done because around these points for some distance sensibly the same latitudinal passage is determined and because the moon, at those times being near the zenith in the parallel of Alexandria where we made the observations, has very nearly the same apparent position as true position. In every case the moon's centre was observed in these passages to be very nearly $2\frac{1}{8}°$ from the zenith so that, from this examination, its greatest latitudinal passage on either side of the ecliptic is demonstrated to be 5°. And this is almost exactly the difference between the 23°51', the arc from the equator to the summer tropic point, and the 30°58' from the zenith to the equator in Alexandria less $2\frac{1}{8}°$.

But for getting the inquiry into the parallaxes done, we again in the same way observed the moon about the winter tropic for reasons already given and because also (being at that time away from the zenith by a similar passage along the meridian) it provides a greater and more easily observed parallax. And, from many parallaxes observed by us in such passages, we shall again set out one by means of which we shall at once both present the manner of calculation and demonstrate the other things as immediate consequences.

13. DEMONSTRATION OF THE MOON'S DISTANCES

For we observed the moon culminating in the year 20 of Hadrian, Egyptianwise Athyr 13, $5+\frac{1}{2}+\frac{1}{3}$ equatorial hours after noon, as the sun was about to set; its centre appeared to us through the instrument at a distance of $(50+\frac{1}{2}+\frac{1}{3}+\frac{1}{12})°$ from the zenith. The distance on the small light rod was $50+\frac{1}{2}+\frac{1}{12}$ parts to the 60 parts of the radius of the circle of revolution, and a chord of this length subtends an arc of $(50+\frac{1}{2}+\frac{1}{3}+\frac{1}{12})°$. But the time from the epochs in the year 1 of Nabonassar, up to this observation, is 882 Egyptian years, 72 days, and $5+\frac{1}{2}+\frac{1}{3}$ equatorial hours simply considered, but $5\frac{1}{3}$ hours accurately considered. And at this time we find the sun's mean position to be 7°31' within the Balance, but its true position 5°28'; and the moon's mean position to be 25°44' within the Archer, its elongation 78°13', its distance from the epicycle's mean apogee 262°20', and its distance from the northern limit of latitude 354°40'. Therefore the anomalistic difference taken out of the proper table all along the line added on 7°26', so that at that hour the moon's true position in longitude was 3°10' within the Goat, in latitude on its oblique circle 2°6' from the northern limit, and 4°59' north of the ecliptic along the circle through the ecliptic's poles, then very nearly culminating.

But 3°10' within the Goat is 23°49' south of the equator along that same circle. And the equator is 30°58′ from the zenith in Alexandria, and likewise south of it. Therefore the moon's centre was truly 49°48′ from the zenith, but it appeared to be 50°55′ from it. Therefore the moon displayed a parallax, for the distance at this passage, of 1°7′ along the great circle drawn through the moon and the horizon's poles, its true position being 49°48′ from the zenith.

Now that this is clear, in the plane of the circle through the horizon's poles and the moon let the following great circles be drawn concentric: the earth's great circle $AB;$ that through the moon's centre at the observation, $CD;$ and the circle $EFGH$ to which the earth has the ratio of a point. And let K be the common centre of them all, and $KACE$ the straight line through the zenith points. And let the moon's true position be supposed at the point D 49°48′ from the zenith as in the preceding instance; and let KDG and ADH be joined. Moreover, from A, which is the observer's eye, let AL be drawn perpendicular to KB, and AF parallel to KG.

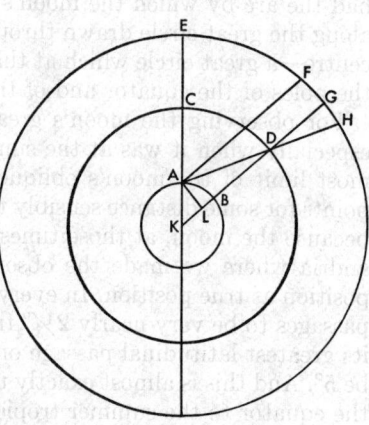

It is clear that the moon displays a parallax of arc GH for those observing from A, so that

$$\text{arc } GH = 1°7′$$

as gotten by observation. But since arc FH is not appreciably greater than GH because of the whole earth's being in the ratio of a point to the circle $EFGH$, therefore

$$\text{arc } FGH \doteqdot 1°7′.$$

And so, again because the point A is indistinguishable from the centre with respect to circle FH,

$$\text{angle } FAH = 1°7′$$
$$= 2°14′ \text{ to } 2 \text{ rt.}$$

And

$$\text{angle } ADL = \text{angle } FAH = 2°14′ \text{ to } 2 \text{ rt.}$$

And therefore, on the circle about right triangle ADL,

$$\text{arc } AL = 2°14′,$$
$$\text{chord } AL = 2^{\text{p}}21′$$

where

$$\text{hypt. } AD = 120^{\text{p}}.$$

And DL is indistinguishably less than AD. Therefore

$$DL = 120^{\text{p}}$$

where

$$AL = 2^{\text{p}}21′.$$

Again, since it is assumed

$$\text{arc } CD = 49°48′,$$

therefore, being at the centre,

$$\text{angle } CKD = 49°48′.$$
$$= 99°36′ \text{ to } 2 \text{ rt.}$$

And so, on the circle about right triangle ALK,
$$\text{arc } AL = 99°36',$$
and, as remainder of the semicircle,
$$\text{arc } LK = 80°24'.$$
And therefore
$$\text{chord } AL = 91^{\mathrm{p}}39',$$
$$\text{chord } KL = 77^{\mathrm{p}}27'$$
where
$$\text{hypt. } AK = 120^{\mathrm{p}}.$$
And so
$$AL = 0^{\mathrm{p}}46',$$
$$KL = 0^{\mathrm{p}}39'$$
where, as the earth's radius,
$$AK = 1^{\mathrm{p}}.$$
But it was shown that
$$DL = 120^{\mathrm{p}}$$
where
$$AL = 2^{\mathrm{p}}21',$$
and therefore
$$DL = 39^{\mathrm{p}}6'$$
where
$$AL = 0^{\mathrm{p}}46'.$$
And, of the same parts,
$$KL = 0^{\mathrm{p}}39'$$
and, as the earth's radius,
$$AK = 1^{\mathrm{p}}.$$

Therefore the whole line KLD, embracing the moon's distance at the observation, will be $39^{\mathrm{p}}45'$ to the 1^{p} of AK, the earth's radius.

Now that this has been shown, let there be the moon's eccentric circle ABC with centre D and diameter ADC, on which

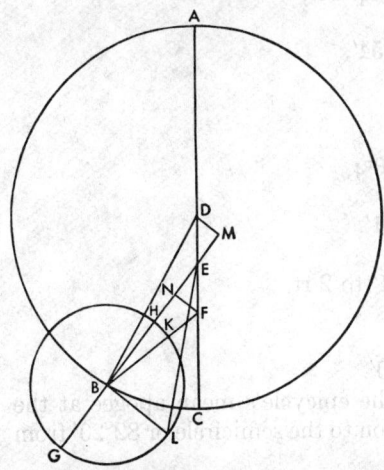

let there be the ecliptic's centre E, and the epicycle's point of inclination F. With the epicycle $GHKL$ drawn about the point B, let the straight lines $GBHE$, BD, and BKF be joined. And let the moon in this observation be supposed at the point L. Let LE and LB be joined, and let line DM be drawn from point D, and FN from point F, both perpendicular to BE.

Since, then, at the time of the observation the number of the elongation was $78°13'$, therefore, through things already seen,
$$\text{angle } AEB = 156°26',$$
and, as supplementary angles,
$$\text{angle } FEN = \text{angle } DEM = 23°34'$$
$$= 47°8' \text{ to 2 rt.}$$

And so, on circles about these right triangles

$$\text{arc } DM = \text{arc } FN = 47°8'$$

because

$$DE = EF;$$

and

$$\text{arc } EM = \text{arc } EN = 132°52'.$$

And therefore

$$\text{chord } DM = \text{chord } FN = 47^{\text{p}}59'$$

and

$$\text{chord } EM = \text{chord } EN = 110^{\text{p}}$$

where

$$\text{hypt. } DE = \text{hypt. } EF = 120^{\text{p}}.$$

And so

$$DM = FN = 4^{\text{p}}8',$$
$$EM = EN = 9^{\text{p}}27'$$

where

$$DE = EF = 10^{\text{p}}19'$$

and

$$\text{ecc. rad. } BD = 49^{\text{p}}41'.$$

And since

$$\text{sq. } BD - \text{sq. } DM = \text{sq. } BM,$$

we shall have, in length,

$$BM = 49^{\text{p}}31',$$

and likewise

$$BE = 40^{\text{p}}4'$$

and, by subtraction,

$$BN = 30^{\text{p}}37'$$

where

$$FN = 4^{\text{p}}8'.$$

And since

$$\text{sq. } BN + \text{sq. } FN = \text{sq. } BF,$$

we shall have, in length,

$$\text{hypt. } BF = 30^{\text{p}}54'.$$

And so

$$FN = 16^{\text{p}}2'$$

where

$$\text{hypt. } BF = 120^{\text{p}};$$

and, on the circle about right triangle BFN,

$$\text{arc } FN = 15°21'.$$

And therefore

$$\text{angle } FBN = 15°21' \text{ to } 2 \text{ rt.}$$
$$\doteqdot 7°40'.$$

Therefore, on the epicycle,

$$\text{arc } HK = 7°40'.$$

Again, since the moon was 262°20′ from the epicycle's mean apogee at the time of the observation, and clearly the addition to the semicircle or 82°20′ from the mean perigee K, therefore also

$$\text{arc } KL = 82°20',$$

and, by addition,

arc $HKL = 90°$.

Therefore

angle HBL = rt. angle.

And so, since it was shown that

$$BE = 40^{\mathrm{p}}4'$$

where

ecc. rad. $BD = 49^{\mathrm{p}}41'$

and

epic. rad. $BL = 5^{\mathrm{p}}15'$,

and since

$$\text{sq. } BL + \text{sq. } BE = \text{sq. } EL,$$

we shall also have, in length,

$$EL = 40^{\mathrm{p}}25'.$$

The moon's linear distance at the observation is hence $40^{\mathrm{p}}25'$ to the assumed $5^{\mathrm{p}}15'$ of the epicycle's radius $BL;$ to the 60^{p} of EA, the radius from the earth's centre to the eccentric's apogee; and to the $39^{\mathrm{p}}22'$ of EC, the radius from the earth's centre to the eccentric's perigee.

But it was shown that the moon's distance at the observation (that is, the straight line EL) was $39^{\mathrm{p}}45'$ to the 1^{p} of the earth's radius. And, therefore, the straight line EA or the mean distance at the syzygies is 59^{p}; and EC or the mean distance at the first and third quarters is $38^{\mathrm{p}}43'$; and the epicycle's radius $5^{\mathrm{p}}10'$ to the $39^{\mathrm{p}}45'$ of the straight line EL, or the moon's distance at the observation. Which things it was required to show.

And now that the moon's distances have been shown in the manner described, it would next be in order to demonstrate at the same time the sun's distance too, since it is readily accessible geometrically if, in addition to the moon's distances at the syzygies, there should be given the magnitudes of the angles at the eye in the syzygies, subtended by the diameters of the sun, moon, and shadow.

14. On the Magnitude of the Apparent Diameters of the Sun, Moon, and Shadow during the Syzygies

Of the methods for such an inquiry, we rejected all those which measure these luminaries by means of waterclocks or the times of equatorial ascensions, because of the impossibility of getting what is proposed by such means. But constructing ourself the four-cubit rod dioptra described by Hipparchus,[1] and making observations with it, we find the sun's diameter everywhere contained

[1]Pappus in his *Commentary* on Book v gives a description of the waterclock, and the following description of the dioptra.

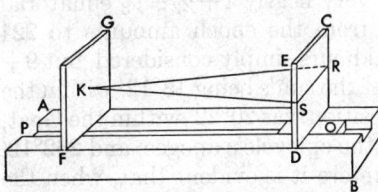

"For let there be a rod not less than 4 cubits in length and of width and thickness sufficient to keep the rod rigid. Let its upper lateral surface be conceived as the parallelogram AB. And let there be a groove on it along the straight line PO through the middle of it, so that a little block is easily moved as we wish along the whole length of the rod without falling from it. And let a suitable prism CD be added on, perpendicular to the rod and stable, having RSD as its side toward the block and the straight line CE at the top of the prism. Let there be another suitable perpendicular prism FG at one end of the rod, and let it have a small hole, not at the rod, but in the middle like K, so that, when our eye is placed at it for

by very nearly the same angle with no variation worthy of mention resulting from its distances. But we find the moon's diameter contained by the same angle as the sun's, then, only when during the full moons it is at its greatest distance from the earth, being at the epicycle's apogee; and not when it is at the mean distance as in the hypotheses of older astronomers. Moreover, we also found these angles a good deal smaller than those handed down, and that without using the measurement on the rod, but by calculating with lunar eclipses. For it was easy to see when each of the diameters subtends the same angle, from the fact that no comparative measurement is available in such a situation. But how large they were seemed very doubtful to us since, even when the comparison is greatest in the to-and-fro movements of the covering width along the length from the eye to the prism, it can be off the true one. But once the moon at its greatest distance appeared to make an angle at the eye equal to the sun's, by means of the lunar eclipses observed at that distance we calculated the angle subtended by the moon, and immediately we had that of the sun also. And, again, by two eclipses set out below, we shall render the method of this general theory very understandable.

For in the year 5 of Nabopollassar (which is the year 127 of Nabonassar, Egyptianwise Athyr 27-28 at the end of the eleventh hour) the moon began to be eclipsed in Babylon; and the greatest extent of the eclipse was ¼ of the diameter from the south. Since, then, the beginning of the eclipse took place 5 seasonal hours after midnight, and the middle very nearly 6 hours after midnight which in Babylon amounted to $5 + \frac{1}{2} + \frac{1}{3}$ equatorial hours because of the sun's true position's being 27°3′ within the Ram, therefore it is clear that the middle of the eclipse, when the greatest part of the diameter fell within the shadow, took place in Babylon $5 + \frac{1}{2} + \frac{1}{3}$ equatorial hours after midnight, but in Alexandria only 5 hours after. And the total time from the epoch amounts to 126 Egyptian years, 86 days, and 17 equatorial hours simply considered, but in terms of mean solar days $16 + \frac{1}{2} + \frac{1}{4}$ equatorial hours. The moon's mean longitudinal passage was thus 25°32′ within the Balance, and its true position 27°5′; also it was 340°7′ from the epicycle's apogee and 80°40′ from the northern limit of the oblique circle. And it is evident that, when the moon's centre (the moon now being near its greatest distance) is $9\frac{1}{3}°$ along the oblique circle from the nodes, and when the shadow's centre lies on the great circle drawn through the moon at right angles to the oblique circle in which position the greatest obscurations take place, then a quarter of the diameter falls within the shadow.

Again, in the year 7 of Cambyses (which is the year 225 of Nabonassar, Egyptianwise Phamenoth 17-18 one hour before midnight) the moon was eclipsed in Babylon to the extent of a half of its diameter from the north. Therefore the eclipse also took place in Alexandria very nearly $1 + \frac{1}{2} + \frac{1}{3}$ equatorial hours before midnight. And the total time from the epoch amounts to 224 Egyptian years, 196 days, and $10\frac{1}{6}$ equatorial hours simply considered, but $9 + \frac{1}{2} + \frac{1}{3}$ hours accurately considered, because of the sun's being 18°12′ within the Crab. And so the moon's mean longitudinal position was 20°22′ within the Goat, but its true one 18°14′; also it was 28°5′ from the epicycle's apogee, and 262°12′ from the oblique circle's northern limit. Therefore it is evident that, when the moon's centre (the moon being near the same greatest distance) is $7\frac{4}{5}°$ along

use, the straight lines drawn from it to the moving prism *CD* through its side edges can contain the whole apparent diameter of the sun, touching it at its extremities."

the oblique circle from the nodes, and the shadow's centre has the position we just described with respect to the moon's centre, one half of the moon's diameter falls within the shadow.

But if the moon's centre is 9⅓° along the oblique circle from the nodes, it is 0°48½′ from the ecliptic along the great circle drawn through itself at right angles to the oblique circle. And when it is 7⅘° along the oblique circle from the nodes, it is 0°40⅔′ from the ecliptic along the great circle drawn through itself at right angles to the oblique circle. Since, then, the difference between the two eclipses embraces a quarter of the moon's diameter, and since the difference between the two distances of its centre from the ecliptic, that is from the shadow's centre, is (7+½+⅓)′, therefore it is evident the whole diameter of the moon subtends an arc of a great circle amounting to 0°31⅓′.

It is immediately easy to see that the radius of the shadow at the moon's greatest distance subtends 0°40⅔′. For, when the moon's centre was that distance from the shadow's centre, it was tangent to the shadow's circle, half of the moon's diameter being eclipsed. And the shadow's radius is very little less than 2⅗ times as great as the moon's radius which is 0°15⅔′. By means of several other such observations we got very nearly these same magnitudes, and we have used them for other things about eclipses. We now use one of them which Hipparchus also followed, for the demonstration of the sun's distance to be made in this same way, since the circles intercepted by the cones on the sun, moon, and earth are not appreciably different from the great circles themselves described on those spheres and their diameters.[1]

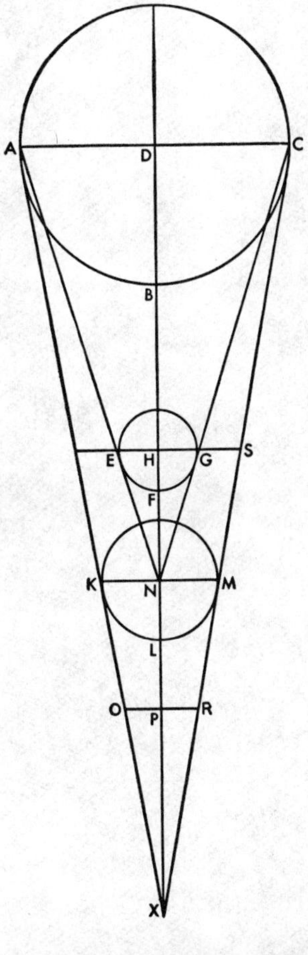

15. On the Sun's Distance and Demonstrations Related Thereto

Now that these things are given, and seeing that the moon's greatest distance is 64ᴾ10′ to the 1ᴾ of the earth's radius because it has been shown the mean distance is 59ᴾ and the epicycle's radius 5ᴾ10′, let us find out also how great is the sun's distance.

For let there be the great circles of the spheres in the same plane: ABC the sun's with centre D, EFG the moon's at its greatest distance with centre H, and KLM the earth's with centre N. Of the planes through the centres, let AXC be that containing the earth's and the sun's, and ANC that containing the sun's and the moon's. Let there be the common axis $DHNX$; and let there be the parallel lines through the points of tangency, clearly equal to the diameters as far as the senses are con-

[1]This demonstration in all its details for the case of the moon is given by Aristarchus in his *Treatise on the Sizes and Distances of the Sun and Moon.*

cerned: that of the sun's circle, ADC; that of the moon's circle, EHG; that of the earth's circle, KNM; and OPR of the shadow's circle into which the moon falls at its greatest distance. And so

$$HN = NP = 64^\text{p}10'$$

where, as earth's radius,

$$LN = 1^\text{p}.$$

Then it is required to find what ratio the line DN, the sun's distance, has to LN, the earth's radius.

Now let EGS be produced. And since we have shown that the moon's diameter at the given greatest distance in the syzygies subtends an arc of $0°31'20''$ on the circle drawn through the moon about the earth's centre, it follows that

$$\text{angle } ENG = 0°31'20''$$

and, as half of it,

$$\text{angle } HNG = 0°31'20'' \text{ to } 2 \text{ rt.}$$

And so, on the circle about right triangle HGN,

$$\text{arc } GH = 0°31'20''$$

and, as remainder of the semicircle,

$$\text{arc } HN = 179°28'40''.$$

And therefore

$$\text{chord } GH = 0^\text{p}32'48''$$

where

$$\text{diam. } GN = 120^\text{p}$$

and

$$\text{chord } HN \doteqdot 120^\text{p}.$$

And so also

$$GH = 0^\text{p}17'33''$$

where

$$HN = 64^\text{p}10'$$

and

$$\text{earth's rad. } MN = 1^\text{p}.$$

But since, very nearly,

$$PR : GH : : 2^\text{p}36' : 1^\text{p},$$

therefore

$$PR = 0^\text{p}45'38''.$$

Therefore

$$GH + PR = 1^\text{p}3'11''$$

where

$$MN = 1^\text{p}.$$

But

$$HS + PR = 2^\text{p},$$

because

$$HS + PR = 2MN.$$

For, as we said, they are all parallel, and

$$NP = HN.$$

And therefore, by subtraction,

$$GS = 0^\text{p}56'49''$$

where

$$MN = 1^\text{p}.$$

And
$$MN : GS :: CN : CG :: DN : DH.$$
Therefore also
$$DH = 0^\mathrm{p}56'49''$$
and, by subtraction,
$$HN = 0^\mathrm{p}3'11''$$
where
$$DN = 1^\mathrm{p}.$$
And so we shall have also, as the sun's distance,
$$DN = 1210^\mathrm{p}$$
where
$$HN = 64^\mathrm{p}10'$$
and
$$MN = 1^\mathrm{p}.$$
And since likewise it was shown that
$$PR = 0^\mathrm{p}45'38''$$
where
$$MN = 1^\mathrm{p},$$
and since
$$MN : PR :: NX : PX,$$
therefore
$$PX = 0^\mathrm{p}45'38'',$$
and, by subtraction,
$$NP = 0^\mathrm{p}14'22''$$
where
$$NX = 1^\mathrm{p}.$$
And therefore
$$PX \doteqdot 203^\mathrm{p}50',$$
$$NX = 268^\mathrm{p}$$
where
$$NP = 64^\mathrm{p}10'$$
and
$$\text{earth's rad. } MN = 1^\mathrm{p}.$$

Therefore, to the 1 of the earth's radius, we have concluded that the moon's mean distance in the syzygies is 59, the sun's 1210, and from the earth's centre to the vertex of the shadow's cone 268.

16. On the Magnitudes of the Sun, Moon, and Earth

Furthermore, the ratio of these solid magnitudes is easily and immediately seen from the diameters of the sun, moon, and earth.

For since it has been shown that
$$\text{moon's rad. } GH = 0^\mathrm{p}17'33'',$$
and
$$HN = 64^\mathrm{p}10'$$
where
$$\text{earth's rad. } MN = 1^\mathrm{p},$$
and since
$$HN : GH :: DN : CD,$$

therefore, having shown

$$DN = 1210^{\mathrm{p}},$$

we shall also have

$$\text{sun's rad. } CD = 5\tfrac{1}{2}^{\mathrm{p}}.$$

And, therefore, the ratios of the diameters will be the same.

The earth's diameter will hence be very nearly $3\tfrac{2}{5}$, and the sun's $18\tfrac{4}{5}$, to the moon's 1. Therefore the earth's diameter is $3\tfrac{2}{5}$ times as great as the moon's, and the sun's $18\tfrac{4}{5}$ times as great as the moon's, and very nearly $5\tfrac{1}{2}$ times as great as the earth's. Accordingly, since the cube of 1 is 1, and the cube of $3\tfrac{2}{5}$ is very nearly $39\tfrac{1}{4}$, and the cube of $18\tfrac{4}{5}$ likewise very nearly $6644\tfrac{1}{2}$, therefore we have concluded [Eucl. XII, 18] that the earth's solid magnitude is $39\tfrac{1}{4}$, and the sun's $6644\tfrac{1}{2}$, to the moon's 1. Therefore the sun's solid magnitude is very nearly 170 times the earth's.

17. On the Particular Parallaxes of the Sun and Moon

Now, with these things supposed in this way, it would next follow that we show in addition and very briefly how one could compute, from the distances of the sun and moon, their particular parallaxes—and, first of all, those considered on the great circle drawn through the zenith and themselves.

Again, then, let there be in the plane of this great circle the earth's great circle AB, the circle at the sun or moon CD, and the circle $EFGH$ to which the earth has the ratio of a point; and let K be the centre of them all, and $KACE$ the diameter through the zenith points. With arc CD cut off from the zenith C at 30° as an example, again let KDG and ADH be joined; and from A let AF be drawn parallel to KG, and AL perpendicular to it.

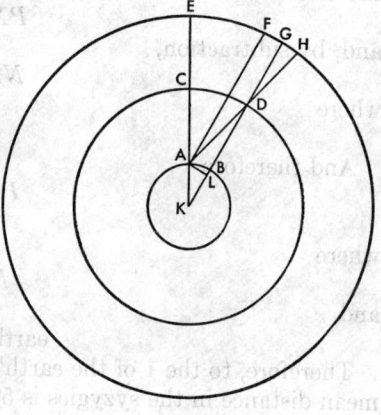

Now, since the distance of each of these luminaries is not always the same, and since the difference of the parallaxes resulting from this cause will be, for the sun, altogether small and imperceptible because its circle's eccentricity is small and its distance great, but since for the moon it would be quite perceptible both because of its epicyclic motion and because of the epicycle's movement on the eccentric which makes a considerable difference at either distance, we shall show the sun's parallaxes only in the one ratio (I mean the ratio of 1210 to 1) and the moon's in those four ratios which will be the more accessible to successive calculations. Of these four distances we have taken, first, those two which result from the epicycle's being at the eccentric's apogee; and, of these two, first the distance to the epicycle's apogee which we have already shown to be 64ᵖ10′ to the 1ᵖ of the earth's radius, and second the distance to the epicycle's perigee found to be 53ᵖ50′. The remaining two we have taken when the epicycle is at the eccentric's perigee; and again, of these, first the distance to the epicycle's apogee which was found (as already shown) to be 43ᵖ53′ to the 1ᵖ of the earth's radius, and second to the epicycle's perigee found to be 33ᵖ33′.

Since then
$$\text{arc } CD = 30°,$$
therefore also
$$\text{angle } CKD = 30°$$
$$= 60° \text{ to 2 rt.}$$
And so, on the circle about right triangle AKL,
$$\text{arc } AL = 60°$$
and, as remainder of the semicircle,
$$\text{arc } KL = 120°.$$
And therefore
$$\text{chord } AL = 60^\text{p}$$
$$\text{chord } KL = 103^\text{p}55'$$
where
$$\text{diam. } AK = 120^\text{p}.$$

And therefore
$$AL = 0^\text{p}30'$$
$$KL = 0^\text{p}52'$$
where
$$AK = 1^\text{p}.$$
And, for the sun's distance,
$$KLD = 1210^\text{p};$$
and, for the lunar distances, at the first term
$$KLD = 64^\text{p}10';$$
at the second term
$$KLD = 53^\text{p}50';$$
at the third term
$$KLD = 43^\text{p}53';$$
and at the fourth term
$$KLD = 33^\text{p}33'.$$
Therefore, since the remainder, line LD, differs from AD by an indistinguishable amount, for the solar distance,
$$AD = 1209^\text{p}8';$$
and for the lunar distances, at the first term
$$AD = 63^\text{p}18';$$
at the second term
$$AD = 52^\text{p}58';$$
at the third term
$$AD = 43^\text{p}1';$$
and at the fourth term
$$AD = 32^\text{p}41'.$$
And so, in the same order to avoid repetition,
$$AL = 0^\text{p}2'59'',$$
$$AL = 0^\text{p}56'52'',$$
$$AL = 1^\text{p}7'58'',$$
$$AL = 1^\text{p}23'41'',$$
and
$$AL = 1^\text{p}50'9'',$$
where
$$\text{hypt. } AD = 120^\text{p}.$$

And, therefore, on the circle about right triangle ADL,

$$\text{arc } AL = 0°2'50'',$$
$$\text{arc } AL = 0°54'18'',$$
$$\text{arc } AL = 1°4'54'',$$
$$\text{arc } AL = 1°20',$$

and

$$\text{arc } AL \fallingdotseq 1°45'.$$

And, since

$$\text{angle } ADB = \text{angle } FAH,$$

therefore

$$\text{angle } FAH = 0°2'50'' \text{ to 2 rt.,}$$
$$= 0°1'25'';$$
$$\text{angle } FAH = 0°54'18'' \text{ to 2 rt.,}$$
$$= 0°27'9'';$$
$$\text{angle } FAH = 1°4'54'' \text{ to 2 rt.,}$$
$$= 0°32'27'';$$
$$\text{angle } FAH = 1°20' \text{ to 2 rt.,}$$
$$= 0°40';$$

and

$$\text{angle } FAH = 1°45' \text{ to 2 rt.}$$
$$= 0°52'30''.$$

And so—since the point A is indistinguishable from the center K, and arc FGH is not appreciably greater than arc GH because of the whole earth's being in the ratio of a point to circle $EFGH$—arc GH of the parallax will be, for the solar distance, $0°1'25''$; and for the lunar distances, at the first term $0°27'9''$, at the second term $0°32'27''$, at the third term $0°40'$, and at the fourth term $0°52'30''$. Which it was required to show.

In the same way, for the other distances from the zenith, we calculated the resulting parallaxes for each term at intervals of 6° up to the quadrant of 90°, and we drew up a table for the determination of parallaxes, again in 45 rows and 9 columns. In the first column we put the 90° of the quadrant making them increase by 2°; in the second column, the sixtieths of the solar parallaxes corresponding to each section; in the third column, the moon's parallaxes at the first term; in the fourth, the excesses of the second term's parallaxes over the first term's; in the fifth, the parallaxes at the third term; and in the sixth, the excesses of the fourth term's parallaxes over the third term's.

For example, compared to 30° there is the sun's $0°1'25''$, then next the $0°27'9''$ of the moon's first term, and then $0°5'18''$ which is the excess of the second term over the first, then again the third term's $0°40'$, and next $0°12'30''$ which is the excess of the fourth term over the third. And in order to find easily and systematically the parallaxes in the distances between the apogees and perigees proportionate to the particular sections, from the parallaxes at the four terms, by comparing the sixtieths, we added the remaining three columns for comparing such differences as were calculated in the following way:

Let there be the moon's epicycle $ABCD$ about E as centre; and let F be the

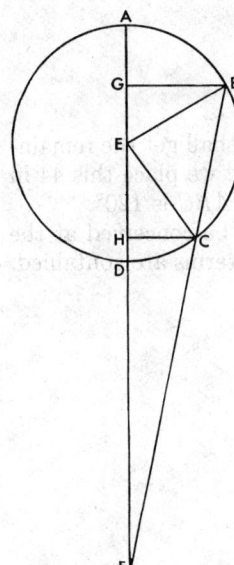

centre of the earth and the ecliptic. With $AEDF$ joined,
let FCB be drawn, and BE and CE joined. And let BG
be drawn from B, and CH from C, perpendicular to AD.
First let the moon be supposed the distance of arc AB
from the true apogee at A considered relative to centre
F. And let the arc be 60°, for example, so that

$$\text{angle } BEG = 60°$$
$$= 120° \text{ to 2 rt.}$$

And so, on the circle about right triangle BEG,

$$\text{arc } BG = 120°$$

and, as remainder of the semicircle,

$$\text{arc } EG = 60°.$$

And therefore

$$\text{chord } BG = 103°55',$$
$$\text{chord } EG = 60^\text{p}$$

where

$$\text{diam. } BE = 120^\text{p}.$$

But, when the epicycle's centre E is at the eccentric's
apogee,

$$EF : BE : : 60^\text{p} : 5^\text{p}15'.$$

And therefore

$$BG = 4^\text{p}33',$$
$$EG = 2^\text{p}38',$$
$$GEF = 62^\text{p}38',$$

where

$$BE = 5^\text{p}15'.$$

And, since

$$\text{sq. } FG + \text{sq. } BG = \text{sq. } BF,$$

therefore

$$BF = 62^\text{p}48'$$

where, as the first term's distance,

$$AF = 65^\text{p}15',$$

and, as the second term's distance,

$$DF = 54^\text{p}45',$$

and, as the difference between the two terms,

$$AD = 10^\text{p}30'.$$

And therefore the difference at B with respect to the first term's distance is $2^\text{p}27'$
to the whole difference's $10^\text{p}30'$.

And so the difference at that time will be 14 to the whole difference's 60.
Therefore we shall place this 14 in column 7 in the row containing half the number 60 (that is, opposite 30) because the whole 90° in the first column of the
table are only half the 180° from A to D.

In the same way, if we suppose

$$\text{arc } CD = 60°,$$

then it will be shown that

$$CH = 4^\text{p}33',$$
$$EH = 2^\text{p}38',$$

and, by subtraction,

$$FH = 57^\text{p}22'$$

where
$$\text{rad. } CE = 5^p15'.$$
And likewise
$$\text{hypt. } CF = 57^p33'.$$

Again subtracting these from the first term's $65^p15'$, we shall get the remainder $7^p42'$ which is 44 sixtieths of the whole difference. And we place this 44 in the same column opposite the number 60 because the arc ABC is 120°.

Again, with the same things assumed, let the centre E be conceived at the eccentric's perigee, in which position the third and fourth terms are contained. Since, then, at this position
$$EF : BE : : 60 : 8,$$
therefore, whenever it is assumed
$$\text{arc } AB = 60°$$
or
$$\text{arc } CD = 60°,$$
then
$$BG = 6^p56'$$
or
$$CH = 6^p56'$$
where
$$BE = 8^p$$
and
$$EF = 60^p.$$
And
$$EG = 4^p$$
or
$$EH = 4^p.$$
And so, with
$$FG = 64^p$$
and
$$FH = 56^p,$$
likewise also
$$\text{hypt. } BF = 64^p23',$$
$$\text{hypt. } CF = 56^p26'$$
where the third term's
$$AF = 68^p$$
and, as difference between the third and fourth term,
$$AD = 16^p.$$

Therefore, if we subtract $64^p23'$ from 68^p, we shall have left $3^p37'$ which is 13 and 33' sixtieths of the whole difference's 16^p. And we shall place this likewise opposite the number 30 in column 8. And if we subtract $56^p26'$ from the same 68^p, we shall have left $11^p34'$ which is 43 and 24' sixtieths of the whole difference's 16^p. And we shall likewise place this opposite the number 60 in column 8.

The differences resulting from the moon's movement on the epicycle will be set out by us in this way, and we shall systematically handle those resulting from the epicycle's passage on the eccentric in the following manner:

Let there be the moon's eccentric circle $ABCD$ with centre E and diameter

AEC, on which let there be conceived the ecliptic's centre *F*. And with *BFD* drawn, again let each of the angles *AFB* and *CFD* be 60°. This takes place if the elongation is 30° when the epicycle's centre is at *B*, and 120° when at *D*. And, with *BE* and *DE* joined, let the straight line *EG* be drawn from *E* perpendicular to *BFD*.

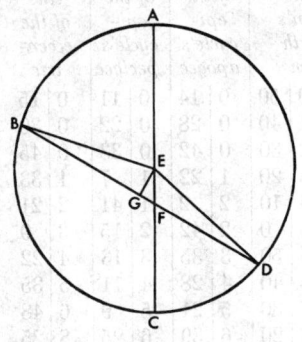

Now, since
$$\text{angle } AFB = 120° \text{ to 2 rt.,}$$
therefore, on the circle about right triangle *EFG*,
$$\text{arc } EG = 120°$$
and, as remainder of the semicircle,
$$\text{arc } FG = 60°.$$
And therefore
$$\text{chord } EG = 103^{\text{p}}55',$$
$$\text{chord } FG = 60^{\text{p}}.$$
where
$$\text{hypt. } EF = 120^{\text{p}}.$$
And so
$$EG = 8^{\text{p}}56',$$
$$FG = 5^{\text{p}}10'$$
where
$$\text{1. betw. c. } EF = 10^{\text{p}}19'$$
and
$$\text{ecc. rad. } 49^{\text{p}}41'.$$
And since
$$\text{sq. } BE - \text{sq. } EG = \text{sq. } BG,$$
therefore
$$BG = DG = 48^{\text{p}}53'.$$
And so, by addition,
$$BF = 54^{\text{p}}3'$$
where, for the first pair of limits,
$$AF = 60^{\text{p}}$$
and, for the second pair of limits,
$$CF = 39^{\text{p}}22',$$
and the difference between them is $20^{\text{p}}38'$. Also, by subtraction,
$$DF = 43^{\text{p}}43'.$$

Since, then, 60^{p} exceeds $54^{\text{p}}3'$ by $5^{\text{p}}57'$ which is 17 18' sixtieths of the whole difference's $20^{\text{p}}38'$, and exceeds $43^{\text{p}}43'$ by $16^{\text{p}}17'$ which is 47 21' sixtieths of $20^{\text{p}}38'$, we place the 17 and 18' in column 9 opposite number 30 of the elongation and the 47 and 21' opposite the number 120 (or, rather, 60, because the elongation of 60° is equal in distance to that of 120° when the perigee is at 90°).

For the other arcs we calculate in this same way the resulting sixtieths of the differences according to the three differences just set out, by sections of twelve which become sections of six for the numbers in the table, the 180 parts from the apogees to the perigees corresponding to the 90 parts in the table. And we have put down for each of the numbers given the corresponding sixtieths all worked out. Those corresponding to the parts in between these we have worked out according to the regular increase of the sixth parts of the difference; for there is no discrepancy worth mentioning between those so gotten and those derived geometrically for differences of this size, either in the sixtieths or in the parallaxes themselves. And here is the table:

18. Parallactic Table

1	2			3			4			5			6			7		8		9	
Numbers	Sun's Parallaxes			Parallaxes of the moon's first term			Differences of the moon's second term			Parallaxes of the moon's third term			Differences of the moon's fourth term			Sixtieths of the epicycle's apogee		Sixtieths of the epicycle's perigee		Sixtieths of the eccentric	
2	0	0	7	0	1	54	0	0	23	0	3	0	0	0	50	0	14	0	11	0	15
4	0	0	13	0	3	48	0	0	45	0	6	0	0	1	40	0	28	0	22	0	30
6	0	0	19	0	5	41	0	1	7	0	9	0	0	2	30	0	42	0	33	0	45
8	0	0	25	0	7	34	0	1	29	0	11	40	0	3	20	1	22	1	7	1	33
10	0	0	31	0	9	27	0	1	51	0	14	20	0	4	10	2	2	1	41	2	21
12	0	0	37	0	11	19	0	2	12	0	17	0	0	5	0	2	42	2	15	3	9
14	0	0	42	0	13	10	0	2	33	0	19	40	0	5	50	3	35	3	13	4	22
16	0	0	48	0	15	0	0	2	54	0	22	20	0	6	40	4	28	4	11	5	35
18	0	0	53	0	16	49	0	3	15	0	25	0	0	7	30	5	21	5	9	6	48
20	0	0	58	0	18	36	0	3	36	0	27	40	0	8	20	6	39	6	25	8	25
22	0	1	4	0	20	22	0	3	57	0	30	20	0	9	10	7	57	7	41	10	2
24	0	1	9	0	22	6	0	4	18	0	33	0	0	10	0	9	15	8	57	11	39
26	0	1	14	0	23	49	0	4	39	0	35	20	0	10	50	10	50	10	29	13	32
28	0	1	20	0	25	30	0	4	59	0	37	40	0	11	40	12	25	12	1	15	25
30	0	1	25	0	27	9	0	5	18	0	40	0	0	12	30	14	0	13	33	17	18
32	0	1	30	0	28	46	0	5	37	0	42	20	0	13	20	15	52	15	22	19	23
34	0	1	35	0	30	21	0	5	55	0	44	40	0	14	10	17	44	17	11	21	28
36	0	1	40	0	31	54	0	6	13	0	47	0	0	15	0	19	36	19	0	23	33
38	0	1	44	0	33	24	0	6	30	0	49	0	0	15	40	21	36	20	59	25	40
40	0	1	49	0	34	51	0	6	47	0	51	0	0	16	20	23	36	22	58	27	47
42	0	1	54	0	36	14	0	7	4	0	53	0	0	17	0	25	36	24	57	29	54
44	0	1	58	0	37	37	0	7	20	0	55	0	0	17	40	27	40	27	1	32	0
46	0	2	3	0	38	57	0	7	35	0	57	0	0	18	20	29	44	29	5	34	6
48	0	2	8	0	40	14	0	7	49	0	59	0	0	19	0	31	48	31	9	36	12
50	0	2	12	0	41	28	0	8	3	1	0	40	0	19	40	33	52	33	14	38	9
52	0	2	16	0	42	39	0	8	16	1	2	20	0	20	20	35	56	35	19	40	6
54	0	2	20	0	43	45	0	8	29	1	4	0	0	21	0	38	0	37	24	42	3
56	0	2	23	0	44	48	0	8	42	1	5	20	0	21	20	40	0	39	24	43	49
58	0	2	26	0	45	48	0	8	53	1	6	40	0	21	40	42	0	41	24	45	35
60	0	2	29	0	46	46	0	9	3	1	8	0	0	22	0	44	0	43	24	47	21
62	0	2	32	0	47	40	0	9	13	1	9	20	0	22	20	45	50	45	13	48	49
64	0	2	34	0	48	30	0	9	22	1	10	40	0	22	40	47	40	47	2	50	17
66	0	2	36	0	49	15	0	9	31	1	12	0	0	23	0	49	30	48	51	51	45
68	0	2	38	0	49	57	0	9	39	1	13	0	0	23	10	50	56	50	24	52	57
70	0	2	40	0	50	36	0	9	46	1	14	0	0	23	20	52	22	51	57	54	9
72	0	2	42	0	51	11	0	9	53	1	15	0	0	23	30	53	48	53	30	55	41
74	0	2	44	0	51	44	0	9	59	1	15	40	0	23	40	54	57	54	41	56	12
76	0	2	46	0	52	12	0	10	4	1	16	20	0	23	50	56	6	55	52	57	3
78	0	2	47	0	52	34	0	10	8	1	17	0	0	24	0	57	15	57	3	57	54
80	0	2	48	0	52	53	0	10	11	1	17	20	0	24	10	57	57	57	47	58	26
82	0	2	49	0	53	9	0	10	14	1	17	40	0	24	20	58	39	58	31	58	58
84	0	2	50	0	53	21	0	10	16	1	18	0	0	24	30	59	21	59	15	59	30
86	0	2	50	0	53	29	0	10	16	1	18	20	0	24	40	59	34	59	30	59	40
88	0	2	51	0	53	33	0	10	17	1	18	40	0	24	50	59	47	59	45	59	50
90	0	2	51	0	53	34	0	10	17	1	19	0	0	25	0	60	0	60	0	60	0

19. On the Determination of Parallaxes

Whenever we wish to determine what parallax the moon displays in each of its passages—first along the great circle through itself and the zenith—we shall look to see how many equatorial hours it is from the meridian of the given parallel. And taking the number found to the Table of Angles of the proper parallel and of the proper sign [Chap. 13, Book II],[1] we shall find in the second column the degrees corresponding to that hour either entire or in proportion to the part of the hour. These are the degrees of the moon's distance from the zenith along the great circle drawn through them both. And carrying this number to the Table of Parallaxes, we shall look to see what row of the first column it falls in, and we shall note down each of the numbers corresponding to it in the four successive columns following the solar parallaxes—that is, columns 3, 4, 5, and 6.

Then, taking the anomalistic number determined for that hour with respect to the true apogee, either the number itself or (if it exceeds 180°) the difference between it and 360°, we carry the half of the number of the degrees so obtained to the same numbers [in column 1], and we look to see how many sixtieths in columns 7 and 8 correspond to that number. As many sixtieths as are found in column 7, just so many sixtieths shall we take of the difference in column 4, always adding it in turn to the parallax in column 3. And as many sixtieths as are found in column 8, just so many sixtieths shall we take of the difference in column 6, always adding it in turn to the parallax of column 5. And we shall set out the difference of the two parallaxes gotten in this way.

Next, taking the number of degrees of the moon's mean distance either from the sun or from the point diametrically opposite according to whichever yields the nearer distance, we shall also carry these to the numbers in column 1. And again, as many sixtieths as correspond in the ninth and last column, just so many sixtieths shall we take of the difference between the parallaxes set out, always adding the result to the lesser of the two parallaxes—that is, to the parallax determined from columns 3 and 4.[2] And we shall have the total parallax the moon displays along the great circle through itself and the zenith.

For solar eclipses, the solar parallax simply considered is immediately obtained at the similar position from the degrees in column 2 corresponding to the magnitude of the arc from the zenith.

[1]To use this table with accuracy, the moon must be supposed at the beginning of the sign and to be on the ecliptic.

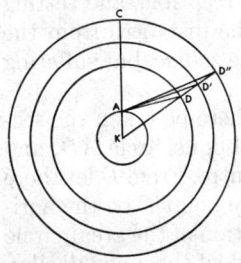

[2]Here, as in the preceding paragraph, the procedure is practically true, not strictly and mathematically true. Ptolemy, here and in the preceding paragraph, is supposing that, between the smaller parallax at the greater distance and the larger parallax at the lesser distance, the differences in the parallaxes are proportional to the differences in the distances.

Thus, consider the centre of the earth K, the observer's eye A, the zenith point C, and the three distances of the moon, D, D', and D'' with the three corresponding parallactic angles ADK, $AD'K$, and $AD''K$. The supposition is that

angle $AD'K$ — angle $AD''K$: angle ADK — $AD''K$: : KD' — $KD : KD'' — KD$, or that

angle $D''AD'$: angle $D''AD$: : $D''D' : D''D$.

Now, to determine also the parallax displayed at that time with respect to the ecliptic, longitudinally and latitudinally, we shall take again the same equatorial hours of the moon's distance from the meridian to the same part of the Table of Angles. And we shall look for the number of degrees corresponding to the number of hours, in column 3 if the moon is antemeridian, but in column 4 if the moon is postmeridian. If it is within 90°, we shall write it down; if above 90°, we shall write down what is left from 180°. For the lesser of these angles about the intersection will be just so many degrees to one right angle's 90°. Then, doubling the number of degrees noted down, we carry it to the Table of Chords, the number itself and the remainder from 180°. And whatever ratio the chord subtending the arc of twice the number of degrees has to the chord subtending the remainder of the semicircle, that ratio the latitudinal parallax has to the longitudinal, since arcs of such size do not differ appreciably from their chords. Then, multiplying the numbers of the corresponding chords by the parallax found on the great circle drawn through the zenith, and dividing the result by 120, we analytically derive the degrees resulting from the division as the degrees of the particular parallax.

In general, in the case of the latitudinal parallax, whenever the zenith is farther north on the meridian than the point of the ecliptic then culminating, the parallax will be to the south of it; and whenever the zenith is farther south than the point of the ecliptic culminating, the latitudinal parallax will be to the north. In the case of the longitudinal parallaxes, since the magnitudes of the angles laid out in the table contain the northern angle of the two angles contained by the eastward section of the ecliptic to either side of it, when the latitudinal parallax is to the north (if the angle in question is greater than a right angle) the longitudinal parallax will be westward; if less than a right angle, eastward. But, contrawise, when the latitudinal parallax is to the south, if the angle in question is greater than a right angle, the longitudinal parallax is eastward; if less than a right angle, westward.

Now, we have used the things previously demonstrated concerning the sun as if it displayed no sensible parallax—not because we were unaware that its parallax when later worked out would make some difference in these matters, but because we did not think any appreciable error would follow from this with respect to the appearances, so as to make it necessary to change any of the details worked out already and without regard to this small difficulty. Likewise, with respect to the moon's parallaxes, we were satisfied with the arcs and angles made with the ecliptic by the great circle drawn through the horizon's poles in the place of those considered with respect to the moon's oblique circle. For the difference resulting at the ecliptic syzygies would be imperceptible, and setting them out requires many proofs and long calculations, the distances from the nodes not being fixed for each of the moon's passages in the zodiac, but suffering various changes in magnitude and position.

For an easy understanding of what has been said, let there be taken the section of the ecliptic ABC, and the section of the moon's oblique circle AD; and let the point A be supposed the node, and D the moon's centre. From D let there be drawn the arc DB perpendicular to the ecliptic. Let the point E be the horizon's pole, and let there be drawn through it EDF as a section of the great circle through the moon's centre, and section EB through B. And let the moon display a parallax of arc DG, and let the arcs GH and GK be drawn through G perpen-

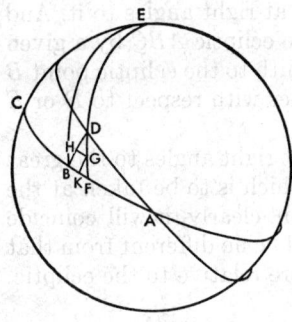

dicular to the arcs *BD* and *BF* so that, of the longitudinal distances from the node, arc *AB* is the true one, and *AK* the apparent one; and, of the latitudinal distances from the ecliptic, the true one is arc *BD* and the apparent one *KG*; so that, of the parallaxes from *DG* considered with respect to the ecliptic, the longitudinal is equal to *HG* and the latitudinal to *DH*.

Now, since the parallax *DG* is found by the means presented above when arc *ED* is given, and since each of the parallaxes *DH* and *HG* is found when angle *CFE* is given, and since we previously demonstrated the angles and arcs of the great circle through the zenith with respect to given points on the ecliptic and thus we have only point *B* of the ecliptic given, it is clear that we are using arc *EB* instead of arc *ED*, and angle *CBE* instead of angle *CFE*.

Hipparchus tried to make this correction, and he appears to have attacked the problem in an ill-considered and illogical fashion. For, first, he used one distance *AD*, and not all or several distances as would have been consequent upon his desire to be exact in small things. Then, too, he failed to notice that he was falling into several absurdities. For after he himself has already demonstrated the arcs and angles considered with respect to the ecliptic, and had

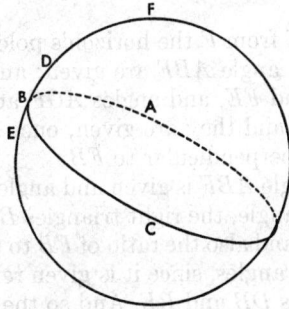

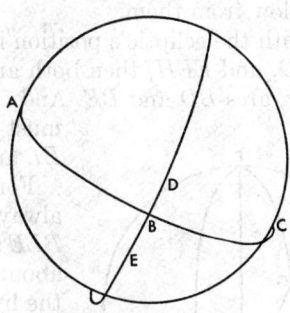

demonstrated that, when arc *ED* is given, arc *DG* is gotten (for he demonstrates this in Book I of his *Treatise on Parallaxes*), he uses arc *EF* and angle *EFC* as given for getting arc *ED*. Thus in Book II, after having calculated arc *FD*, he assumes the remainder *ED;* and he came to these conclusions because he did not notice that the point *B*, and not *F*, is given on the ecliptic; and therefore arc *EB* is given and not arc *EF*, and angle *EBC* is given and not *EFC*. Therefore, to make a partial correction, he had upset everything. For there is quite a sensible difference between arcs *ED* and *EF*, the latter being much less given than the former. But since actually *BE* is given, the difference with respect to *ED* will be at most only the magnitude of arc *BD* for each of the distances from the node.[1]

Now we can see what follows from the correction rightly made, in this way:

---

[1]For *BD* would always be less than *DF*, and *BE* in nearly all cases would differ from *DE* by less than *BD*.

Let there be the ecliptic ABC and the circle DBE at right angles to it. And let the moon, either at D or at E, be distant from the ecliptic ABC by a given arc, such as BD and BE, so that the arcs from the zenith to the ecliptic point B and the angles at B are given, and the arcs and angles with respect to D or E are sought.

If, then, the ecliptic has a position such that it is at right angles to the great circle drawn through the point B and the point F, which is to be taken at the horizon's pole (for example the great circle FB), then, clearly, it will coincide with arc DE, and the angle considered at D and E will be no different from that supposed at B. For they are right angles and therefore relative to the ecliptic. And arc FD will be less than arc FB by arc BD, and arc FE greater by arc BE, with arcs BD and BE given.

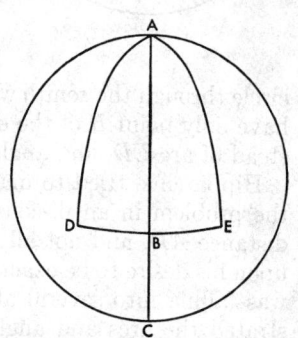

Furthermore, if the ecliptic ABC coincides with the great circle drawn through the zenith, and if (assuming A to be the horizon's pole) we join the arcs AD and AE, they will differ from arc AB, and the angles BAD and BAE will differ from the angle which in the former case did not exist. But arcs AD and AE are given, since they are as straight lines very nearly, from arcs AB, and BD and BE which are given. For the sums of their squares give the squares on AD and AE. And angles BAD and BAE follow from them.

But with the ecliptic's position inclined, if from F the horizon's pole we join FB, FGD, and FEH, then both arc FB and angle ABF are given; and again, certainly, arcs BD and BE. And arcs FD and FE, and angles AGF and AHF must be given; and they are given, once DK and EL are drawn perpendicular to FB.

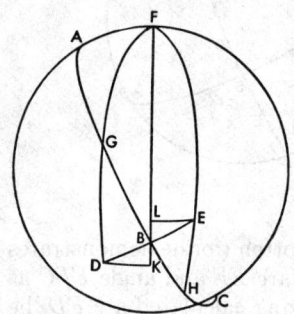

For, since angle ABF is given and angle ABE is always a right angle, the right triangles BKD and BLE are given and also the ratio of FB to the sides about the right angles, since it is given relative to the hypotenuses DB and BE. And so the hypotenuses FD and FE are given, and therefore also angles DFK and EFL which are the differences with the angles desired. For angle AGF is greater than angle ABF by angle DFB; and angle AHF is less than angle ABF by angle EFL.

It is clear that, with the same latitudinal distance supposed, the greatest difference between the angles occurs when the point B itself is the zenith. For with no angle at B, the arcs from the zenith to D and E make right angles with the ecliptic. The greatest difference between the arcs occurs when the position is the same; for again, with no arc at B, the arcs at D and E will be as great as those of the moon's latitudinal passage; and also when the great circle through the zenith is at right angles to the ecliptic. For, again, arcs FD and FE will differ from FB by the whole latitudinal passage. But in the other positions with DE inclined to FB, the differences of both the arcs and angles will come to less. Therefore, when the moon is distant 5° in latitude from the ecliptic, the greatest difference of the parallaxes will be very nearly 10 sixtieths, the 5° of the greatest difference in arcs making just this many sixtieths of parallax in the case of the greatest excesses and least distances. But when the moon is at its greatest distance in the solar eclipses and the latitudinal passage is very nearly 1½°, then the difference of parallax will be the same number of sixtieths, 1½, which rarely happens.

Now, the method for the correction of the angles and arcs (for those who wish it for such small ratios) would be available as follows: In general, doubling the number of the angles, we take it to the Table of Chords; and multiplying the numbers corresponding to it and to its supplement by the degrees of latitude, we write down $\frac{1}{120}$ of each.[1] And we subtract the resulting number for the first angle from the given arc from the zenith when the moon is on the same side of the ecliptic as the zenith; and we shall add when it is on the opposite side of the ecliptic. And squaring the result and adding to the square from the supplement, we shall have the arc required by taking the square root of this sum.

Then multiplying the numbers of the second or supplementary angle by 120, and dividing the results by the arcs just found, we take the halves of the arcs corresponding to these numbers in the Table of Chords and add them to the arcs of the original angle if the corrected arc is greater; and we subtract, if less. And thus we have the corrected angle.

As an example, let the arc FB of the last figure be supposed 45°, the angle ABF 30°, and each of the arcs DB and BE 5° in latitude.

Now, since a chord of 60ᵖ corresponds to double 30°, or 60°, and a chord of very nearly 104ᵖ to the supplement or 120°, therefore

$$BL : BE : : BK : DK : : 60 : 120$$

where

$$\text{hypt.} = 120.$$

Then, multiplying each of the numbers by the 5° of the hypotenuse and taking $\frac{1}{120}$ of the results, we have

$$\text{arc } BK = \text{arc } BL = 2°30',$$
$$\text{arc } DK = \text{arc } KL = 4°20'.$$

Then first we subtract the 2°30', if the moon is supposed at point E, from the 45° of arc FB because the moon's latitudinal distance is on the same side as the zenith—that is, because they are both either north or south of the ecliptic. And we have

$$\text{arc } FL = 42°30'.$$

And if the moon is at D, we add to it because of the contrary situation, and we have

$$\text{arc } FK = 47°30'.$$

Then, adding the square of FL to the square of LE, and the square of FK to the square of DK (that is, the square of 4°20' to the square of 42°30', and the square

---

[1]For in the last figure angle LEB equals angle AFB, angle LBE equals 90° less angle AFB. If we now conceive a circle about right triangle BLE, considering it to be rectilinear for the small arcs, we shall have the values of BL and LE in terms of the chords where BE equals 120. Let BL be s. But we know BE is so many degrees of arc, say n. Therefore, if x is the number of degrees of BL to be found,

$$x : n = s : 120.$$

Whence

$$120\,x = n \cdot s.$$

The same kind of calculation is used in the next paragraph.

of 4°20′ to the square of 47°30′) and taking the square roots of the results, we have

$$\text{arc } EF \doteqdot 42°46',$$
$$\text{arc } DF \doteqdot 47°44'.$$

Finally, multiplying 4°20′ by 120 and dividing separately by 42°46′ and by 47°44′, we have

$$\text{chord } EL \doteqdot 12^{\text{p}}8'$$

where

$$\text{hypt. } EF = 120^{\text{p}};$$

and

$$\text{chord } DK \doteqdot (10+\tfrac{1}{2}+\tfrac{1}{3})^{\text{p}}$$

where

$$\text{hypt. } DF = 120^{\text{p}}.$$

An arc of $11\tfrac{3}{5}°$ corresponds to the chord of $12^{\text{p}}8'$, and an arc of very nearly $10\tfrac{1}{3}°$ corresponds to the chord of $(10+\tfrac{1}{2}+\tfrac{1}{3})^{\text{p}}$. Taking the halves of these arcs, on the one hand we subtract the $5\tfrac{4}{5}°$ of angle EFL from the 30° of angle ABF, because arc EF is less than arc BF, and we have

$$\text{angle } AHF = 24\tfrac{1}{5}°.$$

On the other hand, if we add it to the same 30° because arc DF is greater than arc BF, we have

$$\text{angle } AGF = 35\tfrac{1}{6}°.$$

Which it was required to work out systematically.

BOOK SIX

1. On Conjunctions and Full Moons

THE treatment of the ecliptic syzygies of the sun and moon comes next in order, and this in turn is preceded by the examination of the conjunctions and full moons truly considered. For a first understanding of such things, we think that the periodic and irregular movements already demonstrated for each of the luminaries are sufficient. By means of these it is possible, for anyone sufficiently industrious, to determine their particular positions each time, and to calculate the places and times of the future syzygies—both those taken with respect to mean movements and the true ones with the anomaly. Nevertheless, to have them at hand systematically, we first set out the times and places of the periodic conjunctions and full moons, and the moon's anomalistic and latitudinal positions at the mid-eclipses. For by means of these last the correction for the true syzygies is effected, and from these the correction for the ecliptic syzygies. And we built tables of the following kind for such an examination.

2. Construction of the Tables of the Mean Syzygies

First, to establish the epochs of the months (like the other epochs, from the year 1 of Nabonassar), we took the surplus of the noon elongation, 70°37′, already demonstrated for the first of the Egyptians' Thoth, and we found 5 days 47′ 33″ of mean movement of elongation corresponding to it; so that by just so much time had the mean conjunction preceded noon of the first day of Thoth. And the next one, therefore, took place very nearly 23 days 44′ 17″ after that same midday—that is, 44′ 17″ of a day after noon of the 24th. But in 23 days 44′ 17″ the sun's mean movement is 23°23′ 50″, and the moon moves 310° 8′ 13″ of anomaly and 314° 2′ 21″ in latitude. Furthermore, at noon of the first of Thoth, the sun's mean position was 0° 45′ within the Fishes and, for greater facility, 265°15′ from its apogee, while the moon's position in anomaly was 268°49′ from the epicycle's apogee, and 354°15′ in latitude from the oblique circle's northern limit. Therefore, at the time of the mean conjunction after the first of the month, the sun and moon were both 288°38′50″ in mean movement from the sun's apogee—that is, 5°30′ within the Twins; and the moon was 218°57′15″ of anomaly from the apogee and 308°17′21″ in latitude from the northern limit.

Now, we shall first arrange a synodic table, again in 45 rows and 5 columns. For the first row we shall place, in the first column, the first year of Nabonassar; and, in the second column, the 24 days 44′17″ of Thoth since the extra sixtieths are from noon of the 24th. In the third column we shall place the 288°38′50″ of the mean position from the sun's apogee; in the fourth, the 218°57′15″ from the apogee of the lunar anomaly; and, in the fifth, the 308°17′21″ from the northern limit of latitude.

Since, moreover, in half a mean month's time there are contained very nearly

14 days 45′55″, 14°33′12″ of solar position, 192°54′30″ of lunar anomaly, and 195°20′6″ of latitude, we shall subtract these numbers from those of the conjunction first given; and we shall arrange the remainders in a second and similar table, which will be plenilunar, in the same way as before. And there are left 9 days 58′22″, 274°5′38″ from the sun's apogee, 26°2′45″ of anomaly from the moon's apogee, and 112°57′15″ in latitude from the northern limit.

And since, in 25 Egyptian years, whole months less $2^i47^{ii}5^{iii}$ of a day very nearly are completed, and the sun adds on in mean movement (once and above complete circles) $353°52^i34^{ii}13^{iii}$, and the moon $57°21^i44^{ii}1^{iii}$ of anomaly and $117°12^i49^{ii}54^{iii}$ in latitude, we shall increase the first columns of the two tables by successive additions of 25 years, the second columns we shall successively decrease by $0°2^i47^{ii}5^{iii}$, and of the rest we shall successively increase the third by $353°52^i34^{ii}13^{iii}$, the fourth by $57°21^i44^{ii}1^{iii}$, and the fifth by $117°12^i49^{ii}54^{iii}$.

Following these, we shall arrange a table by years in 24 rows and another by months in 12 rows, each of them with as many columns as the first tables. And, in the case of the table by months, for the first row, we place in the first column the first month; in the second column the 29 days $31^i50^{ii}8^{iii}20^{iv}$; in the third the total $29°6^i23^{ii}1^{iii}$ of the sun for that much time; in the fourth the $25°49^i0^{ii}8^{iii}$ of the moon's anomaly; and in the fifth the $30°40^i14^{ii}9^{iii}$ in latitude. And we successively increase these by these same numbers of the first row.

In the case of the table by years, for the first row, we place in the first column the first year; in the second the 18 days $53^i52^{ii}48^{iii}$ additional in 13 months; in the third the $18°22^i59^{ii}18^{iii}$ of the solar surplus for that much time; in the fourth the $335°37^i1^{ii}51^{iii}$ of lunar anomaly; and in the fifth the $38°43^i3^{ii}51^{iii}$ in latitude. With a view to setting out the first syzygy following upon the whole Egyptian years, we also successively increase at one time by the thirteen-month surplus already given, and at another by the twelve-month surplus which comes to 354 days $22^{ii}1^{ii}40^{iii}$, to $349°16^i36^{ii}16^{iii}$ in solar position, to $309°48^i1^{ii}42^{iii}$ in lunar anomaly, and to $8°2^i49^{ii}42^{iii}$ in latitude. Nevertheless it will suffice to take the tabulated numbers out to the second sixtieths. And here is the result reduced to tables:

3. TABLE OF CONJUNCTIONS

1 25-Year Periods	2 Days of Thoth			3 Degrees of Solar Position			4 Degrees of Lunar Anomaly			5 Degrees of Latitude		
				°	′	″	°	′	″	°	′	″
1	24	44	17	288	38	50	218	57	15	308	17	21
26	24	41	30	282	31	24	276	18	59	65	30	11
51	24	38	43	276	23	58	333	40	43	182	43	1
76	24	35	56	270	16	33	31	2	27	299	55	51
101	24	33	9	264	9	7	88	24	11	57	8	41
126	24	30	22	258	1	41	145	45	55	174	21	31
151	24	27	35	251	54	15	203	7	39	291	34	20
176	24	24	47	245	46	50	260	29	23	48	47	10
201	24	22	0	239	39	24	317	51	7	166	0	0
226	24	19	13	233	31	58	15	12	51	283	12	50
251	24	16	26	227	24	32	72	34	35	40	25	40
276	24	13	39	221	17	6	129	56	19	157	38	30
301	24	10	52	215	9	41	187	18	3	274	51	20
326	24	8	5	209	2	15	244	39	47	32	4	10
351	24	5	18	202	54	49	302	1	31	149	17	0
376	24	2	31	196	47	23	359	23	15	266	29	50
401	23	59	44	190	39	57	56	44	59	23	42	39
426	23	56	57	184	32	32	114	6	43	140	55	29
451	23	54	10	178	25	6	171	28	27	258	8	19
476	23	51	23	172	17	40	228	50	11	15	21	9
501	23	48	35	166	10	14	286	11	55	132	33	59
526	23	45	48	160	2	49	343	33	39	249	46	49
551	23	43	1	153	55	23	40	55	23	6	59	39
576	23	40	14	147	47	57	98	17	7	124	12	29
601	23	37	27	141	40	31	155	38	51	241	25	19
626	23	34	40	135	33	5	213	0	35	358	38	9
651	23	31	53	129	25	40	270	22	19	115	50	58
676	23	29	6	123	18	14	327	44	3	233	3	48
701	23	26	19	117	10	48	25	5	47	350	16	38
726	23	23	32	111	3	22	82	27	31	107	29	28
751	23	20	45	104	55	57	139	49	16	224	42	18
776	23	17	57	98	48	31	197	11	0	341	55	8
801	23	15	10	92	41	5	254	32	44	99	7	58
826	23	12	23	86	33	39	311	54	28	216	20	48
851	23	9	36	80	26	13	9	16	12	333	33	38
876	23	6	49	74	18	48	66	37	56	90	46	28
901	23	4	2	68	11	22	123	59	40	207	59	17
926	23	1	15	62	3	56	181	21	24	325	12	7
951	22	58	28	55	56	30	238	43	8	82	24	57
976	22	55	41	49	49	4	296	4	52	199	37	47
1001	22	52	54	43	41	39	353	26	36	316	50	37
1026	22	50	7	37	34	13	50	48	20	74	3	27
1051	22	47	20	31	26	47	108	10	4	191	16	17
1076	22	44	32	25	19	21	165	31	48	308	29	7
1101	22	41	45	19	11	56	222	53	32	65	41	57

TABLE OF FULL MOONS

1 25-Year Periods	2 Days of Thoth			3 Degrees of Solar Position			4 Degrees of Lunar Anomaly			5 Degrees of Latitude		
	°	′	″	°	′	″	°	′	″	°	′	″
1	9	58	22	274	5	38	26	2	45	112	57	15
26	9	55	35	267	58	12	83	24	29	230	10	5
51	9	52	48	261	50	46	140	46	13	347	22	55
76	9	50	1	255	43	21	198	7	57	104	35	45
101	9	47	14	249	35	55	255	29	41	221	48	35
126	9	44	27	243	28	29	312	51	25	339	1	25
151	9	41	40	237	21	3	10	13	9	96	14	14
176	9	38	52	231	13	38	67	34	53	213	27	4
201	9	36	5	225	6	12	124	56	37	330	39	54
226	9	33	18	218	58	46	182	18	21	87	52	44
251	9	30	31	212	51	20	239	40	5	205	5	34
276	9	27	44	206	43	54	297	1	49	322	18	24
301	9	24	57	200	36	29	354	23	33	79	31	14
326	9	22	10	194	29	3	51	45	17	196	44	4
351	9	19	23	188	21	37	109	7	1	313	56	54
376	9	16	36	182	14	11	166	28	45	71	9	44
401	9	13	49	176	6	45	223	50	29	188	22	33
426	9	11	2	169	59	20	281	12	13	305	35	23
451	9	8	15	163	51	54	338	33	57	62	48	13
476	9	5	27	157	44	28	35	55	41	180	1	3
501	9	2	40	151	37	2	93	17	25	297	13	53
526	8	59	53	145	29	37	150	39	9	54	26	43
551	8	57	6	139	22	11	208	0	53	171	39	33
576	8	54	19	133	14	45	265	22	37	288	52	23
601	8	51	32	127	7	19	322	44	21	46	5	13
626	8	48	45	120	59	53	20	6	5	163	18	3
651	8	45	58	114	52	28	77	27	49	280	30	52
676	8	43	11	108	45	2	134	49	33	37	43	42
701	8	40	24	102	37	36	192	11	17	154	56	32
726	8	37	37	96	30	10	249	33	1	272	9	22
751	8	34	50	90	22	45	306	54	45	29	22	12
776	8	32	2	84	15	19	4	16	29	146	35	2
801	8	29	15	78	7	53	61	38	14	263	47	52
826	8	26	28	72	0	27	118	59	58	21	0	42
851	8	23	41	65	53	1	176	21	42	138	13	32
876	8	20	54	59	45	36	233	43	26	255	26	22
901	8	18	7	53	38	10	291	5	10	12	39	11
926	8	15	20	47	30	44	348	26	54	129	52	1
951	8	12	33	41	23	18	45	48	38	247	4	51
976	8	9	46	35	15	52	103	10	22	4	17	41
1001	8	6	59	29	8	27	160	32	6	121	30	31
1026	8	4	12	23	1	1	217	53	50	238	43	21
1051	8	1	25	16	53	35	275	15	34	355	56	11
1076	7	58	37	10	46	9	332	37	18	113	9	1
1101	7	55	50	4	38	44	29	59	2	230	21	51

Yearly Surpluses at Conjunctions and Full moons

1 Single Years	2 Days			3 Degrees of Solar Position			4 Degrees of Lunar Anomaly			5 Degrees of Latitude		
				°	′	″	°	′	″	°	′	″
1	18	53	52	18	22	59	335	37	2	38	43	4
2	8	15	53	7	39	36	285	25	4	46	45	54
3	27	9	45	26	2	35	261	2	5	85	28	57
4	16	31	47	15	19	11	210	50	7	93	31	47
5	5	53	49	4	35	47	160	38	9	101	34	37
6	24	47	40	22	58	47	136	15	11	140	17	41
7	14	9	42	12	15	23	86	3	12	148	20	30
8	3	31	44	1	31	59	35	51	14	156	23	20
9	22	25	36	19	54	59	11	28	16	195	6	24
10	11	47	37	9	11	35	321	16	18	203	9	14
11	1	9	39	358	28	11	271	4	19	211	12	3
12	20	3	31	16	51	10	246	41	21	249	55	7
13	9	25	32	6	7	47	196	29	23	257	57	57
14	28	19	24	24	30	46	172	6	25	296	41	1
15	17	41	26	13	47	22	121	54	27	304	43	50
16	7	3	28	3	3	59	71	42	28	312	46	40
17	25	57	19	21	26	58	47	19	30	351	29	44
18	15	19	21	10	43	34	357	7	32	359	32	34
19	4	41	23	0	0	10	306	55	33	7	35	23
20	23	35	14	18	23	10	282	32	35	46	18	27
21	12	57	16	7	39	46	232	20	37	54	21	17
22	2	19	18	356	56	22	182	8	39	62	24	7
23	21	13	10	15	19	22	157	45	41	101	7	10
24	10	35	11	4	35	58	107	33	42	109	10	0

Mean Passages { Solar limits from 69°19′ to 101°22′ and from 258°38′ to 290°41′

Lunar limits from 74°48′ to 105°12′ and from 254°48′ to 285°12′

Months	Days			Solar Position			Lunar Anomaly			Latitude		
1	29	31	50	29	6	23	25	49	0	30	40	14
2	59	3	40	58	12	46	51	38	0	61	20	28
3	88	35	30	87	19	9	77	27	0	92	0	42
4	118	7	21	116	25	32	103	16	1	122	40	57
5	147	39	11	145	31	55	129	5	1	153	21	11
6	187	11	1	174	38	18	154	54	1	184	1	25
7	206	42	51	203	44	41	180	43	1	214	41	39
8	236	14	41	232	51	4	206	32	1	245	21	53
9	265	46	31	261	57	27	232	21	1	276	2	7
10	295	18	21	291	3	50	258	10	1	306	42	21
11	324	50	12	320	10	13	283	59	2	337	22	36
12	354	22	2	349	16	36	309	48	2	8	2	50

4. How to Locate the Periodic and True Syzygies

Now, whenever we wish to get the mean syzygies for some one of the required years, we calculate how far the supposed year is from the year 1 of Nabonassar. And looking to see which rows of either of the first two 25-year tables together with the third table's years contain that number of years, we add the corresponding numbers in each of the columns of the two rows: for the synodic syzygies those from the first table to those from the third, and, for the plenilunar syzygies, those from the second table to those from the third. From the sums in the second column we shall have the time of the syzygy from the beginning of that year: for instance, if they add up to 24 days 44', then 44 sixtieths of a day after midday of Thoth 24; and again, if they add up to 34 days 44', then the same sixtieths of a day after midday of Pleophi 4. From the third column we shall have the degrees from the sun's apogee; from the fourth, the degrees from the apogee of the moon's anomaly; and, from the fifth, the degrees from the northern limit of latitude.

Accordingly, we can readily calculate those that follow, whether we wish to get them all or some of them, through the proper sums in the fourth or monthly table, having changed the times, for greater facility, from the sixtieths of a day to equatorial hours. The resulting surplus of hours will be as of regular solar days, for the surplus taken seasonally is not always the same, but as of irregular solar days. And then we shall correct this by estimating the difference, subtracting it from the mean sum if the surplus of time for the irregular interval is greater, and adding it to it if it is less.

Now, once the synodic or plenilunar date considered with respect to mean passages has been gotten in this way along with the anomalies for each of the luminaries, it will be very easy to get the date and place of the true syzygy, and even the moon's latitudinal passage, from the combination of both anomalies. For in each case we examine the true passage of the sun, moon, and latitude at that periodic time by means of the addition-subtraction obtained. And if they are found to be at the same degree or directly opposite, we also have the time of the true syzygy; and if not, taking the degrees of the interval between them and adding to them a twelfth of them[1], we see in how many equatorial hours the moon will move that number of degrees. If the moon's true passage is less than the sun's, we add that number of hours to the periodic time; and if greater, we subtract it. And thus, if the moon's true passage at the periodic time is less than the sun's, we add the degrees of the interval between, together with the twelfth of them to the moon's true passage both in longitude and latitude; and if greater, we subtract them. In this way we shall have the time of the true syzygy and very nearly the moon's true passage on its oblique circles.

Now, the moon's hourly irregular movement at the syzygies is each time gotten in this way. Carrying the number of anomalistic degrees for the supposed date to the Table of the Moon's Anomaly, we take from the excess of the addition-subtractions lying opposite it the difference belonging to one degree of anom-

[1]That is, the number of degrees between them if the syzygy is synodic; between one of them and the point opposite the others, if the syzygy is plenilunar. Now while the moon moves along the ecliptic nearly 13°, the sun moves nearly 1°, or the moon moves thirteen times as fast. And while the moon moves that 1° the sun again 1/13°. Therefore, for all practical purposes, 1/13° is 1/12 of the original 13°. This approximation is even truer for the smaller numbers involved here. See Chapter 5.

aly. This difference we multiply by the hourly mean movement of anomaly which is $0°32^{i}40^{ii}0^{iii}$. If the anomalistic number is in the rows above the greatest addition-subtraction, we subtract this product from the hourly mean movement in longitude which is $0°32^{i}56^{ii}0^{iii}$; and if it is below, we add it. And we have, as a result, how much the moon moves irregularly in longitude in one equatorial hour at that particular time[1].

The time of the true syzygies for Alexandria will be gotten systematically by us in this way, because all the epochs have their hours established with respect to the meridian through Alexandria. And it is easy from the times in Alexandria to find the times which will result in any region for the same syzygy, given the number of hours of its distance from that meridian. For, if, from the difference of the localities, we consider the meridian through the place required, then, by as many degrees as it differs from that through Alexandria, by just so much time later will the appearance seem to be observed if the meridian through the place required is east of that through Alexandria; but by so much earlier if west of it, with fifteen time-degrees still making, of course, one equatorial hour.

5. On the Ecliptic Limits of the Sun and Moon

Now that these things have been worked out, the next job it to present those matters having to do with the ecliptic limits of the occultations of the sun and moon, so that, even if we do not choose to compute all the periodic syzygies but only those which can fall within the zone of ecliptic markings, we can have ready to hand a discrimination of this kind from the moon's mean latitudinal passage for each of the periodic syzygies.

Now, in the preceding Book, we have shown that the moon's diameter subtends at its greatest an arc of the great circle drawn about the ecliptic's centre equal to $0°31'20''$, calculating it to be such by two eclipses which occured at the apogee of its epicycle. Since we now wish to get the greatest limits of the ecliptic syzygies, and since these occur when the moon is about the perigee of its epicycle, we shall show by means of two eclipses observed near the perigee (for the proof of these things would be more certain by means of their appearances)

---

[1]This description of the method by Ptolemy is far from clear. Theo of Alexandria in his Commentary on Book V gives a better one as follows:

"For taking the anomalistic number . . . he carries it to the Table of the Moon's Simple Anomaly. And taking the difference of the numbers lying in a line with the nearest anomalistic numbers greater and less than it, he divides it by the difference of the common [i.e., anomalistic] numbers. For example, if the anomalistic number is 33°, taking the 2°19′ corresponding to 30° and the 2°44′ corresponding to 36°, he finds their difference which is 0°25′. And dividing this 0°25′ by the difference between 30° and 36° (that is, by 6) he gets 0°4′24″; and this is the difference belonging to one degree of the anomaly. And multiplying 0°4′24″ by the 0°32′40″ of the mean hourly movement of anomaly, we subtract the product from the hourly mean movement in longitude of 0°32′56″ if the given anomalistic number is in the rows above the greatest addition-subtraction—that is, from 1 to 96 and from 264 to 360. But if it is from 96 to 180 and from 180 to 264, or in the rows below the greatest addition-subtraction, we shall add it to the 0°32′ 56″.''

Theo of Alexandria goes on to give the reasoning behind this method. But it is clear from the method itself. One finds the average change along the ecliptic affected by a degree of anomaly for the section of the anomaly the moon happens to be at. This, being multiplied by the number of degrees of anomaly the moon moves in one hour, becomes the change produced along the ecliptic for an hour's movement in anomaly at that particular section of the epicycle. It can, of course, only be approximate. This hourly change is then added to or subtracted from, as the case may be, the moon's mean movement along the ecliptic.

how much of an arc the moon's diameter likewise intercepts at this point.

In the year 7 of Philometor then, (*i. e.*, the year 574 of Nabonassar, Egyptianwise Phamenoth 27-28 from the beginning of the eighth hour to the end of the tenth hour), in Alexandria the moon was eclipsed up to 7 digits from the north. Now, the middle occurred $2\frac{1}{2}$ seasonal hours after midnight (or $2\frac{1}{3}$ equatorial hours, because of the sun's true position's being 6°4′ within the Bull). And the time from the epoch to the middle of the eclipse comes to 573 Egyptian years, 206 days, and $14\frac{1}{3}$ equatorial hours simply considered but only 14 with respect to regular solar days. And for this much time the mean position of the moon's centre was 7°49′ within the Scorpion but its true position 6°16′; and its centre was 163°40′ from the epicycle's apogee and 98°20′ from the northern limit of the oblique circle. Therefore it is evident that, when the moon's centre, being near its least distance, is 8°20′ from the nodes along the oblique circle, and the shadow's centre is on the great circle drawn through the moon's centre at right angles to the oblique circle at which passage the greatest shadowings are effected, then $\frac{1}{2}+\frac{1}{12}$ of its diameter falls within the shadow.

Once again, in the year 37 of the Third Callippic Period (which is the year 607 of Nabonassar, Egyptianwise Tybi 2-3), the moon began to be eclipsed at the beginning of the fifth hour in Rhodes and was obscured at the most 3 digits from the south. Here once more the beginning of the eclipse occurred two seasonal hours before midnight, which were $2\frac{1}{3}$ equatorial hours both in Rhodes and in Alexandria because of the sun's true position's being 5°8′ within the Water Bearer, and the middle (when it was obscured the most) occurred very nearly $1+\frac{1}{2}+\frac{1}{3}$ equatorial hours before midnight. And here the time from the epoch to the middle of the eclipse adds up to 606 Egyptian years, 121 days, and $10\frac{1}{6}$ equatorial hours considered both simply and with respect to regular solar days. And for this much time the mean position of the moon's centre was 5°16′ within the Lion, but its true position 5°8′; and its centre was 178°46′ from the epicycle's apogee and 280°36′ from the northern limit on the oblique circle. It is therefore evident that, when the moon's centre, being near its same least distance, is 10°36′ from the nodes along the oblique circle, with the shadow's centre situated on the common section of the ecliptic, and the great circle drawn through the moon's centre at right angles to the oblique circle, then the fourth part of the moon's diameter will fall within the shadow.

But if the moon's centre is $8\frac{1}{3}°$ from the nodes along the oblique circle, it is $43\frac{1}{20}$ sixtieths of one degree [*i. e.*, 43′3″] from the ecliptic along the great circle drawn through the oblique circle's poles; and, when it is $10\frac{3}{5}°$ from the nodes along the oblique circle, it is $54+\frac{1}{2}+\frac{1}{3}$ sixtieths of one degree from the ecliptic along the great circle drawn through the oblique circle's poles. Now, since the difference between the two eclipses contains a third of the moon's diameter, and since the difference of the two distances of its centre along the same great circle from the same ecliptic point (that is, from the shadow's centre) is 0°11′47″, it is clear that the moon's whole diameter, at its least distance, subtends an arc of very nearly $35\frac{1}{3}$ sixtieths of one degree on the great circle drawn about the ecliptic's centre. And since also in the second of the eclipses (in which $\frac{1}{4}$ of the moon's diameter was eclipsed) the moon's centre was $54+\frac{1}{2}+\frac{1}{3}$ sixtieths from the shadow's centre, and $\frac{1}{4}$ of the moon's diameter or $8+\frac{1}{2}+\frac{1}{3}$ sixtieths from the point where the line joining their centres cuts the shadow's circumference, it is immediately evident that the shadow's radius at the moon's least distance is the remainder, 46 sixtieths. This is hardly greater than two and three-fifths times the moon's radius, which is 0°17⅔'. But the sun's radius likewise subtends an arc of 0°15'40" on the great circle drawn through the sun about the ecliptic's centre. For the sun and moon were shown to measure off equally on their circles in the syzygies at the greatest distance. Therefore, when the moon's apparent centre is 0°33'20" from the sun's centre on either side of the ecliptic, it will first be possible for the moon's apparent position to be one of tangency to the sun.

For example, if we conceive arc AB of the ecliptic and arc CD of the moon's

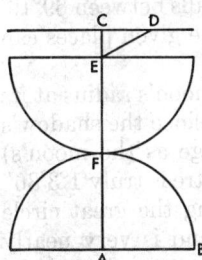

oblique circle as being sensibly parallel as far as the passages at eclipse times, and if we draw arc AEC of the great circle through the poles of the oblique circle, and conceive the sun's semicircle about point A and the moon's apparent semicircle about E so that it is just touching the sun's at point F, then arc AE, the distance of the moon's apparent centre E from the sun's centre A, can become the 0°33'20" just given.

But in the places from Meroë, where the longest day is 13 equatorial hours, to the mouth of the Borysthenes, where the longest day is 16 equatorial hours, the moon, at its least distance in the syzygies, displays a northward parallax of at most very nearly 0°8' (the sun's parallax being taken into account), and likewise a southward parallax of at most 0°58'. And when it displays its northward parallax of 0°8', it displays its greatest longitudinal parallax of very nearly 0°30' about the Lion and the Twins; but when it displays its greatest southward parallax, it displays its greatest longitudinal of very nearly 0°15' about the Scorpion and the Fishes.

Therefore—if we suppose the moon's true centre at D and we join the DE of the whole parallax—the arc CD will be very nearly the arc of the longitudinal parallax, and CE that of the latitudinal. And so, whenever the moon is north of the sun and displays its greatest southward parallax,

$$\text{arc } CD = 0°15',$$
$$\text{arc } AEC = 1°31'.$$

Since the ratio of the arc from the node to C to the arc AC at the distance between the ecliptic limit is that which 11½ has to 1 (this being easily understood from things already demonstrated on the obliquity of the lunar circle), the arc from the node to C will be 17°26', and added to CD it will be 17°41'. But when it is south of the sun and displays its greatest northward parallax,

$$\text{arc } CD = 0°30',$$
$$\text{arc } AEC = 0°41';$$

and for the same reasons the arc from the node to C will be 7°52', and added to CD it will be 8°22'. Therefore, whenever the moon's centre is truly 17°41' from either of the nodes northward along the oblique circle, first in the given places of the inhabited world can its apparent position become one of tangency to the sun.

Again, inasmuch as the greatest difference of solar anomaly was demonstrated to be 2°23', and the greatest difference of lunar anomaly about the syzygies 5°1', it is possible at times for the moon to be truly 7°24' from the sun at the periodic syzygies. But while the moon is traversing that many degrees, the sun will traverse ¹⁄₁₃ that many, or very nearly 0°34'; and again, while the moon moves these 0°34', the sun will traverse also ¹⁄₁₃ that many, or very nearly 0°3'; and

$\frac{1}{13}$ of this is not worthy of mention. If, therefore, we add to the 2°23′ of solar anomaly the total of 0°37′ which is $\frac{1}{12}$ of the original 7°24′, we shall then have the 3° by which the true syzygies differ very nearly the most from the mean longitudinal and latitudinal passages in the periodic syzygies. Consequently, whenever the mean passage of the moon's centre is 20°41′ from the nodes northward along the oblique circle and 11°22′ southward, then first, in the given places of the inhabited world, can its apparent position become one of tangency to the sun. Therefore, whenever the number of degrees from the northern limit of the moon's oblique circle corresponding to the periodic syzygies falls between 69°19′ and 101°22′ or between 258°38′ and 209°41′, then only in the given places can the proposed thing happen.

Yet again, respecting the moon's ecliptic limits: since the moon's radius at its least distance was shown to subtend an arc of 0°17′40″, and since the shadow's radius (being very nearly two and three fifths times as large as the moon's) comes to 45°56′, it is also clear that, whenever the moon's centre is truly 1°3′36″ from the shadow's centre on either side of the ecliptic along the great circle drawn through the centres and the oblique circle's poles, and is very nearly 12°12′ from either of the nodes along the moon's oblique circle (according to the ratio of 1 to 11½) then first can the moon be tangent to the shadow. For the same reasons as already demonstrated concerning the anomaly, whenever the moon's centre taken at the mean passage is 15°12′ from the nodes along the oblique circle—so that, for numbers indicating distance from the northern limit, it falls between 74°48′ and 105°12′ and between 254°48′ and 285°12′, then first can the moon be tangent to the shadow.

We shall now place beside the appointed tables of the syzygies the numbers belonging to the solar and lunar limits of the moon's latitude so that we can readily judge those capable of falling within an eclipse.

6. ON THE INTERVAL OF ECLIPTIC MONTHS

And to these things it would be useful to add how many months apart, in general, the ecliptic syzygies can occur, so that, if we take the position of one ecliptic syzygy, by an examination of the terms we may get not all the syzygies which follow but only those at month-intervals in which an eclipse can occur.

Now, it would be immediately clear that the sun and moon can be eclipsed at six-month intervals, since the moon's mean latitudinal passage comes to 184°1′25″ in six months, and since the arcs between the ecliptic limits, both for the sun and moon, embrace fewer degrees than this when they are within a semicircle and more when they are above a semicircle. For, as demonstrated, since the solar limits cut off 20°41′ from either of the nodes northward along the moon's oblique circle, and southward 11°22′, the northern anecliptic arc is 138°38′, and the southern is 157°16′. As the lunar limits cut off to either side of the ecliptic 15°12′ from the nodes along the same circle, each of the anecliptic arcs comes to 149°36′.

That by means of these hypotheses it is possible for an eclipse of the moon to occur at an interval of the greatest five months—that is, when the sun is making its greatest passage and the moon its least—we can see as follows:

Since in the mean five-month interval we find the longitudinal passage of each luminary adding on 145°32′ in terms of mean movement, and the moon 129°5′

of anomaly on the epicycle; since at its greatest passage either side of the perigee the sun's 145°32' add 4°38' to the mean passage; and since at its least passage either side of the apogee the 129°5' of the moon's epicycle, subtract 8°40'
from the mean passage, it follows that in the time of the mean five-month period,
whenever the sun effects its greatest and the moon its least passage, the moon
will be west of the sun by the combined anomalies of both: 13°18'. Again, taking
$\frac{1}{12}$ of this for reasons already demonstrated, we shall have very nearly the 1°6'
which the sun moves forward until it is overtaken by the moon.

Now, since it had added on 4°38' from its own anomaly and another 1°6' from
the time required for overtaking at the true syzygy, the greatest five-month interval will have added on 5°44' in longitude beyond the mean. Therefore the
moon's latitudinal passage along the oblique circle will have added on just that
many degrees to very nearly 153°21' in latitude resulting for the five-month
interval. And so the latitudinal passage, truly considered in the greatest five-
month interval, will come to 159°5'.

But the moon's ecliptic limits either side of the ecliptic circle, at the moon's
mean distance, embrace very nearly 1° on the great circle drawn through the
poles of the oblique circle, since at the least distance it is 1°3'36" and at the
greatest distance 0°56'24"; and they embrace 11°30' from the nodes along the
oblique circle. Therefore the anecliptic arc between them comes to 157°, which
for the greatest five-month interval is less by 2°5' than the additional 159°5'
of the oblique circle. Now, it is clear for these reasons that it is possible
for the moon, within the greatest five-month interval, to be eclipsed at the
first full moon in its withdrawal from either node, and to be eclipsed again
at the last full moon in its approach to the opposite node. For in both eclipses
the occultation occurs on the same side of the ecliptic, and never on opposite sides.

In this way we have seen how the greatest five-month period can produce two
lunar eclipses. And that it is impossible for the same thing to happen in a seven-
month interval even if we suppose the least seven-month interval (that is, during which the sun effects its least passage and the moon its greatest) we can see
by working in the same way as before.

For since, again, in the mean seven-month interval, the mean longitudinal
passage of both luminaries takes on an additional 203°45', that of the moon on
its epicycle 180°43'; since the sun's 103°45' at its least passage either side of the
apogee subtracts 4°42' from the mean movement; and since the 180°43' of the
moon's epicycle at its greatest passage either side of the perigee adds 9°58' to
the mean movement, it follows that in the time of a mean seven-month interval,
whenever the sun effects its least passage and the moon its greatest, the moon
will have passed the sun by the combined 14°40' of both anomalies. For the
same reasons, taking $\frac{1}{12}$ of this and adding it to the 4°42' of the subtractive
solar anomaly, we shall have all told very nearly 5°55' by which the longitudinal
passage in the least seven-month interval will lag behind that in the mean, and
just so will the latitudinal passage fail of the total 214°42' for the mean seven-
month interval. Therefore in the least seven-month interval the moon will have
added on 208°47' in latitude along the oblique circle, whereas the whole greatest
arc on the oblique circle between the moon's ecliptic limits at its mean distance,
from the approach to one of the nodes to the withdrawal from the opposite
node, is 203°. It is consequently not possible for the moon, in the least seven-

month interval, to be eclipsed ever so little at the first full moon and again at the last.

Then again it must be shown that it is possible for the sun to be eclipsed twice in the greatest five-month interval for the same people and in all parts of the world inhabited by us.

For we demonstrated the moon's latitudinal passage in the greatest five-month interval to be 159°5′ while the anecliptic arc for the sun, at the moon's mean distance, is 167°36′. For the ecliptic limits are 0°32′20″ from the ecliptic along the oblique circle. Therefore it is clear that, if the moon displays no parallax, the required result is impossible, because the anecliptic arc is greater than the passage in the greatest five-month interval by 8°31′ along the oblique circle, and by very nearly 0°45′ along the circle at right angles to the ecliptic, but that, wherever it can display a parallax such that the parallaxes in either of the extreme conjunctions or the parallaxes of both together exceed 0°45′, in such a place both of the extreme conjunctions can be ecliptic.

Now, since we showed that, in the time of the greatest five-month interval, whenever the moon effects its least passage and the sun effects its greatest from two-thirds within the Virgin to two-thirds within the Water Bearer, the moon falls west of the sun by the 13°18′ of both anomalies, and since the moon moves in mean terms this much and $\frac{1}{12}$ as much more in 1 day and $2\frac{1}{4}$ hours, it is clear that, while the time of the mean five-month interval is 147 days and very nearly $15+\frac{1}{2}+\frac{1}{4}$ hours, the time of the greatest five-month interval is 148 days and 18 hours. And, for this reason, if the first conjunction is nearly two-thirds within the Virgin, the last one nearly two-thirds within the Water Bearer will be earlier by the six hours lacking to fill out the whole days. Therefore one must seek where and when the moon can display a parallax of more than these 0°45′, either in one or the other of these two dodecatemories or in both, at a position 6 hours earlier in the Water Bearer than in the Virgin.

Now nowhere in the world inhabited by us is the moon found to display such a parallax northward, as we have said. Whence it is impossible for the sun to be twice eclipsed in the greatest five-month interval with the moon's passage south of the ecliptic—that is, whenever the moon at the first conjunction is withdrawing from the descending node and at the last conjunction is approaching the ascending node. But it can display just such a parallax southward, for those living below the equator northward, in both these dodecatemories at a position six hours earlier whenever two-thirds the Virgin is supposed setting at the first conjunction and two-thirds the Water Bearer is culminating at the second. For in such positions we find the moon, in its mean distance, displaying a southward parallax (the sun's parallax being accounted for) of very nearly 0°22′ at the equator when it is in the Virgin, and of 0°14′ when it is in the Water Bearer; but where the longest day is $12\frac{1}{2}$ hours, 0°27′ when it is in the Virgin, and 0°22′ when it is in the Water Bearer; so that in this case the two parallaxes together exceed the 0°45′ by 4 sixtieths. And since the southward parallax becomes greater for the still more northern places, therefore it is evident that it will be even more possible for the sun to appear twice eclipsed in the least five-month interval for those inhabiting these places, but only at the moon's passage north of the ecliptic—that is, when the moon in the first eclipse withdraws from the ascending node and, in the second, approaches the descending node.

Thus I say again that, also in the least seven-month interval, it is possible for the sun to be twice eclipsed for the same people. For in the least seven-month interval we demonstrated the moon's latitudinal passage to be 208°47′. And since the greatest arc of the oblique circle cut off between the ecliptic limits is that from the limit at the approach to one node to the limit at the withdrawal from the other, therefore, in the case of the sun this distance will come to 192°24′ at the moon's mean distance. Therefore it is clear that, if the moon displays no parallax, the required appearance will be impossible, because the oblique circle's arc of the least seven-month interval is greater than the greatest arc cut off by the sun's ecliptic limits which is 16°23′ along the oblique circle and 1°25′ along the circle drawn through the ecliptic's poles. But wherever it can display a parallax such that the parallaxes in either of the extreme conjunctions or both parallaxes together exceed this 1°25′, in such a place can both extreme conjunctions be ecliptic.

Now since we showed that, in the time of the mean seven-month interval, whenever the moon effects its greatest passage, and the sun its least passage from the last part of the Water Bearer to the middle of the Virgin, the moon has already truly passed the sun by 14°40′. Since the moon moves in mean terms just that many degrees together with $\frac{1}{12}$ of them in 1 day and 5 hours, therefore it is evident that, while the time of the mean seven-month interval embraces 206 days and very nearly 17 hours, the time of the least seven-month interval will be 205 days and 12 hours. For this reason the time of the last conjunction near the middle of the Virgin will be 12 hours later than the first near the end of the Water Bearer. Therefore one must seek where and when the moon can display a parallax of more than 1°25′, either in one or the other of the given dodecatemories or in both at positions 12 hours apart—that is, when the one is setting and the other is rising. For not otherwise could both eclipses occur above the earth.

Now again, in the world inhabited by us, the moon is nowhere found in any position displaying such a parallax northward; and even to those living under the equator a parallax of not more than the 23 sixtieths of the latitudinal parallax at the greatest distance. Whence it is impossible for the sun to be twice eclipsed in the least seven-month interval with the moon's passage south of the ecliptic; that is, whenever it approaches the ascending node at the first conjunction and withdraws from the descending node at the last. But we find such a parallax effected southward from around the parallel through Rhodes whenever the last of the Water Bearer is rising and the middle of the Virgin setting. For at its mean distance in Rhodes and in places under the same parallel, the moon displays in either position a southward parallax (the solar parallax being subtracted) up to very nearly 0°46′, so that the parallaxes at both conjunctions are together greater than the 1°25′. Now, since the southward parallax is even greater in those places north of this parallel, it is evident that, for those inhabiting these places, it is possible for an eclipse of the sun to appear twice in the least seven-month interval, but again only at the moon's passage north of the ecliptic—that is, when the moon in the first eclipse approaches the descending node and in the second withdraws from the ascending node.

It remains further to be shown, moreover, that at an interval of one month it is not possible for the sun to be twice eclipsed in the world inhabited by us, either in the same parallel or in different parallels, even if one supposes all to-

gether those things which cannot concur, but as combined to make the required
appearance possible; I mean, even if we suppose the moon at its least distance
so that it may display a parallax (the month the least so that the monthly latitudinal passage may be greater, by as little as possible) that is greater than that
embraced by the sun's ecliptic limits, using indifferently hours and dodecatemories in which it appears to make the greatest parallaxes.

Since, then, in the mean month the longitudinal passage of each of the luminaries takes on 29°6′ in mean terms, and the passage on the moon's epicycle
takes on 25°49′; and since of these the sun's 29°6′ at its least passage either side
of the apogee subtract 1°8′ from the mean, and the 25°49′ of the moon's epicycle
at its greatest passage either side of the perigee add 2°28′ to the mean—if, according to what has already been demonstrated, we combine the addition-subtractions of both anomalies which come to 3°36′ and add on a twelfth or 0°18′
to what the sun lacked, we shall have 1°26′. And by just this amount we shall
have the least month's passage less than the longitudinal and latitudinal in the
mean month. And so, since the mean month's latitudinal passage is 30°40′, the
least month's passage is 29°14′, which makes very nearly 2°33′ along the great
circle at right angles to the ecliptic. But the whole passage of the sun's ecliptic
limits comes to 1°6′ when the moon is at its least distance, so that the least
month's passage is greater by 1°27′.

Now, if the sun were to be twice eclipsed in one month, it would be absolutely
necessary, either that the moon display no parallax at one of the conjunctions
and one greater than 1°27′ at the other; or that it display parallaxes in the same
direction at both conjunctions with the difference between the parallaxes greater
than 1°27′; or that both parallaxes come to something greater when the parallax
at one conjunction is northward and at the other southward. But nowhere on
the earth in the syzygies—not even at its least distance—will the moon display
(the sun's parallax being accounted for) a parallax greater than one degree.
Therefore it is not possible in the least month for the sun to be twice eclipsed,
either when the moon displays no parallax at one of the conjunctions, or when
it displays one in the same direction at both, since their difference is never
greater than one degree although it needs to be greater than 1°27′.

The required appearance could happen only if the total number of degrees
from both parallaxes, one being in an opposite direction to the other, should
total more than 1°27′. And this is possible in different regions because the moon
can display, to those north of the equator in the regions inhabited by us, a
southward parallax, and to those south of the equator in what is called the
antichthones, a northward parallax of from 0°25′ to 1° beyond the sun's parallax. But this could never happen for the same region. Because the moon displays
in like manner a greatest parallax northward and southward of not more than
0°25′ for those under the equator; and to the most northern and most southern
not more than the stated 1° in the opposite directions, so that in this way both
parallaxes still total less than 1°27′. Inasmuch as each of the opposite parallaxes
would always be much less in the case of regions between the equator and one of
the limits, the impossibility would be even greater for them.

Nowhere on the earth for the same latitude, therefore, can the sun be twice
eclipsed in one month; and for different latitudes nowhere in the same inhabited
region. Which things we were required to show.

7. Construction of Ecliptic Tables

It has now become clear to us what intervals of syzygies we must take for a research into the eclipses. In order that, when the mean times at them have been distinguished and the moon's passages for those times calculated both in the case of the apparent conjunctive syzygies and in the case of the true plenilunar ones we might (by means of the moon's latitudinal positions) be able easily to review those of the syzygies certain to be ecliptic, their magnitudes, and the times of the obscurities, we constructed tables for so distinguishing them: two for solar eclipses and two for lunar ones, both at the moon's greatest and least distance, supposing the increase of the obscurations through twelve parts of the obscured diameter of each of the luminaries.

Now, the first table of the solar eclipses, which contains the ecliptic limits at the moon's greatest distance, we have arranged in 25 rows and 4 columns. The first two columns contain the moon's apparent latitudinal passage along the oblique circle for each of the obscurations. Since the sun's diameter is 0°31′20″, and the moon's was shown to be also 0°31′20″ at its greatest distance—and since, therefore, whenever the moon's apparent centre was 0°31′20″ from the sun's centre along the great circle through both centres, and 6° from the node along the oblique circle according to the ratio previously set out of 11½ to 1, then first will the moon be in a position of tangency to the sun, therefore, in the first rows of the columns we shall place 84° for the first, and 206° for the second; and, in the last rows, 96° for the first, and 264° for the second. And since very nearly 30 sixtieths of one degree along the oblique circle correspond to one-twelfth of the sun's diameter, we shall continually increase and decrease these two columns by just so much, beginning from the extremes and going to the middle. At the middle rows we shall put 90° and 270°. The third column will contain the magnitudes of the obscurations: in the case of the end rows, the corresponding zero of tangency; and in those following them one digit for each ¹⁄₁₂ of the diameter; and thus for the rest a continual increase of one digit to the middle row, to which the number of twelve digits will correspond. And the fourth column will contain the resulting passages of the moon's centre for each obscuration, without any calculations of the added movements of the sun or of the added parallaxes of the moon.

The second table of solar eclipses, which contains the ecliptic limits at the moon's least distance, we shall arrange as to other things like the first, but in 27 rows and 4 columns. Because the moon's radius at its least distance has been shown to be 17°40′ to the 15°40′ of the sun's radius; and whenever the moon first becomes tangent to the sun, then its apparent centre is 0°33′20″ from the sun's centre and 6°24′ from the nodes along the oblique circle. The numbers of apparent latitude in the end rows are 83°36′ and 206°24′ and again 96°24′ and 263°36′, and for the middle row of the digits, the number is twelve digits and, because of a like excess, four fifths of a digit for the delay of occultation.

Each of the two lunar tables is arranged in 45 rows and 5 columns, the first table being furnished with latitudinal numbers as of the moon at its greatest distance. For, since the moon's radius was shown to be 0°15′40″ at its greatest distance and the shadow's radius 0°40′44″ (so that, whenever the moon is first tangent to the shadow, its centre is 0°56′24″ from the shadow's centre along the great circle through both centres, and 1°48′ from the nodes along the oblique circle), therefore, in the first rows we shall place the numbers 79°12′ and 280°48′, and, in the last rows, the numbers 100°48′ and 259°12′. For the same reasons as the first we shall continually increase and decrease them by the 30 sixtieths corresponding to $\frac{1}{12}$ of the lunar diameter at that time.

The second table we shall furnish with latitudinal numbers as of the moon at its least distance, at which distance its radius was shown to be 0°17′40″ and the shadow's radius 0°45′56″ so that, whenever the moon first touches the shadow, then its centre is likewise 1°3′36″ from the shadow's centre and 12°12′ from the node along the oblique circle. Now, therefore, putting the numbers 77°48′ and 282°12′ in the first rows, and the numbers 202°12′ and 257°48′ in the last, we shall again continually increase and decrease them by the 34 sixtieths corresponding to $\frac{1}{12}$ of the lunar diameter at that time.

And they will contain third columns of digits like the solar tables; and likewise succeeding columns containing the moon's passages for each obscuration, those of immersion and those of emersion, and further those of half the delay of occultation.

We calculated geometrically for each obscuration the given passages of the moon. But we treated the proofs as if in one plane and in straight lines, because arcs of that magnitude differ insensibly from their chords, and the moon's passage along the oblique circle differs hardly at all from that considered along the ecliptic. Let no one suppose that we do not know that, in general, with respect to the moon's latitudinal passage, there is a difference in using the arcs of the oblique circle for those of the ecliptic; furthermore it does not follow that the times of the syzygies are exactly the same as the mid-eclipses.

For if we cut off from the node A two equal arcs AB and AC of the proposed circles, and, joining BC, draw BD from B at right angles to AC, then it will be immediately evident that, with the moon supposed at B, if we use arc AC of the ecliptic instead of the AD used because of considering the passages relative to it 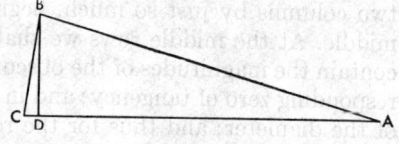 with respect to circles through the ecliptic's poles, then the difference due to the inclination of the lunar circle will be CD. Again, if the sun or the shadow's centre is conceived at B, the time of the syzygy, in accordance with the little difference between the circles, will be when the moon is at C; and the mid-eclipse will be when the moon is at D, because the mid-times of the obscurations are considered with respect to the circles through the poles of the lunar circle. And the time of the syzygy will differ from the mid-eclipse by arc CD.

The cause of our not calculating these arcs in detail is that their differences are small and insensible, and that (while not knowing this is absurd) yet, because of the difficulty in working out each case, this willing neglect of something which can be overlooked both in the hypotheses and the observations makes the greatest difference in the usefulness of a simple method, and no difference or very little in the discrepancy with appearances. Now, we find the arc similar to CD to be, in general, not greater than 5 sixtieths of one degree. This is proved by the same theorem as that by which we calculated the differences of the equatorial arcs with respect to those of the ecliptic for circles drawn through the equator's poles. But in the case of the eclipses we find it to be not greater than 2 sixtieths, since BD is almost 1° to the 12 ° of each of the arcs AB and AC. For the moon's passages at eclipses reach almost that far. Therefore arc AD is very nearly 11°58′, and that leaves CD equal to 2 sixtieths of a degree, which does not make one sixteenth of an equatorial hour. Concern over such a fractional degree is more vanity than love of truth.

Now, by these means, we also worked out the required passages of the moon's obscurations as if the circles differed insensibly. And our calculation for one or two examples is as follows:

Let there be the sun's or the shadow's centre A, and the straight line BCD in

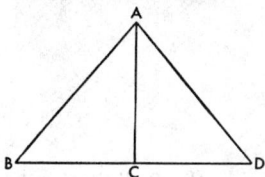

place of the lunar circle's arc. And let B be supposed the moon's centre when it first touches the sun or shadow as it approaches; and D as it withdraws. And with AB and AD joined, let AC be drawn from A perpendicular to BD.

Now, that the mid-time of the eclipse and the greatest obscuration occurs when the moon's centre is at C is evident from AB's being equal to AD; and, therefore, the passage BC's being equal to CD, and from AC's being less than all the lines joining the two centres to BD. It is clear also that either of the lines AB and AD contains both the radius of the moon and of the sun or shadow, and that line AC is less than either of them by that part of the diameter of the body being eclipsed which is cut off by the obscuration.

With these things so, let the obscuration be 3 digits as an example, and let A be first supposed the sun's centre. Now, therefore, when the moon is at its greatest distance,

$$AB = 31'20'',$$

and

$$\text{sq. } AB = 981'47''.$$

And

$$AC = 23'30'',$$

for it is less than AB by the 3 twelfths of the sun's diameter, or 7ᵖ50′. And

$$\text{sq. } AC = 552'15''.$$

And so

$$\text{sq. } BC = 429'32'',$$

and, in length,

$$BC = 20'43'',$$

which we shall place in the first table of the solar eclipses beside the 3 digits in the fourth column.

Again, in the case of the moon's least distance,

$$AB = 33'20'',$$

and

$$\text{sq. } AB = 1111'7'';$$

and

$$AC = 25'30'',$$

$$\text{sq. } AC = 650'15'';$$

and, by subtraction,

$$\text{sq. } BC = 460'52'',$$

and therefore, in length,

$$BC = 21'28''$$

which we shall place in the second table of the solar eclipses beside the 3 digits in the fourth column.

Yet again, let A be supposed the shadow's centre and the obscuration the

same ¼ of the moon's diameter. Therefore, for the moon's greatest distance,
$$AB = 56'24''$$
and
$$\text{sq. } AB = 3180'58''.$$
And
$$AC = 48'34'',$$
for it is less than AB by ¼ of the lunar diameter or, at the greatest distance, by 7'50''. And
$$\text{sq. } AC = 2358'43''.$$
And so, by subtraction,
$$\text{sq. } BC = 822'15'',$$
and, in length,
$$BC = 28'41'',$$
which we shall place in the first of the lunar tables beside the 3 digits in the fourth column and which contain the passage of immersion, sensibly the same as that of emersion.

And, in the case of the least distance,
$$AB = 63'36''$$
and
$$\text{sq. } AB = 4044'58''.$$
And
$$AC = 54'46'',$$
for the 8'50'' difference is again ¼ of the lunar diameter at the least distance. And
$$\text{sq. } AC = 2999'23''.$$
And so, by subtraction,
$$\text{sq. } BC = 1045'35'',$$
and, in length,
$$BC = 32'20'',$$
which we shall place likewise beside the 3 digits in the fourth column in the second of the lunar tables.

Once more, because the lunar obscurations have a time of delay, let the point A be the shadow's centre, and let the straight line $BCDEF$ be in place of the arc of the moon's oblique circle. Let B be supposed the point where the moon's centre will be when the moon, as approaching, first touches the shadow from without; and C where the moon's centre will be when the totally eclipsed moon will first touch the shadow's circle from within. And let E be the point where the moon's centre will be again when the moon, as withdrawing, first touches the shadow's circle from within; and F where the moon's centre will be when, taking its departure, it touches the shadow from without for the last time. And again let AD be drawn from A perpendicular to BF.

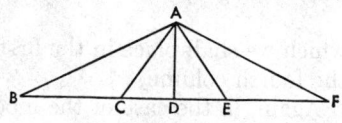

Now, given here those things already demonstrated as remaining true, it is also evident that either of the straight lines AC and AE bounds the difference by which the shadow's radius exceeds the moon's radius, so that the passage CD equals the passage DE, and each contains half the delay, and the remainder BC of immersion is equal to the remainder EF of emersion.

So let there be supposed an eclipse in which 15 digits of the moon are available

—that is, in which its centre D is within the bound of the ecliptic limits by one lunar diameter plus a fourth of it; in other words when AD is less than either AB or AF by the given one lunar diameter plus a fourth of it, and less than either AC or AE by a fourth of one lunar diameter.

Therefore, when the moon is at its greatest distance,
$$AB = 56'24''$$
and
$$\text{sq. } AB = 3180'58''.$$
And
$$AC = 25'4'',$$
for the moon's diameter at its greatest distance is $31'20''$. And
$$\text{sq. } AC = 628'20''.$$
And likewise
$$AD = 17'14''$$
and
$$\text{sq. } AD = 396'59''.$$
And so, by subtraction,
$$\text{sq. } BD = 2883'59''$$
and, in length,
$$BD = 53'42''.$$
And, by subtraction,
$$\text{sq. } CD = 331'21''$$
and, in length,
$$CD = 18'12'';$$
and, by subtraction,
$$BC = 35'30''.$$
Now we shall place these $35'30''$ of immersion, equal to those of emersion, beside the number of 15 digits, in the fourth column of the first table of lunar eclipses; and the $18'12''$ of the half-time of delay, in the fifth column.

When the moon is at its least distance, then again
$$AB = 63'36''$$
and
$$\text{sq. } AB = 4044'56''.$$
And
$$AC = 28'16'',$$
for the moon's diameter at the least distance was shown to be $35'20''$. And
$$\text{sq. } AC = 799'.$$
And likewise
$$AD = 19'26''$$
and
$$\text{sq. } AD = 377'39''.$$
And so also, by subtraction,
$$\text{sq. } BD = 3667'19''$$
and, in length,
$$BD = 60'34''.$$
And, by subtraction,
$$CD = 421'21''$$
and, in length,
$$CD = 20'32''.$$
And, by subtraction,
$$BC = 40'2''.$$

Therefore we shall also place these 40′2″ of immersion, again equal to those of emersion, beside the number of 15 digits, in the fourth column of the second table of lunar eclipses; and the 20′32″ of the half-time of delay in the fifth column.

But, for the moon's passages on its epicycle between the greatest and least distances, in order that we might easily obtain by the method of sixtieths the corresponding parts of the whole difference for each passage, we placed under the foregoing tables another short table containing the numbers of the passage on the epicycle and the corresponding sixtieths for each of the apparent excesses from the first and second tables of the eclipses. And the quantity of these sixtieths has been worked out by us and placed in the seventh column of the moon's Parallactic Table, for the epicycle is assumed to be at the eccentric's apogee throughout the syzygies.

Since most of those who observe the ecliptic markings do not measure the magnitudes of the obscurations by the circles' diameters but in general by the whole plane figures (the eye comparing in a rough way the whole apparent part with that not appearing), we have added to these also another short table of 12 rows and 3 columns. In the first column we placed the 12 digits, each digit containing $\frac{1}{12}$ of the diameter of each luminary as in the ecliptic tables; and in the next columns in turn the twelfths of the whole areas corresponding to them—in the second the sun's, in the third the moon's. These impositions we calculated only for the magnitudes of the moon's mean distance (for very nearly the same ratio is established for such increases and decreases of the diameters) and with the ratio of the circumferences to the diameters being as $3^p8′30″$ to 1^p. For this ratio is between (very nearly) a triple plus a seventh part and a triple plus ten seventy-firsts, both of which Archimedes used for greater simplicity.

Then first, for the solar eclipses, let there be the sun's circle $ABCD$ about centre E; and the moon's circle, as its mean distance, $AFCG$ about centre H cutting the sun's circle at points A and C. And with $BEHG$ joined, let it be supposed that $\frac{1}{4}$ of the sun's diameter has been eclipsed, so that
$$FD = 3^p$$
where
$$\text{diam. } BD = 12^p$$
and
$$\text{moon's diam. } FG \doteq 12^p20′$$
in the ratio of $15^p40′$ to $16^p40′$. And therefore
$$EH = 9^p10′,$$
With the perimeters in the ratio of 1^p to $3^p8′30″$, that of the sun's circle is $37^p42′$, and that of the moon's $38^p46′$. Likewise of the whole areas, since the radius multiplied by the perimeter gives twice the circle's area, that of the sun's circle will come to $113^p6′$, and that of the moon's to $119^p32′$.

Then, these things being so, it is required to find how great is the area contained by $ADCF$ where the whole area of the sun's circle is 12^p.

Let AE and AH, and CE and CH be joined, and further the perpendicular AKC.

Now, since it is supposed
$$AE = CE = 6^p,$$
$$AH = CH = 6^p10′$$

where
$$EH = 9^p10',$$
and the angle at K is right, therefore, if we apply the excess by which the square on AH exceeds the square on AE, or $2^p2'$, to the line EH, we shall have the difference between EK and HK of $13'3''$[1]. And
$$EK = 4^p28',$$
$$HK = 4^p42';$$
and therefore
$$AK = CK = 4^p.$$
And consequently we shall have
$$\text{trgl. } AEC = 17^p52',$$
and
$$\text{trgl. } AHC = 18^p48'.$$

Again, since
$$AC = 8^p$$
where
$$\text{diam. } BD = 12^p$$
and likewise
$$\text{diam. } FG = 12^p20',$$
and hence
$$AC = 80^p$$
where
$$\text{diam. } BD = 120^p,$$
and
$$AC = 77^p50'$$
where
$$\text{diam. } FG = 120^p,$$
therefore
$$\text{arc } ADC = 83°37'$$
where circle $ABCD$ is 360°, and
$$\text{arc } AFC = 80°52'$$
where circle $AFCG$ is 360°.

And so, since the ratio of circles to arcs is the same as the circles' areas to the areas of the sectors of the arcs, therefore
$$\text{sect. } AECD = 26^p16'$$
where it was shown
$$\text{circle } ABCD = 113^p6';$$
and
$$\text{sect. } AHCF = 26^p51'$$
for
$$\text{circle } AFCG = 119^p32'.$$
But it was shown also that
$$\text{trgl. } AEC = 17^p52'$$
and likewise
$$\text{trgl. } AHC = 18^p48'.$$
And therefore, by subtraction, we shall have
$$\text{seg. } ADCK = 8^p24',$$
$$\text{seg. } AFCK = 8^p3'.$$
And therefore the whole area contained by arcs AF, CD is $16^p27'$ where the area

[1]Application is here equivalent to division. The geometric proof of this statement is simple.

of circle $ABCD$ is supposed 113ᵖ6'. Thus, where the area of the sun's circle is 12, the area contained by the eclipsed segment is very nearly 1¾ which we shall place in the table just mentioned, along the 3-digits row, in the second column.

Again, in the same figure for the lunar eclipses, let $ABCD$ be supposed the moon's circle, and $AFCG$ the shadow's circle at mean distance. And likewise let there be an eclipse to ¼ of the moon's diameter so that, where diameter BD is 12ᵖ, diameter DF of the eclipse is 3ᵖ and diameter FG of the shadow is 31ᵖ12' according to the ratio of 1ᵖ to 2ᵖ36'. And therefore

$$EKH = 18ᵖ36'.$$

And therefore again, of the perimeters, that of the lunar circle is 37ᵖ42' and that of the shadow's 98ᵖ1'; and, of the areas, that of the lunar circle 113ᵖ6' and that of the shadow's 764ᵖ32'.

Now, since here it is supposed

$$AE = CE = 6ᵖ,$$
$$AH = CH = 15ᵖ36'$$

where

$$EH = 18ᵖ36',$$

therefore, if likewise we apply to EH the excess by which AH exceeds AE, we shall have

$$HK - EK = 11ᵖ8'.$$

And so

$$EK = 3ᵖ44',$$
$$HK = 14ᵖ52',$$

and therefore

$$AK = CK = 4ᵖ42'.$$

And consequently we shall have

$$\text{trgl. } AEC = 17ᵖ33'$$

and

$$\text{trgl. } AHC = 69ᵖ52'.$$

Again, since

$$AC = 9ᵖ24'$$

where

$$\text{diam. } BD = 12ᵖ$$

and likewise

$$\text{diam. } FG = 31ᵖ12',$$

and

$$AC = 94ᵖ$$

where

$$\text{diam. } BD = 120ᵖ,$$

and

$$AC = 36ᵖ9'$$

where

$$\text{diam. } FG = 120ᵖ,$$

therefore

$$\text{arc } ADC = 103°8'$$

where circle $ABCD$ is 360°, and

$$\text{arc } AFC = 35°4'$$

where circle $AFCG$ is 360°.

And so, by means of things already said, we shall have

$$\text{sect. } AECD = 32ᵖ24'$$

where it was shown

$$\text{circle } ABCD = 113^{\text{p}}6';$$

and

$$\text{sect. } ACHF = 74^{\text{p}}28'$$

for

$$\text{circle } AFCG = 764^{\text{p}}32'.$$

But it was shown also

$$\text{trgl. } AEC = 17^{\text{p}}33'$$

and likewise

$$\text{trgl. } AHC = 69^{\text{p}}52'.$$

And therefore, by subtraction, we shall have

$$\text{seg. } ADCK = 14^{\text{p}}51',$$
$$\text{seg. } AFCK = 4^{\text{p}}36'.$$

Consequently, the whole area contained by arcs AF, CD is $19^{\text{p}}27'$ where the area of circle $ABCD$ is supposed $113^{\text{p}}6'$. Where the area of the moon's circle is 12, therefore, that contained by the eclipsed segment will be very nearly $2\frac{1}{15}$, which we shall place in the same table, along the 3-digits row, in the third column belonging to the moon. And here is the exposition of the tables:

8. TABLE OF SOLAR ECLIPSES

At Greatest Distance					At Least Distance				
Numbers of Latitude			Digits	Fraction of Immersion	Numbers of Latitude			Digits	Fraction of Immersion
1		2	3	4	1		2	3	4
84	0	276	0	0	0 0	83	36	276	24	0	0 0
84	30	275	30	1	12 32	84	6	275	54	1	12 57
85	0	275	0	2	17 19	84	36	275	24	2	17 54
85	30	274	30	3	20 43	85	6	274	54	3	21 28
86	0	274	0	4	23 27	85	36	274	24	4	24 14
86	30	273	30	5	25 38	86	6	273	54	5	26 27
87	0	273	0	6	27 8	86	36	273	24	6	28 16
87	30	272	30	7	28 29	87	6	272	54	7	29 45
88	0	272	0	8	29 32	87	36	272	24	8	30 55
88	30	271	30	9	30 20	88	6	271	54	9	31 51
89	0	271	0	10	30 54	88	36	271	24	10	32 33
89	30	270	30	11	31 13	89	6	270	54	11	33 1
90	0	270	0	12	31 20	89	36	270	24	12	33 16
90	30	269	30	11	31 13	90	0	270	0	12	33 22
91	0	269	0	10	30 54	90	24	269	36	12	33 16
91	30	268	30	9	30 20	90	54	269	6	11	33 1
92	0	268	0	8	29 32	91	24	268	36	10	32 33
92	30	267	30	7	28 29	91	54	268	6	9	31 51
93	0	267	0	6	27 8	92	24	267	36	8	30 55
93	30	266	30	5	25 38	92	54	267	6	7	29 45
94	0	266	0	4	23 27	93	24	266	36	6	28 16
94	30	265	30	3	20 43	93	54	266	6	5	26 27
95	0	265	0	2	17 19	94	24	265	36	4	24 14
95	30	264	30	1	12 32	94	54	265	6	3	21 28
96	0	264	0	0	0 0	95	24	264	36	2	17 54
						95	54	264	6	1	12 57
						96	24	263	36	0	0 0

TABLE OF LUNAR ECLIPSES

At Greatest Distance									At Least Distance								
Numbers of Latitude				Dig-its	Fraction of Im-mersion		Half Delay		Numbers of Latitude				Dig-its	Fraction of Im-mersion		Half Delay	
1		2		3	4		5		1		2		3	4		5	
79	12	280	48	0	0	0			77	48	282	12	0	0	0		
79	42	280	18	1	16	59			78	22	281	38	1	19	9		
80	12	279	48	2	23	43			78	56	281	4	2	26	45		
80	42	279	18	3	28	41			79	30	280	30	3	32	20		
81	12	278	48	4	32	42			80	4	279	56	4	36	53		
81	42	278	18	5	36	6			80	38	279	22	5	40	42		
82	12	277	48	6	39	1			81	12	278	48	6	43	59		
82	42	277	18	7	41	34			81	46	278	14	7	46	53		
83	12	276	48	8	43	50			82	20	277	40	8	49	25		
83	42	276	18	9	45	48			82	54	277	6	9	51	40		
84	12	275	48	10	47	35			83	28	276	32	10	53	39		
84	42	275	18	11	49	9			84	2	275	58	11	55	25		
85	12	274	48	12	50	31			84	36	275	24	12	57	59		
85	42	274	18	13	40	35	11	9	85	10	274	50	13	45	47	12	34
86	12	273	48	14	37	28	15	20	85	44	274	16	14	42	15	17	17
86	42	273	18	15	35	30	18	12	86	18	273	42	15	40	2	20	32
87	12	272	48	16	34	6	20	22	86	52	273	8	16	38	28	22	58
87	42	272	18	17	33	7	22	0	87	26	272	34	17	37	20	24	49
88	12	271	48	18	32	23	23	14	88	0	272	0	18	36	37	26	1
88	42	271	18	19	31	51	24	8	88	34	271	26	19	35	55	27	13
89	12	270	48	20	31	32	24	43	89	8	270	52	20	35	34	27	42
89	42	270	18	21	31	22	23	1	89	42	270	18	21	35	22	28	12
90	0	270	0	Complete	31	20	23	4	90	0	270	0	Complete	35	20	28	6
90	18	269	42	21	31	22	23	1	90	18	269	42	21	35	22	28	12
90	48	269	12	20	31	32	24	43	90	52	269	8	20	35	34	27	42
91	18	268	42	19	31	51	24	8	91	26	268	34	19	35	55	27	13
91	48	268	12	18	32	23	23	14	92	0	268	0	18	36	37	26	1
92	18	267	42	17	33	7	22	0	92	34	267	26	17	37	20	24	49
92	48	267	12	16	34	6	20	22	93	8	266	52	16	38	28	22	58
93	18	266	42	15	35	30	18	12	93	42	266	18	15	40	2	20	32
93	48	266	12	14	37	28	15	20	94	16	265	44	14	42	15	17	17
94	18	265	42	13	40	35	11	9	94	50	265	10	13	45	47	12	34
94	48	265	12	12	50	31			95	24	264	36	12	57	59		
95	18	264	42	11	49	9			95	58	264	2	11	55	25		
95	48	264	12	10	47	35			96	32	263	28	10	53	39		
96	18	263	42	9	45	48			97	6	262	54	9	51	40		
96	48	263	12	8	43	50			97	40	262	20	8	49	25		
97	18	262	42	7	41	34			98	14	261	46	7	46	53		
97	48	262	12	6	39	1			98	48	261	12	6	43	59		
98	18	261	42	5	36	6			99	22	260	38	5	40	42		
98	48	261	12	4	32	42			99	56	260	4	4	36	53		
99	18	260	42	3	28	41			100	30	259	30	3	32	20		
99	48	260	12	2	23	43			101	4	258	56	2	26	45		
100	18	259	42	1	16	59			101	38	258	22	1	19	9		
100	48	259	12	0	0	0			102	12	257	48	0	0	0		

	TABLE OF CORRECTION				TABLE OF SUN'S AND MOON'S MAGNITUDE	
Numbers of Anomaly 1	*Numbers of Anomaly* 2	*Sixtieths of Differences* 3		*Digits*	*Digits of Sun*	*Digits of Moon*
6	354	0	21	1	0⅓	0½
12	348	0	42	2	1	1⅙
18	342	1	42	3	1¾	2¹⁄₁₅
24	336	2	42	4	2⅔	3⅙
30	330	4	1	5	3⅔	4⅓
36	324	5	21	6	4⅔	5½
42	318	7	18	7	5⅚	6¾
48	312	9	15	8	7	8
54	306	11	37	9	8⅓	9⅙
60	300	14	0	10	9⅔	10⅓
66	294	16	48	11	10⅚	11⅓
72	288	19	36	12	12	12
78	282	22	36			
84	276	25	36			
90	270	28	42			
96	264	31	48			
102	258	34	54			
108	252	38	0			
114	246	41	0			
120	240	44	0			
126	234	46	45			
132	228	49	30			
138	222	51	39			
144	216	53	48			
150	210	55	32			
156	204	57	15			
162	198	58	18			
168	192	59	21			
174	186	59	41			
180	180	60	0			

9. DETERMINATION OF LUNAR ECLIPSES

Now, with these things set out beforehand, we shall study the lunar eclipses in this way. For we set out the resulting number of degrees of the required full moon for the hour of the mid-syzygy in Alexandria, both the number of degrees from the so-called anomalistic epicycle's apogee and the number of degrees in latitude from the northern limit after determination of the addition-subtraction. We first carry the latitudinal number to the Tables of Lunar Eclipses, and, if it falls in the numbers of the first two columns, we take down separately each of those lying in the row with the latitudinal number in either table, both those in the columns of passages and those in the columns of digits. Then we carry the anomalistic number to the Table of Correction. And as many sixtieths as lie in the same row with it, just so many do we take of the difference between the digits and sixtieths taken down for either table, and we add this to the numbers gotten from the first Table. If it happens that the latitudinal number falls only in the second Table, we set out that number of sixtieths of the digits and fractions lying in a row with them.[1]

Whatever number of digits we get from this correction, we say the obscuration of the moon's diameter at mid-eclipse embraces just so many twelfths. And to the resulting sixtieths in the same correction we always add $\frac{1}{12}$ of them for the sun's added movement. Dividing them by the moon's hourly irregular movement at that time, to whatever the division comes, just so many equatorial hours shall we have for each passage-time of the eclipse: those calculated from the fourth table giving separately the time of immersion and the time of emersion, those from the fifth the time of half the delay of occultation. The hour-positions at the beginnings and ends of incidence and restoration are immediately evident from the addition-subtraction of particular passages with respect to the middle of the delay—that is, very nearly the time of the true full moon. And immediately, if we carry the twelfths of the diameter to the shortest table, we shall also find the twelfths of the whole areas of the moon from the corresponding numbers in the third column, and likewise those of the sun's in the second column.

Now, reason proves that the time from the beginning of the eclipse to the middle is not always equal to the time from the middle to the end, because of the irregularity of the sun and moon. Equal passages are effected for that reason in unequal times. But supposing these times not unequal would work no discrepancy perceptible to sense in the appearances. For even if they were near the mean courses where the differences of the increases are greater, a passage for the number of hours of a whole eclipse would make the difference of the excess in no way sensible.

But we would think that probably we find the moon's latitudinal period shown by Hipparchus to be mistaken, since, by his hypothesis, the surplus is less than the surplus between the given eclipses but greater taken according to our calculations, although we start from the same things.

For he takes for this demonstration two lunar eclipses which occurred at an interval of 7,160 months, in both of which the quarter of the moon's diameter was eclipsed at the same passage from the ascending node: the first having been observed in the year 2 of Mardokempad, and the second in the year 37 of the Third Callippic Period. Hipparchus avails himself of the same latitudinal passage's being contained consistently in either eclipse with respect to the demonstration of return, because of the fact that the first eclipse occurred with the moon at the epicycle's apogee and the second with it at the perigee, and therefore of no anomalistic difference's having resulted as he thought. But he is mistaken first to this extent that, since an appreciable difference results from the irregularity, the regular passage is found greater than the true by an amount not

[1]The obscurity here is cleared up by Theo's *Commentary*. If the latitudinal number falls only in the second Table, we carry the anomalistic number to the Table of Correction as before; but we take the number of sixtieths, not of the difference which does not exist in this second case, but of the digits and fraction of immersion found in the second Table. In the first case, we added the result to the digits and fraction of the first Table; here we simply take that fraction of the second Table's numbers. This method is valid here because, for a latitudinal number to fall only in the second Table, the anomalistic number must lie between 150 and 210. The corresponding fraction for such numbers must lie between 55/60 and 1. Then if we let a represent the digits or immersion at the least distance and b those at the greatest, by the first method we should have $55/60 \, (a - b) + b$ or $55/60 \, a + 5/60 \, b$; and by the second method $55/60a$. But b does not exist, therefore the two methods give the same result.

equal in the two eclipses. But in the first it is by very nearly 1° and in the second
⅛°, so that according to this the latitudinal period lacks ⅞° of whole returns
where the moon's oblique circle is 360°.

Next he did not calculate the difference occurring in the magnitudes of the
obscurations because of the moon's distances. And the greatest possible of these
differences occurred in the case of these eclipses because the first took place with
the moon at its greatest distance, and the second with it at its least. For necessarily the obscuration of the same quarter part followed at a less distance from
the ascending node at the first eclipse and at a greater at the second. We demonstrated that the difference between them amounts to 1⅕° [Tables of Lunar
Eclipses], so that in this case the latitudinal period added just that much to
complete returns. Now the periodic return in latitude would have erred by the
approximately 2° of both mistakes together if both had happened to involve a
difference towards the greater or towards the less. But since, by happy chance,
the one makes the return fail of completion and the other makes it exceed, the
result obtained appeared greater than the return by only the ⅓° of the excess
of one error over the other.

10. Determination of Solar Eclipses

Now, the study of lunar eclipses would proceed soundly, therefore, only in the
ways we have described, with the calculations made accurate. But next we shall
make a determination of the solar eclipses—a much harder thing to do because
of the moon's parallaxes.

First we look up the time of the true conjunction in Alexandria to see how
many equatorial hours before or after midday it occurred. Then, if the supposed
longitude of the required region is different—that is, if its meridian is not the
same as that through Alexandria—we add or subtract the longitudinal difference in equatorial hours between the two meridians. And since we know how
many equatorial hours before or after this the time of the true conjunction fell,
we determine first the time of the apparent conjunction for the required longitude, which will be very nearly the same as the middle of the eclipse, by the
method of parallaxes already explained. For we take out of the Table of Angles
and the Table of Parallaxes its parallax first along the great circle drawn through
the zenith and the moon's centre and proper to the latitude, to the hour-interval
from the meridian, and further to the conjunctive part of the ecliptic, and in
addition to the moon's distance. Always subtracting from this the sun's parallax
lying in the same row, we determine within the remainder, as we have shown,
by means of the angle obtained at the intersection of the ecliptic and the great
circle through the zenith, the parallax computed with respect to the longitudinal
passage alone. And we always add to this the difference of added parallax corresponding to the equatorial time embraced by the first, that is of the excess,
obtained in the same table, between the two parallaxes—one corresponding to
the first interval of the zenith, and the other to the interval with the addition of
the equatorial time, again using only the parts belonging to the longitudinal
parallax alone, together with as great a part of them (if it is sensible) as they are
of the first parallax.[1] And to the degrees of the whole longitudinal parallax thus

[1]First the moon's longitudinal parallax at the true conjunction is computed. The problem
is to find the length of time to the apparent conjunction. The moon must move the distance
of this parallax plus the difference between this parallax and the different parallax it will have

combined we shall again add $\frac{1}{12}$ of them for the sun's movement, and we shall reduce the result to equatorial hours by dividing by the degrees of the moon's irregular hourly courses about the conjunction (for we have shown above how we obtain this determination). If the longitudinal parallax is eastward, we subtract the degrees we reduced to equatorial hours from the moon's degrees already determined separately for longitude, latitude, and anomaly at the true time of the conjunction, and we shall have the moon's true passages at the time of the apparent conjunction. And we shall have found the number of hours by which the apparent conjunction precedes the true. But if the longitudinal parallax is found to be westward, we shall then add the degrees to the passages already determined separately for longitude, latitude, and anomaly at the true time of the conjunction; and we shall have the hours by which the apparent conjunction will follow the true.

Now again, by the same methods, we look to see first how great a parallax the moon displays along the great circle drawn through itself and the zenith, at the apparent conjunction's interval of equatorial hours from the meridian. And subtracting from the number of degrees found the sun's parallax lying in the row with that same number, we determine within the remainder (likewise by means of the angle found for that time at the intersection of the circles) the latitudinal parallax lying along the circle at right angles to the ecliptic. The resulting number of degrees we change to the corresponding number along the oblique circle—that is, we multiply them by 12. And if the latitudinal parallax is effected to the north of the ecliptic, we shall add the product to the latitudinal passage already determined for the time of the apparent conjunction, when the moon is about the ascending node; but we subtract it likewise when it is about the descending node. And if the latitudinal parallax is effected to the south of the ecliptic, contrariwise we subtract the degrees resulting from the parallax from the degrees in latitude already determined at the time of the apparent conjunction, when the moon is about the ascending node; but we likewise add when it is about the descending node. Thus we shall have the number of apparent latitude at the time of the apparent conjunction. And carrying this to the Tables of Solar Eclipses, if it falls in the numbers of the first two columns, we shall say there will be an eclipse of the sun, whose mid-time very nearly coincides with the apparent conjunction. Now we set out the quantity of digits lying in the row with that number of apparent latitude, and also the degrees of immersion and emersion separately from each table. And we carry the number representing the degrees from the apogee of lunar anomaly to the Table of Correction. And taking as many sixtieths of each excess noted down as lie in the row with this number, we always add that much to the numbers taken from the first Table. By this correction we shall have the resulting digits, and in turn for that many twelfths of the sun's diameter there will be an obscuration, at very nearly the mid-eclipse. Again, adding to the degrees of each passage $\frac{1}{12}$ of them for the sun's movement, and changing this sum into equatorial hours by means of the moon's irregular movement, we shall have just so much time for immersion and emersion each, supposing no difference occurs for that time because of the parallaxes.

But since there is a sensible inequality about these times, because of the

_____

when it has moved the first parallax; and so on in an unending series. The approximation is good enough after the first or second time. To this, of course, must be added also the movement of the sun during this time.

moon's parallaxes and not because of the luminaries' irregularity, according to which both the immersions and emersions predicted turn out to be greater and in general unequal to each other, we shall not know this, even if it happens to be small. Now this circumstance arises from there always being in the moon's apparent passage certain regressive appearances due to the parallaxes, as if it were not shifted by its proper movement forward to the east. For if it appears to be passing before the meridian, rising little by little and displaying a continually shorter parallax eastward, it appears to move more slowly forward to the east. And if it be passing beyond the meridian, descending now little by little and displaying a continually longer parallax westward, likewise it will again appear to move more slowly forward to the east. Now, because of this, the aforesaid times will always be greater than those taken simply. And since the difference in the excesses of the parallaxes is always greater in the passages nearer the meridian, the times of the eclipses near the meridian are fulfilled more slowly. For this reason, whenever the mid-eclipse falls at midday, then only is the time of immersion very nearly equal to that of emersion, since the regressive appearance due to the parallaxes happens then to be very nearly equal on either side. But, when it precedes midday, then the time of emersion being nearer the meridian becomes greater; and when it follows midday, then the time of immersion being nearer the meridian becomes greater.

Now, in order to make this correction of the times, we shall look, in the way we demonstrated, for the time worked out before this correction for each of the passages set out, and for the distance from the zenith at the mid-eclipse.

For example, let either time be one equatorial hour and the distance from the zenith 75°. Now we shall look in the Parallactic Table for the sixtieths of parallax corresponding to the number of 75°, with the moon, for instance, at its greatest distance, at which distance those in the third column are taken. And we find 52 sixtieths corresponding to 75°. Since both the time of immersion and the time of emersion are supposed one equatorial hour considered in mean terms, or 15° in time, therefore subtracting these from the 75° of the distance, we find, in the same column, 47 sixtieths of parallax corresponding to the remaining 60°, so that at the mid-passage near the meridian there results from the parallax a regression of 5 sixtieths. Now adding these to the 75° we find in the same column, corresponding to the sum of 90°, the 53½ sixtieths of the whole parallax, so that here the regression of the passage near the horizon comes to 1½ sixtieths. Now taking from these differences the correspondences in longitude, and reducing each in turn to a part of an equatorial hour by means of the moon's irregular movement, as shown, we shall add the result from each, properly to each of the times taken in mean and simple terms, the greater to the time at the passage nearer the meridian and the less to the time at the passage nearer the horizon. And it is clear that the difference of these times was 3½ sixtieths or very nearly ⅑ of one equatorial hour, for the moon will move just that many sixtieths of mean movement in that much time. There is then left the easy task, if we wish, of reducing the equatorial hours for each interval to the particular seasonal hours in the way we have already shown above.

11. On the Directions in the Eclipses

The examination of the directions of the obscurations comes next. And this study is established both from the direction of the obscurations with respect to the ecliptic, and from the inclination of the ecliptic to the horizon. Either of these in each of the ecliptic times would suffer the greatest indefinite variation at the shifts if one wished to work out the inclinations which would take place during the whole time; but such prediction is neither necessary nor useful. For the ecliptic's configuration relative to the horizon is considered from the position of its rising and setting points at the horizon; and necessarily throughout the time of the eclipse, as different parts of the ecliptic become continuously rising and setting, the sections of the horizon bounded by them become continuously different. Likewise the inclination of the obscurations relative to the ecliptic is considered along the great circle drawn through both centres, the moon's and the sun's or shadow's; and again necessarily, throughout the passage of the moon's centre at the time of the eclipse, the circle drawn through both centres also takes a position continuously other relative to the ecliptic and makes the angles contained by their intersection continuously unequal.

Now, since this examination will be sufficient if it is taken for only the obscurations having some significance and more generally for the arcs considered relative to the horizon, it will be possible for those appraising the situation with their eyes to estimate immediately the particular directions by attending to both inclinations. For, as we said, in these matters a general judgment is sufficient. Yet, not to pass over this subject entirely, we shall try to expound ways as easy as possible for getting at this.

Of the obscurations, we have chosen as significant markings that of the first part eclipsed, which occurs at the beginning of the whole time of eclipse; that of the last part eclipsed, which occurs at the beginning of the time of delay; that of the greatest part eclipsed, which occurs at the mid-eclipse without the delay; that of the first part restored, which occurs at the end of the whole time of delay; and that of the last part restored which occurs at the end of the whole time of eclipse. And of the directions we have chosen again, as the more reasonable and expressible, those defined by the meridian and by the risings and settings of the ecliptic's equinoxial and tropic points. For the principle of directions could be differently understood by many people at many times, and could, if one wished, be designated by the given angles of the horizon. Now of the intersections of the meridian with the horizon, let us understand by ἄρκτοι the northern, and by μεσημβρίος the southern; and of the rising and setting intersections, let us understand by equatorial rising and setting those intersections made with the horizon by the beginning of the Ram and of the Balance and which are always an equal quadrant from those produced at the meridian; by summer rising and setting, those made by the beginning of the Crab; and, by winter rising and setting, those made by the beginning of the Goat. These intervals are different according to latitude, and the determination of the directions is sufficient when they have been shown to be either at or between these limits.

Therefore, to have every configuration of the ecliptic with the horizon, we calculated (in the first part of the Composition as already shown) the intervals produced on the horizon at risings and settings by the beginning of each one of the dodecatemories either side of the intersections produced by the equator and for each latitude from the Borysthenes to Meroë for which we laid out the angles. And, for an easy understanding, we have drawn, instead of a table, 8 concentric circles conceived in the horizon's plane and containing the intervals and names of the 7 latitudes. Then, drawing two straight lines through all the circles at right angles to each other—the horizontal one as the common section of the planes of the horizon and equator, and the vertical one as the common section of the planes of the horizon and meridian—we have designated the extremities of the horizontal line at the outside circles as equatorial rising and equatorial setting; and of the vertical line as north and south. Likewise we have drawn straight lines at equal intervals on either side of the equatorial line and again through all the circles, and we have placed on the lines within the seven intervals the distances, found for each latitude, of the tropic points from the equator along the horizon, a quadrant being 90°. On those at the inner extremities of the circles we have placed, to the south, winter rising and winter setting; and to the north, summer rising and summer setting. For the intervening dodecatemories (further inserting, within each of the four intervals, two other lines) we have placed on these also the distances along the horizon from the equator for the particular dodecatemories, with the name of each written at the outside circle. And about the meridian line we have indicated the names of the parallels, the hourly magnitudes, and the heights of the pole, making the list in order of northerliness from the greater and encompassing circle.

In order that we may also have set out the apparent directions of the obscurations with respect to the ecliptic (that is, the angles produced at each of the aforesaid markings by the intersection of the ecliptic and the great circle through both the centres indicated), we calculated them for each of the moon's passages for differences of 1 digit of obscuration, and only for those at the mean distance as being sufficient. And it is supposed the arcs of the ecliptic and of the moon's oblique circle are sensibly parallel in the obscurations.

For, again as an example, let there be the straight line AB in place of the

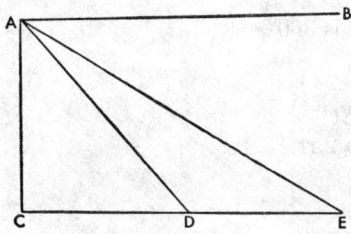

ecliptic's arc, and on it let A be supposed the centre of the sun or shadow. And let there be the straight line CDE in place of the arc of the moon's oblique circle. And let C be the point where the moon's centre lies at mid-eclipse; D the point where again its centre will be when the whole moon is first eclipsed or first begins to be restored (that is, when it touches the shadow's circle from within); and E the point where its centre lies when either the sun or moon first begins to be eclipsed or finishes being restored—that is, when the circles touch each other from without. And let AC, AD, and AE be joined.

Now, it is evident that the angles BAC and ACE embracing the mid-eclipses are sensibly right, that angle BAE contains that at the first part eclipsed and the last part restored, and that angle BAD contains that at the last part eclipsed and the first part restored. It is also immediately clear that the line AE embraces the radii of both circles, and AD their difference.

Now as an example, let the eclipse be supposed one in which at the middle the half of the sun's diameter will be obscured. And let A be the sun's centre, so that, by supposing the moon at its mean distance,
$$AE = 32^\mathrm{p}20';$$
and, since it is less by half the sun's diameter,
$$AC = 16^\mathrm{p}40'.$$

Since, then, according to the given magnitude of the obscuration,
$$AC = 16^p40'$$
where
$$\text{hypt. } AE = 32^p20',$$
therefore
$$AC = 61^p51'$$
where
$$\text{hypt. } AE = 120^p;$$
and, where the circle about right triangle ACE is 360°,
$$\text{arc } AC = 62°2'.$$
And so also
$$\text{angle } BAE = \text{angle } AEC$$
$$= 62°2' \text{ to 2 rt.}$$
$$= 31°1'.$$

Again, for the lunar eclipses, let A be the shadow's centre, so that, since the moon's mean's distance is likewise supposed, always
$$AE = 60^p,$$
and likewise
$$AD = 26^p40'.$$
And let the moon be eclipsed to 18 digits, so that again AC is less than AD by half the diameter, and by subtraction
$$AC = 10^p.$$
Since, then,
$$AC = 20^p$$
where
$$\text{hypt. } AE = 120^p,$$
and, where the circle about right triangle ACE is 360°,
$$\text{arc } AC = 19°12';$$
therefore
$$\text{angle } BAE = \text{angle } AEC$$
$$= 19°12' \text{ to 2 rt.}$$
$$= 9°36'.$$
And, likewise, since
$$AC = 45^p$$
where
$$\text{hypt. } AD = 120^p,$$
and, where the circle about right triangle ACD is 360°,
$$\text{arc } AC = 44°2';$$
therefore
$$\text{angle } BAD = \text{angle } ADC$$
$$= 44°2' \text{ to 2 rt.}$$
$$= 22°1'.$$

Then, in the same way, in the case of the other digits taking the sizes of the angles less than a right angle which is 90° (and which is also what a quadrant of the horizon is taken to be), we arranged a table in 22 rows and 4 columns. The first column contains the digits of the diameter's obscuration found at the mid-eclipse; the second contains the angles produced in solar eclipses at the time of the first part eclipsed and the last part restored; the third contains the angles produced in lunar eclipses at the time of the first part eclipsed and the last part restored; and the fourth contains the angles produced, again in lunar eclipses at the time of the last part eclipsed and the first part restored. And here are the diagrams of the table and of the circles:

12. Exposition of the Diagrams for the Directions

1	2		3		4	
	Sun's		Moon's			
	First Point of		First Point of		Last Point of	
	Eclipse and Last		Eclipse and Last		Eclipse and First	
Digits	Point of Emersion		Point of Emersion		Point of Emersion	
0	90	0	90	0		
1	66	50	72	30		
2	56	59	65	10		
3	49	16	59	27		
4	42	36	54	27		
5	36	35	50	14		
6	31	1	46	15		
7	25	46	42	31		
8	20	44	39	2		
9	15	51	35	42		
10	11	6	32	29		
11	6	25	29	23		
12	1	47	26	23	90	0
13			23	28	63	37
14			20	36	52	24
15			17	48	43	26
16			15	1	35	41
17			12	18	28	38
18			9	36	22	1
19			6	55	15	43
20			4	15	9	36
21			1	36	3	35

13. Determination of Directions

We now have in our hands, already determined in the way we showed, the times of each of the given markings; from the times, of course, the ecliptic's rising and setting parts at those times; and from the figure, their positions on the horizon. And whenever the moon's centre (either the apparent as for the solar eclipses, or the true as for the lunar) is on the ecliptic, we shall have, from the horizon-position of the part then setting, the direction of the sun's first part eclipsed and, further, the direction at the moon's last part eclipsed and restored. Moreover, from the horizon-position of the part then rising, we shall have the direction of the sun's last part restored and, further, the direction of the moon's first part eclipsed and restored.

But whenever the moon's centre is not on the ecliptic, we take the numbers of the angles lying in the same row and proper to the number of digits, counting them from the common sections of the horizon and ecliptic. If the moon's centre is north of the ecliptic, for the sun's first part eclipsed and for the moon's last

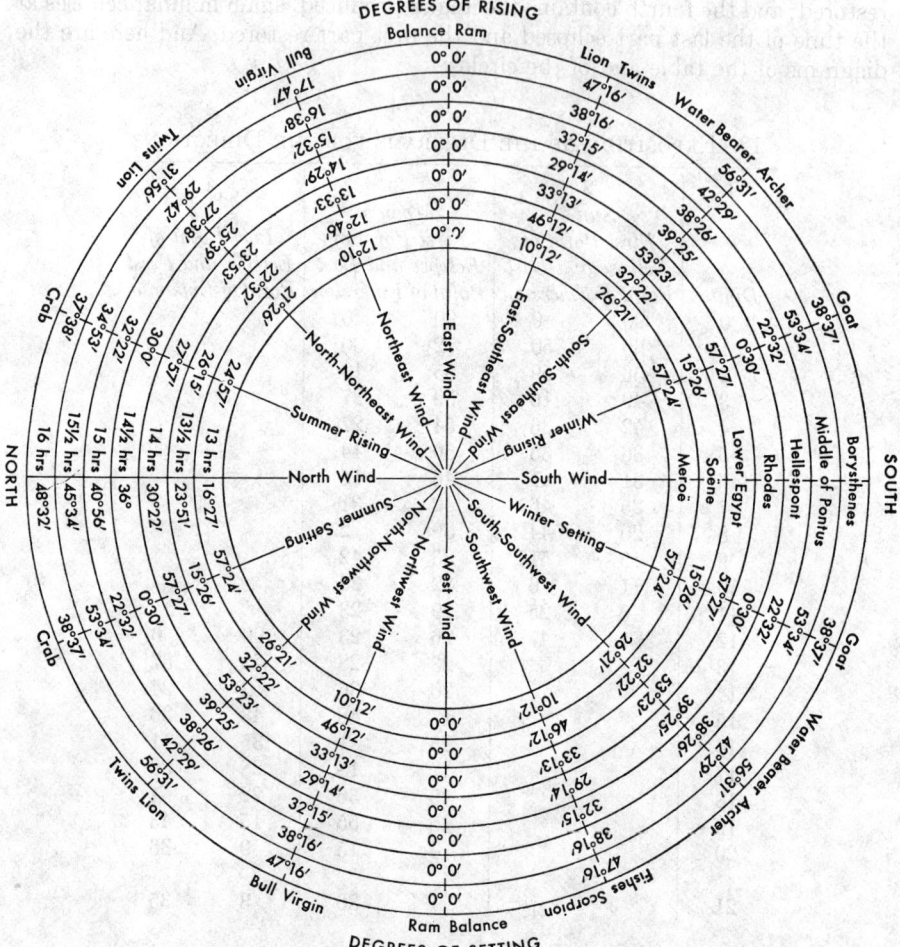

part eclipsed, we count them northward from the setting intersection; for the sun's last part restored and the moon's first part restored, northward from the rising intersection; and again, for the moon's first part eclipsed, southward from the rising intersection, and, for the moon's last part restored, southward from the setting intersection. And if the moon's centre is south of the ecliptic, for the sun's first part eclipsed and the moon's last part eclipsed, we count them southward from the setting intersection; for the sun's last part restored and the moon's first part restored, southward from the rising intersection; and again, for the moon's first part eclipsed, northward from the rising intersection, and, for the moon's last part restored, northward from the setting intersection. We shall thus have, established from this correction, that part of the horizon in general to which are directed the parts of the luminaries receiving the first and last markings of the eclipses and restorations.

BOOK SEVEN

1. That the Fixed Stars Always Keep the Same Position with Respect to Each Other

So far in this treatise, Syrus, we have gone through the accidents relative to the right and oblique sphere, and then those relative to the hypotheses of the movements of the sun and moon and of the configurations considered according to those movements. Now, for the theory to follow, we shall begin a discussion of the stars—and first, naturally, of those called fixed.

This must first of all be understood: that, as far as this term is concerned, because the stars always appear to keep similar figures and equal distances with respect to each other, we would do well to call them "fixed." But, because the whole sphere of them, on which they hang (as it were) and revolve, appears itself to move eastward toward the prime movement's rising with a proper ordered motion, it would not be right to call that sphere "fixed." For we find both of these views to be true, judging from the results of a great stretch of time. And Hipparchus first, from the appearances he had, suspected both of these things; but for the most part conjectured rather than affirmed them because of the very few observations on the fixed stars that had been made before him, which were only those recorded by Aristyllus and Timocharis and which were uncertain and not worked over. And we, from a comparison of what is observed now with what was observed then, have come to the same conclusion, but more sure because the examination has taken place over a longer time, and because Hipparchus' own laborious records concerning the fixed stars (with respect to which we, for the most part, made the comparisons) have been furnished us.

If the present appearances agree with the records of Hipparchus, then it would be clear to anyone wishing to pursue the investigation and truthfully examine, that no change has hitherto taken place in their position with respect to each other, but the configurations observed by Hipparchus are seen to be absolutely the same now. This is true not only of those inside the zodiac with respect to each other or those outside (which would be the case if, as Hipparchus first supposed, only those stars around the zodiac made an eastward change in the order of the signs) but also of those inside with respect to those outside and far off.

And we shall now set out here, for an easy test, a few of the records which can be most readily grasped and which can bring to view the complete comparison by which it is shown that the observed configurations contained by those outside are the same with respect to each other and those inside the zodiac.

In the case of the stars in the Crab, he writes that the star in the southern claw of the Crab, the bright star west of this and of the head of the Water Snake [Hydra], and the bright star among those in the Little Dog [Procyon] are very nearly on the same straight line. For the middle one lies to the north and east of the straight line between the ends of 1½ digit, and the distances between are equal.

In the case of the stars in the Lion, he writes that, of the four in the Lion's head, the eastern two and the one at the beginning of the Water Snake's neck are on the same straight line; and again, that the straight line drawn through the Lion's tail and the star at the tip of the Bear's tail leaves the bright star under the Bear's tail 1 digit to the west; likewise that the straight line through the star under the Bear's tail and through the Lion's tail joins the western stars in Berenice's Hair.

In the case of the stars in the Virgin, he says that, between the Virgin's northern foot and the Ploughman's [Boötes] right foot, lie two stars of which the southern and bright one (like that in the Ploughman's foot) lies west of the straight line through the feet, and the northern and half bright one is on a straight line with the feet. He further says that, west of the half bright one of these two, there are two bright ones making with it an isosceles triangle whose vertex is the half bright one; and they are on a straight line with Arcturus and the Virgin's southern foot. Again, he says that between Spica and the second from the end of the Water Snake's tail lie three stars in a straight line with one another; and the middle one of these is in a straight line with Spica and the second star from the end of the Water Snake's tail.

In the case of the stars in the Balance [*i.e.*, the claws of the Scorpion], he says that very nearly in a straight line with the bright stars of the Balance, to the north, is a bright triple star. For on each side of it lies a small one.

In the case of the stars of the Scorpion, he says that the straight line drawn through the eastern one in the center of the Scorpion and through the right knee of Serpentarius bisects the distance between the western stars in the right foot of Serpentarius. He also says that the fifth and seventh joints are in a straight line with the bright star in the middle of the Censer [Ara]; moreover, that the more northern of those in the Censer's base is almost in a straight line with the fifth joint and the star in the middle of the Censer, being nearly equidistant from both.

In the case of the stars in the Archer, he says that in the Circle [Southern Crown] under the Archer toward the east lie two bright stars about three cubits from each other; moreover, that the more southern and brighter, in the Archer's foot, is very nearly in a straight line with the middle star of those three bright ones in the Circle lying eastward and with the eastern star of the opposite bright ones in the Quadrilateral; and the two distances between them are equal. The northern one of them is off the straight line to the east, but is in a straight line with the bright and opposite ones in the Quadrilateral.

In the case of the stars in the Water Bearer, he says that the two consecutive stars in the Horse's head and the eastern shoulder of the Water Bearer are very nearly in a straight line, to which is parallel the straight line drawn from the western shoulder of the Water Bearer to the star in the Horse's jaws. And again he says that the Water Bearer's western shoulder and the bright star of the two in the Horse's [Pegasus] throat and the star in the horse's navel are in a straight line, and the distances equal; and that the straight line through the Horse's muzzle and through the eastern star of the four in the Urn very nearly bisects at right angles the straight line between the two consecutive stars in the Horse's head.

In the case of the stars in the Fishes, he says that the star in the mouth of the southern Fish, the bright star in the Horse's shoulders, and the bright star in his breast are in a straight line.

In the case of the stars in the Ram, he says that the western star of the Triangle's base lies one digit east of the straight line drawn through the star in the Ram's jaw and the left foot of Andromeda; and also that the western stars in the Ram's head and the midpoint of the Triangle's base are in a straight line.

In the case of the stars in the Bull, he says that the eastern stars of the Hyades and the sixth star, counting from the south, of the hide which Orion holds in his left hand are in a straight line; and that the straight line drawn through the Bull's western eye and the seventh from the south of those in the hide leaves the bright star of the Hyades a digit to the north.

In the case of the stars in the Twins, he says that in a straight line with the Twin's heads there is a star east of the eastern head by a distance three times that between the heads, and that this same star is in a straight line with the more southern of those about the little nebula.

Now, in these and similar configurations affording a comparison for nearly the whole sphere we see nothing changed up to now. And such a change would have been certainly sensible in the intervening two hundred and sixty years if only those stars about the ecliptic had made a movement to the east.

In order that those after us may make a comparison over a longer time from more configurations of the same kind, beginning with the stars in the Ram, we shall also set out those configurations most easily grasped of all those not given in the older record but obtained by us.

Now, of the three stars in the Ram's head the more northern two, the bright one in the southern knee of Perseus and the star called Capella are in a straight line. Again the straight line joining Capella and the bright star of the Hyades [Aldebaran] leaves a little to the east the star in the Charioteer's [Auriga] western foot. And Capella, and the star common to the Charioteer's eastern foot and the northern end of the Bull's horns, and the star in Orion's western shoulder are in a straight line. Again, the bright stars in the Twins' heads and the bright star in the Water Snake's throat are very nearly in a straight line. Yet again, the two consecutive stars in the Bear's forefoot, the star at the top of the Scorpion's northern claw, and the more southern of the Asses are in a straight line. Likewise the southern Ass, the bright star in the Little Dog [Procyon], and the bright star between them, west of the Water Snake's head, are very nearly in a straight line. Furthermore, the straight line drawn from the middle star of the bright ones in the Lion's throat to the bright star in the Water Snake leaves the star of the Lion's heart a little to the east. The straight line from the bright star in the Lion's loin to the bright star in the back of the Bear's thigh, which is south of the eastern side of the quadrilateral, leaves a little to the west the two consecutive stars in the Bear's eastern foot. Again, the straight line from the star in the back of the Virgin's thigh to the second star from the end of the Water Snake's tail leaves a bit to the west the star called Spica. The straight line from Spica to the star in the Ploughman's head leaves Arcturus a bit to the east. Spica and the stars on the Raven's wings are in a straight line. Spica, the star in the back of the Virgin's thigh, and the bright northern star in the Ploughman's western calf are in a straight line. Again, the bright stars in the Balance and the star at the tip of the Water Snake's tail are very nearly in a straight line. The bright star in the southern Claw, Arcturus, and the middle star of the three in the Big Bear's tail are in a straight line. The bright star in the northern Claw, Arcturus, and the star in the back of the Bear's thigh are in a straight line. Again the star on the eastern shin of Serpentarius, the star in the Scorpion's fifth joint, and the western star of the two consecutive ones in its centre are in a straight line. The western star of the three in the Scorpion's breast and the two in Serpentarius' knees makes an isosceles triangle, whose vertex is the western star of the three in the breast. Again, the star on the Archer's southern and forward ankle and of second magnitude, the star on the barb, and the star in Serpentarius' eastern knee are in a straight line. The star in the knee of the Archer's same foot, near the Crown, the star on the barb, and the star in Serpentarius' western knee are in a straight line. Again, the straight line joined from the bright star [Vega] in the Lyre to the star in the Goat's [Capricorn] horns leaves a little to the east the bright star in the Eagle [Aquila]. The straight line from the bright star in the Eagle to the star of the first magnitude in the mouth of the southern Fish nearly bisects the distance between the two bright stars in the Goat's tail. Moreover, the straight line from the star of the first magnitude in the mouth of the southern Fish to the star in the Horse's muzzle leaves a little to the east the bright star in the Water Bearer's eastern shoulder. Again, the stars in the mouths of the two southern Fishes and the western stars of the square in the Horse are in a straight line.

And finally, if one should compare these configurations with those of the constellations on Hipparchus' solid sphere, he would find the positions gotten by the observations of that time and recorded on the sphere to be very nearly the same as those gotten now.

2. That the Sphere of the Fixed Stars Makes a Movement Eastward on the Ecliptic

By means of the foregoing and similar comparisons we can show that the relation and movement of the so-called fixed stars is one and the same. And that their sphere makes its own proper movement in the direction contrary to the motion of the whole—that is, eastward in the order of the signs from the great circle drawn through both sets of poles, those of the equator and those of the ecliptic—becomes evident to us especially through the fact that the same stars do not keep the same distances formerly and in our time with respect to the tropic and equinoctial points, but are always found in later times to be a greater distance eastward than the first from those same points.

For Hipparchus, in his treatise *On the Precession of the Tropic and Equinoctial Points*, compares the lunar eclipses from those carefully observed by him and from those observed earlier by Timocharis, and he calculates that Spica is 6° west of the autumn equinox in his time, but very nearly 8° in the time of Timocharis. Finally he says this: "If then, for example, Spica was formerly 8° in longitude west of the fall equinox, and is now 6° west" and so forth. And similarly, in the case of the other planets of which he made a comparison, he shows just about the same eastward shift accomplished. And we, comparing the apparent distances of the fixed stars relative to the tropic and equinoctial points in our time with those observed and recorded by Hipparchus, find their shift eastward along the ecliptic the same proportionately to the foregoing one. This research we have made by means of the instrument we prepared for the observation of the moon's particular elongations from the sun, placing one circle of the astrolabe at the moon's apparent passage falling at the hour of the observation, and carrying the other circle to the star being sighted so that the moon and star may be sighted together in their proper places. And thus, from its distance to the moon, we get the position of each one of the bright stars.

For one example, in the year 2 of Antonine, Egyptianwise Pharmouthi 9, as the sun was about to set in Alexandria and the last section of the Bull was culminating (that is, $5\frac{1}{2}$ equatorial hours after noon of the ninth) we observed the apparent moon to be $92\frac{1}{8}°$ from the sun which was sighted about 3° within the Fishes. And a half hour after the sun had set, with the first quarter of the Twins culminating and the apparent moon sighted in the same position as before, the star in the Lion's heart [Regulus] appeared, with the aid of the other circle of the astrolabe, to be $57\frac{1}{6}°$ from the moon eastward along the ecliptic. But in the first observation the sun's true position was very nearly $3\frac{1}{20}°$ within the Fishes, so that the apparent moon was then a distance of $92\frac{1}{8}°$ eastward or very nearly $5\frac{1}{6}°$ within the Twins, where, according to our hypotheses, it should have been. A half hour later, the moon must have moved eastward very nearly $\frac{1}{4}°$ and have displayed a westward parallax of very nearly $\frac{1}{12}°$ at the first position. Therefore the half hour after the apparent moon was $5\frac{1}{8}°$ within the Twins, so that the star in the heart (since it appeared to be $57\frac{1}{6}°$ eastward from it) was situated $2\frac{1}{2}°$ within the Lion, and was a distance of $32\frac{1}{2}°$ from the summer tropic.

But in the year 50 of the Third Callippic Period, as Hipparchus observes and records, it [Regulus] was then $(29+\frac{1}{2}+\frac{1}{3})°$ eastward from the same summer tropic point. Therefore, the star in the Lion's heart had shifted eastward along the ecliptic $2\frac{2}{3}°$ in the years from Hipparchus' observation to the beginning of Antonine's reign when we observed most of the passages of the fixed stars, a period which comes to about 265 years. And so from this it is found that there is an eastward shift of 1° in very nearly 100 years, as Hipparchus seems to have guessed when he says his treatise *On the Magnitude of the Solar Year:* "If for this cause the tropics and equinoxes shifted westward not less than $\frac{1}{100}°$ in a year, then they would have to shift not less than 3° in 300 years." And having sighted Spica and the brightest stars about the ecliptic in their distance from the moon in this same way, then finally from these more accessible ones the other also, we find their distances with respect to each other very nearly the same as those observed by Hipparchus but their distances with respect to the tropic and equinoctial points to have shifted eastward very nearly $2\frac{1}{2}°$ compared to the record of Hipparchus.

3. That the Eastward Movement of the Sphere of the Fixed Stars Takes Place About the Pole of the Ecliptic[1]

It has now become clear to us that the sphere of the fixed stars makes an eastward motion of very nearly this amount. And the next thing is to find out the direction of this movement—that is, whether it takes place about the poles of equator or of the ecliptic. And this would become evident to us from the

[1]The history of the interpretation of the appearance called the precession of the equinoxes is one of the most beautiful in the development of astronomy and physics.

In the Copernican theory, it is explained by having the restoration of the annual declination of the earth's axis with respect to the plane through the earth and the sun anticipate the

longitudinal shift. For the great circles drawn through the poles of one of these cut off unequal arcs on the other unless the difference due to this cause should be altogether indistinguishable to the senses because of such a small shift's taking place in this amount of time. But it would be very easily gotten from their latitudinal shift then and now. For with respect to whichever of the circles, the equator or ecliptic, they always appear to keep their latitudinal distances, it is clear that the movement of the sphere will be effected about that circle.

Now Hipparchus also agrees to the movement's being about the ecliptic's poles. For in his treatise *On the Precession of the Tropic and Equinoctial Points* he in turn concludes, from the things observed by Timocharis and by himself, that Spica keeps unchanged; not relative to the equator, but relative to the ecliptic, the magnitude of its latitudinal distance of 2° south of the ecliptic. Therefore in his treatise *On the Magnitude of the Solar Year* he supposes only the movement about the poles of the ecliptic. And yet he still has doubts, as he himself says, because the trustworthy observations of Timocharis have not been taken in a general enough way and because the intervening time has not been long enough for a conclusive observation.

However, since we find over a longer time and for nearly all the fixed stars just this thing, we can reasonably suppose their movement about the poles of the ecliptic to be fairly sure. For, observing the latitudinal distance of each on the great circle drawn through its poles, we find nearly the same distances contained as were recorded and brought together by Hipparchus, or else disagreeing so little that the discrepancy could be neglected as the result of the observations themselves. But in the case of the distances observed with respect to the equator along the great circle drawn through its poles, neither do we find those gotten by us agreeing with those recorded in the same way by Hipparchus, nor these with those gotten still earlier by Timocharis. And from these themselves we find even more thoroughly confirmed the identity of the latitude with respect to the ecliptic. For the stars in the hemisphere from the winter tropic through the spring equinox to the summer tropic are always found farther north than the earlier distance with respect to the equator; but those in the opposite hemisphere farther south, those near the equinoctial points having greater differences, and those near the tropic points having less—almost in proportion as the ecliptic's eastward sections in their longitudinal progression get farther north or farther south of the equator.

restoration of the earth's centre in its revolution about the sun. Copernicus thought there was an irregularity in the rate of the precession. Neither Ptolemy nor the moderns find this appearance.

In Newton's *Principles*, the precession is deduced by an extraordinary analogy with the three body problem in the famous Proposition 66 of Book I, particularly in the first eleven corollaries and in Corollaries 20, 21, and 22.

It is in this last corollary also that it is brought out that from Newtonian principles it must follow that the rotation of a body on its axis is a regular motion and no centripetal force will change the velocity of this rotation. Thus the Ptolemaic assumption of the regularity of the two motions which made up the apparent motion of the fixed stars is, at least for the first one, in effect the same as the Newtonian. The astronomers before Hipparchus had simply considered the revolution of the fixed stars as regular.

The choice of regular motion is one that is arbitrary. But the very fact that one can and must choose a regular motion, and that the apparent motions are so ambiguous as to allow any one of them to be chosen as such is the sign for St. Augustine that points to a non-sensible theory of time and of memory. See the *Confessions*, Books x and xi.

In order to state this more clearly in a few easily understood cases, we shall set out, for either hemisphere, their recorded latitudinal distances from the equator along the great circle drawn through its poles, those gotten by Timocharis, those by Hipparchus, and those gotten in the same way by ourselves.

Now, Timocharis records the bright star in the Eagle [Altair] as being $5\frac{4}{5}°$ north of the equator, and Hipparchus the same; but we find it to be $(5+\frac{1}{2}+\frac{1}{3})°$. And Timocharis records the centre of the Pleiades as being $14\frac{1}{2}°$ north of the equator, Hipparchus $15\frac{1}{6}°$, and we find it to be $16\frac{1}{4}°$. Again, Timocharis records the bright star of the Hyades [Aldebaran] as being $(8+\frac{1}{2}+\frac{1}{4})°$ north of the equator, and Hipparchus $(9+\frac{1}{2}+\frac{1}{4})°$, and we find it to be 11°. Aristyllus records the brightest star in the Charioteer, called the Goat [Capella] as being 40° north of the equator, Hipparchus $40\frac{2}{5}°$, and we find it to be $41\frac{1}{6}°$. Timocharis records the star in the western shoulder of Orion as being $1\frac{1}{5}°$ north of the equator, Hipparchus $1\frac{4}{5}°$, and we find it to be $2\frac{1}{2}°$. Timocharis records the star in the eastern shoulder of Orion [Betelgeuse] as being $(3+\frac{1}{2}+\frac{1}{3})°$ north of the equator, Hipparchus $4\frac{1}{3}°$, and we find it to be $5\frac{1}{4}°$. Timocharis records the bright star in the Dog's mouth [Sirius] as being $16\frac{1}{3}°$ south of the equator, Hipparchus 16°, and we find it to be $(15+\frac{1}{2}+\frac{1}{4})°$. Aristyllus records the western star of the bright ones in the Twins' heads [Castor] to be 33° north of the equator, Hipparchus $33\frac{1}{6}°$, and we find it to be $33\frac{2}{5}°$. And Aristyllus records the eastern one [Pollux] as being 30° north of the equator, Hipparchus the same, and we find it to be $30\frac{1}{6}°$.

Of all these distances intercepted longitudinally within the hemisphere containing the spring equinox, the later ones have become all more northern in latitude with respect to the equator than the earlier ones, those near the tropic sections by a very small amount and those near the equinoctial sections by a considerable amount. This is consequent upon the precession eastward about the ecliptic's poles, because the eastward sections of this semicircle always get more northern than the western, those near the equinoctial points with greater differences and those near the tropic points with smaller.

In the opposite hemisphere, Timocharis records the star in the Lion's heart [Regulus] as being $21\frac{1}{3}°$ north of the equator, Hipparchus $20\frac{2}{3}°$, and we find it to be $(19+\frac{1}{2}+\frac{1}{3})°$. Timocharis records Spica as being $1\frac{2}{5}°$ north of the equator, Hipparchus only $\frac{3}{5}°$, and we find it to be $\frac{1}{2}°$ south of the equator. Aristyllus records that of the three stars in the Big Bear's tail the one at the tip is $61\frac{1}{2}°$ north of the equator, Hipparchus $(60+\frac{1}{2}+\frac{1}{4})°$, and we find it to be $59\frac{2}{3}°$. Aristyllus records the second from the end, in the middle of the tail, as being $67\frac{1}{4}°$ north of the equator, Hipparchus $66\frac{1}{2}°$, and we find it to be 65°. Aristyllus records the third from the end, at the beginning of the tail, as being $68\frac{1}{2}°$ north of the equator, Hipparchus $67\frac{3}{5}°$, and we find it to be $66\frac{1}{4}°$. Timocharis records Arcturus as being $31\frac{1}{2}°$ north of the equator, Hipparchus 31°, and we find it to be $(29+\frac{1}{2}+\frac{1}{3})°$. Timocharis records that, of the bright stars in the Scorpion's claws, the one in the southern tip is 5° south of the equator, Hipparchus $5\frac{3}{5}°$, and we find it to be $7\frac{1}{6}°$. Timocharis records the star in the tip of the northern claw as being $1\frac{1}{5}°$ north of the equator, Hipparchus only $\frac{2}{5}°$, and we find it to be 1° south of the equator. And Timocharis records the bright star in the Scorpion's breast, called Antares, as being $18\frac{1}{3}°$ south of the equator, Hipparchus 19°, and we find it to be $20\frac{1}{4}°$.

Now, of all these passages, in the opposite way, the later have become proportionately more southern in latitude with respect to the equator than the earlier. Therefore it could be concluded that the eastward longitudinal shift of the sphere of the fixed stars is 1°, as we said before, in very nearly 100 years, and $2\frac{2}{3}$° in the 265 years between the observation of Hipparchus and our own. And this conclusion is reached through the latitudinal difference found for those stars about the equinoctial points.

For the centre star of the Pleiades, found by Hipparchus to be $15\frac{1}{6}$° north of the equator and by us $16\frac{1}{4}$°, has become more northern in the intervening time by $1\frac{1}{12}$°. And the $2\frac{2}{3}$° on the ecliptic for stars at the end of the Ram, resulting from the eastward longitudinal shift over the same amount of time, gives just that difference in latitude with respect to the equator. Again, the star called Goat [Capella], found by Hipparchus to be $40\frac{2}{5}$° north of the equator and by us $41\frac{1}{6}$°, has become more northern by $\frac{4}{5}$°, the $2\frac{2}{3}$° on the ecliptic for stars at the middle of the Bull again giving just that difference in latitude with respect to the equator. In the western shoulder of Orion, the star found by Hipparchus to be $1\frac{4}{5}$° north of the equator and by us $2\frac{1}{2}$° has become more northern by very nearly $\frac{2}{3}$°, the $2\frac{2}{3}$° on the ecliptic for stars two-thirds within the Bull giving just that difference in latitude with respect to the equator.

Likewise for the opposite hemisphere, Spica, found by Hipparchus to be $\frac{3}{5}$° north of the equator and by us $\frac{1}{2}$° south, has become more southern by $1\frac{1}{10}$°. Again, the $2\frac{2}{3}$° on the ecliptic for stars at the end of the Virgin give just that difference in latitude with respect to the equator. The star at the tip of the Big Bear's tail, found by Hipparchus to be $60\frac{3}{4}$° north of the equator and by us $59\frac{2}{3}$°, has become more southern by $1\frac{1}{12}$°; and the $2\frac{2}{3}$° on the ecliptic for stars at the beginning of the dodecatemory of the Balance give just this difference in latitude with respect to the equator. And Arcturus, found by Hipparchus to be 31° north of the equator and by us $(29+\frac{1}{2}+\frac{1}{3})$°, has become more southern by $1\frac{1}{6}$°, the $2\frac{2}{3}$° on the ecliptic for stars at the beginning of the Balance likewise giving very nearly this difference in latitude with respect to the equator.

And what is required will be even clearer to us from the following observations.

For Timocharis, having observed these things in Alexandria, records that in the year 47 of the first Callippic Period of 76 years (Anthesterion 8, Egyptian-wise Athyr 29), at the end of the third hour, the southern half of the moon appeared to have advanced eastward one-third or one-half the way through the Pleiades, in true position. And this date is the year 465 of Nabonassar, Egyptianwise Athyr 29-30, 3 seasonal hours before midnight and $3\frac{1}{3}$ equatorial hours. For the sun was 7° within the Water Bearer, and with respect to regular solar days the amount of time before midnight adds up to that many hours. According to hypotheses already demonstrated by us, the moon at that hour had its true position 0°20′ within the Bull—that is, it was 30°20′ from the spring equinox and 3°45′ north of the ecliptic. In Alexandria it appeared to be 29°20′ within the Ram in longitude, and 3°35′ north of the ecliptic, since the second third of the Twins was culminating. Therefore, the eastern limit of the Pleiades was then very nearly $29\frac{1}{2}$° east of the spring equinox, since the moon's centre was still west of it and very nearly $3\frac{2}{3}$° north of the ecliptic. For this limit was, in turn, a little more north than the moon's centre.

And Agrippa who observed in Bithynia records that, in the year 12 of Domitian (in their fashion Metroius 7), at the beginning of the third hour of the night, the moon occulted with its southern horn the southeastern part of the Pleiades. This date is the year 840 of Nabonassar, Egyptianwise Tybi 2-3, 4 seasonal hours before midnight, and 5 equatorial hours. Because the sun was 6° within the Archer. Therefore, with respect to the meridian of Alexandria, the observation was 5⅓ equatorial hours before midnight, and relative to regular solar days 5¾ hours, at which time the true position of the moon's centre was 3°7′ within the Bull and (4+½+⅓)° north of the ecliptic. In Bithynia it appeared to be 3°15′ in longitude within the Bull and 4° north of the ecliptic because the point two-thirds within the Fishes was culminating. Therefore the eastern part of the Pleiades was then 33¼° east of the spring equinox and 3⅔° north of the ecliptic. So it is evident that, in latitude, the eastern part of the Pleiades was then and now 3⅔° north of the ecliptic along the great circle drawn through its poles, and, in longitude, has moved 3°45′ eastward from the spring equinox. Because at the first observation it was 29½° from it, and at the second 33¼°; and the time between the two observations embraces 365 years. And, therefore, the eastern part of the Pleiades has moved eastward 1° in 100 years.

Again having observed in Alexandria, Timocharis records that in the year 36 of the First Callippic Period (Elaphebolion 15 or Tybi 5), at the beginning of the third hour, the moon reached Spica with the midpoint of its disc toward the equatorial rising, and Spica went behind it cutting off exactly one-third of the diameter towards the north. And this date is the year 454 of Nabonassar, Egyptianwise Tybi 5-6, very nearly 4 seasonal and equatorial hours before midnight, because the sun was about 15° within the Fishes. With respect to regular solar days, the determination comes to just about that many hours before. And at that hour the true position of the moon's centre was again 21°21′ in longitude within the Virgin—that is, it was 81°21′ east of the summer tropic and (1+½+⅓)° south of the ecliptic. But it appeared to be 82°12′ in longitude from the summer tropic and very nearly 2° south of the ecliptic. For the middle of the Crab was culminating. And therefore, for these reasons, Spica was at that time 82⅓° from the summer tropic and 2° south of the ecliptic.

Timocharis likewise says that in the year 48 of the same period (on the sixth of Pyanepsion waning, or Thoth 7), at half-past the ninth hour, the moon having risen above the horizon, Spica appeared to be exactly touching the northern part of it. And this date is the year 466 of Nabonassar, Egyptianwise Thoth 7-8, as he himself says, 3½ seasonal hours after midnight, and very nearly 3⅛ equatorial hours, since the sun was near the middle of the Scorpion. Consequently, it was 2½ hours after midnight. For at just that many equatorial hours after midnight the point 22½° within the Twins was culminating, and about the same point within the Virgin was rising. And the moon was in this position when it rose, as he says. With respect to regular solar days we find it to be only 2 equatorial hours after midnight. Again, at this time the true position of the moon's centre was 81°30′ from the summer equinoxes and 2⅙° south of the ecliptic; but it appeared to be 82°30′ in longitude away from it and 2¼° south of the ecliptic. And therefore Spica, by this observation, was in turn very nearly 2° south of the ecliptic and 82½° from the summer tropic. Consequently, in the 12 years between the two observations, it has moved very nearly ⅙° eastward from the summer tropic.

And Menelaus, the geometer, says that he observed in Rome, in the year 1 of Trajan (Mechir 15-16), at the end of the tenth hour, Spica occulted by the moon; for it could not be seen; but that at the end of the eleventh hour he observed it west of the moon's centre equally distant from the horns by less than a diameter. And this date is the year 845 of Nabonassar, Egyptianwise Mechir 15-16, 4 seasonal hours after midnight when the moon's centre overtook Spica, but 5 equatorial hours because the sun was 20° within the Goat; with respect to the meridian through Alexandria, it was 6⅓ hours after, and with respect to regular solar days was 6¼ hours after or a little more. At this hour the true position of the moon's centre was 85¾° from the summer tropic and very nearly 1⅓° south of the ecliptic, but it appeared to be 86¼° in longitude from it and 2° south. For the first quarter of the Balance was culminating. Therefore Spica had that position at that time.

It is clear that, according both to Timocharis and to ourselves, Spica was the same distance south of the ecliptic (that is, 2°) but that since the observation in the year 36 it has shifted 3°55' during the 391 intervening years; and, since the observation in the year 48, 3°45' during the 379 intervening years. And so, from this the eastward shift of Spica in 100 years comes to very nearly 1°.

Again, Timocharis says he observed in Alexandria that in the year 36 of the First Callippic Period (Poseidon 25, or Phaophi 16), exactly at the beginning of the tenth hour, the moon appeared to overtake with its northern arc the northern star of those in the Scorpion's forehead. And this date is the year 454 of Nabonassar, Egyptianwise Phaophi 16-17, 3 seasonal hours after midnight and 3⅖ equatorial hours, because the sun was 26° within the Archer, but 3⅙ hours with respect to regular solar days. At that hour the true position of the moon's centre was 31¼° from the autumn equinox and 1⅓° north of the ecliptic, but it appeared to be 32° in longitude and 1°12' north of the ecliptic. For the middle of the Lion was culminating. And, therefore, the northernmost star in the Scorpion's forehead was at that time 32° in longitude from the autumn equinox and very nearly 1⅓° north of the ecliptic.

Likewise Menelaus says he observed in Rome that in the year 1 of Trajan, Mechir 18-19, at the end of the eleventh hour, the moon's southern horn appeared in a straight line with the middle and southern stars of those in the Scorpion's forehead. But its centre lay east of this line and was as far from the middle star as the middle star was from the southern star; and its centre seemed to have overtaken the northern star of those in the forehead. For it made no appearance whatsoever. This date is again the year 845 of Nabonassar, Egyptianwise Mechir 18-19, 5 seasonal hours after midnight and 6½ equatorial hours, because the sun was 23° within the Goat; but 7½ hours after with respect to the meridian through Alexandria, and very nearly the same with respect to regular solar days. At this hour the true position of the moon's centre was 35⅓° from the autum equinox and 2⅙° north of the ecliptic. But it appeared to be 35°55' in longitude and 1⅓° north. For the end of the Balance was culminating. Therefore, the northernmost star in the Scorpion's forehead, at that time, had very nearly that same position.

It is thus evident that also in the case of this star the same latitudinal distance has been observed then and now, but that the longitudinal distance has shifted 3°55' eastward from the autumn equinox for the total of 391 years between the observations. Again it follows from this that the eastward shift of the star is 1° in 100 years.

4. On the Manner of Recording the Fixed Stars

And now, from the similar observation and comparison of these and other bright stars and from the constant distance of the rest with respect to the stars observed, we find it certain, to the extent that the time elapsed allows, that the sphere of the fixed stars makes a shift of this amount eastward from the tropic and equinoctial points, and moreover that this movement is effected about the poles of the ecliptic and not about the poles of the equator—that is, those of the prime movement. We therefore thought it proper, for each of these and of the other fixed stars, to make observations and records of their epochs observed at the present time, considered in longitude and latitude, not with respect to the equator but defined with respect to the ecliptic by the great circles drawn through its poles and each one of the stars. In accord with the given hypothesis on the movement, it is necessary that their latitudinal passages with respect to the ecliptic remain always the same, and that the longitudinal shifts eastward cut off equal arcs in equal times. And so again, using the same instrument, by the turning of the armillary circles in it about the ecliptic's poles we observed as many stars as we could, up to those of the sixth magnitude. We always directed one of these armillary circles towards one of the bright stars gotten by means of the moon, according to its proper section on the ecliptic; another armillary circle, graduated and capable of turning on the ecliptic's poles, we directed towards the desired star until, like the first one, it also was sighted through the hole of its own proper circle. When this took place, both passages of the stars desired were immediately evident to us on the armillary circle, since the longitudinal position was defined by its intersection with the ecliptic and the latitudinal positions by the arc on it cut off between this intersection and the upper hole.

Now, to have the solid sphere's arrangement of constellations expounded in this way, we set it up tablewise in 4 parts, placing in the first part the configurations for each one of the stars by constellation. In the second we placed the positions according to longitude within the dodecatemories as they are gotten from observations at the start of Antonine's reign, the beginning of the quadrants again being taken at the tropic and equinoctial points. In the third we placed the latitudinal distances from the ecliptic for both the northern and southern sides. And in the fourth we placed the order of magnitude. Now, the latitudinal distances are always the same. But the longitudinal positions can easily provide the passage for other dates, if we subtract the degrees corresponding to the time between the date of the position and the date sought, at the rate of 1° in a hundred years, from the degrees of the position in the case of an earlier date; and if we add in the case of a later date.

The designations by configurations, therefore, must be understood in accordance with the convention of constellations and by the determinations of the ecliptic's poles. For by "stars preceding certain stars" and by "stars following certain stars" we mean those having their positions in the preceding western or following eastern sections of the ecliptic; and by "more southern" or "more northern" we mean those nearer the corresponding pole of the ecliptic.

We have not used for each of the stars altogether the same formations as our predecessors, just as they did not use the same as their predecessors. But often we use others according to the greater propriety and fittingness of the configurations—as, for example, when those stars which Hipparchus places in the shoulders of the Virgin, we call her sides because their distance from the stars in the head appears greater than that from the hands, and thus they better fit the sides and are quite different from the shoulders. But the correspondence of the differently designated stars would be easy to ascertain by the comparison of their recorded positions. And here is the exposition of the records:

5. TABULAR EXPOSITION OF THE CONSTELLATIONS OF THE NORTHERN HEMISPHERE

Configurations	Longitude	Latitude	Magn.
Constellation of the Little Bear			
The star on the tip of the tail	Twins 0°⅙′	N66°	3
The next one in the tail	Twins 2½°	N70°	4
The next one, before the beginning of the tail	Twins 16°	N74⅓°	4
The southern one on the western side of the rectangle	Twins 29⅔°	N75⅔°	4
The northern one on the same side	Crab 3⅔°	N77⅔°	4
The southern one of those on the eastern side	Crab 17½°	N72⅚°	2
The northern one on the same side	Crab 26⅙°	N74⅚°	2
In all, 7 stars of which 2 are of 2nd magnitude, 1 of 3rd, 4 of 4th.			
The unfigured star near it, that is the more southern star of first magnitude in a straight line with those on the eastern side	Crab 13°	N71⅙°	4
Constellation of the Big Bear			
The star at the tip of the muzzle	Twins 25⅓°	N39⅚°	4
The western star of those in the two eyes	Twins 25⅚°	N43°	5
The eastern one of these	Twins 26⅓°	N43°	5
The western star of the two in the forehead	Twins 26⅙°	N47⅙°	5
The eastern one of these	Twins 26⅔°	N47°	5
The star at the end of the western ear	Twins 28⅙°	N50½°	5
The western star of the 2 in the neck	Crab ½°	N43⅚°	4
The eastern one of these	Crab 2½°	N44⅓°	4
The northern star of the 2 in the breast	Crab 9°	N42°	4
The southern one of these	Crab 11°	N44°	4−
The star in the left knee	Crab 10⅔°	N35°	3
The northern star at the end of the left forefoot	Crab 5½°	N29⅓°	3
The southern one of these	Crab 6⅓°	N28⅓°	3
The star above the right knee	Crab 5⅔°	N36°	4
The star below the right knee	Crab 5⅚°	N33°	4
Of those in the quadrilateral, the star on the back	Crab 17⅔°	N49°	2
Of these, the star on the flank	Crab 22⅙°	N44½°	2
The star at the beginning of the tail	Lion 3⅙°	N51°	3
The remaining star in the left thigh	Lion 3°	N46½°	2
The western star of those at the end of the left hindfoot	Crab 22⅔°	N29⅓°	3
The star east of this one	Crab 24⅙°	N28¼°	3
The star in the left ham	Lion 1⅔°	N35¼°	4+
The northern star of those at the end of the right hindfoot	Lion 9⅚°	N25⅚°	3
The southern star of these	Lion 10⅓°	N25°	3
The first star of the 3 in the tail after the beginning	Lion 12⅙°	N53½°	2
The middle one of these	Lion 18°	N55⅔°	2
The third one at the end of the tail	Lion 29⅚°	N25°	3
In all, 27 stars of which 6 are of 2nd magnitude, 8 of 3rd, 8 of 4th, 5 of 5th.			

Configurations	*Longitude*		*Latitude*	*Magn.*
Of the Unfigured Stars beneath it				
The star under the tail far to the south	Lion	27⅚°	N39¾°	3
The dimmer star west of it	Lion	20⅙°	N41⅓°	5
The more southern star of those between the forefeet of the Bear and the head of the Lion	Crab	15°	N17¼°	4
The star north of this	Crab	13⅓°	N19⅙°	4
The star east of the other 3 dim ones	Crab	16⅙°	N20°	dim
The star west of this last	Crab	12⅙°	N22½°	dim
The star still farther west than this last	Crab	11⅙°	N23°	dim
The star between the forefeet and the Twins	Crab	0°	N22¼°	dim
In all, 8 unfigured stars of which 1 is of 3rd magnitude, 2 of 4th, 1 of 5th, and 4 dim.				
Constellation of the Dragon				
The star on the tongue	Balance	26⅔°	N76½°	4
The star in the mouth	Scorpion	11⅚°	N78½°	4+
The star above the eye	Scorpion	13⅙°	N75⅔°	3
The star in the jaw	Scorpion	27⅓°	N80⅓°	4
The star above the head	Scorpion	29⅔°	N75½°	3
The northern star of the 3 in a straight line in the first fold of the neck	Archer	24⅔°	N82⅓°	4
The southern one of these	Goat	2⅓°	N78¼°	4
The middle star of these	Archer	28⅚°	N80⅓°	4
The star east of this one	Goat	19½°	N81½°	4
The southern star of the western side of the square in the next turn	Fishes	8°	N81⅔°	4
The northern star of the western side	Fishes	20½°	N83°	4
The northern star of the eastern side	Ram	7⅔°	N78⅚°	4
The southern star of the eastern side	Fishes	22⅚°	N77⅚°	4
The southern star of the triangle in the next turn	Ram	10⅔°	N80½°	5
The western star of the remaining 2 of the triangle	Ram	21⅔°	N81⅓°	5
The eastern star of these	Ram	26⅙°	N80¼°	5
The eastern star of those in the next triangle west of this	Twins	13⅓°	N84½°	4
The southern star of the remaining 2 of the triangle	Bull	20⅓°	N87½°	4
The northern star of the remaining two	Bull	11⅚°	N84⅚°	4
The eastern star of the 2 small stars west of the triangle	Crab	28⅔°	N87½°	6
The western one of these	Crab	21⅔°	N86⅚°	6
The more northern of the next 3 in a straight line	Virgin	9°	N81¼°	5
The middle one of the 3	Virgin	9⅓°	N80⅓°	5
The northern one of these	Virgin	8⅓°	N84⅚°	3
The northern one of the next 2 to the west	Virgin	10°	N78°	3
The southern one of these	Virgin	10⅓°	N74⅔°	4+
The western star of those to the west in the turn near the tail	Virgin	12⅔°	N70°	3
The western star of the 2 rather distant from the last one	Lion	7⅓°	N64⅔°	4
The eastern star of these	Lion	11⅙°	N65½°	3
The star near them by the tail	Crab	19⅙°	N61¼°	3
The remaining star at the end of the tail	Crab	13⅙°	N56¼°	3
In all, 31 stars of which 8 are of 3rd magnitude, 16 of 4th, 5 of 5th, 2 of 6th.				
Constellation of Cepheus				
The star in the right foot	Bull	5°	N75⅔°	4
The star in the left foot	Bull	3°	N64¼°	4
The star under the belt on the right side	Ram	7⅓°	N71⅙°	4

Configurations	*Longitude*	*Latitude*	*Magn.*
The star touching the right shoulder from above	Fishes 16⅔°	N69°	3
The star touching the right elbow from above	Fishes 9⅓°	N72°	4
The star touching the same elbow from below	Fishes 10°	N74°	4
The star in the chest	Fishes 28½°	N65½°	5
The star in the left arm	Ram 7½°	N62½°	4+
The southern star of the 3 in the tiara	Fishes 16⅓°	N60¼°	5
The middle one of the 3	Fishes 17⅓°	N61¼°	4
The northern one of the 3	Fishes 19°	N61⅓°	5

In all, 11 stars of which 1 is of 3rd magnitude, 7 of 4th, 3 of 5th.

Of the Unfigured Stars About Cepheus

The star west of the tiara	Fishes 13⅔°	N64°	5
The star east of the tiara	Fishes 21⅓°	N59½°	4

In all, 2 unfigured stars of which 1 is of 4th magnitude, 1 of 5th.

Constellation of the Ploughman

The star west of the 3 in the left hand	Virgin 2⅓°	N58⅔°	5
The middle and southern one of the 3	Virgin 4⅙°	N58⅓°	5
The eastern one of the 3	Virgin 5⅓°	N60⅙°	5
The star in the left elbow	Virgin 9⅔°	N54⅔°	5
The star in the left shoulder	Virgin 19⅔°	N49°	3
The star in the head	Virgin 26⅔°	N53⅚°	4+
The star in the right shoulder	Balance 5⅔°	N48⅔°	4+
The star north of these and in the crook	Balance 5⅔°	N53¼°	4
The star north of this at the tip of the crook	Balance 5°	N57½°	4
The northern one of the 2 below the shoulder in the cudgel	Balance 7⅔°	N46½°	4+
The southern one of these	Balance 8½°	N45½°	5
The star at the tip of the right hand	Balance 8⅙°	N41⅓°	5
The western one of the 2 in the wrist	Balance 6⅔°	N41⅔°	5
The eastern one of these	Balance 7°	N42½°	5
The star at the end of the crook's haft	Balance 7⅓°	N40⅓°	5
The star in the right thigh in the girdle	Balance 0°	N40¼°	3
The eastern one of the two in the girdle	Virgin 25⅔°	N41⅔°	4
The western one of these	Virgin 25°	N42⅙°	4+
The star in the right heel	Balance 5⅓°	N28°	3
The northern one of the 3 in the left shank	Virgin 21⅓°	N28°	3
The middle one of the 3	Virgin 20½°	N26½°	4
The southern one of these	Virgin 21⅓°	N25°	4

In all, 22 stars of which 4 are of 3rd magnitude, 9 of 4th, 9 of 5th

One Unfigured Star Under This of 1st Mag.

The fiery star called Arcturus between the thighs	Virgin 27°	N31½°	1

Constellation of the Northern Crown

The bright star in the Crown	Balance 14⅔°	N44½°	2+
The most western of all	Balance 11⅔°	N46½°	4+
The one east and north of this one	Balance 11⅚°	N48°	5
The one again east and north of this last	Balance 13⅔°	N50½°	6
The star east of the bright one southwards	Balance 17⅙°	N44¾°	4
The star east of this last and nearby	Balance 19⅙°	N44⅚°	4
The star still east of these	Balance 21⅓°	N46⅙°	4
The star east of all those in the Crown	Balance 21⅔°	N49⅓°	4

In all, 8 stars of which 1 is of 2nd magnitude, 5 of 4th, 1 of 5th, 1 of 6th.

Configurations	Longitude	Latitude	Magn.
Constellation of Man Kneeling			
The star in the head	Scorpion 17⅔°	N37½°	3
The star in the right shoulder beside the armpit	Scorpion 3⅔°	N43°	3
The star in the right arm	Scorpion 1⅔°	N40⅙°	3
The star in the right elbow	Balance 28°	N37⅙°	4
The star in the left shoulder	Scorpion 16⅔°	N48°	3
The star in the left arm	Scorpion 22°	N49½°	4+
The star in the left elbow	Scorpion 27⅔°	N52°	4+
The eastern one of the 3 in the left wrist	Archer 5½°	N52⅚°	4+
The northern one of the remaining 2	Archer 1⅔°	N54°	4+
The southern one of these	Archer 1½°	N53°	4
The star in the right side	Scorpion 3⅚°	N50⅔°	3
The star in the left side	Scorpion 10⅙°	N53½°	5
The one north of this last in the left buttock	Scorpion 10°	N56½°	5
The star at the beginning of the same thigh	Scorpion 11⅙°	N58½°	3
The western star of the 3 in the left thigh	Scorpion 14°	N59⅚°	4
The one east of this last	Scorpion 15⅓°	N60⅓°	4
The star again east of this one	Scorpion 16⅓°	N61¼°	4+
The star in the left knee	Archer ⅚°	N61°	4
The star in the left shin	Scorpion 22⅙°	N69⅓°	4
The western one of the 3 in the foot	Scorpion 15⅓°	N70¼°	6
The middle one of the 3	Scorpion 16⅚°	N71¼°	6
The eastern one of these	Scorpion 19⅔°	N72¼°	6
The star at the beginning of the right thigh	Scorpion ⅔°	N60¼°	4+
The one north of this and in the same thigh	Balance 25⅓°	N63°	4
The star in the right knee	Balance 15⅔°	N65½°	4+
The southern star of the 2 under the right knee	Balance 13⅔°	N63⅔°	4
The northern one of these	Balance 10⅙°	N64¼°	4
The star in the right shank	Balance 11⅙°	N60°	4
The star at the end of the right foot which is the same as that at the tip of the crook			

Except for this last, in all 28 stars of which 6 are of 3rd magnitude, 17 of 4th, 2 of 5th, 3 of 6th.

The Unfigured Star Beyond This			
The star south of that in the right arm	Scorpion 2⅔°	N38⅙°	5

In all 1 star of 5th magnitude.

Constellation of the Lyre			
The bright star on the shell called the Lyre	Archer 17⅓°	N62°	1
The northern one of the 2 lying next it	Archer 20⅓°	N62⅔°	4+
The southern one of these	Archer 20⅓°	N61°	4+
The star east of these and at the beginning of the horns	Archer 23⅔°	N60°	4
The northern one of the two near the eastern side of the shell	Goat 2°	N61⅓°	4
The southern one of these	Goat 1⅔°	N60⅓°	4
The northern one of the two western stars in the crossbar	Archer 21°	N56⅙°	3
The southern one of these	Archer 20⅚°	N55°	4−
The northern one of the 2 in the cross-bar	Archer 24⅙°	N55⅓°	3
The southern one of these	Archer 24°	N54¾°	4−

In all, 10 stars of which 1 is of 1st magnitude, 2 of 3rd, 7 of 4th.

Constellation of the Bird			
The star in the beak	Goat 4½°	N49°	3
The one east of this and in the head	Goat 9°	N50½°	5

Configurations	*Longitude*	*Latitude*	*Magn.*
The star in the middle of the throat	Goat 16⅓°	N54½°	4+
The star in the breast	Goat 28½°	N57⅓°	3
The bright star in the tail	Water Bearer 9⅙°	N60°	2
The star in the elbow of the right wing	Goat 19⅓°	N64⅔°	3
The southern star of the 3 in the right wing-spread	Goat 22½°	N69⅔°	4
The middle one of the 3	Goat 21⅙°	N71½°	4+
The northern one at the edge of the wing-spread	Goat 16⅔°	N74°	4+
The star in the elbow of the left wing	Water Bearer ⅚°	N49½°	3
The star north of these and in the middle of the same wing	Water Bearer 3⅚°	N52⅙°	4+
The star at the edge of the left wing-spread	Water Bearer 6⅔°	N44°	3
The star in the left foot	Water Bearer 10°	N55⅙°	4+
The star in the left knee	Water Bearer 14½°	N57°	4+
The western one of the 2 in the right foot	Water Bearer 1⅙°	N64°	4
The eastern one of these	Water Bearer 2⅔°	N64½°	4
The star in the nebula of the right knee	Water Bearer 12⅙°	N64¾°	5

In all, 17 stars of which 1 is of 2nd magnitude, 5 of 3rd, 9 of 4th, 2 of 5th.

The Unfigured Stars About It

The southern star of the 2 under the left wing	Water Bearer 10⅔°	N49⅔°	4+
The northern one of these	Water Bearer 13⅚°	N51⅔°	4+

In all, 2 stars of 4th magnitude.

Constellation of Cassiopeia

The star in the head	Ram 7⅚°	N45⅓°	4+
The star in the breast	Ram 10⅚°	N46¾°	3
The star north of this and in the girdle	Ram 13°	N47⅚°	4
The star above the chair along the thighs	Ram 16⅔°	N49°	3+
The star in the knees	Ram 20⅔°	N45½°	3
The star in the shank	Ram 27°	N47¾°	4
The star at the tip of the foot	Bull 1⅔°	N47⅓°	4
The star in the left arm	Ram 14⅔°	N44⅓°	4
The star below the left elbow	Ram 17⅔°	N45°	5
The star in the right forearm	Ram 2⅓°	N50°	6
The star above the foot of the throne	Ram 15°	N52⅔°	4−
The star in the middle of the back of the chair	Ram 7⅚°	N51⅔°	3
The star at the end of the back	Ram 3⅔°	N51⅔°	6

In all, 13 stars, of which 4 are of 3rd magnitude, 6 of 4th, 1 of 5th, 2 of 6th.

Constellation of Perseus

The nebula in the right hand	Ram 26⅔°	N40½°	neb.
The star in the right elbow	Bull 1⅙°	N37½°	4
The star in the right shoulder	Bull 2⅔°	N34½°	3
The star in the left shoulder	Ram 27½°	N32⅓°	4
The star in the head	Bull ⅔°	N34½°	4
The star in the broad of the back	Bull 1½°	N31⅙°	4
The bright star in the right side	Bull 4⅚°	N30°	2
The western one of the 3 after the one in the side	Bull 5⅓°	N27⅚°	4
The middle one of the 3	Bull 7°	N27⅔°	4
The eastern one of these	Bull 7⅔°	N27⅓°	3
The star in the left elbow	Bull ½°	N27°	4
The bright star in the Gorgon's head	Ram 29⅔°	N23°	2
The star east of this	Ram 29⅙°	N21°	4
The star west of the bright one	Ram 27⅔°	N21°	4
The star left farther west than this	Ram 26⅚°	N22¼°	4
The star in the right knee	Bull 14⅚°	N28°	4

Configurations	Longitude		Latitude	Magn.
The star west of this and above the knee	Bull	13°	N28⅙°	4
The western star of the 2 above the joint	Bull	12⅓°	N25°	4
The eastern one in the joint itself	Bull	14°	N26¼°	4
The star in the right calf	Bull	14⅙°	N24½°	5
The star in the right ankle	Bull	16⅓°	N18¾°	5
The star in the left thigh	Bull	6⅚°	N21⅚°	4+
The star in the left knee	Bull	8⅔°	N19¼°	3
The star in the left shank	Bull	8⅓°	N14¾°	4
The star in the left heel	Bull	4⅙°	N12°	3−
The star east of it in the left foot	Bull	6⅓°	N11°	3+

In all, 26 stars, of which 2 are of 2nd magnitude,
5 of 3rd, 16 of 4th, 2 of 5th, a nebula.

The Unfigured Stars about Perseus

The star east of the one in the knee	Bull	11⅚°	N18°	5
The star north of those in the right knee	Bull	15°	N31°	5
The western star of those in the Gorgon's Head	Ram	24⅔°	N20⅔°	dim

In all, 3 stars, of which 2 are of 5th magnitude,
1 indistinct.

Constellation of the Charioteer

The southern one of the 2 at the head	Twins	2½°	N30°	4
The northern one and above the head	Twins	2⅓°	N31⅚°	4
The star in the left shoulder called Capella	Bull	25°	N22½°	1
The star in the right shoulder	Twins	2⅚°	N20°	2
The star in the right elbow	Twins	1⅙°	N15¼°	4
The star in the right wrist	Twins	2⅚°	N13⅓°	4+
The star in the left elbow	Bull	22°	N20⅔°	4+
The eastern one of the 2 in the left wrist called the Kids	Bull	22⅙°	N18°	4+
The western one of these	Bull	22°	N18°	4
The star in the left ankle	Bull	19⅚°	N10⅙°	3−
The star common to the right ankle and the horn	Bull	25⅔°	N5°	3+
The star north of this near the foot	Bull	26°	N8½°	5
The star still north of this in the buttock	Bull	26⅓°	N12⅙°	5
The little star above the left foot	Bull	20⅔°	N16°	6

In all, 14 stars, of which 1 is of 1st magnitude,
1 of 2nd, 2 of 3rd, 7 of 4th, 2 of 5th, 1 of 6th.

Constellation of Serpentarius

The star in the head	Scorpion 24⅚°	N36°	3+
The western one of the 2 in the right shoulder	Scorpion 28°	N27¼°	4+
The eastern one of these	Scorpion 29°	N26½°	4
The western star of the 2 in the left shoulder	Scorpion 13⅓°	N33°	4
The eastern one of these	Scorpion 14⅔°	N31⅚°	4
The star in the left elbow	Scorpion 8⅓°	N24½°	4
The western star of the 2 in the left hand	Scorpion 5°	N17°	3
The eastern one of these	Scorpion 6°	N16½°	3
The star in the right elbow	Scorpion 26⅔°	N15°	4
The western star of the 2 in the right hand	Archer 2⅓°	N13⅔°	4−
The eastern one of these	Archer 3⅓°	N14⅓°	4
The star in the right knee	Scorpion 21⅙°	N7½°	3
The star in the right shank	Scorpion 26⅔°	N2¼°	4+
The western star of the 4 in the right foot	Scorpion 23°	S2¼°	4
The one east of this one	Scorpion 24⅓°	S1½°	4+
The star still east of this last	Scorpion 25°	S⅓°	4
The remaining and easternmost of the 4	Scorpion 25⅚°	S¼°	5
The one east of these and touching the heel	Scorpion 27⅙°	N1°	5
The star in the left knee	Scorpion 12⅙°	N11⅚°	3

Configurations	*Longitude*	*Latitude*	*Magn.*
The northern one of the 3 in a straight line in the left shank	Scorpion 11⅔°	N5⅓°	5+
The middle one of these	Scorpion 10⅔°	N3⅙°	5
The southern one of the 3	Scorpion 9⅚°	N1⅔°	5+
The star in the left heel	Scorpion 12⅓°	N⅔°	5
The star touching the hollow of the left foot	Scorpion 10⅔°	S¾°	4

In all, 24 stars, of which 5 are of 3rd magnitude, 13 of 4th, 6 of 5th.

The Unfigured Stars about the Serpentarius

The northern one of the 3 east of the right shoulder	Archer 2°	N28⅙°	4
The middle one of the 3	Archer 2⅔°	N26⅓°	4
The southern one of these	Archer 3°	N25°	4
The star east of the 3 above the middle one	Archer 3⅔°	N27°	4
The lone star north of the 4	Archer 4⅔°	N33°	4

In all, 5 stars of 4th magnitude.

Constellation of the Serpent of Serpentarius

Of the square in the head, the star at the end of the jaw	Balance 18⅚°	N38°	4
The star touching the nostrils	Balance 21⅔°	N40°	4
The star in the temple	Balance 24⅓°	N36°	3
The star at the beginning of the throat	Balance 22°	N34¼°	3
The star in the middle of the square and in the jaw	Balance 21⅓°	N37¼°	4
The star outside and north of the head	Balance 26⅙°	N42½°	4
The star after the first curve of the neck	Balance 21⅔°	N29¼°	3
The northern one of the 3 following this	Balance 24⅚°	N26½°	4
The middle one of the 3	Balance 24⅓°	N25⅓°	3
The southern one of these	Balance 26⅓°	N24°	3
The star after the next curve, west of the Serpentarius' left hand	Balance 28⅚°	N16½°	4
The star east of those in the hand	Scorpion 8⅙°	N13¼°	5
The star after the Serpentarius' right thigh	Scorpion 23⅔°	N10½°	4
The southern one of the 2 east of this	Scorpion 27°	N8½°	4+
The northern one of these	Scorpion 27⅚°	N10⅚°	4
The star after the right hand in the tail's curve	Archer 3⅔°	N20°	4
The star east of this likewise in the tail	Archer 8⅔°	N21⅙°	4+
The star at the tip of the tail	Archer 18⅓°	N27°	4

In all, 18 stars, of which 5 are of 3rd magnitude, 12 of 4th, 1 of 5th.

Constellation of the Arrow

The lone star in the point	Goat 10⅙°	N39⅓°	4
The eastern one of the 3 in the shaft	Goat 6⅔°	N39⅙°	6
The middle one of these	Goat 5⅚°	N39½°	5
The western one of the 3	Goat 4⅔°	N39°	5
The star at the extremity of the notched end	Goat 3⅓°	N38⅔°	5

In all, 5 stars, of which 1 is of 4th magnitude, 3 of 5th, 1 of 6th.

Constellation of the Eagle

The star in the middle of the head	Goat 7⅙°	N26⅚°	4
The star west of this and in the neck	Goat 4⅚°	N27⅙°	3
The bright one in the broad of the back called the Eagle	Goat 3⅚°	N29⅙°	2+
The one near this to the north	Goat 4⅔°	N30°	3−
The western one of the 2 in the left shoulder	Goat 3⅙°	N31½°	3
The eastern one of these	Goat 6°	N31½°	5

Configurations	*Longitude*	*Latitude*	*Magn.*
The western one of the 2 in the right shoulder	Archer 29⅔°	N28⅔°	5
The eastern one of these	Goat 1⅙°	N26⅔°	5+
The star farther off under the Eagle's tail touching the Milky Way	Archer 22⅙°	N36⅔°	3
In all, 9 stars, of which 1 is of 2nd magnitude, 4 of 3rd, 1 of 4th, 3 of 5th.			
The Unfigured Stars about the Eagle			
The western star of the 2 south of the Eagle's head	Goat 3⅔°	N21⅔°	3
The eastern one of these	Goat 8⅚°	N19⅙°	3
The star southwest of the Eagle's right shoulder	Archer 26°	N25°	4+
The star south of this	Archer 28½°	N20°	3
The star still south of this	Archer 29⅔°	N15½°	5
The star west of all these	Archer 21⅙°	N18⅙°	3
In all, 6 stars, of which 4 are of 3rd magnitude, 1 of 4th, 1 of 5th.			
Constellation of the Dolphin			
The western star of the 3 in the tail	Goat 17⅔°	N29⅙°	3−
The northern one of the remaining 2	Goat 18⅔°	N29°	4−
The southern one of these	Goat 18⅔°	N27¾°	4
The southern one of the western side of those stars in the rhomboidal figure of 4 sides	Goat 18½°	N32°	3−
The northern one of the western side	Goat 20⅙°	N33⅚°	3−
The southern one of the eastern side of the rhombus	Goat 21⅓°	N32°	3−
The northern one of the eastern side	Goat 23⅙°	N33⅙°	3−
The southern one of the 3 between the tail and the rhombus	Goat 17½°	N30¼°	6
The western one of the remaining 2 northern ones	Goat 17½°	N31⅚°	6
The remaining eastern one of these	Goat 19°	N31½°	6
In all, 10 stars, of which 5 are of 3rd magnitude, 2 of 4th, 3 of 6th.			
Constellation of Forepart of Horse			
The western one of the 2 in the head	Goat 26⅓°	N20½°	dim
The eastern one of these	Goat 28°	N20⅔°	dim
The western one of the 2 in the jaw	Goat 26⅓°	N25½°	dim
The eastern one of these	Goat 27⅔°	N25°	dim
In all, 4 dim stars.			
Constellation of the Horse			
The star common to the Horse's navel and Andromeda's head	Fishes 17⅚°	N26°	2−
The star in the loin and at the end of the wing	Fishes 12⅙°	N12½°	2−
The star in the right shoulder and at the beginning of the foot	Fishes 2⅙°	N31°	2−
The star in the broad of the back, and shoulder of the wing	Water Bearer 26⅔°	N19⅔°	2−
The northern one of the 2 in the body under the wing	Fishes 4½°	N25½°	4
The southern one of these	Fishes 5°	N25°	4
The northern one of the 2 in the right knee	Water Bearer 29°	N35°	3
The southern one of these	Water Bearer 28½°	N34½°	5
The western one of the 2 close together in the chest	Water Bearer 26⅙°	N29°	4
The eastern one of these	Water Bearer 27°	N29½°	4
The western one of the 2 close together in the neck	Water Bearer 18⅚°	N18°	3
The eastern one of these	Water Bearer 20½°	N19°	4
The southern one of the 2 in the mane	Water Bearer 21⅓°	N15°	5
The northern one of these	Water Bearer 20½°	N16°	5
The northern one of the 2 close together in the head	Water Bearer 9⅓°	N16½°	3

Configurations	Longitude	Latitude	Magn.
The southern one of these	Water Bearer 8°	N16°	4
The star in the muzzle	Water Bearer 5⅓°	N22½°	3+
The star in the right ankle	Water Bearer 23⅓°	N41⅙°	4+
The star in the left knee	Water Bearer 17⅓°	N34¼°	4+
The star in the left ankle	Water Bearer 12⅓°	N36⅚°	4+

In all, 20 stars, of which 4 are of 2nd magnitude,
4 of 3rd, 9 of 4th, 3 of 5th.

Constellation of Andromeda

The star in the broad of the back	Fishes 25⅓°	N24½°	3
The star in the right shoulder	Fishes 26⅓°	N27°	4
The star in the left shoulder	Fishes 24⅓°	N23°	4
The southern star of the 3 in the right arm	Fishes 23⅔°	N32°	4
The northern one of these	Fishes 24⅔°	N33½°	4
The middle one of the 3	Fishes 25°	N32⅓°	5
The southern star of the 3 at the end of the right hand	Fishes 19⅔°	N41°	4
The middle one of these	Fishes 20⅔°	N42°	4
The northern one of the three	Fishes 22⅙°	N44°	4
The star in the left arm	Fishes 24⅙°	N17½°	4
The star in the left elbow	Fishes 25⅔°	N15⅚°	4
The southern one of the 3 above the girdle	Ram 3⅚°	N26⅓°	3
The middle one of these	Ram 1⅚°	N30°	4
The northern one of the 3	Ram 2°	N32½°	4
The star above the left foot	Ram 16⅚°	N28°	3
The star in the right foot	Ram 17⅙°	N37⅓°	4−
The star south of this one	Ram 15⅙°	N35⅔°	4+
The northern one of the 2 in the left bend of the knee	Ram 12⅓°	N29°	4
The southern one of these	Ram 12°	N28°	4
The star in the right knee	Ram 10⅙°	N35½°	5
The northern one of the 2 in the train	Ram 12⅔°	N34½°	5
The southern one of these	Ram 14⅙°	N32½°	5
The star outside and west of the 3 in the right hand	Fishes 11⅔°	N44°	3

In all, 23 stars, of which 4 are of 3rd magnitude,
15 of 4th, 4 of 5th.

Constellation of the Triangle

The star at the vertex of the Triangle	Ram 11°	N16½°	3
The western one of the 3 in the base	Ram 16°	N20⅔°	3
The middle one of these	Ram 16⅓°	N19⅔°	4
The eastern one of the 3	Ram 16⅚°	N19°	3

In all, 4 stars, of which 3 of 3rd magnitude, 1 of 4th.
—Thus, in all, 360 stars for the northern part,
of which 3 are of 1st magnitude, 18 of 2nd,
81 of 3rd, 177 of 4th, 58 of 5th, 13 of 6th,
9 dim. 1 nebular.

CONSTELLATIONS OF THE STARS IN THE ZODIAC

Constellation of the Ram

The western star of the 2 in the horn	Ram 6⅔°	N7⅓°	3−
The eastern one of these	Ram 7⅔°	N8⅓°	3
The northern one of the 2 in the muzzle	Ram 11°	N7⅔°	5
The southern one of these	Ram 11½°	N6°	5
The star in the neck	Ram 6½°	N5½°	5
The star in the loins	Ram 17⅔°	N6°	6
The star at the beginning of the tail	Ram 21⅓°	N4⅚°	5
The western one of the 3 in the tail	Ram 23⅚°	N1⅔°	4
The middle one of the 3	Ram 25⅓°	N2½°	4

Configurations	*Longitude*	*Latitude*	*Magn.*
The eastern one of these	Ram 27°	N1⅚°	4
The star in the calf	Ram 19⅔°	N1½°	5
The star under the bend of the knee	Ram 18°	S1½°	5
The star in the hind-foot	Ram 15°	S5¼°	4+

In all, 13 stars, of which 2 are of 3rd magnitude,
4 of 4th, 6 of 5th, 1 of 6th.

The Unfigured Stars about the Ram

The star above the head which Hipparchus placed in the muzzle	Ram 10⅔°	N10½°	3+
The eastern and brightest one of the 4 above the loins	Ram 21⅔°	N10⅙°	4
The northern one of the remaining fainter 3	Ram 21⅓°	N12⅔°	5
The middle one of the 3	Ram 19⅔°	N11⅙°	5
The southern one of these	Ram 19⅙°	N10⅔°	5

In all, 5 stars, of which 1 is of 3rd magnitude,
1 of 4th, 3 of 5th.

Constellation of the Bull

The northern star of the 4 in the section	Ram 26⅙°	S6°	4
The one next it	Ram 26°	S7¼°	4
The one again next to this last	Ram 24⅓°	S8½°	4
The southernmost one of the 4	Ram 24⅓°	S9¼°	4
The one east of these in the right shoulder blade	Ram 29⅔°	S9½°	5
The star in the chest	Bull 3⅔°	S8°	3
The star in the right knee	Bull 6⅔°	S12⅔°	4
The star in the right ankle	Bull 3°	S14⅚°	4
The star in the left knee	Bull 12⅙°	S10°	4
The star in the left forearm	Bull 13°	S13°	4
Of those in the face called the Hyades, the one on the nostrils	Bull 9°	S5¾°	3−
The star between this last and the northern eye	Bull 10⅓°	S4¼°	3−
The star between this last one and the southern eye	Bull 10⅚°	S5⅚°	3−
The bright red star of the Hyades in the southern eye	Bull 12⅔°	S5⅙°	1
The other one in the northern eye	Bull 11⅚°	S3°	3−
The star at the beginning of the southern horn and the ear	Bull 17½°	S4°	4
The southern one of the 2 in the southern horn	Bull 20⅓°	S5°	5
The northern one of these	Bull 20°	S3½°	5
The star at the tip of the southern horn	Bull 27⅔°	S2½°	3
The star at the beginning of the northern horn	Bull 15⅔°	S¼°	4
The star at the tip of the northern horn the same as the one in the Charioteer's right foot	Bull 25⅔°	N5°	3
The northern one of the 2 close together in the northern ear	Bull 12°	N½°	5
The southern one of these	Bull 11⅔°	N¼°	5
The western one of the 2 small ones in the neck	Bull 7°	N⅔°	5
The eastern one of these	Bull 9°	S1°	6
The southern one of the western side of the square in the neck	Bull 8°	N5°	5
The northern one of the western side	Bull 8½°	N7⅓°	5
The southern one of the eastern side	Bull 12°	N3°	5
The northern one of the eastern side	Bull 11⅔°	N5°	5
The northern limit of the eastern side of the Pleiads	Bull 2⅙°	N4½°	5
The southern limit of the eastern side	Bull 2½°	N3⅔°	5
The eastern and narrowest limit of the Pleiads	Bull 3⅔°	N3⅓°	5
The small star outside and north of the Pleiads	Bull 3⅔°	N5°	4

In all, 33 stars, of which 1 of 1st magnitude, 7 of
3rd, 11 of 4th, 13 of 5th, 1 of 6th.

Configurations	*Longitude*	*Latitude*	*Magn.*
The Unfigured Stars about the Bull			
The star below the right foot and the shoulder-blade	Ram 25°	S17½°	4
The western one of the 3 above the southern horn	Bull 20°	S2°	5
The middle one of the 3	Bull 21°	S1¾°	5
The eastern one of these	Bull 26°	S2°	5
The northern one of the 2 below the tip of the southern horn	Bull 29°	S6⅓°	5
The southern one of these	Bull 29°	S7⅔°	5
The western star of the 5 eastern ones under the northern horn	Bull 27°	N⅔°	5
The one east of this	Bull 29°	N1°	5
The one again east of this	Twins 1°	N1⅓°	5
The northern one of the 2 remaining eastern ones	Twins 2⅓°	N3⅓°	5
The southern one of these	Twins 3⅓°	N1¼°	5
In all, 11 stars, of which 10 of 4th magnitude, 1 of 5th.			

Constellation of the Twins			
The star in the head of the western Twin	Twins 23⅓°	N9½°	2
The red star in the head of the eastern Twin	Twins 26⅔°	N6¼°	2
The star in the left forearm of the western Twin	Twins 16⅔°	N10°	4
The star in the same arm	Twins 18⅔°	N7⅓°	4
The star east of this one and in the broad of the back	Twins 22°	N5½°	4
The one east of this in the right shoulder of the same Twin	Twins 24°	N4⅚°	4
The star in the eastern shoulder of the eastern Twin	Twins 26⅔°	N2⅔°	4
The star in the right side of the western Twin	Twins 21⅔°	N2⅔°	5
The star in the left side of the eastern Twin	Twins 23⅙°	N⅓°	5
The star in the left knee of the western Twin	Twins 13°	N1½°	3
The star under the left knee of the eastern Twin	Twins 18¼°	S2½°	3
The star in the left testicle of the eastern Twin	Twins 21⅔°	S½°	3
The star under the bend of the right knee of the same Twin	Twins 21⅔°	S6°	3
The star in the forward foot of the western Twin	Twins 6½°	S1½°	4+
The star east of this in the same foot	Twins 8½°	S1¼°	4+
The star at the end of the right foot of the western Twin	Twins 10⅙°	S3½°	4+
The star at the end of the left foot of the eastern Twin	Twins 12°	S7½°	3
The star in the right foot of the eastern Twin	Twins 14⅔°	S10½°	4
In all, 18 stars, of which 2 are of 2nd magnitude, 5 of 3rd, 9 of 4th, 2 of 5th.			

The Unfigured Stars about the Twins			
The western star of the forward foot of the western Twin	Twins 4⅙°	S⅔°	4
The bright western star of the western knee	Twins 6½°	N5⅚°	4+
The western star of the left knee of the eastern Twin	Twins 15⅙°	S2¼°	5
The northern star of the 3 in a straight line east of the right hand of the eastern Twin	Twins 28⅓°	S1⅓°	5
The middle one of the 3	Twins 26⅓°	S3⅓°	5
The southern one of these between the forearm and hand	Twins 26°	S4½°	5
The bright one east of these 3	Crab ⅔°	S2⅔°	4
In all, 7 stars, of which 3 are of 4th magnitude, 4 of 5th.			

Configurations	*Longitude*	*Latitude*	*Magn.*
Constellation of the Crab			
The middle of the nebula called the Crab, in the breast	Crab 10⅓°	N⅓°	neb.
The northern star of the 2 western ones of the square about the nebula	Crab 7⅔°	N1¼°	4−
The southern star of the 2 western ones	Crab 8°	S1⅙°	4−
The northern star of the 2 eastern ones of the square called the Asses	Crab 10⅓°	N2⅔°	4+
The southern one of these 2	Crab 11⅓°	S⅙°	4+
The star in the southern claw	Crab 16½°	S5½°	4
The star in the northern claw	Crab 8⅓°	N11⅚°	4
The star in the northern hind-foot	Crab 2⅔°	N1°	5
The star in the southern hind-foot	Crab 7⅙°	S7½°	4+

In all, 9 stars, of which 7 are of 4th magnitude,
1 of 5th, 1 nebula.

The Unfigured Stars about the Crab			
The star above the joint of the southern claw	Crab 19⅔°	S2⅓°	4−
The star east of the tip of the southern claw	Crab 21⅙°	S5⅔°	4−
The western star of the 2 above the nebula	Crab 14°	N4⅚°	5
The eastern one of these	Crab 17°	N7¼°	5

In all, 4 stars, of which 2 are of 4th magnitude,
2 of 5th.

Constellation of the Lion			
The star at the tip of the nostril	Crab 18⅓°	N10°	4
The star in the open mouth	Crab 21⅙°	N7½°	4
The northern one of the 2 in the head	Crab 24⅓°	N12°	3
The southern one of these	Crab 24⅙°	N9½°	3+
The northern one of the 3 in the throat	Lion ⅙°	N11°	3
The middle one of the 3, nearby	Lion 2⅙°	N8½°	2
The southern one of these	Lion ⅔°	N4½°	3
The one at the heart called Regulus	Lion 2½°	N⅙°	1
The one south of this, in the chest	Lion 3½°	S1⅚°	4
The star a little west of the one in the heart	Lion 0°	S4°	5
The star in the right knee	Crab 27⅓°	0°	5
The star in the right foreclaw	Crab 24⅙°	S3⅔°	5
The star in the left foreclaw	Crab 27⅓°	S4⅙°	4
The star in the left knee	Lion 2½°	S4¼°	4
The star in the left armpit	Lion 9⅙°	S⅙°	4
The western star of the 3 in the belly	Lion 7°	N4°	6
The northern one of the other eastern 2	Lion 10⅓°	N5⅓°	6
The southern one of these	Lion 12⅙°	N2⅓°	6
The western one of the 2 in the loin	Lion 11⅓°	N12¼°	6
The eastern one of these	Lion 14⅙°	N13⅔°	2−
The northern one of the 2 in the buttocks	Lion 14⅓°	N11⅙°	5
The southern one of these	Lion 16⅓°	N9⅔°	3
The star in the calfs of the legs	Lion 20⅓°	N5⅚°	3
The star in the hind-leg joints	Lion 21⅔°	N1¼°	4
The star south of this one, in the forelegs	Lion 24⅔°	S⅚°	4
The star in the hind-claws	Lion 27½°	S3⅕°	5
The star at the tip of the tail	Lion 24½°	N11⅚°	1−

In all, 27 stars, of which 2 are of 1st magnitude,
2 of 2nd, 6 of 3rd, 8 of 4th, 5 of 5th, 4 of 6th.

The Unfigured Stars about the Lion			
The western star of the 2 above the back	Lion 6°	N13⅓°	5
The eastern one of these	Lion 8⅙°	N15½°	5

Configurations	*Longitude*		*Latitude*	*Magn.*
The northern one of the 3 above the flank	Lion	17½°	N1⅙°	4 −
The middle one of these	Lion	17⅙°	S½°	5
The southern one of these	Lion	18°	S2⅔°	5
The northernmost part of the nebula called the Hair, lying between the extremities of the Lion and the Bear	Lion	24⅚°	N30°	dim
The western one of the eminent southern stars of the Hair	Lion	24⅓°	N25°	dim
The eastern one of those in the figure of the ivy leaf	Lion	28½°	N25½°	dim

In all, 5 stars, of which 1 is of 4th magnitude, 4 of 5th, and the Hair.

Constellation of the Virgin

	Longitude		*Latitude*	*Magn.*
The southern star of the 2 in the tip of the skull	Lion	26⅓°	N4¼°	5
The northern one of these	Lion	27°	N5⅔°	5
The northern one of the 2 in the face east of these	Virgin	⅔°	N8°	5
The southern one of these	Virgin	½°	N5½°	5
The star at the tip of the southern and left wing	Lion	29°	N⅓°	3
The western star of the 4 in the left wing	Virgin	8¼°	N1½°	3
The one east of this	Virgin	13⅙°	N2⅚°	3
The star east of this again	Virgin	17½°	N2½°	5
The last and eastern one of these 4	Virgin	21°	N1⅔°	4
The star in the right side under the girdle	Virgin	14⅓°	N8½°	3
The western star of the 3 in the right and northern wing	Virgin	8⅙°	N13½°	5
The southern of the 2 remaining ones	Virgin	10⅙°	N11⅔°	6
The northern one of these called Vindemiatrix	Virgin	12⅙°	N15⅙°	3+
The star in the left hand called Spica	Virgin	26⅔°	S2°	1
The star under the girdle on the right buttock	Virgin	24⅚°	N8⅔°	3
The northern star of the western side of the square in the left thigh	Virgin	26⅓°	N3⅓°	5
The southern star of the western side	Virgin	27¼°	N⅙°	6
The northern star of the 2 of the eastern side	Balance	0°	N1½°	4 −
The southern one of the eastern side	Virgin	28°	S3°	5
The star in the left knee	Balance	1⅔°	S1½°	5
The star in the hinder part of the right thigh	Virgin	28°	N8½°	5
The middle one of the 3 in the train about the feet	Balance	6⅔°	N7⅙°	4
The southern one of these	Balance	7⅓°	N2⅔°	4
The northern one of the 3	Balance	8⅓°	N11⅔°	4
The star in the left and southern foot	Balance	10°	N½°	4
The star in the right and northern foot	Balance	12⅔°	N9⅚°	4

In all, 26 stars, of which 1 is of 1st magnitude, 6 of 3rd, 7 of 4th, 10 of 5th, 2 of 6th.

The Unfigured Stars about the Virgin

	Longitude		*Latitude*	*Magn.*
The western star of the 3 in a straight line under the left forearm	Virgin	14⅔°	S3½°	5
The middle one of these	Virgin	19°	S3½°	5
The eastern one of the 3	Virgin	22¼°	S3⅓°	5
The western one of the 3 in a straight line under Spica	Virgin	27⅙°	S7⅙°	6
The middle one of these which is double	Virgin	28⅙°	S8⅓°	5
The eastern one of these	Balance	5°	S7⅚°	6

In all, 6 stars, of which 4 are of 5th magnitude, 2 of 6th.

BOOK EIGHT

1. Tabular Exposition of the Constellations of the Southern Hemisphere

Configurations	Longitude	Latitude	Magn.
Constellation of the Balance			
The bright star at the end of the southern claw (of the Scorpion)	Balance 18°	N⅔°	2
The one north of and dimmer than this last	Balance 17°	N2½°	5
The bright star of those at the end of the northern claw	Balance 22⅙°	N8⅚°	2
The dim one west of this	Balance 17⅔°	N8½°	5
The star in the middle of the southern claw	Balance 24°	S1⅔°	4
The star west of this in the same claw	Balance 21⅓°	N1¼°	4
The star in the middle of the northern claw	Balance 27⅚°	N4¾°	4
The one east of this in the same claw	Scorpion 3°	N3½°	4 −

In all, 8 stars, of which 2 are of 2nd magnitude, 4 of 4th, 2 of 5th.

The Unfigured Stars about the Balance			
The western star of the 3 northern ones in the northern claw	Balance 26⅙°	N9°	5
The southern star of the 2 eastern ones	Scorpion 3⅔°	N6⅔°	4 −
The northern one of these	Scorpion 4⅓°	N9¼°	4 −
The eastern one of the 3 between the claws	Scorpion 3½°	N½°	6
The northern one of the 2 remaining eastern ones	Scorpion ⅔°	N⅓°	5
The southern one of these	Scorpion 1⅙°	S1½°	4
The western star of the more southern 3 of the southern claw	Balance 23°	S7½°	3
The northern one of the 2 remaining eastern ones	Scorpion 1⅙°	S8½°	4
The southern one of these	Scorpion 2°	S9⅔°	4

In all, 9 stars, of which 1 is of 3rd magnitude, 5 of 4th, 2 of 5th, 1 of 6th.

Constellation of the Scorpion			
The northern one of the 3 bright ones in the forehead	Scorpion 6⅓°	N1⅓°	3
The middle one of these	Scorpion 5⅔°	S1⅔°	3
The southern of the 3	Scorpion 5⅔°	S5°	3
The star south of this again, in one of the feet	Scorpion 6°	S7⅚°	3
The northern one of the 2 lying beside the northernmost of the bright ones	Scorpion 7°	N1⅔°	4
The southern one of these	Scorpion 6⅓°	N½°	4
The western star of the 3 bright ones in the body	Scorpion 10⅔°	S3¾°	3
The red middle one of these called Antares	Scorpion 12⅔°	S4°	2
The eastern one of the 3	Scorpion 14½°	S5½°	3
The western one of the 2 beneath these in the farthest foot	Scorpion 9⅓°	S6½°	5
The eastern one of these	Scorpion 10⅔°	S6⅔°	5
The star in the first joint from the body	Scorpion 18½°	S11°	3
The star after this one in the 2nd joint	Scorpion 18⅚°	S15°	3
The northern one of the double star in the 3rd joint	Scorpion 20°	S18⅔°	4

247

Configurations	Longitude	Latitude	Magn.
The southern one of the double	Scorpion 20⅙°	S18°	4
The next one in the 4th joint	Scorpion 23⅙°	S19½°	3
The star after this one in the 5th joint	Scorpion 28⅙°	S18⅚°	3
The star next to this last in the 6th joint	Archer ½°	S16⅔°	3
The star in the 7th joint near the center	Scorpion 29°	S15⅙°	3
The eastern one of the 2 in the center	Scorpion 27½°	S13⅓°	3
The western one of these	Scorpion 27°	S13½°	4

In all, 21 stars, of which 1 is of 2nd magnitude,
13 of 3rd, 5 of 4th, 2 of 5th.

The Unfigured Stars about the Scorpion

The nebula east of the center	Archer 1⅙°	S13¼°	neb.
The western star of the 2 north of the center	Scorpion 25½°	S6⅙°	5+
The eastern one of these	Scorpion 25½°	S4⅙°	5

In all, 3 stars, of which 2 are of 5th magnitude,
a nebula.

Constellation of the Archer

The star at the tip of the arrow	Archer 4½°	S6½°	3
The star in the grip of the left hand	Archer 7⅔°	S6½°	3
The star in the southern part of the bow	Archer 8°	S10⅚°	3
The southern star of those in the northern part of the bow	Archer 9°	S1½°	3
The northern of these, at the tip of the bow	Archer 6⅔°	N2⅚°	4
The star in the left shoulder	Archer 15⅓°	S3⅙°	3
The star west of this in the arrow	Archer 13°	S3½°	4
The nebular and double star in the eye	Archer 15⅙°	N¾°	neb.
The western star of the 3 in the head	Archer 15⅔°	N2⅙°	4
The middle one of these	Archer 17⅔°	N1½°	4
The eastern one of the 3	Archer 19⅙°	N2°	4
The southern one of the 3 in the northern part of cloak	Archer 21⅓°	N2⅚°	5
The middle one of these	Archer 22⅓°	N4½°	4
The northern one of the 3	Archer 22⅚°	N6½°	4
The dim one east of these 3	Archer 25⅔°	N5½°	6
The northern one of the 2 in the southern part of cloak	Archer 29½°	N5⅚°	5
The southern one of these	Archer 27⅔°	N2°	6
The star in the right shoulder	Archer 22⅔°	S1⅚°	5
The star in the right elbow	Archer 24⅚°	S2⅚°	4
Of the 3 in the back, the star in the broad of the back	Archer 20°	S2½°	5
The middle one of these in the shoulder blade	Archer 17⅔°	S4½°	4+
The remaining one below the armpit	Archer 16⅓°	S6¾°	3
The star in the left fore-ankle	Archer 17⅔°	S23°	2
The star in the knee of the same foot	Archer 17°	S18°	2−
The star in the right fore-ankle	Archer 6⅔°	S13°	3
The star in the left thigh	Archer 27⅓°	S13½°	3
The star in the right forearm behind	Archer 23⅚°	S20⅙°	3
The western star of the northern side of the 4 at the beginning of the tail	Archer 27⅔°	S4⅚°	5
The eastern star of the northern side	Archer 28⅚°	S4⅚°	5
The western star of the southern side	Archer 28⅚°	S5⅚°	5
The eastern star of the southern side	Archer 29⅔°	S6½°	5

In all, 31 stars, of which 2 are of 2nd magnitude,
9 of 3rd, 9 of 4th, 8 of 5th, 2 of 6th, a nebula.

Constellation of the Goat

The northern star of 3 in the eastern horn	Goat 7⅓°	N7⅓°	3
The middle star of these	Goat 7⅔°	N6⅔°	6

Configurations	*Longitude*		*Latitude*	*Magn.*
The southern one of the 3	Goat	7⅓°	N5°	3
The star at the tip of the western horn	Goat	5°	N8°	6
The southern star of the 3 in the muzzle	Goat	9°	N¾°	6
The western one of the remaining 2	Goat	8⅔°	N1¾°	6
The eastern one of these	Goat	8⅚°	N1½°	6
The western one of the 3 under the right eye	Goat	6⅙°	N⅔°	5
The northern one of the 2 in the neck	Goat	11⅔°	N3⅚°	6
The southern one of these	Goat	11⅚°	N⅚°	5
The star in the left bent knee	Goat	11⅔°	S8⅔°	4
The star under the right knee	Goat	10⅚°	S6½°	4
The star in the left shoulder	Goat	16⅔°	S7⅔°	4
The western star of the 2 close together under the belly	Goat	20⅙°	S6⅚°	4
The eastern one of these	Goat	20⅓°	S6°	5
The eastern one of the 3 in the middle of the body	Goat	18½°	S4¼°	5
The southern one of the 2 remaining western stars	Goat	16⅔°	S4°	5
The northern one of these	Goat	16⅔°	S2⅚°	5
The western one of the 2 in the back	Goat	16⅔°	0°	4
The eastern one of these	Goat	21°	S⅚°	4
The western one of the 2 in the southern part of the thorn	Goat	23⅓°	S4¾°	4
The eastern one of these	Goat	25°	S4¼°	4
The western star of the 2 near the tail	Goat	24⅚°	S2⅙°	3
The eastern one of these	Goat	26⅓°	S2°	3
The western one of the 4 in the northern part of the tail	Goat	26⅚°	N⅓°	4
The southern one of the remaining 3	Goat	28⅔°	0°	5
The middle one of these	Goat	27⅔°	N2⅚°	5
The northern one of these at the tail end	Goat	28⅔°	N4⅓°	5

In all, 28 stars, of which 4 of 3rd magnitude, 9 of
4th, 9 of 5th, 6 of 6th.

Constellation of the Water Bearer

The star in the head of the Water Bearer	Water Bearer	⅓°	N15¾°	5
The brighter of the 2 in the right shoulder	Water Bearer	6⅓°	N11°	3
The dimmer one beneath this	Water Bearer	5⅙°	N9⅔°	5
The star in the left shoulder	Goat	26½°	N8⅚°	3
The star under it in the back, as if under the armpit	Goat	27⅓°	N6¼°	5
The eastern one of the 3 in the left hand in the strap	Goat	17⅔°	N5½°	3
The middle one of these	Goat	16⅙°	N8°	4
The western one of the 3	Goat	14⅔°	N8⅔°	3
The star in the right forearm	Water Bearer	9½°	N8¾°	3
The northern one of the 3 in the end of the right hand	Water Bearer	11⅔°	N10¾°	3
The western one of the remaining 2 northern ones	Water Bearer	12°	N9°	3
The eastern one of these	Water Bearer	13⅓°	N8½°	3
The western star of the 2 close together in the right socket	Water Bearer	6⅙°	N3°	4
The eastern one of these	Water Bearer	7°	N3⅙°	5
The star in the right buttock	Water Bearer	8⅔°	S⅚°	4
The southern star of the 2 in the left buttock	Water Bearer	1⅔°	S1⅔°	4
The northern one of these	Water Bearer	3⅙°	N¼°	6
The southern star of the 2 in the right shin	Water Bearer	11⅔°	S7½°	3
The northern one of these below the bend of the knee	Water Bearer	11⅓°	S5°	4
The star in the left calf	Water Bearer	4⅔°	S5⅔°	5
The southern one of the 2 in the left shin	Water Bearer	8⅓°	S10°	5
The northern one of these under the knee	Water Bearer	7⅚°	S9°	5
The western one of those in the flow of water from the hand	Water Bearer	15°	N2°	4

Configurations	Longitude	Latitude	Magn.
The star near this last southwards	Water Bearer 15⅚°	N⅙°	4
The star near this last after the curve	Water Bearer 17⅔°	S1⅙°	4
The star still east of this	Water Bearer 20°	S½°	4
The star in the curve south of this last	Water Bearer 20½°	S1⅔°	4
The northern one of the 2 south of this	Water Bearer 19°	S3½°	4
The southern one of the 2	Water Bearer 19⅚°	S4⅙°	4
The lone star distant from these towards the south	Water Bearer 20⅚°	S8¼°	5
The western star of the 2 close together after this one	Water Bearer 22⅔°	S11°	5
The eastern one of these	Water Bearer 23⅙°	S10⅚°	5
The northern one of the 3 in the nearby stream	Water Bearer 21⅔°	S14°	5
The middle one of the 3	Water Bearer 22⅙°	S14¾°	5
The eastern one of these	Water Bearer 23⅙°	S15⅔°	5
The northern one of the next 3, in like manner	Water Bearer 17°	S14⅙°	4
The southern one of the 3	Water Bearer 18⅓°	S15¾°	4
The middle one of these	Water Bearer 17½°	S15°	4
The western one of the 3 in the remaining stream	Water Bearer 11⅚°	S14¾°	4
The southern one of the remaining 2	Water Bearer 12⅓°	S15⅓°	4
The northern one of these	Water Bearer 13⅙°	S14°	4
The last star in the water and in the southern Fish's mouth	Water Bearer 7°	S20⅓°	1

In all, 42 stars, of which 1 is of 1st magnitude, 9 of 3rd, 18 of 4th, 13 of 5th, 1 of 6th.

The Unfigured Stars about the Water Bearer

Configurations	Longitude	Latitude	Magn.
The western star of the 3 stars east of the water's curve	Water Bearer 26⅔°	S15½°	4+
The northern one of the remaining 2	Water Bearer 29⅔°	S14⅔°	4+
The southern one of these	Water Bearer 29°	S18¼°	4+

In all, 3 stars of 4th magnitude.

Constellation of the Fishes

Configurations	Longitude	Latitude	Magn.
The star in the mouth of the western Fish	Water Bearer 21⅔°	N9¼°	4
The southern one of the 2 in the top of his head	Water Bearer 24⅙°	N7½°	4
The northern one of these	Water Bearer 26°	N9⅓°	4
The western one of the 2 in the back	Water Bearer 28⅙°	N9½°	4
The eastern one of these	Fishes ⅔°	N7½°	4
The western one of the 2 in the belly	Water Bearer 26°	N4½°	4
The eastern one of these	Water Bearer 29⅔°	N3½°	4
The star in the tail of the same Fish	Fishes 6°	N6⅓°	4
The first star from the tail, in the cord	Fishes 11°	N5¾°	6
The eastern one of these	Fishes 13°	N3¾°	6
The western star of the 3 bright ones following	Fishes 17⅙°	N2¼°	4
The middle one of these	Fishes 20½°	N1⅙°	4
The eastern one of the 3	Fishes 23°	S⅙°	4
The northern one of the 2 little ones in the curve under these	Fishes 22⅓°	S2°	6
The southern one of these	Fishes 23°	S5°	6
The western one of the 3 after the curve	Fishes 26½°	S2⅓°	4
The middle one of these	Fishes 28⅔°	S4⅔°	4
The eastern one of the 3	Ram ⅔°	S7¾°	4
The star in the knot of the 2 cords	Ram 2½°	S8½°	3
The star west of the knot, in the northern cord	Ram ½°	S1⅔°	4
The southern one of the next 3 after it	Ram ⅙°	N1⅚°	5
The middle one of these	Ram ⅔°	N5⅓°	3
The northern one of the 3, and at the tail's end	Ram ½°	N9°	4
The northern one of the 2 in the mouth of the eastern Fish	Ram 2°	N21¾°	5
The southern one of these	Ram 1⅔°	N21⅔°	5
The eastern of the 3 little ones in the head	Fishes 28⅔°	N20°	6

Configurations	*Longitude*	*Latitude*	*Magn.*
The middle one of these	Fishes 27⅔°	N19⅚°	6
The western one of the 3	Fishes 27°	N20⅓°	6
The western star of the 3 in the southern fin after the star in Andromeda's elbow	Fishes 25⅔°	N14⅓°	4
The middle one of these	Fishes 26⅓°	N13¼°	4
The eastern one of the 3	Fishes 27⅔°	N12°	4
The northern one of the 2 in the belly	Ram 2⅙°	N17°	4
The southern one of these	Fishes 29⅚°	N15⅓°	4
The star in the eastern fin near the tail	Ram 0°	N11¾°	4

In all, 34 stars, of which 2 are of the 3rd magnitude, 22 of the 4th, 3 of the 5th, 7 of the 6th.

The Unfigured Stars about the Fishes

The western star of the 2 northern ones of the square under the western Fish	Fishes 1⅙°	S2⅔°	4
The eastern one of these	Fishes 2¼°	S2½°	4
The western star of the southern side	Fishes ⅔°	S5½°	4
The eastern one of the southern side	Fishes 2⅓°	S5½°	4

In all 4 stars of 4th magnitude.

—Thus, in all, 346 stars of the zodiac, of which 5 are of 1st magnitude, 9 of 2nd, 64 of 3rd, 133 of 4th, 105 of 5th, 27 of 6th, 3 nebulae, and the Hair.

Constellation of the Sea-Monster

The star at the nostril tip	Ram 17⅔°	S7¾°	4
The eastern star of the 3 in the muzzle, at the tip of the jaw	Ram 17⅔°	S12⅓°	3
The middle one of these in the middle of the mouth	Ram 12⅔°	S11½°	3
The western one of the 3, in the cheek	Ram 10½°	S14°	3
The star in the brow and eye	Ram 10⅙°	S8⅙°	4
The star north of this in the hair of the head	Ram 12⅔°	S6⅓°	4
The star west of these in the flowing hair	Ram 7⅔°	S4⅙°	4
The northern star of the western side of the square in the chest	Ram 3°	S24½°	4
The southern star of the western side	Ram 3⅓°	S28°	4
The northern star of the eastern side	Ram 6⅔°	S25⅙°	4
The southern star of the eastern side	Ram 7°	S27½°	3
The middle one of the 3 in the body	Fishes 22°	S25⅓°	3
The southern one of these	Fishes 23°	S30⅚°	4
The northern one of the 3	Fishes 25°	S20°	3
The eastern one of the 2 near the tail	Fishes 19⅔°	S15⅔°	3
The western one of these	Fishes 15°	S15⅔°	3
The northern star of the eastern side of the square near the tail	Fishes 11°	S13⅔°	5
The southern one of the eastern side	Fishes 10⅔°	S14⅔°	5
The northern star of the western side	Fishes 9⅓°	S13°	5+
The southern one of the western side	Fishes 9°	S14°	5+
The northern star of the 2 at the tail's tip	Fishes 4⅓°	S9⅔°	3−
The star at the tail's southern end	Fishes 5⅔°	S20⅓°	3

In all, 22 stars, of which 10 are of 3rd magnitude, 8 of 4th, 4 of 5th.

Constellation of Orion

The nebula in Orion's head	Bull 27°	S13⅓°	neb.
The bright red star in the right shoulder	Twins 2°	S17°	1−
The star in the left shoulder	Bull 24°	S17½°	2
The eastern star below this	Bull 25°	S18°	4−

Configurations	*Longitude*	*Latitude*	*Magn.*
The star in the right elbow	Twins 4⅓°	S14½°	4
The star in the right forearm	Twins 6⅓°	S11⅚°	6
The eastern double star of the southern side of the square in the right hand	Twins 6½°	S10°	4
The western star of the southern side	Twins 6°	S9¾°	4
The eastern star of the northern side	Twins 7⅓°	S8¼°	6
The western star of the northern side	Twins 6⅔°	S8¼°	6
The western star of the 2 in the club	Twins 1⅔°	S3¾°	5
The eastern one of these	Twins 4⅔°	S4¼°	5
The eastern one of the 4 stars in a straight line in the back	Bull 27⅚°	S19⅔°	4
The star west of this one	Bull 26⅓°	S20°	6
The star still west of this last	Bull 25⅓°	S20⅙°	6
The last and western one of the 4	Bull 24⅙°	S20⅔°	5
The northern one of those in the skin held by the left hand	Bull 20½°	S8°	4
The 2nd one from the northernmost	Bull 19⅓°	S8⅙°	4
The 3rd from the northernmost	Bull 18°	S10¼°	4
The 4th from the northernmost	Bull 16⅓°	S12⅚°	4
The 5th from the northernmost	Bull 15⅙°	S14¼°	4
The 6th from the northernmost	Bull 14⅚°	S15⅚°	3
The 7th from the northernmost	Bull 14⅚°	S17⅙°	3
The 8th from the northernmost	Bull 15⅓°	S20⅓°	3
The last and southernmost of those in the skin	Bull 16⅓°	S21½°	3
The western star of the 3 in the belt	Bull 25⅓°	S24⅙°	2
The middle one of these	Bull 27⅓°	S24⅚°	2
The eastern one of the 3	Bull 28⅙°	S25⅔°	2
The star in the handle of the dagger	Bull 23⅚°	S25⅚°	3
The northern one of the 3 bunched at the tip of the dagger	Bull 26½°	S28⅓°	4
The middle one of these	Bull 26⅔°	S29⅙°	3−
The southern one of the 3	Bull 27°	S29⅚°	3
The eastern star of the 2 under the tip of the handle	Bull 27⅔°	S30⅔°	4
The western one of these	Bull 26½°	S30⅚°	4
The bright star in the left foot common with the Water	Bull 19⅚°	S31½°	1
The northern one of those above the ball of the anklejoint in the shin	Bull 21°	S30¼°	4+
The star outside under the left heel	Bull 23⅓°	S31⅙°	4
The star under the right and eastern knee	Twins ⅙°	S33½°	3+

In all, 38 stars, of which 2 are of the 1st magnitude, 4 of the 2nd, 8 of the 3rd, 15 of the 4th, 3 of the 5th, 5 of the 6th, a nebula.

Constellation of the River

The star after the star in the foot of Orion at the beginning of the River	Bull 18⅓°	S31⅚°	4+
The star north of this one in the bend near Orion's shin	Bull 18½°	S28¼°	4
The eastern one of the 2 after this one	Bull 18°	S29⅚°	4
The western one of these	Bull 14⅔°	S28¼°	4
Again the eastern one of the next 2	Bull 13⅙°	S25⅚°	4
The western one of these	Bull 10⅙°	S25⅓°	4
The eastern one of the 3 after this last	Bull 6⅓°	S26°	5
The middle one of these	Bull 5½°	S27°	4
The western one of the 3	Bull 2⅚°	S27⅚°	4
The eastern star of the 4 in the next interval	Ram 27°	S32⅚°	3
The star west of this one	Ram 24⅓°	S31°	4
The star west again of this last	Ram 24⅙°	S28⅚°	3

Configurations	*Longitude*	*Latitude*	*Magn.*
The western one of the 4	Ram 22°	S28°	3
Likewise the eastern one of the 4 in the next interval	Ram 17⅙°	S25½°	3
The star west of this last	Ram 14½°	S23⅚°	4
The star again west of this	Ram 12⅙°	S23½°	3
The western one of the 4	Ram 10½°	S23¼°	4
The first star in the bend of the River and touching the chest of the Sea-Monster	Ram 5⅙°	S32⅙°	4
The star east of this	Ram 5⅚°	S34⅚°	4
The western one of the next 3	Ram 8⅚°	S38½°	4
The middle one of these	Ram 13⅚°	S38⅙°	4
The eastern one of the 3	Ram 17½°	S39°	4
The northern one of the western side of the 4 in a trapezium	Ram 21⅓°	S41⅓°	4
The southern one of the western side	Ram 21½°	S42½°	5
The western one of the eastern side	Ram 22⅙°	S43¼°	4
The eastern one of this side and last of the 4	Ram 24⅔°	S43⅓°	4
The northern one of the 2 distant stars to the east and close together	Bull 4⅙°	S50⅓°	4
The southern one of these	Bull 5°	S51¾°	4
The eastern one of the next 2 after the turn	Ram 28⅙°	S53⅚°	4
The western one of these	Ram 25⅚°	S53⅙°	4
The eastern one of the 3 in the next interval	Ram 17⅚°	S53°	4
The middle one of these	Ram 14⅚°	S53½°	4
The western one of the 3	Ram 11⅚°	S52½°	4
The last and bright star of the River	Ram ⅙°	S53½°	1

In all, 34 stars, of which 1 is of 1st magnitude, 5 of 3rd, 26 of 4th, 2 of 5th.

Constellation of the Hare

The northern star of the western side of the square down over the ears	Bull 19⅔°	S35°	5
The southern one of the western side	Bull 19⅚°	S36½°	5
The northern one of the eastern side	Bull 21⅓°	S35⅔°	5
The southern one of the eastern side	Bull 21⅓°	S36⅔°	5
The star in the chin	Bull 19⅙°	S39¼°	4+
The star in the left forefoot	Bull 16⅙°	S45¼°	4+
The star in the middle of the body	Bull 25⅚°	S41½°	3
The star under the belly	Bull 24⅚°	S44⅓°	3
The northern one of the 2 in the hind-feet	Twins 1°	S44⅙°	4+
The southern one of these	Bull 29°	S45⅚°	4+
The star in the loin	Twins 0°	S38⅓°	4+
The star at the tail's tip	Twins 2⅔°	S38⅙°	4+

In all, 12 stars, of which 2 are of 3rd magnitude, 6 of 4th, 4 of 5th.

Constellation of the Dog

The brightest and red star in the face called the Dog	Twins 17⅔°	S39⅙°	1
The star in the ears	Twins 19⅔°	S35°	4
The star in the head	Twins 21⅓°	S36½°	5
The northern one of the 2 in the neck	Twins 23⅓°	S37¾°	4
The southern one of these	Twins 25⅓°	S40°	4
The star in the chest	Twins 20½°	S42⅔°	5
The northern one of the 2 in the right knee	Twins 16⅙°	S41¼°	5
The southern one of these	Twins 16°	S42½°	5
The star at the end of the forefoot	Twins 11°	S41⅓°	3
The western star of the 2 in the left knee	Twins 14⅔°	S46½°	5
The eastern one of these	Twins 16⅙°	S45⅚°	5
The eastern star of the 2 in the left shoulder	Twins 24⅔°	S46⅙°	4
The western one of these	Twins 21⅔°	S47°	5

Configurations	*Longitude*	*Latitude*	*Magn.*
The star at the beginning of the left thigh	Twins 26⅔°	S48¾°	3−
The star under the belly betwen the thighs	Twins 23⅔°	S51½°	3
The star in the joint of the right foot	Twins 23°	S55⅙°	4
The star at the tip of the right foot	Twins 9⅔°	S53¾°	3
The star in the tail	Crab 2⅙°	S50⅔°	3−

In all, 18 stars, of which 1 is of 1st magnitude, 5 of 3rd, 5 of 4th, 7 of 5th.

The Unfigured Stars about the Dog

The star north of the Dog's head	Twins 19½°	S25¼°	4
The southernmost one of the 4 in a straight line under the hind-feet	Twins 10°	S61½°	4
The star north of this	Twins 11⅓°	S58¾°	4
The star still north of this	Twins 13°	S57°	4
The last and northern star of the 4	Twins 14⅙°	S56°	4
The western star of the 3 in a straight line east of these 4	Bull 28°	S55½°	4
The middle one of these	Twins ⅓°	S57⅔°	4
The eastern one of the 3	Twins 2⅓°	S59⅚°	4
The eastern star of the 2 bright ones under these	Bull 29°	S59⅔°	2
The western star of these	Bull 26°	S57⅔°	2
The last and southern star of the foregoing	Bull 22⅙°	S59½°	4

In all, 11 stars, of which 2 are of 2nd magnitude, 9 of 4th.

Constellation of Procyon (Little Dog)

The star in the neck	Twins 25°	S14°	4
The bright star in the hinder parts called Procyon	Twins 29⅙°	S16⅙°	1

In all, 2 stars, of which 1 is of 1st magnitude, 1 of 4th.

Constellation of the Argus

The western star of the 2 in the stern-post ornament	Crab 10⅓°	S42½°	5
The eastern one of these	Crab 14⅓°	S43⅓°	3
The northern one of the 2 close together above the Shield in the stern	Crab 8⅚°	S45°	4
The southern one of these	Crab 8⅔°	S46⅙°	4
The star west of these	Crab 5⅓°	S45½°	4
The bright star in the middle of the Shield	Crab 6⅓°	S47¼°	3
The western star of the 3 below the Shield	Crab 5⅓°	S49¾°	4
The eastern one of these	Crab 9⅓°	S49½°	4
The middle one of the 3	Crab 8½°	S49¼°	4
The star in the goose neck of the stern	Crab 14°	S49⅚°	4
The northern one of the 2 in the stern-keel	Crab 4°	S53°	4
The southern one of these	Crab 4°	S58⅔°	3
The northern of those in the deck of the poop	Crab 10⅙°	S55½°	5
The western one of the next 3	Crab 12⅙°	S58⅔°	5
The middle one of these	Crab 13⅔°	S57¼°	4
The eastern one of the 3	Crab 16½°	S57⅚°	4
The bright one east of these, on the deck	Crab 21⅙°	S58⅔°	2
The western one of the 2 dim stars under the bright one	Crab 18⅙°	S60°	5
The eastern one of these	Crab 21°	S59⅓°	5
The eastern star of the 2 above the bright one	Crab 23⅙°	S56⅔°	5
The western one of these	Crab 24⅓°	S57⅔°	5
The northern star of the 3 in the shields near the mastholder	Lion 5⅔°	S51½°	4+
The middle one of these	Lion 6⅙°	S55⅔°	4+
The southern one of the 3	Lion 4°	S57⅙°	4+

Configurations	*Longitude*		*Latitude*	*Magn.*
The northern one of the 2 close together under these	Lion	9⅙°	S60°	4+
The southern one of these	Lion	9°	S61¼°	4
The southern one of the 2 in the middle of the mast	Lion	⅙°	S51⅚°	3
The northern one of these	Crab	29⅓°	S49°	3
The western star of the 2 near the tip of the mast	Crab	28°	S43⅓°	4
The eastern one of these	Crab	29°	S43½°	4
The star below the 3rd and eastern shield	Lion	14⅙°	S54½°	2
The star on the section of the deck	Lion	17½°	S51¼°	2−
The star between the oars in the keel	Crab	11⅙°	S63°	4
The dim star east of this	Crab	19°	S64½°	6
The bright star east of this below the deck	Lion	0°	S63⅚°	2
The bright star south of this in the lower keel	Lion	8½°	S69⅔°	2
The western star of the 3 east of this	Lion	15⅙°	S65⅔°	3
The middle one of these	Lion	21⅓°	S65⅚°	3
The eastern one of the 3	Lion	26°	S67⅓°	2
Of the 2 east of these, the western one near the section	Virgin	1°	S62⅚°	3
The eastern one of these	Virgin	8°	S62¼°	3
The western one of the 2 in the northern and western oar	Twins	4°	S65⅚°	4+
The eastern one of these	Twins	20⅙°	S65⅔°	3+
Of the 2 in the remaining oar the western star called Canopus	Twins	17⅙°	S75°	1
The last and eastern one of these	Twins	29°	S71¾°	3+

In all, 45 stars, of which 1 is of 1st magnitude, 6 of 2nd, 11 of 3rd, 19 of 4th, 7 of 5th, 1 of 6th.

Constellation of the Water-Snake

Of the 2 western stars in the head, the southern one in the nostrils	Crab	14°	S15°	4
The northern one of these, above the eye	Crab	13⅓°	S13⅙°	4
Of the 2 stars east of these, the northern one near the top of the head	Crab	15⅓°	S11½°	4
The southern one of these, in the open mouth	Crab	15½°	S14¼°	4
The star east of them all in the jaw	Crab	17½°	S12¼°	4
The western one of the 2 at the beginning of the neck	Crab	20⅓°	S11⅚°	5
The eastern one of these	Crab	23⅓°	S13⅔°	4
The middle one of the next 3 in the curve of the neck	Crab	28⅚°	S15⅓°	4
The eastern one of the 3	Lion	⅔°	S14⅚°	4
The southernmost of these	Crab	28½°	S17⅙°	4
The dim northern star of the 2 close together in the south	Crab	29⅙°	S19¾°	6
The bright one of these 2	Lion	0°	S20½°	2
The western star of the 3 east of the curve	Lion	6°	S26½°	4
The middle one of these	Lion	8⅔°	S26°	4
The eastern one of the 3	Lion	11⅙°	S23¼°	4
The western one of the next 3 almost in a straight line	Lion	18°	S24⅔°	3
The middle one of these	Lion	20°	S23¼°	4
The eastern one of the 3	Lion	23°	S22⅙°	3
The northern one of the 2 after the base of the Bowl	Virgin	1½°	S25¾°	4+
The southern one of these	Virgin	2⅓°	S30⅙°	4
The western one of the 3 in the triangle after these	Virgin	12⅙°	S31⅓°	4
The middle and southern one of these	Virgin	14½°	S33⅙°	4
The eastern one of the 3	Virgin	16⅙°	S31⅓°	3
The star behind the Raven near the tail	Balance	0°	S13⅔°	4+
The star at the tip of the tail	Balance	13½°	S17⅔°	4+

In all, 25 stars, of which 1 is of 2nd magnitude, 3 of 3rd, 19 of 4th, 1 of 5th, 1 of 6th.

Configurations	*Longitude*		*Latitude*	*Magn.*

The Unfigured Stars about the Water-Snake

The star in the southern part of the head	Crab	12½°	S23¼°	3
The star far east of those in the neck	Lion	11°	S16⅓°	3
In all, 2 stars of 3rd magnitude.				

Constellation of the Bowl

The star in the base of the Bowl common to the Water-Snake	Lion	26⅓°	S23°	4
The southern one of the 2 in the middle of the Bowl	Virgin	2½°	S19½°	4
The northern one of these	Virgin	0°	S18°	4
The star on the southern edge of the face	Virgin	7°	S18½°	4+
The star on the northern edge	Lion	29⅓°	S13⅔°	4
The star on the southern handle	Virgin	9⅙°	S16⅙°	4−
The star on the northern handle	Virgin	1⅔°	S11½°	4
In all, 7 stars of 4th magnitude.				

Constellation of the Raven

The star in the beak and common with the Water-snake	Virgin	15⅓°	S21⅔°	3
The star in the neck near the head	Virgin	14⅓°	S19⅔°	3
The star in the breast	Virgin	16⅔°	S18⅙°	5
The star in the western and right wing	Virgin	13½°	S14⅚°	3
The western star of the 2 in the eastern wing	Virgin	16⅔°	S12½°	3
The eastern one of these	Virgin	17°	S11¾°	4
The star at the end of the foot, common with the Water-Snake	Virgin	20½°	S18⅙°	3
In all, 7 stars, of which 5 are of 3rd magnitude, 1 of 4th, 1 of 5th.				

Constellation of the Centaur

The southernmost of the 4 in the head	Balance	10½°	S21⅔°	5+
The northernmost of these	Balance	10°	S18⅚°	5+
The western star of the remaining 2 middles ones	Balance	9⅙°	S20½°	4+
The eastern and last one of these 4	Balance	10°	S20°	5+
The star on the left and western shoulder	Balance	6⅙°	S25⅔°	3
The star on the right shoulder	Balance	15⅔°	S22½°	3
The star on the left shoulder blade	Balance	9⅙°	S27½°	4
The northern star of the 2 western ones of the 4 in the wand	Balance	18⅙°	S22⅓°	4
The southern one of these	Balance	19⅙°	S23¾°	4
Of the remaining 2, the star at the tip of the wand	Balance	22°	S18¼°	4
The remaining one south of this	Balance	22½°	S20⅚°	4
The western one of the 3 in the right side	Balance	13⅓°	S28⅓°	4+
The middle one of these	Balance	14°	S29⅓°	4+
The eastern one of the 3	Balance	15⅙°	S28°	4+
The star in the right arm	Balance	16⅓°	S26½°	4+
The star in the right forearm	Balance	22⅚°	S25¼°	3
The star at the tip of the right hand	Balance	27½°	S24¼°	4
The bright star at the beginning of the human body	Balance	18°	S33½°	3+
The eastern star of the 2 dim stars north of this one	Balance	17⅔°	S31°	5
The western one of these	Balance	16⅚°	S33°	5
The star at the beginning of the back	Balance	12⅙°	S34⅚°	5
The star west of this last on the horse's back	Balance	9°	S37⅔°	5
The eastern star of the 3 in the loins	Balance	5⅚°	S40°	3
The middle one of these	Balance	5°	S43°	4
The western one of the 3	Balance	2⅔°	S41°	5
The western star of the 2 close together in the right thigh	Balance	2⅔°	S46⅙°	3
The eastern one of these	Balance	3½°	S46¾°	4

Configurations	*Longitude*	*Latitude*	*Magn.*
The star in the chest under the horse's armpit	Balance 18⅓°	S40¾°	4
The western star of the 2 under the belly	Balance 16⅓°	S43°	2
The eastern one of these	Balance 17⅔°	S43¾°	3
The star in the bend of the right foot	Balance 10°	S51⅙°	2
The star in the ankle of the same foot	Balance 15⅓°	S51⅔°	2
The star under the ankle of the left foot	Balance 6⅓°	S55⅙°	4
The star in the frog of the same foot	Balance 11⅙°	S55⅓°	2
The star at the tip of the right forefoot	Scorpion 8⅓°	S41⅙°	1
The star in the knee of the left foot	Balance 24⅙°	S45⅓°	2
The star outside under the right hind-foot	Balance 14⅔°	S49⅙°	4
In all, 37 stars, of which 1 is of 1st magnitude, 5 of 2nd, 7 of 3rd, 16 of 4th, 8 of 5th.			
Constellation of the Wild Beast (Lupus)			
The star at the end of the hind-foot near the Centaur's hand	Balance 28°	S24⅚°	3
The star in the hand of the same foot	Balance 25⅚°	S29⅙°	3
The western star of the 2 on the shoulder-blade	Scorpion 1°	S21¼°	4
The eastern one of these	Scorpion 4⅙°	S21°	4
The star in the middle of Wild Beast's body	Scorpion 3°	S25⅙°	4
The star in the belly under the flank	Scorpion ⅙°	S27°	5
The star in the thigh	Scorpion ½°	S29°	5
The northern one of the 2 near the beginning of the thigh	Scorpion 4⅔°	S28½°	5
The southern one of these	Scorpion 3⅔°	S30⅙°	5
The star at the end of the loins	Scorpion 5⅔°	S33⅙°	5
The southern star of the 3 at the tip of the tail	Balance 22°	S31⅓°	5
The middle one of the 3	Balance 21⅚°	S30½°	4
The northern one of these	Balance 23°	S29⅓°	4+
The southern star of the 2 in the neck	Scorpion 8⅚°	S17°	4
The northern one of these	Scorpion 9⅓°	S15⅓°	4+
The western one of the 2 in the muzzle	Scorpion 5⅔°	S13⅓°	4
The eastern one of these	Scorpion 6⅔°	S11⅚°	4
The southern one of the 2 in fore-foot	Balance 27⅙°	S11⅚°	4+
The northern one of these	Balance 26½°	S10°	4+
In all, 19 stars, of which 2 are of 3rd magnitude, 11 of 4th, 6 of 5th.			
Constellation of the Censer (Ara)			
The northern star of the 2 in the base	Scorpion 27⅔°	S22⅔°	5
The southern one of these	Archer 3°	S25¾°	4
The star in the middle of the altar-like vessel	Scorpion 26⅓°	S26½°	4+
The northern one of the 3 in the brazier	Scorpion 20⅔°	S1⅓°	5
The southern one of the remaining 2 contiguous ones	Scorpion 25⅙°	S34⅙°	4+
The northern one of these	Scorpion 25°	S33⅓°	4
The star at the end of the burning	Scorpion 20⅚°	S34¼°	4
In all, 7 stars, of which 5 are of 4th magnitude, 2 of 5th.			
Constellation of the Southern Crown			
The outside western star of the southern edge	Archer 9⅙°	S21½°	4
The eastern star of those on the Crown	Archer 11⅔°	S21°	5
The star east of this one	Archer 13⅙°	S23°	5
The star again east of this one	Archer 14⅚°	S20°	4
The star after this one in front of the Archer's groin	Archer 16⅙°	S18½°	5
The star after this one and north of the bright one in the knee	Archer 17°	S17⅙°	4
The star north of this one	Archer 16⅚°	S16°	4
The star still north of this one	Archer 16½°	S15⅙°	4

Configurations	*Longitude*	*Latitude*	*Magn.*
The eastern one of the 2 western ones following this last on the northern edge	Archer 15⅙°	S15⅓°	6
The western one of these 2 dim ones	Archer 14⅔°	S14⅚°	6
The star rather west of this one	Archer 11⅚°	S14⅔°	5
The star still west of this	Archer 9⅔°	S15⅚°	5
The last one south of this last	Archer 9⅙°	S18½°	5
In all, 13 stars, of which 5 are of 4th magnitude, 6 of 5th, 2 of 6th.			
Constellation of the Southern Fish			
The star in the mouth, the same as that at the beginning of the Water	Water Bearer 7°	S20⅓°	1
The western star of the 3 at the southern edge of the head	Water Bearer ⅔°	S20⅓°	4
The middle one of these	Water Bearer 4⅙°	S22¼°	4
The eastern one of the 3	Water Bearer 5⅓°	S22½°	4
The star near the gills	Water Bearer 4⅓°	S16¼°	4+
The star in the southern spinal fin	Goat 25⅙°	S19½°	5
The eastern one of the 2 in the belly	Water Bearer 1⅙°	S15⅙°	5
The western one of these	Goat 28⅚°	S14⅔°	4
The eastern one of the 3 in the northern fin	Goat 25⅙°	S15°	4
The middle one of these	Goat 21⅚°	S16½°	4
The western one of the 3	Goat 21°	S18⅙°	4
The star at the tip of the tail	Goat 20⅙°	S22¼°	4
In all, 12 stars, of which 1 is of the 1st magnitude, 9 of 4th, 2 of 5th.			
The Unfigured Stars about the Southern Fish			
The western one of the 3 bright stars west of the Fish	Goat 8°	S22⅓°	3−
The middle one of these	Goat 11⅙°	S22⅙°	3−
The eastern one of the 3	Goat 11°	S21⅙°	3−
The dim star west of this	Goat 12°	S20⅚°	5
The southern star of the remaining 2 to the north	Goat 13⅚°	S17°	4
The northern one of these	Goat 13⅚°	S14⅚°	4
In all, 6 stars, of which 3 are of 3rd magnitude, 2 of 4th, 1 of 5th.			

Thus there are 316 stars in the southern part, of which 7 are of 1st magnitude, 18 of 2nd, 63 of 3rd, 164 of 4th, 54 of 5th, 9 of 6th, and 1 nebula.

Thus altogether there are 1022 stars, of which 15 are of 1st magnitude, 45 of 2nd, 208 of 3rd, 474 of 4th, 217 of 5th, 49 of 6th, 9 dim ones, 5 nebulae, and the Hair.

2. On the Position of the Milky Way

Now this is the exposition we give of the fixed stars, and next we add on the things having to do with the position of the Milky Way as far as we can and to the extent we have observed each of its parts, trying to represent its particular appearances.

It is easily seen that the Milky Way is not simply a circle but a zone having quite the color of milk, whence its name; and that it is not regular and ordered, but different in width, color, density, and position; and that in one part it is double. These particulars we find needing careful observation.

Now, the double part of this zone has one of its junctions near the Censer [Ara] and the other at the Bird [Cygnus]. The western zone nowhere touches the other, for it divides at the junction at the Censer and at the junction at the Bird, the eastern zone joining the other part of the Milky Way and making one zone which the great circle drawn in its middle would traverse. We shall first discuss this zone beginning with its southernmost parts.

These parts go through the Centaur's feet, and are thinner and fainter. The star in the bend of the right hind-foot is a little south of the northern line of the Milky Way; likewise the star in the left fore-knee and the star under the right hind-ankle. The star in the left hind shank lies in the middle of the Milky Way, the star in the same ankle and the star in the right fore-ankle being very nearly 2° north of the southern arc. And the parts about the hind-feet are rather denser.

Next, the northern arc of the Milky Way is very nearly 1½° from the star in the loin of the Beast [Lupus], and the southern arc intercepts the star at the Censer's ember, touching the more northern of the two consecutive stars in the brazier, and the more southern of the two in the base. The star in the northern part of the brazier and the star in the middle of the brazier lie in the Milky Way itself. And these parts are thinner.

Next, the northern part of the Milky Way intercepts the three joints preceding the Scorpion's centre and the nebular mass following the centre. The southern arc touches the star in the Archer's right fore-ankle and intercepts the star in his left hand. The star in the southern part of the Archer is outside the Milky Way, and the star at the arrow's point is in the middle of it. In the northern part of the Archer each of the stars lies a little more than 1° from either arc: the southern one from the southern arc, and the northern one from the opposite arc. And the parts about the three joints are slightly denser, the parts about the arrow's point appearing quite dense and smoky.

The following parts are slightly thinner, and extend along the Eagle, keeping the same width. The star in the tip of the tail of the Serpent which the Serpentarius [Ophiouchus] holds, lies in the open sky a little more than 1° from the western arc of the Milky Way. The two western stars of the bright ones lying under it lie in the Milky Way itself, the more southern one 1° from the eastern arc and the more northern 2°. Of those in the Eagle's right shoulder the eastern star touches the same arc; and the western one is cut off within it, and likewise the bright western star of those in the left wing. And the bright star in the back and the two in a straight line with it just fail to touch the same arc.

After these parts, the whole Arrow [Sagitta] is enclosed in the Milky Way, and the star at the point is 1° from the eastern arc, and the star at the notched end is 2° from the western arc. The parts near the Eagle are slightly denser, and the rest slightly thinner.

The Milky Way next passes through the Bird. The northerwestern arc is bounded in its curve by the star in the Bird's southern shoulder, by the star under it in the wing, and by the two stars in the southern foot. The southeastern arc is bounded by the star in the tip of the southern flat of the wing and it encloses within itself the two figured stars under the same wing which are nearly 2° from it. The parts about the wings are slightly thicker.

The parts following are included in this zone and are much denser and as if coming from another beginning. For they lean to the extreme parts of the other zone, and, making a gap with it on the southern side, they now join with the zone we have just spoken of which is very thin at the junction. After the gap in density with respect to the other zone, they begin from the bright star in the Bird's rump and from the nebular mass in the northern knee. Then, turning slightly as far as the star in the southern knee, they extend this density, a bit thinned out, as far as the tiara of Cepheus, and are bounded on the northern side by the southern star of the three in the tiara and by the star east of these three at which they make two eminences, one pointing to the northeast, the other to the southeast.

After these parts, the Milky Way encloses the whole of Cassiopeia except the star at the tip of the foot. The southern arc is bounded by the star in Cassiopeia's head, and the northern arc by the star in the foot of the throne by the star in Cassiopeia's calf. The other stars about her all lie in the Milky Way. Near the arcs the parts are of a thinner mass, while those in the middle of Cassiopeia show an extended density.

And next, the right side of Perseus is enveloped by the Milky Way, the lone star outside Perseus' right knee bounds the northern side which is the thinnest, and the bright star in the right rib and the two eastern stars of the three south of it bound the southern side which is the densest. The nebular mass in the handle, the star in the head, the star in the right shoulder, and the star in the right elbow are all enveloped in it. The quadrilateral in the right knee and again the star in the calf of the same leg lie in the middle of the Milky Way, the star in the right heel being itself a little within the southern side.

And after these parts the zone, showing a slightly thinner mass, goes through the Charioteer. The star in the right shoulder called the Goat [Capella] and the two in the right forearm just fail to touch the northeastern arc of the Milky Way. The little star above the left foot in the part around the feet bounds the southwestern side, and the star $\frac{1}{2}°$ above the right foot is within the same side. In the left forearm the two consecutive stars, called the Kids, lie in the middle of the zone.

And, next, the Milky Way goes through the feet of the Twins, showing a rather extensive density below the stars in the tip of the feet. The eastern star of the three in a straight line under the right foot of the Charioteer, the eastern star of the two in Orion's club, and the northern stars of the four in his hand, bound the western arc of the Milky Way. The bright star under the Charioteer's right hand and the star in the eastern foot of the eastern Twin are very nearly 1° within the eastern side. And the stars in the other extremities of the feet lie in the middle of the Milky Way.

From there the zone passes by the Little Dog and the Dog, leaving the whole of the Little Dog quite far outside the Milky Way to the east, and the Dog almost wholly outside to the west. For a cloud here envelops the star on the back, and next it almost touches the three east of it in the Dog's neck. And the lone star above the Dog's head, outside and farther off, is very nearly $2\frac{1}{2}°$ within the eastern arc; and the mass here is rather rarer.

After these parts, the Milky Way goes through the Argus. And the northwestern star of those in the small shield of the poop bounds the western arc of the zone; and the star in the middle of the shield, the two consecutive stars under it, the bright star at the beginning of the deck near the rudder, and the middle star of the three in the keel, nearly touch the same side. The northern star of the three in the mast-holder bounds the eastern arc, and the bright star in the terminal ornament is 1° within the same side. And the bright star under the eastern shield on the deck is the same 1° outside the same side. And the southern star of the two bright ones in the middle of the mast touches the same side, and the two bright stars in the same piece of the keel are very nearly 2° within the western arc.

From these the Milky Way now joins with the zone through the Centaur's feet. And the mass through the Argus is rather light, but the parts about the little shield are thicker than it, and likewise those about the sailholder and about the segment of the keel.

The zone we have just spoken of, dividing off as we said from the zone described at the Censer and beginning from these, envelops the three joints of the Scorpion's body and leaves the eastern star of the three in the body 1° outside the western arc. And the star in the fourth joint lies in the clear space between the two zones, nearly equidistant from both and a little more than 1° away.

And after this, the western zone turns eastward 1° likewise, and bounds the western side of the Milky Way with the star in the right knee of Ophiuchus and the eastern side with the star in the same shin. The western star in the end of the same foot touches the same side. And next again the star under the right elbow of the Serpentarius bounds the western arc, and the principal star of the two in the tip of the same hand bounds the eastern arc. At the point there is a rather large gap of clear space in which lie the two stars in the Serpent's tail after the one in the tip. And the whole part of the zone just given is a mass quite rare and air-like except for the part enveloping the three joints. For that part is slightly dense.

And after this gap the Milky Way again begins from the four stars east of the right shoulder of the Serpentarius, and the bright line star touching the Eagle's tail bounds the eastern arc of this zone, the farthest away to the north of the four stars spoken of above bounding the opposite arc.

From here the zone, after this, narrows into the western parts of the Bird's beak so that it gives the appearance of a gap. But the rest of it from the star in the Bird's beak to the star in the Bird's breast is rather wider and denser. The star in the Bird's throat lies in the middle of the concentration. But a rarer part runs northward from the stars in the breast to the star in the shoulder of the right wing and the two consecutive stars in the tip of the right foot from whence, as we said before, there is a clear gap relative to the other zone from the aforementioned stars of the Bird to the bright star in the Rump.

3. ON THE CONSTRUCTION OF THE SOLID SPHERE

Now, the appearances of the Milky Way have this position. And in order that we may construct, by means of a solid sphere, a model in accord with the hypotheses demonstrated with respect to the sphere of the fixed stars—according to which it appeared to be revolved, along with the planets, by the prime movement from east to west about the poles of the equator and also moved in the opposite direction about the poles of the sun's circle or ecliptic—we shall set up the construction of it and the arrangement of the constellations in the following manner:

We shall make the color of this sphere rather deep so as to be not the atmosphere of day but the night's in which the stars appear. And taking on it two points exactly opposite each other, with these as poles we shall describe a great circle which will always be in the plane of the ecliptic and at right angles to it through its poles another circle. Beginning from one of its intersections with the first circle, we divide the ecliptic into 360 sections and subdivide these into as many sections as appear feasible. Then, making out of a strong tensile material two circles with surfaces at right angles and everywhere accurately turned (the lesser everywhere touching the curved surface of the sphere, and the other a bit larger) we shall draw lines in the middle of the curved surface of each, dividing their widths exactly in two. By means of these lines, cutting one or the other of the sides so defined into semicircles, we shall divide the semicircles resulting from these cuts into 180 sections. This done, we suppose the lesser circle always to be through both sets of poles—that is, of the equator and of the ecliptic, and also through the tropic points on the surface of this cut. Boring it in the middle diametrically opposite at the limits of the cut, we shall fit it on pins at the poles of the ecliptic taken on the sphere so that it can revolve over the whole spherical surface.

Now, to get some constant beginning for the constellations of the fixed stars, since it is not plausible to mark the tropic and equinoctial points on the sphere's ecliptic (for the distance of the constellations to them is not preserved), we shall mark the brightest of them, I mean the star in the Dog's mouth [Sirius], on the circle drawn at right angles to the ecliptic at the section beginning the division, at the given latitude from the ecliptic in the direction of its south pole. For each of the other fixed stars, according to the sequence of the Catalogue, we shall make marks by the turning the circle which is divided by the cut, about the ecliptic's poles. For we always carry the surface of its cut side to the point on the ecliptic as many degrees away from the beginning of the numbers at the section of the Dog as the desired star is in longitude from the Dog according to the Catalogue. And we go to the point of the side which has been divided and swung about, according as the star in the Catalogue is either towards the north or south pole of the ecliptic. And there we mark the point of the star, affixing a yellow or some other distinct color in proportion and in accordance with the size of the magnitudes of each.

Now, we shall make the figures of each of the constellations as simple as possible, enclosing the stars under the same contour, only with lines not differing much from the color of the whole sphere so that the advantage in distinguishing them may not be lost and the juxtaposition of many colors may not blot out the likeness to the true picture; and so that we may easily retain the comparison made in our observations when we have become habituated to the original image of the stars in the spherical representation.

We also arrange the position of the Milky Way in accordance with the places and figures and further in accordance with the densities and gaps, already explained. And we fit the greater circle, which is always to be the meridian, on the smaller one which is enveloping the sphere, about the same poles as those of the equator. And the pole-points are inserted, diametrically opposite, in the greater circle or meridian, at the extremities of the side which has been cut and divided and which is to lie above. But the pole-points are inserted in the smaller circle, which passes through both sets of poles, at the extremities diametrically opposite of arcs extending the 23°51′ of inclination either side of the ecliptic's poles. And little solids are put at the cuts of the circle where the holes of the poles are[1].

---

[1]The smaller circle is attached to the solid sphere, and these poles are the ecliptic's and do not change with respect to the fixed stars. But the larger circle is attached to the smaller at points 23°51′ away from these. These are the poles of the equator which change with respect to the fixed stars.

Each time we place the cut side of the smaller circle, which is always the same of course as the meridian through the tropic points, at that point of division of the ecliptic which is as far away from the beginning of the Dog as the Dog at the given time is from the summer tropic. At the beginning of the reign of Antonine that is 12⅓° west. We fit the meridian circle at right angles to the horizon, which is the base plane, so that it cuts its apparent surface in two and can revolve in its own plane in such a way that each time we can raise the north pole above the horizon by the amount proper to the given latitudes. And this is done with the help of the division of the meridian circle.

It makes no difference if we cannot put the equator and tropic points on the sphere itself. For the point on the divided side of the meridian circle, between the poles of the equator and lying the 90° of a quadrant's distance from either one, will serve the same purpose as the points of the equator. And the points lying 23°51′ either side of this point will serve the same purpose as either of the tropics, the northern one the same as the summer tropic, and the southern one the same as the winter tropic. And so, when the desired stars are carried by the prime east-west revolution to the divided side of the meridian circle, then, by means of that division, their distances with respect to the equator and tropics can be gotten as if on the circle through the poles of the equator.

4. On the Configurations Proper to the Fixed Stars

Now that the character of the constellations of the fixed stars has been demonstrated, there remains the discussion of their configurations. Of the configurations concerning the fixed stars besides those dealing only with their relations to each other (as when they are in a straight line or in a triangular figure or some such thing), there are those which are considered with respect only to the planets and sun and moon or parts of the ecliptic, and those which are considered with respect only to the earth. And then there are those which are considered with respect to the earth, and at the same time with respect to the planets and sun and moon or parts of the ecliptic.

Those configurations of the fixed stars which are with respect only to the planets and parts of the ecliptic, are gotten in general whenever the fixed stars and the planets are on one and the same great circle drawn through the ecliptic's poles, or on a different one but forming triangular or tetragonal or hexagonal distances—that is, forming an angle which is either right or greater or less than the third of a right angle. And they are gotten in particular in the case of those fixed stars over which some one of the planets can pass (and these are those arranged in the band of the zodiac containing the latitudinal passages of the planets): with respect to the five planets, at their apparent appulses or occultations, and with respect to the sun and moon, at the heliacal or lunar settings, conjunctions, and heliacal or lunar risings. We call heliacal or lunar setting any star begins to disappear in the rays of the luminaries; conjunction whenever the star is in a straight line with the centre; and heliacal or lunar rising whenever it begins to appear from the rays.

There are four configurations of the fixed stars with respect to the earth alone: by some they are called in general "centres," and in particular, they are rising, upper culmination, setting, and lower culmination. Where the equator is at the zenith, all the fixed stars both rise and set, and once at each revolution have an upper and lower culmination; for then the equator's poles touch the horizon, making none of the parallel circles either one of perpetual apparition or one of perpetual occultation. Where the poles are at the zenith, no one of the fixed stars either rises or sets; for then the equator has the horizon's position and one of the hemispheres formed by it revolves always above the earth and the other always below the earth, so that each of the fixed stars culminates twice in one revolution, those above the earth and those below. In the other latitudes between these, where there are some circles always visible and some always invisible, the stars enclosed by these relative to the poles neither rise nor set, and two culminations are effected at each revolution—those within the circle of perpetual apparition above the earth, and those within the circle of perpetual occultation below the earth. And the rest on the greater parallels both rise and set, culminating once above and once below in each revolution.

And their time from one of these centres back again to the same is always the same. For it embraces sensibly one revolution. And the time from one of the centres to the diametrically opposite one relative to the meridian is always the same, for it embraces half a revolution. With respect to the horizon, when the equator is at the zenith, the same is again true. For the time of each embraces half a revolution, since each of the parallels is bisected not only by the meridian but also by the horizon. But in the case of the other inclinations neither the time above nor the time below is itself equal for all, nor in each case is the time above equal to the time below, except for those on the equator itself which alone in the oblique sphere is bisected by the horizon; for all the other parallels are cut in dissimilar and unequal arcs. Consequently, the time from the rising or setting to one of the culminations is in each case equal to the time from the same culmination to the rising or setting, because the meridian divides the sections of the parallels above the earth and those below into equal parts. But the times from the rising or setting to either culmination are unequal in the inclined sphere, and equal in the right sphere, since there only are the lower sections equal to the upper sections. Therefore, in the right sphere, the stars which culminate together always rise and set together in so far as their shift about the poles of the ecliptic is imperceptible. But in the oblique sphere those stars which culminate together neither rise nor set together, the more southern always rising later than the more northern and set earlier.

And the configurations of the fixed stars, considered with respect to the earth or planets or parts of the ecliptic together, are gotten in general from the simultaneous risings or culminations or settings either with one of the planets or with some part of the ecliptic; and in particular they are considered with respect to the sun according to nine kinds.

The first kind of configuration, called early morning east wind, is when the star at rising is with the sun. And of this there is a kind called invisible morning after-rising when the star, beginning its heliacal setting, rises immediately after the sun. And there is a kind called true morning co-rising when the star rises together with and at the same time as the sun on the horizon. And there is a kind called visible morning fore-rising when the star, beginning its heliacal rising, rises before the sun.

The second configuration, called early morning culmination, is when the star, with the sun rising at the horizon, is culminating either above or below the earth. And again of this there is a kind called invisible morning after-culmination when the star culminates immediately after sunrise. And there is a kind called true morning co-culmination when the star culminates as the sun rises. And there is a kind called morning fore-culmination when the sun rises immediately after the star's culmination.

The third kind of configuration, called early morning west wind, is when the star is on the western horizon while the sun is on the eastern. Again of this there is a kind called invisible morning after-setting when the star sets immediately after the sun rises. And there is a kind called true morning co-setting when the star sets at the same time the sun rises. And there is a kind called visible morning fore-setting when the sun rises immediately after the star sets.

The fourth configuration, called noontide east wind, is when the star is on the eastern horizon while the sun is on the meridian. And again of this there is a kind called invisible daytime when the star rises as the sun culminates above the earth; and a kind called visible night time when the star rises as the sun culminates below the earth.

The fifth configuration called noontide culmination is when the sun and star are on the meridian together. And of this there are two invisible daytime kinds when, with the sun culminating above the earth, the star either culminates with it above the earth or culminates diametrically opposite below the earth. And there are two night-time kinds with the sun culminating below the earth. Of these there is the invisible when the star culminates with the sun below the earth, and the visible when the star culminates diametrically opposite above the earth.

The sixth configuration, called noontide west wind, is when the star is on the western horizon while the sun is on the meridian. And again of this there is the invisible daytime kind when the star sets as the sun culminates above the earth, and there is the visible night-time kind when the star sets as the sun culminates below the earth.

The seventh configuration, called late east wind, is when the star is on the eastern horizon while the sun is on the western. And again of this there is the kind called visible evening after-rising when the star rises immediately after sunset. And there is the kind called true evening co-rising when the star rises exactly as the sun sets. And there is the kind called invisible evening fore-rising when the sun sets immediately after the star rises.

The eighth configuration, called late culmination, is when, with the sun on the western horizon, the star is on the meridian either above or below the earth. And of this again there is the kind called visible evening after-culmination when the star culminates immediately after sunset. And there is the kind called true evening co-culmination when the star culminates exactly as the sun sets. And there is the kind called invisible evening fore-culmination when the sun sets immediately after the star culminates.

The ninth configuration, called late west wind, is when the star is on the western horizon together with the sun. And of this kind again there is the kind called visible evening fore-setting when the star, beginning its heliacal setting, sets immediately after the sun. And there is the kind called true evening co-setting when the star sets exactly with the sun. And there is the kind called invisible evening fore-setting when the star, beginning its heliacal rising, sets before the sun.

5. On the Co-risings, Co-culminations, and Co-settings of the Fixed Stars

Now with matters this way, the times of the true co-risings, co-culminations, and co-settings considered with respect to the sun's centre can be gotten geometrically by us from their position according to the star catalogue. Because the points on the ecliptic with which each of the fixed stars culminates, rises, and sets, can be shown geometrically by the following theorems.

For first, with a view to the co-culminations, let there be the circle *ABCD* through both sets of poles, the equator's and the ecliptic's; and let there be the semicircle *AEC* of the equator about the pole *F*, and the semicircle *BED* of the ecliptic about the pole *G*. Let the segment *GHKL* of a great circle be drawn through the poles of the ecliptic. And let the fixed star in question be thought at the point *H* on it. For their positions with respect to the circles so drawn are available from our observation and record. And let the segment *FHMN* of the great circle through the poles of the equator and through the star at *H* be drawn.

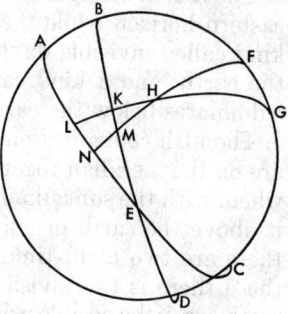

Fig. viii, 1.

Now, it is evident that the star at *H* culminates with the points *M* and *N* of the equator and ecliptic; and that these points and the arc *HN* are given will be clear from these considerations. For, by things demonstrated in the first part of the Composition, since the arcs *GL* and *NF* of great circles are drawn through to the arcs *AG* and *AN* of two great circles,

chord 2 arc *GA* : chord 2 arc *AF* comp. chord 2 arc *GL* : chord 2 arc *LH*, chord 2 arc *NH* : chord 2 arc *FN*.

But each of the arcs *AF*, *FN*, and *GK* is supposed a quadrant, and from the star's record are given the arc *KH* in latitude, the arc *KB* in longitude, and arcs *FG* and *KL* from the inclination of the ecliptic already demonstrated. Therefore it is clear that the desired arcs *GA*, *AF*, *GL*, *LH*, and *NF* are given, and the remaining arc *NH* is hence given.

Again, since

chord 2 arc *FG* : chord 2 arc *GA* comp. chord 2 arc *FH* : chord 2 arc *HN*, chord 2 arc *NL* : chord 2 arc *LA*

and the desired arcs *FG*, *GA*, *FH*, and *HN* are given by the preceding steps, and the arc *LA* from the arc *KB* by means of the co-risings of the equator and ecliptic in the right sphere, therefore the remaining arc *NL* is given.

The points of the equator and ecliptic co-rising and co-setting with the fixed stars are easily gotten from the co-culminations in this way.

For let there be the meridian circle *ABCD*, the semicircle of the equator *AEC* about pole *F*, and the semicircle of the horizon *BED*. And let the star rise at the point *G* of the horizon. Through the points *F* and *G* let the quadrant *FGH* of a great circle be drawn.

Now, since again the arcs *FH* and *EB* have been drawn through to the arcs of two great circles *AF* and *AE*, therefore

chord 2 arc *FB* : chord 2 arc *BA* comp. chord 2 arc *FG* : chord 2

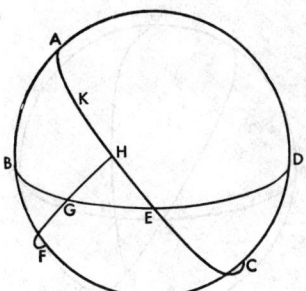

arc *GH*, chord 2 arc *HE* : chord 2 arc *AE*.

But each of the desired arcs *FA*, *FH*, and *EA* embraces a quadrant, and the arc *FB* is given from the elevation of the poles, and the equator's point *H* and the arc *HG* by means of the co-culminations. And, therefore, the remaining arc *HE* is given.

It is easily understood that in the case of the co-settings—if we take an arc equal to arc *HE* west of *H*, such as *HK*—the star will set with the point *K* of the equator because the setting at that time takes place on the arc equal to *BG*, and an angle west of the meridian is intercepted equal to that contained, according to this figure, to the east by the arcs *AF* and *FH*.

From the things demonstrated for the co-risings and co-settings of the equator and ecliptic for each latitude, the part of the ecliptic rising with the point *E* of the equator and with the star will be given; and the part setting with point *K* and the star also. It is clear that, at the times the sun is truly at those points of the ecliptic, the risings, culminations, and settings of the fixed stars considered with respect to its centre, and called the true co-centerings, will be accomplished.

6. On the Heliacal Risings and Settings of the Fixed Stars

Now, in the case of the heliacal risings and settings we no longer find the geometrical method worked out from their positions alone sufficient (since, for example, with whatever point of the ecliptic the star is shown to rise by these means, it is still impossible similarly to find out at what distance of the sun from the horizon beneath the earth it will first appear or be hidden). For this distance of arc cannot be equal for all the stars nor for the same everywhere, but differs according to the magnitudes of the stars, their latitudinal elongations from the sun, and the change in the inclinations of the ecliptic.

If we suppose *ABCD* to be the meridian circle, *AEFC* the semicircle of the ecliptic, and *BED* the semicircle of the horizon about pole *G*, then it is clear that (when the stars are rising at point *E* of the ecliptic) if the greater begins to appear when the sun, for instance, is below the earth a distance of arc *EF*, then the smaller (if it has an equal latitudinal elongation from the sun) will first appear when the sun is distant by a greater arc *EF* and makes thinner rays. Again, in the case of stars of equal magnitude, if the star nearer the point *E* in latitude appears first at a distance *EF*, then the one farther away will appear at a less distance, because, with the sun the same distance below the earth, there are more rays near the ecliptic and the sun than remote from them. And, in the case of stars of equal magnitude and rising at the same latitudinal elongation, the more the ecliptic is inclined to the horizon and makes a less angle *DEF*, at so much greater a distance *EF* will the star first appear.

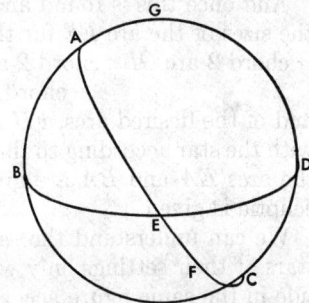

For if we add on, as in the following figure, the semicircle *HFK* through the poles of the horizon and through the sun at *F* (which is, of course, at right angles to the horizon) then the sun's distance under the earth for the same stars is always equal to arc *FH*. For the rays above the earth are similar for equal distances considered in this way. And, with arc *HF* remaining the same as we said, arc *EF* will be less when the ecliptic is perpendicular to the horizon, and greater when it is inclined.

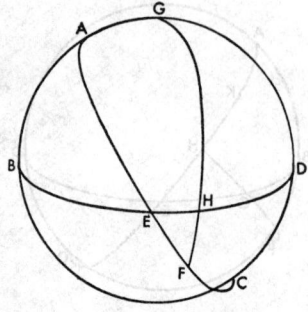

It is therefore necessary to take observations for each of the stars to get the sun's distance beneath the earth along the ecliptic. If, now, the distance along the circle at right angles to the horizon (as arc *FH* in the above figure) does not remain the same in all places for the same stars because similar rays do not shine the same in the denser air of the northern climate, then we shall need observations for not only one climate, but also for each of the rest. But if the arc corresponding to *FH* remains everywhere the same for the same stars, as is likely (for the stars' rays would necessarily suffer in the same way from the difference in the air) then the distances observed for one climate will suffice for examining the rest geometrically, whether the inclination of the ecliptic changes because of difference in place or because of the demonstrated shift of the sphere of the fixed stars towards its eastern parts.

For let the distance *EF* be given from observation in some latitude. Since then again the arcs *BH* and *FA* have been drawn through to the arcs *GB* and *GF* of two great circles, therefore,

chord 2 arc *AB* : chord 2 arc *BG* comp. chord 2 arc *AE* : chord 2 arc *EF*,
chord 2 arc *FH* : chord 2 arc *HG*.

But of the desired arcs, *BG* and *HG* are each a quadrant. And since point *E* is supposed to be that with which the star rises, the point *A* of culmination is also given from the Table of Ascensions, so that arc *AE* is therefore given and *EF* from observation. The arc *AG* is given by calculation of the distance of the point *A* from the equator which, in turn, is given in the Table of Obliquity, and from the distance of the equator from the zenith along the same meridian, which is equal to the pole's elevation. And, therefore, the remaining arc *FH* will be given.

And once this is found and is kept the same, we shall get, by means of this, the sizes of the arc *EF* for the other inclinations. For again

chord 2 arc *GB* : chord 2 arc *AB* comp. chord 2 arc *GH* : chord 2 arc *FH*,
chord 2 arc *FE* : chord 2 arc *EA*;

and of the desired arcs, *FH* is now assumed, and the point *E* is given as rising with the star according to the latitude in question as shown before; and likewise the arcs *EA* and *BA* are given. And, therefore, the remaining arc *EF* of the ecliptic is given.

We can understand the same kind of method for the disappearances of the stars at their settings only with the position of the ecliptic drawn on the other side in the same figure according to the inclination so that *BD* is taken as the western horizon.

Not to pass this subject by entirely, we think we have treated it sufficiently to show the methods used in this theory. And because the generality induced from such predictions is so fluctuating not only from the great difference of the places and inclinations of the ecliptic but also from the multitude of the stars and the difficulty in observing their heliacal risings, since the observers and the atmosphere for the places observed can make the time of the first glimpse unlike and unsure (as I know from trial and from the differences in the observations) and besides these things because, through the shift of the sphere of the fixed stars, the co-risings, co-culminations, and co-settings cannot remain constant, even for one latitude, with those calculated with the present numbers and proofs, therefore we have avoided such a waste of time, being content for the present with the approximations which can be gotten each time from the catalogue or from the arrangement of the sphere. For we see that the signs of the condition of the atmosphere gotten from the heliacal risings and settings almost never keep any order or unchangeableness, if one attributes the cause of the differences to the weather and not to the places of the ecliptic; so that this cause acts only in a very general way and is not established by the beginnings of the heliacal risings and settings as it is by the configurations of the moon with respect to the sun in its general distances, and by the moon's inclinations in the particular distances.

BOOK NINE

1. Concerning the Order of the Spheres of the Sun and Moon and Five Planets

Now, certainly whatever one could say in general about the fixed stars, to the extent that the appearances up until now fall under our apprehension, would be pretty much like this. But since this Composition still lacks a treatment of the five planets, we shall give an exposition of them, going as far as possible with what they have in common to avoid repetition, and then adding on the plan of each one in particular.

First, then, concerning the order of their spheres, all of which have their positions about the poles of the ecliptic, we see the foremost mathematicians agree that all these spheres are nearer the earth than the sphere of the fixed stars, and farther from the earth than that of the moon; that the three—of which Saturn's is the largest, Jupiter's next earthward, and Mars' below that—are all farther from the earth than the others and that of the sun. On the other hand, the spheres of Venus and Mercury are placed by the earlier mathematicians below the sun's, but by some of the later ones above the sun's because of their never having seen the sun eclipsed by them. But this judgment seems to us unsure since these planets could be below the sun and never yet have been in any of the planes through the sun and our eye but in another, and therefore not have appeared in a line with it; just as in the case of the moon's conjunctive passages there are for the most part no eclipses.

Since there is no other way of getting at this because of the absence of any sensible parallax in these stars, from which appearance alone linear distances are gotten, the order of the earlier mathematicians seems the more trustworthy, using the sun as a natural dividing line between those planets which can be any angular distance from the sun and those which cannot but which always move near it. Besides, it does not place them far enough at their perigees to produce a sensible parallax.

2. On the Aim of the Planetary Hypotheses

So much, then, for the orders of the spheres. Now, since our problem is to demonstrate, in the case of the five planets as in the case of the sun and moon, all their apparent irregularities as produced by means of regular and circular motions (for these are proper to the nature of divine things which are strangers to disparities and disorders) the successful accomplishment of this aim as truly belonging to mathematical theory in philosophy is to be considered a great thing, very difficult and as yet unattained in a reasonable way by anyone. For, since, in the case of the researches about the periodic movements of each planet, whatever slight error the eye makes in systematic observations produces a sensible difference more quickly when the examination has been over a shorter interval than when over a greater one, the time for which we have observations of the planets recorded (being short for grasping such a considerable lay-out, furnishes an unsure prediction over long periods. In the case of research about the anomalies, the fact that there are two anomalies appearing for each of the planets, and that they are unequal in magnitude and in the times of their returns, works a good deal of confusion. For one of the anomalies is seen to have relation to the sun, and the other to the parts of the zodiac, but both are mixed together so it is very hard to determine what belongs to each[1]; and most of the old observations were thrown together carelessly and grossly. The more continuous of them contain stations and apparitions, and the apprehension of these properties is not certain. The stations cannot indicate the exact time, since the planet's local motion remains imperceptible for many days before and after its station; and the apparitions not only make the places immediately disappear along with the stars as they are seen for the first or last time, but also can be utterly misleading as to the times because of the differences in the atmosphere and in the eye of the observer. In general, the observations made with reference to some fixed star at a rather great angular distance, unless because of these things one attends to them wisely and clear-sightedly, furnish a magnitude from their measurements hard to calculate and subject to guesswork. And this is so, not only because the lines between the observed stars make different angles with the ecliptic and by no means right angles—whence in the variety of the zodiac's inclinations a great uncertainty is apt to follow in the determination of the longitudinal and latitudinal positions—but also because the same angular distances appear to the eye greater near the horizon and smaller near the culminations, and so they can be measured as sometimes greater and sometimes smaller than the real angular distance.

[1]It is important to notice that all the five planets, just like the moon, have an anomaly with respect to the sun as well as an anomaly with respect to the zodiac. Since Ptolemy merely expounds the theory as a deduction, it might be well to explain the appearances from which these things could be gotten. It must be remembered that Ptolemy had long astronomical tables of data which had been kept for nearly a thousand years, and which served as appearances over a long period of time.

The appearances of Venus and Mercury are fairly simple. These two stars move on the ecliptic, more or less, and swing back and forth from one side of the sun to the other, Mercury never getting more than some 25° from the sun, and Venus never more than some 45°. This makes them alternately morning and evening stars. This swinging in the heliacal anomaly and, from a greatest elongation from the mean sun (say eastern) back to the next greatest eastern elongation, is called one cycle of heliacal anomaly. Furthermore the time from a western elongation to an eastern is longer than from the eastern to the next western. It is also observed that, for different positions of the mean sun on the ecliptic, the greatest elongations are smaller or larger, but always the same for the same position.

It is further observed that, if one considers the sum of the greatest eastern and greatest western elongation for each position of the mean sun, this sum is greatest at one position, and on either side gets smaller and smaller until it is least at the position exactly opposite on the ecliptic. This variation of the apparent heliacal anomaly is called the zodiacal anomaly.

The appearances of Mars, Jupiter, and Saturn are more complicated. These planets move generally from west to east along the ecliptic more or less at different speeds, Mars making a complete circuit through the fixed stars in about 2 years, Jupiter in about 11, and Saturn in about 30. They can be at any angular distance from the sun, unlike Venus and Mercury which are constrained to remain within certain bounds. But they are tied to the sun in a different way. Whenever the mean sun is nearly opposite any one of these three planets, the planet stops its eastward motion, and this is called a station. And then, as the mean sun gets more directly opposite, the planet moves westward, and this is called a regression or retrogradation. As the mean sun moves on, the planet appears to stop again, and then move eastward again. As the mean sun moves toward the planet, the planet moves faster and faster

And so I consider Hipparchus to have been most zealous after the truth, both because of all these things and especially because of his having left us more examples of accurate observations than he ever got from his predecessors. He sought out the hypotheses of the sun and moon, and demonstrated as far as possible and by every available means that they were accomplished through uniform circular movements, but he did not attempt to give the principle of the hypotheses of the five planets, as far as we can tell from those memoirs of his which have come down to us, but only arranged the observations in a more useful way and showed the appearances to be inconsistent with the hypotheses of the mathematicians of that time. For not only did he think it necessary as it seemed to declare that, because of the double anomaly of each planet, the regressions of each are unequal and of such and such a magnitude, while the other mathematicians gave their geometrical demonstrations on one and the same anomaly and regression, but he also thought that these movements could not be effected either by eccentric circles, or by circles concentric with the ecliptic but bearing epicycles, or even by both together, although the zodiacal anomaly was of one magnitude and the anomaly with respect to the sun of another. For these are the means used by nearly all those who have wished to demonstrate uniform circular movement by the so-called perpetual table, but in a false and inconsequential way, some getting nowhere at all, some following the problem to a limited extent. But Hipparchus reasoned that no one who has progressed through the whole of mathematics to such a point of accuracy and zeal for truth would be content to stop at this like the rest; but that anyone who was to persuade himself and those in touch with him would have to demonstrate the magnitude and periods of each of the anomalies by clear and consistent appearances; and, putting both together, he would have to find out the position and order of the circles by which these anomalies are produced and the mode of their movement and finally show about all the appearances to be consistent with the peculiar property of this hypothesis of the circles. I think this is difficult, and it seemed so to him. We have said all this not through ostentation, but in order that, if we are forced by the problem itself either (1) to use something contrary to the general argument, as when, for example, for ease we make our demonstrations of the circles described by the movement in the planetary spheres as if they were simple and in the same plane with the ecliptic; or if we are forced (2) to presuppose something without immediate foundation in the appearances, an apprehension gotten from continuous trial and adjustment; or (3) to suppose not everywhere the same mode of movement or inclination of the circles—in order that, I say, we may then reasonably agree that (1) using something of the sort that no appreciable difference is to result from it will not falsify the subject in hand; (2) that things supposed without proof, once they are conceived in such a way as to be consistent with appearances, cannot be

---

eastward until the mean sun has overtaken it; then it moves more and more slowly eastward until it again appears to stop. The time from a station to a corresponding station is one cycle of heliacal anomaly. Furthermore, the time from a station through the eastward motion of the planet to the next station is much longer than that from a station through the westward or regressive motion of the planet to the next station.

Again these speeds vary for different positions of the mean sun on the ecliptic. And this variation is called the zodiacal anomaly.

All the planets wander slightly from one side of the ecliptic to the other. The theory of this latitudinal anomaly is explained in Book XIII.

found without some plan and knowledge even if the way of getting hold of them is hard to explain (after all, generally speaking, the cause of first principles is either nothing or hard to interpret in its nature); and (3) that, since the appearances relative to the stars are also found to be dissimilar, one should not reasonably think it strange or absurd to vary the mode of the hypotheses of the circles, especially when, along with saving the regular circular movement absolutely everywhere, each of the appearances is demonstrated in its more lawful and general character.

And so we have used for the demonstrations of each planet only those observations which cannot be disputed, that is those taken at contact or great proximity with the stars or even with the moon, and above all those taken with the astrolabe where the eye is lined up with the diametrically opposite sights in the circles, sees on every side equal angular distances by means of similar arcs, and can accurately apprehend the passages relative to the middle of each star in longitude and latitude by moving to and fro to the observed stars the astrolabe's ecliptic circle and the diametrically opposite sights in the circles through its poles.

3. On the Periodic Returns of the Five Planets

Now that these things have been explained in advance, we shall first set out the least periodic joint returns (that is very nearly joint) of each of the five planets as calculated by Hipparchus, with a correction of our own gotten from the comparison of the positions made after the demonstrations of the anomalies, as we shall show in that place. We have put them first in order to have set out at hand, for the calculations of the anomalies, the particular mean movements of each one, both in longitude and in anomaly, since there would be no appreciable difference even if one should use the mean passages in their more approximate form. In general, one is to understand by movement in longitude the movement of the epicycle's centre on the eccentric, and by anomaly the movement of the star on the epicycle.

Now, we find 57 cycles of anomaly of Saturn exactly completed in 59 solar years of our kind (that is from one tropic or equinoctial point back to the same) plus $1+\frac{1}{2}+\frac{1}{4}$ day very nearly, and in 2 revolutions of the star plus $(1+\frac{2}{3}+\frac{1}{20})°$ of a revolution; for, in the case of the three stars continually being overtaken by the sun, the number of revolutions run by the sun in the time of return of each is equal to the number of longitudinal revolutions of the star together with the number of its returns in anomaly.[1] And we find 65 cycles of anomaly of Jupiter exactly completed in 71 solar years of the same kind less $4+\frac{1}{2}+\frac{1}{3}+\frac{1}{15}$ days very nearly, and in 6 revolutions of the star less $(4+\frac{1}{2}+\frac{1}{3})°$ of a revolution, counting from a tropic point back to the same. Likewise we find 37 cycles of anomaly of Mars in 79 of our solar years plus $3+\frac{1}{6}+\frac{1}{20}$ days very nearly, and in 42 revolutions of the star plus $3\frac{1}{6}°$ of a revolution, counting from a tropic

---

[1]This fact that, for the planets Mars, Jupiter, and Saturn, the number of revolutions of the mean sun is always equal to the number of longitudinal revolutions of the star plus the number of its returns of anomaly, is of great importance later on in Book X, Chapter 6. It also becomes important in the heliocentric theories. For while it remains a useful accident for Ptolemy, it is a necessary consequence of the primary assumptions of Copernicus.

The fact, again, that even these three planets, which are not tied to the sun by an immediate appearance as Venus and Mercury, yet have an anomaly which is referred to the sun, is a sign pointing towards a heliocentric hypothesis.

point back to the same; 5 cycles of anomaly of Venus in 8 of our solar years less $2+\frac{1}{4}+\frac{1}{20}$ days, and in 8 revolutions of the star less $2\frac{1}{4}°$ of a revolution, equal in number to the revolutions of the sun; and 145 cycles of anomaly of Mercury in 46 years of the same kind plus $1\frac{1}{30}$ day, and in 46 revolutions of the star plus $1°$ of a revolution, again equal in number to the revolutions of the sun.

But if, for each one, we reduce the time of return into days in accordance with the year's time as already given by us, and the number of cycles of anomaly into the $360°$ of a circle, then we shall have, in the case of Saturn, $21,551\frac{18}{60}$ days and $20,520°$ of anomaly; in the case of Jupiter, $25,927\frac{37}{60}$ days and $27,400°$ of anomaly; in the case of Mars, $28,857\frac{53}{60}$ days and $13,320°$ of anomaly; in the case of Venus, $2,919\frac{4}{60}$ days and $1,800°$ of anomaly; and in the case of Mercury, $16,802\frac{24}{60}$ days and $52,200°$ of anomaly.

Dividing, then, in each case, the number of degrees of anomaly by the number of days, we shall have the daily mean movement of anomaly: very nearly $57^{i}7^{ii}43^{iii}41^{iv}43^{v}40^{vi}$ for Saturn, $54^{i}9^{ii}2^{iii}46^{iv}26^{v}$ for Jupiter, $27^{i}41^{ii}40^{iii}19^{iv}20^{v}58^{vi}$ for Mars, $36^{i}59^{ii}25^{iii}53^{iv}11^{v}28^{vi}$ for Venus, and $3^{i}6^{ii}24^{iii}6^{iv}59^{v}35^{vi}50^{vi}$ for Mercury.

Taking a twenty-fourth of each of these, we shall have the hourly mean movement of anomaly: $2^{i}22^{ii}49^{iii}19^{iv}14^{v}19^{vi}10^{vii}$ for Saturn, $2^{i}15^{ii}22^{iii}36^{iv}56^{v}5^{vi}$ for Jupiter, $1^{i}9^{ii}14^{iii}10^{iv}48^{v}22^{vi}25^{vii}$ for Mars, $1^{i}32^{ii}28^{iii}34^{iv}42^{v}58^{vi}40^{vii}$ for Venus, and $7^{i}46^{ii}0^{iii}17^{iv}28^{v}59^{vi}35^{vii}$ for Mercury.

Again, multiplying the daily mean movements of each by thirty, we shall have the monthly mean movement of anomaly: $28^{i}33^{ii}51^{iii}50^{iv}51^{v}50^{v}$ for Saturn, $27°4^{i}31^{ii}23^{iii}13^{iv}$ for Jupiter, $13°50^{i}50^{ii}9^{iii}40^{iv}29^{v}$ for Mars, $18°29^{i}42^{ii}56^{iii}35^{iv}44^{v}$ for Venus, and $93°12^{i}3^{ii}29^{iii}47^{iv}55^{v}$ for Mercury.

And likewise multiplying the daily mean movements by the 365 days of the Egyptian year, we shall have the yearly mean movement of anomaly: $347°32^{i}0^{ii}48^{iii}50^{iv}38^{v}20^{vi}$ for Saturn, $329°25^{i}1^{ii}52^{iii}28^{iv}10^{v}$ for Jupiter, $168°28^{i}30^{ii}17^{iii}42^{iv}32^{v}50^{vi}$ for Mars, $225°1^{i}32^{ii}28^{iii}34^{iv}39^{v}15^{vi}$ for Venus, and a surplus of $53°56^{i}42^{ii}32^{iii}32^{iv}59^{v}10^{vi}$ for Mercury.

In the same way, multiplying also each of the yearly movements by 18, as in the case of the tables of the sun and moon, we shall have the mean surplus of anomaly of the Egyptian 18-year period: $135°36^{i}14^{ii}39^{iii}11^{iv}30^{v}$ for Saturn, $169°30^{i}33^{ii}44^{iii}27^{iv}$ for Jupiter, $152°33^{i}5^{ii}18^{iii}45^{iv}51^{v}$ for Mars, $90°27^{i}44^{ii}34^{iii}23^{iv}46^{v}30^{vi}$ for Venus, and $251°0^{i}45^{ii}45^{iii}53^{iv}45^{v}$ for Mercury.

From these numbers we shall get the mean movements in longitude so that, without reducing the number of revolutions to degrees, we may, in each case, divide them into the time proposed. It is clear that for Venus and Mercury the mean movements in longitude will be the same as those already set out for the sun, and for the other three stars they will be, for each number, the difference between the mean movement of anomaly and the sun's mean movement in longitude. And in this way we shall find Saturn's daily mean movement in longitude to be $2^{i}0^{ii}33^{iii}31^{iv}28^{v}51^{vi}$, Jupiter's $4^{i}59^{ii}14^{iii}26^{iv}46^{v}31^{vi}$, and Mars' $31^{i}26^{ii}36^{iii}53^{iv}51^{v}33^{vi}$; Saturn's hourly mean movement in longitude $5^{ii}1^{iii}23^{iv}48^{v}42^{vi}7^{vii}30^{viii}$, Jupiter's $12^{ii}28^{iii}6^{iv}6^{v}56^{vi}17^{vii}30^{viii}$, and Mars' $1^{i}18^{ii}36^{iii}32^{iv}14^{v}39^{vi}$; Saturn's monthly mean movement in longitude $1°0^{i}16^{ii}45^{iii}44^{iv}25^{v}30^{vi}$, Jupiter's $2°29^{i}37^{ii}13^{iii}23^{iv}15^{v}30^{vi}$, and Mars' $15°43^{i}18^{ii}26^{iii}55^{iv}46^{v}30^{vi}$; Saturn's yearly mean movement in longitude $12°13^{i}23^{ii}56^{iii}30^{iv}30^{v}15^{vi}$, Jupiter's $30°20^{i}22^{ii}52^{iii}52^{iv}38^{v}35^{vi}$, and Mars' $191°16^{i}54^{ii}27^{iii}38^{iv}35^{v}45^{vi}$; and Saturn's mean movement in longitude over 18 years to be $220°1^i10^{ii}57^{iii}9^{iv}4^v30^{vi}$, Jupiter's a surplus of $186°6^i51^{ii}51^{iii}53^{iv}34^v30^{vi}$, and Mars' a surplus of $203°4^i20^{ii}17^{iii}34^{iv}43^v30^{vi}$.

Now we shall again arrange, in the order of the stars for the ready use of each, the tables of these mean movements, in 45 rows and in lots of three like the others. The first lots will contain the combinations of 18-year periods, the second the yearly and hourly combinations, and the third the monthly and daily ones. And here follow the tables:

4. TABLES OF THE MEAN MOVEMENTS IN LONGITUDE
AND IN ANOMALY OF THE FIVE STARS
SATURN, Anomaly at epoch, 34°2′

18-years	Longitude at epoch, Goat 26°43′ Degrees in longitude							Apogee at epoch, Scorpion 14°10′ Degrees of anomaly						
	°	I	II	III	IV	V	VI	°	I	II	III	IV	V	VI
18	220	1	10	57	9	4	30	135	36	14	39	11	30	0
36	80	2	21	54	18	9	0	271	12	29	18	23	0	0
54	300	3	32	51	27	13	30	46	48	43	57	34	30	0
72	160	4	43	48	36	18	0	182	24	58	36	46	0	0
90	20	5	54	45	45	22	30	318	1	13	15	57	30	0
108	240	7	5	42	54	27	0	93	37	27	55	9	0	0
126	100	8	16	40	3	31	30	229	13	42	34	20	30	0
144	320	9	27	37	12	36	0	4	49	57	13	32	0	0
162	180	10	38	34	21	40	30	140	26	11	52	43	30	0
180	40	11	49	31	30	45	0	276	2	26	31	55	0	0
198	260	13	0	28	39	49	30	51	38	41	11	6	30	0
216	120	14	11	25	48	54	0	187	14	55	50	18	0	0
234	340	15	22	22	57	58	30	322	51	10	29	29	30	0
252	200	16	33	20	7	3	0	98	27	25	8	41	0	0
270	60	17	44	17	16	7	30	234	3	39	47	52	30	0
288	280	18	55	14	25	12	0	9	39	54	27	4	0	0
306	140	20	6	11	34	16	30	145	16	9	6	15	30	0
324	0	21	17	8	43	21	0	280	52	23	45	27	0	0
342	220	22	28	5	52	25	30	56	28	38	24	38	30	0
360	80	23	39	3	1	30	0	192	4	53	3	50	0	0
378	300	24	50	0	10	34	30	327	41	7	43	1	30	0
396	160	26	0	57	19	39	0	103	17	22	22	13	0	0
414	20	27	11	54	28	43	30	238	53	37	1	24	30	0
432	240	28	22	51	37	48	0	14	29	51	40	36	0	0
450	100	29	33	48	46	52	30	150	6	6	19	47	30	0
468	320	30	44	45	55	57	0	285	42	20	58	59	0	0
486	180	31	55	43	5	1	30	61	18	35	38	10	30	0
504	40	33	6	40	14	6	0	196	54	50	17	22	0	0
522	260	34	17	37	23	10	30	332	31	4	56	33	30	0
540	120	35	28	34	32	15	0	108	7	19	35	45	0	0
558	340	36	39	31	41	19	30	243	43	34	14	56	30	0
576	200	37	50	28	50	24	0	19	19	48	54	8	0	0
594	60	39	1	25	59	28	30	154	56	3	33	19	30	0
612	280	40	12	23	8	33	0	290	32	18	12	31	0	0
630	140	41	23	20	17	37	30	66	8	32	51	42	30	0
648	0	42	34	17	26	42	0	201	44	47	30	54	0	0
666	220	43	45	14	35	46	30	337	21	2	10	5	30	0
684	80	44	56	11	44	51	0	112	57	16	49	17	0	0
702	300	46	7	8	53	55	30	248	33	31	28	28	30	0
720	160	47	18	6	3	0	0	24	9	46	7	40	0	0
738	20	48	29	3	12	4	30	159	46	0	46	51	30	0
756	240	49	40	0	21	9	0	295	22	15	26	3	0	0
774	100	50	50	57	30	13	30	0	58	30	5	14	30	0
792	320	52	1	54	39	18	0	206	34	44	44	26	0	0
810	180	53	12	51	48	22	30	342	10	59	23	37	30	0

Saturn, *Continued*

Single Years	Saturn's Degrees in longitude						Saturn's Degrees of anomaly					
	°	I	II	III	IV	V	VI	°	I	II	III	IV	V	VI
1	12	13	23	56	30	30	15	347	32	0	48	50	38	20
2	24	26	47	53	1	0	30	335	4	1	37	41	16	40
3	36	40	11	49	31	30	45	322	36	2	26	31	55	0
4	48	53	35	46	2	1	0	310	8	3	15	22	33	20
5	61	6	59	42	32	31	15	297	40	4	4	13	11	40
6	73	20	23	39	3	1	30	285	12	4	53	3	50	0
7	85	33	47	35	33	31	45	272	44	5	41	54	28	20
8	97	47	11	32	4	2	0	260	16	6	30	45	6	40
9	110	0	35	28	34	32	15	247	48	7	19	35	45	0
10	122	13	59	25	5	2	30	235	20	8	8	26	23	20
11	134	27	23	21	35	32	45	222	52	8	57	17	1	40
12	146	40	47	18	6	3	0	210	24	9	46	7	40	0
13	158	54	11	14	36	33	15	197	56	10	34	58	18	20
14	171	7	35	11	7	3	30	185	28	11	23	48	56	40
15	183	20	59	7	37	33	45	173	0	12	12	39	35	0
16	195	34	23	4	8	4	0	160	32	13	1	30	13	20
17	207	47	47	0	38	34	15	148	4	13	50	20	51	40
18	220	1	10	57	9	4	30	135	36	14	39	11	30	0

Hours	Degrees in longitude						Degrees of anomaly					
	°	I	II	III	IV	V	VI	°	I	II	III	IV	V	VI
1	0	0	5	1	23	48	42	0	2	22	49	19	14	19
2	0	0	10	2	47	37	24	0	4	45	38	38	28	38
3	0	0	15	4	11	26	6	0	7	8	27	57	42	57
4	0	0	20	5	35	14	48	0	9	31	17	16	57	17
5	0	0	25	6	59	3	31	0	11	54	6	36	11	36
6	0	0	30	8	22	52	13	0	14	16	55	55	25	55
7	0	0	35	9	46	40	55	0	16	39	45	14	40	14
8	0	0	40	11	10	29	37	0	19	2	34	33	54	33
9	0	0	45	12	34	18	19	0	21	25	23	53	8	52
10	0	0	50	13	58	7	1	0	23	48	13	12	23	12
11	0	0	55	15	21	55	43	0	26	11	2	31	37	31
12	0	1	0	16	45	44	25	0	28	33	51	50	51	50
13	0	1	5	18	9	33	8	0	30	56	41	10	6	9
14	0	1	10	19	33	21	50	0	33	19	30	29	20	28
15	0	1	15	20	57	10	32	0	35	42	19	48	34	47
16	0	1	20	22	20	59	14	0	38	5	9	7	49	7
17	0	1	25	23	44	47	56	0	40	27	58	27	30	26
18	0	1	30	25	8	36	38	0	42	50	47	46	17	45
19	0	1	35	26	32	25	20	0	45	13	37	5	32	4
20	0	1	40	27	56	14	2	0	47	36	26	24	46	23
21	0	1	45	29	20	2	45	0	49	59	15	44	0	42
22	0	1	50	30	43	51	27	0	52	22	5	3	15	2
23	0	1	55	32	7	40	9	0	54	44	54	22	29	21
24	0	2	0	33	31	28	51	0	57	7	43	41	43	40

Saturn, *Continued*

Months	Degrees in longitude							Degrees of anomaly						
	°	I	II	III	IV	V	VI	°	I	II	III	IV	V	VI
30	1	0	16	45	44	25	30	28	33	51	50	51	50	0
60	2	0	33	31	28	51	0	57	7	43	41	43	40	0
90	3	0	50	17	13	16	30	85	41	35	32	35	30	0
120	4	1	7	2	57	42	0	114	15	27	23	27	20	0
150	5	1	23	48	42	7	30	142	49	19	14	19	10	0
180	6	1	40	34	26	33	0	171	23	11	5	11	0	0
210	7	1	57	20	10	58	30	199	57	2	56	2	50	0
240	8	2	14	5	55	24	0	228	30	54	46	54	40	0
270	9	2	30	51	39	49	30	257	4	46	37	46	30	0
300	10	2	47	37	24	15	0	255	38	38	28	38	20	0
330	11	3	4	23	8	40	30	314	12	30	19	30	10	0
360	12	3	21	8	53	6	0	342	46	22	10	22	0	0

Days	Degrees in longitude							Degrees of anomaly						
	°	I	II	III	IV	V	VI	°	I	II	III	IV	V	VI
1	0	2	0	33	31	28	51	0	57	7	43	41	43	40
2	0	4	1	7	2	57	42	1	54	15	27	23	27	20
3	0	6	1	40	34	26	33	2	51	23	11	5	11	0
4	0	8	2	14	5	55	24	3	48	30	54	46	54	40
5	0	10	2	47	37	24	15	4	45	38	38	28	38	20
6	0	12	3	21	8	53	6	5	42	46	22	10	22	0
7	0	14	3	54	40	21	57	6	39	54	5	52	5	40
8	0	16	4	28	11	50	48	7	37	1	49	33	49	20
9	0	18	5	1	43	19	39	8	34	9	33	15	33	0
10	0	20	5	35	14	48	30	9	31	17	16	57	16	40
11	0	22	6	8	46	17	21	10	28	25	0	39	0	20
12	0	24	6	42	17	46	12	11	25	32	44	20	44	0
13	0	26	7	15	49	15	3	12	22	40	28	2	27	40
14	0	28	7	49	20	43	54	13	19	48	11	44	11	20
15	0	30	8	22	52	12	45	14	16	55	55	25	55	0
16	0	32	8	56	23	41	36	15	14	3	39	7	38	40
17	0	34	9	29	55	10	27	16	11	11	22	49	22	20
18	0	36	10	3	26	39	18	17	8	19	6	31	6	0
19	0	38	10	36	58	8	9	18	5	26	50	12	49	40
20	0	40	11	10	29	37	0	19	2	34	33	54	33	20
21	0	42	11	44	1	5	51	19	59	42	17	36	17	0
22	0	44	12	17	32	34	42	20	56	50	1	18	0	40
23	0	46	12	51	4	3	33	21	53	57	44	59	44	20
24	0	48	13	24	35	32	24	22	51	5	28	41	28	0
25	0	50	13	58	7	1	15	23	48	13	12	23	11	40
26	0	52	14	31	38	30	6	24	45	20	56	4	55	20
27	0	54	15	5	9	58	57	25	42	28	39	46	39	0
28	0	56	15	38	41	27	48	26	39	36	23	28	22	40
29	0	58	16	12	12	56	39	27	36	44	7	10	6	20
30	1	0	16	45	44	25	30	28	33	51	50	51	50	0

JUPITER, Anomaly at epoch, 146°4′

18-years	Longitude at epoch, Balance 4°41′ Degrees in longitude							Apogee at epoch, Virgin 2°9′ Degrees of anomaly						
	°	I	II	III	IV	V	VI	°	I	II	III	IV	V	VI
18	186	6	51	51	53	34	30	169	30	33	44	27	0	0
36	12	13	43	43	47	9	0	339	1	7	28	54	0	0
54	198	20	35	35	40	43	30	148	31	41	13	21	0	0
72	24	27	27	27	34	18	0	318	2	14	57	48	0	0
90	210	34	19	19	27	52	30	127	32	48	42	15	0	0
108	36	41	11	11	21	27	0	297	3	22	26	42	0	0
126	222	48	3	3	15	1	30	106	33	56	11	9	0	0
144	48	54	54	55	8	36	0	276	4	29	55	36	0	0
162	235	1	46	47	2	10	30	85	35	3	40	3	0	0
180	61	8	38	38	55	45	0	255	5	37	24	30	0	0
198	247	15	30	30	49	19	30	64	36	11	8	57	0	0
216	73	22	22	22	42	54	0	234	6	44	53	24	0	0
234	259	29	14	14	36	28	30	43	37	18	37	51	0	0
252	85	36	6	6	30	3	0	213	7	52	22	18	0	0
270	271	42	57	58	23	37	30	22	38	26	6	45	0	0
288	97	49	49	50	17	12	0	192	8	59	51	12	0	0
306	283	56	41	42	10	46	30	1	39	33	35	39	0	0
324	110	3	33	34	4	21	0	171	10	7	20	6	0	0
342	296	10	25	25	57	55	30	340	40	41	4	33	0	0
360	122	17	17	17	51	30	0	150	11	14	49	0	0	0
378	308	24	9	9	45	4	30	319	41	48	33	27	0	0
396	134	31	1	1	38	39	0	129	12	22	17	54	0	0
414	320	37	52	53	32	13	30	298	42	56	2	21	0	0
432	146	44	44	45	25	48	0	108	13	29	46	48	0	0
450	332	51	36	37	19	22	30	277	44	3	31	15	0	0
468	158	58	28	29	12	57	0	87	14	37	15	42	0	0
486	345	5	20	21	6	31	30	256	45	11	0	9	0	0
504	171	12	12	13	0	6	0	66	15	44	44	36	0	0
522	357	19	4	4	53	40	30	235	46	18	29	3	0	0
540	183	25	55	56	47	15	0	45	16	52	13	30	0	0
558	9	32	47	48	40	49	30	214	47	25	57	57	0	0
576	195	39	39	40	34	24	0	24	17	59	42	24	0	0
594	21	46	31	32	27	58	30	193	48	33	26	51	0	0
612	207	53	23	24	21	33	0	3	19	7	11	18	0	0
630	34	0	15	16	15	7	30	172	49	40	55	45	0	0
648	220	7	7	8	8	42	0	342	20	14	40	12	0	0
666	46	13	59	0	2	16	30	151	50	48	24	39	0	0
684	232	20	50	51	55	51	0	321	21	22	9	6	0	0
702	58	27	42	43	49	25	30	130	51	55	53	33	0	0
720	244	34	34	35	43	0	0	300	22	29	38	0	0	0
738	0	41	26	27	36	34	30	109	53	3	22	27	0	0
756	256	48	18	19	30	9	0	279	23	37	6	54	0	0
774	82	55	10	11	23	43	30	88	54	10	51	21	0	0
792	269	2	2	3	17	18	0	258	24	44	35	48	0	0
810	95	8	53	55	10	52	30	67	55	18	20	15	0	0

JUPITER, *Continued*

Single years	Degrees in longitude							Degrees of anomaly					
	°	I	II	III	IV	V	IV	°	I	II	III	IV	V	VI
1	30	20	22	52	52	58	35	329	25	1	52	28	10	0
2	60	40	45	45	45	57	10	298	50	3	44	56	20	0
3	91	1	8	38	38	55	45	268	15	5	37	24	30	0
4	121	21	31	31	31	54	20	237	40	7	29	52	40	0
5	151	41	54	24	24	52	55	207	5	9	22	20	50	0
6	182	2	17	17	17	51	30	176	30	11	14	49	0	0
7	212	22	40	10	10	50	5	145	55	13	7	17	10	0
8	242	43	3	3	3	48	40	115	20	14	59	45	20	0
9	273	3	25	55	56	47	15	84	45	16	52	13	30	0
10	303	23	48	48	49	45	50	54	10	18	44	41	40	0
11	333	44	11	41	42	44	25	23	35	20	37	9	50	0
12	4	4	34	34	35	43	0	353	0	22	29	38	0	0
13	34	24	57	27	28	41	35	322	25	24	22	6	10	0
14	64	45	20	20	21	40	10	291	50	26	14	34	20	0
15	95	5	43	13	14	38	45	261	15	28	7	2	30	0
16	125	26	6	6	7	37	20	230	40	29	59	30	40	0
17	155	46	28	59	0	35	55	200	5	31	51	58	50	0
18	186	6	51	51	53	34	30	169	30	33	44	27	0	0

Hours	Degrees in longitude							Degrees of anomaly					
	°	I	II	III	IV	V	VI	°	I	II	III	IV	V	IV
1	0	0	12	28	6	6	56	0	2	15	22	36	56	5
2	0	0	24	56	12	13	52	0	4	30	45	13	52	10
3	0	0	36	24	18	20	48	0	6	46	7	50	48	15
4	0	0	49	52	24	27	45	0	9	1	30	27	44	20
5	0	1	2	20	30	34	41	0	11	16	53	4	40	25
6	0	1	14	48	36	41	37	0	13	32	15	41	36	30
7	0	1	27	16	42	48	34	0	15	47	38	18	32	35
8	0	1	39	44	48	55	30	0	18	3	0	55	28	40
9	0	1	52	12	55	2	26	0	20	18	23	32	24	45
10	0	2	4	41	1	9	22	0	22	33	46	9	20	50
11	0	2	17	9	7	16	19	0	24	49	8	46	16	55
12	0	2	29	37	13	23	15	0	27	4	31	23	13	0
13	0	2	42	5	19	30	11	0	29	19	54	0	9	5
14	0	2	54	33	25	37	8	0	31	35	16	37	5	10
15	0	3	7	1	31	44	4	0	33	50	39	14	1	15
16	0	3	19	29	37	51	0	0	36	6	1	50	57	20
17	0	3	31	57	43	57	56	0	38	21	24	27	53	25
18	0	3	44	25	50	4	53	0	40	36	47	4	49	30
19	0	3	56	53	56	11	49	0	42	52	9	41	45	35
20	0	4	9	22	2	18	45	0	45	7	32	18	41	40
21	0	4	21	50	8	25	42	0	47	22	54	55	37	45
22	0	4	34	18	14	32	38	0	49	38	17	32	33	50
23	0	4	46	46	20	39	34	0	51	53	40	9	29	55
24	0	4	59	14	26	46	31	0	54	9	2	46	26	0

JUPITER, *Continued*

Months	Degrees in longitude							Degrees of anomaly						
	°	I	II	III	IV	V	VI	°	I	II	III	IV	V	VI
30	2	29	37	13	23	15	30	27	4	31	23	13	0	0
60	4	59	14	26	46	31	0	54	9	2	46	26	0	0
90	7	28	51	40	9	46	30	81	13	34	9	39	0	0
120	9	58	28	53	33	2	0	108	18	5	32	52	0	0
150	12	28	6	6	56	17	30	135	22	36	56	5	0	0
180	14	57	43	20	19	33	0	162	27	8	19	18	0	0
210	17	27	20	33	42	48	30	189	31	39	42	31	0	0
240	19	56	57	47	6	4	0	216	36	11	5	44	0	0
270	22	26	35	0	29	19	30	243	40	42	28	57	0	0
300	24	56	12	13	52	35	0	270	45	13	52	10	0	0
330	27	25	49	27	15	50	30	297	49	45	15	23	0	0
360	29	55	26	40	39	6	0	324	54	16	38	36	0	0

Days	Degrees in longitude							Degrees of anomaly						
	°	I	II	III	IV	V	VI	°	I	II	III	IV	V	VI
1	0	4	59	14	26	46	31	0	54	9	2	46	26	0
2	0	9	58	28	53	33	2	1	48	18	5	32	52	0
3	0	14	57	43	20	19	33	2	42	27	8	19	18	0
4	0	19	56	57	47	6	4	3	36	36	11	5	44	0
5	0	24	56	12	13	52	35	4	30	45	13	52	10	0
6	0	29	55	26	40	39	6	5	24	54	16	38	36	0
7	0	34	54	41	7	25	37	6	19	3	19	25	2	0
8	0	39	53	55	34	12	8	7	13	12	22	11	28	0
9	0	44	53	10	0	58	39	8	7	21	24	57	54	0
10	0	49	52	24	27	45	10	9	1	30	27	44	20	0
11	0	54	51	38	54	31	41	9	55	39	30	30	46	0
12	0	59	50	53	21	18	12	10	49	48	33	17	12	0
13	1	4	50	7	48	4	43	11	43	57	36	3	38	0
14	1	9	49	22	14	51	14	12	38	6	38	50	4	0
15	1	14	48	36	41	37	45	13	32	15	41	36	30	0
16	1	19	47	51	8	24	16	14	26	24	44	22	56	0
17	1	24	47	5	35	10	47	15	20	33	47	9	22	0
18	1	29	46	20	1	57	18	16	14	42	49	55	48	0
19	1	34	45	34	28	43	49	17	8	51	52	42	14	0
20	1	39	44	48	55	30	20	18	3	0	55	28	40	0
21	1	44	44	3	22	16	51	18	57	9	58	15	6	0
22	1	49	43	17	49	3	22	19	51	19	1	1	32	0
23	1	54	42	32	15	49	53	20	45	28	3	47	58	0
24	1	59	41	46	42	36	24	21	39	37	6	34	24	0
25	2	4	41	1	9	22	55	22	33	46	9	20	50	0
26	2	9	40	15	36	9	26	23	27	55	12	7	16	0
27	2	14	39	30	2	55	57	24	22	4	14	53	42	0
28	2	19	38	44	29	42	28	25	16	13	17	40	8	0
29	2	24	37	58	56	28	59	26	10	22	20	26	34	0
30	2	29	37	13	23	15	30	27	4	31	23	13	0	0

MARS, Anomaly at epoch, 327°13'

18-years	Longitude at epoch, Ram 3°32' Degrees in longitude						Apogee at epoch, Crab 16°40' Degrees of anomaly						
	°	I	II	III	IV	V	VI	°	I	II	III	IV	V	VI
18	203	4	20	17	34	43	30	152	33	5	18	45	51	0
36	46	8	40	35	9	27	0	305	6	10	37	31	42	0
54	249	13	0	52	44	10	30	97	39	15	56	17	33	0
72	92	17	21	10	18	54	0	250	12	21	15	3	24	0
90	295	21	41	27	53	37	30	42	45	26	33	49	15	0
108	138	26	1	45	28	21	0	195	18	31	52	35	6	0
126	341	30	22	3	3	4	30	347	51	37	11	20	57	0
144	184	34	42	20	37	48	0	140	24	42	30	6	48	0
162	27	39	2	38	12	31	30	292	57	47	48	52	39	0
180	230	43	22	55	47	15	0	85	30	53	7	38	30	0
198	73	47	43	13	21	58	30	238	3	58	26	24	21	0
216	276	52	3	30	56	42	0	30	37	3	45	10	12	0
234	119	56	23	48	31	25	30	183	10	9	3	56	3	0
252	323	0	44	6	6	9	0	335	43	14	22	41	54	0
270	166	5	4	23	40	52	30	128	16	19	41	27	45	0
288	9	9	24	41	15	36	0	280	49	25	0	13	36	0
306	212	13	44	58	50	19	30	73	22	30	18	59	27	0
324	55	18	5	16	25	3	0	225	55	35	37	45	18	0
342	258	22	25	33	59	46	30	18	28	40	56	31	9	0
360	101	26	45	51	34	30	0	171	1	46	15	17	0	0
378	304	31	6	9	9	13	30	323	34	51	34	2	51	0
396	147	35	26	26	43	57	0	116	7	56	52	48	42	0
414	350	39	46	44	18	40	30	268	41	2	11	34	33	0
432	193	44	7	1	53	24	0	61	14	7	30	20	24	0
450	36	48	27	19	28	7	30	213	47	12	49	6	15	0
468	239	52	47	37	2	51	0	6	20	18	7	52	6	0
486	82	57	7	54	37	34	30	158	53	23	26	37	57	0
504	286	1	28	12	12	18	0	311	26	28	45	23	48	0
522	129	5	48	29	47	1	30	103	59	34	4	9	39	0
540	332	10	8	47	21	45	0	256	32	39	22	55	30	0
558	175	14	29	4	56	28	30	49	5	44	41	41	21	0
576	18	18	49	22	31	12	0	201	38	50	0	27	12	0
594	221	23	9	40	5	55	30	354	11	55	19	13	3	0
612	64	27	29	57	40	39	0	146	45	0	37	58	54	0
630	267	31	50	15	15	22	30	299	18	5	56	44	45	0
648	110	36	10	32	50	6	0	91	51	11	15	30	36	0
666	313	40	30	50	24	49	30	244	24	16	34	16	27	0
684	156	44	51	7	59	33	0	36	57	21	53	2	18	0
702	359	49	11	25	34	16	30	189	30	27	11	48	9	0
720	202	53	31	43	9	0	0	342	3	32	30	34	0	0
738	45	57	52	0	43	43	30	134	36	37	49	19	51	0
756	249	2	12	18	18	27	0	287	9	43	8	5	42	0
774	92	6	32	35	53	10	30	79	42	48	26	51	33	0
792	295	10	52	53	27	54	0	232	15	53	45	37	24	0
810	138	15	13	11	2	37	30	24	48	59	4	23	15	0

Mars, *Continued*

Single years	Degrees in longitude							Degrees of anomaly						
	°	I	II	III	IV	V	VI	°	I	II	III	IV	V	VI
1	191	16	54	27	38	35	45	168	28	30	17	42	32	50
2	22	33	48	55	17	11	30	336	57	0	35	25	5	40
3	213	50	43	22	55	47	15	145	25	30	53	7	38	30
4	45	7	37	50	34	23	0	313	54	1	10	50	11	20
5	236	24	32	18	12	58	45	122	22	31	28	32	44	10
6	67	41	26	45	51	34	30	290	51	1	46	15	17	0
7	258	58	21	13	30	10	15	99	19	32	3	57	49	50
8	90	15	15	41	8	46	0	267	48	2	21	40	22	40
9	281	32	10	8	47	21	45	76	16	32	39	22	55	30
10	112	49	4	36	25	57	30	244	45	2	57	5	28	20
11	304	5	59	4	4	33	15	53	13	33	14	48	1	10
12	135	22	53	31	49	9	0	221	42	3	32	30	34	0
13	326	39	47	59	21	44	45	30	10	33	50	13	6	50
14	157	56	42	27	0	20	30	198	39	4	7	55	39	40
15	349	13	36	54	38	56	15	7	7	34	25	38	12	30
16	180	30	31	22	17	32	0	175	36	4	43	20	45	20
17	11	47	25	49	56	7	45	344	4	35	1	3	18	10
18	203	4	20	17	34	43	30	152	33	5	18	45	51	0

Hours	Degrees in longitude							Degrees of anomaly						
	°	I	II	III	IV	V	VI	°	I	II	III	IV	V	VI
1	0	1	18	36	32	14	39	0	1	9	14	10	48	22
2	0	2	37	13	4	29	18	0	2	18	28	21	36	44
3	0	3	55	49	36	43	6	0	3	27	42	32	25	7
4	0	5	14	26	8	58	35	0	4	36	56	43	13	29
5	0	6	33	2	41	13	14	0	5	46	10	54	1	52
6	0	7	51	39	13	27	53	0	6	55	25	4	50	14
7	0	9	10	15	45	42	32	0	8	4	39	15	38	36
8	0	10	28	52	17	57	11	0	9	13	53	26	26	59
9	0	11	47	28	50	11	49	0	10	23	7	37	15	21
10	0	13	6	5	22	26	28	0	11	32	21	48	3	44
11	0	14	24	41	54	41	7	0	12	41	35	58	52	6
12	0	15	43	18	26	55	46	0	13	50	50	9	40	29
13	0	17	1	54	59	10	25	0	15	0	4	20	28	51
14	0	18	20	31	31	25	4	0	16	9	18	31	17	13
15	0	19	39	8	3	39	43	0	17	18	32	42	5	36
16	0	20	57	44	35	54	22	0	18	27	46	52	53	58
17	0	22	16	21	8	9	0	0	19	37	1	3	42	21
18	0	23	34	57	40	23	39	0	20	46	15	14	30	43
19	0	24	53	34	12	38	18	0	21	55	29	25	19	5
20	0	26	12	10	44	52	57	0	23	4	43	36	7	28
21	0	27	30	47	17	7	36	0	24	13	57	46	55	50
22	0	28	49	23	49	22	15	0	25	23	11	57	44	13
23	0	30	8	0	21	36	54	0	26	32	26	8	32	35
24	0	31	26	36	53	51	33	0	27	41	40	19	20	58

Mars, *Continued*

Months	Degrees in longitude							Degrees of anomaly						
	o	I	II	III	IV	V	VI	o	I	II	III	IV	V	VI
30	15	43	18	26	55	4t	30	13	50	50	9	40	29	0
60	31	26	36	53	51	33	0	27	41	40	19	20	58	0
90	47	9	55	20	47	19	30	41	32	30	29	1	27	0
120	62	53	13	47	43	6	0	55	23	20	38	41	56	0
150	78	36	32	14	38	52	30	69	14	10	48	22	25	0
180	94	19	50	41	34	39	0	83	5	0	58	2	54	0
210	110	3	9	8	30	25	30	96	55	51	7	43	23	0
240	125	46	27	35	26	12	0	110	46	41	17	23	52	0
270	141	29	46	2	21	58	30	124	37	31	27	4	21	0
300	157	13	4	29	17	45	0	138	28	21	36	44	50	0
330	172	56	22	56	13	31	30	152	19	11	46	25	19	0
360	188	39	41	23	9	18	0	166	10	1	56	5	48	0

Days	Degrees in longitude							Degrees of anomaly						
	o	I	II	III	IV	V	VI	o	I	II	III	IV	V	VI
1	0	31	26	36	53	51	33	0	27	41	40	19	20	58
2	1	2	53	13	47	43	6	0	55	23	20	38	41	56
3	1	34	19	50	41	34	39	1	23	5	0	58	2	54
4	2	5	46	27	35	26	12	1	50	46	41	17	23	52
5	2	37	13	4	29	17	45	2	18	28	21	36	44	50
6	3	8	39	41	23	9	18	2	46	10	1	56	5	48
7	3	40	6	18	17	0	51	3	13	51	42	15	26	46
8	4	11	32	55	10	52	24	3	41	33	22	34	47	44
9	4	42	59	32	4	43	57	4	9	15	2	54	8	42
10	5	14	26	8	58	35	30	4	36	56	43	13	29	40
11	5	45	52	45	52	27	3	5	4	38	23	32	50	38
12	6	17	19	22	46	18	36	5	32	20	3	52	11	36
13	6	48	45	59	40	10	9	6	0	1	44	11	32	34
14	7	20	12	36	34	1	42	6	27	43	24	30	53	32
15	7	51	39	13	27	53	15	6	55	25	4	50	14	30
16	8	23	5	50	21	44	48	7	23	6	45	9	35	28
17	8	54	32	27	15	36	21	7	50	48	25	28	56	26
18	9	25	59	4	9	27	54	8	18	30	5	48	17	24
19	9	57	25	41	3	19	27	8	46	11	46	7	38	22
20	10	28	52	17	57	11	0	9	13	53	26	26	59	20
21	11	0	18	54	51	2	33	9	41	35	6	46	20	18
22	11	31	45	31	44	54	6	10	9	16	47	5	41	16
23	12	3	12	8	38	45	39	10	36	58	27	25	2	14
24	12	34	38	45	32	37	12	11	4	40	7	44	23	12
25	13	6	5	22	26	28	45	11	32	21	48	3	44	10
26	13	37	31	59	20	20	18	12	0	3	28	23	5	8
27	14	8	58	36	14	11	51	12	27	45	8	42	26	6
28	14	40	25	13	8	3	24	12	55	26	49	1	47	4
29	15	11	51	50	1	54	57	13	23	8	29	21	8	2
30	15	43	18	26	55	46	30	13	50	50	9	40	29	0

VENUS, Anomaly at epoch, 71°7′

18-years	Longitude at epoch, Fishes 45° Degrees in longitude							Apogee at epoch, Bull 16°10′ Degrees of anomaly						
	°	I	II	III	IV	V	VI	°	I	II	III	IV	V	VI
18	355	37	25	36	20	34	30	90	27	44	34	23	46	30
36	351	14	51	12	41	9	0	180	55	29	8	47	33	0
54	346	52	16	49	1	43	30	271	23	13	43	11	19	30
72	342	29	42	25	22	18	0	1	50	58	17	35	6	0
90	338	7	8	1	42	52	30	92	18	42	51	58	52	30
108	333	44	33	38	3	27	0	182	46	27	26	22	39	0
126	329	21	59	14	24	1	30	273	14	12	0	46	25	30
144	324	59	24	50	44	36	0	3	41	56	35	10	12	0
162	320	36	50	27	5	10	30	94	9	41	9	33	58	30
180	316	14	16	3	25	45	0	184	37	25	43	57	45	0
198	311	51	41	39	46	19	30	275	5	10	18	21	31	30
216	307	29	7	16	6	54	0	5	32	54	52	45	18	0
234	303	6	32	52	27	28	30	96	0	39	27	9	4	30
252	298	43	58	28	48	3	0	186	28	24	1	32	51	0
270	294	21	24	5	8	37	30	276	56	8	35	56	37	30
288	289	58	49	41	29	12	0	7	23	53	10	20	24	0
306	285	36	15	17	49	46	30	97	51	37	44	44	10	30
324	281	13	40	54	10	21	0	188	19	22	19	7	57	0
342	276	51	6	30	30	55	30	278	47	6	53	31	43	30
360	272	28	32	6	51	30	0	9	14	51	27	55	30	0
378	268	5	57	43	12	4	30	99	42	36	2	19	16	30
396	263	43	23	19	32	39	0	190	10	20	36	43	3	0
414	259	20	48	55	53	13	30	280	38	5	11	6	49	30
432	254	58	14	32	13	48	0	11	5	49	45	30	36	0
450	250	35	40	8	34	22	30	101	33	34	19	54	22	30
468	246	13	5	44	54	57	0	192	1	18	54	18	9	0
486	241	50	31	21	15	31	30	282	29	3	28	41	55	30
504	237	27	56	57	36	6	0	12	56	48	3	5	42	0
522	233	5	22	33	56	40	30	103	24	32	37	29	28	30
540	228	42	48	10	17	15	0	193	52	17	11	53	15	0
558	224	20	13	46	37	49	30	284	20	1	46	17	1	30
576	219	57	39	22	58	24	0	14	47	46	20	40	48	0
594	215	35	4	59	18	58	30	105	15	30	55	4	34	30
612	211	12	30	35	39	33	0	195	43	15	29	28	21	0
630	206	49	56	12	0	7	30	286	11	0	3	52	7	30
648	202	27	21	48	20	42	0	16	38	44	38	15	54	0
666	198	4	47	24	41	16	30	107	6	29	12	39	40	30
684	193	42	13	1	1	51	0	197	34	13	47	3	27	0
702	189	19	38	37	22	25	30	288	1	58	21	27	13	30
720	184	57	4	13	43	0	0	18	29	42	55	51	0	0
738	180	34	29	50	3	34	30	108	57	27	30	14	46	30
756	176	11	55	26	24	9	0	199	25	12	4	38	33	0
774	171	49	21	2	44	43	30	289	52	56	39	2	19	30
792	167	26	46	39	5	18	0	20	20	41	13	26	6	0
810	163	4	12	15	25	52	30	110	48	25	47	49	52	30

Venus, *Continued*

Single years	Degrees in longitude							Degrees of anomaly						
	°	I	II	III	IV	V	VI	°	I	II	III	IV	V	VI
1	359	45	24	45	21	8	35	225	1	32	28	34	39	15
2	359	30	49	30	42	17	10	90	3	4	57	9	18	30
3	359	16	14	16	3	25	45	315	4	37	25	43	57	45
4	359	1	39	1	24	34	20	180	6	9	54	18	37	0
5	358	47	3	46	45	42	55	45	7	42	22	53	16	15
6	358	32	28	32	6	51	30	270	9	14	51	27	55	30
7	358	17	53	17	28	0	5	135	10	47	20	2	34	45
8	358	3	18	2	49	8	40	0	12	19	48	37	14	0
9	357	48	42	48	10	17	15	225	13	52	17	11	53	15
10	357	34	7	33	31	25	50	90	15	24	45	46	32	30
11	357	19	32	18	52	34	25	315	16	57	14	21	11	45
12	357	4	57	4	13	43	0	180	18	29	42	55	51	0
13	356	50	21	49	34	51	35	45	20	2	11	30	30	15
14	356	35	46	34	56	0	10	270	21	34	40	5	9	30
15	356	21	11	20	17	8	45	135	23	7	8	39	48	45
16	356	6	36	5	38	17	20	0	24	39	37	14	28	0
17	355	52	0	50	59	25	55	225	26	12	5	49	7	15
18	355	37	25	36	20	34	30	90	27	44	34	23	46	30

Hours	Degrees in longitude							Degrees of anomaly						
	°	I	II	III	IV	V	VI	°	I	II	III	IV	V	VI
1	0	2	27	50	43	3	1	0	1	32	28	34	42	58
2	0	4	55	41	26	6	2	0	3	4	57	9	25	57
3	0	7	23	32	9	9	3	0	4	37	25	44	8	56
4	0	9	51	22	52	12	5	0	6	9	54	18	51	54
5	0	12	19	13	35	15	6	0	7	42	22	53	34	53
6	0	14	47	4	18	18	7	0	9	14	51	28	17	52
7	0	17	14	55	1	21	9	0	10	47	20	3	0	50
8	0	19	42	45	44	24	10	0	12	19	48	37	43	49
9	0	22	10	36	26	26	11	0	13	52	17	12	26	48
10	0	24	38	27	10	30	12	0	15	24	45	47	9	46
11	0	27	6	17	53	33	14	0	16	57	14	21	52	45
12	0	29	34	8	36	36	15	0	18	29	42	56	35	44
13	0	32	1	59	19	39	16	0	20	2	11	31	18	42
14	0	34	29	50	2	42	18	0	21	34	40	6	1	41
15	0	36	57	40	45	45	19	0	23	7	8	40	44	40
16	0	39	25	31	28	48	20	0	24	39	37	15	27	38
17	0	41	53	22	11	51	21	0	26	12	5	50	10	37
18	0	44	21	12	54	54	23	0	27	44	34	24	53	36
19	0	46	49	3	37	57	24	0	29	17	2	59	36	34
20	0	49	16	54	21	0	25	0	30	49	31	34	19	33
21	0	51	44	45	4	3	27	0	32	22	0	9	2	32
22	0	54	12	35	47	6	28	0	33	54	28	43	45	30
23	0	56	40	26	30	9	29	0	35	26	57	18	28	29
24	0	59	8	17	13	12	31	0	36	59	25	53	11	28

VENUS, *Continued*

Months	Degrees in longitude							Degrees of anomaly						
	°	I	II	III	IV	V	VI	°	I	II	III	IV	V	VI
30	29	34	8	36	36	15	30	18	29	42	56	35	44	0
60	59	8	17	13	12	31	0	36	59	25	53	11	28	0
90	88	42	25	49	48	46	30	55	29	8	49	47	12	0
120	118	16	34	26	25	2	0	73	58	51	46	22	56	0
150	147	50	43	3	1	17	30	92	28	34	42	58	40	0
180	177	24	51	39	37	33	0	110	58	17	39	34	24	0
210	206	59	0	16	13	48	30	129	28	0	36	10	8	0
240	236	33	8	52	50	4	0	147	57	43	32	45	52	0
270	266	7	17	29	26	19	30	166	27	26	29	21	36	0
300	295	41	26	6	2	35	0	184	57	9	25	57	20	0
330	325	15	34	42	38	50	30	203	26	52	22	33	4	0
360	354	49	43	19	15	6	0	221	56	35	19	8	48	0

Days	Degrees in longitude							Degrees of anomaly						
	°	I	II	III	IV	V	VI	°	I	II	III	IV	V	VI
1	0	59	8	17	13	12	31	0	36	59	25	53	11	28
2	1	58	16	34	26	25	2	1	13	58	51	46	22	56
3	2	57	24	51	39	37	33	1	50	58	17	39	34	24
4	3	56	33	8	52	50	4	2	27	57	43	32	45	52
5	4	55	41	26	6	2	35	3	4	57	9	25	57	20
6	5	54	49	43	19	15	6	3	41	56	35	19	8	48
7	6	53	58	0	32	27	37	4	18	56	1	12	20	16
8	7	53	6	17	45	40	8	4	55	55	27	5	31	44
9	8	52	14	34	58	52	39	5	32	54	52	58	43	12
10	9	51	22	52	12	5	10	6	9	54	18	51	54	40
11	10	50	31	9	25	17	41	6	46	53	44	45	6	8
12	11	49	39	26	38	30	12	7	23	53	10	38	17	36
13	12	48	47	43	51	42	43	8	0	52	36	31	29	4
14	13	47	56	1	4	55	14	8	37	52	2	24	40	32
15	14	47	4	18	18	7	45	9	14	51	28	17	52	0
16	15	46	12	35	31	20	16	9	51	50	54	11	3	28
17	16	45	20	52	44	32	47	10	28	50	20	4	14	56
18	17	44	29	9	57	45	18	11	5	49	45	57	26	24
19	18	43	37	27	10	57	49	11	42	49	11	50	37	52
20	19	42	45	44	24	10	20	12	19	48	37	43	49	20
21	20	41	54	1	37	22	51	12	56	48	3	37	0	48
22	21	41	2	18	50	35	22	13	33	47	29	30	12	16
23	22	40	1	36	3	47	53	14	10	46	55	23	23	44
24	23	39	18	53	17	0	24	14	47	46	21	16	35	12
25	24	38	27	10	30	12	55	15	24	45	47	9	46	40
26	25	37	35	27	43	25	26	16	1	45	13	2	58	8
27	26	36	43	44	56	37	57	16	38	44	38	56	9	36
28	27	35	52	2	9	50	28	17	15	44	4	49	21	4
29	28	35	0	19	23	2	59	17	52	43	30	42	32	32
30	29	34	8	36	36	15	30	18	29	42	56	35	44	0

MERCURY, Anomaly at epoch, 21°55′

18-years	Longitude at epoch, Fishes 0°45 Degrees in longitude							Apogee at epoch, Balance 1°10 Degrees of anomaly						
	°	I	II	III	IV	V	VI	°	I	II	III	IV	V	VI
18	355	37	25	36	20	34	30	251	0	45	45	53	45	0
36	351	14	51	12	41	9	0	142	1	31	31	47	30	0
54	346	52	16	49	1	43	30	33	2	17	17	41	15	0
72	342	29	42	25	22	18	0	284	3	3	3	35	0	0
90	338	7	8	1	42	52	30	175	3	48	49	28	45	0
108	333	44	33	38	3	27	0	66	4	34	35	22	30	0
126	329	21	59	14	24	1	30	317	5	20	21	16	15	0
144	324	59	24	50	44	36	0	208	6	6	7	10	0	0
162	320	36	50	27	5	10	30	99	6	51	53	3	45	0
180	316	14	16	3	25	45	0	350	7	37	38	57	30	0
198	311	51	41	39	46	19	30	241	8	23	24	51	15	0
216	307	29	7	16	6	54	0	132	9	9	10	45	0	0
234	303	6	32	52	27	28	30	23	9	54	56	38	45	0
252	298	43	58	28	48	3	0	274	10	40	42	32	30	0
270	294	21	24	5	8	37	30	165	11	26	28	26	15	0
288	289	58	49	41	29	12	0	56	12	12	14	20	0	0
306	285	36	15	17	49	46	30	307	12	58	0	13	45	0
324	281	13	40	54	10	21	0	198	13	43	46	7	30	0
342	276	51	6	30	30	55	30	89	14	29	32	1	15	0
360	272	28	32	6	51	30	0	340	15	15	17	55	0	0
378	268	5	57	43	12	4	30	231	16	1	3	48	45	0
396	263	43	23	19	32	39	0	122	16	46	49	42	30	0
414	259	20	48	55	53	13	30	13	17	32	35	36	15	0
432	254	58	14	32	13	48	0	264	18	18	21	30	0	0
450	250	35	40	8	34	22	30	155	19	4	7	23	45	0
468	246	13	5	44	54	57	0	46	19	49	53	17	30	0
486	241	50	31	21	15	31	30	297	20	35	39	11	15	0
504	237	27	56	57	36	6	0	188	21	21	25	5	0	0
522	233	5	22	33	56	40	30	79	22	7	10	58	45	0
540	228	42	48	10	17	15	0	330	22	52	56	52	30	0
558	224	20	13	46	37	49	30	221	23	38	42	46	15	0
576	219	57	39	22	58	24	0	112	24	24	28	40	0	0
594	215	35	4	59	18	58	30	3	25	10	14	33	45	0
612	211	12	30	35	39	33	0	254	25	56	0	27	30	0
630	206	49	56	12	0	7	30	145	26	41	46	21	15	0
648	202	27	21	48	20	42	0	36	27	27	32	15	0	0
666	198	4	47	24	41	16	30	287	28	13	18	8	45	0
684	193	42	13	1	1	51	0	178	28	59	4	2	30	0
702	189	19	38	37	22	25	30	69	29	44	49	56	15	0
720	184	57	4	13	43	0	0	320	30	30	35	50	0	0
738	180	34	29	50	3	34	30	211	31	16	21	43	45	0
756	176	11	55	26	24	9	0	102	32	2	7	37	30	0
774	171	49	21	2	44	43	30	353	32	47	53	31	15	0
792	167	26	46	39	5	18	0	244	33	33	39	25	0	0
810	163	4	12	15	25	52	30	135	34	19	25	18	45	0

Mercury, *Continued*

Single years	°	I	II	III	IV	V	VI	°	I	II	III	IV	V	VI
			Degrees in longitude							*Degrees of anomaly*				
1	359	45	24	45	21	8	35	53	56	42	32	32	59	10
2	359	30	49	30	42	17	10	107	53	25	5	5	58	20
3	359	16	14	16	3	25	45	161	50	7	37	38	57	30
4	359	1	39	1	24	34	20	215	46	50	10	11	56	40
5	358	47	3	46	45	42	55	269	43	32	42	44	55	50
6	358	32	28	32	6	51	30	323	40	15	15	17	55	0
7	358	17	53	17	28	0	5	17	36	57	47	50	54	10
8	358	3	18	2	49	8	40	71	33	40	20	23	53	20
9	357	48	42	48	10	17	15	125	30	22	52	56	52	30
10	357	34	7	33	31	25	50	179	27	5	25	29	51	40
11	357	19	32	18	52	34	25	233	23	47	58	2	50	50
12	357	4	57	4	13	43	0	287	20	30	30	35	50	0
13	356	50	21	49	34	51	35	341	17	13	3	8	49	10
14	356	35	46	34	56	0	10	35	13	55	35	41	48	20
15	356	21	11	20	17	8	45	89	10	38	8	14	47	30
16	356	6	36	5	38	17	20	143	7	20	40	47	46	40
17	355	52	0	50	59	25	55	197	4	3	13	20	45	50
18	355	37	25	36	20	34	30	251	0	45	45	53	45	0

Hours	°	I	II	III	IV	V	VI	°	I	II	III	IV	V	VI
			Degrees in longitude							*Degrees of anomaly*				
1	0	2	27	50	43	3	1	0	7	46	0	17	28	59
2	0	4	55	41	26	6	2	0	15	32	0	34	57	59
3	0	6	23	32	9	9	3	0	23	18	0	52	26	58
4	0	9	51	22	52	12	5	0	31	4	1	9	55	58
5	0	12	19	13	35	15	6	0	38	50	1	27	24	57
6	0	14	47	4	18	18	7	0	46	36	1	44	53	57
7	0	17	14	55	1	21	9	0	54	22	2	2	22	57
8	0	19	42	45	44	24	10	1	2	8	2	19	51	56
9	0	22	10	36	27	27	11	1	9	54	2	37	20	56
10	0	24	38	27	10	30	12	1	17	40	2	54	49	55
11	0	27	6	17	53	33	14	1	25	26	3	12	18	55
12	0	29	34	8	36	36	15	1	33	12	3	29	47	55
13	0	32	1	59	19	39	16	1	40	58	3	47	16	54
14	0	34	29	50	2	42	18	1	48	44	4	4	45	54
15	0	36	57	40	45	45	19	1	56	30	4	22	14	53
16	0	39	25	31	28	48	20	2	4	16	4	39	43	53
17	0	41	53	22	11	51	21	2	12	2	4	57	12	52
18	0	44	21	12	54	54	23	2	19	48	5	14	41	52
19	0	46	49	3	37	57	24	2	27	34	5	32	10	52
20	0	49	16	54	21	0	25	2	35	20	5	49	39	51
21	0	51	44	45	4	3	27	2	43	6	6	7	8	51
22	0	54	12	35	47	6	28	2	50	52	6	24	37	50
23	0	56	40	26	30	9	29	2	58	38	6	42	6	50
24	0	59	8	17	13	12	31	3	6	24	6	59	35	50

MERCURY, *Continued*

Months	Degrees in longitude							Degrees of anomaly						
	°	I	II	III	IV	V	VI	°	I	II	III	IV	V	VI
30	29	34	8	36	36	15	30	93	12	3	29	47	55	0
60	59	8	17	13	12	31	0	186	24	6	59	35	50	0
90	88	42	25	49	48	46	30	279	36	10	29	23	45	0
120	118	16	34	26	25	2	0	12	48	13	59	11	40	0
150	147	50	43	3	1	17	30	106	0	17	28	59	35	0
180	177	24	51	39	37	33	0	199	12	20	58	47	30	0
210	206	59	0	16	13	48	30	292	24	24	28	35	25	0
240	236	33	8	52	50	4	0	25	36	27	58	23	20	0
270	266	7	17	29	26	19	30	118	48	31	28	11	15	0
300	295	41	26	6	2	35	0	212	0	34	57	59	10	0
330	325	15	34	42	38	50	30	305	12	38	27	47	5	0
360	354	49	43	19	15	6	0	38	24	41	57	35	0	0

Days	Degrees in longitude							Degrees of anomaly						
	°	I	II	III	IV	V	VI	°	I	II	III	IV	V	VI
1	0	59	8	17	13	12	31	3	6	24	6	59	35	50
2	1	58	16	34	26	25	2	6	12	48	13	59	11	40
3	2	57	24	51	39	37	33	9	19	12	20	58	47	30
4	3	56	33	8	52	50	4	12	25	36	27	58	23	20
5	4	55	41	26	6	2	35	15	32	0	34	57	59	10
6	5	54	49	43	19	15	6	18	38	24	41	57	35	0
7	6	53	58	0	32	27	37	21	44	48	48	57	10	50
8	7	53	6	17	45	40	8	24	51	12	55	56	46	40
9	8	52	14	34	58	52	39	27	57	37	2	56	22	30
10	9	51	22	52	12	5	10	31	4	1	9	55	58	20
11	10	50	31	9	25	17	41	34	10	25	16	55	34	10
12	11	49	39	26	38	30	12	37	16	49	23	55	10	0
13	12	48	47	43	51	42	43	40	23	13	30	54	45	50
14	13	47	56	1	4	55	14	43	29	37	37	54	21	40
15	14	47	4	18	18	7	45	46	36	1	44	53	57	30
16	15	46	12	35	31	20	16	49	42	25	51	53	33	20
17	16	45	20	52	44	32	47	52	48	49	58	53	9	10
18	17	44	29	9	57	45	18	55	55	14	5	52	45	0
19	18	43	37	27	10	57	49	59	1	38	12	52	20	50
20	19	42	45	44	24	10	20	62	8	2	19	51	56	40
21	20	41	54	1	37	22	51	65	14	26	26	51	32	30
22	21	41	2	18	50	35	22	68	20	50	33	51	8	20
23	22	40	10	36	3	47	53	71	27	14	40	50	44	10
24	23	39	18	53	17	0	24	74	33	38	47	50	20	0
25	24	38	27	10	30	12	55	77	40	2	54	49	55	50
26	25	37	35	27	43	25	26	80	46	27	1	49	31	40
27	26	36	43	44	56	37	57	83	52	51	8	49	7	30
28	27	35	52	2	9	50	28	86	59	15	15	48	43	20
29	28	35	0	19	23	2	59	90	5	39	22	48	19	10
30	29	34	8	36	36	15	30	93	12	3	29	47	55	0

5. Preliminaries of the Hypotheses of the Five Planets

Now, the relation of the anomalies to the longitudinal passage of the five planets follows the exposition of these mean movements, and we have attempted a general outline of it in the following way.

For, as we said, the very simple movements together sufficient for the problem in hand are two: one effected by circles eccentric to the ecliptic, and the other by circles concentric with the ecliptic but bearing epicycles. And likewise also the apparent anomalies for each star considered singly are two: one observed with respect to the parts of the zodiac and the other with respect to the configurations of the sun. In the case of this latter anomaly, we find, from different configurations observed in contiguity and in the same parts of the zodiac, that, for the five planets, the time from the greatest movement to the mean movement is always longer than from the mean to the least. And such a property (σύμπτωμα) cannot follow from the hypothesis of eccentricity, but its contrary follows, because the greatest passage is always effected at the perigee, and in both hypotheses the arc from the perigee to the point of mean passage is less than that from this point to the apogee. But it can occur in the hypothesis of epicycles when the greatest passage is not effected at the perigee as in the case of the moon, but at the apogee—that is, when the star, starting from the apogee, moves not westward as the moon, but eastward in the opposite direction. And so we suppose this anomaly to be produced by epicycles.

But in the case of the anomaly observed with respect to the parts of the zodiac, we find, by means of the arcs of the zodiac taken at the same phases or configurations, that, on the contrary, the time from the least movement to the mean is always greater than the time from the mean movement to the greatest. But this property can follow from either hypothesis, and at the beginning of the composition of the sun [III, 3] we showed how they were alike in this. But since it is more proper to the eccentric hypothesis, we suppose this anomaly is effected according to it, and also because the other anomaly is peculiar to the epicyclic hypothesis.

But immediately on applying the particular positions observed to the courses constructed from the combination of both hypotheses and continually examining them together, we find things cannot proceed so simply: (1) The planes in which we describe the eccentric circles are not immobile, so that the straight line through both their centres and the ecliptic's centre, along which the apogees and perigees are sighted, always remains at the same angular distances from the tropic and equinoctial points. (2) The epicycles do not have their centres borne on the eccentric circles whose centres are those with respect to which the epicycles' centres revolve in a regular eastward motion and cut off equal angles in equal times. But (1) the eccentrics' apogees make a slight regular shift eastward from the tropic points around the ecliptic's centre and nearly as much for each planet as the sphere of the fixed stars is found to make—that is, one degree in a hundred years, as far as one can detect from present data. And (2) the epicycles' centres are borne on circles equal to the eccentrics effecting the anomaly, but described about other centres. And these other centres, in the case of all except Mercury, bisect the straight lines between the centres of the eccentrics effecting the anomaly and the centre of the ecliptic.[1] But in the case of Mercury

[1]These three points—the centre of the equant, the centre of the deferent, and the centre of the ecliptic—with the deferent's centre midway between the other two, by means of the

alone, this other centre is the same distance from the centre revolving it [centre of equant] as this centre revolving it is in turn from the centre effecting the anomaly on the side of the apogee, and as this last centre effecting the anomaly is in turn from the centre placed at the eye. For, in the case of that star alone as also with the moon, we find the eccentric circle revolved by the aforesaid centre, contrariwise to the epicycle, back westward one revolution in a year's time, since it appears to be twice perigee in one revolution, just as the moon is also twice so in one month's time.

6. On the Mode and Difference of these Hypotheses

The mode of the hypotheses just derived would be more easy to understand in this way:

In the case of the hypothesis of all the planets except Mercury, first let there be conceived the eccentric circle ABC about the centre D, and the diameter ADC through D and the centre of the eclip-
tic. And on this diameter let E be made the centre of the ecliptic, the point A the apogee, and C the perigee. And let DE be bisected at F; and with F as centre and DA as radius, let circle GHK be drawn, equal of course to circle ABC. And with H as centre let the epicycle LM be drawn, and let the straight line $LHMD$ be joined.

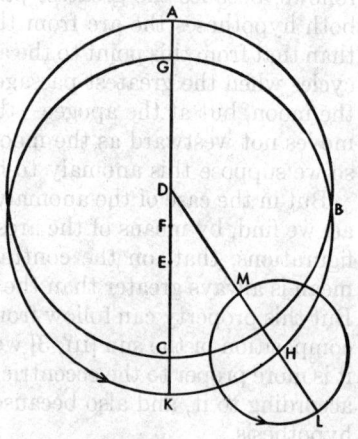

Then first we suppose the plane of the eccentric circles to be inclined to that of the ecliptic, and again the plane of the epicycle to that of the eccentric, because of the latitudinal passage of the stars to be demonstrated by us hereafter. But to make things easy as far as the longitudinal passages are concerned, we suppose that they are all conceived in the one plane of the ecliptic, since there will be no appreciable difference in longitude resulting from such inclinations as will be found for each of the stars.

Then we say that the whole plane revolves eastward in the direction of the signs about centre E, moving the apogees and perigees one degree in a hundred years; that the epicycle's diameter LHM in turn is revolved regularly by centre D eastward in the direction of the signs at the rate of the star's longitudinal return; and that at the same time it revolves the points of the epicycle L and M, its centre H always borne on the eccentric GHK, and the star itself. And the star in turn moves on the epicycle LM, regularly with respect to the diameter always pointing to centre D, and makes its returns at the rate of the mean cycle

Copernican transformation, come to represent the two foci and the centre of the Keplerian ellipse with exactly the same ratios preserved.

It is to be remarked that this broadening of the principle of celestial mechanics to allow an epicycle's centre to move regularly about a point other than the centre of its deferent was for Copernicus the major scandal of the Ptolemaic system and one which his own allowed him to remove only at the expense of the appearances, as Kepler well saw.

All this is explained in more detail in the first note of Book XII and in Appendix B to this work.

of the anomaly with respect to the sun, moving eastward in the order of the signs at the apogee *L*.

And we could visualize the characteristic property of the hypothesis of Mercury in this way.

For let there be the eccentric circle of anomaly *ABC* about centre *D*, and the

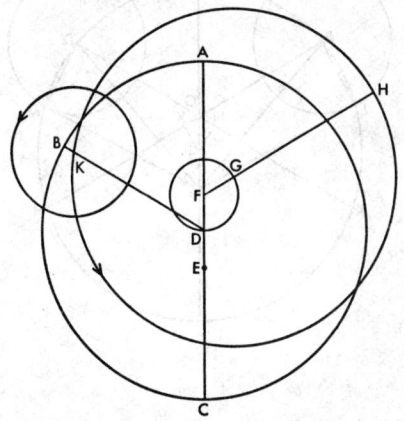

diameter *ADEC* through *D*, the ecliptic's centre *E*, and the apogee *A*. And let *DF* be taken on *AC* in the direction of the apogee *A* and equal to *DE*.

Then, other things remaining the same (that is, the whole plane shifting the apogee eastward about *E* as a centre the same amount as for the other stars, and the epicycle being revolved regularly eastward about *D* as centre by the straight line *DB*, and again the star moving on the epicycle in the same way as the others), here the centre of the other eccentric, equal to the first and on which the epicycle's centre will always lie, will be revolved by the straight line *FGH* about point *F* contrariwise to the epicycle—that is, westward in the direction opposite to the signs—regularly and at the same speed as the epicycle, so that each of the straight lines *DB* and *FGH*, in one year's time, is restored once with respect to the points of the ecliptic, and twice with respect to each other. And this centre of the other eccentric will always be a distance from the point *F* equal to either of the straight lines *ED* or *DF* (for instance, *FG*) so that the little circle described by its movement westward, with *F* as centre and *FG* as radius, is always bounded by the centre of the first eccentric which remains fixed; and the moving eccentric is described in every case with *G* as centre and with radius *GH*, equal to *DA*, as for instance here *HK*, and the epicycle always has its centre on it, as here at point *K*.

We can follow the suppositions even more precisely from the demonstrations we are to give of the magnitudes for each planet. In these demonstrations the motives for formulating the hypotheses will somehow show up in clearer outline.

Yet one must premise that, since the longitudinal cycles do not make their returns with the points of the zodiac and with the apogees or perigees of the eccentric circles, because of their shift, therefore the longitudinal movements set out by us in the foregoing manner do not contain returns considered with respect to the apogees of the eccentrics but returns that are relative to the tropic and equinoctial points in accordance with our year.

Then it must be shown first that, also according to these hypotheses, whenever the mean longitudinal position of the star is equidistant from the apogees and perigees in either direction, the difference of zodiacal anomaly is equal for either distance, and also the greatest elongation on the epicycle on the corresponding side of the mean position.

For about centre *E* and diameter *AEC*, let there be the eccentric circle *ABC* on which the epicycle's centre is borne. On this diameter let *F* be taken as the ecliptic's centre, and *G* as the centre of the eccentric making the anomaly—that is, the centre around which we say the epicycle's mean passage is regularly effected. And let the straight lines BGH and DGK be drawn through, both the same angular distance from the apogee A, so that angles AGB and AGD are equal. And let epicycles be described about points B and D, and let straight lines BF and BD be joined, and from F the eye-point let the straight lines FL and FM be drawn tangent to the epicycles on the corresponding sides.

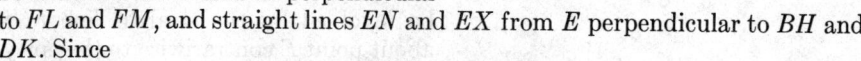

I say that angle FBG of the difference of zodiacal anomaly is equal to angle GDF; and that angle BFL, the greatest elongation on the epicycle, is likewise equal to angle DFM. For in this way the magnitudes of the elongations resulting from the combination of the eccentric and of the greatest elongations from the mean position will also be equal.

Then let the straight lines BL and DM be drawn from B and D perpendicular to FL and FM, and straight lines EN and EX from E perpendicular to BH and DK. Since

$$\text{angle } XGE = \text{angle } NGE,$$

and the angles at N and X are right, and EG is common to the equiangular triangles, therefore

$$NG = XG,$$
$$EN = EX.$$

Therefore BH and DK are chords equidistant from the centre E; therefore they are equal and their halves also. And so, by subtraction,

$$BG = DG.$$

But GF is common, and

$$\text{angle } BGF = \text{angle } DGF,$$

and are within equal sides; therefore also

$$\text{base } BF = \text{base } DF,$$

and

$$\text{angle } GBF = \text{angle } DGF.$$

And also, as radii of the epicycles,

$$BL = DM,$$

and the angles at L and M are right; therefore also

$$\text{angle } BFL = \text{angle } DFM.$$

Which things it was required to prove.

Then again, for the hypothesis of Mercury, let there be the diameter ABC through the circles' centres and apogee; and let A be supposed the centre of the ecliptic; B the centre of the eccentric effecting the anomaly, and C the point about which moves the centre of the eccentric bearing the epicycle. And again let the straight lines BD and BE of the epicycle's regular eastward motion be drawn through on either side, and the straight lines CF and CG of the eccentric's westward revolution at the same rate, so that of course the angles at C and B are

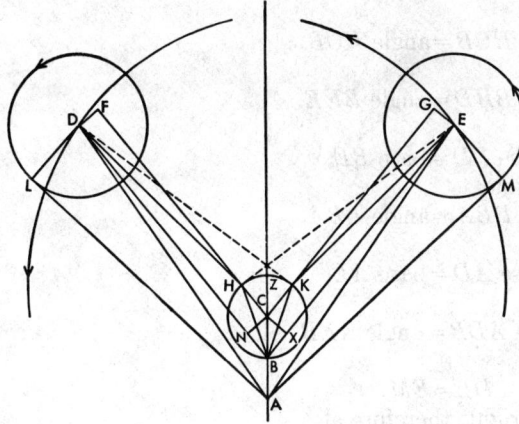

equal, and *BD* parallel to *CF*, and *BE* to *CG*. And let the centres of the eccentrics be taken on *CF* and *CG*, and let them be *H* and *K*. And let the eccentrics described about these centres, eccentrics bearing the epicycles, pass through the points *D* and *E*. Again, with equal epicycles described about points *D* and *E*, let the straight lines *AD* and *AE* be joined, and let the straight lines *AL* and *AM* be drawn tangent to the corresponding sides of the epicycles.

Then it must be proved that the angle of zodiacal anomaly *ADB* is equal to angle *AEB;* and that the angle of greatest elongation for the epicycle *DAL* is equal to angle *EAM*.

For let the straight lines *BH, BK, HD,* and *KE* be joined; and let *CN* and *CX* be drawn from *C* perpendicular to *BD* and *BE;* and *DF* and *EG* from *D* and *E* perpendicular to *CF* and *CG;* and *DL* and *EM* perpendicular to *AL* and *AM*. Since then

$$\text{angle } CBN = \text{angle } CBX,$$

and the angles at *N* and *X* are right, and the straight line *CB* is common, therefore

$$CN = CX,$$

that is

$$DF = EG.$$

But also

$$HD = KE,[1]$$

and the angles at *F* and *G* are right. And so

$$\text{angle } DHF = \text{angle } EKG;$$

and

$$\text{angle } CHB = \text{angle } CKB,$$

because it is supposed

$$HC = CK,$$

[1]For, as below,

$$HB = KB,$$

and as radii of the same moving eccentric

$$HE = KD.$$

And by hypothesis

$$\text{angle } DBC = \text{angle } EBC;$$

and, since by hypothesis

$$\text{arc } HZ = \text{arc } ZK,$$

therefore

$$\text{angle } HBC = \text{angle } KBC,$$

and by addition

$$\text{angle } DBZ = \text{angle } EBZ.$$

Hence, by congruent triangles *DKB* and *EHB*,

$$HD = KE.$$

CB is common, and

$$\text{angle } HCB = \text{angle } KCB.$$

And so also, by subtraction,

$$\text{angle } BHD = \text{angle } BKE,$$

and

$$\text{base } BD = \text{base } BE.$$

But again *BA* is also common, and

$$\text{angle } DBA = \text{angle } EBA.$$

And so

$$\text{base } AD = \text{base } AE,$$

and

$$\text{angle } ADB = \text{angle } AEB$$

And in the same way, since

$$DL = EM,$$

and the angles at *L* and *M* are right, therefore also

$$\text{angle } DAL = \text{angle } EAM.$$

Which things it was required to prove.[1]

7. DEMONSTRATION OF MERCURY'S APOGEE AND OF ITS SHIFT

With this theory established, we first took this way of finding the whereabouts on the ecliptic of Mercury's apogee. For we examined the observations of the greatest elongations in which the morning positions of the star were equal to the evening ones in their angular distance from the mean position of the sun. When these had been found, it followed from what we have shown that the point midway between the two positions included the eccentric's apogee.

Then we took some observations for this purpose, few because such combinations are seldom met with, but capable of showing up the subject in hand. Here are the more recent of them.

For in the year 16 of Hadrian, Egyptianwise Phamenoth 16-17 in the evening, we observed Mercury, by the manipulation of the astrolabe, at its greatest elongation from the sun's mean position. And then, being sighted with the bright star of the Hyades [Aldebaran], it appeared to be 1° within the Fishes. But at that time the mean position of the sun $(9+\frac{1}{2}+\frac{1}{4})°$ within the Water Bearer. Therefore the greatest evening elongation from the mean position was $21\frac{1}{4}°$.

And in the year 18 of Hadrian, Egyptianwise Epiphi 18-19 at dawn, Mercury was at its greatest elongation, appeared very slight and dim, was sighted with the bright star of the Hyades [Aldebaran], and appeared to be $(18+\frac{1}{2}+\frac{1}{4})°$ within the Bull. But at that time the mean sun was 10° within the Twins. And therefore at that time the greatest morning elongation from the mean position was equally $21\frac{1}{4}°$. And so, since in one observation the star's mean position was $(9+\frac{1}{2}+\frac{1}{4})°$ within the Water Bearer, and in the other 10° within the Twins, and since the point on the ecliptic midway between them is $(10-\frac{1}{8})°$ within

[1]In other words, Ptolemy has proved that if the epicycle's centre is equidistant on either side from the apogee, then the angles are equal. It cannot be proved in the case of the hypotheses of Mercury that the converse is true, since as we shall see later Mercury has two perigees and, therefore, there are other points of symmetry. Ptolemy, however, will use the converse as true for his observations. This is possible because he knows about where the apogee of the eccentric lies and, within a limited range on either side of that approximate point, the converse is true.

the Ram, the diameter through the apogee would be in that position at that time.

Again, in the year 1 of Antonine, Egyptianwise Epiphi 20-21 in the evening, with the astrolabe we observed Mercury at its greatest elongation from the sun's mean position. Being sighted at that time with the star of the Lion's heart [Regulus], it appeared to be 7° within the Crab. But at that time the mean sun was $10\frac{1}{2}$° within the Twins. Therefore the greatest evening elongation from the mean position was $26\frac{1}{2}$°.

And likewise also in the year 4 of Antonine, Egyptianwise Phamenoth 18-19 at dawn, Mercury was again at its greatest elongation, was sighted with the star called Antares, and appeared to be $13\frac{1}{2}$° within the Goat, while the mean sun was 10° within the Water Bearer. And therefore at that time the greatest morning elongation from the mean position was likewise $26\frac{1}{2}$°. And so, since at one of the observations the mean position of the star was $10\frac{1}{2}$° within the Twins, and at the other 10° within the Water Bearer, therefore the point of the ecliptic midway between them is $10\frac{1}{4}$° within the Balance, and at that time the diameter through the apogee would be in that position.

From these observations, then, we find the apogee falling very nearly 10° within the Ram or the Balance; and from the old observations of the greatest elongations, about 6° within the same signs, just as one would calculate it to be.

For in the year 23 according to Dionysius, Hydron 29 in the morning, Mercury was three moon's to the north of the brightest star in the Goat's tail. But this fixed star was then, according to our starting points (that is, the tropic and equinoctial points), $22\frac{1}{3}$° within the Goat, the same evidently as Mercury. And it is evident the mean sun was $18\frac{1}{6}$° within the Water Bearer; for that time was the year 486 of Nabonassar, Egyptianwise Choïak 17-18 at dawn. Therefore, the greatest morning elongation from the mean position was $(25+\frac{1}{2}+\frac{1}{3})$°.

We did not find a greatest evening elongation exactly equal to this one in any of the observations that have come down to us, but from two of them we calculated one very nearly equal in the following manner.

For in the same year 23 according to Dionysius, Tauron 4 in the evening, Mercury was three moons beyond the straight line through the horns of the Bull, and seemed to be passing more than three moons south of the common star.[1] And so again, according to our starting points, it was $23\frac{2}{3}$° within the Bull. And that was again the year 486 of Nabonassar, Egyptianwise Phamenoth 30-Pharmouthi 1 in the evening, when the mean sun was $29\frac{1}{2}$° within the Ram. Therefore, the greatest evening elongation from the mean position was $24\frac{1}{6}$°.

In the year 28 according to Dionysius, Didymon 7 in the evening, Mercury was in a straight line with the heads of the Twins, and was to the south of the southern one by a third part of a moon less than double the distance between the heads. And so again at that time Mercury was, according to our starting points, $29\frac{1}{3}$° within the Twins. And that was the year 491 of Nabonassar, Egyptianwise Pharmouthi 5-6 in the evening, at which time the mean sun was $(2+\frac{1}{2}+\frac{1}{3})$° within the Twins. And therefore the elongation itself was $26\frac{1}{2}$°.

Since, when the mean position was $29\frac{1}{2}$° within the Ram, the greatest elongation was $24\frac{1}{6}$°, and, when the mean position was $(2+\frac{1}{2}+\frac{1}{3})$° within the Twins, the elongation was $26\frac{1}{2}$°, and since the greatest morning elongation whose cor-

[1]The star described in the Catalogue of the Stars as "the star at the tip of the northern horn, the same as the star in the Charioteer's right foot."

respondent we sought was $(25+\frac{1}{2}+\frac{1}{3})°$, we extracted from the difference of the two observations just reported, where the mean position would have to be in order for the greatest evening elongation to be $(25+\frac{1}{2}+\frac{1}{3})°$. For the difference between the two mean positions comes to $33\frac{1}{3}°$, and between the greatest elongations to $2\frac{1}{3}°$, so that very nearly 24° corresponds to the $1\frac{2}{3}°$ difference between $(25+\frac{1}{2}+\frac{1}{3})°$ and $24\frac{1}{6}°$. If we add these 24° to the $29\frac{1}{2}°$ within the Ram, we shall have the mean position where the greatest evening elongation will be equal to the greatest morning elongation of $(25+\frac{1}{2}+\frac{1}{3})°$, and that will be $23\frac{1}{2}°$ within the Bull. And the point midway between $18\frac{1}{6}°$ within the Water Bearer and $23\frac{1}{2}°$ within the Bull is about $(5+\frac{1}{2}+\frac{1}{3})°$ within the Ram.

Again, in the year 24 according to Dionysius, Leonton 28 in the evening, Mercury was west of Spica, according to Hipparchus' calculations, by little more than 3°. And so it was then $19\frac{1}{2}°$ within the Virgin according to our starting points. And that was the year 486 of Nabonassar, Egyptianwise Paÿni 30 in the evening, at which time the mean sun was $(27+\frac{1}{2}+\frac{1}{3})°$ within the Lion. Therefore, the greatest evening elongation from the mean position was $21\frac{2}{3}°$, whose exact morning correspondent we again calculate by means of the following observations.

For in the year 75 according to the Chaldeans, Dius 14 in the morning, Mercury was half a cubit on the upper side of the southern Balance. And so it was then, according to our starting points, $14\frac{1}{6}°$ within the Balance. And that was the year 512 of Nabonassar, Egyptianwise Thoth 9-10, at dawn, at which time the mean sun was $5\frac{1}{2}°$ within the Scorpion. Therefore, the greatest morning elongation was 21°.

In the year 67 according to the Chaldeans, Apellaius 5 in the morning, Mercury was half a cubit on the upper side of the northern forehead of the Scorpion. And so at that time, in our terms, it was $2\frac{1}{3}°$ within the Scorpion. And that was the year 504 of Nabonassar, Egyptianwise Thoth 27-28 at dawn, at which time the mean sun was $(24+\frac{1}{2}+\frac{1}{3})°$ within the Scorpion. Therefore the elongation itself was $22\frac{1}{2}°$. Then again—since in these two observations the difference between the mean positions comes to $19\frac{2}{3}°$, and between the greatest elongations to $1\frac{1}{2}°$, and since for this reason 9° corresponds to the $\frac{2}{3}°$ by which the $21\frac{2}{3}°$ of the elongation required exceed the 21° of the smaller elongation—if we add these 9° to the $5\frac{1}{2}°$ within the Scorpion, we shall have the mean position at which the greatest morning elongation is equal to the $21\frac{2}{3}°$ of the evening elongation. And this mean position is $14\frac{1}{6}°$ within the Scorpion. And again, the point midway between $(27+\frac{1}{2}+\frac{1}{3})°$ within the Lion and $14\frac{1}{6}°$ within the Scorpion is very nearly 6° within the Balance.

From these appearances, then, and from the agreement of the appearances particular to the other stars, we find it consistent for the diameters through the perigees and apogees of the five planets to make a shift about the ecliptic's centre eastward in the order of the signs, and for that shift to be at the same rate as that of the sphere of the fixed stars. For, as we showed [VII, 2], it shifts very nearly 1° in a hundred years, and so the time from the old observations, where Mercury's apogee was about 6°, to our own observations, where it has come to be about 10°, is found to embrace nearly 400 years.

8. That Mercury also Becomes Twice Perigee in One Revolution

Following on this, we examined the magnitudes of the greatest elongations produced when the sun's mean position was at the apogee itself, and again when it was diametrically opposite. And here one can very well understand the usefulness of this kind of sighting [*i.e.*, with the astrolabe], since, even if some observed stars do not appear near each other because of their predetermined positions (and this happens for the most part in the case of Mercury because most of the fixed stars can rarely appear at a distance from the sun equal to Mercury's), yet by sighting with the far distant stars it is possible to get accurately their longitudinal and latitudinal positions.

Now in the year 19 of Hadrian, Egyptianwise Athyr 14-15, the morning Mercury was at its greatest elongation, and, sighted with the star of the Lion's heart, it appeared to be $20\frac{1}{5}°$ within the Virgin, while the mean sun was about $9\frac{1}{4}°$ within the Balance. And so the greatest elongation came to $19\frac{1}{20}°$.

And in the same year, Pachon 19 in the evening, it was at a greatest elongation, and, sighted with the bright star of the Hyades [Aldebaran], appeared to be $4\frac{1}{3}°$ within the Bull, while the mean sun was $11\frac{1}{2}°$ within the Ram. And so the greatest elongation in this case came to $23\frac{1}{4}°$, and from that it was clear the eccentric's apogee was in the Balance and not in the Ram.

Now, these things being given, let the straight line ABC be the diameter through the apogee; and let the point B be supposed the ecliptic's centre where the eye is; A the point 10° within the Balance; and C the point 10° within the Ram. Let equal epicycles be described about A and C, one with point D on it, the other with point E; and let the straight lines BD and BE be produced from B tangent to them; and let the perpendiculars AD and CE be drawn from the centres to the points of contact.

Since, then, the greatest morning elongation in the Balance was observed to be $19\frac{1}{20}°$ from the mean position,

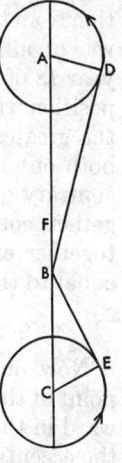

$$\text{angle } ABD = 19°3'$$
$$= 38°6' \text{ to 2 rt.}$$

And so, on the circle about right triangle ABD,

$$\text{arc } AD = 38°6',$$

and

$$\text{chord } AD = 39^{\text{p}}9'$$

where

$$\text{hypt. } AB = 120^{\text{p}}.$$

Again, since the greatest evening elongation in the Ram was observed to be $23\frac{1}{4}°$ from the mean position,

$$\text{angle } CBE = 23°15'$$
$$= 46°30' \text{ to 2 rt.}$$

And so also, on the circle about right triangle CBE,

$$\text{arc } CE = 46°30'$$

and

$$\text{chord } CE = 47^{\text{p}}22'$$

where

$$\text{hypt. } CB = 120^{\text{p}}.$$

And because as radii of the epicycles

$$AD = CE,$$

therefore
$$BC = 99^\text{p}9'$$
and, by addition,
$$ABC = 219^\text{p}9'$$
where
$$CE = 39^\text{p}9'$$
and
$$AB = 120^\text{p}.$$

And so, if the straight line ABC be bisected at F, then as half of ABC
$$AF = 109^\text{p}34',$$
and
$$BF = 10^\text{p}25'.$$

Then it is clear that either the point F is the centre of the eccentric or the centre around which the centre of that eccentric circle is revolved. For in this way only could the epicycle's centre be equidistant from F for either of the diametrically opposite positions, as was proved. But since, if F were itself the centre of that eccentric on which the epicycle's centre always lies, that eccentric would be fixed, and of all the positions that in the Ram would alone be perigee because BC is the least of all the straight lines from B to the circle described about F; and since the position in the Ram is not to be the nearest the earth, but positions in the Twins and the Water Bearer are even nearer the earth than it and very nearly equal to each other, therefore it is clear that the centre of this eccentric is carried about point F in the direction contrary to that of the epicycle's revolution — that is, westward contrary to the order of the signs — once in one cycle. For in this way the epicycle's centre will be twice perigee in that cycle.

It is immediately understandable from the observations just set out [ix, 7], that the epicycle is nearer the earth in the Twins and the Water Bearer than in the Ram. For in the observation of the year 16 of Hadrian, Phamenoth 16, the greatest evening elongation from the mean position was $21\frac{1}{4}°$; and in the observation of the year 4 of Antonine, Phamenoth 18, the greatest morning elongation from the mean position was $26\frac{1}{2}°$, while the mean sun for both observations was about $10°$ within the Water Bearer. And again, in the observation of the year 18 of Hadrian, Epiphi 19, the greatest morning elongation from the mean position was $21\frac{1}{4}°$; and in the observation of the year 1 of Antonine, Epiphi 20, the greatest evening elongation from the mean position was $26\frac{1}{2}°$, while for both observations the mean sun was about $10°$ within the Twins. And so the contrary greatest elongations in the Water Bearer and in the Twins, added together, come to $(47+\frac{1}{2}+\frac{1}{4})°$, while both the greatest elongations in the Ram together embrace $46\frac{1}{2}°$, because the evening elongation was observed to be equal to the morning one of $23\frac{1}{4}°$.

9. On the Ratio and Magnitude of Mercury's Anomalies

Now, once these things have been dealt with, it remains to show around what point of the straight line AB the epicycle's yearly return in regular motion eastward in the order of the signs takes place; and how far from F is the centre of the eccentric making its return at an equal speed westward. We have also used for this research two observations of greatest elongations both morning and evening, with the mean position in either case situated a quadrant's distance from the apogee on the same side, for in this position very nearly the greatest difference of zodiacal anomaly is produced.

For in the year 14 of Hadrian, Egyptianwise Mesore 18 in the evening, as we find in the observations taken by Theon, "Mercury," he says, "was at its greatest elongation from the sun, being $(3+\frac{1}{2}+\frac{1}{3})°$ east of the star in the Lion's heart [Regulus]." And so, according to our starting points, it was very nearly $6\frac{1}{3}°$ within the Lion, while the mean sun at that time was about $10\frac{1}{12}°$ within the Crab. And so the greatest elongation was $26\frac{1}{4}°$.

And in the year 2 of Antonine, Egyptianwise Mesore 24 at dawn, observing its greatest elongation with the astrolabe and sighting it with the bright star of the Hyades [Aldebaran], we found Mercury to be $20\frac{1}{12}°$ within the Twins, while the mean sun was again about $10\frac{1}{3}°$ within the Crab. And so the greatest morning elongation was $20\frac{1}{4}°$.

Now, with these things supposed, again let there be the diameter $AFBC$

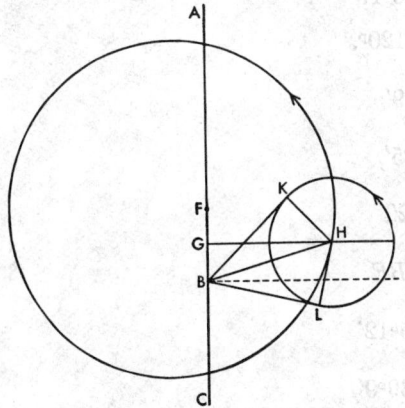

through the points 10° within the Balance and the Ram. And as in the last figure, let A be supposed the point where the epicycle's centre lies when it is 10° within the Balance; C the point where it lies when it is 10° within the Ram; B the centre of the ecliptic; and F the point about which the eccentric's centre makes its westward shift.

First let it be required to find how far from the point B is the centre about which we say the epicycle's regular eastward movement takes place.

Then let it be the point G, and let a straight line be drawn through G at right angles to AC, so that it will be a quadrant's distance from the apogee A; and let H be taken on it as the centre of the epicycle, according to the observations just set forth, because in these the mean position was a quadrant's distance from the apogee, the mean sun being about 10° within the Crab. And with the epicycle KL described about H, let the straight lines BK and BL be drawn from B tangent to it. And let HK, HL, and BH be joined.[1]

Now, since at the mean position just taken, the greatest morning elongation is supposed $20\frac{1}{4}°$, and the evening $26\frac{1}{4}°$, therefore

$$\text{angle } KBL = 46°30';$$

and therefore, being half of angle KBL,

$$\text{angle } KBH = 46°30' \text{ to 2 rt.}$$

And so also, on the circle about right triangle BHK,

$$\text{arc } HK = 46°30',$$

and

$$\text{chord } HK = 47^{\text{p}}22'$$

where

$$\text{hypt. } BH = 120^{\text{p}}.$$

[1] We have added to the figure a broken line through B parallel to GH to represent the line to the mean sun which moves regularly, of course, about the earth or the centre of the ecliptic.

And therefore where
$$\text{epic. rad. } HK = 39^\text{p}9'$$
and it was shown [p. 300]
$$BF = 10°25',$$
there
$$BH = 99^\text{p}9'.$$

Again, since the difference of 6° between these greatest elongations embraces twice the difference of zodiacal anomaly, and since this difference is contained by angle BHG (for we have proved that before [p. 295]), therefore
$$\text{angle } BHG = 3°$$
$$= 6° \text{ to 2 rt.}$$
And so, on the circle about right triangle BGH,
$$\text{arc } BG = 6°,$$
and
$$\text{chord } BG = 6^\text{p}17'$$
where
$$\text{hypt. } BH = 120^\text{p}.$$

And where
$$BH = 99^\text{p}9'$$
and likewise
$$BF = 10^\text{p}25',$$
there
$$BG = 5^\text{p}12'.$$
Therefore
$$BG \doteqdot \text{half } BF$$
and
$$BG \doteqdot BF \doteqdot 5^\text{p}12'$$
where
$$\text{epic. rad.} = 39^\text{p}9'.$$

Again, in the same figure, let the straight line FMN be drawn through F at right angles to AC on the side opposite GH. And it is clear the centre of that eccentric on which the epicycle's centre H lies will be on this straight line FMN, because of the equal period of joint return in opposite directions made by GH and FN. And let

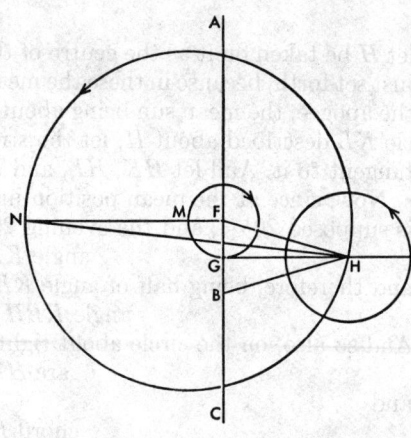

$$\cdot FN = FA,$$
so that FN like FA is composed of the eccentric's radius and of the straight line between the eccentric's centres and the point F. And let the eccentric's centre be taken on it and let it be M. And let FH be joined.

Then, since angle MFG is right, and since angle HFG hardly differs at all from a right angle so that NFH does not differ appreciably from a straight line, and since it has been shown [p. 300] that, if
$$\text{epic. rad.} = 39^\text{p}30',$$

then
$$NF = AF = 109^{\text{p}}34'$$
and
$$FH = BH = 99^{\text{p}}9',$$
therefore, by addition,
$$NFH = 208^{\text{p}}43'$$
and the eccentric's radius will be the half of NFH, that is
$$NM \doteq 104^{\text{p}}22'$$
and, by subtraction,
$$1. \text{ btw. c. } FM \doteq 5^{\text{p}}12'.$$
But it was shown [p. 302]
$$BG = 5^{\text{p}}12',$$
$$GF = 5^{\text{p}}12'$$
where the parts are the same.

Therefore we have proved that, to the $104^{\text{p}}22'$ of the eccentric's radius, each of the straight lines between the centres is $5^{\text{p}}12'$, and the epicycle's radius $39^{\text{p}}9'$. And therefore, to the 60^{p} of the eccentric's radius, each of the straight lines between the centers will be 3^{p}, and the epicycle's radius $22^{\text{p}}30'$. Which it was required to prove.

And we can discover in the following way that, these things being supposed, the greatest elongations at the perigees are consistent with the observations;[1]

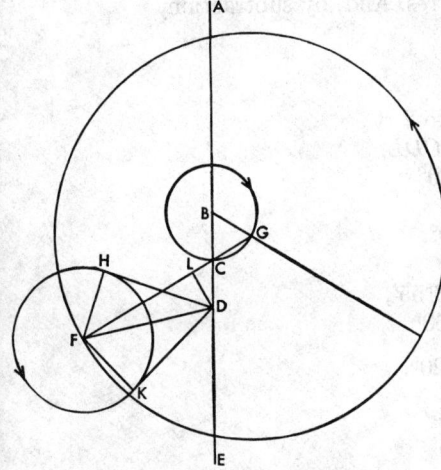

that is, that, when the mean position is $10°$ within the Water Bearer or $10°$ within the Twins and is distant from the apogee the side of the inscribed equilateral triangle, then the angle at the eye subtending the epicycle is very nearly $(47 + \frac{1}{2} + \frac{1}{4})°$.

For let there be the diameter through the apogee $ABCDE$, and let point A on it be supposed at the apogee; B the point about which the eccentric's centre moves westward; C the point about which the epicycle's centre moves eastward; and D the centre of the ecliptic. And let both movements be taken about their proper centres, regularly and equally, in opposite directions from the apogee A, through an angular distance equal to the side of the inscribed equilateral triangle. And let CF be the straight line revolving the epicycle, and BG the straight line revolving the

[1] That these points should be the perigees of the moving eccentric must have been known to Ptolemy through empirical mathematical methods—that is, by trying points very small distances away from the given point on either side and calculating the distances. For instance, if we calculate the square of the distance BH (*i.e.*, the distance of the epicycle's centre to the earth) first when the epicycle's center is $118°$ from the apogee, secondly when it is $120°$ from the apogee, and thirdly when it is $122°$ from the apogee, we get the following values respectively: 3,101.49, 3,101.04, and 3,101.99. According to Mr. George Comenetz who has worked on this problem, it is evident from the methods of the differential calculus that the perigee's being at or very near the point $120°$ from the apogee is dependent on the particular ratio of the line between the centres to the eccentric's radius. Therefore, there is no general geometric proof.

eccentric's centre. And let G be the eccentric's centre, and F the epicycle's. And with the epicycle described about F, let DH and DK be drawn tangent to it; and let CG, DF, FH, and FK be joined. And let DL be drawn from D perpendicular to CF.

It is required to prove that

$$\text{angle } HDK = (47 + \tfrac{1}{2} + \tfrac{1}{4})°.$$

Since, then, each of the angles ABG and ACL subtends a side of the inscribed equilateral triangle and equals 120°, so that

$$\text{angle } CBG = \text{angle } DCL = 60°,$$

and since

$$\text{angle } BGC = \text{angle } BCG$$

because it is supposed

$$BC = BG,$$

and since the other two angles together are 120°, and each of them 60°, the triangle BCG is equiangular and equilateral. And also

$$\text{angle } DCL = \text{angle } BCG;$$

therefore G, C, and F are points on the same straight line.

And so

$$\text{ecc. rad. } GF = 60^\text{p}$$

where

$$CG = CD = 3^\text{p},$$

CD being the straight line between the centres. And, by subtraction,

$$CF = 57^\text{p}.$$

Again, since

$$\text{angle } DCL = 60°$$
$$= 120° \text{ to 2 rt.,}$$

therefore, on the circle about right triangle CDL,

$$\text{arc } DL = 120°$$

and, by subtraction from the semicircle,

$$\text{arc } CL = 60°.$$

And therefore

$$\text{chord } DL = 103^\text{p}55',$$
$$\text{chord } CL = 60^\text{p}$$

where

$$\text{hypt. } CD = 120^\text{p}.$$

And so

$$DL = 2^\text{p}36',$$
$$CL = 1^\text{p}30',$$

and, by subtraction,

$$LF = 55^\text{p}30'$$

where

$$DC = 3^\text{p}$$

and likewise

$$CF = 57^\text{p}.$$

And since

$$\text{sq. } LF + \text{sq. } DL = \text{sq. } DF,$$

therefore

$$DF = 55^\text{p}34'$$

where it was supposed

$$FH = FK = 22^\text{p}30',$$

that being the epicycle's radius.

And therefore

$$FH = FK = 48^p35'$$

where

$$\text{hypt. } DF = 120^p;$$

and

$$\text{angle } FDH = \text{angle } FDK = 47°46' \text{ to 2 rt.}$$

so that, by addition,

$$\text{angle } HDK = 47°46'.$$

Which it was required to prove.

10. ON THE CORRECTION OF MERCURY'S PERIODIC MOVEMENTS

Now, the establishing of Mercury's periodic movements and its epochs follows next. And we have the longitudinal movements—that is, those carrying the epicycle regularly about C—immediately given from those of the sun; and the movements of anomaly—that is, those carrying the star on the epicycle about the epicycle's centre—we have taken from two sure observations, one from those recorded by us, the other from old ones.

For in the year 2 of Antonine, which was the year 886 of Nabonassar, Egyptianwise Epiphi 2-3, we observed Mercury with the astrolabe when it had not yet come to its greatest evening elongation, and being sighted with the star in the Lion's heart [Regulus] it appeared to be $17\frac{1}{2}°$ within the Twins. At that time it was past the moon's centre to the east by $1\frac{1}{6}°$, and in Alexandria the time was $4\frac{1}{2}$ equatorial hours before midnight of the third, since on the astrolabe the point $12°$ within the Virgin was culminating and the sun was about $23°$ within the Bull. But the sun's mean position at that hour, according to the hypotheses demonstrated by us, was $22°34'$ within the Bull. The moon's mean position was $12°14'$ within the Twins, and the moon was $281°20'$ in anomaly from the epicycle's apogee, so that the true position of the moon's centre came to $17°10'$ within the Twins, and its apparent position $16°20'$ within the Twins. Therefore Mercury, since it was $1\frac{1}{6}°$ beyond the moon's centre, was $17\frac{1}{2}°$ within the Twins.

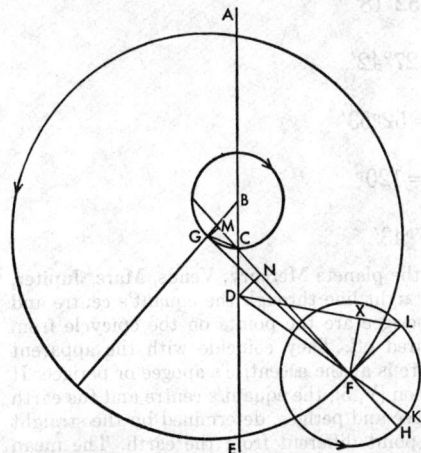

With this assumed, let $ABCDE$ be the diameter through the apogee and perigee. And let A be supposed its point at the apogee; B the point about which the eccentric's centre moves westward; C the point about which the epicycle's centre moves eastward; and D the centre of the ecliptic. And let the epicycle's centre F have been moved through angle ACF about point C by the straight line CF; and let the eccentric's centre G have been moved about B by the straight line BG to the extent of angle ABG, of course always equal to angle ACF because of the equal rate of the movements. And, with the epicycle HKL described about F, let the star be supposed at L. And let CG, GF, DF, FL, and DL be joined; and let GM and DN be drawn from G and D perpendicular to CFH produced, and FX from F perpendicular to DL.

And it is required to find the epicycle's arc from the apogee H^1 to the star at L.

Since, then, the mean sun at that time was 22°34′ within the Bull, and the star's perigee very nearly 10° within the Ram so that its mean longitudinal position was 42°34′ from the perigee, therefore

$$\text{angle } CBG = 42°34′$$
$$= 85°8′ \text{ to 2 rt.,}$$

and, because always

$$BC = BG,$$
$$\text{angle } BGC = \text{angle } BCG = 137°26′ \text{ to 2 rt.}$$

And so, on the circle about triangle BCG,

$$\text{arc } GC = 85°8′$$

and

$$\text{arc } BC = 137°26′.$$

And therefore

$$\text{chord } GC = 81^p10′$$
$$\text{chord } BC = 111^p49′.$$

And so

$$GC = 2^p11′$$

where

$$BC = 3^p.$$

Again, since

$$\text{angle } BCG = 137°26′ \text{ to 2 rt.}$$

and

$$\text{angle } BCM = 85°8′ \text{ to 2 rt.,}$$

therefore also, by subtraction,

$$\text{angle } GCM = 52°18′ \text{ to 2 rt.}$$

And so also, on the circle about right triangle CGM,

$$\text{arc } GM = 52°18′$$

and, by subtraction from the semicircle,

$$\text{arc } CM = 127°42′.$$

And therefore

$$\text{chord } GM = 52^p53′$$

where

$$\text{hypt. } CG = 120^p$$

and

$$CM = 107^p43′.$$

---

[1]The regular epicyclic apogee and perigee, for the planets Mercury, Venus, Mars, Jupiter, and Saturn, are determined as always by the straight line through the equant's centre and the epicycle's centre. The regular apogee and perigee are the points on the epicycle from which the anomalistic angle is regularly measured off. They coincide with the apparent apogee and perigee only when the epicycle's centre is at the eccentric's apogee or perigee. It should be recalled here that, in the case of the moon [V, 5], the equant's centre and the earth coincide, and that there is the moon's mean apogee and perigee, determined by the straight line through the epicycle's centre and another point different from the earth. The mean apogee and perigee in the case of the moon are the points from which the anomalistic angle is measured off.

And so also
$$GM = 0^\mathrm{p}58'$$
and
$$CM = 1^\mathrm{p}58'$$
where
$$GC = 2^\mathrm{p}11'$$
and
$$GF = 60^\mathrm{p},$$
GF being the radius of the eccentric bearing the epicycle. And being for this reason inappreciably less than the hypotenuse GF,
$$MF = 60^\mathrm{p},$$
and, by subtraction,
$$CF = 58^\mathrm{p}2'.$$

Likewise, since
$$\text{angle } DCN = 85°8' \text{ to } 2 \text{ rt.,}$$
therefore, on the circle about right triangle CDN,
$$\text{arc } DN = 85°8',$$
and, by subtraction from the semicircle,
$$\text{arc } CN = 94°52'.$$
And so
$$\text{chord } DN = 81^\mathrm{p}10'$$
and
$$\text{chord } CN = 88^\mathrm{p}23'$$
where
$$\text{hypt. } CD = 120^\mathrm{p}.$$

And therefore
$$DN = 2^\mathrm{p}2'$$
and
$$CN = 2^\mathrm{p}13'$$
and, by subtraction,
$$NF = 55^\mathrm{p}49'$$
where
$$CD = 3^\mathrm{p}$$
and, as was shown,
$$CF = 58^\mathrm{p}2'.$$

And for this reason
$$\text{hypt. } DF = 55^\mathrm{p}51'$$
where
$$\text{epic. rad.} = 22^\mathrm{p}30'.$$

And therefore
$$DN = 4^\mathrm{p}22'$$
where
$$\text{hypt. } DF = 120^\mathrm{p}.$$
And, on the circle about right triangle DFN,
$$\text{arc } DN = 4°11',$$
so that also
$$\text{angle } DFN = 4°11' \text{ to } 2 \text{ rt.}$$
and, by addition,
$$\text{angle } EDF = 89°19' \text{ to } 2 \text{ rt. [Eucl. i, 32],}$$

and, also by addition,

$$\text{angle } EDL = 135° \text{ to 2 rt.}$$

because the star at that time appeared to be 67°30′ from the apogee; and, by subtraction,

$$\text{angle } FDL = 45°41′ \text{ to 2 rt.}$$

And therefore, on the circle about right triangle DFX,

$$\text{arc } FX = 45°41′;$$

and

$$\text{chord } FX = 46^{\text{p}}35′$$

where

$$\text{hypt. } DF = 120^{\text{p}}.$$

And so also

$$FX = 21^{\text{p}}41′$$

where

$$DF = 55^{\text{p}}51′$$

and

$$\text{epic. rad. } FL = 22^{\text{p}}30′.$$

And again

$$FX = 115^{\text{p}}39′$$

where

$$\text{hypt. } FL = 120^{\text{p}}.$$

And therefore, on the circle about triangle FLX,

$$\text{arc } FX = 149°2′$$

and

$$\text{angle } FLX = 149°2′ \text{ to 2 rt.}$$

And it was proved that

$$\text{angle } FDL = 45°41′ \text{ to 2 rt.}$$

and likewise

$$\text{angle } HFK = 4°11′ \text{ to 2 rt.}$$

And so, by addition,

$$\text{angle } HFL = 198°54′ \text{ to 2 rt.}$$
$$= 99°27′.$$

And therefore the arc HKL of the epicycle, which is Mercury's distance from the apogee H at the observation, is 99°27′. Which it was required to prove.

And again, in the year 21 according to Dionysius, which was the year 484 of Nabonassar, Scorpion 22, Egyptianwise Thoth 18-19, the morning Mercury was the distance of a moon east of the straight line through the northern and middle stars of the Scorpion's forehead, and was 2 moons north of the northern star of the forehead. But the middle star of the Scorpion's forehead was at that time, according to our starting points, 1⅔° within the Scorpion and the same number of degrees south of the ecliptic. And the most northern star was 2⅓° within the Scorpion and 1⅓° north of the ecliptic. Therefore Mercury was very nearly 3⅓° within the Scorpion. It is also evident that it had not yet come to its greatest morning elongation, because 4 days later, Scorpion 26, it is recorded that it was a moon and a half east of the same straight line. For the elongation was greater, since the sun had moved nearly 4°, and the star a half moon. And the mean sun, Thoth 19 at dawn, was (20+½+⅓)° within the Scorpion according to our ways of counting, and the star's apogee was 6° within the Balance because the 400 years or so between the observations made the apogee shift very nearly 4°.

Now, with these things supposed, let a figure similar to the one above be again constructed. But because of the dissimilarity of the positions, let the angles at the apogee A be drawn acute, and let the straight lines joining the star be drawn to the west of the epicycle, and let the perpendicular FX be drawn above the epicycle's radius FL.

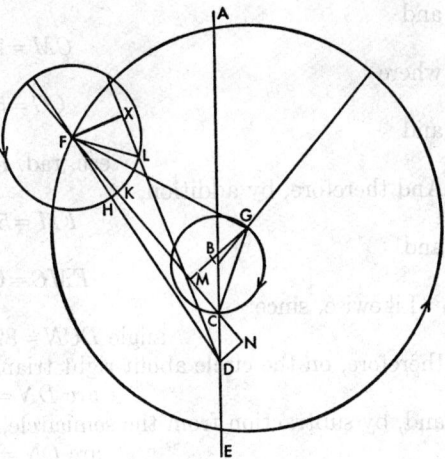

Since, then, the mean position of the star was 44°50′ from the apogee,

$$\text{angle } ABG = 44°50'$$
$$= 89°40' \text{ to } 2 \text{ rt.}$$

And so, by subtraction,

$$\text{angle } CBG = 270°20' \text{ to } 2 \text{ rt.,}$$

and

$$\text{angle } BCG = \text{angle } BGC = 44°50'$$
$$\text{to } 2 \text{ rt.}$$

And therefore

$$\text{chord } CG = 84^\text{p}36'$$

and

$$BC = BG = 45^\text{p}46'$$

where, in the circle about triangle BCG,

$$\text{the diameter} = 120^\text{p}.$$

And therefore

$$CG = 5^\text{p}33'$$

where

$$BC = BG = 3^\text{p}.$$

Again, since it is supposed

$$\text{angle } ACF = 89°40' \text{ to } 2 \text{ rt.}$$

and

$$\text{angle } BCG = 44°50' \text{ to } 2 \text{ rt.,}$$

and by addition

$$\text{angle } FCG = 134°30' \text{ to } 2 \text{ rt.,}$$

therefore, on the circle about right triangle CGM,

$$\text{arc } GM = 134°30'$$

and, by subtraction from the semicircle,

$$\text{arc } CM = 45°30'.$$

And therefore

$$\text{chord } GM = 110^\text{p}40',$$

and

$$\text{chord } CM = 46^\text{p}24'$$

where

$$\text{hypt. } CG = 120^\text{p}.$$

And so

$$GM = 5^\text{p}7'$$

and
$$CM = 2^p 10',$$
where
$$CG = 5^p 33'$$
and

ecc. rad. $FG = 60^p$.

And therefore, by addition,
$$FM = 59^p 47'$$
and
$$FMC = 61°57'.$$

Likewise, since
$$\text{angle } DCN = 89°40' \text{ to 2 rt.,}$$
therefore, on the circle about right triangle CDN,
$$\text{arc } DN = 89°40'$$
and, by subtraction from the semicircle,
$$\text{arc } CN = 90°20'.$$

And therefore
$$\text{chord } DN = 84^p 36',$$
$$\text{chord } CN = 85^p 6'$$
where
$$\text{hypt. } CD = 120^p.$$

And so also
$$DN = 2^p 7',$$
$$CN = 2^p 8',$$
and by addition
$$FCN = 64^p 7'$$
where
$$CD = 3^p.$$

And therefore
$$DN = 3^p 58'$$
where
$$FD = 120^p.$$
And, on the circle about right triangle DFN,
$$\text{arc } DN = 3°48'.$$

And so also
$$\text{angle } DFN = 3°48' \text{ to 2 rt.,}$$
and, by subtraction,
$$\text{angle } ADF = 85°52' \text{ to 2 rt.}$$

But also it is supposed
$$\text{angle } ADL = 54°40' \text{ to 2 rt.}$$
because, according to the observation, the star was 27°20′ from the apogee.
And so, by subtraction,
$$\text{angle } FDL = 31°12' \text{ to 2 rt.}$$
And therefore, on the circle about right triangle FDX,
$$\text{arc } FX = 31°12',$$
and
$$\text{chord } FX = 32^p 16'$$
where
$$\text{hypt. } DF = 120^p.$$

And therefore
$$FX = 17^p15'$$
where
$$DF = 64^p7'$$
or
$$\text{epic. rad. } FL = 22^p30'.$$
And
$$FX \doteq 92^p$$
where
$$FL = 120^p.$$
And so also, on the circle about right triangle FLX,
$$\text{arc } FX = 100°8'$$
and
$$\text{angle } FLX = 100°8' \text{ to 2 rt.}$$
And it was also shown that
$$\text{angle } FDL = 31°12' \text{ to 2 rt.}$$
And
$$\text{angle } HFK = 3°48' \text{ to 2 rt.}$$
and so also, by subtraction,
$$\text{angle } KFL = 65°8' \text{ to 2 rt.}$$
$$= 32°34'.$$

Therefore, at this observation, the star was 32°34′ from K the epicycle's perigee, and of course 212°34′ from the apogee. At the time of our own observation, it was shown to be 99°27′ from the epicycle's apogee; the time from one observation to the other is 402 Egyptian years, 283 days, and very nearly 13½ hours; and that time embraces 1,268 of the star's returns in anomaly, since, with 20 Egyptian years making very nearly 63 cycles, the 400 years add up to 1,260 cycles, and the 2 years with the days added on give 8 whole cycles more. Therefore it is clear to us that, in 402 Egyptian years, 283 days, and 13½ hours, Mercury added on, over and above the 1,268 returns in anomaly, the 246°53′ by which its position at our own observation exceeds its position at the older one. And just about that number of degrees result in the tables set out by us, since we made the correction of Mercury's periodic movements from these very observations, reducing the proposed time to days and the cycles of anomaly plus the surplus to degrees. For when the number of degrees had been divided over the number of days, we got Mercury's daily movement of anomaly as we gave it.

11. On the Epoch of its Periodic Movements

In order, then, as with the sun and moon, to establish the epoch for the five planets at the year 1 of Nabonassar, Egyptianwise Thoth 1 at noon, we took the time from it to the older and nearer of the observations. The time came to 483 Egyptian years, 17 days, and very nearly 18⅓ hours. And a surplus of 190°39′ in mean movement of anomaly corresponds to this amount of time. If we subtract these from the 212°34′ representing the distance from the apogee at the observation, we shall have the epoch in the year 1 of Nabonassar, Egyptianwise Thoth 1 at noon (1) 21°55′ from the epicycle's apogee for anomaly; (2) for longitude the same as the sun, that is 45′ within the Fishes; (3) and the apogee of eccentricity 1⅙° within the Balance, since the number of years in hundreds comes to about 4+½+⅓, just the number by which the 6° within the Balance at the observation exceeds 1⅙°.

BOOK TEN

1. Demonstration of Venus' Apogee

Therefore we have ascertained in this way the hypotheses of Mercury, the magnitudes of its anomalies, and further the quantity of its periodic movements and of their epochs. In the case of Venus, we again sought, from equal greatest elongations on corresponding sides, in what parts of the ecliptic the apogee and perigee of eccentricity are. For this purpose we did not have any old observations exactly corresponding, but we have made just such an addition from our own observations.

For among those given us from Theo the mathematician, we found an observation recorded in the year 16 of Hadrian, Egyptianwise Pharmouthi 21-22, in which he says the evening Venus was at its greatest elongation from the sun, being west of the middle star of the Pleiades by as much as the length of the Pleiades. It seemed also to be passing by a little to the north. Now, since the middle star of the Pleiades was at that time, by our starting points, 3° within the Bull, and since their length is very nearly $1\frac{1}{2}°$, it is evident Venus was then $1\frac{1}{2}°$ within the Bull. And so, since the mean sun was then $14\frac{1}{4}°$ within the Fishes, the greatest evening elongation from the mean position was $47\frac{1}{4}°$.

And in the year 14 of Antonine, Egyptianwise Thoth 11-12, we observed the morning Venus at its greatest elongation from the sun; and it was north of the star in the middle of the Twins' knees, and east of it by half a full moon. At that time that fixed star, by our starting points, was $18\frac{1}{4}°$ within the Twins so that Venus was very nearly $18\frac{1}{2}°$ within the Twins, while the mean sun was $(5+\frac{1}{2}+\frac{1}{4})°$ within the Lion. Therefore, the greatest morning elongation was also $47\frac{1}{4}°$.

Then, since the mean position at the first observation was $14\frac{1}{4}°$ within the Fishes, and at the second observation $(5+\frac{1}{2}+\frac{1}{4})°$ within the Lion, and since the point midway between them falls 25° within the Bull and 25° within the Scorpion, the diameter through the apogee and perigee would be at these points.

Likewise, among the observations from Theo, we found that in the year 12 of Hadrian, Egyptianwise Athyr 21-22, the morning Venus was at its greatest elongation from the sun, being east of the star at the tip of Virgin's southern wing by the length of the Pleiades, or this length less Venus' own magnitude. And it seemed to be passing north of the star by one moon. Now, since this fixed star was at that time, according to us, $(28+\frac{1}{2}+\frac{1}{3}+\frac{1}{12})°$ within the Lion so that Venus was very nearly $\frac{1}{3}°$ within the Virgin, and since the mean sun was $(17+\frac{1}{2}+\frac{1}{3}+\frac{1}{30})°$ within the Balance, the greatest elongation from the mean position was $(47+\frac{1}{2}+\frac{1}{30})°$.

And in the year 21 of Hadrian, Egyptianwise Mechir 9-10 in the evening, we ourselves observed Venus at its greatest elongation from the sun. It was very nearly $\frac{2}{3}$ a full moon west of the northernmost star of the four in a square, following the star to the east of, and in a line with, the Water Bearer's testicles; and it seemed to outshine the star. And so since this fixed star was then, accord-

312

ing to us, 20° within the Water Bearer, and therefore Venus was about 19⅗°
within the Water Bearer, and since the mean sun was 2¹⁄₁₅° within the Goat, the
greatest evening elongation was (47+½+¹⁄₃₀)°. And the points midway between the (17+½+⅓+¹⁄₃₀)° within the Balance of the first observation and
the 2¹⁄₁₅° within the Goat of the second are again very nearly 25° within the
Scorpion and within the Bull.

2. On the Magnitude of its Epicycle

In this way, therefore, we took the apogee and perigee of eccentricity for our
time at 25° within the Bull and within the Scorpion. And next we again examined the greatest elongations when the sun's mean position was about 25°
within the Bull and about 25° within the Scorpion.

For, among the observations given us from Theo, we find that in the year 13
of Hadrian, Egyptianwise Epiphi 2-3, the morning Venus was at its greatest
elongation from the sun, being 1⅖° west of the straight line through the principal star of the three in the Ram's head and through the star of the hind-leg. Its
distance from the principal star in the Ram's head was very nearly double that
from the star in the leg. And at that time, according to us, the principal star of
the three in the Ram's head was 6⅗° within the Ram and 7⅓° north of the
ecliptic; and the star in the hind-leg was (14+½+¼)° within the Ram and
5¼° south of the ecliptic. Therefore Venus was 10⅗° within the Ram and 1½°
south of the ecliptic. And so, since the mean sun was then 25⅖° within the Bull,
the greatest elongation from the mean position was 44¼°.

And in the year 21 of Hadrian, Egyptianwise Tybi 2-3 in the evening, we observed Venus at its greatest elongation from the sun; and, sighted with the stars
in the Goat's horns, it appeared to be (12+½+⅓)° within the Goat, while the
mean sun was 25½° within the Scorpion. And so the greatest elongation from
the mean position came to 47⅓°. It is clear that the apogee is 25° within the
Bull and the perigee 25° within the Scorpion. And
it is evident to us that there is only the eccentric
bearing Venus' epicycle, because nowhere on the
ecliptic is the sum of both the greatest elongations
on either side found to be either less than the sum
of both those in the Bull or greater than the sum
of both those in the Scorpion.

Then, with these things assumed, let there be
the eccentric circle ABC on which Venus' epicycle
is always borne; and let this circle be about diameter AC on which let D be supposed the eccentric's centre, E the ecliptic's centre, and A the
point 25° within the Bull. About points A and
C let equal epicycles be described with points
F and G on them. And let the tangents EF and
EG be drawn through, and AF and CG joined.

Since, then, angle AEF, at the ecliptic's centre,
subtends the greatest elongation at the star's apogee which is assumed to be 44⅘°, therefore

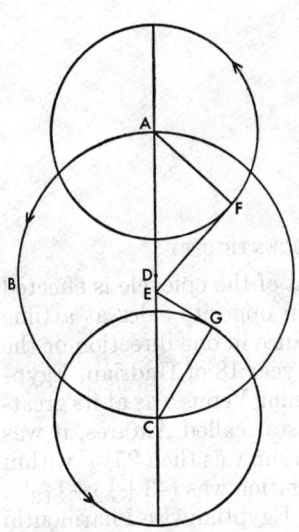

angle $AEF = 44°48'$
$= 89°36'$ to 2 rt.

And so, on the circle about right triangle AEF,

$$\text{arc } AF = 89°36',$$

and

$$\text{chord } AF \doteq 84^p33',$$

where

$$\text{hypt. } AE = 120^p.$$

Likewise, since angle CEG subtends the greatest elongation at the perigee which is assumed to be $47\frac{1}{3}°$, therefore

$$\text{angle } CEG = 47°20'$$
$$= 94°40' \text{ to 2 rt.}$$

And so, on the circle about right triangle CEG,

$$\text{arc } CG = 94°40',$$

and

$$\text{chord } CG \doteq 88^p13'$$

where

$$\text{hypt. } CE = 120^p.$$

And therefore, where

$$\text{rad. epic. } CG = \text{rad. epic. } AF$$
$$= 84^p33'$$

and

$$AE = 120^p,$$

there

$$EC = 115^p1'$$

and clearly, by addition,

$$AC = 235°1',$$

and, half of AC

$$AD \doteq 117^p30',$$

and, by subtraction,

$$\text{1. betw. c. } DE = 2^p29'.$$

And so also

$$\text{1. betw. c. } DE \doteq 1\frac{1}{4}^p,$$
$$\text{epic. rad. } AF = 43^p6'$$

where

$$\text{ecc. rad. } AD = 60^p.$$

3. On the Ratios of the Star's Eccentricity

Since it is not clear whether the regular movement of the epicycle is effected about point D, we took two greatest elongations on opposite sides at a time when the sun's mean position was a quadrant's distance in one direction or the other from the apogee. One of them we made in the year 18 of Hadrian, Egyptianwise Pharmouthi 2-3, according to which the morning Venus was at its greatest elongation from the sun; and, sighted with the star called Antares, it was $(11+\frac{1}{2}+\frac{1}{3}+\frac{1}{12}°)$ within the Goat, while the mean sun was then $25\frac{1}{2}°$ within the Water Bearer. And so the greatest morning elongation was $(43+\frac{1}{2}+\frac{1}{12}°)$.

The other one we made in the year 3 of Antonine, Egyptianwise Pharmouthi 4-5 in the evening, according to which Venus was at its greatest elongation from the sun; and, sighted with the bright star of the Hyades [Aldebaran] was $(13+$

½+⅓)° within the Ram, while the mean sun was again 25½° within the Water Bearer. And so, therefore, the greatest evening elongation from the mean position was 48⅓°.

With these things assumed, let there be the diameter ABC through the apogee and perigee of eccentricity; and let A be supposed the point 25° within the Bull, and B the ecliptic's centre.

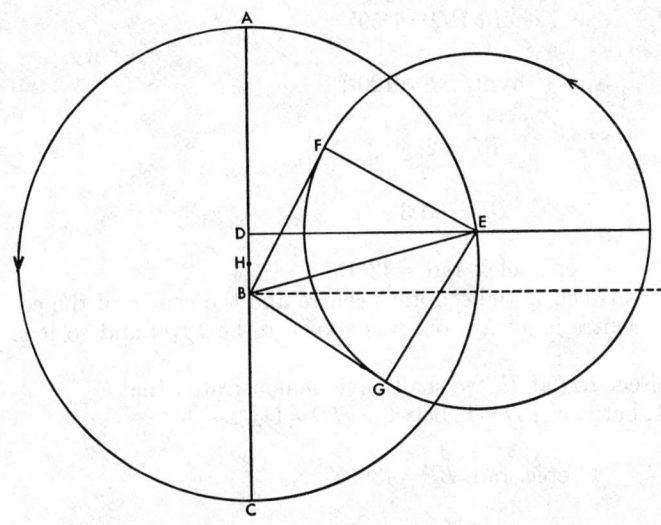

Let it be required to find the centre around which we say the epicycle's regular movement is effected.

Then let it be the point D, and let DE be drawn through it perpendicular to AC in order that the epicycle's mean position may be a quadrant's distance from the apogee as in the observations. And let the epicycle's centre E be taken on DE according to the observations given. With epicycle FG described about E, let BF and BG be drawn from B tangent to it, and let BF, EF, and EG be joined. Since, then, for the proposed mean position, the greatest morning elongation is assumed to be $(43+½+\frac{1}{12})°$, and the evening one $48⅓°$, therefore, by addition,

$$\text{angle } FBG = 91°55';$$

and therefore, angle FBE being half of it,

$$\text{angle } FBE = 91°55' \text{ to 2 rt.}$$

And so, on the circle about right triangle BEF,

$$\text{arc } EF = 91°55',$$

and

$$\text{chord } EF = 86^{\text{p}}16'$$

where

$$\text{hypt. } BE = 120^{\text{p}}.$$

And therefore where

$$\text{epic. rad. } EF = 43^{\text{p}}10',$$

there

$$BE = 60^{\text{p}}3'.$$

Again, since the difference between these greatest elongations, which is $4°45'$, embraces twice the difference of zodiacal anomaly for that time which is contained in angle BED, therefore angle $BED = 2°22\frac{1}{2}'$

$= 4°45'$ to 2 rt.

And so also, on the circle about right triangle BDE,

arc $BD = 4°45'$,

and

chord $BD \doteq 4^\text{p}59'$

where

hypt. $BE = 120^\text{p}$.

And therefore

$BD \doteq 2\frac{1}{2}^\text{p}$

where

$BE = 60^\text{p}3'$,

and

epicycle's rad. $= 43^\text{p}10'$.

But the straight line between B the ecliptic's centre and the centre of the eccentric the epicycle's centre is always on, was shown to be $1\frac{1}{4}^\text{p}$; and so it is half BD.

If, therefore, we bisect BD at H, we shall have demonstrated that

1. betw. c. $BH = 1$. betw. c. $HD = 1\frac{1}{4}^\text{p}$,

and

epic. rad. $EF = 43^\text{p}10'$

where

$AH = 60^\text{p}$,

AH being radius of the eccentric bearing the epicycle.

4. On the Correction of the Star's Periodic Movements

Now, the mode of the hypothesis and the ratios of the anomalies were gotten by us in this way. But again, for the periodic movements of the star and its epochs, we took two sure observations from among our own and from among the old ones.

With the astrolabe, in the year 2 of Antonine, Egyptianwise Tybi 29-30, we observed the morning Venus with Spica, after its greatest elongation. And it appeared to be $6\frac{1}{2}°$ within the Scorpion. At that time it was between, and on a straight line with, the northernmost star in the Scorpion's forehead and the moon's apparent centre; and it was west of the moon's centre by one-and-a-half times its distance east of the northernmost star in the forehead. But this fixed star was then, by our starting points, $6°20'$ within the Scorpion and $1°20'$ north of the ecliptic. And the time was $4 + \frac{1}{2} + \frac{1}{4}$ equatorial hours after midnight, since, with the sun about $23°$ within the Archer, the point on the astrolabe $2°$ within the Virgin was culminating. At this time the sun's mean position was $22°9'$ within the Archer; and in mean longitude the moon was $11°24'$ within the Scorpion, in anomaly $87°30'$ from the apogee, and in latitude $12°22'$ from the northern limit. Therefore, the moon's centre had its true position $5°45'$ within the Scorpion, and $5°$ north of the ecliptic; and in Alexandria it appeared to be $6°45'$ within the Scorpion in longitude, and $4°40'$ north of the ecliptic. Therefore Venus, for these reasons, was $6°30'$ within the Scorpion and $2°40'$ north of the ecliptic.

With these things assumed, let $ABCDE$ be the diameter through the apogee.

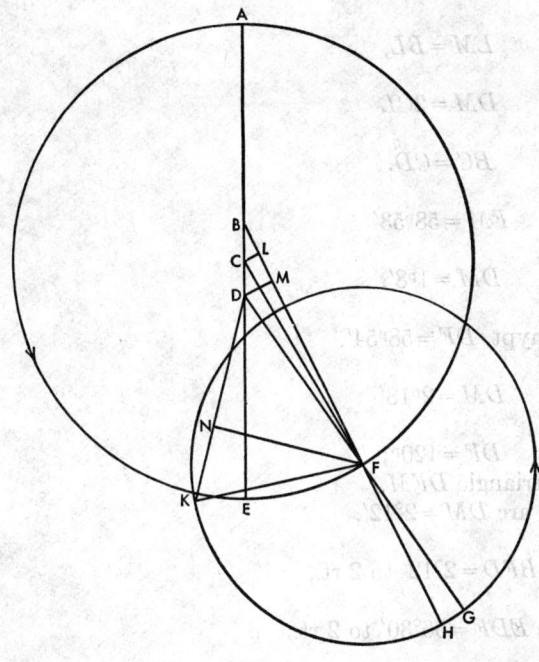

And let A be supposed the point 25° within the Bull; B the point about which the epicycle moves regularly; C the centre of the eccentric on which the epicycle's centre is borne; and D the centre of the ecliptic. Since in the observation the mean sun was 22°9′ within the Archer, so that the epicycle's mean position was 27° 9′ east of the perigee at E, let the epicycle's centre be supposed at F; and, with epicycle GHK described about it, let DFG, CF, and BFH be joined. Let CL and DM be drawn from C and D perpendicular to BF. And, with the star put at point K, let DK and FK be joined, and FN drawn perpendicular.

It is required to find the arc HK, the distance of the star from the epicycle's apogee.

Since, then,
$$\text{angle } EBF = 27°9′$$
$$= 54°18′ \text{ to 2 rt.,}$$
therefore also, on the circle about right triangle BCL,
$$\text{arc } CL = 54°18′$$
and, by subtraction from the semicircle,
$$\text{arc } BL = 125°42′.$$

And therefore
$$\text{chord } CL = 54^{\text{p}}46′,$$
$$\text{chord } BL = 106^{\text{p}}47′$$
where
$$\text{hypt. } BC = 120^{\text{p}}.$$

And so also
$$CL = 0^{\text{p}}34′,$$
$$BL = 1^{\text{p}}7′$$
where
$$BC = 1^{\text{p}}15′$$
and
$$\text{ecc. rad. } CF = 60^{\text{p}}.$$

And since
$$\text{sq. } CF - \text{sq. } CL = \text{sq. } FL,$$
$$FL = 60^{\text{p}}.$$

Also
$$LM = BL,$$
and
$$DM = 2CL$$
because
$$BC = CD.$$
And so also, by subtraction,
$$FM = 58^{p}53'$$
and
$$DM = 1^{p}8'.$$
And consequently
$$\text{hypt. } DF = 58^{p}54'.$$
And therefore
$$DM = 2^{p}18'$$
where
$$DF = 120^{p};$$
and, on the circle about right triangle DFM,
$$\text{arc } DM = 2°12'.$$
And so also
$$\text{angle } BFD = 2°12' \text{ to 2 rt.,}$$
and, by addition,
$$\text{angle } EDF = 56°30' \text{ to 2 rt.}$$
And also
$$\text{angle } EDK = 18°30'$$
because by just so much, according to the observations, is the star west of the perigee at E—that is, west of 25° within the Scorpion; and
$$\text{angle } EDK = 37° \text{ to 2 rt.}$$
And therefore, by addition,
$$\text{angle } FDK = 93°30' \text{ to 2 rt.;}$$
and, on the circle about right triangle DFN,
$$\text{arc } FN = 93°30'.$$
And therefore
$$\text{chord } FN = 87^{p}25'$$
where
$$FD = 120^{p}.$$
But
$$FN = 42^{p}54'$$
where
$$DF = 58^{p}54',$$
that is, where
$$\text{epic. rad. } FK = 43^{p}10' \text{ [p. 316].}$$
And so also
$$FN = 119^{p}18'$$
where
$$\text{hypt. } FK = 120^{p};$$
and, on the circle about right triangle FKN,
$$\text{arc } FN = 167°38'.$$
And therefore
$$\text{angle } DKF = 167°38' \text{ to 2 rt.}$$

just as it is supposed

angle $FDK = 93°30'$ to 2 rt.;

and, by addition,

angle $GFK = 261°8'$ to 2 rt.

And it was also proved that

angle $BFD = 2°12'$ to 2 rt.,

that is, that

angle $GFH = 2°12'$ to 2 rt.

And therefore, by subtraction,

angle $HFK = 258°56'$ to 2 rt.

$= 129°28'$.

Therefore, Venus at the stated time was 129°28' west of the epicycle's apogee H; and, by subtraction from the circle, 230°32' east of it according to the movement consequent upon the hypothesis. Which it was required to find.

Of the old observation's, we took one which Timocharis records thus: In the year 13 of Philadelphus, Egyptianwise Mesore 17-18 at the twelfth hour, Venus appeared to have exactly overtaken the star opposite Vindemiatrix. And this star, according to us, is beyond the star on the tip of the Virgin's southern wing, and, in the year 1 of Antonine, was 8¼° within the Virgin. Since, then, the year of the observation is the year 406 of Nabonassar, and since the beginning of the reign of Antonine is the year 884, (so as to add on very nearly a 4¹⁄₁₂° movement of the fixed stars and apogees for the 408 intervening years) it is evident that Venus was 4⅙° within the Virgin, and the eccentric's perigee $(20+½+⅓+¹⁄₁₂)°$ within the Scorpion. And at this time Venus had passed its greatest morning elongation. For 4 days after this observation, Mesore 21-22, from what

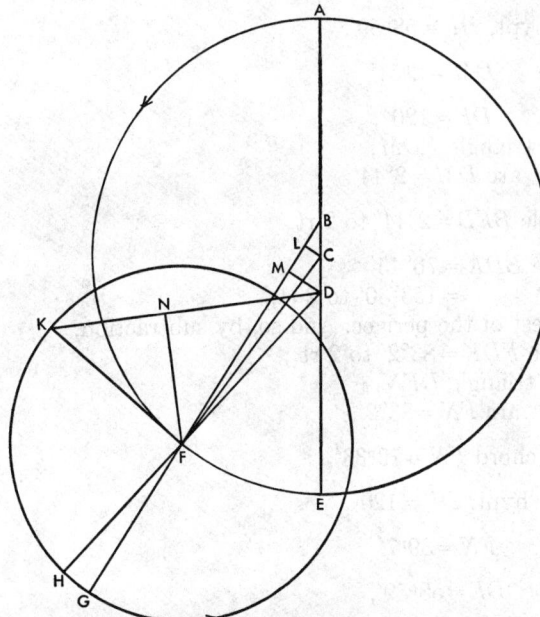

Timocharis says, Venus was, by our starting points, $(8+½+⅓)°$ within the Virgin, while the sun's mean position at the first observation was 17°3' within the Balance, and at the second 20°59' within the Balance. And so the elongation of the first observation comes to 42°53', and of the second to 42°9'.

Then, with these things given, let a similar figure be again set out, but having the epicycle to the west of the perigee because of the epicycle's mean position's being 17°3' within the Balance and the eccentric's perigee's being 20°55' within the Scorpion.

Since, then, for this reason

$$\text{angle } EBF = 33°52'$$
$$= 67°44' \text{ to } 2 \text{ rt.},$$

therefore, on the circle about right triangle BCL,

$$\text{arc } CL = 67°44',$$

and, by subtraction from the semicircle,

And therefore

$$\text{arc } BL = 112°16'.$$

$$\text{chord } CL = 66^{\mathrm{p}}52',$$
$$\text{chord } BL = 99^{\mathrm{p}}38'$$

where

And so also

$$\text{hypt. } BC = 120^{\mathrm{p}}.$$

$$CL = 0^{\mathrm{p}}42',$$
$$BL = 1^{\mathrm{p}}2'$$

where

and

$$BC = 1^{\mathrm{p}}15'$$

And since

$$\text{ecc. rad. } CF = 60^{\mathrm{p}}.$$

in length

$$\text{sq. } CF - \text{sq. } CL = \text{sq. } FL,$$

$$FL = 60^{\mathrm{p}}.$$

And, for the same reason as before,

and

$$BL = LM$$

And so, by subtraction,

$$DM = 2CL.$$

$$FM = 58^{\mathrm{p}}58',$$
$$DM = 1^{\mathrm{p}}24'.$$

And consequently

And therefore

$$\text{hypt. } DF = 58^{\mathrm{p}}59'.$$

where

$$DM = 2^{\mathrm{p}}51'$$

$$DF = 120^{\mathrm{p}};$$

and, on the circle about right triangle FDM,

And so also

$$\text{arc } DM = 2°44'.$$

And

$$\text{angle } BFD = 2°44' \text{ to } 2 \text{ rt.}$$

$$\text{angle } EDK = 76°45'$$
$$= 153°30' \text{ to } 2 \text{ rt.},$$

which is the star's distance west of the perigee. And so, by subtraction,

$$\text{angle } FDK = 83°2' \text{ to } 2 \text{ rt.};$$

and, on the circle about right triangle DFN,

And therefore

$$\text{arc } FN = 83°2'.$$

where

$$\text{chord } FN = 79^{\mathrm{p}}33'$$

But

$$\text{hypt. } DF = 120^{\mathrm{p}}.$$

where

$$FN = 39^{\mathrm{p}}7'$$

$$DF = 58^{\mathrm{p}}59',$$

that is, where

$$\text{epic. rad. } FK = 43^{\mathrm{p}}10' \text{ [p. 316].}$$

And so also
$$FN = 108^{\mathrm{p}}45'$$
where
$$\text{hypt. } FK = 120^{\mathrm{p}};$$
and, on the circle about right triangle FKN,
$$\text{arc } FN = 130°.$$
And therefore
$$\text{angle } DKF = 130° \text{ to 2 rt.}$$
just as it is supposed
$$\text{angle } FDK = 83°2' \text{ to 2 rt.,}$$
and, by addition,
$$\text{angle } HFK = 213°2' \text{ to 2 rt.}$$
And it was also proved that
$$\text{angle } BFD = 2°42' \text{ to 2 rt.,}$$
that is, that
$$\text{angle } GFH = 2°42' \text{ to 2 rt.}$$
And therefore, by addition,
$$\text{angle } GFK = 215°46' \text{ to 2 rt.}$$
$$= 107°53'.$$

And therefore at that time Venus was, by subtraction from the whole circle, 252°7′ east of the epicycle's apogee at G. Which was to be proved.

Since, then, at the time of our own observation, it was likewise 230°32′ from the epicycle's apogee, and since the time from one observation to the other embraces 409 Egyptian years and very nearly 167 days, and 255 complete returns in anomaly (for with 8 Egyptian years making very nearly 5 cycles, 408 years add up to 255 cycles, and the year left over taken with the days does not fill out the time of one return), it is evident to us that, in 409 Egyptian years and 167 days, Venus added on, over and above the 255 complete returns in anomaly, 338°25′ on the epicycle, by which amount its position at our observation exceeded that of the earlier one. Just about that number of degrees turn up in the tables of mean movement established by us, because the correction of them was made from the cyclic surplus we have just found, the time being reduced to days and the returns together with the surplus to degrees. For when the number of degrees has been divided over the number of days, there results the daily mean movement in anomaly we have already set forth.

5. On the Epoch of its Periodic Movements

Since it remains now to establish the epochs of its periodic movements at the year 1 of Nabonassar's reign, Egyptianwise Thoth 1 at noon, we again took the time from this date to the older of the observations. And it comes to 475 Egyptian years and very nearly $346 + \frac{1}{2} + \frac{1}{4}$ days. According to the columns of anomaly, the surplus of mean movement corresponding to this amount of time is very nearly 181°. If we subtract this from the 252°7′ at the observation, we shall have the epoch at the year 1 of Nabonassar, Egyptianwise Thoth 1 at noon; 71°7′ from the epicycle's apogee for anomaly, with the mean position in longitude again supposed the same as the sun's—that is, 45′ within the Fishes. It is evident that, since at the observation the apogee is about 20°55′ within the Bull, and since the intervening 476 years add on about $(4 + \frac{1}{2} + \frac{1}{4})°$, at the proposed time of the epoch the apogee will be about 16°10′ within the Bull.

6. Preliminaries to the Demonstrations concerning the Other Stars

In the case of the two stars Mercury and Venus, we have used such methods as these for getting hold of the hypotheses and demonstrating the anomalies. In the case of the other three—Mars, Jupiter, and Saturn—we find the one and the same hypothesis as that apprehended for Venus; that is, the hypothesis according to which the eccentric circle the epicycle's centre is always borne on is described with its centre at the point bisecting the straight line between the centres of the ecliptic and of the circle effecting the epicycle's uniform revolution. For in the case of each of these stars, the difference in general found at the point of greatest difference of zodiacal anomaly turns out to be very nearly double the difference of the eccentricity calculated from the magnitude of the epicycle's regressions at the greatest and least distances.[1] And we find that demonstrations, by means of which we establish each of the magnitudes of the anomalies and of the apogees, cannot be worked out for these stars in the same way as for the other two, because they can be at any angular distance from the sun and because it is not evident from the observations—as in the case of the greatest elongations of Mercury and Venus, when the star is at the point of contact of the straight line drawn from our eye tangent to the epicycle. Since, then, this method does not work here, we have used the positions observed when diametrically opposite the sun's mean position, and from these we show the ratios of eccentricity and the apogees, since only in the positions so considered do we find the zodiacal anomaly set off by itself. For then there is no anomalistic difference with respect to the sun.

For let ABC be the star's eccentric circle on which the epicycle's centre is borne, and let it be about centre D. And let AC be the diameter through the apogee; and point E on it the ecliptic's centre; and F the centre of the eccentric with respect to which the mean longitudinal position of the epicycle is considered. With the epicycle $GHKL$ described about B, let the straight lines $FLBH$ and $GBKEM$ be joined.

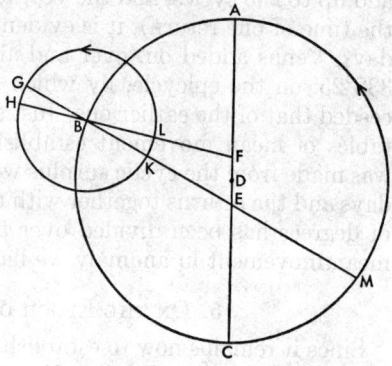

I say, first, that when the star appears along the straight line EG through the epicycle's centre B the sun's mean position will always be in the same straight line: when the star is at G, it is in conjunction with the sun's mean position seen at

[1]The eccentricity of the planets Mars, Jupiter, and Saturn is established by the theory of regressions in Book XII, where the angle of regression is computed for each planet at each of the three principal distances: mean, greatest, and least. The angle of regression obviously appears larger or smaller according as the star is closer or farther from the eye of the observer. It is therefore shown in Book XII that the assumption that the deferent's centre lies half way between the earth and the equant's centre saves the appearances of the angles of regression.

In the following chapters of this Book and of Book XI, this assumption concerning the position of the deferent's centre is made without more ado, and this sentence is the lone reference to the manner of its justification. For the demonstrations that follow are solely concerned with finding the centres of the equants.

G, and when it is at K, it will be diametrically opposite the sun's mean position seen at M.

For since in the case of each of these stars the mean angular distances from the apogee both in longitude and in anomaly, when added together, give the mean passage of the sun from the same starting point; and since the angle at B embracing the star's regular passage on its epicycle is always the difference between the angle at centre F which embraces the star's regular movement in longitude and the angle at E which embraces its apparent movement; therefore is it clear that, when the star is at point G, it will fall short of its return to apogee H by angle GBH, the angle which combined with angle AFB (that is, subtracted from it) gives angle AEG, the angle contained by the mean solar passage and the same as the star's apparent passage. And it is clear that, when the star is at point K, again it will have moved on the epicycle through angle HBK which, added to angle AFB, will equal the sun's mean passage from apogee A. For the sun's mean passage embraces the semicircle plus the difference between angle AFB and angle KBL—that is, angle CEM, the angle vertical to the angle of the star's apparent passage.

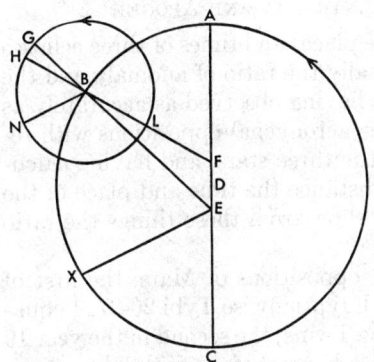

For this reason, in the case of these configurations, the straight line drawn from the epicycle's centre B to the star and that drawn from the point E at our eye to the sun's mean position fall both along the same straight line. And, in the case of all the other distances, they are directed to different points, but are always parallel to each other.[1]

For if, at any position on the figure just given, we draw a straight line from B to the star—for example, BN, and another from E to the sun's mean position, for instance EX—then, for the same reasons as

[1]There is a most important tacit assumption made here. In order for this theorem to apply, it is evident that we must assume that at least once in the past or future the sun, the mean sun, the earth, Mars (for example) and the centre of Mars' epicycle have been, or will be, in a straight line. Then, given the fact that the cycles of mean longitude plus the cycles of anomaly equal the cycles of the mean sun, it is proved here that those four points will always be in a straight line whenever three of them—Mars, the earth, and the mean sun—are in a straight line.

Now, Ptolemy probably referred to just this assumption and the one discussed in the previous note when, in IX, 2 , he said, "or if we are forced (2) to presuppose something without immediate foundation in the appearances, an apprehension gotten from continuous trial and adjustment." This assumption becomes a necessity in the Copernican system where the outer planet's epicycle becomes the circular orbit of the earth about the mean sun and the outer planet's eccentric circle becomes the circular orbit of the outer planet's mean longitudinal movement about the mean sun. Since, under the Copernican hypothesis, the earth continually passes between the outer planet and the mean sun, and the centre of the outer planet's epicycle has under this hypothesis become the mean sun, it is obvious that there will be a time when the earth, the planet, and the mean sun will be in a straight line; and that will be precisely when the planet is nearest the earth—that is, in the Ptolemaic system at the apparent perigee of its epicycle. Hence the above assumption of Ptolemy points almost by an inner necessity to a heliocentric theory. In Book I of this treatise Ptolemy asserts, it must be remembered, that the heliocentric hypothesis is simpler.

just given,

$$\text{angle } AEX = \text{angle } AFH + \text{angle } NBH$$

and

$$\text{angle } AFH = \text{angle } AEG + \text{angle } GBH.$$

By the subtraction of the common angle AEG,

$$\text{angle } GEX = \text{angle } GBN.$$

Therefore, straight line EX is parallel to BN.

Since, then, at the configurations of conjunctions and oppositions considered in relation to the sun's mean position, we find the star to be seen in a line with the epicycle's centre as if it had no movement whatsoever on the epicycle but had its position on the circle ABC and were revolved regularly by the straight line FB in the same way as the epicycle's centre, therefore it is clear that it will be possible by means of these positions to demonstrate the ratios of eccentricity of zodiacal anomaly in themselves. But since the conjunctive configurations do not appear, it is clear that it remains only to get at the demonstrations by means of the oppositions.

7. Demonstration of Mars' Eccentricity and Apogee

Just as, in the case of the moon, we took the places and times of three eclipses at the full moon and demonstrated geometrically the ratio of anomaly and the place of the apogee, so here in the same way, having observed as accurately as possible with the astrolabe the places of three acronychal oppositions with respect to the sun's mean position for each of the three stars, and having calculated beforehand to a fine degree of angular distance the time and place of the sun's mean positions at the observations, we show from these things the ratio of eccentricity and the apogee.

In the first place, therefore, we took three oppositions of Mars: the first of which we observed in the year 15 of Hadrian, Egyptianwise Tybi 26-27, 1 equatorial hour after midnight, about 21° within the Twins; the second in the year 19 of Hadrian, Egyptianwise Pharmouthi 6-7, 3 hours before midnight, about 28°50′ within the Lion; and the third in the year 2 of Antonine, Egyptianwise Epiphi 12-13, 2 equatorial hours before midnight, about 2°34′ within the Archer. Now, the time of the interval from the first opposition to the second embraces 4 Egyptian years, 69 days, and 20 equatorial hours; and from the second to the third, likewise, 4 years, 96 days, and 1 equatorial hour. From the first interval of time there adds up 81°44′ in longitudinal movement, over and above complete circles; and from the second, 95°28′. For there will be no appreciable difference even if we calculate the mean movements for this amount of time from the periodic returns set out in the rough. And it is clear that, for the first interval, the apparent star has moved 67°50′ over and above complete circles, and, for the second, 93°44′.

Then let three equal circles be described in the plane of the ecliptic. Let ABC about centre D be the one bearing the epicycle's centre; EFG about centre H the eccentric of regular movement; KLM about centre N, concentric with the ecliptic; and let the straight line $KOPR$ be the diameter through all the centres. Moreover, let A be supposed the point where the epicycle's centre was at the first opposition, B where it was at the second, and C where it was at the third. And let HAE, HBF, HGC, NKA, NLB, and NCM be joined, so that arc EF of the eccentric is the 81°44′ of the first periodic angular distance, and arc FG the

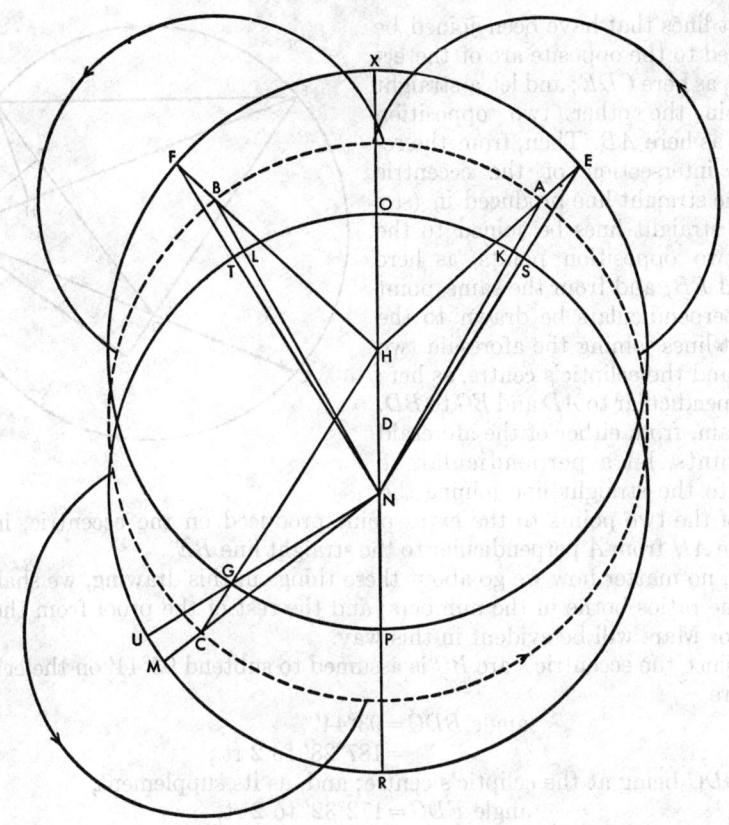

95°28' of the second; and again so that arc KL of the ecliptic is the 67°60' of the first apparent angular distance, and arc LM the 93°44' of the second.

If, then, the eccentric's arcs EF and FG were subtended by the ecliptic's arcs KL and LM, we should need nothing more for the demonstration of the eccentricity. But since they subtend arcs AB and BC of the middle eccentric which are not given, and since, if we join NSE, NTF, and NGU, again arcs ST and TU of the ecliptic (clearly not given) subtend arcs EF and FG of the eccentric, it will be necessary, first, that the differences KS, LT, and MU be given, in order for the ratio of eccentricity to be accurately demonstrated from the corresponding arcs EF, FG and ST, TU. But since it is not possible to get these accurately prior to the ratio of eccentricity and the apogee—and yet since they will be given approximately, even if not accurately given before, because the differences are not great—we shall first make our calculation as if the arcs ST, TU did not differ appreciably from arcs KL, LM.

For let ABC be the eccentric circle of Mars' regular passage [the equant], and let A be supposed the point of the first opposition, B of the second, and C of the third. Within this circle let D be taken as the centre of the ecliptic where our eye is; and let all the straight lines be joined from the three opposition points to the eye—in this case AD, BD, and CD. And let one of the three

straight lines that have been joined be
produced to the opposite arc of the eccentric, as here *CDE*; and let a straight
line join the other two opposition
points, as here *AB*. Then, from the resulting intersection of the eccentric
with the straight line produced in (say
E), let straight lines be joined to the
other two opposition points, as here
EA and *EB;* and from the same point
E let perpendiculars be drawn to the
straight lines joining the aforesaid two
points and the ecliptic's centre, as here
EF perpendicular to *AD* and *EG* to *BD*.
Yet again, from either of the aforesaid
two points, let a perpendicular be
drawn to the straight line joining the
other of the two points to the extra point produced on the eccentric, in this
instance *AH* from *A* perpendicular to the straight line *BE*.

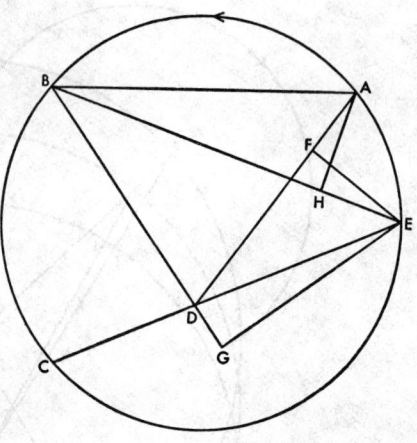

Now, no matter how we go about these things in this drawing, we shall find
the same ratios borne in the numbers; and the rest of the proof from the arcs
given for Mars will be evident in this way.

For since the eccentric's arc *BC* is assumed to subtend 93°44′ on the ecliptic,
therefore

$$\text{angle } BDC = 93°44′$$
$$= 187°28′ \text{ to 2 rt.,}$$

angle *BDC* being at the ecliptic's centre; and, as its supplement,
$$\text{angle } EDG = 172°32′ \text{ to 2 rt.}$$
And so also, on the circle about right triangle *DEG*,
$$\text{arc } EG = 172°32′,$$
and
$$\text{chord } EG = 119^{\text{p}}45′$$
where
$$\text{hypt. } DE = 120^{\text{p}}.$$

Likewise, since
$$\text{arc } BC = 95°28′,$$
therefore, being an angle at the circumference,
$$\text{angle } BEC = 95°28′ \text{ to 2 rt.}$$
And
$$\text{angle } BDE = 172°32′ \text{ to 2 rt.;}$$
therefore, by subtraction,
$$\text{angle } EBG = 92° \text{ to 2 rt.}$$
And so also, on the circle about right triangle *BEG*,
$$\text{arc } EG = 92°,$$
and
$$\text{chord } EG = 86^{\text{p}}19′$$
where
$$\text{hypt. } BE = 120^{\text{p}}.$$

And therefore

$$BE = 166^p29'$$

where it was proved

$$EG = 119^p45'$$

and

$$DE = 120^p.$$

Again, since the whole arc ABC of the eccentric is assumed to subtend on the ecliptic $161°34'$, the sum of both intervals, therefore

$$\text{angle } ADC = 161°34',$$

and, by subtraction,

$$\text{angle } ADE = 18°26'$$
$$= 36°52' \text{ to 2 rt.}$$

And so also, on the circle about right triangle DEF,

$$\text{arc } EF = 36°52',$$

and

$$\text{chord } EF = 37^p57'$$

where

$$\text{hypt. } DE = 120^p.$$

Likewise, since

$$\text{arc } ABC = 177°12',$$

ABC being an arc on the eccentric, therefore

$$\text{angle } AEC = 177°12' \text{ to 2 rt.}$$

And we saw

$$\text{angle } ADE = 36°52' \text{ to 2 rt.}$$

Therefore, by subtraction,

$$\text{angle } DAE = 145°56' \text{ to 2 rt.}$$

And so also, on the circle about right triangle AEF,

$$\text{arc } EF = 145°56',$$

and

$$\text{chord } EF = 114^p44'$$

where

$$\text{hypt. } AE = 120^p.$$

And therefore

$$AE = 39^p42'$$

where it was proved

$$EF = 37^p57'$$

and

$$ED = 120^p.$$

Again, since

$$\text{arc } AB = 81°44',$$

AB being an arc on the eccentric, therefore

$$\text{angle } AEB = 81°44' \text{ to 2 rt.}$$

And so also, on the circle about right triangle AEH,

$$\text{arc } AH = 81°44'$$

and, by subtraction from the semicircle,

$$\text{arc } EH = 98°16'.$$

And therefore

$$\text{chord } AH = 78^p31',$$
$$\text{chord } EH = 90^p45'$$

where
$$\text{hypt. } AE = 120^{\text{p}}.$$

And so
$$AH = 25^{\text{p}}58',$$
$$EH = 30^{\text{p}}2'$$

where it was proved
$$AE = 39^{\text{p}}42'$$

supposing
$$ED = 120^{\text{p}}.$$

And it was also proved, with the same parts, that
$$\text{whole } BE = 166^{\text{p}}29';$$

and therefore, by subtraction,
$$BH = 136^{\text{p}}27'$$

where
$$AH = 25^{\text{p}}58'.$$

And
$$\text{sq. } BH = 18,615^{\text{p}}16'$$

and likewise
$$\text{sq. } AH = 674^{\text{p}}16',$$

which added together make
$$\text{sq. } AB = 19,289^{\text{p}}32';$$

in length, therefore,
$$AB = 138^{\text{p}}53',$$
$$AE = 39^{\text{p}}42',$$

where
$$DE = 120^{\text{p}}.$$

And
$$AB = 78^{\text{p}}31'$$

where
$$\text{ecc. diam.} = 120^{\text{p}};$$

for AB subtends an arc of $81°44'$. And therefore
$$DE = 67^{\text{p}}50',$$
$$AE = 22^{\text{p}}44'$$

where
$$AB = 78^{\text{p}}31'$$

and
$$\text{ecc. diam.} = 120^{\text{p}}.$$

And so also, AE being an arc on the eccentric,
$$\text{arc } AE = 21°41'$$

and, by addition,
$$\text{arc } EABC = 198°53',$$

and, by subtraction,
$$\text{arc } CE = 161°7'.$$

And
$$\text{chord } CDE = 118^{\text{p}}22'$$

where
$$\text{ecc. diam.} = 120^{\text{p}}.$$

If, then, the straight line CE had been found equal to the eccentric's diameter,

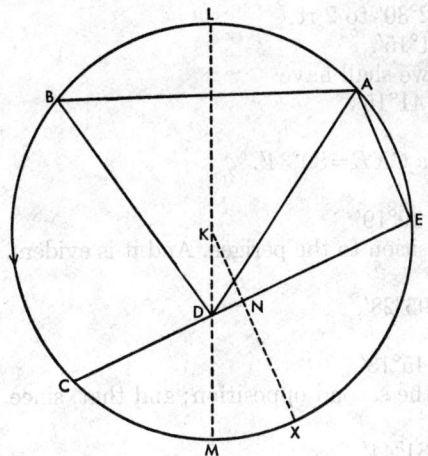

it is clear that the eccentric's centre would be on it, and the ratio of eccentricity would be immediately apparent. But since it has not come out equal, and has made segment *EABC* greater than a semicircle, it is evident that the eccentric's centre will fall on that side. Then let it be supposed the point *K*, and let the diameter *LKDM* through both centres be drawn through *K* and *D*; and from *K* let *KNX* be drawn perpendicular to *CE*.

Since, then, it was shown
$$CE = 118^p22',$$
$$DE = 67^p50'$$
where
$$\text{diam. } LM = 120^p,$$
therefore also, by subtraction,
$$CD = 50^p32'.$$

And so, since
$$\text{rect. } ED, DC = \text{rect. } LD, DM,$$
we shall find
$$\text{rect. } LD, DM = 3,427^p51'.$$
But also
$$\text{rect. } LD, DM + \text{sq. } DK = \text{sq. } LK$$
which is the square on half the whole diameter. Therefore, if we subtract from the $3,600^p$ of the square on *LK* the $3,427^p51'$ of the rectangle *LD, DM*, then we shall have left the $172^p9'$ of the square on *DK*. And therefore we shall have in length
$$\text{1. btw. c. } DK = 13^p7'$$
where
$$\text{ecc. rad. } LK = 60^p.$$

Again, since
$$\text{half } CE \text{ or } CN = 59^p11',$$
and it was proved
$$DC = 50^p32'$$
where
$$\text{diam. } LM = 120^p,$$
therefore, by subtraction,
$$DN = 8^p39'$$
where it was found
$$DK = 13^p7'.$$

And so also
$$DN = 79^p8'$$
where
$$\text{hypt. } DK = 120^p;$$
and, on the circle about right triangle *DKN*,
$$\text{arc } DN = 82°30.$$
Therefore also

angle $DKN = 82°30'$ to 2 rt.
$$= 41°15'.$$
And since it is at the eccentric's centre, we shall have
$$\text{arc } MX = 41°15'.$$
And also, by addition,
$$\text{arc } CMX = \text{half arc } CXE = 80°34'.$$
Therefore also, by subtraction,
$$\text{arc } CM = 39°19'$$
where CM is the arc from the third opposition to the perigee. And it is evident that, since it was assumed
$$\text{arc } BC = 95°28',$$
by subtraction,
$$\text{arc } BL = 45°13'$$
where LB is the arc from the apogee to the second opposition; and that, since it was assumed
$$\text{arc } AB = 81°44',$$
therefore, by subtraction,
$$\text{arc } AL = 36°31'$$
where CL is the arc from the first opposition to the apogee.

Now, with these things assumed, let us find out in the following way what differences they yield at each opopsition for the required arcs of the ecliptic.

From the figure of the three oppositions given above [p. 325], let the drawing of the first opposition alone be laid out. And after AD has been joined, let DV and NY be drawn from points D and N perpendicular to AH produced.

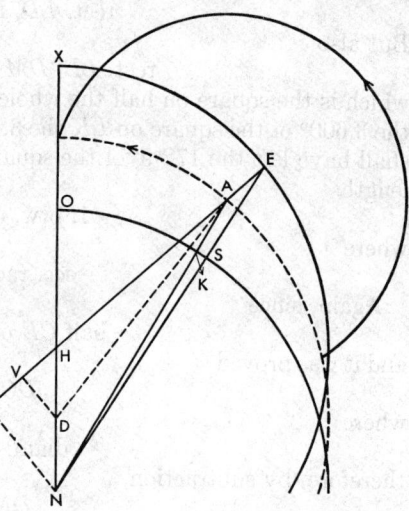

Since, then,
$$\text{arc } EX = 36°31',$$
therefore
$$\text{angle } EHX = 36°31',$$
and, being the angle vertical to it,
$$\text{angle } DHV = 73°2' \text{ to 2 rt.}$$
And so also, on the circle about right triangle DHV,
$$\text{arc } DV = 73°2',$$
and, by subtraction from the semicircle,
$$\text{arc } HV = 106°58'.$$
And therefore
$$\text{chord } DV = 71^{\text{p}}25'$$
$$\text{chord } HV = 96^{\text{p}}27'$$
where

And so also
$$\text{hypt. } DH = 120^{\text{p}}.$$
$$DV = 3^{\text{p}}54',$$
$$HV = 5^{\text{p}}16'$$
where

and
$$DH = 6^{\text{p}}33\tfrac{1}{2}'$$

$$\text{ecc. rad. } AD = 60^{\text{p}}.$$

And since
$$\text{sq. } AD - \text{sq. } DV = \text{sq. } AV,$$
therefore, in length,
$$AV = 59^\text{p}52';$$
and since
$$VY = HV,$$
therefore, by addition,
$$AY = 65^\text{p}8'$$
where, since
$$NY = 2DV,$$
$$NY = 7^\text{p}48'.$$
And consequently
$$\text{hypt. } AN = 65^\text{p}36'.$$

And therefore
$$NY = 14^\text{p}16'$$
where
$$AN = 120^\text{p};$$
and, on the circle about right triangle ANY,
$$\text{arc } NY = 13°40'.$$
And so also
$$\text{angle } NAY = 13°40' \text{ to 2 rt.}$$

Again, since it was shown
$$NY = 7^\text{p}48',$$
$$HY = 10^\text{p}32'$$
where
$$\text{ecc. rad. } EH = 60^\text{p},$$
therefore, by addition,
$$EHY = 70^\text{p}32'$$
and consequently
$$\text{hypt. } EN = 71^\text{p}.$$

And therefore
$$NY = 13^\text{p}10'$$
where
$$EN = 120^\text{p};$$
and, on the circle about right triangle ENY,
$$\text{arc } NY = 12°36'.$$
And so also
$$\text{angle } NEY = 12°36' \text{ to 2 rt.}$$
But
$$\text{angle } NAY = 13°40' \text{ to 2 rt.};$$
and therefore, by subtraction,
$$\text{angle } ANE = 1°4' \text{ to 2 rt.}$$
$$= 32'.$$
Therefore on the ecliptic
$$\text{arc } KS = 32'.$$
Then let there be laid out the similar figure containing the drawing of the

second opposition. Since it is assumed
$$\text{arc } FX = 45°13',$$
therefore
$$\text{angle } FHX = 45°13',$$
and, being the angle vertical to it,
$$\text{angle } DHV = 90°26' \text{ to 2 rt.}$$
And so also, on the circle about right triangle DHV,
$$\text{arc } DV = 90°26',$$
and, by subtraction from the semicircle,
$$\text{arc } HV = 89°34'.$$
And therefore
$$\text{chord } DV = 85^{p}10',$$
$$\text{chord } HV = 84^{p}32'$$
where
$$\text{hypt. } DH = 120^{p}.$$
And so also
$$DV = 4^{p}39',$$
$$HV = 4^{p}38'$$
where
$$DH = 6^{p}33\tfrac{1}{2}'$$
and
$$\text{ecc. rad. } BD = 60^{p}.$$
And since
$$\text{sq. } BD\text{—sq. } DV = \text{sq. } BV,$$
therefore, in length,
$$BV = 59^{p}49';$$
and, because
$$VY = HV,$$
therefore, by addition,
$$BY = 64^{p}27'$$
where, since
$$NY = 2DV,$$
$$NY = 9^{p}18'.$$
And consequently, also,
$$\text{hypt. } BN = 69^{p}6'.$$
And therefore
$$NY = 17^{p}9'$$
where
$$BN = 120^{p};$$
and, on the circle about right triangle BNY,
$$\text{arc } NY = 16°26'.$$
And so also
$$\text{angle } NBY = 16°26' \text{ to 2 rt.}$$
Again, since it was proved
$$NY = 9^{p}18',$$
$$HY = 9^{p}16'$$
where
$$\text{ecc. rad. } FH = 60^{p},$$
therefore, by addition,

$$FHY = 69^{\text{p}}16'$$

and consequently

$$\text{hypt. } FN = 69^{\text{p}}52'.$$

And therefore

$$NY \eqcirc 16^{\text{p}}$$

where

$$\text{hypt. } FN = 120^{\text{p}};$$

and, on the circle about right triangle FNY,

$$\text{arc } NY = 15°20'.$$

And so also

$$\text{angle } NFY = 15°20' \text{ to 2 rt.}$$

But

$$\text{angle } NBY = 16°26' \text{ to 2 rt.}$$

And therefore, by subtraction,

$$\text{angle } BNF = 1°6' \text{ to 2 rt.}$$
$$= 33'.$$

Therefore on the ecliptic

$$\text{arc } KS = 33'.$$

Since, then, at the first opposition we found arc KS to be 32', it is clear that the first interval of the apparent movement considered with respect to the eccentric will be greater by the segments of both arcs, 1°5', and will contain 68°55'.

Then let the drawing of the third opposition be laid out. Since then it is supposed

$$\text{arc } GP = 39°19',$$

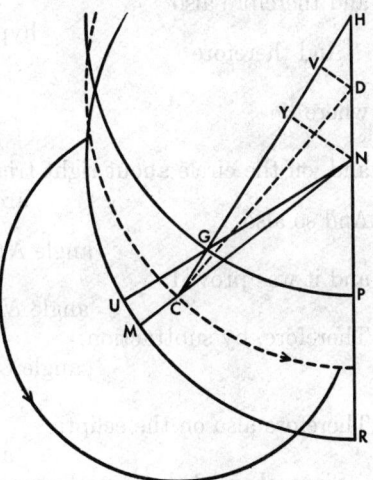

therefore

$$\text{angle } GPH = 39°19'$$
$$= 78°38' \text{ to 2 rt.}$$

And so also, on the circle about right triangle DHV,

$$\text{arc } DV = 78°38',$$

and, by subtraction from the semicircle,

$$\text{arc } HV = 101°22'.$$

And therefore

$$\text{chord } DV = 76^{\text{p}}2',$$
$$\text{chord } HV = 92^{\text{p}}50'$$

where

$$\text{hypt. } DH = 120^{\text{p}}.$$

And so also

$$DV = 4^{\text{p}}9',$$
$$HV = 5^{\text{p}}4'$$

where

$$\text{1. btw. c. } DH = 6^{\text{p}}33\tfrac{1}{2}',$$

and

$$\text{ecc. rad. } CD = 60^{\text{p}}.$$

And since

$$\text{sq. } CD - \text{sq. } DV = \text{sq. } CV,$$

therefore

$$CV = 59^{\text{p}}51';$$

and, because

$$HV = VY,$$

by subtraction

$$CY = 54^\text{p}47'$$

where, since

$$NY = 2DV,$$
$$NY = 8^\text{p}18'.$$

And consequently also

hypt. $CN = 55^\text{p}25'.$

And therefore

$$NY = 17^\text{p}59'$$

where

$$CN = 120^\text{p};$$

and, on the circle about right triangle CNY,

arc $NY = 17°14'.$

And so also

angle $NCY = 17°14'$ to 2 rt.

Again, since it was shown

$$NY = 8^\text{p}18',$$
$$HY = 10^\text{p}8'$$

where

ecc. rad. $GH = 60^\text{p},$

therefore, by subtraction,

$$GY = 49^\text{p}52',$$

and therefore also

hypt. $GN = 50^\text{p}33'.$

And therefore

$$NY = 19^\text{p}42'$$

where

$$GN = 120^\text{p};$$

and, on the circle about right triangle GNY,

arc $NY = 18°54'.$

And so also

angle $NGY = 18°54'$ to 2 rt.,

and it was proved

angle $NCY = 17°14'$ to 2 rt.

Therefore, by subtraction,

angle $CNG = 1°40'$ to 2 rt.
$$= 50'.$$

Therefore also on the ecliptic

arc $MU = 50'.$

Since, then, at the second opposition, we found the arc LT to be 33', it is clear that the second interval of the apparent movement, considered with respect to the eccentric, will be less by the segments of both arcs, 1°23', and will contain 92°21'.

With these arcs of the ecliptic calculated for the two intervals, we again go through the theorem for demonstrating the apogee and the ratio of eccentricity, and find (not to make this treatise too long by repition)

1. btw. c. $DK^1 = 11^\text{p}50'$

[1]DK here refers to the fourth figure back. It is the distance between the ecliptic's centre or the earth and the equant's centre. As it has been pointed out before, the deferent's centre is assumed to be midway between the two, an assumption established and justified by the theory of regressions in Book XII.

where

$$\text{ecc. rad.} = 60^\text{p};$$

and, on the eccentric,

$$\text{arc } CM = 45°33',$$

CM being the arc from the third opposition to the perigee. And again from this

$$\text{arc } BL = 38°59',$$
$$\text{arc } AL = 42°45'.$$

Likewise when we had used these numbers in the proofs of each opposition, we finally found the accurate magnitudes of each of the required arcs:

$$\text{arc } KS = 28',$$
$$\text{arc } LT = 28',$$
$$\text{arc } MU = 30'.$$

And putting together the differences at the first and second oppositions and adding the resulting 56' to the 67°50' of the first interval on the ecliptic, we had the distance of 68°46' accurately considered with respect to the eccentric; and putting together those at the second and third oppositions and subtracting the resulting 1°8' from the apparent 93°44' of the second interval on the ecliptic, again we found the distance of 92°36' accurately considered with respect to the eccentric. Finally from these results, using the same proof, we accurately ascertained the ratio of eccentricity and the apogee.

And we found

$$\text{1. btw. c. } DK \doteqdot 12^\text{p}$$

where

$$\text{ecc. rad. } KL = 60^\text{p};$$

and on the eccentric

$$\text{arc } CM = 44°21'$$

from which, in turn, it results that

$$\text{arc } BL = 40°11',$$
$$\text{arc } AL = 41°33'.$$

By these same means we shall also show that the observed apparent intervals of the three oppositions agree with these last magnitudes.

For let there be set out the drawing of the first opposition, containing only the eccentric circle the epicycle's centre is always borne on [the deferent].

Since then

$$\text{angle } AHE = 41°33',$$

and, being the angle vertical to it,

$$\text{angle } DHV = 83°6' \text{ to 2 rt.,}$$

therefore, on the circle about right triangle DHV,

$$\text{arc } DV = 83°6'$$

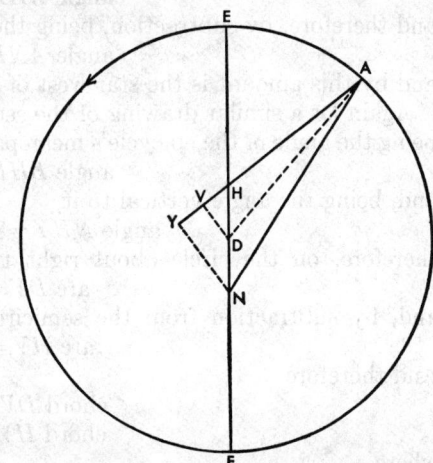

and, by subtraction from the semicircle,

$$\text{arc } HV = 96°54'.$$

And therefore

$$\text{chord } DV = 79^\text{p}35',$$
$$\text{chord } HV = 89^\text{p}50'$$

where

$$\text{hypt. } DH = 120^\text{p}.$$

And so also

$$DV = 3^p 58\tfrac{1}{2}',$$
$$HV = 4^p 30'$$

where

$$DH = 6^p,$$

and

$$AD = 60^p.$$

And since

$$\text{sq. } AD - \text{sq. } DV = \text{sq. } AV,$$

therefore, in length,

$$AV = 59^p 50'.$$

Again, since

$$HV = VY$$

and

$$NY = 2DV,$$

we shall have, by addition,

$$AY = 64^p 20'$$

where

$$NY = 7^p 57'.$$

And consequently also

$$\text{hypt. } AN = 64^p 52'.$$

And so also

$$NY = 14^p 44'$$

where

$$AN = 120^p;$$

and, on the circle about right triangle ANY,

$$\text{arc } NY = 14°6',$$

and therefore

angle $NAY = 14°6'$ to 2 rt.
$$= 7°3'.$$

But

angle $AHE = 41°33',$

and therefore, by subtraction, being the angle of apparent passage,

angle $ANE = 34°30',$

and by this amount is the star west of the apogee at the first opposition.

Again let a similar drawing of the second opposition be set out. Since, then, being the angle of the epicycle's mean passage

angle $BHE = 40°11',$

and, being the angle vertical to it,

angle $NHY = 80°22'$ to 2 rt.,

therefore, on the circle about right triangle DHV,

$$\text{arc } DV = 80°22'$$

and, by subtraction from the semicircle,

$$\text{arc } HV = 99°38'.$$

And therefore

chord $DV = 77^p 26',$
chord $HV = 91^p 41'$

where

$$\text{hypt. } DH = 120^p.$$

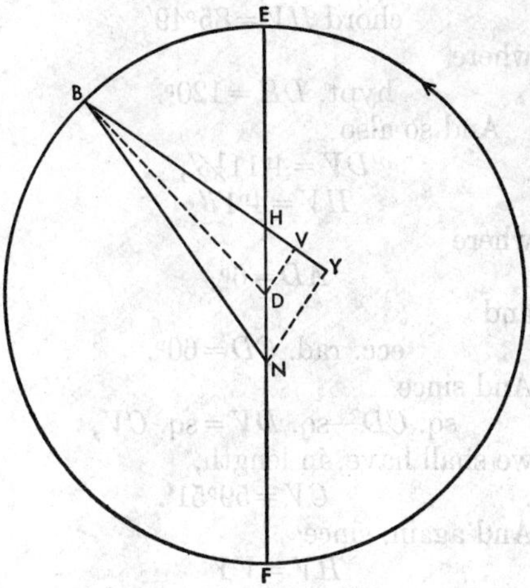

And also
$$DV = 3^p52',$$
$$HV = 4^p35'$$
where
$$DH = 6^p$$
and
$$\text{hypt. } BD = 60^p.$$
And since
$$\text{sq. } BD - \text{sq. } DV = \text{sq. } BV,$$
therefore, in length,
$$BV = 59^p53'.$$
And in the same way, since
$$HV = VY$$
and
$$NY = 2DV,$$
therefore, by addition
$$BY = 64^p28'$$
where
$$NY = 7^p44'.$$
And consequently
$$\text{hypt. } BN = 64^p56'.$$
And therefore
$$NY = 14^p19'$$
where
$$\text{hypt. } BN = 120^p;$$
and, on the circle about right triangle BNY,
$$\text{arc } NY = 13°42'.$$
And so also
$$\text{angle } NBY = 13°42' \text{ to 2 rt.}$$
$$= 6°51'.$$
And
$$\text{angle } BHE = 40°11'.$$
Therefore, by subtraction, being the angle of apparent passage,
$$\text{angle } BNE = 33°20'.$$
By this distance the star hence appeared east of the apogee at the second opposition. It had already been proved 34°30' west of the apogee at the first opposition; therefore the whole interval from the first to the second opposition comes to 67°50', in agreement with the amount gotten by the observations.

Then let the drawing of the third opposition be set out in the same way. Since in this case, being the angle of the epicycle's regular passage,
$$\text{angle } CHF = 44°21'$$
$$= 88°42' \text{ to 2 rt.,}$$
therefore, on the circle about right triangle DHV,
$$\text{arc } DV = 88°42'$$
and, by subtraction from the semicircle,
$$\text{arc } HV = 91°18'.$$
And therefore
$$\text{chord } DV = 83^p53',$$

chord $HV = 85^p49'$

where

hypt. $DH = 120^p$.

And so also
$$DV = 4^p11\tfrac{1}{2}',$$
$$HV = 4^p17'$$

where

$$AD = 6^p$$

and

ecc. rad. $CD = 60^p$.

And since
$$\text{sq. } CD - \text{sq. } DV = \text{sq. } CV,$$
we shall have, in length,
$$CV = 59^p51'.$$

And again, since
$$HV = VY$$

and

$$NY = 2DV,$$

we shall have, by subtraction,
$$CY = 55^p34'$$

where

$$NY = 8^p23'.$$

And consequently we shall have
$$\text{hypt. } CN = 56^p12'.$$

And therefore

$$NY = 17^p55'$$

where

hypt. $CN = 120^p$;
and, on the circle about right triangle CNY,
$$\text{arc } NY = 17°10'.$$

And so also

$$\text{angle } HCN = 17°10' \text{ to 2 rt.}$$
$$= 8°35'.$$

But

$$\text{angle } CHF = 44°21';$$
and therefore, by addition,
$$\text{angle } CNF = 52°56'.$$

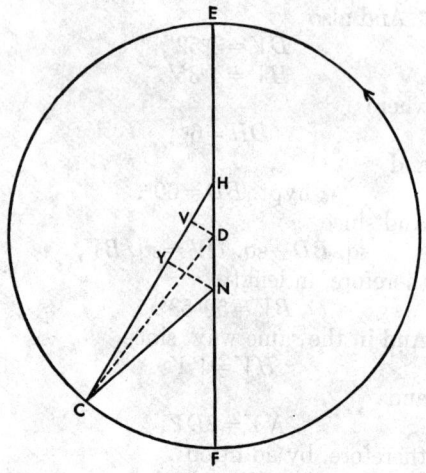

At the third opposition, therefore, the star appeared west of the perigee by just that much. And therefore, by subtraction, the resulting 93°44′ from the second to the third opposition was found to agree with the amount observed in the second interval. It is also clear that, when the star, sighted along the straight line CN, was according to observation 2°34′ within the Archer and angle CNF at the ecliptic's centre was proved to be 52°56′, then the perigee of eccentricity at point F was 25°30′ within the Goat, and the apogee diametrically opposite 25°30′ was within the Crab.

Also, if we describe the epicycle of Mars about centre C and produce straight line CN, we shall have the epicycle's mean passage of 135°39′ from the eccentric's apogee at the time of the third opposition; for it was proved

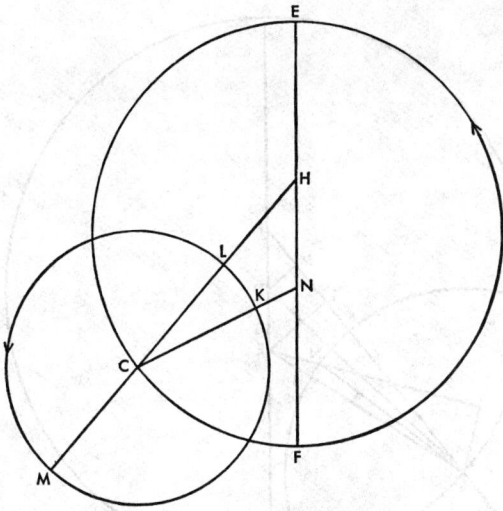

angle $CHF = 44°21'$
which is the remainder of the
semicircle. And we shall have
arc $KM = 171°25'$
which is the star's mean passage from the epicycle's apogee
M^1; because it was proved
angle $HCN = 8°35'$,
HCN being an angle at the epicycle's centre; because
arc $KL = 8°35'$,
KL being the arc from the star
K to the perigee $L;$ and because, therefore, the arc from
apogee M to star K is $171°25'$
as proposed.

With the other results it is
now clear to us that, at the
time of the third opposition—
that is, in the year 2 of Antonine, Egyptianwise Epiphi 12-13, 2 equatorial
hours before midnight—Mars was $135°39'$ in mean longitude from the eccentric's apogee, and $171°25'$ in anomaly from the epicycle's apogee. Which
things it was required to prove.

8. Demonstration of the Magnitude of Mars' Epicycle

Since the next thing was to demonstrate the ratio of the epicycle's magnitude,
we took for this purpose an observation which we made very nearly 3 days after
the third opposition (that is, in the year 2 of Antonine, Egyptianwise month 15-16,
3 equatorial hours before midnight), for the point on the astrolabe 20° within the
Balance was culminating and the sun was then according to its mean passage
$5°27'$ within the Twins. In comparison with the point corresponding to Spica
and sighted with its position, Mars appeared to be $1\frac{3}{5}°$ within the Archer, and
at the same time appeared to be equally $1\frac{3}{5}°$ east of the moon's centre. The
moon's mean position was then about $4°20'$ within the Archer; and its true one
was $29°20'$ within the Scorpion, since in anomaly the moon was $92°$ from the
epicycle's apogee. And the apparent moon was at the beginning of the Archer
so that, consequently, Mars was then consistently, just as sighted, $1°36'$ within
the Archer—and, of course, $53°54'$ west of the perigee. From the time of the
third opposition to that of this observation there is contained $1°32'$ in longitude, and very nearly $1°21'$ in anomaly. And if we add these to the positions
already demonstrated for the third opposition, we shall have Mars, at the time
of this observation, in longitude $137°11'$ from the eccentric's apogee, and in
anomaly $172°46'$ from the epicycle's apogee.

With these things assumed, about centre D and diameter ADC let there be
the eccentric circle ABC bearing the epicycle's centre. And on the diameter let E be supposed the ecliptic's centre, and F the centre of the greater

---

[1] The star at K is, of course, at the apparent perigee. L and M are, respectively, the regular
perigee and regular apogee, but in planetary theory they are often referred to simply as the
perigee and apogee of the planet's epicycle.

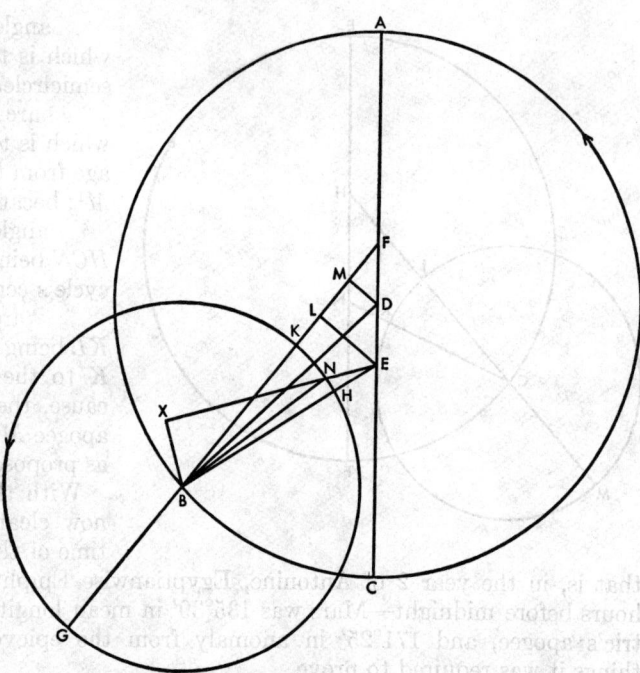

eccentricity. **And**
with epicycle *GHK*
described about *B*,
let *FKBG*, *EHB*,
and *DB* be drawn
through, and let *EL*
and *DM* be drawn
from points *D* and
E perpendicular to
FB. Let the star be
supposed at point
N on the epicycle;
and, with *EN* and
BN joined, let *BX*
be drawn from *B*
perpendicular to
EN produced.

Since, then, the
star is 137°11′ from
the eccentric's apo-
gee so that
angle *BFC* = 42°49′
= 85°38′ to 2 rt.,

therefore, on the circle about right triangle *DFM*,

$$\text{arc } DM = 85°38',$$

and, by subtraction from the semicircle,

$$\text{arc } FM = 94°22'.$$

And therefore

$$\text{chord } DM = 81^{p}34',$$
$$\text{chord } FM = 88^{p}1'$$

where

$$\text{hypt. } DF = 120^{p}.$$

And so also

$$DM = 4^{p}5',$$
$$FM = 4^{p}24'$$

where

$$\text{l. btw. c. } DF = 6^{p}$$

and

$$\text{ecc. rad. } BD = 60^{p}.$$

And since

$$\text{sq. } BD—\text{sq. } DM = \text{sq. } BM,$$

therefore

$$BM = 59^{p}52'.$$

And likewise, since

$$FM = LM$$

and

$$EL = 2\ DM,$$

therefore, by subtraction,

$$BL = 55^{\mathrm{p}}28',$$
$$EL = 8^{\mathrm{p}}10'.$$

And consequently

$$\text{hypt. } BE = 56^{\mathrm{p}}4'.$$

And therefore

$$EL = 17^{\mathrm{p}}28'$$

where

$$BE = 120^{\mathrm{p}};$$

and, on the circle about right triangle BEL,

$$\text{arc } EL = 16°44'.$$

And so also

$$\text{angle } EBF = 16°44' \text{ to 2 rt.}$$

Again, since it is supposed

$$\text{angle } CEX = 53°54',$$
$$= 107°48' \text{ to 2 rt.,}$$

the angle by which Mars appeared west of the perigee C, and since

$$\text{angle } BEC = 102°22' \text{ to 2 rt.}$$

(because

$$\text{angle } BEC = \text{angle } EBF + \text{angle } BFC,$$

it having been proved

$$\text{angle } EBF = 16°42' \text{ to 2 rt.}$$

and assumed

$$\text{angle } BFC = 85°38' \text{ to 2 rt.),}$$

therefore, by subtraction,

$$\text{angle } BEX = 5°26' \text{ to 2 rt.}$$

And, on the circle about right triangle BEX,

$$\text{arc } BX = 5^{\mathrm{p}}26'.$$

And consequently

$$\text{chord } BX = 5^{\mathrm{p}}41'$$

where

$$\text{hypt. } BE = 120^{\mathrm{p}}.$$

And therefore

$$BX = 2^{\mathrm{p}}39'$$

where it was proved

$$BE = 56^{\mathrm{p}}4'$$

and

$$\text{ecc. rad.} = 60^{\mathrm{p}}.$$

Likewise, since the point N was $172°46'$ from G the epicycle's apogee, and $7°14'$ from K the perigee, therefore

$$\text{angle } KBN = 7°14'$$
$$= 14°28' \text{ to 2 rt.}$$

And

$$\text{angle } HBK = 16°44' \text{ to 2 rt.;}$$

and therefore, by subtraction,
$$\text{angle } HBN = 2°16' \text{ to 2 rt.}$$

and, by addition,
$$\text{angle } BNX = 7°42' \text{ to 2 rt.}$$
And so also, on the circle about right triangle BNX,
$$\text{arc } BX = 7°42',$$

and
$$\text{chord } BX = 8^p3'$$

where
$$\text{hypt. } BN = 120^p.$$

And therefore
$$\text{epic. rad. } BN \doteq 39^p30'$$

where
$$BX = 2^p39'$$

and
$$\text{ecc. rad.} = 60^p.$$

Therefore, the ratio of the eccentric's radius to the epicycle's radius is 60ᵖ to 39ᵖ30'. Which it was required to find.

9. On the Correction of Mars' Periodic Movements

For the correction of the periodic mean movements we took one of the old observations according to which it is quite clear that in the year 13 according to Dionysius, Aigon 25 in the morning, Mars seemed to occult the Scorpion's northern forehead. Now, the date of this observation is the year 42 after the death of Alexander (that is, the year 476 of Nabonassar, Egyptianwise Athyr 20-21 in the morning) at which times we find the sun, in its mean passage, 23°54' within the Goat. According to us, the star of the Scorpion's northern forehead was observed to be 6⅓° within the Scorpion. And so, again, since the 409 years from the observation to the reign of Antonine makes very nearly a 4°5' change in the fixed stars and since then, at the time of the observation, this fixed star must have been 2¼° within the Scorpion, clearly Mars must have been in the same position. And likewise, since for us—that is, at the beginning of the reign of Antonine—Mars' apogee was 25°30' within the Crab, at the observation it must have been 21°25' within the Crab. And it is clear that the apparent star was then 100°50' from the apogee; the mean sun 182°29' from the same apogee, and of course 2°29' from the perigee.

With these things assumed, about centre D and diameter ADC let ABC be the eccentric circle bearing the epicycle's centre. On the diameter let E be supposed the ecliptic's centre; and F the centre of the greater eccentricity [of the equant]. With the epicycle GH described about centre B, let FBG and DB be drawn through, and let FK be drawn from F perpendicular to the straight line DB. Let the star be supposed at point H on the epicycle; and with BH joined, let EL be drawn from E parallel to it. Clearly, from what we have already proved, the sun's mean position will be seen along EL. And with EH joined, let DM and BN be drawn from D and B perpendicular to it; and again from D let DX be drawn perpendicular to BN, so that the figure $DMNX$ turns out to be a right parallelogram.

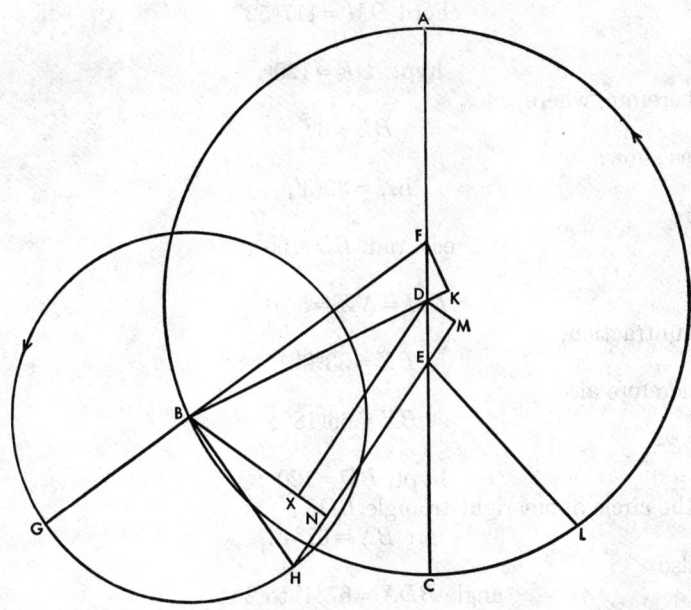

Since, then, being the angle of the star's apparent passage from the apogee,

angle $AEH = 100°50'$,

and, being the angle of the sun's mean passage,

angle $CEL = 2°29'$,

therefore

angle HEL = angle $BHE = 81°39'$
$= 163°18'$ to 2 rt.

And so also, on the circle about right triangle BHN,

arc $BN = 163°18'$,

and

chord $BN = 118^p43'$

where

hypt. $BH = 120^p$.

And therefore

$BN = 39^p3'$

where

epic. rad. $BH = 39^p30'$

and

1. btw. c. $DE = 6^p$.

Again, since

angle $AEH = 100°50'$
$= 201°40'$ to 2 rt.

and consequently, as its supplement,

angle $DEM = 158°20'$ to 2 rt.,

therefore, on the circle about right triangle DEM,

arc $DM = 158°20'$,

and $\qquad$ chord $DM = 117^\text{p}52'$
where

$$\text{hypt. } DE = 120^\text{p}.$$

And therefore, where

$$DE = 6^\text{p}$$

and it was shown

$$BN = 39^\text{p}3',$$

and where

$$\text{ecc. rad. } BD = 60^\text{p},$$

there

$$DM = NX = 5^\text{p}54'$$

and, by subtraction,

$$BX = 33^\text{p}9'.$$

And therefore also

$$BX = 66^\text{p}18'$$

where

$$\text{hypt. } BD = 120^\text{p};$$

and, on the circle about right triangle BDX,

$$\text{arc } BX = 67°4'.$$

And so also

$$\text{angle } BDX = 67°4' \text{ to 2 rt.,}$$

and, by addition,

$$\text{angle } BDM = 247°4' \text{ to 2 rt.}$$

And, because it was shown

$$\text{angle } DEM = 158°20' \text{ to 2 rt.,}$$

therefore

$$\text{angle } EDM = 21°40' \text{ to 2 rt.}$$

And therefore, by subtraction,

$$\text{angle } BDE = 225°24' \text{ to 2 rt.,}$$

and as its supplement

$$\text{angle } BDA = 134°36' \text{ to 2 rt.}$$

And so also, on the circle about right triangle DFK,

$$\text{arc } FK = 134°36'$$

and, by subtraction from the semicircle,

$$\text{arc } DK = 45°24'.$$

And therefore

$$\text{chord } FK = 110^\text{p}42',$$
$$\text{chord } DK = 46^\text{p}18'$$

where

$$\text{hypt. } DF = 120^\text{p}.$$

And therefore

$$FK = 5^\text{p}32',$$
$$DK = 2^\text{p}19'$$

and, by subtraction,

$$BK = 57^\text{p}41'$$

where

$$DF = 6^\text{p}$$

and

$$\text{ecc. rad. } DB = 60^\text{p}.$$

And consequently also

$$\text{hypt. } BF \stackrel{.}{=} 57^{\text{p}}57'.$$

And therefore

$$FK = 11^{\text{p}}28'$$

where

$$BF = 120^{\text{p}};$$

and, on the circle about right triangle BKF,

$$\text{arc } FK = 10°58'.$$

And so also

$$\text{angle } DBF = 10°58' \text{ to 2 rt.}$$

But also

$$\text{angle } ABD = 134°36' \text{ to 2 rt.};$$

and therefore, by addition,

$$\text{angle } AFB = 145°34' \text{ to 2 rt.}$$
$$= 72°47'.$$

Therefore, at the time of this observation, the star's mean longitudinal position—that is, the epicycle's centre B—was $72°47'$ from the apogee, and consequently $4°12'$ within the Balance. Since it is also supposed that

$$\text{angle } CEL = 2°29'$$

(which together with the semicircle of 2 right angles, ABC, is equal to the sum of AFB, the angle of mean longitude, and GBH, the angle of anomaly—that is, the star's movement on the epicycle), we shall have, by subtraction,

$$\text{angle } GBH = 109°42'.$$

Therefore, at the time of the observation, the star was in anomaly that very $109°42'$ from the epicycle's apogee. Which things it was required to find.

And we had already proved that the star, at the time of the third opposition, was in anomaly $171°25'$ from the epicycle's apogee. Therefore, in the time between the observations (embracing 410 Egyptian years and very nearly $231\frac{2}{3}$ days) it added on, over and above the 192 complete circles, $61°43'$. This is very nearly the surplus we find in the tables of the star's mean movements set up by us, since we established the daily movement from these numbers, dividing the sum of the circles and surplus reduced to degrees over the total number of days in the time between the two observations.

10. On the Epoch of its Periodic Movements

Again, since the time from the year 1 of Nabonassar, Egyptianwise Thoth 1 at noon, to this observation is 475 Egyptian years and very nearly $79 + \frac{1}{2} + \frac{1}{4}$ days, and since that amount of time embraces $180°40'$ surplus in longitude and $142°29'$ surplus in anomaly, if we subtract them from each of the corresponding positions at the observation—that is, from the $4°12'$ within the Balance in longitude and from the $109°42'$ in anomaly—we shall have the epoch of the periodic movements of Mars in the year 1 of Nabonassar, Egyptianwise Thoth 1 at noon: (1) in longitude, $3°32'$ within the Ram; (2) in anomaly, $327°13'$ from the epicycle's apogee. And consequently, since in 475 years there comes to be a $(\frac{1}{4} + \frac{1}{2} + \frac{1}{4})°$ shift in apogees, and since Mars' apogee at the observation was about $21°25'$ within the Crab, it will evidently be, at the time of the epoch, $16°40'$ within the Crab.

BOOK ELEVEN

1. Demonstration of Jupiter's Eccentricity

Now that Mars' periodic movements, anomalies, and epochs have been shown, we shall next work out Jupiter's also, and in the same way, taking first again, for the demonstration of the apogee and eccentricity, 3 acronychal oppositions relative to the sun's mean passage. We observed the first of these by the astrolabe in the year 17 of Hadrian, Egyptianwise Epiphi 1-2, 1 hour before midnight, about 23°11′ within the Scorpion. The second in the year 21, Phaophi 13-14, 2 hours before midnight, about 7°54′ within the Fishes. And the third in the year 1 of Antonine, Athyr 20-21, 5 hours after midnight, about 14°23′ within the Ram. Now, of the two intervals, that from the first acronychal opposition to the second embraces 3 Egyptian years, 106 days, and 23 hours, and 104°43′ of the star's apparent passage; and that from the second to the third, 1 Egyptian year, 37 days, and 7 hours, and similarly 36°29′. And the mean longitudinal passage comes to 99°55′ for the time of the first interval, and 33°26′ for that of the second. From these intervals, in consequence of the methods propounded by us in the case of Mars, we first construct the proof of the things we are required to find, again with the one eccentric circle, in this way:

Let there be the eccentric circle *ABC;* and let *A* be supposed the point where the epicycle's centre was at the first achronychal opposition, *B* at the second, and *C* at the third. Within the eccentric *ABC* let *D* be taken as the centre of the ecliptic; and let *AD, BD,* and *CD* be joined. And, with *CDE* produced, let *AE, BE,* and *AB* be joined. Let *EF* and *EG* be drawn from *E* perpendicular to *AD* and *BD;* and *AH* from *A* perpendicular to *EB.*

Since, then, the eccentric's arc *BC* is assumed to subtend 36°39′ of the ecliptic,

angle *EDG* = angle *BDC*
= 36°29′
= 72°58′ to 2 rt.,

angle *BDC* being at the centre. And so also, on the circle about right triangle *EDG,*

arc *EG* = 72°58′,

and

chord *EG* = 71ᵖ21′

where

hypt. *DE* = 120ᵖ.

Likewise, since

arc *BC* = 33°26′,

therefore, being an angle at the circumference,

angle *BEC* = 33°26′ to 2 rt.,

and, by subtraction,
$$\text{angle } EBG = 39°32'.$$
And so also, on the circle about right triangle BEG,
$$\text{arc } EG = 39°32',$$
and
$$\text{chord } EG = 40^{\text{p}}35'$$
where
$$\text{hypt. } BE = 120^{\text{p}}.$$
And therefore
$$BE = 210^{\text{p}}58'$$
where it was shown
$$EG = 71^{\text{p}}21'$$
and
$$DE = 120^{\text{p}}.$$

Again, since the eccentric's whole arc ABC is assumed to subtend on the ecliptic $141°12'$, the sum of both intervals; therefore, being at the ecliptic's centre,
$$\text{angle } ADC = 141°12'$$
$$= 282°24' \text{ to } 2 \text{ rt.}$$
and, being adjacent to it,
$$\text{angle } ADE = 77°36' \text{ to } 2 \text{ rt.}$$
And so also, on the circle about right triangle DEF,
$$\text{arc } EF = 77°36',$$
and
$$\text{chord } EF = 75^{\text{p}}12'$$
where
$$\text{hypt. } DE = 120^{\text{p}}.$$

Likewise, since the eccentric's arc ABC adds up to $133°21'$, therefore, being an angle at the circumference,
$$\text{angle } AEC = 133°21' \text{ to } 2 \text{ rt.}$$
But
$$\text{angle } ADE = 77°36' \text{ to } 2 \text{ rt.}$$
And therefore, by subtraction,
$$\text{angle } EAF = 149°3'.$$
And so, on the circle about right triangle AEF,
$$\text{arc } EF = 149°3',$$
and
$$\text{chord } EF = 115^{\text{p}}39'$$
where
$$\text{hypt. } AE = 120^{\text{p}}.$$
And therefore
$$AE = 78^{\text{p}}2'$$
where it was shown
$$EF = 75^{\text{p}}12'$$
and it is supposed
$$DE = 120^{\text{p}}.$$

Again, since the eccentric's arc AB is $99°55'$, therefore, being at the circumference,
$$\text{angle } AEB = 99°55'.$$

And so, on the circle about right triangle AEH,

$$\text{arc } AH = 99°55'$$

and as supplement

$$\text{arc } EH = 80°5'.$$

And therefore

$$\text{chord } AH = 91^{\text{p}}52',$$
$$\text{chord } EH = 77^{\text{p}}12'$$

where

$$\text{hypt. } AE = 120^{\text{p}}.$$

And so

$$AH = 59^{\text{p}}44'$$

and likewise

$$EH = 50^{\text{p}}12'$$

where it was shown

$$AE = 78^{\text{p}}2'$$

and

$$DE = 120^{\text{p}}.$$

It had already been shown

$$BE = 210^{\text{p}}58'.$$

And therefore, by subtraction,

$$BH = 160^{\text{p}}46'$$

where

$$AH = 59^{\text{p}}44'.$$

And

$$\text{sq. } BH = 25,845^{\text{p}}55'$$

and likewise

$$\text{sq. } AH = 3,568^{\text{p}}4',$$

which, added together, make

$$\text{sq. } AB = 29,413^{\text{p}}59';$$

in length, therefore,

$$AB = 171^{\text{p}}30'$$

where

$$DE = 120^{\text{p}},$$

and likewise

$$AE = 78^{\text{p}}2'.$$

And also

$$AB = 91^{\text{p}}52'$$

where

$$\text{ecc. diam.} = 120^{\text{p}};$$

for AB subtends an arc of $99°55'$. And therefore

$$DE = 64^{\text{p}}17',$$
$$AE = 41^{\text{p}}47'$$

where

$$AB = 91^{\text{p}}52'$$

and

$$\text{ecc. diam.} = 120^{\text{p}}.$$

And so also, AE being an arc on the eccentric,

$$\text{arc } AE = 40°45',$$

and, by addition,

$$\text{arc } EABC = 174°6'.$$

And therefore

$$\text{chord } EDC = 119^{\text{p}}50'$$

where
$$\text{ecc. diam.} = 120^p.$$

Since, then, segment $EABC$ is less than a semicircle, and therefore the eccentric's centre falls outside it, let it be supposed the point K. And let the diameter through both centres be drawn through it and D, and let KNX be drawn from K perpendicular to CE and produced.

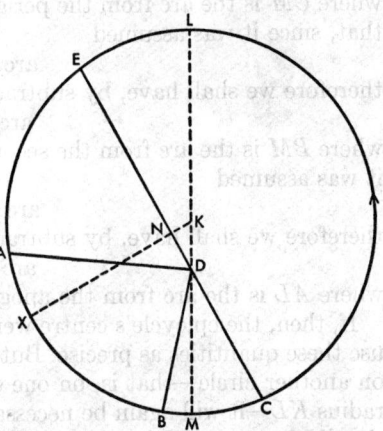

Since, then, it was shown
$$CE = 119^p50',$$
$$DE = 64^p17'$$
where
$$\text{diam. } LM = 120^p,$$
therefore, by subtraction, we shall have
$$CD = 55^p33'.$$
And so, since
$$\text{rect. } ED, DC = \text{rect. } LD, DM,$$
we shall have
$$\text{rect. } LD, DM = 3{,}570^p56'$$
where
$$\text{diam. } LM = 120^p.$$
But
$$\text{rect. } LD, DM + \text{sq. } DK = \text{sq. half diam.}$$
$$= \text{sq. } KL.$$
Therefore, if we subtract the rectangle LD, DM or $3{,}570^p56'$ from the square on half the diameter or $3{,}600^p$, we shall have left the square on DK as $29^p4'$. And therefore we shall have
$$\text{l. betw. c. } DK = 5^p23'$$
where
$$\text{ecc. rad. } KL = 60^p.$$

Again, since
$$\text{half } CE \text{ or } CN = 59^p55'$$
where
$$\text{diam. } LM = 120^p,$$
and it was shown also
$$CD = 55^p33',$$
therefore also, by subtraction,
$$DN = 4^p22'$$
where
$$DK = 5^p23'.$$
And so also
$$DN = 97^p20'$$
where
$$DK = 120^p;$$
and, on the circle about right triangle DKN,
$$\text{arc } DN = 108°24'.$$
And therefore
$$\text{angle } DKN = 108°24' \text{ to 2 rt.}$$
$$= 54°12'.$$
And since it is at the eccentric's centre, we shall have also
$$\text{arc } MX = 54°12'.$$

And also, by addition,

$$\text{arc } CMX = \text{half arc } CXE = 87°3'.$$

Therefore also, by subtraction,

$$\text{arc } CM = 32°51'$$

where CM is the arc from the perigee to the third opposition. And it is evident that, since it was assumed

$$\text{arc } BC = 33°26',$$

therefore we shall have, by subtraction

$$\text{arc } BM = 0°35'$$

where BM is the arc from the second opposition to the perigee; and that, since it was assumed

$$\text{arc } AB = 99°55',$$

therefore we shall have, by subtraction,

$$\text{arc } AL = 79°30'$$

where AL is the arc from the apogee to the first opposition.

If, then, the epicycle's centre were borne on this eccentric, it would suffice to use these quantities as precise. But since, according to the hypothesis, it moves on another circle—that is, on one drawn with a centre bisecting DK and with radius KL—it will again be necessary, as in the case of Mars, to calculate first the differences resulting for the apparent distances, and to show of what size they would be, considering the ratios of eccentricity very nearly the same as if the epicycle's centre were borne, not on another eccentric, but on the first also embracing the zodiacal anomaly; that is, on the one drawn about centre K.

Then let the circle LM about centre D be the eccentric bearing the epicycle's centre. And let the circle NX about centre F and equal to LM be the circle of its regular movement. With the diameter NLM through the centres joined, let E be taken on it as the ecliptic's centre. And first let the epicycle's centre be supposed at point A for the first opposition. Let DA, EA, FAX, and EX be joined; and let DG and EH be drawn from points D and E perpendicular to AF produced.

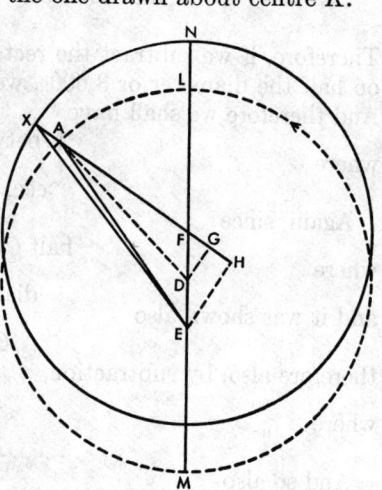

Since, then, angle NFX of the regular longitudinal movement was shown to be 79°30', therefore, being the angle vertical to it,

$$\text{angle } DFG = 79°30'$$
$$= 159° \text{ to 2 rt.}$$

And so also, on the circle about right triangle DFG,

$$\text{arc } DG = 159°$$

and, as its supplement,

$$\text{arc } FG = 21°.$$

And therefore

$$\text{chord } DG = 117^\text{p}59',$$
$$\text{chord } FG = 21^\text{p}52'$$

where

$$\text{hypt. } DF = 120^\text{p}.$$

And so also
$$DG = 2^{\text{p}}39'$$
and likewise
$$FG = 0^{\text{p}}30'$$
where
$$DF = \text{half } EF \doteqdot 2^{\text{p}}42'$$
and
$$\text{ecc. rad. } AD = 60^{\text{p}}.$$
And since
$$\text{sq. } AD — \text{sq. } DG = \text{sq. } AG,$$
therefore we shall have also
$$AG = 59^{\text{p}}56'.$$
And likewise, since
$$FG = GH$$
and
$$EH = 2\ DG,$$
therefore also, by addition,
$$AH = 60^{\text{p}}26'$$
where
$$EH = 5^{\text{p}}18',$$
and therefore
$$\text{hypt. } AE = 60^{\text{p}}40'.$$
And therefore
$$EH = 10^{\text{p}}29'$$
where
$$AE = 120^{\text{p}};$$
and, on the circle about right triangle AEH,
$$\text{arc } EH \doteqdot 10°1'.$$
And so also
$$\text{angle } EAH = 10°1' \text{ to 2 rt.}$$

Again, since
$$\text{rad. ecc. } FX = 60^{\text{p}},$$
$$FH = 1^{\text{p}}$$
and, by addition, clearly
$$HX = 61^{\text{p}}$$
where
$$EH = 5^{\text{p}}18',$$
therefore we shall have also
$$\text{hypt. } EX = 61^{\text{p}}14'.$$
And so also
$$EH = 10^{\text{p}}23'$$
where
$$EX = 120^{\text{p}};$$
and, on the circle about right triangle EHX,
$$\text{arc } EH = 9°55'.$$
And therefore
$$\text{angle } EXH = 9°55' \text{ to 2 rt.}$$
But it was shown
$$\text{angle } EAH = 10°1' \text{ to 2 rt.}$$
And therefore, by subtraction,
$$\text{angle } AEX = 0°6' \text{ to 2 rt.}$$
$$= 0°3',$$
which is the difference sought.

But the star, sighted along the straight line AE, appeared, at the first opposition, to be situated 23°11′ within the Scorpion. It is hence evident that, if the epicycle's centre were not borne on the eccentric LM but on NX, it would be at point X on it and the star would appear along straight line EX, differing by 3 sixtieths and being situated 23°14′ within the Scorpion.

Again, in a like figure, let also the drawing of the second opposition be laid down in a position a little west of the perigee.

Since the eccentric's arc NX was shown to be 35 sixtieths, therefore

$$\text{angle } NFX = 0°35'$$
$$= 1°10' \text{ to } 2 \text{ rt.}$$

And so also, on the circle about right triangle DFG,

$$\text{arc } DG = 1°10',$$

and, as its supplement,

$$\text{arc } FG = 178°50'.$$

And therefore

$$\text{chord } DG = 1^{\text{p}}13',$$
$$\text{chord } FG = 120^{\text{p}}$$

where

$$\text{hypt. } DF = 120^{\text{p}}.$$

And so also

$$DG = 0^{\text{p}}2'$$

and likewise

$$FG = 2^{\text{p}}42'$$

where

$$DF = 2^{\text{p}}42'$$

and

$$\text{ecc. rad. } BD = 60^{\text{p}}.$$

And likewise also, since it is indistinguishable from the hypotenuse BD,

$$BG = 60^{\text{p}}.$$

And again, since

$$GH = FG,$$

and

$$EH = 2 DG,$$

we shall also have, by subtraction,

$$BH = 57^{\text{p}}18'$$

where

$$EH = 0^{\text{p}}4',$$

and therefore also

$$\text{hypt. } BE = 57^{\text{p}}18'.$$

And so also

$$EH = 0^{\text{p}}8'$$

where

$$BE = 120^{\text{p}};$$

and, on the circle about right triangle BEH, again

$$\text{arc } EH = 0°8'.$$

And therefore
$$\text{angle } EBH = 0°8' \text{ to 2 rt.}$$
Likewise, since it was shown
$$FH = 5^{\text{p}}24'$$
where
$$\text{ecc. rad. } FX = 60^{\text{p}},$$
therefore, by subtraction, we shall also have
$$HX = 54^{\text{p}}36'$$
where
$$EH = 0^{\text{p}}4'$$
and therefore
$$\text{hypt. } EX = 54^{\text{p}}36'.$$

And therefore
$$EH \fallingdotseq 0^{\text{p}}10'$$
where
$$EX = 120^{\text{p}};$$
and, on the circle about right triangle EHX,
$$\text{arc } EH = 0°10'.$$
And so also
$$\text{angle } EXH = 0°10' \text{ to 2 rt.,}$$
and, by subtraction,
$$\text{angle } BEX = 0°2' \text{ to 2 rt.}$$
$$= 0°1'.$$

And now it is evident, therefore, that, since, at the second opposition, the star as it appeared along EB was situated 7°54' within the Fishes, if in turn it appeared along EX it would be only 7°53' within the Fishes.

And now let the drawing of the third opposition be laid out in a position east of the perigee. Since the eccentric's arc NX is assumed to be 32°51', therefore
$$\text{angle } NFX = 32°51'$$
$$= 65°42' \text{ to 2 rt.}$$
And so also, on the circle about right triangle DFG,
$$\text{arc } DG = 65°42',$$
and as its supplement
$$\text{arc } FG = 114°18'.$$
And therefore
$$\text{chord } DG = 65^{\text{p}}6',$$
$$\text{chord } FG = 100^{\text{p}}49'$$
where
$$\text{hypt. } DF = 120^{\text{p}}.$$

And so also
$$DG = 1^{\text{p}}28'$$
and likewise
$$FG = 2^{\text{p}}16'$$

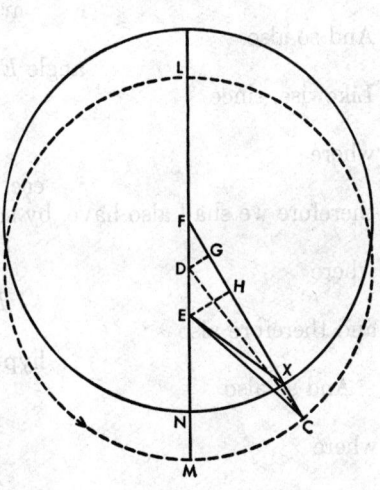

where
$$DF = 2^p42'$$
and
$$\text{ecc. rad. } CD = 60^p.$$
And since
$$\text{sq. } CD - \text{sq. } DG = \text{sq. } CG,$$
we shall also have
$$CG = 59^p59'.$$
And likewise, since
$$GH = FG$$
and
$$EH = 2\,DG,$$
we shall also have, by subtraction,
$$CH = 57^p43'$$
where
$$EH = 2^p56',$$
and therefore also
$$\text{hypt. } CE = 57^p47'.$$
And therefore
$$EH = 6^p5'$$
where
$$CE = 120^p;$$
and, on the circle about right triangle CEH,
$$\text{arc } EH = 5°48'.$$
And so also
$$\text{angle } ECH = 5°48' \text{ to 2 rt.}$$
Likewise, since
$$FH = 4^p32'$$
where
$$\text{ecc. rad. } FX = 60^p,$$
therefore we shall also have, by subtraction,
$$HX = 55^p28',$$
where
$$EH = 2^p56';$$
and therefore also
$$\text{hypt. } EX = 55^p33'.$$
And so also
$$EH = 6^p20'$$
where
$$EX = 120^p,$$
and, on the circle about right triangle EHX,
$$\text{arc } EH = 6°2'.$$
And therefore
$$\text{angle } EXH = 6°2' \text{ to 2 rt.,}$$
and, by subtraction,
$$\text{angle } CEX = 0°14' \text{ to 2 rt.}$$
$$= 0°7'.$$

And so, since at the third opposition the star sighted along EC was situated $14°23'$ within the Ram, it is evident that, if it were along the straight line EX, it would be situated 14°30′ within the Ram. And it was shown that at the first opposition it was 23°14′ within the Scorpion, and at the second 7°53′ within the Fishes. Therefore, if the star's apparent intervals were considered—not with respect to the eccentric bearing the epicycle's centre, but with respect to that embracing its regular movement—they would come to 104°39′ from the first opposition to the second, and to 36°37′ from the second to the third. Following these with the theorem already shown, we find the intervals between the centres of the ecliptic and of the eccentric embracing the epicycle's regular movement to be very nearly 5ᵖ30′ where the eccentric's diameter is 120ᵖ. Of the eccentric's arcs, we find that from the apogee to the first opposition to be 77°15′, that from the second opposition to the perigee to be 2°50′, and that from the perigee to the third opposition to be 30°36′.

That these quantities have been here taken accurately because the differences of the intervals are very nearly the same as the first and are calculated through them—all this is evident from the fact that the star's apparent intervals are found, by means of the discovered ratios, to be the same as the observed ones, as will be clear to us from what follows.

For again let the drawing of the first opposition be set out having only the eccentric bearing the epicycle's centre.

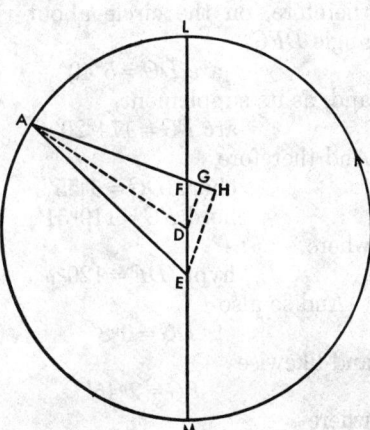

Since it was shown
$$\text{angle } LFA = 77°15′$$
$$= 154°30′ \text{ to 2 rt.},$$
and, being vertical to it,
$$\text{angle } DFG = 154°30′ \text{ to 2 rt.},$$
therefore, on the circle about right triangle DFG,
$$\text{arc } DG = 154°30′,$$
and, as its supplement,
$$\text{arc } FG = 25°30′.$$
And therefore
$$\text{chord } DG = 117ᵖ2′$$
$$\text{chord } FG = 26ᵖ29′$$
where
$$\text{hypt. } DF = 120ᵖ.$$
And so also
$$DG = 2ᵖ41′$$
and likewise
$$FG = 0ᵖ36′$$
where
$$DF = 2ᵖ45′$$
and
$$\text{ecc. rad. } AD = 60ᵖ.$$
And, for the same reasons as shown before,
$$AG = 59ᵖ56′,$$
and
$$AH = 60ᵖ32′$$
where
$$EH = 2\,DG = 5ᵖ22′;$$

and so it is calculated
$$AE = 60^\mathrm{p}46'.$$
And therefore
$$EH = 10^\mathrm{p}36'$$
where
$$AE = 120^\mathrm{p};$$
and, on the circle about right triangle AEH,
$$\text{arc } EH = 10°8'.$$
And therefore
$$\text{angle } EAH = 10°8' \text{ to 2 rt.}$$
and, by subtraction,
$$\text{angle } LEA = 144°22' \text{ to 2 rt.}$$
$$= 72°11'.$$
Therefore, by just so many degrees was the star distant from the ecliptic's apogee at the first opposition.

Again, let the drawing of the second opposition be set out. Since it is assumed
$$\text{angle } BFM = 2°50'$$
$$= 5°40' \text{ to 2 rt.,}$$
therefore, on the circle about right triangle DFG,
$$\text{arc } DG = 5°40'$$
and, as its supplement,
$$\text{arc } FG = 174°20'.$$
And therefore
$$\text{chord } DG = 5^\mathrm{p}55'$$
$$\text{chord } FG = 119^\mathrm{p}51'$$
where
$$\text{hypt. } DF = 120^\mathrm{p}.$$
And so also
$$DG = 0^\mathrm{p}8'$$
and likewise
$$FG = 2^\mathrm{p}45'$$
where
$$DF = 2^\mathrm{p}45'$$
and
$$\text{ecc. rad. } BD = 60^\mathrm{p}.$$ 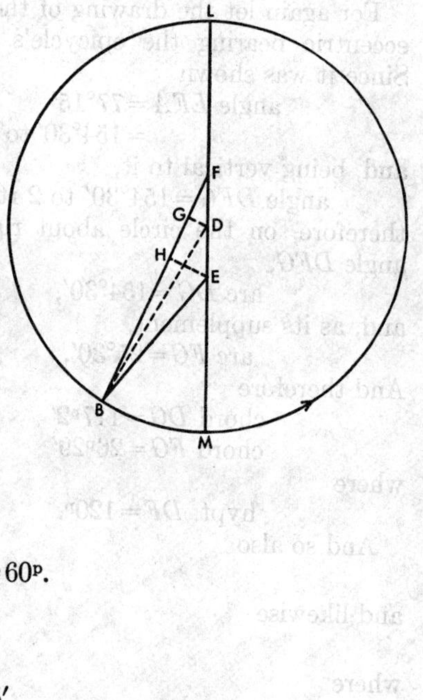
And for the same reasons also
$$BG = 60^\mathrm{p},$$
and, by subtraction,
$$BH = 57^\mathrm{p}15'$$
where
$$EH = 0^\mathrm{p}16'.$$
And so also it is calculated
$$\text{hypt. } BE = 57^\mathrm{p}15'.$$
And therefore
$$EH = 0^\mathrm{p}33'$$
where
$$BE = 120^\mathrm{p};$$
and, on the circle about right triangle EBH,

arc $EH = 0°32'$.

And so also

angle $EBH = 0°32'$ to 2 rt.

and, by addition,

angle $BEM = 6°12'$ to 2 rt.
$$= 3°6'.$$

Therefore the star at the second opposition was also 3°6' west of the perigee. But it was also shown to be 72°11' east of the apogee at the first. Therefore the apparent distance from the first opposition to the second is calculated to be the 104°43' of the remainder of the semicircle, in accord with the distance gotten from the observations.

Then also let the drawing of the third opposition be set out. Since it was shown

angle $MFC = 30°36'$
$$= 61°12' \text{ to 2 rt.},$$

therefore, on the circle about right triangle DFG

arc $DG = 61°12'$,

and, as its supplement,

arc $FG = 118°48'$.

And therefore

chord $DG = 61^p6'$,
chord $FG = 103^p17'$

where

hypt. $DF = 120^p$.

And so also

$$DG = 1^p24'$$

and likewise

$$FG = 2^p22'$$

where

$$DF = 2^p45'$$

and

ecc. rad. $CD = 60^p$.

And for the same reasons also

$$CG = 59^p59'$$

and, by subtraction,

$$CH = 57^p37'$$

where it is calculated

$$EH = 2^p48'$$

And so also

hypt. $CE = 57^p41'$.

And therefore

$$EH = 5^p50'$$

where

$$CE = 120^p;$$

and, on the circle about right triangle CEH,

arc $EH = 5°34'$.

And so also

angle $ECH = 5°34'$ to 2 rt.,

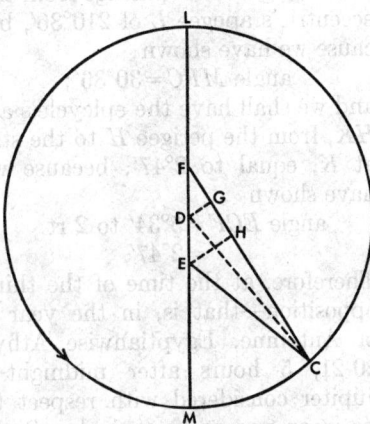

and, by addition,

$$\text{angle } MEC = 66°46' \text{ to } 2 \text{ rt.}$$
$$= 33°23'.$$

By just as many degrees was the star east of the perigee, therefore, at the third opposition. And it was shown to be 3°6′ west of the same perigee at the second. Consequently, the apparent distance from the second to the third comes to the same result of 36°29′, again in accord with things observed.

It is immediately clear that since, at the third opposition, the star was situated by observation 14°23′ within the Ram (at a distance, as was shown, of 33°23′ east of the perigee), the perigee of the eccentricity at that time was 11° within the Fishes, and the apogee exactly opposite 11° within the Virgin.

If we draw the epicycle GHK about centre C, we shall have immediately the mean longitudinal passage from the eccentric's apogee L of 210°36′, because we have shown

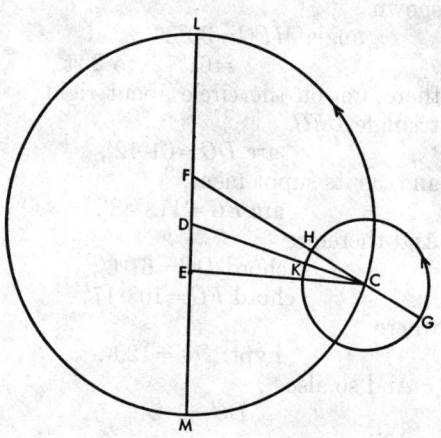

$$\text{angle } MFC = 30°36';$$

and we shall have the epicycle's arc HK, from the perigee H to the star at K, equal to 2°47′, because we have shown

$$\text{angle } ECF = 5°34' \text{ to } 2 \text{ rt.}$$
$$= 2°47'.$$

Therefore, at the time of the third opposition—that is, in the year 1 of Antonine, Egyptianwise Athyr 20-21, 5 hours after midnight— Jupiter considered with respect to its mean passages was in longitude 210°36′ from the eccentric's apogee (that is, it was situated 11°36′ within the Ram) and in anomaly 182°47′ from G, the epicycle's apogee.

2. Demonstration of the Size of Jupiter's Epicycle

Again in what follows for the demonstration of the epicycle's size we took the observation we sighted in the year 2 of Antonine, Egyptianwise Mesore 26-27 before the rising of the sun—that is, very nearly 5 equatorial hours after midnight, when the sun's mean passage was 16°11′ within the Crab and the second degree of the Ram was culminating in the astrolabe. At that time, Jupiter, sighted relative to the bright star in the Hyades [Aldebaran], appeared to be 15¾° within the Twins, and it appeared at the same longitude as the centre of the moon which was more to the south. But at that hour, by calculations already set forth, we find the moon's mean position to be 9° within the Twins, and in anomaly we find it to be 272°5′ from the epicycle's apogee; and therefore its true passage to be about 14°50′ within the Twins, and its apparent passage in Alexandria to be about 15°45′. Therefore Jupiter was in this way situated 15¾° within the Twins.

Again, since the time from the third opposition to the given observation is 1 Egyptian year and 276 days, and since that amount of time embraces 53°17′ in longitude and 218°31′ in anomaly (for there will be no sensible difference even if this amount is taken more or less roughly), if we add these to the demonstrated positions at the third opposition we shall have at the time of the observation very nearly 263°53′ in longitude from the same apogee and 41°18′ in anomaly from the epicycle's apogee.

Then, with these things supposed, let there be laid out again the drawing of a proof similar to that of Mars, hav-
ing the epicycle's position east of the eccentric's perigee and the star's just after the epicycle's apogee in accord with the mean passages in longitude and anomaly here laid out.

Since, then, the mean passage in longitude from the eccentric's apogee is 263°53′, therefore

angle $BFC = 83°53′$
$= 167°46′$ to 2 rt.

And so also, on the circle about right triangle DFM,

arc $DM = 167°46′$

and, as its supplement,

arc $FM = 12°14′$.

And therefore

chord $DM = 119^p19′$,
chord $FM = 12^p47′$

where

hypt. $DF = 120^p$.

And so also

$DM \doteqdot 2^p44′$,

and likewise

$FM = 0^p18′$

where

$DF = 2^p45′$

and

ecc. rad. $BD = 60^p$.

And since

sq. BD—sq. $DM =$ sq. BM,

therefore

$BM = 59^p56′$.

And likewise, since

$FM = LM$

and

$EL = 2\ DM$,

therefore, by subtraction,

$BL = 59^p38′$

where it is calculated

$EL = 5^p28′$,

and therefore

hypt. $BE = 59^p52′$.

And therefore

$EL \doteqdot 10^p58′$

where
$$BE = 120^p;$$
and, on the circle about right triangle BEL,
$$\text{arc } EL = 10°30'.$$
And so also
$$\text{angle } EBF = 10°30' \text{ to 2 rt.}$$
But
$$\text{angle } BFC = 167°46' \text{ to 2 rt.}$$
And therefore, by addition,
$$\text{angle } BEC = 178°16' \text{ to 2 rt.}$$
Again since the perigee is very nearly 11° within the Fishes and the star appeared along EK 15°45' within the Twins, therefore
$$\text{angle } KEC = 94°45'$$
$$= 189°30' \text{ to 2 rt.,}$$
and, by subtraction,
$$\text{angle } BEK = 11°14' \text{ to 2 rt.}$$
And so also, on the circle about right triangle BEN,
$$\text{arc } BN = 11°14',$$
and
$$\text{chord } BN = 11^p44'$$
where
$$\text{hypt. } BE = 120^p.$$
And therefore
$$BN = 5^p50'$$
where
$$BE = 59^p52'$$
and
$$\text{ecc. rad.} = 60^p.$$
And likewise, since
$$\text{arc } GK = 41°18',$$
therefore
$$\text{angle } GBK = 41°18'$$
$$= 82°36' \text{ to 2 rt.}$$
But
$$\text{angle } GBH = \text{angle } EBF$$
$$= 10°30' \text{ to 2 rt.}$$
And therefore, by subtraction,
$$\text{angle } HBK = 72°6' \text{ to 2 rt.}$$
But it was shown also
$$\text{angle } HEK = 11°14' \text{ to 2 rt.,}$$
and therefore, by subtraction,
$$\text{angle } BKN = 60°52' \text{ to 2 rt.}$$
And so also, on the circle about right triangle BKN,
$$\text{arc } BN = 60°52',$$
and
$$\text{chord } BN = 60^p47'$$
where
$$\text{hypt. } BK = 120^p.$$

And therefore

$$\text{epic. rad. } BK \doteq 11^{\text{p}}30'$$

where

$$BN = 5^{\text{p}}50'$$

and

$$\text{ecc. rad.} = 60^{\text{p}}$$

Which it was required to find.

3. On the Correction of Jupiter's Periodic Movements

Next, for the periodic movements, we again took one of the ancient observations very faithfully recorded, according to which it is quite clear that in the year 45 of Dionysius, Parthenon 10, Jupiter at sunrise occulted the Southern Ass. Now, this time is the year 83 after Alexander's death, Egyptianwise Epiphi 17-18 in the morning, at which time we find the sun's mean passage 9°56' within the Virgin. But the star called the Southern Ass of those about the nebula of the Crab was at the time of our observation 11⅓° within the Crab, but clearly at that observation 7°33', since 3°47' correspond to the 378 years between the observations. And therefore Jupiter at that time (since it occulted the star) was 7°33' within the Crab. Likewise also, since the apogee according to us was about 11° within the Virgin, at the observation it must have been 7°13' within the Virgin. It is clear that the apparent star was 300°20' from the eccentric's apogee at that time, and the mean sun was 2°43' from the same apogee.

Now, with these things supposed, again let the drawing of the similar proof

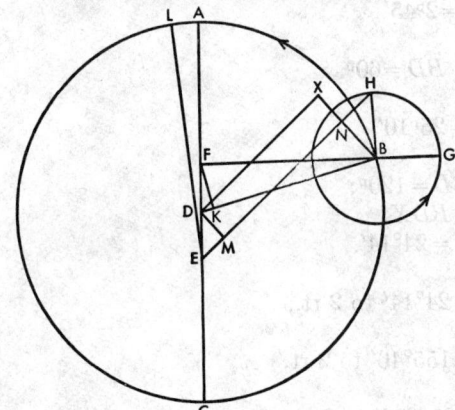

for Mars be laid out, only here according to the passages given at the observation, having the epicycle's position at B before the apogee A and that of the sun's mean situation at L a little after the same apogee. And therefore it also has the position of the star at H after the epicycle's apogee G. Likewise let FBG, DB, BH, and EH still be joined; and let FK be drawn perpendicular to DB, DM and BN to EH, and here DX to NB produced to make the rectangular parallelogram $DMNX$.

Now since, containing as it does the remainder of 300°20' from the one circle of the ecliptic,

$$\text{angle } AEH = 59°40'$$

and

$$\text{angle } AEL = 2°43',$$

therefore, by addition,

$$\text{angle } LEH \text{ or angle } BHE = 62°23'$$
$$= 124°46' \text{ to } \mathbf{2 \text{ rt.}}$$

And so also, on the circle about right triangle BHN,

$$\text{arc } BN = 124°46',$$

and

$$\text{chord } BN = 106^{\text{p}}20'$$

where

$$\text{hypt. } BH = 120^{\text{p}}.$$

And therefore

$$BN = 10^{\text{p}}12'$$

where

$$\text{epic. rad.} = 11^{\text{p}}30'.$$

Again, since it is assumed

$$\text{angle } DEM = 59°40'$$
$$= 119°20' \text{ to 2 rt.}$$

and, by subtraction,

$$\text{angle } MDE = 60°40' \text{ to 2 rt.,}$$

therefore also, on the circle about right triangle DEM,

$$\text{arc } DM = 119°20',$$

and

$$\text{chord } DM = 103^{\text{p}}34'$$

where

$$\text{hypt. } DE = 120^{\text{p}}.$$

And therefore

$$DM = 2^{\text{p}}23'$$

and, by addition,

$$BNX = 12^{\text{p}}35'$$

where

$$DE = 2^{\text{p}}45'$$

and

$$\text{ecc. rad. } BD = 60^{\text{p}}.$$

And so also

$$BX = 25^{\text{p}}10'$$

where

$$\text{hypt. } BD = 120^{\text{p}};$$

and, on the circle about right triangle BDX,

$$\text{arc } BX = 24°14'.$$

And therefore

$$\text{angle } BDX = 24°14' \text{ to 2 rt.,}$$

and, as its complement,

$$\text{angle } BDM = 155°46' \text{ to 2 rt.}$$

and likewise, by addition,

$$\text{angle } BDE = 216°26' \text{ to 2 rt.}$$

and again, as its supplement,

$$\text{angle } BDF = 143°34' \text{ to 2 rt.}$$

And so also, on the circle about right triangle FDK,

$$\text{arc } FK = 143°34',$$

and, as its supplement,

$$\text{arc } DK = 36°26'.$$

And therefore also

$$\text{chord } FK = 113^{\text{p}}59',$$
$$\text{chord } DK = 37^{\text{p}}31'$$

where
$$\text{hypt. } DF = 120^p.$$

And therefore
$$FK = 2^p37'$$

and likewise
$$DK = 0^p52'$$

and, by subtraction,
$$BK = 59^p8'$$

where
$$DF = 2^p45'$$

and
$$\text{ecc. rad. } BD = 60^p.$$

And therefore also
$$\text{hypt. } BF = 59^p12'.$$

And so also
$$FK = 5^p18'$$

where
$$BF = 120^p;$$
and, on the circle about right triangle BFK,
$$\text{arc } FK = 5°4'.$$

And therefore
$$\text{angle } FBD = 5°4' \text{ to 2 rt.}$$
and by addition, embracing the regular longitude,
$$\text{angle } AFB = 148°38' \text{ to 2 rt.}$$
$$= 74°19'.$$

And since also angle GBH combined with angle BFC and the semicircle (that is, less angle AFB here) gives
$$\text{angle } AEL = 2°43',$$
therefore we shall also have angle GBH, which contains the star's passage from the epicycle's apogee, equal to 77°2′. We have hence shown that, at the time of the given observation, Jupiter considered according to its mean passage was in longitude 285°41′ from the eccentric's apogee or in mean position 22°54′ within the Twins, and in anomaly 77°2′ from the epicycle's apogee.

But we had also proved that, at the time of the third opposition, it was 182°47′ from the epicycle's apogee. Therefore, in the time between the two observations (embracing 377 Egyptian years and 128 days less very nearly 1 hour) it added on, with 345 complete circles, 105°45′ in anomaly. The surplus of degrees in anomaly from the mean movements worked out by us comes to very nearly this amount, because we established the daily movement from these, dividing the total number of degrees from the circle and surplus by the total number of days of that time.

4. On the Epoch of Jupiter's Periodic Movements

Now here again, since the time from the year 1 of Nabonassar, Egyptianwise Thoth 1 at midday, to the given ancient eclipse is 506 Egyptian years and very nearly 316¾ days, and since that amount of time embraces surpluses of 258°13′ in longitude and 290°58′ in anomaly, therefore, if we subtract these from the proper given positions at the observation, we shall have, at the time of the epoch the same as for the others, Jupiter's mean longitudinal position

4°41′ within the Balance, and its anomalistic position 146°41′ from the epicycle's apogee. Also for the same reasons the apogee of its eccentricity will be 2°9′ within the Virgin.

5. Demonstration of Saturn's Eccentricity and Apogee

And now that it was left at this place to demonstrate the anomalies of Saturn and its positions, first for the examination of its apogee and eccentricity, we again, as for the others, took the acronychal oppositions relative to the sun's mean passage. The first of these we observed with the astrolabe in the year 11 of Hadrian, Egyptianwise, Pachons 7-8 in the evening, 1°13′ within the Balance; and the second in the year 17 of Hadrian likewise, Egyptianwise Epiphi 18; and we calculated the time and place of the true opposition, by observations on it, to be 4 hours after noon of the 18th, 9°40′ within the Archer. Observing the third opposition in the year 20 of Hadrian again, Egyptianwise Mesore 24, we likewise calculated the time of the true opposition to have been at the very noon of the 24th, and its place to have been 14°14′ within the Goat.

Now, of the two intervals, the one from the first opposition to the second embraces 6 Egyptian years, 70 days, and 22 hours, and 68°27′ of the star's apparent passage; and that from the second to the third, 3 Egyptian years, 35 days, and 20 hours, and likewise 34°34′. And 75°43′ of mean longitudinal passage are calculated in the rougher way[1] for the first interval, and 37°52′ for the second. With these intervals supposed, we again show what is required by the same theorem that is first on one eccentric in this way.

For, not to repeat, let there be laid out the drawing similar to those of the same proof. And since the eccentric's arc BC is assumed to subtend 34°34′ of the ecliptic, therefore, being at the ecliptic's centre

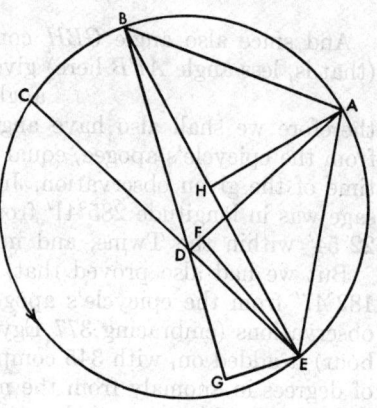

$$\text{angle } EDG = \text{angle } BDC$$
$$= 34°34′$$
$$= 69°8′ \text{ to 2 rt.}$$

And so also, on the circle about right triangle DEG,

$$\text{arc } EG = 69°8′;$$

and

$$\text{chord } EG = 68^\text{p}5′$$

where

$$\text{hypt. } DE = 120^\text{p}.$$

Likewise, since

$$\text{arc } BC = 37°52′,$$

therefore, being at the circumference,

$$\text{angle } BEC = 37°52′ \text{ to 2 rt.}$$

and, by subtraction,

$$\text{angle } EBG = 31°16′ \text{ to 2 rt.}$$

And so also, on the circle about right triangle EBG,

$$\text{arc } EG = 31°16′,$$

and

$$\text{chord } EG = 32^\text{p}20′$$

[1] That is, without correction. For such a small angular distance it would make no difference.

where
$$\text{hypt. } BE = 120^\text{p}.$$
And therefore
$$BE = 252^\text{p}41'$$
where it was shown
$$EG = 68^\text{p}5'$$
and
$$DE = 120^\text{p}.$$

Again, since the whole arc ABC subtends on the ecliptic the 103°1′ all told of both distances, therefore, being at the ecliptic's centre,
$$\text{angle } ADC = 103°1'.$$
And for this reason also, as adjacent to it,
$$\text{angle } ADE = 76°59'$$
$$= 153°58' \text{ to 2 rt.}$$
And so also, on the circle about right triangle DEF,
$$\text{arc } EF = 153°58'$$
and
$$\text{chord } EF = 116^\text{p}55'$$
where
$$\text{hypt. } DE = 120^\text{p}.$$
And likewise, since the eccentric's arc ABC totals 113°35′, therefore, being at the circumference,
$$\text{angle } AEC = 113°35' \text{ to 2 rt.}$$
But
$$\text{angle } ADE = 153°58' \text{ to 2 rt.}$$
And therefore, by subtraction,
$$\text{angle } FAE = 92°27' \text{ to 2 rt.}$$
And so also, on the circle about right triangle AEF,
$$\text{arc } EF = 92°27',$$
and
$$\text{chord } EF = 86^\text{p}39'$$
where
$$\text{hypt. } AE = 120^\text{p}.$$
And therefore
$$AE = 161^\text{p}55'$$
where it was shown
$$EF = 116^\text{p}55'$$
and
$$DE = 120^\text{p}.$$

Again, since the eccentric's arc AB is 75°43′, therefore also, being at the circumference,
$$\text{angle } AEB = 75°43' \text{ to 2 rt.}$$
And so also, on the circle about right triangle AEH,
$$\text{arc } AH = 75°43'$$
and as its supplement
$$\text{arc } EH = 104°17'.$$
And therefore
$$\text{chord } AH = 73^\text{p}39',$$
$$\text{chord } EH = 94^\text{p}45'$$

where

$$\text{hypt. } AE = 120^p.$$

And so also

$$AH = 99^p43'$$

and likewise

$$EH = 127^p51'$$

where it was shown

$$AE = 161^p55'$$

and

$$DE = 120^p.$$

And it has been shown

$$BE = 252^p41';$$

and therefore, by subtraction,

$$BH = 124^p50'$$

where

$$AH = 99^p43'.$$

And

$$\text{sq. } BH = 15,583^p22'$$

and likewise

$$\text{sq. } AH = 9,877^p3',$$

which, added together, make

$$\text{sq. } AB = 25,460^p25'.$$

Therefore, in length,

$$AB = 159^p34'$$

where

$$DE = 120^p$$

and likewise

$$AE = 161^p55'.$$

But also

$$AB = 73^p39'$$

where

$$\text{ecc. diam.} = 120^p,$$

for AB subtends an arc of $75°43'$. And therefore

$$DE = 55^p23'$$

and

$$AE = 74^p43'$$

where

$$AB = 73^p39'$$

and

$$\text{ecc. diam.} = 120^p.$$

And so also

$$\text{ecc. arc } AE = 77°1'$$

and, by addition,

$$\text{arc } EABC = 190°36',$$

and clearly, by subtraction,

$$\text{arc } CE = 169°24'.$$

And for this reason also

$$\text{chord } CDE = 119^p28'$$

where
$$\text{ecc. diam.} = 120^\text{p}.$$

Then let the eccentric's centre be taken within the segment EAC since it is greater than a semicircle, and let it be K. Through it and D let the eccentric's diameter through both centres $LKDM$ be drawn. And let KNX be drawn perpendicular to CE and produced.

Since, then, it was shown
$$CE = 119^\text{p}28'$$
and
$$DE = 55^\text{p}23'$$
where
$$\text{diam. } LM = 120^\text{p},$$
therefore we shall also have, by subtraction,
$$CD = 64^\text{p}5'.$$
And so, since
$$\text{rect. } ED, DC = \text{rect. } LD, DM,$$
we shall also have
$$\text{rect. } LD, DM = 3,549^\text{p}9'$$
where
$$\text{diam. } LM = 120^\text{p}.$$
But also
$$\text{rect. } LD, DM + \text{sq. } DK = \text{sq. half diam.}$$
$$= \text{sq. } LK.$$
If, therefore, we subtract $3,549^\text{p}9'$ from the square on half the diameter or $3,600^\text{p}$, we shall have left the square on DK as $50^\text{p}51'$. And therefore we shall have, in length,
$$\text{l. betw. c. } DK = 7^\text{p}8'$$
where
$$\text{ecc. diam.} = 120^\text{p}.$$

Again, since
$$\text{half } CE \text{ or } EN = 59^\text{p}44'$$
where
$$\text{diam. } LM = 120^\text{p}$$
and it was shown also
$$DE = 55^\text{p}23',$$
therefore we shall also have, by subtraction,
$$DN = 4^\text{p}21'$$
where
$$DK = 7^\text{p}8'.$$

And so also
$$DN = 73^\text{p}11'$$
where
$$\text{hypt. } DK = 120^\text{p};$$
and, on the circle about right triangle DKN,
$$\text{arc } DN = 75°10'.$$

And therefore

$$\text{angle } DKN = 75°10' \text{ to 2 rt.}$$
$$= 37°35'.$$

And since it is at the eccentric's centre, we shall also have

$$\text{arc } MX = 37°35'.$$

And

$$\text{arc } CX = \text{half arc } CXE = 84°42'.$$

And therefore, by subtraction,

$$\text{arc } CL = 57°43'$$

where CL is the arc from the apogee to the third opposition. But also it is assumed

$$\text{arc } BC = 37°52';$$

And therefore, by subtraction,

$$\text{arc } BL = 19°51'$$

where BL is the arc from the apogee to the second opposition. And likewise, since it is assumed

$$\text{arc } AB = 75°43',$$

therefore we shall also have

$$\text{arc } AL = 55°52'$$

where AL is the arc from the first opposition to the apogee.

Now, since again the epicycle's centre is not borne on this eccentric, but on the eccentric drawn with a centre bisecting DK and with radius KL, we calculated accordingly, as for the others, the resulting differences of the apparent distances on the ecliptic, considering the ratios very nearly the same if one should change the epicycle's passage to the eccentric effecting the zodiacal anomaly.

For let the drawing of the first opposition for the similar proof be laid out in a position west of the apogee L. Since, then, angle NFX of the regular longitudinal passage, (that is, angle DFG) was shown to be $55°52'$ or $111°42'$ to 2 right angles' $360°$, therefore, on the circle about right triangle DFG,

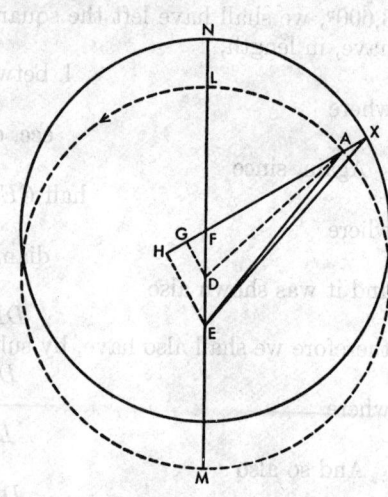

$$\text{arc } DG = 111°42'$$

and, as its supplement,

$$\text{arc } FG = 68°16'.$$

And therefore

$$\text{chord } DG = 99^p20',$$
$$\text{chord } FG = 67^p20'$$

where

$$\text{hypt. } DF = 120^p.$$

And so also

$$DG = 2^p57'$$

and likewise

$$FG = 2^p$$

where

$$\text{l. betw. c. } DF = 3^p34'$$

and

$$\text{ecc. rad. } AD = 60^p.$$

And since
$$\text{sq. } AD - \text{sq. } DG = \text{sq. } AG,$$
we shall have
$$AG = 59^{\text{p}}56'.$$
And likewise, since
$$FG = GH$$
and
$$EH = 2\, DG,$$
therefore, by addition,
$$AH = 61^{\text{p}}56'$$
where
$$EH = 5^{\text{p}}54'.$$
And for this reason also
$$\text{hypt. } AE = 62^{\text{p}}13'.$$
And so also
$$EH = 11^{\text{p}}21'$$
where
$$\text{hypt. } AE = 120^{\text{p}};$$
and, on the circle about right triangle AEH,
$$\text{arc } EH \doteq 10°51'.$$
And therefore
$$\text{angle } EAH = 10°51' \text{ to 2 rt.}$$
Again, since
$$\text{ecc. rad. } FX = 60^{\text{p}},$$
$$FH = 4^{\text{p}}$$
and, by addition, clearly
$$HX = 64^{\text{p}}$$
where
$$EH = 5^{\text{p}}54';$$
therefore we shall also have
$$\text{hypt. } EX = 64^{\text{p}}16'.$$
And therefore
$$EH = 11^{\text{p}}2'$$
where
$$\text{hypt. } EX = 120^{\text{p}};$$
and, on the circle about right triangle EHX,
$$\text{arc } EH = 10°33'.$$
And so also
$$\text{angle } EXH = 10°33' \text{ to 2 rt.}$$
But it was also shown
$$\text{angle } EAH = 10°51' \text{ to 2 rt.};$$
and therefore, by subtraction,
$$\text{angle } AEX = 0°18' \text{ to 2 rt.}$$
$$= 0°9'$$
which is the difference sought.

But at the first opposition the star appeared along straight line AE, situated 1°13' within the Balance. Now, it is clear that, if the epicycle's centre were not borne on the epicycle AL but on NX, it would be at point X on it, and the star would appear along straight line EX, 9 sixtieths west of the position at A, and it would be situated 1°4′ within the Balance.

Again, for the same proof, let the drawing of the second opposition be laid out east of the apogee.

Since the eccentric's arc NX was shown to be 19°51′, therefore angle NFX and angle DFG, vertical to it, would each equal 19°51′, or 39°42′ to 2 right angles' 360°. And so also, on the circle about right triangle DFG,

$$\text{arc } DG = 39°42′$$

and, as its supplement,

$$\text{arc } FG = 140°18′.$$

And therefore

$$\text{chord } DG = 40^{\text{p}}45′,$$
$$\text{chord } FG = 112^{\text{p}}52′$$

where

$$\text{hypt. } DF = 120^{\text{p}}.$$

And so also

$$DG = 1^{\text{p}}13′$$

and likewise

$$FG = 3^{\text{p}}21′$$

where

$$DF = 3^{\text{p}}34′$$

and

$$\text{ecc. rad. } BD = 60^{\text{p}}.$$

And since

$$\text{sq. } BD - \text{sq. } DG = \text{sq. } BG,$$

therefore

$$BG = 59^{\text{p}}59′.$$

And likewise, since

$$FG = GH$$

and

$$EH = 2\, DG,$$

therefore, by addition, we shall have

$$BH = 63^{\text{p}}20′$$

where

$$EH = 2^{\text{p}}26′;$$

and therefore also

$$\text{hypt. } BE = 63^{\text{p}}23′.$$

And therefore

$$EH = 4^{\text{p}}36′$$

where

$$\text{hypt. } BE = 120^{\text{p}};$$

and, on the circle about right triangle BEH,

$$\text{arc } EH = 4°24′.$$

And so also

$$\text{angle } EBH = 4°24′ \text{ to 2 rt.}$$

Likewise, since
$$FH = 6^\text{p}42'$$
where
$$\text{ecc. rad. } FX = 60^\text{p},$$
therefore we shall have, by addition,
$$HX = 66^\text{p}42'$$
where it was supposed
$$EH = 2^\text{p}26',$$
and therefore
$$\text{hypt. } EX = 66^\text{p}45'.$$

And so also
$$EH = 4^\text{p}23'$$
where
$$\text{hypt. } EX = 120^\text{p};$$
and, on the circle about right triangle EHX,
$$\text{arc } EH = 4°12'.$$

And therefore
$$\text{angle } EXH = 4°12' \text{ to 2 rt.}$$
But it had already been shown also
$$\text{angle } EBH = 4°24' \text{ to 2 rt.}$$
And therefore, by subtraction,
$$\text{angle } BEX = 0°12' \text{ to 2 rt.}$$
$$= 0°6'.$$

Now, it is clear here that, since at the second opposition the star appearing along EB was situated 9°40′ within the Archer, if in turn it appeared along EX it would be situated 9°46′ within the Archer. But it was shown that, at the first opposition, it was situated likewise 1°4′ within the Balance. Hence it is evident that the apparent distance from the first opposition to the second would amount to 68°42′ on the ecliptic if it were considered with respect to the eccentric NX.

And likewise let the drawing of the third opposition be laid out according to the same general figure as that of the second.

Since arc NX was shown to be 57°43′, therefore angle NFX or angle DFG is 57°43′, or 115°26′ to 2 right angles' 360°. And so also, on the circle about right triangle DFG,
$$\text{arc } DG = 115°26'$$
and as its supplement
$$\text{arc } FG = 64°34'.$$
And therefore
$$\text{chord } DG = 101^\text{p}27',$$
$$\text{chord } FG = 64^\text{p}6'$$
where
$$\text{hypt. } DF = 120^\text{p}.$$
And so also
$$DG = 3^\text{p}1'$$
and likewise
$$FG = 1^\text{p}54'$$

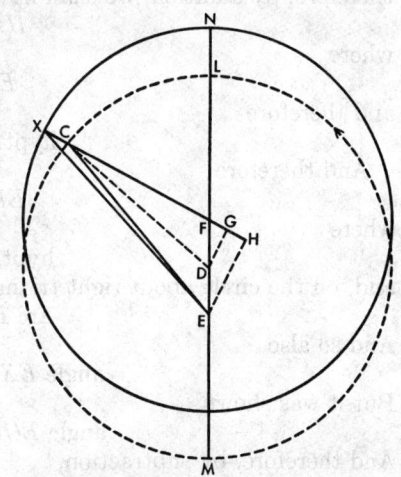

where
$$DF = 3^p34'$$
and
$$\text{ecc. rad. } CD = 60^p.$$
And again, since
$$\text{sq. } CD - \text{sq. } DG = \text{sq. } CG,$$
we shall also have
$$CG = 59^p56'.$$
And likewise, since
$$FG = GH$$
and
$$EH = 2\ DG,$$
therefore, by addition, we shall have
$$CH = 61^p50'$$
where
$$EH = 6^p2',$$
and therefore
$$\text{hypt. } CE = 62^p8'.$$
   And therefore
$$EH = 11^p39'$$
where
$$\text{hypt. } CE = 120^p;$$
and, on the circle about right triangle CEH,
$$\text{arc } EH = 11°9'.$$
And so also
$$\text{angle } ECH = 11°9' \text{ to 2 rt.}$$
   Likewise, since
$$FH = 3^p48'$$
where
$$\text{ecc. rad. } FX = 60^p,$$
therefore, by addition, we shall have
$$HX = 63^p48'$$
where
$$EH = 6^p2',$$
and therefore
$$\text{hypt. } EX = 64^p5'.$$
   And therefore
$$EH = 11^p18'$$
where
$$\text{hypt. } EX = 120^p;$$
and, on the circle about right triangle EHX,
$$\text{arc } EH = 10°49'.$$
And so also
$$\text{angle } EXH = 10°49' \text{ to 2 rt.}$$
But it was shown
$$\text{angle } ECH = 11°9' \text{ to 2 rt.}$$
And therefore, by subtraction,
$$\text{angle } CEX = 0°20' \text{ to 2 rt.}$$
$$= 0°10'.$$

And so, since, at the third opposition, the star appearing along *EC* was situated 14°14′ within the Goat, it is evident that, if it were on straight line *EX*, it would be 14°24′ within the Goat, and in turn the apparent distance from the second opposition to the third, considered relative to the eccentric *NX*, would be 34°38′.

Working with these distances in the same theorem, we find the distance between the centres of the ecliptic and of the eccentric embracing the epicycle's regular movement (or the distance equal to *EF*) to be very nearly 6ᴾ50′ where the eccentric's diameter is 120ᴾ. And, of the same eccentric's arcs, we find that from the first opposition to the apogee is 57°5′; that from the apogee to the second opposition is 18°38′; and that from the apogee to the third opposition is 56°30′.

Here again these quantities have been accurately taken because the differences of the ecliptic's arcs amount to very nearly the same as the former ones, by using these arcs, and because the star's apparent distances are found to be in accord with those observed, as will be clear to us from similar proofs.

For let the figure of the first opposition be laid out for only the eccentricity bearing the epicycle's centre.

Since, then, angle *AFL*, subtending as it does 57°5′ of the eccentric, is 57°5′, and it and the vertical angle *DFG* are each 114°10′ to 2 right angles' 360°, therefore, on the circle about right triangle *DFG*,

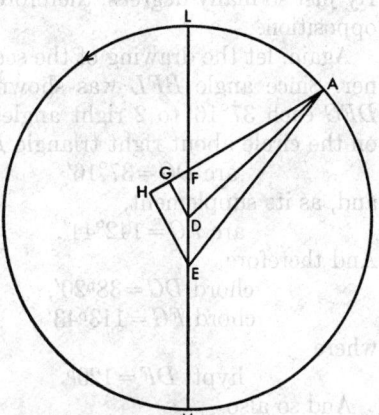

arc *DG* = 114°10′,

and as its supplement

arc *FG* = 65°50′.

And therefore

chord *DG* = 100ᴾ44′,
chord *FG* = 65ᴾ13′

where

hypt. *DF* = 120ᴾ.

And so also

DG = 2ᴾ52′

and likewise

FG = 1ᴾ51′

where

1. betw. c. *DF* = 3ᴾ25′

and

ecc. rad. *AD* = 60ᴾ.

And again, since

sq. *AD* − sq. *DG* = sq. *AG*,

we shall also have

AG = 59ᴾ56′.

And likewise, since

FG = *GH*

and

EH = 2 *DG*,

therefore, by addition, we shall have

AH = 61ᴾ47′

where
$$EH = 5^p44',$$
and therefore also
$$\text{hypt. } AE = 62^p3'.$$

And therefore
$$EH = 11^p5'$$
where
$$\text{hypt. } AE = 120^p;$$
and, on the circle about right triangle AEH,
$$\text{arc } EH = 10°36'.$$
And so also
$$\text{angle } EAF = 10°36' \text{ to 2 rt.}$$
But it was supposed
$$\text{angle } AFL = 114°10' \text{ to 2 rt.}$$
And therefore, by subtraction,
$$\text{angle } AEL = 103°34' \text{ to 2 rt.}$$
$$= 51°47'.$$
By just so many degrees, therefore, the star was west of the apogee at the first opposition.

Again, let the drawing of the second opposition be laid out in a similar manner. Since angle BFL was shown to be 18°38', and it and the vertical angle DFG each 37°16' to 2 right angles' 360°, on the circle about right triangle DFG,
$$\text{arc } DG = 37°16'$$
and, as its supplement,
$$\text{arc } FG = 142°44'.$$ 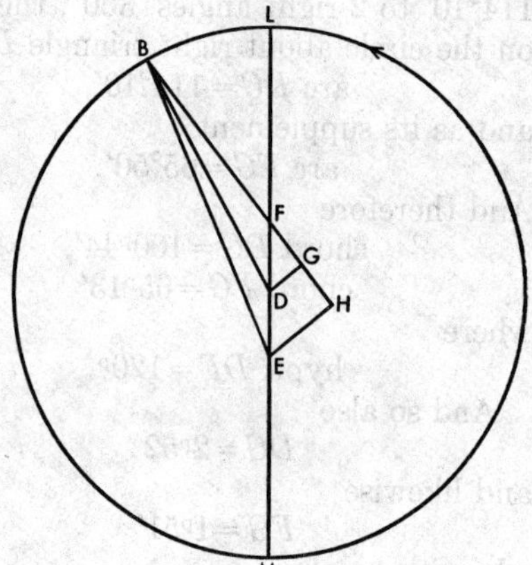
And therefore
$$\text{chord } DG = 38^p20',$$
$$\text{chord } FG = 113^p43'$$
where
$$\text{hypt. } DF = 120^p.$$
And so also
$$DG = 1^p5'$$
and likewise
$$FG = 3^p14'$$
where
$$DF = 3^p25'$$
and
$$\text{ecc. rad. } BD = 60^p.$$

And since
$$\text{sq. } BD - \text{sq. } DG = \text{sq. } BG,$$
therefore we shall have
$$BG = 59^p59'.$$
And likewise, since
$$FG = GH$$
and
$$EH = 2\, DG,$$
therefore we shall have, by addition,
$$BH = 63^p13'$$

where
$$EH = 2^p 10',$$
and therefore also
$$\text{hypt. } BE = 63^p 15'.$$
And therefore
$$EH = 4^p 7'$$
where
$$\text{hypt. } BE = 120^p;$$
and, on the circle about right triangle BEH,
$$\text{arc } EH = 3°56'.$$
And so also
$$\text{angle } EBF = 3°56' \text{ to } 2 \text{ rt.}$$
But it was supposed
$$\text{angle } BFL = 37°16' \text{ to } 2 \text{ rt.}$$
And therefore, by subtraction,
$$\text{angle } BEL = 33°20' \text{ to } 2 \text{ rt.}$$
$$= 16°40'.$$

Therefore at the second opposition the star appeared 16°40′ east of the apogee. But it was shown, at the first opposition, to be 51°47′ west of the same apogee. Hence the apparent distance from the first opposition to the second comes to a total of 68°27′ in accord with the number obtained from the observations.

Then let the drawing of the third opposition be laid out also. Since angle CFL was shown to be 56°30′, and it and the vertical angle DFG each 113° to 2 right angles' 360°, therefore, on the circle about right triangle DFG,

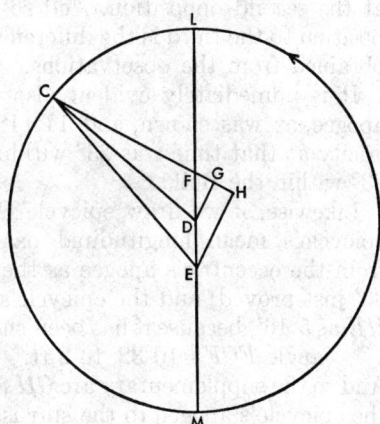

$$\text{arc } DG = 113°$$
and as its supplement
$$\text{arc } FG = 67°.$$
And therefore
$$\text{chord } DG = 100^p 4',$$
$$\text{chord } FG = 66^p 14'$$
where
$$\text{hypt. } DF = 120^p.$$
And so also
$$DG = 2^p 51'$$
and likewise
$$FG = 1^p 53'$$
where
$$DF = 3^p 25'$$
and
$$\text{ecc. rad. } CD = 60^p.$$
And since again
$$\text{sq. } CD - \text{sq. } DG = \text{sq. } CG,$$
we shall also have
$$CG = 59^p 56'.$$

And likewise, since
$$FG = GH$$
and
$$EH = 2\ DG,$$
therefore we shall also have, by addition,
$$CH = 61^{\mathrm{p}}49'$$
where
$$EH = 5^{\mathrm{p}}42',$$
and therefore also
$$\text{hypt. } CE = 62^{\mathrm{p}}5'.$$

And therefore
$$EH = 11^{\mathrm{p}}10'$$
where
$$\text{hypt. } CE = 120^{\mathrm{p}};$$
and, on the circle about right triangle CEH,
$$\text{arc } EH = 10°32'.$$
And so also
$$\text{angle } ECH = 10°32' \text{ to 2 rt.}$$
But it is supposed
$$\text{angle } CFA = 113° \text{ to 2 rt.}$$
And therefore, by subtraction,
$$\text{angle } CEL = 102°28' \text{ to 2 rt.}$$
$$= 51°14'.$$

Therefore by just so many degrees, at the third opposition, did the star appear east of the apogee. But it was also shown to be 16°40′ east of the apogee at the second opposition. And so the apparent distance from the second opposition to the third is the difference of 34°34′, again in accord with the number obtained from the observations.

It is immediately evident also that, since the star was 51°14′ east of the apogee, as was shown, and 14°14′ within the Goat, the apogee of its eccentricity at that time was 23° within the Scorpion, and its perigee just opposite 23° within the Bull.

Likewise, if we draw epicycle GH about centre C, then we shall have the epicycle's mean longitudinal passage from the eccentric's apogee as the 56° 30′ just proved; and the epicycle's arc HK as 5°16′, because it has been shown

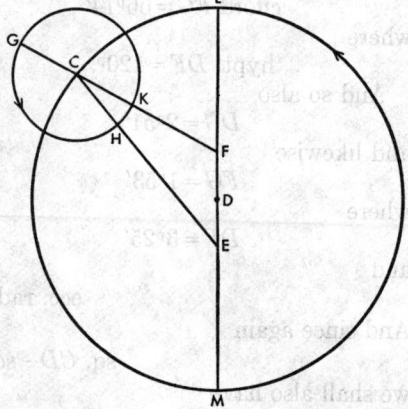

$$\text{angle } ECF = 10°32' \text{ to 2 rt.}$$

And so the supplementary arc GH from the epicycle's apogee to the star is left to be 174°44′. Therefore, at the time of the third opposition—that is, in the year 20 of Hadrian, Egyptianwise Mesore 24 at midday—Saturn considered with respect to its mean passages was 56°30′ in longitude from the eccentric's apogee or 19°30′ within the Goat, and 174°44′ in anomaly from the epicycle's apogee. Which it was required to find.

6. Demonstration of the Size of Saturn's Epicycle

And then again for showing the epicycle's size we took an observation we made in the year 2 of Antonine, Egyptianwise Mechir 6-7, 4 equatorial hours before midnight, when the last degree of the Ram was culminating in the astrolabe, with the mean sun 28°41' within the Archer. At that time Saturn, sighted relative to the bright star of the Hyades [Aldebaran], appeared to be 9⅕° within the Water Bearer and was very nearly ½° east of the moon's centre. For it was just that far from its northern horn. But at that hour the moon, according to its mean passage, was 8°55' within the Water Bearer, and in anomaly was 174°15' from the epicycle's apogee. Therefore its true passage must have been 9°40' within the Water Bearer, and its apparent passage in Alexandria 8°34'. Consequently, since it was very nearly ½° east of its centre Saturn must have been 9⅕° within the Water Bearer. And it was 76°4' from the eccentric's same apogee because in that amount of time it did not change appreciably.

Since the time from the third opposition to this observation is 2 Egyptian years, 167 days, and 8 hours, and since again Saturn, in that amount of time, moves approximately in longitude 30°3' and in anomaly 134°24', it follows that if we add these to the position given at the third opposition we shall have, for the time of the given observation, in longitude 86°33' from the eccentric's apogee and in anomaly 309°8' from the epicycle's apogee.

Now, with these things supposed, let the drawing of the similar proof be laid out, having the epicycle's position to the east of the eccentric's apogee, and the star's position before the epicycle's apogee according to the passages supposed.

Since, then, it is supposed
angle AFB or
angle $DFM = 86°33'$
$= 173°6'$ to 2 rt.,
therefore, on the circle about right triangle DFM,
arc $DM = 173°6'$
and, as its supplement,
arc $FM = 6°54'$.
And therefore
chord $DM = 119^\mathrm{p}47'$,
chord $FM = 7^\mathrm{p}13'$

where

hypt. $DF = 120^\mathrm{p}$.

And so also

$DM \doteqdot 3^\mathrm{p}25'$

and likewise

$FM = 0^\mathrm{p}12'$

where

l. betw. c. $DF = 3^\mathrm{p}25'$

and

$$\text{ecc. rad. } BD = 60^{\text{p}}.$$

And since

$$\text{sq. } BD - \text{sq. } DM = \text{sq. } BM,$$

we shall also have

$$BM = 59^{\text{p}}54'.$$

And likewise, since

$$FM = LM,$$

and

$$EL = 2 \, DM,$$

therefore also we shall have, by addition,

$$BL = 60^{\text{p}}6'$$

where

$$EL = 6^{\text{p}}50',$$

and therefore also

$$\text{hypt. } BE = 60^{\text{p}}29'.$$

And therefore

$$EL = 13^{\text{p}}33'$$

where

$$\text{hypt. } BE = 120^{\text{p}};$$

and, on the circle about right triangle BEL,

$$\text{arc } EL = 12°58'.$$

And so also

$$\text{angle } EBF = 12°58' \text{ to 2 rt.}$$

And it is also supposed

$$\text{angle } AFB = 173°6' \text{ to 2 rt.}$$

And therefore, by subtraction,

$$\text{angle } AEB = 160°8' \text{ to 2 rt.}$$

But also, as the angle containing the star's apparent distance from the apogee,

$$\text{angle } AEK = 76°4'$$
$$= 152°8' \text{ to 2 rt.}$$

And therefore we shall have, by subtraction,

$$\text{angle } KEB = 8°0' \text{ to 2 rt.}$$

And so also, on the circle about right triangle BEN,

$$\text{arc } BN = 8°,$$

and

$$\text{chord } BN = 8^{\text{p}}22'$$

where

$$\text{hypt. } BE = 120^{\text{p}}.$$

And therefore

$$BN = 4^{\text{p}}13'$$

where

$$BE = 60^{\text{p}}29'$$

and

$$\text{ecc. rad.} = 60^{\text{p}}.$$

Again, since the star was 309°8′ from the epicycle's apogee G, therefore, by subtraction, arc $GK = 50°52'$.

And therefore
$$\text{angle } GBK = 50°52'$$
$$= 101°44' \text{ to 2 rt.}$$

But
$$\text{angle } EBF = \text{angle } GBH = 12°58' \text{ to 2 rt.}$$

And therefore, by subtraction,
$$\text{angle } HBK = 88°46' \text{ to 2 rt.}$$

where it was shown
$$\text{angle } KEB = 8° \text{ to 2 rt.}$$

And therefore, by subtraction, we shall have
$$\text{angle } BKN = 80°46' \text{ to 2 rt.}$$

And so also, on the circle about right triangle BKN,
$$\text{arc } BN = 80°46'$$

and
$$\text{chord } BN = 77^\text{p}45'$$

where
$$\text{hypt. } BK = 120^\text{p}.$$

And therefore we shall have
$$\text{epic. rad. } BK \doteq 6\tfrac{1}{2}^\text{p}$$

where it was shown
$$BN = 4^\text{p}13'$$

and
$$\text{ecc. rad.} = 60^\text{p}.$$

We have concluded that Saturn's apogee at these dates near the beginning of Antonine's reign was 23° within the Scorpion. Where the radius of the eccentric bearing the epicycle is 60ᵖ, there the line between the centres of the ecliptic and of the eccentric effecting the regular movement comes to 6ᵖ50', and the epicycle's radius to 6ᵖ30'. Which it was required to find.

7. ON THE CORRECTION OF SATURN'S PERIODIC MOVEMENTS

Now that it is left to show the correction of the periodic movements, we took for this again one of the faithfully recorded ancient observations, according to which it is clear that in the year 82 of the Chaldeans, Xanthicus 5, in the evening, Saturn was 2 digits below the Virgin's southern shoulder. This date is the year 519 of Nabonassar, Egyptianwise Tybi 14 in the evening, at which time we find the mean sun 6°10' within the Fishes. But the fixed star of the Virgin's northern shoulder at the time of our observation was 13⅙° within the Virgin. At the time of the given observation, since very nearly 3⅔° of the fixed star's movement correspond to the intervening 366 years, it was clearly 9½° within the Virgin; and also Saturn, since it was south of the fixed star by 2 digits. Likewise, since its apogee was shown in our time to be nearly 23° within the Scorpion, at that time it must have been 19⅓° within the Scorpion. By means of these things it is concluded that at the given time the apparent star was 290°10' along the ecliptic from the apogee at that time, and the mean sun was 106°50' from the same apogee.

With these things supposed, again let there be set out the drawing for a

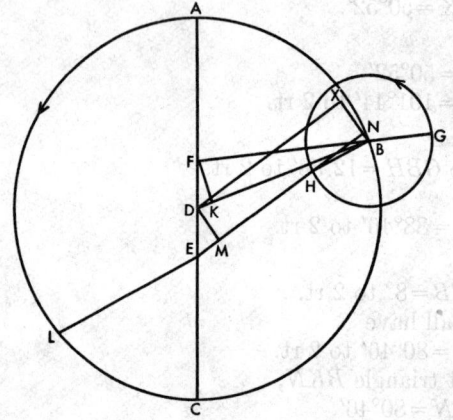

similar proof, having the epicycle's position west of the eccentric's apogee and the sun's
west of the perigee and parallel
to it the line from the epicycle's
centre to the star.

Now, since Saturn appeared
west of the apogee by the 69°50'
failing one complete circle, therefore, being at the ecliptic's centre,

angle $AEH = 69°50'$
$= 139°40'$ to 2 rt.

But also the angle AEL of the
solar distance is assumed to be
106°50' or 213°40' to 2 right
angles' 360°. And therefore, by
addition,

angle HEL or angle $BHE = 353°20'$ to 2 rt.

because BH is parallel to EL, And by subtraction

angle $BHN = 6°40'$ to 2 rt.

And so also, on the circle about right triangle BHN,

arc $BN = 6°40'$,

and

chord $BN = 6^p58'$

where

hypt. $BH = 120^p$.

And therefore

$BN = 0^p23'$

where

epic. rad. $BH = 6^p30'$.

Likewise, since

angle $AEH = 139°40'$ to 2 rt.

and

angle $EDM = 40°20'$ to 2 rt.

therefore also, on the circle about right triangle DEM,

arc $DM = 139°40'$,

and

chord $DM = 112^p39'$

where

hypt. $DE = 120^p$.

And therefore

$DM = XN = 3^p12'$

where

l. betw. c. $DE = 3^p25'$

and

ecc. rad. $BD = 60^p$;

and, by addition,

$BNX = 3^p35'$

where

hypt. $BD = 60^p$.

And therefore
$$BX = 7^p10'$$
where
$$BD = 120^p;$$
and, on the circle about right triangle BDX,
$$\text{arc } BX = 6°52'.$$
And so also
$$\text{angle } BDX = 6°52' \text{ to } 2 \text{ rt.,}$$
and as its complement
$$\text{angle } BDM = 173°8' \text{ to } 2 \text{ rt.,}$$
and likewise by addition
$$\text{angle } BDE = 213°28' \text{ to } 2 \text{ rt.,}$$
and as its supplement
$$\text{angle } BDA = 146°32' \text{ to } 2 \text{ rt.}$$
And so also, on the circle about right triangle DFK,
$$\text{arc } FK = 146°32'$$
and, as its supplement,
$$\text{arc } DK = 33°28'.$$
And therefore
$$\text{chord } FK = 114^p55',$$
$$\text{chord } DK = 34^p33'$$
where
$$\text{hypt. } DF = 120^p.$$
And therefore
$$FK = 3^p17'$$
and likewise
$$DK = 0^p59'$$
where
$$\text{l. betw. c. } DF = 3^p25'$$
and
$$\text{ecc. rad. } BD = 60^p;$$
and, by subtraction,
$$BK = 59^p1'$$
where
$$FK = 3^p17',$$
and therefore
$$\text{hypt. } BF = 59^p6'.$$
And so also
$$FK = 6^p40'$$
where
$$\text{hypt. } BF = 120^p;$$
and, on the circle about right triangle BFK,
$$\text{arc } FK = 6°22'.$$
And therefore
$$\text{angle } FBK = 6°22' \text{ to } 2 \text{ rt.}$$
But
$$\text{angle } ADB = 146°32' \text{ to } 2 \text{ rt.}$$
And therefore, by addition, we shall have
$$\text{angle } AFB = 152°54' \text{ to } 2 \text{ rt.}$$
$$= 76°27',$$
the angle which embraces the regular longitudinal passage.

Therefore, at the time of the given observation, Saturn, according to its mean longitudinal passage, was 283°33′ from the apogee, or situated 2°53′

within the Virgin. Since, moreover, the sun's mean passage is supposed 106°
50′, if we add to this the 360° of one circle and from the resulting 466°50′
subtract the 283°33′ in longitude, we shall have, for that same time, the
183°17′ of anomaly from the epicycle's apogee.

At the time of the given observation, which was in the year 519 of Nabonassar, Tybi 14 in the evening, Saturn was shown to be 183°17′ from the epicycle's apogee, and at the time of the third opposition, which was in the year
883 of Nabonassar, Mesore 24 at midday, it was 174°44′; therefore it is evident
that in the time between the two observations, which embraces 364 Egyptian
years and 219¾ days, Saturn has moved 351°27′ above 351 complete circles
of anomaly. And again the surplus from the mean movements worked out by
us comes to very nearly this much. For the daily mean movement was established by dividing the total number of degrees resulting from the number
of circles and the surplus by the total number of days of the time.

8. On the Epoch of Saturn's Periodic Movements

But since also the time from the year 1 of Nabonassar, Thoth 1, at midday
to the given ancient observation is 518 Egyptian years and 133¼ days, and
since this amount of time embraces surpluses of 216°9′ in longitude and 149° 15′
in anomaly, if we subtract these from the given positions at the observations,
we shall have, again for this time of the epoch, Saturn's mean longitudinal
position 26°44′ within the Goat, its anomalistic position 34°2′ from the epicycle's apogee, and therefore the apogee of its eccentricity about 14°10′ within
the Scorpion. Which it was required to find.

9. How the True Passages are Gotten Geometrically from the Periodic Movements

By means of the same things it will be clear to us that conversely, if the periodic arcs of the eccentric embracing the regular movement and of the epicycle
are given, then also the stars' apparent passages are easily obtained by geometry.

For if, in the simple drawing of the eccentric and epicycle, we join FBH and
EBG, then, given the mean longi-
tudinal passage (that is, angle AFB)
angle AEB, and angle EBF or angle
GBH are also given according to
both hypotheses, from things already shown. Furthermore, the ratio
of the straight line BE to the epicy-
cle's radius is given.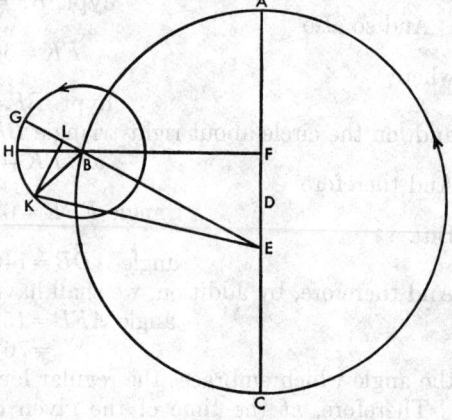

Let the star be supposed, for instance, at point K on the epicycle,
and EK and BK be joined. And let
arc HK be given. Now, if we no longer (as in the converse proof) draw
a straight line from the epicycle's
centre B perpendicular to EK but
rather from the star at K perpendicular to EB (as here KL) then the

whole angle *GBK* is given, and therefore also the ratio of *KL* and *LB* to *BK* and *EB;* and, accordingly, the ratio of the whole *EBL* to *LK*. And so also, given the angle *LEK*, we get the angle *AEK* containing the star's apparent distance from the apogee.

10. TREATMENT OF THE CONSTRUCTION OF TABLES FOR THE ANOMALIES

Yet in order that we may not always calculate the apparent passages geometrically (although this way alone accurately obtains what is required, but is too difficult for ease in researches), we have constructed tables as convenient and as nearly accurate as possible, for each of the five stars, and containing their particular anomalies combined in such a way that, when the periodic movements from the proper apogees are given, we may readily calculate from them the apparent passages for any time.

Each of these tables we have arranged again in 45 rows, for symmetry's sake, and in 8 columns. Of these columns, the first two contain the numbers of the mean passages, as in the case of the sun and the moon, with the 180° from the apogee arranged downwards in the first and the remaining 180° of the semicircle arranged upwards in the second, so that the number 180 has been put in the last row in both, and their increase for the first 15 rows downwards is by intervals of 6° and for the remaining 30 under them by intervals of 3°. For the differences of the sections of anomaly with respect to each other are less appreciable at the apogees, but they change more rapidly at the perigees.

Of the next two columns, the third contains the addition-subtractions resulting for the corresponding number of mean longitudinal passage through the greatest eccentricity, yet taken simply as if the epicycle's centre were borne on the eccentric embracing the regular movement. The fourth column contains the differences of the addition-subtractions resulting from the fact that the epicycle's centre is not borne on that circle but on another. And the way in which each of these two is obtained geometrically, at the same time and separately, can be readily understood through the many theorems already propounded by us. It was fitting that at this point in this treatise such an analysis of the zodiacal anomaly be displayed and therefore set forth in two columns; but, for actual use, one column combined from the addition-subtraction of them both would suffice.

Of the next three columns, each contains the addition-subtractions due to the epicycle, again taken simply, with the apogees and perigees considered relative to the distance from our eye. For the method of this kind of proof can be easily understood by us with the help of theorems already set out. The middle one of these three columns, or the sixth from the first, contains the addition-subtractions calculated according to the ratios of the mean distances. But the fifth contains, for the same sections, the differences of the addition-subtractions at the greatest distance with respect to those at the mean; and the seventh contains the differences of the addition-subtractions at the least distance with respect to those at the mean.

For we have shown that, where the epicycle's radius is 6ᵖ30' in the case of Saturn (for it would be well finally to begin from the top down), 11ᵖ30' for Jupiter, 39ᵖ30' for Mars, 43ᵖ10' for Venus, and 22ᵖ30' for Mercury, there the mean distance of all is 60ᵖ—that is, the distance considered with respect to the radius of the eccentric bearing the epicycle; and the greatest distance with respect to the ecliptic's centre is for Saturn 63ᵖ25', for Jupiter 62ᵖ45', for Mars 66ᵖ, for

Venus 61ᴘ15′, and for Mercury 69ᴘ; and likewise the least distance is for Saturn 56ᴘ35′, for Jupiter 57ᴘ15′, for Mars 54ᴘ, for Venus 58ᴘ45′, and for Mercury 55ᴘ34′.

We have arranged the eighth and last column for obtaining the corresponding parts of the difference, set out when the stars' epicycles are neither at the mean, greatest, or least distances, but in the passages between. We have arranged the calculation of this correction for each distance between, only with respect to the greatest addition-subtractions at the tangents from our eye to the epicycle, since there is no appreciable deviation in the proportion of the differences for the other sections of the epicycle relative to those for the greatest addition-subtractions.

To make what is here said still clearer, and to have the method of proportions stand out in evidence, let there be laid out the straight line ABCD through the centres of the eclip- 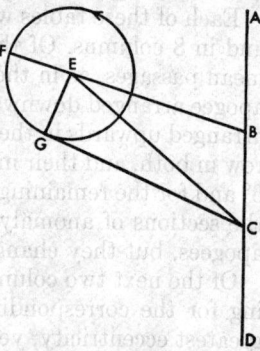 tic and of the eccentric embracing the regular move- ment of the epicycle. Let C be supposed the ecliptic's centre, and B the centre of the epicycle's regular movement. With BEF produced, let the epicycle FG be drawn about centre E; and let straight line CG be drawn from C tangent to it, letting CE and the per- pendicular EG be joined. For an example, let the epi- cycle's centre for each of the five stars be supposed 30° in regular movement from the apogee of eccen- tricity.

Now (not to draw out the calculations by proving the same things again) it was shown by many theo-

Fig. xi, 24.

rems preceding this, both for the hypothesis of Mer- cury and the rest, that, when angle ABE is given, the ratio of CE to the epicy- cle's radius or GE is also given; and, when angle ABE is assumed to be 30°, by calculations for each case, the ratio becomes 63ᴘ2′ to 6ᴘ30′ for Saturn, 62ᴘ26′ to 11ᴘ30′ for Jupiter, 65ᴘ24′ to 39ᴘ30′ for Mars, 61ᴘ26′ to 43ᴘ10′ for Venus, and 66ᴘ35′ to 22ᴘ30′ for Mercury. Therefore we shall have angle ECG which contains the greatest addition-subtraction due to the epicycle at that time: 5°55½′ for Saturn, 10°36½′ for Jupiter, 37°9′ for Mars, 44°56½′ for Venus, and 19°45′ for Mercury.

According to the ratios just expounded, the greatest addition-subtractions at the mean distances, become 6°13′, 11°3′, 41°10′, 46°, and 22°2′, in the order of the stars just given, to avoid repetition. At the greatest distances they become 5°53′, 10°34′, 36°45′, 44°48′, and 19°2′; and at least distances they become 6°36′, 11°35′, 47°1′, 47°17′, and 23°53′. Those at the greatest distances hence differ from those at the mean by 0°20′, 0°29′, 4°25′, 1°12′, and 3°; and those at the least differ from them by 0°23′, 0°32′, 5°51′, 1°17′, and 1°51′.

Now, the addition-subtractions of the distances sought are less than those of the mean distances and differ from them by 0°17½′, 0°26½′, 4°1′, 1°3½′, and 2°17′. These are, for Saturn, 52 and 30′ sixtieths of the given whole differences between those at the mean distances and those at the greatest; for Jupiter, 54 and 50′ sixtieths; for Mars, 54 and 34′; for Venus 52 and 55′; and for Mercury, 45 and 40′. And therefore in the eighth column in each table we have placed just that number of sixtieths in the row containing the number 30 of periodic longitude. And in the case of distances having addition-subtractions greater than those at the mean distances, we likewise analysed their differences into sixtieths again, but relative to whole differences with those at the least distances and no longer with those at the greatest. In the same way we calculated, for the other positions at intervals of 6° mean longitude, the resulting sixtieths of the whole differences, and we put them beside the proper numbers. For, as we said, the proportion of the differences is sensibly the same, even if the passages of the stars are not at the epicycle's greatest addition-subtractions, but at other parts of it. And here is the exposition presented in the following five tables [pp. 386–390].

12. On Calculating the Longitudes of the Five Planets

Now, whenever we wish to know the apparent passages of each of the stars, from their periodic movements in longitude and anomaly, by means of the foregoing tables, we shall make the calculation, one and the same for the five stars, in this way:

Calculating, from the tables of mean movement, the regular positions of longitude and anomaly above whole circles produced in the time required, we first carry the degrees from the eccentric's apogee at that time to the mean longitudinal passage, to the table of anomaly proper to the star. If the longitudinal number set out is in the first column, we subtract from the degrees of longitude the quantities in the third column of the truly determined longitude corresponding to the number, along with the addition-subtraction of sixtieths in the fourth column; and we add them to the degrees of anomaly. But if the longitudinal number is in the second column, we add them to the longitudinal and subtract them from the anomalistic, so that we may have both passages truly determined.

Then we carry the number of degrees from the anomaly's apogee, analysed out, again to the first two tables, and we record the corresponding addition-subtraction of the mean distance in the sixth column. Likewise carrying the original number of regular longitude, brought over, to the same numbers, if it is in the first rows more apogee than that of the mean distance (which becomes clear from the sixtieths in the eighth column), then, whatever number of sixtieths in the eighth column correspond to it, we take just that many of the difference, corresponding to the recorded mean addition-subtraction, in the fifth column of the greatest distance, and we subtract the result from what we recorded. But if the number of the aforesaid longitude is in the lower rows more perigee than that at the mean distance, then likewise, whatever number of sixtieths correspond to it in the eighth column, we take just that many of the difference, corresponding to the recorded mean addition-subtraction, in the seventh column of the least distance, and we add the results to what we recorded.

The total number of degrees of the addition-subtraction so determined we add to the degrees of longitude, truly determined, if the truly determined anomalistic number is in the first column; and we subtract them from the longitudinal degrees, if it is in the second column. And counting the resulting number of degrees from the star's apogee at that time, we come to its apparent passage.

11. Tables for the Anomalies
SATURN, Apogee, 14°10′ within the Scorpion

1	2	3		4		5		6		7		8	
Common Numbers		Longitudinal Addition-Subtraction		Differences of Addition-Subtraction		Differences of Subtraction		Addition-Subtraction of Anomaly		Differences of Addition		Sixtieths of Subtraction	
6	354	0	37	0	2	0	2	0	36	0	2	60	0
12	348	1	13	0	4	0	4	1	11	0	4	58	30
18	342	1	49	0	6	0	5	1	45	0	7	57	0
24	336	2	23	0	8	0	7	2	18	0	9	55	30
30	360	2	57	0	9	0	8	2	50	0	11	52	30
36	324	3	29	0	10	0	10	3	20	0	13	49	30
42	318	3	59	0	11	0	11	3	49	0	15	46	30
48	312	4	28	0	11	0	12	4	17	0	17	43	30
54	306	4	55	0	10	0	14	4	42	0	19	39	0
60	300	5	20	0	9	0	15	5	4	0	20	34	30
66	294	5	42	0	8	0	17	5	25	0	20	30	0
72	288	6	0	0	7	0	18	5	42	0	21	24	0
78	282	6	14	0	5	0	18	5	55	0	21	18	0
84	276	6	24	0	3	0	19	6	5	0	22	12	0
90	270	6	30	0	1	0	19	6	12	0	22	4	30
93	267	6	31	0	0	0	20	6	12	0	23	0	45
				Addition								*Subtraction*	
96	264	6	32	0	2	0	20	6	13	0	23	2	32
99	261	6	31	0	3	0	20	6	12	0	24	5	51
102	258	6	30	0	4	0	21	6	12	0	24	9	8
105	255	6	27	0	5	0	21	6	9	0	24	11	45
108	252	6	23	0	6	0	20	6	5	0	25	14	21
111	249	6	19	0	7	0	20	6	0	0	25	16	58
114	246	6	14	0	8	0	20	5	55	0	24	19	31
117	243	6	7	0	9	0	19	5	48	0	24	22	11
120	240	5	59	0	10	0	19	5	40	0	23	24	47
123	237	5	50	0	10	0	19	5	31	0	23	27	24
126	234	5	39	0	11	0	18	5	21	0	22	30	0
129	231	5	27	0	11	0	18	5	10	0	22	32	37
132	228	5	14	0	12	0	17	4	58	0	21	35	13
135	225	5	0	0	12	0	17	4	45	0	20	37	50
138	222	4	45	0	12	0	16	4	31	0	19	40	26
141	219	4	29	0	12	0	15	4	16	0	18	43	3
144	216	4	12	0	12	0	14	4	0	0	17	45	39
147	213	3	54	0	12	0	14	3	43	0	15	47	37
150	210	3	35	0	11	0	12	3	25	0	14	49	34
153	207	3	16	0	11	0	11	3	7	0	13	51	32
156	204	2	56	0	10	0	10	2	48	0	12	53	29
159	201	2	36	0	9	0	9	2	29	0	11	54	49
162	198	2	15	0	8	0	7	2	9	0	10	56	6
165	195	1	53	0	7	0	6	1	48	0	8	57	24
168	192	1	31	0	6	0	5	1	27	0	7	58	42
171	189	1	9	0	5	0	5	1	6	0	5	59	21
174	186	0	47	0	3	0	4	0	45	0	4	60	0
177	183	0	24	0	2	0	2	0	23	0	2	60	0
180	180	0	0	0	0	0	0	0	0	0	0	60	0

11. TABLES FOR THE ANOMALIES
JUPITER, Apogee, 2°9' within the Virgin

1	2	3		4		5		6		7		8	
Common Numbers		Longitudinal Addition-Subtraction		Differences of Addition-Subtraction		Differences of Subtraction		Addition-Subtraction of Anomaly		Differences of Addition		Sixtieths of Subtraction	
6	354	0	30	0	1	0	2	0	58	0	2	60	0
12	348	1	0	0	2	0	5	1	56	0	5	58	58
18	342	1	30	0	3	0	7	2	52	0	7	57	56
24	336	1	58	0	4	0	9	3	48	0	9	56	54
30	330	2	26	0	5	0	11	4	42	0	11	54	50
36	324	2	52	0	6	0	13	5	34	0	13	51	43
42	318	3	17	0	7	0	15	6	25	0	15	47	35
48	312	3	40	0	7	0	17	7	12	0	18	43	27
54	306	4	1	0	7	0	19	7	57	0	20	39	19
60	300	4	20	0	6	0	21	8	37	0	22	35	8
66	294	4	37	0	5	0	23	9	14	0	24	28	58
72	288	4	51	0	4	0	24	9	46	0	26	22	45
78	282	5	2	0	3	0	25	10	13	0	28	17	35
84	276	5	9	0	2	0	26	10	35	0	30	11	23
90	270	5	14	0	1	0	26	10	51	0	31	4	40
93	267	5	15	0	0	0	27	10	57	0	31	1	8
				Subtraction								Addition	
96	264	5	16	0	1	0	27	11	0	0	32	1	52
99	261	5	15	0	1	0	27	11	2	0	32	5	9
102	258	5	14	0	2	0	28	11	3	0	32	8	26
105	255	5	12	0	2	0	28	11	1	0	33	11	43
108	252	5	9	0	3	0	29	10	59	0	33	15	0
111	249	5	5	0	4	0	29	10	53	0	33	17	49
114	246	5	0	0	5	0	30	10	45	0	34	20	37
117	243	4	54	0	5	0	30	10	35	0	34	23	26
120	240	4	47	0	6	0	30	10	24	0	34	26	15
123	237	4	39	0	6	0	29	10	10	0	33	29	4
126	234	4	10	0	7	0	29	9	54	0	33	31	52
129	231	4	20	0	7	0	28	9	36	0	32	34	41
132	228	4	9	0	8	0	28	9	16	0	32	37	30
135	225	3	58	0	8	0	27	8	54	0	31	40	19
138	222	3	46	0	8	0	26	8	30	0	30	43	7
141	219	3	33	0	8	0	25	8	4	0	28	45	28
144	216	3	20	0	7	0	23	7	36	0	26	47	49
147	213	3	6	0	7	0	22	7	6	0	25	49	42
150	210	2	51	0	6	0	21	6	34	0	23	51	31
153	207	2	36	0	6	0	19	6	0	0	21	52	58
156	204	2	20	0	5	0	17	5	24	0	19	54	22
159	201	2	4	0	5	0	15	4	47	0	17	55	47
162	198	1	47	0	4	0	13	4	9	0	15	57	11
165	195	1	30	0	3	0	11	3	29	0	13	57	40
168	192	1	13	0	2	0	9	2	49	0	10	58	13
171	189	0	55	0	2	0	7	2	7	0	8	58	40
174	186	0	37	0	1	0	5	1	25	0	5	59	4
177	183	0	18	0	1	0	3	0	43	0	3	59	32
180	180	0	0	0	0	0	0	0	0	0	0	60	0

11. TABLES FOR THE ANOMALIES
MARS, Apogee, 16°40′ within the Crab

1	2	3		4		5		6		7		8	
Common Numbers		Longitudinal Addition-Subtraction		Differences of Addition-Subtraction		Differences of Subtraction		Addition-Subtraction of Anomaly		Differences of Addition		Sixtieths of Subtraction	
6	354	1	0	0	5	0	8	2	24	0	9	59	53
12	348	2	0	0	10	0	16	4	46	0	18	58	59
18	342	2	58	0	15	0	24	7	8	0	28	57	51
24	336	3	56	0	20	0	33	9	30	0	37	56	36
30	330	4	52	0	24	0	42	11	51	0	46	54	34
36	324	5	46	0	27	0	51	14	11	0	56	52	11
42	318	6	39	0	28	1	0	16	29	1	6	49	28
48	312	7	28	0	29	1	9	18	46	1	16	46	17
54	306	8	14	0	28	1	18	21	0	1	28	42	38
60	300	8	57	0	27	1	27	23	13	1	40	38	8
66	294	9	36	0	24	1	37	25	22	1	53	33	26
72	288	10	9	0	20	1	49	27	29	2	6	28	20
78	282	10	38	0	15	2	1	29	32	2	19	22	47
84	276	11	2	0	10	2	14	31	30	2	33	16	33
90	270	11	19	0	4	2	28	33	22	2	45	10	5
93	267	11	25	0	0	2	35	34	15	2	57	6	34
				Subtraction									
96	264	11	29	0	4	2	42	35	6	3	6	3	3
												Addition	
99	261	11	32	0	8	2	49	35	56	3	15	0	5
102	258	11	32	0	12	2	56	36	43	3	25	3	13
105	255	11	31	0	16	3	4	37	27	3	36	6	1
108	252	11	28	0	19	3	13	38	9	3	47	8	49
111	249	11	22	0	22	3	22	38	48	3	58	11	44
114	246	11	14	0	25	3	32	39	24	4	9	14	38
117	243	11	5	0	28	3	43	39	56	4	21	17	33
120	240	10	53	0	31	3	54	40	23	4	35	20	27
123	237	10	39	0	33	4	4	40	44	4	50	23	35
126	234	10	23	0	35	4	14	40	59	5	5	26	42
129	231	10	4	0	37	4	24	41	7	5	21	29	31
132	228	9	42	0	39	4	35	41	9	5	37	32	20
135	225	9	21	0	40	4	45	41	2	5	55	35	9
138	222	8	55	0	41	4	56	40	45	6	14	37	58
141	219	8	27	0	41	5	7	40	16	6	34	40	35
144	216	7	59	0	41	5	18	39	37	6	53	43	12
147	213	7	27	0	41	5	28	38	40	7	12	45	26
150	210	6	54	0	38	5	34	37	25	7	30	47	39
153	207	6	19	0	36	5	38	35	52	7	45	49	50
156	204	5	41	0	33	5	38	33	53	7	58	52	1
159	201	5	3	0	30	5	34	31	30	8	3	53	47
162	198	4	22	0	27	5	18	28	35	7	58	55	32
165	195	3	41	0	23	4	52	25	3	7	47	56	44
168	192	2	58	0	19	4	18	21	0	7	6	57	55
171	189	2	14	0	15	3	32	16	25	5	59	58	49
174	186	1	30	0	10	2	27	11	19	4	26	59	43
177	183	0	45	0	5	1	16	5	45	2	20	59	52
180	180	0	0	0	0	0	0	0	0	0	0	60	0

11. TABLES FOR THE ANOMALIES
VENUS, Apogee, 16°10′ within the Bull

1	2	3		4		5		6		7		8	
Common Numbers		Longitudinal Addition-Subtraction		Differences of Addition-Subtraction		Differences of Subtraction		Addition-Subtraction of Anomaly		Differences of Addition		Sixtieths of Subtraction	
6	354	0	14	0	1	0	1	2	31	0	2	59	10
12	348	0	28	0	1	0	3	5	1	0	4	57	55
18	342	0	42	0	1	0	5	7	31	0	6	56	40
24	336	0	56	0	2	0	7	10	1	0	8	55	0
30	330	1	9	0	2	0	9	12	30	0	10	52	55
36	324	1	21	0	2	0	11	14	58	0	12	49	35
42	318	1	32	0	3	0	13	17	25	0	14	45	50
48	312	1	43	0	3	0	15	19	51	0	16	42	5
54	306	1	53	0	3	0	18	22	15	0	18	37	5
60	300	2	1	0	2	0	20	24	38	0	20	31	40
66	294	2	8	0	2	0	22	26	37	0	23	26	15
72	288	2	14	0	2	0	24	29	14	0	25	20	25
78	282	2	18	0	1	0	27	31	27	0	28	14	35
84	276	2	21	0	1	0	29	33	38	0	30	8	20
90	270	2	23	0	1	0	31	35	44	0	33	1	40
				Subtraction								*Addition*	
93	267	2	23	0	0	0	33	36	40	0	36	1	31
96	264	2	23	0	1	0	35	37	43	0	38	4	42
99	261	2	22	0	1	0	38	38	40	0	40	7	39
102	258	2	21	0	1	0	40	39	35	0	43	10	35
105	255	2	20	0	1	0	42	40	29	0	45	13	32
108	252	2	18	0	1	0	45	41	20	0	47	16	28
111	249	2	16	0	1	0	47	42	9	0	50	19	25
114	246	2	13	0	2	0	49	42	54	0	52	22	21
117	243	2	10	0	2	0	52	43	35	0	55	25	18
120	240	2	6	0	2	0	54	44	12	0	58	28	14
123	237	2	2	0	2	0	57	44	45	1	1	31	0
126	234	1	58	0	2	1	0	45	14	1	4	33	44
129	231	1	51	0	2	1	3	45	36	1	8	36	18
132	228	1	49	0	3	1	6	45	51	1	11	38	50
135	225	1	44	0	3	1	10	45	55	1	14	41	11
138	222	1	39	0	3	1	14	45	57	1	18	43	32
141	219	1	33	0	3	1	19	45	45	1	22	45	42
144	216	1	27	0	2	1	24	45	20	1	27	47	51
147	213	1	21	0	2	1	29	44	40	1	32	49	37
150	210	1	14	0	2	1	33	43	39	1	38	51	23
153	207	1	7	0	2	1	37	42	18	1	43	52	46
156	204	1	0	0	2	1	39	40	28	1	58	54	8
159	201	0	53	0	2	1	41	38	7	1	51	55	18
162	198	0	46	0	1	1	42	35	7	1	52	56	26
165	195	0	39	0	1	1	38	31	24	1	50	57	28
168	192	0	32	0	1	1	31	26	46	1	43	58	26
171	189	0	24	0	1	1	19	21	15	1	27	59	1
174	186	0	16	0	1	0	58	14	47	1	5	59	36
177	183	0	8	0	1	0	31	7	38	0	35	59	58
180	180	0	0	0	0	0	0	0	0	0	0	60	0

11. Tables for the Anomalies
MERCURY, Apogee, 1°10′ within the Balance

1	2	3		4		5		6		7		8	
Common Numbers		Longitudinal Addition-Subtraction		Differences of Addition-Subtraction		Differences of Subtraction		Addition-Subtraction of Anomaly		Differences of Addition		Sixtieths of Subtraction	
6	354	0	18	0	1	0	10	1	38	0	5	59	20
12	348	0	34	0	2	0	20	3	16	0	11	57	20
18	342	0	51	0	4	0	22	4	53	0	17	54	40
24	336	1	7	0	5	0	39	6	29	0	23	50	40
30	330	1	22	0	5	0	49	8	4	0	28	45	40
36	324	1	37	0	4	0	59	9	36	0	34	39	40
42	318	1	51	0	4	1	8	11	6	0	40	33	0
48	312	2	4	0	3	1	18	12	33	0	45	25	40
54	306	2	15	0	1	1	28	13	58	0	50	18	0
60	300	2	25	0	0	1	39	15	18	0	56	10	20
				Addition									
66	294	2	34	0	2	1	49	16	33	1	4	2	20
												Addition	
72	288	2	41	0	4	1	59	17	43	1	11	9	14
78	282	2	46	0	6	2	9	18	47	1	17	20	0
84	276	2	50	0	7	2	19	19	44	1	23	29	44
90	270	2	52	0	9	2	29	20	33	1	29	39	28
93	267	2	52	0	10	2	34	20	54	1	32	43	31
96	264	2	52	0	10	2	39	21	14	1	35	47	34
99	261	2	51	0	11	2	44	21	29	1	38	50	0
102	258	2	50	0	10	2	48	21	42	1	41	52	26
105	255	2	48	0	10	2	53	21	52	1	44	54	52
108	252	2	46	0	10	2	58	21	59	1	46	57	18
111	249	2	44	0	9	3	2	22	2	1	49	58	23
114	246	2	41	0	9	3	4	22	1	1	52	59	28
117	243	2	37	0	9	3	6	21	56	1	55	59	44
120	240	2	33	0	8	3	8	21	47	1	57	60	0
123	237	2	28	0	7	3	9	21	33	1	59	59	44
126	234	2	23	0	7	3	10	21	15	2	0	59	23
129	231	2	18	0	6	3	12	20	53	2	0	58	39
132	228	2	12	0	6	3	12	20	25	2	1	57	50
135	225	2	6	0	5	3	9	19	50	2	1	56	46
138	222	2	0	0	4	3	6	19	10	2	0	55	41
141	219	1	53	0	4	3	2	18	24	2	0	54	3
144	216	1	46	0	3	2	57	17	32	1	58	52	26
147	213	1	38	0	3	2	51	16	35	1	53	50	48
150	210	1	30	0	2	2	42	15	31	1	47	49	11
153	207	1	22	0	2	2	32	14	20	1	41	47	34
156	204	1	13	0	2	2	21	13	3	1	34	45	57
159	201	1	5	0	1	2	9	11	41	1	26	44	36
162	198	0	56	0	1	1	55	10	13	1	17	43	15
165	195	0	46	0	1	1	38	8	40	1	7	42	26
168	192	0	38	0	0	1	19	7	1	0	56	41	37
171	189	0	28	0	0	1	1	5	19	0	43	40	48
174	186	0	19	0	0	0	42	3	35	0	28	40	0
177	183	0	9	0	0	0	21	1	48	0	14	39	44
180	180	0	0	0	0	0	0	0	0	0	0	39	28

BOOK TWELVE

1. ON THE PRELIMINARIES TO THE REGRESSIONS

Now that these things have been demonstrated, it would follow that the greatest and least regressions for each of the five planets be examined and that, from the given hypotheses, their sizes be shown as much in accord as possible with those gotten from observations.

For the understanding of this, the other mathematicians and Apollonius of Perga first demonstrate, as in the case of the one anomaly relative to the sun, that if it is taken care of according to the epicyclic hypothesis (with the epicycle making its longitudinal passage eastward about the circle concentric with the ecliptic and with the star on the epicycle making its anomalistic passage about its centre eastward from the apogee), and if a straight line is drawn from our eye cutting the epicycle in such a way that the half of its segment intercepted within the epicycle has to the straight line from our eye to its intersection at the epicycle's perigee the ratio which the speed of the epicycle has to the speed of the star, then the point produced by the straight line so drawn on the epicycle's perigeal arc divides the progressions and regressions so that the star at the point itself makes the appearance of a station.

If the anomaly relative to the sun is taken care of by the hypothesis of eccentricity (this can be done only in the case of the three stars capable of any elongation from the sun), with the eccentric's centre carried eastward about the ecliptic's centre at a speed equal to the sun's and with the star moving on the eccentric about its centre westward at a speed equal to the anomalistic passage, and if a straight line is drawn to the eccentric circle through the ecliptic's centre (that is, through our eye), in such a way that one-half of the whole line has to the lesser of the segments produced by our eye the ratio which the eccentric's speed has to the star's speed, then the star at the point at which the straight line cuts the eccentric's perigeal arc will make the appearance of stations.

Editorial Note. This second theory for the three planets capable of any elongation from the sun is not mentioned anywhere else in the *Almagest*. It is of greater importance than it might at first seem. For it is almost equivalent to the conversion theorem by which one passes from the Ptolemaic theory to the Copernican theory of the outer planets. The ratio of the radius of the circle the eccentric's centre moves on to the eccentric's radius is the same as that of the epicycle's radius to the radius of the deferent in the epicyclic theory. This is apparent from the theorem which follows in the text.

Since this equivalence is so important we shall proceed to give its proof, and then show the immediate resemblance to the conversion theorem. We shall ignore the anomaly of the equant and deferent in this.

Let us consider the epicyclic theory first. Suppose the planet first at A, and then at C. Then angle AEB is the angle of longitude, and angle DBC the angle of anomaly. And angle AEC is the angle of apparent distance between the two positions of the planet.

391

Now
        angle AEC = angle AEB = angle BEC
        angle AEB = angle CBD — angle BCE
since
        angle CBD = angle BCE + angle BEC.

Let us next consider the eccentric hypothesis. Let
$K'E'$, the radius of the circle on which the eccentric's
centre moves, be equal to the epicycle's radius; and
let $A'K'$, the eccentric's radius, be equal to the deferent's radius. Let the planet be first at A' and

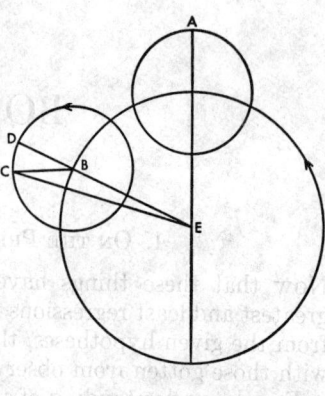

then at C'. Now,
according to the
hypothesis, angle
$A'E'D'$ is equal to
the angle of the
mean sun's mo-
tion, angle $C'B'D'$ is equal to the angle of anomaly,
and angle $A'E'C'$ is the angle of apparent distance.
        But

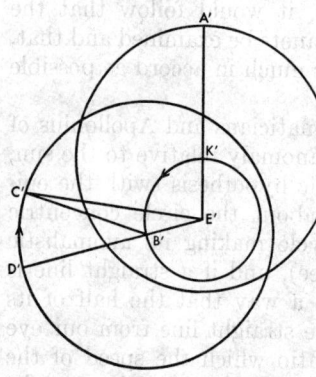

                        angle $A'E'C'$ = angle
                        $A'E'D'$ — angle $B'C'E'$.
And, since angle of mean sun's movement minus the
angle of anomaly is equal to the angle of longitude,
therefore
        angle of longitude = angle $A'E'D'$ — angle
                        $C'E'B'$ — angle $B'C'E'$.
Hence
        angle $A'E'C'$ = angle $A'E'D'$ — angle $C'E'B'$
        = angle of longitude + angle $C'B'D'$ — angle $C'E'B'$.
But because triangle $E'B'C'$ is congruent with triangle EBC in the epicyclic hypothesis,
therefore
                        angle $C'E'B'$ = angle BCE,
and
                        angle $A'E'C'$ = angle AEC,
because angle AEB represents the angle of longitude in the epicyclic hypothesis. Hence
the angle of apparent distance is the same in both hypotheses.

The step from this last hypothesis to the Copernican is fairly immediate. The centre
of the planet's eccentric moves eastward about the earth at the rate of the mean sun.
Suppose, then, that the earth moves about the centre of the planet's eccentric at the
same rate: nothing will be changed in the appearances. And then the centre of the
planet's eccentric would be the mean sun. Then suppose the planet to move about the
eccentric's centre at the rate of the longitudinal movement. We can now demonstrate
the equivalence of these last two hypotheses.

Thus suppose the earth first at E and the planet first at
A; then the earth at D moving about K at the rate of the
mean sun and the planet at C moving about K at the
mean longitudinal rate of the planet. Thus angle EKD is
the movement of the mean sun, angle AKC the longitudinal movement of the planet, and angle ARC the apparent distance between the two positions of the planet.

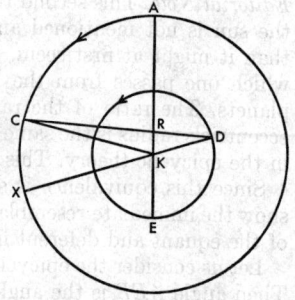

        Now
                angle EKD — angle XKC = angle AKC.
But since angle EKD is the mean sun's movement and
angle AKC the longitudinal movement, and since the
sun's mean movement minus the anomalistic movement
is equal to the longitudinal, therefore angle XKC is the

angle of anomaly. Hence angle CKD equals $C'B'E'$ of the hypothesis of the stationary earth, since in both cases these angles are 2 right angles minus the anomalistic angle. Hence the two triangles CKD and $C'B'E'$ are congruent and

$$\text{angle } CDK = \text{angle } C'E'B'.$$

But

$$\text{angle } ARC = \text{angle } AKC + \text{angle } DCK$$
$$= \text{angle } AKC + \text{angle } CKX - \text{angle } CDK$$

And, since angle AKC is the angle of longitude and angle CKX that of anomaly, therefore

$$\text{angle } ARC = \text{angle } A'E'C'$$

of the former hypothesis. And so in both hypotheses the apparent distances are the same, and they are equivalent for saving the appearances.

The equant and deferent of the Ptolemaic hypothesis is taken care of in the Copernican by making the planet's orbit eccentric to the mean sun and putting the planet on a small epicycle. The proportions are given without explanation by Copernicus in Book V of *The Revolutions of the Celestial Spheres*. Their equivalence will be explained in Appendix B to this book.

The passage from the Ptolemaic to Copernican hypothesis for Venus and Mercury is immediately evident. Hence it is not too daring to say that this hypothesis of eccentricity for the other planets indicates how the Greeks handled their heliocentric theories, no different from the manner of Copernicus. It is not a vague statement Ptolemy is making when he says in Book I of this treatise that the heliocentric theory is simpler for saving astronomical appearances. R. C. T.

Nevertheless we also shall set out briefly and more carefully the required point, using a common proof combined from both hypotheses for showing the accord and similarity in their ratios.

Let there be the epicycle $ABCD$ about centre E, and let AEC be its diameter

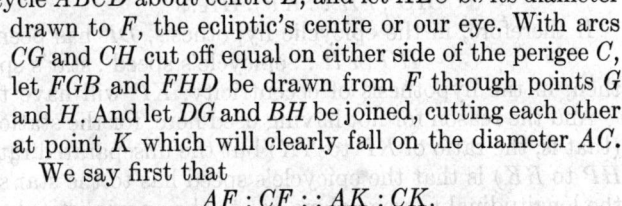

drawn to F, the ecliptic's centre or our eye. With arcs CG and CH cut off equal on either side of the perigee C, let FGB and FHD be drawn from F through points G and H. And let DG and BH be joined, cutting each other at point K which will clearly fall on the diameter AC. We say first that

$$AF : CF : : AK : CK.$$

For let AD and DC be joined. And through C parallel to AD let LCM be drawn, clearly at right angles to DC, since angle ADC is also right. Now since

$$\text{angle } CDG = \text{angle } CDH,$$

therefore

$$CL = CM.$$

And therefore

$$AD : CL : : AD : CM.$$

But

$$AD : CM : : AF : CF,$$

and

$$AD : CL : : AK : CK.$$

And therefore

$$AF : CF : : AK : CK.$$

Therefore, if we conceive the epicycle $ABCD$ as the eccentric in the hypothesis of eccentricity, the point K will be the ecliptic's centre and the diameter AC will be divided by it in the same ratio of the epicyclic hypothesis, since we showed that, for the epicycle, whatever ratio the greatest distance AF has to the least distance CF, that ratio, for the eccentric, the greatest distance AK has to the least distance CK.

And we say that also

$$DF : FH :: BK : HK.$$

For in a similar drawing let there be joined the straight line BND clearly at right angles to diameter $AC;$ and from H let HX be drawn parallel to it.

Since, then,

$$BN = DN,$$

therefore

$$BN : HX :: DN : HX.$$

But

$$DN : HX :: DF : FH,$$

and

$$BN : HX :: BK : HK.$$

And therefore

$$DF : FH :: BK : HK.$$

And *componendo*

$$DF + FH : FH :: BH : HK,$$

and *dividendo*, with the perpendiculars EO and EP drawn,

$$FO : FH :: HP : HK.$$

And further, *separando*,

$$HO : FH :: KP : HK.$$

If therefore, in the epicyclic hypothesis, DF has been so drawn that

$$HO : FH :: \text{epicycle's speed : star's speed},$$

then, in the hypothesis of eccentricity, KP will have to HK the same ratio.

And the reason for not having used here, for the stations, the separated ratio (that is, the ratio of KP to HK) but the unseparated ratio (that is, the ratio of HP to HK) is that the epicycle's speed has to the star's speed the ratio which the longitudinal passage alone has to the anomalistic; but the eccentric's speed has to the star's the ratio which the sun's mean passage (that is, the star's longitudinal and anomalistic passages combined) has to the anomalistic. And so, for example, in the case of Mars, the ratio of the epicycle's speed to the star's speed is very nearly 42 to 37. For we demonstrated the ratio of the longitudinal passage to the anomalistic to be very nearly that. And, therefore, HO to FH is in that ratio. But the eccentric's speed to the star's speed is that of the sum 79 to 37 (that is, of the combined HP to HK) since the separated ratio of KP to HK was the same as the ratio of HO to FH that is, as the ratio of 42 to 37.

Let us consider the things up to this point as preliminary theorems. It is left to show that, when the straight lines taken in either hypothesis are divided in this ratio, then the points G and H will embrace the appearances of stations, and the arc GCH is necessarily regressive and the rest progressive. And Apollonius first

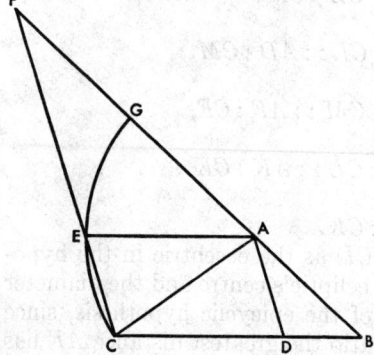

takes this little lemma that, if, in the triangle ABC having BC greater than AC, CD is cut off not less than AC, then

$$CD : BD > \text{angle} : ABC \text{ angle } BCA.$$

And he proves it in this way. For, he says, let the parallelogram $ADCE$ be completed, and let AB and CE produced meet at point F. Since AE is not less than AC, the circle drawn about centre A and with radius AE will pass either through C or beyond C. Then let the circle GEC be drawn through C.

And since

$$\text{trgl. } AEF > \text{sect. } AEG,$$

and

$$\text{trgl. } AEC < \text{sect. } AEC,$$

therefore

$$\text{trgl. } AEF : \text{trgl. } AEC > \text{sect. } AEG : \text{sect. } AEC.$$

But

$$\text{sect. } AEG : \text{sect. } AEC :: \text{angle } EAF : \text{angle } EAC,$$

and

$$\text{trgl. } AEF : \text{trgl. } AEC :: \text{base } EF : \text{base } CE;$$

therefore

$$EF : CE > \text{angle } EAF : \text{angle } EAC.$$

But

$$EF : CE :: CD : BD,$$

and

$$\text{angle } EAF = \text{angle } ABC,$$
$$\text{angle } EAC = \text{angle } ACB.$$

Therefore

$$CD : BD > \text{angle } ABC : \text{angle } ACB.$$

And it is evident that the ratio will be much greater if CD or AE is not supposed equal to AC, but greater.

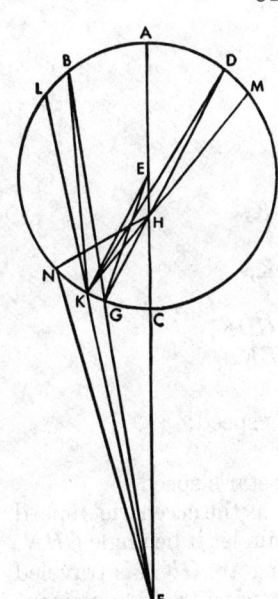

Now, with this first understood, let there be the epicycle $ABCD$ about centre E and diameter AEC. And let the diameter be extended to point F our eye in such a way that

$$CE : CF > \text{epicycle's speed : star's speed.}$$

Therefore it is possible to draw through straight line FGB in such a way that

half $BG : FG ::$ epicycle's speed : star's speed.[1]

If, because of things already proved, we take arc AD equal to arc AB and join DHG, then point H in the hypothesis of eccentricity will be conceived as our eye and

half $DG : HG ::$ eccentric's speed : star's speed.

Then we say that the star at point G, in either hypothesis, will effect the appearance of a station; and, whatever arc we take on either side of G, we shall find the arc taken towards the apogee progressive and that towards the perigee regressive.

For first let there be cut off an arc at random KG

---

[1]For BG takes on every magnitude between CA and nothing, and FG increases from FC to the length of the tangent from F to the epicycle. Therefore the ratio of half BG to FG can be any ratio less than CE to CF. This can be proved on Euclidean principles similar to, and yet different from, those of Dedekind.

towards the apogee. And let FKL and KHM be drawn through; and let BK and DK, and also EK and EG, be joined. Since, then, in triangle BKF,

$$BG > BK,$$

therefore

$$BG : FG > \text{angle } GFK : \text{angle } GBK.$$

And so also

$$\text{half } BG : FG > \text{angle } GFK : 2 \text{ angle } GBK,$$
$$> \text{angle } GFK : \text{angle } GEK.$$

But

$$\text{half } BG : FG :: \text{epicycle's speed : star's speed;}$$

therefore

$$\text{angle } GFK : \text{angle } GEK < \text{epicycle's speed : star's speed.}$$

Therefore the angle, having to angle GEK the same ratio as the epicycle's speed to the star's speed, is greater than angle GFK. Then let it be angle GFN.

Since, then, while the star moves through the epicycle's arc KG, the epicycle's centre has made a passage in the contrary direction equal to the distance from FG to FN, it is evident that in the same time the epicycle's arc KG has carried the star westward through an angle at our eye GFK less than that through which the epicycle has moved it eastward—that is, angle GFN. And so the star has progressed through angle KFN.

Likewise also, if we reason it out with the eccentric circle, since

$$BG : FG > \text{angle } GFK : \text{angle } GBK,$$

therefore *componendo*

$$BF : FG > \text{angle } BKL : \text{angle } GBK.$$

But

$$BF : FG :: DH : GH,$$

and

$$\text{angle } BKL = \text{angle } DKM,[1]$$
$$\text{angle } GBK = \text{angle } GDK.$$

Therefore

$$DH : GH > \text{angle } DKM : \text{angle } GDK.$$

And so also *componendo*

$$DG : GH > \text{angle } GHK : \text{angle } GDK;$$

and therefore *dividendo*

$$\text{half } DG : GH > \text{angle } GHK : 2 \text{ angle } GDK,$$
$$> \text{angle } GHK : \text{angle } GEK.$$

But

$$\text{half } DG : GH :: \text{eccentric's speed : star's speed;}$$

therefore

$$\text{angle } GHK : \text{angle } GEK < \text{eccentric's speed : star's speed.}$$

Therefore the angle, having to angle GEK the same ratio as the eccentric's speed to the star's speed, is greater than angle GHK. Then again let it be angle GHN.

Since, then, in the same time, the star itself describing arc GK has traveled westward angle GEK, and is carried eastward by the eccentric's movement through angle GHN which is greater than angle GHK, it is evident that the star will thus appear to progress through KHN.

---

[1]For arc LB is equal to arc DM, since, in the eccentric theory, the star moves on the eccentric according to the anomalistic speed—that is, as the star moves on the epicycle in the epicyclic theory.

It can be seen at once that by the same means the contrary will also be shown, if in the same drawing we suppose

half KL : FK : : epicycle's speed : star's speed,

so that

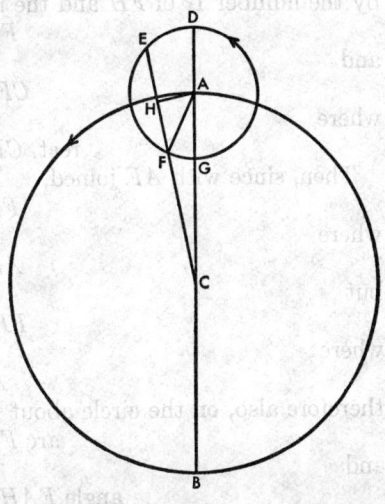

half KM : HK : : eccentric's speed : star's speed,

if we conceive arc GK as having been cut off in the direction of the perigee from straight line FL. For, with LG joined and producing triangle LFG in which FK is cut off greater than FG,

KL : FK < angle GFK : angle GLK.

And so also

half KL : FK < angle GFK : 2 angle GLK
< angle GFK : angle GEK,

conversely to what was shown before. By the same means the contrary can be concluded that

angle GEK : angle GFK < star's speed :
epicycle's speed,

and

angle GEK : angle GHK < star's speed :
eccentric's speed.

And so, since an angle greater than angle GEK would have the same ratio, therefore the regressive shift would turn out greater than the progressive.

For those distances where CE does not have to CF a ratio greater than the ratio of the epicycle's speed to the star's speed, it is evident that it will not be possible to draw another line through in the same ratio, nor will the star appear to pause or to regress. For since, in triangle EKF, the straight line CE is not cut off less than EK, therefore

angle CFK : angle CEK < CE : CF.

But

CE : CF > epicycle's speed : star's speed;

therefore

angle CFK : angle CEK < epicycle's speed : star's speed.

And so, since we have shown the star to progress wherever this happens, we shall find no arc of the epicycle and eccentric for which it will appear to regress.

2. DEMONSTRATION OF SATURN'S REGRESSIONS

With these things so, we shall finally set out the calculation of the regressions for each of the stars in accordance with the hypotheses already demonstrated, beginning with Saturn in this way.

Let the circle bearing the epicycle's centre be the circle AB about diameter ACB, on which let the ecliptic's centre or our eye be supposed. And with the epicycle *DEFG* drawn about centre *A*, let the straight line *CFE* be drawn through in such a way that, if *AH* is drawn perpendicular to it, then

half *EF* or *FH* : *CF* : : epicycle's speed : star's speed.

And first let the epicycle be supposed in the position of the mean distance so that the periodic movements of longitude and anomaly are very nearly the same as those considered with respect to the ecliptic's centre.

Now since, in the case of Saturn, we showed

epic. rad. $AD = 6\frac{1}{2}^\text{p}$

where the mean distance *AC* equals 60ᵖ,
so that, by addition,

$$CD = 66^\text{p}30',$$

and, by subtraction,

$$CG = 53^\text{p}30',$$

and

rect. $CD, CG = 3{,}557^\text{p}45',$

and

rect. $CD, CG = $ rect. $CE, CF,$

therefore we shall also have

rect. $CE, CF = 3{,}557^\text{p}45'.$

Again, since, according to the mean passages,

star's speed or $CF = 28^\text{p}25'\ 46''$

where

epicycle's speed or $FH = 1^\text{p},$

so that, by addition,

$$CE = 30^\text{p}25'46''$$

and

rect. $CE, CF = 865^\text{p}5'32'',$

therefore, if we apply [divide] 3,557ᵖ45' to [by] 865ᵖ5'32'', take the square root 2ᵖ1'40'' of the 4ᵖ6'45'' resulting from the application, and multiply it by the number 1ᵖ of *FH* and the number 28ᵖ25'46'' of *CF*, then we shall have

$$FH = 2^\text{p}1'40''$$

and

$$CF = 57^\text{p}38'55''$$

where

rect. $CE, CF = 3{,}557^\text{p}45'.$

Then, since with *AF* joined,

$$FH = 2^\text{p}1'40''$$

where

$$AF = 6^\text{p}30',$$

but

$$FH = 37^\text{p}26'9''$$

where

$$AF = 120^\text{p},$$

therefore also, on the circle about right triangle *AFH*,

arc $FH = 36°21'15'',$

and

angle $FAH = 36°21'15''$ to 2 rt.
$$\doteqdot 18°10'38''.$$

Again, since by addition
$$CFH = 59^{\mathrm{p}}40'35''$$
where
$$\text{hypt. } CGA = 60^{\mathrm{p}},$$
and
$$CFH = 119^{\mathrm{p}}21'10''$$
where
$$\text{hypt. } CGA = 120^{\mathrm{p}},$$
therefore also, on the circle about right triangle ACH,
$$\text{angle } CAH = 168°5'39'' \text{ to 2 rt.}$$
$$\doteqdot 84°2'50''.$$
And therefore we shall also have, by subtraction, from a right angle,
$$\text{angle } ACH = 5°57'10'',$$
and, by subtraction of angle FAH,
$$\text{angle } FAG = 65°52'12''.$$

Since, then, at the first station, the star appears along CF and, at the acronychal opposition, along CG, it is clear that, if the epicycle's centre were not moving eastward, the 65°52'12'' of arc FG would embrace the 5°57'10'' of angle ACF in regression. But since, according to the given ratio of the epicycle's speed to the star's speed, very nearly 2°19' of longitude corresponds to the required 65°52'12'' of anomaly, from one of the stations to the opposition we shall thus have by subtraction 3°38'10'' and the 69 days in which the star moves very nearly 2°19' of periodic longitude; and we shall have the whole regression of 7°16'20'' and 138 days.

And next we shall examine with the same means the quantities about the greatest distance; that is, when the acronychal opposition midway the stations puts the epicycle's centre at the eccentric's apogee and when each of the stations is clearly at a distance somewhere near the 2°19' demonstrated for the mean distance, from the opposition or the apogee of the longitude truly determined.[1] At this position the straight line AC of the distance for that time is taken as indistinguishable from the greatest, because of theorems already given by us; and an addition-subtraction of very nearly 0°6'30'' is taken as corresponding to 1° of longitude. And so the longitude truly determined to the anomaly truly determined—that is, the epicycle's apparent speed at that time to the star's apparent speed[2] is in the ratio of 0°53'30'' to 28°32'16''.

Now, with the same drawing set out, since, being no different from the greatest distance,
$$AC = 63^{\mathrm{p}}25'$$

[1]To find the longitude truly determined—that is, the change of the epicycle's centre for a particular part of the ecliptic—Ptolemy here uses the same method as for the moon in Book VI, Chap. 4. Going to the Tables of Anomaly in Book XI, we find that for the first 6° in mean longitude there is, in the third column, an addition-subtraction of 0°37' due to the epicycle's centre being moved regularly with respect to an equant not concentric with the ecliptic. This addition-subtraction is taken as if the equant and deferent were the same. But in the fourth column we find an addition of 0°2' due to their not being the same. Hence there is a difference of 0°39' for 6° of the mean longitude, or a difference of 0°6½' for each 1° of mean longitude. Therefore, while the epicycle's centre makes a mean movement of 1°, at this part of the ecliptic it makes an apparent movement of only 0°53½'.

[2]The anomaly truly determined or star's apparent speed on the epicycle is the star's speed taken over a certain distance relative to the epicycle's apparent apogee and perigee rather than its regular apogee and perigee. In planetary theory, the apparent apogee is that defined

where

ecc. rad. $AD = 6^p30'$;

and since for that reason, by addition,

$CD = 69^p55'$

and, by subtraction,

$CG = 56^p55'$

and

rect. CE, CF = rect. CD, CG
$$= 3,979^p25'25'';$$

and since

star's speed or $CF = 28^p32'16''$

where it is supposed

epicycle's speed or $FH = 0^p53'30''$

and, by addition,

$CE = 30^p19'16''$

and

rect. $CE, CF = 865^p17'50''$

therefore, if again we apply [divide] $3,979^p25'25''$ to [by] $865^p17'50''$, and if we multiply the square root $2^p8'40''$ of the $4^p35'56''$ resulting from the application by the $0^p53'30''$ of straight line FH and the $28^p32'16''$ of CF each separately, then we shall have

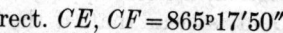

$$FH = 1^p54'44'',$$
$$AC = 63^p25',$$
$$CF = 61^p11'52'',$$

and, by addition,

$$CH = 63^p6'36''$$

where

And therefore

$$AF = 6^p30'.$$
$$FH = 35^p18'9''$$

---

with respect to the ecliptic's centre or the earth; the regular apogee is that defined with respect to the equant's centre.

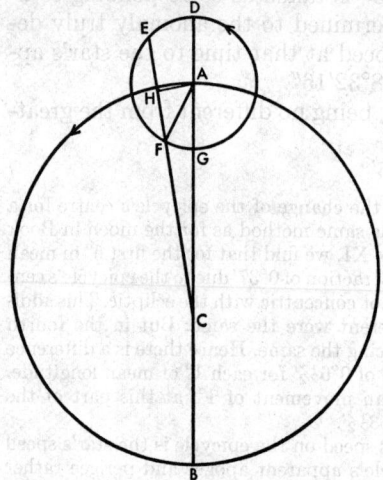

If, now, we wish to get the star's speed from a station preceding the perigee to an acronychal opposition at the greatest distance, consider the figure where E is the ecliptic's centre, D the equant's centre, and F the apogee of eccentricity. Furthermore, A is the epicycle's regular perigee and B its apparent perigee. Now consider the star moving on the epicycle toward A from the side opposite B, while the epicycle's centre C moves toward F. But as C moves towards F, the apparent apogee B moves towards the regular apogee A. Hence the star moves faster toward B than it does toward A. But its regular anomalistic movement is with respect to A, and therefore we add the difference of angle ACB to the regular anomalistic movement for the period of longitudinal movement from C to F, or, as we found above for Saturn, an average of $0°6\frac{1}{2}'$ for each $1°$ of mean longitude and for each $0°53\frac{1}{2}'$ of longitude truly determined.

About the least distance, the difference of apparent anomaly is subtractive for the same reasons.

where
$$\text{hypt. } AF = 120^{\text{p}};$$
and
$$CH = 119^{\text{p}}25'11''$$
where
$$\text{hypt. } AC = 120^{\text{p}}.$$
And therefore, on the circle about right triangle AFH,
$$\text{arc } FH = 34°13'4'';$$
and, on the circle about right triangle ACH,
$$\text{arc } CH = 168°43'38''.$$
And therefore
$$\text{angle } FAH = 34°13'4'' \text{ to 2 rt.}$$
$$= 17°6'32'';$$
and
$$\text{angle } CAH = 168°43'38'' \text{ to 2 rt.}$$
$$= 84°21'49''.$$
And so, by subtraction, we would have
$$\text{angle } ACH = 5°38'11''$$
as the angle from one of the stations to the opposition, if the epicycle did not
lag behind the regression; and, by subtraction, we would have
$$\text{angle } FAG = 67°15'17''$$
as the apparent passage on the epicycle for that distance. Since to these angles,
according to the ratios of the speeds at the apogee, there corresponds $2°6'6''$ of
truly determined longitude, we shall have, by subtraction, half of the whole regression as $3°32'5''$ and $70\frac{1}{3}$ days in which the star very nearly moves the periodic $2°21'25''$ corresponding to the $2°6'6''$ of truly determined longitude required; and we shall have the whole regression as $7°4'10''$ and $140\frac{2}{3}$ days.

Again, through similar means and with the same drawing, we shall examine

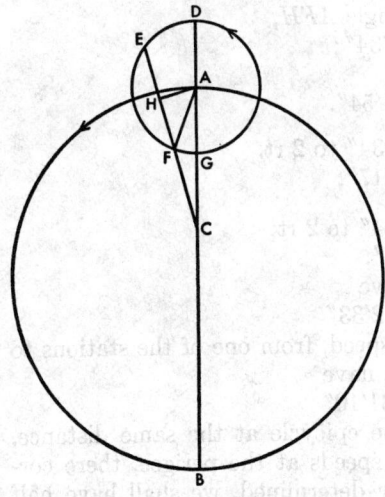

the quantities about the least distance,
when the acronychal opposition midway
the stations is at the eccentric's perigee
and each of the stations is somewhere near
the given longitudinal distance from the
opposition or perigee. And AC, the distance at that time, is taken in this position
as not differing from the least distance,
and the addition-subtraction corresponding to 1° of longitude is taken as very nearly $0°7'20''$. And so here the epicycle's apparent speed to the star's apparent speed
is in the ratio of $1°7'20''$ to $28°18'26''$, and
therefore
$$CF = 28^{\text{p}}18'26''$$
where
$$FH = 1^{\text{p}}7'20'',$$
and by addition
$$CE = 30^{\text{p}}33'6'',$$
and
$$\text{rect. } CE, CF = 864^{\text{p}}49'50''.$$

Now since also, not differing from the least distance,

$$AC = 56^{\text{p}}35'$$

where

$$\text{epic. rad. } AD = 6^{\text{p}}30';$$

and therefore by addition

$$CD = 63^{\text{p}}5'$$

and by subtraction

$$CG = 50^{\text{p}}5'$$

and

$$\text{rect. } CE, CF = \text{rect. } CD, CG$$
$$= 3{,}159^{\text{p}}25'25'',$$

therefore, if in the same way we apply [divide] 3,159ᵖ25′25″ to [by] 864ᵖ49′58″ and, taking the square root 1ᵖ54′42″ of the 3ᵖ39′12″ resulting from the application, multiply by the 1ᵖ7′20″ of the straight line FH and the 28ᵖ18′26″ of CF, each separately, then we shall have

$$FH = 2^{\text{p}}8'43'',$$
$$CF = 54^{\text{p}}6'22'',$$

and by addition

$$CH = 56^{\text{p}}15'5''$$

where

$$\text{epic. rad. } AF = 6^{\text{p}}30'$$

and, as the distance at that time,

$$AC = 56^{\text{p}}35'.$$

And therefore

$$FH = 39^{\text{p}}36'18''$$

where

$$\text{hypt. } HF = 120^{\text{p}};$$

and

$$CH = 119^{\text{p}}17'46''$$

where

$$\text{hypt. } AC = 120^{\text{p}}.$$

And therefore, on the circle about right triangle AFH,

$$\text{arc } FH = 38°32'34'';$$

and, on the circle about right triangle ACH,

$$\text{arc } CH = 167°34'54''.$$

And so also

$$\text{angle } FAH = 38°32'34'' \text{ to 2 rt.}$$
$$= 19°16'17'';$$

and

$$\text{angle } CAH = 167°34'54'' \text{ to 2 rt.}$$
$$= 83°47'27''.$$

And therefore, by subtraction, we shall have

$$\text{angle } ACH = 6°12'33''$$

as the angle of regression, due to the star's speed, from one of the stations to the opposition; and, by subtraction, we shall have

$$\text{angle } FAG = 64°31'10''$$

as the angle of the apparent passage on the epicycle at the same distance. Since to this, according to the ratio of the speeds at the perigee, there corresponds the 2°33′28″ of the longitude truly determined, we shall have half the whole regression of 3°39′5″ and 68 days in which the star very nearly makes a mean movement of 2°16′45″ corresponding to the given 2°33′28″ of the longitude truly determined; and we shall have the whole regression of 7°18′10″ and 136 days.

3. Demonstration of Jupiter's Regressions

In the case of Jupiter, according to the calculations for the mean distance,

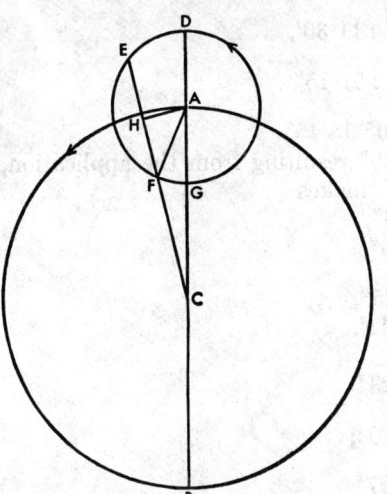

$$FH : CF :: 1^\text{p} : 10^\text{p}51'29'',$$

and

$$CE : CF :: 12^\text{p}51'29'' : 10^\text{p}51'29'',$$

and

$$\text{rect. } CE, CF = 139^\text{p}37'39'';$$

and again

$$AC : AD :: 60^\text{p} : 11^\text{p}30',$$

and

$$CD : CG :: 71^\text{p}30' : 48^\text{p}30',$$

and

$$\text{rect. } CD, CG = 3{,}467^\text{p}45'.$$

And the square root $4^\text{p}59'1''$ of the 24^p $50'9''$ resulting from the application, multiplied by the given ratio of FH and CF, makes

$$FH = 4^\text{p}59'1'',$$
$$CF = 54^\text{p}6'44'',$$

and by addition

$$CH = 59^\text{p}5'45'',$$

relative to the given quantities of AC and AF. And therefore

$$FH = 52^\text{p}0'10''$$

where

$$\text{hypt. } AF = 120^\text{p};$$

and

$$CH = 118^\text{p}11'30''$$

where

$$\text{hypt. } AC = 120^\text{p}.$$

And

$$\text{arc } FH = 51°21'41'',$$
$$\text{arc } CH = 160°4'55''.$$

And accordingly also

$$\text{angle } FAH = 25°40'50'',$$
$$\text{angle } CAH = 80°2'28''.$$

And, by subtraction,

$$\text{angle } FCA = 9°57'32''$$

as the angle of regression due to the star's speed; and

$$\text{angle } FAG = 54°21'38''$$

as the angle of the apparent anomaly. Since to this, according to the given ratio, there corresponds $5°1'24''$ of longitudinal passage, half of the regression is $4°56'8''$ and very nearly $60\frac{1}{2}$ days; and the whole regression is $9°52'16''$ and 121 days.

But the distance at an interval of 5° from the apogee and perigee is hardly less than the greatest and hardly greater than the least.

According to the calculations near the greatest distance, the addition-subtraction of true determination is found to be $0°5'6''$. And therefore

$$FH : CF :: 0^\text{p}54'50'' : 10^\text{p}56'39'',$$

and

$$CE : CF :: 12^\text{p}46'19'' : 10^\text{p}56'39'',$$

and
$$\text{rect. } CE, CF = 139^{\text{p}}46'42''.$$
And again
$$AC : AD :: 62^{\text{p}}45' : 11^{\text{p}}30',$$
and
$$CD : CG :: 74^{\text{p}}15' : 51^{\text{p}}15',$$
and
$$\text{rect. } CD, CG = 3,805^{\text{p}}18'45''.$$
And the square root $5^{\text{p}}13'4''$ of the $27^{\text{p}}13'26''$ resulting from the application, multiplied by the given ratio of FH and CF, makes
$$FH = 4^{\text{p}}46'6'',$$
$$CF = 57^{\text{p}}6'19'',$$
and, by addition,
$$CH = 61^{\text{p}}52'25'',$$
relative to the given quantities of AC and AF.

And therefore also
$$FH = 49^{\text{p}}45'23''$$
where
$$\text{hypt. } AF = 120^{\text{p}};$$
and
$$CH = 118^{\text{p}}19'27''$$
where
$$\text{hypt. } AC = 120^{\text{p}}.$$
and
$$\text{arc } FH = 48°59'34'',$$
$$\text{arc } CH = 160°49'36''.$$

And consequently
$$\text{angle } FAH = 24°29'47'',$$
$$\text{angle } CAH = 80°24'48''.$$
And, by subtraction,
$$\text{angle } FCA = 9°35'12''$$
as the angle of regression due to the star's speed; and
$$\text{angle } FAG = 55°55'1''$$
as the angle of apparent anomaly. Since to this, according to the apogeal ratios, there corresponds $4°40'35''$ of longitude truly determined and $5°6'35''$ of periodic longitude, half of the regression is $4°54'37''$ and very nearly $61\frac{1}{2}$ days, and the whole regression is $9°49'14''$ and 123 days.

According to the calculations near the least distance, the addition-subtraction of true determination is found to be $0°5\frac{2}{3}'$. And therefore
$$FH : CF :: 1^{\text{p}}5'40'' : 10^{\text{p}}45'49'',$$
and
$$CE : CF :: 12^{\text{p}}57'9'' : 10^{\text{p}}45'49'',$$
and
$$\text{rect. } CE, CF = 139^{\text{p}}24'56''.$$
And again
$$AC : AD :: 57^{\text{p}}15' : 11^{\text{p}}30',$$
and
$$CD : CG :: 68^{\text{p}}45' : 45^{\text{p}}45',$$
and
$$\text{rect. } CD, CG = 3,145^{\text{p}}18'45''.$$
And the square root $4^{\text{p}}45'0''$ of the $22^{\text{p}}33'39''$ resulting from the application, multiplied by the given ratio of FH and CF, makes
$$FH = 5^{\text{p}}11'55'',$$
$$CF = 51^{\text{p}}7'38'',$$

and, by addition,
$$CH = 56^\mathrm{p}19'33'',$$
relative to the given quantities of AC and AF.

And therefore also
$$FH = 54^\mathrm{p}14'47''$$
where
$$\text{hypt. } AF = 120^\mathrm{p};$$
and
$$CH = 118^\mathrm{p}3'46''$$
where
$$\text{hypt. } AC = 120^\mathrm{p}.$$
And
$$\text{arc } FH = 53°45'4'',$$
$$\text{arc } CH = 159°22'40''.$$
And consequently also
$$\text{angle } FAH = 26°52'32'',$$
$$\text{angle } CAH = 79°41'20''.$$
And, by subtraction,
$$\text{angle } FCA = 10°18'40''$$
as the angle of regression due to the star's speed; and
$$\text{angle } FAG = 52°48'48''$$
as the angle of the apparent anomaly. Since to this, according to the ratios at the perigee, there corresponds 5°21'20" of longitude truly determined and 4°54'20" of periodic longitude, half of the regression comes to 4°57'20" and very nearly 59 days; and the whole regression comes to 9°54'40" and 118 days.

4. Demonstration of Mars' Regressions

Again, in the case of Mars, according to the calculations for the mean distance

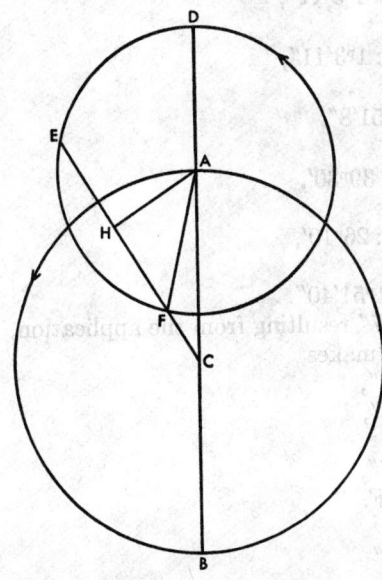

$$FH : CF : : 1^\mathrm{p} : 0^\mathrm{p}52'51'',$$
and
$$CE : CF : : 2^\mathrm{p}52'51'' : 0^\mathrm{p}52'51'',$$
and
$$\text{rect. } CE, CF = 2^\mathrm{p}32'15''.$$
And again
$$AC : AG : : 60^\mathrm{p} : 39^\mathrm{p}30',$$
and
$$CD : CG : : 99^\mathrm{p}30' : 20^\mathrm{p}30',$$
and
$$\text{rect. } CD, CG = 2{,}039^\mathrm{p}45'.$$
And the square root 28ᵖ21'8" of the 803ᵖ 50'50" resulting from the application, multiplied by the given ratio of FH and CF, makes
$$FH = 28^\mathrm{p}21'8'',$$
$$CF = 24^\mathrm{p}58'25'',$$
and, by addition,
$$CH = 53^\mathrm{p}19'33'',$$
relative to the given quantities of AC and AF.

And therefore also

$$FH = 86^{\text{p}}8'0''$$

where

$$\text{hypt. } AF = 120^{\text{p}};$$

and

$$CH = 106^{\text{p}}39'6''$$

where

$$\text{hypt. } AC = 120^{\text{p}}.$$

And

$$\text{arc } FH = 91°44'34'',$$
$$\text{arc } CH = 125°26'10''.$$

And consequently also

$$\text{angle } FAH = 45°52'17'',$$
$$\text{angle } CAH = 62°43'5''.$$

And, by subtraction,

$$\text{angle } FCA = 27°16'55''$$

as the angle of regression due to the star's speed; and

$$\text{angle } FAG = 16°50'48''$$

as the angle of the anomaly. Since to this, according to the given ratio, there corresponds 19°7'33'' of longitudinal passage, half of the regression is 8°9'22'' and very nearly 36½ days; and the whole regression is 16°18'44'' and 73 days.

But the distance, at the interval of the stations from the apogee and perigee, is less than the greatest and greater than the least by very nearly 20 sixtieths.

And according to the calculations near the greatest distance, the addition-subtraction of true determination is found to be 0°10⅓' in proportion to 1°. And therefore

$$FH : CF : : 0^{\text{p}}49'40'' : 1^{\text{p}}3'11'',$$

and

$$CE : CF : : 2^{\text{p}}42'31'' : 1^{\text{p}}3'11'',$$

and

$$\text{rect. } CE, CF = 2^{\text{p}}51'8''.$$

And again

$$AC : AG : : 65^{\text{p}}40' : 39^{\text{p}}30',$$

and

$$CD : CG : : 105^{\text{p}}10' : 26^{\text{p}}10',$$

and

$$\text{rect. } CD, CG = 2{,}751^{\text{p}}51'40''.$$

And the square root 31ᵖ3'41'' of the 964ᵖ48'47'' resulting from the application, multiplied by the given ratio of FH and CF, makes

$$FH = 25^{\text{p}}42'43'',$$
$$CF = 32^{\text{p}}42'34'',$$

and, by addition,

$$CH = 58^{\text{p}}25'17'',$$

relative to the given quantities of AC and AF.

And therefore also

$$FH = 78^{\text{p}}6'44''$$

where

$$\text{hypt. } AF = 120^{\text{p}};$$

and
$$CH = 106^{\text{p}}45'36''$$
where
$$\text{hypt. } AC = 120^{\text{p}}.$$
And
$$\text{arc } FH = 81°13'8'',$$
$$\text{arc } CH = 125°39'46''.$$
And consequently
$$\text{angle } FAH = 40°36'34'',$$
$$\text{angle } CAH = 62°49'53''.$$
And, by subtraction,
$$\text{angle } FCA = 27°10'7''$$
as the angle of regression due to the star's speed; and
$$\text{angle } FAG = 22°13'19''$$
as the angle of the apparent anomaly. Since to this, according to the apogee's ratios, there corresponds 17°13'21'' of longitude truly determined and 20°58'21'' of periodic longitude, half of the regression comes to 9°56'46'' and very nearly 40 days; and the whole regression comes to 19°53'32'' and 80 days.

According to the calculations near the least distance, the addition-subtraction of true determination is found to be 0°12⅔'.
And therefore
$$FH : CF :: 1^{\text{p}}12'40'' : 0^{\text{p}}40'11'',$$
and
$$CE : CF :: 3^{\text{p}}5'31'' : 0^{\text{p}}40'11'',$$
and
$$\text{rect. } CE, CF = 2^{\text{p}}4'14''.$$
And again
$$AC : AG :: 54^{\text{p}}20' : 39^{\text{p}}30',$$
and
$$CD : CG :: 93^{\text{p}}50' : 14^{\text{p}}50',$$
and
$$\text{rect. } CD, CG = 1,391^{\text{p}}51'40''.$$
And the square root 25^{\text{p}}55'38'' of the 672^{\text{p}}12' resulting from the application, multiplied by the ratio of FH and CF, makes
$$FH = 31^{\text{p}}24'3'',$$
$$CF = 17^{\text{p}}21'51'',$$
and by addition
$$CH = 48^{\text{p}}45'54'',$$
relative to the given quantities of AC and AF.
And therefore
$$FH = 95^{\text{p}}23'42''$$
where
$$\text{hypt. } AF = 120^{\text{p}};$$
and
$$CH = 107^{\text{p}}42'7''$$
where
$$\text{hypt. } AC = 120^{\text{p}}.$$
And
$$\text{arc } FH = 105°18'10'',$$
$$\text{arc } CH = 127°40'22''.$$

And consequently

$$\text{angle } FAH = 52°39'5''$$
$$\text{angle } CAH = 63°50'11''.$$

And, by subtraction,

$$\text{angle } FCA = 26°9'49''$$

as the angle of regression due to the star's speed; and

$$\text{angle } FAG = 11°11'6''$$

as the angle of the apparent anomaly. Since to this, according to the ratios at the perigee, there corresponds 20°33'42'' of longitude truly determined and 16°52'52'' of periodic longitude, half of the regression comes to 5°36'7'' and very nearly 32¼ days; and the whole regression comes to 11°12'14'' and 64½ days.

5. Demonstration of Venus' Regressions

Again, in the case of Venus, according to calculations near the mean distance,

$$FH : CF :: 1^p : 0^p37'31'',$$

and

$$CE : CF :: 2^p37'31'' : 0^p37'31'',$$

and

$$\text{rect. } CE, CF = 1^p38'30''.$$

And again

$$AC : AG :: 60^p : 43^p10',$$

and

$$CD : CG :: 103^p10' : 16^p50',$$

and

$$\text{rect. } CD, CG = 1,736^p38'20''.$$

And the square root 32^p31'29'' of the 105^p50'6'' resulting from the application, multiplied by the given ratio of FH and CF, makes

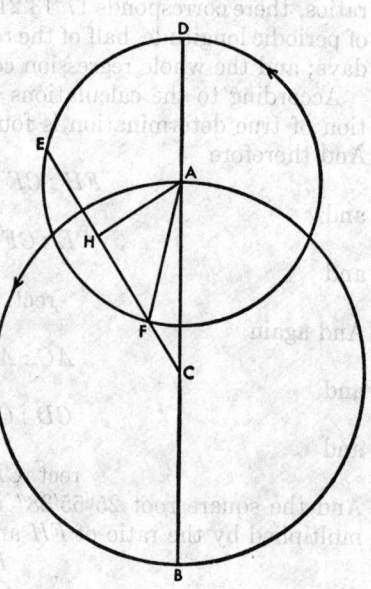

$$FH = 32^p31'29'',$$
$$CF = 20^p20'11'',$$

and, by addition,

$$CH = 52^p51'40'',$$

relative to the given quantities of AC and AF.

And therefore also

$$FH = 90^p24'58'',$$

where

$$\text{hypt. } AF = 120^p;$$

and

$$CH = 105^p43'20''$$

where

$$\text{hypt. } AC = 120^p.$$

And

$$\text{arc } FH = 97°47'0'',$$
$$\text{arc } CH = 123°31'49''.$$

And consequently also

$$\text{angle } FAH = 48°53'30'',$$
$$\text{angle } CAH = 61°45'54''.$$

And, by subtraction,
$$\text{angle } FCA = 28°14'6''$$
as the angle of regression due to the star's speed; and
$$\text{angle } FAG = 12°52'24''$$
as the angle of the anomaly. Since to this, according to the given mean ratio, there corresponds 20°35'19'' of the longitudinal passage, half of the regression comes to 7°38'47'' and very nearly $20 + \frac{1}{2} + \frac{1}{3}$ days; and the whole regression comes to 15°17'34'' and $41\frac{2}{3}$ days.

And the distance at the interval of the stations from the apogee and perigee is less than the greatest and greater than the least, by very nearly 5 sixtieths of the mean distance.

According to the calculations near the greatest distance, the addition-subtraction of true determination is found to be 0°2⅓'. And therefore
$$FH : CF :: 0^{\text{p}}57'40'' : 0^{\text{p}}39'51'',$$
$$CE : CF :: 2^{\text{p}}35'11'' : 0^{\text{p}}39'51'',$$
and
$$\text{rect. } CE, CF = 1^{\text{p}}43'4''.$$
And again
$$AC : AG :: 61^{\text{p}}10' : 43^{\text{p}}10',$$
and
$$CD : CG :: 104^{\text{p}}20' : 18^{\text{p}}0',$$
and
$$\text{rect. } CD, CG = 1,878^{\text{p}}0'.$$

And the square root 33ᵖ3'53'' of the 1,093ᵖ16'23'' resulting from the application, multiplied by the given ratio of FH and CF, makes
$$FH = 31^{\text{p}}46'44'',$$
$$CF = 21^{\text{p}}57'38'',$$
and, by addition,
$$CH = 53^{\text{p}}44'22'',$$
relative to the given quantities of AC and AF.

And therefore also
$$FH = 88^{\text{p}}20'34''$$
where
$$\text{hypt. } AF = 120^{\text{p}};$$
and
$$CH = 105^{\text{p}}25'44''$$
where
$$\text{hypt. } AC = 120^{\text{p}}.$$
And
$$\text{arc } FH = 94°48'54'',$$
$$\text{arc } CH = 122°56'27''.$$
And consequently
$$\text{angle } FAH = 47°24'27'',$$
$$\text{angle } CAH = 61°28'14''.$$

And, by subtraction,
$$\text{angle } FCA = 28°31'46''$$
as the angle of regression due to the star's speed; and
$$\text{angle } FAG = 14°3'47''$$
as the angle of the apparent anomaly. Since to this, according to the ratios at the apogee, there corresponds 20°19'3'' of longitude truly determined and 21°9'

3″ of periodic longitude, half of the regression comes to 8°12′43″ and very nearly 21½ days; and the whole regression comes to 16°25′26″ and 43 days.

According to the calculations near the least distance, the addition-subtraction of true determination is found to be 0°2⅓′.
And therefore

$$FH : CF :: 1^{\mathrm{p}}2′20″ : 0^{\mathrm{p}}35′11″,$$

and

$$CE : CF :: 2^{\mathrm{p}}39′51″ : 0^{\mathrm{p}}35′11″,$$

and

$$\text{rect. } CE, CF = 1^{\mathrm{p}}33′44″.$$

And again

$$AC : AD :: 58^{\mathrm{p}}50′ : 43^{\mathrm{p}}10′,$$

and

$$CD : CG :: 102^{\mathrm{p}}0′ : 15^{\mathrm{p}}40′,$$

and

$$\text{rect. } CD, CG = 1{,}598^{\mathrm{p}}0′.$$

And the square root $31^{\mathrm{p}}58′58″$ of the $1{,}022^{\mathrm{p}}54′7″$ resulting from the application, multiplied by the given ratio of FH and CF, makes

$$FH = 33^{\mathrm{p}}13′36″,$$
$$CF = 18^{\mathrm{p}}45′16″,$$

and, by addition,

$$CH = 51^{\mathrm{p}}58′52″,$$

relative to the supposed quantities of AC and AF.

And therefore also

$$FH = 92^{\mathrm{p}}22′3″$$

where

$$\text{hypt. } AF = 120^{\mathrm{p}};$$

and

$$CH = 106^{\mathrm{p}}1′23″$$

where

$$\text{hypt. } AC = 120^{\mathrm{p}}.$$

And

$$\text{arc } FH = 100°39′34″,$$
$$\text{arc } CH = 124°8′22″.$$

And consequently

$$\text{angle } FAH = 50°19′47″,$$
$$\text{angle } CAH = 62°4′11″.$$

And, by subtraction,

$$\text{angle } FCA = 27°55′49″$$

as the angle of regression due to the star's speed; and

$$\text{angle } FAG = 11°44′24″$$

as the angle of the apparent anomaly. Since to this, according to the ratios at the perigee, there corresponds 20°53′30″ of longitude truly determined and 20°4′30″ of periodic longitude, half of the regression consequently comes to 7°2′19″ and very nearly 20⅓ days; and the whole regression comes to 14°4′38″ and 40⅔ days.

6. Demonstration of Mercury's Regressions

And again, in the case of Mercury, according to the calculations near the mean distance,

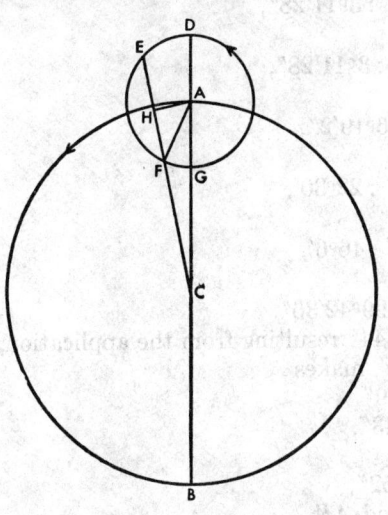

$$FH : CF :: 1^p : 3^p9'8'',$$

and

$$CE : CF :: 5^p9'8'' : 3^p9'8'',$$

and

$$\text{rect. } CE, CF = 16^p14'27''.$$

And again

$$AC : AG :: 60^p : 22\tfrac{1}{2}^p,$$

and

$$CD : CG :: 82^p30' : 37^p30',$$

and

$$\text{rect. } CD, CG = 3,093^p45'.$$

And the square root $13^p48'7''$ of the 190^p $29'31''$ resulting from the application, multiplied by the give ratio of FH and CF, makes

$$FH = 13^p48'7'',$$
$$CF = 43^p30'24'',$$

and, by addition,

$$CH = 57^p18'31'',$$

relative to the supposed quantities of AC and AF.

And therefore also

$$FH = 73^p36'37''$$

where

$$\text{hypt. } AF = 120^p;$$

and

$$CH = 114^p37'2''$$

where

$$\text{hypt. } AC = 120^p.$$

And

$$\text{arc } FH = 75°40'28'',$$
$$\text{arc } CH = 145°32'52''.$$

And consequently

$$\text{angle } FAH = 37°50'14'',$$
$$\text{angle } CAH = 72°46'26''.$$

And, by subtraction,

$$\text{angle } FCA = 17°13'34''$$

as the angle of regression due to the star's speed; and

$$\text{angle } FAG = 34°56'12''$$

as the angle of anomaly. Since to this, according to the given ratio, there corresponds $11°4'59''$ of longitudinal passage, half of the regression is left to be $6°8'35''$ and very nearly $11\tfrac{1}{4}$ days; and the whole regression is left to be $12°17'$ $10''$ and $22\tfrac{1}{2}$ days.

According to the calculations near the greatest distance, that is, when the longitude truly determined is about $11°$ from the apogee (to which there corresponds very nearly 11½° of regular longitude), the addition-subtraction of true determination is found to be very nearly 0°2⅓′ in proportion to 1°. And therefore

$$FH : CF :: 0^\text{p}57'40'' : 3^\text{p}11'28'',$$

and

$$CE : CF :: 5^\text{p}6'48'' : 3^\text{p}11'28'',$$

and

$$\text{rect. } CE, CF = 16^\text{p}19'2''.$$

And again

$$AC : AG :: 68^\text{p}36' : 22^\text{p}30',$$

and

$$CD : CG :: 91^\text{p}6' : 46^\text{p}6',$$

and

$$\text{rect. } CD, CG = 4,199^\text{p}42'36''.$$

And the square root 16ᵖ2′35″ of the 257ᵖ22′44″ resulting from the application, multiplied by the given ratio of FH and CF, makes

$$FH = 15^\text{p}25'9'',$$
$$CF = 51^\text{p}11'43'',$$

and, by addition,

$$CH = 66^\text{p}36'52'',$$

relative to the supposed quantities of AC and AF.

And therefore also

$$FH = 82^\text{p}14'8''$$

where

$$\text{hypt. } AF = 120^\text{p};$$

and

$$CH = 116^\text{p}31'36''$$

where

$$\text{hypt. } AC = 120^\text{p}.$$

And

$$\text{arc } FH = 86°31'4'',$$
$$\text{arc } CH = 152°27'56''.$$

And consequently

$$\text{angle } FAH = 43°15'32'',$$
$$\text{angle } CAH = 76°13'58''.$$

And, by subtraction,

$$\text{angle } FCA = 13°46'2''$$

as the angle of regression due to the star's speed; and

$$\text{angle } FAG = 32°52'26''$$

as the angle of apparent anomaly. And since to this, according to the ratios at the apogee, there corresponds 9°48′51″ of longitude truly determined, and 10°16′51″ of periodic longitude, half of the regression is left to be 3°57′11″ and very nearly 10½ days; and the whole regression to be 7°54′22″ and 21 days.

According to the calculations near the least distances, which are at the intervals of 120° in periodic longitude from the apogee, the addition-subtraction of true determination for the rate 11° either side of the perigees is found to be very nearly 0°1½′. And therefore

$$FH : CF :: 1^\text{p}1'30'' : 3^\text{p}7'38'',$$

and
$$CE : CF :: 5^p10'38'' : 3^p7'38'',$$
and
$$\text{rect. } CE, CF = 16^p11'25''.$$

And again, very nearly,
$$AC : AG :: 55^p42' : 22^p30',$$
and
$$CD : CG :: 78^p12' : 33^p12',$$
and
$$\text{rect. } CD, CG = 2,596^p14'24''.$$

And the square root $12^p39'48''$ of the $160^p21'29''$ resulting from the application, multiplied by the given ratio of FH and CF separately, makes
$$FH = 12^p58'47'',$$
$$FC = 39^p36'4'',$$
and by addition
$$CH = 52^p34'51'',$$
relative to the supposed quantities of AC and AF.

And therefore also
$$FH = 69^p13'31''$$
where
$$\text{hypt. } AF = 120^p;$$
and
$$CH = 113^p16'48''$$
where
$$\text{hypt. } AC = 120^p.$$

And
$$\text{arc } FH = 70°27'44'',$$
$$\text{arc } CH = 141°28'14''.$$

And consequently
$$\text{angle } FAH = 35°13'52'',$$
$$\text{angle } CAH = 70°44'7''.$$

And, by subtraction,
$$\text{angle } FCA = 19°15'53''$$
as the angle of regression due to the star's speed; and
$$\text{angle } FAG = 35°30'15''$$
as the angle of the apparent anomaly. Since to this, according to the given ratios, there corresponds $11°39'30''$ of longitude truly determined, and $11°$ $21'30''$ of periodic longitude, half of the regression is left to be $7°36'23''$ and very nearly $11\frac{1}{2}$ days; and the whole regression to be $15°12'46''$ and 23 days.

The quantities which have been shown are in each case very nearly in accord with those taken from the appearances.

And we got the rates of longitudinal passage about the greatest and least distances in this way: for example, in the case of those about the greatest distance of Mars we showed the epicycle's apparent arc from one of the stations to the opposition (that is, the arc considered with respect to the ecliptic's centre) to be $22°13'19''$. The approximately $21°10'$ of periodic longitude corresponding to these in the ratio of 1^p to $1^p3'11''$, although they are not exact because the speeds given at the stations do not remain unchanged throughout the whole regressions, yet do not differ enough to make the corresponding addition-subtraction differ appreciably from very nearly 3°45′. And we subtracted these from the 22°13′19″ of the epicycle, since at the greatest distances the apparent passages on the epicycle are greater than the periodic, and we found the corresponding periodic passage of anomaly from one of the stations to the opposition to be 18°28′19″. Since, by the ratio of the mean movements, 20°58′21″ of periodic longitude correspond to them, we used these as exact instead of the 21°10′. Subtracting from them the 3°45′ of addition-subtraction which remained almost the same here (for at the greatest distances the apparent passages in longitude are less than the periodic) we found the apparent passage in longitude for the given interval to be 17°13′21″.

7. Construction of a Table for the Stations

And again, in order that we may be able easily to see at what sections of the epicycle each of the stars makes the appearance of stations for the distances between the mean distance and the greatest and least distances, we arrange this table of 31 rows and 12 columns. The first two columns contain the numbers of periodic longitude at intervals of 6° according to the developments of the other tables. And the ten columns following contain, for each of the five stars, the intervals of anomaly truly determined from the epicycles' apparent apogees—the first one in each case containing those of the first stations and the second those of the second. We took the quantities of these from what was demonstrated above for the mean, least, and greatest distances, and from those differences in the distances between which we have already explained for the comparison by sixtieths in the eighth column of the Tables of Anomalies, Book XI, chap. 11. The epicycles' distances, relative to which the difference of the stations is most especially considered, are there demonstrated for each passage of periodic longitude with the quantity of greatest anomalistic difference.

Since the regressions shown about the apogees and perigees do not contain the stations resulting when the epicycles' centres are at the apogees and perigees but only when they are a certain distance away, for each star we first of all got from these quantities the quantities corresponding to the apogees and perigees in this way.

Now, in the case of Saturn and Jupiter—since the epicycles' distances at the apogees and perigees differ hardly at all from those at the given intervals from them—we placed, in the proper rows, the anomalistic numbers from the epicycles' apparent apogees, obtained in these cases; that is, those of the apogees in the rows containing the number 360, and those of the perigees in the rows containing the number 180. In the case of Saturn the distance from the epicycle's perigee, at the apogee of eccentricity, was shown to be very nearly 67°15′, and at the perigee 64°31′; in the case of Jupiter, the distance at the apogee 55°55′, and at the perigee 52°49′. For convenience we arranged the numbers from the epicycles' apogees corresponding to these in the subsequent four columns along the proper rows: along the row containing the apogee's number of 360°, in the third column, the 112°45′ of Saturn's first station; in the fourth, the 247°15′ of its second station; likewise, in the fifth, the 124°5′ of Jupiter's first station; and, in the sixth, the 235°55′ of its second station. And along the row containing the perigee's number of 180°, according to the same order, 115°29′ and 244°31′; and likewise 127°11′ and 232°49′.

In the case of Mars, we showed that, whenever the epicycle's centre is 20°58' of periodic movement from the eccentric's apogee, the star makes its stations at a distance of 22°13' from the epicycle's apparent perigee. But the passage at the mean distance contains 16°51', so that there is a difference of 5°22'. And where the mean distance is 60ᵖ, the greatest is 66ᵖ, and the difference relative to the mean is 6ᵖ. But at the given angular distance from the apogee, it is 65ᵖ40', and the difference relative to the mean 5ᵖ40'. Now, multiplying the 6ᵖ by the 5°22', and applying [dividing] the result to [by] the 5ᵖ40', we found the distance at the apogee over the mean distance to be very nearly 5°41'. And so the angular distance from the epicycle's apparent perigee comes to 22°32', and the angular distance of the first station from the apogee comes to 157°28' which we place in the seventh column in the row of 360°; and of the second station to 202°32' which we place in the eighth column in the same row.

Likewise, when the epicycle's centre is 16°53' in mean movement from the perigee, the star makes its stations at a distance of 11°11' from the epicycle's apparent perigee, so that the difference relative to the mean distance comes to 5°40'. But of the linear distances, the least is 54ᵖ according to the difference of 6ᵖ relative to the mean, and that of the given angular distance from the eccentric's perigee 54ᵖ20'; and the difference relative to the mean 5ᵖ40'. Therefore we shall have the whole difference at the perigee to be 6°, and the passage from the epicycle's apparent perigee 10°51'; and the passage of the first station from the apogee 169°9', and of the second, 190°51', which we place in the 180° row in the proper columns.

In the case of Venus, we showed that, when the epicycle's centre is 21°9' in periodic longitude from the apogee, the star makes its stations 14°4' from the epicycle's apparent perigee. But the passage at the mean distance contains 12° 52', so that there is a difference of 1°12'. Where the mean distance is 60ᵖ, the greatest is 61ᵖ15' and the difference relative to the mean 1ᵖ15'. But at the given angular distance from the apogee, the distance is 61ᵖ10' and the difference relative to the mean 1ᵖ10'. And again, multiplying 1ᵖ15' by 1°12' and applying [dividing] the result to [by] 1ᵖ10', we found the difference at the apogee over the mean distance to be 1°17'. And so the angular distance from the epicycle's apparent perigee comes to 14°9', and the angular distance of the first station from the apogee comes to 165°51' which we place in the ninth column in the row of 360°; and of the second station to 194°9', which we place in the tenth column along the same row.

And likewise, when the epicycle is very nearly 20° according to regular longitudinal passage from the eccentric's perigee, the star makes its stations at a distance of 11°44' from the epicycle's apparent perigee, so that the difference relative to the mean distance comes to 1°8'. Of the linear distances, the least is 58ᵖ45' where the mean is 60ᵖ, and the difference between them 1ᵖ15'; but that of the given angular distance from the eccentric's perigee 58ᵖ50', and its difference relative to the mean 1ᵖ10'. And nultiplying the 1ᵖ15' by the 1°8' and applying [dividing] the result to [by] 1ᵖ10', we found the difference at the apogee over the mean distance to be 1ᵖ13'. Therefore we found the passage from the epicycle's apparent perigee to be 11°39', and the passage of the first station from the apogee to be 168°21', and of the second station 191°39', which we place in the same columns by the number 180°.

In the case of Mercury, we demonstrated that, when the epicycle is 10°17' in periodic longitude from the eccentric's apogee, the star makes its stations 32°52′ from the epicycle's apparent perigee. But the passage at the mean distance contains 34°56′, so that there is a difference of 2°4′. Where the mean distance is 60^p, the greatest is 69^p and the difference between them 9^p; but at the given angular distance from the apogee, it is 68^{p}36′ and the difference relative to the mean 8^{p}36′. And in the same way as before, multiplying the 9^p by 2°4′ and applying [dividing] the result to [by] 8^{p}36′, we found the difference at the apogee over the mean distance to be very nearly 2^{p}10′. And so the angular distance from the epicycle's apparent perigee comes to 32°46′, and the angular distance of the first station from the apogee comes to 147°14′ which we place in the eleventh column beside the number of 360°; and, of the second station, to 212°46′, which we place in the twelfth column along the same row.

And likewise, when the epicycle is 11°22′ in periodic movement from the perigee, then the star makes its stations 35°30′ from the epicycle's apparent perigee so that the difference relative to the mean distance is 0°34′. Of the linear distances, the least is 55^{p}34′ where the mean is 60^p, and their difference is 4^{p}26′; but at the given angular distance from the eccentric's perigee is very nearly 55^{p}42′, and the difference relative to the mean 4^{p}18′. Again multiplying the 4^{p}26′ by 0°34′ and applying [dividing] the result to [by] the 4^{p}18′, we found the difference at the perigee relative to the mean to be 0^{p}35′. Therefore we found the passage from the epicycle's apparent perigee to be 35°31′, and the perigee of the first station from the apogee to be 144°29′, and, of the second, 215°31′, which we place in the same columns; yet not beside the number 180° in longitude but beside 120° and 240°, since the perigees of Mercury's eccentricity have been demonstrated to be at those places.

Now with these things first set forth, the differences of the intervening passages are established according to the same methods.

For, as an example, let it be required to find the corresponding positions of the apparent anomaly for the first stations when the mean longitudinal passage is 30° from the apogee. In this position, where the mean distance is in every case 60^p, the epicycle's distance is established, by means already formulated, to be 63^{p}2′ for Saturn, 62^{p}26′ for Jupiter, 65^{p}24′ for Mars, 61^{p}6′ for Venus, and 66^{p}35′ for Mercury. And so, relative to the mean, the differences in each case are (in the same order, to avoid repetition) 3^{p}2′, 2^{p}26′, 5^{p}24′, 1^{p}6′, and 6^{p}35′. But the differences between the mean and apogeal distances (for in every case the given numbers of the distances are greater than the mean) are 3^{p}25′, 2^{p}45′, 6^{p}0′, 1^{p}15′, and 9^{p}0′. Now, since the whole differences of the degrees of apparent anomaly at the apogees, relative to the mean distances, come to 1°23′, 1°33′, 5°41′, 1°17′, and 2°10′, in the same order, therefore, multiplying each of them by the difference between the distance at that time and the mean, proper to each star (for example, 1°23′ by 3^{p}2′), and applying [dividing] the result to [by] the difference of the greatest distance (for instance 3^{p}25′), we shall have, for each case at the given longitudinal passage, the excess of the degrees of anomaly over those for the mean distance: 1°14′, 1°22′, 5°7′, 1°8′, and 1°35′. But, for the mean distances, the intervals from the epicycle's apparent apogee are 114°8′, 135°38′, 163°9′, 167°8′, and 145°4′; and the intervals for the greatest distances are less than these in all cases except Mercury where it is more. And so, for the other cases, subtracting the differences found for the given distances from intervals at the mean distances, but adding them in the case of Mercury, we shall have, corresponding to 30° of periodic longitude in the columns of the first stations, the degrees of apparent anomaly from the epicycle's apogee: 112°54′ for Saturn, 124° 16′ for Jupiter, 158°2′ for Mars, 166° for Venus, and 146°39′ for Mercury. We fill in the columns of the second stations immediately by placing the differences between the numbers of the first stations and 360° in the same rows in the columns of the second stations: in the case of the given longitude, 247°6′, 235°44′, 201°58′, 194°0′, and 213°21′.

It is easily understood that, even if we do not choose to set out the degrees of anomaly considered with respect to the epicycle's apparent apogee, but, for greater convenience, those not truly determined considered relative to the periodic, we can immediately establish such a table by taking the total addition-subtraction in the Tables of Anomaly corresponding to each number of periodic longitude and subtracting it from the degrees of apparent anomaly found for those up to 180° from the eccentric's apogee and adding it for those beyond 180°. And here is the outlay of the table:

8. Numbers of Anomaly Truly Determined

Common Numbers		SATURN First Station	SATURN Second Station	JUPITER First Station	JUPITER Second Station	MARS First Station	MARS Second Station	VENUS First Station	VENUS Second Station	MERCURY First Station	MERCURY Second Station
0	360	112 45	247 15	124 5	235 55	157 28	202 32	165 51	194 9	147 14	212 46
6	354	112 45	247 15	124 6	235 54	157 29	202 31	165 52	194 8	147 13	212 47
12	348	112 46	247 14	124 7	235 53	157 34	202 26	165 53	194 7	147 8	212 52
18	342	112 48	247 12	124 9	235 51	157 41	202 19	165 55	194 5	147 1	212 59
24	336	112 51	247 9	124 12	235 48	157 50	202 10	165 57	194 3	146 51	213 9
30	330	112 54	247 6	124 16	235 44	158 2	201 58	166 0	194 0	146 39	213 21
36	324	112 58	247 2	124 21	235 39	158 18	201 42	166 4	193 56	146 25	213 35
42	318	113 3	246 57	124 26	235 34	158 34	201 26	166 9	193 51	146 11	213 49
48	312	113 8	246 52	124 32	235 28	158 55	201 5	166 15	193 45	145 55	214 5
54	306	113 15	246 45	124 39	235 21	159 17	200 43	166 22	193 38	145 39	214 21
60	300	113 22	246 38	124 47	235 13	159 42	200 18	166 29	193 31	145 23	214 37
66	294	113 29	246 31	124 55	235 5	160 10	199 50	166 35	193 25	145 8	214 52
72	286	113 36	246 24	125 3	234 57	160 39	199 21	166 42	193 18	144 58	215 2
78	282	113 44	246 16	125 12	234 48	161 10	198 50	166 50	193 10	144 52	215 8
84	276	113 53	246 7	125 22	234 38	161 44	198 16	166 58	193 2	144 46	215 14
90	270	114 1	245 59	125 32	234 28	162 18	197 42	167 7	192 53	144 40	215 20
96	264	114 10	245 50	125 41	234 19	162 54	197 6	167 14	192 46	144 36	215 24
102	258	114 18	245 42	125 51	234 9	163 31	196 29	167 21	192 39	144 33	215 27
108	252	114 27	245 33	126 0	234 0	164 9	195 51	167 28	192 32	144 30	215 30
114	246	114 35	245 25	126 10	233 50	164 47	195 13	167 35	192 25	144 30	215 30
120	240	114 43	245 17	126 19	233 41	165 25	194 35	167 43	192 17	144 29	215 31
126	234	114 51	245 9	126 28	233 32	166 3	193 57	167 50	192 10	144 29	215 31
132	228	114 58	245 2	126 36	233 24	166 37	193 23	167 56	192 4	144 30	215 30
138	222	115 5	244 55	126 44	233 16	167 8	192 52	168 1	191 59	144 31	215 29
144	216	115 11	244 49	126 51	233 9	167 39	192 21	168 6	191 54	144 33	215 27
150	210	115 16	244 44	126 57	233 3	168 4	191 56	168 10	191 50	144 35	215 25
156	204	115 21	244 39	127 2	232 58	168 28	191 32	168 14	191 46	144 37	215 23
162	198	115 25	244 35	127 6	232 54	168 46	191 14	168 17	191 43	144 38	215 22
168	192	115 27	244 33	127 8	232 52	168 59	191 1	168 19	191 41	144 39	215 21
174	186	115 29	244 31	127 10	232 50	169 8	190 52	168 20	191 40	144 40	215 20
180	180	115 29	244 31	127 11	232 49	169 9	190 51	168 21	191 39	144 40	215 20

9. Demonstration of Venus' and Mercury's Greatest Elongations from the Sun

Now that we have arranged things having to do with the regressions, it would be reasonable next to demonstrate for each dodecatemory the greatest elongations from the sun of Venus and Mercury as established from the given hypotheses. We have the expositions of these with respect to the sun's apparent passage, with the stars at the beginnings of the dodecatemories, and with their apogees in position with respect to the tropic and equinoctial points for our times—that is, with Venus' 25° within the Bull and Mercury's 10° within the Balance. There will be a change in the greatest elongations because of the movement of the apogees and this can be easily corrected by the same methods as before; otherwise it will remain without any appreciable difference for a long time. And that the manner of our methods may be easily understood, it is necessary to show first, as an example, the greatest morning and evening elongations of Venus when it is in the spring equinox and at the beginning of the Ram.

Then let there be through the apogee of eccentricity A the straight line $ABCDE$. And on it let B be supposed the centre of regular movement, C the centre of the eccentric bearing the epicycle, and D the ecliptic's centre. And, with the eccentric's radius CF drawn through, let the epicycle GH be described about F; and let DH be drawn tangent to its morning and western parts. And let BFG and FH be joined; and let CK, CL, and BM be drawn as perpendiculars.

Now, since DA is 25° within the Bull, and DH at the beginning of the Ram, therefore

$$\text{angle } ADH = 55°$$
$$= 110° \text{ to 2 rt.}$$

and its complement

$$\text{angle } DCK = 70° \text{ to 2 rt.}$$

And so also, on the circle about right triangle CDK,

$$\text{arc } CK = 110°,$$

and

$$\text{chord } CK = 98^\text{p}18'$$

where

$$\text{hypt. } CD = 120^\text{p}.$$

And therefore

$$CK = HL = 1^\text{p}1'$$

where

$$CD = 1^\text{p}15'$$

and

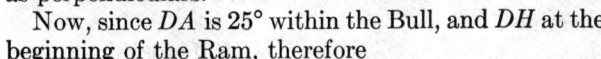

$$\text{epic. rad. } FH = 43^\text{p}10';$$

and, by subtraction,

$$FL = 42^\text{p}9'$$

where it is supposed

$$\text{ecc. rad. } CF = 60^\text{p}.$$

And therefore

$$FL = 84^{\text{p}}18'$$

where

$$\text{hypt. } CF = 120^{\text{p}};$$

and, on the circle about right triangle CFL,

$$\text{arc } FL = 89°16'.$$

And so also

$$\text{angle } FCL = 89°16' \text{ to 2 rt.}$$

And

$$\text{angle } DCK = 70° \text{ to 2 rt.,}$$

and angle LCK is right. Therefore, by addition,

$$\text{angle } FCD = 339°16' \text{ to 2 rt.,}$$

and, by subtraction,

$$\text{angle } ACF = 20°44' \text{ to 2 rt.}$$

And so also, on the circle about right triangle BCM,

$$\text{arc } BM = 20°44'$$

and as its supplement

$$\text{arc } CM = 159°16'.$$

And therefore

$$\text{chord } BM = 21^{\text{p}}35',$$
$$\text{chord } CM = 118^{\text{p}}2'$$

where

$$\text{hypt. } BC = 120^{\text{p}}.$$

And so also, where

$$BC = 1^{\text{p}}15'$$

and

$$\text{ecc. rad. } CF = 60^{\text{p}},$$

there also

$$BM = 0^{\text{p}}13',$$
$$CM = 1^{\text{p}}14',$$

and, by subtraction,

$$FM = 58^{\text{p}}46'.$$

And therefore also

$$\text{hypt. } BF = 58^{\text{p}}46'.$$

And therefore

$$BM = 0^{\text{p}}27'$$

where

$$BF = 120^{\text{p}};$$

and, on the circle about right triangle BFM,

$$\text{arc } BM = 0^{\text{p}}26'.$$

And so also

$$\text{angle } BFC = 0°26' \text{ to 2 rt.}$$

But it was shown that

$$\text{angle } ACF = 20°44' \text{ to 2 rt.}$$

And therefore, by addition, as the angle of regular longitudinal passage,

$$\text{angle } ABF = 21°10' \text{ to 2 rt.}$$
$$= 10°35'.$$

The sun's mean passage will therefore be 10°35' westward from the apogee A and its position, of course, 14°25' within the Bull; while the true sun will be 15°14' within the Bull. And so the star, when it is at the beginning of the

Ram, will have a greatest western elongation from the true sun of 45°14′.

Again, let the following drawing be laid out: the tangent drawn to the evening and eastern parts of the epicycle and the star likewise supposed at the beginning of the Ram.

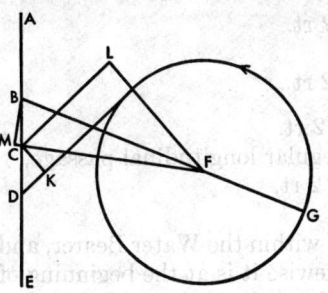

By means of things already demonstrated and with angle ADH remaining the same,

angle $DCK = 70°$ to 2 rt.,

and

chord $CK = LH = 1^{\mathrm{p}}1′$

where

ecc. rad. $CF = 60^{\mathrm{p}}$

and

epic. rad. $FH = 43^{\mathrm{p}}10′$.

And so, by addition,

$$FL = 44^{\mathrm{p}}11′.$$

And it is clear that

$$FL = 88^{\mathrm{p}}22′$$

where

hypt. $CF = 120^{\mathrm{p}}$;

and, on the circle about right triangle CFL,

arc $FL = 94°51′$.

And so also

angle $FCL = 94°51′$ to 2 rt.,

and as its complement

angle $FCK = 85°9′$ to 2 rt.,

and, by addition,

angle FCD = angle $BCM = 155°9′$ to 2 rt.

And therefore, on the circle about right triangle BCM,

arc $BM = 155°9′$,

and as its supplement

arc $CM = 24°51′$.

And therefore

chord $BM = 117^{\mathrm{p}}11′$,
chord $CM = 25^{\mathrm{p}}49′$

where

hypt. $BC = 120^{\mathrm{p}}$.

And so also, where

there also

$$BC = 1^{\mathrm{p}}15′,$$

$$BM = 1^{\mathrm{p}}13′,$$
$$CM = 0^{\mathrm{p}}16′,$$

and, by addition,

$$FM = 60^{\mathrm{p}}16′;$$

and therefore also

hypt. $BF = 60^{\mathrm{p}}17′$.

And therefore

$$BM = 2^{\mathrm{p}}25′$$

where

$$BF = 120^{\mathrm{p}};$$

and, on the circle about right triangle BFM,

And so also
$$\text{arc } BM = 2°19'.$$

$$\text{angle } BFM = 2°19' \text{ to 2 rt.}$$
And since it has been shown

therefore
$$\text{angle } DCF = 155°9' \text{ to 2 rt.,}$$

$$\text{angle } BCF = 204°51' \text{ to 2 rt.}$$
And therefore, by addition, as the angle of the regular longitudinal passage,
$$\text{angle } ABF = 207°10' \text{ to 2 rt.}$$
$$= 103°35'.$$

The sun's mean passage will therefore be 11°25' within the Water Bearer, and its true passage 13°38'. And so the star, when likewise it is at the beginning of the Ram, will have a greatest eastern elongation from the true sun of 46°22'.

And for Mercury, let it be supposed as an evening star at the beginning of the Scorpion and as a morning star at the beginning of the Bull; because, with reference to the demonstrations of its heliacal risings on the ecliptic which will follow, it is easier to find the star's greatest elongations from the true sun in these positions. Now, according to Mercury's hypothesis, when the star's apparent passage is given, the mean longitudinal passage is not obtained, because the straight line CF does not always remain the same with and equal to the eccentric's radius as in the hypothesis of the others. But when the regular longitudinal passage is given, the apparent is shown. Therefore, supposing there are two longitudinal positions for each dodecatemory which can carry the star at the beginning of the dodecatemory in question, and calculating the greatest elongations resulting in the passages obtained, in this way we find the greatest elongation for the beginning of the dodecatemory, as will be easily understood through the means set forth. And this will be done first for the greatest eastern elongation at the beginning of the Scorpion.

For let there be the diameter $ABCD$ through the apogee A. And on it let C be supposed the ecliptic's centre and B the centre of the epicycle's regular movement. First let the epicycle's centre be conceived at the apogee itself, so that the sun's mean longitudinal passage is 10° within the Balance, and its true one 8°. And with epicycle FG described about A, let CG be drawn from C tangent to it at the eastern parts; and let the perpendicular AG be joined.

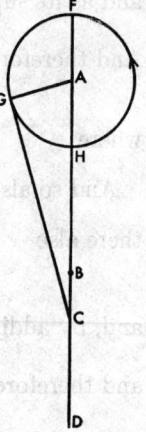

Now, since it has been shown by means already formulated that
$$\text{epic. rad. } AG = 22\tfrac{1}{2}^{\text{p}}$$
where, as the greatest distance,
$$AC = 69^{\text{p}},$$
therefore
$$AG = 39^{\text{p}}8'$$
where
$$\text{hypt. } AC = 120^{\text{p}}.$$
And so, on the circle about right triangle ACG,
$$\text{arc } ACG = 38°4',$$
and
$$\text{angle } ACG = 38°4' \text{ to 2 rt.}$$
$$= 19°2'.$$

And AC is 10° within the Balance. Therefore the star will be 29°2′ within the Balance when it is at its greatest elongation of 21°2′ from the true sun.

Again, let the mean longitude be supposed 3° from the apogee so that the mean sun is 13° within the Balance, and the true sun 11°4′. And with BE continued through, let epicycle FG be described about centre E. With CG drawn tangent in the same way, let EC and EG be joined. Since, in this position (that is, when it is supposed

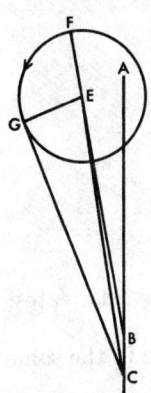

$$\text{angle } ABE = 3°)$$

it is shown by means already formulated that, as the angle of difference of eccentricity,

$$\text{angle } ACE = 2°52′,$$

and, as the epicycle's distance at that time,

$$CE \doteqdot 68^\text{p}58′$$

where

$$\text{epic. rad. } EG = 22^\text{p}30′;$$

therefore

$$EG = 39^\text{p}9′$$

where

$$\text{hypt. } CE = 120^\text{p}.$$

And so, on the circle about right triangle CEG,

$$\text{arc } EG = 38°5′,$$

and

$$\text{angle } ECG = 38°5′ \text{ to 2 rt.}$$
$$\doteqdot 19°3′;$$

and therefore, by addition,

$$\text{angle } ACG = 21°25′.$$

Therefore, when the star is 1°55′ within the Scorpion, it will have a greatest elongation from the true sun of 20°21′. But it was shown that, when it is 29°2′ within the Balance, it will have a greatest elongation of 21°2′ from the true sun. Since, then, the difference between the positions is 2°53′, and the difference of the greatest elongations 0°11′ so that very nearly 0°4′ correspond to the 0°58′ from the first position to the beginning of the Scorpion, we subtract these from the 21°2′ and thus have for the beginning of the Scorpion the greatest eastern elongation from the true sun of 20°58′.

And next, for the greatest western elongation at the beginning of the Bull, first let the mean longitudinal passage be 39° east of the perigee so that the mean sun is 19° within the Bull, and the true 19°38′. Let a similar drawing be laid out with the epicycle in a position east of the perigee and the tangent drawn to the western parts of the epicycle.

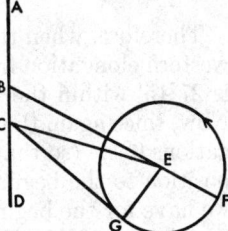

Now since, at this passage (that is, when it is supposed

$$\text{angle } DBF = 39°)$$

it is shown by means already formulated that

$$\text{angle } DCE = 40°57′,$$

and as the distance at that time

$$CE = 55^\text{p}59′$$

where

$$\text{epic. rad. } EG = 22^\text{p}30',$$

therefore

$$EG = 48^\text{p}14'$$

where

$$\text{hypt. } CE = 120^\text{p};$$

and, on the circle about right triangle CEG,

$$\text{arc } EG = 47^\circ24'.$$

And so also

$$\text{angle } ECG = 47^\circ24' \text{ to 2 rt.}$$
$$= 23^\circ42',$$

and, by subtraction,

$$\text{angle } GCD = 17^\circ15'.$$

And therefore when Mercury is 27°15′ within the Ram, it will have a greatest western elongation from the true sun of 22°23′.

Again, let the mean longitude be supposed 42° from the perigee in the same direction, so that the sun's mean position is 22° within the Bull, and its true 22°31′.

Now since, for this same passage (that is, when it is supposed

$$\text{angle } DBF = 42^\circ)$$

it is shown that

$$\text{angle } DCE = 44^\circ4',$$

and, as the distance at that time,

$$CE = 55^\text{p}50'$$

where

$$\text{epic. rad. } EG = 22^\text{p}30';$$

therefore

$$EG = 48^\text{p}19'$$

where

$$\text{hypt. } CE = 120^\text{p};$$

and, on the circle about right triangle ECG,

$$\text{arc } EG = 47^\circ30'.$$

And so also

$$\text{angle } ECG = 47^\circ30' \text{ to 2 rt.}$$
$$= 23^\circ45',$$

and, by subtraction,

$$\text{angle } GCD = 20^\circ19'.$$

Therefore, when the Mercury is 0°19′ within the Bull, it will have a greatest western elongation from the true sun of 22°12′. But it was shown that, when it is 27°15′ within the Ram, it will have a similar greatest elongation of 22°23′. Now, since again the difference of the positions is 3°4′, and of the greatest elongations 0°11′ (so that very nearly 0°10′ correspond to the 2°45′ from the first position to the beginning of the Bull), we subtract these from the 22°23′, and we have for the beginning of the Bull the greatest western elongation from the true sun of 22°13′. Which things it was required to find.

For the other dodecatemories, calculating in the same way the greatest western and eastern elongations of both stars, we arranged a table of them in 12 rows and 5 columns. In the first column we arranged the beginnings of the dodecatemories beginning with the Ram. And in the next four we placed the greatest elongations from the true sun as calculated: the second containing the western elongations of Venus and the third the eastern; and again the fourth the western elongations of Mercury and the fifth the eastern. And here is the table:

10. GREATEST ELONGATIONS WITH RESPECT TO THE TRUE SUN

Beginnings of the Signs	VENUS		MERCURY	
	Western	Eastern	Western	Eastern
Ram	45 14	46 22	24 14	19 36
Bull	45 17	45 31	22 13	21 7
Twins	45 34	44 49	20 18	23 41
Crab	45 56	44 25	18 17	26 16
Lion	46 20	44 31	16 35	27 37
Virgin	46 38	44 55	16 8	26 17
Balance	46 45	45 41	17 46	23 31
Scorpion	46 47	46 30	21 32	20 58
Archer	46 30	47 13	26 9	19 28
Goat	46 7	47 35	28 37	19 14
Water Bearer	45 41	47 34	28 17	18 51
Fishes	45 20	47 7	26 24	19 0

BOOK THIRTEEN

1. On the Hypotheses for the Latitudinal Passages
of the Five Planets

Two matters are still left for the treatise on the five planets: (1) their latitudinal passage with respect to the ecliptic, and (2) the business of the distances of the heliacal risings and settings. The latitudinal distance of each of them must be first cleared up here, since from this there result noteworthy differences in the risings and settings. Therefore we shall again present first whatever we suppose as common to the obliquities of their circles.

Now, because each planet appears to effect a double latitudinal difference just like the longitudinal anomaly—one due to the eccentric circle relative to parts of the ecliptic, and the other due to the epicycle relative to the sun—in each case we suppose the eccentric inclined to the ecliptic's plane and the epicycle to the eccentric's plane, although (as we said) there is no noteworthy change resulting from this in the longitudinal passage or in the demonstrations of the anomalies for such obliquities as we shall show in what follows. And because, through observations made on each of them, the stars appear in the plane of the ecliptic when the number of truly determined longitude and of truly determined anomaly are each very nearly a quadrant (the one from the eccentric's northern or southern limit, and the other from its own apogee) we suppose the inclinations of the eccentrics about the ecliptic's centre, as in the case of the moon, and relative to the diameters through the northern or southern limits; and we suppose those of the epicycles relative to their diameters directed to the ecliptic's centre and along which the apparent apogees and perigees are observed.

And again, in the case of the three planets Saturn, Jupiter, and Mars, we observed that, when their longitudinal passages are near the eccentric's apogee, then they always appear the farthest north of the ecliptic and farther north at the passages in the epicycle's perigees than at those in their apogees; but when their longitudinal passages are at the eccentric's perigee, on the contrary they appear farther south than the ecliptic. In the case of Saturn and Jupiter, we observed that the eccentric's northernmost limits are near the beginning of the dodecatemory of the Balance, but in the case of Mars near the end of Cancer and almost at its apogee. And so we concluded from these things that the points of the eccentrics at these parts of the ecliptic are inclined towards the north, whereas the points diametrically opposite are equally inclined to the south; and that the perigees of the epicycles are always inclined in the direction of the eccentrics' inclination, while the diameters at right angles to those through their apogees always remain parallel to the plane of the ecliptic.

In the case of Venus and Mercury, we observed that, when their longitudinal passages are at the eccentric's apogees or perigees, the movements at the epicycle's perigees do not differ latitudinally from those at the apogees, but are alike either north or south of the ecliptic: in the case of Venus always north; and in the case of Mercury, on the contrary, always south. But the passages at the greatest elongations differ most from each other (that is, the western from the eastern) and from those at the epicycle's apogees and perigees (that is, the difference with respect to the eccentric), while the greatest eastern and evening elongation, in the case of Venus, is north at the eccentric's apogee and south at its perigee; and in the case of Mercury, on the contrary, south at the apogee and north at the perigee. But when their passages of truly determined longitude are at the nodes, then the quadrant distances on each epicycle from the apogees or perigees are both in the plane of the ecliptic, and the passages at the perigees differ most from those at the apogees, and, in the case of Venus, make the inclination for the node in the subtractive semicircle southward and for the opposite one northward. But, in the case of Mercury, again the contrary: for the node in the subtractive semicircle northward and for the opposite southward. And so we concluded from this that the eccentrics move their obliquities and make their returns with the periods of the epicycles, being in the same plane with the ecliptic when the epicycles are at the nodes, and, when it is around the apogees and perigees, throwing the epicycle the farthest north in the case of Venus and the farthest south in the case of Mercury. And we concluded that the two epicycles effect differences by inclining their diameters through the apparent apogees the most at the eccentric's nodes, and slanting the diameters perpendicular to these the most at the eccentrics' perigees and apogees (for let us distinguish this inclination by that name), thus contrariwise putting the first diameters in the eccentric's plane at its apogees and perigees, and the second in the ecliptic's plane at the nodes.[1]

[1]These appearances of latitudinal variation can be understood in the heliocentric theory. Kepler, in the *Commentaries on Mars* (Part V, Chapters 67 and 68) and again in the *Epitome of Copernican Astronomy* (Book VI, Parts 2 and 3) gives good accounts of the transformation from the Ptolemaic appearances and theory to his own theory which will be that of Newton in the *Principia*. The latitudinal variations are caused by the inclination of the plane of each planet's orbit to that of the earth with the sun as centre. These inclinations, according to Kepler, are fixed. Newton deduces their fixity except for very slight perturbations in the *Principles*, Book I, Section II, Proposition I.

It is now obvious that for the outer planets there will be greatest variations in latitude at opposite points on the ecliptic and no variation at the quadrants representing the nodes. Furthermore, this variation or inclination will appear greater the nearer the earth and the planet, and therefore when the planet is at the perigee of its epicycle in Ptolemaic theory.

In the case of the lower planets, Venus and Mercury, it is evident that, since its Ptolemaic epicycle represents its Copernican orbit about the sun, there will be two opposite points on the ecliptic where the greatest difference in latitude will be at the greatest elongations and none at the apogee and perigee. And at the quadrants relative to these two points, on the contrary, the greatest difference in latitude will be at the perigee and apogee of the epicycle. The fact that the planet at the apogee and perigee of the epicycle in the case of the first two points has a small latitudinal deviation on the same side of the ecliptic is explained by referring the line of the nodes to the true sun, according to Kepler. This is an argument for the Keplerian dynamical theory of the sun as the centre of the universe. Thus is explained the Ptolemaic inclination of the eccentric which serves to throw the latitude more one side than the other.

2. On the Manner of the Movement of the Obliquities and Slantings According to the Hypotheses

The general conclusion of the hypotheses is, then, that the eccentric circles of the five planets are inclined to the ecliptic's plane about the ecliptic's centre: without movement in the case of the three, Saturn, Jupiter, and Mars, so that diametrically opposite passages of the epicycles are borne in contrary latitudinal directions; but in the case of Venus and Mercury, changing simultaneously with the epicycles towards the same latitude, always towards the north for Venus and always towards the south for Mercury; and that those diameters of the epicycles through their apparent apogees, starting somewhere in the eccentric's plane, are carried aside by little circles lying beside the perigeal limits, say, proportionate in size to the latitudinal deviation, perpendicular to the eccentrics' planes, and having their centres on them. These little circles are revolved regularly and in accord with the longitudinal passages starting from an intersection of the planes with the epicycles (say towards the north) and at the same time carrying the epicycles' planes in the first quadrant's turn to the northernmost limit, of course, then back again to the eccentric's plane; and in the third quadrant's turn to the southernmost limit; and, finally, at the return to the starting point. The beginning and return of this circuit are established—for Saturn, Jupiter, and Mars—from the intersection at the ascending node; in the case of Venus, from the eccentric's perigee; and in the case of Mercury, from the eccentric's apogee.

In the case of the three stars, the diameters perpendicular to these first diameters remain, as we said, always parallel to the ecliptic's plane or have an inappreciable slant to it. But in the case of Mercury and Venus, starting again from some point in the ecliptic's plane, they are carried aside by little circles lying beside, say, their eastern limits, again proportionate in size to the latitudinal deviation, perpendicular to the ecliptic's plane, and having their centres on diameters parallel to the ecliptic's plane. These little circles are revolved at the same speed as the others starting from an intersection of the planes and the epicycles again northwards (let us say), carrying the eastern extremities of these diameters in the same order as before. And again for these stars, the beginning and return of the similar circuit are established, for Venus, from the node in the additive semicircle, and, for Mercury, from the node in the subtractive semicircle.

Now, concerning these little circles by which the oscillations of the epicycles are effected, it is necessary to assume that they are bisected by the planes about which we say the swayings of the obliquities take place; for only in this way can equal latitudinal passages be established on either side of them. Yet they do not have their revolutions with respect to regular movement effected about the proper centre, but about another which has the same eccentricity for the little circle as the star's longitudinal eccentricity for the ecliptic. For the returns on the ecliptic and the little circle are supposed isochronous and the quarterly passages on each apparently agree. But if the little circle's revolutions take place about its proper centre, that which is required can in no way come about, since the passages for the little circle travel each quadrant in equal time, but the epicycle's passages with respect to the ecliptic do not because of the eccentricity assumed in each case. But if they take place about a centre similar in position to that of the eccentric, and of the quadrants, the returns of the obliquities will traverse corresponding parts of the ecliptic and of the little circle in equal times.

Let no one, seeing the difficulty of our devices, find troublesome such hypotheses. For it is not proper to apply human things to divine things nor to get beliefs concerning such great things from such dissimilar examples. For what is more unlike than those which are always alike with respect to those which never are, and than those which are impeded by anything with those which are not even impeded by themselves? But it is proper to try and fit as far as possible the simpler hypotheses to the movements in the heavens; and if this does not succeed, then any hypotheses possible. Once all the appearances are saved by the consequences of the hypotheses, why should it seem strange that such complications can come about in the movements of heavenly things? For there is no impeding nature in them, but one proper to the yielding and giving way to movements according to the nature of each planet, even if they are contrary, so that they can all penetrate and shine through absolutely all the fluid media; and this free action takes place not only about the particular circles, but also about the spheres themselves and the axes of revolution. We see the complication and sequence in their different movements difficult and hard to come by for the freedom of the movements in the likely stories constructed by us, but in the heavenly thing never anywhere impeded by this mixture. Or rather it is not proper to judge the simplicity of heavenly things by those which seem so with us, when here not even to all of us does the same thing seem likewise simple. For in this way not one of the heavenly occurrences would seem simple to those studying them, not even the unchangeableness of the first motion, since always to be the same is not difficult here with us but impossible. We should instead judge their simplicity from the unchangeableness of the natures in the heavens and their movements. For thus they would all appear simple, more than those things which seem so here with us, since no difficulty or trouble could be conjectured concerning their periods.

3. On the Size of Each of the Obliquities and Slantings

Now, from these things, one could calculate the general position and order of the circles of obliquity. In the case of Venus and Mercury, the apparent passages at the given positions of latitude render easily calculable for each star the particular quantities of the arcs which the obliquities cut off on the great circle drawn through the inclined circle's poles at right angles to the ecliptic, and according to which the latitudinal passages are considered. For when their longitudinal movements are at the eccentrics' apogees and perigees, then, as we declared from nearby observations of the addition resulting for us, the stars, as they pass through the epicycle's perigees and apogees, appear either north or south of the ecliptic by an equal amount, Venus always being north by $\frac{1}{6}°$, and Mercury always south by $\frac{3}{4}°$, so that from this the obliquities of each of the eccentrics are just about those amounts. But at the greatest elongations from the sun they both appear in mean terms about 5° north or south of the opposite greatest elongations. For, when it effects this latitudinal opposition at the eccentric's apogee, Venus appears very little less than 5°, and, when at the eccentric's perigee, very little more than 5°; and Mercury by at most $\frac{1}{2}°$ more or less. And so the slantings of the epicycle from one side or the other of the eccentric planes subtend, in mean terms, about $2\frac{1}{2}°$ of the circle at right angles to the ecliptic, from which are taken the quantities of the angles resulting from the epicycles' slant to the eccentrics' planes. This will be clear from later demonstrations about them in what follows, not to interrupt at present what we have to say in common about the five planets.

But when the movements of truly determined longitude are at the nodes and mean distances, then, as Venus makes its passage about the epicycle's apogee, it appears 1° north and south of the ecliptic, and, about the epicycle's perigee, very nearly $6\frac{1}{3}°$; so that from this it is concluded the epicycle's obliquity cuts off $2\frac{1}{2}°$ on the circle drawn through its poles in the way we have described. For as a result of the epicyclic anomaly at the mean distances we find that many degrees subtend, for the epicycle's apogee, an angle at the eye of 1°2′, and, for the epicycle's perigee, an angle of 6°22′. And, as Mercury makes its passage about the epicycle's apogee, one would calculate from its heliacal risings that it is very nearly $1\frac{3}{4}°$ north and south of the ecliptic, and, about the epicycle's perigee, very nearly 4°; so that from this the obliquity is established as $6\frac{1}{4}°$. For again, as a result of the epicyclic anomaly at the distances of the greatest obliquities (that is, when the truly determined longitude is a quadrant's distance from the apogee), we find just that many degrees subtend, for the epicycle's apogee, an angle at the eye of 1°46′, and, for the epicycle's perigee, an angle of 4°5′.

In the case of the others—Saturn, Jupiter, and Mars—one could not immediately apprehend the quantities of the obliquities which are both always mixed together, that effected by the eccentric with that effected by the epicycle. But from the latitudinal passages again observed at the perigees and apogees of the eccentrics and epicycles, we separate out each of the two obliquities in this way:

In the plane at right angles to the plane of the ecliptic, let AB be its intersection with the ecliptic's plane, and CD its intersection with the eccentric's plane. And let point E be the ecliptic's centre. About the eccentric's apogee C and perigee D on the intersection of the planes, let there be drawn in the plane of reference the equal circles $FGHK$ and $LMNX$ through the poles of the epicycles. And on these circles let the epicycles' planes be inclined at lines GCK and MDX with equal angles—of course, at C and D. Let also straight lines be drawn from the ecliptic's centre E where the eye is to the epicycles' apogees and perigees: EG and EM to the epogees, and EK and EX to the perigees; for the points K and X embrace, of course, the passages of acronychal opposition, and G and M the synodic passages.

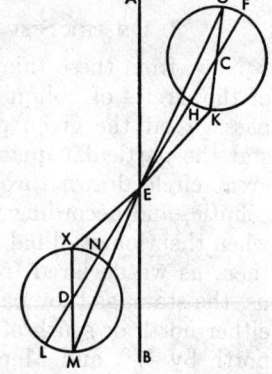

Now, in the case of Mars, we took the latitudinal passages about the acronychal oppositions established at the eccentric's apogee (that is, those about the point K of the epicycle) and those at the eccentric's perigee (that is, those about the point X of the epicycle), because their difference is quite sensible. In the oppositions about the apogee it is $4\frac{1}{3}°$

north of the ecliptic, and in the oppositions about the perigee very nearly 7°
south of the ecliptic, so that
$$\text{angle } AEK = 4\tfrac{1}{3}°,$$
$$\text{angle } BEX = 7°.$$

Now, with these things supposed, we find the angle contained by the eccentric's obliquity (that is, angle AEC) and that contained by the epicycle's (that is, angle GCF) in this way. For since, from what we have demonstrated concerning the anomalies of Mars, it is easily seen that, of those angles subtended by equal arcs about the epicycle's perigeal parts, those about the passages at the eccentric's apogee have to those about the passages at the perigee the ratio which very nearly 5 has to 9[1], and since arcs HK and NX are equal, therefore
$$\text{angle } CEK : \text{angle } DEX : : 5 : 9.$$
And so, since angles AEK and BEX are given, and the ratio of angle CEK to angle DEX is given, and
$$\text{angle } AEC = \text{angle } BED,$$
therefore, if whatever part the difference of the whole quantities is of the difference of the terms of the ratio, we take just that part of the terms of the ratio, and then shall have the quantity in the proper ratio. For this is shown by a short arithmetical lemma.[2] Since the quantities are $4\tfrac{1}{3}$ and 7 and their difference $2\tfrac{2}{3}$, and the ratio is 5 to 9 and their difference 4, and $2\tfrac{2}{3}$ is two-thirds of 4, therefore, taking two-thirds of 5 and 9, we shall have
$$\text{angle } CEK = 3\tfrac{1}{3}°,$$
$$\text{angle } DEX = 6°,$$
and accordingly, by subtraction, as the angles of the eccentric's obliquity,
$$\text{angle } AEC = \text{angle } BED = 1°.$$
And from these we shall have as the arc of the epicycle's obliquity
$$\text{arc } HK = 2\tfrac{1}{4}°,$$
because, according to the Tables of Anomaly, the quantities found for angles CEK and DEX embrace just that many degrees.

And in the case of Saturn and Jupiter—since we find the passages about the apogeal sections of the eccentrics sensibly no different from those about the perigeal sections just opposite—we calculated what was required, in another way, from the comparison of those about the epicycles' apogees with those about their perigees. As we could easily see from particular observations, in the passages about the heliacal risings and settings, Saturn was at most very nearly 2° north and south, and Jupiter 1°; and in the passages about the acronychal oppositions, Saturn about 3°, Jupiter about 2°. Now, since it is evident from their

[1]For the distances to the star in those two positions would be as $(60 - 39\tfrac{1}{2} + 6)$ to $(60 - 39\tfrac{1}{2} - 6)$ or as very nearly 9 to 5. Now, the arcs being small and equal can be considered as perpendiculars to the lines representing the distances from the eye to the star. Then, since for small angles the angles are as their sines, the angles are as 5 to 9 very nearly. The same principle is used for Saturn and Jupiter in the next few pages; but since their epicycles are relatively small and their eccentricities also, it is necessary to make the comparison between the epicycle's apogee and perigee.

[2]For we have
$$(7° - \text{angle } BED) : (4\tfrac{3}{4}° - \text{angle } BED) : : 9 : 5,$$
separando
$$(7° - 4\tfrac{1}{3}°) : (4\tfrac{1}{3}° - \text{angle } BED) : : (9 - 5) : 5$$
or convertendo
$$(7° - 4\tfrac{1}{3}°) : (7° - \text{angle } BED) : : (9 - 5) : 9.$$

anomaly that, of the angles subtended at the eye by equal arcs about the perigeal and apogeal parts of the epicycle, those formed by arcs about the apogees have to those formed by arcs about the perigees, in the case of Saturn, the ratio of 18 to 23, and, in the case of Jupiter, of 29 to 43, and since FG and HK are equal arcs of the epicycle, therefore, in the case of Saturn,

$$\text{angle } FEG : \text{angle } FEK :: 18 : 23;$$

in the case of Jupiter

$$\text{angle } FEG : \text{angle } FEK :: 29 : 43.$$

But angle GEK is the difference between the two latitudinal passages for both stars and is a remainder of 1°. Therefore, if the 1° is divided according to these ratios, we shall have, in the case of Saturn,

$$\text{angle } FEG = 0°26';$$

and, in the case of Jupiter,

$$\text{angle } FEG = 0°24'.$$

And we shall have, in the case of Saturn,

$$\text{angle } FEK = 0°34';$$

and, in the case of Jupiter,

$$\text{angle } FEK = 0°36'.$$

And so, by subtraction, there will remain, as the angle of the eccentric's obliquity for Saturn,

$$\text{angle } AEC = 2°26';$$

and, for Jupiter,

$$\text{angle } AEC = 1°24'.$$

For convenience we use, instead of these quantities, $2\frac{1}{2}°$ and $1\frac{1}{2}°$. And immediately it is concluded that, as the arc of the epicycle's obliquity, for Saturn,

$$\text{arc } HK = 4\frac{1}{2}°;$$

and, for Jupiter,

$$\text{arc } HK = 2\frac{1}{2}°.$$

For, again, just this number of degrees in each case embrace very nearly, according to the Tables of Anomaly, the quantities found for angles FEG and FEK. Which things it was required to find.

4. Construction of Tables for Particular Latitudinal Passages

By these means we have now established the general quantities of the epicycles' and eccentrics' greatest obliquities. But that we may also be able to work out easily at any time the latitudinal passages of the particular distances, we constructed five tables for the five planets, each having as many rows as the Tables of Anomaly and five columns. The first two columns contain the same numbers as in those. The third columns contain the latitudinal deviations from the ecliptic corresponding to sections of the epicycles with the epicycles at their point of greatest obliquity: in the case of Venus and Mercury, at the nodes of the eccentrics, and, for the other three stars, at the northern limits of the eccentrics. In the case of these latter, the fourth columns contain the similar additions about the eccentrics' southern limits. At the same time the greatest deviation of the eccentrics is calculated for these three stars. And, in the case of Venus and Mercury, we worked out the sections, again through one theorem in this way:

In the plane at right angles to the ecliptic's plane, let ABC be its intersection

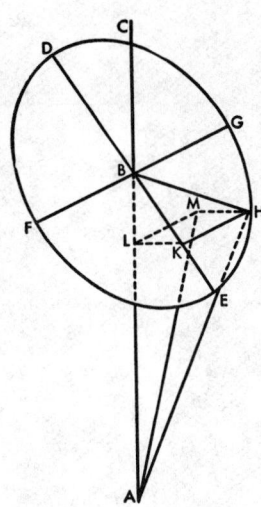

with the ecliptic's plane, and *DBE* its intersection with the epicycle's plane. Let *A* be the ecliptic's centre, *B* the epicycle's, and let *AB* be the distance about the greatest obliquities of the epicycles. With epicycle *DFEG* drawn about *B*, let diameter *FBG* be joined perpendicular to *DE*. And let the epicycle's plane be supposed perpendicular to the plane of reference, so that, of the straight lines drawn perpendicular to *DE*, only *FG* lies in the ecliptic's plane and all the rest are parallel to it.

Given the ratio of *AB* to *BE* and the quantity of the obliquity (that is, angle *ABE*), let it be required to find the stars' latitudinal passages when, for example, they are 45° from *E* the epicycle's perigee. For we wish to demonstrate at the same time, by means of these inclinations, the differences resulting in the longitudinal passages. But these differences must be the greatest about the passages between the perigee *E* and *F* and *G* because they turn out to be the same as those effected without the obliquity.

Then let arc *EH* be taken as 45°. Let *HK* be drawn perpendicular to *BE*, and *KL* and *HM* to the ecliptic's plane. And let *HB, LM, AM,* and *AH* be joined.

Now, it would be immediately evident that the quadrilateral *LKHM* is a rectangular parallelogram because of *KH*'s being parallel to the ecliptic's plane; and that angle *LAM* embraces the longitudinal addition-subtraction and angle *HAM* the latitudinal passage, while angles *ALM* and *AMH* are right angles because of *AM*'s falling in the ecliptic's plane. It is now necessary to show how great the required passages are for each of these stars, and first for Venus.

Now, since

$$\text{arc } EH = 45°,$$

being at the epicycle's centre,

$$\text{angle } EBH = 45°$$
$$= 90° \text{ to 2 rt.}$$

And so, on the circle about right triangle *BHK*,

$$\text{arc } BK = \text{arc } HK = 90°.$$

And therefore

$$\text{chord } BK = \text{chord } HK = 84^{\text{p}}52'$$

where

$$\text{hypt. } BH = 120^{\text{p}}.$$

And so also

$$BK = HK = 30^{\text{p}}32'$$

where

$$\text{epic. rad. } BH = 43^{\text{p}}10'$$

and, as mean distance,

$$AB = 60^{\text{p}};$$

for at this distance occurs the epicycle's greatest obliquity.

Again, since it is supposed that, as the angle of obliquity,

$$\text{angle } ABE = 2°30'$$
$$= 5° \text{ to 2 rt.,}$$

therefore, on the circle about right triangle BLK,
$$\text{arc } KL = 5°,$$
and, as its supplement,
$$\text{arc } BL = 175°.$$
And therefore
$$\text{chord } KL = 5^\text{p}14',$$
$$\text{chord } BL = 119^\text{p}53'$$
where
$$\text{hypt. } BK = 120^\text{p}.$$
And so also, where
$$\text{hypt. } BK = 30^\text{p}32',$$
and
$$AB = 60^\text{p},$$
there
$$KL = 1^\text{p}20',$$
$$BL = 30^\text{p}30',$$
and, by subtraction,
$$AL = 29^\text{p}30'.$$
And
$$LM = HK = 30^\text{p}32'.$$
And so it is concluded that
$$\text{hypt. } AM = 42^\text{p}27'.$$
And therefore, where
$$\text{hypt. } AM = 120^\text{p},$$
there
$$LM = 86^\text{p}19';$$
and, as the angle of longitudinal addition-subtraction for that time,
$$\text{angle } LAM = 92°0' \text{ to 2 rt.}$$
$$= 46°0'.$$
And likewise, since
$$HM = KL = 1^\text{p}20'$$
where
$$AM = 42^\text{p}27',$$
and the squares on them added together give the square on AH, therefore in length
$$AH = 42^\text{p}29'.$$
And
$$HM = 3^\text{p}46'$$
where
$$\text{hypt. } AH = 120^\text{p};$$
and, as the angle of latitudinal deviation,
$$\text{angle } HAM = 3°36' \text{ to 2 rt.}$$
$$= 1°48'.$$
And we place this in the third column of Venus' table in the row containing the number 135°.

For measuring the resulting difference of the longitudinal addition-subtrac-

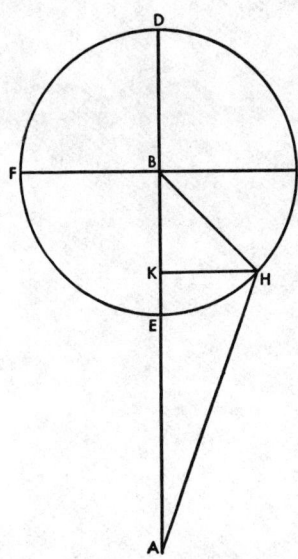

tion, let a similar drawing be laid out having the epicycle not inclined.

Since we demonstrated that
$$BK = HK = 30^p 32'$$
where
$$AB = 60^p,$$
so that, by subtraction,
$$AK = 29^p 28';$$
and since
$$\text{sq. } AK + \text{sq. } HK = \text{sq. } AH,$$
therefore, in length,
$$AH = 42^p 26'.$$
And therefore
$$HK = 86^p 21'$$
where
$$\text{hypt. } AH = 120^p;$$
and, as the angle of longitudinal addition-sub-traction,
$$\text{angle } HAK = 92°3' \text{ to 2 rt.}$$
$$\doteqdot 46°2'$$

But with the obliquity it was shown to be 46°. Therefore the longitudinal addition-subtraction, because of the epicycle's obliquity, is less by 0°2'. Which it was required to find.

Again, to show the passages of Mercury, let there be laid out a drawing similar to the one before this, with the supposition that
$$\text{arc } EH = 45°;$$
so that again
$$BK = HK = 84^p 22'$$
where
$$\text{hypt. } BH = 120^p.$$
And therefore
$$BK = HK = 15^p 55'$$
where
$$\text{epic. rad. } BH = 22^p 30'$$
and, as the distance at the greatest obliquities,
$$AB = 56^p 40';$$
for we have demonstrated all these things before.

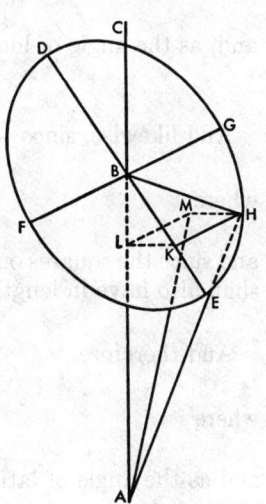

Again, since, as the angle of the epicycle's obliquity, it is supposed
$$\text{angle } ABE = 6°15'$$
$$= 12°30' \text{ to 2 rt.,}$$
therefore, on the circle about right triangle BKL,
$$\text{arc } KL = 12°30'$$
and, as its supplement,
$$\text{arc } BL = 167°30'.$$

And therefore
$$\text{chord } KL = 13^p 4',$$
$$\text{chord } BL = 119^p 17'$$

where

$$\text{hypt. } BK = 120^{\text{p}}.$$

And so also, where it was shown

$$BK = 15^{\text{p}}55'$$

and it is supposed

$$AB = 56^{\text{p}}40',$$

there also

$$KL = 1^{\text{p}}44',$$
$$BL = 15^{\text{p}}49'$$

and, by subtraction,

$$AL = 40^{\text{p}}51'.$$

And

$$LM = KH = 15^{\text{p}}55'.$$

And since

$$\text{sq. } AL + \text{sq. } LM = \text{sq. } AM,$$

we shall have in length

$$AM = 43^{\text{p}}50'$$

where

$$LM = 15^{\text{p}}55'.$$

And therefore

$$LM = 43^{\text{p}}34'$$

where

$$\text{hypt. } AM = 120^{\text{p}};$$

and, as the angle of longitudinal addition-subtraction,

$$\text{angle } LAM = 42°34' \text{ to 2 rt.}$$
$$= 21°17'.$$

And likewise, since

$$HM = KL = 1^{\text{p}}44'$$

where

$$AM = 43^{\text{p}}50',$$

and since the squares on both of them added together give the square on AH, we shall also have in length

$$AH = 43^{\text{p}}52'.$$

And therefore

$$HM = 4^{\text{p}}44'$$

where

$$\text{hypt. } AH = 120^{\text{p}};$$

and as the angle of latitudinal deviation

$$\text{angle } HAM = 4°32' \text{ to 2 rt.}$$
$$= 2°16'.$$

And again we shall place this in the third column of Mercury's table in the same row—that is, in the row containing the number of 135°.

Again, for the comparison of the addition-subtraction, let the drawing be laid out without the obliquity.

And since it was shown that, where

$$AB = 56^{\text{p}}40',$$

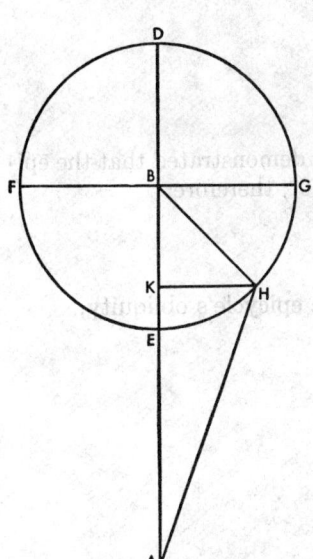

there
$$HK = BK = 15^{\text{p}}55'$$
and, by subtraction, clearly
$$AK = 40^{\text{p}}45',$$
and since
$$\text{sq. } AK + \text{sq. } HK = \text{sq. } AH,$$
therefore we shall have in length
$$AH = 43^{\text{p}}45'$$
where
$$HK = 15^{\text{p}}45'.$$
And therefore
$$HK = 43^{\text{p}}39'$$
where
$$\text{hypt. } AH = 120^{\text{p}};$$
and as the angle of longitudinal addition-subtraction,
$$\text{angle } KAH = 42°40' \text{ to 2 rt.}$$
$$= 21°20'.$$
But it was shown to be 21°17′ with the obliquity. Therefore, in this case, the longitudinal addition-subtraction, because of the epicycle's obliquity, is less by 0°3′. Which was to be found.

Now, for these two stars we worked out the latitudinal passages at the greatest obliquities by taking them when the eccentric is in the same plane with the ecliptic. But, for the other three stars, we used another geometrical theorem since the epicycles' greatest obliquities come about at the eccentrics' greatest obliquities, and it would be helpful to have the latitudinal passages combined from both obliquities calculated out together.

For again, in the plane at right angles to the ecliptic's, let AB be its intersection with the ecliptic's plane, AC its intersection with the eccentric's plane, and DCE its intersection with the epicycle's plane. Let A be supposed the ecliptic's centre, and C the epicycle's. About C let the epicycle $DFEG$ be drawn again so that, of the straight lines drawn perpendicular to DE, the diameter FCG is in the eccentric's plane and parallel to the ecliptic's, and all the rest are parallel to both these planes. Likewise let arc EH be supposed cut off at 45°. And with HK drawn perpendicular from the star's point H, and KB and HL from the points H and K perpendicular to the ecliptic's plane, let BL and AL be joined.

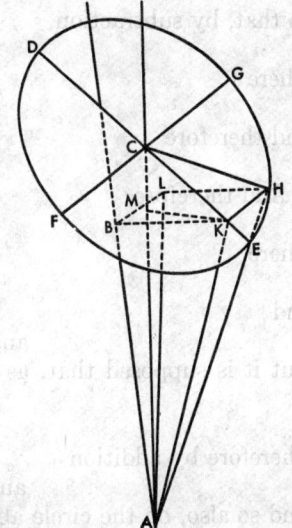

It is required to find the longitudinal addition-subtraction contained by angle BAL, and the latitudinal passage contained by angle HAL.

Then let KM be drawn from K perpendicular to AC, and let CH and AK be joined. And again, because of things already shown, let it be supposed that

$$CK = HK = 84^{\text{p}}52'$$

where

$$\text{hypt. } CH = 120^{\text{p}}.$$

Then, first in the case of Saturn, since it has been demonstrated that the epicycle's radius is 6ᵖ30′ where the mean distance is 60ᵖ, therefore

$$CK = HK = 4^{\text{p}}36'$$

where

$$\text{hypt. } CH = 6^{\text{p}}30'.$$

And since it is supposed that, as the angle of the epicycle's obliquity,

$$\text{angle } ACE = 4°30'$$
$$= 9° \text{ to 2 rt.,}$$

therefore, on the circle about right triangle CKM,

$$\text{arc } KM = 9°,$$

and, as its supplement,

$$\text{arc } CM = 171°.$$

Therefore

$$\text{chord } KM = 9^{\text{p}}25',$$
$$\text{chord } CM = 119^{\text{p}}38'$$

where

$$\text{hypt. } CK = 120^{\text{p}}.$$

And therefore

$$KM = 0°22',$$
$$CM = 4^{\text{p}}35'$$

where

$$CK = 4^{\text{p}}36'.$$

But, for the greatest obliquity in the apogeal semicircle, from theorems already worked out for the anomalies, it is calculated that, as the distance about the beginning of the Balance,

$$AC = 62^{\text{p}}10',$$

so that, by subtraction,

$$AM = 57^{\text{p}}35'$$

where

$$KM = 0^{\text{p}}22';$$

and therefore

$$\text{hypt. } AK = 57^{\text{p}}35'.$$

And therefore

$$KM = 0^{\text{p}}46'$$

where

$$\text{hypt. } AK = 120^{\text{p}};$$

and

$$\text{angle } KAM = 0°44' \text{ to 2 rt.}$$

But it is supposed that, as the angle of the eccentric's obliquity,

$$\text{angle } BAC = 2° \ 30'$$
$$= 5° \text{ to 2 rt.}$$

Therefore by addition

$$\text{angle } BAK = 5°44' \text{ to 2 rt.}$$

And so also, on the circle about right triangle BAK,

$$\text{arc } BK = 5°44',$$

and, as its supplement,
$$\text{arc } AB = 174°16'.$$
And therefore
$$\text{chord } BK = 6^{\text{p}}0',$$
$$\text{chord } AB = 119^{\text{p}}51'$$
where
$$\text{hypt. } AK = 120^{\text{p}}.$$

And so also, where
$$AK = 57^{\text{p}}35',$$
there
$$BK = 2^{\text{p}}53',$$
$$AB = 57^{\text{p}}31',$$
and
$$BL = HK = 4^{\text{p}}36'.$$
And since
$$\text{sq. } AB + \text{sq. } BL = \text{sq. } AL,$$
therefore we shall have in length
$$AL = 57^{\text{p}}42'.$$
And likewise, since
$$HL = BK = 2^{\text{p}}53',$$
and
$$\text{sq. } AL + \text{sq. } LH = \text{sq. } AH,$$
therefore we shall have in length
$$AH = 57^{\text{p}}46'.$$

And so also
$$LH = 5^{\text{p}}59'$$
where
$$\text{hypt. } AH = 120^{\text{p}};$$
and, as the angle of latitudinal deviation,
$$\text{angle } HAL = 5°44' \text{ to } 2 \text{ rt.}$$
$$= 2°52'.$$
And we place this in the third column of Saturn's table alongside of 135°.

For the greatest obliquity in the perigeal semicircle, since, as the distance at the beginning of the Ram,
$$AC = 57^{\text{p}}40'$$
where it was shown
$$KM = 0^{\text{p}}22';$$
and likewise
$$CM = 4^{\text{p}}35',$$
and therefore, by subtraction,
$$AM = 53^{\text{p}}5';$$
and because it is hardly at all greater than AM,

$$\text{hypt. } AK = 53^{\text{p}}5',$$
therefore
$$KM = 0^{\text{p}} \, 50'$$
where
$$\text{hypt. } AK = 120^{\text{p}};$$

and
$$\text{angle } KAM = 0°48' \text{ to 2 rt.}$$
And it is supposed
$$\text{angle } BAC = 5° \text{ to 2 rt.}$$
And therefore, by addition,
$$\text{angle } BAK = 5°48' \text{ to 2 rt.}$$
And so also, on the circle about right triangle BAK,
$$\text{arc } BK = 5°48',$$
and, as its supplement,
$$\text{arc } AB = 174°12'.$$
And therefore
$$\text{chord } BK = 6^p4',$$
$$\text{chord } AB = 119^p51'$$
where
$$\text{hypt. } AK = 120^p.$$
And so also
$$BK = 2^p41',$$
$$AB = 53^p1'$$
where
$$AK = 53^p5'.$$
And since
$$\text{sq. } AB + \text{sq. } BL = \text{sq. } AL$$
and it was shown that of the same parts
$$BL = 4^p36',$$
therefore we shall have in length
$$AL = 53^p13'.$$
And therefore
$$BL = 10^p23'$$
where
$$\text{hypt. } AL = 120^p;$$
and, as the angle of the longitudinal addition-subtraction,
$$\text{angle } BAL = 9°56' \text{ to 2 rt.}$$
$$= 4°58'.$$
Again, since
$$HL = BK = 2^p41'$$
where
$$AL = 53^p13',$$
and the squares on both added together give the square on AH, therefore we shall have in length
$$AH = 53^p17'.$$
And therefore
$$HL = 6^p3'$$
where
$$\text{hypt. } AH = 120^p;$$
and, as the angle of latitudinal deviation,
$$\text{angle } HAL = 5°46' \text{ to 2 rt.}$$
$$= 2°53'.$$
And we place this in the fourth column of the table beside 135°.

Then, to make the comparison of the longitudinal addition-subtraction for

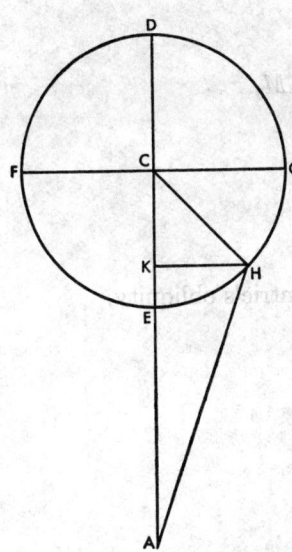

the perigeal obliquity, again let the figure be drawn as having no obliquity.

And since, where, as the distance at that time,
$$AC = 57^p40',$$
there it is supposed
$$CK = HK = 4^p36'$$
and, by subtraction,
$$AK = 53^p4',$$
and since
$$\text{sq. } AK + \text{sq. } HK = \text{sq. } AH,$$
therefore we shall have in length
$$AH = 53^p16'.$$
And so also
$$HK = 10^p22'$$
where
$$\text{hypt. } AH = 120^p;$$
and, as the angle of longitudinal addition-subtraction,
$$\text{angle } HAK = 9°54' \text{ to 2 rt.}$$
$$= 4°57'.$$

But with the obliquities it was shown to be 4°58'. Therefore the longitudinal addition-subtraction, because of both obliquities, is greater by 0°1'. Which was to be found.

Again, let there be first laid out the drawing with the obliquities, containing the ratios we have already demonstrated for Jupiter, so that
$$CK = HK = 8^p8'$$
where
$$\text{epic. rad. } CH = 11^p30'.$$

Now since, as the angle of the epicycle's obliquity, it is supposed that
$$\text{angle } ACE = 2°30'$$
$$= 5° \text{ to 2 rt.,}$$
therefore, on the circle about right triangle CKM,
$$\text{arc } KM = 5°,$$
and, as its supplement,
$$\text{arc } CM = 175°.$$
And therefore
$$\text{chord } KM = 5^p14',$$
$$\text{chord } CM = 119^p53'$$
where
$$\text{hypt. } CK = 120^p.$$
And so also, where
$$CK = 8^p8'$$
and, as the distance about the beginning of the Balance,
$$AC = 62^p30',$$
there also
$$KM = 0^p21',$$
$$CM = 8^p8',$$

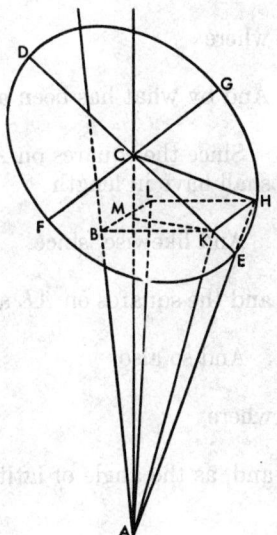

and, by subtraction,
$$AM = 54^{\mathrm{p}}22';$$
and therefore, since it is hardly at all greater than AM,
$$\text{hypt. } AK = 54^{\mathrm{p}}22'.$$
And therefore
$$KM = 0^{\mathrm{p}}46'$$
where
$$\text{hypt. } AK = 120^{\mathrm{p}};$$
and
$$\text{angle } KAM = 0°44' \text{ to 2 rt.}$$
But it is also supposed that, as the angle of the eccentric's obliquity,
$$\text{angle } BAC = 1°30'$$
$$= 3° \text{ to 2 rt.}$$
And therefore, by addition,
$$\text{angle } BAK = 3°44' \text{ to 2 rt.}$$
And so also, on the circle about right triangle BAK,
$$\text{arc } BK = 3°44',$$
and, as its supplement,
$$\text{arc } AB = 176°16'.$$
And therefore
$$\text{chord } BK = 3^{\mathrm{p}}54',$$
$$\text{chord } AB = 119^{\mathrm{p}}56'$$
where
$$\text{hypt. } AK = 120^{\mathrm{p}}.$$
And so also
$$BK = 1^{\mathrm{p}}46',$$
$$AB = 54^{\mathrm{p}}20'$$
where
$$AK = 54^{\mathrm{p}}22'.$$
And by what has been already demonstrated
$$BL = 8^{\mathrm{p}}8'.$$
Since the squares on AB and BL added together give the square on AL, we shall have in length
$$AL = 54^{\mathrm{p}}56'.$$
And likewise, since
$$HL = 1^{\mathrm{p}}46',$$
and the squares on AL and HL together give the square on AH, we shall have
$$AH = 54^{\mathrm{p}}58'.$$
And so also
$$HL = 3^{\mathrm{p}}52'$$
where
$$\text{hypt. } AH = 120^{\mathrm{p}};$$
and, as the angle of latitudinal deviation,
$$\text{angle } HAL = 3°42' \text{ to 2 rt.}$$
$$= 1°51'.$$
This we place in the third column of Jupiter's table beside 135°.

Likewise, since again as the distance at the beginning of the Ram
$$AC = 57^{\mathrm{p}}30',$$
$$CM = 8^{\mathrm{p}}8'$$
where it was shown
$$KM = 0^{\mathrm{p}}21',$$

so that, by subtraction, and since it is hardly at all greater than AK,
$$AM = AK = 49^\text{p}22'.$$

And therefore also
$$KM = 0^\text{p}51'$$
where
$$\text{hypt. } AK = 120^\text{p};$$
and
$$\text{angle } KAM = 0°49' \text{ to 2 rt.,}$$
and, by addition,
$$\text{angle } BAK = 3°49' \text{ to 2 rt.}$$
And so also, on the circle about right triangle AKB,
$$\text{arc } BK = 3°49',$$
and, as its supplement,
$$\text{arc } AB = 176°11'.$$

And therefore
$$\text{chord } BK = 3^\text{p}59',$$
$$\text{chord } AB = 119^\text{p}56'$$
where
$$\text{hypt. } AK = 120^\text{p}.$$

And so also
$$BK = 1^\text{p}39',$$
$$AB = 49^\text{p}20'$$
where
$$AK = 49^\text{p}22'.$$

And therefore, since
$$BL = 8^\text{p}8',$$
and the squares on AB and BL added together make the square on AL, therefore we shall have in length
$$AL = 50^\text{p}0'.$$

And so also
$$BL = 19^\text{p}31'$$
where
$$\text{hypt. } AL = 120^\text{p};$$
and, as the angle of longitudinal addition-subtraction,
$$\text{angle } BAL = 18°44' \text{ to 2 rt.}$$
$$= 9°22'.$$

Again, since
$$HL = 1^\text{p}39'$$
where
$$AL = 50^\text{p},$$
and the squares on them added together give the square on AH, therefore we shall have in length
$$AH = 50^\text{p}2'.$$

And therefore
$$HL = 3^\text{p}57'$$
where
$$\text{hypt. } AH = 120^\text{p};$$
and as the angle of latitudinal distance
$$\text{angle } HAL = 3°46' \text{ to 2 rt.}$$
$$= 1°53'.$$

This we place in the fourth column of the table beside 135°.

For the comparison of the longitudinal addition-subtractions, let the drawing be laid out without the obliquities.

Since, at the given distance, where

$$HK = CK = 8^{p}8',$$

there by addition

$$AC = 57^{p}30'$$

and, by subtraction,

$$AK = 49^{p}22';$$

and since

$$\text{sq. } AK + \text{sq. } HK = \text{sq. } AH,$$

therefore we shall have in length

$$AH = 50^{p}2'.$$

And so also

$$HK = 19^{p}30'$$

where

$$\text{hypt. } AH = 120^{p};$$

and, as the angle of longitudinal addition-subtraction,

$$\text{angle } HAK = 18°42' \text{ to 2 rt.}$$
$$= 9°21'.$$

But with the obliquities it was shown to be 9°22'.
Therefore, again, the longitudinal addition-subtraction, because of both obliquities, is more by 0°1'. Which it was required to find.

Next for the ratios of Mars, first let the drawing of the obliquities be laid out, and again let it be concluded that

$$CK = HK = 27^{p}56'$$

where

$$\text{epic. rad. } CH = 39^{p}30'.$$

Now, since as the angle of the epicycle's obliquity it is supposed that

$$\text{angle } ACE = 2°15'$$
$$= 4°30' \text{ to 2 rt.,}$$

therefore, on the circle about right triangle CMK,

$$\text{arc } KM = 4°30'$$

and, as its supplement,

$$\text{arc } CM = 175°30'.$$

And therefore

$$\text{chord } KM = 4^{p}43',$$
$$\text{chord } CM = 119^{p}54'$$

where

$$\text{hypt. } CK = 120^{p}.$$

And so, where

$$CK = 27^{p}56',$$

and as greatest distance

$$AC = 66^{p},$$

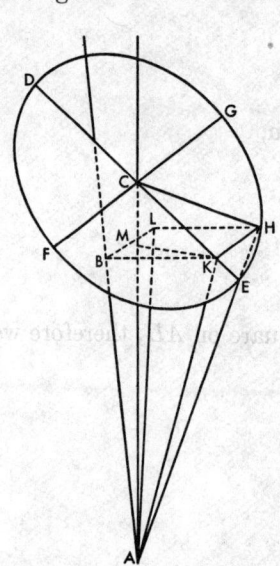

there also
$$KM = 1^p6',$$
$$CM = 27^p54',$$

and, by subtraction,
$$AM = 38^p6';$$

and therefore also
$$\text{hypt. } AK = 38^p7'.$$

And therefore
$$KM = 3^p28'$$

where
$$\text{hypt. } AK = 120^p;$$

and
$$\text{angle } KAM = 3°19' \text{ to 2 rt.}$$
But it is supposed that, as the angle of the eccentric's obliquity,
$$\text{angle } BAC = 1°$$
$$= 2° \text{ to 2 rt.}$$

And therefore, by addition,
$$\text{angle } BAK = 5°19' \text{ to 2 rt.}$$
And so also, on the circle about right triangle BAK,
$$\text{arc } BK = 5°19'$$

and, as its supplement,
$$\text{arc } AB = 174°41'.$$

And therefore
$$\text{chord } BK = 5^p34',$$
$$\text{chord } AB = 119^p52'$$

where
$$\text{hypt. } AK = 120^p.$$

And so also, where
$$AK = 38^p7',$$

there also
$$BK = 1^p46',$$

and
$$AB = 38^p5'.$$

But
$$BL = 27^p56'.$$

And since
$$\text{sq. } AB + \text{sq. } BL = \text{sq. } AL,$$
we shall have in length
$$AL = 47^p14'.$$

And since of like parts
$$HL = 1^p46'$$

and
$$\text{sq. } AL + \text{sq. } HL = \text{sq. } AH,$$
therefore we shall have in length
$$AH = 47^p16'.$$

And so also
$$HL = 4^p29'$$

where
$$\text{hypt. } AH = 120^p;$$
and as the angle of latitudinal distance
$$\text{angle } HAL = 4°18' \text{ to 2 rt.}$$
$$= 2°9'.$$
This we place in the third column of Mars' table beside 135°.

Likewise, for the obliquities at the least distance, since
$$AC = 54^p,$$
$$CM = 27^p54'$$
where it was shown
$$KM = 1^p6',$$
so that, by subtraction,
$$AM = 26^p6'$$
and it is calculated that
$$\text{hypt. } AK = 26^p7';$$
therefore
$$KM = 5^p3'$$
where
$$\text{hypt. } AK = 120^p;$$
and
$$\text{angle } KAM = 4°49' \text{ to 2 rt.}$$
And for that reason, by addition,
$$\text{angle } BAK = 6°49' \text{ to 2 rt.}$$
And so also, on the circle about right triangle ABK,
$$\text{arc } BK = 6°49'$$
and, as its supplement,
$$\text{arc } AB = 173°11'.$$
And therefore
$$\text{chord } BK = 7^p8',$$
$$\text{chord } AB = 119^p47'$$
where
$$\text{hypt. } AK = 120^p.$$
And so also
$$BK = 1^p33'$$
and
$$AB = 26^p4'$$
where
$$AK = 26^p7'.$$
And again, of like parts,
$$BL = 27^p56'.$$
And since
$$\text{sq. } AB + \text{sq. } BL = \text{sq. } AL,$$
we shall have in length
$$AL = 38^p12'.$$
And so also
$$BL = 87^p45'$$

where
$$\text{hypt. } AL = 120^p;$$
and, as the angle of longitudinal addition-subtraction,
$$\text{angle } BAL = 94° \text{ to 2 rt.}$$
$$= 47°.$$

Likewise, since
$$HL = 1^p33'$$
where
$$AL = 38^p12',$$
and since the squares on them added together give the square on AH, therefore we shall have in length
$$AH = 38^p14'.$$

And so also
$$HL = 4^p52'$$
where
$$\text{hypt. } AH = 120^p;$$
and as the angle of latitudinal distance
$$\text{angle } HAL = 4°40' \text{ to 2 rt.}$$
$$= 2°20'.$$
This we place in the fourth column of the table beside the 135°.

And now again, for the comparison of the longitudinal addition-subtractions, if we lay out the drawing without the obliquities, then, at the least distance where the difference is necessarily most sensible,

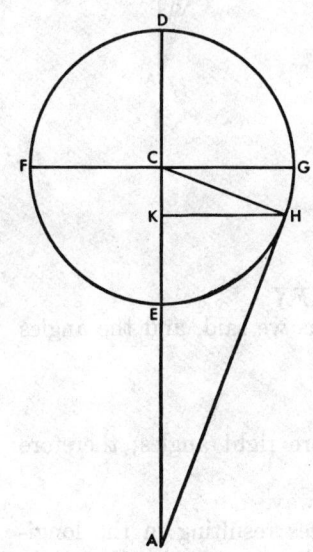

$$AC : CK \text{ or } HK : : 54^p : 27^p56';$$
so that for this reason, by subtraction,
$$AK = 26^p4'$$
and it is calculated
$$\text{hypt. } AH = 38^p12'.$$
And therefore also, again,
$$HK = 87^p45'$$
where
$$\text{hypt. } AH = 120^p;$$
and, as the angle of longitudinal addition-sub-traction,
$$\text{angle } HAK = 94° \text{ to 2 rt.}$$
$$= 47°.$$
But from calculations with the obliquities it was shown to be just that much. Therefore, in the case of Mars, the longitudinal addition-subtraction does not differ as a result of the obliquities of the circles. Which was to be found.

The fourth columns of the two tables of Venus and Mercury will contain the latitudinal passages embraced by the greatest slantings of the epicycles which occur at the eccentrics' apogees and perigees. But these passages have been worked out by us independently and separate from the difference due to the eccentrics' obliquities. Otherwise we should need more tables and a difficult calculus, since the evening and morning passages will be unequal and never at the same parts of the ecliptic; and besides, since the obliquity of the eccentrics varies, the differences in the decreases for the greatest obliquities would not agree with those in the decreases for the greatest slantings. But with the difference separated out, each case can be more easily handled as will be clear from what we are going to add.

Let AB be the intersection of the ecliptic's plane and the epicycle's plane, point A being supposed the ecliptic's centre and B the epicycle's centre. And let epicycle $CDEFG$ be drawn about B slanting to the ecliptic's plane—that is, so that the straight lines drawn in them perpendicular to the intersection CG make equal all the angles resulting at the points CG. Let AE be produced tangent to the epicycle, and AFD cutting it at random. And let DH, EK, and FL be drawn from points D, E, and F perpendicular to CG; and DM, EN, and FX perpendicular to the ecliptic's plane. And let HM, KN, and LX be joined; and also AN and AXM. For AXM is one straight line, since the three points are in two planes—that of the ecliptic and that through AFD at right angles to the ecliptic's.

Now, it is evident that, for the given slanting, angles HAM and KAN contain the longitudinal addition-subtractions of the stars, and angles DAM and EAN the latitudinal addition-subtractions.

It is first necessary to show that the latitudinal passage (angle EAN) formed at the tangent is greater than any others, just like the longitudinal addition-subtraction.

For, since angle EAK is greater than any others,
$$EK : AE > DH : AD$$
$$> FL : AF.$$
But
$$EK : EN :: DH : DM :: FL : FX.$$
For the triangles thus formed are all equiangular as we said, and the angles at M, N, and X are right. And, therefore,
$$EN : AE > DM : AD$$
$$> FX : AF.$$
And, again, the angles DMA, ENA, and FXA are right angles; therefore
$$\text{angle } EAN > \text{angle } DAM$$
and greater than all the others formed in the same way.

It is immediately evident that, of the differences resulting in the longitudinal addition-subtractions from the slanting, the greatest is effected in the greatest passages at E, since they are contained by the angles subtending the differences of HD, KE, and LF over HM, KN, and LX. Since the same ratio holds for each, it follows, relative to the differences, that the difference between EK and KN has a greater ratio to EA than those of any others to lines similar to AD. It is immediately clear also that, whatever ratio the greatest longitudinal addition-subtraction has to the greatest latitudinal passage, that ratio the longitudinal addition-subtractions in each case have to the latitudinal passages for all sections of the epicycle, since as *EK* is to *EN* so are all lines like *FL* and *DH* to those like *FX* and *DM*. Which it was required to show.

Now, with these things worked out, let us see first how great an angle is contained, for each of the stars, by the slant of the planes, if we suppose, according to postulates already assumed at the beginning, that about midway between the greatest and least distance each of them is at the most 5° north and south of the opposite passage on the epicycle. For Venus appears to make a deviation at the eccentric's perigee and apogee of hardly more or less than 5°, and Mercury of ½° more and less than 5°.

Now, again, let *ABC* be the intersection of the ecliptic and the epicycle.

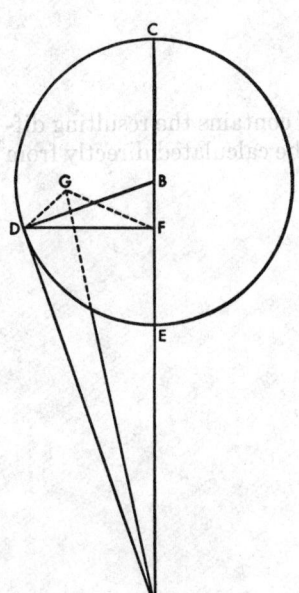

With the epicycle drawn about point *B* aslant the ecliptic's plane as we have described, let *AD* be joined tangent to the epicycle from the ecliptic's centre *A*. From *D* let *DF* be drawn perpendicular to *CBE*, and *DG* perpendicular to the ecliptic's plane. And let *BD*, *FG*, and *AG* be joined.

And let angle *DAG*, containing half of the given latitudinal deviation, be supposed to be 2½° for either of the stars. And let it be required to find the slant of the two planes—that is, the size of angle *DFG*.

Now, in the case of Venus, since where
$$\text{epic. rad.} = 43^{\text{p}}10',$$
there
$$\text{greatest dist.} = 61^{\text{p}}15',$$
$$\text{least dist.} = 58^{\text{p}}45'$$
and
$$\text{mean dist.} = 60^{\text{p}},$$
therefore
$$AB : BD :: 60^{\text{p}} : 43^{\text{p}}10'.$$
And since
$$\text{sq. } AB — \text{sq. } BD = \text{sq. } AD,$$
we shall have in length
$$AD = 41^{\text{p}}40'.$$

And likewise, since
$$AB : AD :: BD : DF,$$
we shall have
$$DF = 29^{\text{p}}58'.$$

Again, since it is supposed that
$$\text{angle } DAG = 2°30'$$
$$= 5° \text{ to } 2 \text{ rt.,}$$
therefore, on the circle about right triangle *ADG*,
$$\text{arc } DG = 5°$$
and
$$\text{chord } DG = 5^{\text{p}}14'$$

where

$$\text{hypt. } AD = 120^{\text{p}}.$$

And therefore

$$DG = 1^{\text{p}}50'$$

where

$$AD = 41^{\text{p}}40'.$$

But it was shown

$$DF = 29^{\text{p}}58'.$$

And so also

$$DG = 7^{\text{p}}20'$$

where

$$\text{hypt. } DF = 120^{\text{p}};$$

and, as the angle of slant,

$$\text{angle } DFG = 7° \text{ to } 2 \text{ rt.}$$
$$= 3°30'.$$

But since the excess of angle DAF over angle GAF contains the resulting difference of longitudinal addition-subtraction, it must be calculated directly from their size. For since it was shown that

$$\text{hypt. } AD = 31^{\text{p}}40'$$

and

$$DF = 29^{\text{p}}58'$$

where

$$DG = 1^{\text{p}}50';$$

and since

$$\text{sq. } AD - \text{sq. } DG = \text{sq. } AG,$$
$$\text{sq. } FD - \text{sq. } DG = \text{sq. } FG,$$

therefore we shall have in length

$$AG = 41^{\text{p}}37',$$
$$FG = 29^{\text{p}}55'.$$

And so also

$$FG = 86^{\text{p}}16'$$

where

$$\text{hypt. } AG = 120^{\text{p}};$$

and

$$\text{angle } FAG = 91°56' \text{ to } 2 \text{ rt.}$$
$$= 45°58'.$$

And likewise, since

$$DF = 86^{\text{p}}18'$$

where

$$\text{hypt. } AD = 120^{\text{p}};$$

and we shall have

$$\text{angle } DAF = 91°58' \text{ to } 2 \text{ rt.}$$
$$= 45°59'.$$

Therefore the longitudinal addition-subtraction, as a result of the slant, is less by 0°1'.

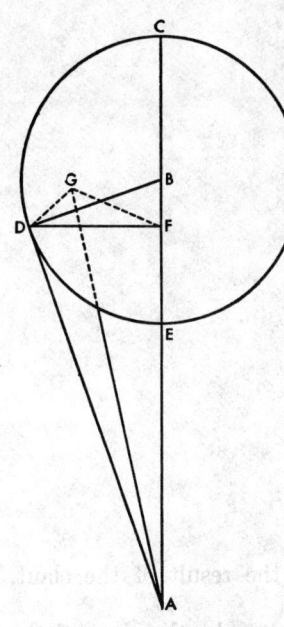

And, in the case of Mercury, since where
epic. rad. = 22ᵖ30′,

there it was shown
greatest dist. = 69ᵖ,
least dist. = 57ᵖ,

and
mean dist. = 63ᵖ,

therefore
$$AB : BD : : 63^\text{p} : 22^\text{p}30'.$$

And since
$$\text{sq. } AB - \text{sq. } BD = \text{sq. } AD,$$

we shall have also in length
$$AD = 58^\text{p}51'.$$

And likewise, since
$$AB : AD : : BD : DF,$$

therefore of the same parts
$$DF = 21^\text{p}1'.$$

Again, since it is supposed that
angle $DAG = 5°$ to 2 rt.,

therefore, on the circle about right triangle ADG,
arc $DG = 5°$;

and
chord $DG = 5^\text{p}14'$

where
hypt. $AD = 120^\text{p}.$

And therefore

where
$$DG = 2^\text{p}34'$$

$$AD = 58^\text{p}51'.$$

But also it was shown
$$DF = 21^\text{p}1'.$$

And so also
$$DG = 14^\text{p}40'$$

where
hypt. $DF = 120^\text{p}$;

and as the angle of slant
angle $DFG = 14°$ to 2 rt.
$= 7°.$

Likewise, for the comparison of the angles of addition-subtraction, since again it was shown
hypt. $AD = 58^\text{p}51'$

and
$$DF = 21^\text{p}1'$$

where
$$DG = 2^\text{p}34',$$

and since
$$\text{sq. } AD - \text{sq. } DG = \text{sq. } AG,$$

$$\text{sq. } DF - \text{sq. } DG = \text{sq. } FG,$$

therefore we shall have in length

$$AG = 58^\text{p}47',$$
$$FG = 20^\text{p}53'.$$

And so also

$$FG = 42^\text{p}38'$$

where

$$\text{hypt. } AG = 120^\text{p};$$

and

$$\text{angle } FAG = 41°38' \text{ to 2 rt.}$$
$$= 20°49'.$$

And in the same way, since

$$DF = 42^\text{p}50'$$

where

$$\text{hypt. } AD = 120^\text{p},$$

therefore we shall have

$$\text{angle } DAF = 41°50' \text{ to 2 rt.}$$
$$= 20°55'.$$

Therefore the longitudinal addition-subtraction, as the result of the slant, is less by 0°6'. Which it was required to find.

Following this, let us see if, when we suppose these to be the sizes of the slants, we find the latitudinal passages at the greatest and least distances consistent with those gotten by observations.

Again, with the same drawing, let Venus' greatest distance be supposed first—that is, let

$$AB : BD : : 61^\text{p}15' : 43^\text{p}10',$$

so that, since

$$\text{sq. } AB - \text{sq. } BD = \text{sq. } AD,$$

therefore it is concluded

$$AD = 43^\text{p}27'.$$

But

$$AB : AD : : BD : DF;$$

and therefore

$$DF = 30^\text{p}37'.$$

Again, since it is supposed that, as the angle of slant,

$$\text{angle } DFG = 7° \text{ to 2 rt.}$$

and that

$$DG = 7^\text{p}20'$$

where

$$DF = 120^\text{p},$$

therefore

$$DG = 1^\text{p}52'$$

where

$$DF = 30^\text{p}37'$$

and

$$AD = 43^\text{p}27'.$$

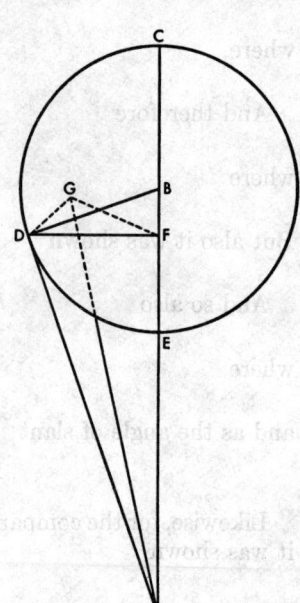

And so also
$$DG = 5^p9'$$
where
$$\text{hypt. } AD = 120^p;$$
and, as the angle of greatest latitudinal deviation,
$$\text{angle } DAG = 4°54' \text{ to 2 rt.}$$
$$= 2°27'.$$
And at the least distance, since it is supposed that
$$AB = 58^p45'$$
where
$$\text{epic. rad. } BD = 43^p10',$$
and since
$$\text{sq. } AB - \text{sq. } BD = \text{sq. } AD,$$
therefore we shall have in length
$$AD = 39^p51'.$$
And likewise, since
$$AB : AD :: BD : DF,$$
therefore
$$DF = 29^p17'.$$
But it is supposed that
$$DF : DG :: 120^p : 7^p20'.$$
And therefore
$$DG = 1^p47'$$
where
$$DF = 29^p17'$$
and
$$AD = 39^p51'.$$
And so also
$$DG = 5^p22'$$
where
$$\text{hypt. } AD = 120^p;$$
and as the angle of greatest latitudinal deviation
$$\text{angle } DAG = 5°8' \text{ to 2 rt.}$$
$$= 2°34'.$$

Therefore the latitudinal deviation is insensibly less at the apogee, and insensibly more at the perigee, than the deviation of $2\frac{1}{2}°$ assumed in mean terms. For at the greatest distance it is less by 0°3′, and at the least distance more by 0°4′, which obviously cannot be gotten by observations.

Again, let the greatest distance of Mercury be supposed—that is, let
$$AB : BD :: 69^p : 22^p30',$$
so that by the same means as above it is concluded that of the same parts
$$AD = 65^p14'$$
and
$$DF = 21^p16'.$$
But here we have, as the supposed angle of slant,
$$\text{angle } DFG = 14° \text{ to 2 rt.,}$$
and therefore we have
$$DG = 14^p40'$$

where
$$\text{hypt. } DF = 120^{\text{p}}.$$
And therefore
$$DG = 2^{\text{p}}36'$$
where
$$DF = 21^{\text{p}}16'$$
and
$$AD = 65^{\text{p}}14'.$$
And so also
$$DG = 4^{\text{p}}47'$$
where
$$\text{hypt. } AD = 120^{\text{p}};$$
and, as the angle of greatest latitudinal deviation,
$$\text{angle } DAG = 4°34' \text{ to 2 rt.}$$
$$= 2°17'.$$
At the least distance it is supposed that
$$AB : BD : : 57^{\text{p}} : 22^{\text{p}}30'.$$
And since because of the same slant it is supposed
that
$$DF : DG : : 120^{\text{p}} : 14^{\text{p}}40',$$
therefore
$$DG = 2^{\text{p}}32'$$
where
$$DF = 20^{\text{p}}40'$$
and
$$AD = 52^{\text{p}}22'.$$
And so also
$$DG = 5^{\text{p}}48'$$
where
$$\text{hypt. } AD = 120^{\text{p}};$$
and
$$\text{angle } DAG = 5°32' \text{ to 2 rt.}$$
$$= 2°46'.$$

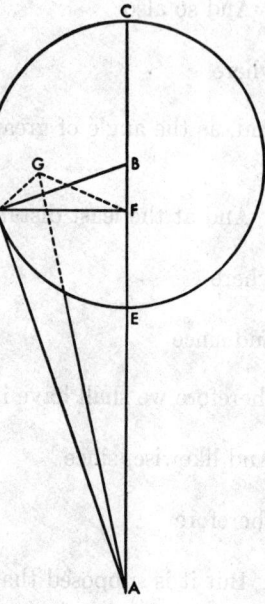

Therefore the latitudinal deviation at the apogee differs at the least by
0°13′ and at the perigee at the most by 0°16′ from the deviation of 2½° assumed in mean terms. In place of these we shall use, for the mean correction
in the calculus, the sensible ¼° difference of the observations.

With these things demonstrated—and because, as the greatest longitudinal
addition-subtractions are to the greatest latitudinal passages, so are the particular longitudinal addition-subtractions for the other sections of the epicycle
to the particular latitudinal passages—the filling in of the latitudinal passages
due to slanting, in these fourth columns of Venus' and Mercury's tables, is
immediately available to us, although these passages, as we said, are calculated with only the slanting of the epicycles and from the mean addition.
Because of greater ease in the calculus which will be given, the difference for
Mercury, due to the eccentrics' obliquity at the apogee and perigee, will provide the correction.

Since, according to the given mean terms, the greatest latitudinal passage
of both stars on either side of the ecliptic was shown to be 2°30′, due to slant-

ing; since the greatest longitudinal addition-subtraction for Venus is 46° and for Mercury very nearly 22°; and since we have given in their Tables of Anomaly the addition-subtractions corresponding to the particular sections of the epicycles, it follows that whatever part these latter are of the greatest longitudinal addition-subtractions as wholes, we take that part of the 2°30' for each star, placing the result in the fourth columns of the Tables of Latitude beside the same numbers.

We have the fifth columns for truly determining, by the method of corresponding sixtieths, the latitudinal deviations in the other passages of the eccentrics. For since, as we said, the obliquities and slantings of the epicycles make their return of increase and decrease proportionately with the eccentric return, by the interposition of little circles, and the quantities of all the obliquities and slantings are not very different from that of the moon's oblique circle, and since the particular deviations for obliquities of such amounts are very nearly proportional and we have those of the moon all worked out geometrically, we multiplied each of the entries there by twelve (because the greatest addition there is 5° and here we are considering it as 60°). The results we have placed beside the proper numbers in each of the fifth columns. The tabulated exposition follows:

5. Exposition of the Tables of Latitude

		SATURN'S OBLIQUITIES			JUPITER'S OBLIQUITIES			MARS' OBLIQUITIES		
1	2	3	4	5	3	4	5	3	4	5
Numbers from Apogee		From Northern Limit	From Southern Limit	Six-tieths	From Northern Limit	From Southern Limit	Six-tieths	From Northern Limit	From Southern Limit	Six-tieths
6	354	2 4	2 2	59 36	1 7	1 5	59 36	0 8	0 4	59 36
12	348	2 5	2 3	58 36	1 8	1 6	58 36	0 9	0 4	58 36
18	342	2 6	2 3	57 0	1 8	1 6	57 0	0 11	0 5	57 0
24	336	2 7	2 4	54 36	1 9	1 7	54 36	0 13	0 6	54 36
30	330	2 8	2 5	52 0	1 10	1 8	52 0	0 14	0 7	52 0
36	324	2 10	2 7	48 24	1 11	1 9	48 24	0 15	0 9	48 24
42	318	2 11	2 8	44 24	1 12	1 10	44 24	0 18	0 12	44 24
48	312	2 12	2 10	40 0	1 13	1 11	40 0	0 21	0 15	40 0
54	306	2 14	2 12	35 12	1 14	1 13	35 12	0 24	0 18	35 12
60	300	2 16	2 15	30 0	1 16	1 16	30 0	0 28	0 22	30 0
66	294	2 18	2 18	24 24	1 18	1 18	24 24	0 32	0 26	24 24
72	288	2 21	2 21	18 24	1 21	1 21	18 24	0 36	0 30	18 24
78	282	2 24	2 24	18 24	1 24	1 24	12 24	0 41	0 36	12 24
84	276	2 27	2 27	6 24	1 27	1 27	6 24	0 46	0 42	6 24
90	270	2 30	2 30	0 0	1 30	1 30	0 0	0 52	0 49	0 0
93	267	2 31	2 31	3 12	1 31	1 31	3 12	0 55	0 52	3 12
96	264	2 33	2 33	6 24	1 33	1 33	6 24	0 59	0 56	6 24
99	261	2 34	2 34	9 24	1 34	1 34	9 24	1 3	1 0	9 24
102	258	2 36	2 36	12 24	1 36	1 36	12 24	1 6	1 4	12 24
105	255	2 37	2 37	15 24	1 37	1 37	15 24	1 10	1 8	15 24
108	252	2 39	2 39	18 24	1 39	1 39	18 24	1 14	1 13	18 24
111	249	2 40	2 40	21 24	1 40	1 40	21 24	1 18	1 18	21 24
114	246	2 42	2 42	24 24	1 42	1 42	24 24	1 23	1 24	24 24
117	243	2 43	2 43	27 12	1 43	1 43	27 12	1 28	1 30	27 12
120	240	2 45	2 45	30 0	1 45	1 45	30 0	1 34	1 37	30 0
123	237	2 46	2 46	32 36	1 46	1 46	32 36	1 41	1 44	32 36
126	234	2 47	2 48	35 12	1 47	1 48	35 12	1 48	1 51	35 12
129	231	2 49	2 49	37 36	1 49	1 49	37 36	1 54	2 0	37 36
132	228	2 50	2 51	40 0	1 50	1 51	40 0	2 1	2 10	40 0
135	225	2 52	2 53	42 12	1 51	1 53	42 12	2 9	2 20	42 12
138	222	2 53	2 54	44 22	1 52	1 54	44 24	2 16	2 32	44 24
141	219	2 54	2 55	46 36	1 53	1 55	46 36	2 25	2 44	46 36
144	216	2 55	2 56	48 24	1 55	1 57	48 24	2 34	2 56	48 24
147	213	2 56	2 57	50 12	1 56	1 59	50 12	2 44	3 12	50 12
150	210	2 57	2 58	52 0	1 58	2 0	52 0	2 54	3 29	52 0
153	207	2 58	2 59	53 12	1 59	2 1	53 12	3 5	3 46	53 12
156	204	2 59	3 0	54 36	2 0	2 3	54 36	3 16	4 9	54 36
159	201	2 59	3 1	56 0	2 1	2 4	56 0	3 27	4 32	56 0
162	198	3 0	3 2	57 0	2 2	2 5	57 0	3 38	4 55	57 0
165	195	3 0	3 2	57 48	2 2	2 6	57 48	3 49	5 24	57 48
168	192	3 1	3 3	58 36	2 3	2 6	58 36	4 0	5 53	58 36
171	189	3 1	3 3	59 12	2 3	2 7	59 12	4 10	6 21	59 12
174	186	3 2	3 4	59 36	2 4	2 7	59 36	4 14	6 36	59 36
177	183	3 2	3 4	59 48	2 4	2 8	59 48	4 18	6 51	59 48
180	180	3 2	3 5	60 0	2 4	2 8	60 0	4 21	7 7	60 0

TABLE 5—*Continued*

1	2	3		4		5		3		4		5	
		VENUS' OBLIQUITIES						MERCURY'S OBLIQUITIES					
Numbers from Apogee		*Obliquity*		*Slanting*		*Sixtieths*		*Obliquity*		*Slanting*		*Sixtieths*	
6	354	1	2	0	8	59	36	1	45	0	11	59	36
12	348	1	1	0	16	58	36	1	44	0	22	58	36
18	342	1	0	0	25	57	0	1	43	0	33	57	0
24	336	0	59	0	33	54	36	1	40	0	44	54	36
30	330	0	57	0	41	52	0	1	36	0	55	52	0
36	324	0	55	0	49	48	24	1	30	1	6	48	24
42	318	0	51	0	57	44	24	1	23	1	16	44	24
48	312	0	46	1	5	40	0	1	16	1	26	40	0
54	360	0	41	1	13	35	12	1	8	1	35	35	12
60	300	0	35	1	20	30	0	0	59	1	44	30	0
66	294	0	29	1	28	24	24	0	49	1	52	24	24
72	288	0	23	1	35	18	24	0	38	2	0	18	24
78	282	0	16	1	42	12	24	0	26	2	7	12	24
84	276	0	8	1	50	6	24	0	16	2	14	6	24
90	270	0	0	1	57	0	0	0	0	2	20	0	0
93	267	0	5	2	0	3	12	0	8	2	23	3	12
96	264	0	10	2	3	6	24	0	15	2	25	6	24
99	261	0	15	2	6	9	24	0	23	2	27	9	24
102	258	0	20	2	9	12	24	0	31	2	28	12	24
105	255	0	26	2	12	15	24	0	40	2	29	15	24
108	252	0	32	2	15	18	24	0	48	2	29	18	24
111	249	0	38	2	17	21	24	0	57	2	30	21	24
114	246	0	44	2	20	24	24	1	6	2	30	24	24
117	243	0	50	2	22	27	12	1	16	2	30	27	12
120	240	0	59	2	24	30	0	1	25	2	29	30	0
123	237	1	8	2	26	32	36	1	35	2	28	32	36
126	234	1	18	2	27	35	12	1	45	2	26	35	12
129	231	1	28	2	29	37	36	1	55	2	23	37	36
132	228	1	38	2	30	40	0	2	6	2	20	40	0
135	225	1	48	2	30	42	12	2	16	2	16	42	12
138	222	1	59	2	30	44	24	2	27	2	11	44	24
141	219	2	11	2	29	46	36	2	37	2	6	46	36
144	216	2	23	2	28	48	24	2	47	2	0	48	24
147	213	2	43	2	26	50	12	2	57	1	53	50	12
150	210	3	3	2	22	52	0	3	7	1	46	52	0
153	207	3	23	2	18	53	12	3	17	1	38	53	12
156	204	3	44	2	12	54	36	3	26	1	29	54	36
159	201	4	5	2	4	56	0	3	34	1	20	56	0
162	198	4	26	1	55	57	0	3	42	1	10	57	0
165	195	4	49	1	42	57	48	3	48	0	59	57	48
168	192	5	13	1	27	58	36	3	54	0	48	58	36
171	189	5	36	1	9	59	12	3	58	0	36	59	12
174	186	5	52	0	48	59	36	4	2	0	24	59	36
177	183	6	7	0	25	59	48	4	4	0	12	59	48
180	180	6	22	0	0	60	0	4	5	0	0	60	0

6. CALCULUS OF THE LATITUDINAL DEVIATION OF THE FIVE PLANETS

With these things so established, we shall work out the latitudinal calculus of the five planets in this way.

In the case of the three stars, Saturn, Jupiter, and Mars, we carry the truly determined longitude to the numbers of the proper table, that of Mars as it is, Jupiter's with a subtraction of 20°, and Saturn's with an addition of 50°. We record the sixtieths in the fifth columns of latitude corresponding to it, and likewise we carry the truly determined number of anomaly to the same numbers. If the truly determined longitude is in the first 15 rows, we multiply the corresponding latitudinal difference in the third column by the given number of sixtieths; but if it is in the rows following, we multiply that in the fourth column. We shall have the star north of the ecliptic by the number of degrees resulting from these operations if we have taken the latitudinal difference from the third column; but south of it by that much if we have taken it from the fourth column.

But in the case of Venus and Mercury, we first carry the truly determined number of anomaly to the numbers of the proper table, and we record separately the corresponding numbers in the third and fourth columns of latitude—those in three of the columns as they are, but those in the fourth column of Mercury with a subtraction of 10° if the truly determined longitude is in the first 15 rows, and with an addition of 10° if below. Then, for Venus, we always add 90° to the truly determined longitude, and for Mercury 270°, subtracting a circle if we can. The result we carry to the same numbers; and whatever number of sixtieths in the fifth column correspond to these numbers, just so many do we take of the numbers recorded from the third column. When the longitude with the given addition is in the first 15 rows, we shall set out the result as south, if the truly determined number of anomaly is in the first 15 rows, but as north if it is in those that follow. And when this number of longitude falls in the rows below the first 15, we shall set out the result as north if the number of anomaly is in the first 15 rows, but as south if it is in those that follow.

Next we carry the truly determined longitude to the same numbers: in the case of Venus, simply as it is, but in the case of Mercury, with an addition of 180°. Whatever number of sixtieths lie beside it in the fifth column, just so many do we take of the numbers recorded from the fourth column. And when, as we said, the longitude we carried over falls in the first 15 rows, we shall set out the result as north if the truly determined number of anomaly is among those up to 180°, but as south if above 180°. When this longitude falls below these 15 rows, we shall set back the result as south if the anomalistic number is among those up to 180°, but as north if above.

Finally taking, of these sixtieths found from the second carrying over the longitude, the same part as they were of 60, we shall set forth, for Venus, ⅙ of the result always to the north, and for Mercury, ¾ of the result always to the south. Thus, from the mixture of the three settings forth, we get their apparent latitudinal passage with respect to the ecliptic.

7. ON THE HELIACAL RISINGS AND SETTINGS OF THE FIVE PLANETS

Now that we have worked through the latitudinal deviation of the five stars, we have left the filling out of those things which must be considered concerning their heliacal risings and settings. For, just as we described them in detail in the treatise on the fixed stars, it turns out that their elongations on the ecliptic with respect to the sun are differently unequal in the case of their risings and settings for many causes. The first of these is due to the inequality in their magnitudes; the second to the dissimilarity of the ecliptic's inclinations to the horizon's; and the third to their latitudinal passages.

For if, again, we consider the sections of great circles (AB of the horizon and

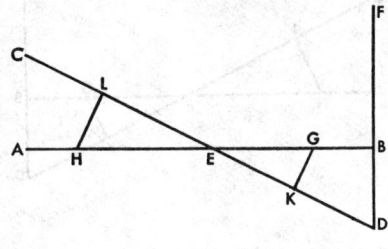

CD of the ecliptic); if we suppose the point E their intersection either eastern or western, and points C and A lying on the meridian, and D the sun's centre; and if we draw through it and the horizon's pole section DBF of a great circle, and suppose the star to rise or set on the horizon AEB (clearly at E when on the ecliptic; at G when north of the ecliptic; and at H when south of it), and draw from G and H the perpendiculars GK and HL, then again we shall have arc BD, as always, equal to the arc of the sun's distance below the earth when the star will first be seen or disappear. For at equal distances below the earth, along the great circle so drawn, the sun's rays give the same light. But since first this distance is established later on to be unequal for the different unequal stars, necessarily, even if all the other things are the same, the ecliptic arcs subtending the right angle subtending the right angle (that is, the distances similar to ED) are different, evidently less for the larger stars, and greater for the smaller.

Likewise, if BD is the same for the same star, and BED the angle of inclination of the ecliptic is unequal either from the differences of the dodecatemories or from those of the latitudes, again the arc ED will differ and will be greater when the given angle is decreased, and smaller when it is increased. And likewise even if the inclination is first presupposed the same, but the star not on the ecliptic but north at G or south at H, then it will no longer appear or disappear first when it is arc DE away; but, when it is north of the ecliptic, DK will be less, and when south, DEL will be greater.

Therefore it is necessary for the examination of particular cases that general sizes of the arcs BD be first given, for each of the five planets, from carefully observed risings. Such would be those in summer about the Crab because of the lightness and clearness of the air at that season, and because of the mean value of the ecliptic's inclination to the horizon. Then we find by this examination of the morning observations that, at the beginning of the Crab, Saturn rises generally when it is 14° from the true sun; Jupiter likewise when it is 12¾° away; and the evening Mercury when it is 11½° away.

With these things supposed, let the figure of the preceding drawing be laid out since there is no difference in the case of arcs of this size if, for facility in calculation, we take the ratios of the chords (for they are sensibly no different). And let point E of intersection of the ecliptic and the horizon be the rising point in the foregoing appearances at the beginning of the Crab for the three morning planets Saturn, Jupiter, and Mars; and the setting point, of course, for the evening planets Venus and Mercury. And let the latitude be taken as the parallel through Phoenicia where the longest day is 14¼ equatorial hours, since especially at and near this parallel the most and trustworthy observations have been made, those of the Chaldeans on it, and those of Greece and Egypt near it.

Since, then, from the previous demonstration concerning angles [II, 13], when the beginning of the Crab rises in the given latitude, we find

angle $BED = 103°$ to 2 rt.,

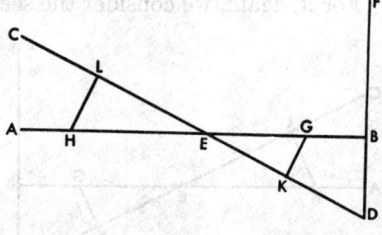

and therefore the ratio of the sides about the right angles is very nearly 94 to 75 to the hypotenuse's 120; and since by means of the latitudinal theory, when the three lone stars rise near the beginning of the Crab (that is, are passing near the apogees of the epicycle so as never to be farther from the apogee than a dodecatemory), we find Saturn and Jupiter practically on the ecliptic, but Mars nearly $\frac{1}{5}°$ north; therefore DE will be the elongation of Saturn and Jupiter from the sun along the ecliptic, but DK that of Mars because of its being farther north by the 12' of arc KG.

And since

$$KG : KE : : 94 : 75,$$

therefore

$$KE = 0°10'.$$

And it is assumed in the case of Mars

$$DK = 14\frac{1}{2}°,$$

so that altogether

$$DE = 14°40'.$$

In the case of Saturn, it is 14°; and of Jupiter, $12\frac{3}{4}°$. And so, since again

$$DE : DB : : 120 : 94,$$

we shall have arc DB of the great circle drawn through the poles of the horizon equal to 11° in the case of Saturn, 10° in the case of Jupiter, and very nearly $11\frac{1}{2}°$ in the case of Mars.

Likewise in the case of Venus and Mercury—since, when the beginning of the Crab sets, it makes the same angle and inclination with the horizon as the foregoing, and it is supposed that about this part the evening Venus rises $5\frac{2}{3}°$ from the true sun and Mercury $11\frac{1}{2}°$—the true sun will be situated at their risings $24\frac{1}{3}°$ within the Twins in the case of Venus, $18\frac{1}{2}°$ in the case of Mercury; the mean sun, 25° in the case of Venus, and very nearly 19° in the case of Mercury. Therefore, the mean longitudinal movement of these stars was that number of degrees. When with this longitude they appear at the beginning of the Crab, Venus is found to be about 14° from the epicycle's apogee, and Mercury about 32°. This is shown by the theorems already expounded on the anomaly. Consequently, in these passages, Venus is found 1° north of the ecliptic and Mercury very nearly $1\frac{2}{3}°$, which of course is KG. And so, since

$$KG : EK : : 94 : 75 : : 1 : \frac{3}{4},$$

or very nearly

$$KG : EK : : 1\frac{2}{3} : 1\frac{1}{3},$$

in the case of Venus we shall have

$$EK = \frac{3}{4}°;$$

in the case of Mercury
$$EK = 1\tfrac{1}{3}°.$$
And it is supposed, in the case of Venus,
$$DK = 5\tfrac{2}{3}°$$
where DK is the elongation of either planet from the sun; and in the case of Mercury
$$DK = 11\tfrac{1}{2}°.$$
Therefore we shall have altogether
$$DKE = 6\tfrac{2}{5}°$$
in the case of Venus; and in the case of Mercury
$$DKE = 12\tfrac{5}{6}°.$$
And so, since again
$$ED : BD : : 120 : 94 : : 6\tfrac{2}{5} : 5,$$
or very nearly
$$ED : BD : : 12 \ \tfrac{5}{6} : 10,$$
we shall have the arc BD, the value of the general distance as 5° in the case of Venus, and 10° in the case of Mercury. Which it was required to find.

8. That the Particularities of the Heliacal Risings and Settings of Venus and Mercury Agree with the Hypotheses

We can thus understand that even the extraordinary things concerning the heliacal risings and settings of Venus and Mercury are consequent upon these hypotheses; that is, that in the case of Venus the time from the evening setting to the morning rising about the beginning of the Fishes is about 2 days, but about the beginning of the Virgin 16 days; and that in the case of Mercury the evening risings are eclipsed when it should appear at the beginning of the Scorpion; and the morning risings when it should appear at the beginning of the Bull. And first the case of Venus.

For let a drawing of the apparitions similar to the preceding one be laid out.

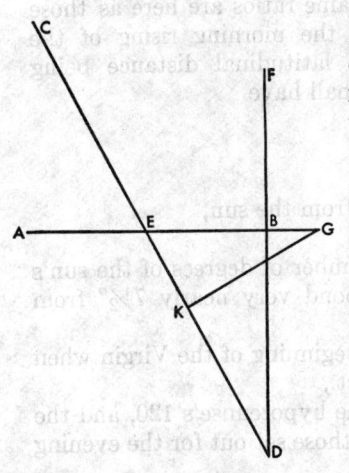

Let point E be first supposed near the beginning of the Fishes where Venus, when at the perigee of its epicycle, is north of the ecliptic by very nearly $6\tfrac{1}{3}°$. Let it also be supposed [to represent] the figure of the evening setting where angle BED in the given latitude totals 154° to 2 right angles' 360°, with the greater side of those about the right angle as 117 to the hypotenuse's 120, and the lesser side very nearly 27. Therefore, where the arc DB of the general distance is 5°, there
$$DE = 5°8'.$$
But since the star is $6\tfrac{1}{3}°$ north of the ecliptic or arc KG, and
$$117 : 27 : : 6\tfrac{1}{3} : 1\tfrac{1}{2}$$
very nearly, therefore
$$KE = 1\tfrac{1}{2}°,$$
and, by subtraction,
$$KD = 3°38'$$
which is the elongation of the star eastward from the sun, in its evening setting.

Again, in a similar drawing, since in the morning rising

angle $BED = 69°$ to 2 rt.,

therefore the lesser of the sides about the right
angle is 68 to the hypotenuse's 120, and the
greater is 99. And

$$68° : 120° : : 5° : 8°49',$$
$$68° : 99° : : 6\tfrac{1}{3}° : 9°13';$$

therefore we shall have

$$DE = 8°49',$$

and the difference due to latitude

$$KE = 9°13';$$

and, by subtraction, eastward of the sun,

$$DK = 0°24'.$$

And at the evening setting it was likewise eastward 3°38'. Therefore it has
moved, in the time from the evening setting to the morning rising, less than
the sun's movement—that is, less than its proper longitudinal passage, because of the epicyclic retrogression of 3°14'. Since, then, the star moves westward by so many degrees, as is easily seen from the Table of Anomaly, when
it has moved $1\tfrac{1}{4}°$ at the perigee of the epicycle, and passes through these
in mean motion in very nearly 2 days, it is evident that just so much time
would be taken for that distance in conformity with the appearances.

Again, in a similar drawing, let the point E be supposed at the beginning

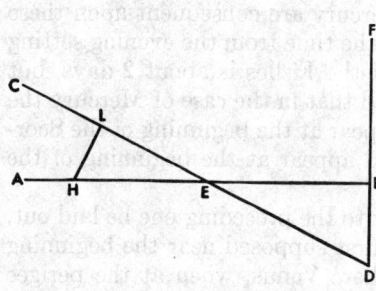

of the Virgin where Venus, when at the
epicycle's perigee, appears very nearly
$6\tfrac{1}{3}°$ south of the ecliptic. And let the
evening setting be first proposed when
angle $BED = 69°$ to 2 rt.,
and the lesser of the sides about the
right angle is 68 to the hypotenuse's
120, and the greater very nearly 99.
Since the same ratios are here as those
relative to the morning rising of the
Fishes, the latitudinal distance being
equal, we shall have

$$\text{arc } ED = 8°49',$$

and, as difference due to latitude,

$$LE = 9°13',$$

and, as the total elongation of the star eastward from the sun,

$$DL = 18°2'.$$

By the Table of Anomaly, as we said, to that number of degrees of the sun's
and star's retrogression in mean motion correspond very nearly $7\tfrac{1}{2}°$ from
the epicycle's perigee.

Likewise since, at the morning rising near the beginning of the Virgin when
angle $BED = 154°$ to 2 rt.,
the greater side about the right angle is 117 to the hypotenuse's 120, and the
lesser side 27, and the same ratios are deduced as those set out for the evening
setting in the Fishes, we shall have

$$\text{arc } DE = 5°8',$$

and as difference in latitude

$$EL = 1°30',$$

and, as the total elongation of the star westward from the sun,
$$DL = 6°38'.$$
In the same way to these correspond very nearly $2\frac{1}{2}°$ from the epicycle's perigee. Therefore Venus, from the evening setting to the morning rising, will move 10° which it passes through in very nearly 16 days in conformity with the appearances.

These things being proved, it is necessary to consider the incidents of Mercury regarding the eclipsed risings; and first that, at the beginning of the Scorpion, even if it is at its greatest elongation eastward from the sun, the evening rising cannot appear.

For let the drawing of these risings be laid out, E being supposed the point on the ecliptic near the beginning of the Scorpion, where at the setting

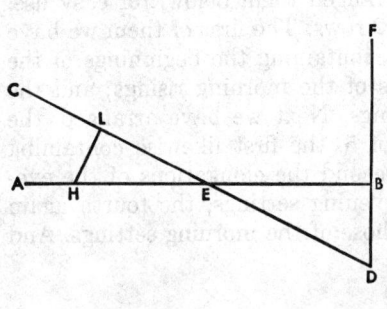

angle $BED = 69°$ to 2 rt.,

and the lesser side about the right angle is 68 to the hypotenuse's 120, and the greater 99. Therefore where BD, the general distance, is 10°, there
$$DE = 17°39'.$$
But when the star has that position, it is very nearly 3° south of the ecliptic. And so, since for the given ratios
$$LE = 4°22'$$
where, as arc of latitude,
$$LH = 3°,$$
and the total
$$DEL \doteq 22°.$$
This is the elongation of the star from the true sun necessary for its first appearing. And so, since its greatest elongation from the true sun in the beginning of the Scorpion is only 20°58' (for this was proved by us in the demonstrations concerning the greatest elongations), it is evident that such risings are eclipsed.

But again if—with a similar drawing of the risings set out—we suppose the point E the beginning of the Bull at the morning rising, then, when the star in the given passages is very nearly $3\frac{1}{6}°$ south of the ecliptic and the ratios about the right angles are the same as before, we shall have
$$DE = 17°39',$$
and
$$LE = 4°37'$$
where as arc of latitude
$$HL = 3°10',$$
and the total
$$DEL = 22°16'.$$
And so the star will have to have an elongation from the true sun of just that amount to be first seen. Since at the most its elongation does not exceed 22°13' as shown above [Book XII], risings of this kind are eclipsed. And the things proposed have been shown by us to be consonant with the appearances and with the given hypotheses.

9. The Method for the Particular Distances from the Sun of the Risings and Settings

It is immediately evident that, in general (arcs *BD* being supposed for each of the stars and the beginning of the dodecatemories being given at the intersection *E* and therefore angle *BED*), *DE* will also be given and the star's latitudinal passage at this elongation—that is, *KG* or *HL;* and, therefore, *KE* or *EL*, and also the apparent distance *DK* or *DL*. In this way we have calculated for every dodecatemory (not to make the treatise long) the apparent elongations of the risings and settings from the true sun for each of the 5 stars, and for the given latitude only, as being sufficient. Using only the beginnings of the dodecatemories, we have arranged them below, for easy use, in 5 tables for the 5 stars, each containing 12 rows. The first of them we have arranged in columns of 3, the first columns containing the beginnings of the dodecatemories; the second, the elongations of the morning risings; and the third the elongations of the evening settings. Next we have arranged the tables of Venus and Mercury in columns of 5, the first likewise containing the beginnings of the dodecatemories, the second the elongations of the evening risings, the third again those of the evening settings, the fourth again those of the morning risings, and the fifth those of the morning settings. And here is the exposition presented in tables:

10. Exposition of the Tables Containing the Heliacal Risings and Settings of the Five Planets

Beginnings of the Dodecatemories	SATURN Morning Rising		SATURN Evening Setting		JUPITER Morning Rising		JUPITER Evening Setting		MARS Morning Rising		MARS Evening Setting	
Ram	23	1	11	28	20	10	10	19	21	12	11	40
Bull	21	57	11	41	19	6	10	29	20	8	11	48
Twins	17	52	12	26	15	51	11	10	17	21	12	30
Crab	14	2	14	2	12	46	12	46	14	33	14	33
Lion	11	34	15	34	10	40	14	31	12	28	17	19
Virgin	10	53	16	53	10	1	16	12	11	46	20	5
Balance	10	48	17	6	9	57	16	34	11	38	21	1
Scorpion	10	53	16	53	10	1	16	12	11	48	20	19
Archer	11	34	15	34	10	40	14	31	12	34	17	32
Goat	14	2	14	2	12	46	12	46	14	45	14	45
Water Bearer	17	52	12	26	15	51	11	10	17	35	12	36
Fishes	21	57	11	41	19	6	10	29	20	26	11	49

Beginnings of the Dodecatemories	VENUS Evening Rising		VENUS Evening Setting		VENUS Morning Rising		VENUS Morning Setting		MERCURY Evening Rising		MERCURY Evening Setting		MERCURY Morning Rising		MERCURY Morning Setting	
Ram	5	10	4	9	3	0	10	28	9	58	9	43	23	58	23	38
Bull	5	8	4	16	6	16	9	40	10	4	10	15	22	15	22	15
Twins	5	12	5	7	9	15	7	36	10	18	11	47	18	0	16	44
Crab	5	36	8	23	9	50	5	59	12	22	15	34	14	4	12	30
Lion	6	16	13	3	8	2	5	5	13	43	19	59	11	25	10	21
Virgin	7	22	18	2	6	38	4	54	18	1	23	13	10	21	9	59
Balance	7	53	17	43	5	41	4	54	22	49	23	16	9	51	10	0
Scorpion	8	20	13	47	5	28	4	55	20	1	22	1	9	44	10	19
Archer	7	49	8	1	4	39	5	16	18	11	17	25	9	25	11	19
Goat	6	25	4	8	2	43	6	35	13	54	12	10	9	36	14	5
Water Bearer	5	51	3	16	0	30	8	33	11	10	9	50	12	27	17	50
Fishes	5	22	3	38	0	24	10	16	10	11	9	43	19	15	21	46

11. Epilogue

Now that these things have been added, Syrus, and to my mind about all things which ought to be considered in such a treatise have been worked out as much as the time to the present affords for discovery and more accurate revision, and annals suggest as useful for the theory and not just as demonstration, it is therefore fitting and proper that this treatise end here.

APPENDIX A

1. Ptolemaic Dates, the Era of Nabonassar, and the Christian Era

The following is a translation from the Greek of the *Chronological Table of the Kings,* published by Halma in his edition of the *Almagest,* and by F. K. Grinzel in his *Handbuch der Mathematischen und Technischen Chronologie* (3 Vols., Leipzig, 1906).

Years of the Kings before the Death of Alexander and the Years of Alexander[1]

Of the Assyrians and Medes	Years	Totals
Nabonassar	14	14
Nadius	2	16
Chinzer and Porus	5	21
Iloulaius	5	26
Mardokempad	12	38
Arkean	5	43
First Interregnum	2	45
Bilib	3	48
Aparanad	6	54
Rhegebel	1	55
Mesesimordak	4	59
Second Interregnum	8	67
Asaradin	13	80
Saosdouchin	20	100
Kinelanadan	22	122
Nabopolassar	21	143
Nabokolassar	43	186
Illoaroudam	2	188
Nerigasolassar	4	192
Nabonadius	17	209

Of the Persian Kings		
Cyrus	9	218
Cambyses	8	226
Darius I	36	262
Xerxes	21	283
Artaxerxes I	41	324
Darius II	19	343
Artaxerxes II	46	389
Ochus	21	410
Arogus	2	412
Darius III	4	416
Alexander of Macedonia	8	424

Years of the Macedonian Kings after the Death of Alexander the King

Of the Macedonian Kings	Years	Totals
Philip	7	7
Alexander II	12	19
Ptolemy Lagus	20	39
Philadelphus	38	77
Euergetes I	25	102
Philopator	17	119
Epiphanes	24	143
Philometor	35	178
Euergetes II	29	207
Soter	36	243
Dionysius the Younger	29	276
Cleopatra	22	294

Of the Roman Kings		
Augustus	43	337
Tiberius	22	359
Gaius	4	363
Claudius	14	377
Nero	14	391
Vespasian	10	401
Titus	3	404
Domitian	15	419
Nerva	1	420
Trajan	19	439
Hadrian	21	460
Alelius-Antonine	23	483

A year is counted from Thoth 1 preceding the beginning of the king's reign. Kings not ruling a year are not mentioned.

[1]The names of the Assyrian kings, as rendered by modern scholars, are as follows: (1) Nabu-nasir, (2) Nabu-nadin-zer, (3) Ukinzer and Pulu, (4) Ululai, (5) Marduk-apal-iddin, (6) Sargon, (7) Bel-ibni, (8) Ashur-nadin-shum, (9) Nergal-usheziib, (10) Mushezib-Marduk, (11) Esarhaddon, (12) Shamash-shim-ukin, (13) Kandalanu, (14) Nabu-apal-usur, (15) Nebuchadrezzar, (16) Amel-Marduk, (17) Nergal-shar-usur (Neriglissar), (18) Nabu-na'id (Nabonidius). Among the Persian kings, Arogus is called Arses.

The Egyptian year used by Ptolemy consists of 365 days. This contains 12 months of 30 days each, followed by 5 intercalary days. This year, of course, changes with respect to the equinoxes and soltices. But it is simpler and more practical than any other. The months occur in the following order:

1. Thoth	4. Choiak	7. Phamenoth	10. Payni
2. Phaophi	5. Tybi	8. Pharmouthi	11. Epiphi
3. Athyr	6. Mechir	9. Pachom	12. Mesore

FIVE INTERCALARY DAYS

The era used by Ptolemy is the so-called Era of Nabonassar, whose beginnings or epoch is Thoth 1, midday, the year 1 of the reign of Nabonassar. The table just given permits one to calculate the years from the epoch to the given date.

If one wishes to pass from the Era of Nabonassar to the Christian Era, certain complications arise. For the Christian Era is computed in two styles, the Julian and the Gregorian. The Christian Era up to October 4, 1582, is computed in terms of the Julian year, which is the year made up of 365 days ordinarily and every fourth year or leap year of 366 days; that is, the Julian year averages $365\frac{1}{4}$ days. Since, however, the solar year is approximately 365 days 14' 48" according to Ptolemy's calculations in Book III of the *Almagest*, the Julian year will fall behind the solar year. Thus in the year A.D. 325 (after the birth of Christ), the year of the Council of Nicea, the spring equinox fell on March 21. In the year A.D. 1582, the spring equinox fell on March 11.

And so, in order to make the calendar year more nearly equal to the solar year for liturgical reasons, Pope Gregory XIII ordered the day following October 4, 1582, to be counted as October 15, 1582. Further, the years ending in two zeros which were not divisible by 400 were no longer to be leap years. Thus the years A.D. 1700, 1800, 1900 would not be leap years. The Gregorian reform was followed at first only by southern Europe, but since the eighteenth century it has been followed by the whole of Europe and the New World.

The Christian Era, therefore, is counted by Julian Years before and after the birth of Christ, up until October 4, 1582; thereafter by the Julian year modified according to the reform instituted by Gregory, as just explained.

But the Christian Era is also counted in two ways: the historical and the astronomical. In the historical way, there is no year between the year 1 B.C. (before the birth of Christ) and the year A.D. 1 (after the birth of Christ). In the astronomical way, since the years before Christ are written as negative numbers, the first year before Christ or the year 1 B.C. (historical way) is the year 0. And so, up until A.D. 1582, all years divisible by 4 are leap years both according to the historical and to the astronomical ways of counting. Respecting the years before Christ, those years are leap years which are divisible by 4 with a remainder of 1 in the historical way; in the astronomical way, those years which are divisible by 4 as for the years after Christ.

The Julian year is made up of 12 unequal months as follows:

1. January, 31 days	7. July, 31 days
2. February, 28 days (leap year 29 days)	8. August, 31 days
3. March, 31 days	9. September, 30 days
4. April, 30 days	10. October, 31 days
5. May, 31 days	11. November, 30 days
6. June, 30 days	12. December, 31 days.

The correspondence of the Era of Nabonassar and the Christian Era is as follows:—Thoth 1, midday, the year of Nabonassar corresponds to February 27, midday, 747 B.C. (historical way), or 746 B.C. (astronomical way).

But a further distinction has to be made. Since Ptolemy, the astronomical day begins with midday and the civil day with midnight. Therefore February 27, midday (civil style) corresponds to February 26, midday (astronomical style). And so Thoth 1, midday, the year 1 of Nabonassar corresponds to February 26, midday (astronomical style), 747 B.C. (historical way).

One can now pass safely from Ptolemy's dates, which are always given finally in terms of Egyptian years and the Era of Nabonassar, to dates of the Christian Era.

The Julian year and Julian style, explained above, are not to be confused with the Julian Period, an era constructed by Joseph Scaliger in the 17th century. The Julian Period is a cycle of 7980 Julian years. The first year of the Julian Period is January 1, 4713 B.C., or 4712 B.C. (astronomical way). This period is the product of 28, 19, and 15—representing, respectively, the solar cycle, lunar cycle, and indiction. The solar cycle of 28 Julian years is the period in which the same day of the week falls again on the same day of the month of the Julian year. The lunar cycle of 19 Julian years is a period in which the solar years and the synodic months fall together again.

2. Equivalent Modern Terms for Determining the Positions of Stars, and for the Solar and Lunar Cycles

We shall now set down the modern astronomical terms and their Ptolemaic equivalents for those who wish to pass easily from ancient to modern literature. In doing this, we get a brief review of the astronomical appearances and the Ptolemaic measurements which are very close to the modern ones when they are not exactly the same.

First, we must remember that there are three systems of coördinates for determining the positions of the stars: (1) *With respect to the equator and the great circle through the equator's poles and the equinoxes'*, that is, the meridian through the equinoxes. In modern terms, the arc of the equator cut off by the meridian through the star and by the spring equinox, taken eastward from the spring equinox, is called the star's right ascension. And the smaller arc of the meridian cut off by the equator and by the star is called its declination. (2) *With respect to the ecliptic and to the great circle through the ecliptic's poles and the spring equinox*. This is the system most used by Ptolemy. The ancient and modern terms are the same. The arc of the ecliptic cut off by the great circle through the ecliptic's poles and the star and by the spring equinox, taken eastward from the spring equinox, is called the star's longitude. And the smaller arc of the great circle through the ecliptic's poles and the star, cut off by the ecliptic and by the star, is called its latitude. (3) *With respect to the horizon and the meridian or great circle through the zenith and the equator's poles*. In modern terms, the arc of the horizon cut off by the great circle through the zenith and the star and by the intersection of the meridian with the horizon nearer the southern pole taken clockwise is called the star's azimuth. It is indeterminate, of course, when either of the poles is the zenith. And the smaller arc of the great circle through the zenith and the star, cut off by the star and the horizon, is called the star's height or altitude.

Now, the sun is considered in two cycles: (1) *Its passage from one equinoctial point back to the same.* This is called the solar year both by Ptolemy and by the moderns. (2) *Its passage from one fixed star back to the same.* This is now called the sidereal year. These two cycles are not equal, since the spring equinox moves from east to west along the ecliptic about 1° in 100 years according to Ptolemy, or 1.396° in 100 years according to modern calculations. Hence the sidereal year is a bit longer than the solar year. By Ptolemy's calculations, in 36,000 solar years there would be 35,999 sidereal years. At that time the solar year and the sidereal year would finish at the same point, if one considered them as beginning from the same point. This is the period of those two cycles.

The difference between the mean sun and true sun reduced to time is called in modern terms *the equation of time.* The method of calculating it is given by Ptolemy in Book III, Section 9.

As described in Books IV and V, the moon has a great many cycles. For it must be considered in its movement (1) with respect to the sun, (2) with respect to the fixed stars, (3) with respect to its irregularity of movement longitudinally about the ecliptic, and (4) with respect to its movement latitudinally back and forth across the ecliptic. There is also (5) its cycle of anomaly with respect to its movement relative to the sun, and (6) the inclination of the epicycle.

The first four are spoken of as four kinds of months. We shall state their modern names and add the Ptolemaic name when it is different. We also add their magnitude in terms of mean solar days; the modern calculations of these magnitudes are carried to five decimals, the same as those of Ptolemy.

(1) The lunar month is the period from full moon to full moon—that is, from the moon's opposition to the sun to its next opposition. The mean lunar month is 29.53059 mean solar days.

(2) The sidereal month is the period from the moon's conjunction with a fixed star to its next conjunction with the same fixed star. The mean sidereal month is 27.32166 mean solar days. It is called by Ptolemy the longitudinal cycle.

(3) The anomalistic month is the cycle of the moon's irregular motion in longitude; it is called by Ptolemy the moon's first anomaly or longitudinal anomaly. The mean anomalistic month is 27.55455 mean solar days.

(4) The nodical month is the period from the moon's passage at one node back to its next passage at the same node. The moon's nodes are the points where its oblique circle crosses the ecliptic. These nodes move westward along the ecliptic about 1½° in a lunar month. Ptolemy gives it as 3′ a day. The mean nodical month is 27.21222 mean solar days. This is called by Ptolemy the latitudinal cycle.

Since all these cycles overlap and impinge on each other, any given one of these months is longer or shorter than the mean because of the intertwining of the other cycles. To get them separated out in their purity, it is necessary to find the period at the end of which they all finish out together, or nearly so. It is to be remembered that in Book IV Ptolemy reports that Hipparchus found that in 126,007 mean solar days and 1 hour there occurred 4,267 lunar months, 4,573 anomalistic months, and 4,612 sidereal months less 7½° of a month, where each month is taken as 360°. In this time the sun made 345 revolutions about the ecliptic, less $7\frac{1}{2}°$. All of this is with respect to the fixed stars rather than the spring equinox. Hipparchus also found that there occurred 5,923 nodical months in 5,458 lunar months. Except for slight corrections in the case of the anomalistic and nodical months, Ptolemy uses these figures of Hipparchus to calculate the mean periods of the respective months as we have given them above.

APPENDIX B

The Passage from the Ptolemaic to the Copernican System, and thence to that of Kepler

The passage from Ptolemy to Copernicus depends on the interpretation of certain fundamental numbers resulting from observation and from the Ptolemaic system. And furthermore certain laws of Kepler come from a scrutiny of these same numbers and a certain correlation of them. The great revolutions in astronomical theory have not depended as much as one might think on more accurate observations or on better instruments, but rather on the reinterpretation of the symbols presented by the appearances and of the numbers immediately symbolizing these symbols. Indeed, we have already indicated in our Introduction and in our commentary to the third section of Book XII that the Copernican system was known in its essentials to the Greeks. Here the matter will be shown in detail; and also how Kepler, by considering these same numbers, formulated his law that the periodic times of the planets are in the triplicate of the subduplicate ratios of their distances from the sun—a law which first set up an interdependence of time and space and led to the possibility of formulating a celestial dynamics.

We shall set out these numbers in the following fundamental table:

	1	2	3	4	5	6
Planets	Cycles of Anomaly	Revolutions of longitude	Solar years	Radius of Eccentric	Radius of Epicycle	Line between centers
Saturn	57	$2+(1+\frac{2}{3}+\frac{1}{20})°$	$59+(1+\frac{1}{2}+\frac{1}{4})$	60	$6\frac{1}{2}$	$35\frac{1}{12}$
Jupiter	65	$6—(4+\frac{1}{2}+\frac{1}{3})°$	$71—(4+\frac{1}{2}+\frac{1}{3}+\frac{1}{15})$	60	$11\frac{1}{2}$	$2\frac{3}{4}$
Mars	37	$42+(3\frac{1}{6})°$	$79+(3+\frac{1}{6}+\frac{1}{20})$	60	$39\frac{1}{2}$	6
Sun	1	1	1	60		$2\frac{1}{2}$
Venus	5	$8—(2\frac{1}{4})°$	$8—(2+\frac{1}{4}+\frac{1}{20})$	60	$43\frac{1}{6}$	$1\frac{1}{4}$
Mercury	145	$46+(1)°$	$46+(1\frac{1}{30})$	60	$22\frac{1}{2}$	3

The numbers in parentheses in the column of Revolutions of longitude represent three-hundred-and-sixtieths of a complete circle; and those in parentheses in the next column represent days or three-hundred-and-sixty-fifths of a cycle.

In the case of Venus and Mercury, the numbers in the second and third columns should be equal and any discrepancy is due to the fact that the cycles have not been taken at periods of complete returns with all the cycles in the same position as at the starting point. This error is always taken care of by Ptolemy in the case of each planet by a chapter on the correction of the planet's periodic movements.

In the case of Saturn, Jupiter and Mars, Ptolemy remarks that the first column plus the second column gives the third column. Any discrepancy is again due to the same error as mentioned in the preceding paragraph. This property of the numbers is an accident in the Ptolemaic system, but it is already evident in the commentary on Paragraph 3, Book XII, that it is essential for passing to the Copernican system. But it can be seen more directly as follows:—

In the first place, according to the Ptolemaic planetary theory, the planets move on the epicycle in the same direction that the epicycle moves on the deferent. This means, in the Copernican theory, that the earth and the planets move about the sun in the same direction and not in opposite directions.

For let S be the sun, E the earth on its nearly circular orbit about the sun,

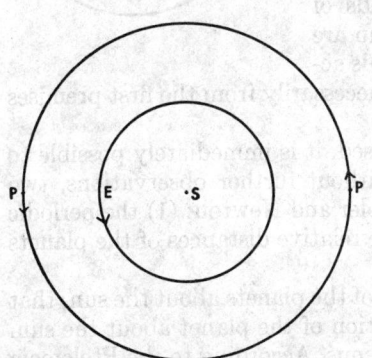

and P one of the three outer planets (Mars, Jupiter, Saturn) on its nearly circular orbit about the sun. Now, when E and P are on the same side of S and in a straight line with it, then P is at its perigee; and when E and P are on opposite sides of S and in a straight line with it, then P is at its apogee (the assumption of Ptolemy in Book X). Perigee and apogee are here spoken of relative to the epicycle only and not to the zodiacal anomaly. Now, if P and E, when on the same side of S, moved in opposite directions with respect to each other, then they would move in opposite directions with respect to S. It follows that they would move in the same direction with respect to each other when on opposite sides of S. Hence the fastest movement of P with respect to E would be at the perigee, and the slowest at the apogee. But the reverse is the case according to the Ptolemaic theory and according to the appearances. Hence, in the Copernican theory, this means that the planet moves about the sun in the same direction as the earth.

By interchanging P and E the reader can easily prove for himself that the same thing holds for the inner planets, Mercury and Venus. Kepler will use these facts to advance a dynamical theory of the planet's motions. Since, by the observation of sun spots, the sun seems to whirl on its axis in that same direction, he supposes that the sun thus possesses a motor virtue which whirls the planets about it.

Further, it must be remarked that for the outer planets Saturn, Jupiter, and Mars, the Ptolemaic cycles of anomaly, in the Copernican system, represent the earth's movement on its orbit with respect to the sun. To see this, the reader should first imagine himself on the sun. The planet would then appear to move, about the ecliptic more or less, in a regular motion (except for the minor zodiacal anomalies). This would be the planet's longitudinal motion with respect to the sun. If now, instead of standing on the sun, the reader imagines himself to be on the earth moving around the sun, on an orbit well within the orbit of the planet, then, from the point of view of the earth, the planet will appear to add an epicyclic motion to its regular longitudinal motion. Thus, for the outer planets, the cycles of anomaly are, according to the Copernican theory, produced by the earth's motion about the sun.

If, on the other hand, the earth's orbit lies outside that of the planet, the cycle of anomaly, on the contrary, is produced by the planet's own motion about the sun; and it is also immediately evident why the inner planets, Venus and Mercury, have limited elongations from the sun. See the figure. For, from the point of view of the earth, the sun and planet represent a system moving about the earth. On the other hand, the outer planets can be at any angular distance with respect to the sun as seen from the earth. And so, again, this distinction between the two kinds of planets—those whose elongations from the sun are limited, and those whose elongations are not—is accidental in the Ptolemaic system but follows necessarily from the first premises of the Copernican.

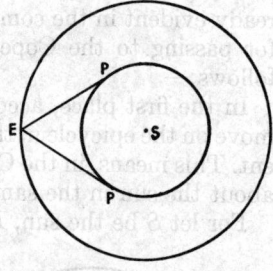

Now, once the Copernican system is supposed, it is immediately possible to deduce from the Ptolemaic numbers, and without further observations, two things which are extremely important for Kepler and Newton: (1) the periodic times of the planets about the sun and (2) the relative distances of the planets from the sun.

First, we can now deduce the periodic times of the planets about the sun; that is, the time of a complete longitudinal revolution of the planet about the sun. Let us first consider an inner planet such as Venus. According to the Ptolemaic numbers, there are 5 cycles of anomaly for Venus in nearly 8 solar years; that is, Venus appears to make 5 longitudinal revolutions about the sun while the earth makes nearly 8. Therefore Venus either moves faster or slower about the sun than the earth. But we know it must move faster, for otherwise it would have to move in the opposite direction on the epicycle from the direction of the epicycle's movement on the deferent in the Ptolemaic system. But this is contrary to the appearances; therefore, in the Copernican hypothesis, Venus moves about the sun at an angular velocity greater than that of the earth. Now, if from the earth Venus appears to make 5 revolutions about the sun while the earth makes nearly 8, and since Venus moves faster than the earth, then in nearly 8 revolutions of the earth, Venus has overtaken the earth exactly 5 times. Hence in nearly 8 revolutions of the earth about the sun, or in nearly 8 solar years, Venus has made 13 revolutions about the sun. The periodic time of Venus about the sun is therefore very nearly $\frac{8}{13}$ of a solar year or, roughly, $224\frac{10}{13}$ days. Likewise, Mercury has a periodic time about the sun of very nearly $\frac{46}{191}$ of a solar year or, roughly, $87\frac{84}{191}$ days.

Next let us consider an outer planet such as Mars. Mars makes 42 longitudinal revolutions and 37 cycles of anomaly in very nearly 79 solar years. In other words, since the cycles of anomaly are a reflection of the earth's motion with respect to the sun, Mars makes 42 revolutions about the sun in 79 solar years, while the earth overtakes Mars 37 times. Therefore the periodic time of Mars about the sun is very nearly $1\frac{37}{42}$ of a solar year or roughly 1 year and $321\frac{32}{42}$ days or $687\frac{1}{84}$ days. Likewise Jupiter's periodic time is very nearly $11\frac{9}{10}$ solar years or 4,345 days. And Saturn's periodic time is very nearly $29\frac{43}{100}$ solar years, or 10,750 days. In the case of Jupiter and Saturn, the fractions in columns 2 and 3 have been taken into account.

Now, since the earth overtakes Mars 37 times while Mars makes 42 revolutions about the sun, it is evident that in overtaking Mars 37 times, the earth makes $37+42$ revolutions about the sun. Hence, while in the Ptolemaic system it is accidental that for the planets Mars, Jupiter and Saturn the sum of the numbers in the first two columns is equal to the numbers in the third, on the contrary in the Copernican system this follows necessarily from the fundamental premisses of the system.

Secondly, we can find the ratio of the mean distances of the different planets from the sun. For in the case of Venus and Mercury the radius of the epicycle represents the planet's mean distance from the sun as compared with the radius of the eccentric which represents the earth's mean distance from the sun. Hence the mean distances of Venus and Mercury are respectively $43\frac{1}{6}$ and $22\frac{1}{2}$ to the earth's distance of 60. In the case of the other planets, however, the epicycle's radius represents the earth's mean distance from the sun as compared with the eccentric's radius which represents the planet's mean distance. Thus the mean distance of Mars from the sun is 60 to the earth's $39\frac{1}{2}$; of Jupiter, 60 to $11\frac{1}{2}$; and of Saturn, 60 to the earth's $6\frac{1}{2}$.

We can now present a table of the periodic times and relative mean distances from the sun, the earth now being considered a planet instead of the sun:

Planets	Periodic Times	Distances from Sun
Saturn	10,750	553.84
Jupiter	4,345	313.04
Mars	687	91.14
Earth	365.25	60.00
Venus	225	43.16
Mercury	88	22.50

The mean distances of the outer planets are here easily deduced from the formula in the case of Mars,

$$60 : 39\frac{1}{2} :: x : 60;$$

and *mutatis mutandis* for the others.

For Kepler, these numbers must have some unifying relationship, since it is not sufficient for numbers merely to save the appearances. Hence in his first work, *The Cosmographical Mystery*, he shows that these mean distances are in the ratio of the radii of the spheres inscribing and circumscribing the five regular solids of Plato and Euclid, if the solids are placed one within another, from the outside inwards (in the order of cube, tetrahedron, dodecahedron, icosahedron, octohedron) and if the inscribed sphere of one becomes the circumscribed sphere of the next.

This theory fits quite well except for the earth which lies on the sphere inscribed in the dodecahedron and circumscribed about the icosahedron. Moreover, the periodic times are in the ratio of the string-lengths of important musical harmonies, if they are properly considered, as demonstrated in the treatise *On the Harmonies of the World*, where even the eccentricities of the orbits are shown to serve the harmonious whole. These eccentricities manifest themselves in the numbers of column 6 of the first table. If, then, the distances and times were the ones a function of the others in terms of some intelligible law, the deviation of the earth would be mathematically necessary for the harmony of the whole. And this deviation would be a real necessity, tolerated only in view of the greater harmony achieved, as in the *Timaeus*. This is exactly the view of Kepler in *The Epitome of Copernican Astronomy*, Book IV. It is here also that the function or law relating the distances and times is finally given.

This is the celebrated Third Law of Kepler which states that the squares of the periodic times are as the cubes of the mean distances. Thus, in the case of the earth and Mercury,

$$(87)^2 : (365.25)^2 : : (22.50)^3 : (60.00)^3;$$

and this is very nearly true, even with these approximations. This law was later deduced by Newton from his more general three laws and the assumption of an inverse-square field of force.

We have now finished with the passage from Ptolemy's geocentric system to Copernicus' heliocentric system as far as the planetary heliacal anomalies are concerned. Both of these systems were known to the Greeks of the times of Hipparchus and Aristarchus. The originality of Ptolemy seems to consist in the additional anomalies of the eccentric and equant. We can therefore safely assume that the originality of Copernicus lies mainly in the translation he gives of these in his own system. Since the epicycles of Ptolemy have disappeared in Copernicus' system, Copernicus now has two instruments, the epicycle and the eccentric, with which to take care of the two remaining anomalies. He can therefore avoid the use of the equant, and this, in his eyes, is the greatest merit of his system.

We have already remarked that, in the case of the outer planets, the movement of the epicycle's centre about the deferent in the Ptolemaic system corresponds to the revolution of the planet about the mean sun in the Copernican; and that the radius of the deferent corresponds to the planet's mean distance from the sun. Hence, in periodic time and radius, the orbit of the epicycle's centre about the earth in the Ptolemaic system is exactly that of the planet about the mean sun in the Copernican, if no account is taken of the two zodiacal anomalies. The problem of Copernicus, therefore, is to find a combination of epicycle and eccentric with reference to the mean sun which will be exactly equivalent to Ptolemy's eccentric and equant with respect to the earth. The following is the solution which Copernicus devised, equivalent in all respects save one which did not seem important since it had to do with linear distance rather than angular distance. But it is this very difference which proved the undoing of the Copernican system and helped to bring about the Keplerian revolution with its elliptical orbits, the so-called First Law of Kepler.

Consider, first, the Ptolemaic system of Mars without the epicycle. Let A be the earth, B the centre of the eccentric, C the centre of the equant, E the apogee, and D the perigee. Now since

$$AB = BC$$

and

$$AB : BE :: 6 : 60,$$

we can let AB and BC be each 1000 and BE 10,000 according to the decimal system used by Copernicus. Then

$$AE = 11,000 \qquad AD = 9,000;$$

and, if we draw CF perpendicular to DE, then F and G represent the positions of the epicycle's centre at the quadrants of the periodic time. Then

$$AF = \sqrt{(10,000^2 - 1,000^2) + 2,000^2},$$

since

$$CF^2 = BF^2 - BC^2.$$

Now consider the Copernican equivalent. Let A' be the mean sun, B' the centre of the eccentric, and let the radius of the eccentric

$$B'\,1 = 10,000$$

and

$$A'B' = \tfrac{3}{4}\,(2,000) = 1500.$$

Let 1 be the aphelion and 3 the perihelion. Let the planet be placed on an epicycle whose radius is equal to $\tfrac{1}{4}$ (2,000) or 500. When the epicycle's centre is at the aphelion 1, let the planet be at the perihelion of the epicycle E', and let the planet move on the epicycle in the same direction as the epicycle on the deferent and at the same angular velocity, so that at the quadrants and at the half of the periodic time the planet occupies the positions F', D', and G'. Then

$$A'E' = 11,000 \qquad A'D' = 9,000$$

just as in the Ptolemaic system. Furthermore, at the quadrants of the

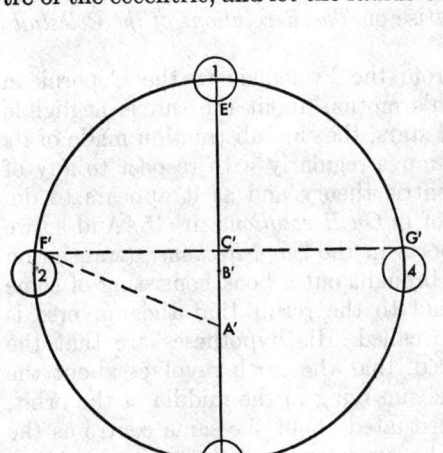

periodic time 2 and 4, the planet occupies the positions F' and G' which are on the perpendicular to $E'D'$ at C' which is exactly 2,000 from A', 8,000 from E', and 12,000 from D', just as in the Ptolemaic C is 2,000 from A, 8,000 from E, and 12,000 from D. The fact that the position of C' with respect to

B' is different from that of C with respect to B makes no difference, for B' and B have no immediate physical significance.

But the distance

$$A' F' = 10,000^2 + 2,000^2,$$

which is considerably larger than the corresponding distance AF in the Ptolemaic system. The orbit of the planet in the Copernican system bulges at the quadrants of the periodic time compared to that of the Ptolemaic. The appearances here favor the Ptolemaic system as Kepler points out. But even the Ptolemaic system does not draw the planet in enough at these quadrants. This is one of the dilemmas which led Kepler to conjecture an elliptical orbit as worked out in the *Commentaries on Mars* and later in the *Epitome*. It is easy to see from the first table why Mars should be the planet chosen. For of all the planets it has the largest eccentricity, and the discrepancies would be most manifest.

Hence, in the case of the outer planets, the three Ptolemaic points, (1) the earth, (2) the centre of the eccentric, and (3) the centre of the equant, are exactly transformed in the Keplerian theory into (1) the sun at one focus of the ellipse, (2) the centre of the ellipse, and (3) the other focus of the ellipse. The numbers remain approximately the same. But a new definition of regular motion is needed: it must be supposed that the planet on the ellipse sweeps across equal areas in equal times with respect to the sun at the focus. This is the so-called Second Law of Kepler. All this is worked out in detail and with the proper deductions in the *Commentaries on Mars* and in the *Epitome*.

In the case of the inner planets, Venus and Mercury, the Copernican solution of the zodiacal anomalies is necessarily different, for here the epicycles are the orbits of the planets about the sun. The details of this solution are worked out in the latter part of Book V of the treatise on *The Revolutions of the Celestial Spheres*.

One difficulty remains in passing from the Ptolemaic to the Copernican system. Unless the radius of the earth's motion about the sun is negligible with respect to its distance to the fixed stars, the sun, abstraction made of its eccentric anomaly, would not seem to move regularly with respect to any of the fixed stars as it does in the geocentric theory and as it appears to do. Copernicus gives the detail of this proof in *On Revolutions* III, 15. And so we are not surprised that Archimedes reports in the *Sand-Reckoner* (translation of Heath): "But Aristarchus of Samos brought out a book consisting of some hypotheses, in which the premisses lead to the result that the universe is many times greater than that now so called. His hypotheses are that the fixed stars and the sun remain unmoved, that the earth revolves about the sun in the circumference of a circle, the sun lying in the middle of the orbit, and that the sphere of the fixed stars, situated about the same centre as the sun, is so great that the circle in which he supposes the earth to revolve bears such a proportion to the distance of the fixed stars as the centre of the sphere bears to its surface."

APPENDIX C

Since this understanding of the *Timaeus* is followed by few scholars, we stop to outline the arguments for it. Timaeus says first that the planets are placed in circles the ratios of whose radii (presumably) are as 1, 2, 3, 4, 8, 9, 2. . . . With respect to what as centre these circles and the distances are taken and which planets are placed in which, is carefully left unexplained. Their motions are then described for an observer on the earth (36d, 5—). Later the planets are named and placed in these circles from the point of view of the earth, but no connection is made with the series of numbers:

ὁ θεὸς ἔθηεν . . . σελήνην μεν ἐις τὸν περὶ γῆν πρῶτον, ἥλεον δὲ ἐις τὸν δεύτεσον ὑπες γῆς . . .

Then follow Mercury and Venus and their peculiar motions with respect to the sun as seen from the earth; the others are described as too complicated to give here (38c9-d8). The angular speeds of the different planets are then given, *abstraction made of their daily revolution with the fixed stars*, exactly contrary to Aristotle's account in the *Heavens* II, 8 which follows the completely geocentric Eudoxean hypothesis. It is again mentioned that the sun has been placed in the second circle relative to the earth as a measure of all these movements:

φῶς ὁ θεος ἀνῆψεν εν τῇ προς γῆν δευτρα τῶν περιόδων (39a, b).

Now follows the famous passage (40b8-d4) which for the first time gives in an absolute point of reference:

γῆν δε τροφὸν μὲν ἡμετέραν, εἰλλομενην δὲ περὶ τον διὰ παντὸς πόλον τεταμένον φύλακα καὶ δημιουργὸν νυκτός τε καὶ ἡμέρας ἐμηχανήσατο . . . ,

"and he contrived the earth revolving about the pole set through the universe as the guardian and creator of night and day . . ." We here translate εἰλλομενην as did Aristotle, the earliest commentator on the passage, in the *Heavens*, II, 13, 14. Then follows a description of the appearances which such a revolution of the earth would be used to explain the change of the planets, their progressions and regressions which, for the planets other than Mercury and Venus, are explained most easily by the swinging of the earth about the sun as centre of the universe. For in the heliocentric theory the regressions of the outer planets Mars, Jupiter, and Saturn are only the reflections of the earth's motion about the sun. And it was well known at the time that the speeds of all the planets along the ecliptic, their regressions and stations, are tied to their oppositions to and conjunctions with the sun, for such things were incorporated in the system of Eudoxus.

If the sun is taken as centre, then it is extremely easy to compute the relative distances of the planets from the sun by means of their regressions. This is shown in Appendix B to this book. The ratios of the distances of Mercury, Venus, the Earth, Mars, Jupiter, and Saturn are nearly as 1, 2, 3, 4, 14, 25. Jupiter's 14 is the only one far off from the series assigned by Timaeus. The moon would be assigned 8 completely without justification except that this series is fundamental to the musical scale of the great diatonic, but it is very unlikely there were any calculations of the relative distances of the sun and moon at that time. With the heliocentric hypothesis it is easy to assign fairly accurate ratios; it is impossible to do so in a purely geocentric theory like Ptolemy's with the instruments the Greeks possessed, and that is why, perhaps, no such numerical assignment is made in the *Republic*.

We can now get the force of that strange and isolated statement in the *Laws* (VII, 822a) that each planet's motion is one and simple and not the resultant as it appears of many different motions. This is only possible in the heliocentric theory and if the apparently faster planets are considered the slower.

Introduction,
Symbols and Abbreviations,
and a Short Bibliography to
Copernicus and Kepler

TRANSLATOR'S INTRODUCTION

Why did Copernicus refrain so long from publishing De revolutionibus orbium coelestium?

Because, at least in part, he feared that at a time of ecclesiastical jitteriness, which arose out of the dissensions between Catholics and Protestants, his work might occasion sufficient scandal for him to be charged with impugning the authority of the Church on the grounds that the assertion that the earth was neither at rest nor at the centre of the world might be construed as contradicting one possible literal interpretation of certain passages in the Bible. But he does not explicitly foresee that anyone would be scandalized by construing as a loss to man's dignity the assertion that the corporeal heavens do not revolve around man's domicile. And, as a matter of fact, in scholastic theological thought man was a rather humble creature: the highest of the animals but the lowest of the created intellects, one whose original dignity had been corrupted by original sin, and whose present little dignity arose from the assumption of human nature by the Word of God in the Incarnation and not from any supposed revolution of the corporeal heavens about man's domicile.

But was not the humanistic effect of the Copernican revolution actually to lower the dignity of man in the imaginations of men?

Maybe so. But do not forget that the so-called Copernican revolution may only be a part of a story we have constructed in order to explain why we no longer understand in what the real dignity of man might consist. If we wish to talk poetically and humanistically, we may still ask out of what feeling about man's rank in the universe can the assertion of the earth's motion be said to spring.

How shall we go about answering that question?

First, let us try to find out how "true" Copernicus considered the mobility of the earth to be; then, let us look into the workings of the history of astronomy itself; and, thirdly, the relation of the mobility of the earth to certain larger ideas which entered into the speculation of the times. And I shall leave it up to you to apply our discussion of these topics to the burning question of the dignity of man.

Will you first say something about what the job of an astronomer is?

Let us define the job of the astronomer in the classical phrase as "saving the appearances" of the celestial movements. Now we may distinguish two sides to saving the appearances. First, an astronomical theory must "save" in the sense of "preserve"—that is to say, it must not deny any of the apparent celestial movements as appearances, and in this bare sense, it might merely comprise a record of observed positions of the planets. But, if that were all, it would not be taking into account all the apparent movements but would be merely including past movements and leaving out future movements and thus, in order to take into account all the apparent movements, it must be able to predict apparent movements in the future from those observed in the past. But in order to be able to look backwards and forwards beyond recorded positions of the planets, it must arrange the celestial movements in a pattern of orderly recurrence. And by setting up this pattern of order, it saves the appearances in a second sense; I mean to say, that it gives them salvation, as it were, by making them intelligible and by explicating them in terms of a permanent order.

Does Copernicus lay down any general rules or principles as to how appearances must best be saved?

He talks as if the principle of intelligibility and order can be fulfilled only if the astronomer takes the movements of the celestial bodies to be regular, circular, everlasting, or compounded out of circular movements; that is to say, in case the moving planetary body does not appear to describe a perfect circle, its path must be reconstructed as the resultant of a configuration of purely circular movements, whereof in any given circle equal arcs are traversed in equal times. Those are the general limits within which there is a field free for the further delimitations demanded by given apparent movements. That is to say, the moving circles which combine with one another may be homocentric (circles of equal radii and of the same centre but of different axes of revolution), or eccentric (circles or equal radii but of different centres), or epicyclical (where the centre of one circle is located on the circumference of another), or related according to any number of permutations and combinations of those elements.

Now, the formulation of those general limits has been called classically by the name of "axioms" or "principles," and the further determinations within those limits by the name of "hypotheses." As Copernicus always employs the term *principia* in conjunction with *hypotheses* and as he refers to the proposition that the movements of the celestial bodies are regular and circular as an axiom, I shall employ the term "axiom" to denote the formulation of the limiting conditions of intelligible order. But he clearly uses the term "hypothesis" to signify any determination made within the field delimited by the axiom, in order to explain given apparent movements and to provide a geometric basis for computation and prediction.

How true does Copernicus consider the axioms and hypotheses to be?

He argues at some length to the effect that the state of affairs defined by the axiom of regular and circular movement must really exist in the heavens and that the mind would shudder at any other supposition.

Now an hypothesis must fulfil two conditions: first, it must conform to the axiom; and second, it must underlie particular propositions about the combination of regular, circular movements and the planetary tables. That is to say, it further delimits the ground covered by the axiom; for example, the generality of regular circular movement may, in a given case, be further determined as movement on the second epicycle of an eccentric circle, where the magnitudes of the circles and directions and periods of the movements are given; and by this delimitation the hypothesis makes possible the accurate prediction of particular movements. Thus within the single field of the axiom there is room for many equivalent or alternative hypotheses: these hypotheses are equivalent in that the same set of appearances may be saved formally just as well by one hypothesis as by another; for example, an epicycle on a homocentric circle or an eccentric circle whose eccentricity is equal to the radius of the epicycle may be the geometric formal causes which account for the same apparent movement; they are alternative in the sense that, if interpreted physically, in terms of solid circles or something else necessary for the mechanical explanation of the phenomena by efficient causes (in contradistinction to the geometric explanation through formal causes), the two configurations of circles cannot both exist in the heavens, for example, a planet cannot wheel around on the rim of an epicycle revolving on an homocentric at the same time that it wheels around on the rim of a rotating eccentric, even if the path described in space by the planet affixed to the epicycle coincide with the circumference of the eccentric circle.

Now, just as Copernicus regarded the axiom of regular circular movement as designating a reality in the heavens, so too he regarded alternative hypotheses not merely as devices for prediction, whereof the one or the other might be relatively more convenient for use in constructing planetary tables, but as designating real possibilities within the field of physical actuality defined by the axiom—although, as he admits, it is difficult or impossible to determine, in a given case, whether it is eccentric or epicycle which really exists in the heavens.

Now, what about the mobility of the earth?

Ptolemy had remarked that although it would be possible to save the appearances by treating the earth as if it were in motion but that such a supposition would be no more than a convenient device for computation, since Aristotle's cosmology demanded an unmoving earth at the centre of the world; he preferred to make the supposition which would be physically true in the light of the Aristotelian analysis.

Osiander's unauthorized preface to *De revolutionibus* tries to reduce the mobility of the earth to a point of mere convenience in constructing tables of movements; but that attempt is clearly at variance with the intentions of the author as exhibited in the body of the text itself. For if Copernicus had looked upon the mobility of the earth merely as a fiction useful as a computing device, he would have had, on the outside, no reason to fear that his book would occasion a scandal; and, on the inside, no reason for composing arguments on behalf of the natural possibility of the movement of the earth.

Then, is the movement of the earth to be regarded as the one of two hypotheses designating alternative real possibilities which is chosen, say, for the sake of convenience? That is to say, supposing the movement of the earth is really possible, does Copernicus find it hard to determine whether it is actually the case in the heavens?

No. Copernicus looked upon it as more certain than that. For he appears to find the astronomical consequences following from the supposition of the mobility of the earth sufficiently weighty to place it in the same order of truth as the sphericity of the earth, since he insinuates that his opponents are to be classed with Lactantius, who had denied that there were antipodes.

Then if Copernicus regarded the motion of the earth as certain, why did he refer to it as an hypothesis?

Because it underlies all his other hypotheses, as he indicates in speaking of the movement of the earth as a *principium* and *hypothesis*—a starting point in reference to which he maps out his hypotheses as to the given apparent movements of other bodies besides the earth. The application of the term "hypothesis" signifies not that the motion of the earth is advanced merely as a tentative proposal to be taken or left but that it forms an underlying principle from which further determinations of celestial movements may be deduced.

Why did time wait so long for a man to declare that the earth was in movement?

That is not wholly the case. The school of Pythagoras had held that the earth as well as the sun were in motion around the central fire. Herakleides of Pontus, who may have studied under Plato, taught the daily rotation of the earth, and Aristarchus of Samos, who studied under a student of a student of Aristotle's, suggested that the annual movement as well, belonged to the earth and not to the sun. And some early Renaissance philosophers, of whom I shall speak later, also imputed movement to the earth in various ways. But none of these men used that supposition as a starting point for giving a detailed and systematic account of the apparent celestial movements.

Why did not Ptolemy himself do so?

Because, as I have said, the supposition of the earth's motion was contrary to the conclusions of Aristotelian physics. Now Aristotelian cosmology might be termed an hypothetical construction designed, among other reasons, to save the appearances given by the following simple experiment: if you light a fire, the flame rises upwards through the air; and if you shake earth, air, and water together in a closed container and then allow them to settle, the air will rise in bubbles to the surface and the earth will sink to the bottom. Therefore the earth, as the heaviest element, will always be at the bottom of things, or, in a spherical cosmos, at the centre, which is the earth's natural place, just as the elements of water, air, and fire belong to concentric spheres arranged around the earth. Now since the earth is in its natural place, it is in possession of its end, and therefore there is no reason for it to move, either by rotating or in any other fashion; while conversely, the stars, the sun, and the five planets (which are unchangeable except with respect to place) attain certain natural ends by their diurnal and other movements.

The general outlines of Aristotelian cosmology were acceptable to Ptolemy as a framework within which to work out a detailed account of the movements of the celestial bodies, because Aristotle's physics on the whole was more sophisticated than that of the atomists and was more fully elaborated and less oracular in statement than Plato's physics (in, say, the *Timaeus*, which was itself perhaps even more sophisticated than Aristotle's in its grasp of fundamental problems). Ptolemaic astronomy however differed specifically from the Aristotelian in that Aristotle constructed an elaborate system (based on that of Eudoxus, Plato's pupil) of many solid spheres having the same centre but different axes of rotation in order to account both geometrically and mechanically for the apparent celestial movements, while Ptolemy, employing systems of circles on circles and circles off centre, left it doubtful as to whether these epicycles and eccentrics, were to be accorded a physical and mechanical interpretation as well as the geometrical, with respect to saving the phenomena.

Do you want to say something about the history of astronomy between Ptolemy and Copernicus?

Most of the astronomers of Islam were more concerned with the problem of efficient causation than Ptolemy had been in the *Syntaxis* (which was translated into Arabic about A.D. 820), and they endeavored to reformulate any plane geometry of planetary motions as the projection on a plane of the movements of a system of spheres. Thus Al Kaswini, Abu'l Faraj, and Al Jagmini—three astronomers probably of the thirteenth century—would transform an epicycle on a homocentric into an epicyclic sphere between two homocentric crystalline spheres, which was tangent to the inner surface of the outer and to the outer surface of the inner sphere and which rolled around within their space in between—with further permutations and combinations of eccentric, epicyclic, and homocentric spheres for apparent movements of greater irregularity.

In similar fashion, Al Betrugi, an astronomer of the twelfth century, tried to renovate the homocentric spheres of Aristotle and Eudoxus so as to take care of the irregularities in celestial movements which had made their appearance to observers since the time of Aristotle. And in the thirteenth century a great and very ingenious astronomer, Al Tusi, constructed a system of spheres, within which a single configuration would involve two homocentric spheres with an episphere in between and a series of spheres internally tangent within the episphere. But as far as formal causes go; Al Betrugi's system was not better at saving the appearances than Ptolemy's; nor was Al Tusi's more intrinsically simple than Ptolemy's.

The important astronomers of Christendom at first followed closely after Ptolemy but with an eye on the astronomers of Islam. The *Syntaxis* was translated from the Arabic into Latin by Gerard of Cremona in 1175. Amateurs at astronomy were more inclined than professionals to play with the supposition that the sun was at the center of some planetary movements or that the earth was in motion. The encyclopedist Martianus Capella, in the *Wedding of Philology and Mercury*, had placed the orbits of Venus and Mercury around the sun, and in the ninth century, John Scot Erigena, the great neo-Platonist theologian, extended this heliocentricity to Jupiter and Mars as well.

In the fifteenth century theological reasons led Nicholas, Cardinal of Cues, to assert that the world, although not infinite, was without centre or circumference and that consequently everything in the world participated in motion to some extent. In *On Learned Ignorance* he goes no further than to suggest that the earth has some movement of rotation but none of translation; but a note of his on the fly-leaf of another man's work draws a fuller sketch of a system of solar and terrestrial motion, as follows: there is a general proviso that there are no perfect circles described by bodies or absolutely fixed poles of rotation. The appearances of the diurnal movement are saved by making the sphere of the fixed stars and the stars revolve from east to west twice in twenty-four hours, and the earth in the same direction once in twenty-four hours. The apparent annual movement of the sun is accounted for by two hypotheses: first, it lags slightly behind the heavens in the daily rotation: but that retardation by itself would give the sun merely an annual motion in a plane identical with or parallel to the celestial equator, hence there is need of some other movement to account for the oblique direction along the ecliptic. Therefore, secondly, there are situated in the plane of the equator two poles, around which the earth revolves once in twenty-four hours (and the sphere of the fixed stars in slightly less time, in order, unsuccessfully, to account for precession), while the sun is on a small circle about 23° distant from one of the poles and revolves in slightly less time than the earth wherefrom the sun thus appears, in its annual passage around the heavens, to move from the tropic of Cancer to the tropic of Capricorn and back again. Nicholas' numbers here were a little off, as he made the sun's retardation in both cases equal to $\frac{1}{164}$th of a circle instead of $\frac{1}{165}$th. Although it is unlikely that Copernicus was acquainted with this particular theory, that is the sort of thing which was germinating in the seed-bed of the times out of which Copernicus' own system grew.

A younger contemporary of the Cardinal's, George Peurbach, published a highly reputed textbook, *New Theories of the Planets*, wherein he adapted solid spheres to the accepted Ptolemaic planetary theory; and he was engaged in the search for Greek manuscripts of Ptolemy, as the available translation from the Arabic were not wholly trustworthy. It was not until 1515 that the twelfth-century translation of Ptolemy's *Syntaxis* was printed for the first time, and in 1528 was published a new translation, made from the Greek by George of Trebizond; and finally the original, together with Theo of Alexandria's *Commentary*, was printed at Basle in 1538. A pupil of Peurbach's, John Regiomontanus, collected Greek astronomical manuscripts in Italy, settled in Nuremberg, where he erected an observatory and started a printing press, and completed a textbook begun by Peurbach, *Epitome of Ptolemy's Almagest*. Men like Peurbach and Regimontanus were instrumental in keeping alive the scientific grammar, which a great talent like that of Copernicus had to have before him in order to transform it.

In the third decade of the sixteenth century, just before the publication of *De revolutionibus*, were printed two works which tried to renovate systems of homocentric spheres, namely Fracastoro's *Homocentrica*, which had the novelty of employing spheres whose axes of movement were situated at right angles to one another and which demanded seventy-nine spheres, all in all, in order to account for the celestial phenomena, and *On the Movements of the Celestial Bodies according to Peripatetic Principles without Eccentrics and Epicycles* by Giovanni Amici, a brilliant young man, who, incidentally, was murdered before he was thirty.

But by now the unpublished work of Copernicus had acquired an underground reputation; Celio Calagnini, once a soldier of fortune and now a cleric, who had visited at Cracow in 1518, composed before 1524 a highly periphrastic essay in which he attempted to argue that all the apparent movements in the heavens could be saved by rotatory movements of the earth!

What induced Copernicus himself to think of the earth's being in motion?

You will read Copernicus' own answer to that in Book I of *De revolutionibus*, insofar as it was occasioned by astronomical considerations.

You are implying that it was occasioned by other considerations besides the astronomical?

Yes. For in any given age distinct arts and sciences may share in formal patterns which are not the peculiar property of any single one of them. Or there may be a certain leading idea which serves to organize apparently diverse materials: I speak roughly, but consider the continuum as a master-builder idea which has received varying embodiments in modern biology, mathematics, physics, psychology, metaphysics, and the novel; or the modern preoccupation with time from Calvin's theology and Galileo's physics to Proust's *Remembrance of Things Past*. Sometimes some special science lays claim as to its own property to the discovery and analysis of these formal patterns or leading ideas, and sets up rules for the reduction of many other disciplines to some single one which is viewed as architectonic. For example, the Marxists today have contrived a method of exegesis which reads poetry, theology, mathematics, and politics as symbols for economic realities, just at St. Augustine saw human nature as made up of mirror-images of the Trinity, and St. Bonaventura found foot-prints of the Incarnation, the Christian way of life, and the beatific vision in all the arts which human beings practice. Similarly, the Freudians would like to reduce the world that man constructs for himself to a number of erotic categories, the most justly famous of which is the Oedipus complex.

What analogous architectonic idea do you find at the time of Copernicus?

As formulated mythologically, it is the doctrine of the microcosm and the macrocosm, the "little world" and the "big world." Pico della Mirandola tells the story of it as follows: "God by the laws of his hidden wisdom had constructed the world. Creation was complete: everything was filled up; all things had been laid out in the highest, the lowest, and the mean orders. He had adorned the supercelestial region with intelligences, and He had animated the celestial globes with immortal souls and with the primal animals. But now that the work was all done, the Master-Builder desired some creature that should contemplate the organization of the created world, love its beauty, and wonder at its greatness. But there was nothing left among the archetypal ideas from which He could form a new sprout nor anything in his storehouses which He could bestow as an heritage upon this new son nor an empty judiciary seat where this contemplator of the universe could sit. But the paternal power could not fail in the final birth-throes, as if worn out through child-bearing; wisdom, in a case of necessity, could not be at a loss for want of a plan, the loving-kindness which would praise liberality in others could not be forced to condemn itself. Finally, the Master-Builder decided that that to which nothing which should be its very own could be given should be, in composite fashion, whatsoever had belonged individually to each and every thing." Therefore He made man to be a mirror of the whole universe, a creature whose nature was distinguished from all other natures by being limited to no single nature but embracing all natures in the world: a body which tends towards the centre of the earth, a growing vegetable rooted in one place, an animal having desire and local movement, and an angel uniting contrary forms in oneness of intuition.

I can see how man may be regarded poetically as a small world which mirrors the great world of which he is a part. But what does that have to do with Copernicus?

As you will see, Copernicus substituted the daily rotation of the earth for the rotation of the total heavens, made the precession of the equinoxes depend upon a conical revolution of the axis of the terrestrial ecliptic around the axis of the terrestrial equator (rather than upon a conical revolution, so to speak, of the axis of the celestial ecliptic around the axis of the celestial equator), and transferred the annual revolution from the sun to the earth. By this last step he telescoped into one circle (viz., the annual orbit of the earth) five planetary circles (viz., the eccentric circles of Mercury and Venus and the major epicycles of Mars, Jupiter, and Saturn). Thus the Copernican earth is to the Ptolemaic heavens as microcosm is to macrocosm; or, to keep the metaphor sharp, perhaps we should say that the Copernican earth is a little heaven, or *microüranus*, while the Ptolemaic heavens are a big earth, or *macrogë*. If you choose to interpret either system literally, you may read the other as a mirror-symbol of the first by way of the microcosm-macrocosm transformation.

Do any anologies hold between Copernican astronomy and any other sciences of the times?

There is an anology between Copernican astronomy and the analytic geometry developed out of the work of Descartes. Or, more fully, as Copernicus is to Ptolemy, so is analytic to the synthetic geometry of Euclid or Apollonius of Perga.

Now Ptolemy, as you have seen, built up separately his schemes for each of the planets and established the relative magnitudes of the major epicycle and the epicycle-bearing circle of one and the same planet. But, on his own grounds, he had no way of determining the relative magnitude of the epicycle-bearing circle of one planet in comparison with that of another, and therefore no way of determining intrinsically the distances and order of the planets. Later on, Proclus—the disciple of Plotinus and commentator on Plato and Euclid—proposed the rule which was adopted by the Moslem and Renaissance astronomers, namely, that, if the order of the planets be taken according to the speed of their revolutions, then, within that order, their relative distances should be determined by making the apogee of the nearest planet immediately precede the perigee of the next planet and so on, the apogee of the higher immediately following the perigee of the lower. But that was a surmise or an extrinsic hypothesis. However, within the Ptolemaic set-up, it was remarkable and unexplained that the period of the epicycle-bearing circles of Mercury and Venus should be equal to a year and the sun should always be on a line with the centre of the epicycle, and that in the case of Mars, Jupiter, and Saturn (within any cycle of time common to the epicycle-bearing circle and to the epicycle), the sum of the revolutions of the two circles should be equal to the number of solar years, the number of revolutions of the sun within that same cycle of time.

Now Copernicus, as you will see and as I shall not explain right now, interpreted as mirror-images of the earth's annual movement the epicycle-bearing circles of Venus and Mercury and the epicycles of the upper planets (in such fashion that the difference between the movement of an upper planet on its epicycle in one year and the movement on the epicycle-bearing circle is redefined as the difference between the earth's movement and the planet's during that same time). In this way, by telescoping five circles into one, he set up an hypothesis which should underlie the Ptolemaic hypotheses and from it was able to deduce the distances of the planets in comparison with one another.

Similarly, Apollonius of Perga had built up elaborate demonstrations, for example, of the constructibility of conic sections, separate and distinct demonstrations for the circle, parabola, hyperbola, and ellipse, which analytic geometry redefines with greater symbolical and operational simplicity, in the general equation of the second degree:

$$ax^2 + bxy + cy^2 + dx + ey + f = 0.$$

That is to say, the operational unity of symbols to which analytics reduces synthetic Euclidean geometry is like the notorious Copernican simplification of Ptolemaic hypotheses.

Do analogies hold between Copernican astronomy and anything else outside the strict, scientific field?

Yes, for his astronomical system is neo-classical, in a way that the tragedies of Corneille and Racine were neo-classical a century later. For Renaissance literary critics rigorously interpreted Aristotle's unity of action, which was merely the explicit statement of a property which would be found in any good tragedy, as a formal rule for the construction of a plot, and from it deduced unity of time and unity of place. Thus they transformed a generalization about existing tragedies into a law which must be obeyed by all future tragedies and an insight into a system.

Similarly, Copernicus interpreted the axiom of regular circular motion with a neo-classical rigor that Ptolemy had not employed. For example, in his lunar and planetary hypotheses, Ptolemy would set up a circle, on the circumference of which regular movement took place. But (to state the simplest case) the regularity of the movement would be measured, not according as equal angles at the centre measured equal times but according as equal angles around some other fixed point measured equal times; that is to say, the "centre of distance" was not the same as the "centre of regular motion." Ptolemy found that all right: there was one circle on whose circumference the motion took place, and another circle around whose centre the regularity of the motion could be measured. Hence the requirement of regular and circular motion was fulfilled.

But Copernicus argued that such a reading of the axiom destroyed it while purporting to save it, that the notion of regular, circular movement was parodied by having the movement on one circle and the regularity on another, and that the axiom strictly demanded that equality of distance and regularity of motion be measured on one circumference—or, in other words, that the circles of distance and regular movement be one and the same.

How was De revolutionibus *received by the men of the times?*

People were divided for and against it. Those who received it favorably numbered astronomers and ecclesiastics; those who received it unfavorably numbered ecclesiastics and astronomers. The objections raised against the mobility of the earth had to do both with theology and with natural science. One hundred years or more earlier all theologians would have been more sophisticated in their literal interpretation of certain parts of Scripture (just as St. Thomas Aquinas had remarked that analogical arguments raised by speculative reason for the doctrine of the Trinity were of no greater probability than the epicycles and eccentrics of Ptolemy) and would not have found the motion of the earth in contradiction with Job's "who shaketh the earth out of her place and the pillars thereof tremble." But the dissensions between Catholics and Protestants made both sects fearful of any scandal which might appear to undermine respect for the Church of the Bible, and consequently they became over-literal in their reading of Scripture and were inclined to condemn any assertion which could be construed as contradicting any literal interpretation of any passage in the Bible. Luther blustered that "the fool will upset the whole science of astronomy, but as the Holy Scripture shows, it was the sun and not the earth which Joshua ordered to stand still." And even Melanchthon condemned Copernicus' opinion.

Giordano Bruno, however, the ecclesiastical reformer and philosopher, who in 1600 was burned at the stake for heresy, in his cosmology praised Copernicus highly; while Diego de Stuñiga, a doctor of divinity of the University of Toledo, in a commentary on Job interpreted the aforementioned passage in the light of Copernican astronomy. But in 1616 the Inquisition at Rome declared the assertion of the earth's motion to be heretical, and the Sacred Congregation solemnly suspended *De revolutionibus* and Stuñiga's commentary "until they should be corrected." Copernicus' book, along with Kepler's *Epitome* and Galileo's *Dialogue on the Two Chief Systems of the World* wherein he had sophistically ignored the existence of Tycho Brahe's system, were not removed from the Index until 1822.

The main difficulty raised by physicists was to the effect that, if the earth were in rotation, then falling bodies would not appear to describe a plumb-line but some other curve in relation to the merely apparent stillness of the earth. Galileo was probably the first experimenter to drop a stone from the top to the foot of the mast of a moving ship. There was no philosophic solution to the difficulty before Galilean kinetics: with respect to a short fall in a brief time, the motion of a body falling to the earth could be explained by analogy with the rectangle of movement of a projectile, where the rotation of the earth (as if the horizontal component) does not interfere with the pull of gravity towards the centre of the earth (as if the vertical component).

Tycho Brahe, nearly as great an astronomer as Copernicus or Kepler, found unanswerable the objections based on the Scriptures and on the apparent course of falling bodies; but approved the simplification introduced into the planetary theories by making a point around the sun the centre of all the planets' orbits. Accordingly, he adopted the Copernican system with a slight revision: he centred all the planets around the sun but kept the sun revolving round the earth, which remained motionless at the centre of the world. Tycho's main work, however, lay less in the construction of a new system of the heavenly motions (for the Tychonic is derived by a simple transformation of the Copernican) than in taking new observations in order to determine with greater accuracy the apparent course of the planets—and it was out of Tycho's observations as material that Kepler built his system.

As a young man, Tycho had met Pierre de la Ramée, professor of philosophy and rhetoric at the College Royal at Paris, who had been intellectually nursed in scholasticism but ever afterwards was a violent Orestes towards any Aristotelian Clytemnaestra. De la Ramée, who thought epicycles and eccentrics too arbitrary a way of saving the appearances, demanded an "astronomy without hypotheses." Tycho pointed out to him the unsophistication of his demand, inasmuch as motions would always need to be represented by geometric figures, and the simplest astronomical conception—that of a recurrence or cycle of movements, without which no science would be possible—presupposes something like a circle; but he agreed with de la Ramee that some other figures besides the epicycles and eccentrics of the ancients might form a more convenient or more beautiful way of saving the appearances; and consequently he gathered together his "storehouse of observations" not merely for the sake of making precise the eccentricities and the number of epicycles, but also for the sake of any revolutions in theory which they might make possible.

Among scientists who were not primarily astronomers the most influential Corpernican was William Gilbert, a physician of London, who in 1600 published *On the Loadstone and Magnetic Bodies and on the Great Magnet the Earth*, the first great treatise on magnetism.

The loadstone or natural magnet, he argues, is of the same nature as iron or iron ore. The attraction subsisting between a loadstone and iron is not due merely to the action of the loadstone but is the joint work of the two. The force of attraction, or "coition" (as he prefers to call it), is strongest at the poles of the loadstone but is present throughout its whole body, since a needle brought into contact with a loadstone will not move towards a pole, although it will turn until it is directed in line with the poles. On two magnetized iron bodies the force of coition proceeds from unlike pole to unlike pole. But principally, the loadstone is of the same nature as the earth and is but a part of the earth homogeneous with the whole; and a spherical loadstone is a little earth, or *microgë*, while the earth itself (which possesses magnetic poles, meridians, and equator) is a big magnet or macromagnes—on the grounds that a piece of iron or a loadstone behaves in the same way towards the whole earth as a piece of iron or small loadstone does towards a larger spherical loadstone. And just as the human soul is the principle which gives order and unity to the various powers and operations of man, so the magnetic force of a loadstone is like a soul which underlies the diverse magnetic powers of coition and direction. As a spherical loadstone has the power of rotating (as witnessed by the fact that it can rotate around the axis of a meridian, if one of its poles faces the like pole on another loadstone), then the daily rotation of the earth is probably due to its magnetic energy and to the influence of the sun; and more universally still, all the planetary motions may be due to magnetism. Although in neither case does he give a detailed explanation as to how celestial movements may be conditioned magnetically, yet he is here giving the bare suggestion for the transformation of the heavens into a *macrogë*, which Kepler attempted with more specificity and Newton carried out in a different fashion.

How did Kepler conceive of the task of saving the appearances?

He held a view of the nature of empirical science which is not fashionable today, nor was it fashionable among his contemporaries. As a pious Christian Kepler believed that the world had been created according to an archetypal plan in the intellect of God; and, as a philosopher, he held that the human mind was adequate to comprehend the order of the natural world by observation through the senses and by understanding; and that this order, when discovered and understood, could be formulated with precision and certainty in a deductive system whose governing principle would be that nature was created according to an archetypal plan which was itself in the image of God.

Did he not affirm with dogmatic extravagance that he had deduced the appearances a priori from archetypal principles?

In so far as he seems to say that, he was carried away more by poetic enthusiasm than by unlicensed dogmatism. While he held that the appearances would ultimately be deducible from archetypal principles, he laid no claim to having made any final deductions. He calls upon any one to improve upon his work who can do so. His own deductions are designed to be tentative and exemplary rather than final. For example, in searching for some law that would bind together the distances of the planets, after a series of trials and errors he hit upon the circumscribed and inscribed spheres of the five regular solids as a measuring rod. And again, after many trials and errors, he at last discerned an aspect of the planetary movements that could be measured by the ratios of musical harmonies. But he judged that insofar as his particular conclusions were true, they must fit together into a final deductive system. And he himself merely strove to build up what should be a logical and rhetorical foreshadowing of the same. A reading of Book v of the *Harmonies* will make all that clear.

But is it not arbitrary to try to measure the distances of the planets according to the spheres in and around the five regular solids and fantastic to apply musical ratios to celestial movements?

In what way are the spheres of the five solids a more arbitrary measuring rod for the distances of the planets than successive increments of whole numbers as in "Bode's Law," or than an hyperbola as a measuring-rod for the relation between the volume and pressure of a gas under constant temperature?

Similarly, it would have struck Kepler as obscure that the set of numbers which measured the relative lengths of harmonically tuned strings should be said to be limited to them alone.

But does not Kepler also pretend to account for the number of the planets by means of the five solids? What would he say about the planets more recently discovered through the telescope?

Well, as Peter Johannides aptly remarked, do not the five regular solids save the appearances of all the primary planets which are visible to the naked, untutored eye?

Why have you chosen to translate these particular works?

De revolutionibus orbium caelestium is Copernicus' major and almost single work. I have not translated his *Commentariolus*, which is a brief sketch of his system, written at an earlier date, or the *Letter Against Werner*, which is concerned with the variation in the precession of the equinoxes, because these works are themselves of secondary importance and are already available in English.

In the case of Kepler, there might be some doubt as to why I have translated the *Epitomes astronomiae* rather than the *Astronomia nova*, and a part of the *Epitomes* rather than the whole. Now the *Astronomia nova* is a work designed for study by the professional astronomer—one which presupposes in the reader a technical knowledge of astronomy and is, so to speak, built directly up out of observations and computations—while the *Epitomes*, as written for the educated amateur as well as for the practitioners, comprehends a fuller and more explicit account of the elements of Keplerian astronomy and is less wrapped up in the interplay of observation and computation. I have omitted Books I–III, because they deal merely with spherical astronomy (that is to say, the phenomena arising from the daily rotation) and add nothing to Ptolemy and Copernicus. I have omitted Books VI–VII principally for reasons of space and time. They can, without too great loss, be omitted, because they are subordinate to Books IV and V, as being concerned with the application of the general hypotheses and calculus established in Books IV and V to the specific details of the planetary movements. I have also included Book V of the *Harmonies* becuase it is the work which Kepler himself set most store by, because it is a model of elegance and dramatic suspense in scientific exposition, because it contains the original presentation of Kepler's "third law," because its discussion of the "music of the spheres" forms a needed supplement to, and explication of, parts of Book IV of the *Epitomes*, because it shows most clearly the role that Kepler conceived technical astronomy to play in a complete science of nature, because it shows very clearly the method followed by Kepler as a practising astronomer, and because it presents a system of mathematical measurement which is self-contained, speculative, and non-practical. I have been able to omit Books I-IV of the *Harmonices mundi* with a relatively clear conscience, because they are not concerned directly with astronomy.

What has been your method of translating?

There are two methods of translating which I have employed according to the topic of the discourse in the originals. One, in the case of expository passages which do not involve numerical computation to any great extent, I have used a straight prose and have not been concerned if I stayed very close to the syntax of the original. For while the job of a translator is not to reconstruct in one language the word-patterns of another but to put across into the new language the ideas expressed in the old, still only a presumptuous translator would suppose that he can recover all the interrelations among ideas which are as it were co-signified by the specific syntax of the original statements: therefore a certain strict awkwardness of English syntax may serve to roughen too smooth a flow of words and thus to remind the hurrying reader that there are relations of ideas that elegance must gloss over. On the other hand, in places where numerical computations occur at length, I have schematized the verbal format to the end that "he who runs may read," which is the manner whereby passages of computation should be read.

Are there any sign-posts so that the reader, if need be, can check the translation against the original text?

The pagination of the originals is indicated by bracketed numbers within the English text. In the cases of *De revolutionibus* and *Epitomes Astronomiae* the page-numbers are those of the first editions, while in the case of *Harmonices mundi* the page-numbers are those of Frisch's edition. In translating explicit page-references made by Kepler himself in the body of the text, I have used the term *folium* to signify that the page-number refers to the original edition and not to the translation.

In conclusion, I should like to express my gratitude to Mr. Elliott Carter, who patiently read through my manuscript translation of Book v of *The Harmonies of the World*, suggested improvements in the musical terminology, and liberally placed at my disposal a set of notes on Kepler's musical system, which are incorporated in the present text; but needless to say, all the failings of the present translation are my own. I should also like to acknowledge my indebtedness to Dr. R. Catesby Taliaferro, to Dr. George Comenetz, to Dr. Jacob Klein, and especially to Mr. Peter H. Jackson for criticisms and suggestions as to the revision of the earlier drafts of these translations, and also for various kinds of labour in the preparation of these earlier drafts, which were published in mimeographed form at St. John's College, Annapolis, in 1938-9, to Mrs. Edward F. Lathrop, Mr. Hirsh Nadel, Mr. Lee M. Mace, and to Mr. Harvey Dubinsky.

C. G. WALLIS

SYMBOLS AND ABBREVIATIONS

The translator here appends a list of examples of symbols and abbreviations which have been used in these works:

♄ *for* Saturn   ☉ *for* Earth
♃ *for* Jupiter   ♀ *for* Venus
♂ *for* Mars   ☿ *for* Mercury

♈ *for* Ram (Aries)   ♎ *for* Balance (Libra)
♉ *for* Bull (Taurus)   ♏ *for* Scorpion (Scorpio)
♊ *for* Twins (Gemini)   ♐ *for* Archer (Sagittarius)
♋ *for* Crab (Cancer)   ♑ *for* Goat (Capricornus)
♌ *for* Lion (Leo)   ♒ *for* Waterboy (Aquarius)
♍ *for* Virgin (Virgo)   ♓ *for* Fishes (Pisces)

sq. *AB for* square on *AB*

rect. *AB, CD for* rectangle *AB, CD*

trgl. *for* triangle

sect. *for* sector

$AB : CD \ \ EF : GH$ for *AB* has to *CD* a greater ratio than *EF* to *GH*

ch. *AB for* chord *AB*

½ ch. 2 *AB for* one half the chord subtending twice arc *AB*

dmt. sph. *for* diameter of the sphere

AB gr. circ. sph. *for* arc *AB* on the great circle of the sphere

$AB : CD = AB : BC$ comp. $BC : CD$ *for* the ratio of *AB* to *CD* is equal to the ratio of *AB* to *BC* compounded with the ratio of *BC* to *CD*.

$AB = CD$ *for AB* is equal to *CD*

$AB \eqsim CD$ *for AB* is approximately equal to *CD*

$AB > CD$ *for AB* is not less than *CD*

add. $AB = 6°42'$ *for* addition-subtraction *AB* is equal to 6°42′

add. *for* additive addition-subtraction

-add. *for* subtractive addition-subtraction

5°10′12″ *for* 5 degrees 10 minutes 12 seconds of the given circle of 360 degrees
6ᴾ5′14″ *for* 6 degrees 5 minutes 14 seconds of the given diameter (or radius) of
  60 degrees
seg. circ. *ABC for* segment *ABC* of the circle
ecc. *for* eccentricity
rad. ep. *for* radius of epicycle
gnom. *ABC for* gnomon *ABC*
comp. area *ABC for* composite area *ABC*
sag. *AB for* sagitta *AB*

Short Bibliography of Copernicus and Kepler

Nicolai Copernici Torinensis. *De revolutionibus orbium coelestium.* Norimbergae,
  1543.
Nicolai Copernici Torinensis. *Astronomia instaurata. Restituta notisque illus-
  trata, opera et studio D.* Nicolai Mulerii. Amstelrodami, 1617.
Nicolai Copernici Torinensis. *De Revolutionibus Orbium Caelestium. Ex auctoris
  autographo recudi curavit Societas Copernicana Thorunensis.* Thoruni, 1873.
Joanne Kepplero. *Epitomes Astronomiae Copernicanae Liber Quartus.* Lentus ad
  Danubium, 1620.
Joanne Kepplero. *Epitomes Astronomiae Copernicanae Libri V, VI, VII.* Fran-
  cofurti, 1621.
Joannis Kepleri Opera Omnia, ed. Dr. Cl. Frisch. Volumen V. *Harmonices
  Mundi Libri V.* Francofurti, 1864.

Nicolaus Copernicus

ON THE REVOLUTIONS OF
THE HEAVENLY SPHERES

BIOGRAPHICAL NOTE
Nicolaus Copernicus, 1473-1543

COPERNICUS was born February 19, 1473, at Torun, Poland, the youngest of the four children of a prosperous merchant. Upon the father's death in 1484, the children were adopted by their maternal uncle, Lucas Watzelrode, a priest of some scholarly attainments who became Bishop of Ermland in 1489; it was decided that Nicolaus should be trained for the church.

At the University of Cracow, which he entered in 1491, Copernicus first became seriously interested in mathematics. He studied particularly with Albert Brudzewski, the author of a commentary on Peurbach's text-book of Ptolemaic astronomy, and the leader of the humanist faction at the university. From him Copernicus not only learned mathematics and astronomy, but also acquired an attraction for the new humanistic studies. He left Cracow in 1494, without taking his examinations for a degree.

After it had become apparent that his uncle would provide him with a sinecure, Copernicus went to Italy. He remained there from 1496 to 1506 perfecting his education in many different fields. He first attended the University of Bologna, where he followed the course in canon law as a preparation for administrative work in the church. But mathematics and astronomy continued to be his particular interest, and he became closely associated with Domenico Maria de Novara, a Platonist who had detected the diminution in the obliquity of the ecliptic and the variation in latitude. Although he obtained his appointment as canon of the cathedral of Frauenburg in 1497, he immediately obtained a leave of absence to continue his studies. In the jubilee year of 1500 he visited Rome and lectured on mathematics. The following year he returned to Ermland and obtained an extension of his leave of absence so that he might study medicine at Padua. Except for the interval in 1503 when he completed his doctorate in canon law at Ferrara, Copernicus studied from 1501 to 1505 in

the medical school at Padua. When he returned to Poland the following year, he was not only a humanist learned in Greek, mathematics, and astronomy, but also a jurist and a physician.

Copernicus did not actively assume his duties as a canon until six years after his departure from Italy. Until 1512 he resided at the episcopal palace of Heilsberg as physician to his uncle, the bishop. Upon the death of his uncle in that year he took up residence as a canon of the rich cathedral of Frauenburg on the Baltic. Although he never took holy orders, and only those vows necessary for his office as a canon, he was the official representative of the cathedral chapter in the many disputes in which it was involved. After the war between Poland and the Teutonic Knights from 1519 to 1521, he planned and aided the reconstruction of Ermland. He served as commissary for the diocese of Ermland, and his medical skill was always at the service of the poor and frequently in demand by the rich. In 1522 he presented a scheme for the reform of the currency before the Diet of Graudenz. He never became personally involved in the conflicts of the Reformation.

While engaged in many practical duties, Copernicus continued his intellectual pursuits. His first work, published in 1509, was a Latin translation of the fictitious correspondence of famous men written by Theophylact Simocatta, a seventh-century Byzantine historian. The introductory poem written by a college friend provided the first public praise of Copernicus as an astronomer, who "explores the rapid course of the moon and the changing movements of the fraternal star and the whole firmament with the planets." Copernicus himself said that it was in 1506, immediately after his return from Italy, that he began to develop his astronomical system and to write it down. The astronomical observations, which he had begun in Italy, were continued in Poland, particularly at Frauenburg, where he established an observatory. By 1514 his reputation as an astronomer led to his being invited by the Lateran Council to give his opinion on the proposed reform of the calendar. He declined on the ground that the movements of the sun and the moon had not yet been determined with sufficient accuracy. Although continually making observations and elaborating his own doctrine, Copernicus showed great reluctance to publish the result of his work. His *Letter Against Werner*, which appeared in 1524, tried to demolish the old explanation of the alleged variation in the precession of the equinoxes but revealed nothing of his new theory.

It was not until 1530 that Copernicus provided in the *Commentariolus* a preliminary outline of his heliocentric theory. It immediately attracted great attention. At Rome, Johann Albrecht Widmanstadt lectured upon the new doctrine; Pope Clement VII gave his approval;

Cardinal Schönberg entreated the author to make public his full thought upon the subject. In the spring of 1539 Copernicus was visited by Joachim Rheticus, a protegé of Melanchthon and at the age of twenty-five professor of mathematics at the University of Wittenberg. Rheticus stayed for some time, studied the details of Copernicus' planetary system, and in 1540 composed and published, with Copernicus' approval, a general account of it entitled *Narratio Prima*. At length Copernicus was prevailed upon by his friends to allow Rheticus to publish the *De revolutionibus orbium coelestium*. Copernicus lived only long enough to witness its appearance. Towards the close of 1542 he was seized with apoplexy and paralysis; on May 24, 1543, an advance copy of his work was presented to him, and on the same day he died. He was buried in the Frauenburg Cathedral.

CONTENTS

BOOK SIX

INTRODUCTION

To the Reader Concerning the Hypotheses of this Work[1]

[i[b]][2]Since the newness of the hypotheses of this work—which sets the earth in motion and puts an immovable sun at the centre of the universe—has already received a great deal of publicity, I have no doubt that certain of the savants have taken grave offense and think it wrong to raise any disturbance among liberal disciplines which have had the right set-up for a long time now. If, however, they are willing to weigh the matter scrupulously, they will find that the author of this work has done nothing which merits blame. For it is the job of the astronomer to use painstaking and skilled observation in gathering together the history of the celestial movements, and then—since he cannot by any line of reasoning reach the true causes of these movements—to think up or construct whatever causes or hypotheses he pleases such that, by the assumption of these causes, those same movements can be calculated from the principles of geometry for the past and for the future too. This artist is markedly outstanding in both of these respects: for it is not necessary that these hypotheses should be true, or even probably; but it is enough if they provide a calculus which fits the observations—unless by some chance there is anyone so ignorant of geometry and optics as to hold the epicycle of Venus as probable and to believe this to be a cause why Venus alternately precedes and follows the sun at an angular distance of up to 40° or more. For who does not see that it necessarily follows from this assumption that the diameter of the planet in its perigee should appear more than four times greater, and the body of the planet more than sixteen times greater, than in its apogee? Nevertheless the experience of all the ages is opposed to that.[3] There are also other things in this discipline which are just as absurd, but it is not necessary to examine them right now. For it is sufficiently clear that this art is absolutely and profoundly ignorant of the causes of the apparent irregular movements. And if it constructs and thinks up causes—and it has certainly thought up a good

---

[1]This foreword, at first ascribed to Copernicus, is held to have been written by Andrew Osiander, a Lutheran theologian and friend of Copernicus, who saw the *De Revolutionibus* through the press.

[2]The numbers within the brackets refer to the pages of the first edition, published in 1543 at Nuremberg.

[3]Ptolemy makes Venus move on an epicycle the ratio of whose radius to the radius of the eccentric circle carrying the epicycle itself is nearly three to four. Hence the apparent magnitude of the planet would be expected to vary with the varying distance of the planet from the Earth, in the ratios stated by Osiander.

Moreover, it was found that, whenever the planet happened to be on the epicycle, the mean position of the sun appeared in line with *EPA*.

And so, granted the ratios of epicycle and eccentric, Venus would never appear from the Earth to be at an angular distance of much more than 40° from the centre of her epicycle, that is to say, from the mean position of the sun, as it turned out by observation.

505

many—nevertheless it does not think them up in order to persuade anyone of their truth but only in order that they may provide a correct basis for calculation. But since for one and the same movement varying hypotheses are proposed from time to time, as eccentricity or epicycle for the movement of the sun, the astronomer much prefers to take the one which is easiest to [ii^a] grasp. Maybe the philosopher demands probability instead; but neither of them will grasp anything certain or hand it on, unless it has been divinely revealed to him. Therefore let us permit these new hypotheses to make a public appearance among old ones which are themselves no more probable, especially since they are wonderful and easy and bring with them a vast storehouse of learned observations. And as far as hypotheses go, let no one expect anything in the way of certainty from astronomy, since astronomy can offer us nothing certain, lest, if anyone take as true that which has been constructed for another use, he go away from this discipline a bigger fool than when he came to it. Farewell.

Preface and Dedication to Pope Paul III

[ii^b] I can reckon easily enough, Most Holy Father, that as soon as certain people learn that in these books of mine which I have written about the revolutions of the spheres of the world I attribute certain motions to the terrestrial globe, they will immediately shout to have me and my opinion hooted off the stage. For my own works do not please me so much that I do not weigh what judgments others will pronounce concerning them. And although I realize that the conceptions of a philosopher are placed beyond the judgment of the crowd, because it is his loving duty to seek the truth in all things, in so far as God has granted that to human reason; nevertheless I think we should avoid opinions utterly foreign to rightness. And when I considered how absurd this "lecture" would be held by those who know that the opinion that the Earth rests immovable in the middle of the heavens as if their centre had been confirmed by the judgments of many ages—if I were to assert to the contrary that the Earth moves; for a long time I was in great difficulty as to whether I should bring to light my commentaries written to demonstrate the Earth's movement, or whether it would not be better to follow the example of the Pythagoreans and certain others who used to hand down the mysteries of their philosophy not in writing but by word of mouth and only to their relatives and friends—witness the letter of Lysis to Hipparchus. They however seem to me to have done that not, as some judge, out of a jealous unwillingness to communicate their doctrines but in order that things of very great beauty which have been investigated by the loving care of great men should not be scorned by those who find it a bother to expend any great energy on letters—except on the money-making variety—or who are provoked by the exhortations and examples of others to the liberal study of philosophy but on account of their natural [iii^a] stupidity hold the position among philosophers that drones hold among bees. Therefore, when I weighed these things in my mind, the scorn which I had to fear on account of the newness and absurdity of my opinion almost drove me to abandon a work already undertaken.

But my friends made me change my course in spite of my long-continued hestitation and even resistance. First among them was Nicholas Schonberg, Cardinal of Capua, a man distinguished in all branches of learning; next to him was my devoted friend Tiedeman Giese, Bishop of Culm, a man filled with the greatest zeal for the divine and liberal arts: for he in particular urged me frequently and even spurred me on by added reproaches into publishing this book and letting come to light a work which I had kept hidden among my things for not merely nine years, but for almost four times nine years. Not a few other learned and distinguished men demanded the same thing of me, urging me to refuse no longer—on account of the fear which I felt—to contribute my work to the common utility of those who are really interested in mathematics: they said that the absurder my teaching about the movement of the Earth now seems to very many persons, the more wonder and thanksgiving will it be the object of, when after the publication of my commentaries those same persons see the fog of absurdity dissipated by my luminous demonstrations. Accordingly I was led by such persuasion and by that hope finally to permit my friends to undertake the publication of a work which they had long sought from me.

But perhaps Your Holiness will not be so much surprised at my giving the results of my nocturnal study to the light—after having taken such care in working them out that I did not hesitate to put in writing my conceptions as to the movement of the Earth—as you will be eager to hear from me what came into my mind that in opposition to the general opinion of mathematicians and almost in opposition to common sense I should dare to imagine some movement of the Earth. And so I am unwilling to hide from Your Holiness that nothing except my knowledge that mathematicians have not agreed with one another in their researches moved me to think out a different scheme of drawing up the movements of the spheres of the world. For in the first place mathematicians are so uncertain about the movements of the sun and moon that they can neither demonstrate nor observe the unchanging magnitude of the [iii^{b}] revolving year. Then in setting up the solar and lunar movements and those of the other five wandering stars, they do not employ the same principles, assumptions, or demonstrations for the revolutions and apparent movements. For some make use of homocentric circles only, others of eccentric circles and epicycles, by means of which however they do not fully attain what they seek. For although those who have put their trust in homocentric circles have shown that various different movements can be composed of such circles, nevertheless they have not been able to establish anything for certain that would fully correspond to the phenomena. But even if those who have thought up eccentric circles seem to have been able for the most part to compute the apparent movements numerically by those means, they have in the meanwhile admitted a great deal which seems to contradict the first principles of regularity of movement. Moreover, they have not been able to discover or to infer the chief point of all, i.e., the form of the world and the certain commensurability of its parts. But they are in exactly the same fix as someone taking from different places hands, feet, head, and the other limbs—shaped very beautifully but not with reference to one body and without correspondence to one another—so that such parts made up a monster rather than a man. And so, in the process of demonstration which they call "method," they are found either to have omitted something necessary or to have admitted something foreign which by no means pertains to the matter; and they would by no means have been in this fix, if they had followed sure principles. For if the hypotheses they assumed were not false, everything which followed from the hypotheses would have been verified without fail; and though what I am saying may be obscure right now, nevertheless it will become clearer in the proper place.

Accordingly, when I had meditated upon this lack of certitude in the traditional mathematics concerning the composition of movements of the spheres of the world, I began to be annoyed that the philosophers, who in other respects had made a very careful scrutiny of the least details of the world, had discovered no sure scheme for the movements of the machinery of the world, which has been built for us by the Best and Most Orderly Workman of all. Wherefore I took the trouble to reread all the books by philosophers which I could get hold of, to see if any of them even supposed that the movements of the spheres of the world [iv^a] were different from those laid down by those who taught mathematics in the schools. And as a matter of fact, I found first in Cicero that Nicetas thought that the Earth moved. And afterwards I found in Plutarch that there were some others of the same opinion: I shall copy out his words here, so that they may be known to all:

Some think that the Earth is at rest; but Philolaus the Pythagorean says that it moves around the fire with an obliquely circular motion, like the sun and moon. Herakleides of Pontus and Ekphantus the Pythagorean do not give the Earth any movement of locomotion, but rather a limited movement of rising and setting around its centre, like a wheel.[1]

Therefore I also, having found occasion, began to meditate upon the mobility of the Earth. And although the opinion seemed absurd, nevertheless because I knew that others before me had been granted the liberty of constructing whatever circles they pleased in order to demonstrate astral pheonmena, I thought that I too would be readily permitted to test whether or not, by the laying down that the Earth had some movement, demonstrations less shaky than those of my predecessors could be found for the revolutions of the celestial spheres.

And so, having laid down the movements which I attribute to the Earth farther on in the work, I finally discovered by the help of long and numerous observations that if the movements of the other wandering stars are correlated with the circular movement of the Earth, and if the movements are computed in accordance with the revolution of each planet, not only do all their phenomena follow from that but also this correlation binds together so closely the order and magnitudes of all the planets and of their spheres or orbital circles and the heavens themselves that nothing can be shifted around in any part of them without disrupting the remaining parts and the universe as a whole.

Accordingly, in composing my work I adopted the following order: in the first book I describe all the locations of the spheres or orbital circles together with the movements which I attribute to the earth, so that this book contains as it were the general set-up of the universe. But afterwards in the remaining books I correlate all the movements of the other planets and their spheres or orbital circles with the mobility of the Earth, so that it can be gathered from that how far the apparent movements of the remaining planets and their orbital circles can be saved by being correlated with the movements of the Earth. And I have no doubt that talented and learned mathematicians will agree with me, if—as philosophy [iv^b] demands in the first place—they are willing to give not superficial but profound thought and effort to what I bring

―――――――
[1] *De placitis philosophorum,* III. 13.

forward in this work in demonstrating these things. And in order that the unlearned as well as the learned might see that I was not seeking to flee from the judgment of any man, I preferred to dedicate these results of my nocturnal study to Your Holiness rather than to anyone else; because, even in this remote corner of the earth where I live, you are held to be most eminent both in the dignity of your order and in your love of letters and even of mathematics; hence, by the authority of your judgment you can easily provide a guard against the bites of slanderers, despite the proverb that there is no medicine for the bite of a sycophant.

But if perchance there are certain "idle talkers" who take it upon themselves to pronounce judgment, although wholly ignorant of mathematics, and if by shamelessly distorting the sense of some passage in Holy Writ to suit their purpose, they dare to reprehend and to attack my work; they worry me so little that I shall even scorn their judgments as foolhardy. For it is not unknown that Lactantius, otherwise a distinguished writer but hardly a mathematician, speaks in an utterly childish fashion concerning the shape of the Earth, when he laughs at those who have affirmed that the Earth has the form of a globe. And so the studious need not be surprised if people like that laugh at us. Mathematics is written for mathematicians; and among them, if I am not mistaken, my labours will be seen to contribute something to the ecclesiastical commonwealth, the principate of which Your Holiness now holds. For not many years ago under Leo X when the Lateran Council was considering the question of reforming the Ecclesiastical Calendar, no decision was reached, for the sole reason that the magnitude of the year and the months and the movements of the sun and moon had not yet been measured with sufficient accuracy. From that time on I gave attention to making more exact observations of these things and was encouraged to do so by that most distinguished man, Paul, Bishop of Fossombrone, who had been present at those deliberations. But what have I accomplished in this matter I leave to the judgment of Your Holiness in particular and to that of all other learned mathematicians. And so as not to appear to Your Holiness to make more promises concerning the utility of this book than I can fulfill, I now pass on to the body of the work.

BOOK ONE[1]

AMONG the many and varied literary and artistic studies upon which the natural talents of man are nourished, I think that those above all should be embraced and pursued with the most loving care which have to do with things that are very beautiful and very worthy of knowledge. Such studies are those which deal with the godlike circular movements of the world and the course of the stars, their magnitudes, distances, risings and settings, and the causes of the other appearances in the heavens; and which finally explicate the whole form. For what could be more beautiful than the heavens which contain all beautiful things? Their very names make this clear: *Caelum* (heavens) by naming that which is beautifully carved; and *Mundus* (world), purity and elegance. Many philosophers have called the world a visible god on account of its extraordinary excellence. So if the worth of the arts were measured by the matter with which they deal, this art—which some call astronomy, others astrology, and many of the ancients the consummation of mathematics—would be by far the most outstanding. This art which is as it were the head of all the liberal arts and the one most worthy of a free man leans upon nearly all the other branches of mathematics. Arithmetic, geometry, optics, geodesy, mechanics, and whatever others, all offer themselves in its service. And since a property of all good arts is to draw the mind of man away from the vices and direct it to better things, these arts can do that more plentifully, over and above the unbelievable pleasure of mind [which they furnish]. For who, after applying himself to things which he sees established in the best order and directed by divine ruling, would not through diligent contemplation of them and through a certain habituation be awakened to that which is best and would not wonder at the Artificer of all things, in Whom is all happiness and every good? For the divine Psalmist surely did not say gratuitously that he took pleasure in the workings of God and rejoiced in the works of His hands, unless by means of these things as by some sort of vehicle we are transported to the contemplation of the highest Good.

Now as regards the utility and ornament which they confer upon a commonwealth—to pass over the innumerable advantages they give to private citizens —Plato makes an extremely good point, for in the seventh book of the *Laws* he says that this study should be pursued in especial, that through it the orderly arrangement of days into months and years and the determination of the times for solemnities and sacrifices should keep the state alive and watchful; and he says that if anyone denies that this study is necessary for a man who is going to take up any of the highest branches of learning, then such a person is thinking foolishly; and he thinks that it is impossible for anyone to become godlike or be called so who has no necessary knowledge of the sun, moon, and the other stars.

However, this more divine than human science, which inquires into the high-

[1]The three introductory paragraphs are found in the Thorn centenary and Warsaw editions.

est things, is not lacking in difficulties. And in particular we see that as regards its principles and assumptions, which the Greeks call "hypotheses," many of those who undertook to deal with them were not in accord and hence did not employ the same methods of calculation. In addition, the courses of the planets and the revolution of the stars cannot be determined by exact calculations and reduced to perfect knowledge unless, through the passage of time and with the help of many prior observations, they can, so to speak, be handed down to posterity. For even if Claud Ptolemy of Alexandria, who stands far in front of all the others on account of his wonderful care and industry, with the help of more than forty years of observations brought this art to such a high point that there seemed to be nothing left which he had not touched upon; nevertheless we see that very many things are not in accord with the movements which should follow from his doctrine but rather with movements which were discovered later and were unknown to him. Whence even Plutarch in speaking of the revolving solar year says, "So far the movement of the stars has overcome the ingenuity of the mathematicians." Now to take the year itself as my example, I believe it is well known how many different opinions there are about it, so that many people have given up hope of making an exact determination of it. Similarly, in the case of the other planets I shall try—with the help of God, without Whom we can do nothing—to make a more detailed inquiry concerning them, since the greater the interval of time between us and the founders of this art—whose discoveries we can compare with the new ones made by us—the more means we have of supporting our own theory. Furthermore, I confess that I shall expound many things differently from my predecessors—although with their aid, for it was they who first opened the road of inquiry into these things.

1. The World is Spherical

[1ª] In the beginning we should remark that the world is globe-shaped; whether because this figure is the most perfect of all, as it is an integral whole and needs no joints; or because this figure is the one having the greatest volume and thus is especially suitable for that which is going to comprehend and conserve all things; or even because the separate parts of the world i.e., the sun, moon, and stars are viewed under such a form; or because everything in the world tends to be delimited by this form, as is apparent in the case of drops of water and other liquid bodies, when they become delimited of themselves. And so no one would hesitate to say that this form belongs to the heavenly bodies.

2. The Earth is Spherical Too

The Earth is globe-shaped too, since on every side it rests upon its centre. But it is not perceived straightway to be a perfect sphere, on account of the great height of its mountains and the lowness of its valleys, though they modify its universal roundness to only a very small extent.

That is made clear in this way. For when people journey northward from anywhere, the northern vertex of the axis of daily revolution gradually moves overhead, and the other moves downward to the same extent; and many stars situated to the north are seen not to set, and many to the south are seen not to rise any more. So Italy does not see Canopus, which is visible to Egypt. And Italy sees the last star of Fluvius, which is not visible to this region situated in a more frigid zone. Conversely, for people who travel southward, the second group of stars becomes higher in the sky; while those become lower which for us are high up.

Moreover, the inclinations of the poles have everywhere the same ratio with places at equal distances from the poles of the Earth and that [1ᵇ] happens in no other figure except the spherical. Whence it is manifest that the Earth itself is contained between the vertices and is therefore a globe.

Add to this the fact that the inhabitants of the East do not perceive the evening eclipses of the sun and moon; nor the inhabitants of the West, the morning eclipses; while of those who live in the middle region—some see them earlier and some later.

Furthermore, voyagers perceive that the waters too are fixed within this figure; for example, when land is not visible from the deck of a ship, it may be seen from the top of the mast, and conversely, if something shining is attached to the top of the mast, it appears to those remaining on the shore to come down gradually, as the ship moves from the land, until finally it becomes hidden, as if setting.

Moreover, it is admitted that water, which by its nature flows, always seeks lower places—the same way as earth—and does not climb up the shore any farther than the convexity of the shore allows. That is why the land is so much higher where it rises up from the ocean.

3. How Land and Water Make Up a Single Globe

And so the ocean encircling the land pours forth its waters everywhere and fills up the deeper hollows with them. Accordingly it was necessary for there to be less water than land, so as not to have the whole earth soaked with water—since both of them tend toward the same centre on account of their weight—and so as to leave some portions of land—such as the islands discernible here and there—for the preservation of living creatures. For what is the continent itself and the *orbis terrarum* except an island which is larger than the rest? We should not listen to certain Peripatetics who maintain that there is ten times more water than land and who arrive at that conclusion because in the transmutation of the elements the liquefaction of one part of earth results in ten parts of water. And they say that land has emerged for a certain distance because, having hollow spaces inside, it does not balance everywhere with respect to weight and so the centre of gravity is different from the centre of magnitude. But they fall into error through ignorance of geometry; for they do not know that there cannot be seven times more water than land and some part of the land still remain dry, unless the land abandon its centre of gravity and give place to the waters as being heavier. For spheres are to one another as the cubes of their diameters. If therefore there were seven parts of water and one part of land, [2ᵃ] the diameter of the land could not be greater than the radius of the globe of the waters. So it is even less possible that the water should be ten times greater. It can be gathered that there is no difference between the centres of magnitude and of gravity of the Earth from the fact that the convexity of the land spreading out from the ocean does not swell continuously, for in that case it would repulse the sea-waters as much as possible and would not in any way allow interior seas and huge gulfs to break through. Moreover, from the seashore outward the depth of the abyss would not stop increasing, and so no island or reef or any spot of land would be met with by people voyaging out very far. Now it is well known that there is not quite the distance of two miles —at practically the centre of the *orbis terrarum*—between the Egyptian and the Red Sea. And on the contrary, Ptolemy in his *Cosmography* extends inhabitable lands as far as the median circle, and he leaves that part of the Earth as unknown, where the moderns have added Cathay and other vast regions as far as 60° longitude, so that inhabited land extends in longitude farther than the rest of the ocean does. And if you add to these the islands discovered in our time under the princes of Spain and Portugal and especially America—named after the ship's captain who discovered her—which they consider a second *orbis terrarum* on account of her so far unmeasured magnitude—besides many other islands heretofore unknown, we would not be greatly surprised if there were antipodes or antichthones. For reasons of geometry compel us to believe that America is situated diametrically opposite to the India of the Ganges.

And from all that I think it is manifest that the land and the water rest upon one centre of gravity; that this is the same as the centre of magnitude of the land, since land is the heavier; that parts of land which are as it were yawning are filled with water; and that accordingly there is little water in comparison with the land, even if more of the surface appears to be covered by water.

Now it is necessary that the land and the surrounding waters have the figure which the shadow of the Earth casts, for it eclipses the moon by projecting a perfect circle upon it. Therefore the Earth is not a plane, as Empedocles and Anaximenes opined; or a tympanoid, as Leucippus; or a scaphoid, as Heracleitus; or hollowed out in any other way, as Democritus; or again a cylinder, as Anaximander; and it is not infinite in its lower part, with the density increasing rootwards, as Xenophanes thought; but it is perfectly round, as the philosophers perceived.

4. The Movement of the Celestial Bodies Is Regular, Circular, and Everlasting—Or Else Compounded of Circular Movements

[2ᵇ] After this we will recall that the movement of the celestial bodies is circular. For the motion of a sphere is to turn in a circle; by this very act expressing its form, in the most simple body, where beginning and end cannot be discovered or distinguished from one another, while it moves through the same parts in itself.

But there are many movements on account of the multitude of spheres or orbital circles[1]. The most obvious of all is the daily revolution—which the Greeks call νυχθήμερον; *i.e.*, having the temporal span of a day and a night. By means of this movement the whole world—with the exception of the Earth—is supposed to be borne from east to west. This movement is taken as the common measure of all movements, since we measure even time itself principally by the number of days.

Next, we see other as it were antagonistic revolutions; *i.e.*, from west to east, on the part of the sun, moon, and the wandering stars. In this way the sun gives us the year, the moon the months—the most common periods of time; and each of the other five planets follows its own cycle. Nevertheless these movements are

---

[1]The "orbital circle" (*orbis*) is the great circle whereon the planet moves in its sphere (*sphaera*). Copernicus uses the word *orbis* which designates a circle primarily rather than a sphere because, while the sphere may be necessary for the mechanical explanation of the movement, only the circle is necessary for the mathematical.

manifoldly different from the first movement. First, in that they do not revolve around the same poles as the first movement but follow the oblique ecliptic; next, in that they do not seem to move in their circuit regularly. For the sun and moon are caught moving at times more slowly and at times more quickly. And we perceive the five wandering stars sometimes even to retrograde and to come to a stop between these two movements. And though the sun always proceeds straight ahead along its route, they wander in various ways, straying sometimes towards the south, and at other times towards the north—whence they are called "planets." Add to this the fact that sometimes they are nearer the Earth —and are then said to be at their perigee—and at other times are farther away— and are said to be at their apogee.

We must however confess that these movements are circular or are composed of many circular movements, in that they maintain these irregularities in accordance with a constant law and with fixed periodic returns: and that could not take place, if they were not circular. For it is only the circle which can bring back what is past and over with; and in this way, for example, the sun by a movement composed of circular movements brings back to us the inequality of days and nights and the four seasons of the year. [3ª] Many movements are recognized in that movement, since it is impossible that a simple heavenly body should be moved irregularly by a single sphere. For that would have to take place either on account of the inconstancy of the motor virtue—whether by reason of an extrinsic cause or its intrinsic nature—or on account of the inequality between it and the moved body. But since the mind shudders at either of these suppositions, and since it is quite unfitting to suppose that such a state of affairs exists among things which are established in the best system, it is agreed that their regular movements appear to us as irregular, whether on account of their circles having different poles or even because the earth is not at the centre of the circles in which they revolve. And so for us watching from the Earth, it happens that the transits of the planets, on account of being at unequal distances from the Earth, appear greater when they are nearer than when they are farther away, as has been shown in optics: thus in the case of equal arcs of an orbital circle which are seen at different distances there will appear to be unequal movements in equal times. For this reason I think it necessary above all that we should note carefully what the relation of the Earth to the heavens is, so as not—when we wish to scrutinize the highest things—to be ignorant of those which are nearest to us, and so as not—by the same error—to attribute to the celestial bodies what belongs to the Earth.

5. Does the Earth Have a Circular Movement? And of Its Place

Now that it has been shown that the Earth too has the form of a globe, I think we must see whether or not a movement follows upon its form and what the place of the Earth is in the universe. For without doing that it will not be possible to find a sure reason for the movements appearing in the heavens. Although there are so many authorities for saying that the Earth rests in the centre of the world that people think the contrary supposition inopinable and even ridiculous; if however we consider the thing attentively, we will see that the question has not yet been decided and accordingly is by no means to be scorned. For every apparent change in place occurs on account of the movement either of the thing seen or of the spectator, or on account of the necessarily unequal movement of both. For no movement is perceptible relatively to things moved equally in the same directions—I mean relatively to the thing seen and the spectator. Now it is from the Earth that the celestial circuit is beheld and presented to our sight. Therefore, if some movement should belong to the Earth [3b] it will appear, in the parts of the universe which are outside, as the same movement but in the opposite direction, as though the things outside were passing over. And the daily revolution in especial is such a movement. For the daily revolution appears to carry the whole universe along, with the exception of the Earth and the things around it. And if you admit that the heavens possess none of this movement but that the Earth turns from west to east, you will find—if you make a serious examination—that as regards the apparent rising and setting of the sun, moon, and stars the case is so. And since it is the heavens which contain and embrace all things as the place common to the universe, it will not be clear at once why movement should not be assigned to the contained rather than to the container, to the thing placed rather than to the thing providing the place.

As a matter of fact, the Pythagoreans Herakleides and Ekphantus were of this opinion and so was Hicetas the Syracusan in Cicero; they made the Earth to revolve at the centre of the world. For they believed that the stars set by reason of the interposition of the Earth and that with cessation of that they rose again. Now upon this assumption there follow other things, and a no smaller problem concerning the place of the Earth, though it is taken for granted and believed by nearly all that the Earth is the centre of the world. For if anyone denies that the Earth occupies the midpoint or centre of the world yet does not admit that the distance [between the two] is great enough to be compared with [the distance to] the sphere of the fixed stars but is considerable and quite apparent in relation to the orbital circles of the sun and the planets; and if for that reason he thought that their movements appeared irregular because they are organized around a different centre from the centre of the Earth, he might perhaps be able to bring forward a perfectly sound reason for movement which appears irregular. For the fact that the wandering stars are seen to be sometimes nearer the Earth and at other times farther away necessarily argues that the centre of the Earth is not the centre of their circles. It is not yet clear whether the Earth draws near to them and moves away or they draw near to the Earth and move away

And so it would not be very surprising if someone attributed some other movement to the earth in addition to the daily revolution. As a matter of fact, Philolaus the Pythagorean—no ordinary mathematician, whom Plato's biographers say Plato went to Italy for the sake of seeing—is supposed to have held that the Earth moved in a circle and wandered in some other movements and was one of the planets.

Many however have believed that they could show by geometrical reasoning that the Earth is in the middle of the world; that it has the proportionality of a point in relation to the immensity of the heavens, occupies the central position, and for this reason is immovable, because, when the universe moves, the centre [4a] remains unmoved and the things which are closest to the centre are moved the most slowly.

6. On the Immensity of the Heavens in Relation to the Magnitude of the Earth

It can be understood that this great mass which is the Earth is not comparable with the magnitude of the heavens, from the fact that the boundary circles —for that is the translation of the Greek ὁρίζοντες—cut the whole celestial sphere into two halves; for that could not take place if the magnitude of the Earth in comparison with the heavens, or its distance from the centre of the world, were considerable. For the circle bisecting a sphere goes through the centre of the sphere, and is the greatest circle which it is possible to circumscribe.

Now let the horizon be the circle *ABCD*, and let the Earth, where our point of view is, be *E*, the centre of the horizon by which the visible stars are separated from those which are not visible. Now with a dioptra or horoscope or level placed at *E*, the beginning of Cancer is seen to rise at point *C;* and at the same moment the beginning of Capricorn appears to set at *A*. Therefore, since *AEC* is in a straight line with the dioptra, it is clear that this line is a diameter of the ecliptic, because the six signs bound a semicircle, whose centre *E* is the same as that of the horizon. But when a revolution has taken place and the beginning of Capricorn arises at *B*, then the setting of Cancer will be visible at *D*, and *BED* will be a straight line and a diameter of the ecliptic. But it has already been seen that the line *AEC* is a diameter of the same circle; therefore, at their common section, point *E* will be their centre. So in this way the horizon always bisects the ecliptic, which is a great circle of the sphere. But on a sphere, if a circle bisects one of the great circles, then the circle bisecting is a great circle. Therefore the horizon is a great circle; and its centre is the same as that of the ecliptic, as far as appearance goes; although nevertheless the line passing through the centre of the Earth and the line touching to the surface are necessarily different; but on account of their immensity in comparison with the Earth they are like parallel lines, which on account of the great distance between the termini appear to be one line, when the space contained between them [4b] is in no perceptible ratio to their length, as has been shown in optics.

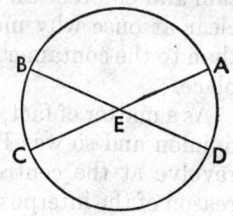

From this argument it is certainly clear enough that the heavens are immense in comparison with the Earth and present the aspect of an infinite magnitude, and that in the judgment of sense-perception the Earth is to the heavens as a point to a body and as a finite to an infinite magnitude. But we see that nothing more than that has been shown, and it does not follow that the Earth must rest at the centre of the world. And we should be even more surprised if such a vast world should wheel completely around during the space of twenty-four hours rather than that its least part, the Earth, should. For saying that the centre is immovable and that those things which are closest to the centre are moved least does not argue that the Earth rests at the centre of the world. That is no different from saying that the heavens revolve but the poles are at rest and those things which are closest to the poles are moved least. In this way Cynosura [the pole star] is seen to move much more slowly than Aquila or Canicula because, being very near to the pole, it describes a smaller circle, since they are all on a single sphere, the movement of which stops at its axis and which does not allow any of its parts to have movements which are equal to one another. And nevertheless the revolution of the whole brings them round in equal times but not over equal spaces.

The argument which maintains that the Earth, as a part of the celestial sphere and as sharing in the same form and movement, moves very little because very near to its centre advances to the following position: therefore the Earth will move, as being a body and not a centre, and will describe in the same time arcs similar to, but smaller than, the arcs of the celestical circle. It is clearer than daylight how false that is; for there would necessarily always be noon at one place and midnight at another, and so the daily risings and settings could not take place, since the movement of the whole and the part would be one and inseparable.

But the ratio between things separated by diversity of nature is so entirely different that those which describe a smaller circle turn more quickly than those which describe a greater circle. In this way Saturn, the highest of the wandering stars, completes its revolution in thirty years, and the moon which is without doubt the closest to the Earth completes its circuit in a month, and finally the Earth itself will be considered to complete a circular movement in the space of a day and a night. So this same problem concerning the daily revolution comes up again. And also the question about the place of the Earth becomes even less certain on account of what was just said. For that demonstration proves nothing except that the heavens are of an indefinite magnitude with respect to the Earth. But it is not at all clear how far this immensity stretches out. On the contrary, since the minimal and indivisible corpuscles, which are called atoms, are not perceptible to sense, they do not, when taken in twos or in some small number, constitute a visible body; but they can be taken in such a large quantity that there will at last be enough to form a visible magnitude. So it is as regards the place of the earth; for although it is not at the centre of the world, nevertheless the distance is as nothing, particularly in comparison with the sphere of the fixed stars.

7. WHY THE ANCIENTS THOUGHT THE EARTH WAS AT REST AT THE MIDDLE OF THE WORLD AS ITS CENTRE

[5ª] Wherefore for other reasons the ancient philosophers have tried to affirm that the Earth is at rest at the middle of the world, and as principal cause they put forward heaviness and lightness. For Earth is the heaviest element; and all things of any weight are borne towards it and strive to move towards the very centre of it.

For since the Earth is a globe towards which from every direction heavy things by their own nature are borne at right angles to its surface, the heavy things would fall on one another at the centre if they were not held back at the surface; since a straight line making right angles with a plane surface where it touches a sphere leads to the centre. And those things which are borne toward the centre seem to follow along in order to be at rest at the centre. All the more then will the Earth be at rest at the centre; and, as being the receptacle for falling bodies, it will remain immovable because of its weight.

They strive similarly to prove this by reason of movement and its nature. For

Aristotle says that the movement of a body which is one and simple is simple, and the simple movements are the rectilinear and the circular. And of rectilinear movements, one is upward, and the other is downward. As a consequence, every simple movement is either toward the centre, *i.e.*, downward, or away from the centre, *i.e.*, upward, or around the centre, *i.e.*, circular. Now it belongs to earth and water, which are considered heavy, to be borne downward, *i.e.*, to seek the centre: for air and fire, which are endowed with lightness, move upward, *i.e.*, away from the centre. It seems fitting to grant rectilinear movement to these four elements and to give the heavenly bodies a circular movement around the centre. So Aristotle. Therefore, said Ptolemy of Alexandria, if the Earth moved, even if only by its daily rotation, the contrary of what was said above would necessarily take place. For this movement which would traverse the total circuit of the Earth in twenty-four hours would necessarily be very headlong and of an unsurpassable velocity. Now things which are suddenly and violently whirled around are seen to be utterly unfitted for reuniting, and the more unified are seen to become dispersed, unless some constant force constrains them to stick together. And a long time ago, he says, the scattered Earth would have passed beyond the heavens, as is certainly ridiculous; [5^b] and *a fortiori* so would all the living creatures and all the other separate masses which could by no means remain unshaken. Moreover, freely falling bodies would not arrive at the places appointed them, and certainly not along the perpendicular line which they assume so quickly. And we would see clouds and other things floating in the air always borne toward the west.

8. ANSWER TO THE AFORESAID REASONS AND THEIR INADEQUACY

For these and similar reasons they say that the Earth remains at rest at the middle of the world and that there is no doubt about this. But if someone opines that the Earth revolves, he will also say that the movement is natural and not violent. Now things which are according to nature produce effects contrary to those which are violent. For things to which force or violence is applied get broken up and are unable to subsist for a long time. But things which are caused by nature are in a right condition and are kept in their best organization. Therefore Ptolemy had no reason to fear that the Earth and all things on the Earth would be scattered in a revolution caused by the efficacy of nature, which is greatly different from that of art or from that which can result from the genius of man. But why didn't he feel anxiety about the world instead, whose movement must necessarily be of greater velocity, the greater the heavens are than the Earth? Or have the heavens become so immense, because an unspeakably vehement motion has pulled them away from the centre, and because the heavens would fall if they came to rest anywhere else?

Surely if this reasoning were tenable, the magnitude of the heavens would extend infinitely. For the farther the movement is borne upward by the vehement force, the faster will the movement be, on account of the ever-increasing circumference which must be traversed every twenty-four hours: and conversely, the immensity of the sky would increase with the increase in movement. In this way, the velocity would make the magnitude increase infinitely, and the magnitude the velocity. And in accordance with the axiom of physics that *that which is infinite cannot be traversed or moved in any way*, then the heavens will necessarily come to rest.

But they say that beyond the heavens there isn't any body or place or void or anything at all; and accordingly it is not possible for the heavens to move outward: in that case it is rather surprising that something can be held together by nothing. But if the heavens were infinite and were finite only with respect to a hollow space inside, then it will be said with more truth that there is nothing outside the heavens, since anything [6ᵃ] which occupied any space would be in them; but the heavens will remain immobile. For movement is the most powerful reason wherewith they try to conclude that the universe is finite.

But let us leave to the philosophers of nature the dispute as to whether the world is finite or infinite, and let us hold as certain that the Earth is held together between its two poles and terminates in a spherical surface. Why therefore should we hesitate any longer to grant to it the movement which accords naturally with its form, rather than put the whole world in a commotion—the world whose limits we do not and cannot know? And why not admit that the appearance of daily revolution belongs to the heavens but the reality belongs to the Earth? And things are as when Aeneas said in Virgil: "We sail out of the harbor, and the land and the cities move away." As a matter of fact, when a ship floats on over a tranquil sea, all the things outside seem to the voyagers to be moving in a movement which is the image of their own, and they think on the contrary that they themselves and all the things with them are at rest. So it can easily happen in the case of the movement of the Earth that the whole world should be believed to be moving in a circle. Then what would we say about the clouds and the other things floating in the air or falling or rising up, except that not only the Earth and the watery element with which it is conjoined are moved in this way but also no small part of the air and whatever other things have a similar kinship with the Earth? whether because the neighbouring air, which is mixed with earthly and watery matter, obeys the same nature as the Earth or because the movement of the air is an acquired one, in which it participates without resistance on account of the contiguity and perpetual rotation of the Earth. Conversely, it is no less astonishing for them to say that the highest region of the air follows the celestial movement, as is shown by those stars which appear suddenly—I mean those called "comets" or "bearded stars" by the Greeks. For that place is assigned for their generation; and like all the other stars they rise and set. We can say that that part of the air is deprived of terrestrial motion on account of its great distance from the Earth. Hence the air which is nearest to the Earth and the things floating in it will appear tranquil, unless they are driven to and fro by the wind or some other force, as happens. For how is the wind in the air different from a current in the sea?

But we must confess that in comparison with the world the movement of falling and of rising bodies is twofold and is in general compounded of the rectilinear and the circular. As regards things which move downward on account of their weight [6ᵇ] because they have very much earth in them, doubtless their parts possess the same nature as the whole, and it is for the same reason that fiery bodies are drawn upward with force. For even this earthly fire feeds principally on earthly matter; and they define flame as glowing smoke. Now it is a property of fire to make that which it invades to expand; and it does this with such force that it can be stopped by no means or contrivance from breaking prison and completing its job. Now expanding movement moves away from the

centre to the circumference; and so if some part of the Earth caught on fire, it
would be borne away from the centre and upward. Accordingly, as they say,
a simple body possesses a simple movement—this is first verified in the case of
circular movement—as long as the simple body remain in its unity in its natural
place. In this place, in fact, its movement is none other than the circular, which
remains entirely in itself, as though at rest. Rectilinear movement, however, is
added to those bodies which journey away from their natural place or are shov-
ed out of it or are outside it somehow. But nothing is more repugnant to the
order of the whole and to the form of the world than for anything to be outside
of its place. Therefore rectilinear movement belongs only to bodies which are
not in the right condition and are not perfectly conformed to their nature—
when they are separated from their whole and abandon its unity. Furthermore,
bodies which are moved upward or downward do not possess a simple, uniform,
and regular movement—even without taking into account circular movement.
For they cannot be in equilibrium with their lightness or their force of weight.
And those which fall downward possess a slow movement at the beginning but
increase their velocity as they fall. And conversely we note that this earthly
fire—and we have experience of no other—when carried high up immediately
dies down, as if through the acknowledged agency of the violence of earthly
matter.

Now circular movement always goes on regularly, for it has an unfailing
cause; but [in rectilinear movement] the acceleration stops, because, when the
bodies have reached their own place, they are no longer heavy or light, and so
the movement ends. Therefore, since circular movement belongs to wholes and
rectilinear to parts, we can say that the circular movement stands with the rectilinear, as does animal with sick. And the fact that Aristotle divided simple
movement into three genera: away from the centre, toward the centre, and
around the centre, will be considered merely as an act of reason, just as we distinguish between line, point, and surface, though none of them can subsist without the others or [7ª] without body.

In addition, there is the fact that the state of immobility is regarded as more
noble and godlike than that of change and instability, which for that reason
should belong to the Earth rather than to the world. I add that it seems rather
absurd to ascribe movement to the container or to that which provides the place
and not rather to that which is contained and has a place, i.e., the Earth. And
lastly, since it is clear that the wandering stars are sometimes nearer and sometimes farther away from the Earth, then the movement of one and the same
body around the centre—and they mean the centre of the Earth—will be both
away from the centre and toward the centre. Therefore it is necessary that
movement around the centre should be taken more generally; and it should be
enough if each movement is in accord with its own centre. You see therefore that
for all these reasons it is more probable that the Earth moves than that it is at
rest—especially in the case of the daily revolution, as it is the Earth's very own.
And I think that is enough as regards the first part of the question.

9. Whether Many Movements Can Be Attributed to the Earth, and Concerning the Centre of the World

Therefore, since nothing hinders the mobility of the Earth, I think we should
now see whether more than one movement belongs to it, so that it can be re-

garded as one of the wandering stars. For the apparent irregular movement of the planets and their variable distances from the Earth—which cannot be understood as occurring in circles homocentric with the Earth—make it clear that the Earth is not the centre of their circular movements. Therefore, since there are many centres, it is not foolhardy to doubt whether the centre of gravity of the Earth rather than some other is the centre of the world. I myself think that gravity or heaviness is nothing except a certain natural appetency implanted in the parts by the divine providence of the universal Artisan, in order that they should unite with one another in their oneness and wholeness and come together in the form of a globe. It is believable that this affect is present in the sun, moon, and the other bright planets and that through its efficacy they remain in the spherical figure in which they are visible, though they nevertheless accomplish their circular movements in many different ways. Therefore if the Earth too possesses movements different from the one around its centre, then they will necessarily be movements which similarly appear on the outside in the many bodies; and we find the yearly revolution among these movements. For if the annual revolution were changed from being solar to being terrestrial, and immobility were granted to the sun, [7ᵇ] the risings and settings of the signs and of the fixed stars—whereby they become morning or evening stars—will appear in the same way; and it will be seen that the stoppings, retrogressions, and progressions of the wandering stars are not their own, but are a movement of the Earth and that they borrow the appearances of this movement. Lastly, the sun will be regarded as occupying the centre of the world. And the ratio of order in which these bodies succeed one another and the harmony of the whole world teaches us their truth, if only—as they say—we would look at the thing with both eyes.

10. On the Order of the Celestial Orbital Circles

I know of no one who doubts that the heavens of the fixed stars is the highest up of all visible things. We see that the ancient philosophers wished to take the order of the planets according to the magnitude of their revolutions, for the reason that among things which are moved with equal speed those which are the more distant seem to be borne along more slowly, as Euclid proves in his *Optics*. And so they think that the moon traverses its circle in the shortest period of time, because being next to the Earth, it revolves in the smallest circle. But they think that Saturn, which completes the longest circuit in the longest period of time, is the highest. Beneath Saturn, Jupiter. After Jupiter, Mars.

There are different opinions about Venus and Mercury, in that they do not have the full range of angular elongations from the sun that the others do[1]. Wherefore some place them above the sun, as Timaeus does in Plato; some, beneath the sun, as Ptolemy and a good many moderns. Alpetragius makes Venus higher than the sun and Mercury lower. Accordingly, as the followers of Plato suppose that all the planets—which are otherwise dark bodies—shine with light received from the sun, they think that if the planets were below the sun, they would on account of their slight distance from the sun be viewed as only half—or at any rate as only partly—spherical. For the light which they receive is re-

[1]The greatest angular elongation of Venus from the sun is approximately 45°; that of Mercury, approximately 24°; while Saturn, Jupiter, and Mars have the full range of possible angular elongation, *i.e.*, up to 180°.

flected by them upward for the most part, *i.e.*, towards the sun, as we see in the
case of the new moon or the old. Moreover, they say that necessarily the sun
would sometimes be obscured through their interposition and that its light
would be eclipsed in proportion to their magnitude; and as that has never appeared to take place, they think that these planets cannot by any means be below the sun[1].

On the contrary, those who place Venus and Mercury below the sun claim as
a reason the amplitude of the space which they find between the sun and the
moon. [8ª] For they find that the greatest distance between the Earth and the
moon, *i.e.*, 64⅙ units, whereof the radius of the Earth is one, is contained almost
18 times in the least distance between the sun and the Earth. This distance is
1160 such units, and therefore the distance between the sun and the moon is
1096 such units. And then, in order for such a vast space not to remain empty,
they find that the intervals between the perigees and apogees—according to
which they reason out the thickness of the spheres[2]—add up to approximately
the same sum: in such fashion that the apogee of the moon may be succeeded by
the perigee of Mercury, that the apogee of Mercury may be followed by the
perigee of Venus, and that finally the apogee of Venus may nearly touch the
perigee of the sun. In fact they calculate that the interval between the perigee
and the apogee of Mercury contains approximately 177½ of the aforesaid units
and that the remaining space is nearly filled by the 910 units of the interval between the perigee and apogee of Venus[3]. Therefore they do not admit that these
planets have a certain opacity, like that of the moon; but that they shine either
by their own proper light or because their entire bodies are impregnated with
sunlight, and that accordingly they do not obscure the sun, because it is an extremely rare occurrence for them to be interposed between our sight and the
sun, as they usually withdraw [from the sun] latitudinally. In addition, there is
the fact that they are small bodies in comparison with the sun, since Venus even

[1]The transit of Venus across the face of the sun was first observed—
by means of a telescope—in 1639.
[2]That is to say, the thickness of the sphere would be measured by the
ratio of the diameter of the epicycle to the diameter of the sphere, or, in
the accompanying diagram, by the distance between the inmost and the
outmost of the three homocentric circles.
[3]The succession of the orbital circles according to their perigees and
apogees may be represented in the following diagram, which has been
drawn to scale.

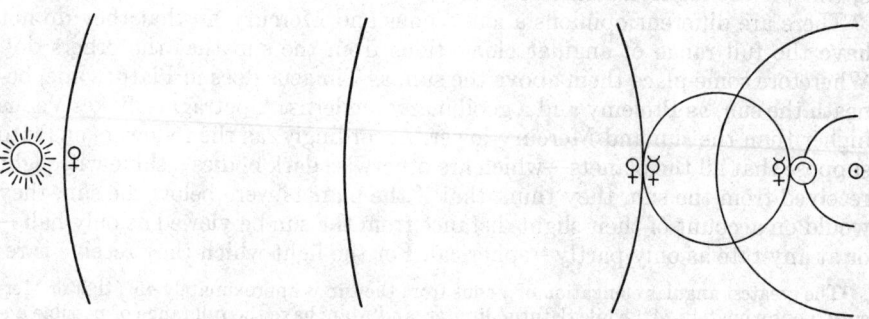

though larger than Mercury can cover scarcely one one-hundredth part of the sun, as al-Battani the Harranite maintains, who holds that the diameter of the sun is ten times greater, and therefore it would not be easy to see such a little speck in the midst of such beaming light. Averroes, however, in his paraphrase of Ptolemy records having seen something blackish, when he observed the conjunction of the sun and Mercury which he had computed. And so they judge that these two planets move below the solar circle.

But how uncertain and shaky this reasoning is, is clear from the fact that though the shortest distance of the moon is 38 units whereof the radius of the Earth is one unit—according to Ptolemy, but more than 49 such units by a truer evaluation, as will be shown below—nevertheless we do not know that this great space contains anything except air, or if you prefer, what they call the fiery element.

Moreover, there is the fact that the diameter of the epicycle of Venus—by reason of which Venus has an angular digression of approximately 45° on either side of the sun—would have to be six times greater than the distance from the centre of the Earth to its perigee, as will be shown in the proper place[1]. Then what will they say is contained in all this apace, which [8ᵇ] is so great as to take in the Earth, air, ether, moon and Mercury, and which moreover the vast epicycle of Venus would occupy if it revolved around an immobile Earth?

Furthermore, how unconvincing is Ptolemy's argument that the sun must occupy the middle position between those planets which have the full range of angular elongation from the sun and those which do not is clear from the fact that the moon's full range of angular elongation proves its falsity.

But what cause will those who place Venus below the sun, and Mercury next, or separate them in some other order—what cause will they allege why these planets do not also make longitudinal circuits separate and independent of the sun, like the other planets[2]—if indeed the ratio of speed or slowness does not falsify their order? Therefore it will be necessary either for the Earth not to be the centre to which the order of the planets and their orbital circles is referred, or for there to be no sure reason for their order and for it not to be apparent why the highest place is due to Saturn rather than to Jupiter or some other planet. Wherefore I judge that what Martianus Capella—who wrote the *Encyclopedia* —and some other Latins took to be the case is by no means to be despised. For they hold that Venus and Mercury circle around the sun as a centre; and they hold that for this reason Venus and Mercury do not have any farther elongation

---

[1]According to Ptolemy, the ratio of the radius of Venus' epicycle to the radius of its eccentric is between 2 to 3 and 3 to 4, or approximately 43⅙ to 60. Now since at perigee the epicycle subtracts from the mean distance, or radius of the eccentric circle, that which at apogee it adds to the mean distance, the ratio of Venus' distance at perigee to its distance at apogee is approximately 1 to 6. That is to say, in the passage from apogee to perigee, the ratio of increase in the apparent magnitude of the planet should be approximately 36 to 1, as the apparent magnitude varies inversely in the ratio of the square of the distance. But no such increase in the magnitude of the planet is apparent. This opposition between an appearance and the consequences of an hypothesis made to save another appearance is still present within Copernicus' own scheme.

[2]Ptolemy makes the centres of the epicycles of Venus and Mercury travel around the Earth longitudinally at the same rate as the mean sun, and in such fashion that the mean sun is always on the straight line extending from the centre of the Earth through the centres of their epicycles, while the centres of the epicycles of the upper planets may be at any angular distance from the mean sun.

from the sun than the convexity of their orbital circles permits; for they do not make a circle around the earth as do the others, but have perigee and apogee interchangeable [in the sphere of the fixed stars]. Now what do they mean except that the centre of their spheres is around the sun? Thus the orbital circle of Mercury will be enclosed within the orbital circle of Venus— which would have to be more than twice as large—and will find adequate room for itself within that amplitude[1]. Therefore if anyone should take this as an occasion to refer Saturn, Jupiter, and Mars also to this same centre, provided he understands the magnitude of those orbital circles to be such as to comprehend and encircle the Earth remaining within them, he would not be in error, as the table of ratios of their movements makes clear[2]. For it is manifest that the planets are always nearer the Earth at the time of their evening rising, *i.e.*, when they are opposite to the sun and the Earth is in the middle between them and the sun. But they are farthest away from the Earth at the time of their evening setting, *i.e.*, when they are occulted in the neighbourhood of the sun, namely, when we have the sun between them and the Earth. All that shows clearly enough that their centre is more directly related to the sun and is the same as

---

[1]As in the following diagram which has been drawn to scale.

[2]Take the case of Mars. In Ptolemy, the ratio of its epicycle to its eccentric is $39\frac{1}{2}$ to 60, or approximately 2 to 3. Mars has 37 cycles of anomaly, or movement on the epicycle, and 42 cycles of longitude, or movement of the epicycle on the eccentric, in 79 solar years; or for the sake of easiness let us say that the ratio

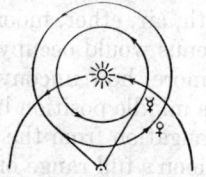

of the sun's movement to either of the planets' two movements is 2 to 1. Copernicus is here suggesting that if the centre of the planet's movement is placed around the moving sun, then the Ptolemaic cycles of anomaly will represent the number of times the sun has overtaken the planet in longitude: thus the 37 cycles of anomaly plus the 42 cycles of longitude add up to the 79 solar revolutions. That is to say, the sun will now be traveling around the Earth on a circle which has the same relative magnitude as the Martian epicycle in Ptolemy and bears an epicycle having the same relative magnitude as Ptolemy's Martian eccentric circle, on which epicycle Mars travels in the opposite direction at half the speed of the sun. Under both hypotheses the appearances from the Earth will be the same, as can be seen in the following diagrams.

For according to the Ptolemaic hypothesis, let the Earth be at the center of the approximately homocentric circles of the sun, Mars, and the ecliptic. Let the radius of the planet's epicycle be to the radius of the planet's eccentric as 2 to 3. Now, first, let the sun be viewed at the beginning of Leo, and let the planet at the perigee of its epicycle be viewed at the beginning of Aquarius, in opposition to the sun. Next, let the sun move 240° eastwards, to the beginning of Aries; and during the same interval let the epicycle move 120° eastwards, to the beginning of Gemini, and the planet 120° eastwards on the epicycle. Now the planet will be found to appear in Taurus, about 36° west of the sun.

But if according to the semi-Copernican hypothesis, the sun is made to revolve around the Earth on a circle having the same relative magnitude as Mars' Ptolemaic epicycle, while Mars is placed on an epicycle which has the same relative magnitude as its Ptolemaic eccentric and has its centre at the sun; and if the apparent positions of Mars and the sun are first the same as before, and the sun moves 240° eastwards, bearing along the deferent of that to which Venus and Mercury refer their revolutions[1]. But as they all have one common centre, it is necessary that the space left between the convex orbital circle of Venus and the concave orbital circle of Mars should be viewed as an orbital circle [9ª] or sphere homocentric with them in respect to both surfaces, and that it should receive the Earth and its satellite the moon and whatever is contained beneath the lunar globe. For we can by no means separate the moon from the Earth, as the moon is incontestably very near to the Earth—especially since we find in this expanse a place for the moon which is proper enough and sufficiently large. Therefore we are not ashamed to maintain that this totality— which the moon embraces—and the centre of the Earth too traverse that great orbital circle among the other wandering stars in an annual revolution around the sun; and that the centre of the world is around the sun. I also say that the sun remains forever immobile and that whatever apparent movement belongs to it can be verified of the mobility of the Earth; that the magnitude of the world is such that, although the distance from the sun to the Earth in relation

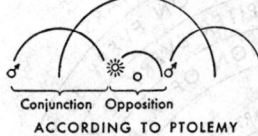

Conjunction   Opposition
ACCORDING TO PTOLEMY

[1]Copernicus is asking what reason there is why the planets are always found to be at their apogees at the time of conjunction with the sun, and at their perigees at the time of opposition, since according to the Ptolemaic scheme the reverse is also possible—as is evident from the accompanying diagram.

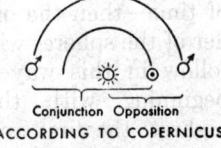

Conjunction   Opposition
ACCORDING TO COPERNICUS

But if the sun and not the Earth is the centre of the planet's movements, the reason is obvious.

Mars, while Mars moves 120° westwards on its epicycle; then Mars will once more be found to appear in Taurus, approximately 36° west of the sun.

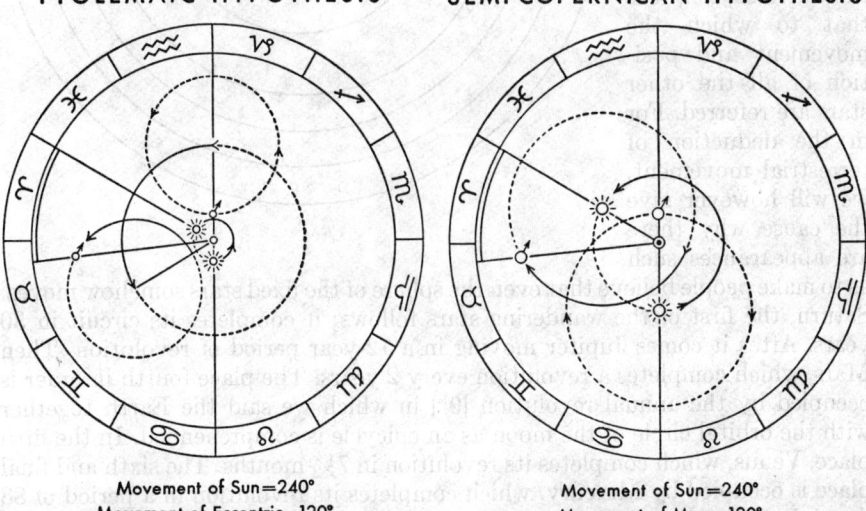

PTOLEMAIC HYPOTHESIS   SEMI-COPERNICAN HYPOTHESIS

Movement of Sun=240°
Movement of Eccentric=120°
Movement of Epicycle=120°

Movement of Sun=240°
Movement of Mars=120°

to whatsoever planetary sphere you please possesses magnitude which is sufficiently manifest in proportion to these dimensions, this distance, as compared with the sphere of the fixed stars, is imperceptible. I find it much more easy to grant that than to unhinge the understanding by an almost infinite multitude of spheres—as those who keep the earth at the centre of the world are forced to do. But we should rather follow the wisdom of nature, which, as it takes very great care not to have produced anything superfluous or useless, often prefers to endow one thing with many effects. And though all these things are difficult, almost inconceivable, and quite contrary to the opinion of the multitude, nevertheless in what follows we will with God's help make them clearer than day—at least for those who are not ignorant of the art of mathematics.

Therefore if the first law is still safe—for no one will bring forward a better one than that the magnitude of the orbital circles should be measured by the magnitude of time—then the order of the spheres will follow in this way—beginning with the highest: the first and highest of all is the sphere of the fixed stars, which comprehends itself and all things, and is accordingly immovable. In fact it is the place of the universe, *i.e.*, it is that to which the movement and position of all the other stars are referred. For in the deduction of terrestrial movement, we will however give the cause why there are appearances such

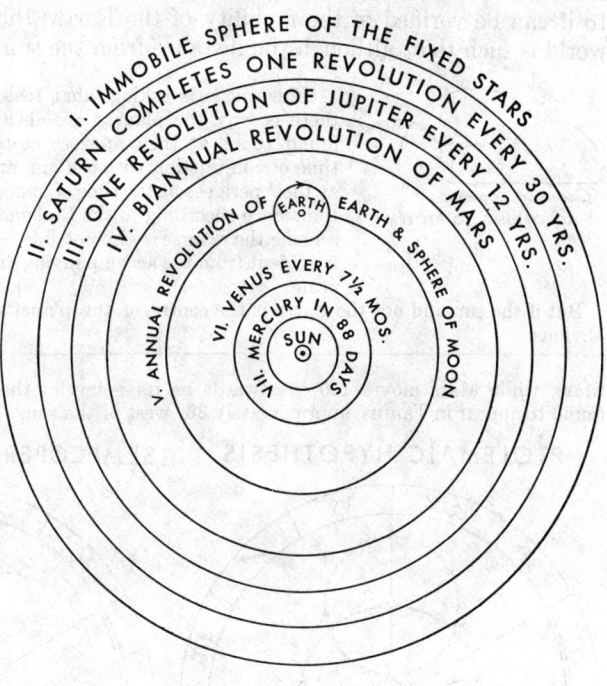

as to make people believe that even the sphere of the fixed stars somehow moves. Saturn, the first of the wandering stars follows; it completes its circuit in 30 years. After it comes Jupiter moving in a 12-year period of revolution. Then Mars, which completes a revolution every 2 years. The place fourth in order is occupied by the annual revolution [9^{b}] in which we said the Earth together with the orbital circle of the moon as an epicycle is comprehended. In the fifth place, Venus, which completes its revolution in 7½ months. The sixth and final place is occupied by Mercury, which completes its revolution in a period of 88 days[1]. In the center of all rests the sun. For who would place this lamp of a very

[1]In order to see how Copernicus derived the length of his periods of revolution, consider the following Ptolemaic ratios for the lower planets:

beautiful temple in another or better place than this wherefrom it can illuminate everything at the same time? As a matter of fact, not unhappily do some call it the lantern; others, the mind and still others, the pilot of the world. Trismegistus calls it a "visible god"; Sophocles' Electra, "that which gazes up-

	Cycles of anomaly	Cycles of longitude	Solar years
Mercury	145	46+	46+
Venus	5	8−	8−

It is noteworthy that the number of cycles of longitude in one year is equal to the number of solar cycles. Moreover, the two planets have a limited angular elongation from the sun. In order to explain these two peculiar appearances Copernicus sets the Earth in motion on the circumference of a circle which encloses the orbits of Venus and Mercury, with the sun at the centre of all three orbits. Thus the planet's cycles of anomaly in so many years become the number of times the planet has overtaken the Earth, as they revolve around the sun. That is to say, in so many solar years the planet will have traveled around the sun a number of times which is equal to the sum of its cycles of anomaly and its cycles in longitude. Thus, for example, Venus travels around the sun approximately 13 times in 8 solar years; hence its period of revolution is approximately 7½ months; and similarly, that of Mercury is approximately 88 days—although for some obscure reason Copernicus actually writes down 9 months for Venus (*nono mense reducitur*) and 80 days for Mercury (*octaginta dierum spatio circumcurrens*).

The reader may intuit from the following diagrams the equipollence, with respect to the appearances, of the Ptolemaic and the Copernican explanations of the movement of Venus.

COPERNICAN HYPOTHESIS

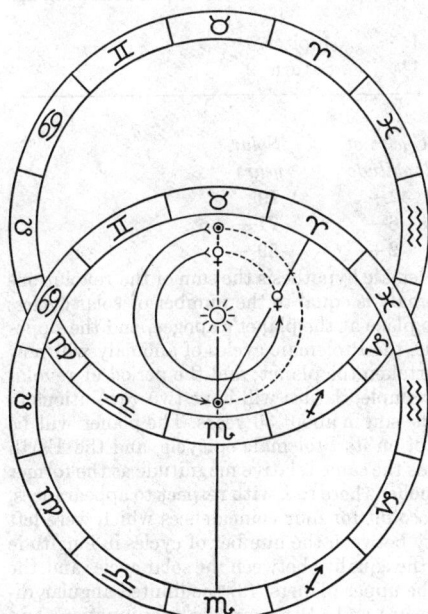

Movement of Earth=180°
Movement of Venus=292½°

Now, on Ptolemy's hypothesis, let the Earth be placed at the centre of the ecliptic, the solar circle, and the orbital circle of Venus, which carries the planetary epicycle. The radius of the epicycle is to that of the orbital circle approximately as 3 is to 4. First let the sun be situated at the middle of Scorpio, and let Venus be in conjunction with the sun and at the perigee of its epicycle. Next let the sun move 180° eastwards to the middle of Taurus, and similarly the centre of the epicycle; during this same interval the planet will move 112½° eastwards on its epicycle and will be found to appear in the middle of Aries approximately, or 30° west of the sun.

But according to the Copernican hypothesis, let us place the sun at the centre of the orbital circles of Venus and the Earth, which preserve the relative magnitudes of the Ptolemaic epicycle and orbital circle of Venus, but let us keep the Earth at the centre of the ecliptic, as far as appearances go, since the distance between the Earth and the sun is imperceptible in comparison with the magnitude of the sphere of the fixed stars. Now if the Earth is placed in the middle of Taurus, as viewed from the sun, and the planet at its perigee between the Earth and the sun, in such fashion that Venus and the sun would appear in the middle of Scorpio, while Venus moves eastwards 292½°, then the sun will be found to appear in the middle of Taurus, and the planet itself in middle of Aries or 30° west of the sun.

on all things." And so the sun, as if resting on a kingly throne, governs the family of stars which wheel around. Moreover, the Earth is by no means cheated of the services of the moon; but, as Aristotle says in the *De Animalibus*, the earth has the closest kinship with the moon. The Earth moreover is fertilized by the sun and conceives offspring every year.

Therefore in this ordering we find [10ª] that the world has a wonderful commensurability and that there is a sure bond of harmony for the movement and magnitude of the orbital circles such as cannot be found in any other way[1]. For now the careful observer can note why progression and retrogradation appear greater in Jupiter than in Saturn and smaller than in Mars; and in turn greater

[1]Let us recall the Ptolemaic ratios between the radius of the epicycle and that of the eccentric circle, and also the eccentricity.

	Epicycle	Eccentric	Eccentricity
Mercury	22½	60	3
Venus	43⅙	60	1¼
Mars	39½	60	6
Jupiter	11½	60	2⅔
Saturn	6½	60	3¼

By the Ptolemaic scheme it is impossible to compute the magnitudes of the eccentric circles themselves relative to one another, as there is no common measure. But now that the eccentric circles of Mercury and Venus and the epicycles of Mars, Jupiter, and Saturn have all been reduced to the orbital circle of the Earth, it is easy to calculate the relative magnitudes of the orbital circles—heretofore the epicycles of the lower planets and the eccentric circles of the upper—since, by reason of the necessary commensurability between epicycle and eccentric, they are all commensurable with the orbital circle of the Earth. Thus, for example, if we take the distance from the Earth to the sun as 1, the planets will observe the following approximate distances from the sun.

Mercury ⅓	Earth 1	Jupiter 5
Venus ¾	Mars 1½	Saturn 9

But let us turn to the three upper planets.

	Cycles of anomaly	Cycles of longitude	Solar years
Mars	37	42+	79
Jupiter	65	6—	71—
Saturn	57	2+	59—

It is here noteworthy that according to the Ptolemaic hypothesis the sum of the revolutions of the eccentric circle and the revolutions in anomaly is equal to the number of solar cycles; and also that, the conjunctions with the sun take place at the planet's apogee, and the oppositions at its perigee. But according to Copernicus the Ptolemaic cycles of anomaly will now represent the number of times the Earth has overtaken the planet; and the period of revolution in longitude will stay the same. Thus, for example, Saturn will have two revolutions in longitude in 59 years, or one revolution around the sun in about 30 years. The planet will be revolving directly on its eccentric circle instead of on its Ptolemaic epicycle, and the Earth will now be revolving on an inner circle which has the same relative magnitude as the former epicycle. The two hypotheses, of course, are equipollent here too, with respect to appearances.

In other words, in constructing a theory to account for four coincidences which were left unexplained by Ptolemy, namely, (1) the equality between the number of cycles in longitude and the solar cycles, in the two lower planets; (2) the equality between the solar cycles and the sum of the cycles of anomaly and longitude, in the upper planets; (3) the limited angular digressions of Mercury and Venus away from the sun; and (4) the apogeal conjunctions and perigeal oppositions of Saturn, Jupiter, and Mars; Copernicus has telescoped the eccentric circle of Venus and that of Mercury into one circle carrying the Earth; and he has furthermore collapsed the three epicycles of Saturn, Jupiter, and Mars into this same one circle. That is to say, one circle is now doing the work of five.

in Venus than in Mercury[1]. And why these reciprocal events appear more often in Saturn than in Jupiter, and even less often in Mars and Venus than in Mercury[2]. In addition, why when Saturn, Jupiter, and Mars are in opposition [to the mean position of the sun] they are nearer to the Earth than at the time of their occultation and their reappearance. And especially why at the times when Mars is in opposition to the sun, it seems to equal Jupiter in magnitude and to be distinguished from Jupiter only by a reddish color, but when discovered through careful observation by means of a sextant is found with difficulty among the stars of second magnitude[3]? All these things proceed from the same cause, which resides in the movement of the Earth.

But that there are no such appearances among the fixed stars argues that they are at an immense height away, which makes the circle of annual movement or its image disappear from before our eyes since every visible thing has a certain distance beyond which it is no longer seen, as is shown in optics. For the brilliance of their lights shows that there is a very great distance between Saturn the highest of the planets and the sphere of the fixed stars. It is by this mark in particular that they are distinguished from the planets, as it is proper to have the greatest difference between the moved and the unmoved. How exceedingly fine is the godlike work of the Best and Greatest Artist!

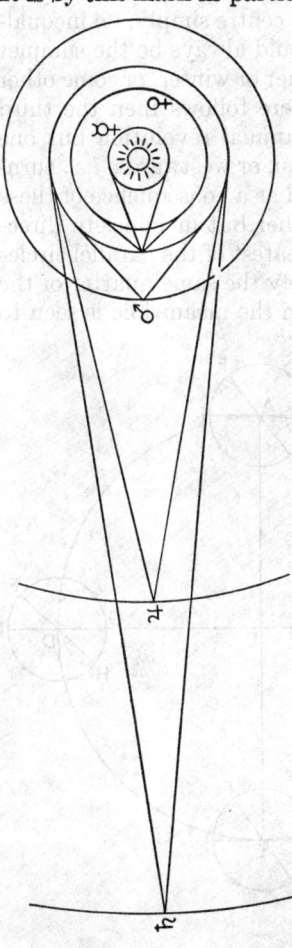

11. A Demonstration of the Threefold Movement of the Earth

Therefore since so much and such great testimony on the part of the planets is consonant with the mobility of the Earth, we shall now give a summary of its movement, insofar as the appear-

[1]In the three upper planets, the angles which measure the apparent progression and retrogradation have as their vertex the centre of the planet and as their sides the tangents drawn to the orbital circle of the Earth. In the two lower planets, however, the vertex of the angle is at the centre of the Earth and the sides are the tangents drawn to the orbital circle of the planet. It is easy to see that, on account of the relative magnitudes of the orbital circles, the arcs of progression and retrogradation will appear smaller in Saturn than in Jupiter, and smaller in Jupiter than in Mars, and greater in Venus than in Mercury.

[2]The interchanges of progression and retrogradation are proportional to the number of times the Earth overtakes the outer planets and the inner planets overtake the Earth. Now the Earth overtakes Saturn more often than Jupiter, Jupiter more often than Mars, Mars more often than overtaken by Venus, and overtaken less often by Venus than by Mercury. Hence the frequency of progression and retrogradation is in that order.

[3]According to the Ptolemaic scheme, it can be inferred only from the changes in magnitude of the planet Mars what its relative distances from the Earth are at perigee and apogee. But according to the Copernican scheme, it follows from the relative distances of the planet at perigee and at apogee—which are as 1 to 5—that the apparent diameter of the planet should vary inversely in that ratio— assuming that the planet could be seen when in conjunction with the sun.

ances can be shown forth by its movement as by an hypothesis. We must allow a threefold movement altogether.

The first—which we said the Greeks called νυχΘημέρινος— is the proper circuit of day and night, which goes around the axis of the earth from west to east —as the world is held to move in the opposite direction—and describes the equator or the equinoctial circle—which some, imitating the Greek expression [10ᵇ] ἰσηέρινος, call the equidial.

The second is the annual movement of the centre, which describes the circle of the [zodiacal] signs around the sun similarly from west to east, *i.e.*, towards the signs which follow [from Aries to Taurus] and moves along between Venus and Mars, as we said, together with the bodies accompanying it. So it happens that the sun itself seems to traverse the ecliptic with a similar movement. In this way, for example, when the centre of the Earth is traversing Capricorn, the sun seems to be crossing Cancer; and when Aquarius, Leo, and so on, as we were saying.

It has to be understood that the equator and the axis of the Earth have a variable inclination with the circle and the plane of the ecliptic. For if they remained fixed and only followed the movement of the centre simply, no inequality of days and nights would be apparent, but it would always be the summer solstice or the winter solstice or the equinox, or summer or winter, or some other season of the year always remaining the same. There follows then the third movement, which is the declination: it is also an annual revolution but one towards the signs which precede [from Aries to Pisces], or westwards, *i.e.*, turning back counter to the movement of the centre; and as a consequence of these two movements which are nearly equal to one another but in opposite directions, it follows that the axis of the Earth and the greatest of the parallel circles on it, the equator, always look towards approximately the same quarter of the world, just as if they remained immobile. The sun in the meanwhile is seen to move along the oblique ec-

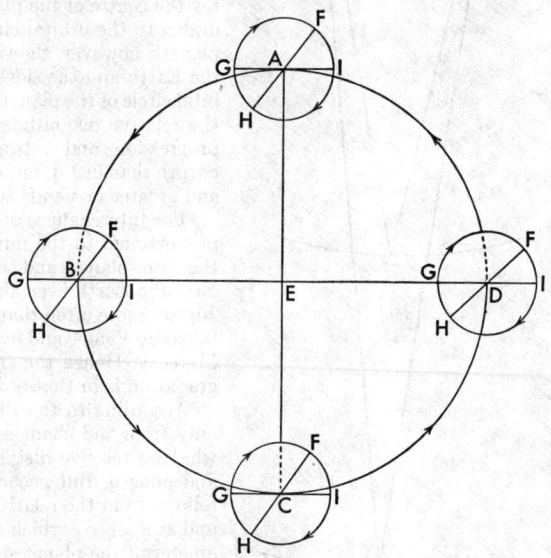

liptic with that movement with which the centre of the earth moves, just as if the centre of the earth were the centre of the world—provided you remember that the distance between the sun and the earth in comparison with the sphere of the fixed stars is imperceptible to us.

Since these things are such that they need to be presented to sight rather than merely to be talked about, let us draw the circle *ABCD*, which will represent the annual circuit of the centre of the earth in the plane of the ecliptic, and let *E* be the sun around its centre. I will cut this circle into four equal parts by means of the diameters AEC and BED. Let the point A be the beginning of Cancer; B of Libra; E of Capricorn; and D of Aries. Now let us put the centre of the earth first at A, around which we shall describe the terrestrial equator $FGHI$, but not in the same plane [as the ecliptic] except that the diameter GAI is the common section of the circles, i.e., of the e-quator and the ecliptic. Also let the diameter FAH be drawn at right angles to GAI; and let F be the limit of the greatest southward declination [of the equa-tor], and H of the northward declination. With this set-up, the Earth-dweller will see the sun—which is at the centre E—at the point of the winter solstice in Capricorn—[11a] which is caused by the greatest northward declination at H being turned toward the sun; since the inclination of the equator with respect to line AE describes by means of the daily revolution the winter tropic, which is parallel to the equator at the distance comprehended by the angle of inclination EAH. Now let the centre of the Earth proceed from west to east; and let F, the limit of greatest declination, have just as great a movement from east to west, until at B both of them have traversed quadrants of circles. Meanwhile, on ac-count of the equality of the revolutions, angle EAI will always remain equal to angle AEB; the diameters will always stay parallel to one another—FAH to FBH and GAI to GBI; and the equator will remain parallel to the equator. And by reason of the cause spoken of many times already, these lines will appear in the immensity of the sky as the same. Therefore from the point B the beginning of Libra, E will appear to be in Aries, and the common section of the two circles [of the ecliptic and the equator] will fall upon line $GBIE$, in respect to which the daily revolution has no declination; but every declination will be on one side or the other of this line. And so the sun will be soon in the spring equinox. Let the centre of the Earth advance under the same conditions; and when it has completed [11b] a semicircle at C, the sun will appear to be entering Cancer. But since F the southward declination of the equator is now turned toward the sun, the result is that the sun is seen in the north, traversing the summer tropic in accordance with angle of inclination ECF. Again, when F moves on through the third quadrant of the circle, the common section GI will fall on line ED; whence the sun, seen in Libra, will appear to have reached the autumn equinox. But then as, in the same progressive movement, HF gradually turns in the direction of the sun, it will make the situation at the beginning return, which was our point of departure.

In another way: Again in the underlying plane let AEC be both the diameter [of the ecliptic] and its common section with the circle perpendic-ular to its plane. In this circle let $DGFI$, the meri-dian passing through the poles of the Earth be

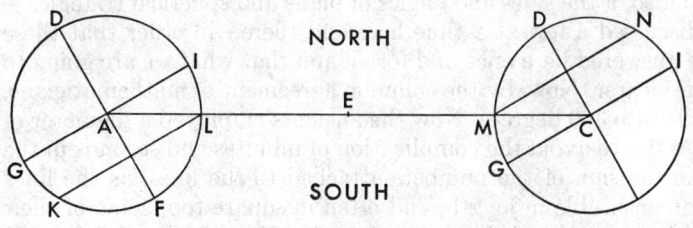

described around A and C, in turn, i.e., in Cancer and in Capricorn. And let the axis of the Earth be DF, the north pole D, the south pole F, and GI the di-ameter of the equator. Therefore when F is turned in the direction of the sun, which is at E, and the inclination of the equator is northward in proportion to angle *IAE*, then the movement around the axis will describe—with the diameter *KL* and at the distance *LI*—parallel to the equator the southern circle, which appears with respect to the sun as the tropic of Capricorn. Or—to speak more correctly—this movement around the axis describes, in the direction of *AE*, a conic surface, which has the centre of the earth as its vertex and a circle parallel to the equator as its base[1]. Moreover in the opposite sign, *C*, the same things take place but conversely. Therefore it is clear how the two mutually opposing movements, *i.e.*, that of the centre and that of the inclination, force the axis of the Earth to remain balanced in the same way and to keep a similar position, and how they make all things appear as if they were movements of the sun.

Now we said that the yearly revolutions of the centre and of the declination were approximately equal, because if they were exactly so, then the points of equinox and solstice and the obliquity of the ecliptic in relation to the sphere of the fixed stars could not change at all. But as the difference is very slight, [12ª] it is not revealed except as it increases with time: as a matter of fact, from the time of Ptolemy to ours there has been a precession of the equinoxes and solstices of about 21°. For that reason some have believed that the sphere of the fixed stars was moving, and so they choose a ninth higher sphere. And when that was not enough, the moderns added a tenth, but without attaining the end which we hope we shall attain by means of the movement of the Earth. We shall use this movement as a principle and a hypothesis in demonstrating other things.

12. On the Straight Lines in a Circle

Because the proofs which we shall use in almost the entire work deal with straight lines and arcs, with plane and spherical triangles, and because Euclid's *Elements*, although they clear up much of this, do not have what is here most required, namely, how to find the sides from the angles and the angles from the sides, since the angle does not measure the subtending straight line—just as the line does not measure the angle—but the arc does, there has accordingly been found a method whereby the lines subtending any arc may become known. By means of these lines, or chords, it is possible to determine the arc corresponding to the angle: and conversely by means of the arc to determine the straight line, or chord, which subtends the angle. So it does not seem irrelevant, if we treat of these lines, and also of the sides and angles of plane and spherical triangles— which Ptolemy discussed a few at a time here and there—in order that these questions may be answered here once and for all and that what we are going to teach may become clearer. Now, by the common agreement of mathematicians, we divide the circle into 360 degrees. Now the ancients employed a diameter of 120 parts. But in order to avoid the complication of minutes and seconds in the multiplication and division of the numbers attached to the lines, as the lines are usually incommensurable in length, and often in square too; some of their successors established a rational diameter of 1,200,000 parts or of 2,000,000 parts, or of some other rational quantity—from the time when Arabic numerals

---

[1]Or, in other words, the axis of the terrestrial equator describes around the axis of the terrestrial ecliptic a double conic surface having its vertices at the centre of the Earth, in a period of revolution equal approximately to that of the Earth's centre.

came into general use. This mathematical notation surpasses any other—Greek or Latin—[12^b] in a certain singular ease of employment and readily accommodates itself to every class of computation. For that reason we too have taken a division of the diameter into 200,000 parts as sufficient to exclude any very noticeable error. For as regards things which are not related as number to number, it is enough to attain a close approximation. But we will unfold this in six theorems and a problem—following Ptolemy fairly closely.

FIRST THEOREM

The diameter of a circle being given, the sides of the triangle, tetragon, hexagon, and decagon, which the same circle circumscribes, are also given.

Half the diameter, or the radius, is equal to the side of the hexagon, [Euclid, IV, 15]; the square on the side of the triangle is three times the square on the side of the hexagon, [Euclid, XIII, 12]; and the square on the side of the tetragon is twice the square on the side of the hexagon, Euclid as is shown in Euclid's *Elements* [IV, 9 and I, 47]. Therefore the side of a hexagon is given in length as 100,000 parts, that of the tetragon as 141,422 parts, and that of the triangle as 173,205 parts.

Now let AB be the side of the hexagon; and by Euclid, II, 11, or VI, 30, let it be cut in mean and extreme ratio at point C; and let CB be the greater segment to which its equal BD is added. Therefore the whole ABD will have been cut in extreme and mean ratio, and the lesser segment BD will be the side of the decagon inscribed in the circle, and AB will be the side of the inscribed hexagon, as is made clear by Euclid, XIII, 5 and 9.

But BD will be given in this way: let AB be bisected at E, and it will be clear from Euclid, XIII, 3 that

$$\text{sq. } EBD = 5 \text{ sq. } EB.$$

But

$$EB = 50,000.$$

Whence

$$5 \text{ sq. } EB \text{ is given.}$$

Hence

$$EBD = 111,803.$$

And

$$BD = EBD - EB = 111,803 - 50,000 = 61,803,$$

which is the side of the decagon sought.

Moreover the side of the pentagon, the square on which is equal to the sum of the squares on the side of the hexagon and on the side of the decagon [*Elements*, XIII, 10], is given as 117,557 parts.

Therefore the diameter of the circle being given, the sides of the triangle, tetragon, pentagon, hexagon and decagon, which may be inscribed in the same circle, have been given—as was to be shown.

PORISM

Furthermore, it is clear that when the chord subtending an arc has been given, that chord too can be found which subtends the rest [13^a] of the semicircle.

Since the angle in a semicircle is right, and in right triangles the square on the chord subtending the right angle, *i.e.*, the square on the diameter, is equal to the sum of the squares on the sides comprehending the right angle; therefore —since the side of the decagon, which subtends 36° of the circumference, has been shown to have 61,803 parts whereof the diameter has 200,000 parts—the chord which subtends the remaining 144° of the semicircle has 190,211 parts.

And in the case of the side of the pentagon, which is equal to 117,557 parts of the diameter and subtends an arc of 72°, a straight line of 161,803 parts is given, and it subtends remaining 108° of the circle.

SECOND THEOREM

If a quadrilateral is inscribed in a circle, the rectangle comprehended by the diagonals is equal to the two rectangles which are comprehended by the two pairs of opposite sides.

For let the quadrilateral $ABCD$ be inscribed in a circle; I say that the rectangle comprehended by the diagonals AC and DB is equal to those comprehended by AB, CD and by AD, BC.

For let us make

$$\text{angle } ABE = \text{angle } CBD.$$

Therefore by addition

$$\text{angle } ABD = \text{angle } EBC,$$

taking angle EBD as common to both. Moreover

$$\text{angle } ACB = \text{angle } BDA.$$

because they stand on the same segment of the circle; and accordingly the two similar triangles BCE and BDA will have their sides proportional. Hence

$$BC : BD = EC : AD.$$

And

$$\text{rect. } EC, BD = \text{rect. } BC, AD.$$

But also the triangles ABE and CBD are similar, because

$$\text{angle } ABE = \text{angle } CBD.$$

And

$$\text{angle } BAC = \text{angle } BDC,$$

because they intercept the same arc of the circle. So again,

$$AB : BD = AE : CD$$

And

$$\text{rect. } AB, DC = \text{rect. } AE, BD.$$

But it has already been made clear that

$$\text{rect. } AD, BC = \text{rect. } BD, EC.$$

Accordingly, taken as a whole,

$$\text{rect. } BD, AC = \text{rect. } AD, BC + \text{rect. } AB, CD,$$

as it was opportune to have shown.

THIRD THEOREM

Hence if straight lines subtending unequal arcs in a semicircle are given, the chord subtending the arc whereby the greater arc exceeds the smaller is also given.

[13ᵇ] In the semicircle $ABCD$ with diameter AD, let the straight lines AB and AC subtending unequal arcs be given. To us, who wish to discover the chord subtending BC, there are given by means of the aforesaid the chords BD and CD subtending the remaining arcs of the semicircle, and these chords bound

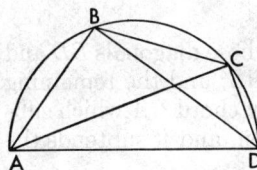

the quadrilateral $ABCD$ in the semicircle. The diagonals AC and BD have been given together with the three sides AB, AD, and CD. And, as has already been shown,

rect. AC, BD = rect. AB, CD + rect. AD, BC.

Therefore,

rect. AD, BC = rect. AC, BD − rect. AB, CD.

Accordingly, in so far as the division may be carried out,

$$(AC\text{·}BD - AB\text{·}CD) \div AD = BC,$$

which was sought.

Further when, for example, the sides of the pentagon and hexagon are given from the above, by this computation a line is given subtending 12°—which is the difference between the arcs—and it is equal to 20,905 parts of the diameter.

Fourth Theorem

Given a chord subtending any arc, the chord subtending half of the arc is also given.

Let us describe the circle ABC, whose diameter is AC, and let the arc BC be given together with the chord subtending it, and let the line EF from the centre E cut BC at right angles. Accordingly by Euclid, III, 3, it will bisect chord BC at F, and the arc at D. Let the chords subtending arcs AB and BD be drawn. Since the triangles ABC and EFC are right and also similar—for they have angle ECF in common; therefore, as

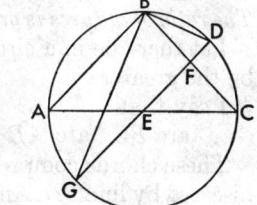

$$CF = \tfrac{1}{2}\,BFC,$$

so

$$EF = \tfrac{1}{2}\,AB.$$

But chord AB is given, for it subtends the remaining arc of the semicircle. Therefore EF is given; and so is line DF the remainder of the radius. Let the diameter DEG be completed, and let BG be joined. Therefore in triangle BDG line BF falls from the right angle at B perpendicular to the base. Accordingly,

rect. GD, DF = sq. BD.

Therefore BD is given in length, and it subtends half of the arc BDC.

And since a chord subtending 12° has already been given, the chord subtending 6° is given as 10,467 parts; that subtending 3°, as 5235 parts; that subtending $1\tfrac{1}{2}°$, as 2618 parts; and that subtending 45', as 1309 parts.

[14ª] Fifth Theorem

Again, when chords are given subtending two arcs, the chord subtending the whole arc made up of them is also given.

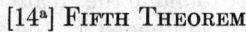
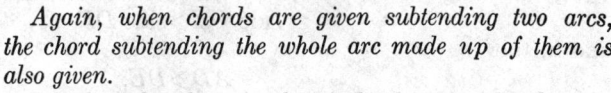

Let there be given in the circle the two chords subtending the arcs AB and BC; I say that the chord subtending the whole arc ABC is also given.

For let the diameters AFD and BFE be drawn, and also the chords BD and CE, which are given by means of the foregoing, on account of chords AB and BC being given; and chord DE = chord AB.

The joining of CD completes the quadrilateral $BCDE$, whose diagonals BD and CE are given together with the three sides BC, DE, and BE; and the remaining side CD will be given by the second theorem; accordingly chord CA which subtends the remaining part of the semicircle will be given, and it subtends the whole arc ABC and is what was sought.

Furthermore, since so far there have been discovered chords which subtend $3°$, $1\frac{1}{2}°$, and $\frac{3}{4}°$; by means of these intervals a table can be constructed with the most exact ratios. Nevertheless if we ascend through the degrees and add one arc to another arc either by halves or by some other mode, there is not unjustified doubt concerning the chords subtending those arcs, as the graphical ratios by which they can be shown are lacking to us. Nothing, however, prevents us from going on with that by some mode which is this side of error perceptible to sense and which is least unconsonant with the assumed number. This was what Ptolemy too sought as regards the chords subtending arcs of $1°$ or of $\frac{1}{2}°$; and he admonished us in the first place.

Sixth Theorem

The ratio of the arcs is greater than the ratio of the greater to the smaller of the chords.

Let there be in a circle two unequal successive arcs AB and BC, and let BC be the greater.

I say that

arc BC : arc AB > chord BC : chord AB.

These chords comprehend angle B, and let that be bisected by line BD. And let AC be joined, which cuts BD at point E. Similarly let AD and CD be joined; then

$$AD = CD,$$

because they subtend equal arcs.

Accordingly, since in triangle ABC, the line which bisects the angle also cuts AC [14b] at E, then

EC, segment of base : $AE = BC : AB$ [Euclid, vi, 3)

and since

$$BC > AB,$$

then

$$EC > EA.$$

Let DF be erected perpendicular to AC; it will bisect AC at point F. And F must necessarily be found in the greater segment EC. And since in every triangle the greater angle is subtended by the greater side, in the triangle DEF

$$\text{side } DE > \text{side } DF,$$

and further,

$$AD > DE,$$

wheretofore the circumference described with D as center and DE as radius will cut AD and pass beyond DF. Therefore let it cut AD at H, and let it be extended in the straight line DFI.

Since

$$\text{sect. } EDI > \text{trgl. } EDF,$$

while

$$\text{trgl. } DEA > \text{sect. } DEH,$$

therefore

　　　　trgl. DEF : trgl. DEA < sect. DEI : sect. DEH.

But sectors are proportional to their arcs or to the angles at the centre; while triangles under the same vertex are proportional to their bases. Accordingly

　　　　angle EDF : angle ADE > base EF : base AE.

Therefore, *componendo*,

　　　　angle FDA : angle ADE > base AF : base AE.

And, in the same way,

　　　　angle CDA : angle ADE > base AC : base AE.

But, *separando*,

　　　　angle CDE : angle EDA > base CE : base EA.

But

　　　　angle CDE : angle EDA = arc CB : arc AB.

And

　　　　base CE : base AE = chord CB : chord AB.

Therefore

　　　　arc CB : arc AB > chord BC : chord AB,

as was to be shown.

PROBLEM

But since the arc is always greater than the straight line subtending it—as the straight line is the shortest of those lines which have the same termini— nevertheless in going from greater to lesser sections of the circle, the inequality approaches equality, so that finally the circular line and the straight line go out of existence simultaneously at the point of tangency on the circle. Therefore it is necessary that just before that moment they differ from one another by no discernible difference.

For example, let arc AB be $3°$ and arc AC $1\frac{1}{2}°$. It has been shown that

　　　　ch. $AB = 5235$,

　　　　where diameter $= 200,000$,

and that

　　　　ch. $AC = 2618$.

And though

　　　　arc $AB = 2$ [15ª] arc AC,

Yet

　　　　ch. $AB < 2$ ch. AC

and

　　　　ch. AC—$2617 = 1$.

But if we make

　　　　arc $AB = 1\frac{1}{2}°$

and

　　　　arc $AC = \frac{3}{4}°$,

then

　　　　ch. $AB = 2618$

and

　　　　ch. $AC = 1309$,

and even though chord AC ought to be greater than half of chord AD, it is seen to be no different from the half. And the ratios of the arcs and the straight lines are now apparently the same. Therefore, since we see that we have come so far that the difference between the straight and the circular line evades sense-perception as completely as if there were only one line, we do not hesitate to take 1309 as subtending $\frac{3}{4}°$ and in the same ratio to fit the chord to the degree and to the remaining parts [of the degree]; and so with the addition of $\frac{1}{4}°$ to the $\frac{3}{4}°$ we establish 1° as subtended by 1745, $\frac{1}{2}°$ by 872$\frac{1}{2}$, and $\frac{1}{3}°$ by approximately 582.

Nevertheless I think it will be enough if in the table we give only the halves of the chords subtending twice the arc, whereby we may concisely comprehend in the quadrant what it used to be necessary to spread out over the semicircle; and especially because the halves come more frequently into use in demonstration and calculation than the whole chords do. Now we have set forth a table increasing by $\frac{1}{6}°$'s and having three columns. In the first column are the degrees and sixth parts of a degree. The second contains the numerical length of half the chord subtending twice the arc. The third contains the difference between the numerical lengths of each half chord, and by means of these differences we can make proportional additions in taking half-chords of a particular number of minutes. The table follows:

TABLE OF THE CHORDS IN A CIRCLE

Arcs (Deg.)	Arcs (Min.)	Halves of the chords subtending twice the arcs	Differences between each half-chord	Arcs (Deg.)	Arcs (Min.)	Halves of the chords subtending twice the arcs	Differences between each half-chord	Arcs (Deg.)	Arcs (Min.)	Halves of the chords subtending twice the arcs	Differences between each half-chord
0	10	291	291	7	40	13341	288	15	10	26163	280
0	20	582	291	7	50	13629	288	15	20	26443	281
0	30	873	290	8	0	13917	288	15	30	26724	280
0	40	1163	291	8	10	14205	288	15	40	27004	280
0	50	1454	291	8	20	14493	288	15	50	27284	280
1	0	1745	291	8	30	14781	288	16	0	27564	279
1	10	2036	291	8	40	15069	287	16	10	27843	279
1	20	2327	290	8	50	15356	287	16	20	28122	279
1	30	2617	291	9	0	15643	288	16	30	28401	279
1	40	2908	291	9	10	15931	287	16	40	28680	279
1	50	3199	291	9	20	16218	287	16	50	28959	278
2	0	3490	291	9	30	16505	287	17	0	29237	278
2	10	3781	290	9	40	16792	286	17	10	29515	278
2	20	4071	291	9	50	17078	287	17	20	29793	278
2	30	4362	291	10	0	17365	286	17	30	30071	277
2	40	4653	290	10	10	17651	286	17	40	30348	277
2	50	4943	291	10	20	17937	286	17	50	30625	277
3	0	5234	290	10	30	18223	286	18	0	30902	276
3	10	5524	290	10	40	18509	286	18	10	31178	276
3	20	5814	291	10	50	18795	286	18	20	31454	276
3	30	6105	290	11	0	19081	285	18	30	31730	276
3	40	6395	290	11	10	19366	286	18	40	32006	276
3	50	6685	290	11	20	19652	285	18	50	32282	275
4	0	6975	290	11	30	19937	285	19	0	32557	275
4	10	7265	290	11	40	20222	285	19	10	32832	274
4	20	7555	290	11	50	20507	284	19	20	33106	275
4	30	7845	290	12	0	20791	285	19	30	33381	274
4	40	8135	290	12	10	21076	284	19	40	33655	274
4	50	8425	290	12	20	21360	284	19	50	33929	273
5	0	8715	290	12	30	21644	284	20	0	34202	273
5	10	9005	290	12	40	21928	284	20	10	34475	273
5	20	9295	290	12	50	22212	283	20	20	34748	273
5	30	9585	289	13	0	22495	283	20	30	35021	272
5	40	9874	290	13	10	22778	284	20	40	35293	272
5	50	10164	289	13	20	23062	282	20	50	35565	272
6	0	10453	289	13	30	23344	283	21	0	35837	271
6	10	10742	289	13	40	23627	283	21	10	36108	271
6	20	11031	289	13	50	23910	282	21	20	36379	271
6	30	11320	289	14	0	24192	282	21	30	36650	270
6	40	11609	289	14	10	24474	282	21	40	36920	270
6	50	11898	289	14	20	24756	282	21	50	37190	270
7	0	12187	289	14	30	25038	281	22	0	37460	270
7	10	12476	288	14	40	25319	282	22	10	37730	269
7	20	12764	289	14	50	25601	281	22	20	37999	269
7	30	13053	288	15	0	25882	281	22	30	38268	269

TABLE OF THE CHORDS IN A CIRCLE—(Continued)

Arcs		Halves of the chords subtending twice the arcs	Differences between each half-chord	Arcs		Halves of the chords subtending twice the arcs	Differences between each half-chord	Arcs		Halves of the chords subtending twice the arcs	Differences between each half-chord
Deg.	Min.			Deg.	Min.			Deg.	Min.		
22	40	38587	268	30	10	50252	251	37	40	61107	230
22	50	38805	268	30	20	50503	251	37	50	61337	229
23	0	39073	268	30	30	50754	250	38	0	61566	229
23	10	39341	267	30	40	51004	250	38	10	61795	229
23	20	39608	267	30	50	51254	250	38	20	62024	227
23	30	39875	266	31	0	51504	249	38	30	62251	228
23	40	40141	267	31	10	51753	249	38	40	62479	227
23	50	40408	266	31	20	52002	248	38	50	62706	226
24	0	40674	265	31	30	52250	248	39	0	62932	226
24	10	40939	265	31	40	52498	247	39	10	63158	225
24	20	41204	265	31	50	52745	247	39	20	63383	225
24	30	41469	265	32	0	52992	246	39	30	63608	224
24	40	41734	264	32	10	53238	246	39	40	63832	224
24	50	41998	264	32	20	53484	246	39	50	64056	223
25	0	42262	263	32	30	53730	245	40	0	64279	222
25	10	42525	263	32	40	53975	245	40	10	64501	222
25	20	42788	263	32	50	54220	244	40	20	64723	222
25	30	43051	262	33	0	54464	244	40	30	64945	221
25	40	43313	262	33	10	54708	243	40	40	65166	220
25	50	43575	262	33	20	54951	243	40	50	65386	220
26	0	43837	261	33	30	55194	242	41	0	65606	219
26	10	44098	261	33	40	55436	242	41	10	65825	219
26	20	44359	261	33	50	55678	241	41	20	66044	218
26	30	44620	260	34	0	55919	241	41	30	66262	218
26	40	44880	260	34	10	56160	240	41	40	66480	217
26	50	45140	259	34	20	56400	241	41	50	66697	216
27	0	45399	259	34	30	56641	239	42	0	66913	216
27	10	45658	259	34	40	56880	239	42	10	67129	215
27	20	45917	258	34	50	57119	239	42	20	67344	215
27	30	46175	258	35	0	57358	238	42	30	67559	214
27	40	46433	257	35	10	57596	237	42	40	67773	214
27	50	46690	257	35	20	57833	237	42	50	67987	213
28	0	46947	257	35	30	58070	237	43	0	68200	212
28	10	47204	256	35	40	58307	236	43	10	68412	212
28	20	47460	256	35	50	58543	236	43	20	68624	211
28	30	47716	255	36	0	58779	235	43	30	68835	211
28	40	47971	255	36	10	59014	234	43	40	69046	210
28	50	48226	255	36	20	59248	234	43	50	69256	210
29	0	48481	254	36	30	59482	234	44	0	69466	209
29	10	48735	254	36	40	59716	233	44	10	69675	208
29	20	48989	253	36	50	59949	232	44	20	69883	208
29	30	49242	253	37	0	60181	232	44	30	70091	207
29	40	49495	253	37	10	60413	232	44	40	70298	207
29	50	49748	252	37	20	60645	231	44	50	70505	206
30	0	50000	252	37	30	60876	231	45	0	70711	205

TABLE OF THE CHORDS IN A CIRCLE—(*Continued*)

Arcs		Halves of the chords subtending twice the arcs	Differences between each half-chord	Arcs		Halves of the chords subtending twice the arcs	Differences between each half-chord	Arcs		Halves of the chords subtending twice the arcs	Differences between each half-chord
Deg.	Min.			Deg.	Min.			Deg.	Min.		
45	10	70916	205	52	40	79512	176	60	10	86747	145
45	20	71121	204	52	50	79688	176	60	20	86892	144
45	30	71325	204	53	0	79864	174	60	30	87036	142
45	40	71529	203	53	10	80038	174	60	40	87178	142
45	50	71732	202	53	20	80212	174	60	50	87320	142
46	0	71934	202	53	30	80386	172	61	0	87462	141
46	10	72136	201	53	40	80558	172	61	10	87603	140
46	20	72337	200	53	50	80730	172	61	20	87743	139
46	30	72537	200	54	0	80902	170	61	30	87882	138
46	40	72737	199	54	10	81072	170	61	40	88020	138
46	50	72936	199	54	20	81242	169	61	50	88158	137
47	0	73135	198	54	30	81411	169	62	0	88295	136
47	10	73333	198	54	40	81580	168	62	10	88431	135
47	20	73531	197	54	50	81748	167	62	20	88566	135
47	30	73728	196	55	0	81915	167	62	30	88701	134
47	40	73924	195	55	10	82082	166	62	40	88835	133
47	50	74119	195	55	20	82248	165	62	50	88968	133
48	0	74314	194	55	30	82413	164	63	0	89101	131
48	10	74508	194	55	40	82577	164	63	10	89232	131
48	20	74702	194	55	50	82741	163	63	20	89363	130
48	30	74896	194	56	0	82904	162	63	30	89493	129
48	40	75088	192	56	10	83066	162	63	40	89622	129
48	50	75280	191	56	20	83228	161	63	50	89751	128
49	0	75471	190	56	30	83389	160	64	0	89879	127
49	10	75661	190	56	40	83549	159	64	10	90006	127
49	20	75851	189	56	50	83708	159	64	20	90133	125
49	30	76040	189	57	0	83867	158	64	30	90258	125
49	40	76299	188	57	10	84025	157	64	40	90383	124
49	50	76417	187	57	20	84182	157	64	50	90507	124
50	0	76604	187	57	30	84339	156	65	0	90631	122
50	10	76791	186	57	40	84495	155	65	10	90753	122
50	20	76977	185	57	50	84650	155	65	20	90875	121
50	30	77162	185	58	0	84805	154	65	30	90996	120
50	40	77347	184	58	10	84959	153	65	40	91116	119
50	50	77531	184	58	20	85112	152	65	50	91235	119
51	0	77715	182	58	30	85264	151	66	0	91354	118
51	10	77897	182	58	40	85415	151	66	10	91472	118
51	20	78079	182	58	50	85566	151	66	20	91590	116
51	30	78261	181	59	0	85717	149	66	30	91706	116
51	40	78442	180	59	10	85866	149	66	40	91822	114
51	50	78622	179	59	20	86015	148	66	50	91936	114
52	0	78801	179	59	30	86163	147	67	0	92050	114
52	10	78980	178	59	40	86310	147	67	10	92164	112
52	20	79158	177	59	50	86457	145	67	20	92276	112
52	30	79335	177	60	0	86602	145	67	30	92388	111

TABLE OF THE CHORDS IN A CIRCLE—(Continued)

Arcs		Halves of the chords sub-tending twice the arcs	Differences be-tween each half-chord	Arcs		Halves of the chords sub-tending twice the arcs	Differences be-tween each half-chord	Arcs		Halves of the chords sub-tending twice the arcs	Differences be-tween each half-chord
Deg.	Min.			Deg.	Min.			Deg.	Min.		
67	40	92499	110	75	10	96667	75	82	40	99182	37
67	50	92609	109	75	20	96742	73	82	50	99219	36
68	0	92718	109	75	30	96815	72	83	0	99255	35
68	10	92827	108	75	40	96887	72	83	10	99290	34
68	20	92935	107	75	50	96959	71	83	20	99324	33
68	30	93042	106	76	0	97030	69	83	30	99357	32
68	40	93148	105	76	10	97099	70	83	40	99389	32
68	50	93253	105	76	20	97169	68	83	50	99421	31
69	0	93358	104	76	30	97237	67	84	0	99452	30
69	10	93462	103	76	40	97304	67	84	10	99482	29
69	20	93565	102	76	50	97371	66	84	20	99511	28
69	30	93667	102	77	0	97437	65	84	30	99539	28
69	40	93769	101	77	10	97502	64	84	40	99567	27
69	50	93870	99	77	20	97566	64	84	50	99594	26
70	0	93969	99	77	30	97630	62	85	0	99620	24
70	10	94068	99	77	40	97692	62	85	10	99644	24
70	20	94167	97	77	50	97754	61	85	20	99668	24
70	30	94264	97	78	0	97815	60	85	30	99692	22
70	40	94361	96	78	10	97875	59	85	40	99714	22
70	50	94457	95	78	20	97934	58	85	50	99736	20
71	0	94552	94	78	30	97992	58	86	0	99756	20
71	10	94646	93	78	40	98050	57	86	10	99776	19
71	20	94739	93	78	50	98107	56	86	20	99795	18
71	30	94832	92	79	0	98163	55	86	30	99813	17
71	40	94924	91	79	10	98218	54	86	40	99830	17
71	50	95015	90	79	20	98272	53	86	50	99847	16
72	0	95105	90	79	30	98325	53	87	0	99863	15
72	10	95195	89	79	40	98378	52	87	10	99878	14
72	20	95284	88	79	50	98430	51	87	20	99892	13
72	30	95372	87	80	0	98481	50	87	30	99905	12
72	40	95459	86	80	10	98531	49	87	40	99917	11
72	50	95545	85	80	20	98580	49	87	50	99928	11
73	0	95630	85	80	30	98629	47	88	0	99939	10
73	10	95715	84	80	40	98676	47	88	10	99949	9
73	20	95799	83	80	50	98723	46	88	20	99958	8
73	30	95882	82	81	0	98769	45	88	30	99966	7
73	40	95964	81	81	10	98814	44	88	40	99973	6
73	50	96045	81	81	20	98858	44	88	50	99979	6
74	0	96126	80	81	30	98902	42	89	0	99985	4
74	10	96206	79	81	40	98944	42	89	10	99989	4
74	20	96285	78	81	50	98986	41	89	20	99993	3
74	30	96363	77	82	0	99027	40	89	30	99996	2
74	40	96440	77	82	10	99067	39	89	40	99998	1
74	50	96517	75	82	20	99106	38	89	50	99999	1
75	0	96592	75	82	30	99144	38	90	0	100000	0

13. ON THE SIDES AND ANGLES OF PLANE RECTILINEAR TRIANGLES

I

[19^b] *The sides of a triangle whose angles are given are given.*

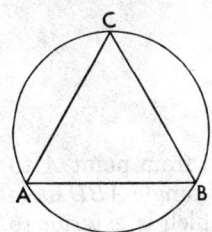

I say let there be the triangle *ABC*, around which a circle is circumscribed, by Euclid, IV, 5. Therefore arcs *AB*, *BC*, and *CA* will be given in degrees whereof 360° are equal to two right angles. Now given the arcs, the subtending sides of the triangle inscribed in the circle are also given by the table drawn up, where the diameter is assumed to have 200,000 parts.

II

But if two sides of the triangle are given together with one of the angles, the remaining side and the remaining angles may become known.

For the given sides are either equal or unequal. But the given angle is either right or acute or obtuse. Again, the given sides either comprehend the angle or they do not comprehend it.

Therefore in triangle *ABC* first let the two given sides *AB* and *AC* be equal, and let them comprehend the given angle *A*.

Therefore the remaining angles at base *BC* are also given— since they are equal—as half of the remainder, when *A* is sub-tracted from two right angles. And if the angle given first was at the base, then its equal is soon given, and from the two of them the remaining angle that goes to make up two right angles. But given the angles of a triangle, the sides are given: and moreover the base *BC* is given from the table in the parts whereof *AB* or *AC* as radius has 100,000 parts or whereof the diameter has 200,000 parts.

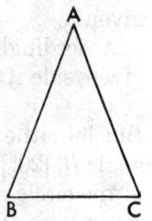

III

But if the angle BAC comprehended by the given sides is right, the same thing will result.

Since it is obvious that

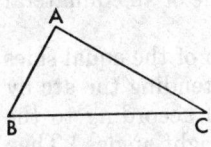

$$[20^a] \text{ sq. } AB + \text{sq. } AC = \text{sq. } BC;$$

therefore *BC* is given in length and the sides in their ratio to one another. But the segment of a circle which compre-hends a right triangle is a semicircle, and base *BC* is the di-ameter. Therefore *AB* and *AC* as subtending the remain-ing angles *C* and *B* will be given in the parts whereof *BC* has 200,000 parts. And the ratio of the table will reveal the angles in the degrees whereof 180° are equal to two right angles.

The same thing will result if *BC* is given together with one of the sides com-prehending the right angle, as I judge has been clearly established.

IV

But now let the given angle ABC be acute, and also let it be comprehended by the given sides AB and BC.

And from point *A* drop a perpendicular to *BC* extended, if necessary, accord-ing as it falls inside or outside the triangle, and let it be *AD*. By this perpen-dicular the two right triangles *ABD* and *ADC* are distinguished, and since the angles in *ABD* are given—for D is a right angle, and *B* is given by hypothesis; therefore AD and BD are given by the table as subtending angles A and B in the parts whereof AB, the diameter of the circle, has 200,000 parts. And in the same ratio wherein AB was given in length, AD and BD are given similarly; and CD, which is the difference between BC and BD, is given also.

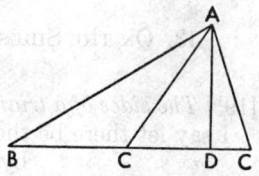

Therefore in the right triangle ADC, the sides AD and CD being given, AC the side sought and angle ACD are given according to what has been shown above.

V

And it will not turn out differently, if angle B is obtuse.

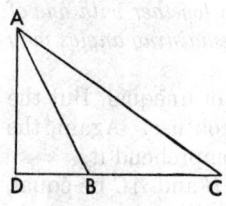

For the perpendicular AD dropped from point A to straight line BC extended makes the triangle ABD have its angles given. For angle ABD, which is exterior to angle ABC, is given; and

angle $D = 90°$.

Therefore sides BD and AD are given in the parts whereof AB has 200,000. And since BA and BC have a given ratio to one another, therefore AB too is given in the same parts, wherein BD and the whole CBD are given.

Accordingly in the right triangle ADC, since the two sides AD and CD are given, side AC and angles BAC and ACB, which were sought for, are also given.

VI

But let either of the given sides, AC or AB, be the one subtending the given angle B. [20b] Therefore AC is given by the table in parts whereof the diameter of the circle circumscribing the triangle ABC has 200,000 and according to the given ratio of AC to AB. AB is given in similar parts, and by the table the angle ACB is given together with the remaining angle BAC, by which chord CB is also given. And by this ratio they are given in any magnitude.

VII

Given all the sides of the triangle, the angles are given.

It is too well known to be worth mentioning that each angle of an equilateral triangle is one third of two right angles.

It is also clear in the case of an isosceles triangle. For each of the equal sides is to the third side as half of the diameter is to the side subtending the arc by which the angle comprehended by the equal sides is given according to the table, wherein the 360° around the centre are equal to four right angles.[1] Then the two angles at the base are given as half of the supplementary angle.

Therefore it now remains to show this in the case of scalene triangles, which we divide in the same way into right triangles. Therefore let there be the scalene triangle ABC of which the sides are given, and upon the side which is the longest, namely BC, drop the perpendicular AD. Now Euclid, II, 13 tells us that if AB subtends the acute angle, then

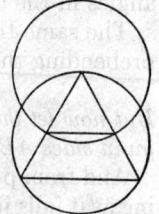

(sq. AC+sq. BC)—sq. $AB = 2$ rect. BC, CD.

Now it is necessary for angle C to be acute; for otherwise AB

[1]As in the subjoined figure:

would be the longest side contrary to the hypotheses, according to Euclid, I, 17-19. Therefore BD and DC are given, and there will be the right triangles ABC and ADC with their sides and angles given—as has so often happened before—and so the angles of triangle ABC which were sought become established.

Another way. Similarly Euclid, III, 36 will perhaps give us an easy method, if with BC the shorter side as radius and with point C as centre, we describe a circle which will cut either one or both of the remaining sides.

First, let it cut both: AB at point E and AC at D; and let line ADC extended to point F in order to complete the diameter DCF. And with this construction it is clear from that proposition of Euclid that

$$[21^a] \quad \text{rect. } FA, AD = \text{rect. } BA, AE,$$

since each is equal to the square on the tangent to the circle from A. But the whole AF is given, as all its segments are given, since

$$\text{radius } CF = \text{radius } CD = BC,$$

and

$$AD = CA - CD.$$

Wherefore, as the rectangle BA, AE is given, AE also is given in length; and so is the remainder BE subtending arc BE. By joining EC we shall have the isosceles triangle BCE with all its sides given. Therefore the angle EBC is given. Hence in the triangle ABC the remaining angles at C and at A may become known by means of what has been shown above.

However, let the circle not cut AB as in the other figure, where AB falls upon the concave circumference; nevertheless BE will be given, and in the isosceles triangle BCE angle CBE will be given and also the exterior angle ABC. And by the same method as before the remaining angles are given.

And we have said enough concerning rectilinear triangles, in which a great part of geodesy consists. Now let us turn to spherical triangles.

14. On Spherical Triangles

In this place we take that triangle as spherical which is comprehended by three arcs of great circles on a spherical surface. But we take the difference and magnitude of the angles from the arc of a great circle, *i.e.*, a great circle described with the point of section as a pole; and this arc is the arc intercepted by the quadrants of the circles comprehending the angle. For as the arc thus intercepted is to the whole circumference, so is the angle of section to four right angles—which we have said contain 360 equal degrees.

I

[21ᵇ] *If there are three arcs of the great circles of a sphere, and if any two of them joined together are longer than the third; it is clear that a spherical triangle can be constructed from them.*

For Euclid, XI, 23 shows in the case of angles what is here proposed in the case of arcs. Since there is the same ratio between angles as between arcs, and since the great circles are those circles which pass through the centre of the sphere; it is manifest that those three sectors of circles, *i.e.*, the sectors to which the three arcs belong, form a solid angle at the centre of the sphere. There-fore what was proposed has been established.

II

Any arc of a [spherical] triangle must be less than a semicircle.

For the semicircle makes no angle at the centre but falls upon it in a straight line. But the remaining two angles which intercept the arcs cannot complete a solid angle at the centre, and so they cannot complete a spherical triangle.

And I think this is the reason why Ptolemy in his exposition of triangles of this genus, especially as regards the figure of the spherical sector, argues that none of the arcs taken together must be greater than a semicircle.

III

In spherical triangles having a right angle, the chord subtending twice the side op-posite the right angle is to a chord subtending twice one of the sides comprehending the right angle as the diameter of the sphere is to the chord which subtends the angle comprehended in the great circle of the sphere by the first side and by the remaining side.

For let there be the spherical triangle ABC, of which the angle at C is right. I say that

ch. 2 AB : ch. 2 BC = dmt. sph. : ch. 2 BAC gr. circ. sph.

With A as a pole draw DE the arc of a great circle, and let ABD and ACE the quadrants of the circles be completed. And from the centre F of the sphere draw the common sections of the circles: FA the common section of circles ABD and ACE, [22ª] FE of circles ACE and DE, and FD of cir-cles ABD and DE; and moreover, FC of the circles AC and BC. Then draw BG at right angles to FA, BI at right angles to FC, and DK at right angles to FE; and let GI be joined.

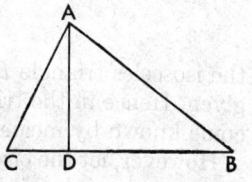

Since if a circle cuts a circle described through its poles, it cuts it at right angles; therefore the angle AED will be right; and angle ACB is right by hypothesis; and each of the planes EDF and BCF is perpen-dicular to plane AEF. Wherefore if a line be erected in the underlying plane of AFE at right angles to point K in the common section, this line and KD will comprehend a right angle, by the definition of planes which are perpendicular to one another. Wherefore, by Euclid, XI, 4, line KD is perpendicular to circle AEF. But BI was erected in the same relation to the same plane; and so by Euclid, XI, 6, DK is parallel to BI and FD is parallel to GB, because

angle FGB = angle GFD = 90°.

And by Euclid, XI, 10,

angle FDK = angle GBI.

But

angle FKD = 90°,

and by definition

GI is perpendicular to IB.

Accordingly the sides of similar triangles are proportional; and

$DF : BG = DK : BI$.

But

BI = ½ ch. 2 CB,

since it is at right angles to the radius from center F; and for the same reason,

$$BG = \tfrac{1}{2} \text{ ch. } 2\ BA,$$
$$DK = \tfrac{1}{2} \text{ ch. } 2\ DE, \text{ or } \tfrac{1}{2} \text{ ch. } 2\ DAE,$$

and

$$DF = \tfrac{1}{2} \text{ dmt. sph.},$$

Therefore it is clear that

$$\text{ch. } 2\ AB : \text{ch. } 2\ BC = \text{dmt.} : \text{ch. } 2\ DAE \text{ (or ch. } 2\ DE),$$

as it was time to show.

IV

In any triangle having a right angle, if another angle and any side are given, the remaining angle and the remaining sides will be given.

For let there be the triangle ABC having the angle A right and having one of the other two angles, namely B, given.

Let us take three cases of the given side. For it is either adjacent to both the given angles, as AB, or only to the right angle, as AC, or is opposite the right angle, as BC.

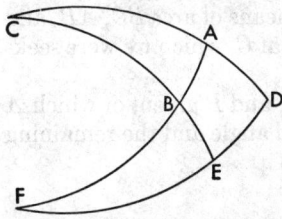

Therefore let AB be the side given first; and with C as a pole let arc [22^b] DE of the great circle be described. Let the quadrants CAD and CBE be completed; and let AB and DE be extended, until they cut one another at point F. Therefore conversely the pole of CAD will be at F, because

angle A = angle $D = 90°$.

And since, if in a sphere the great circles cut one another at right angles, they will bisect one another and pass through the poles of one another; therefore ABF and DEF are quadrants of circles. And since AB is given, BF the remainder of the quadrant is also given; and the vertical angle EBF is equal to the given angle ABC. But by what has been shown above

$$\text{ch. } 2\ BF : \text{ch. } 2\ EF = \text{dmt. sph.} : \text{ch. } 2\ EBF.$$

But three of the chords have been given:

dmt. sph.,

ch. 2 BF,

ch. 2 EBF,

or the half-chords; and therefore by Euclid, VI, 15, there is also given

$$\tfrac{1}{2} \text{ ch. } 2\ EF;$$

and by the table the arc EF itself and DE the remainder of the quadrant, or the angle at C, which was sought. Similarly and alternately,

$$\text{ch. } 2\ DE : \text{ch. } 2\ AB = \text{ch. } 2\ EBC : \text{ch. } 2\ CB.$$

But DE, AB, and CE on the quadrants of the circle have already been given; and therefore the fourth chord, subtending twice arc CB, will be given, and also the side CB, which was sought.

And since

$$\text{ch. } 2\ CB : \text{ch. } 2\ CA = \text{ch. } 2\ BF : \text{ch. } 2\ EF,$$

because they both have the ratio of

dmt. sph. : ch. 2 CBA,

and because things which have the same ratio to one and the same thing have the same ratio to one another; therefore with the three chords BF, EF, and CB given, the fourth chord CA is also given; and arc CA is the third side of the triangle ABC.

But now let AC be the side assumed as given, and let our problem be to find the sides AB and BC together with the remaining angle C. Again similarly and by inversion,

$$\text{ch. } 2\ CA : \text{ch. } 2\ CB = \text{ch. } 2\ ABC : \text{dmt.}$$

Hence the side CB is given, and also AD and BE the remainders of the quadrants of the circles. And so again,

$$\text{ch. } 2\ AD : \text{ch. } 2\ BE = \text{ch. } 2\ ABF,\ i.e.,\ \text{dmt.}, : \text{ch. } 2\ BF.$$

Therefore arc BF is given, and the side AB, which is the remainder. And similarly,

$$\text{ch. } 2\ BC : \text{ch. } 2\ AB = 2\ \text{ch. } CBE : \text{ch. } 2\ DE.$$

Hence arc DE, or twice the remaining angle at C, will be given.

Furthermore, if it was BC which was assumed, again as before, AC and the remainders AD and BE will be given. Hence arc BF and the remaining side AB are given by means of the diameter and the chords [23a] subtending them, as has often been said. And as in the preceding theorem, by means of arcs BC, AB, and CBE being given, the arc ED, i.e., the remaining angle at C, which we were seeking, is discovered.

And so again in the triangle ABC with two angles A and B given, of which A is right, and with one of the three sides given, the third angle and the remaining sides are given, as was to be shown.

V

The sides of a right triangle, of which the angles are given, are also given.

Let the preceding diagram be kept. On account of the angle C being given, the arc DE and EF the remainder of the quadrant are given. And since BEF is a right angle, because BE was let fall from the pole of arc DEF; and since angle EBF is equal to its vertical angle, which was given; therefore the triangle BEF, having the right angle E and the angle at B given together with the side EF, has its sides and angles given by the preceding theorem. Therefore BF is given, and so is AB the remainder of the quadrant. And similarly in the triangle ABC the remaining sides AC and BC are shown as above.

VI

If in the same sphere two triangles have right angles and another angle equal to another angle and one side equal to one side—whether the sides be adjacent to the equal angles or lie opposite one of the equal angles—they will have the remaining sides equal to the remaining sides and the remaining angle equal to the remaining angle.

Let there be the hemisphere ABC, in which the two triangles ABD and CEF are taken. Let the angles at A and C be right; and furthermore let the angle ADB be equal to CEF, and one side to one side. And first let the equal sides be adjacent to the equal angles, i.e., let AD be equal to CE. I say moreover that side AB is equal to side CF, side BD to EF, and the remaining angle ABD to the remaining angle CFE.

For with B and F as poles, draw GHI and IKL the quadrants of the great circles. And

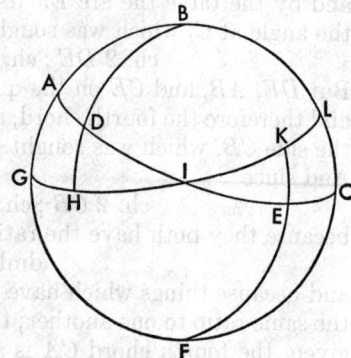

let quadrants ADI and CEI be completed. They necessarily cut one another at the pole of the hemisphere, point I, [23^b] because

$$\text{angle } A = \text{angle } C = 90°$$

and quadrants GHI and CEI have been drawn through the poles of the circle ABC.

Therefore, since it has been assumed that

$$\text{side } AD = \text{side } CE$$

then by subtraction

$$\text{arc } DI = \text{arc } EI.$$

And

$$\text{angle } IDH = \text{angle } IEK;$$

for they are placed at the vertices of the angles assumed as equal; and

$$\text{angle H} = \text{angle K} = 90°.$$

As things which have the same ratio to the same are in the same ratio; and since by Theorem III in this chapter,

$$\text{ch. 2 } ID : \text{ch. 2 } HI = \text{dmt. sph.} : \text{ch. 2 } IDH,$$

and

$$\text{ch. } EI : \text{ch. 2 } KI = \text{dmt. sph.} : \text{ch. 2 } IEK;$$

therefore

$$\text{ch. 2 } ID : \text{ch. 2 } HI = \text{ch. 2 } EI : \text{ch. 2 } IK.$$

And by Euclid's *Elements*, v, 14, since

$$\text{ch. 2 } DI = \text{ch. 2 } IE$$

therefore

$$\text{ch. 2 HI} = \text{ch. 2 } IK.$$

And as in equal circles equal chords cut off equal arcs, and as the parts of multiples are in the same ratio [as the multiples]; therefore the plain arcs IH and IK will be equal; and so will GH and KL the remainders of the quadrants. Whence it is clear that

$$\text{angle } B = \text{angle } F,$$

and since, by the inverse of the third theorem,

$$\text{ch. 2 AD} : \text{ch. 2 } BD = \text{ch. 2 } HG : \text{ch 2 } BDH, \text{ or dmt.,}$$

and

$$\text{ch. 2 } EC : \text{ch. 2 } EF = \text{ch. 2 } KL : \text{ch. 2 } FEK, \text{ or dmt.,}$$

wherefore

$$\text{ch. 2 } AD : \text{ch. 2 } BD = \text{ch. 2 } EC : \text{ch. 2 } EF$$

and

$$AD = CE.$$

Therefore, by Euclid's *Elements*, v, 14,

$$\text{arc } BD = \text{arc } EF,$$

on account of the chords subtending twice the arcs being equal.

In the same way with BD and EF equal, we will show that the remaining sides and angles are equal.

And in turn, if sides AB and CF are assumed to be equal, the results will follow the same identity of ratio.

VII

Now also even if there is no right angle, but provided that the sides which are adjacent to the equal angles are equal to one another, the same thing will be shown.

In this way if in the two triangles ABD and CEF

$$\text{angle } B = \text{angle F}$$

and
$$\text{angle } D = \text{angle } E,$$
and if side BD is adjacent to the equal [24ª]
angles and
$$\text{side } BD = \text{side } EF,$$
I say that again the triangles are equilateral
and equiangular.

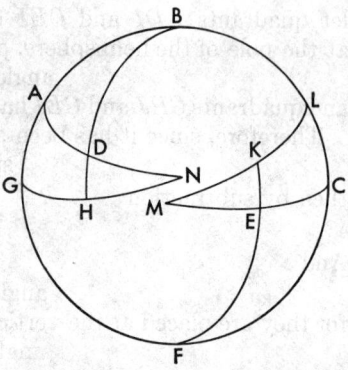

For once more with B and F as poles, describe GH and KL, the arcs of the great circles. And let AD and GH extended intersect at
N; and let EC and LK similarly extended intersect at M.

Therefore since in the two triangles HDN
and EKM
$$\text{angle } HDN = \text{angle } KEM,$$
because they are placed at the vertex of the angles assumed equal; and since
$$\text{angle } H = \text{angle } K = 90°$$
on account of the intersection of circles described through the poles of one
another; and
$$\text{side } DH = \text{side } EK;$$
therefore the triangles are equiangular and equilateral by the preceding proof.
And again because
$$\text{arc } GH = \text{arc } KL$$
on account of its being assumed that
$$\text{angle } B = \text{angle } F;$$
therefore by addition
$$\text{arc } GHN = \text{arc } MKL,$$
by the axiom concerning the addition of equals. And therefore there are these
two triangles AGN and MCL where
$$\text{side } GN = \text{side } ML,$$
$$\text{angle } ANG = \text{angle } CML,$$
and
$$\text{angle } G = \text{angle } L = 90°.$$
So the triangles will have their sides and angles equal. Therefore when equals
have been subtracted from equals, the remainders will be equal:
$$\text{arc } AD = \text{arc } CE,$$
$$\text{arc } AB = \text{arc } CF,$$
and
$$\text{angle } BAD = \text{angle } ECF,$$
as was to be shown.

VIII

*Now further, if two triangles have two sides equal to two sides and an angle equal
to an angle, whether the angle which the equal sides comprehend, or an angle at the
base, they will also have base equal to base and the remaining angles equal to the
remaining angles.*

As in the preceding diagram, let
$$\text{side } AB = \text{side } CF$$
and
$$\text{side } AD = \text{side } CE.$$

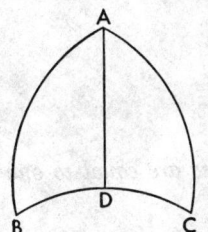

And first let

$$\text{angle } A = \text{angle } C,$$

which is comprehended by the equal sides. I say also that

$$\text{base } BD = \text{base } EF,$$
$$\text{angle } B = \text{angle } F,$$

and

$$\text{angle } BDA = \text{angle } CEF.$$

For we shall have the two triangles AGN and CLM, where

$$\text{angle } G = \text{angle } L = 90°.$$

And since

$$\text{angle } GAN = 180° - \text{angle } BAD,$$

and

$$\text{angle } MCL = 180° - \text{angle } ECF,$$

then

$$\text{angle } GAN = \text{angle } MCL.$$

Therefore the triangles are equiangular and equilateral. Wherefore since

$$\text{arc } AN = \text{arc } CM$$

and

$$\text{arc } AD = \text{arc } CE,$$

then by subtraction

$$\text{arc } DN = \text{arc } ME.$$

But it has already been made clear that

$$\text{angle } DNH = \text{angle } EMK,$$

and

$$\text{angle } H = \text{angle } K = 90°.$$

Therefore the two triangles DHN and EMK will also be equiangular and equilateral. [24$^\text{b}$] Hence [by the subtraction of equals]

$$\text{arc } BD = \text{arc } EF$$

and

$$\text{arc } GH = \text{arc } KL.$$

Hence

$$\text{angle } B = \text{angle } F,$$

and

$$\text{angle } ADB = \text{angle } FEC.$$

But if instead of sides AD and CE it be assumed that

$$\text{base } BD = \text{base } EF,$$

which are opposite the equal angles; and if the rest stays the same; then the proof will be similar. For since

$$\text{exterior angle } GAN = \text{exterior angle } MCL,$$
$$\text{angle } G = \text{angle } L = 90°,$$

and

$$\text{side } AG = \text{side } CL;$$

in the same way as before we shall have the two triangles AGN and MCL as equiangular and equilateral. And moreover, as parts of them,

$$\text{trgl. } DNH = \text{trgl. } MEK,$$

because

$$\text{angle } H = \text{angle } K = 90°,$$
$$\text{angle } DNH = \text{angle } KME,$$

and by subtraction from the quadrant
$$\text{side } DH = \text{side } EK.$$
Whence the same things follow as before.

IX

Moreover, in isosceles spherical triangles the angles at the base are equal to one another.

Let there be triangle ABC, where
$$\text{side } AB = \text{side } AC.$$
I say that on the base
$$\text{angle } ABC = \text{angle } ACB.$$

From the vertex A drop a great circle which will cut the base at right angles, *i.e.*, a circle through the poles of the base; and let this circle be AD. Therefore, since in the two triangles ABD and ADC
$$\text{side } BA = \text{side } AC,$$
and
$$\text{side } AD = \text{side } AD,$$
and
$$\text{angle } BDA = \text{angle } CDA = 90°,$$
it is clear from what was shown above that
$$\text{angle } ABC = \text{angle } ACB,$$
as was to be shown.

PORISM

Hence it follows that the arc from the vertex of an isosceles triangle which falls at right angles upon the base will at the same time bisect the base and the angle comprehended by the equal sides, and vice versa. And that is clear from what has been shown above.

X

If two triangles in the same sphere have the sides of the one severally equal to the sides of the other, they will have the angles of the one severally equal to the angles of the other.

For in each triangle the three segments of great circles form pyramids which have as their apexes the centre of the sphere and as their bases the plane triangles which are comprehended by the straight lines subtending the arcs of the convex triangles. And those pyramids are similar and [25ᵃ] equal by the definition of similar and equal solid figures [Euclid, XI, Def. 10]; now the ratio of similarity is that the angles taken in any order will be severally equal to one another. Therefore the triangles will have their angles equal to one another.

In particular, those who define similarity of figures more generally say that similar figures are those which have similar declinations, and have corresponding angles equal to one another. Whence I think it is manifest that in a sphere the triangles which are equilateral are similar, just as in the case of plane triangles.

XI

Every triangle which has two sides and an angle given will have the remaining sides and angles given.

For if the two sides are given as equal, the angles at the base will be equal, and by drawing an arc from the vertex at right angles to the base, what is sought will easily be found by means of the Porism to the ninth theorem.

But if however the sides given are unequal, as in triangle ABC, where angle A is given together with two sides, the sides either comprehend the given angle or do not comprehend it: First, let the given sides AB and AC comprehend it. And with C as a pole draw arc DEF of a great circle; and let the quadrants CAD and CBE be completed; and let AB extended cut DE at point F. So also in the triangle ADF,

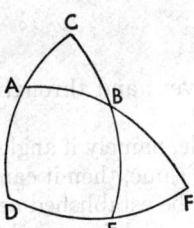

$$\text{side } AD = 90° - \text{arc } AC;$$

and

$$\text{angle } BAD = 180° - \text{angle } CAB.$$

For the ratios and dimensions of these angles are the same as those of angles occurring at the intersection of straight lines and planes. And

$$\text{angle } D = 90°.$$

Therefore by the fourth theorem of this chapter, triangle ADF will have its sides and angles given. And again in triangle BEF angle F has been found, and

$$\text{angle } E = 90°$$

on account of the intersection of circles through the poles of one another; and

$$\text{side } BF = \text{arc } ABF - \text{arc } AB.$$

Therefore by the same theorem triangle BEF also will have its angles and sides given. Whence BC the side sought is given, as

$$BC = 90° - BE,$$

and BC is the side sought. And

$$\text{arc } DE = \text{arc } DEF - \text{arc } EF.$$

And so angle C is given. Any by means of angle EBF, the vertical angle ABC, which was sought, is given.

But if in place of side AB, side CB which is opposite to the given angle is assumed, the same thing will result. For AD and BE the remainders of quadrants are given; and by the same argument the two triangles ADF and BEF will have their sides and angles given, as before.

Whence, as was intended, ABC the triangle set before us will have its sides and angles given.

[25ᵇ] XII

Furthermore, if any two angles are given together with one side, there will be the same result.

For let the construction in the previous figure stay; and in triangle ABC let the two angles ACB and BAC be given together with side AC, which is adjacent to both angles. Now if one of the angles given were right, then everything else would follow from the ratios by the preceding fourth theorem. But we wish to keep the theorems different and to have neither of the angles right. Therefore

$$AD = 90° - AC.$$

And

$$\text{angle } BAD = 180° - \text{angle } BAC.$$

And

$$\text{angle } D = 90°.$$

Therefore by the fourth theorem in this chapter, triangle AFD will have its angles and sides given. But through angle C being given, the arc DE is given, and so is the remainder

$$\text{arc } EF = 90° - \text{arc } DE.$$

And

angle $BEF = 90°$;

and

angle F = angle F.

In the same way by the fourth theorem BE and BF are given; and through them we can discover sides AB and BC, which were sought.

Moreover, if one of the given angles is opposite the given side, namely if angle ABC is given in place of angle ACB, and if the rest stayed the same, then it can be shown in similar fashion that the whole triangle ADF will be established as having its sides and angles given; and similarly the part of it which is triangle BEF; since on account of angle F being common to both, angle EBF being at the vertex of the given angle, and angle E being right, it is shown as above that all the sides are given. And from that there follows what I said. For all these things are always tied together by a mutual and perpetual bond, as befits the form of a globe.

XIII

Finally, all the sides of a triangle being given, the angles are given.

Let all the sides of triangle ABC be given: I say that all the angles too are found.

For the triangle either will have equal sides or it will not. First therefore let AB and AC be equal. It is clear that the halves of chords subtending twice those sides will be equal. And let these halves be BE and CE, which on account of being at an equal distance from the centre of the sphere will cut one another at point E in DE the common section of the circles, as is clear from Euclid, III, Def. 4, [26ᵃ] and its converse.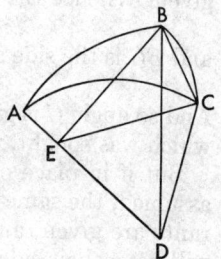

But by Euclid, III, 3, in plane ABD

angle $DEB = 90°$;

and in plane ACD similarly

angle $DEC = 90°$.

Therefore by Euclid, XI, Def. 3, BEC is the angle of inclination of the planes; and we shall find it as follows; for since there is a straight line subtending BC, we shall have a rectilinear triangle BEC with its sides given on account of their arcs being given; and then since the angles may be found, we shall have the angle BEC, which was sought, *i.e.*, we shall have the spherical angle BAC; and we shall have the others as above.

But if the triangle is scalene, as in the second figure, it is clear that the halves of the chords subtending twice the sides will by no means touch one another. For if

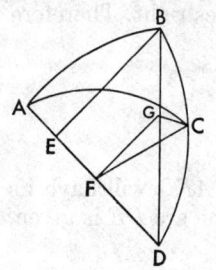

arc $AC >$ arc AB,

then, as

$CF = ½$ ch. $2\ AC$,

CF will fall lower down. But if

arc $AC <$ arc AB,

then CF will fall higher up, according as such lines become nearer and farther away from the centre, by Euclid, III, 15. Now however let FG be drawn parallel to BE; and at

point G let it cut BD the common section of the two circles [AB and BC]. And let GC be joined. Therefore it is clear that
$$\text{angle } EFG = \text{angle } AEB = 90°$$
And too
$$\text{angle } EFC = 90°;$$
for
$$CF = \tfrac{1}{2} \text{ ch. } 2\, AC.$$
Therefore angle CFG will be the angle of section of circles AB and AC; and we shall find this angle too. For
$$DF : FG = DE : EB,$$
since triangles DFG and DEB are similar. Therefore FG is given in the parts wherein FC is also given; and
$$DG : DB = DE : EB.$$
Hence DG will be given in the same parts whereof DC has 100,000. But as the angle GDC is given through the arc BC, therefore by the second theorem on plane triangles the side GC is given in the same parts wherein the remaining sides of the plane triangle GFC are given. Therefore by the last theorem on plane triangles we shall have the angle GFC, i.e., the spherical angle BAC, which was sought; and then we shall find the remaining angles by the eleventh theorem on spherical triangles.

XIV

If a given arc of a circle is cut anywhere so that both of the segments together are less than a semicircle, and if the ratio of half of the chord subtending twice one segment to the half of the chord subtending twice the other segment is given, [26ᵇ] the arcs of those segments will also be given.

For let arc ABC be given, around centre D; and let ABC be cut at point B
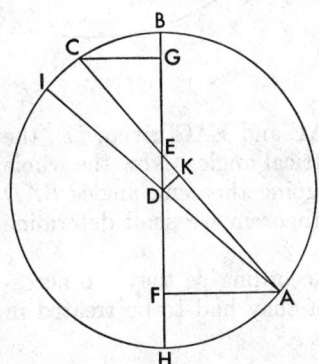
anywhere, but in such a way that the segments are less than a semicircle; and let
$$\tfrac{1}{2} \text{ ch. } 2\, AB : \tfrac{1}{2} \text{ ch. } 2\, BC$$
be somehow given in length: I say that the arcs AB and BC are also given.

For let the straight line AC be drawn, which the diameter cuts at point E; and from the termini A and C let the perpendiculars AF and CG fall upon the diameter. And of necessity
$$AF = \tfrac{1}{2} \text{ ch. } 2\, AB$$
and
$$CG = \tfrac{1}{2} \text{ ch. } 2\, BC.$$
Therefore in the right triangles AEF and CEG
$$\text{angle } AEF = \text{angle } CEG,$$
because they are vertical angles. And the triangles which are therefore equiangular and similar have the sides opposite the equal angles proportional:
$$AF : CG = AE : EC.$$
Therefore we shall have AE and EC in the parts wherein AF or GC has been given. But the chord subtending arc ABC is given in the parts wherein the radius DEB, AK the half of chord AC, and the remainder EK are given. Let DA and DK be joined, and they will be given in the parts wherein BD is given: DK will be given as half of the chord subtending the remaining segment which

is supplementary to arc *ABC* and is comprehended by angle *DAK*. And therefore angle *ADK* is given, which comprehends half of arc *ABC*. But in the triangle *EDK* having two sides given and angle *EKD* right, angle *EDK* will also be given. Hence the whole angle *EDA* comprehending the arc *AB* will be given. Thereby also the remainder *CB* will be manifest. And it was this that we were trying to show.

xv

If all the angles of a triangle are given, even though none is a right angle, all the sides are given.

Let there be the triangle *ABC*, all the angles of which are given but none of which is right. I say that all the sides are given too.

For from some one of the angles, say *A*, drop the arc *AD* through the poles of *CB*. *AD* will cut *BC* at right angles, and it will fall within the triangle, unless one of the angles at the base—angle *B* or angle *C*—is obtuse and the other acute. If that were the case, the arc would have to be drawn from the obtuse angle to the base. So with the quadrants *BAF*, *CAG*, and *DAE* completed and with *B* and *C* as poles, let the arcs *EF* and *EG* [27a] be drawn. Therefore

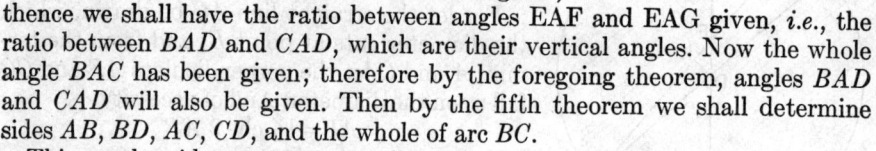

angle *F* = angle *G* = 90°.

Therefore in the right triangle *EAF*

½ ch. 2 *AE* : ½ ch. 2 *EF* = ½ dmt. sph. : ½ ch. 2 *EAF*.

Similarly in right triangle *AEG*

½ ch. 2 *AE* : ½ ch. 2 *EG* = ½ dmt. sph. : ½ ch. 2 *EAG*.

Therefore, *ex aequali*,

½ ch. 2 *EF* : ½ ch. 2 *EG* = ½ ch. 2 *EAF* : ½ ch. 2 *EAG*.

And because arcs *FE* and *EG* are given, since

arc *FE* = 90° − angle B

and

arc *EG* = 90° − angle *C*;

thence we shall have the ratio between angles EAF and EAG given, *i.e.*, the ratio between *BAD* and *CAD*, which are their vertical angles. Now the whole angle *BAC* has been given; therefore by the foregoing theorem, angles *BAD* and *CAD* will also be given. Then by the fifth theorem we shall determine sides *AB*, *BD*, *AC*, *CD*, and the whole of arc *BC*.

This much said enroute concerning triangles, according as they are necessary for our undertaking, will be sufficient. For if they had to be treated in greater detail, the work would be of unusual size.

SINCE we have expounded briefly the three terrestrial movements, by means of which we promised to demonstrate all the planetary appearances, now we shall fulfil our promise by proceeding from the whole to the parts and examining and investigating particular questions to the extent of our powers. Now we shall begin with the best-known movement of all, the revolution of day and night—which we said the Greeks called νυχθήμερος and which we have taken as belonging wholly and immediately to the terrestrial globe, since from this movement arise the months, years, and other variously named periods of time, as number from unity. Therefore we shall say only a few words about the inequality of days and nights, the rising and setting of the sun and of the parts of the ecliptic and the signs, and the consequences of this type of revolution; for many people have written about these subjects copiously enough and what they say is in harmony and agreement with our conceptions. It is of no importance if we take up in an opposite fashion what others have demonstrated by means of a motionless earth and a giddy world and race with them toward the same goal, since things related reciprocally happen to be inversely in harmony with one another. Nevertheless we shall omit nothing necessary. But no one should be surprised if we still speak of the rising and setting of the sun and stars, *et cetera*; but he should realize that we are speaking in the usual manner of speech which can be recognized by all and that we are nevertheless always keeping in mind that: "To us who are being carried by the Earth, the sun and the moon seem to pass over; and the stars return to their former positions and again move away."

1. ON THE CIRCLES AND THEIR NAMES

We have said that the equator is the greatest of the parallel circles on the terrestrial globe described around the axis of its daily revolution and that the ecliptic is the circle through the middle [28ᵃ] of the signs under which the centre of the Earth moves in a circle in its annual revolution.

But since the ecliptic crosses the equator obliquely; in proportion to the inclination of the axis of the Earth to it, it describes in the course of the daily revolution two circles which touch it on either side of the equator, as if the farthest limits to its obliquity. These circles are called the tropics. For on them the sun appears to make its "tropes," *i.e.*, its winter and summer changes of direction. Whence the northern circle used to be called the tropic of the summer solstice and the other the tropic of the shortest day, as was set forth in our summary exposition of the circular movements of the Earth.

Next follows the so-called horizon, which the Latins call the boundary circle; for it is the boundary between that part of the world which is visible to us and that part which lies hidden. All stars which set are seen to have their rising on it; and it has its centre on the surface of the Earth and its pole at the point directly overhead. But since it is impossible to compare the Earth with the immensity of the heavens—for according to our hypothesis even the total distance between the sun and the moon is indiscernible beside the magnitude of the heavens—the circle of the horizon appears to bisect the heavens, as if it went through the centre of the world, as we demonstrated in the beginning.

But when the horizon is oblique to the equator, it too touches on either side of the equator twin parallel circles, *i.e.*, the northern circle of the always visible stars and the southern circle of the always hidden stars. The first circle was called the arctic, and the second the antarctic by Proclus and the Greeks; and they become greater or smaller in proportion to the obliquity of the horizon or the elevation of the pole of the equator[1].

There remains the meridian circle which passes through the poles of the horizon and through the poles of the equator too and hence is perpendicular to both circles. The sun's reaching it gives us midday and midnight.

But these two circles which have their centres on the surface of the Earth, *i.e.*, the horizon and the meridian, are wholly consequent upon the movement of the Earth and upon our sight at some particular place. For the eye everywhere becomes as it were the centre of the sphere of all things which are visible to it on all sides.

Furthermore all the circles assumed on the Earth produce circles in the heavens as their likenesses and images, as will be shown more clearly in cosmography and in connection with the dimensions of the Earth. And these circles at any rate are the ones having proper names, though there are infinite ways of designating and naming others.

2. On the Obliquity of the Ecliptic and the Distance of the Tropics and How They Are Determined

[28ᵇ] Since the ecliptic lies between the tropics and crosses the equator obliquely, I therefore think that we should now try to observe what the distance between the tropics is and hence what the angle of section between the equator and the ecliptic is. For in order to perceive this by sense with the help of artificial instruments, by means of which the job can be done best, it is necessary to have a wooden square prepared, or preferably a square made from some other more solid material, from stone or metal; for the wood might not stay in the same condition on account of some alteration in the atmosphere and might mislead the observer. Now one surface of it should be very carefully planed, and it should be of sufficient area to admit being divided into sections, that is, a side should be about 5 or 6 feet long. Now with one of the corners [of the square] as centre and with a side as radius, let a quadrant of a circle be drawn and divided into 90 equal degrees; and let each of the degrees be subdivided into 60 minutes, or whatever number can be taken. Next let a cylindrical pointer which has been well turned on a lathe be set up at the centre (of the quadrant) and fixed in such a way as to be perpendicular to the surface and to extend out from it a little, say perhaps a finger's width or less.

When the instrument has been prepared in this way, the next thing to do is to exhibit the line of the meridian on a piece of flooring which lies in the plane of the horizon and which has been made even as carefully as is possible by means

---

[1]That is to say, the magnitude of the circle of the always visible stars varies inversely with the obliquity of the horizon and directly with the elevation of the poles of the equator.

of a hydroscope or ground-level, so as not to have a slope in any part of it. The piece of flooring should have a circle drawn on it and a cylinder erected at the center of the circle: we shall take observations and mark the point where at some time before midday the extremity of the shadow of the cylinder touches the circumference of the circle. We shall do the same thing in the afternoon, and then shall bisect the arc of the circle lying between the two points we have already marked. In this way a straight line drawn from the centre through the point of section will indicate infallibly for us the south and the north.

Accordingly the plane surface of the instrument should be set up on this piece of flooring as a base and fixed perpendicular to it with the centre [of the quadrant] to the south, so that a plumb-line from the centre would fall exactly at right angles to the meridian line. For it comes about in this way that the surface of the instrument exhibits the meridian circle. Hence on the days of summer and winter solstice the shadows of the sun at noon [29^a] are to be observed according as they are cast by the pointer, or cylinder, from the centre [of the quadrant]; and some mark is to be made on the arc of the quadrant, so that the place of the shadow may be kept more surely. And we shall note down the centre of the shadow in degrees and minutes as accurately as is possible. For if we do this, the arc between the marked shadows—the summer—and winter—solstitial shadows —will be found and will show us the distance between the tropics and also the total obliquity of the ecliptic[1]. By taking half of the arc, we shall have the distance of the tropics from the equator, and it will be clear what the angle of inclination is between the equator and the ecliptic.

Now Ptolemy took the interval between the aforesaid limits—the northern and the southern—as 47°42′40″, whereof the circle has 360°, as he found had been observed by Hipparchus and Eratosthenes before his time; and there are 11ᵖ whereof the whole circle has 83ᵖ. Hence half the arc—and half the arc has 23°51′20″, whereof the circle has 360°—showed the distance of the tropics from the equator and what the angle of section with the ecliptic was. Accordingly Ptolemy believed that these things were invariably such and would always remain so. But these distances have been found to have decreased continually from that time down to ours. For it has already been discovered by us and some of our contemporaries that the distance between the tropics is not more than 46°58′ approximately and that the angle of section is 23°29′. Hence it is clear enough that the obliquity of the ecliptic is not fixed. More on this below, where we shall show by a probable enough conclusion that it was never greater than 23°52′ and will not ever be less than 23°28′.

3. On the Arcs and Angles of the Intersections of the Equator, Ecliptic, and Meridian, By Means of Which Declinations and Right Ascensions Are Determined, and on the Computation of These Arcs and Angles

Accordingly as we were saying in the case of the horizon that the parts of the world have their risings and settings on it, we say that the meridian circle [29^b] halves the heavens. During the space of twenty-four hours this circle is crossed by both the ecliptic and the equator and divides both of their circumferences

[1]Since the distance between the sun and the Earth is imperceptible in relation to the radius of the sphere of the fixed stars, the centre of the quadrant may be taken as the centre of the sphere of the fixed stars.

by cutting them at the spring and at the autumnal intersection and in turn has its circumference divided by the arc intercepted by those two circles. Since they are all great circles, they form a spherical right triangle; for the angle is right where the meridian circle by definition cuts the equator described through its poles. Now the arc of the meridian circle, or any arc of a circle passing through the poles [of the equator] and intercepted in this way is called the declination of a segment of the ecliptic; and the corresponding arc on the equator is called the right ascension occurring at the same time as the similar arc on the ecliptic.

All this is easily demonstrated in a convex triangle. For let the circle *ABCD* be a circle passing simultaneously through the poles of the ecliptic and of the equator—most people call this circle the "colure"—let the semicircle of the ecliptic be *AEC*, the semicircle of the equator *BED*; let the spring equinox be at point *E*, the summer solstice at *A*, and the winter solstice at *C*. Now let *F* be taken as the pole of daily revolution, and on the ecliptic let

arc *EG* = 30°,

for example, and let it be cut off by *FGH* the quadrant of a circle.

Then it is clear that in triangle *EGH*

side *EG* = 30°,

angle *GEH* is given,

since at its least, in conformity with the greatest declination *AB*,

angle *GEH* = 23°28′,

and

where 4 rt. angles = 360°;

angle *GHE* = 90°.

Therefore by the fourth theorem on sphericals, triangle *EHG* will have its sides and angles given. For it was shown that

ch. 2 *EG* : ch. 2 *GH* = ch. 2 *AGE*, or dmt. sph. : ch. 2 *AB*

and their halves are in the same ratio. And since

½ ch. 2 *AGE* = radius = 100,000,

½ ch. 2 *AB* = 39,822,

and

½ ch. 2 *EG* = 50,000;

and since, if four numbers are proportional, the product of the means is equal to the product of the extremes; therefore

½ ch. 2 *GH* = 19,911,

and hence, by the table,

arc *GH* = 11°29′,

which is the declination of segment *EG*,

side *FG* = 78°31′,

side *AG* = 60°,

since they are the remainders of the quadrants, and

angle *FAG* = 90°.

In the same way

[30ª] ½ ch. 2 *FG* : ½ ch. 2 *AG* = ½ ch. 2 *FGH* : ½ ch. 2 *BH*.

Now since three of these chords are given, the fourth will also be given, that is to say,

arc *BH* = 62°6′,

which is the right ascension from the summer solstice, and
$$HE = 27°54'$$
from the spring equinox. Similarly, since
$$\text{side } FG = 78°31',$$
$$\text{side } AF = 64°30',$$
and
$$AGE = 90°;$$
then, since angles AGF and HGE are vertical angles,
$$\text{angle } AGF = \text{angle } HGE = 63°29\tfrac{1}{2}'.$$

In the rest we shall do as in this example. But we should not be ignorant of the fact that the meridian circle cuts the ecliptic at right angles in the signs where the ecliptic touches the tropics, for then the meridian circle cuts it through its poles, as we said. But at the equinoctial points the meridian makes an angle less than a right angle by the angle of inclination of the ecliptic, so that in conformity with the least inclination of the ecliptic it makes an angle of 66°32'.

Moreover we should note that equal sides and equal angles of the triangles follow upon equal arcs of the ecliptic being taken from the points of solstice or equinox. In this way if we draw the equatorial arc ABC and the ecliptic BDE as intersecting at point B, where the equinox is, and if we take as equal the arcs FB and BG and also arcs KFL and HGM two quadrants of circle described through the poles of daily revolution; there will be the two triangles FLB and BMG, wherein

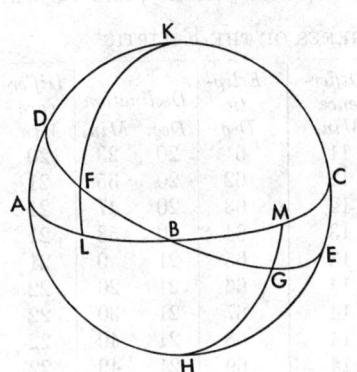

$$\text{side } BF = \text{side } BG$$
$$\text{angle } FLB = \text{angle } GBM$$
and
$$\text{angle } FLB = \text{angle } GMB = 90°.$$
Therefore by the sixth theorem on spherical triangles the sides and angles are equal. Hence
$$\text{declination } FL = \text{declination } GM$$
$$\text{rt. ascension } LB = \text{rt. ascension } BM$$
and
$$\text{angle } LFB = \text{angle } MGB.$$

This same fact will be manifest upon the assumption of equal arcs described from a point of solstice, for example, when AB and BC on different sides of their point of contact B, the solstice, are equally distant from it. For when the arcs DA and DB [and DC] have been drawn from the pole of the equator, there will similarly be the two triangles ABD and DBC.

Then
$$\text{base } AB = \text{base } BC$$
$$\text{side } BD \text{ is common}$$
and
$$\text{angle } ABD = \text{angle } CBD = 90°.$$
Accordingly by the eighth theorem on sphericals the triangles will be shown to have equal sides and angles. It is clear from this that such

angles and arcs laid out in one quadrant of the ecliptic [30b] are in accord with the remaining quadrants of the full circle.

We shall subjoin an example of these things in the tables. In the first column are placed the degrees of the ecliptic; in the following column, the declinations answering to those degrees; and in the third column the minutes, which are the differences between the particular declinations and the declinations which occur at the time of greatest obliquity of the ecliptic: the greatest of these differences is 24'.

We shall do the same thing in the table of ascensions and the table of meridian angles. For it is necessary for all things which are consequences of the obliquity of the ecliptic to be changed with a change in it. Furthermore, in the right ascensions an extremely slight difference is found, one which does not exceed $\frac{1}{10}$ "time" and which in the space of an hour makes only $\frac{1}{150}$ 'time.''—The ancients give the name of "time" to the parts of the equator which arise together with the parts of the ecliptic. Each of these circles, as we have often said, has 360 parts; but in order to distinguish between them, most of the ancients called the parts of ecliptic "degrees" and those of the equator "times"; and we will

TABLE OF DECLINATIONS OF THE DEGREES OF THE ECLIPTIC

Ecliptic Deg.	Declination Deg.	Declination Min.	Difference Min.	Ecliptic Deg.	Declination Deg.	Declination Min.	Difference Min.	Ecliptic Deg.	Declination Deg.	Declination Min.	Difference Min.
1	0	24	0	31	11	50	11	61	20	23	20
2	0	48	1	32	12	11	12	62	20	35	21
3	1	12	1	33	12	32	12	63	20	47	21
4	1	36	2	34	12	52	13	64	20	58	21
5	2	0	2	35	13	12	13	65	21	9	21
6	2	23	2	36	13	32	14	66	21	20	22
7	2	47	3	37	13	52	14	67	21	30	22
8	3	11	3	38	14	12	14	68	21	40	22
9	3	35	4	39	14	31	14	69	21	49	22
10	3	58	4	40	14	50	14	70	21	58	22
11	4	22	4	41	15	9	15	71	22	7	22
12	4	45	4	42	15	27	15	72	22	15	23
13	5	9	5	43	15	46	16	73	22	23	23
14	5	32	5	44	16	4	16	74	22	30	23
15	5	55	5	45	16	22	16	75	22	37	23
16	6	19	6	46	16	39	17	76	22	44	23
17	6	41	6	47	16	56	17	77	22	50	23
18	7	4	7	48	17	13	17	78	22	55	23
19	7	27	7	49	17	30	18	79	23	1	24
20	7	49	8	50	17	46	18	80	23	5	24
21	8	12	8	51	18	1	18	81	23	10	24
22	8	34	8	52	18	17	18	82	23	13	24
23	8	57	9	53	18	32	19	83	23	17	24
24	9	19	9	54	18	47	19	84	23	20	24
25	9	41	9	55	19	2	19	85	23	22	24
26	10	3	10	56	19	16	19	86	23	24	24
27	10	25	10	57	19	30	20	87	23	26	24
28	10	46	10	58	19	44	20	88	23	27	24
29	11	8	10	59	19	57	20	89	23	28	24
30	11	29	11	60	20	10	20	90	23	28	24

copy them for the remainder of the work.—Therefore since the difference is so small that it can be properly neglected, we are not peeved at having to place it in a separate column.

Hence these tables can be made to apply to any other obliquity of the ecliptic, if in conformity with the ratio of difference between the least and greatest obliquity of the ecliptic we make the proper corrections. For example, if with an obliquity of 23°34′ we wish to know how great a declination follows from taking a distance of 30° from the equator along the ecliptic, we find that in the table there are 11°29′ in the column of declinations and 11′ in the column of differences. These 11′ would be all added in the case of the greatest obliquity of the ecliptic, which is, as we said, an obliquity of 23°52′. But it has already been laid down that the obliquity is 23°34′ and is accordingly greater than the least obliquity by 6′, which are one quarter of 24′, which is the excess of the greatest obliquity over the least. Now

$$3' : 11' \fallingdotseq 6' : 24'.$$

When I add 3′ to the 11°29′, I shall have 11°32′, which will then measure the declination of the arc of the ecliptic 30° from the equator.

TABLE OF RIGHT ASCENSIONS

Ecliptic Deg.	Equator Times Min.		Difference Min.	Ecliptic Deg.	Equator Times Min.		Difference Min.	Ecliptic Deg.	Equator Times Min.		Difference Min.
1	0	55	0	31	28	54	4	61	58	51	4
2	1	50	0	32	29	51	4	62	59	54	4
3	2	45	0	33	30	50	4	63	60	57	4
4	3	40	0	34	31	46	4	64	62	0	4
5	4	35	0	35	32	45	4	65	63	3	4
6	5	30	0	36	33	43	5	66	64	6	3
7	6	25	1	37	34	41	5	67	65	9	3
8	7	20	1	38	35	40	5	68	66	13	3
9	8	15	1	39	36	38	5	69	67	17	3
10	9	11	1	40	37	37	5	70	68	21	3
11	10	6	1	41	38	36	5	71	69	25	3
12	11	0	2	42	39	35	5	72	70	29	3
13	11	57	2	43	40	34	5	73	71	33	3
14	12	52	2	44	41	33	6	74	72	38	2
15	13	48	2	45	42	32	6	75	73	43	2
16	14	43	2	46	43	31	6	76	74	47	2
17	15	39	2	47	44	32	5	77	75	52	2
18	16	34	3	48	45	32	5	78	76	57	2
19	17	31	3	49	46	32	5	79	78	2	2
20	18	27	3	50	47	33	5	80	79	7	2
21	19	23	3	51	48	34	5	81	80	12	1
22	20	19	3	52	49	35	5	82	81	17	1
23	21	15	3	53	50	36	5	83	82	22	1
24	22	10	4	54	51	37	5	84	83	27	1
25	23	9	4	55	52	38	4	85	84	33	1
26	24	6	4	56	53	41	4	86	85	38	0
27	25	3	4	57	54	43	4	87	86	43	0
28	26	0	4	58	55	45	4	88	87	48	0
29	26	57	4	59	56	46	4	89	88	54	0
30	27	54	4	60	57	48	4	90	90	0	0

The same thing can be done in the table of meridian angles and right ascensions, except that we must always add the differences in the case of right ascensions but subtract them in the case of the meridian angles, so that everything may proceed correctly in conformity with the time.

TABLE OF THE MERIDIAN ANGLES

Ecliptic Deg.	Angle Deg.	Angle Min.	Difference Min.	Ecliptic Deg.	Angle Deg.	Angle Min.	Difference Min.	Ecliptic Deg.	Angle Deg.	Angle Min.	Difference Min.
1	66	32	24	31	69	35	21	61	78	7	12
2	66	33	24	32	69	48	21	62	78	29	12
3	66	34	24	33	70	0	20	63	78	51	11
4	66	35	24	34	70	13	20	64	79	14	11
5	66	37	24	35	70	26	20	65	79	36	11
6	66	39	24	36	70	39	20	66	79	59	10
7	66	42	24	37	70	53	20	67	80	22	10
8	66	44	24	38	71	7	19	68	80	45	10
9	66	47	24	39	71	22	19	69	81	9	9
10	66	51	24	40	71	36	19	70	81	33	9
11	66	55	24	41	71	52	19	71	81	58	8
12	66	59	24	42	72	8	18	72	82	22	8
13	67	4	23	43	72	24	18	73	82	46	7
14	67	10	23	44	72	39	18	74	83	11	7
15	67	15	23	45	72	55	17	75	83	35	6
16	67	21	23	46	73	11	17	76	84	0	6
17	67	27	23	47	73	28	17	77	84	25	6
18	67	34	23	48	73	47	17	78	84	50	5
19	67	41	23	49	74	6	16	79	85	15	5
20	67	49	23	50	74	24	16	80	85	40	4
21	67	56	23	51	74	42	16	81	86	5	4
22	68	4	22	52	75	1	15	82	86	30	3
23	68	13	22	53	75	21	15	83	86	55	3
24	68	22	22	54	75	40	15	84	87	19	3
25	68	32	22	55	76	1	14	85	87	53	2
26	68	41	22	56	76	21	14	86	88	17	2
27	68	51	22	57	76	42	14	87	88	41	1
28	69	2	21	58	77	3	13	88	89	6	1
29	69	13	21	59	77	24	13	89	89	33	0
30	69	24	21	60	77	45	13	90	90	0	0

4. HOW TO DETERMINE THE DECLINATION AND RIGHT ASCENSION OF ANY STAR WHICH IS PLACED OUTSIDE THE ECLIPTIC BUT WHOSE LONGITUDE AND LATITUDE HAVE BEEN ESTABLISHED; AND WITH WHAT DEGREE OF THE ECLIPTIC IT HALVES THE HEAVENS

[32ᵇ] These things have been set down concerning the ecliptic and the equator and their intersections. But as regards the daily revolution, it is of interest not only to know what parts of the ecliptic appear, by means of which the causes of the sun's appearing where it does are discovered, but also to know that there is a similar demonstration of the declination from the equator and of the right ascension in the case of those fixed or wandering stars which are outside the ecliptic but whose longitude and latitude have been given.

Therefore let the circle ABCD be described through the poles of the equator

and of the ecliptic; let AEC be the semicircle
of the equator above pole F; let BED be the
semicircle of the ecliptic about pole G; and let
its intersection with the equator be at point
E. Now from the pole G let the arc $GHKL$ be
drawn through a star, and let the position of
the star be given as point H, and let $FHMN$ a
quadrant of a circle fall through H from the
pole of daily movement.

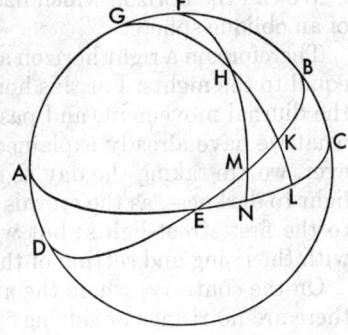

Then it is clear that the star which is at H
falls upon the meridian at the same time as
points M and N do, and that arc HMN is the
declination of the star from the equator, and
EN is its ascension in the right sphere, and those are what we are seeking.
Accordingly since in triangle KEL

side KE is given,

angle KEL is given,

and

angle $EKL = 90°$,

therefore by the fourth theorem on spherical triangles,

side KL is given,

side EL is given,

and

angle KLE is given.

Therefore by addition

arc HKL is given.

And on that account, in triangle HLN,

angle HLN is given,

angle $LNH = 90°$,

and

side HL is given.

Therefore by the same fourth theorem on sphericals there are also given the remaining sides: HN the declination of the star, and LN, and the remaining distance NE, the right ascension, which measures the distance the sphere turns
from the equinox to the star.

—Or in another way. If in the foregoing you take KE the arc of the ecliptic
as the right ascension of LE, conversely LE will be given by the table of right
ascensions; and so will LK, as the declination corresponding to LE; [33a] and
the angle KLE will be given by the table of meridian angles; and hence the
remaining sides and angles, as we have showed, may be learned.—

Then by means of the right ascension EN, the number of degrees of EM the
arc of the ecliptic are given. And in conformity with these things the star together with point M halves the heavens.

5. On the Sections of the Horizon

Now the horizon of a right sphere is different from the horizon of an oblique
sphere. For the horizon to which the equator is perpendicular, or which passes
through the poles of the equator, is called a right horizon.

We call the horizon which has some inclination with the equator the horizon of an oblique sphere.

Therefore on a right horizon all the stars rise and set, and the days are always equal to the nights. For this horizon bisects all the parallel circles described by the diurnal movement, and passes through their poles; and there occurs there what we have already explained in the case of the meridian circle. Here, however, we are taking the day as extending from sunrise to sunset, and not from light to darkness, as the crowds understand it, *i.e.*, from early morning twilight to the first street lights; but we shall say more on this subject in connection with the rising and setting of the signs.

On the contrary, where the axis of the Earth is perpendicular to the horizon there are no risings or settings, but all the stars turn in a gyre and are always visible or hidden, unless they are affected by some other motion, such as the annual movement around the sun. Consequently, there day lasts perpetually for the space of half a year and night for the rest of the time; and there is nothing else to differentiate summer and winter, since there the horizon coincides with the equator.

Furthermore, in an oblique sphere certain stars rise and set; and certain others are always visible or always hidden; and meanwhile the days and nights are unequal there where an oblique horizon touches two parallel circles in proportion to its inclination. And of these circles, the one nearer the visible pole is the boundary of the always visible stars, and conversely the circle nearer the hidden pole is the boundary for the always hidden stars. Therefore the horizon, as falling completely between these boundaries, cuts all the parallel circles in the middle into unequal arcs, except the equator, which is the greatest of the parallels; and great circles bisect one another. Therefore an oblique horizon in the upper hemisphere cuts off arcs of parallels in the direction of the visible pole which are greater than the arcs which are toward the southern and hidden [33b] pole; and the converse is the case in the hidden hemisphere. The sun becomes visible in these horizons by reason of the diurnal movement and causes the inequality of days and nights.

6. What the Differences Between the Midday Shadows Are

There are differences between the midday shadows on account of which some people are called periscian, others amphiscian, and still others heteroscian. The periscian are those whom we might call "circumumbratile," that is to say, "throwing the shadow of the sun on every side." And they live where the distance between the vertex, or pole, of the horizon and the pole of the Earth is less or no greater than that between the tropic and the equator. For there the parallels which the horizon touches as the boundaries of the always apparent or always hidden stars are greater than, or equal to, the tropics. And so the summer sun high up among the always apparent stars at that time throws the shadow of a pointer in every direction. But where the horizon touches the tropics, the tropics become the boundaries of the always apparent and the always hidden stars. Wherefore instead of there being midnight the sun at its [winter] solstice seems to graze the Earth, at which time the whole circle of the ecliptic coincides with the horizon; and straightway six signs rise at the same time, and on the opposite side six signs set at the same time, and the pole of the ecliptic coincides with the pole of the horizon.

The amphiscian, who cast midday shadows on both sides, are those who live between the tropics. This is the space which the ancients called the middle zone. And since throughout that whole tract the circle of the ecliptic passes directly over head twice, as is shown in the second theorem of the *Phaenomena* of Euclid, the shadows of pointers are cast in two directions there: for as the sun moves back and forth, the pointers throw their shadows sometimes to the south and sometimes to the north.

The rest of us who inhabit the region between the two others are heteroscian, because we cast our midday shadows in only one direction. *i.e.*, towards the north.

Now the ancient mathematicians were accustomed to divide the world into seven climates, through Meroë, Siona, Alexandria, Rhodes, the Hellespont, the middle of the Pontus, Boristhenes, Byzantium, and so on with the single parallel circles taken according to the differences between the longest days and according to the lengths of the shadows, which they observed by means of pointers at noon on the days of equinoxes and solstices, and [34a] according to the elevation of the pole or the latitude of some segment. Since these things have partly changed through time, they are not exactly the same as they once were, on account of the variable obliquity of the ecliptic, as we said, of which the ancients were ignorant; or, to speak more correctly, on account of the variable inclination of the equator to the plane of the ecliptic, upon which these things depend. But the elevations of the pole or the latitudes of the places and the equinoctial shadows agree with those which antiquity discovered and made note of. That would necessarily take place, since the equator depends upon the pole of the terrestrial globe. Wherefore those segments are not accurately enough designated and defined by shadows falling on special days, but more correctly by their distances from the equator, which remain perpetually. But although this variability of the tropics, because very slight, admits but slight diversity of days and of shadows in southern places, it becomes more apparent to those who are moving northward. Therefore as regards the shadows of pointers, it is clear that for any given altitude of the sun the length of the shadow is derivable and vice versa.

In this way if there is the pointer AB which casts a shadow BC; since the pointer is perpendicular to the plane of the horizon, angle ABC must always be right, by the definition of lines perpendicular to a plane. Wherefore if AC be joined, we shall have a right triangle ABC; and for a given altitude of the sun we shall have angle ACB given. And by the first theorem on plane triangles the ratio of the pointer AB to its shadow BC will be given, and BC will be given in length. Conversely, moreover, when AB and BC are given, it will be clear from the third theorem on plane triangles what angle ACB is and what the elevation of the sun making that shadow at that time is. In this way the ancients in describing the regions of the terrestrial globe gave the lengths of the midday shadows sometimes at the equinoxes and sometimes at the solstices.

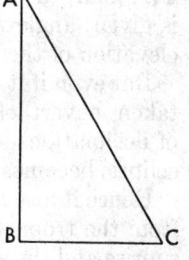

7. How the Longest Day, the Distance of Rising, and the Inclination of the Sphere Are Derived from One Another, and on the Differences Between Days

[34[b]] In this way too for any obliquity of the sphere or inclination of the horizon we will demonstrate simultaneously the longest and the shortest day together with the distance of rising [of the sun] and the difference of the remaining days. Now the distance of rising is the arc of the horizon intercepted between the summer solstitial and the winter solstitial sunrises, or the sum of the distances of the solstitial from the equinoctial sunrise.

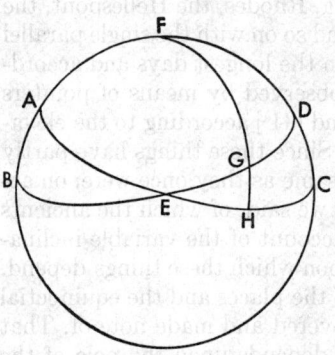

Therefore let $ABCD$ be the meridian circle, and let BED be the semicircle of the horizon in the eastern hemisphere, and let AEC be the similar semicircle of the equator with F as its northern pole. Let point G be taken as the rising of the sun at the summer solstice, and let FGH the arc of a great circle be drawn. Therefore since the motion of the terrestrial sphere takes place around pole F of the equator, then necessarily points G and H will fit onto the meridian $ABCD$ at the same time, since parallel circles are around the same poles through which pass the great circles which intercept similar arcs on the parallel circles. Wherefore the selfsame time from the rising at G to midday measures also the arc AEH; and the time from midnight to sunrise measures CH the remaining and subterranean arc of the semicircle. Now AEC is a semicircle; and AE and EC are quadrants of circles, since they are drawn through the pole of $ABCD$. On that account, EH will be half the difference between the longest day and the equinox; and EG will be the distance between the equinoctial and the solstitial sunrise. Therefore since in triangle EHG angle GEH, the obliquity of the sphere, is established by means of arc AB, and angle GHE is right, and side GH is given as the distance from the summer tropic to the equator; the remaining sides are also given by the fourth theorem on sphericals: side EH as half the difference between the longest day and the equinox, and side GE as the distance of sunrise. Moreover, if together with side GH side EH, [half] the difference between the longest day and the equinox, or else EG, is given; angle E of the inclination of the sphere is given, and hence FD the elevation of the pole above the horizon.

But even if it is not the tropic but some other point G in the ecliptic which is taken, nevertheless arcs EG and EH will become manifest: since by the table of declinations set out above GH the arc of declination for that degree of the ecliptic becomes known, and the rest can be demonstrated in the same way.

Hence it also follows that the degrees of the ecliptic which are equally distant from the tropic cut off equal arcs of the horizon [35[a]] between the equinoctial sunrise and the same degrees and make the lengths of days and nights inversely equal. And that is so because the parallels which pass through each of those degrees of the ecliptic are equal, since each of the degrees has the same declination.

But when equal arcs are taken between the equinoctial intersection and the two degrees [on the ecliptic], again the distances of rising are equal but in different directions; and the duration of days and nights are inversely equal, because on each side of the equinox the durations describe equal arcs of parallels, according as the signs themselves which are equally distant from the equinox have equal declinations from the equator.

For in the same figure let GM and KN the arcs of parallels be described cutting the horizon BED at points G and K, and let LKO a quadrant of a great circle be drawn from the south pole L. Therefore since

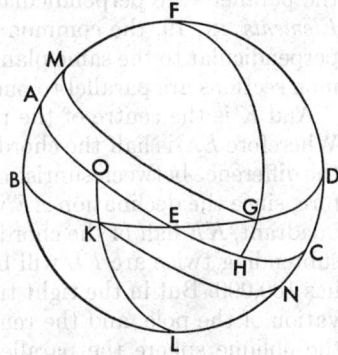

declination HG = declination KO, there will be two triangles DFG and BLK, wherein two sides of the one are equal to two sides of the other:
$$FG = LK$$
and the elevations of the poles are equal,
$$FD = LB,$$
and
$$\text{angle } D = \text{angle } B = 90°.$$
Therefore
$$\text{base } DG = \text{base } BK;$$
and hence, as the distances of sunrise are the remainders of the quadrants
$$GE = EK.$$
Wherefore since here too,
$$\text{side } EG = \text{side } EK,$$
$$\text{side } GH = \text{side } KO,$$
and
$$\text{vertical angle } KEO = \text{vertical angle } GEH;$$
$$\text{side } EH = \text{side } EO.$$
And
$$EH + 90° = OE + 90°.$$
Hence
$$\text{arc } AEH = \text{arc } OEC.$$
But since great circles described through the poles of parallel circles cut off similar arcs, GM and KN will be similar and equal, as was to be shown.

But all this can be shown differently. In the same way let the meridian circle $ABCD$ be described with centre E. Let the diameter of the equator and the common section of the two circles be AEC; let BED be the diameter of the horizon and the meridian line, let LEM be the axis of the sphere; and let L be the apparent pole and M the hidden. Let AF be taken as the distance of the summer solstice or as some other declination; and to AF let GF be drawn as the diameter of a parallel and its common section with the meridian; FG will cut the axis at K and the meridian line at N.

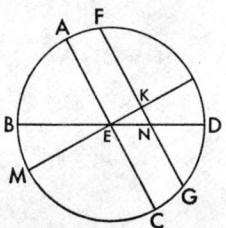

Therefore, [35ᵇ] since by the definition of Posidonius those lines are parallel which neither move toward nor move away from one another but which everywhere make the perpindicular lines between them equal,

$$KE = \tfrac{1}{2} \text{ ch. 2 } AF.$$

Similarly KN will be half of the chord subtending twice the arc of the parallel circle whose radius is FK. And twice this arc is the difference between the equinoctial day and the other day. And this is true because all the semicircles of which these lines are the common sections and diameters—namely, BED of the oblique horizon, LEM of the right horizon, AEC of the equator, and FKG of the parallel—are perpendicular to the plane of circle $ABCD$. And by Euclid's *Elements*, xi, 19, the common sections which they make with one another are perpendicular to the same plane at points E, K, and N: and by xi, 6, these common sections are parallel to one another.

And K is the centre of the parallel circle; and E is the centre of the sphere. Wherefore EN is half the chord subtending twice the arc of the horizon which is the difference between sunrise on the parallel and the equinoctial sunrise. Therefore, since the declination AF was given together with FL the remainder of the quadrant, KE half of the chord subtending twice arc AF and FK half the chord subtending twice arc FL will be established in terms of the parts whereof AE has 100,000. But in the right triangle EKN angle KEN is given by DL the elevation of the pole, and the remaining angle KNE is equal to AEB, because in the oblique sphere the parallels are equally inclined to the horizon; and the sides are given in the same parts whereof the radius has 100,000. Therefore KN will be given in the parts whereof FK the radius of the parallel has 100,000; for KN is equal to half the chord subtending the arc which measures the distance between the equinoctial day and a day on the parallel; and this arc is similarly given in the degrees whereof the parallel circle has 360°.

From this it is clear that

$$FK : KN = \tfrac{1}{2} \text{ ch. 2 } FL : \tfrac{1}{2} \text{ ch. 2 } AF \text{ comp. } \tfrac{1}{2} \text{ ch. 2 } AB : \tfrac{1}{2} \text{ ch. 2 } DL$$

and

$$\tfrac{1}{2} \text{ ch. 2 } FL : \tfrac{1}{2} \text{ ch. 2 } AF \text{ comp. } \tfrac{1}{2} \text{ ch. 2 } AB : \tfrac{1}{2} \text{ ch. 2 } DL =$$
$$FK : KE \text{ comp. } EK : KN.$$

That is to say, EK is taken as a mean between FK and KN. Similarly too

$$BE : EN = BE : EK \text{ comp. } KE : EN,$$

as Ptolemy shows in greater detail by means of spherical segments. So I think that not only the inequality of days and nights can be determined; but also that in the case of the moon and the stars whose declination on the parallels described through them by the daily movement has been given, the segments [of the parallels] which are above the horizon can be distinguished from those which are below; and hence the risings and settings [of the moon or stars] can be easily understood.

TABLE OF DIFFERENCE OF THE ASCENSIONS IN AN OBLIQUE SPHERE

Decli-nation	Elevation of the Pole										
	31°		32°		33°		34°		35°		36°	
	Times	Min.	Times	Min.	Times	Min.	Times	Min.	Times	Min.	Times	Min.
1	0	36	0	37	0	39	0	40	0	42	0	44
2	1	12	1	15	1	18	1	21	1	24	1	27
3	1	48	1	53	1	57	2	2	2	6	2	11
4	2	24	2	30	2	36	2	42	2	48	2	55
5	3	1	3	8	3	15	3	23	3	31	3	39
6	3	37	3	46	3	55	4	4	4	13	4	23
7	4	14	4	24	4	34	4	45	4	56	5	7
8	4	51	5	2	5	14	5	26	5	39	5	52
9	5	28	5	41	5	54	6	8	6	22	6	36
10	6	5	6	20	6	35	6	50	7	6	7	22
11	6	42	6	59	7	15	7	32	7	49	8	7
12	7	20	7	38	7	56	8	15	8	34	8	53
13	7	58	8	18	8	37	8	58	9	18	9	39
14	8	37	8	58	9	19	9	41	10	3	10	26
15	9	16	9	38	10	1	10	25	10	49	11	14
16	9	55	10	19	10	44	11	9	11	25	12	2
17	10	35	11	1	11	27	11	54	12	22	12	50
18	11	16	11	43	12	11	12	40	13	9	13	39
19	11	56	12	25	12	55	13	26	13	57	14	29
20	12	38	13	9	13	40	14	13	14	46	15	20
21	13	20	13	53	14	26	15	0	15	36	16	12
22	14	3	14	37	15	13	15	49	16	27	17	5
23	14	47	15	23	16	0	16	38	17	17	17	58
24	15	31	16	9	16	48	17	29	18	10	18	52
25	16	16	16	56	17	38	18	20	19	3	19	48
26	17	2	17	45	18	28	19	12	19	58	20	45
27	17	50	18	34	19	19	20	6	20	54	21	44
28	18	38	19	24	20	12	21	1	21	51	22	43
29	19	27	20	16	21	6	21	57	22	50	23	45
30	20	18	21	9	22	1	22	55	23	51	24	48
31	21	10	22	3	22	58	23	55	24	53	25	53
32	22	3	22	59	23	56	24	56	25	57	27	0
33	22	57	23	54	24	19	25	59	27	3	28	9
34	23	55	24	56	25	59	27	4	28	10	29	21
35	24	53	25	57	27	3	28	10	29	21	30	35
36	25	53	27	0	28	9	29	21	30	35	31	52

Table of Difference of the Ascensions in an Oblique Sphere

Decli-nation	Elevation of the Pole										
	37°		38°		39°		40°		41°		42°
	Times	Min.	Times	Min.	Times	Min.	Times	Min.	Times	Min.	Times	Min.
1	0	45	0	47	0	49	0	50	0	52	0	54
2	1	31	1	34	1	37	1	41	1	44	1	48
3	2	16	2	21	2	26	2	31	2	37	2	42
4	3	1	3	8	3	15	3	22	3	29	3	37
5	3	47	3	55	4	4	4	13	4	22	4	31
6	4	33	4	43	4	53	5	4	5	15	5	26
7	5	19	5	30	5	42	5	55	6	8	6	21
8	6	5	6	18	6	32	6	46	7	1	7	16
9	6	51	7	6	7	22	7	38	7	55	8	12
10	7	38	7	55	8	13	8	30	8	49	9	8
11	8	25	8	44	9	3	9	23	9	44	10	5
12	9	13	9	34	9	55	10	16	10	39	11	2
13	10	1	10	24	10	46	11	10	11	35	12	0
14	10	50	11	14	11	39	12	5	12	31	12	58
15	11	39	12	5	12	32	13	0	13	28	13	58
16	12	29	12	57	13	26	13	55	14	26	14	58
17	13	19	13	49	14	20	14	52	15	25	15	59
18	14	10	14	42	15	15	15	49	16	24	17	1
19	15	2	15	36	16	11	16	48	17	25	18	4
20	15	55	16	31	17	8	17	47	18	27	19	8
21	16	49	17	27	18	7	18	47	19	30	20	13
22	17	44	18	24	19	6	19	49	20	34	21	20
23	18	39	19	22	20	6	20	52	21	39	22	28
24	19	36	20	21	21	8	21	56	22	46	23	38
25	20	34	21	21	22	11	23	2	23	55	24	50
26	21	34	22	24	23	16	24	10	25	5	26	3
27	22	35	23	28	24	22	25	19	26	17	27	18
28	23	37	24	33	25	30	26	30	27	31	28	36
29	24	41	25	40	26	40	27	43	28	48	29	57
30	25	47	26	49	27	52	28	59	30	7	31	19
31	26	55	28	0	29	7	30	17	31	29	32	45
32	28	5	29	13	30	54	31	31	32	54	34	14
33	29	18	30	29	31	44	33	1	34	22	35	47
34	30	32	31	48	33	6	34	27	35	54	37	24
35	31	51	33	10	34	33	35	59	37	30	39	5
36	33	12	34	35	36	2	37	34	39	10	40	51

TABLE OF DIFFERENCE OF THE ASCENSIONS IN AN OBLIQUE SPHERE

Decli-nation	Elevation of the Pole										
	43°		44°		45°		46°		47°		48°
	Times	Min.	Times	Min.	Times	Min.	Times	Min.	Times	Min.	Times	Min.
1	0	56	0	58	1	0	1	2	1	4	1	7
2	1	52	1	56	2	0	2	4	2	9	2	13
3	2	48	2	54	3	0	3	7	3	13	3	20
4	3	44	3	52	4	1	4	9	4	18	4	27
5	4	41	4	51	5	1	5	12	5	23	5	35
6	5	37	5	50	6	2	6	15	6	28	6	42
7	6	34	6	49	7	3	7	18	7	34	7	50
8	7	32	7	48	8	5	8	22	8	40	8	59
9	8	30	8	48	9	7	9	26	9	47	10	8
10	9	28	9	48	10	9	10	31	10	54	11	18
11	10	27	10	49	11	13	11	37	12	2	12	28
12	11	26	11	51	12	16	12	43	13	11	13	39
13	12	26	12	53	13	21	13	50	14	20	14	51
14	13	27	13	56	14	26	14	58	15	30	16	5
15	14	28	15	0	15	32	16	7	16	42	17	19
16	15	31	16	5	16	40	17	16	17	54	18	34
17	16	34	17	10	17	48	18	27	19	8	19	51
18	17	38	18	17	18	58	19	40	20	23	21	9
19	18	44	19	25	20	9	20	53	21	40	22	29
20	19	50	20	35	21	21	22	8	22	58	23	51
21	20	59	21	46	22	34	23	25	24	18	25	14
22	22	8	22	58	23	50	24	44	25	40	26	40
23	23	19	24	12	25	7	26	5	27	5	28	8
24	24	32	25	28	26	26	27	27	28	31	29	38
25	25	47	26	46	27	48	28	52	30	0	31	12
26	27	3	28	6	29	11	30	20	31	32	32	48
27	28	22	29	29	30	38	31	51	33	7	34	28
28	29	44	30	54	32	7	33	25	34	46	36	12
29	31	8	32	22	33	40	35	2	36	28	38	0
30	32	35	33	53	35	16	36	43	38	15	39	53
31	34	5	35	28	36	56	38	29	40	7	41	52
32	35	38	37	7	38	40	40	19	42	4	43	57
33	37	16	38	50	40	30	42	15	44	8	46	9
34	38	58	40	39	42	25	44	18	46	20	48	31
35	40	46	42	33	44	27	46	23	48	36	51	3
36	42	39	44	33	46	36	48	47	51	11	53	47

TABLE OF DIFFERENCE OF THE ASCENSIONS IN AN OBLIQUE SPHERE

Decli-nation	Elevation of the Pole										
	49°		50°		51°		52°		53°		54°	
	Times	Min.	Times	Min.	Times	Min.	Times	Min.	Times	Min.	Times	Min.
1	1	9	1	12	1	14	1	17	1	20	1	23
2	2	18	2	23	2	28	2	34	2	39	2	45
3	3	27	3	35	3	43	3	51	3	59	4	8
4	4	37	4	47	4	57	5	8	5	19	5	31
5	5	47	5	50	6	12	6	26	6	40	6	55
6	6	57	7	12	7	27	7	44	8	1	8	19
7	8	7	8	25	8	43	9	2	9	23	9	44
8	9	18	9	38	10	0	10	22	10	45	11	9
9	10	30	10	53	11	17	11	42	12	8	12	35
10	11	42	12	8	12	35	13	3	13	32	14	3
11	12	55	13	24	13	53	14	24	14	57	15	31
12	14	9	14	40	15	13	15	47	16	23	17	0
13	15	24	15	58	16	34	17	11	17	50	18	32
14	16	40	17	17	17	56	18	37	19	19	20	4
15	17	57	18	39	19	19	20	4	20	50	21	38
16	19	16	19	59	20	44	21	32	22	22	23	15
17	20	36	21	22	22	11	23	2	23	56	24	53
18	21	57	22	47	23	39	24	34	25	33	26	34
19	23	20	24	14	25	10	26	9	27	11	28	17
20	24	45	25	42	26	43	27	46	28	53	30	4
21	26	12	27	14	28	18	29	26	30	37	31	54
22	27	42	28	47	29	56	31	8	32	25	33	47
23	29	14	30	23	31	37	32	54	34	17	35	45
24	31	4	32	3	33	21	34	44	36	13	37	48
25	32	26	33	46	35	10	36	39	38	14	39	59
26	34	8	35	32	37	2	38	38	40	20	42	10
27	35	53	37	23	39	0	40	42	42	33	44	32
28	37	43	39	19	41	2	42	53	44	53	47	2
29	39	37	41	21	43	12	45	12	47	21	49	44
30	41	37	43	29	45	29	47	39	50	1	52	37
31	43	44	45	44	47	54	50	16	52	53	55	48
32	45	57	48	8	50	30	53	7	56	1	59	19
33	48	19	50	44	53	20	56	13	59	28	63	21
34	50	54	53	30	56	20	59	42	63	31	68	11
35	53	40	56	34	59	58	63	40	68	18	74	32
36	56	42	59	59	63	47	68	26	74	36	90	0

TABLE OF DIFFERENCE OF THE ASCENSIONS IN AN OBLIQUE SPHERE

Decli-nation	Elevation of the Pole										
	55°		56°		57°		58°		59°		60°	
	Times	Min.	Times	Min.	Times	Min.	Times	Min.	Times	Min.	Times	Min.
1	1	26	1	29	1	32	1	36	1	40	1	44
2	2	52	2	58	3	5	3	12	3	20	3	28
3	4	17	4	27	4	38	4	49	5	0	5	12
4	5	44	5	57	6	11	6	25	6	41	6	57
5	7	11	7	27	7	44	8	3	8	22	8	43
6	8	38	8	58	9	19	9	41	10	4	10	29
7	10	6	10	29	10	54	11	20	11	47	12	17
8	11	35	12	1	12	30	13	0	13	32	14	5
9	13	4	13	35	14	7	14	41	15	17	15	55
10	14	35	15	9	15	45	16	23	17	4	17	47
11	16	7	16	45	17	25	18	8	18	53	19	41
12	17	40	18	22	19	6	19	53	20	43	21	36
13	19	15	20	1	20	50	21	41	22	36	23	34
14	20	52	21	42	22	35	23	31	24	31	25	35
15	22	30	23	24	24	22	25	23	26	29	27	39
16	24	10	25	9	26	12	27	19	28	30	29	47
17	25	53	26	57	28	5	29	18	30	35	31	59
18	27	39	28	48	30	1	31	20	32	44	34	19
19	29	27	30	41	32	1	33	26	34	58	36	37
20	31	19	32	39	34	5	35	37	37	17	39	5
21	33	15	34	41	36	14	37	54	39	42	41	40
22	35	14	36	48	38	28	40	17	42	15	44	25
23	37	19	39	0	40	49	42	47	44	57	47	20
24	39	29	41	18	43	17	45	26	47	49	50	27
25	41	45	43	44	45	54	48	16	50	54	53	52
26	44	9	46	18	48	41	51	19	54	16	57	39
27	46	41	49	4	51	41	54	38	58	0	61	57
28	49	24	52	1	54	58	58	19	62	14	67	4
29	52	20	55	16	58	36	62	31	67	18	73	46
30	55	32	58	52	62	45	67	31	73	55	90	0
31	59	6	62	58	67	42	74	4	90	0		
32	63	10	67	53	74	12	90	0				
33	68	1	74	19	90	0						
34	74	33	90	0								
35	90	0										
36												

The vacant spaces go to the stars which neither rise nor set

8. On the Hours and Parts of the Day and Night

[38ᵇ] Accordingly it is clear from this that if from the table we take the difference of days which correspond to the declination of the sun and is found under the given elevation of the pole and add it to a quadrant of a circle in the case of a northern declination and subtract it in the case of a southern declination, and then double the result, we shall have the length of that day and the span of night, which is the remainder of the circle.

Any of these segments divided by 15 "times" will show how many equal hours there are [in that day]. But by taking a twelfth part of the segment we shall have the duration of one seasonal hour. Now the hours get their name from their day, whereof each hour is always the twelfth part. Hence the hours are found to have been called summer-solstitial, equinoctial, and winter-solstitial by the ancients.

But there were not any others in use at first except the twelve hours from sunrise to sunset; and they divided the night into four vigils or watches. This set-up of the hours lasted a long time by the tacit consent of mankind. And for its sake were water-clocks invented: by the addition and subtraction of dripping water people adjusted the hours to the different lengths of days, so as not to have distinctions in time obscured by a cloud. But afterwards when equal hours common to day and night came into general use, as making it easier to tell the time, then the seasonal hours became obsolete, so that if you asked any ordinary person whether it was the first, third or sixth, ninth, or eleventh hour of the day, he would not have any answer to make or would make one which had nothing to do with the matter. Furthermore, at present some measure the number of equal hours from noon, some from sunset, some from midnight, and others from sunrise, according as it is instituted by the state.

9. On the Oblique Ascension of the Parts of the Ecliptic and How the Degree Which Is in the Middle of the Heavens Is Determined with Respect to the Degree Which Is Rising

[39ᵃ] Now that the lengths and differences of days and nights have been expounded, there follows in proper order an exposition of oblique ascensions, that is to say, together with what "times" [of the equator] the dodekatemoria, *i.e.*, the twelve parts of the ecliptic, or some other arcs of it, cross the horizon. For the differences between right and oblique ascensions are the same as the differ-

ences between the equinox and a different day, as we set forth. Furthermore, the ancients borrowed the names of animals for twelve constellations of unmoving stars, and, beginning at the spring equinox, called them Aries, Taurus, Gemini, Cancer, and so on in order.

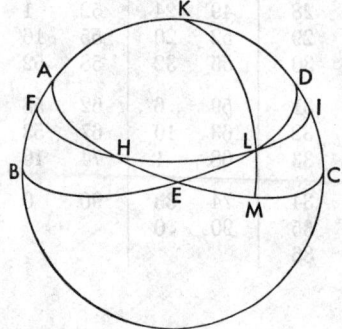

Therefore for the sake of greater clearness let the meridian circle *ABCD* be repeated; and the equatorial semicircle *AEC* and the horizon *BED*, which cut one another at point *E*. Now let point *H* be taken as the equinox. Let the ecliptic *FHI* pass through this point and cut the horizon at *L*; and through this intersection let *KLM* the quadrant of a great circle fall from *K* the pole of the equator. Thus it is perfectly clear that arc *HL* of the ecliptic and arc *HE* of the equator cross the horizon together, but that in the right sphere [arc *HL*] was rising together with arc *HEM*. Arc *EM* is the difference between these ascensions; and we have already shown that it is half the difference between the equinox and the different day. But in a northern declination what was there added [to the quadrant of a circle] is here subtracted [from the right ascension]; but in a southern declination it is added to the right ascension, so that the ascension may become oblique. And hence the extent that the whole sign or some other arc of the ecliptic has emerged may become manifest by means of the numbered ascensions from beginning to end.

From this it follows that when some degree of the ecliptic is given, the rising of which has been measured from the equinox, the degree which is in the middle of the heavens is also given. For when the declination of a degree rising at *L* has been given as corresponding to arc *HL* the distance from the equinox, and arc *HEM* is the right ascension, and the whole *AHEM* is the arc of half a day: then the remainder *AH* is given. And *AH* is the right ascension of arc *FH*, which is also given by the table, or because angle *AHF* the angle of section is given together with side *AH*, and angle *FAH* is right. And so *FHL* the whole arc between the degree rising and the degree in the middle of the heavens is given.

Conversely, if the degree which is in the middle of the heavens, namely arc *FH*, is given first, we shall also know the sign which [39[b]] is rising. For arc *AF* the declination will be known; and by means of the angle of obliquity of the sphere, arc *AFB* and arc *FB* the remainder will become known. Now in triangle *BFL* angle *BFL* and side *FB* are given by the above, and angle *FBL* is right. Therefore side *FHL*, which was sought, is given; or by a different method, as below.

10. On the Angle of Section of the Ecliptic with the Horizon

Moreover, as the ecliptic is oblique to the axis of the sphere, it makes various angles with the horizon. For we have already said in the case of the differences of the shadows that two opposite degrees of the ecliptic pass through the axis of the horizon of those who live between the tropics. But I think it will be sufficient for our purpose if we demonstrate the angles which we the heteroscian inhabitants find. By means of these angles the universal ratio of them may easily be understood. Accordingly I think it is clear enough that in the oblique sphere when the equinox or the beginning of Aries is rising, the more the greatest southward declination increases—and this declination is measured from the beginning of Capricorn which is in the middle of the heavens at this time—the more the ecliptic is inclined and verges towards the horizon; and conversely, when the ecliptic has a greater elevation [above the horizon], it makes a greater eastern angle, when the beginning of Libra is emerging and the beginning of Cancer is in the middle of the heavens; since these three circles, the equator, the ecliptic, and the horizon, coincide in one common section at the poles of the meridian circle, and the arcs of the meridian circle intercepted by them show how great the angle of rising should be judged to be.

But in order that the way of taking the measurements of the other parts of the ecliptic may be clear, again let *ABC* be the meridian circle, let *BED* be the semicircle of the horizon, let *AEC* be the semi-circle of the ecliptic, and let any degree of the ecliptic be rising at E.

Our problem is to find how great angle AEB is, according as four right angles are equal to 360°. Therefore since E is given as the rising degree, there are given by the foregoing the degree which is in the middle of the heavens and the arc AE.

And since

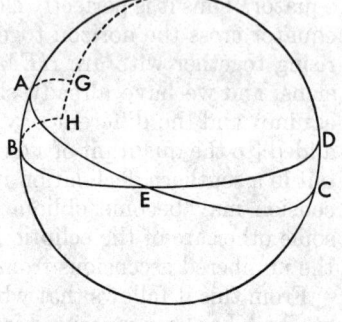

$$\text{angle } ABE = 90°;$$
$$\text{ch. } 2\,AE : \text{ch. } 2\,AB = \text{dmt. sph.} : \text{ch. } 2\,AEB.$$

[40ª] Therefore too

$$\text{angle } AEB \text{ is given.}$$

But if the degree given is not rising but the degree in the middle of the heavens—and let it be A—nevertheless angle AEB will be the measure of the eastern angle or angle of rising. For with E as pole, let FGH the quadrant of a great circle be described, and let the quadrants EAG and EBH be completed.

Therefore since

$$\text{meridian altitude } AB \text{ is given,}$$

and

$$AF = 90° - AB,$$

and by the foregoing

$$\text{angle } FAG \text{ is given,}$$

and

$$\text{angle } FGA = 90°;$$

therefore

$$\text{arc } FG \text{ is given,}$$

and

$$90° - FG = GH,$$

which measures the sought angle of rising. Similarly, it is also made evident here how for the degree which is in the middle of the heavens the degree which is rising is given, because

$$\text{ch. } 2\,GH : 2\,AB = \text{dmt. sph.} : \text{ch. } 2\,AE,$$

as in spherical triangles.

We are subjoining three sets of tables of these things. The first will be the table of ascensions in the right sphere, beginning with Aries and increasing by by sixtieth parts of the ecliptic. The second will be that of ascensions in the oblique sphere, proceeding by steps of 6° in the ecliptic, from the parallel for which there is a polar elevation of 39° to the parallel which has a polar elevation of 57°—increasing the elevation by 3°'s each time. The remaining table contains the angles made with the horizon and proceeds through the ecliptic by steps of 6° beneath the same seven segments. These tables have been set up in accordance with the least obliquity of the ecliptic, namely 23°28′, which is approximately right for our age.

TABLE OF THE ASCENSIONS OF THE SIGNS IN THE REVOLUTION OF THE RIGHT SPHERE

Ecliptic Signs	Deg.	Ascensions Times Min.		One Degree Times Min.		Ecliptic Signs	Deg.	Ascensions Times Min.		One Degree Times Min.	
Aries	6	5	30	0	55	Libra	6	185	30	0	55
♈	12	11	0	0	55	♎	12	191	0	0	55
	18	16	34	0	56		18	196	34	0	56
	24	22	10	0	56		24	202	10	0	56
	30	27	54	0	57		30	207	54	0	57
Taurus	6	33	43	0	58	Scorpio	6	213	43	0	58
♉	12	39	35	0	59	♏	12	219	35	0	59
	18	45	32	1	0		18	225	32	1	0
	24	51	37	1	1		24	231	37	1	1
	30	57	48	1	2		30	237	48	1	2
Gemini	6	64	6	1	3	Sagittarius	6	244	6	1	3
♊	12	70	29	1	4	♐	12	250	29	1	4
	18	76	57	1	5		18	256	57	1	5
	24	83	27	1	5		24	263	27	1	5
	30	90	0	1	5		30	270	0	1	5
Cancer	6	96	33	1	5	Capricornus	6	276	33	1	5
♋	12	103	3	1	5	♑	12	283	3	1	5
	18	109	31	1	5		18	289	31	1	5
	24	115	54	1	4		24	295	54	1	4
	30	122	12	1	3		30	302	12	1	3
Leo	6	128	23	1	2	Aquarius	6	308	23	1	2
♌	12	134	28	1	1	♒	12	314	28	1	1
	18	140	25	1	0		18	320	25	1	0
	24	146	17	0	59		24	326	17	0	59
	30	152	6	0	58		30	332	6	0	58
Virgo	6	157	50	0	57	Pisces	6	337	50	0	57
♍	12	163	26	0	56	♓	12	343	26	0	56
	18	169	0	0	56		18	349	0	0	56
	24	174	30	0	55		24	354	30	0	55
	30	180	0	0	55		30	360	0	0	55

TABLE OF THE ASCENSIONS IN THE OBLIQUE SPHERE

Ecliptic Signs	Elevation of the Pole of the Equator												
	39°		42°		45°		48°		51°		54°		57°
	Ascension		Ascension		Ascension		Ascension		Ascension		Ascension		Ascension
	Times	Min.	Times	Min.	Times	Min.	Times	Min.	Times	Min.	Times	Min.	Times	Min.
♈ 6	3	34	3	20	3	6	2	50	2	32	2	12	1	49
12	7	10	6	44	6	15	5	44	5	8	4	27	3	40
18	10	50	10	10	9	27	8	39	7	47	6	44	5	34
24	14	32	13	39	12	43	11	40	10	28	9	7	7	32
30	18	26	17	21	16	11	14	51	13	26	11	40	9	40
♉ 6	22	30	21	12	19	46	18	14	16	25	14	22	11	57
12	26	39	25	10	23	32	21	42	19	38	17	13	14	23
18	31	0	29	20	27	29	25	24	23	2	20	17	17	2
24	35	38	33	47	31	43	29	25	26	47	23	42	20	2
30	40	30	38	30	36	15	33	41	30	49	27	26	23	22
♊ 6	45	39	43	31	41	7	38	23	35	15	31	34	27	7
12	51	8	48	52	46	20	43	27	40	8	36	13	31	26
18	56	56	54	35	51	56	48	56	45	28	41	22	36	20
24	63	0	60	36	57	54	54	49	51	15	47	1	41	49
30	69	25	66	59	64	16	61	10	57	34	53	28	48	2
♋ 6	76	6	73	42	71	0	67	55	64	21	60	7	54	55
12	83	2	80	41	78	2	75	2	71	34	67	28	62	26
18	90	10	87	54	85	22	82	29	79	10	75	15	70	28
24	97	27	95	19	92	55	90	11	87	3	83	22	78	55
30	104	54	102	54	100	39	98	5	95	13	91	50	87	46
♌ 6	112	24	110	33	108	30	106	11	103	33	100	28	96	48
12	119	56	118	16	116	25	114	20	111	58	109	13	105	58
18	127	29	126	0	124	23	122	32	120	28	118	3	115	13
24	135	4	133	46	132	21	130	48	128	59	126	56	124	31
30	142	38	141	33	140	23	139	3	137	38	135	52	133	52
♍ 6	150	11	149	19	148	23	147	20	146	8	144	47	143	12
12	157	41	157	1	156	19	155	29	154	38	153	36	153	24
18	165	7	164	40	164	12	163	41	163	5	162	24	162	47
24	172	34	172	21	172	6	171	51	171	33	171	12	170	49
30	180	0	180	0	180	0	180	0	180	0	180	0	180	0

TABLE OF THE ASCENSIONS IN THE OBLIQUE SPHERE

Ecliptic Signs	Elevation of the Pole of the Equator													
	39° Ascension		42° Ascension		45° Ascension		48° Ascension		51° Ascension		54° Ascension		57° Ascension	
	Times	Min.	Times	Min.	Times	Min.	Times	Min.	Times	Min.	Times	Min.	Times	Min.
♎ 6	187	26	187	39	187	54	188	9	188	27	188	48	189	11
12	194	53	195	19	195	48	196	19	196	55	197	36	198	23
18	202	21	203	0	203	41	204	30	205	24	206	25	207	36
24	209	49	210	41	211	37	212	40	213	52	215	13	216	48
30	217	22	218	27	219	37	220	57	222	22	224	8	226	8
♏ 6	224	56	226	14	227	38	229	12	231	1	233	4	235	29
12	232	56	234	0	235	37	237	28	239	32	241	57	244	47
18	240	31	241	44	243	35	245	40	248	2	250	47	254	2
24	247	36	249	27	251	30	253	49	256	27	259	32	263	12
30	255	36	257	6	259	21	261	52	264	47	268	10	272	14
♐ 6	262	8	264	41	267	5	269	49	272	57	276	38	281	5
12	269	50	272	6	274	38	277	31	280	50	284	45	289	32
18	276	58	279	19	281	58	248	58	288	26	292	32	297	34
24	283	54	286	18	289	0	292	5	295	39	299	53	305	5
30	290	75	293	1	295	45	298	50	302	26	306	42	311	58
♑ 6	297	0	299	24	302	6	305	11	308	45	312	59	318	11
12	303	4	305	25	308	4	311	4	314	32	318	38	323	40
18	308	52	311	8	313	40	316	33	319	52	323	47	328	34
24	314	21	316	29	318	53	321	37	324	45	328	26	332	53
30	319	30	321	30	323	45	326	19	329	11	332	34	336	38
♒ 6	324	21	326	13	328	16	330	35	333	13	336	18	339	58
12	330	0	330	40	332	31	334	36	336	58	339	43	342	58
18	333	21	334	50	336	27	338	18	340	22	342	47	345	37
24	337	30	338	48	340	3	341	46	343	35	345	38	348	3
30	341	34	342	39	343	49	345	9	346	34	348	20	350	20
♓ 6	345	29	346	21	347	17	348	20	349	32	350	53	352	28
12	349	11	349	51	350	33	351	21	352	14	353	16	354	26
18	352	50	353	16	353	45	354	16	354	52	355	33	356	20
24	356	26	356	40	356	23	357	10	357	53	357	48	358	11
30	360	0	360	0	360	0	360	0	360	0	360	0	360	0

TABLE OF ANGLES MADE BY THE ECLIPTIC WITH THE HORIZON

Elevation of the Pole of the Equator

Ecliptic Sign	39° Deg.	39° Min.	42° Deg.	42° Min.	45° Deg.	45° Min.	48° Deg.	48° Min.	51° Deg.	51° Min.	54° Deg.	54° Min.	57° Deg.	57° Min.	Ecliptic Sign
♈ 0	27	32	24	32	21	32	18	32	15	32	12	32	9	32	♓ 30
♈ 6	27	37	24	36	21	36	18	36	15	35	12	35	9	35	♓ 24
♈ 12	27	49	24	39	21	47	18	47	15	45	12	43	9	41	♓ 18
♈ 18	28	13	25	9	22	3	19	3	15	59	12	56	9	53	♓ 12
♈ 24	28	45	25	40	22	34	19	29	16	23	13	18	10	13	♓ 6
♈ 30	29	27	26	15	23	11	20	5	16	56	13	45	10	31	♒ 30
♉ 6	30	19	27	9	23	48	20	48	17	34	14	20	11	2	♒ 24
♉ 12	31	21	28	9	24	56	20	41	18	23	15	3	11	40	♒ 18
♉ 18	32	35	29	20	26	3	22	43	19	21	15	56	12	26	♒ 12
♉ 24	34	5	30	43	27	23	24	2	20	41	16	59	13	20	♒ 6
♉ 30	35	40	32	17	28	52	25	26	21	52	18	14	14	26	♑ 30
♊ 6	37	29	34	1	30	37	27	5	23	11	19	42	15	48	♑ 24
♊ 12	39	32	36	4	32	32	28	56	25	15	21	25	17	23	♑ 18
♊ 18	41	44	38	14	34	41	31	3	27	18	23	25	19	16	♑ 12
♊ 24	44	8	40	32	37	2	33	22	29	35	25	37	21	26	♑ 6
♊ 30	46	41	43	11	39	33	35	53	32	5	28	6	23	52	♐ 30
♋ 6	49	18	45	51	42	35	38	35	34	44	30	50	26	36	♐ 24
♋ 12	52	3	48	34	45	8	41	8	37	55	33	43	29	34	♐ 18
♋ 18	54	44	51	20	47	13	44	13	40	31	36	40	32	39	♐ 12
♋ 24	57	30	54	5	50	6	47	6	43	33	39	43	35	50	♐ 6
♋ 30	60	4	56	42	53	54	49	54	46	21	42	43	38	56	♏ 30
♌ 6	62	40	59	27	56	34	52	34	49	9	45	37	41	57	♏ 24
♌ 12	64	59	61	44	58	7	55	7	51	46	48	19	44	48	♏ 18
♌ 18	67	7	63	56	60	26	57	26	54	6	50	47	47	24	♏ 12
♌ 24	68	59	65	52	62	20	59	20	56	17	53	7	49	47	♏ 6
♌ 30	70	38	67	27	64	42	61	42	58	9	54	50	52	38	♎ 30
♍ 6	72	0	68	53	65	46	62	46	59	37	56	27	53	16	♎ 24
♍ 12	73	4	70	2	66	56	63	56	60	53	57	50	54	46	♎ 18
♍ 18	73	51	70	50	67	48	64	48	61	46	58	45	55	44	♎ 12
♍ 24	74	19	71	20	68	20	65	20	62	18	59	17	56	16	♎ 6
♍ 30	74	28	71	28	68	28	65	28	62	28	59	28	56	28	♎ 0

11. On the Use of These Tables

[42ᵇ] Now the use of these tables is clear from the demonstrations, since if we take the right ascension corresponding to the known degree of the sun and if for every equal hour measured from noon we add 15 "times" to it—not counting the 360° of the whole circle, if there is more than that—the sum of the right ascensions will show the degree of the ecliptic in the middle of the heavens at the proposed hour.

Similarly if you do the same thing in the case of the oblique ascension of your region, you will have the rising degree of the ecliptic for the hour measured from sunrise.

Moreover, in the case of certain stars which are outside the ecliptic but of which the right ascension has been established—as we taught above—by their right ascension from the beginning of Aries the degrees of the ecliptic which are in the middle of the heavens together with them are given according to the table; and by their oblique ascension the degree of the ecliptic which arises with them, according as the ascensions and parts of the ecliptic are placed in corresponding regions of the tables. It is possible to operate with the setting similarly but by means of the position opposite.

Moreover, if to the right ascension in the middle of the heavens a quadrant of a circle is added, the sum is the oblique ascension of the rising degree. Wherefore the rising degree is given by means of the degree in the middle of the heavens, and vice versa.

There follows the table of the angles of the ecliptic and the horizon, which are measured at the rising degree of the ecliptic. Hence it is understood how great the elevation of the 90th degree of the ecliptic is above the horizon; and it is particularly necessary to know that in the case of solar eclipses.

12. On the Angles and Arcs of the Circles Which Pass Through the Poles of the Horizon and Intersect the Same Circle of the Ecliptic

In what follows we shall expound the ratio of the angles and arcs made by the intersection of the ecliptic with the circles through the vertex of the horizon, in the cases wherein the intersections have some altitude above the horizon. But we spoke above concerning the meridian altitude of the sun or of any degree of the ecliptic which is in the middle of the heavens, and concerning the angle of section with the meridian, since [43ᵃ] the meridian circle is also one of those circles which pass through the vertex of the horizon. Moreover we have already talked about the angle of the rising sign, the complementary angle to which is the angle which is comprehended by a great circle passing through the vertex of the horizon and by the rising ecliptic. Therefore there remain to be considered the mean sections, that is, the mean sections of the meridian circle with the semicircles of the ecliptic and the horizon.

Let the above figure be repeated. Let G be taken as any point on the ecliptic between midday and the point of rising or setting. Through G from F the pole of the horizon let fall FGH a quadrant of a circle.

"Hour" AGE is given

as the whole arc of the ecliptic between the meridian and the horizon, and by hypothesis

AG is given.

Similarly, because

meridian altitude AB is given,

and

meridian angle FAG is given;

therefore

AF is given.

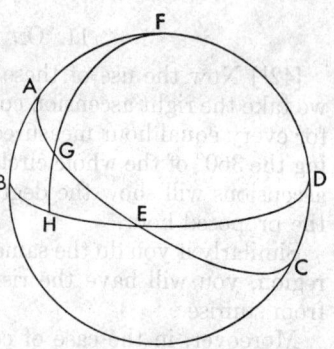

And by what has been shown concerning spherical triangles,

arc FG is given.

And hence

altitude of G is given,

because

$90° - FG = GH$.

And

meridian angle FAG is given.

And those are what we were looking for.

En route, we have taken from Ptolemy these truths about the angles and intersections of the ecliptic, and have referred ourselves to the geometry of spherical triangles. If anyone wishes to pursue this study at length, he can find by himself more utilities than we have given examples of.

13. On the Rising and Setting of the Stars

The rising and setting of the stars also seems to depend upon the daily revolution, not only the simple risings and settings of which we have just spoken but also those which occur in the morning or evening; because although their occurrence is affected by the course of the annual revolution, it will be better to speak of them here.

The ancient mathematicians distinguish the true risings and settings from the apparent. The morning rising of the star is true when the star rises at the same time as the sun; and the morning setting is true, when the star sets at sunrise; for morning is said to occur at the midpoint of this time. But the evening rising is true when the star rises at sunset; and the evening setting is true when the star sets at the same time as the sun; for evening is said to occur at the midpoint of this time, namely the time [43^b] between the time which is beginning and the time which ceases with night.

But the morning rising of a star is apparent when it rises first in the twilight before sunrise and begins to be apparent; and the morning setting is apparent when the star is seen to set very early before the sun rises. The evening rising is apparent when the star is seen to rise first in the evening; and the evening setting is apparent, when the star ceases to be apparent some time after sunset, and the star is occulted by the approach of the sun, until they come forth in their previous order at the morning rising.

This is true of the fixed stars and of the planets Saturn, Jupiter, and Mars. But Venus and Mercury rise and set in a different fashion. For they are not occulted by the approach of the sun, as the higher planets are; and they are not uncovered again by its departure. But, coming in front, they mingle with the radiance of the sun and free themselves. But when the higher planets have an evening rising and a morning setting, they are not obscured at any time, so as not to traverse the night with their illumination. But the lower planets remain hidden indifferently from sunset to sunrise, and cannot be seen anywhere. There is still another difference, namely that in higher planets the true morning risings and settings are prior to the apparent ones; and the evening risings and settings are posterior to the apparent, according as in the morning they precede the rising of the sun and in the evening follow its setting. But in the lower planets the apparent morning and evening risings are posterior to the true, while the apparent settings are prior to the true.

Now it can be understood from the above, where we expounded the oblique ascension of any star having a known position, how [the risings and settings] may be discerned, and together with what degree of the ecliptic the star rises or sets and at what position, or degree opposite—if the sun has become apparent by that time—the star has its true morning or evening rising or setting. The apparent risings and settings differ from the true according to the clarity and magnitude of the star, so that the stars which give a more powerful light are less dimmed by the rays of the sun than those which are less luminous. And the boundaries of occultation and apparition are determined in the lower hemisphere, between the horizon and the sun, on the arcs of circles which pass through the poles of the horizon. And the limits are 12° for the primary stars, 11° for Saturn, 10° for Jupiter, 11½° for Mars, 5° for Venus, and 10° for Mercury. But in this whole period during which what is left of daylight yields to night—this period embraces twilight, or dusk—there are 18° of the aforesaid circle. When the sun has traversed these degrees, the smaller stars too begin ro be apparent. By this distance the mathematicians determine [44ᵃ] a parallel below the horizon in the lower hemisphere, and they say that when the sun has reached this parallel, day has ended and night has begun. Therefore when we have learned with what degree of the ecliptic the star rises or sets and what the angle of section of the ecliptic with the horizon at that point is, and if then too we find as many degrees of the ecliptic between the rising degree and the sun as are sufficient to give the sun an altitude below the horizon in accord with the prescribed limits of the star in question; we shall pronounce that the first emergence or occultation of the star has taken place.

But what we have expounded, in the foregoing explanation, in the case of the altitude of the sun above the Earth agrees in all respects with its descent below the Earth. For there is no difference in the corresponding positions; and consequently those stars which are setting in the visible hemisphere are rising in the hidden hemisphere; and everything is the converse, and is easy to understand. What has been said concerning the rising and setting of the stars and the daily revolution of the terrestrial globe shall be sufficient.

14. On Investigating the Positions of the Stars and the Catalogue of the Fixed Stars

After the daily revolution of the terrestrial globe and its consequences have been expounded by us, the demonstrations relating to the annual circuit ought to follow now. But since some of the ancient mathematicians thought the phenomena of the fixed stars ought to come first as being the first beginnings of this art, accordingly we decided to act in accordance with this opinion, as among our principles and hypotheses we had assumed that the sphere of the fixed stars, to which the wanderings of all the planets are equally referred, is wholly immobile.

But no one should be surprised at our following this order, although Ptolemy in his *Almagest* held that an explanation of the fixed stars could not be given, unless knowledge of the positions of the sun and moon had preceded it, and accordingly he judged that whatever had to do with the fixed stars should be put off till then. We think that this opinion must be opposed. But if you understand it of the numbers with which the apparent motion of the sun and moon is computed perhaps the opinion will stand. For Menelaus the geometer discovered the positions of many stars by means of the numbers relating to their conjunctions with the moon. [44ᵇ] But we shall do a much better job if we determine a star by the aid of instruments after examining carefully the positions of the sun and moon, as we will show how in a little while. We are even admonished by the wasted attempt of those who thought that the magnitude of the solar year could be defined simply by the equinoxes or solstices without the fixed stars. We shall never agree with them on that, so much so that there will nowhere be greater discord. Ptolemy called our attention to this: when he had evaluated the solar year in his time not without suspicion of an error which might emerge with the passage of time, he admonished posterity to examine the further certainty of the thing later on. Therefore it seemed to us to be worth the trouble to show how by means of artificial instruments the positions of the sun and moon may be determined, that is, how far distant they are from the spring equinox or some other cardinal points of the world. The knowledge of these positions will afford us some facilities for investigating the other stars, and thus we shall be able to set forth before your eyes the sphere of the fixed stars and an image of it embroidered with constellations.

Now we have set forth above with what instruments the distance of the tropics, the obliquity of the ecliptic, and the inclination of the sphere, or the altitude of the pole of the equator, may be determined. In the same way we can determine any other altitude of the sun at midday. This altitude will exhibit to us through its difference from the inclination of the sphere how great the declination of the sun from the equator is. Then by means of this declination the position of the sun at midday will become clear as measured from the solstice or the equinox. Now the sun seems to traverse approximately 1° during the space of 24 hours; 2½′ come as the hourly allotment. Hence its position at any other definite hour will easily be determined.

But for observing the positions of the moon and stars another instrument is constructed, which Ptolemy calls the astrolabe. For let two circles, or rather four-sided rims of circles, be constructed in such a way that they may have their concave and convex surfaces at right angles to the plane sides. These rims are to be equal and similar in every respect and of a suitable size, in order not to become hard to handle through being too large, though they must be of sufficient amplitude to be divided into degrees and minutes. Their width and thickness [45ᵃ] should be at least one thirtieth of the diameter. Therefore they are to be fitted together and joined at right angles to one another, having their convex sides as it were on the surface of the same sphere, and their concave sides on the surface of another single sphere. Now one of the circles should have the relative position of the ecliptic; and the other, that of the circle which passes through both poles, *i.e.*, the poles of the equator and of the ecliptic. Therefore the circle of the ecliptic is to be divided along its sides into the conventional number of 360°, which are again to be subdivided according to the capacity of the instrument. Moreover, when quadrants on the other circle have been measured from the ecliptic, the poles of the ecliptic should be marked on it; and when a distance proportionate to the obliquity has been measured from those points, the poles of the equator are also to be marked down. When these circles are finished, two other circles should be prepared and constructed around the same poles of the ecliptic: they will move about these poles, one circle inside and one circle outside. They should be of equal thicknesses between their plane surfaces, and the width of their plane surfaces should be equal to that of the others; and they should be so constructed that at all points the concave surface of the larger will touch the convex surface of the ecliptic; and the convex surface of the smaller, the concave surface of the ecliptic. Nevertheless do not let their revolutions be impeded, but have them able to traverse freely and easily both the ecliptic together with its meridian circle and one another. Therefore we shall make holes in these circles diametrically opposite the poles of the ecliptic, and pass axles through these holes, so that by means of these axles the circles will be bound together and carried along. Moreover, the inside circle should be divided into 360° in such fashion that the single quadrant of 90° will be at the poles. Furthermore, within the concavity of the inside circle a fifth circle should be placed which can be turned in the same plane and which has an apparatus fixed to its plane surfaces which has openings diametrically opposite and reflectors or eyepieces, through which the light of the sun, as in a dioptra, can break through and go out along the diameter of the circle. And certain appliances or pointers for numbers are fitted on to this fifth circle at opposite points for the sake of observing the latitudes on the container circle. Finally, a sixth circle is to be applied which will embrace and support the whole astrolabe, which is hung on to it by means of fastenings at the poles of the equator; this last circle is to be placed upon some sort of column, or stand, and made to rest upon it perpendicular to the plane of the horizon. Moreover, the poles [of the equator] should be adjusted to the inclination of the sphere, so that the outmost circle will have a position similar to that of a natural meridian and will by no means waver from it.

Therefore after the instrument has been prepared in this way, when we wish to determine the position of some star, then in the evening or at the approach of sunset and at a time when the moon too is visible, we shall adjust the outer circle to the degree of the ecliptic, in which [45ᵇ] we have determined—by the methods spoken of—that the sun is at that time. And we shall turn the intersection of the [ecliptic and the outer] circle towards the sun itself, until both of them—I mean the ecliptic and the outer circle which passes through its poles—cast shadows on themselves evenly.[1] Then we shall turn the inner circle towards the moon; and with the eye placed in its plane we shall mark its position on the ecliptic part of the instrument there where we shall view the moon as opposite, or as it were bisected by the same plane. That will be the position of the moon as seen in longitude. For without the moon there is no way of discovering the positions of the stars, as the moon alone among all is a partaker of both day and night. Then after nightfall, when the star whose position we are seeking is visible, we shall adjust the outer circle to the position of the moon; and thus, as we did in the case of the sun, we shall bring the position of the astrolabe into relation with the moon. Then also we shall turn the inner circle towards the star, until the star seems to be in contact with the plane surfaces of the circle and is viewed

[1] i.e., until the shadows intersect as two straight lines at right angles to one another.

through the eyepieces which are on the little circle contained [by the inner circle]. For in this way we shall have discovered the longitude and latitude of the star. When this is being done, the degree of the ecliptic which is in the middle of the heavens will be before the eyes; and accordingly it will be obvious at what hour the thing itself was done.[1]

For example, in the 2nd year of the Emperor Antoninus Pius, on the 9th day of Pharmuthi, the 8th month by the Egyptian calendar, Ptolemy, who was then at Alexandria and wished to observe at the time of sunset the position of the star which is in the breast of Leo and is called Basiliscus or Regulus, adjusted his astrolabe to the setting sun at 5 equatorial hours after midday. At this time the sun was at $3\frac{1}{24}°$ of Pisces, and by moving the inner circle he found that the moon was $92\frac{1}{8}°$ east of the sun: hence it was seen that the position of the moon was then at $5\frac{1}{6}°$ of Gemini. After half an hour—which made six hours since noon—when the star had already begun to be apparent and 4°

[1]Legend:
1. Circle through poles of ecliptic
2. Ecliptic
3. Outer circle
4. Inner circle
5. Little circle
6. Meridian circle
A and A_1. Poles of equator
BCC_1B_1. Axis of ecliptic
D. Zenith, or pole of horizon

The astrolabe is constructed as an image of the Ptolemaic heavens, or as a "smaller world." Accordingly the astrolabe in operation is an imitation of the revolving heavens on a reduced scale.

The astrolabe is set up with the meridian circle (6) fixed in the meridian line and with the northern and southern poles of the equator (A and A_1) pointing towards the celestial poles above and below the horizon, as the meridian does not change during the course of the daily revolution. The degrees of the celestial ecliptic are marked off on the ecliptic circle (2), with the solstices or equinoxes at the intersections of the ecliptic (2) and the circle through the poles of the ecliptic (1). The outer circle (3) is turned to that point on the ecliptic where the position of the sun is computed to be,

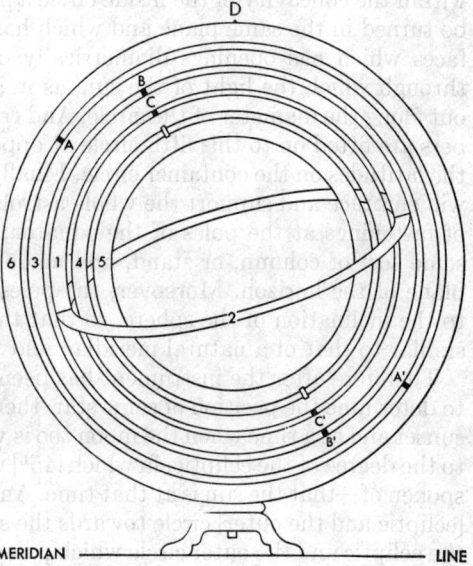

COPERNICUS' ASTROLABE

MERIDIAN ———————————————— LINE

and then this intersection of the outer circle and the ecliptic is turned towards the sun itself, until each circle casts its shadow in the form of a straight line intersecting the other shadow at right angles. Now as the revolution of the outer circle around the axis of the equator makes the axis of the ecliptic, the circle through the poles of the ecliptic, the inner circle, and the little circle swing round the axis of the equator, and as the pole of the ecliptic revolves around the pole of the equator during the daily revolution; the turning towards the sun of the intersection of the two circles seves to bring the yearly and daily movements of the sun into proper ratio with one another; and the cruciform shadow is a sign that the wooden ecliptic occupies the relative position in the astrolabe that the celestial ecliptic occupies at this moment of the daily revolution. The inner circle (4) can now be turned towards the moon in order to mark on the ecliptic the lunar longitude, and the little circle (5) can be wheeled around in the plane of the inner circle, in order to mark the lunar latitude on the graduated inner circle.

of Gemini was in the middle of the heavens, he turned the outer circle of the instrument to the already determined position of the moon. Proceeding with the inner circle, he took the distance of the star from the moon as $57\frac{1}{10}°$ to the east. Accordingly the moon had been found at $92\frac{1}{8}°$ from the setting sun, as was said—which placed the moon at $5\frac{1}{6}°$ of Gemini; but it was correct for the moon to have moved $\frac{1}{4}°$ in the space of half an hour; since the hourly allotment in the movement of the moon is more or less $\frac{1}{2}°$; but on account of the then subtractive parallax of the moon it must have been slightly less than $\frac{1}{4}°$, [46ª] that is to say, about $\frac{1}{6}°$: hence the moon was at $5\frac{1}{3}°$ of Gemini. But when we have discussed the parallaxes of the moon, the difference will not appear to have been so great; and hence it will be evident enough that the position of the moon viewed was more than $5\frac{1}{3}°$ but a little less than $5\frac{2}{5}°$. The addition of $57\frac{1}{10}°$ to this locates the position of the star at $2°30'$ of Leo at a distance of about $32\frac{1}{2}°$ from the summer solstice of the sun and with a northern latitude of $\frac{1}{6}°$. This was the position of Basiliscus; and consequently the way was laid open to the other fixed stars. This observation of Ptolemy's was made in the year of Our Lord 139 by the Roman calendar, on the 24th day of February, in the 1st year of the 229th Olympiad.

That most outstanding of mathematicians took note of what position at that time each of the stars had in relation to the spring equinox, and catalogued the constellations of the celestial animals. Thus he helps us not a little in this our enterprise and relieves us of some difficult enough labour, so that we, who think that the positions of the stars should not be referred to the equinoxes which change with time but that the equinoxes should be referred to the sphere of the fixed stars, can easily draw up a description of the stars from any other unchanging starting-point. We decided to begin this description with the Ram as being the first sign, and with its first star, which is in its head—so that in this way a configuration which is absolute and always the same will be possessed by those stars which shine together as if fixed and clinging perpetually and at the same time to the throne which they have seized. But by the marvellous care and industry of the ancients the stars were distributed into forty-eight constellations with the exception of those which the circle of the always hidden stars removed from the fourth climate, which passes approximately through Rhodes; and in this way the unconstellated stars remained unknown to them. According to the opinion of Theo the Younger in the *Aratean Treatise* the stars were not arranged in the form of images for any other reason except that their great multitude might be divided into parts and that they might be designated separately by certain names in accordance with an ancient enough custom, since even in Hesiod and Homer we read the names of the Pleiades, Hyas, Arcturus, and Orion. Accordingly in the description of the stars according to longitude we shall not employ the "twelve divisions," or dodekatemoria, which are measured from the equinoxes or solstices, but the simple and conventional number of degrees. We shall follow Ptolemy as to the rest with the exception of a few cases, where we have either found some corruption or a different state of affairs. We shall however teach you in the following book how to find out what their distances are from those cardinal points [*i.e.*, the equinoxes].

CATALOGUE OF THE SIGNS AND OF THE STARS
And First Those of the Northern Region

Constellations	Longitude Deg. Min.			Latitude Deg. Min.		Magnitude
URSA MINOR, OR THE LITTLE BEAR, OR CYNOSURA						
The [star] at the tip of the tail	53	30	N	66	0	3
The [star] to the east in the tail	55	50	N	70	0	4
The [star] at the base of the tail	69	20	N	74	0	4
The more southern [star] on the western side of the quadrilateral	83	0	N	75	20	4
The northern [star] on the same side	87	0	N	77	40	4
The more southern of the stars on the eastern side	100	30	N	72	40	2
The more northern on the same side	109	30	N	74	50	2
7 stars: 2 of second magnitude, 1 of third, 4 of fourth						
The most southern unconstellated star near the Cynosure, in a straight line with the eastern side	103	20	N	71	10	4
URSA MAJOR, OR THE GREAT BEAR						
The star in the muzzle	78	40	N	39	50	4
The western star in the two eyes	79	10	N	43	0	5
The star to the east of that	79	40	N	43	0	5
The more western star of the two in the forehead	79	30	N	47	10	5
The star to the east in the forehead	81	0	N	47	0	5
The western star in the right ear	81	30	N	50	30	5
The more western of the two in the neck	85	50	N	43	50	4
The eastern	92	50	N	44	20	4

NORTHERN SIGNS

	Longitude Deg. Min.			Latitude Deg. Min.		Magnitude
The more northern of the two in the breast	94	20	N	44	0	4
The more southern	93	20	N	42	0	4
The star at the knee of the left foreleg	89	0	N	35	0	3
The more northern of the two in the left forefoot	89	50	N	29	0	3
The more southern	88	40	N	28	30	3
At the knee of the right foreleg	89	0	N	36	0	4
The star below the knee	101	10	N	33	30	4
The star on the shoulder	104	0	N	49	0	2
The star on the flanks	105	30	N	44	30	2
The star at the base of the tail	116	30	N	51	0	3
The star in the left hind leg	117	20	N	46	30	2
The more western of the two in the left hind foot	106	0	N	29	38	3
The star to the east of that	107	30	N	28	15	3
[47ᵃ] The star in the hollow of the left leg	115	0	N	35	15	4
The more northern of the two which are in the right hind foot	123	10	N	25	50	3

NORTHERN SIGNS

Constellations	Longitude Deg.	Min.		Latitude Deg.	Min.	Magnitude
The more southern	123	40	N	25	0	3
The first of the three in the tail after the base	125	30	N	53	30	2
The middle star	131	20	N	55	40	2
The star which is last and at the tip of the tail	143	10	N	54	0	2
27 stars: 6 of second magnitude, 8 of third, 8 of fourth, and 5 of fifth						

UNCONSTELLATED STARS NEAR THE GREAT BEAR

	Longitude Deg.	Min.		Latitude Deg.	Min.	Magnitude
The star to the south of the tail	141	10	N	39	45	3
The more obscure star to the west	133	30	N	41	20	5
The star between the forefeet of the Bear and the head of the Lion	98	20	N	17	15	4
The star more to the north than that one	96	40	N	19	10	4
The last of the three obscure stars	99	30	N	20	0	obscure
The one to the west of that	95	30	N	22	45	obscure
The one more to the west	94	30	N	23	15	obscure
The star between the forefeet and the Twins	100	20	N	22	15	obscure
8 unconstellated stars: 1 of third magnitude, 2 of fourth, 1 of fifth, 4 obscure						

DRACO, OR THE DRAGON

	Longitude Deg.	Min.		Latitude Deg.	Min.	Magnitude
The star in the tongue	200	0	N	76	30	4
On the jaws	215	10	N	78	30	4 greater
Above the eye	216	30	N	75	40	3
In the cheek	229	40	N	75	20	4
Above the head	233	30	N	75	30	3
The most northern star in the first curve of the neck	258	40	N	82	20	4
The most southern	295	50	N	78	15	4
The star in between	262	10	N	80	20	4
The star to the east of them at the second curve	282	50	N	81	10	4
The more southern star on the western side of the quadrilateral	331	20	N	81	40	4
The more northern star on the same side	343	50	N	83	0	4
The more northern star on the eastern side	1	0	N	78	50	4
The more southern on the same side	346	10	N	77	50	4
The more southern star in the triangle at the third curve	4	0	N	80	30	4
The more western of the other two in the triangle	15	0	N	81	40	5
The star to the east	19	30	N	80	15	5
<The star to the east> in the triangle to the west	66	20	N	83	30	4
The more southern of the remaining two in the same triangle	43	40	N	83	30	4

NORTHERN SIGNS

Constellations	Longitude Deg. Min.			Latitude Deg. Min.		Magnitude
[47^b] The star which is more northern than the two above	35	10	N	84	50	4
Of the small stars west of the triangle, the more eastern	200	0	N	87	30	6
The more western	195	0	N	86	50	6
The most southern of the three which are in a straight line towards the east	152	30	N	81	15	5
The one in the middle	152	50	N	83	0	5
The most northern	151	0	N	84	50	3
The more northern of the two which follow towards the west	153	20	N	78	0	3
The more southern	156	30	N	74	40	4 greater
The star to the west of them, in the coil of the tail	156	0	N	70	0	3
The more western of the two rather distant from that one	120	40	N	64	40	4
The star to the east of it	124	30	N	65	30	3
The star to the east in the tail	192	30	N	61	15	3
At the tip of the tail	186	30	N	56	15	3
Therefore 31 stars: 8 of third magnitude, 16 of fourth, 5 of fifth, 2 of sixth						

CEPHEUS

In the right foot	28	40	N	75	40	4
In the left foot	26	20	N	64	15	4
On the right side beneath the belt	0	40	N	71	10	4
The star which touches the top of the right shoulder	340	0	N	69	0	3
The star which touches the right joint of the elbow	332	40	N	72	0	4
The star to the east which touches the same elbow	333	20	N	74	0	4
The star on the chest	352	0	N	65	30	5
On the right arm	1	0	N	62	30	4 greater
The most southern of the three on the tiara	339	40	N	60	15	5
The one in the middle	340	40	N	61	15	4
The most northern	342	20	N	61	30	5
11 stars: 1 of third magnitude, 7 of fourth, 3 of fifth						
Of the two unconstellated stars, the one to the west of the tiara	337	0	N	64	0	5
The one to the east of the tiara	344	40	N	59	30	4

BOÖTES, OR ARCTURUS

The more western of the three in the left hand	145	40	N	58	40	5
The middle one of the three, the more southern	147	30	N	58	20	5
The more eastern of the three	149	0	N	60	10	5
The star in the left joint of the elbow	143	0	N	54	40	5

Northern Signs

Constellations	Longitude Deg.	Min.		Latitude Deg.	Min.	Magnitude
On the left shoulder	163	0	N	49	0	3
On the head	170	0	N	53	50	4 greater
On the right shoulder	179	0	N	48	40	4
[48ª] The more southern of the two on the crook	179	0	N	53	15	4
The star more to the north, at the tip of the crook	178	20	N	57	30	4
The more northern of the two under the shoulder and on the spear	181	0	N	46	10	4 greater
The more southern	181	50	N	45	30	5
At the extremity of the right hand	181	35	N	41	20	5
The more western of the two in the palm	180	0	N	41	40	5
The one to the east	180	20	N	42	30	5
At the extremity of the handle of the crook	181	0	N	40	20	5
On the right leg	183	20	N	40	15	3
The more eastern of the two in the belt	169	0	N	41	40	4
The more western	168	20	N	42	10	4 greater
At the right heel	178	40	N	28	0	3
The more northern of the three on the left ham	164	40	N	28	0	3
The middle one of the three	163	50	N	26	30	4
The more southern of them	164	50	N	25	0	4
22 stars: 4 of third magnitude, 9 of fourth, 9 of fifth						
The unconstellated star between the thighs, which they call Arcturus	170	20	N	31	30	1
CORONA BOREALIS, OR THE NORTHERN CROWN						
The brilliant star in the crown	188	0	N	44	30	2 greater
The most western of all	185	0	N	46	10	4 greater
The eastern star towards the north	185	10	N	48	0	5
The eastern star more to the north	193	0	N	50	30	6
The star to the south-east of the brilliant one	191	30	N	44	45	4
The next star to the east	190	30	N	44	50	4
The star farther to the east	194	40	N	46	10	4
The most eastern of all in the crown	195	0	N	49	20	4
8 stars: 1 of second magnitude, 5 of fourth, 1 of fifth, 1 of sixth						
ENGONASI, OR THE KNEELING MAN						
On the head	221	0	N	37	30	3
At the right arm-pit	207	0	N	43	0	3
On the right arm	205	0	N	40	10	3
In the right flank	201	20	N	37	10	4
On the left shoulder	220	20	N	49	30	4 greater
[48ᵇ] In the left flank	231	0	N	42	0	4

Northern Signs

Constellations	Longitude Deg. Min.		Latitude Deg. Min.		Magnitude
\<The more eastern\> of the three in the left palm	238 50	N	52 50		4 greater
The more northern of the remaining two	235 0	N	54 0		4 greater
The more southern	234 50	N	53 0		4
On the right side	207 10	N	56 10		3
On the left side	213 30	N	53 30		4
On the \<lower part of the\> left buttock	213 20	N	56 10		5
At the beginning of the left leg	214 30	N	58 30		5
The most western of the three in the left ham	217 20	N	59 50		3
The more eastern	218 40	N	60 20		4
The most eastern	219 40	N	61 15		4
At the left knee	237 10	N	61 0		4
On the \<upper part of the\>left buttock	225 30	N	69 20		4
The most western of the three in the left foot	188 40	N	70 15		6
The middle star	220 10	N	71 15		6
The most eastern of the three	223 0	N	72 0		6
At the beginning of the right leg	207 0	N	60 15		4 greater
The more northern on the right ham	198 50	N	63 0		4
At the right knee	189 0	N	65 30		4 greater
The more southern of the two under the right knee	186 40	N	63 40		4
The more northern	183 30	N	64 15		4
On the right shin	184 30	N	60 0		4
At the extremity of the right foot, the same as the tip of Boötes' crook	178 20	N	57 30		4
Besides that last one, 28 stars: 6 of third magnitude, 17 of fourth, 2 of fifth, 3 of sixth					
The unconstellated star to the south of the right arm	26 0	N	38 10		5
Lyra, or the Lyre					
The brilliant star which is called Lyra or Fidicula	250 40	N	62 0		1
The more northern of the two adjacent stars	253 40	N	62 40		4 greater
The more southern	253 40	N	61 0		4 greater
The star which is at the centre of the beginning of the horns	262 0	N	60 0		4
The more northern of the two which are next and to the east	265 20	N	61 20		4
The more southern	265 0	N	60 20		4
The more northern of the two westerly stars on the cross-piece	254 20	N	56 10		3
The more southern	254 10	N	55 0		4 smaller
The more northern of the two easterly stars on the cross-piece	257 30	N	55 20		3
The more southern	258 20	N	54 45		4 smaller

NORTHERN SIGNS

Constellations	Longitude Deg. Min.		Latitude Deg. Min.		Magnitude
10 stars: 1 of first magnitude, 2 of third magnitude, 7 of fourth					
[49ª] CYGNUS, OR THE SWAN					
At the mouth	267	50 N	49	20	3
On the head	272	20 N	50	30	5
In the middle of the neck	279	20 N	54	30	4 greater
In the breast	291	50 N	56	20	3
The brilliant star in the tail	302	30 N	60	0	2
In the elbow of the right wing	282	40 N	64	40	3
The most southern of the three in the flat of the wing	285	50 N	69	40	4
The middle star	284	30 N	71	30	4 greater
The last of the three, and at the tip of the wing	310	0 N	74	0	4 greater
At the elbow of the left wing	294	10 N	49	30	3
In the middle of the left wing	298	10 N	52	10	4 greater
At the tip of the same	300	0 N	74	0	3
In the left foot	303	20 N	55	10	4 greater
At the left knee	307	50 N	57	0	4
The more western of the two in the right foot	294	30 N	64	0	4
The more eastern	296	0 N	64	30	4
The nebulous star at the right knee	305	30 N	63	45	5
17 stars: 1 of second magnitude, 5 of third, 9 of fourth, 2 of fifth					
AND TWO UNCONSTELLATED STARS NEAR THE SWAN					
The more southern of the two under the left wing	306	0 N	49	40	4
The more northern	307	10 N	51	40	4
CASSIOPEIA					
On the head	1	10 N	45	20	4
On the breast	4	10 N	46	45	3 greater
On the girdle	6	20 N	47	50	4
Above the seat, at the hips	10	0 N	49	0	3 greater
At the knees	13	40 N	45	30	3
On the leg	20	20 N	47	45	4
At the extremity of the foot	355	0 N	48	20	4
On the left arm	8	0 N	44	20	4
On the left forearm	7	40 N	45	0	5
On the right forearm	357	40 N	50	0	6
At the foot of the chair	8	20 N	52	40	4
At the middle of the settle	1	10 N	51	40	3 smaller
At the extremity	27	10 N	51	40	6
13 stars: 4 of third magnitude, 6 of fourth, 1 of fifth, 2 of sixth					

Northern Signs

Constellations	Longitude Deg. Min.		Latitude Deg. Min.		Magnitude
[49^b] Perseus					
The nebulous star at the extremity of the right hand	21	0	N 40	30	nebulous
On the right forearm	24	30	N 37	30	4
On the right shoulder	26	0	N 34	30	4 smaller
On the left shoulder	20	50	N 32	20	4
On the head, or a nebula	24	0	N 34	30	4
On the shoulder-blades	24	50	N 31	10	4
The brilliant star on the right side	28	10	N 30	0	2
The most western of the three on the same side	28	40	N 27	30	4
The middle one	30	20	N 27	40	4
The remaining one of the three	31	0	N 27	30	3
On the left forearm	24	0	N 27	0	4
The brilliant star in the left hand and in the head of Medusa	23	0	N 23	0	2
The easterly star on the head of the same	22	30	N 21	0	4
The more western on the head of the same	21	0	N 21	0	4
The most western	20	10	N 22	15	4
On the right knee	38	10	N 28	15	4
The one to the west of this one at the knee	37	10	N 28	10	4
The more western of the two on the belly	35	40	N 25	10	4
The more eastern	37	20	N 26	15	4
On the right hip	37	30	N 24	30	5
On the right calf	39	40	N 28	45	5
On the left hip	30	10	N 21	40	4 greater
On the left knee	32	0	N 19	50	3
On the left calf	31	40	N 14	45	3 greater
On the left heel	24	30	N 12	0	3 smaller
On the top part of the left foot	29	40	N 11	0	3 greater
26 stars: 2 of second magnitude, 5 of third, 16 of fourth, 2 of fifth, 1 nebulous					
Unconstellated Stars Around Perseus					
To the east of the left hand	34	10	N 31	0	5
To the north of the right hand	38	20	N 31	0	5
To the west of Medusa's head	18	0	N 20	40	obscure
3 stars: 2 of fifth magnitude, 1 obscure					
[50^a] Auriga, or the Charioteer					
The more southern of the two on the head	55	50	N 30	0	4
The more northern	55	40	N 30	50	4
The brilliant star on the left shoulder, which is called Capella	48	20	N 22	30	1
On the right shoulder	56	10	N 20	0	2
On the right forearm	54	30	N 15	15	4
On the palm of the right hand	56	10	N 13	30	4 greater
On the left forearm	45	20	N 20	40	4 greater
The star to the west of the Haedi	45	30	N 18	0	4 smaller

NORTHERN SIGNS

Constellations	Longitude Deg. Min.			Latitude Deg. Min.			Magnitude
The star on the palm of the left hand which is to the east of the Haedi	46	0	N	18	0		4 greater
On the left calf	53	10	N	10	10		3 smaller
On the right calf and at the tip of the northern horn of Taurus	49	0	N	5	0		3 greater
At the ankle	49	20	N	8	30		5
On the buttocks	49	40	N	12	20		5
The small star on the left foot	24	0	N	10	20		6
14 stars: 1 of first magnitude, 1 of second, 2 of third, 7 of fourth, 2 of fifth, 1 of sixth							
OPHIUCHUS, OR THE SERPENT-HOLDER							
On the head	228	10	N	36	0		3
The more western of the two on the right shoulder	231	20	N	27	15		4 greater
The more eastern	232	20	N	26	45		4
The more western of the two on the left shoulder	216	40	N	33	0		4
The more eastern	218	0	N	31	50		4
At the left elbow	211	40	N	34	30		4
The more western of the two in the left hand	208	20	N	17	0		4
The more eastern	209	20	N	12	30		3
At the right elbow	220	0	N	15	0		4
The more western in the right hand	205	40	N	18	40		4 smaller
The more eastern	207	40	N	14	20		4
At the right knee	224	30	N	4	30		3
On the right shin	227	0	N	2	15		3 greater
The most western of the four on the right foot	226	20	S	2	15		4 greater
The more easterly	227	40	S	1	30		4 greater
The next to the east	228	20	S	0	20		4 greater
The most easterly	229	10	S	1	45		5 greater
The star which touches the heel	229	30	S	1	0		5
[50ᵇ] At the left knee	215	30	N	11	50		3
The most northern of the three in a straight line on the lower part of the left leg	215	0	N	5	20		5 greater
The middle one	214	0	N	3	10		5
The most southern of the three	213	10	N	1	40		5 greater
The star on the left heel	215	40	N	0	40		5
The star touching the hollow of the left foot	214	0	S	0	45		4
24 stars: 5 of third magnitude, 13 of fourth, 6 of fifth							
UNCONSTELLATED STARS AROUND OPHIUCHUS							
The most northern of the three to the east of the right shoulder	235	20	N	28	10		4
The middle one	236	0	N	26	20		4
The most southern of the three	233	40	N	25	0		4
Another one, farther to the east of the three	237	0	N	27	0		4

Northern Signs

Constellations	Longitude Deg.	Min.		Latitude Deg.	Min.	Magnitude
A star separate from the four, to the north	238	0	N	33	0	4
Therefore 5 unconstellated stars: all of fourth magnitude						
SERPENS-OPHIUCHI, OR THE SERPENT						
On the quadrilateral, the star in the cheeks	192	10	N	38	0	4
The star touching the nostrils	201	0	N	40	0	4
On the temples	197	40	N	35	0	3
At the beginning of the neck	195	20	N	34	15	3
At the middle of the quadrilateral, and on the jaws	194	40	N	37	15	4
To the north of the head	201	30	N	42	30	4
At the first curve of the neck	195	0	N	29	15	3
The most northern of the three to the east	198	10	N	26	30	4
The middle one	197	40	N	25	20	3
The most southern of the three	199	40	N	24	0	3
The star to the west of the left hand of Ophiuchus	202	0	N	16	30	4
The star to the east of the same hand	211	30	N	16	15	5
The star to the east of the right hip	227	0	N	10	30	4
The more southern of the two to the east of that	230	20	N	8	30	4 greater
The more northern	231	10	N	10	30	4
To the east of the right hand, in the coil of the tail	237	0	N	20	0	4
Farther east in the tail	242	0	N	21	10	4
At the tip of the tail	251	40	N	27	0	4 greater
18 stars: 5 of third magnitude, 12 of fourth, 1 of fifth						
[51ᵃ] SAGITTA, OR THE ARROW						
At the head	273	30	N	39	20	4
The most eastern of the three on the shaft	270	0	N	39	10	6
The middle one	269	10	N	39	50	5
The most western of the three	268	0	N	39	0	5
At the notch	266	40	N	38	45	5
5 stars: 1 of fourth magnitude, 3 of fifth, 1 of sixth						
AQUILA, OR THE EAGLE						
In the middle of the head	270	30	N	26	50	4
On the neck	268	10	N	27	10	3
The brilliant star on the shoulder-blades, which is called Aquila	267	10	N	29	10	2 greater
The star to the north which is very near	268	0	N	30	0	3 smaller
The more western on the left shoulder	266	30	N	31	30	3
The more eastern	269	20	N	31	30	5
The star to the west in the right shoulder	263	0	N	28	40	5
The star to the east	264	30	N	26	40	5 greater

NORTHERN SIGNS

Constellations	Longitude Deg. Min.		Latitude Deg. Min.		Magnitude
The star in the tail, which touches the milky circle	265	30	N	26	30	3
9 stars: 1 of second magnitude, 4 of third, 1 of fourth, 3 of fifth						
UNCONSTELLATED STARS AROUND AQUILA						
The more western star south of the head	272	0	N	21	40	3
The more eastern	272	20	N	29	10	3
Away from the right shoulder and to the south-west	259	20	N	25	0	4 greater
To the south	261	30	N	20	0	3
Farther south	263	0	N	15	30	5
West of all	254	30	N	18	10	3
6 unconstellated stars: 4 of third magnitude, 1 of fourth, and 1 of fifth						
DELPHINUS, OR THE DOLPHIN						
The most western of the three in the tail	281	0	N	29	10	3 smaller
The more northern of the two remaining	282	0	N	29	0	4 smaller
The more southern	282	0	N	26	40	4
The more southern on the western side of the rhomboid	281	50	N	32	0	3 smaller
The more northern on the same side	283	30	N	33	50	3 smaller
The more southern on the eastern side	284	40	N	32	0	3 smaller
The more northern on the same side	286	50	N	33	10	3 smaller
The most southern of the three between the tail and the rhombus	280	50	N	34	15	6
The more western of the other two to the north	280	50	N	31	50	6
The more eastern	282	20	N	31	30	6
10 stars: 5 of third magnitude, 2 of fourth, 3 of sixth						
[51b] EQUI SECTIO, OR THE SECTION OF THE HORSE						
The more western of the two on the head	289	40	N	20	30	obscure
The more eastern	292	20	N	20	40	obscure
The more western of the two at the mouth	289	40	N	25	30	obscure
The more eastern	291	21	N	25	0	obscure
4 stars: all obscure						
PEGASUS, OR THE WINGED HORSE						
Within the open mouth	298	40	N	21	30	3 greater
The more northern of the two close together on the head	302	40	N	16	50	3
The more southern	301	20	N	16	0	4
The more southern of the two on the mane	314	40	N	15	0	5
The more northern	313	50	N	16	0	5
The more western of the two on the neck	312	10	N	18	0	3
The more eastern	313	50	N	19	0	4

NORTHERN SIGNS

Constellations	Longitude Deg.	Min.		Latitude Deg.	Min.	Magnitude
On the left pastern	305	40	N	36	30	4 greater
On the left knee	311	0	N	34	15	4 greater
On the right pastern	317	0	N	41	10	4 greater
The more western of the two close together on the breast	319	30	N	29	0	4
The more eastern	320	20	N	29	30	4
The more northern of the two on the right knee	322	20	N	35	0	3
The more southern	321	50	N	24	30	5
The more northern of the two beneath the wing, on the body	327	50	N	25	40	4
The more southern	328	20	N	25	0	4
At the shoulder-blades and juncture of the wing	350	0	N	19	40	2 smaller
On the right shoulder and at the beginning of the leg	325	30	N	31	0	2 smaller
At the tip of the wing	335	30	N	12	30	2 smaller
At the navel, and on the head of Andromeda too	341	10	N	26	0	2 smaller
20 stars: 4 of second magnitude, 4 of third, 9 of fourth, 3 of fifth						

ANDROMEDA

Constellations	Longitude Deg.	Min.		Latitude Deg.	Min.	Magnitude
On the shoulder-blades	348	40	N	24	30	3
On the right shoulder	349	40	N	27	0	4
On the left shoulder	347	40	N	23	0	4
The most southern of the three on the right arm	347	0	N	32	0	4
The most northern	348	0	N	33	30	4
The middle one of the three	348	20	N	32	20	5
The most southern of the three on the top of the right hand	343	0	N	41	0	4
The middle star	344	0	N	42	0	4
[52ª] The most northern of the three	345	30	N	44	0	4
On the left arm	347	30	N	17	30	4
At the left elbow	349	0	N	15	50	3
The most southern of the three on the girdle	357	10	N	25	20	3
The middle one	355	10	N	30	0	3
The most northern	355	20	N	32	30	3
On the left foot	10	10	N	23	0	3
On the right foot	10	30	N	37	10	4 greater
To the south of those two	8	30	N	35	20	4 greater
The more northern of the two under the hamstrings	5	40	N	29	0	4
The more southern	5	20	N	28	0	4
At the right knee	5	30	N	35	30	5
The more northern of the two on the flowing robe	6	0	N	34	30	5
The more southern	7	30	N	32	30	5

Northern Signs

Constellations	Longitude Deg. Min.		Latitude Deg. Min.		Magnitude
The unconstellated star west of the right hand	5	0	N	44	0	3
23 stars: 7 of third magnitude, 12 of fourth, 4 of fifth						
TRIANGULUM, OR THE TRIANGLE						
At the vertex of the triangle	4	20	N	16	30	3
The most western of the three on the base	9	20	N	20	40	3
The middle one	9	30	N	20	20	4
The most eastern of the three	10	10	N	19	0	3
4 stars: 3 of third magnitude, 1 of fourth						

Therefore in the northern region there are 360 stars, all in all: 3 of first magnitude, 18 of second, 81 of third, 177 of fourth, 58 of fifth, 13 of sixth, 1 nebulous, and 9 obscure.

THE SIGNS AND STARS WHICH ARE IN THE MIDDLE AND AROUND THE ECLIPTIC

Constellations	Longitude Deg. Min.		Latitude Deg. Min.		Magnitude
ARIES, OR THE RAM						
The star which is first of all and the more western of the two on the horn	0	0	N	7	20	3 smaller
The more eastern on the horn	1	0	N	8	20	3
The more northern of the two in the opening of the jaws	4	20	N	7	40	5
The more southern	4	50	N	6	0	5
On the neck	9	50	N	5	30	5
On the kidneys	10	50	N	6	0	6
At the beginning of the tail	14	40	N	4	50	5
The most western of the three on the tail	17	10	N	1	40	4
The middle one	18	40	N	2	30	4
[52b] The most eastern	20	20	N	1	50	4
On the hips	13	0	N	1	10	5
On the ham	11	20	S	1	30	5
At the tip of the hind foot	8	10	S	5	15	4 greater
13 stars: 2 of third magnitude, 4 of fourth, 6 of fifth, 1 of sixth						
UNCONSTELLATED STARS AROUND ARIES						
The brilliant star over the head	3	50	N	10	0	3 greater
The very northerly star above the back	15	0	N	10	10	4
The most northern of the remaining three small stars	14	40	N	12	40	5
The middle one	13	0	N	10	40	5
The most southern	12	30	N	10	40	5
5 stars: 1 of third magnitude, 1 of fourth, 3 of fifth						
TAURUS, OR THE BULL						
The most northern of the four in the section	19	40	S	6	0	4
The next after that	19	20	S	7	15	4
The third	18	0	S	8	30	4

In the Middle, and Around the Ecliptic

Constellations	Longitude Deg.	Min.		Latitude Deg.	Min.		Magnitude
The fourth and most southern	17	50	S	9	15	4	
On the right shoulder	23	0	S	9	30	5	
In the breast	27	0	S	8	0	3	
At the right knee	30	0	S	12	40	4	
On the right pastern	26	20	S	14	50	4	
At the left knee	35	30	S	10	0	4	
On the left pastern	36	20	S	13	30	4	
Of the five called Hyades and on the face, the one at the nostrils	32	0	S	5	45	3 smaller	
Between that star and the northern eye	33	40	S	4	15	3 smaller	
Between that same star and the southern eye	34	10	S	8	50	3 smaller	
The brilliant star, in the very eye, called Palilicius by the Romans	36	0	S	5	10	1	
On the northern eye	35	10	S	3	0	3 smaller	
The star south of the horn between the base and the ear	40	30	S	4	0	4	
The more southern of the two on the same horn	43	40	S	5	0	4	
The more northern	43	20	S	3	30	5	
At the extremity of the same	50	30	S	2	30	3	
To the north of the base of the horn	49	0	S	4	0	4	
At the extremity of the horn and on the right foot of Auriga	49	0	N	5	0	3	
The more northern of the two in the north ear	35	20	N	4	30	5	
The more southern	35	0	N	4	30	5	Apogee of Venus: 48°20′
[53ª] The more western of the two small stars on the neck	30	20	N	0	40	5	
The more eastern	32	20	N	1	0	6	
The more southern on the western side of the quadrilateral on the neck	31	20	N	5	0	5	
The more northern on the same	32	10	N	7	10	5	
The more southern on the eastern side	35	20	N	3	0	5	
The more northern on the same side	35	0	N	5	0	5	
The northern limit of the western side of the Pleiades	25	30	N	4	30	5	
The southern limit of the same side	25	50	N	4	40	5	
The very narrow limit of the eastern side of the Pleiades	27	0	N	5	20	5	
A small star of the Pleiades, separated from the limits	26	0	N	3	0	5	
32 stars, apart from that which is at the tip of the northern horn: 1 of first magnitude, 6 of third, 11 of fourth, 13 of fifth, 1 of sixth							

Unconstellated Stars around Taurus

Between the foot and below the shoulder	18	20	S	17	30	4	

IN THE MIDDLE, AND AROUND THE ECLIPTIC

Constellations	Longitude Deg. Min.			Latitude Deg. Min.		Magnitude
The most western of the three to the south						
of the horn	43	20	S	2	0	5
The middle one	47	20	S	1	45	5
The most eastern of the three	49	20	S	2	0	5
The more northern of the two under the tip						
of the same horn	52	20	S	6	20	5
The more southern	52	20	S	7	40	5
The most western of the five under the						
northern horn	50	20	N	2	40	5
The next to the east	52	20	N	1	0	5
The third and to the east	54	20	N	1	20	5
The more northern of the remaining two	55	40	N	3	20	5
The more southern	56	40	N	1	15	5
11 unconstellated stars: 1 of fourth magnitude, 10 of fifth						

GEMINI, OR THE TWINS

Constellations	Longitude Deg. Min.			Latitude Deg. Min.		Magnitude
On the head of the western Twin, Castor	76	40	N	9	30	2
The reddish star on the head of the eastern						
Twin, Pollux	79	50	N	6	15	2
At the left elbow of the western Twin	70	0	N	10	0	4
On the left arm	72	0	N	7	20	4
At the shoulder-blades of the same Twin	75	20	N	5	30	4
On the right shoulder of the same	77	20	N	4	50	4
On the left shoulder of the eastern Twin	80	0	N	2	40	4
On the right side of the western Twin	75	0	N	2	40	5
On the left side of the eastern Twin	76	30	N	3	0	5
[53^b] At the left knee of the western Twin	66	30	N	1	30	3
At the left knee of the eastern	71	35	S	2	30	3
On the left groin of the same	75	0	S	0	30	3
At the hollow of the right knee of the same	74	40	S	0	40	3
The more western star in the foot of the						
western Twin	60	0	S	1	30	4 greater
The more eastern star in the same foot	61	30	S	1	15	4
At the extremity of the foot of the western						
Twin	63	30	S	3	30	4
On the top of the foot of the eastern Twin	65	20	S	7	30	3
On the bottom of the foot of the same	68	0	S	10	30	4
18 stars: 2 of second magnitude, 5 of third, 9 of fourth, 2 of fifth						

UNCONSTELLATED STARS AROUND GEMINI

Constellations	Longitude Deg. Min.			Latitude Deg. Min.		Magnitude
The star west of the top of the foot of the						
western Twin	57	30	S	0	40	4
The brilliant star to the west of the knee of						
the same	59	50	N	5	50	4 greater
To the west of the left knee of the eastern						
Twin	68	30	S	2	15	5
The most northern of the three east of the						
right hand of the eastern Twin	81	40	S	1	20	5

In the Middle, and Around the Ecliptic

Constellations	Longitude Deg. Min.		Latitude Deg. Min.		Magnitude
The middle one	79 40	S	3 20		5
The most southern of the three, and in the neighbourhood of the right arm	79 20	S	4 30		5
The brilliant star to the east of the three	84 0	S	2 40		4
7 unconstellated stars: 3 of fourth magnitude, 4 of fifth					
CANCER, OR THE CRAB					
The nebulous star in the breast, which is called Praeses	93 40	N	0 40		nebulous
The more northern of the two west of the quadrilateral	91 0	N	1 15		4 smaller
The more southern	91 20	S	1 10		4 smaller
The more northern of the two to the east, which are called the Asses	93 40	N	2 40		4 greater
The southern Ass	94 40	S	0 10		4 greater
On the claws or the southern arm	99 50	S	5 30		4
On the northern arm	91 40	N	11 50		4
At the extremity of the northern foot	86 0	N	1 0		5
At the extremity of the southern foot	90 30	S	7 30		4 greater
9 stars: 7 of fourth magnitude, 1 of fifth, 1 nebulous					
UNCONSTELLATED STARS AROUND CANCER					
Above the elbow of the southern claw	103 0	S	2 40		4 smaller
East of the extremity of the same claw	105 0	S	5 40		4 smaller
[54ª] The more western of the two above the little cloud	97 20	N	4 50		5
The more eastern	100 20	N	7 15		5
4 unconstellated stars: 2 of fourth magnitude, 2 of fifth					
LEO, OR THE LION					
At the nostrils	101 40	N	10 0		4
At the opening of the jaws	104 30	N	7 30		4
The more northern of the two on the head	107 40	N	12 0		3
The more southern	107 30	N	9 30		3 greater
The most northern of the three on the neck	113 30	N	11 0		3 Apogee of Mars: 109°50′
The middle one	115 30	N	8 30		2
The most southern of the three	114 0	N	4 30		3
At the heart, the star called Basiliscus or Regulus	115 50	N	0 10		1
The more southern of the two on the breast	116 50	S	1 50		4
A little to the west of the star at the heart	113 20	S	0 15		5
At the knee of the right foreleg	110 40		0 0		5
On the right pad	117 30	S	3 40		6
At the knee of the left foreleg	122 30	S	4 10		4
On the left pad	115 50	S	4 15		4

IN THE MIDDLE, AND AROUND THE ECLIPTIC

Constellations	Longitude Deg. Min.			Latitude Deg. Min.		Magnitude
At the left arm-pit	122	30	S	0	10	4
The most western of the three on the belly	120	20	N	4	0	6
The more northern of the two to the east	126	20	N	5	20	6
The more southern	125	40	N	2	20	6
The more western of the two on the loins	124	40	N	12	15	5
The more eastern	127	30	N	13	40	2
The more northern of the two on the rump	127	40	N	11	30	5
The more southern	129	40	N	9	40	3
At the hips	133	40	N	5	50	3
At the hollow of the knee	135	0	N	1	15	4
On the lower part of the leg	135	0	S	0	50	4
On the hind foot	134	0	S	3	0	5
At the tip of the tail	137	50	N	11	50	1 smaller
27 stars: 2 of first magnitude, 2 of second, 6 of third, 8 of fourth, 5 of fifth, 4 of sixth						
UNCONSTELLATED STARS AROUND LEO						
The more western of the two above the back	119	20	N	13	20	5
The more eastern	121	30	N	15	30	5
The most northern of the three below the belly	129	50	N	1	10	4 smaller
[54b] The middle one	130	30	S	0	30	5
The most southern of the three	132	20	S	2	40	5
The star farthest north between the extremities of Leo and the nebulous complex called Coma Berenices	138	10	N	30	0	luminous
The more western of the two to the south	133	50	N	25	0	obscure
The star to the east, in the shape of an ivy leaf	141	50	N	25	30	obscure
8 unconstellated stars: 1 of fourth magnitude, 4 of fifth, 1 luminous, 2 obscure						
VIRGO, OR THE VIRGIN						
The more southwestern of the two on the top of the head	139	40	N	4	15	5
The more northeastern	140	20	N	5	40	5
The more northern of the two on the face	144	0	N	8	0	5
The more southern	143	30	N	5	30	5
At the tip of the left and southern wing	142	20	N	6	0	3
The most western of the four on the left wing	151	35	N	1	10	3
The next to the east	156	30	N	2	50	3
The third	160	30	N	2	50	5
The last and most eastward of the four	164	20	N	1	40	4
On the right side beneath the girdle	157	40	N	8	30	3
The most western of the three on the right and northern wing	151	30	N	13	50	5
The more southern of the two remaining	153	30	N	11	40	6 Apogee of Jupiter: 154°20′

In the Middle, and Around the Ecliptic

Constellations	Longitude Deg. Min.		Latitude Deg. Min.		Magnitude
The more northern of them, called Vinde-					
miator	155	30 N	15	10	3 greater
On the left hand, called Spica	170	0 S	2	0	1
Beneath the girdle and on the right buttock	168	10 N	8	40	3
The more northern of the two on the west-					
ern side of the quadrilateral on the left					
hip	169	40 N	2	20	5
The more southern	170	20 N	0	10	6
The more northern of the two on the east-					
ern side	173	20 N	1	30	4
The more southern	171	20 N	0	20	5
At the left knee	175	0 N	1	30	5
On the posterior side of the right hip	171	20 N	8	30	5
On the flowing robe, in the middle	180	0 N	7	30	4
More to the south	180	40 N	2	40	4
More to the north	181	40 N	11	40	4 Apogee of Mer-cury: 183°20'
On the left and southern foot	183	20 N	0	30	4
On the right and southern foot	186	0 N	9	50	3

26 stars: 1 of first magnitude, 7 of third, 6 of fourth, 10 of fifth, 2 of sixth

Unconstellated Stars around Virgo

	Longitude Deg. Min.		Latitude Deg. Min.		Magnitude
[55ª] The most western of the three in a					
straight line under the left arm	158	0 S	3	30	5
The middle one	162	20 S	3	30	5
The most eastern	165	35 S	3	20	5
The most western of the three in a straight					
line under Spica	170	30 S	7	20	6
The middle one, which is also a double star	171	30 S	8	20	5
The most eastern of the three	173	20 S	7	50	6

6 unconstellated stars: 4 of fifth magnitude, 2 of sixth

Chelae, or the Claws

	Longitude Deg. Min.		Latitude Deg. Min.		Magnitude
The bright one of the two at the extremity					
of the southern claw	191	20 N	0	40	2 greater
The more obscure star to the north	190	20 N	2	30	5
The bright one of the two at the extremity					
of the northern claw	195	30 N	8	30	2
The more obscure star to the west of that	191	0 N	8	30	5
In the middle of the southern claw	197	20 N	1	40	4
In the same claw, but to the west	194	40 N	1	15	4
At the middle of the northern claw	200	50 N	3	45	4
In the same claw, but to the east	206	20 N	4	30	4

8 stars: 2 of second magnitude, 4 of fourth, 2 of fifth

IN THE MIDDLE, AND AROUND THE ECLIPTIC

Constellations	Longitude Deg. Min.		Latitude Deg. Min.		Magnitude
UNCONSTELLATED STARS AROUND THE CHELAE					
The most western of the three north of the northern claw	199	30	N	9	0	5
The more southern of the two to the east	207	0	N	6	40	4
The more northern	207	40	N	9	15	4
The most eastern of the three between the claws	205	50	N	5	30	6
The more northern of the remaining two to the west	203	40	N	2	0	4
The more southern	204	30	N	1	30	5
The most western of the three beneath the southern claw	196	20	S	7	30	3
The more northern of the remaining two to the east	204	30	S	8	10	4
The more southern	205	20	S	9	40	4
9 unconstellated stars: 1 of third magnitude, 5 of fourth, 2 of fifth, 1 of sixth					
SCORPIO, OR THE SCORPION					
The most northern of the three bright stars on the forehead	209	40	N	1	20	3 greater
The middle one	209	0	S	1	40	3
The most southern of the three	209	0	S	5	0	3
More to the south and in the foot	209	20	S	7	50	3
The more northern of the two adjacent bright stars	210	20	N	1	40	4
The more southern	210	40	N	0	30	4
The most western of the three bright stars on the body	214	0	S	3	45	3
The reddish star in the middle, called Antares	216	0	S	4	0	2 greater
The most eastern of the three	217	50	S	5	30	3
[55b] The more western of the two at the extremity of the foot	212	40	S	6	10	5
The more eastern	213	50	S	6	40	5
At the first vertebra of the body	221	50	S	11	0	3
At the second vertebra	222	10	S	15	0	4
The more northern of the double at the third	223	20	S	18	40	4
The more southern of the double	223	30	S	18	0	3
At the fourth vertebra	226	30	S	19	30	3 Apogee of Saturn: 226°30′
At the fifth	231	30	S	18	50	3
At the sixth vertebra	233	50	S	16	40	3
At the seventh, and next to the sting	232	20	S	15	10	3
The more eastern of the two on the sting	230	50	S	13	20	3
The more western	230	20	S	13	30	4
21 stars: 1 of second magnitude, 13 of third, 5 of fourth, 2 of fifth					

IN THE MIDDLE, AND AROUND THE ECLIPTIC

Constellations	Longitude Deg.	Min.		Latitude Deg.	Min.	Magnitude
UNCONSTELLATED STARS AROUND SCORPIO						
The nebulous star to the east of the sting	234	30	S	12	15	nebulous
The more western of the two north of the sting	228	50	S	6	10	5
The more eastern	232	50	S	4	10	5
3 unconstellated stars: 2 of fifth magnitude, 1 nebulous						
SAGITTARIUS, OR THE ARCHER						
At the head of the arrow	237	50	S	6	30	3
In the palm of the left hand	241	0	S	6	30	3
On the southern part of the bow	241	20	S	10	50	3
The more southern of the two to the north	242	20	S	1	30	3
More northward, at the extremity of the bow	240	0	N	2	50	4
On the left shoulder	248	40	S	3	10	3
To the west and on the dart	246	20	S	3	50	4
The nebulous double star in the eye	248	30	N	0	45	nebulous
The most western of the three on the head	249	0	N	2	10	4
The middle one	251	0	N	1	30	4 greater
The most eastward	252	30	N	2	0	4
The most southern of the three on the northern garment	254	40	N	2	50	4
The middle one	255	40	N	4	30	4
The most northern	256	10	N	6	30	4
The obscure star east of the three	259	0	N	5	30	6
The most northern of the two on the southern garment	262	50	N	5	0	5
The more southern	261	0	N	2	0	6
On the right shoulder	255	40	S	1	50	5
[56ᵃ] At the right elbow	258	10	S	2	50	5
At the shoulder-blades	253	20	S	2	30	5
At the foreshoulder	251	0	S	4	30	4 greater
Beneath the arm-pit	249	40	S	6	45	3
On the pastern of the left foreleg	251	0	S	23	0	2
At the knee of the same leg	250	20	S	18	0	2
On the pastern of the right foreleg	240	0	S	13	0	3
At the left shoulder blade	260	40	S	13	30	3
At the knee of the right foreleg	260	0	S	20	10	3
The more western on the northern side of the quadrilateral at the beginning of the tail	261	0	S	4	50	5
The more eastern on the same side	261	10	S	4	50	5
The more western on the southern side	261	50	S	5	50	5
The more eastern on the same side	263	0	S	6	50	5
31 stars: 2 of second magnitude, 9 of third, 9 of fourth, 8 of fifth, 2 of sixth, 1 nebulous						

IN THE MIDDLE, AND AROUND THE ECLIPTIC

Constellations	*Longitude* Deg. Min.		*Latitude* Deg. Min.		*Magnitude*
CAPRICORNUS, OR THE GOAT					
The most northern of the three on the western horn	270	40	N	7	30	3
The middle one	271	0	N	6	40	6
The most southern of the three	270	40	N	5	0	3
At the extremity of the eastern horn	272	20	N	8	0	6
The most southern of the three at the opening of the jaws	272	20	N	0	45	6
The more western of the two remaining	272	0	N	1	45	6
The more eastern	272	10	N	1	30	6
Under the right eye	270	30	N	0	40	5
The more northern of the two on the neck	275	0	N	4	50	6
The more southern	275	10	S	0	50	5
At the right knee	274	10	S	6	30	4
At the left knee, which is bent	275	0	S	8	40	4
On the left shoulder	280	0	S	7	40	4
The more western of the two contiguous stars below the belly	283	30	S	6	50	4
The more eastern	283	40	S	6	0	5
The most eastern of the three in the middle of the body	282	0	S	4	15	5
The more southern of the two remaining to the west	280	0	S	7	0	5
The more northern	280	0	S	2	50	5
The more western of the two on the back	280	0		0	0	4
The more eastern	284	20	S	0	50	4
The more western of the two on the southern part of the spine	286	40	S	4	45	4
[56ᵇ] The more eastern	288	20	S	4	30	4
The more western of the two at the base of the tail	288	40	S	2	10	3
The more eastern	289	40	S	2	0	3
The more western of the four in the northern part of the tail	290	10	S	2	20	4
The most northern of the remaining three	292	0	S	5	0	5
The middle one	291	0	S	2	50	5
The most northern, at the extremity of the tail	292	0	N	4	20	5
28 stars: 4 of third magnitude, 9 of fourth, 9 of fifth, 6 of sixth					
AQUARIUS, OR THE WATER-BOY					
On the head	293	40	N	15	45	5
The brighter of the two on the right shoulder	299	40	N	11	0	3
The more obscure	298	30	N	9	40	5
On the left shoulder	290	0	N	8	50	3
Under the arm-pit	290	40	N	6	15	5
The most eastern of the three under the left hand and on the coat	280	0	N	5	30	3
The middle one	279	30	N	8	0	4

In the Middle, and Around the Ecliptic

Constellations	Longitude Deg.	Min.		Latitude Deg.	Min.	Magnitude
The most western of the three	278	0	N	8	30	3
At the right elbow	302	50	N	8	45	3
The farthest north on the right hand	303	0	N	10	45	3
The more western of the two remaining to the south	305	20	N	9	0	3
The more eastern	306	40	N	8	30	3
The more western of the two adjacent stars on the right hip	299	30	N	3	0	4
The more eastern	300	20	N	2	10	5
On the right buttock	302	0	S	0	50	4
The more southern of the two on the left buttock	295	0	S	1	40	4
The more northern	295	30	N	4	0	6
The more southern of the two on the right shin	305	0	S	6	30	3
The more northern	304	40	S	5	0	4
On the left hip	301	0	S	5	40	5
The more southern of the two on the left shin	300	40	S	10	0	5
The northern star beneath the knee	302	10	S	9	0	5
The first star in the fall of water from the hand	303	20	N	2	0	4
More to the south-east	308	10	N	0	10	4
To the east at the first bend in the water	311	0	S	1	10	4
To the east of that	313	20	S	0	30	4
In the second and southern bend	313	50	S	1	40	4
The more northern of the two to the east	312	30	S	3	30	4
The more southern	312	50	S	4	10	4
Farther off to the south	314	10	S	8	15	5
[57ª] Eastward, the more western of the two adjacent	316	0	S	11	0	5
The more eastern	316	30	S	10	50	5
The most northern of the three at the third bend in the water	315	0	S	14	0	5
The middle one	316	0	S	14	45	5
The most eastern of the three	316	30	S	15	40	5
The most northern of three in a similar figure to the east	310	20	S	14	10	4
The middle one	310	50	S	15	0	4
The most southern of the three	311	40	S	15	45	4
The most western of the three at the last bend in the water	305	10	S	14	50	4
The more southern of the two to the east	306	0	S	15	20	4
The more northern	306	30	S	14	0	4
The last in the water, and in the mouth of the southern Fish	300	20	S	23	0	1
42 stars: 1 of first magnitude, 9 of third, 18 of fourth, 13 of fifth, 1 of sixth						

In the Middle, and Around the Ecliptic

Constellations	Longitude Deg. Min.		Latitude Deg. Min.		Magnitude
Unconstellated Stars around Aquarius					
The most western of the three east of the bend in the water	320	0	S 15	30	4
The more northern of the two remaining	323	0	S 14	20	4
The more southern	322	20	S 18	15	4
3 stars: greater than fourth magnitude					
Pisces, or the Fish					
In the mouth of the western Fish	315	0	N 9	15	4
The more southern of the two on the occiput	317	30	N 7	30	4 greater
The more northern	321	30	N 9	30	4
The more western of the two on the back	319	20	N 9	20	4
The more eastern	324	0	N 7	30	4
The more western one on the belly	319	20	N 4	30	4
The more eastern	323	0	N 2	30	4
On the tail of the same Fish	329	20	N 6	20	4
On the fishing-line, the first star from the tail	334	20	N 5	45	6
To the east of that	336	20	N 2	45	6
The most western of the three bright stars to the east	340	30	N 2	15	4
The middle one	343	50	N 1	10	4
The most eastern	346	20	S 1	20	4
The more northern of the two small stars on the curvature	345	40	S 2	0	6
The more southern	346	20	S 5	0	6
The most western of the three after the curvature	350	20	S 2	20	4
The middle one	352	0	S 4	40	4
The most eastern one	354	0	S 7	45	4
[57b] At the knot of the two fishing-lines	356	0	S 8	30	3
In the northern line, west of the knot	354	0	S 4	20	4
The most southern of the three to the east	353	30	N 1	30	5
The middle one	353	40	N 5	20	3
The most northern of the three and the last in the line	353	50	N 9	0	4
The Eastern Fish					
The more northern of the two in the mouth	355	20	N 21	45	5
The more southern	355	0	N 21	30	5
The most eastern of the three small stars on the head	352	0	N 20	0	6
The middle one	351	0	N 19	50	6
The most western of the three	350	20	N 23	0	6
The most western of the three on the southern fin, near the left elbow of Andromeda	349	0	N 14	20	4
The middle one	349	40	N 13	0	4
The most eastern of the three	351	0	N 12	0	4
The more northern of the two on the belly	355	30	N 17	0	4
The more southern	352	40	N 15	20	4

In the Middle, and Around the Ecliptic

Constellations	Longitude Deg. Min.		Latitude Deg. Min.		Magnitude
On the eastern fin, near the tail	353 20	N	11 45		4
34 stars: 2 of third magnitude, 22 of fourth, 3 of fifth, 7 of sixth					
UNCONSTELLATED STARS AROUND PISCES					
The more western on the northern side of the quadrilateral under the western Fish	324 30	S	2 40		4
The more eastern	325 35	S	2 30		4
The more western on the southern side	324 0	S	5 50		4
The more eastern	325 40	S	5 30		4
4 unconstellated stars: of fourth magnitude					

Therefore, all in all, there are 348 stars in the zodiac: 5 of first magnitude, 9 of second, 65 of third, 132 of fourth, 105 of fifth, 27 of sixth, 3 nebulous, 2 obscure; and, over and above the count, the Coma, which we said above was called Coma Berenices by Conon the mathematician.

The Stars of the Southern Region

CETUS, OR THE WHALE					
At the extremity of the nose	11 0	S	7 45		4
The most eastern of the three in the jaws	11 0	S	11 20		3
The middle one, in the middle of the mouth	6 0	S	11 30		3
The most western of the three, on the cheek	3 50	S	14 0		3
In the eye	4 0	S	8 10		4
Northward, in the hair	5 30	S	6 20		4
[58ª] Westward, in the mane	1 0	S	4 10		4
The more northern on the western side of the quadrilateral in the breast	355 20	S	24 30		4
The more southern	356 40	S	28 0		4
The more northern of the two to the east	0 0	S	25 10		4
The more southern	0 0	S	27 30		3
The middle one of the three on the body	345 20	S	25 20		3
The most southern	346 20	S	30 30		4
The most northern of the three	348 20	S	20 0		3
The more eastern of the two at the tail	343 0	S	15 20		3
The more western	338 20	S	15 40		3
The more northern on the eastern side of the quadrilateral in the tail	335 0	S	11 40		5
The more southern	334 0	S	13 40		5
The more northern of the two remaining to the west	332 40	S	13 0		5
The more southern	332 20	S	14 0		5
At the northern extremity of the tail	327 40	S	9 30		3
At the southern extremity of the tail	329 0	S	20 20		3
22 stars: 10 of third magnitude, 8 of fourth, 4 of fifth					

SOUTHERN SIGNS

Constellations	Longitude Deg. Min.		Latitude Deg. Min.		Magnitude
ORION					
The nebulous star on the head	50	20	S	16	30	nebulous
The bright, reddish star on the right shoulder	55	20	S	17	0	1
On the left shoulder	43	40	S	17	30	2 greater
East of that star	48	20	S	18	0	4 smaller
At the right elbow	57	40	S	14	30	4
On the right forearm	59	40	S	11	50	6
The more eastern on the southern side of the quadrilateral in the right hand	59	50	S	10	40	4
The more western	59	20	S	9	45	4
The more eastern on the northern side	60	40	S	8	15	6
The more western on the same side	59	0	S	8	15	6
The more western of the two on the club	55	0	S	3	45	5
The more eastern	57	40	S	3	15	5
The most eastern of the four in a straight line on the back	50	50	S	19	40	4
More western	49	40	S	20	0	6
Still more western	48	40	S	20	20	6
Most western	47	30	S	20	30	5
The most northern of the nine on the shield	43	50	S	8	0	4
The second	42	40	S	8	10	4
The third	41	20	S	10	15	4
The fourth	39	40	S	12	50	4
The fifth	38	30	S	14	15	4
The sixth	37	50	S	15	50	3
[58b] The seventh	38	10	S	17	10	3
The eighth	38	40	S	20	20	3
The last and most southern	39	40	S	21	30	3
The most western of the three bright stars on the sword-belt	48	40	S	24	10	2
The middle one	50	40	S	24	50	2
The most eastern of the three in a straight line	52	40	S	25	30	2
On the hilt of the sword	47	10	S	25	50	3
The most northern of the three on the sword	50	10	S	28	40	4
The middle one	50	0	S	29	30	3
The most southern one	50	20	S	29	50	3 smaller
The more eastern of the two at the tip of the sword	51	0	S	30	30	4
The more western	49	30	S	30	50	4
On the left foot, the bright star which belongs to Fluvius too	42	30	S	31	30	1
On the left shin	44	20	S	30	15	4 greater
At the right heel	46	40	S	31	10	4
At the right knee	53	30	S	33	30	3
38 stars: 2 of first magnitude, 4 of second, 8 of third, 15 of fourth, 3 of fifth, 5 of sixth, and 1 nebulous					

Southern Signs

Constellations	Longitude Deg. Min.		Latitude Deg. Min.		Magnitude
FLUVIUS, OR THE RIVER					
After the left foot of Orion, and at the beginning of Fluvius	41	40	S	31	50	4
The most northern star within the bend of Orion's leg	42	10	S	28	15	4
The more eastern of the two after that	41	20	S	29	50	4
The more western	38	0	S	28	15	4
The more eastern of the next two	36	30	S	25	15	4
The more western	33	30	S	25	20	4
The most eastern of the three after them	29	40	S	26	0	4
The middle one	29	0	S	27	0	4
The most western of the three	26	18	S	27	50	4
The most eastern of the four after the interval	20	20	S	32	50	3
More western	18	0	S	31	0	4
Still more western	17	30	S	28	50	3
The most western of all four	15	30	S	28	0	3
Again similarly, the most eastward of the four	10	30	S	25	30	3
More westward	8	10	S	23	50	4
Still more westward	5	30	S	23	10	3
The most westward of the four	3	50	S	23	15	4
The star in the bend of Fluvius which touches the breast of Cetus	358	30	S	32	10	4
East of that	359	10	S	34	50	4
The most westward of the three to the east	2	10	S	38	30	4
[59ᵃ] The middle one	7	10	S	38	10	4
The most eastward of the three	10	50	S	39	0	5
The more northern of the two on the western side of the quadrilateral	14	40	S	41	30	4
The more southern	14	50	S	42	30	4
The more western on the eastern side	15	30	S	43	20	4
The most eastward of those four	18	0	S	43	20	4
The more northern of the two contiguous stars towards the east	27	30	S	50	20	4
The more southern	28	20	S	51	45	4
The more eastern of the two at the bend	21	30	S	53	50	4
The more western	19	10	S	53	10	4
The most eastern of the three in the remaining space	11	10	S	53	0	4
The middle one	8	10	S	53	30	4
The most western of the three	5	10	S	52	0	4
The bright star at the extremity of the river	353	30	S	53	30	1
34 stars: 1 of first magnitude, 5 of third, 27 of fourth, 1 of fifth						
LEPUS, OR THE RABBIT					
The more northern one on the western side of the quadrilateral at the ears	43	0	S	35	0	5
The more southern	43	10	S	36	30	5
The more northern one on the eastern side	44	40	S	35	30	5

SOUTHERN SIGNS

Constellations	Longitude Deg.	Min.		Latitude Deg.	Min.	Magnitude
The more southern	44	40	S	36	40	5
At the chin	42	30	S	39	40	4 greater
At the extremity of the left forefoot	39	30	S	45	15	4 greater
In the middle of the body	48	50	S	41	30	3
Beneath the belly	48	10	S	44	20	3
The more northern of the two on the hind feet	54	20	S	44	0	4
The more southern	52	20	S	45	50	4
On the loins	53	20	S	38	20	4
At the tip of the tail	56	0	S	38	10	4
12 stars: 2 of third magnitude, 6 of fourth, 4 of fifth						
CANIS, OR THE DOG						
The very bright star called Canis, in the mouth	71	0	S	39	10	1 very great
On the ears	73	0	S	35	0	4
On the head	74	40	S	36	30	5
The more northern of the two on the neck	76	40	S	37	45	4
The more southern	78	40	S	40	0	4
On the breast	73	50	S	42	30	5
The more northern of the two at the right knee	69	30	S	41	15	5
The more southern	69	20	S	42	30	5
At the extremity of the forefoot	64	20	S	41	20	3
[59[b]] The more western of the two on the left knee	68	0	S	46	30	5
The more eastern	69	30	S	45	50	5
The more eastern of the two on the left shoulder	78	0	S	46	0	4
The more western	75	0	S	47	0	5
On the left hip	80	0	S	48	45	3 smaller
Beneath the belly between the thighs	77	0	S	51	30	3
In the hollow of the right foot	76	20	S	55	10	4
At the extremity of the same foot	77	0	S	55	40	3
At the tip of the tail	85	30	S	50	30	3 smaller
18 stars: 1 of first magnitude, 5 of third, 5 of fourth, 7 of fifth						
UNCONSTELLATED STARS AROUND CANIS						
North of the head of the Dog	72	50	S	25	15	4
The most southern in a straight line under the hind feet	63	20	S	60	30	4
The more northern	64	40	S	58	45	4
Still more northern	66	20	S	57	0	4
The last and farthest north of the four	67	30	S	56	0	4
The most western of the three westward as it were in a straight line	50	20	S	55	30	4
The middle one	53	40	S	57	40	4
The most eastern of the three	55	40	S	59	30	4

Southern Signs

Constellations	Longitude Deg.	Min.		Latitude Deg.	Min.	Magnitude
The more western of the two bright stars beneath them	52	20	S	59	40	2
The more western	49	20	S	57	40	2
The remaining star, more southern	45	30	S	59	30	4
11 stars: 2 of second magnitude, 9 of fourth						
CANICULA, OR PROCYON, OR THE LITTLE BITCH						
On the neck	78	20	S	14	0	4
The bright star on the thigh, that is, Προκύων or Canicula, the Dog-star	82	30	S	16	10	1
2 stars: 1 of first magnitude, 1 of fourth						
ARGO, OR THE SHIP						
The more western of the two at the extremity of the Ship	93	40	S	42	40	5
The more eastern	97	40	S	43	20	3
The more northern of the two on the stern	92	10	S	45	0	4
The more southern	92	10	S	46	0	4
West of the two	88	40	S	45	30	4
The bright star in the middle of the shield	89	40	S	47	15	4
The most western of the three beneath the shield	88	40	S	49	45	4
The most eastern	92	40	S	49	50	4
The middle one of the three	91	40	S	49	15	4
At the extremity of the rudder	97	20	S	49	50	4
The more northern of the two on the stern keel	87	20	S	53	0	4
The more southern	87	20	S	58	30	3
[60ᵃ] The most northern on the cross-bank of the stern	93	30	S	55	30	5
The most western of the three on the same cross-bank	95	30	S	58	30	5
The middle one	96	40	S	57	15	4
The most eastern	99	50	S	57	45	4
The bright star to the east on the cross-bank	104	30	S	58	20	2
The more western of the two obscure stars beneath that	101	30	S	60	0	5
The more eastern	104	20	S	59	20	5
The more western of the two east of the aforesaid bright star	106	30	S	56	40	5
The more eastern	107	40	S	57	0	5
The most northern of the three on the small shields and at the foot of the mast	119	0	S	51	30	4 greater
The middle one	119	30	S	55	30	4 greater
The most southern of the three	117	20	S	57	10	4
The more northern of the two contiguous stars beneath them	122	30	S	60	0	4
The more southern	122	20	S	61	15	4

SOUTHERN SIGNS

Constellations	Longitude Deg. Min.			Latitude Deg. Min.		Magnitude
The more southern of the two in the middle of the mast	113	30	S	51	30	4
The more northern	112	40	S	49	0	4
The more western of the two at the top part of the sail	111	20	S	43	20	4
The more eastern	112	20	S	43	30	4
Below the third star east of the shield	98	30	S	54	30	2 smaller
In the section of the bridge	100	50	S	51	15	2
Between the oars in the keel	95	0	S	63	0	4
The obscure star east of that	102	20	S	64	30	6
The bright star, east of that and below the cross-bank	113	20	S	63	50	2
The bright star to the south, more within the keel	121	50	S	69	40	2
The most western of the three to the east of that	128	30	S	65	40	3
The middle one	134	40	S	65	50	3
The most eastern	139	20	S	65	50	2
The more western of the two in the section	144	20	S	62	50	3
The more eastern	151	20	S	62	15	3
The more western in the northwestern oar	57	20	S	65	50	4 greater
The more eastern	73	30	S	65	40	3 greater
The more western one in the remaining oar, Canopus	70	30	S	75	0	1
The remaining star east of that	82	20	S	71	50	3 greater
45 stars: 1 of first magnitude, 6 of second, 8 of third, 22 of fourth, 7 of fifth, 1 of sixth						

HYDRA

	Longitude Deg. Min.			Latitude Deg. Min.		Magnitude
Of the two more western of the five on the head, the more southern, at the nostrils	97	20	S	15	0	4
The more northern of the two, and in the eye	98	40	S	13	40	4
On the occiput, the more northern of the two to the east	99	0	S	11	30	4
[60b] The more southern, and at the jaws	98	50	S	14	45	4
East of all those and on the cheeks	100	50	S	12	15	4
The more western of the two at the beginning of the neck	103	40	S	11	50	5
The more eastern	106	40	S	13	30	4
The middle one of the three at the curve of the neck	111	40	S	15	20	4
East of that	114	0	S	14	50	4
The most southern	111	40	S	17	10	4
The obscure and northern star of the two contiguous to the south	112	30	S	19	45	6
The bright one and to the south-east	113	20	S	20	30	2
The most western of the three after the curve in the neck	119	20	S	26	30	4

SOUTHERN SIGNS

Constellations	Longitude Deg. Min.			Latitude Deg. Min.		Magnitude
The most eastern	124	30	S	23	15	4
The middle one	122	0	S	24	0	4
The most western of the three in a straight line	131	20	S	24	30	3
The middle one	133	20	S	23	0	4
The most eastern one	136	20	S	23	10	3
The more northern of the two beneath the base of the Cup	144	50	S	25	45	4
The more southern	145	40	S	30	10	4
East of them, the most western of the three on the triangle	155	30	S	31	20	4
The most southern	157	50	S	34	10	4
The most eastern of the same three	159	30	S	31	40	3
East of the Crow, near the tail	173	20	S	13	30	4
At the extremity of the tail	186	50	S	17	30	4
25 stars: 1 of second magnitude, 3 of third, 19 of fourth, 1 of fifth, 1 of sixth						

UNCONSTELLATED STARS AROUND HYDRA

South of the head	96	0	S	23	15	3
East of those on the neck	124	20	S	26	0	3
2 unconstellated stars: of third magnitude						

CRATER, OR THE CUP

On the base of the Cup and in Hydra too	139	40	S	23	0	4
The more southern of the two in the middle of the Cup	146	0	S	19	30	4
The more northern of them	143	30	S	18	0	4
On the southern rim of the Cup	150	20	S	18	30	4 greater
On the northern part of the rim	142	40	S	13	40	4
On the southern part of the stem	152	30	S	16	30	4 smaller
On the northern part	145	0	S	11	50	4
7 stars: of fourth magnitude						

[61ᵃ] CORVUS, OR THE CROW

On the beak, and in Hydra too	158	40	S	21	30	5
On the neck	157	40	S	19	40	5
In the breast	160	0	S	18	10	5
On the right wing, the western wing	160	50	S	14	50	3
The more western of the two on the eastern wing	160	0	S	12	30	3
The more eastern	161	20	S	11	45	4
At the extremity of the foot, and in Hydra too	163	50	S	18	10	3
7 stars: 5 of third magnitude, 1 of fourth, 1 of fifth						

CENTAURUS, OR THE CENTAUR

The most southern of the four on the head	183	50	S	21	20	5
The more northern	183	20	S	13	50	5

SOUTHERN SIGNS

Constellations	Longitude Deg.	Min.		Latitude Deg.	Min.	Magnitude
The more western of the two in the middle	182	30	S	20	30	5
The more eastern and last of the four	182	20	S	20	0	5
On the left and western shoulder	179	30	S	25	30	3
On the right shoulder	189	0	S	22	30	3
On the left forearm	182	30	S	17	30	4
The more northern of the two on the western side of the quadrilateral on the shield	191	30	S	22	30	4
The more southern	192	30	S	23	45	4
Of the remaining two, the one at the top of the shield	195	20	S	18	15	4
The more southern	196	50	S	20	50	4
The most western of the three on the right side	186	40	S	28	20	4
The middle one	187	20	S	29	20	4
The most eastern	188	30	S	28	0	4
On the right arm	189	40	S	26	30	4
On the right elbow	196	10	S	25	15	3
At the extremity of the right hand	200	50	S	24	0	4
The bright star at the junction of the human body	191	20	S	33	30	3
The more eastern of the two obscure stars	191	0	S	31	0	5
The more western	189	50	S	30	20	5
At the beginning of the back	185	30	S	33	50	5
West of that, on the horse's back	182	20	S	37	30	5
The most eastern of the three on the loins	179	10	S	40	0	3
The middle one	178	20	S	40	20	4
The most western of the three	176	0	S	41	0	5
The more western of the two contiguous stars on the right hip	176	0	S	46	10	2
The more eastern	176	40	S	46	45	4
On the breast, beneath the horse's wing	191	40	S	40	45	4
[61b] The more western of the two under the belly	179	50	S	43	0	2
The more eastern	181	0	S	43	45	3
In the hollow of the right hind foot	183	20	S	51	10	2
On the pastern of the same	188	40	S	51	40	2
In the hollow of the left <hind> foot	188	40	S	55	10	4
Under the muscle of the same foot	184	30	S	55	40	4
On top of the right forefoot	181	40	S	41	10	1
At the left knee	197	30	S	45	20	2
The unconstellated star below the right thigh	188	0	S	49	10	3

37 stars: 1 of first magnitude, 5 of second, 7 of third, 15 of fourth, 9 of fifth

BESTIA QUAM TENET CENTAURUS, OR THE BEAST HELD BY THE CENTAUR—THE WOLF

At the top of the hind foot and in the hand of the Centaur	201	20	S	24	50	3

SOUTHERN SIGNS

Constellations	Longitude Deg. Min.		Latitude Deg. Min.		Magnitude
On the hollow of the same foot	199	10	S 20	10	3
The more western of the two on the fore shoulder	204	20	S 21	15	4
The more eastern	207	30	S 21	0	4
In the middle of the body	206	20	S 25	10	4
On the belly	203	30	S 27	0	5
On the hip	204	10	S 29	0	5
The more northern of the two at the beginning of the hip	208	0	S 28	30	5
The more southern	207	0	S 30	0	5
The upmost part of the loins	208	40	S 33	10	5
The most southern of the three at the extremity of the tail	195	20	S 31	20	5
The middle one	195	10	S 30	0	4
The most northern of the three	196	20	S 29	20	4
The more southern of the two at the throat	212	10	S 17	0	4
The more northern	212	40	S 15	20	4
The more western of the two at the opening of the jaws	209	0	S 13	30	4
The more eastern	210	0	S 12	50	4
The more southern of the two on the forefoot	240	40	S 11	30	4
The more northern	239	50	S 10	0	4
19 stars: 2 of third magnitude, 11 of fourth, 6 of fifth					

ARA OR THURIBULUM, THE ALTAR OR THE CENSER

	Longitude Deg. Min.		Latitude Deg. Min.		Magnitude
The more northern of the two at the base	231	0	S 22	40	5
The more southern	233	40	S 25	45	4
At the center of the altar	229	30	S 26	30	4
[62ª] The most northern of the three on the hearth	224	0	S 30	20	5
The more southern of the remaining two contiguous stars	228	30	S 34	10	4
The more northern	228	20	S 33	20	4
In the midst of the flames	224	10	S 34	10	4
7 stars: 5 of fourth magnitude, 2 of fifth					

CORONA AUSTRINA, OR SOUTHERN CROWN

	Longitude Deg. Min.		Latitude Deg. Min.		Magnitude
The more western star on the outer periphery	242	30	S 21	30	4
East of that on the crown	245	0	S 21	0	5
East of that too	246	30	S 20	20	5
Farther east of that also	248	10	S 20	0	5
East of that and west of the knee of Sagittarius	249	30	S 18	30	5
The bright star to the north on the knee	250	40	S 17	10	4
The more northern	250	10	S 16	0	4
Still more northern	249	50	S 15	20	4

SOUTHERN SIGNS

Constellations	Longitude Deg. Min.		Latitude Deg. Min.			Magnitude
The more eastern of the two on the northern part of the periphery	248	30	S	15	50	6
The more western	248	0	S	14	50	6
Some distance west of those	245	10	S	14	40	5
Still west of that	243	0	S	15	50	5
The last star, more towards the south	242	30	S	18	30	5
13 stars: 5 of fourth magnitude, 6 of fifth, 2 of sixth						
PISCIS AUSTRINUS, OR THE SOUTHERN FISH						
In the mouth, and the same as at the extremity of Aqua	300	20	S	23	0	1
The most western of the three on the head	294	0	S	21	20	4
The middle one	297	30	S	22	15	4
The most eastern	299	0	S	22	30	4
At the gills	297	40	S	16	15	4
On the southern and dorsal fin	288	30	S	19	30	5
The more eastern of the two in the belly	294	30	S	15	10	5
The more western	292	10	S	14	30	4
The most eastern of the three on the northern fin	288	30	S	15	15	4
The middle one	285	10	S	16	30	4
The most western of the three	284	20	S	18	10	4
At the extremity of the tail	289	20	S	22	15	4
11 stars beside the first: 9 of fourth magnitude, 2 of fifth						
[62b] UNCONSTELLATED STARS AROUND PISCIS AUSTRINUS						
The most western of the bright stars west of Piscis	271	20	S	22	20	3
The middle one	274	30	S	22	10	3
The most eastern of the three	277	20	S	21	0	3
The obscure star west of that	275	20	S	20	50	5
The more southern of the two remaining to the north	277	10	S	16	0	4
The more northern	277	10	S	14	50	4
6 stars: 3 of third magnitude, 2 of fourth, 1 of fifth						

In the southern region 316 stars: 7 of first magnitude, 18 of second, 60 of third, 167 of fourth, 54 of fifth, 9 of sixth, and 1 nebulous. And so there are altogether 1024 stars: 15 of first magnitude, 45 of second, 206 of third, 476 of fourth, 217 of fifth, 49 of sixth, 11 obscure, and 5 nebulous.

BOOK THREE

1. On the Precessions of the Solstices and Equinoxes

[63ᵃ] Having depicted the appearance of the fixed stars in relation to the annual revolution, we must pass on; and we shall treat first of the change of the equinoxes, by reason of which even the fixed stars are believed to move. Now we find that the ancient mathematicians made no distinction between the "turning" or natural year, which begins at an equinox or solstice, and the year which is determined by means of some one of the fixed stars. That is why they thought the Olympic years, which they measured from the rising of Canicula, were the same as the years measured from the summer solstice, since they did not yet know the distinction between the two.

But Hipparchus of Rhodes, a man of wonderful acumen, was the first to call attention to the fact that there was a difference in the length of these two kinds of year. While making careful observations of the magnitude of the year, he found that it was longer as measured from the fixed stars than as measured from the equinoxes or solstices. Hence he believed that the fixed stars too possessed a movement eastward, but one so slow as not to be immediately perceptible. But now through the passage of time, the movement has become very evident. By it we discern a rising and setting of the signs and stars which are already far different from those risings and settings described by the ancients; and we see that the twelve parts of the ecliptic have receded from the signs of the fixed stars by a rather great interval, although in the beginning they agreed in name and in position.

Moreover, an irregular movement has been found; and wishing to assign the cause for its irregularity, astronomers have brought forward different theories. Some maintained that there was a sort of swinging movement of the suspended world—like the movement in latitude which we find in the case of the planets—and that back and forth within fixed limits as far out as the world has gone forward in one direction it will come back again in the other at some time,[1] and that the extent of its digression from the middle on either side was not more than 8°. But this already outdated theory can no longer hold, especially because [63ᵇ] it is already clear enough that the head of the constellation of Aries has become more than three times 8° distant from the spring equinox—and similarly for other stars—and no trace of a regression has been perceived during so many ages. Others indeed have opined that the sphere of the fixed stars moves forward but does so by irregular steps; and nevertheless they have failed to define any fixed mode of movement.

Moreover, there is an additional surprise of nature, in that the obliquity of the ecliptic does not appear so great to us as before Ptolemy—as we said above.

For the sake of a cause for these facts some have thought up a ninth sphere

[1]*i.e.*, the sphere of the world has rotated westward and will at some time rotate eastward the same distance.

and others a tenth: they thought these facts could be explained through those spheres; but they were unable to produce what they had promised. Already an eleventh sphere has begun to see the light of day; and in talking of the movement of the Earth we shall easily prove that this number of circles is superfluous.

For, as we have already set out separately in Book I, the two revolutions, that is, of the annual declination and of the centre of the Earth, are not altogether equal, namely because the restoration of the declination slightly anticipates the period of the centre, whence it necessarily follows that the equinoxes seem to arrive before their time—not that the sphere of the fixed stars is moved eastward, but rather that the equator is moved westward, as it is inclined obliquely to the plane of the ecliptic in proportion to the amount of deflexion of the axis of the terrestrial globe. For it seems more accurate to say that the equator is inclined obliquely to the ecliptic than that the ecliptic, a greater circle, is inclined to the equator, a smaller. For the ecliptic, which is described by the distance between the sun and the Earth during the annual circuit, is much greater than the equator, which is described by the daily movement of the Earth around its axis. And in this way the common sections of the equator and the oblique ecliptic are perceived, with the passage of time, to get ahead, while the stars are perceived to lag behind. But the measure of this movement and the ratio of its irregularity were hidden from our predecessors, because the period of revolution was not yet known on account of its surprising slowness—I mean that during the many ages after it was first noticed by men, it has advanced through hardly a fifteenth part of a circle, or 24°. Nevertheless, we shall state things with as much certitude as possible, with the aid of what we have learned concerning these facts from the history of observations down to our own time.

2. History of the Observations Confirming the Irregular Precession of the Equinoxes and Solstices

[64ª] Accordingly in the 36th year of the first of the seventy-six-year periods of Callippus, which was the 30th year after the death of Alexander the Great, Timochares the Alexandrian, who was the first to investigate the positions of the fixed stars, recorded that Spica, which is in the constellation of Virgo, had an angular elongation of $82\frac{1}{3}°$ from the point of summer solstice with a southern latitude of 2°; and that the star in the forehead of Scorpio which is the most northward of the three and is first in the order of formation of the sign had a latitude of $1\frac{1}{3}°$ and a longitude of 32° from the autumn equinox.

And again in the 48th year of the same period he found that Spica in Virgo had a longitude of $82\frac{1}{2}°$ from the summer solstice but had kept the same latitude.

Now Hipparchus in the 50th year of the third period of Callippus, in the 196th year since the death of Alexander, found that the star called Regulus, which is in the breast of Leo, was $29\frac{5}{6}°$ to the east of the summer solstice.

Next Menelaus, the Roman geometer, in the first year of Trajan's reign, i.e., in the 99th year since the birth of Christ, and in the 422nd year since the death of Alexander, recorded that Spica in Virgo had a longitude of $86\frac{1}{4}°$ from the [summer] solstice and that the star in the forehead of Scorpio had a longitude of $35\frac{11}{12}°$ from the autumn equinox.

Following them, Ptolemy, in the second year of the reign of Antoninus Pius, in the 462nd year since the death of Alexander, discovered that Regulus in Leo had a longitude of 32½° from the [summer] solstice; Spica, 86½°; and that the star in the forehead of Scorpio had a longitude of 36⅓° from the autumn equinox, with no change in latitude—as was set forth above in drawing up the tables. And we have passed these things in review, just as they were recorded by our predecessors.

After a great lapse of time, however, in the 1202nd year after the death of Alexander, came the observations of al-Battani the Harranite; and we may place the utmost confidence in them. In that year Regulus, or Basiliscus, was seen to have attained a longitude of 44°5′ from the [summer] solstice; and the star in the forehead of Scorpio, one of 47°50′ [64ᵇ] from the autumn equinox. The latitude of these stars stayed completely the same, so that there is no longer any doubt on that score.

Wherefore in the year of Our Lord 1525, in the year after leap-year by the Roman calendar and 1849 Egyptian years after the death of Alexander, we were taking observations of the often mentioned Spica, at Frauenburg, in Prussia. And the greatest altitude of the star on the meridian circle was seen to be approximately 27°. We found that the latitude of Frauenburg was 54°19½′. Wherefore its declination from the equator stood to be 8°40′. Hence its position became known as follows:

For we have described the meridian circle *ABCD* through the poles of the ecliptic and the equator. Let *AEC* be the diameter and common section with the equator; and *BED* is the diameter and common section with the ecliptic. Let *F* be the north pole of the ecliptic and *FEG* its axis; and let *B* be the beginning of Capricorn and *D* of Cancer. Now let

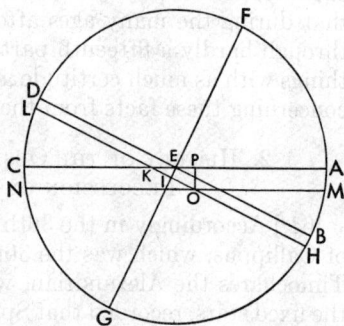

$$\text{arc } BH = 2°,$$

which is the southern latitude of the star. And from point *H* let *HL* be drawn parallel to *BD*; and let *HL* cut the axis of the ecliptic at *I* and the equator at *K*. Moreover, let

$$\text{arc } MA = 8°40′,$$

in proportion to the southern declination of the star; and from point *M* let *MN* be drawn parallel to *AC*.

MN will cut *HIL* the parallel to the ecliptic; therefore let *MN* cut *HIL* at point *O*; and if the straight line *OP* is drawn at right angles to *MN* and *AC*, then

$$OP = \tfrac{1}{2} \text{ ch. } 2 \, AM.$$

But the circles having the diameters *FG*, *HL*, and *MN* are perpendicular to plane *ABCD*; and by Euclid's *Elements*, XI, 19, their common sections are at right angles to the same plane in points *O* and *I*. Hence by XI, 6, they [the common sections] are parallel to one another. And since *I* is the centre of the circle whose diameter is *HL*, therefore line *OI* will be equal to half the chord subtending twice an arc in a circle of diameter *HL*—an arc similar to the arc which measures the longitude of the star from the beginning of Libra, and this arc is what we are looking for. It is found in this way:

Since the exterior angle is equal to its interior and opposite,

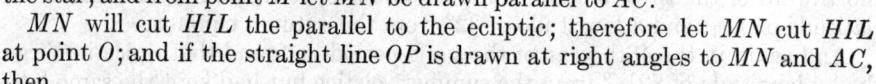

$$\text{angle } AEB = \text{angle } OKP$$

and
$$\text{angle } OPK = 90°.$$
Accordingly
[65ᵃ] $OP : OK = \frac{1}{2}$ ch. $2\ AB : BE = \frac{1}{2}$ ch. $2\ AH : HIK$.
For the lines comprehend triangles similar to OPK.
But
$$\text{arc } AB = 23°28\frac{1}{2}',$$
and
$$\frac{1}{2} \text{ ch. } 2\ AB = 39{,}832,$$
$$\text{where } BE = 100{,}000.$$
And
$$\text{arc } ABH = 25°28\frac{1}{2}',$$
$$\frac{1}{2} \text{ ch. } 2\ ABH = 43{,}010,$$
$$\text{arc } MA = 8°40',$$
which is the declination,
and
$$\frac{1}{2} \text{ ch. } 2\ MA = 15{,}069.$$
It follows from this that
$$HIK = 107{,}978,$$
$$OK = 37{,}831,$$
and by subtraction
$$HO = 70{,}147.$$
But
$$HOI = \frac{1}{2} \text{ ch. } HGL$$
and
$$\text{arc } HGL = 176°.$$
Then
$$HOI = 99{,}939,$$
$$\text{where } BE = 100{,}000.$$
And therefore by subtraction,
$$OI = HOI - HO = 29{,}792.$$
But in so far as $HOI = $ radius $= 100{,}000$,
$$OI = 29{,}810$$
$$= \frac{1}{2} \text{ ch. } 2 \text{ arc } 17°21'.$$

This was the distance of Spica in [the constellation] Virgo from the beginning of Libra; and the position of the star was here. Moreover, ten years before, in 1515, we found that it had a declination of 8°36'; and its position was 17°14' distant from the beginning of the Balances.

Now Ptolemy recorded that it had a declination of only $\frac{1}{2}°$. Therefore its position was at 26°40' of the [zodiacal sign] Virgo, which seems to be more or less true in comparison with the previous observations.

Hence it appears clearly enough that during nearly the whole period of 432 years from Timochares to Ptolemy the equinoxes and solstices were moved according to a precession of 1° per 100 years—if a constant ratio is set up between the time and the amount of precession, which added up to $4\frac{1}{3}°$. For in the 266 years between Hipparchus and Ptolemy the longitude of Basiliscus in Leo from the summer solstice moved $2\frac{2}{3}°$, so that here too, by taking the time into comparison, there is found a precession of 1° per 100 years.

Moreover, because during the 782 mean years between the observation of

Menelaus and that of al-Battani the first star in the forehead of Scorpio had a change in longitude of 11°55′, it will certainly seem that 1° should be assigned not to 100 years but rather to 66 years; but for the 741 years after Ptolemy, 1° to only 65 years.

If finally the remaining space of 645 years is compared with the difference of 9°11′ given by our observation, there will be 71 years allotted to 1°.

From this it is clear that the precession of the equinoxes was slower [65ᵇ] during the 400 years before Ptolemy than during the time between Ptolemy and al-Battani, and that the precession in this middle period was speedier than in the time from al-Battani to us.

Moreover, there is found a difference in the movement of obliquity, since Aristarchus of Samos found that the obliquity of the ecliptic and the equator was 23°51′20″, just as Ptolemy did; al-Battani, 23°35′; 190 years later Arzachel the Spaniard, 23°34′. And similarly after 230 years Prophatius the Jew found that the obliquity was approximately 2′ smaller. And in our time it has not been found greater than 23°28½′. Hence it is also clear that the movement was least from the time of Aristarchus to that of Ptolemy and greatest from that of Ptolemy to that of al-Battani.

3. The Hypotheses by Means of Which the Mutation of the Equinoxes and of the Obliquity of the Ecliptic and the Equator are Shown

Accordingly it seems clear from this that the solstices and equinoxes change around in an irregular movement. No one perhaps will bring forward a better reason for this than that there is a certain deflexion of the axis of the Earth and the poles of the equator. For that seems to follow upon the hypothesis of the movement of the Earth, since it is clear that the ecliptic remains perpetually unchangeable—the constant latitudes of the fixed stars bear witness to that—while the equator moves. For if the movement of the axis of the Earth were simply and exactly in proportion to the movement of the centre, there would not appear at all any precession of the equinoxes and solstices, as we said; but as these movements differ from one another by a variable difference, it was necessary for the solstices and equinoxes to precede the positions of the stars in an irregular movement.

The same thing happens in the case of the movement of declination, which changes the obliquity of the ecliptic irregularly—although this obliquity should be assigned more rightly to the equator.

For this reason you should understand two reciprocal movements belonging wholly to the poles, like hanging balances, since the poles and circles in a sphere imply one another mutually and are in agreement. Therefore there will be one movement which changes the inclination of those circles [66ᵃ] by moving the poles up and down in proportion to the angle of section. There is another which alternately increases and decreases the solstitial and equinoctial precessions by a movement taking place crosswise. Now we call these movements "librations," or "swinging movements," because like hanging bodies swinging over the same course between two limits, they become faster in the middle and very slow at the extremes. And such movements occur very often in connection with the latitudes of the planets, as we shall see in the proper place.

They differ moreover in their periods, because the irregular movement of the equinoxes is restored twice during one restoration of obliquity. But as in every apparent irregular movement, it is necessary to understand a certain mean, through which the ratio of irregularity can be determined; so in this case too it was quite necessary to consider the mean poles and the mean equator and also the mean equinoxes and points of solstice. The poles and the terrestrial equator, by being deflected in opposite directions away from these mean poles, though within fixed limits, make those regular movements appear to be irregular. And so these two librations competing with one another make the poles of the earth in the passage of time describe certain lines similar to a twisted garland.

But since it is not easy to explain these things adequately with words, and

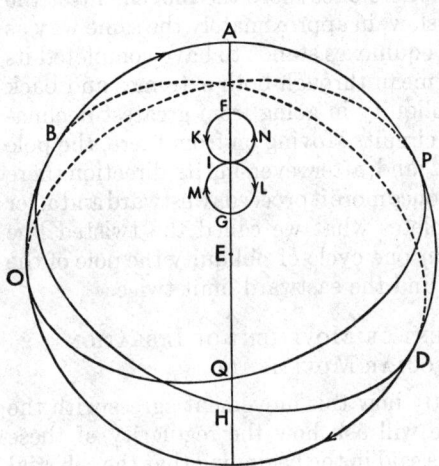

still less—I fear—to have them grasped by the hearing, unless they are also viewed by the eyes, therefore let us describe on a sphere circle *ABCD* which is the ecliptic. Let the north pole [of the ecliptic] be *E*, the beginning of Capricornus *A*, that of Cancer *C*, that of Aries *B*, and that of Libra *D*. And through points *A* and *C* and pole *E* let circle *AEC* be drawn. And let the greatest distance between the north poles of the ecliptic and of the equator be *EF*, and the least *EG*. Similarly let *I* be the pole in the middle position, and around *I* let the equator *BHD* be described, and let that be called the mean equator; and let *B* and *D* be called the mean equinoxes.

Let the poles of the equator, the equinoxes, and the equator be all carried around *E* by an always regular movement westward, *i.e.*, counter to the order of the signs in the sphere of the fixed stars, and with a slow movement, as I said. Now let there be understood two reciprocal movements of the terrestrial poles like hanging bodies—one of them between the limits *F* and *G*, which will be called the movement of anomaly,[1]—*i.e.*, irregularity—of declination; the other from westward to eastward , and from eastward to westward. This second movement, which has twice the velocity of the first, we shall call the anomaly of the equinoxes. As both of these movements belong to the poles of the earth, they deflect the poles in a surprising way.

For first with *F* as the north pole of the earth, [66ᵇ] the equator described around the pole will pass through the same sections *B* and *D*, *i.e.*, through the poles of circle *AFEC*. But it will make greater angles of obliquity in proportion to arc *FI*. Now the second movement supervening does not allow the terrestrial pole, which was about to cross from the assumed starting point *F* to the mean obliquity at *I*, to proceed in a straight line along *FI*, but draws it aside in a circular movement towards its farthest eastward latitude,

---

[1] The term *anomaly* will be used to designate a regular movement the compounding of which with the principal regular movement being considered makes that principal movement appear irregular.

which is at K. The intersection of the apparent equator OQP described around this position will not be in B but to the east of it in O, and the precession of the equinoxes will be decreased in proportion to arc BO. Changing its direction and moving westwards, the pole is carried by the two simultaneously competing movements to the mean position I. And the apparent equator is in all respects identical with the regular or mean equator. Crossing there, the pole of the earth moves westward and separates the apparent equator from the mean equator and increases the precession of the equinoxes up to the other limit L. There changing its direction again, it subtracts what it had just added to the precession of the equinoxes, until, when situated at point G, it causes the least obliquity at the same common section B, where once more the movement of the equinoxes and solstices will appear very slow, in approximately the same way as at F. At this time the irregularity of the equinoxes stands to have completed its revolution, since it has passed rom the mean through both extremes and back to the mean; while the movement of obliquity in going from greatest declination to least has completed only half its circuit. Moving on from there, the pole advances eastward to the farthest limit M; and, after reversing its direction there becomes one with the mean pole I; and once more it proceeds westward and after reaching the limit N finally [67a] completes what we called the twisted line $FKILGMINF$. And so it is clear that in one cycle of obliquity the pole of the Earth reaches the westward limit twice and the eastward limit twice.

4. How the Reciprocal Movement or Movement of Libration Is Composed of Circular Movements

Accordingly we shall make clear exactly how this movement agrees with the appearances. In the meantime someone will ask how the regularity of these librations is to be understood, since it was said in the beginning that the celestial movement was regular, or composed of regular and circular movements. But here in either case of libration two movements are apparent as one movement between two limits, and the two limits necessarily make a cessation of movement intervene. For we acknowledge that there are twin movements, which are demonstrated from regular movements in this way.

Let there be the straight line AB, and let it be cut into four equal parts at

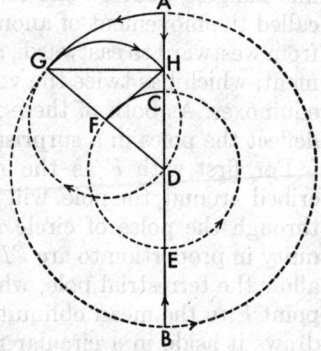

points C, D, and E. Let the homocentric circles ADB and CDE be described around D in the same plane. And in the selfsame plane ADB and CDE, let any point F be taken on the circumference of the inner circle; and with F as centre and radius equal to FD let circle GHD be described. And let it cut the straight line AB at point H; and let the diameter DFG be drawn. We have to show that when the twin movements of circles GHD and CFE compete with one another, the movable point H proceeds back and forth along the same straight line AB by a reciprocal motion.

This will take place if we understand that H is moved in a different direction from F and through twice the distance, since the angle same CDF which is situated at the centre of circle CFE and on the circumference of circle GHD comprehends both arcs of the equal circles: arc FC and arc GH which is twice arc FC.

It is laid down that at some time upon the coincidence of the straight lines ACD and DFG the moving point H will be at G, which will then coincide with A; and F will be at C. Now, however, the centre F has moved towards the right along CF, and H has moved along the circumference to the left twice the distance CF [67^b] or vice versa; accordingly H will be deflected along line AB; otherwise the part would be greater than the whole, as it is easy to see. But H has moved away from its first position along the length AH made by the bent line DFH, which is equal to AD; and H has moved for a distance by which the diameter DFG exceeds chord DH. And in this way H will be made to arrive at centre D, which will be the point of tangency of circle DHG with straight line AB, namely when GD is at right angles to AB; and then H will reach the other limit at B, and from that position it will move back again according to the same ratio.

Therefore it is clear that movement along a straight line is compounded of two circular movements which compete with one another in this way; and that a reciprocal and irregular movement is composed of regular movements; as was to be shown. Moreover it follows from this that the straight line GH will always be at right angles to AB; for lines DH and HG, being in a semicircle, will always comprehend a right angle. And accordingly

$$GH = \tfrac{1}{2} \text{ ch. } 2\,AG;$$

and

$$DH = \tfrac{1}{2} \text{ ch. } 2\,(90° - AG),$$

because circle AGB has twice the diameter of circle HGD.

5. A Demonstration of the Irregularity of the Equinoctial Precession and the Obliquity

For this reason some call this movement of the circle a movement in width, *i.e.*, along the diameter. But they determine its periodicity and its regularity by means of the circumference, and its magnitude by means of the chords subtending. On that account it is easily shown that the movement appears irregular and faster at the centre and slower [68^a] at the circumference.

For let there be the semicircle ABC with centre D and diameter ADC, and let it be bisected at point B. Now let equal arcs AE and BF be taken, and from points F and E let EG and FK be drawn perpendicular to ADC. Therefore, since

$$2\,DK = 2 \text{ ch. } BF,$$

and

$$2\,EG = 2 \text{ ch. } AE,$$

then

$$DK = EG.$$

But by Euclid's *Elements*, III, 7,

$$AG < GE;$$

hence

$$AG < DK.$$

But GA and KD will take up equal time because

$$\text{arc } AE = \text{arc } BF;$$

therefore the movement in the neighbourhood of

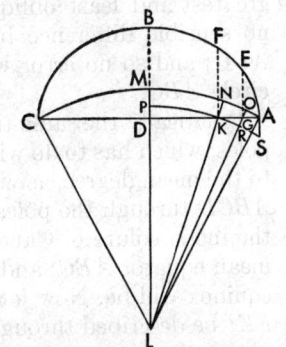

arc A will [appear to] be slower than in the neighbourhood of the centre D.

Having shown this, let us take L as the centre of the Earth, so that the straight line DL is perpendicular to plane ABC of the semicircle; and with L as centre and through points A and C let arc AMC of a circle be described; and let LDM be drawn in a straight line. Accordingly the pole of the semicircle ABC will be at M, and ADC will be the common section of the circles. Let LA and LC be joined; and similarly LK and LG too. And let LK and LG extended in straight lines cut arc AMC at N and O. Therefore, since angle LDK is right, angle LKD is acute. Wherefore too the line LK is longer than LD, and all the more is side LG greater than side LK, and LA than LG in the obtuse triangles. Therefore the circle described with L as centre and LK as radius will fall beyond LD, but will cut LG and LA; let it be described, and let it be $PKRS$. And since

$$\text{trgl. } LDK < \text{sect. } LPK,$$

while

$$\text{trgl. } LGA > \text{sect. } LRS,$$

on that account

$$\text{trgl. } LDK : \text{sect. } LPK < \text{trgl. } LGA : \text{sect. } LRS.$$

Hence, alternately also,

$$\text{trgl. } LDK : \text{trgl. } LGA < \text{sect. } LPK : \text{sect. } LRS.$$

And by Euclid's *Elements*, VI, 1,

$$\text{trgl. } LDK : \text{trgl. } LGA = \text{base } DK : \text{base } AG.$$

But

$$\text{sect. } LPK : \text{sect. } LRS = \text{angle } DLK : \text{angle } RLS = \text{arc } MN : \text{arc } OA.$$

Therefore

$$\text{base } DK : \text{base } GA < \text{arc } MN : \text{arc } OA.$$

But we have already shown that

$$DK > GA.$$

All the more then

$$[68^{\text{b}}] \quad MN > OA.$$

And arcs MN and OA are understood as having been described during equal intervals of time by the poles of the earth in accordance with the equal arcs of anomaly AE and BF—as was to be shown. But since the difference between greatest and least obliquity is so slight as not to exceed $\frac{2}{5}°$, there will be no sensible difference between the curved line AMC and the straight line ADC; and so no error will arise if we work simply with line ADC and semicircle ABC.

Practically the same thing happens in the case of the other movement of the poles, which has to do with the equinoxes, since this movement does not ascend to the mean degree, as will be apparent below. Once more let there be the circle $ABCD$ through the poles of the ecliptic and the mean equator. We may call it the mean colure of Cancer. Let the semicircle of the ecliptic be DEB and the mean equator AEC; and let them cut one another at point E, where the mean equinox will be. Now let the pole of the equator be F, and let the great circle FEI be described through it. On that account it will be the colure of the mean or regular equinoxes.

Therefore for the sake of an easier demonstration let us separate the libration

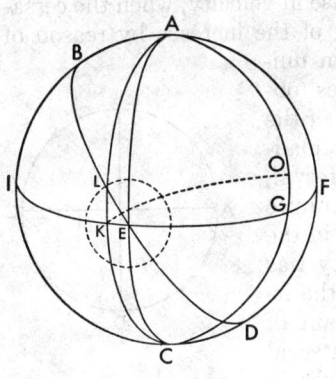

of the equinoxes from the obliquity of the ecliptic. On the colure EF let arc FG be taken, and through that distance let G the apparent pole of the equator be understood as removed from F the mean pole. And with G as a pole let $ALKC$ the semicircle of the apparent equator be described. It will cut the ecliptic at L. Therefore point L will be the apparent equinox; and its distance from the mean equinox will be measured by arc LE, which is produced by arc EK the equal of FG.

But with K as a pole we shall describe circle AGC; and let it be understood that the equatorial pole during the time in which the libration FG takes place does not remain the "true" pole at point G, but, driven by another libration or swinging movement, moves away in the direction of the oblique ecliptic through arc GO. Therefore while ecliptic BED abides, the "true" equator will be changed to the "apparent" in accordance with the transposition of the pole to O. And similarly the movement of intersection L the apparent equinox will be faster in the neighbourhood of the mean [equinox] E and very slow in the neighbourhood of the extreme equinoxes, more or less in proportion to the swinging movement of the poles which we have already demonstrated—as was worth the trouble of our attention.

6. On the Regular Movements of the Precession of the Equinoxes and of the Inclination of the Ecliptic

[69ᵃ] Now every apparent irregular circular movement passes through four termini: there is the terminus where it appears slow and the terminus where it appears fast, as if at the extremes, and the terminus where it appears to have a mean velocity, as if at the means, since from the point which is the end of decrease in velocity and the beginning of increase it passes on to a mean velocity; and from the mean velocity it increases till it becomes fast; again after being fast it approaches a mean velocity, whence for the remainder of the cycle it changes to its former slowness.

By means of that it is possible to know in what part of the circle the position of the non-uniform movement, or irregularity, is at a given time; and too by means of these indications the restitution of the irregularity is perceptible[1]. Accordingly in a quadrisected circle let A be the position of greatest slowness, B the mean of increasing velocity, C the end of the increase and the beginning of the decrease, and D the mean of decreasing velocity. Therefore, since, as was reported above, the apparent movement of the precession of the equinoxes was found to be rather slow in the time between Timochares and Ptolemy in comparison with the other times, and because for a while it appeared regular and uniform, as is shown by the observations of Aristyllus, Hipparchus, Agrippa, and Menelaus which were made at the middle of that time; it argues that the apparent movement of the equinoxes had been simply at its slowest and at the

---

[1]This circle is not the circle of libration, of course, but a circle which typifies the cycle in velocity which results from compounding the libration with the regular movement of precession of the equinoxes.

middle of this time was at the beginning of increase in velocity, when the cessation of the decrease conjoined to the beginning of the increase by reason of
mutual compensation made the movement seem uni-
form for the time being. Accordingly Timochares' observation must be placed in the fourth quadrant of the
circle along DA; but Ptolemy's falls in the first quadrant along AB. Again, because in the second interval,
the one between Ptolemy and al-Battani the Harranite
the movement is found to have been faster than in the
third, it is clear that the point of highest velocity was
passed during the second interval of time, and the irregularity had already reached the third quadrant of
the circle along CD, and that from the third interval
down to us the restoration of the irregularity was nearly

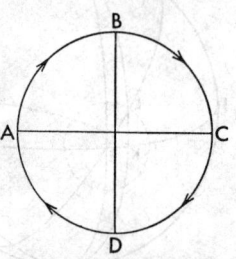

completed and has nearly returned to its starting-point with Timochares. For
if we divide the cycle of 1819 years between Timochares and us into the customary 360 parts, we shall have proportionately an arc of $85\frac{1}{2}°$ for 432 years;
$146°51'$ for 742 years; and the remaining arc of $127°39'$ for the remaining 645
years.

We have made these determinations by an obvious and simple inference;
[69ᵇ] but upon working them over with stricter calculations, to see how exactly
they agree with observations, we find that the movement of irregularity during
the 1819 Egyptian years has already exceeded its complete revolution by $21°24'$,
and that the time of the period comprehends only 1717 Egyptian years. In
accordance with this ratio it is discovered that the first segment of the circle has
$90°35'$; the second, $155°34'$; while the third period of 543 years will comprehend
the remaining $113°51'$ of the circle. Now that these things have been set up in
this way, the mean movement of the precession of the equinoxes is also disclosed; and it is $23°57'$ for these same 1717 years, at the end of which the whole
movement of irregularity was restored to its pristine status, since for the 1819
years we have an apparent movement of approximately $25°1'$.

But in 102 years after Timochares—the difference between the 1717 years
and the 1819 years—the apparent movement must have been about $1°4'$, because it is probable that the apparent movement was then a little greater than
to need only $1°$ per 100 years, since it was decreasing without yet having reached the end of the decrease. Hence, if we subtract $1°4'$ from $25°1'$ there will remain, as we said, for the 1717 Egyptian years a mean and regular movement of
$23°57'$, now corrected according to the apparent and irregular movement: hence
the complete and regular revolution of the precession of the equinoxes arises in
25,816 years, during which time 15 cycles of irregularity are traversed and approximately $\frac{1}{28}$ cycle over and above.

Moreover, the movement of obliquity, whose restoration we said was twice
as slow as the irregular precession of the equinoxes, accords with this ratio. For
the fact that Ptolemy reports that during the 400 years between the time of
Aristarchus of Samos and his own the obliquity of $23°51'20''$ had hardly changed
at all indicates that the obliquity was then close to the limit of greatest obliquity,
namely when the precession of the equinoxes was in its slowest motion.
But now also when the same restoration of slowness is approaching, the inclination of the axis is not at its greatest but is near its least. In the middle of

the time in between, al-Battani the Harranite, as was said, found that the inclination was 23°35'; 190 years after him Arzachel the Spaniard, 23°34'; and similarly 230 years later Prophatius the Jew found it approximately 2' less. Finally as regards our own times, we in 30 years of frequent observation found it approximately 23°28 ⅖'—from which George Peurbach and John of Monteregium, [70ᵃ] our nearest predecessors, differ slightly. Here again it is perfectly obvious that for the 900 years after Ptolemy the change in obliquity was greater than for any other interval of time.

Therefore since we already have the cycle of irregularity of precession in 1717 years, we shall also have half the period of obliquity in that time, and in 3434 years its complete restoration. Wherefore if we divide the 360° by the number of the 3434 years or 180° by 1717, the quotient will be the annual movement of simple anomaly of 6'17"24'''9''''. These in turn distributed through the 365 days give a daily movement of 1"2'''2''''.

Similarly, when the mean precession of equinoxes has been distributed through the 1717 years—and there was 23°57'—an annual movement of 50" 12'''5'''' will be the result; and this distributed through the 365 days will give a daily movement of 8'''15''''.

But in order that the movements may be more in the open and may be found right at hand when there is need of them, we shall draw up their tables or canons by the continuous and equal addition of annual movement—60 parts always being carried over into the minutes or degrees, if the sum exceeds that—and for the sake of convenience we shall keep on adding until we reach the 60th year, since the same configuration of numbers returns every sixty years, only with the denominations of degrees and minutes moved up, so that what were formerly seconds become minutes and so on.[1] By this abridgement in the form of brief tables, it will be possible merely by a double entry to determine and infer the regular movements for the years in question among the 3600 years. This is also the case with the number of days.

Moreover, in our computations of the celestial movements we shall employ the Egyptian years, which alone among the legal years are found equal. For it is necessary for the measure to agree with the measured; but that is not the case with the years of the Romans, Greeks, and Persians, for intercalations are made not in any single way, but according to the will of the people. But the Egyptian year contains no ambiguity as regards the fixed number of 365 days, in which throughout twelve equal months—which they name in order by these names: Thoth, Phaophi, Athyr, Chiach, Tybi, Mechyr, Phamenoth, Pharmuthi, Pachon, Pauni, Epiphi, and Mesori—in which, I say, six periods of 60 days are comprehended evenly together with the five remaining days, which they call the intercalary days. For that reason Egyptian years are most convenient for calculating regular movements. Any other years are easily reducible to them by resolving the days.

---

[1]That is to say, the same configurations of numbers return in multiples of sixty years, because the cycle of movement is divided according to the sexagesimal system—just as it would return in multiples of ten years if the circle were divided according to the decimal system.

REGULAR MOVEMENT OF THE PRECESSION OF THE EQUINOXES IN YEARS AND PERIODS OF SIXTY YEARS

Egyptian Years	60°	°	Longitude '	"	'''		Egyptian Years	60°	°	Longitude '	"	'''
1	0	0	0	50	12		31	0	0	25	56	14
2	0	0	1	40	24		32	0	0	26	46	26
3	0	0	2	30	36		33	0	0	27	36	38
4	0	0	3	20	48		34	0	0	28	26	50
5	0	0	4	11	0		35	0	0	29	17	2
6	0	0	5	1	12		36	0	0	30	7	15
7	0	0	5	51	24		37	0	0	30	57	27
8	0	0	6	41	36		38	0	0	31	47	38
9	0	0	7	31	48		39	0	0	32	37	51
10	0	0	8	22	0		40	0	0	33	28	3
11	0	0	9	12	12		41	0	0	34	18	15
12	0	0	10	2	25		42	0	0	35	8	27
13	0	0	10	52	37		43	0	0	35	58	39
14	0	0	11	42	49		44	0	0	36	48	51
15	0	0	12	33	1		45	0	0	37	39	3
16	0	0	13	23	13		46	0	0	38	29	15
17	0	0	14	13	25		47	0	0	39	19	27
18	0	0	15	3	37		48	0	0	40	9	40
19	0	0	15	53	49		49	0	0	40	59	52
20	0	0	16	44	1		50	0	0	41	50	4
21	0	0	17	34	13		51	0	0	42	40	16
22	0	0	18	24	25		52	0	0	43	30	28
23	0	0	19	14	37		53	0	0	44	20	40
24	0	0	20	4	50		54	0	0	45	10	52
25	0	0	20	55	2		55	0	0	46	1	4
26	0	0	21	45	14		56	0	0	46	51	16
27	0	0	22	35	26		57	0	0	47	41	28
28	0	0	23	25	38		58	0	0	48	31	40
29	0	0	24	15	50		59	0	0	49	21	52
30	0	0	25	6	2		60	0	0	50	12	5

Position at the Birth of Christ—5° 32'

REGULAR MOVEMENT OF THE PRECESSION OF THE EQUINOXES IN DAYS AND PERIODS OF SIXTY DAYS

Days	60°	°	Longitude '	"	'''		Days	60°	°	Longitude '	"	'''
1	0	0	0	0	8		31	0	0	0	4	15
2	0	0	0	0	16		32	0	0	0	4	24
3	0	0	0	0	24		33	0	0	0	4	32
4	0	0	0	0	33		34	0	0	0	4	40
5	0	0	0	0	41		35	0	0	0	4	48
6	0	0	0	0	49		36	0	0	0	4	57
7	0	0	0	0	57		37	0	0	0	5	5
8	0	0	0	1	6		38	0	0	0	5	13
9	0	0	0	1	14		39	0	0	0	5	21
10	0	0	0	1	22		40	0	0	0	5	30
11	0	0	0	1	30		41	0	0	0	5	38
12	0	0	0	1	39		42	0	0	0	5	46
13	0	0	0	1	47		43	0	0	0	5	54
14	0	0	0	1	55		44	0	0	0	6	3
15	0	0	0	2	3		45	0	0	0	6	11
16	0	0	0	2	12		46	0	0	0	6	11
17	0	0	0	2	20		47	0	0	0	6	27
18	0	0	0	2	28		48	0	0	0	6	36
19	0	0	0	2	36		49	0	0	0	6	44
20	0	0	0	2	45		50	0	0	0	6	52
21	0	0	0	2	53		51	0	0	0	7	0
22	0	0	0	3	1		52	0	0	0	7	9
23	0	0	0	3	9		53	0	0	0	7	17
24	0	0	0	3	18		54	0	0	0	7	25
25	0	0	0	3	26		55	0	0	0	7	33
26	0	0	0	3	34		56	0	0	0	7	42
27	0	0	0	3	42		57	0	0	0	7	50
28	0	0	0	3	51		58	0	0	0	7	58
29	0	0	0	3	59		59	0	0	0	8	6
30	0	0	0	4	7		60	0	0	0	8	15

Position at the Birth of Christ—5° 32'

MOVEMENT OF THE SIMPLE ANOMALY OF EQUINOXES IN YEARS AND PERIODS OF SIXTY YEARS

Egyptian Years	60°	°	'	"	'''	Egyptian Years	60°	°	'	"	'''
1	0	0	6	17	24	31	0	3	14	59	28
2	0	0	12	34	48	32	0	3	21	16	52
3	0	0	18	52	12	33	0	3	27	34	16
4	0	0	25	9	36	34	0	3	33	51	41
5	0	0	31	27	0	35	0	3	40	9	5
6	0	0	37	44	24	36	0	3	46	26	29
7	0	0	44	1	49	37	0	3	52	43	53
8	0	0	50	19	13	38	0	3	59	1	17
9	0	0	56	36	36	39	0	4	5	18	42
10	0	1	2	54	1	40	0	4	11	36	6
11	0	1	9	11	25	41	0	4	17	53	30
12	0	1	15	28	49	42	0	4	24	10	54
13	0	1	21	46	13	43	0	4	30	28	18
14	0	1	28	3	38	44	0	4	36	45	42
15	0	1	34	21	2	45	0	4	43	3	0
16	0	1	40	38	26	46	0	4	49	20	31
17	0	1	46	55	50	47	0	4	55	37	55
18	0	1	53	13	14	48	0	5	1	55	19
19	0	1	59	30	38	49	0	5	8	12	43
20	0	2	5	48	3	50	0	5	14	30	7
21	0	2	12	5	27	51	0	5	20	47	31
22	0	2	18	22	51	52	0	5	27	4	55
23	0	2	24	40	15	53	0	5	33	22	20
24	0	2	30	57	39	54	0	5	39	39	44
25	0	2	37	15	3	55	0	5	45	57	8
26	0	2	43	32	27	56	0	5	52	14	32
27	0	2	49	49	52	57	0	5	58	31	56
28	0	2	56	7	16	58	0	6	4	49	20
29	0	3	2	24	40	59	0	6	11	6	45
30	0	3	8	42	4	60	0	6	17	24	9

Position at the Birth of Christ—6° 45'

MOVEMENT OF THE SIMPLE ANOMALY OF EQUINOXES IN DAYS AND PERIODS OF SIXTY DAYS

Days	60°	°	'	"	'''	Days	60°	°	'	"	'''
1	0	0	0	1	2	31	0	0	0	32	3
2	0	0	0	2	4	32	0	0	0	33	5
3	0	0	0	3	6	33	0	0	0	34	7
4	0	0	0	4	8	34	0	0	0	35	9
5	0	0	0	5	10	35	0	0	0	36	11
6	0	0	0	6	12	36	0	0	0	37	13
7	0	0	0	7	14	37	0	0	0	38	15
8	0	0	0	8	16	38	0	0	0	39	17
9	0	0	0	9	18	39	0	0	0	40	19
10	0	0	0	10	20	40	0	0	0	41	21
11	0	0	0	11	22	41	0	0	0	42	23
12	0	0	0	12	24	42	0	0	0	43	25
13	0	0	0	13	26	43	0	0	0	44	27
14	0	0	0	14	28	44	0	0	0	45	29
15	0	0	0	15	30	45	0	0	0	46	31
16	0	0	0	16	32	46	0	0	0	47	33
17	0	0	0	17	34	47	0	0	0	48	35
18	0	0	0	18	36	48	0	0	0	49	37
19	0	0	0	19	38	49	0	0	0	50	39
20	0	0	0	20	40	50	0	0	0	51	41
21	0	0	0	21	42	51	0	0	0	52	43
22	0	0	0	22	44	52	0	0	0	53	45
23	0	0	0	23	46	53	0	0	0	54	47
24	0	0	0	24	48	54	0	0	0	55	49
25	0	0	0	25	50	55	0	0	0	56	51
26	0	0	0	26	52	56	0	0	0	57	53
27	0	0	0	27	54	57	0	0	0	58	55
28	0	0	0	28	56	58	0	0	0	59	57
29	0	0	0	29	58	59	0	0	1	0	59
30	0	0	0	31	1	60	0	0	1	2	2

Position at the Birth of Christ—6° 45'

7. What the Greatest Difference Is Between the Regular and the Apparent Precession of the Equinoxes

[72^{b}] Now that the mean movements have been set out in this way, we must inquire what the greatest difference is between the regular and the apparent movement of the equinoxes, or what the diameter of the small circle is, through which the movement of anomaly turns.[1] For when this is known, it will be easy to discern various other differences in the movements. As was written above, between the observation of Timochares, which came first, and that of Ptolemy in the second year of the reign of Antoninus Pius, there were 432 years; and during that time the mean movement was 6° and the apparent 4°20′. So the difference between them is 1°40′. And the movement of double[2] anomaly was 90°35′. Moreover, it seems that at the middle of this period of time or around there the apparent movement reached its peak of greatest slowness. At that time the [position of the] apparent movement necessarily agreed with the mean movement, and the true equinox and the mean equinox occurred at the same section of the circles.[3] Wherefore if we make a distribution of the movement and the time into two equal parts, there will be in each part as differences between the irregular and the regular movement $1\frac{0}{12}$°, which the circle of anomaly comprehends on either side beneath an arc of 45°17½′. But since all these differences are very small and do not amount to 1½° on the ecliptic, and the straight lines are almost equal to the arcs subtended by them, and there is scarcely any diversity found in the third-minutes: we who are staying within the minutes will make no error if we employ straight lines instead of arcs.

[73^{a}] Let ABC be a part of the ecliptic and on it let the mean equinox be B. And with B as pole let there be described the semicircle ADC, and let it cut the ecliptic at points A and C. Moreover let DB be drawn from the pole of the ecliptic, it will bisect the semicircle at D; and let D be understood to be limit of greatest slowness and beginning of the increase.[4] In the quadrant AD let

$$\text{arc } DE = 45°17½′;$$

and through point E from the pole of the ecliptic, let fall EF; and let

$$BF = 50′.$$

Our problem is to find out from this what the whole BFA is.

Accordingly it is clear that

$$2\ BF = \text{ch. } 2\ DE.$$

[1] *I.e.*, what the diameter of the small circle is, along which the libration takes place back and forth.

[2] The anomaly of precession is called the "double" anomaly because it completes two cycles for one cycle of the anomaly of obliquity.

[3] As Copernicus showed in Chapter 4, the movement of the libration, considered above, appears fastest around the centre of the circle. Hence the apparent movement itself will appear slowest when the fastest movement of libration is in opposition to the mean movement with which it is compounded. And the fastest libration is in opposition to the mean movement when the apparent equinox is swinging eastward and is in the neighbourhood of the centre of the circle or the mean equinox.

[4] Thus, circle ADC is the circle of libration transferred from the pole of the ecliptic to around the equinox—as in the last diagram in Chapter 5.

But
$$FB : AFB = 7107 : 10,000 = 50' : 70'.$$

Hence
$$AB = 1°10',$$

and that is the greatest difference between the mean and the apparent movement of the equinoxes, which we were seeking; and the greatest polar deflexion of 28' follows upon it.

[72ᵇ] For with this set-up let ABC be the arc of the ecliptic, BDE the mean

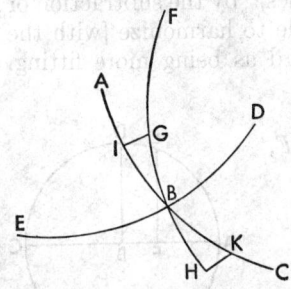

equatorial arc, and B the mean section of the apparent equinoxes, either Aries or Libra, and through the poles of DBE let fall BF. Now along arc ABC on both sides let
$$\text{arc } BI = \text{arc } BK = 1°10';$$
hence, by addition,
$$\text{arc } IBK = 2°20'.$$

Moreover, let there be drawn at right angles to FB extended to FBH the two arcs IG and HK of the apparent equators. Now I say "at right angles," [73ᵃ] though the poles of IG and IK are usually outside of circle BF, since the movement of obliquity gets mixed in, as was seen in the hypothesis, but on account of the distance being very slight—for at its greatest it does not exceed 90°/350—we employ these angles as angles which are right to sense-perception. For no great error will appear on that account. Therefore in triangle IBG
$$\text{angle } IBG = 66°20',$$
since its complement, as being the angle of mean obliquity of the ecliptic,
$$\text{angle } DBA = 23°40'.$$

And
$$\text{angle } BGI = 90°.$$

Moreover,
$$\text{angle } BIG = \text{angle } IBD,$$
because they are alternate angles. And
$$\text{side } IB = 70'.$$

Therefore too
$$\text{arc } BG = 28',$$
and that is the distance between the poles of the mean and the apparent equator. Similarly in triangle BHK,
$$\text{angle } BHK = \text{angle } IGB$$
and
$$\text{angle } HBK = \text{angle } IBG,$$
and
$$\text{side } BK = \text{side } BI.$$

Moreover,
$$BH = BG = 28'.$$
For
$$GB : IB = BH : BK;$$
and the movements will be of the same ratio in the poles as in the intersections.

8. On the Particular Differences in the Movements and the Table of Them

[73ᵇ] Therefore since

$$\text{arc } AB = 70',$$

and since arc AB does not appear to differ from the chord subtending it length-wise, it will not be difficult to exhibit certain other differences between the mean and the apparent movements. The Greeks call the differences προσθαφαιρέσεις, or "additosubtractions," and later writers "aequationes," by the subtraction or addition of which the apparent movements are made to harmonize [with the mean movements]. We shall employ the Greek word as being more fitting. Therefore if

$$\text{arc } ED = 3°,$$

then in accordance with the ratio of AB to the chord BF,

$$\text{arc } BF = 4',$$

which is the additosubtraction. And if

$$ED = 6°,$$

then

$$\text{arc } BF = 7';$$

and if

$$ED = 9°,$$

then

$$BF = 11',$$

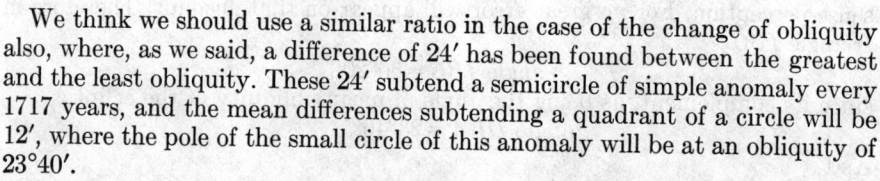

and so on.

We think we should use a similar ratio in the case of the change of obliquity also, where, as we said, a difference of 24′ has been found between the greatest and the least obliquity. These 24′ subtend a semicircle of simple anomaly every 1717 years, and the mean differences subtending a quadrant of a circle will be 12′, where the pole of the small circle of this anomaly will be at an obliquity of 23°40′.

And in this way, as we said, we shall extract the remaining parts of difference approximately in proportion to the aforesaid as in the subjoined table. And if through these demonstrations the apparent movements can be compounded by various modes, nevertheless that mode is better whereby all the particular additosubtractions may be taken separately, that the calculus of their move-ments may be easier to understand and may agree better with the explanations of what has been demonstrated.

Accordingly we have drawn up a table of sixty rows, increasing by 3°'s. For in this way it will not be spread over too much space, and it will not seem to be compressed into too little—as we shall do in the case of the similar remaining tables. The table will have only four main columns, the first two of which will contain the degrees of both semicircles; and we call them the common numbers, because the obliquity of the circle of signs is taken from the simple number, and twice the number applies to the additosubtractions of the movement of the equinoxes; and the numbers have their commencement at the beginning of the increase [74ᵃ] [in velocity].[1] In the third column will be placed the additosub-tractions of the equinoxes corresponding to the single 3°'s; and they are to be added to, or subtracted from, the mean movement—which we measure from the

---

[1] i.e., in the foregoing diagram, the first quadrant comprises the arc DA; and the fourth quadrant the arc CD.

head of Aries at the spring equinox. The subtractive additosubtractions correspond to the numbers in the first semicircle of the anomaly or the first column; and the additive, to those in the second column and the second semicircle. Finally, in the last column are the minutes, which are called the differences in the proportions of obliquity and which go up to 60′, since in place of the difference of 24′ between greatest and least obliquity we are putting 60′, and we adjust the proportional minutes to them in the same ratio in proportion to the other differences of obliquity. On that account we place 60′ as corresponding to the beginning and end of the anomaly; but where the difference of obliquity is 22′, as in the anomaly of 33°, we put 55′ instead. In this way we put 50′ in place of 20′, as in the anomaly of 48°; and so on for the rest, as in the subjoined table.[1]

ADDITIONS-AND-SUBTRACTIONS OF EQUINOXES, OBLIQUITY OF THE ECLIPTIC

Common Numbers		Additions-and-Subtractions of Movement of Equinoxes		Proportional Minutes of Obliquity	Common Numbers		Additions-and-Subtractions of Movement of Equinoxes		Proportional Minutes of Obliquity
Deg.	Deg.	Deg.	Min.		Deg.	Deg.	Deg.	Min.	
3	357	0	4	60	93	267	1	10	28
6	354	0	7	60	96	264	1	10	27
9	351	0	11	60	99	261	1	9	25
12	348	0	14	59	102	258	1	9	24
15	345	0	18	59	105	255	1	8	22
18	342	0	21	59	108	252	1	7	21
21	339	0	25	58	111	249	1	5	19
24	336	0	28	57	114	246	1	4	18
27	333	0	32	56	117	243	1	2	16
30	330	0	35	56	120	240	1	1	15
33	327	0	38	55	123	237	0	59	14
36	324	0	41	54	126	234	0	56	12
39	321	0	44	53	129	231	0	54	11
42	318	0	47	52	132	228	0	52	10
45	315	0	49	51	135	225	0	49	9
48	312	0	52	50	138	222	0	47	8
51	309	0	54	49	141	219	0	44	7
54	306	0	56	48	144	216	0	41	6
57	303	0	9	46	147	213	0	38	5
60	300	1	1	45	150	210	0	35	4
63	297	1	2	44	153	207	0	32	3
66	294	1	4	42	156	204	0	28	3
69	291	1	5	41	159	201	0	25	2
72	288	1	7	39	162	198	0	21	1
75	285	1	8	38	165	195	0	18	1
78	282	1	9	36	168	192	0	14	1
81	279	1	9	35	171	189	0	11	0
84	276	1	10	33	174	186	0	7	0
87	273	1	10	32	177	183	0	4	0
90	270	1	10	30	180	180	0	0	0

[1]Thus, let line *FIG*, as in Chapter 3, represent the colure of the solstices. Point *F* is the limit of greatest obliquity of the ecliptic, point *G* that of the least; and thus the distance *FG* is 28′. The distance *KN* of the libration of the equinoxes is 2°20′. In the foregoing table the anomalies of precession and of obliquity are taken as starting at point *I* and proceeding along the route *INFKILGM*.

9. On the Examination and Correction of That Which Was Set Forth Concerning the Precession of the Equinoxes

[75ᵃ] But since by an inference we took the beginning of increase in the movement of anomaly as occurring in the middle of the time from the 36th year of the first period of Callippus to the 2nd year of Antoninus, and we take the order of the movement of anomaly from that beginning; it is still necessary for us to test whether we did that correctly and whether it agrees with the observations.

Let us consider again the three observations of the stars made by Timochares, Ptolemy, and al-Battani the Harranite: And it is clear that there were 432 Egyptian years in the first interval and 742 years in the second. The regular movement in the first span of time was 6°; the irregular movement 4°20′; and the movement of double anomaly 90°35′, subtracting 1°40′ from the regular movement. During the second interval the regular movement was 10°21′, the irregular 11½°; and the movement of double anomaly was 155°34′, adding 1°9′ to the regular movement.

Now as before let the arc of the ecliptic be ABC, and let B—which is to be the mean spring equinox—be taken as a pole; let

arc $AB = 1°10′$,

and let the small circle $ADCE$ be described. But let the regular movement of B be understood as in the direction of A, i.e., westward; and let A be the westward limit, where the irregular equinox is westernmost; and C the eastern limit, where the irregular equinox is easternmost. Furthermore, from the pole of the ecliptic drop DBE through point B. DBE together with the ecliptic will cut the small circle $ADCE$ into four equal parts, since circles described through the poles of one another

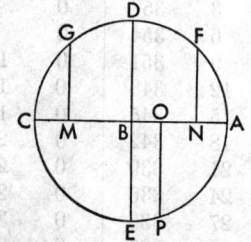

cut one another at right angles. However since the movement in the semicircle ADC is eastward, and the movement remaining in CEA is westward, the extreme slowness of the apparent equinox will be at D on account of its resistance to the forward movement of B; but there will be at E the greatest velocity for the movements moving forwards in the same direction.

Moreover on either side of D let

arc $FD =$ arc $DG = 45°17½′$.

Let F be the first terminus of the anomaly—the one observed by Timochares; G the second—the one observed by Ptolemy; and P the third—the one observed by al-Battani. And through these points let fall great circles FN, GM, and OP through the poles of the ecliptic; and they all]75ᵇ] appear in this very small circle rather much like straight lines. Therefore

arc $FDG = 99°35′$,
where circle $ADCE = 360°$,

wherefrom

−add. $MN = 1°40′$,
where $ABC = 2°20′$.

And

arc $GCEP = 155°34′$,

wherefrom

+add. $MBO = 109′$.

Accordingly, by subtraction,
$$\text{arc } PAF = 113°51'$$
wherefrom
$$+\text{add. } ON = 31'$$
$$\text{where } AB = 70'.$$
But since by addition
$$\text{arc } DGCEP = 200°51'$$
and
$$EP = DGCEP - 180° = 20°51';$$
therefore by the table of chords in a circle, as if a straight line,
$$BO = 356,$$
$$\text{where } AB = 1,000.$$
But
$$BO = 24',$$
$$\text{where } AB = 70';$$
and
$$MB = 50'.$$
Hence, by addition,
$$MBO = 74',$$
and,
$$NO = MN - MBO = 26'.$$
But, in the foregoing,
$$MBO = 69',$$
and
$$NO = 31'.$$
Hence NO has a deficiency of 5'; and MO has an excess of 5'. Accordingly the circle $ADCE$ must be revolved, until there is compensation on both sides.

But this will take place if
$$\text{arc } DG = 42\frac{1}{2}°,$$
so that by subtraction,
$$\text{arc } DF = 48°5'.$$
For by this both errors will seem to be corrected and everything else will be all right, since—with the beginning at D the limit of greatest slowness—
$$\text{arc } DGCEPAF = 311°55',$$
which is the movement of anomaly at the first terminus; at the second terminus
$$\text{arc } DG = 42\frac{1}{2}°;$$
and at the third terminus
$$\text{arc } DGCEP = 198°4'.$$
Now since
$$AB = 70';$$
at the first terminus
$$+\text{add. } BN = 52',$$
by what has been shown; at the second terminus
$$-\text{add. } MB = 47\frac{1}{2}';$$
and at the third terminus again
$$+\text{add. } BO = 21'.$$
Therefore during the first interval
$$\text{arc } MN = 1°40',$$
and during the second interval
$$\text{arc } MBO = 1°9';$$

and they agree exactly with the observations. Moreover, by those means a simple anomaly of 155°57½′ is made evident at the first terminus; at the second terminus, one of 21°15′; and at the third terminus, a simple anomaly of 99°2′—as was to be shown.

10. What the Greatest Difference Is Between the Intersections of the Equator and the Ecliptic

[76ᵃ] In the same way we shall confirm what we expounded concerning the change in obliquity of the ecliptic and the equator and shall find it to be correct. For we have in Ptolemy for the second year of Antoninus Pius a corrected simple anomaly of 21¼°; and a greatest obliquity of 23°51′20″ was found to go with it. From this position down to the observation made by us there have been 1387 years, during which the movement of simple anomaly is reckoned to be 144°4′; and at this time an obliquity of approximately 23°28⅖′ is found.

In connection with this let there be drawn again arc ABC of the ecliptic, or instead of it a straight line on account of the shortness of the arc; and above it the semicircle of simple anomaly around pole B, as before. And let A be the limit of greatest declination and C the limit of least declination; and it is the difference between them which we are examining. Therefore in the small circle let

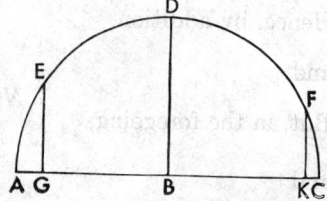

$$\text{arc } AE = 21°15',$$

and,

$$\text{arc } ED = AD - AE = 68°45';$$

while, by calculation,

$$\text{arc } EDF = 144°4'$$

and,

$$\text{arc } DF = EDF - ED = 75°19'.$$

Drop perpendiculars EG and EK upon the diameter ABC.

Now on the great circle

$$\text{arc } GK = 22'56'',$$

on account of the difference in obliquities from Ptolemy to us. But on account of being like a straight line,

$$GB = \tfrac{1}{2} \text{ ch. } 2\, ED = 932,$$

where AC the diameter's image $= 2,000$.

And also

$$KB = \tfrac{1}{2} \text{ ch. } 2\, DF = 967.$$

And

$$GK = 1899,$$

where $AC = 2,000$.

But according as

$$GK = 22'56'',$$
$$AC \doteq 24',$$

the difference between greatest and least obliquity which we have been examining. So it is established that the greatest obliquity which occurred during the time between Timochares and Ptolemy was 23°52′ and a least obliquity of 23°28′ is now approaching. [76ᵇ] Hence also whatever mean inclinations of these circles there happen to be are discovered by the same mathematical reasoning we expounded in connection with the precession.

11. On Determining the Positions of the Regular Movements
of the Equinoxes and of the Anomaly

With all that unfolded, it remains for us to determine the positions of the movements of the spring equinox. Some people call these positions "roots," because computations may be drawn from them for any given time. Ptolemy considered that the farthest point in history to which our knowledge of this question extends was the beginning of the reign of Nabonassar of the Chaldees, whom many people—taken in by the similarity of the names—have thought to be Nabuchodonoso, and whom the ratio of time and the computation of Ptolemy— which according to the historians falls in the reign of Shalmaneser of the Chaldees —declare to have been much later. But we, seeking better known times, have judged it sufficient if we start with the first Olympiad, which—measured from the summer solstice—is found to have preceded Nabonassar by 28 years. At this time Canicula was beginning to rise for the Greeks, and the Olympic games were being held, as Censorinus and other trustworthy authors report. Whence, according to the more exact reckoning of the times which is necessary in calculating the heavenly movements, there are 27 years and 247 days from the first Olympiad at noon on the first day of the month Hekatombaion by the Greek calendar to Nabonassar and noon of the first day of the month of Thoth by the Egyptian calendar.

From this to the death of Alexander there are 424 Egyptian years.

But from the decease of Alexander to the beginning of the years of Julius Caesar, there are 278 Egyptian years 118½ days up to the midnight before the Kalends of January, which Julius Caesar took as the beginning of the year instituted by him; it was in his third year as Pontifex Maximus and during the consulship of Marcus Aemilius Lepidus that he instituted this year. And so the later years have been called Julian from the year as established by Julius Caesar.

And from the fourth consulship of Caesar to Octavius Augustus there are by the Roman calendar 18 years up to the Kalends of January, although it was on the 16th day before the Kalends of February that Augustus was proclaimed Emperor and son of the deified Julius Caesar by the senate and the other citizens according to the decree of Numatius Plancus, in the seventh year of the consulship of Marcus Vipsanus and himself. But inasmuch as two years before this the Egyptians came into the power of the Romans after the fall of Antony [77ᵃ] and Cleopatra, the Egyptians reckon 15 years 246½ days up to noon of the first day of the month Thoth, which by the Roman calendar was the 3rd day before the Kalends of September.

Accordingly from Augustus to the years of Christ, which begin similarly in January, there are 27 years by the Roman calendar but 29 years 130½ days by the Egyptian.

From this to the 2nd year of Antoninus, when, as Claud Ptolemy says, the positions of the stars were observed by him, there are 138 Roman years 55 days. And these years add 34 days to the Egyptian reckoning.

Between the first Olympiad and that moment of time there have been altogether 913 years 101 days, for which time the regular precession of the equinoxes was 12°44', and the simple anomaly was 95°44'.

But in the second year of Antoninus, as has been narrated, the spring equinox was 6°40' to the west of the first of the stars which are in the head of Aries; and since there was a double anomaly of 42½°, there was a subtractive difference of 48′ between the regular and the apparent movement. And when this difference was restored to the 6°40′ of the apparent movement, it made the mean position of the spring equinox to be at 7°28′. If to this we add the 360° of a circle, and from the sum subtract 12°44′, we shall have the mean position of the spring equinox at 354°44′—that is to say, the one which was then 5°16′ east of the first star of Aries—for the first Olympiad which began on noon of the first day of the month Hekatombaion among the Athenians.

In the same way if from the 21°15′ of simple anomaly 95°45′ are subtracted, there will remain a position of simple anomaly of 285°30′ for the same beginning of the Olympiads.

And again by a series of additions of movement made in accordance with the lengths of time—the 360° are not counted where there is an excess above that—we shall have the position or root of the regular movement at the death of Alexander as 1°2′, and the position of the movement of simple anomaly as 332°52′; at the beginning of the years of Caesar a mean movement of 4°55′ and an anomaly of 2°2′; and at the beginning of the years of Christ a position of the mean movement at 5°32′ and an anomaly of 6°45′; and in this way we shall determine the roots of movements for whatever beginnings of time are chosen.

12. On the Computation of the Precession of the Spring Equinox and the Obliquity

[77ᵇ] Therefore, whenever we wish to determine the position of the spring equinox, if the years from the assumed beginning to the given time are unequal, such as those of the Roman calendar, which we use commonly, we shall reduce them to equal or Egyptian years. For we do not use any other years than the Egyptian in calculating the regular movements, on account of the reason which we mentioned. In so far as the number of years is greater than a period of 60 years, we shall divide it into periods of 60 years; and when we enter the tables of movement through these 60-year periods, we shall pass over as supernumerary the first column appearing in the movements; and beginning with the second column, we shall determine the 60°'s, if there are any, together with the other degrees and minutes, which follow.[1] Next as the second entry and from the first column, as they are found, we shall take the 60°'s, degrees and minutes corresponding to the remaining years. We shall do the same thing in the case of days and the periods of 60 days, since we wish to connect the days with their regular movements according to the table of days and minutes, although in this case the minutes of days or even the days themselves are not wrongly neglected on account of the slowness of their movements, as within the daily movement there is a question only of seconds or third minutes. Therefore when we have made a sum of all these together with their root, by adding single numbers to single numbers within the same species—not counting six 60°'s, if they occur—we shall have the mean position of the spring equinox, its distance to the west of the first star of the Ram, or the distance of that star east of the equinox.

In the same way we shall determine the anomaly too.

But we shall find placed in the last column of the table of additosubtractions and corresponding to the simple anomaly the proportional minutes: we shall set them aside and save them. Then, in the third column of the same table and cor-

[1]That is to say, reading the column of degrees as 60°'s, the minutes as degrees, and so on.

responding to the double anomaly we shall find the additosubtraction, *i.e.*, the degrees and minutes by which the true movement differs from the mean. And if the double anomaly is less than a semicircle, we shall subtract the additosubtraction from the mean movement. But if, by having more than 180°, the double anomaly exceeds a semicircle, we shall add [78ᵃ] the additosubtraction to the mean movement. And that which is thus the sum or remainder will comprehend the true and apparent precession of the spring equinox, or in turn the then angular elongation of the first star of Aries from the spring equinox. But if you seek the position of any other star, add its number as assigned in the catalogue of the stars.

But since things which have to do with the laboratory usually become clearer by means of some examples, let our problem be to find the true position of the spring equinox together with the obliquity of the ecliptic for the 16th day before the Kalends of May in the year of Our Lord 1525, and how great the angular distance of Spica in Virgo from the same equinox is. Therefore, it is clear that in the 1524 Roman years 106 days from the beginning of the years of Our Lord up to this time, there has been an intercalation of 381 days, *i.e.*, 1 year 16 days, which in terms of equal years make 1525 years 122 days: there are twenty-five periods of 60 years and 25 years over, and two periods of 60 days and 2 days over. But to the twenty-five periods of 60 years there correspond in the table of mean movement 20°55'2"; to the 25 years, 20'55"; to the two periods of 60 days, 16"; the remaining 2 days are in third minutes. All these together with their root—which was 5°32'—add up to 26°48', the mean precession of the spring equinox. Similarly, the movement of simple anomaly in the twenty-five periods of 60 years has been two 60°'s and 37°15'3"; in the 25 years, 2°37'15"; in the two periods of 60 days, 2'4"; and in the 2 days, 2". There also, together with the root—which is 6°45'—add up to 166°40', the simple anomaly. I shall save as corresponding to this anomaly the proportional minutes found in the last column of the table of the additosubtractions; for they will come into use in investigating the obliquity; and only 1' is found in this case. Next, as corresponding to the double anomaly of 333°20', I find 32' as the additosubtraction, which is additive because the double anomaly is greater than a semicircle. And when it is added to the mean movement, there comes about a true and apparent precession of the spring equinox of 27°21'. And lastly if to that we add the 170° which is the angular distance of Spica in Virgo from the first star in Aries, I shall have its position [78ᵇ] to the east of the spring equinox at 17°21' of Libra, where it was found at approximately the time of our observation.

Now the obliquity of the ecliptic and its declination have the ratio that when there are 60 proportional minutes, the differences located in the table of declinations—I mean the differences at greatest and least obliquity—are added in their entirety to the degrees of the declinations. But in this case, 1' adds only 24" to the obliquity. Wherefore the declinations of the degrees of the ecliptic placed in the table remain as they are throughout this time on account of the least obliquity already approaching us, though at some other time they would be more obviously changeable. In this way, for example, if the simple anomaly were 99°, as it was in the 1380th Egyptian year of Our Lord, there are given by it 25 proportional minutes. But 24' is the difference between greatest and least obliquity and

$$60' : 24' = 25' : 10'.$$

And the addition of 10′ to 28′ gives an obliquity of 23°38′ for that time. If then I should wish to know the declination of any degree on the ecliptic, for example, 3° of Taurus, which is 33° distant from the equinox, I find in the table 12°32′, with a difference of 12′. But

$$60' : 25' = 12' : 5';$$

and the addition of 5′ to 32′ gives 12°37′ for 33° of the ecliptic. We can do the same thing in the case of the angles of section of the ecliptic and the equator and the right ascensions—if it is not better to make use of the ratios of spherical triangles—except that it is always necessary to add in the case of the angles of section and to subtract in the case of the right ascensions, so that all things may be corrected to accord with their time.

13. On the Magnitude and Difference of the Solar Year

But that this is the way it is with the precession of the equinoxes and solstices —the precession being due to the inclination of the Earth's axis, as we said— will also be confirmed by the annual movement of the centre of the Earth, as it affects the appearance of the sun, which we must now discuss. It follows of absolute necessity that the magnitude of the year, when referred to one of the equinoxes or solstices, is found unequal on account of the irregular change of the termini. For these things imply one another mutually.

Wherefore we must separate and distinguish [79ᵃ] the seasonal year from the sidereal year. For we call that the natural year which times the four seasonal changes of the year for us; and that the sidereal, the revolutions of which are referred to some one of the fixed stars. Now the observations of the ancients make clear in many ways that the natural year, which is also called the revolving year, is unequal. For Callippus, Aristarchus of Samos, and Archimedes of Syracuse determined the year as containing a quarter of a day in addition to the 365 whole days—taking the beginning of the year at the summer solstice, after the Athenian manner.

But Claud Ptolemy, realizing that the apprehension of the solstices was detailed and difficult, did not rely upon their observations very much and went over rather to Hipparchus, who left after him records not so much of the solar solstices as of the equinoxes in Rhodes and reported that there was some small deficiency in the quarter-day; and afterwards Ptolemy decided that the deficiency was 1/300th part of a day—as follows. For he took the autumn equinox observed as accurately as possible by Hipparchus at Alexandria in the 177th year after the death of Alexander the Great, at midnight of the third intercalary day by the Egyptian calendar—which the fourth intercalary day follows. Then Ptolemy compared it with the equinox as observed by himself at Alexandria in the third year of Antoninus, which was the 463rd year since the death of Alexander, on the 9th day of Athyr, the third month of the Egyptians, at approximately one hour after the rising of the sun. Accordingly between this observation and that of Hipparchus there were 285 Egyptian years 70 days 7⅕ hours, though there should have been 71 days 6 hours, if the revolving year had a full quarter-day in addition to the whole days. Accordingly the 285 years were deficient by 19⁄20th of a day, whence it follows that a whole day fell out in 300 years. Moreover, he made a similar inference from the spring equinox. For what he recorded as reported by Hipparcchus in the 178th year of Alexander on the 27th day of Mechir, the 6th month by the Egyptian calendar, at sunrise, he himself found in the 463rd year of Alexander on the 7th day of Pachon the 9th month by the Egyptian calendar at a little more than one hour after midday; and in the same way the 285 years were deficient by $1\frac{9}{20}$th of a day. By the aid of these indications Ptolemy determined the revolving year as having 365 days 14 min. [of a day] 48 sec. [or 5 hours 55 min. 12 sec.][1].

Afterwards al-Battani in Arata, Syria, [79b] in the 1206th year after the death of Alexander observed the autumn equinox with no less diligence and found that it occurred after the 7th day of the month Pachon, approximately $7\frac{2}{5}$ hours later in the night, i.e., $4\frac{3}{5}$ hours before the light of the 8th day. Accordingly, comparing his own observation with that of Ptolemy made in the third year of Antoninus one hour after sunrise at Alexandria—which is 10° to the west of Arata—he corrected Ptolemy's observation for the meridian at Arata and found the equinox must have occurred at $1\frac{2}{3}$ hours after sunrise. Accordingly in the period of 743 equal years the sum of the quarter-days amounted to 178 extra days and $17\frac{3}{5}$ hours instead of $185\frac{1}{4}$ days. Accordingly since there was deficiency of 7 days $\frac{2}{5}$ hours, it was seen that the quarter-day was deficient by $\frac{1}{106}$th of a day. Therefore in accordance with the number of years he subtracted one 743rd part of the 7 days $\frac{2}{5}$ hours [which is 13 min. of an hour 36 sec.] from the quarter-day and recorded the natural year as containing 365 days 5 hours 46 min. 24 sec.

We too made observations of the autumn equinox at Frauenburg in the year of Our Lord 1515 on the 18th day before the Kalends of October: but according to the Egyptian calendar it was the 1840th year after the death of Alexander on the 6th day of the month Phaophi, half an hour after sunrise. But since Arata is about 25° to the east of this spot—which makes $1\frac{2}{3}$ hours—therefore during the time between our equinox and that of al-Battani there were 633 Egyptian years and 153 days $6\frac{3}{4}$ hours in place of 158 days 6 hours. But between the observation made by Ptolemy at Alexandria and the place and date of our observation, there were 1376 Egyptian years 332 days $\frac{1}{2}$ hour. For there is about an hour's difference between us and Alexandria. Therefore during the 633 years between al-Battani and us there have fallen out 4 days $23\frac{3}{4}$ hours, or 1 day per 128 years; but during the 1376 years after Ptolemy approximately 12 days, i.e., 1 day per 115 years, and again the year has become unequal on both sides.

[80a] Moreover, we determined the spring equinox, which occurred in the year of Our Lord 1516, $4\frac{1}{3}$ hours after midnight on the 5th day before the Ides of March; and since the spring equinox of Ptolemy—the meridian of Alexandria being corrected for ours—there have been 1376 Egyptian years 332 days $16\frac{1}{3}$ hours, in which it is apparent that the distances between the spring and autumn equinoxes are unequal. And so it is of much importance that the solar year as determined in this way should be equal. For the fact that at the autumnal equinoxes between Ptolemy and us, as was shown, in accordance with the equal distribution of years, the quarter-day should be deficient in the 115th part of a day makes the equinox come half a day later than al-Battani's. And the period from al-Battani to us, where the quarter-day must have been deficient in the 128th part of a day, is not consonant with Ptolemy, but the date precedes by a full day the equinox observed by him, and the equinox of Hipparchus by two days. Similarly the time of al-Battani's equinox as measured from Ptolemy's precedes the equinox of Hipparchus by 2 days.

[1]i.e., Ptolemy found 1/300th part of a day lacking to a full quarter-day.

Therefore the equality of the solar year is more correctly measured from the sphere of the fixed stars, as Thebites ben Chora was the first to find; and its magnitude is 365 days 15 minutes [of a day] 23 seconds (which are approximately 6 hours 9 min. 12 sec.) according to a probable argument taken from the fact that the year appears longer in the slower passage of the equinoxes and solstices than in the faster and in accordance with a fixed proportion; and that could not be the case, if there were no equality with reference to the sphere of the fixed stars. Wherefore Ptolemy is not to be listened to in that part where he thinks that it is absurd and irrelevant to measure the annual regularity of the sun through its restitutions with reference to some one of the fixed stars and that this is no more fitting than if someone were to take Jupiter or Saturn as the measure of that regularity. And so there is a ready reason why the seasonal year was longer before Ptolemy and after him became shorter, by a variable difference.

But also in the case of the astral or sidereal year an error can come about, but nevertheless a very slight one and far less than the one which we have already described; and it occurs because this same movement of the centre of the Earth around the sun appears irregular by reason of a twofold irregularity. [80ᵇ] The first and simple irregularity relates to the annual restoration; the other, which varies the first by changing it around, is perceptible not immediately but after a long stretch of time; and accordingly it is not simple or easy to know the ratio of the equality of the year. For if anyone wishes to determine it simply in relation to the fixed distance of some star having a known position— which can be done by using an astrolabe and with the help of the moon, in the way we described in the case of Basiliscus in Leo—he will not avoid error completely, unless at that time the sun on account of the movement of the Earth either has no additosubtraction or else obtains similar and equal additosubtractions at both termini. But unless this happens and unless there is some difference made manifest in accordance with the irregularity, an equal circuit will certainly not seem to have taken place in equal times. But if in both termini the total difference is subtracted or added proportionally, the job will be perfect. Furthermore, the apprehension of the difference requires a prior knowledge of the mean movement, which we are seeking for that reason; and we are versed in this business as in the Archimedean quadrature of the circle.

Nevertheless in order to arrive at the resolution of this knotty problem some time—we find four causes altogether for the appearance of irregularity. The *first* is the irregular precession of the equinoxes, which we have expounded; the *second* is that whereby the sun seems to traverse unequal arcs on the ecliptic, which occurs approximately annually; the *third* is the one which varies this irregularity which we call the second. There remains the *fourth*, which changes the highest and lowest apsides[1] of the centre of the Earth, as will appear below. Of all these only the second was marked by Ptolemy; and it by itself could not produce the inequality of the year but contributes to it through being involved in the others.

But for demonstrating the difference between the regular and the apparent movement of the sun the most accurate ratio of the year does not seem necessary; and it seems to be enough if in the demonstration we take as the magnitude

[1]The apsides are the positions of greatest and least altitudinal distance of a planet from the sun.

of the year the 365¼ days, in which that movement of the first irregularity is completed, since that which stands out so little, when taken on the total circle, vanishes utterly when taken on a lesser magnitude. But on account of the excellence of the order and the facility in teaching we are here expounding first the regular movements of the annual revolution of the centre of the Earth by means of necessary demonstrations. And then we shall build up the regular movements together with the difference between the regular and the apparent movement.

14. On the Regular and Mean Movements of the Revolutions of the Centre of the Earth

[81ᵃ] We find that the magnitude of the year and its equality is only 1 second 10 thirds greater than Thebith ben Chora recorded it to be, so that it contains 365 days 15 minutes 24 seconds 10 third-minutes—which amounts to 6 hours 9 minutes 40 seconds, and its fixed equality with reference to the sphere of the fixed stars is disclosed.

Therefore, when we have multiplied the 360° of a circle by 365 days and have divided the sum by 365 days 15 minutes 24 seconds 10 third-minutes, we shall have the movement of an Egyptian year as 359°44′49″7‴4⁗ and the movement during 60 similar years—not counting the total circles—will be 344°49′7″4‴. Again, if we divide the annual movement by 365 days, we shall have a daily movement of 59′8″11‴22⁗.

But if we add to these the mean and regular precession of the equinoxes, we shall compose another regular annual movement in seasonal years of 359°45′ 39″19‴9⁗, and a daily movement 59′8″19‴37⁗. And for this reason we can call the former movement of the sun—to use the common expression—the regular and simple movement; and the latter, the regular and composite movement. And we shall set them out in tables, as we did with the precession of the equinoxes. The regular movement of the anomaly of the sun is added to them; but we shall speak of that later.

TABLE OF THE MEAN AND SIMPLE MOVEMENT OF THE SUN IN YEARS AND PERIODS OF SIXTY YEARS

Egyptian Years	Movement 60°	°	'	"	'''		Egyptian Years	Movement 60°	°	'	"	'''
1	5	59	44	49	7		31	5	52	9	22	39
2	5	59	29	38	14		32	5	51	54	11	46
3	5	59	14	27	21		33	5	51	39	0	53
4	5	58	59	16	28		34	5	51	23	50	0
5	5	58	44	5	35		35	5	51	8	39	7
6	5	58	28	54	42		36	5	50	53	28	14
7	5	58	13	43	49		37	5	50	38	17	21
8	5	57	58	32	56		38	5	50	23	6	28
9	5	57	43	22	3		39	5	50	7	55	35
10	5	57	28	11	10		40	5	49	52	44	42
11	5	57	13	0	17		41	5	49	37	33	49
12	5	56	57	49	24		42	5	49	22	22	56
13	5	56	42	38	31		43	5	49	7	12	3
14	5	56	27	27	38		44	5	48	52	1	10
15	5	56	12	16	46		45	5	48	36	50	18
16	5	55	57	5	53		46	5	48	21	39	25
17	5	55	41	55	0		47	5	48	6	28	32
18	5	55	26	44	7		48	5	47	51	17	39
19	5	55	11	33	14		49	5	47	36	6	46
20	5	54	56	22	21		50	5	47	20	55	53
21	5	54	41	11	28		51	5	47	5	45	0
22	5	54	26	0	35		52	5	46	50	34	7
23	5	54	10	49	42		53	5	46	35	23	14
24	5	53	55	38	49		54	5	46	20	12	21
25	5	53	40	27	56		55	5	46	5	1	28
26	5	53	25	17	3		56	5	45	49	50	35
27	5	53	10	6	10		57	5	45	34	39	42
28	5	52	54	55	17		58	5	45	19	28	49
29	5	52	39	44	24		59	5	45	4	17	56
30	5	52	24	33	32		60	5	44	49	7	4

Position at the Birth of Christ—272° 31'

TABLE OF THE REGULAR AND SIMPLE MOVEMENT OF THE SUN IN DAYS AND PERIODS OF SIXTY DAYS

Days	Movement 60°	°	'	"	'''		Days	Movement 60°	°	'	"	'''
1	0	0	59	8	11		31	0	30	33	13	52
2	0	1	58	16	22		32	0	31	32	22	3
3	0	2	57	24	34		33	0	32	31	30	15
4	0	3	56	32	45		34	0	33	30	38	26
5	0	4	55	40	56		35	0	34	29	46	37
6	0	5	54	49	8		36	0	35	28	54	49
7	0	6	53	57	19		37	0	36	28	3	0
8	0	7	53	5	30		38	0	37	27	11	11
9	0	8	52	13	42		39	0	38	26	19	23
10	0	9	51	21	53		40	0	39	25	27	34
11	0	10	50	30	5		41	0	40	24	35	45
12	0	11	49	38	16		42	0	41	23	43	57
13	0	12	48	46	27		43	0	42	22	52	8
14	0	13	47	54	39		44	0	43	22	0	20
15	0	14	47	2	50		45	0	44	21	8	31
16	0	15	46	11	1		46	0	45	20	16	42
17	0	16	45	19	13		47	0	46	19	24	54
18	0	17	44	27	24		48	0	47	18	33	5
19	0	18	43	35	35		49	0	48	17	41	16
20	0	19	42	43	47		50	0	49	16	49	28
21	0	20	41	51	58		51	0	50	15	57	39
22	0	21	41	0	9		52	0	51	15	5	50
23	0	22	40	8	21		53	0	52	14	14	2
24	0	23	39	16	32		54	0	53	13	22	13
25	0	24	38	24	44		55	0	54	12	30	25
26	0	25	37	32	55		56	0	55	11	38	36
27	0	26	36	41	6		57	0	56	10	46	47
28	0	27	35	49	18		58	0	57	9	54	59
29	0	28	34	57	29		59	0	58	9	3	10
30	0	29	34	5	41		60	0	59	8	11	22

Position at the Birth of Christ—272° 31'

TABLE OF THE REGULAR COMPOSITE MOVEMENT OF THE SUN IN YEARS AND PERIODS OF SIXTY YEARS

Egyptian Years	60°	Movement °	'	"	'''	Egyptian Years	60°	Movement °	'	"	'''
1	5	59	45	39	19	31	5	52	34	18	53
2	5	59	31	18	38	32	5	52	21	58	12
3	5	59	16	57	57	33	5	52	6	37	31
4	5	59	2	37	16	34	5	51	52	16	51
5	5	58	48	16	35	35	5	51	38	56	10
6	5	58	33	55	54	36	5	51	23	35	29
7	5	58	19	35	14	37	5	51	9	14	48
8	5	58	5	14	33	38	5	50	55	54	7
9	5	57	50	53	52	39	5	50	40	33	26
10	5	57	36	33	11	40	5	50	26	12	46
11	5	57	22	12	30	41	5	50	11	52	5
12	5	57	7	51	49	42	5	49	57	31	24
13	5	56	53	31	8	43	5	49	43	10	43
14	5	56	39	10	28	44	5	49	28	50	2
15	5	56	24	49	47	45	5	49	14	29	21
16	5	56	10	29	6	46	5	49	0	8	40
17	5	55	56	8	25	47	5	48	45	48	0
18	5	55	41	47	44	48	5	48	31	27	19
19	5	55	27	27	3	49	5	48	17	6	38
20	5	55	13	6	23	50	5	48	2	45	57
21	5	54	58	45	42	51	5	47	48	25	16
22	5	54	44	25	1	52	5	47	34	4	35
23	5	54	30	4	20	53	5	47	19	43	54
24	5	54	15	43	39	54	5	47	5	23	14
25	5	54	1	22	58	55	5	46	51	2	33
26	5	53	47	2	17	56	5	46	36	41	52
27	5	53	32	41	37	57	5	46	22	21	11
28	5	53	18	20	56	58	5	46	8	0	30
29	5	53	4	0	15	59	5	45	53	39	49
30	5	52	48	39	34	60	5	45	39	19	9

Position at the Birth of Christ—278° 2'

TABLE OF THE REGULAR COMPOSITE MOVEMENT OF THE SUN IN DAYS AND PERIODS OF SIXTY DAYS

Days	60°	Movement °	'	"	'''	Days	60°	Movement °	'	"	'''
1	0	0	59	8	19	31	0	30	33	18	8
2	0	1	58	16	39	32	0	31	32	26	27
3	0	2	57	24	58	33	0	32	31	34	47
4	0	3	56	33	18	34	0	33	30	43	6
5	0	4	55	41	38	35	0	34	29	51	26
6	0	5	54	49	57	36	0	35	28	59	46
7	0	6	53	58	17	37	0	36	28	8	5
8	0	7	53	6	36	38	0	37	27	16	25
9	0	8	52	14	56	39	0	38	26	24	45
10	0	9	51	23	16	40	0	39	25	33	4
11	0	10	50	31	35	41	0	40	24	41	24
12	0	11	49	39	55	42	0	41	23	49	43
13	0	12	48	48	15	43	0	42	22	58	3
14	0	13	47	56	34	44	0	43	22	6	23
15	0	14	47	4	54	45	0	44	21	14	42
16	0	15	46	13	13	46	0	45	20	23	2
17	0	16	45	21	33	47	0	46	19	31	21
18	0	17	44	29	53	48	0	47	18	39	41
19	0	18	43	38	12	49	0	48	17	48	1
20	0	19	42	46	32	50	0	49	16	56	20
21	0	20	41	54	51	51	0	50	16	4	40
22	0	21	41	3	11	52	0	51	15	13	0
23	0	22	40	11	31	53	0	52	14	21	19
24	0	23	39	19	50	54	0	53	13	29	39
25	0	24	38	28	10	55	0	54	12	37	58
26	0	25	37	36	30	56	0	55	11	46	18
27	0	26	36	44	49	57	0	56	10	54	38
28	0	27	35	53	9	58	0	57	10	2	57
29	0	28	35	1	28	59	0	58	9	11	17
30	0	29	34	9	48	60	0	59	8	19	37

Position at the Birth of Christ—278° 2'

Table of the Regular Movement of Anomaly[1] of the Sun in Years and Periods of Sixty Years

Egyptian Years	Movement						Egyptian Years	Movement				
	60°	°	′	″	‴			60°	°	′	″	‴
1	5	59	44	24	46		31	5	51	56	48	11
2	5	59	28	49	33		32	5	51	41	12	58
3	5	59	13	14	20		33	5	51	25	37	45
4	5	58	57	39	7		34	5	51	10	2	32
5	5	58	42	3	54		35	5	50	54	27	19
6	5	58	26	28	41		36	5	50	38	52	6
7	5	58	10	53	27		37	5	50	23	16	52
8	5	57	55	18	14		38	5	50	7	41	39
9	5	57	39	43	1		39	5	49	52	6	26
10	5	57	24	7	48		40	5	49	36	31	13
11	5	57	8	32	35		41	5	49	20	56	0
12	5	56	52	57	22		42	5	49	5	20	47
13	5	56	37	22	8		43	5	48	49	45	33
14	5	56	21	46	55		44	5	48	34	10	20
15	5	56	6	11	42		45	5	48	18	35	7
16	5	55	50	36	29		46	5	48	2	59	54
17	5	55	35	1	16		47	5	47	47	24	41
18	5	55	19	26	3		48	5	47	31	49	28
19	5	55	3	50	49		49	5	47	16	14	14
20	5	54	48	15	36		50	5	47	0	39	1
21	5	54	32	40	23		51	5	46	45	3	48
22	5	54	17	5	10		52	5	46	29	28	35
23	5	54	1	29	57		53	5	46	13	53	22
24	5	53	45	54	44		54	5	45	58	18	9
25	5	53	30	19	30		55	5	45	42	42	55
26	5	53	14	44	17		56	5	45	26	7	42
27	5	52	59	9	4		57	5	45	11	32	29
28	5	52	43	33	51		58	5	44	55	57	16
29	5	52	27	58	38		59	5	44	40	22	3
30	5	52	12	23	25		60	5	44	24	46	50

Position at the Birth of Christ—211° 19′

[1] Any regular movement which, when compounded with a mean movement, causes an appearance of irregularity is called a movement of anomaly. In this case, the regular movement of anomaly is the movement of the eccentric circle, or the first epicycle.

Movement of Anomaly of the Sun in Days and Periods of Sixty Days

Days	Movement						Days	Movement				
	60°	°	′	″	‴			60°	°	′	″	‴
1	0	0	59	8	7		31	0	30	33	11	48
2	0	1	58	16	14		32	0	31	32	19	55
3	0	2	57	24	22		33	0	32	31	28	3
4	0	3	56	32	29		34	0	33	30	36	10
5	0	4	55	40	36		35	0	34	29	44	17
6	0	5	54	48	44		36	0	35	28	52	25
7	0	6	53	56	51		37	0	36	28	0	32
8	0	7	53	4	58		38	0	37	27	8	39
9	0	8	52	13	6		39	0	38	26	16	47
10	0	9	51	21	13		40	0	39	25	24	54
11	0	10	50	29	21		41	0	40	24	33	2
12	0	11	49	37	28		42	0	41	23	41	8
13	0	12	48	45	35		43	0	42	22	49	16
14	0	13	47	53	43		44	0	43	21	57	24
15	0	14	47	1	50		45	0	44	21	5	31
16	0	15	46	9	57		46	0	45	20	13	38
17	0	16	45	18	5		47	0	46	19	21	46
18	0	17	44	26	12		48	0	47	18	29	53
19	0	18	43	34	19		49	0	48	17	38	0
20	0	19	42	42	27		50	0	49	16	46	8
21	0	20	41	50	34		51	0	50	15	54	15
22	0	21	40	58	42		52	0	51	15	2	23
23	0	22	40	6	49		53	0	52	14	10	30
24	0	23	39	14	56		54	0	53	13	18	37
25	0	24	38	23	4		55	0	54	12	26	45
26	0	25	37	31	11		56	0	55	11	34	52
27	0	26	36	39	18		57	0	56	10	42	59
28	0	27	35	47	26		58	0	57	9	51	7
29	0	28	34	55	33		59	0	58	8	59	14
30	0	29	34	3	41		60	0	59	8	7	22

Position at the Birth of Christ—211° 19′

15. Theorems Prerequisite for Demonstrating the Apparent Irregularity of the Movement of the Sun

[84ᵇ] But for the sake of making a better determination of the apparent irregular movement of the sun we shall now demonstrate more clearly that—with the sun occupying the central position in the world and with the Earth revolving around it as around a centre—if, as we said, there is a distance between the Earth and the sun which cannot be perceived in relation to the immensity of the sphere of the fixed stars; then the sun will be seen to have a regular motion with reference to any point or star in the same sphere [of the fixed stars].

For let AB be the greatest circle in the world in the plane of the ecliptic. Let

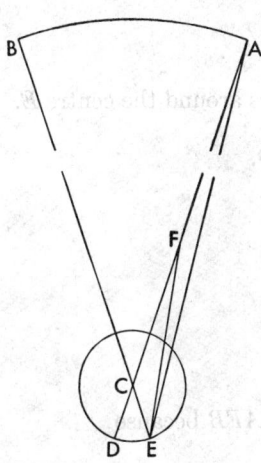

C be its centre, and let the sun be situated there. And in accordance with the distance CD between the sun and the Earth—in comparison with which the depth of the world is immense—let the circle CDE, in which the annual revolution of the centre of the Earth is located, be described in the same plane of the ecliptic: I say that the sun will seem to have a regular motion with reference to any point or star taken on circle AB.

Let some point be taken; and let it be A. And to A let the view of the sun from the Earth—which is at D—be extended as DCA. Now let the Earth be moved anywhere through arc DE; and let AE and DE be drawn from E the position of the Earth. Therefore the sun will now be seen from E at point B. And since AC is immense in comparison with CD or CE its equal, AE too will be immense in comparison with CE. For let any point F be taken on AC, and let EF be joined. Therefore since two straight lines from the termini C and E of the base fall outside triangle EFC on point A; by the converse of Euclid's *Elements*, I, 21,

$$\text{angle } FAE < \text{angle } EFC.$$

Wherefore the straight lines extended to immensity comprehend at last an angle CAE so acute that it is no longer perceptible; and

$$\text{angle } CAE = \text{angle } BCA - \text{angle } AEC.$$

Moreover, on account of the slightness of the difference between them angles BCA and AEC seem to be equal; and lines AC and AE seem to be parallel; and the sun seems to have [85ᵃ] a regular motion with reference to any point on the sphere of the fixed stars, just as if it were revolving around the centre E, as was to be shown.

But its irregular movement is demonstrated, because the movement of the centre of the Earth in its annual revolution is not absolutely around the centre of the sun. That can be understood in two ways, either through an eccentric circle, *i.e.*, one whose centre is not the centre of the sun, or through an epicycle on a homocentric circle.

Now it is made clear through an eccentric in this way. For let $ABCD$ be an eccentric circle in the plane of the ecliptic; and let its centre E be no very slight distance away from the centre of the sun or world. Let the centre of the world be F; and let $AEFD$ be the diameter [of circle $ABCD$] passing through both centres. And let its apogee be at A—which is called the highest apsis by the Romans—the place farthest removed from the centre of the world, and D the perigee, which is nearest [to the centre of the world] and is the lowest apsis.

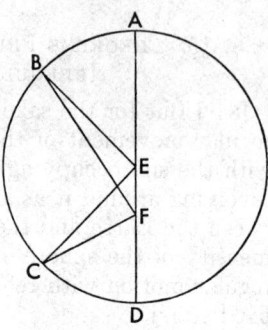

Therefore while the Earth is moved regularly in its orbital circle $ABCD$ around its centre E, as has been already said, there will appear to be an irregular movement around F.

For let
$$\text{arc } AB = \text{arc } CD;$$
and let the straight lines BE, CE, BF, and CF be drawn.
$$\text{Angle } AEB = \text{angle } CED,$$
because angles AEB and CED are intercepting equal arcs around the centre E. But angle CFD is the angle of sight, and
$$\text{ext. angle } CFD > \text{int. angle } CED.$$
But
$$\text{angle } AEB = \text{angle } CED.$$
Hence
$$\text{angle } CFD > \text{angle } AEB.$$
But also
$$\text{ext. angle } AEB > \text{int. angle } AFB;$$
and hence by so much more
$$\text{angle } CFD > \text{angle } AFB.$$
But an equal time produces both angle CFD and angle AFB because
$$\text{arc } AB = \text{arc } CD.$$
Therefore the movement will appear regular from around E and irregular from around F.

Moreover, it is possible to see the same thing more simply, because arc AB is farther away from F than arc CD is. For by Euclid, III, 7, lines AF and BF by which arc AB is intercepted are longer than CF and DF by which arc CD is intercepted, and, as is shown in optics, equal magnitudes which are nearer appear greater than the ones farther away. And so what was proposed in the case of the eccentric circle is manifest.

The same thing will also be made clear by means of an epicycle on a homocentric circle. For let the centre of the homocentric circle $ABCD$ and the centre of the world where the sun is be at E; and in the same plane let A be the centre of epicycle FG. And through both centres let the straight line $CEAF$ be drawn. Let F be the apogee of the epicycle; and I, the perigee. Therefore it is clear that there is regularity [85ᵇ] in A, but apparent irregularity in epicycle FG. For if the movement of A takes place in the direction of B, $i.e.$, eastward, while the movement of the centre of the Earth is from its apogee F westward; then in the perigee—which is I—E will appear to be moving faster, because the two movements of A and I are in the same direction. But in the apogee, which is F, point E will seem to be moved more slowly, namely because it is moved only by the excelling movement out of two contraries; and the Earth situated at G is to the west of the regular movement but at K is to the east of it, and the dis-

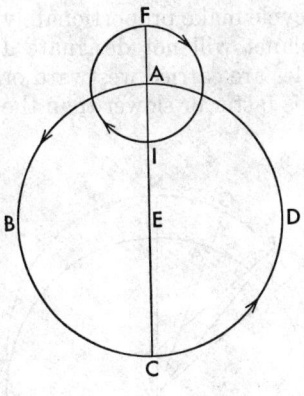

tance of the Earth from the regular movement is measured by arcs AK and AG, in accordance with which the sun will seem to move irregularly.

But whatever things take place by means of the epicycle can happen in the same way by means of the eccentric circle, which the transit of the planet in the epicycle describes equal to the homocentric circle and in the same plane; and the centre of the eccentric circle is at a distance from the centre of the homocentric circle equal to the radius of the epicycle. And all this occurs in three ways, since, if the epicycle on the homocentric circle and the planet on the epicycle made similar revolutions but with movements opposite to one another, the movement of the planet will trace a fixed eccentric circle, *i.e.*, one whose apogee and perigee possess unchanging locations.

In this way let ABC be the homocentric circle, and the centre of the world D, the diameter ADC. And let us put down that, when the epicycle is at A, the planet is in the apogee of the epicycle, which is at G, and its radius is in the straight line DAG. Now let arc AB of the homocentric circle be taken; and with centre B and radius equal to AG, let the epicycle EF be described, and let BD and BE be extended in a straight line; and let the arc EF be similar to arc AB, but let arc EF be taken in the opposite direction. And let the planet or Earth be in F. Let BF be joined. And on line AD let

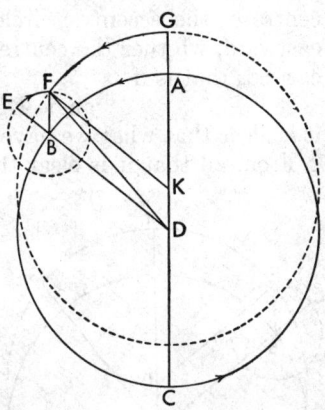

$$DK = BF.$$

Therefore, since

$$\text{angle } EBF = \text{angle } BDA,$$

and for those reasons

$$BF = DK$$

and BF is parallel to DK; and since, if straight lines are joined to equal and parallel straight lines, they are also equal and parallel by Euclid, I, 33; and since

$$DK = AG$$

[86ᵃ] and AK is their common annex;

$$GAK = AKD$$

and therefore

$$GAK = KF.$$

Therefore the circle described with centre K and radius KAG will pass through F. By means of a movement compounded of AB and EF point F describes this circle as eccentric and equal to the homocentric and accordingly fixed too. For when the epicycle makes proportionally equal revolutions with the homocentric circle, the apsides of the eccentric circle so described necessarily remain in the same place.

But if the centre and the circumference of the epicycle make proportionately unequal revolutions, then the movement of the planet will not designate a fixed eccentric circle but one whose centre and apsides are carried westward or eastward, according as the movement of the planet is faster or slower than the centre of its epicycle. In this way if

angle EBF > angle BDA,

let

angle BDM = angle EBF.

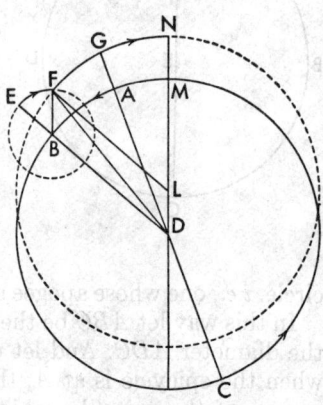

It will similarly be shown that if on line DM there be taken DL equal to BF, the circle described with L as centre and with radius LMN equal to AD will pass through planet F. Hence it is clear that by the composite movement of the planet there is described arc NF of the eccentric circle, whose apogee meanwhile travels from point G westward along arc GN.

On the contrary, if the movement of the planet in the epicycle were slower, then the centre of the eccentric circle should follow it eastward, whither the centre of the epicycle is carried; that is if

angle EBF = angle BDM > angle BDA,

it is clear that what we have spoken of will take place.

From all that it is clear that the same irregularity of appearance is always produced whether by means of an epicycle on a homocentric circle or by means of an eccentric circle equal to the homocentric; and they by no means differ from one another, provided the distance between the centres [of the homocentric and the eccentric] is equal to the radius of the epicycle. Accordingly it is not easy to determine which of them exists in the heavens. Indeed Ptolemy, where he understood simple irregularity and certain and immutable locations for the apsides—as he thought was the case in the sun—judged that the scheme of eccentricity was sufficient. But to the moon and to the five planets which wander in two or more different ways [86^{b}] he applied eccentric circles carrying epicycles.

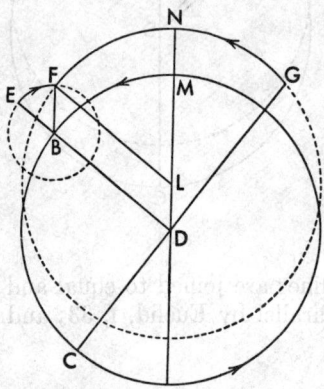

From this moreover it is easily demonstrated that the greatest difference between regularity and appearance is seen at the time when the planet appears in the mean position between the highest and the lowest apsis in the case of the eccentric circle, but in the case of the epicycle at its point of contact [with the circle carrying the epicycle], as in Ptolemy.

In the case of the eccentric circle thus: For let there be the circle $ABCD$ around the centre E; and AEC the diameter through F the sun, which is off centre. Now let line BFD be drawn through F at right angles to the diameter; and let BE and ED be joined. Let A be the apogee and C the perigee; and

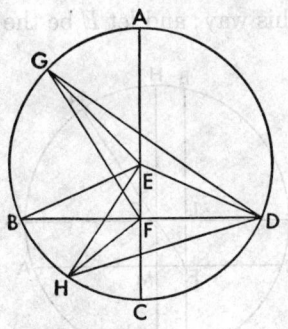

let B and D be the means appearing between them.

I say that no angle greater than angle B or D can be constructed with its vertex on the circumference and line EF as its base.

For let points G and H be taken on either side of B; and let GD, GE, and GF be joined, and also HE, HF, and HD. Since line FG is nearer the centre than line DF,

$$\text{line } FG > \text{line } DF.$$

And therefore

$$\text{angle } GDF > \text{angle } DGF.$$

But

$$\text{angle } EDG = \text{angle } EGD,$$

because sides EG and ED falling upon the base are equal.
And therefore

$$\text{angle } EDF > \text{angle } EGF.$$

But

$$\text{angle } EDF = \text{angle } EBF.$$

Similarly too

$$\text{line } DF > \text{line } FH;$$

and

$$\text{angle } FHD > \text{angle } FDH.$$

But

$$\text{angle } EHD = \text{angle } EDH,$$

because

$$\text{line } EH = \text{line } ED.$$

Therefore, by subtraction,

$$\text{angle } EDF > \text{angle } EHF.$$

But

$$\text{angle } EDF = \text{angle } EBF.$$

Therefore no angle greater than the angles at points B and D will ever be constructed with line EF as base. And so the greatest difference between regularity and appearance is found in the mean position between apogee and perigee.

16. On the Apparent Irregularity of the Sun

These things have been demonstrated generally; and they are applicable not only to the apparent movements of the sun but also to the irregularity of the other planets. Now we shall investigate what relates to the sun and the Earth, first in respect to what has been handed down to us by Ptolemy and the other ancients, and then in respect to what modern times and experience have taught us. Ptolemy found [87a] that $94\frac{1}{2}$ days were comprehended between the spring equinox and the summer solstice, and $92\frac{1}{2}$ between the solstice and the autumn equinox. Therefore in accordance with the ratio of time during the first interval there was a mean and regular movement of $93°9'$; during the second interval, one of $91°11'$.

Let $ABCD$ be the circle of the year as divided in this way; and let E be the centre. Let

$$\text{arc } AB = 93°9'$$

for the first period of time; and let

$$\text{arc } BC = 91°11'$$

for the second. Let the spring equinox be viewed from A; the summer solstice from B; the autumn equinox from C; and the remaining winter solstice from D. Let AC and BD be joined.

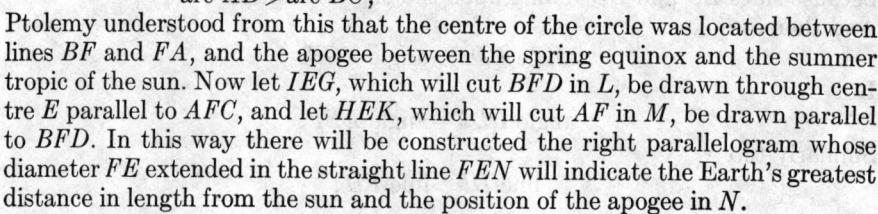

AC and BD cut one another at right angles at F, where we set up the sun. Therefore since

$$\text{arc } ABC > 180°$$

and too

$$\text{arc } AB > \text{arc } BC;$$

Ptolemy understood from this that the centre of the circle was located between lines BF and FA, and the apogee between the spring equinox and the summer tropic of the sun. Now let IEG, which will cut BFD in L, be drawn through centre E parallel to AFC, and let HEK, which will cut AF in M, be drawn parallel to BFD. In this way there will be constructed the right parallelogram whose diameter FE extended in the straight line FEN will indicate the Earth's greatest distance in length from the sun and the position of the apogee in N.

Therefore since

$$\text{arc } ABC = 184°19',$$

and

$$\text{arc } AH = \tfrac{1}{2} \text{ arc } ABC = 92°9\tfrac{1}{2}';$$
$$\text{arc } HB = \text{arc } AGB - \text{arc } AH = 59'.$$

Again

$$\text{arc } AG = \text{arc } AH - 90° = 2°10'.$$

Now

$$LF = \tfrac{1}{2} \text{ ch. } 2\, AG = 377,$$
$$\text{where radius} = 10{,}000.$$

But

$$EL = \tfrac{1}{2} \text{ ch. } 2\, BH = 172.$$

And, as two sides of triangle ELF are given,

$$\text{side } EF = 414 = \tfrac{1}{24} \text{ radius } NE$$
$$\text{where radius } NE = 10{,}000.$$

But

$$EF : EL = NE : \tfrac{1}{2} \text{ ch. } 2\, NH.$$

Therefore

$$\text{arc } NH = 24\tfrac{1}{2}°.$$

And thus

$$\text{angle } NEH \text{ is given,}$$

and

$$\text{angle } NEH = \text{angle } LFE,$$

which is the angle of apparent movement. By such an interval therefore did the highest apsis before Ptolemy precede the summer solstice of the sun. But

$$\text{arc } IK = 90°,$$

and

$$[87^{\text{b}}] \quad \text{arc } IC = \text{arc } AG$$

and
$$\text{arc } DK = \text{arc } HB.$$
Hence
$$\text{arc } CD = \text{arc } IK - (\text{arcs } IC + DK) = 86°51'$$
and
$$\text{arc } DA = \text{arc } CDA - \text{arc } CD = 88°49'.$$
But to the 86°51′ there correspond 88⅛ days; and to the 88°49′, 90 days and 3 hours—the eighth part of a day. During these periods the sun on account of the regular movement of the Earth seemed to cross from the autumn equinox to the winter solstice and for the remainder of the year to return from the winter solstice to the spring equinox. Indeed Ptolemy testifies that he found these things no different from what were reported by Hipparchus before him. Wherefore he judged that for the remainder of time the highest apsis would be 24½° before the summer tropic and that the eccentricity of—as I said—a 24th part of the radius would remain perpetually.

But now it is found that both of them have changed by a manifest difference. Al-Battani noted it as being 93 days 35 minutes [of a day] from the spring equinox to the summer solstice, and 186 days 37 minutes to the autumn, from which by Ptolemy's rule he elicited an eccentricity of not more than 346 parts whereof the radius has 10,000. Arzachel the Spaniard agrees with him in the ratio of eccentricity but reported an apogee 12°10′ west of the solstice, and al-Battani viewed it as 7°43′ west of the same solstice. By these tokens it has been grasped that there still remains another irregularity in the movement of the centre of the Earth, as has been attested by the observations of our time also. For during the ten and more years in which we applied our intelligence to investigating these things and especially in the year of Our Lord 1515, we found that there were 186 days 5½ minutes from the spring equinox to the autumnal. And so as not to deceive ourselves in determining the solstices—which some suspected had happened in the case of our predecessors—we took certain other positions of the sun into consideration in this business which were not difficult to observe even in comparison with the equinoxes, such as the mean positions in the signs of Taurus, Leo, Scorpio, and Aquarius. Therefore we found that there were 45 days 16 minutes from the autumn equinox to the middle point of Scorpio, and 178 days 53½ minutes to the spring equinox. Now the regular movement during the first interval was 44°37′; and during the second interval 176°19′.

[88ᵃ] Now that these preparations have been made, let circle *ABCD* be repeated; and let *A* be the point from which the sun was seen at the spring equinox; *B* the point at which the autumn equinox was viewed; and *C* the midpoint of Scorpio. Let *AB* and *CD*, which cut one another at *F* the centre of the sun, be joined; and let arc *AC* be subtended.

Therefore, since
$$\text{arc } CB = 44°37',$$
$$\text{angle } BAC = 44°37',$$
$$\text{where 2 rt. angles} = 360°.$$
And
$$\text{angle } BFC = 45°,$$
$$\text{where 4 rt. angles} = 360°;$$
and is the angle of apparent movement; but
$$\text{angle } BFC = 90°,$$
$$\text{where 2 rt. angles} = 360°.$$

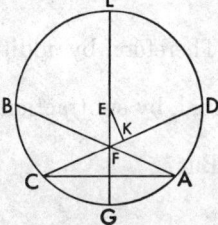

Hence,

$$\text{angle } ACD = 45°23',$$

because

$$\text{arc } AD = 45°23'.$$

But

$$\text{arc } ACB = 176°19',$$

and

$$\text{arc } AC = \text{arc } ACB - \text{arc } BC = 131°42',$$

and

$$\text{arc } CAD = \text{arc } AC + \text{arc } AD = 177°5'.$$

Therefore, since

$$\text{arc } ACB < 180°,$$

and

$$\text{arc } CAD < 180°,$$

it is clear that the centre of the circle is located in the remainder BD. And let the centre be E. And through E let the diameter $LEFG$ be drawn. Let L be the apogee and G the perigee. Let EK be erected perpendicular to CFD. But the chords subtending the given arcs are also given by the table:

$$AC = 182,494$$

and

$$CFD = 199,934,$$

$$\text{where diameter} = 200,000.$$

Accordingly, as triangle ACF has its angles given, the ratio of the sides will be given by the first rule for plane triangles.

$$CF = 97,697,$$

according as

$$AC = 182,494;$$

and for that reason

$$FK = \tfrac{1}{2} CD - CF = 2,000.$$

And since

$$180° - \text{arc } CAD = 2°55';$$

and since

$$EK = \tfrac{1}{2} \text{ ch. } 2°55' = 2,534;$$

then, in triangle EFK, as the two sides FK and KE comprehending the right angle have been given, the triangle will have its sides and angles given:

$$EF = 323,$$

$$\text{where } EL = 10,000;$$

and

$$\text{angle } EFK = 51\tfrac{2}{3}°,$$

$$\text{where 4 rt. angles} = 360°.$$

Therefore, by addition,

$$\text{angle } AFL = 96\tfrac{2}{3}°$$

and, by subtraction,

$$\text{angle } BFL = 83\tfrac{1}{3}°.$$

But

$$EF = 1^p 56',$$

$$\text{where } EL = 60^p.$$

This is the distance of the sun from the centre of the orbital circle; and it has now become approximately $\frac{1}{31}$st [of the radius of the orbital circle], [88ᵇ] though to Ptolemy it seemed to be $\frac{1}{24}$th. And the apogee, which was at that time $24\frac{1}{2}°$ to the west of the summer solstice, is now $6\frac{2}{3}°$ to the east of it.

17. DEMONSTRATION OF THE FIRST AND ANNUAL IRREGULARITY OF THE SUN TOGETHER WITH ITS PARTICULAR DIFFERENCES

Therefore since many differences of the irregular movement of the sun are found, we judge that the difference which occurs annually and is more known than the rest should be deduced first.

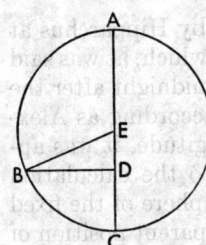

Accordingly let circle ABC be constructed again, around centre E with diameter AEC; apogee at A, perigee at C; and the sun at D. Now it has been shown that the greatest difference between regular and apparent movement occurs at the position which with respect to the apparent movement is midway between the apsides. For that reason let BD be erected perpendicular to AEC, and let it cut the circumference in point B, and let BE be joined. Therefore, since in right triangle BDE two sides have been given, namely BE which is the radius of the circle and DE the distance of the sun from the centre; the triangle will have its angles given. And angle DBE will be given, which is the difference between the angle BEA of regular movement and right angle EDB the angle of apparent movement.

But as DE is made greater or less, the whole species of the triangle changes. Thus, before Ptolemy
$$\text{angle } B = 2°23';$$
in the time of al-Battani and Arzachel
$$\text{angle } B = 1°59';$$
but at present
$$\text{angle } B = 1°51'.$$
And for Ptolemy
$$\text{arc } AB = 92°23',$$
which is intercepted by angle AEB, and
$$\text{arc } BC = 87°37'.$$
For al-Battani
$$\text{arc } AB = 91°59'$$
and
$$\text{arc } BC = 88°1'.$$
And at present
$$\text{arc } AB = 91°51'$$
and
$$\text{arc } BC = 88°9'.$$

Whence too the remaining differences are manifest. For let any other arc AB be taken, as in the following figure: and let angle AEB be given, and the interior angle BED, and the two sides BE and ED. By the calculus of plane triangles there will be given [89ᵃ] angle EBD, the additosubtraction, the difference between the regular and the apparent movement. And it is necessary for these differences to change on account of the change of side ED, as has already been said.

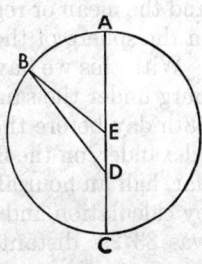

18. On the Examination of the Regular Movement in Longitude

These things have been set forth concerning the annual irregularity of the sun, but not by means of the simple difference so appearing but by means of the difference still mingled with that which the length of time has disclosed.

We shall distinguish them from one another later on. Meanwhile, the mean and regular movement of the centre of the Earth will be given in numbers which will be the more certain the more that movement is separated from any differences of irregularity and the more it extends in time. Now that will be established in this way.

We have taken that autumn equinox which was observed by Hipparchus at Alexandria in the 32nd year of the third period of Callippus—which, as was said above, was the 177th year after the death of Alexander—at midnight after the third intercalary day, which the fourth day followed. But according as Alexandria is approximately 1 hour to the east of Cracow in longitude, it was approximately 1 hour before midnight. Therefore according to the calculation handed on above the position of the autumn equinox in the sphere of the fixed stars was 176°10′ from the head of Aries and that was the apparent position of the sun. It was 114½° distant from the highest apsis.

In accordance with this model let there be traced around centre D the circle ABC which the centre of the Earth describes. Let ADC be the diameter; and let the sun be situated on the diameter at point E; the apogee in A; and the perigee in C. But let B be the point where the sun appears in the autumn equinox, and let the straight lines BD and BE be joined.

Since

$$\text{angle } DEB = 114\tfrac{1}{2}°,$$

and is seen to measure the distance of the sun from the apogee; and

$$\text{side } DE = 414,$$
$$\text{where } BD = 10,000;$$

therefore, by the fourth theorem on plane triangles, triangle BDE has its sides and angles given. And

$$\text{angle } BDE = \text{angle } BDA = \text{angle } BED = 2°10′.$$

[89ᵇ] But

$$\text{angle } BED = 114°30′.$$

Hence

$$\text{angle } BDA = 116°40′;$$

and the mean or regular position of the sun is 178°20′ from the head of the Ram in the sphere of the fixed stars.

With this we have compared the autumn equinox observed by us in Frauenburg under the same meridian of Cracow in the year of Our Lord 1515, on the 18th day before the Kalends of October, in the 1840th year since the death of Alexander, on the 6th day of Phaophi the second month by the Egyptian calendar, half an hour after sunrise. At this time the position of the autumn equinox by calculation and observation was 152°45′ in the sphere of the fixed stars and was 83°29′ distant from the highest apsis in accordance with the preceding demonstration.

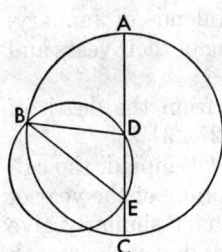

Now let

angle $BEA = 83°20'$

where 2 rt. angles = 180°;

and two sides of the triangle are given:

$BD = 10,000$

and

$DE = 323.$

By the fourth theorem on plane triangles

angle $DBE \doteq 1°50'.$

For, if a circle circumscribes triangle BDE, then, as on the circumference,

angle $BED = 166°40',$

where 2 rt. angles = 360°.

And

ch. $BD = 19,864$

where dmt. = 20,000.

And as

$BD : DE$ is given,

ch. $DE \doteq 640,$

and

$DE = $ ch. DBE

and, as on circumference,

angle $DBE = 1°50';$

but, as at centre,

angle $DBE = 3°40'.$

And this was the additosubtraction and difference between the regular and the apparent movement. And

angle $BDA = $ angle $DBE +$ angle $BED = 1°50' + 83°20' = 85°10',$

the distance of the regular movement from the apogee, and hence the mean position of the sun is 154°35' in the sphere of the fixed stars.

Therefore in the time between both observations there are 1662 Egyptian years 37 days 18 minutes [of a day] 45 seconds. And the mean and regular movement over and above the whole revolutions—of which there were 1660—is approximately 336°15', which is consonant with the number which we set out in the table of regular movements.

19. On Determining the Positions of the Regular Movement of the Sun at the Beginnings [of Years]

[90ᵃ] Accordingly in the flow of time between the death of Alexander the Great and the observation made by Hipparchus there were 176 years 362 days 27½ minutes, in which the mean movement was 312°43', according to calculation. When these degrees are subtracted from the sum of the 178°20' of Hipparchus' observation and from the 360° of the circle, there will remain, for noon of the first day of Thoth the first month of the Egyptians at the beginning of the years named after the death of Alexander, a position of 225°37' beneath the meridian of Cracow and of Frauenburg, the place of our observation.

From this to the beginning of the Roman years of Julius Caesar in 278 years 118½ days the mean movement is 46°27' over and above the complete revolutions. The addition of these degrees to the degrees of the position of Alexander gives 272°4′ as Caesar's position at midnight before the Kalends of January, from which the Romans are accustomed to take the beginning of their years and days.

Then in 45 years 12 days, or in 323 years 130½ days from the death of Alexander the Great, there arises the position of Christ at 272°31′.

And since Christ was born in the third year of the 194th Olympiad, the calculations which give 775 years and 12½ days from the beginning of the year of the first Olympiad to midnight before the Kalends of January similarly give 96°16′ as the position of the first Olympiad at noon of the first day of the month Hekatombaion, the anniversary of which day is now the Kalends of July according to the Roman calendar.

In this way the beginnings of the simple movement of the sun are determined with respect to the sphere of the fixed stars. Moreover, the positions of the composite movement are given by the addition of the precession of the equinoxes and similarly to the others: the Olympic position at 90°59′; the position of Alexander at 226°38′; that of Caesar at 276°59′; and that of Christ at 278°2′. All these things, as we said, are taken with respect to the Cracow meridian.

20. ON THE SECOND AND TWOFOLD IRREGULARITY WHICH OCCURS IN THE CASE OF THE SUN ON ACCOUNT OF THE CHANGE OF THE APSIDES

[90ᵇ] But there is now a greater difficulty in connexion with the inconstancy of the apsis of the sun, since, although Ptolemny thought it to be fixed, others have thought it to follow the movement of the starry sphere, according as they judged that the fixed stars moved too. Arzachel opined that this movement also was irregular, that is to say, as happening to retrograde—from the token that, although, as was said, al-Battani had found the apogee 7°44′ to the west of the solstice (for previously during the 740 years after Ptolemy it had progressed approximately 17°), it seemed to Arzachel 193 years later to have retrograded approximately 4½°. And accordingly he thought there was some other movement made by the centre of the annual orbital circle in a small circle, in accordance with which [movement] the apogee was deflected back and forth and the centre of the circle [of the year] was at unequal distances from the centre of the world. That was a good enough device, but it was not accordingly accepted, because upon a universal comparison it is not consonant with the rest; that is to say, if the succession in the order of movement is considered: namely, that at some time before Ptolemy the movement came to a standstill, that during 740 years or thereabouts it traversed 17°, that in the 200 years thereafter it retrograded 4° or 5°, that in the time remaining down to us it progressed, and that no other retrogradation was perceived during the total time, and no more standstills, though they necessarily intervene in the case of contrary movements back and forth. And this can by no means be understood as occurring in uniform and circular movement. Wherefore it is believed by many that some error had crept into their observations. But each mathematician is alike in his care and industry, so that it is doubtful which one we should follow in preference to the other. At all events, I confess that nowhere is there greater difficulty than in determining the apogee of the sun, where we ratiocinate with very small and hardly perceptible magnitudes, since in the neighbourhood of the perigee and apogee [a movement of] 1° effects only a variation of approximately 2′ in the additosubtraction, but in the neighbourhood of the mean apsides [a movement of] 1' effects 5° or 6° [in the additosubtraction]; and so a slight [91ª] error can propagate itself greatly. Hence in placing the apogee at 6⅔° of Cancer, we were not content to rely upon the instruments of the horoscope, unless the eclipses of the sun and moon gave us more certainty, since if any error lay concealed in our observations, the eclipses would uncover it without fail. Therefore, in accordance with most likelihood, we can apply our intelligence to conceiving the movement as a whole: it is eastward, but irregular, since after that standstill between Hipparchus and Ptolemy the apogee has appeared to be in continuous, orderly, and increased progression down to our time, with the exception of the movement which occurred erroneously—it is believed —between al-Battani and Arzachel, as all the rest seems to be in harmony. For it seems to follow from the same ratio of circular movement that the additosubtraction [of the movement] of the sun similarly does not stop decreasing and that corrections are made for these two irregularities in conjunction with the first and simple anomaly of the obliquity of the ecliptic or something similar.

But in order for this to become more clear, let the circle AB around centre C

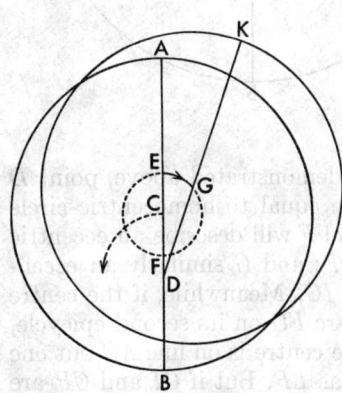

be in the plane of the ecliptic. And let the diameter be ACB, and on ACB let D be the globe of the sun as it were at the centre of the world; and let another quite small circle EF be described around centre C in such a way as not to comprehend the sun. And let it be understood that the centre of the annual revolution of the Earth moves around this small circle with a rather slow progress. And since the small circle EF together with line AD has a rather slow movement eastward and the centre of the annual revolution has a rather slow movement westward along circle EF, sometimes the centre of the annual orbital circle will be found at its greatest distance which is DE, and sometimes at its least which is DF, and with a slower movement at the greatest distance and a faster movement at the least. And along the middle curves the small circle makes the distance between the centres increase and decrease with time, and it makes the highest apsis alternately precede and follow the apsis or apogee which is on line ACD as if in the middle position. In this way, if arc EG is taken and with G as centre a circle equal to AB is described, the then highest apsis will be on line DGK and DG will be a shorter distance than DE, by Euclid, III, 8.

And these things are demonstrated by means of a circle eccentric to an eccentric circle as above; and by means of the epicycle [91ᵇ] on the epicycle as follows: Let circle AB be homocentric with the world and with the sun, and let ABC be the diameter, whereon the highest apsis is. And with A as centre let the epicycle DE be described; and again with D as centre, the epicycle FG, whereon the Earth revolves. And all in the same plane of the ecliptic. Let the movement of the first epicycle be eastward and approximately annual; and that of the second too, i.e., D, be similar but westward. And let both have proportionately equal revolutions with respect to line AC. Moreover, let the centre of the Earth moving westward from F add a little movement to D.

From this it is clear that
when the Earth is at F, it will
make the apogee of the sun to
be farthest away; and when at
G it will make the apogee to be
nearest; but in the mean arcs
of epicycle FG, it will make
the apogee precede or follow,
increased or decreased, greater or less; and hence it will
make the movement appear
irregular, as has been demonstrated before of the epicycle
and the eccentric circle.

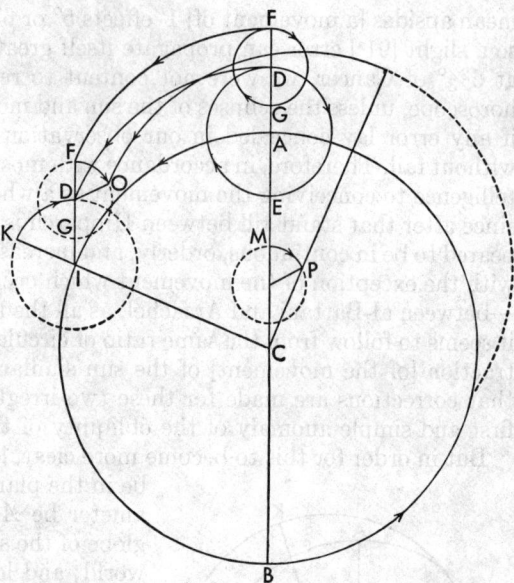

Now let arc AI be taken.
And with point I as centre let
the epicyclical epicycle be
taken again. And let CI be
joined and extended in the
straight line CIK.

angle KID = angle ACI
on account of the revolutions
being proportionately equal. Therefore, as we demonstrated above, point D
will describe around centre L an eccentric circle equal to homocentric circle
AB, and with an eccentricity CL equal to DI; and F will describe an eccentric
circle having an eccentricity CLM equal to IDF; and G similarly an eccentric circle having an eccentricity CN equal to IG. Meanwhile, if the centre
of the Earth has by now measured [92ª] any arc FO on its second epicycle,
point O will not describe an eccentric circle whose centre is on line AC but one
whose centre is on a line parallel [to DO], such as LP. But if OI and CP are
joined,

$$OI = CP,$$

but

$$OI < IF$$

and

$$CP < CM.$$

And

angle DIO = angle LCP,

by Euclid, I, 8. And that is the interval whereby the apogee of the sun on line
CP will be seen to precede A.

From this moreover it is clear that the same thing occurs through the eccentric circle having an epicycle, since with the eccentric circle alone pre-existing
which epicycle D describes around centre L, the centre of the Earth revolves
through arc FO in accordance with the aforesaid conditions, $i.e.$, [in a movement]
less than the annual revolution. For it will describe, as before, another circle
eccentric to the first, around centre P; and the same things will occur again.
And since so many ways lead to the same number, I could not really say which
one is right, except that the perpetual harmony of numbers and appearances
compels us to believe that it is some one of them.

21. How Great the Second Difference in the Irregularity of the Sun Is

Therefore, since it has already been seen that the second irregularity follows after that first first and simple anomaly of the obliquity of the ecliptic or its similitude, we shall have its fixed differences, if some error on the part of past observers does not stand in the way. For according to calculation we have a simple anomaly of approximately 165°39' for the year of Our Lord 1515, and also its beginning by a calculation backwards to approximately 64 years before the birth of Christ, from which time to us there has been a passage of 1580 years. Now the greatest eccentricity of that beginning has been found by us to be 414, whereof the radius is 10,000. But the eccentricity of our time, as was shown, is 323.

Now let AB be a straight line, and on it let B be the sun and centre of the world. Let AB be the greatest eccentricity and BD the least. Let a small circle be described whose diameter is AD, and let

arc $AC = 165°39'$,

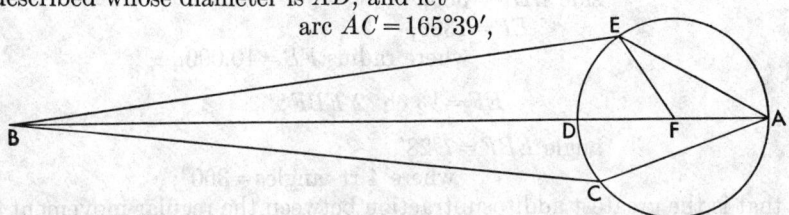

in proportion to the first simple anomaly. Since line AB has [92ᵇ] been found at the beginning of the simple anomaly, *i.e.*, at A, and

line $AB = 414$,

and now

line $BC = 323$,

therefore we shall now have triangle ABC with sides AB and BC given; and also one angle CAD given, because CD the remaining arc of the semicircle is given, *i.e.*,

arc $CD = 14°21'$.

Therefore, by what we have shown concerning plane triangles, there are given the remaining side AC and angle ABC, the difference between the mean and the irregular movement of the apogee; and inasmuch as line AC subtends the given arc, diameter AD of circle ACD will also be given. For since

angle $CAD = 14°21'$,
$CB = 2496$

where diameter of circle circumscribing

and since

triangle $= 20,000$,

$BC : AB$ is given,
$AB = 3225 =$ ch. $ACB =$ ch. $341°26'$.

Hence by subtraction

angle $CBD = 4°13'$,
where 2 rt. angles $= 360°$.

And

Therefore

ch. $CBD = AC = 735$.

$AC \doteq 95$,
where $AB = 414$.

And according as AC subtends the given arc, it will have a ratio to AD as to a diameter. Therefore

$$AD = 96,$$
$$\text{where } ADB = 414;$$

and, by subtraction,

$$DB = 321,$$

and that is the distance of the least eccentricity. But, as on the circumference

$$\text{angle } CBD = 4°13',$$

and as at the centre

$$\text{angle } CBD = 2°6\tfrac{1}{2}',$$

which is the additosubtraction to be subtracted from the regular movement of AB around centre B. Now let there be drawn the straight line BE touching the circle at point E; and with centre F taken, let EF be joined. Therefore, since in right triangle BEF,

$$\text{side } EF = 48,$$

and

$$\text{side } BDF = 369,$$
$$EF = 1300,$$
$$\text{where radius } FB = 10,000.$$

And

$$EF = \tfrac{1}{2} \text{ ch. } 2 \, EBF;$$

and

$$\text{angle } EBF = 7°28',$$
$$\text{where 4 rt. angles} = 360°;$$

and that is the greatest additosubtraction between the regular movement at F and the apparent at E.

Hence the remaining and particular differences can be discovered: for instance, if

$$\text{angle } AFE = 6°.$$

For we shall have the triangle with sides EF and FB and angle EFB given. Hence

$$\text{angle } EBF = 41',$$

which is the additosubtraction. [93ᵃ] But if

$$\text{angle } AFE = 12°,$$
$$\text{add.} = 1°23'.$$

And if

$$\text{angle } AFE = 18°,$$
$$\text{add.} = 2°3';$$

and so for the rest in this way, as was said above in the case of the additosubtractions for the annual revolution.

22. How the Regular Movement of the Apogee of the Sun and the Irregular Movement Are Unfolded

Therefore, since the time in which the greatest eccentricity coincided with the beginning of the first and simple anomaly was the third year of the 178th Olympiad but the 259th year of Alexander the Great by the Egyptian calendar, and on that account the simultaneously true and mean position of the apogee was at $5\tfrac{1}{2}°$ of Gemini, i.e., $65\tfrac{1}{2}°$ from the spring equinox; and since the precession of the equinoxes—the true at that time coinciding with the mean—was $4°38'$: the subtraction of $4°38'$ from $65\tfrac{1}{2}°$ leaves $60°52'$ from the head of Aries in the sphere of the fixed stars as the position of the apogee.

Again in the second year of the 573rd Olympiad and in the 1515th year of Our Lord, the position of the apogee was found at 6⅔° of Cancer. But by calculation the precession of the spring equinox was 27¼°; and the subtraction of 27¼° from 96°40′ leaves 69°25′. Now it was shown that with a first anomaly of 165°39′ existing at that time there was an additosubtraction of 2°7′, by which the true locus preceded the mean. Wherefore it was clear that the mean locus of the apogee of the sun was 71°32′.

Therefore during the middle 1580 Egyptian years the mean and regular movement of the apogee was 10°41′. And when we have divided that by the number of the years, we shall have an annual rate of 24″20‴14⁗.

23. On the Correction of the Anomaly of the Sun and the Determination of Its Prior Positions

[93ᵇ] If we subtract these 24″20‴14⁗ from the simple annual movement, which was 359°44′49″7‴4⁗, there will remain an annual regular movement of anomaly of 359°44′24″46‴50⁗. Again, the distribution of 359°44′24″46‴50⁗ through the 365 days will give a daily rate of 59′8″7‴22⁗ in accord with what was set out above in the tables. Hence we shall have the positions at the established beginnings of years—starting at the 1st Olympiad. For it was shown that on the 18th day before the Kalends of October in the second year of the 573rd Olympiad at half an hour after sunrise the mean apogee of the sun was at 71°32′, from which the sun had a distance of 82°58′. And from the first Olympiad there have been 2290 Egyptian years 281 days 46 minutes, during which the movement of anomaly—the whole cycles not being counted—was 42°33′. The subtraction of 42°33′ from 82°58′ leaves 40°25′ as the position of anomaly for the first Olympaid.

And similarly, as above, the position for the Alexander years is 166°38′; for the Caesar years, 211°11′; and for the years of Our Lord, 211°19′.

24. Table of the Differences Between Regular and Apparent Movement

But in order that those things which we have shown concerning the [additive and subtractive] differences between the regular and apparent movements of the sun may be better fitted up for use, we shall also set out a table of them, having sixty rows and six orders of columns.

For the two first columns of both semicircles—that is to say, of the ascending and the descending semicircles—will contain numbers increasing by 3°'s, as above in the case of the movements of the equinoxes.

In the third column will be inscribed the degrees of additosubtraction arising from the movement [94ᵃ] or anomaly of the solar apogee; and this additosubtraction ascends to the height of approximately 7½°, according as it fits each row of degrees.

The fourth place is given over to the proportional minutes, which go up to 60′; and they are reckoned according to the differences between the greater and the lesser additosubtractions arising from the simple anomaly. For since the greatest of these differences is 32′, the sixtieth part will be 32″. Therefore in accordance with the magnitude of the difference, which we derive from the eccentricity by the mode described above, we put down a number up to 60 to correspond to the single items in the column of the 3°'s.

In the fifth column the single additosubtractions arising from the annual and first anomaly are set up in accordance with the least distance of the sun from the centre.

In the sixth and final column, the differences between these additosubtractions and the additosubtractions which occur at greatest eccentricity.[1] The table is as follows:

TABLE OF THE ADDITIONS-AND-SUBTRACTIONS OF THE MOVEMENT OF THE SUN

Common Numbers		Additions-and-subtractions arising from movement of the centre		Proportional minutes	Additions-and-subtractions arising from eccentric or-bital circle or first epicycle		Differences	Common Numbers		Additions-and-subtractions arising from movement of the centre		Proportional minutes	Additions-and-subtractions arising from eccentric or-bital circle or first epicycle		Differences
Deg.	Deg.	Deg.	Min.		Deg.	Min.	Min.	Deg.	Deg.	Deg.	Min.		Deg.	Min.	Min.
3	357	0	21	60	0	6	1	93	267	7	24	30	1	50	32
6	354	0	41	60	0	11	3	96	264	7	24	29	1	50	33
9	351	1	2	60	0	17	4	99	261	7	24	27	1	50	32
12	348	1	23	60	0	22	6	102	258	7	23	26	1	49	32
15	345	1	44	60	0	27	7	105	255	7	21	24	1	48	31
18	342	2	3	59	0	33	9	108	252	7	18	23	1	47	31
21	339	2	24	59	0	38	11	111	249	7	13	21	1	45	31
24	336	2	44	59	0	43	13	114	246	7	6	20	1	43	30
27	333	3	4	58	0	48	14	117	243	6	58	18	1	40	30
30	330	3	23	57	0	53	16	120	240	6	49	16	1	38	29
33	327	3	41	57	0	58	17	123	237	6	37	15	1	35	28
36	324	4	0	56	1	3	18	126	234	6	25	14	1	32	27
39	321	4	18	55	1	7	20	129	231	6	14	12	1	29	25
42	318	4	35	54	1	12	21	132	228	6	0	11	1	25	24
45	315	4	51	53	1	16	22	135	225	5	44	10	1	21	23
48	312	5	6	51	1	20	23	138	222	5	28	9	1	17	22
51	309	5	20	50	1	24	24	141	219	5	19	7	1	12	21
54	306	5	34	49	1	28	25	144	216	4	51	6	1	7	20
57	303	5	47	47	1	31	27	147	213	4	30	5	1	3	18
60	300	6	3	46	1	34	28	150	210	4	9	4	0	58	17
63	297	6	12	44	1	37	29	153	207	3	46	3	0	53	14
66	294	6	27	42	1	39	29	156	204	3	23	3	0	47	13
69	291	6	33	41	1	42	30	159	201	3	1	2	0	42	12
72	288	6	42	40	1	44	30	162	198	2	37	1	0	36	10
75	285	6	51	39	1	46	30	165	195	2	12	1	0	30	9
78	282	6	58	38	1	48	31	168	192	1	47	1	0	24	7
81	279	7	5	36	1	49	31	171	189	1	21	0	0	18	5
84	276	7	11	35	1	49	31	174	186	0	54	0	0	12	4
87	273	7	16	33	1	50	31	177	183	0	27	0	0	6	2
90	270	7	21	32	1	51	32	180	180	0	0	0	0	0	0

[1]The movements on the homocentric circle, on the first epicycle, and on the second epicycle are proportionately equal. Hence, from the first two columns of the table are to be taken the movement on the second epicycle, or arc KJ; and from the third column, the additosubtraction to be applied to the annual anomaly or movement of the first epicycle;

25. On the Calculation of the Apparent Movement of the Sun

[95^b] From that, I think, it is now sufficiently clear how the apparent position of the sun is calculated for any given time. For we must seek the true position of the spring equinox for that time or its precession together with its first and simple anomaly, as we have set forth above, and then the mean simple movement of the centre of the Earth—or you may call it the movement of the sun—and the annual anomaly, by means of the tables of regular movements; and they are added to their established beginnings. Accordingly you will take the number of the first simple anomaly found in the first or second column of the preceding table; and in the third column[1] you will find the corresponding additosubtraction for correcting the annual anomaly, and in the following column the proportional minutes; save the proportional minutes. Now add the additosubtraction to the annual anomaly, if the first [and simple anomaly]—or its number contained in the first column—is less than a semicircle; otherwise subtract. For the remainder or aggregate will be the corrected anomaly of the sun; now by means of this take the additosubtraction arising from the annual [eccentric] orbital circle [or first epicycle]—which is found in the fifth column—and the difference in the following column. If this difference, when adjusted to the proportional minutes you have saved, amounts to something, it is always added to this additosubtraction, and the additosubtraction thus becomes corrected and is subtracted from the mean position of the sun, if the number of the annual anomaly is found in the first column or is less than a semicircle, but it is added, if the annual anomaly is greater or is found in one of the other columns of numbers. For that which in this way becomes the remainder or aggregate will determine the true position of the sun as measured from the head of the constellation of Aries, and if finally the true precession of the spring equinox is added to this [position of the sun], it will straightway show the distance of the sun from the equinox in degrees of the ecliptic among the twelve signs.

But if you wish to do that in another way, take the regular composite movement instead of the simple, and do the other things we spoke of, except that instead of the precession of the equinox, you add or subtract merely its additosubtraction, as the case demands. And so the rational explanation of the appearance of the sun by means of the mobility of the Earth is consonant with ancient and modern findings; and it is all the more [96^a] presumed to hold for the future.

[1] *i.e.*, since the movements on the first epicycle and on the second epicycle are proportionately equal to one another.

---

this additosubtraction, angle *KFJ*, corrects the mean anomaly from *H* to *I*. (Proportional minutes corresponding to arc *KJ* are to be saved.) Then from the fifth column is to be taken the additosubtraction *GEI*, corresponding to angle *GFI*. But since the true position of the sun is not at *I* but at *J*, the additosubtraction must be corrected for the difference between angle *FEI* and angle *FIJ*. The proportional minutes which have been saved enable one to adjust the final difference, angle *IEJ*, according as chord *FJ* varies in length between *FL* and *FK*: that is to say, the change in eccentricity according to the movement around circle *CO* may be considered as it were a variation in the length of the radius of the corrected epicycle *HK*.

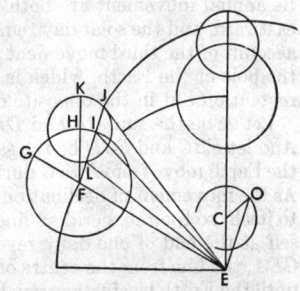

But furthermore, we are not ignorant of the fact that, if anyone thought that the centre of the annual revolutions were fixed as the centre of the world but that the sun moved in accordance with two movements similar and equal to those which we demonstrated in the case of the centre of the eccentric circle, everything will be manifest which was manifest before—the same numbers and the same demonstrations—since nothing else is changed in them except their situation, especially those which have to do with the sun. For then the movement of the centre of the Earth round the centre of the world would be absolute and simple, as the other two movements would be attributed to the sun itself. And on that account there will still remain some doubt as to which of these centres is the centre of the world, as we said ambiguously in the beginning that the centre of the world was at the sun or around the sun. But we shall say more about this question in our explanation of the five wandering stars; and we shall decide the issue to the extent that we are able, holding it enough, if we apply to the apparent movement of the sun calculations which have certitude and are not misleading.

26. On the Ntxөhmepon, i.e., the Difference of the Natural Day

In connection with the sun there still remains some thing to be said about the inequality of the natural day. This time is comprehended by the space of twenty-four hours, which up to now we have used as the common and certain measure of the celestial movements. But some, like the Chaldees and the ancient Jews, define such a day as the time between two sunrises; others, like the Athenians, as that between two sunsets; or like the Romans, from midnight to midnight; or like the Egyptians, from noon to noon. Now it is clear that during this time the revolution proper to the terrestrial globe is completed together with that which is added by the annual revolution in accordance with the apparent movement of the sun[1]. The apparent irregular course of the sun in especial shows that this addition is unequal, as does the fact that the natural day takes place with respect to the poles of the equator, but the year with respect to the ecliptic. Wherefore that apparent time cannot be the common and certain measure of movement, since day does not accord with day in every respect; and so it was necessary to choose among them some mean and equal day, by which it would be possible [96ᵇ] to measure regularity of movement without trouble. Therefore since in the circle of the total year there are 365 revolutions around the poles

---

[1]In Ptolemy the daily revolution and the annual movement were in opposite directions, and thus the solar day was slightly longer than the sidereal day. Here the daily revolution of the Earth and its annual movement are both of them in the same direction, i.e., eastward, and the solar day remains longer than the sidereal day on account of the third movement of the Earth, i.e., the declination of the pole of the Earth, which is approximately equal to the annual revolution but in the opposite direction.

Let A be the sun, CF and DEF the Earth with centre B and G. And let FBC and FGD be the same meridian line. Let the centre of the Earth move from B to G during the space of 24 equatorial hours. As the movement of declination keeps the axis of the Earth parallel to itself, so too the meridian line FBC or FGD will be parallel to itself at the end of one daily revolution, but it will not be one with GEA, the line from the centre of the Earth to the centre of the sun, until the Earth has further revolved through arc DE. That is to say, the solar day is equal to the 360° of sidereal day DEFD plus arc DE.

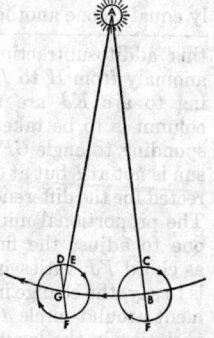

of the Earth, to which there accretes approximately one whole supernumerary revolution on account of the daily addition made by the apparent progress of the sun: consequently one 365th part of that would fill out the natural day upon an equal basis.

Wherefore we must define and separate the equal day from the apparent and irregular. Accordingly we call that the equal day which comprehends the whole revolution of the equator and over and above that the portion which the sun is seen to traverse with regular movement during that time; but the unequal and apparent day that which comprehends the 360 "times"[1] of one revolution of the equator and in addition that which ascends in the horizon or meridian together with the apparent progress of the sun. Although the difference between these days is very slight and not immediately perceptible, nevertheless it becomes evident after the passage of a certain number of days.

There are two causes for this: the irregularity of the apparent movement of the sun and the unequal ascension of the oblique ecliptic. The first cause, which exists by reason of the irregular apparent movement of the sun, has already been explained, since in the case of the semicircle in which the highest apsis holds the midpoint there is a deficiency of $4\frac{3}{4}$ "times" with respect to the ecliptic, according to Ptolemy, and in the case of the other semicircle, in which the lowest apsis is, there is a similar excess of the same amount. Accordingly the total excess of one semicircle over the other was $9\frac{1}{2}$ "times."

But in the case of the other cause—which has to do with the rising and setting —the greatest difference occurs between the semicircles comprehending each solstice. This is the difference which exists between the shortest and the longest day and which is most variable, as being particular to each region. The difference which is measured from noon or midnight is comprehended by four termini everywhere, since from 16° of Taurus to 14° of Leo, 88° [of the ecliptic] cross the meridian together with approximately 93 "times"; and from 14° of Leo to 16° of Scorpio, 92° [of the ecliptic] and 87 "times" pass over the meridian, so that in the latter case there is a deficiency of 5 "times" and in the former case an excess of 5 "times." And so the sum of the days in the first segment exceeds those in the second by ten "times"—which make two thirds of one hour; and the same thing takes place conversely in the other semicircle within the remaining termini set diametrically opposite to these. Now the mathematicians chose [97ª] to take the natural day from noon or midnight rather than from sunrise or sunset. For the difference which is taken from the horizon is more manifold; for it extends to a certain number of hours, and moreover it is not everywhere the same but varies manifoldly according to the obliquity of the sphere. But the one which pertains to the meridian is everywhere the same and is more simple. Therefore the total difference, which is constituted by the aforesaid causes: the apparent irregular progress of the sun and the irregular passage over the meridian, in the time before Ptolemy, took its beginning of decrease at the midpoint of Aquarius and, increasing from the beginning of Scorpio, added up to $8\frac{1}{3}$ "times"; and now decreasing from 20° of Aquarius or thereabouts to 10° of Scorpio and increasing from 10° of Scorpio to 20° of Aquarius, it has contracted to 7 "times" 48'. For these things too are changed on account of the inconstancy of the perigee and the eccentricity with the passage of time. Finally, moreover, if the greatest difference in the precession of the equinoxes is taken

---

[1]The unit parts of the equator are called "times" instead of degrees.

into account, the total difference of the natural days can extend itself to above 10 "times" for a period of years. In this the third cause of the inequality of days was hidden up to now, because the revolution of the equator was found regular in respect to the mean and regular equinox but not in respect to the apparent equinoxes, which—as is clear enough—are not wholly regular. Therefore the doubling of the 10 "times" makes $1\frac{1}{3}$ hours, by which sometimes the longer days can exceed the shorter.

These things can perhaps be neglected this side of manifest error in connexion with the annual progress of the sun and rather slow movement of the fixed stars; but on account of the speed of the moon—by reason of which an inexactitude of $\frac{5}{6}°$ in the movement of the sun can cause error—they are by no means to be neglected. Accordingly, the method of reducing the irregular and apparent time —wherein all differences agree—to the equal time, is as follows.

For any period of time proposed there must be sought in each limit of the time—I mean in the beginning and the end—the mean position of the sun with respect to the mean equinox according to its regular movement which we called composite, and also the true apparent position with respect to the true equinox; and we must consider how many "times" the right ascensions [97^b] at midday or midnight have amounted to, or how many "times" intervened between the first true position and the second true position. For if they are equal to the degrees between the two mean positions, then the apparent time assumed will be equal to the mean time. But if the "times" exceed, the excess should be added to the given time; and if they are deficient, the deficiency should be subtracted from the apparent time. For if we take the sums and remainders, we shall have the time reduced to equality by taking for one "time" four minutes of an hour or ten seconds of a minute of a day. But if the equal time is given, and you want to know how much apparent time corresponds to it, you will do the contrary.

Now for the first Olympiad we have the mean position of the sun at 90°59′ in relation to the mean spring equinox, on noon of the first day of Hekatombaion, the first month by the Athenian calendar, and at 0°36′ of Cancer in relation to the apparent equinox. But for the years of Our Lord we have the mean movement of the sun at 8°2′ of Capricorn and the true movement at 8°48′ of the same. Therefore 178 "times" 54′ ascend in the right sphere from 0°36′ of Cancer to 8°48′ of Capricorn, and they exceed the distance of the mean positions by 1 "times" 51′, which make 7 minutes of an hour. And so for the rest, by means of which the course of the moon can be examined most accurately: we shall speak of that in the following book.

BOOK FOUR

[98ª] Since in the preceding book, to the extent that our mediocrity was able, we explained the appearances due to the movement of the Earth around the sun, and we proposed by that same means to determine the movements of all the planets; the circular movement of the moon interrupts us now and does so of necessity because through her in particular, who shares in both night and day, the positions of the stars are apprehended and examined; then, because she alone of all the planets refers her revolutions however irregular directly to the centre of the earth and is most closely akin to the earth. And on that account, in so far as she is considered in herself, she does not indicate anything about the mobility of the Earth—except perhaps in the case of the daily movement; and for that reason the ancients believed that the Earth was the centre of the world and the centre common to all revolutions. In our explanation of the circular movement of the moon we do not differ from the ancients as regards the opinion that it takes place around the Earth. But we shall bring forward certain things which are different from what we received from our elders and are more consonant; by means of them we shall try to set up the movement of the moon with more certitude, in so far as that is possible.

1. THE HYPOTHESES OF THE CIRCLES OF THE MOON ACCORDING TO THE OPINION OF THE ANCIENTS

Accordingly the movement of the moon has the following property: it does not follow the ecliptic but follows an incline proper to itself, which bisects the ecliptic and is in turn bisected by it, and from this line of intersection the moon crosses over into both latitudes. These facts are as firmly established as the solstices in the annual movement of the sun. As the year belongs to the sun, so the month belongs to the moon. Now the middle positions at the sections are called [by some] ecliptic; by others, nodes—and the conjunctions and oppositions of the sun and moon occurring at those positions are called ecliptic. [98ᵇ] For there are not any other points common to both circles except these in which the eclipses of the sun and moon can take place. For in other places the divagation of the moon keeps the sun and moon from opposing one another with their lights; but, as they pass by, they do not block one another. Moreover, the orbital circle of the moon with its four "hinges" or cardinal points revolves obliquely around the centre of the Earth in a regular movement of approximately 3′ per day, and it completes its revolution in 19 years. Accordingly the moon is perceived always to move eastward in this orbital circle and in its plane, but sometimes with least velocity and at other times with greatest velocity. For it is slower, the higher up it is; and faster, the nearer to Earth; and this fact can be apprehended more easily in the case of the moon than in that of any other planet on account of the nearness of the moon.

Accordingly the ancients understood that change in velocity to occur on account of an epicycle; in running around this epicycle the moon, when in the

675

upper semicircle, subtracts from the regular movement, but when in the lower semicircle, it adds the same amount to it. Besides, it has been demonstrated that those things which take place through an epicycle can take place through an eccentric circle. But the ancients chose the epicycle because the moon seemed to admit to a twofold irregularity. For when it was at the highest or the lowest apsis of the epicycle, there was no apparent difference from regular movement. But around the point of contact of the epicycle and the greater circle there was a variable difference, for the difference was far greater when the half moon was waxing or waning than when there was a full moon; and this in a fixed and orderly succession. Wherefore they thought that the circle in which the epicycle moved was not homocentric with the Earth; but that there was an eccentric circle carrying an epicycle in which the moon was moved in accordance with the law that in all mean oppositions and conjunctions of the sun and moon the epicycle should be at the apogee of the eccentric circle but in the mean quadrants of the [synodic] circle[1] at the perigee of the eccentric circle. Therefore they imagined two equal and mutually opposing movements around the centre of the Earth—namely, that of the epicycle eastward and that of the centre of the eccentric circle and its apsides westward, with the line of the mean position of the sun always half-way between them. And in this way the epicycle traverses the eccentric circle twice a month.

And in order that these things may be brought before our eyes, let ABCD be the oblique lunar circle homocentric with the Earth. Let it be quadrisected by the diameters AEC and BED; and let E be the centre of the Earth. Now on line AC there will be the mean conjunction of the sun and moon and at the same position and time the apogee of the eccentric circle—whose centre is F—and the centre [99a] of the epicycle MN. Now let the apogee of the eccentric circle be moved as far westward as the epicycle eastward, and let them both move regularly around E in regular and monthly revolutions as measured by the mean conjunctions or oppositions of the sun. And let line AEC of the mean position of the sun be always half way between them; and furthermore let the moon move westward from the apogee of the epicycle. For astrono-

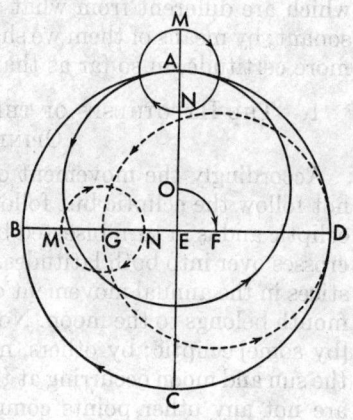

mers think that the appearances agree with this set-up. For since the epicycle in the time of half a month moves the distance of a semicircle away from the sun but completes a full revolution from the apogee of the eccentric circle; as a consequence, at the midpoint of this time—when the moon is half full— the moon and the apogee are in opposition to one another along diameter BD; and the epicycle is at the perigee of the eccentric circle, as at point G where —having become nearer to the Earth—it makes greater differences of irregularity. For when equal magnitudes are set out at unequal intervals, the one which is nearer to the eye appears the greater. Accordingly the differences will be least when the epicycle is at A, but greatest when it is at G, since the diam-

[1]The synodic circle is the lunar cycle of revolution with respect to the sun.

eter MN of the epicycle will be to line AE in its least ratio but will be to GE in a greater ratio than to all the other lines which are found in the rest of the positions, since GE is the shortest line and AE or its equal DE the longest of all those lines which can be extended from the centre of the Earth to the eccentric circle.

2. On the Inadequacy of Those Assumptions

Our predecessors assumed that such a composition of circles was consonant with lunar appearances. But if we consider the thing itself rather carefully, we shall not find this hypothesis very fitting or adequate, as we can prove by reason and sense. For while they admit that the movement of the centre of the epicycle is regular around the centre of the Earth, they must also admit that the movement is irregular on its own eccentric circle which it describes. If—for example—it is

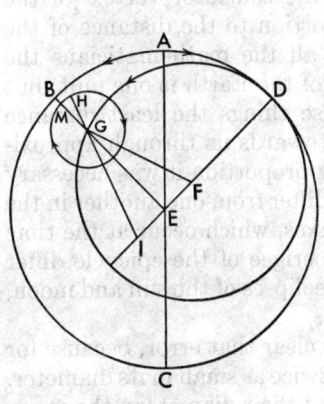

assumed that

angle AEB = angle AED = 45°,

so that by addition

angle BED = 90°;

and if the centre of the epicycle is taken in G [99^{b}] and GF is joined; it is clear that

angle GFD > angle GEF,

the exterior than the interior and opposite angle. Wherefore the dissimilar arcs DAB and DG are both described during one period of time, so that when

arc DAB = 90°;

arc DG > 90°,

and arc DG has been described by the centre of the epicycle during this same time. But it is clear at half moon

arc DAB = arc DG = 180°:

therefore the movement of the epicycle on the eccentric circle which it describes is not regular.

But if this is so, what shall we reply to the axiom: *The movement of the heavenly bodies is regular except for seeming irregular with respect to appearances*; if the apparent regular movement of the epicycle is really irregular and takes place utterly contrary to the principle set up and assumed? But if you say that the epicycle moves regularly around the centre of the Earth and that that takes care sufficiently of the regularity, then what sort of regularity will that be which occurs in a circle foreign to the epicycle, in which its movement does not exist, and not in its own eccentric circle?

We also are amazed at the fact that they mean the regularity of the moon in its epicycle to be understood not in relation to the centre of the Earth, namely, in respect to line EGM, to which the regularity having to do with the centre of the epicycle should rightly be referred, but in relation to some other different point, which has the Earth midway between it and the centre of the eccentric circle, and that line IGH is, as it were, the index of the regularity of the moon in the epicycle. And that shows well enough that this movement is really irregular. For the appearances which in part follow upon this hypothesis force this admission. And now that the moon traverses its own epicycle irregularly, we may mark what the line of reasoning would be like if we should try to con-firm the irregularity of apparent movement by means of real irregularities. For what else shall we be doing except giving a hold to those who detract from this art?

Furthermore, experience and sense-perception teach us that the parallaxes of the moon are not consonant with those which the ratio of the circles promises. For the parallaxes, which are called commutations, take place on account of the magnitude of the Earth being evident in the neighbourhood of the moon. For since the straight lines which are extended from the centre of the Earth and its surface do not appear parallel but [100ª] in accord with a manifest inclination cut one another in the body of the moon, they are necessarily able to make for irregularity in the apparent movement of the moon, so that the moon is seen in a different position by those viewing it obliquely along the convexity of the Earth and by those who behold the moon from the centre or vertex [of the Earth]. Accordingly such parallaxes vary in proportion to the distance of the moon from the Earth. For by the consensus of all the mathematicians the greatest distance is 64⅙ units whereof the radius of the Earth is one unit; but in accordance with the commensurability of these things the least distance should be 33ᵖ33', so that the moon would move towards us through approxi-mately half the total distance—and by the ensuing proportion it was necessary for the parallaxes at greatest and least distance to differ from one another in the ratio of the squares.[1] But we see that those parallaxes, which occur at the time of the half moon waxing or waning, even in the perigee of the epicycle differ slightly or not at all from those which occur at the eclipses of the sun and moon, as we shall show satisfactorily in the proper place.

But the body itself of the moon makes perfectly clear that error, because for the same reason it would appear twice as large and twice as small in its diameter. But just as circles are in the ratio of the squares[1] of their diameters, the moon should seem almost four times greater in its quadratures when nearest the earth than when opposite the sun, if it were a full moon shining; but since a half moon is shining, nevertheless it should shine with twice the area of light as a full moon there—although the contrary of this is self-evident. If someone who is not content with simple sight wishes to make an experiment with the dioptra of Hipparchus or some other instruments by which the diameter of the moon may be determined, he will find that the diameter does not vary except in so far as the epicycle without the eccentric circle demands. For that reason Menelaus and Timochares in investigating the fixed stars by means of the positions of the moon did not hesitate to use the same lunar diameter always as ½°, which the moon was seen to occupy most of the time.

3. Another Theory of the Movement of the Moon

In this way it is perfectly clear that it is not an eccentricity which makes the epicycle appear greater and smaller, but some other relation of circles. [100b] For let AB be the epicycle which we shall call first and greater; and let C be its centre. Let D be the centre of the Earth, and from D let the straight line DC be extended to the highest apsis of the epicycle; and with A as centre let another small epicycle EF also be described—and all this in the same plane of

[1]Literally, in duplicate ratio.

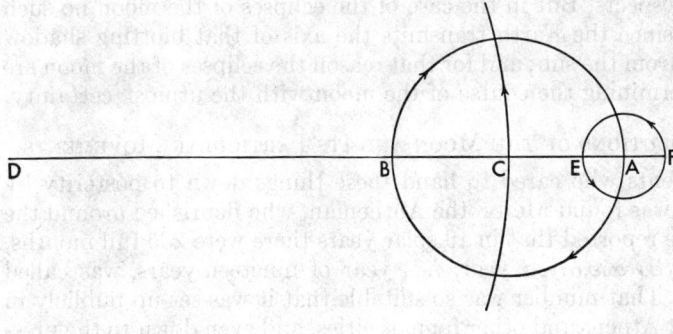

the oblique circle of the moon. Now let C be moved eastward but A westward; and again let the moon be moved eastward from F the upper part of EF. And let such an order be kept that when line DE is one with line of the mean position of the sun, the moon is always nearest to centre C, *i.e.*, is in point E, but in the quadratures is farthest away at F. I say that the lunar appearances agree with this set-up.

For it follows that twice a month the moon runs around epicycle EF, during which time C makes one revolution with respect to the mean position of the sun. And the new and the full moon will be seen to cause the least circle, namely, that whereof the radius is CE; but the moon in its quadratures will cause the greatest circle with radius CF; and thus again in the conjunctions and oppositions it will make lesser differences between the regular and the apparent movement, but in the quadratures greater differences by means of similar but unequal arcs around centre E. And since the centre of the epicycle is always in a circle homocentric with the Earth, it will not exhibit such diverse parallaxes but parallaxes in conformity with the epicycle. And the reason will be evident why the body of the moon is seen somehow similar to itself; and all the other things which are perceived in the movement of the moon will come about in this way.

We shall demonstrate them successively by means of our hypothesis, although the same things can take place through eccentric circles, as in the case of the sun—the due proportion being kept. Now we shall take our start from the regular movements, as we did above, without which the irregular movement cannot be separated out. But here there is no small difficulty on account of the parallaxes, which we mentioned; and for that reason the position [of the moon] is not observable by means of astrolabes and other such instruments. But the kindness of nature makes provision for human longing even in this respect, so that the position [of the moon] is more surely determinable through its eclipses than by means of instruments and without any suspicion of error. [101ᵃ] For since the other parts of the world are pure and are filled with the light of day, it stands to reason that night is nothing except the shadow of the Earth, which has the figure of a cone and ends in a point. Falling upon this cone, the moon is dimmed; add, when placed at the midpoint of its darkness, is understood to have arrived without any doubt at the position opposite the sun. But the eclipses of the sun, which take place when the moon moves in front of it, do not offer such a certain determination of the position of the moon. For it happens that the conjunction of the sun and moon is seen by us at some given time, although in relation to the centre of the Earth the conjunction has passed or has not yet taken place, because of the aforesaid parrallax. And accordingly in different parts of the Earth we view the same eclipse of the sun as unequal in magnitude and duration and

not similar in all respects. But in the case of the eclipses of the moon no such
hindrance occurs, since the Earth transmits the axis of that blotting shadow
through its centre from the sun; and for that reason the eclipses of the moon are
best fitted for determining the course of the moon with the utmost certainty.

4. On the Revolutions of the Moon and Its Particular Movements

Among the ancients who cared to hand these things down to posterity by
means of numbers was found Meton the Anthenian, who flourished around the
37th Olympiad. He reported that in 19 solar years there were 235 full months,
whence that great ἐννεαδεκάτερις year, *i.e.*, year of nineteen years, was called
the Metontic year. That number was so suitable that it was set up publicly in
the market place at Athens and other famous cities, and even down to the present it has remained in common use, because they think that through it the beginnings and ends of the months are established in a sure order and that through
it also the solar year of 365¼ days is commensurable with the months. Hence
the Callippic period of 76 years, in which there is an intercalation of 19 days
and which they call the Callippic year.

But Hipparchus discovered through careful study that in 304 years there was
an excess of a total day, and that [the Callippic year] was verifiable only when
the solar year was 1/300 of a day smaller. And so by some men that year was
called the great year of Hipparchus, [101ᵇ] in which there were 3760 full months.
These years are called more simply and crassly, so to speak, Minerva's, when
the recurrences of anomaly and of latitude are also sought, for the sake of which
that same Hipparchus was making further investigations. For by comparing the
readings which he took in making careful observation of the lunar eclipses with
those which he had got from the Chaldees, he determined the time in which the
revolutions of the months and of the anomaly recurred simultaneously to be 345
Egyptian years 82 days and 1 hour; and during that time there were 4267 full
months and 4573 cycles of anomaly. Therefore when the number of months has
been reduced to days and there are 126,007 days 1 hour, one month is found
equal to 29 days 31 minutes 50 seconds 8 thirds 9 fourths 20 fifths. According to
that ratio the movement during any time is manifest. For the division of the 360°
of revolution of one month by the number of days in a month produces a daily
movement of the moon in relation to the sum of 12°11′26″41‴20⁗18‴‴. The
multiplication of that by 365 makes—in addition to the 12 revolutions—an
annual movement of 129°37′21″28‴29⁗.

Furthermore, since the 4267 months and 4573 cycles of anomaly are given in
numbers which are composite with respect to one another, that is, as being
numbered by the common measure of 17, the ratio of 4267 months to 4573 cycles of anomaly will in least terms be the ratio of 251 to 269; and by Euclid, x,
15, we shall have the proportion of the revolution of the moon to the movement
of anomaly in that ratio. Accordingly, when we have multiplied the [annual]
movement of the moon by 269 and divided the product by 251, the quotient
will be annual movement of anomaly of 13 full revolutions and 88°43′8″40‴-
20⁗, and hence a daily movement of 13°3′53″56‴29⁗.

But the revolution in latitude has another ratio. For it does not agree with
the prescribed time in which the anomaly has recurred; but we understand that
the latitude of the moon has returned only at that time when a later eclipse of
the moon is in every respect similar and equal to an earlier, so that both obscura-

tions are in the same part of the moon and are equal, *i.e.*, in magnitude and duration. And this happens when the distances of the moon from the highest or the lowest apsis are equal. For then the moon is understood to have traversed equal shadows in equal time. [102ᵃ] Now according to Hipparchus such a returning occurs once in 5458 months, to which there correspond 5923 revolutions of latitude. And by that ratio the particular movements of latitude in years and days will be established, as in the case of the others. For when we have multiplied the movement of the moon away from the sun by 5923 months and divided the product by 5458, we shall have an annual movement of the moon in latitude of 13 revolutions 148°42′46″49‴3⁗ and a daily movement of 13°13′45″39‴-40⁗.

Hipparchus gave this as the rate of the regular movements of the moon, and no one before him had made a closer approximation. Nevertheless the succeeding ages did not show these movements absolved by all the same numbers. For Ptolemy found the same mean movement away from the sun as did Hipparchus, but an annual movement of anomaly deficient with respect to the former in 1″11‴39⁗ and an annual movement of latitude with an excess of 53‴41⁗. But now after the passage of many ages since Hipparchus we also found a mean annual movement deficient in 1″2‴49⁗ and a movement of anomaly deficient in only 24‴49⁗. Moreover, there is an excess of 1″1‴44⁗ in the movement in latitude. And so the regular movement of the moon, whereby it differs from the terrestrial movement, will be an annual movement of 129°37′22″32‴40⁗, a movement of anomaly of 88°43′9″5‴9⁗ and a movement in latitude of 148°-42′45″17‴21⁗.

MOVEMENT OF THE MOON IN YEARS AND PERIODS OF SIXTY YEARS

Egyptian Years	Movement					Egyptian Years	Movement				
	60°	°	'	"	'''		60°	°	'	"	'''
1	2	9	37	22	36	31	0	58	18	40	48
2	4	19	14	45	12	32	3	7	56	3	25
3	0	28	52	7	49	33	5	17	33	26	1
4	2	38	29	30	25	34	1	27	10	48	38
5	4	48	6	53	2	35	3	36	48	11	14
6	0	57	44	15	38	36	5	46	25	33	51
7	3	7	21	38	14	37	1	56	2	56	27
8	5	16	59	0	51	38	4	5	40	19	3
9	0	26	36	23	27	39	0	15	17	41	40
10	3	36	13	46	4	40	2	24	55	4	16
11	5	45	31	8	40	41	4	34	32	26	53
12	1	55	28	31	17	42	0	44	9	49	29
13	4	5	5	53	53	43	2	53	47	12	5
14	0	14	43	16	29	44	5	3	24	34	42
15	2	24	20	39	6	45	1	13	1	57	18
16	4	33	58	1	42	46	3	22	39	19	55
17	0	43	35	24	19	47	5	32	16	42	31
18	2	53	12	46	55	48	1	41	54	5	8
19	5	2	50	9	31	49	3	51	31	27	44
20	1	12	27	32	8	50	0	1	8	50	20
21	3	22	4	54	44	51	2	10	46	12	57
22	5	31	42	17	21	52	4	20	23	35	33
23	1	41	19	39	57	53	0	30	0	58	10
24	3	50	57	2	34	54	2	39	38	20	46
25	0	0	34	25	10	55	4	49	15	43	22
26	2	10	11	47	46	56	0	58	53	5	59
27	4	19	49	10	23	57	3	8	30	28	35
28	0	29	26	32	59	58	5	18	7	51	12
29	2	39	3	55	36	59	1	27	45	13	48
30	4	40	41	18	12	60	3	37	22	36	25

Position at the Birth of Christ—209° 58'

MOVEMENT OF THE MOON IN DAYS AND PERIODS OF SIXTY DAYS

Days	Movement					Days	Movement				
	60°	°	'	"	'''		60°	°	'	"	'''
1	0	12	11	26	41	31	6	17	54	47	26
2	0	24	22	53	23	32	6	30	6	14	8
3	0	36	34	20	4	33	6	42	17	40	49
4	0	48	45	46	46	34	6	54	29	7	31
5	1	0	57	13	27	35	7	6	40	34	12
6	1	13	8	40	9	36	7	18	52	0	54
7	1	25	20	6	50	37	7	31	3	27	35
8	1	37	31	33	32	38	7	43	14	54	17
9	1	49	43	0	13	39	7	55	26	20	58
10	2	1	54	26	55	40	8	7	37	47	40
11	2	14	5	53	36	41	8	19	49	14	21
12	2	26	17	20	18	42	8	32	0	41	3
13	2	38	28	47	0	43	8	44	12	7	44
14	2	50	40	13	41	44	8	56	23	34	26
15	3	2	51	40	22	45	9	8	35	1	7
16	3	15	3	7	4	46	9	20	46	27	49
17	3	27	14	33	45	47	9	32	57	54	30
18	3	39	26	0	27	48	9	45	9	21	12
19	3	51	37	27	8	49	9	57	20	47	53
20	4	3	48	53	50	50	10	9	32	14	35
21	4	16	0	20	31	51	10	21	43	41	16
22	4	28	11	47	13	52	10	33	55	7	58
23	4	40	23	13	54	53	10	46	6	34	40
24	4	52	34	40	36	54	10	58	18	1	21
25	5	4	46	7	17	55	11	10	29	28	2
26	5	16	57	33	59	56	11	22	40	54	43
27	5	29	9	0	40	57	11	34	52	21	25
28	5	41	20	27	22	58	11	47	3	48	7
29	5	53	31	54	3	59	11	59	15	14	48
30	6	5	43	20	45	60	12	11	26	41	31

Position at the Birth of Christ—209° 58'

MOVEMENT OF ANOMALY OF THE MOON IN YEARS AND PERIODS OF SIXTY YEARS

Egyptian Years	60°	°	Movement '	"	'''		Egyptian Years	60°	°	Movement '	"	'''
1	1	28	43	9	7		31	3	50	17	42	44
2	2	57	26	18	14		32	5	19	0	51	52
3	4	26	9	27	21		33	0	47	43	0	59
4	5	54	52	36	29		34	2	16	27	10	6
5	1	23	35	45	36		35	3	45	10	19	13
6	2	52	18	54	43		36	5	13	53	28	21
7	4	21	2	3	59		37	0	42	36	37	28
8	5	49	45	12	58		38	2	11	19	46	35
9	1	18	28	22	5		39	3	40	2	55	42
10	2	47	11	31	12		40	5	8	46	4	50
11	4	15	54	40	19		41	0	37	29	13	57
12	5	44	37	49	27		42	2	6	12	23	4
13	1	13	20	58	34		43	3	34	55	32	11
14	2	42	4	7	41		44	5	3	38	41	19
15	4	10	47	16	48		45	0	32	21	50	26
16	5	39	30	25	56		46	2	1	4	59	33
17	1	8	13	35	3		47	3	29	48	8	40
18	2	36	56	44	10		48	4	58	31	17	48
19	4	5	39	53	17		49	0	27	14	26	55
20	5	34	23	2	25		50	1	55	57	36	2
21	1	3	6	11	32		51	3	24	40	45	9
22	2	31	49	20	39		52	4	53	23	54	17
23	4	0	32	29	46		53	0	22	7	3	24
24	5	29	15	38	54		54	1	50	50	12	31
25	0	57	58	48	1		55	3	19	33	21	38
26	2	26	41	57	8		56	4	48	16	30	46
27	3	55	25	6	15		57	0	16	59	39	53
28	5	24	8	15	23		58	1	45	42	49	0
29	0	52	51	24	30		59	3	14	25	58	7
30	2	21	34	33	37		60	4	43	9	7	15

Position at the Birth of Christ—207° 7'

MOVEMENT OF LUNAR ANOMALY IN PERIODS OF SIXTY DAYS

Days	60°	°	Movement '	"	'''		Days	60°	°	Movement '	"	'''
1	0	13	3	53	56		31	6	45	0	52	11
2	0	26	7	47	53		32	5	58	4	46	8
3	0	39	11	41	49		33	7	11	8	40	4
4	0	52	15	35	46		34	7	24	12	34	1
5	1	5	19	29	42		35	7	37	16	27	57
6	1	18	23	23	39		36	7	50	20	21	54
7	1	31	27	17	35		37	8	3	24	15	50
8	1	44	31	11	32		38	8	16	28	9	47
9	1	57	35	5	28		39	8	29	32	3	43
10	2	10	38	59	25		40	8	42	35	57	40
11	2	23	42	53	21		41	8	55	39	51	36
12	2	36	46	47	18		42	9	8	43	45	33
13	2	49	50	41	14		43	9	21	47	39	29
14	3	2	54	35	11		44	9	34	51	33	26
15	3	15	58	29	7		45	9	47	55	27	22
16	3	29	2	23	4		46	10	0	59	21	19
17	3	42	6	17	0		47	10	14	3	15	15
18	3	55	10	10	57		48	10	27	7	9	12
19	4	8	14	4	53		49	10	40	11	3	8
20	4	21	17	58	50		50	10	53	14	57	5
21	4	34	21	52	46		51	11	6	18	51	1
22	4	47	25	46	43		52	11	19	22	44	58
23	5	0	29	40	39		53	11	32	26	38	54
24	5	13	33	34	36		54	11	45	30	32	51
25	5	26	37	28	32		55	11	58	34	26	47
26	5	39	41	22	29		56	12	11	38	20	44
27	5	52	45	16	25		57	12	24	42	14	40
28	6	5	49	10	22		58	12	37	46	8	37
29	6	18	53	4	18		59	12	50	50	2	33
30	6	31	56	58	15		60	13	3	53	56	30

Position at the Birth of Christ—207° 7'

Lunar Movement in Latitude in Years and Periods of Sixty Years

Position at the Birth of Christ—129° 45′

Egyptian Years	60°	°	′	″	‴	Egyptian Years	60°	°	′	″	‴
1	2	28	42	45	17	31	4	50	5	23	57
2	4	57	25	30	34	32	1	18	48	9	14
3	1	26	8	15	52	33	3	47	30	54	32
4	3	54	51	1	9	34	0	16	13	39	48
5	0	23	33	46	26	35	2	44	56	25	6
6	2	52	16	31	44	36	5	13	39	10	24
7	5	20	59	17	1	37	1	42	21	55	41
8	1	49	42	2	18	38	4	11	4	40	58
9	4	18	24	47	36	39	0	39	47	26	16
10	0	47	7	32	53	40	3	8	30	11	33
11	3	15	50	18	10	41	5	37	12	56	50
12	5	44	33	3	28	42	2	5	55	42	8
13	2	13	15	48	45	43	4	34	38	27	25
14	4	41	58	34	2	44	1	3	21	12	42
15	1	10	41	19	20	45	3	32	3	58	0
16	3	39	24	4	37	46	0	0	46	43	17
17	0	8	6	49	54	47	2	29	29	28	34
18	2	36	49	35	12	48	4	58	12	13	52
19	5	5	32	20	29	49	1	26	54	59	8
20	1	34	15	5	46	50	3	55	37	44	26
21	4	2	57	51	4	51	0	24	29	29	44
22	0	31	40	36	21	52	2	53	3	15	1
23	3	0	23	21	38	53	5	21	46	0	18
24	5	29	6	6	56	54	1	50	28	45	36
25	1	57	48	52	13	55	4	19	11	30	53
26	4	26	31	37	30	56	0	47	54	16	10
27	0	55	14	22	48	57	3	16	37	1	28
28	3	23	57	8	5	58	5	45	19	46	45
29	5	52	39	53	22	59	2	14	2	32	2
30	2	21	12	38	40	60	4	42	45	17	21

Movement in Latitude of the Moon in Days and Periods of Sixty Days

Position at the Birth of Christ—129° 45′

Days	60°	°	′	″	‴	Days	60°	°	′	″	‴
1	0	13	13	45	39	31	6	50	6	35	20
2	0	26	27	31	18	32	7	3	20	20	59
3	0	39	41	16	58	33	7	16	34	6	39
4	0	52	55	2	37	34	7	29	47	52	18
5	1	6	8	48	16	35	7	43	1	37	58
6	1	19	22	33	56	36	7	56	15	23	37
7	1	32	36	19	35	37	8	9	29	9	16
8	1	45	50	5	14	38	8	22	42	54	56
9	1	59	3	50	54	39	8	35	56	40	35
10	2	12	17	36	33	40	8	49	10	26	14
11	2	25	31	22	13	41	9	2	24	11	54
12	2	38	45	7	52	42	9	15	37	57	33
13	2	51	58	53	31	43	9	28	51	43	13
14	3	5	12	39	11	44	9	42	5	28	52
15	3	18	26	24	50	45	9	55	19	14	31
16	3	31	40	10	29	46	10	8	33	0	11
17	3	44	53	56	9	47	10	21	46	45	50
18	3	58	7	41	48	48	10	35	0	31	29
19	4	11	21	27	28	49	10	48	14	17	9
20	4	24	35	13	7	50	11	1	28	2	48
21	4	37	48	58	46	51	11	14	41	48	28
22	4	51	2	44	26	52	11	27	55	34	7
23	5	4	16	30	5	53	11	41	9	19	46
24	5	17	30	15	44	54	11	54	23	5	26
25	5	30	44	1	24	55	12	7	36	51	5
26	5	43	57	47	3	56	12	20	50	36	44
27	5	57	11	32	43	57	12	34	4	22	24
28	6	10	25	18	22	58	12	47	18	8	3
29	6	23	39	4	1	59	13	0	31	53	43
30	6	36	25	49	41	60	13	13	45	39	22

5. Demonstration of the First Irregularity of the Moon
Which Occurs at the New and at the Full Moon

[105ᵇ] We have set out the regular movements of the moon, according as they can be known by us at present. Now we must approach the ratio of irregularity which we shall demonstrate by way of the epicycle, and first the irregularity which occurs in the conjunction and oppositions with the sun, in connexion with which the ancient mathematicians exercised their amazing genius in triads of lunar eclipses. We shall also follow the road thus prepared for us by them, and we shall take three eclipses carefully observed by Ptolemy and compare them with three others noted with no less care, in order to examine the regular movements already set out, to see if they have been set out correctly. In explaining them we shall in imitation of the ancients employ as regular the mean movement of the sun and moon away from the position of the spring equinox, since the variation which occurs on account of the irregular precession of equinoxes is not perceptible in such a short time or even in ten years.

Accordingly, Ptolemy took as first the eclipse occurring in the 17th year of Hadrian's reign, after the close of the 20th day of the month Pauni by the Egyptian calendar; and it was the year of Our Lord 133 on the 6th day of May or the day before the Nones. There was a total eclipse, the midtime of which was a quarter of an equal hour before midnight at Alexandria; but at Frauenburg or Cracow it was an hour and a quarter before the midnight which the seventh day followed; and the sun was at $12\frac{1}{4}°$ of Taurus, but according to the mean movement at 12°21′ of Taurus.

He says that the second occurred in the 19th year of Hadrian, when two days of Chiach—the fourth Egyptian month—had passed: that was in the year of Our Lord 134, 13 days before the Kalends of November. There was an eclipse from the north covering ten twelfths of its diameter. The midtime was one equatorial hour before midnight at Alexandria, but two hours before midnight at Cracow; and the sun was at $25\frac{1}{6}°$ of Libra but by its mean movement at 26°43′ of the same.

The third eclipse occurred in the 20th year of Hadrian, when 19 days of Pharmuthi—the eighth Egyptian month—had passed; in the year of Our Lord [106ᵃ] 135, when the 6th day of March had passed. The moon was again eclipsed in the north to the extent of half its diameter. The midtime was four equatorial hours past midnight at Alexandria, but at Cracow it was three hours after midnight, that morning being the Nones of March. At that time the sun was at $14\frac{1}{12}°$ of Pisces, but by its mean movement at 11°44′ of Pisces.

Now it is clear that in the middle space of time between the first and the second eclipse the moon traversed as much space as the sun in its apparent movement—not counting the full circles—i.e., 161°55′; and between the second and the third eclipse, 138°55′. Now in the first interval there were 1 year 166 days $23\frac{3}{4}$ equal hours according to apparent time, but by corrected time $23\frac{5}{8}$ hours; but in the second interval 1 year 137 days 5 hours simply, but $5\frac{1}{2}$ hours correctly.

And during the first interval the regular movement of the sun and the moon measured as one—not counting the circles—was 169°37′, and there was a movement of anomaly of 110°21′; in the second interval the similarly regular movement of the sun and the moon was 137°34′ and there was a movement of anomaly of 81°36′. Therefore it is clear that during the first interval the 110°21′ of the epicycle subtract 7°42′ from the mean movement of the moon; and during the second interval the 81°36′ of the epicycle add 1°21′.

With these things thus before us, let there be described the lunar epicycle

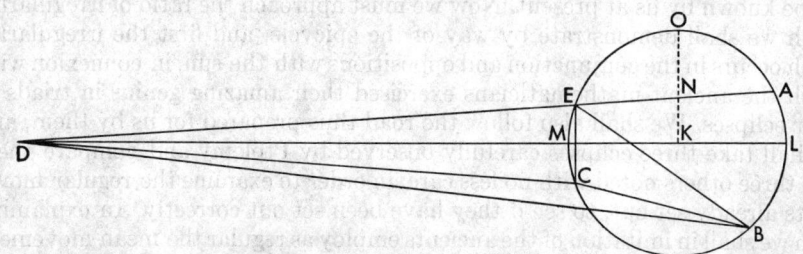

ABC, in which the first eclipse of the moon is at A, the second at B, and the remaining one at C, and in the order as above let the transit of the moon be understood as occurring westward. And let

$$\text{arc } AB = 110°21′,$$

hence

$$-\text{add. } AB = 7°42′,$$

as we said; and let

$$\text{arc } BC = 81°36′,$$

hence

$$+\text{add. } BDC = 1°21′.$$

And, as the remainder of the circle,

$$\text{arc } CA = 168°3′$$

and it adds the remainder of the additosubtraction, $i.e.$,

$$+\text{add. } CDA = 6°21′.$$

Since on the ecliptic

$$\text{arc } AB = 7°42′,$$

therefore

$$\text{angle } ADB = 7°42′,$$
$$\text{where 2 rt. angles} = 180°.$$

But

$$\text{angle } ADB = 15°24′,$$
$$[106^{\text{b}}] \text{ where 2 rt. angles} = 360°.$$

And, as on the circumference and as an exterior angle of triangle BDE,

$$\text{angle } AEB = 110°21′:$$

therefore

$$\text{angle } EBD = 94°57′.$$

But the sides of triangles whose angles are given are themselves given:

and

$$DE = 147,396$$

$$BE = 26,798,$$
where diameter of circle circumscribing triangle = 200,000.

Again, since on the ecliptic

$$\text{arc } AEC = 6°21′,$$
$$\text{angle } EDC = 6°21′,$$
$$\text{where 2 rt. angles} = 180°.$$

But
$$\text{angle } EDC = 12°42',$$
$$\text{where 2 rt. angles} = 360°.$$

And
$$\text{angle } AEC = 191°57'.$$

And
$$\text{angle } ECD = \text{angle } AEC - \text{angle } CDE = 179°15'.$$
Therefore the sides are given:
$$DE = 199,996$$
and
$$CE = 22,120,$$
where the diameter of the circle circumscribing triangle $= 200,000$.

But
$$CE = 16,302$$
and
$$BE = 26,798,$$
$$\text{where } DE = 147,396.$$
Again, since in triangle BEC
$$\text{side } BE \text{ is given,}$$
$$\text{side } EC \text{ is given,}$$
and
$$\text{angle } CEB = 81°36'$$
and hence
$$\text{arc } BC = 81°36':$$
therefore, by the proofs concerning plane triangles,
$$\text{side } BC = 17,960.$$
But since the diameter of the epicycle $= 200,000$,
and
$$\text{arc } BC = 81°36',$$
$$\text{chord } BC = 130,684.$$
And in accordance with the ratio given
$$ED = 1,072,684$$
and
$$CE = 118,637,$$
and
$$\text{arc } CE = 72°46'10''.$$
But, by construction,
$$\text{arc } CEA = 168°3'.$$
Therefore, by subtraction,
$$\text{arc } EA = 95°16'50''$$
and
$$\text{chord } EA = 147,786.$$
Hence by addition
$$\text{line } AED = 1,220,470.$$
But since segment EA is less than a semicircle, the centre of the epicycle will not be in [107^a] it but in the remainder $ABCE$. Therefore let K be the centre, and let $DMKL$ be drawn through both apsides, and let L be the highest apsis and M the lowest. Now, by Euclid, III, 36, it is clear that

rect. AD, DE = rect. LD, DM.

Now since LM, the diameter of the circle—to which DM is added in a straight line—is bisected at K, then

rect. LD, DM + sq. KM = sq. DK.

Therefore

$$DK = 1,148,556$$

where $KL = 100,000$;

and on that account,

$$LK = 8,706$$

where $DKL = 100,000$

and LK is the radius of the epicycle. Having done that, draw KNO perpendicular to AD. Since KD, DE, and EA have their ratios to one another given in the parts whereof $LK = 100,000$, and since

$$NE = \tfrac{1}{2} AE = 73,893:$$

therefore, by addition,

$$DEN = 1,146,577.$$

But in triangle DKN

side DK is given,
side ND is given,

and

angle $N = 90°$;

on that account, at the centre,

angle $NKD = 86°38\tfrac{1}{2}'$

and

Hence,

arc $MEO = 86°38\tfrac{1}{2}'$.

Now

arc $LAO = 180° -$ arc $NEO = 93°21\tfrac{1}{2}'$.

and

arc $OA = \tfrac{1}{2}$ arc $AOE = 47°38\tfrac{1}{2}'$;

arc $LA =$ arc $LAO -$ arc $OA = 45°43'$,

which is the distance—or position of anomaly—of the moon from the highest apsis of the epicycle at the first eclipse. But

arc $AB = 110°21'$.

Accordingly, by subtraction,

arc $LB = 64°38'$,

which is the anomaly at the second eclipse. And by addition

arc $LBC = 146°14'$,

where the third eclipse falls. Now it will also be clear that since

angle $DKN = 86°38\tfrac{1}{2}'$,

where 4 rt. angles = 360°,

angle $KDN = 90° -$ angle $DKN = 3°21\tfrac{1}{2}'$;

and that is the additosubtraction which the anomaly adds at the first eclipse. Now

angle $ADB = 7°42'$;

therefore, by subtraction,

angle $LDB = 4°20\tfrac{1}{2}'$,

which arc LB subtracts from the regular movement of the moon at the second eclipse. And since

[107^{b}] angle $BDC = 1°21'$,

and therefore, by subtraction,

angle $CDM = 2°49'$,

the subtractive additosubtraction caused by arc LBC at the third eclipse; therefore the mean position of the moon, *i.e.*, of centre K, at the first eclipse was 9°53′ of Scorpio, because its apparent position was at 13°15′ of Scorpio; and that was the number of degrees of the sun diametrically opposite in Taurus. And thus the mean movement of the moon at the second eclipse was at $29\frac{1}{2}°$ of Aries; and in the third eclipse, at 17°4′ of Virgo. Moreover, the regular distances of the moon from the sun were 177°33′ for the first eclipse, 182°47′ for the second, 185°20′ for the last. So Ptolemy.

Following his example, let us now proceed to a third trinity of eclipses of the moon, which were painstakingly observed by us. The first was in the year of Our Lord 1511, after October 6th had passed. The moon began to be eclipsed $1\frac{1}{8}$ equal hours before midnight, and was completely restored $2\frac{1}{3}$ hours after midnight, and in this way the middle of the eclipse was at $\frac{7}{12}$ hours after midnight—the morning following being the Nones of October, the 7th. There was a total eclipse, while the sun was in 22°25′ of Libra but by regular movement at 24°13′ of Libra.

We observed the second eclipse in the year of Our Lord 1522, in the month of September, after the lapse of five days. The eclipse was total, and began at $\frac{2}{5}$ equal hours before midnight, but its midpoint occurred $1\frac{1}{3}$ hours after midnight, which the 6th day followed—the 8th day before the Ides of September. The sun was in $22\frac{1}{5}°$ of Virgo but, according to its regular movement, in 23°59′ of Virgo.

We observed the third in the year of Our Lord 1523, at the close of August 25th. It began $2\frac{4}{5}$ hours after midnight, was a total eclipse, and the midtime was $4\frac{5}{12}$ hours after the midnight prior to the 7th day before the Kalends of September. The sun was in 11°21′ of Virgo but according to its mean movement at 13°2′ of Virgo.

And here it is also manifest that the distance between the true positions of the sun and the moon from the first eclipse to the second was 329°47′, [108ᵃ] but from the second to the third it was 349°9′. Now the time from the first eclipse to the second was 10 equal years 337 days $\frac{3}{4}$ hours according to apparent time, but by corrected equal time $\frac{4}{5}$ hours. From the second to the third there were 354 days 3 hours 5 minutes; but according to equal time 3 hours 9 minutes.

During the first interval the mean movement of the sun and the moon measured as one—not counting the complete circles—amounted to 334°47′, and the movement of anomaly to 250°36′, subtracting approximately 5° from the regular movement; in the second interval the mean movement of the sun and moon was 346°10′; and the movement of anomaly was 306°43′, adding 2°59′ to the mean movement.

Now let ABC be the epicycle, and let A be the position of the moon at the

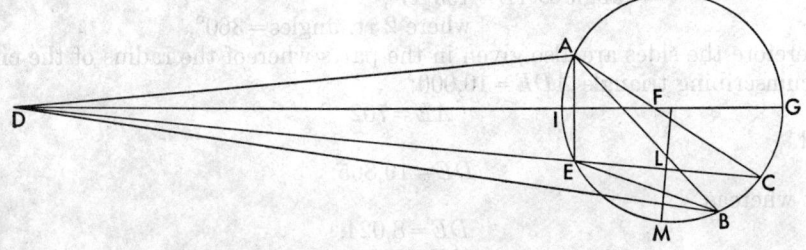

middle of the first eclipse, B at the second, C at the third. And let the movement of the epicycle be understood as proceeding from C to B and from B to A, i.e., from above, westward, and from below, eastward. And

$$\text{arc } ACB = 250°36',$$

and, as we said, it subtracts 5° from the mean movement during the first interval of time. But

$$\text{arc } BAC = 306°43',$$

which adds 2°59' to the mean movement of the moon; and accordingly by subtraction the remainder

$$\text{arc } AC = 197°19',$$

which subtracts the remaining 2°1'. But since arc AC is greater than a semicircle and is subtractive, then it must contain the highest apsis. For the highest apsis cannot be in arcs BA or CBA, which are additive and each less than a semicircle; but the lesser movement is placed by the apogee. Therefore let D be taken opposite as the centre of the Earth; and let AD, DB, DEC, AB, AE, and EB be joined.

Now since in triangle DBE

$$\text{exterior angle } CEB = 53°17',$$

because angle CEB intercepts arc CB, and

$$\text{arc } CB = 360° - \text{arc } BAC;$$

and since, as at the centre,

$$\text{angle } BDE = 2°59',$$

but, as at the circumference,

$$\text{angle } BDE = 5°58';$$

and since, therefore, by subtraction,

$$\text{angle } EBD = 47°19';$$

wherefore

$$\text{side } BE = 1042$$

and

$$\text{side } DE = 8024$$
$$= [108^{\text{b}}] \text{ where radius of circle circumscribing}$$
$$\text{the triangle} = 10,000.$$

Similarly, as standing on arc AC of the circumference,

$$\text{angle } AEC = 197°19',$$

and, as at the centre,

$$\text{angle } ADC = 2°1',$$

but, as on the circumference,

$$\text{angle } ADC = 4°2';$$

therefore, by subtraction,

$$\text{angle } DAE = 193°17',$$
$$\text{where 2 rt. angles} = 360°.$$

Therefore the sides are also given in the parts whereof the radius of the circle circumscribing triangle $ADE = 10,000$:

$$AE = 702$$

and

$$DE = 19,865:$$

but whereas

$$DE = 8,024,$$
$$AE = 283$$

and
$$BE = 1042.$$
Therefore once more we shall have triangle ABE, wherein
side AE is given,
side EB is given,
and
$$\text{angle } AEB = 250°36',$$
where 2 rt. angles $= 360°$.
Accordingly by what we have shown concerning plane triangles
$$AB = 1{,}227$$
where $EB = 1{,}042$.
Accordingly in this way we have got hold of the ratios of the three lines AB, EB, and ED; and hence they will become manifest in terms of the parts whereof the radius of the epicycle $= 10{,}000$:
$$\text{ch. } AB = 16{,}323,$$
$$ED = 106{,}751,$$
and
$$\text{ch. } EB = 13{,}853.$$
Whence also
$$\text{arc } EB = 87°41';$$
and
$$\text{arc } EBC = \text{arc } EB + \text{arc } BC = 140°58';$$
and
$$\text{ch. } CE = 18{,}851,$$
and, by addition,
$$CED = 125{,}602.$$
Now let the centre of the epicycle be set forth: it necessarily falls in segment EAC as being greater than a semicircle. And let F be the centre; and let $DIFG$ be extended in a straight line through both apsides, I the lowest and G the highest. Again it is clear that
$$\text{rect. } CD, DE = \text{rect. } GD, DI.$$
But
$$\text{rect. } GD, DI + \text{sq. } FI = \text{sq. } DF.$$
Therefore
$$DIF = 116{,}226,$$
where $FG = 10{,}000$.
Accordingly
$$FG = 8{,}604,$$
where $DF = 100{,}000$,
—which agrees with what we find reported by most of our predecessors after Ptolemy's time.

[109ᵃ] Now from centre F let FL be drawn at right angles to EC and extended in the straight line FLM. It will bisect CE at point I. Now since
line $ED = 106{,}751$
and
$$\tfrac{1}{2}CE = LE = 9{,}426;$$
therefore, by addition,
$$DEL = 116{,}177$$
where $FG = 10{,}000$
and where $DF = 116{,}226$.

Therefore, in triangle DFL

$$\text{side } DF \text{ is given,}$$
$$\text{side } DL \text{ is given,}$$
$$\text{angle } DFL = 88°21',$$

and, by subtraction,

$$\text{angle } FDL = 1°39';$$

and similarly

$$\text{arc } IEM = 88°21'$$

and

$$\text{arc } MC = \tfrac{1}{2} \text{ arc } EBC = 70°29';$$

hence, by addition,

$$\text{arc } IMC = 158°50',$$

and

$$\text{arc } GC = 180° - \text{arc } IMC = 21°10'.$$

And this was the distance of the moon from the apogee of the epicycle, or the position of anomaly at the third eclipse. And at the second eclipse

$$\text{arc } GCB = 74°27';$$

and at the first eclipse

$$\text{arc } GBA = 183°51'.$$

Again at the third eclipse, and as at the centre,

$$\text{angle } IDE = 1°39',$$

which is the subtractive additosubtraction. And at the second eclipse

$$\text{angle } IDB = 4°38',$$

which is still a subtractive addition-and-subtraction, because

$$\text{angle } IDB = \text{angle } GDC + \text{angle } CDB = 1°39' + 2°59'.$$

And accordingly

$$\text{angle } ADI = \text{angle } ADB - \text{angle } IDB = 5° - 4°38' = 22'$$

which are added to the regular movement at the first eclipse.

For that reason the position of regular movement of the moon in the first eclipse was 22°3' of Aries, but the position of the apparent movement was at 22°25'; and the sun was opposite, at the same number of degrees of Libra. In this way too the mean position of the moon in the second eclipse was at 26°50' of Pisces, but in the third eclipse, at 13° of Pisces, and the mean lunar movement by which it is separated from the annual movement of the Earth, was 177°50' at the first eclipse; at the second eclipse, 182°51'; and at the third eclipse, 179°58'.

6. Confirmation of What Has Been Set Out Concerning the Moon's Movements of Anomaly in Longitude

Moreover, by means of these things which are set out concerning the eclipses of the moon, it will be possible to test whether we have set out the regular movements of the moon correctly. For it was shown that in the second of the two eclipses the distance of the moon from the sun was 182°47', and [the movement] of anomaly was 64°38'; [109ᵇ] but in the second of those eclipses occurring in our time the movement of the moon away from the sun was 182°51' but [the movement] of anomaly was 74°27'. It is clear that in the intervening time there were 17,166 full months and as it were a movement of 4' and a movement of anomaly—not counting the whole cycles—of 9°49'. Now the time which intervenes between the 19th year of Hadrian on the 2nd day of the Egyptian month Chiach 2 hours before midnight, followed by the 3rd day of the month, and the 1522nd year of Our Lord on September 5th, 1⅓ hours after midnight amounts to 1388 Eguptian years 302 days 3⅓ hours by apparent time; and when corrected, 3 hours 34 minutes after midnight.

And in that time after the 17,165 complete revolutions of equal months there was according to Ptolemy and Hipparchus a movement away from the sun of 359°38'. And according to Hipparchus the movement of anomaly was 9°39', but according to Ptolemy 9°11'. Accordingly the lunar movement away from the sun calculated by Hipparchus and Ptolemy is deficient in 26', and the movement of anomaly of Ptolemy and of Hipparchus is deficient in 38'. These minutes swell our movements, and are consonant with the numbers which we have set out.

7. On the Positions of the Moon in Longitude and Anomaly

Now we shall speak of these things, as above; and here we are to determine positions for the established beginnings of calendar years of the Olympiads, of the years of Alexander, Caesar, and Our Lord, and any additional one desired. Therefore if we consider the second of the three ancient eclipses—the one which occurred in the 19th year of Hadrian, on the 2nd day of the Egyptian month Chiach, one equatorial hour before midnight at Alexandria but for us under the Cracow meridian at 2 hours before midnight—we shall find from the beginning of the years of Our Lord to this movement 133 Egyptian years 325 days 22 hours simply, but 21 hours 37 minutes correctly. During this time the movement of the moon according to our calculation was 332°49' and [the movement] of anomaly was 217°32'. [110ᵃ] And when they have been subtracted from the findings for the eclipse, each from its own kind, there remain 209°58' as the mean position of the moon away from the sun, and a position of anomaly of 207°7' at the beginning of the years of Our Lord at midnight before the Kalends of January.

Again [from the 1st Olympiad] to the beginning of the years of Our Lord, there are 193 Olympiads 2 years 194½ days, which make 775 Egyptian years 12½ days, but by corrected time 12 hours 11 minutes. Similarly from the death of Alexander to the birth of Christ, they compute 323 Egyptian years 130½ days by apparent time, but by corrected time 12 hours 16 minutes. And from Caesar to Christ there are 45 Egyptian years 12 days, in which the ratios of equal and apparent time agree.

Accordingly when we have deducted the movements corresponding to the intervals of time from the positions at the birth of Christ, by subtracting single items from single items, we shall have for noon of the 1st day of the month Hekatombaion of the 1st Olympiad a regular lunar distance from the sun of 39°43' and a distance of anomaly of 46°20'.

At the beginning of the years of Alexander at noon on the first day of the month Thoth the moon was 310°44' distant from the sun, and the movement of anomaly was 85°41'.

And at the beginning of the years of Julius Caesar at midnight before the Kalends of January the moon was 350°39' distant from the sun, and the movement of anomaly was 17°58'. All this with reference to the Cracow meridian, since Gynopolis—commonly called Frauenburg—where we took our observations at the mouth of the Vistula, lies under this meridian, as the eclipses of the sun and moon observed in both places at the same time teach us; and Dyrrhachium in Macedonia—which was called Epidamnum in antiquity—is also under this meridian.

8. On the Second Irregularity of the Moon and What Ratio the First Epicycle Has to the Second

Accordingly, in this way the regular movement of the moon together with its first irregularity has been demonstrated. Now we must inquire into what ratio the first epicycle has to the second and both of them to the distance of the centre of the Earth. But, as we said, the greatest difference [between regular and apparent movement] is found in the mean quadratures when the half moon is waxing or waning, and that difference is $7\frac{2}{3}°$, [110^b] as even the observations of the ancients record. For they were making observations of the time in which the half moon had nearly reached the mean distance of the epicycle and was in the neighbourhood of the tangent from the centre of the Earth—and that is easily perceptible by means of the calculus set forth above. And as the moon was then at about 90° of the ecliptic measured from its rising or setting, they were aware of the error which the parallax could bring into the movement of longitude. For at that time the circle through the vertex of the horizon divides the ecliptic at right angles and does not admit any parallax in longitude but the parallax falls wholly in latitude. Then by means of the astrolabe they determined the position of the moon in relation to the sun. When they made their comparison, the moon was found to differ from its regular movement by $7\frac{2}{3}°$, as we said, instead of by 5°.

Now let epicycle AB be described; and let its centre be C. Let the centre of the Earth be D, and from D let the straight line $DBCA$ be extended. Let A be the apogee of the epicycle, B the perigee; and let DE be drawn tangent to

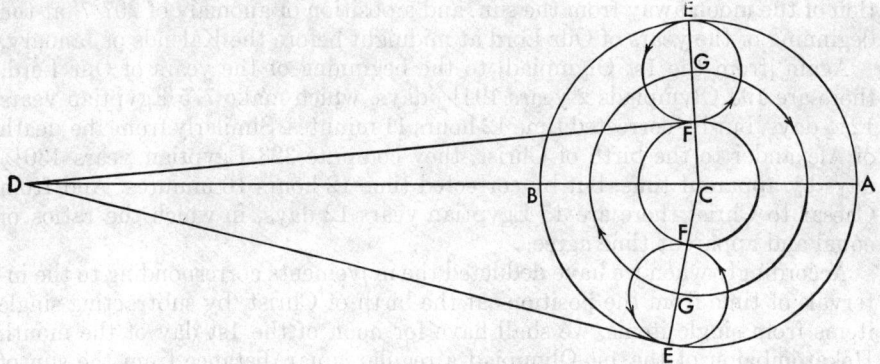

the epicycle, and let CE be joined. Accordingly since the greatest additosubtraction is at the tangent and in this case is $7°40'$, and hence
$$\text{angle } BDE = 7°40',$$
and
$$\text{angle } CED = 90°,$$
as being at the point of tangency of circle AB:
wherefore
$$CE = 1334,$$
$$\text{where radius } CD = 10,000.$$
But at the full moon it was much shorter, that is,
$$CE \doteqdot 860.$$

Let CE be cut again, and let
$$CF = 860.$$
Point F, which the new moon and the full moon occupy, will be circumcurrent around the same centre; and accordingly, by subtraction,
$$FE = 474$$
and is the diameter of the second epicycle. Let FE be bisected at centre G, and by addition
$$CFG = 1097$$
and will be the radius of the circle which the centre of the second epicycle describes. And so it is established that
$$CG : GE = 1097 : 237,$$
$$\text{where } CD = 10,000.$$

9. On the Remaining Difference, by Reason of Which the Moon Seems to Move Irregularly Away from the Highest Apsis of Its Epicycle

[111ᵃ] By this induction it is given to understand how the moon is moved irregularly in its first epicycle, and that its greatest difference occurs when the

half moon is horn-shaped or gibbous. Once more, let AB be that first epicycle, which the centre of the second epicycle describes through its mean movement; let C be the centre, A the highest apsis, and B the lowest. Let point E be taken anywhere in the circumference, and let CE be joined. Now let
$$CE : EF = 1097 : 237.$$
And with radius EF let the second epicycle be described around centre E. And let the straight lines CL and CM be drawn tangent to it on both sides. Let the movement of the small epicycle be from A to E, $i.e.$, from above, westward; and let the movement of the moon be from F to L, still westward. Accordingly it is clear that, since movement AE is regular, the second epicycle by virtue of its motion FL adds arc EL to the regular movement and by virtue of MF subtracts from the regular movement. But since in triangle CEL
$$\text{angle } L = 90°,$$
and
$$EL = 237,$$
$$\text{where } CE = 1,097.$$
Therefore
$$EL = 2,160,$$
$$\text{where } CE = 10,000.$$
And by the table
$$EL = \tfrac{1}{2} \text{ ch. } 2 \ ECL.$$

And
angle ECL = angle MCF,

since the triangles are similar and equal. And that is the greatest difference by which the moon varies in its movement from the highest apsis of the first epicycle. It occurs when the moon by its mean movement is 38°46′ distant on either side of the line of mean movement of the Earth. And so it is perfectly clear that these greatest additosubtractions occur at a mean distance of 38°46′ between the sun and moon, and at the same distance on either side of the mean opposition.

10. How the Apparent Movement of the Moon Is Demonstrated from the Regular Movements

[111ᵇ] Having seen all that first, we now wish to show by means of diagrams how the regular and apparent movements of the moon are separated out from those regular lunar movements which were set before us, taking our example from among the observations of Hipparchus, so that in this way our teaching may at the same time be confirmed experimentally. Accordingly in the 197th year from the death of Alexander, on the 17th day of Pauni, which is the 10th month in the Egyptian calendar, when 9⅓ hours of the day had passed at Rhodes, Hipparchus by an observation of the sun and moon through an astrolabe found that they were 48°6′ distant from one another, and that the moon was to the east of the sun. And since he judged that the position of the sun was in 10⁹⁄₁₀° of Cancer, as a consequence the moon was at 29° of Leo. At that time 29° of Scorpio was rising, and 10° of Virgo was in the middle of the heavens over Rhodes, which has an elevation of the north pole of 36°. By this argument it is clear that the moon, which was situated at 90° of the ecliptic from the meridian had at that time admitted no parallax in vision or else one imperceptible in longitude. But since this observation was made 3⅓ hours after midday of the 17th—which corresponds at Rhodes to four equatorial hours—at Cracow it was 3⅙ equatorial hours after midday in accordance with the distance which makes Rhodes a sixth of an hour nearer to us than Alexandria. Accordingly from the death of Alexander there were 196 years, 286 days, 3⅙ hours simply, but 3⅓ hours by equal time. At that time the sun by its mean movement had arrived at 12°3′ of Cancer, but by its apparent movement at 10°40′ of Cancer, whence the moon appeared in truth to be at 28°37′ of Leo. But the regular movement of the moon according to the monthly revolution was at 45°9′, and the movement of anomaly was 333° away from the highest apsis by our calculations.

With this example before us let us describe the first epicycle AB. Let C be its centre. [112ᵃ] Let ACB be its diameter, and let ACB be extended as ABD in a straight line to the centre of the Earth. And in the epicycle, let

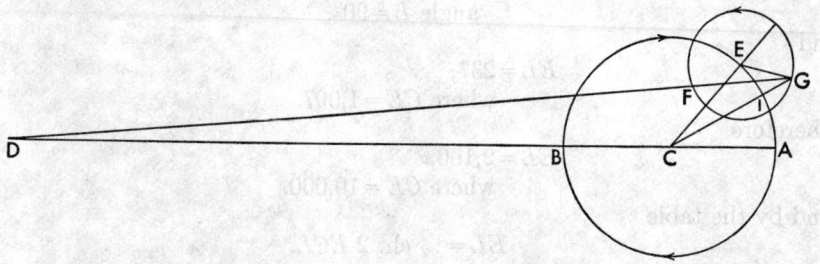

arc $ABE = 333°$.

Let CE be joined and again cut in F, so that
$$EF = 237,$$
where $EC = 1,097$.

And with E as centre and EF as radius, let FG the epicycle of the epicycle be described. Let the moon be at point G; and let
$$\text{arc } FG = 90°18',$$
in the ratio of double to the regular movement away from the sun, which was $45°9'$. And let CG, EG, and DG be joined. Accordingly, since in triangle CEG two sides are given:
$$CE = 1,097$$
and
$$EG = EF = 237;$$
and
$$\text{angle } GEC = 90°18';$$
therefore, by what we have shown concerning plane triangles
$$\text{side } CG = 1,123$$
and
$$\text{angle } ECG = 12°11'.$$

By this means there are determined arc EI and the additive additosubtraction caused by the anomaly; and, by addition,
$$\text{arc } ABEI = 345°11'.$$

And, by subtraction,
$$\text{angle } GCA = 14°49',$$
and is the true distance of the moon from the highest apsis of epicycle AB; and
$$\text{angle } BCG = 165°11'.$$
Wherefore in triangle GDC two sides are given also.
$$GC = 1,123,$$
where $CD = 10,000$;
and
$$\text{angle } GCD = 165°11'.$$

Hence
$$\text{angle } CDG = 1°29',$$
the additosubtraction which was added to the mean movement of the moon. Hence the true distance of the moon from the mean movement of the sun is $46°34'$, and its apparent position is at $28°37'$ of Leo, and is $47°57'$ distant from the true position of the sun. And there is a deficiency of $9'$ according to Hipparchus' observation.

But in order that no one on that account should suspect that either his investigation or ours is wrong—though the deficiency is very slight—nevertheless I shall show that neither he nor we committed any error but that this is the way things rightly are. For if we recollect that the lunar circle which the moon itself follows is oblique, we will admit that it produces some sort of longitudinal irregularity in the ecliptic, especially around the mean positions, which lie between the northern and the southern limits of latitude and the ecliptic sections, in approximately the same way as between the oblique [112^b] ecliptic and the equator, as we expounded in connection with the inequality of the natural day. And so if we transfer the ratios to the orbital circle of the moon, which Ptolemy recorded as being inclined to the ecliptic, we find that at those positions the ratios cause a 7′ difference in longitude in relation to the ecliptic—and twice that difference is 14′; and the difference increases and decreases proportionally, since when the sun and moon are a quadrant of a circle distant from one another, and if the limit of northern or southern latitude is at the midpoint between them, then the arc intercepted on the ecliptic will be 14′ greater than a quadrant of the lunar circle; and conversely in the other quadrants, which the ecliptic sections halve, the circles through the poles of the ecliptic intercept an arc that much less than a quadrant. So in the present case. Since the moon was in the neighbourhood of the mean position between the southern limit of latitude and the ascending ecliptic section— which the moderns call the head of the Dragon—and the sun had already passed by the other descending section—which they call the tail; it is not surprising if when the moon's distance of 47°57′ in its own orbital circle was referred to the ecliptic, it increased by at least 7′, without the fact of the sun declining in the west causing any subtractive parallax of vision. We shall speak more clearly of all that in our explanation of the parallaxes.

And so the distance of the luminaries, which Hipparchus determined by his instrument as being 48°6′, agrees with our calculation perfectly and as it were unanimously.

11. ON THE TABLE OF THE LUNAR ADDITIONS-AND-SUBTRACTIONS OR *Aequationes*

Accordingly, I judge that the mode of determining the motions of the moon is understood generally from this example, since in triangle *CEG*, the two sides *GE* and *CE* always remain the same. But we determine the remaining side *GC* together with angle *ECG*—which is the additosubtraction to be used

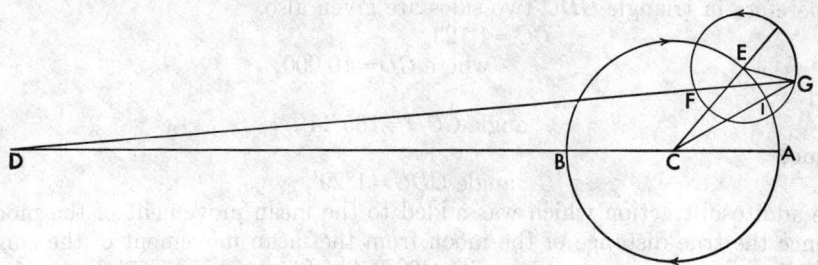

in correcting the anomaly—according to angle *GEC* which changes continually but which is given. Then in triangle *CDG*, since the two sides *DC* and *GC* together with angle *DCG* have been computed, in the same way angle *D* at the centre of the Earth, the angular difference between the true and the regular movement, becomes established.

So that these things may be at hand, [113ᵃ] we shall set out a table of the additosubtractions, which will contain six columns. For after the two columns of common numbers of the circle, in the third column will come the additosubtractions which are caused by the small epicycle and vary the regular movement of the first epicycle in accordance with the bi-monthly revolution. Then, we shall leave the fourth column vacant for the time being, and fill up the fifth column first, in which we shall inscribe the additosubtractions caused by the first and greater epicycle which occur at the mean conjunctions and oppositions of the sun and moon, and the greatest is 4°56′. In the next to the last column will be placed the numbers whereby the additosubtractions which occur at half moon exceed the former additosubtractions, and the greatest of these excesses is 2°44′. But in order that the other excesses may be evaluated, the proportional minutes have been worked out, and this is the ratio of them. For we have taken 2°44′ as 60 minutes in relation to any other excesses occurring at the point of tangency of the [small] epicycle [with the line from the centre of the Earth].

In this way, in the same example,

$$CG = 1123,$$

where $CD = 10,000$.

And that makes the greatest additosubtraction at the point of tangency of the [small] epicycle [with the line from the centre of the Earth] to be 6°29′, which exceeds the first additosubtraction by 1°33′. But

$$2°44′ : 1°33′ = 60′ : 34′;$$

and so we have the ratio of the excess which occurs at the semicircle of the small epicycle to the excess corresponding to the given arc of 90°18′. Therefore we shall write down 34 minutes in that part of the table corresponding to 90°. In this way we shall find the minutes which are proportional to the arcs inscribed in the table; and we shall set them out in the fourth column.

Finally we have added the degrees of northern and southern latitude in the last column, and we shall speak of them below. For convenience and ease of operation advise us to put them in this order.

TABLE OF ADDITIONS-AND-SUBTRACTIONS OF THE MOON

Common Numbers		Additions-and-subtractions caused by small epicycle		Proportional Minutes	Additions-and-subtractions caused by great epicycle		Excesses		Degrees of Northern Latitude	
Deg.	Deg.	Deg.	Min.		Deg.	Min.	Deg.	Min.	Deg.	Min.
3	357	0	51	0	0	14	0	7	4	59
6	354	1	40	0	0	28	0	14	4	58
9	351	2	28	1	0	43	0	21	4	56
12	348	3	15	1	0	57	0	28	4	53
15	345	4	1	2	1	11	0	35	4	50
18	342	4	47	3	1	24	0	43	4	45
21	339	5	31	3	1	38	0	50	4	40
24	336	6	13	4	1	51	0	56	4	34
27	333	6	54	5	2	5	1	4	4	27
30	330	7	34	5	2	17	1	12	4	20
33	327	8	10	6	2	30	1	18	4	12
36	324	8	44	7	2	42	1	25	4	3
39	321	9	16	8	2	54	1	30	3	53
42	318	9	47	10	3	6	1	37	3	43
45	315	10	14	11	3	17	1	42	3	32
48	312	10	30	12	3	27	1	48	3	20
51	309	11	0	13	3	38	1	52	3	8
54	306	11	21	15	3	47	1	57	2	56
57	303	11	38	16	3	56	2	2	2	44
60	300	11	50	18	4	5	2	6	2	30
63	297	12	2	19	4	13	2	10	2	16
66	294	12	12	21	4	20	2	15	2	2
69	291	12	18	22	4	27	2	18	1	47
72	288	12	23	24	4	33	2	21	1	33
75	285	12	27	25	4	39	2	25	1	18
78	282	12	28	27	4	43	2	28	1	2
81	279	12	26	28	4	47	2	30	0	47
84	276	12	23	30	4	51	2	34	0	31
87	273	12	17	32	4	53	2	37	0	16
90	270	12	12	34	4	55	2	40	0	0
93	267	12	3	35	4	56	2	42	0	16
96	264	11	53	37	4	56	2	42	0	31
99	261	11	41	38	4	55	2	43	0	47
102	258	11	27	39	4	54	2	43	1	2
105	255	11	10	41	4	51	2	44	1	18
108	252	10	52	42	4	48	2	44	1	33
111	249	10	35	43	4	44	2	43	1	47
114	246	10	17	45	4	39	2	41	2	2
117	243	9	57	46	4	34	2	38	2	16
120	240	9	35	47	4	27	2	35	2	30
123	237	9	13	48	4	20	2	31	2	44
126	234	8	50	49	4	11	2	27	2	56
129	231	8	25	50	4	2	2	22	3	9
132	228	7	59	51	3	53	2	18	3	21
135	225	7	33	52	3	42	2	13	3	32
138	222	7	7	53	3	31	2	8	3	43
141	219	6	38	54	3	19	2	1	3	53
144	216	6	9	55	3	7	1	53	4	3
147	213	5	40	56	2	53	1	46	4	12
150	210	5	11	57	2	40	1	37	4	20
153	207	4	42	57	2	25	1	28	4	27
156	204	4	11	58	2	10	1	20	4	34
159	201	3	41	58	1	55	1	12	4	40
162	198	3	10	59	1	39	1	4	4	45
165	195	2	39	59	1	23	0	53	4	50
168	192	2	7	59	1	7	0	43	4	53
171	189	1	36	60	0	51	0	33	4	56
174	186	1	4	60	0	34	0	22	4	58
177	183	0	32	60	0	17	0	11	4	59
180	180	0	0	60	0	0	0	0	5	0

12. On the Computation of the Course of the Moon

[114ᵇ] Accordingly the method of computing the apparent movement of the moon is clear from what has been shown and is as follows. We shall reduce to equal time the time for which we are seeking the position of the moon proposed to us. By means of the time we shall deduce the mean movements of longitude, anomaly, and latitude—which last we shall also define soon—as we did in the case of the sun, from the given beginning of the years of Our Lord, or from some other beginning, and we shall declare the positions of the single movements at the time set before us. Then we shall seek in the table twice the regular longitude of the moon or twice its angular distance from the sun and[1] the corresponding additosubtraction found in the third column; and we shall note the proportional minutes which are in the next column. Accordingly if the number with which we entered upon the table was found in the first column or is less than 180°, we shall add the additosubtraction to the lunar anomaly; but if it is greater than 180° or is in the second column, the additosubtraction will be subtracted from the anomaly; and we shall have the corrected anomaly of the moon and its true angular distance from the highest apsis.

And entering the table again with this [distance] we shall determine the corresponding additosubtraction in the fifth column and the excess which follows in the sixth column, which the second [the small] epicycle adds [to the additosubtraction], over and above the first epicycle. The proportional part of this excess taken in accordance with the ratio of the 60 minutes is always added to this additosubtraction. The sum is subtracted from the mean movement of longitude or latitude, if the corrected anomaly is less than 180° or a semicircle; and it is added, if the anomaly is greater. And in this way we shall have the true distance of the moon from the mean position of the sun and the corrected movement of latitude. Wherefore the true position of the moon will not be unknown, either its distance from the first star of Aries in the case of the simple movement of the sun or its distance from the spring equinox in the case of the composite movement or the addition of the precession. Finally by means of the corrected movement in latitude we shall have in the seventh and last place of the table the degrees of latitude which measure the distance of the moon from the ecliptic. That latitude will be northern at the time when the movement of latitude is found in the first part of the table, [115ᵃ] *i.e.*, if it is less than 90° or greater than 270°; otherwise it will be following a southern latitude. And so the moon will be coming down from the north to 180°, and afterwards it will be going up from the southern limit, until it has completed the remaining parts of the circle. Thus the apparent course of the moon has somehow as many affairs around the centre of the Earth as the Earth has around the sun.

13. How the Movement of Lunar Latitude Is Examined and Demonstrated

Now too we must give the ratio of the lunar movement in latitude, and it seems more difficult to discover, as it is complicated by more attendant circumstances. For, as we said before, if two eclipses of the moon were similar and equal in all respects, *i.e.*, with the parts eclipsed having the same position to

---

[1] Because the moon traverses the small epicycle twice during one synodic month, the time of one revolution with respect to the sun.

the north or to the south and at the same ascending or descending ecliptic section: its distance from the Earth or from the highest apsis would be equal,
since in this harmony the moon is understood to have completed its whole
circles of latitude by true movement. For since the shadow of the Earth is
conoid, and if a right cone is cut in a plane parallel with the base, the section is a
circle which is smaller the greater the distance from the base and greater the
shorter the distance from the base, and similarly equal at an equal distance.
And so the moon at equal distances from the Earth traverses equal circles of
shadow and presents to our vision equal disks of itself. Hence the moon, standing out with equal parts in the same direction according to an equal distance
from the centre of the shadow makes us certain of equal latitudes, from which it
necessarily follows that the moon has returned to its former position in latitude
and is now distant from the same ecliptic node by an equal interval. But that
is especially true if the position fulfils two of those conditions. For its approach
to the Earth or withdrawal from it changes the total magnitude of the shadow,
[115^b] but so slightly that it can hardly be grasped. Accordingly the greater the
interval of time between both eclipses, the more definite can we have the movement in latitude of the moon, as was said in the case of the sun.

But since you rarely find two eclipses agreeing in these conditions—and up
to now none have come our way—nevertheless we note there is another method
which will give us the same result, since—the other conditions remaining—if
the moon is eclipsed in different directions and at opposite sections, then it will
signify that at the second eclipse the moon has arrived at a position diametrically
opposite to the former and in addition to the whole circles has described a semicircle; and that will seem to be satisfactory for investigating the thing.

Accordingly we have found two eclipses fairly close in these respects: the
first in the 7th year of Ptolemy Philometor, which was the 150th year of Alexander when—as Claud says—27 days of Phamenoth the 7th month of the
Egyptians had passed, in the night which the 28th day followed. And the moon
was eclipsed from the beginning of the 8th hour till the end of the 10th hour in
Alexandrian nocturnal seasonal hours, to the extent of seven-twelfths of the
lunar diameter, and it was eclipsed from the north around a descending section.
Therefore the midtime of the eclipse was, he says, 2 seasonal hours after midnight, which make 2⅓ equatorial hours, since the sun was at 6° of Taurus, but
1⅓ hours after midnight at Cracow.

We have taken the second eclipse beneath the same Cracow meridian in the
year of Our Lord 1519, after the 4th day before the Nones of June, when the sun
was at 21° of Gemini. The midtime of the eclipse was 11⅗ equatorial hours after
midday; and the moon was eclipsed for approximately eight-twelfths of its diameter, from the south, at an ascending section.

Accordingly, from the beginning of the years of Alexander [to the first eclipse]
there are 149 Egyptian years 206 days 14⅓ hours at Alexandria, but at Cracow
13⅓ hours according to apparent time, but 13½ upon correction. At that time
the position of anomaly by our calculation, which agreed approximately with
Ptolemy's, was at 163°33′ of regular movement; and there was a subtractive
additosubtraction of 1°23′, by which the true position of the moon was exceeded
by the regular. But from the established beginning of the years of Alexander to
the second eclipse [116^a] there are 1832 Egyptian years 295 days 11 hours 45
minutes by apparent time, but by equal time 11 hours 55 minutes: whence the

regular movement of the moon was 182°18'. The position of anomaly was 159°55', but as corrected it was 161°13'; and the additive additosubtraction, by which the regular movement was exceeded by the apparent, was 1°44'.

Accordingly it is clear that in both eclipses the distance of the moon from the Earth was equal, and the sun was approximately at the apogee in both cases, but there was a difference of one-twelfth in the eclipses. But since the diameter of the moon usually occupies approximately $\frac{1}{2}$°, as we will show afterwards, its twelfth part will be $2\frac{1}{2}$', which corresponds to approximately $\frac{1}{2}$° in the oblique circle of the moon at the ecliptic sections. And so the moon was $\frac{1}{2}$° farther away from the ascending section at the second eclipse than from the descending section at the first eclipse. Hence it is clear that the true movement in latitude of the moon was $179\frac{1}{2}$° after the complete revolutions. But the lunar anomaly between the first and second eclipse adds 21'—which is the difference between the additosubtractions—to the regular [movement]. Accordingly we shall have a regular lunar movement in latitude of 179°51' after the full circles. Now the time between the two eclipses was 1683 years 88 days 22 hours 35 minutes by apparent time, which agreed with the equal [time]. During that time there were 40,577 complete equal revolutions and 179°51', which agree with the numbers which we have already set down.

14. On the Positions of Lunar Anomaly in Latitude

However, in order to determine the positions of the moon's movement in relation to the established beginnings of calendar years, we have here also assumed two lunar eclipses, not at the same section and not at diametrically opposite parts, as in the foregoing, but at equal distances north or south, and fulfilling all the other requirements, [116ᵇ] as we said, in accordance with Ptolemy's rule, and in this way we shall solve our problem without any error.

Accordingly, the first eclipse, which we have already used in investigating other movements of the moon, is the one which we said was observed by Claud Ptolemy in the 19th year of Hadrian when two days of the month Chiach had passed, one equatorial hour before midnight at Alexandria, but at Cracow two hours before midnight, which the third day followed. The moon was eclipsed at the midpoint of the eclipse to the extent of ten-twelfths of the diameter, i.e., ten-twelfths from the north, while the sun was at 25°10' of Libra, and the position of lunar anomaly was 64°38' and its subtractive additosubtraction was 4°20' around the descending section.

We made careful observations of the other eclipse at Rome, in the year of Our Lord 1500, after the Nones of November, 2 hours after midnight, and it was the 8th daybreak before the Ides of November. But at Cracow which is 5° to the east, it was $2\frac{2}{5}$ hours after midnight, while the sun was at 23°16' of Scorpio; and once more there was a ten-twelfths eclipse from the north.

Therefore, since the death of Alexander there have passed 1824 Egyptian years 84 days 14 hours 20 minutes by apparent time, but by equal time 14 hours 16 minutes. Accordingly the mean movement of the moon was 174°14', and the lunar anomaly was 294°44', but as corrected it was 291°35'; and there was an additive additosubtraction of 4°27'.

Accordingly it is clear that at both these eclipses the distances of the moon from the highest apsis was approximately equal, and at both times the sun was at its mean apsis, and the magnitude of the shadows was equal. All that makes clear that the latitude of the moon was southern and equal; and hence that the moon was at an equal distance from the sections but was ascending at the second eclipse and descending at the first. Accordingly between both eclipses there are 1366 Egyptian years 358 days 4 hours 20 minutes by apparent time, but by equal time 4 hours 24 minutes, wherein the movement in latitude was 159°55'.

Now let $ABCD$ be the oblique circle of the moon; and let AB be its diameter and common section with the ecliptic. Let C be the northern limit, and D the southern; [117ᵃ] A the ecliptic section descending, and B the ecliptic section ascending. Now let there be taken AF and BE two equal arcs in the south, according as the first eclipse was at point F and the second at E. And again let FK be the subtractive additosubtraction at the first eclipse, and EL the additive additosubtraction at the second. Accordingly, since

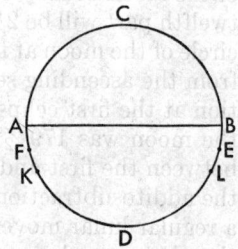

$$\text{arc } KL = 159°55'$$

and

$$\text{arc } FK = 4°20'$$

and

$$\text{arc } EL = 4°27';$$
$$\text{arc } FKLE = \text{arcs } FK + KL + LE = 168°42'.$$

And

$$180° - 168°42' = 11°18'.$$

Now

$$\text{arc } AF = \text{arc } BE = \tfrac{1}{2}(11°18') = 5°39',$$

which is the true distance of the moon from section AB, and on that account

$$\text{arc } AFK = 9°59'.$$

Hence it is clear that K the mean position in latitude is 99°59' away from the northern limit.

From the death of Alexander to this position and time of Ptolemy's observation there are 457 Egyptian years 91 days 10 hours by apparent time, but by equal time 9 hours 54 minutes, during which the mean movement in latitude is 50°59'. And when 50°59' is subtracted from 99°59', there remain 49° for noon on the first day of Thoth the first month by the Egyptian calendar at the beginning of the years of Alexander but on the Cracow meridian. Hence for each of the other beginnings there are given in accordance with the differences of time the positions of the course of the moon in latitude as taken in relation to the northern limit, from which we measure the movement.

Now from the first Olympiad to the death of Alexander there are 451 Egyptian years 247 days—from which in accordance with equality of time 7 minutes of an hour are subtracted—and during that time the progress in latitude was 136°57'. Again from the first Olympiad to Caesar there are 780 Egyptian years 12 hours, but 10 minutes of an hour are added to the equal time; and during that time the movement is 206°53'. Then come 45 years 12 days up to Christ. Accordingly if 136°57' are subtracted from 49° plus the 360° of the circle, there remain 272°3' for noon of the first day of the month Hekatombaion of the first Olympiad.

Now if 206°53' are added to 272°3', the sum will be 118°56' for midnight before the Kalends of January [117ᵇ] at the beginning of the Julian years.

Finally, with the addition of 10°49′ the sum becomes 129°45′ as the position [at the beginning of the years] of Our Lord similarly at midnight before the Kalends of January.

15. Construction of the Instrument for Observing Parallaxes

But chance and the hindrance of the lunar parallaxes did not grant to us, as it had to Ptolemy, the occasion of discovering experimentally that the greatest latitude of the moon—in accordance with the angle of section of its orbital circle and the ecliptic—is 5°, whereof the circle is 360°. For he was watching at Alexandria—which has 30°58′ as the elevation of the north pole— until the moon should come most near to the vertex of the horizon, namely when it was at the beginning of Cancer and at the northern limit, which can be foreknown by means of calculations. Therefore at that time by means of an instrument which he called the parallacticon and which was constructed for measuring the parallaxes of the moon, he found that the least distance was only $2\frac{1}{8}°$ from the vertex, and if any parallax had occurred at this distance it would necessarily have been very slight in such a small spatial interval. Accordingly by the subtraction of $2\frac{1}{8}°$ from 30°58′[1] the remainder is $28°50\frac{1}{2}′$, which exceeds the greatest obliquity of the ecliptic—which at that time was 23°51′20″—by approximately 5°; and this latitude for the moon is found to agree in every respect with the other particulars.

But the instrument for observing parallaxes consists of three straight-edges. Two of them are of equal length and are at least eight or nine feet long; the third is somewhat longer. The latter and one of the former two are joined to both extremities of the remaining straight-edge, by carefully making holes and fitting cylinders or pivots into them in such a way that while the straight-edges are movable in a plane surface they do not wobble at all at the joints. Now in the longer straight-edge a straight line should be drawn from the centre of its place of joining through its total length, and the line is made equal to the distance between the places of joining [on the other straight-edge] measured as accurately as possible. This line is divided into 1,000 equal parts— or into more, if that can be done; and the division of the remainder should be carried on [118ª] in the same unit parts, until it reaches 1414 parts, which subtend the side of a square that may be inscribed in a circle whose radius has 1,000 parts. It will be all right to cut off as superfluous the remainder of the straight-edge over and above this. In the other ruler too, there should be drawn from the centre of the joining-place a line equal to those 1,000 parts or to the distance between the centres of the two joining-places; the ruler should have eyepieces fastened to it on one side, as in a dioptra, which sight may have passage through. The eyepieces should be so adjusted that the sight-passages do not at all swerve away from the line already drawn the length of the straight-edge, but keep at an equal distance; and provided also that the line as extended from its terminus to the longer ruler can touch the divided line. And in this way by means of the rulers an isosceles triangle is made, the base of which will be along the parts of the divided line. Then a pole, which has been divided crosswise in the best manner and well smoothed, should be erected on a firm base. The ruler which has the two joining-places

[1]The elevation of the north pole above the horizon is equal to the declination of the vertex of the horizon from the equator.

should be affixed to this pole by means of pivots, around which the instrument may swing, like a swinging door, but in such a way that the straight line through the centres of the joining-places will always correspond to the plumb-line of the ruler and point towards the vertex of the horizon, as if its axis. Accordingly when a person who wishes to find the distance of some star from the vertex of the horizon has the star itself in full view along a straight line through the eyepieces, then by the application underneath of the ruler with the divided line, he should learn how many unit parts—whereof the diameter of the circle has 20,000—subtend the angle between the line of vision and the axis of the horizon; and by means of the table he will get the sought arc of the great circle passing through the star and the vertex of the horizon.

16. How the Parallaxes of the Moon Are Determined

By means of this instrument, as we said, Ptolemy found the greatest latitude of the moon to be 5°. Next he turned to observing the parallax and said he discovered that at Alexandria its was 1°7', while the sun was at 5°28' of Libra and the mean movement of the moon away from the sun was 78°13', the regular anomaly was 262°20'; the movement in latitude was 354°40'; the additive additosubtraction was 7°26'; [118ᵇ] and accordingly the position of the moon was at 3°9' of Capricorn. The corrected movement in latitude was 2°6'; the northern latitude of the moon was 4°59'; its declination from the equator was 23°49'; and the latitude of Alexandria was 30°58'. The moon, he says, as seen through the instrument, was approximately in the meridian circle at 50°45' from the vertex of the horizon, i.e., 1°7' more than the computation demanded. Hence by the rule of the ancients concerning the eccentric circle and the epicycle, he shows that the distance of the moon from the centre of the Earth was then 39ᵖ45' whereof the radius of the Earth is 1ᵖ; and what next follows from the ratio of the circles, namely that the greatest distance of the moon from the Earth—which they say occurs at a new and at a full moon in the apogee of the epicycle—is 64ᵖ10', but the least distance—at the quadratures and at the half moon in the perigee of the epicycle—is only 33ᵖ33'. Hence he even evaluated the parallaxes, which occur at about 90° from the vertex [of the horizon]: the least at 53'34″, and the greatest at 1°43'—as it is possible to see in a broad outline what he built up concerning them. But now it is perfectly obvious to those wishing to consider the question that these things are far otherwise, as we have found out experimentally very often.

However, we shall review two observations, by which it is again made clear that our hypotheses as to the moon have more certitude than his, because they are found to agree better with the appearances and to leave nothing in doubt. In the 1522nd year since the birth of Christ, on the 5th day before the Kalends of October, after the passage of 5⅔ equal hours since midday, at about sunset at Frauenburg we found by means of the parallactic instrument that the centre of the moon, which was in the meridian circle, was 82°50' distant from the vertex of the horizon. Accordingly from the beginning of the years of Our Lord to this hour there were 1522 Egyptian years 284 days 17⅔ hours by apparent time but by equal time 17 hours 24 minutes. Wherefore the apparent position of the sun was by calculation at 13°29' of Libra and the regular movement of the moon away from the sun [119ᵃ] was 87°6'; the regular anomaly was 357°39'; but the true [the corrected] anomaly was 358°40', and it added 7'; and thus the true position of the moon was at 12°32′ of Aries. The mean movement in latitude was 197°1′ from the northern limit, the true was 197°8′; the southern latitude of the moon was 4°47′; the moon had a declination of 27°41′ from the equator; the latitude of the place of our observation was 54°19′, and the addition of 54°19′ to the lunar declination makes the true distance of the moon from the pole of the horizon to be 82°. Accordingly the 50′ not accounted for belong to the parallax, which by Ptolemy's teaching should be 1°17′.

Once more we made another observation at the same place in the 1524th year of Our Lord on the 7th day before the Ides of August 6 hours after midday; and we saw through the same instrument the moon ar 82° from the vertex of the horizon. Accordingly from the beginning of the years of Our Lord to this hour there were 1524 Egyptian years 234 days 18 hours [by apparent time] and also 18 hours by exact time. The position of the sun was by calculation at 24°14′ of Leo; the mean movement of the moon away from the sun was 97°6′; the regular anomaly was 242°10′; the corrected anomaly was 239°43′, adding approximately 7° to the mean movement; wherefore the true position of the moon was at 9°39′ of Sagittarius; the mean movement of latitude was 193°19′; the true, 200°17′; the southern latitude of the moon was 4°41′; the southern declination was 26°36′, and the addition of 26°36′ to 54°19′ of the latitude of the place of observation makes the distance of the moon from the pole of the horizon to be 80°55′. But there appeared to be 82°. Accordingly the difference of 1°5′ came from the lunar parallax, which according to Ptolemy should have been 1°38′ and also according to the theory of the ancients, as the harmonic ratio, which follows from their hypotheses, forces you to admit.

17. Distance of the Moon from the Earth and Demonstration of Their Ratio in Parts Whereof the Radius of the Earth Is the Unit

[119ᵇ] From this it will now be made apparent how great the distance of the moon from the earth is. And without this distance a sure ratio cannot be given for the parallaxes, for they are mutually related. And it will be established in this way. Let AB be a great circle of the Earth, and let C be its centre. Around C let another circle be described in comparison with which the Earth has considerable magnitude, and let this circle be DE. Let D be the pole of the horizon, and let the centre of the moon be at E, so that DE its distance from the vertex is known. Accordingly, since at the first observation,

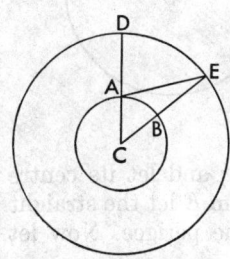

$$\text{angle } DAE = 82°50′$$

and by calculation

$$\text{angle } ACE = 82°,$$

and hence

$$\text{angle } DAE - \text{angle } ACE = 50′,$$

which belonged to the parallax; we have triangle ACE with its angles given and therefore with its sides given. For since

$$\text{angle } CAE \text{ is given,}$$
$$\text{side } CE = 99,219$$

where diameter of circle circumscribing triangle AEC = 100,000

and

$$AC = 1,454;$$

and

$$CE = 68^p,$$

where AC, radius of Earth, = 1^p.

And this was the distance of the moon from the centre of the Earth at the first observation.

But at the second observation

$$\text{angle } DAE = 82°,$$

as the apparent movement; and, by calculation,

$$\text{angle } ACE = 80°55';$$

and, by subtraction,

$$\text{angle } AEC = 1°5'.$$

Accordingly,

$$\text{side } EC = 99,027$$

and

side $AC = 1894$

where diameter of circle circumscribing triangle = 100,000.

And so

$$CE = 56^p42',$$

where the radius of Earth = 1^p.

And that was the distance of the moon.

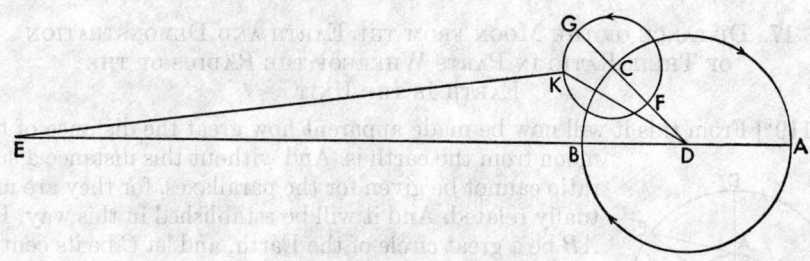

But now let ABC be the greater epicycle of the moon; and let its centre be D. Let E be taken as the centre of the Earth, and from E let the straight line $EBDA$ be drawn, so that A is the apogee and B the perigee. Now let

$$\text{arc } ABC = 242°10',$$

in accordance with the computed regularity of the lunar anomaly.

And with C as centre let epicycle FGK be described, whereon

$$\text{arc } FGK = 194°10',$$

twice the distance of the moon from the sun. And let DK be joined.

Thus,

$$\text{angle } GDK = - \text{add. } [120^a] \ 2°27';$$

and, by subtraction,

$$\text{corr. anomaly} = 59°43',$$

since

$$\text{arc } CDB = \text{arc } ABC - 180° = 62°10',$$

and
$$\text{angle } BEK = 7°,$$
Therefore, in triangle KDE the angles are given in the degrees whereof 2 rt. angles = 180°; and the ratio of the sides is also given:
$$DE = 91,856$$
and
$$EK = 86,354,$$
where diameter of circle circumscribing triangle $KDE = 100,000$.

But
$$KE = 94,010$$
$$\text{where } DE = 100,000.$$
Now it was shown above that
$$DF = 8,600$$
and
$$DFG = 13,340.$$
Accordingly it follows from the given ratio that when, as was shown,
$$EK = 56^{\mathrm{p}}42',$$
where radius of the Earth = 1^{p};

then
$$DE = 60^{\mathrm{p}}18',$$
$$DF = 5^{\mathrm{p}}11',$$
$$DFG = 8^{\mathrm{p}}2';$$
and hence, as extended in a straight line.
$$EDG = 68\tfrac{1}{3}{}^{\mathrm{p}};$$
and that is the greatest altitude of the half moon. Furthermore,
$$ED - DG = 52°17',$$
which is its least distance. And thus, at its greatest,
$$EDF = 65\tfrac{1}{2}{}^{\mathrm{p}},$$
which is the altitude occurring at the bright, full moon; and at its least,
$$EDF - DF = 55^{\mathrm{p}}8'.$$
And we should not be moved by the fact that others—and especially those to whom the parallaxes of the moon could not become known except partially, on account of the location of their places—estimate the greatest distance of the new moon and the full moon to be $64^{\mathrm{p}}10'$. But the greater nearness of the moon to the horizon—for it is clear that the parallaxes are filled out in relation to the horizon—has allowed us to perceive them more perfectly, and we have not found the parallaxes to differ by more than $1'$ on account of the difference caused by the nearness of the moon to the horizon.

18. On the Diameter of the Moon and on the Diameter of the Terrestrial Shadow in the Place of Passage of the Moon

[120^{b}] Moreover, the apparent diameters of the moon and the shadow vary with the distance of the moon from the Earth. Wherefore it is pertinent to speak of them. And although the diameters of the sun and the moon are rightly determined through the dioptra of Hipparchus, nevertheless in the case of the moon astronomers judge that this is done with more certainty through some particular eclipses of the moon, in which the moon is at an equal distance from its highest or lowest apsis, especially if at that time the sun too is in the same relative situation, so that the circle of shadow which the moon passes through is found equal

—unless the eclipses themselves are unequal in extent. For it is clear that the comparison of the difference in extent of the eclipses with the latitude of the moon shows how much of the circle around the centre of the Earth the diameter of the moon subtends. When that has been perceived, the semidiameter of the shadow is also known.

All this will be made clearer by an example. In this way at the midpoint of the first eclipse $3\!\!\not{}\!_{12}$ of the diameter of the moon was eclipsed; and the moon had a latitude of 47′54″; but at the other eclipse $10\!\!\not{}\!_{12}$ of the diameter was eclipsed, and the latitude was 29′37″. The difference between the extent of the eclipses is $7\!\!\not{}\!_{12}$ of the diameter; the difference in latitude is 18′17″; and the $12\!\!\not{}\!_{12}$ are proportional to the 31′20″ which the diameter of the moon subtends. Accordingly it is clear that the centre of the moon at the midpoint of the first eclipse was about a quarter of the moon's diameter—or 7′50″ of latitude—beyond the shadow. If these 7′50″ are subtracted from the 47′54″ of the total latitude, 40′4″ remain as the semidiameter of the shadow; just as at the other eclipse the shadow occupied —in proportion to $1\!\!\not{}\!_{3}$ of the lunar diameter—10′27″ more than the latitude of the centre of the moon. The addition of 29′37″ to 10′27″ similarly makes the semidiameter of the shadow to be 40′4″. And so in accordance with Ptolemy's conclusion, when the sun and moon are in conjunction or opposition at their greatest distance from the Earth, the diameter of the moon is 31′20″— [121ª] as he admits he found the sun's diameter to be through the dioptra of Hipparchus— but the diameter of the shadow is 1°21′ 20″; and he believed that the diameters were in the ratio of 13 to 5, i.e., the ratio of double plus three-fifths.

19. How the Distances of the Sun and Moon from the Earth, Their Diameters and That of the Shadow at the Place of Crossing of the Moon, and the Axis of the Shadow Are Demonstrated Simultaneously

But even the sun has some parallax; and since it is very slight, it is not perceived so easily, except that the following things are related reciprocally: namely the distance of the sun and moon from the Earth, their diameters and that of the shadow at the crossing of the moon, and the axis of the shadow; and for that reason they are mutually productive of one another in analytical demonstrations. First we shall review Ptolemy's conclusions on these things, and how he demonstrated them, and we shall draw out from them what seems the most true. He assumed $31\!\!\not{}\!_{3}′$ as the apparent diameter of the sun, which he employed without any qualification. He assumed as equal to that the diameter of the full and new moon when at its apogee, which he says was at a distance of 64ᴾ10′, whereof the radius of the Earth is 1ᴾ.

From that he demonstrated the rest in this way: Let ABC be the circle of the solar globe around centre D; and let EFG be the circle of the terrestrial globe around its centre K at its greatest distance from the sun. Let AG and CE be straight lines touching both circles, and let them as extended meet at the apex of the shadow, as at point S. And let DKS be a line through the centres of the sun and the Earth. Moreover, let AK and KC be drawn, and let AC and GE be joined, which should hardly differ at all from the diameters on account of the great distance between them. Now on DKS let equal segments LK and KM be taken in proportion to the distance of the moon in the apogee when new and when full: in his opinion 64ᴾ10′, where EK is 1ᴾ. Let QMR be the diameter of

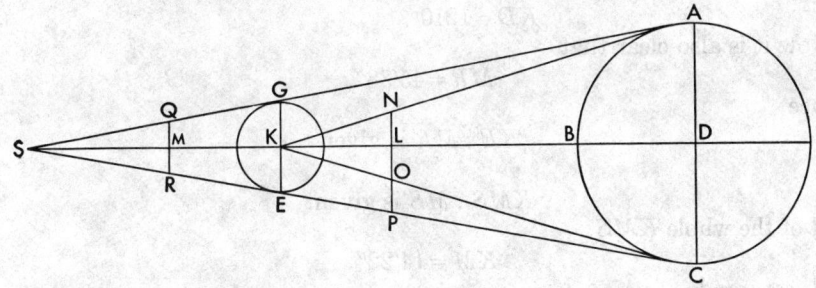

the shadow at this crossing of the moon; and let *NLO* be the diameter of the moon at right angles to *DK*, and let it be extended as *LOP*.

The first problem is to find

$$DK : KE.$$

Accordingly, since

$$\text{angle } NKD = 31\tfrac{1}{3}',$$
$$\text{where 4 rt. angles} = 360°,$$

and [121^b]

$$\text{angle } LKO = \tfrac{1}{2} \text{ angle } NKO,$$
$$\text{angle } LKO = 15\tfrac{2}{3}'.$$

And

$$\text{angle } L = 90°.$$

Accordingly, in triangle *LKO*, which has its angles given,

$$KL : LO \text{ is given,}$$

and

$$LO = 17^p33',$$

and

$$LK = 64^p10',$$
$$\text{where } KE = 1^p.$$

And because

$$LO : MR = 5 : 13,$$
$$MR = 45'38''.$$

But since *LOP* and *MR* are parallel to *KE* at equal intervals, on that account

$$LOP + MR = 2\, KE.$$

And

$$OP = LOP - (MR + LO) = 56'49''.$$

Now by Euclid, VI, 2,

$$EC : PC = KC : OC = KD : LD = KE : OP = 60' : 56'49''.$$

Hence

$$LD = 56'49'',$$
$$\text{where } DLK = 1^p.$$

And accordingly, by subtraction,

$$KL = 3'11''.$$

But according as

$$KL = 64^p10',$$
$$\text{where } FK = 1^p,$$

$$KD = 1210^{\text{p}}.$$

Now it is also clear that

$$MR = 45'38''.$$

Hence

$$KE : MR \text{ is given}$$

and

$$KMS : MS \text{ is given}.$$

And of the whole KMS

$$KM = 14'22''.$$

And, *separando*,

$$KMS = 268^{\text{p}}$$
$$\text{where } KM = 64^{\text{p}}10'.$$

So in truth Ptolemy.

But others after Ptolemy, since they found that these things did not agree sufficiently with the appearances, published other things concerning all this. None the less they admit that the greatest distance of the full moon and the new moon from the Earth is $64^{\text{p}}10'$; and that the apparent diameter of the sun at its apogee is $31\frac{1}{3}'$. They even grant that the diameter of the shadow at the place of crossing of the moon is as 13 to 5, even as Ptolemy himself. Nevertheless they deny that the apparent diameter of the moon at that time is greater than $29\frac{1}{2}'$; and for that reason they put the diameter of the shadow at approximately $1°16\frac{3}{4}'$. They hold that it follows from this that at its apogee the distance of the sun from the Earth is 1146^{p} and that the axis of the shadow is 254^{p}, whereof the radius of the Earth is 1^{p}. [122a] And astronomers attribute these things to the Harranite philosopher [al-Battani] as the discoverer, although they cannot be joined together at all reasonably. We considered that these things must be adjusted and corrected as follows, since we put the apparent diameter of the sun in its apogee at $31'40''$—for it should be somewhat greater now than before Ptolemy—and that of the full or the new moon in its highest apsis at $30'$ and the diameter of the shadow in its crossing at $80\frac{3}{5}'$. For astronomers should have a slightly greater ratio than that of 5 to 13, that is to say 150 to 403. And the whole sun is not covered by the moon, unless the moon is at a lesser distance from the Earth than 62^{p}, whereof the radius of the Earth is 1^{p}. For when these things are put down in this way they seem to be connected with one another and the rest in a sure fashion and to be consonant with the apparent eclipses of the sun and moon. And in accordance with the foregoing demonstration:

$$LO = 17'85''$$
$$\text{where } KE \text{ radius of Earth} = 1^{\text{p}}.$$

And for that reason

$$MR = 46'1'',$$

and

$$OP = 56'51''.$$

And

$$DLK = 1179^{\text{p}},$$

the distance from the Earth of the sun at its apogee; and

$$KMS = 265,$$

which is the axis of the shadow.

20. On the Magnitude of These Three Celestial Bodies: the Sun, Moon, and Earth, and Their Comparison with One Another

Hence it is also manifest that

$$LK : KD = 1 : 18$$

and

$$LO : DC = 1 : 18.$$

Now

$$1 : 18 = 17'8'' : 5^p27'$$
$$\text{where } KE = 1^p.$$

And

$$SK : KE = 265^p : 1^p = SKD : DC = 1444^p : 5^p27'.$$

For they are all proportional; and that will be the ratio of the diameters of the sun and Earth. But, as globes are in the ratio of the cubes[1] of their diameters, accordingly

$$(5^p27')^3 = 161 \; 7\!/\!8^p;$$

and the sun is 161 7⁄8 greater than the terrestrial globe.

Again, since

$$\text{moon's radius} = 17'9''$$
$$\text{where } KE = 1^p,$$

[122^b] Earth's diameter : moon's diameter = 7 : 2, i.e., in the triple sesquialter ratio. When the cube[2] of that ratio is taken, it shows that the Earth is 42⅞ greater than the moon.

And hence the sun will be 6,999 62⁄63 greater than the moon.

21. On the Apparent Diameter of the Sun and Its Parallaxes

But since the same magnitude when farther away appears smaller than when nearer; for that reason it happens that the sun, moon, and the shadow of the Earth vary with their unequal distances from the Earth no less than do their parallaxes. By means of the aforesaid, all these things are easily determinable for any elongation whatsoever. That is first made manifest in the case of the sun. For since we have shown that the Earth at its farthest is 10,323 parts distant from the sun, whereof the radius of the orbital circle of annual revolution = 10,000; and at its nearest the Earth has a distance of 9,678 parts of the remainder of the diameter: accordingly the highest apsis is 1179^p whereof the radius of the Earth is 1^p, the lowest apsis will be 1105^p, and so the mean apsis will be 1142^p. Accordingly in the right triangle[3]

$$1,000,000 \div 1179 = 848^4 = \tfrac{1}{2} \text{ ch. } 2 \; (2'55''),$$

which is the small angle of greatest parallax, and that is found around the horizon. Similarly, as the least distance is 1105^p,

---

[1] *literally,* in the triplicate ratio.

[2] *literally,* the triplicate.

[3] *i.e.,* the right triangle formed by the line joining the centres of the sun and the Earth, the tangent from the centre of the sun to the Earth's surface, and the radius of the Earth to that point of tangency.

[4] *i.e.,* when the highest apsis = 1179^p, 1^p = 848 whereof radius of circle = 1,000,000.

$$1,000,000 - 1105 = 905^1 = \tfrac{1}{2} \text{ ch. } 2 \ (3''7'');$$

and 3''7'' measures the angle of greatest parallax of the lowest apsis. Now it was shown that the diameter of the sun is 5ᵖ27', whereof the diameter of the Earth is 1ᵖ, and that it appears at the highest apsis as 31'48''. For

$$1179^{\text{p}} : 5^{\text{p}} \ 27' = 2,000,000 : 9,245;$$

where diameter of circle = 2,000,000,

and

$$\tfrac{1}{2} \text{ ch. } 2(31'48'') = 9245.$$

It follows that at the least distance of 1105ᵖ there is an apparent diameter of 33'54''. Therefore the difference between them is 2'6''; but there is a difference of only 12'' [123a] between the parallaxes. Ptolemy considered that both of these differences should be ignored on account of their smallness; for 1' or 2' is not easily perceptible to the senses, much less than are a few seconds perceptible. Wherefore if we keep the greatest parallax of the sun at 3' everywhere, we shall be seen to have made no error. Now we shall determine the mean apparent diameters of the sun through its mean distances; or, as do others, through the apparent hourly movement of the sun, which they believe to be to its diameter as 5 to 66 or as 1 to 14⅕. For its hourly movement is approximately proportional to its distance.

22. On the Unequal Apparent Diameter of the Moon and Its Parallaxes

A greater diversity in the apparent diameter and parallaxes appears in the case of the moon as being the nearest planet. For since its greatest distance from the Earth is 65½ᵖ at new moon and full moon, its least distance will by the above demonstrations be 55ᵖ8'; and the greatest [altitudinal] elongation of the half moon will be 68ᵖ21', and the least 52ᵖ17'. Accordingly we shall have the parallaxes of the setting or rising moon at these four termini, when we have divided the radius of the circle by the distances of the moon from the Earth: the parallax of the farthest half moon will be 50'18'' and that of the farthest new or full moon will be 52'24''; the parallax of the nearest full or new moon will be 62'21'' and that of the nearest half moon 65'45''.

Furthermore by this the apparent diameters of the moon are established. For it was shown that the diameter of the Earth is to the diameter of the moon as 7 to 2, and the radius of the Earth will be to the diameter of the moon as 7 to 4. Moreover, the parallaxes are in that ratio to the apparent diameters of the moon, since the straight lines, which comprehend the angles of the greater parallaxes, do not differ at all from the apparent diameters at the same crossing of the moon; and the angles, [or arcs of parallax] are approximately proportional to the chords subtending them; and their difference is not perceptible to sense. By this summary it is clear that at the first limit of the parallaxes which have been already set forth the apparent [123ᵇ] diameter of the moon will be 28¾'; at the second, approximately 30'; at the third, 35'38''; and at the last limit, 37'34''. By the hypothesis of Ptolemy and others the diameter would have been approximately 1°, and so it ought to have been, as the half moon at that time was shedding as much light on the Earth as the full moon would.

¹Similarly, where the lowest apsis = 1105ᵖ, 1ᵖ = 905 whereof radius of circle = 1,000,000.

23. What the Ratio of Difference Between the Shadows of the Earth Is

We have already made clear that
$$\text{shadow's diameter : moon's diameter} = 403 : 150.$$
For that reason at a full or a new moon, when the sun is at its apogee, the shadow's is found to be $80'36''$ at its least and $95'44''$ at its greatest; and the greatest difference is $15'8''$. Moreover, the shadow of the Earth varies, even in the same place of crossing of the moon, on account of the unequal distance of the Earth from the sun, as follows:

For, as in the foregoing diagram, let DKS the straight line through the centres of the sun and the Earth

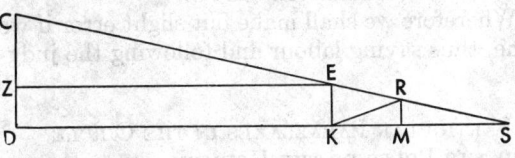

be drawn again, and also CES the line of tangency. As was shown, when
$$\text{distance } DK = 1179^\text{p},$$
$$\text{where } KE = 1^\text{p}$$
and
$$KM = 62^\text{p}$$

then the semidiameter of the shadow
$$MR = 46'1''$$
$$\text{where } KE = 1^\text{p};$$
and [KR being joined]
$$\text{angle } MKR = 42'32'',$$
which is the angle of sight, and the axis of the shadow
$$KMS = 265^\text{p}.$$
Now when the Earth is nearest to the sun, so that
$$DK = 1105^\text{p},$$
we shall evaluate the shadow of the Earth at the same crossing of the moon, as follows: For let EZ be drawn parallel to DK. Then
$$CZ : ZE = EK : KS.$$

But
$$CZ = 4^\text{p}27'$$
and
$$ZE = 1105^\text{p}.$$
For
$$ZE = DK$$
and
$$DZ = KE,$$
as KZ is a parallelogram. Accordingly
$$KS = 248^\text{p}19'$$
$$\text{where } KE = 1^\text{p}.$$

Now
$$KM = 62;$$
and accordingly, by subtraction,
$$MS = 186^\text{p}19'.$$

But since
$$SM : MR = SK : KE,$$
therefore

$$MR = 45'1'',$$
where [124ª] $KE = 1^p.$

And hence

angle $MKR = 41'35'',$

which is the angle of sight. Whence it happens that on account of the approach and withdrawal of the sun and the Earth, the greatest difference in the diameters of the shadow at the same place of crossing of the moon is 1', whereof EK $= 1^p$, in proportion to an angle of sight of 57'', whereof 4 rt. angles $= 360°$. Furthermore, in the first case

shadow's diameter : moon's diameter $> 13 : 5$;

but here

shadow's diameter : moon's diameter $< 13 : 5$,

as 13 : 5 is a sort of mean ratio. Wherefore we shall make but slight error if we employ it as everywhere the same, thus saving labour and following the judgment of the ancients.

24. On the Table of the Particular Parallaxes in the Circle Passing Through the Poles of the Horizon

Moreover, it will not be difficult now to determine all the single parallaxes of the sun and the moon. For let there be drawn again AB the terrestrial circle through the vertex of the horizon, with C as its centre. And in the same plane let DE be the orbital circle of the moon, FG that of the sun, CDF the line through the vertex of the horizon; and let line CEG be drawn, in which the true positions of the sun and the moon are understood to be, and let the lines of sight AG and AE be joined to those points. Therefore the parallaxes of the sun are measured by angle AGC, those of the moon by angle AEC. Moreover, there is a parallax between the sun and moon which is measured by angle GAE, which is determined according to the difference between angles AGC and AEC. Now let us take angle ACG, with which we wish to compare those angles; and, for example, let

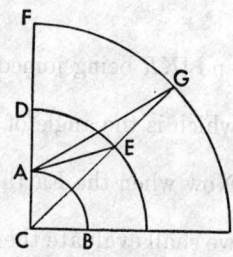

angle $ACG = 30°.$

Now it is clear from what we have shown concerning plane triangles that when

line $CG = 1142^p,$
where $AC = 1^p,$
angle $AGC = 1\frac{1}{2}',$

which is the difference between the true and the seeming altitude of the sun. But when

angle $ACG = 60°,$
angle $AGC = 2'36''.$

Everything will be similarly clear as regards the remaining angles.

But in the case of the moon at its four limits: If at the greatest lunar distance from the Earth, wherein, as we said,

$CE = 68^p21',$
[124ᵇ] where $CA = 1^p,$
angle $DCE = 30°,$
where 4 rt. angles $= 360°,$

we shall have triangle ACE in which the two sides AC and CE together with angle ACE have been given. From that we find that

$$\text{parallax } AEC = 25'28''.$$

And when

$$CE = 65\tfrac{1}{2}^{\mathrm{p}}$$
$$\text{angle } AEC = 26'36''.$$

Similarly in the third case when

$$CE = 55^{\mathrm{p}}8',$$
$$\text{parallax } AEC = 31'42''.$$

Finally, at the least distance when

$$CE = 52^{\mathrm{p}}17',$$
$$\text{angle } AEC = 33'27''.$$

Again, when

$$\text{arc } DE = 60°,$$

the parallaxes in the same order will be as follows:

$$\text{First   parallax} = 43'55'',$$
$$\text{second parallax} = 45'51'',$$
$$\text{third parallax} = 54\tfrac{1}{2}',$$

and

$$\text{fourth parallax} = 57\tfrac{1}{2}'.$$

We shall inscribe all these things after the order of the subjoined table, which for the sake of convenience we shall extend like all the other tables into a series of thirty rows but proceeding by 6°'s by which twice the arcs from the vertex of the horizon—of which the greatest is 90°—are given to be understood. But we have divided the table into nine columns. For in the first and second will be found the common numbers of the circle. We shall put the parallaxes of the sun in the third, and in the next the lunar parallaxes, and in the fifth column the differences, by which the least parallaxes, which occur at the half moon and at the apogee, are deficient as measured by the parallaxes occurring at the apogee of the full moon or the new moon. The sixth column will contain the parallaxes which the full or bright moon produces at its perigee; and in the next column are the minutes of difference, by which the parallaxes which occur at half moon when the moon is nearest to us exceed those occurring at half moon in the apogee. Then, the two spaces which are left are reserved for the proportional minutes, by which the parallaxes between these four limits can be computed. We shall set forth these parallaxes, and first in connection with the apogee and the parallaxes which are between the first two limits—as follows.

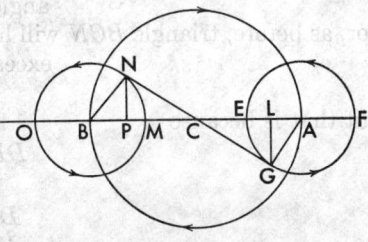

Let circle [125ᵃ] AB be the first epicycle of the moon, and let C be its centre. With D taken as the centre of the Earth, let the straight line $DBCA$ be drawn; and with apogee A as centre let the second epicycle EFG be described. Now let

$$\text{arc } EG = 60°,$$

and let AG and CG be joined. Accordingly, since in the foregoing it was shown that

$$\text{straight line } CE = 5^\text{p}11',$$

where radius of Earth $= 1^\text{p}$,

$$\text{straight line } DC = 60^\text{p}18',$$

and

$$\text{straight line } EF = 2^\text{p}51',$$

then in triangle ACG

$$\text{side } GA = 1^\text{p}25'$$

and

$$\text{side } AC = 6^\text{p}36';$$

and

$$\text{angle } CAG \text{ is given,}$$

which is the angle comprehended by GA and AC. Accordingly, by what has been shown concerning plane triangles,

$$\text{side } CG = 6^\text{p}7'.$$

Accordingly, as extended in a straight line,

$$DCG = DCL = 66^\text{p}25'.$$

But

$$DCE = 65\tfrac{1}{2}^\text{p}.$$

Therefore, by subtraction,

$$EL = 55\tfrac{1}{2}',$$

and that is the excess. Moreover, by this given ratio, when

$$DCE = 60^\text{p};$$
$$EF = 2^\text{p}37',$$

and

$$EL = 46'.$$

Therefore, according as,

$$EF = 60',$$
$$\text{excess } EL = 18'.$$

We shall mark these down in the eighth column of the table as corresponding to 60° [in the first column].

We shall show something similar in the case of perigee B. Let the second epicycle MNO be drawn again around centre B, and let

$$\text{angle } MBN = 60°.$$

For, as before, triangle BCN will have its sides and angles given, and similarly

$$\text{excess } MP = 55\tfrac{1}{2}'$$

where Earth's radius $= 1^\text{p}$.

But that is because

$$DBM = 55^\text{p}8'.$$

If

$$DBM = 60^\text{p};$$
$$MBO = 3^\text{p}7',$$

and
$$\text{excess } MP = 55'.$$
Now
$$3^{\mathrm{p}}7' : 55' = 60' : 18';$$
and so on, the same as before. Nevertheless there is a difference of a few seconds. We shall do this for the rest; and thus we shall fill out the eighth column of the table. But if we were to employ instead of them, those [proportional minutes] which were set out in the table of additosubtractions, we shall make no error. For they are approximately the same—and it is a question of very small numbers. [125^{b}] There remain the proportional minutes which occur at the mean termini, namely between the second and the third termini.

Now let circle AB be the first epicycle at the new or full moon. Let C be its centre; and let D be taken as the centre of the Earth. And let the straight line

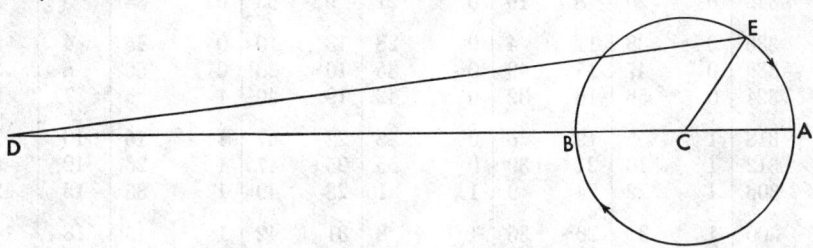

$DBCA$ be extended. Now from apogee A let some arc be taken: for instance, let
$$\text{arc } AE = 60°;$$
and let DE and CE be joined. For we shall have the triangle DCE, in which two sides are given:
$$CD = 60^{\mathrm{p}}19'$$
and
$$CE = 5^{\mathrm{p}}11'.$$
Now angle DCE is an interior angle, and
$$\text{angle } DCE = 180° - \text{angle } ACE.$$
Accordingly, by what we have shown concerning triangles,
$$DE = 63^{\mathrm{p}}4'.$$
But
$$DBA = 65\tfrac{1}{2}^{\mathrm{p}},$$
and
$$DBA - ED = 2^{\mathrm{p}}26'.$$
Now
$$AB = 10^{\mathrm{p}}22';$$
and
$$10^{\mathrm{p}}22' : 2^{\mathrm{p}}26' = 60' : 14'.$$
And they are inscribed in the table in the ninth column opposite 60°. Following this example, we have completed the rest and filled out the table, which follows. And we have added another table of the semidiameters of the sun and the moon, and the shadow of the Earth, so that as far as possible they may be at hand.

TABLE OF THE PARALLAXES OF THE SUN AND MOON

Common Numbers		Parallaxes of the sun		Parallax of the moon at the second limit		Difference between the first and second limit of the moon: to be subtracted		Parallax of the moon at the third limit		Difference between the third and fourth lunar limit: to be added		Proportional minutes of the smaller epicycle	Proportional minutes of the greater epicycle
Deg.	Deg.	Min.	Sec.	Min.	Sec.	Min.	Sec.	Min.	Sec.	Min.	Sec.		
6	354	0	10	2	46	0	7	3	18	0	12	0	0
12	348	0	19	5	33	0	14	6	36	0	23	1	0
18	342	0	29	8	19	0	21	9	53	0	34	3	1
24	336	0	38	11	4	0	28	13	10	0	45	4	2
30	330	0	47	13	49	0	35	16	26	0	56	5	3
36	324	0	56	16	32	0	42	19	40	1	6	7	5
42	318	1	5	19	5	0	48	22	47	1	16	10	7
48	312	1	13	21	39	0	55	25	47	1	26	12	9
54	306	1	22	24	9	1	1	28	49	1	35	15	12
60	300	1	31	26	36	1	8	31	42	1	45	18	14
66	294	1	39	28	57	1	14	34	31	1	54	21	17
72	288	1	46	31	14	1	19	37	14	2	3	24	20
78	282	1	53	33	25	1	24	39	50	2	11	27	23
84	276	2	0	35	31	1	29	42	19	2	19	30	26
90	270	2	7	37	31	1	34	44	40	2	26	34	29
96	264	2	13	39	24	1	39	46	54	2	33	37	32
102	258	2	20	41	10	1	44	49	0	2	40	39	35
108	252	2	26	42	50	1	48	50	59	2	46	42	38
114	246	2	31	44	24	1	52	52	49	2	53	45	41
120	240	2	36	45	51	1	56	54	30	3	0	47	44
126	234	2	40	47	8	2	0	56	2	3	6	49	47
132	228	2	44	48	15	2	2	57	23	3	11	51	49
138	222	2	49	49	15	2	3	58	36	3	14	53	52
134	216	2	52	50	10	2	4	59	39	3	17	55	54
150	210	2	54	50	55	2	4	60	31	3	20	57	56
156	204	2	56	51	29	2	5	61	12	3	22	58	57
162	198	2	58	51	56	2	5	61	47	3	23	59	58
168	192	2	59	52	13	2	6	62	9	3	23	59	59
174	186	3	0	52	22	2	6	62	19	3	24	60	60
180	180	3	0	52	24	2	6	62	21	3	24	60	60

TABLE OF THE SEMIDIAMETERS OF THE SUN, MOON, AND SHADOW

Common Numbers		Semidiameter of the Sun		Semidiameter of the Moon		Semidiameter of the Shadow		Variation of the Shadow
Deg.	Deg.	Min.	Sec.	Min.	Sec.	Min.	Sec.	Min.
6	354	15	50	15	0	40	18	0
12	358	15	50	15	1	40	21	0
18	342	15	51	15	3	40	26	1
24	336	15	52	15	6	40	34	2
30	330	15	53	15	9	40	42	3
36	324	15	55	15	14	40	56	4
42	318	15	57	15	19	41	10	6
48	312	16	0	15	25	41	26	9
54	306	16	3	15	32	41	44	11
60	300	16	6	15	39	42	2	14
66	294	16	9	15	47	42	24	16
72	288	16	12	15	56	42	40	19
78	282	16	15	16	5	43	13	22
84	276	16	19	16	13	43	34	25
90	270	16	22	16	22	43	58	27
96	264	16	26	16	30	44	20	31
102	258	16	29	16	39	44	44	33
108	252	16	32	16	47	45	6	36
114	246	16	36	16	55	45	20	39
120	240	16	39	17	4	45	52	42
126	234	16	42	17	12	46	13	45
132	228	16	45	17	19	46	32	47
138	222	16	48	17	26	46	51	49
144	216	16	50	17	32	47	7	51
150	210	16	53	17	38	47	23	53
156	204	16	54	17	41	47	31	54
162	198	16	55	17	44	47	39	55
168	192	16	56	17	46	47	44	56
174	186	16	57	17	48	47	49	56
180	180	16	57	17	49	47	52	57

25. On Computing the Parallax of the Sun and Moon

[127ª] We shall also set out briefly the mode of computing the parallaxes of the sun and moon by the table. If for the distance of the sun or twice the distance of the moon from the vertex of the horizon we take the corresponding parallaxes in the table—the solar parallaxes simply but the lunar parallaxes at the four limits—and if we take the first proportional minutes corresponding to twice the movement of the moon or twice its distance from the sun; by means of these minutes we shall determine the parts of the difference between the first and the last terminus which are proportional to sixty minutes; we shall always subtract these parts from the parallaxes following next, and we shall always add the later parts to the parallax at the next to the last limit. And we shall have two corrected parallaxes of the moon at the apogee and perigee; the lesser epicycle increases or decreases these parallaxes. Then we shall take the last proportional minutes corresponding to the lunar anomaly; and by means of them we shall determine the proportional part of the difference between the two parallaxes found nearest; we shall always add this proportional part to the first corrected parallax, the parallax at the apogee; and the result will be the parallax of the moon sought for that place and time, as in the following example.

Let the distance of the moon from the vertex [of the horizon] be 54°, the mean movement of the moon 15°, and the corrected anomaly 100°: I wish to find from them by means of the table the lunar parallax. I double the degrees of distance, and the result is 108°, to which in the table there correspond a difference of 1′48″ between the first and second limit, a parallax of 42′50″ at the second limit, a parallax of 50′59″ at the third limit, and a difference of 2′46″ between the third and the fourth limit—which I shall mark down separately. Doubling the movement of the moon makes 30°; I find five of the first proportional minutes corresponding to it, and with them I determine 9″ to be the part of the first difference which is proportional to sixty minutes: I subtract these 9″ from the 42′50″ of the parallax, and the remainder is 42′41″. Similarly the proportional part of the second difference—which was 2′46″—is 14″; and I add it to the 50′59″ of the parallax at the third limit; the sum is 51′13″. The difference between these parallaxes is 8′32″. After this I take the last proportional minutes corresponding to the corrected anomaly, and there are 39′. By means of them I take 4′50″ as the proportional part of the difference of 8′32″; [127ᵇ] I add this 4′50″ to the first corrected parallax, and the sum is 47′31″, which will be the sought parallax of the moon in the circle of altitude.

But since any other parallaxes of the moon differ very little from the parallaxes at full moon and new moon, it would seem to be sufficient if we kept within the mean limits everywhere, for we have great need of them for the sake of predicting eclipses. The rest do not require such great examination, which will be held to offer perhaps less in the way of utility than in the satisfaction of curiosity.

26. How the Parallaxes of Longitude and Latitude Are Distinguished

Now the parallax is divided simply into the parallax of longitude and that of latitude, or the parallax between the sun and moon is distinguished according to the arcs and angles of the intersection of the ecliptic and the circle through the poles of the horizon; since it is clear that when this circle falls at right angles upon the ecliptic, it makes no parallax in longitude, but the parallax is transferred wholly to latitude, as the circle is wholly a circle of latitude and altitude. But where conversely the ecliptic falls at right angles upon the horizon and becomes wholly the same as the circle of altitude; then, if the moon has no latitude, it does not admit anything except a parallax in longitude, but if it has a digression in latitude, it does not escape some parallax in latitude.

In this way let circle ABC be the ecliptic, and let it be at right angles to the horizon, and let A be the pole of the horizon. Accordingly circle ABC will be the same as the circle of altitude of a moon without latitude. Let B be the position of the moon, and BC its total parallax in longitude.

But when it also has latitude, let DBE be the circle described through the poles of the ecliptic and with DB or BE as the latitude of the moon, it is clear that side AD or AE will not be equal to AB; and the angle at D or E will not be right, since DA and EA are not circles through the poles of DBE; and the parallax will participate in latitude, and it will do so all the more the nearer the moon is to the vertex. For let triangle ADE keep the same base, but let sides AD and AE be shorter and comprehend acuter angles at the base; the greater the distance of the moon from the vertex is, the more like right angles will the angles be.

Now let ABC be the ecliptic, and DBE the oblique circle of altitude of a moon not having latitude, as being at an ecliptic section. [128ª] Let B be the ecliptic section, and BE the parallax in the circle of altitude. Let there be drawn EF the arc of a circle through the poles of ABC. Accordingly since in triangle BEF angle EBF is given, as was shown above, and

angle $F = 90°$,

and side BE is also given: by what has been shown concerning spherical triangles, the remaining sides are given: BF the parallax in longitude and FE the parallax in latitude, which agree with parallax BE. But since BE, EF, and FB on account of their shortness differ but slightly and imperceptibly from straight lines, we shall not make an error if we use the right triangle as rectilinear; and on that account the ratio will become easy.

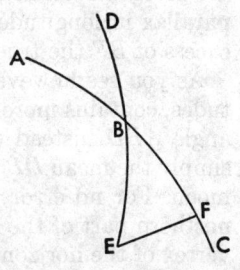

For let circle ABC be drawn as the ecliptic, and let DB the oblique circle through the poles of the horizon fall upon it. Let B be the position in longitude of the moon and FB the northern latitude or BE the southern. Let the vertex of the horizon be D, and from D let fall on the moon the circles of altitude DEK or DFC, whereon are the parallaxes EK and FG. For the true positions of the moon in longitude and latitide will be at points E or F, but the seeming positions will be at K or G. And from K and G let arcs KM and LG be drawn at right angles to the ecliptic ABC. Accordingly, since the longitude and latitude of the moon

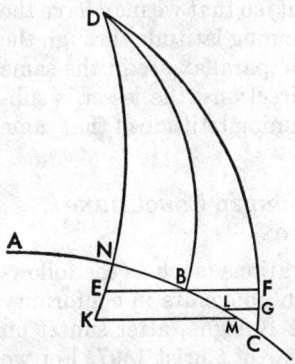

have been established together with the latitude of the region; in triangle *DEB* two sides *DB* and *BE* will be known and also *ABD* the angle of section and angle *DBE* = angle *ABD* + 90°.

Accordingly the remaining side *DE* will be given together with angle *DEB*.

Similarly in triangle *DBF* since two sides *DB* and *BF* are given together with angle *DBF*, which with angle *ABD* makes up a right angle, *DF* will also be given together with angle *DFB*. Accordingly parallaxes *EK* and *FG* on arcs *DE* and *DF* are given by the table, and so is *DE* or *DF*, the true distance of the moon from the vertex, and similarly the seeming distance *DEK* or *DFG*. But in triangle *EBN*, which has the intersection of *DE* with the ecliptic at point *N*, angle *NEB* is given, and base *BE* is given, and angle *NBE* is right: the remaining angle *BNE* will become known too together with the remaining sides *BN* and *NE*. And similarly in the whole triangle *NKM*, as angles *M* and *N* and the whole side *KEN* are given, the base *KM* will be established. *KM* is the seeming southern latitude of the moon, and its excess over *EB* is the parallax of latitude: and the remaining side *NBM* is given: by the subtraction of *NB* from *NBM* the remainder *BM* will be the parallax in longitude.

Moreover, thus in the northern triangle *BFC*, since side *BF* is given together with angle *BFC* [128ᵇ] and angle *B* is right, the remaining sides *BLC* and *FGC* together with the remaining angle *C* are given; and after the subtraction of *FG* from *FGC* there remains *GC*, which is a side given in triangle *GLC* together with the angle *LCG* and angle *CLG*, which is right. Accordingly the remaining sides are given: *GL* and *LC*, and hence *BL* which is the remainder of *BC* and is the parallax in longitude; and *GL* is the seeming latitude, and its parallax is the excess of *BF* the true latitude over *GL*.

As you see however, this computation, which deals with very small magnitudes, contains more labour than fruitfulness. For it will be sufficient if we use angle *ABD* instead of *DCB* and angle *DBF* instead of *DEB*, and as before, simply the mean *DB* instead of arcs *DE* and *DF*—neglecting the latitude of the moon. For no error will appear because of that, especially in regions of the northern part of the Earth; but in very southern regions, where *B* touches the vertex of the horizon at the greatest latitude of 5° and when the moon is at its perigee, there is a difference of approximately 6′. But in the ecliptic conjunctions with the sun, where the latitude of the moon cannot exceed ½°, there can be a difference of merely 1¾′. Accordingly it is clear from this that the parallax is always added to the true position of the moon in the eastern quadrant of the ecliptic and is always subtracted in the other quadrant, so that we may have the seeming longitude of the moon; and may have the seeming latitude through the parallax in latitude, since if the true latitude and the parallax are in the same direction, they are added together; if in different directions, the lesser is subtracted from the greater, and the remainder is the seeming latitude of that same part, to which the greater falls away.

27. Confirmation of What Has Been Expounded Concerning the Parallaxes of the Moon

Accordingly we can confirm by many other observations (such as the following one) that the parallaxes of the moon as set forth above are in conformity with the appearances. We made this observation at Bologna, after sunset on the seventh day before the Ides of March, in the year of Christ 1497. For we observed how long [129ᵃ] the moon would occult the bright star of the Hyades (which the Romans call Paliticium), and with this in mind, we saw the star brought into contact with the shadowy part of the lunar body and already lying hidden between the horns of the moon at the end of the fifth hour of the night, though the star was nearer the southern horn by three quarters as it were of the width or diameter of the moon. And since according to the tables the star was at 2°52′ of Gemini with a southerly latitude of 5⅙°, it was clear that to eyesight the centre of the moon was half a diameter to the west of the star, and accordingly its seen position was 2°36′ in longitude and approximately 5°6′ in latitude.

Accordingly from the beginning of the years of Christ there have been 1497 Egyptian years 76 days 23 hours at Bologna; but at Cracow, which is approximately 8° farther east, 23 hours 36 minutes, to which equal time adds 4 minutes. For the sun was at 28½° of Pisces and therefore the regular movement of the moon away from the sun was 74°, the regular anomaly was 111°10′, the true position of the moon was at 3°24′ of Gemini, the southerly latitude 4°35′, for the true movement of latitude was 203°41′. Moreover, at that time at Bologna, 26° of Scorpio was rising, with an angle of 57½°; and the moon was 83° from the vertex of the horizon, and the angle of section between the circle of altitude and the ecliptic was approximately 29°, the parallax of the moon was 1°51′ in longitude and 30′ in latitude. Those things agree perfectly with the observations; and all the less will anyone doubt that our hypotheses and what results from them are correct.

28. On the Mean Oppositions and Conjunctions of the Sun and Moon

The method of investigating the conjunctions and oppositions of the sun and the moon is clear from what has been said so far concerning their movement. For in relation to that approaching time at which we think this or that conjunction or opposition will take place, we shall seek the regular movement of the moon; and if we find that the regular movement has already completed a circle, we understand a full conjunction at the semicircle. [129ᵇ] But since that rarely presents itself, we shall have to observe the distance between the sun and the moon; and when we have divided it by the daily movement of the moon, we shall know by how much time the one of them is in advance of the other, or how far off in the future the conjunction or the opposition is. Therefore we shall seek out the movements and positions for this time, and with them we shall set up ratios for the true new moons and full moons; and we shall distinguish the ecliptic conjunctions from the others, as we shall indicate below. When we have got these things set up, it will be possible to go on into any number of months and continue through some number of years by means of the table of twelve months, which contains the time and the regular movements of the anomaly of the sun and the moon and the regular movement of the moon in latitude— joining single movements to the single movements already found. But we shall put down the anomaly of the sun as true, so as to have it as corrected immediately. For its difference is not perceptible to sense in one or more years on account of its slowness at its beginning, i.e., at its highest apsis.

TABLE OF THE CONJUNCTION AND OPPOSITION OF SUN AND MOON

Months	Divisions of Time				Movements of Lunar Anomaly				Movement in Latitude of the Moon			
	Days	Min. of Day	Sec.	Thirds	60°	Deg.	Min.	Sec.	60°	Deg.	Min.	Sec.
1	29	31	50	8	0	25	49	0	0	30	40	13
2	59	3	40	16	0	51	38	0	1	1	20	27
3	88	35	30	24	1	17	27	0	1	32	0	41
4	118	7	20	32	1	43	16	0	2	2	40	55
5	147	39	10	40	2	9	5	0	2	33	21	9
6	177	11	0	48	2	34	34	0	3	4	1	23
7	206	42	50	57	3	0	43	0	3	34	41	36
8	236	14	41	25	3	26	32	0	4	5	21	50
9	265	46	31	13	3	52	21	0	4	36	2	4
10	295	18	21	21	4	18	10	0	5	6	42	18
11	324	50	11	29	4	4	59	0	5	37	22	32
12	354	22	1	37	5	9	48	0	0	8	2	46

THE HALF MONTH BETWEEN THE FULL AND NEW MOON

½	14	45	55	4	3	12	54	30	3	15	20	6

MOVEMENT OF SOLAR ANOMALY

Months	60°	°	′	″	Months	60°	°	′	″
1	0	29	6	18	7	3	23	44	6
2	0	58	12	36	8	3	52	50	24
3	1	27	18	54	9	4	21	56	42
4	1	56	25	12	10	4	51	3	0
5	2	25	31	30	11	5	20	9	19
6	2	54	57	48	12	5	49	15	37

THE HALF MONTH

					½	0	14	33	9

29. ON THE CLOSE EXAMINATION OF THE TRUE CONJUNCTIONS AND OPPOSITIONS OF THE SUN AND MOON

]130ᵇ] Since we possess, as was said, the time of mean conjunction or opposition of these heavenly bodies together with their movements, then the true distance between them, whereby they precede or follow one another, will be necessary in order to find their true [conjunctions and oppositions]. For if the [true] moon is prior to the sun in [mean] conjunction or opposition, it is clear that the true one will be in the future; but if the sun, then it is already past the true one which we are seeking. This is made clear by the additosubtractions in the case of both of them, since if there were no additosubtractions, or if they were equal and of the same quality, viz., both additive or both subtractive, it is clear that at the same moment the true conjunctions or oppositions and the mean ones coincide. But if they are unequal, the difference indicates what their distance is and that the star to which the additive or subtractive difference belongs precedes or follows. But when they are in different parts [of their circles] that star all the more precedes whose additosubtraction is subtractive; and the adding together of the additosubtractions shows what the distance between them is. In connection with this we shall decide how many whole hours can be traversed by the moon—taking two hours for every degree of distance.

In this way, if there were about 6° of distance, we should take 12 hours as corresponding to them. Therefore we shall seek the true movement of the moon away from the sun for the interval of time thus set up; and we shall do that easily, when we know that the mean movement of the moon is 1°1′ per 2 hours, but that the true hourly movement of anomaly around the full moon or the new moon is approximately 50′. In 6 hours that makes the regular movement to be 3°3′, and the true movement of anomaly 5°; and in the table of lunar additosubtractions we shall note the difference between the additosubtractions and add it to the mean movement—if the anomaly is in the lower part of the circle—and subtract it if the anomaly is in the upper. For the sum or the remainder is the true movement of the moon for the hours taken. Therefore that movement, if equal to the distance first existing, is sufficient. Otherwise the distance multiplied by the number of estimated hours should be divided by this movement; or else we shall divide the true simple distance by the hourly movement taken. [131ᵃ] For the quotient will be the true difference in time in hours and minutes between the mean and the true conjunction or opposition. We shall add this difference to the mean time of conjunction or opposition, if the moon is west of the sun, or to the position of the sun diametrically opposite: or we shall subtract, if the moon is eastward; and we shall have the time of true conjunction or opposition, although we must confess that the anomaly of the sun too adds or subtracts something, but it is rightly neglected, as in the whole tract and at greatest elongation—which extends beyond 7°—the anomaly cannot fill 1′; and the method of evaluating the lunar movements is more certain.

For those who rely only upon the hourly movement of the moon, which they call the hourly excelling movement, make mistakes sometimes and are forced rather often to repeat their calculations. For the moon is changeable even from hour to hour and does not stay like itself. Accordingly, for the time of true conjunction or opposition, we shall work out the true movement in latitude, so as to learn the latitude of the moon and work out the true position of the sun in relation to the spring equinox, i.e., in the signs, whereby the true position of the moon is known to be the same or opposite to it. And since time is here understood as mean and equal with respect to the Cracow meridian, we shall reduce it to apparent time by the method described above. But if we should wish to set this up for any other place than Cracow, we shall note its longitude and take four minutes of an hour for each degree of longitude and four seconds of an hour for each minute of longitude; and we shall add them to the Cracow time, if the other place is to the east, and subtract them, if it is to the west. And the sum or the remainder will be the time of conjunction or opposition of the sun and moon.

30. How the Ecliptic Conjunctions and Oppositions of the Sun and Moon Are Distinguished from the Others

In the case of the moon it is easily discernible whether or not they are ecliptic; since, if the latitude of the moon is less than half the diameters of the moon and the shadow, it will undergo an eclipse, but if greater, it will not. But there is more than enough bother in the case of the sun, as the parallax of each of them, by which for the most part the visible conjunction differs from the true, is mixed up in it. Accordingly when we have examined [131ᵇ] what the parallax in longitude between the sun and moon is at the time of true conjunction, similarly we shall look for the apparent [angular] elongation of the moon from the sun at the interval of an hour before the true conjunction in the eastern quarter of the ecliptic or after the true conjunction in the western quarter, in order to understand how far the moon seems to move away from the sun in one hour. Therefore when we have divided the parallax by this hourly movement, we shall have the difference in time between the true and the seen conjunction. When that is subtracted from the time of the true conjunction in the eastern part of the ecliptic or added in the western—for in the eastern part the seen conjunction precedes the true, and in the western it follows it—the result will be the time of seen conjunction which we were looking for. Therefore we shall reckon the seen latitude of the moon in relation to the sun for this time, or the distance between the centres of the sun and the moon at the seen conjunction, after deducting the parallax of the sun. If this latitude is greater than half the diameters of the sun and moon, the sun will not undergo an eclipse; but if smaller, it will. From this it is clear that if the moon at the time of true conjunction does not have any parallax in longitude, the seen and the true conjunction will be the same, and the conjunction will take place at 90° of the ecliptic as measured from the east or the west.

31. How Great an Eclipse of the Sun or Moon Will Be

Therefore, after we have learned that the sun or moon will undergo an eclipse, we shall easily come to know how great the eclipse will be—in the case of the sun by means of the seen latitude between the sun and moon at the time of seen conjunction. For if we subtract the latitude from half the diameters of the sun and the moon, the remainder is the eclipse of the sun as measured along its diameter; and when we have multiplied that by twelve and divided the product by the diameter of the sun, we shall have the number of twelfths of the eclipse of the sun. But if there is no latitude between the sun and the moon, there will be a total eclipse of the sun or as much of it as the moon can cover.

Approximately the same method [is used] in the case of a lunar eclipse, except that instead of the seen latitude we employ the simple latitude. When the latitude is subtracted from half the diameters of the moon and shadow, the remainder is the part of [132ᵃ] the moon eclipsed, provided the latitude of the moon is not less than half the diameters of the moon and shadow, as taken along the diameter of the moon. For then there will be a total eclipse. And furthermore the lesser latitude even adds some delay in the darkness; and the delay will be greatest when there is no latitude—as I think is perfectly clear to those who consider it. Accordingly, in the case of a particular eclipse of the moon, when we have multiplied the eclipsed part by twelve and divided the product by the diameter of the moon, we shall have the number of twelfths of the eclipse—just as in the case of the sun.

32. How to Know Beforehand How Long an Eclipse Will Last

It remains to see how long an eclipse will last. It should be noted that we use the arcs which occur in the case of the sun, moon, and shadow as straight lines; for they are so small that they do not seem to be different from straight lines.

Accordingly let us take point A as the centre of the sun or of the shadow, and line BC as the passage of the orb of the moon. And

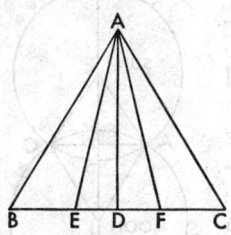

let B be the centre of the moon touching the sun or shadow at the beginning of incidence and C at the end of its transit. Let AB and BC be joined, and let fall AD perpendicular to BC.

It is clear that when the centre of the moon is at D, it will be the middle of the eclipse. For AD is the shortest of the lines falling from A, and

$$BD = DC,$$

since

$$AB = AC,$$

and AB or AC is equal to half the sum of the diameters of the sun and the moon in a solar eclipse and to that of the diameters of the moon and shadow in a lunar eclipse; and AD is the true latitude of the moon or the seen latitude at the middle of the eclipse. Accordingly, when we have subtracted the square on AD from the square on AB, the remainder is the square on BD. Therefore BD will be given in length. When we have divided it by the true hourly movement of the moon during the eclipse of the moon, or by the visible movement in the case of a solar eclipse, we shall have the time of half the duration. But the moon very often delays in the middle of the darkness—that happens when half the sum of the diameters of the moon and the shadow exceeds the latitude of the moon by more than the moon's diameter, as we said. Accordingly when we have placed E the centre of the moon at the starting-point of the total [132^b] obscuration, when the moon touches the concave circumference of the shadow, and F at the other point of contact, when the moon first emerges, and have joined AE and AF, it will be made clear in the same way as before that ED and DF are the halves of the delay in darkness, because AD is the known latitude of the moon, and AE or AF is that whereby the half of the diameter of the shadow is greater than half the diameter of the moon. Therefore DE or DF will be established; and once more when we have divided it by the true hourly movement of the moon, we shall have the time of half the delay, which we were looking for.

Nevertheless we must notice here that since the moon moves in its own orbital circle, it does not, by the mediation of the circles passing through the poles of the ecliptic, cut arcs of longitude on the ecliptic wholly equal to the arcs in its own orbital circle. But the difference is very slight, so that at the total distance of 12° from the ecliptic section, which is approximately the farthest limit of the eclipses of the sun and moon, the arcs of the circles do not differ from one another by 2′, which makes $\frac{1}{15}$ hour; on that account we often use one instead of the other as if they were the same. So too we use the same latitude of the moon at the limits of the eclipses as at the middle of the eclipse, although the latitude of the moon is always increasing or decreasing, and on that account the intervals of incidence and withdrawal are not wholly equal, but the difference is so slight that it seems a waste of time to examine them more closely. In this way the times, durations, and magnitudes of eclipses have been unfolded with respect to the diameters.

But since it is the opinion of many persons that the parts eclipsed should be distinguished not with respect to the diameters but with respect to the surfaces, for it is not lines but surfaces which are eclipsed: accordingly let $ABCD$ be the circle of the sun or of the shadow, and let E be its centre. Let $AFCG$ be the lunar circle, and let I be its centre. Let the circles cut one another in points A and C, let the straight line $BEIF$ be drawn through the centres of both, and let AE, EC, IA, IC be joined and line AKC at right angles to BF. By means of this we wish to examine how great $ADCG$ the surface obscured is, or how many twelfths of the whole surface of the orb of the moon or sun belong to the part eclipsed.

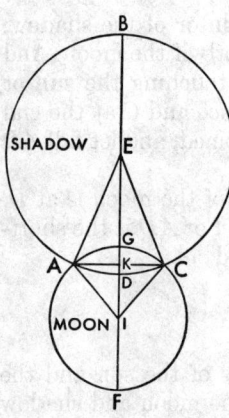

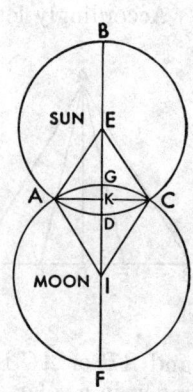

Accordingly since the semidiameters AE and AI of each circle are given by the above, and also EI the distance between their centres or the lunar latitude, we shall have [133ᵃ] triangle AEI with its sides given; and for that reason with its angles given by the demonstrations above; and angle AEI is similar and equal to angle EIC. Accordingly

arcs ADC and AGC will be given,

where the circumference $= 360°$.

Furthermore, in the measurement of the circle Archimedes of Syracuse records that

circumference : diameter $< 3\tfrac{1}{7} : 1$

but

circumference : diameter $> 3\tfrac{10}{71} : 1$.

Ptolemy assumed as a mean between these

3ᴾ8′30″ : 1ᴾ.

By means of this ratio

arcs AGC and ADG will be given,

in terms of the same parts as the semidiameters AE and AI.

And

quad. EA, $AD = $ sector AEC,

and

quad. IA, $AG = $ sector AIC.

But in the isosceles triangles AEC and AIC the common base AKC and the perpendiculars EK and KI are given. And accordingly the quadrilateral AK, KE is given, which is the area of triangle AEC—and similarly the quadrilateral AK, KI is the area of triangle ACI. Accordingly

$$\text{sect. } AFCK - \text{trgl. } AIC = \text{seg. circ. } AFC$$

and

$$\text{sect. } ABCK - \text{trgl. } AEC = \text{seg. circ. } ABC$$

and hence,

figure $ADCG$ is given,

which was sought.

And moreover, the total area of the circle—which is comprehended by BE and BAD in a solar eclipse or by FI and FAG in a lunar eclipse—was given. Accordingly it will be manifest how many twelfths of the total circle of the sun or moon was eclipsed in $ADCG$. Let all this—which has been treated in more detail by others—be enough now concerning the moon: for we are in a hurry to get to the revolutions of the remaining five planets, which will be spoken of in the books following.

BOOK FIVE

[133^b] Up to now we have been explaining to the best of our ability the revolutions of the Earth around the sun and of the moon around the Earth. Now we are turning to the movements of the five wandering stars: the mobility of the Earth binds together the order and magnitude of their orbital circles in a wonderful harmony and sure commensurability, as we said in our brief survey in the first book, when we showed that the orbital circles do not have their centres around the Earth but rather around the sun. Accordingly it remains for us to demonstrate all these things singly and with greater clarity; and let us fulfil our promises adequately, in so far as we can, particularly by measuring the appearances by the experiments which we have got from the ancients or from our own times, in order that the ratio of the movements may be held with greater certainty. Now in Plato's *Timaeus* each of thse five stars is named in accordance with its visible aspect: Saturn, Phaenon—as if to say "shining" or "appearing," for Saturn is hidden less than the others, and emerges more quickly after undergoing occultation by the sun; Jupiter, Phaeton from his radiance; Mars, Pyrois from his fiery glow; Venus sometimes φωσφόρος and sometimes ἕοπερος, *i.e.*, Lucifer and Vesperugo, according as she shines at morning or evening; and finally Mercury, Stilbon from his sparkling and twinkling light. Moreover the planets have greater irregularities in longitude and in latitude than the moon.

1. On Their Revolutions and Mean Movements

Two longitudinal movements which are quite different appear in the planets. One of them is on account of the movement of the Earth, as we said; and the other is proper to each planet. We may rightly call the first the movement of parallax, since it is the one which makes the planets appear to have stoppings, progressions, and retrogradations—[134^a] not that the planet which always progresses by its own movement, is pulled in different directions, but that it appears to do so by reason of the parallax caused by the movement of the Earth taken in relation to the differing magnitudes of their orbital circles.

Accordingly it is clear that the true position of Saturn, Jupiter, and Mars become visible to us only at the time when they are in opposition to the sun; and that occurs approximately in the middle of their retrogradations. For at that time they fall on a straight line with the mean position of the sun, and lay aside their parallax.

Furthermore there is a different ratio in the case of Venus and Mercury: for they are hidden at the time they are in conjunction with the sun, and they show only the digressions which they make on either side away from the sun: hence they are never found without parallax.

Therefore the revolution of parallax—I mean the movement of the Earth with respect to the planet—is private to each planet; and the planet and the Earth are mutually explanatory of it. For we say that the movement of parallax is

732

nothing except that wherein the regular movement of the Earth exceeds their movement, as in the case of Saturn, Jupiter, and Mars, or is exceeded by it, as in the case of Venus and Mercury. But since such periods of parallax are found unequal by a manifest difference, the ancients recognized that the movements of these planets too were irregular and had apsides of circles to which their irregularity returned, and the ancients supposed that these apsides had perpetual seats in the sphere of the fixed stars. By that argument the road is opened for learning their mean movements and equal periods. For when the ancients had recorded in memory the position of some planet with respect to its exact distance from the sun and a fixed star, and after an interval of time found that it had arrived at the same position with an equal distance from the sun; the planet was seen to have completed its whole movement of irregularity and to have returned through all to its former relationship with the Earth. And so by means of the time which intervened they calculated the number of whole and equal revolutions and from them the particular movements of the planet. Ptolemy surveyed the circuits through a number of years, according as, he acknowledged, he got them from Hipparchus. Now he means solar years to be understood as the years measured from an equinox or solstice. But it has already been made clear that such years are not quite equal; on that account we shall use years measured from the fixed stars, and by means of them the movements of these five planets have been reconstituted more correctly by us, according as in our time [134ᵇ] we found there was some deficiency in them or excess, as follows.

For the Earth has 57 revolutions in respect to Saturn—we call this the movement of parallax—in 59 of our solar years 1 day 6 minutes of a day 48 seconds approximately: during this time the planet has by its own movement completed two circuits plus 1°6'6".

Jupiter is outrun by the Earth 65 times in 71 solar years minus 5 days 45 minutes 27 seconds: during this time the planet by its own movement has 6 revolutions minus 5°41'2½".

Mars has 37 revolutions of parallax in 79 solar years 2 days 27 minutes 3 seconds: during this time the planet by its own movement completes 42 periods plus 2°24'56".

Venus outruns the movement of the Earth 5 times in 8 solar years minus 2 days 26 minutes 46 seconds. And during this time it has 13 revolutions minus 2°24'40" around the sun.

Finally, Mercury completes 145 periods of parallax, by which it outruns the movement of the Earth, in 46 solar years plus 34 minutes of a day 23 seconds. And it has 191 revolutions around the sun in that time plus 34 minutes of a day 23 seconds approximately.

Accordingly the single circuits of parallax are as follows: for the single planets:

Saturn: 378 days   5 min. 32 sec. 11 thirds
Jupiter: 398 days 23 min. 25 sec. 56 thirds
Mars: 779 days 56 min. 19 sec.   7 thirds
Venus: 583 days 45 min. 17 sec. 24 thirds
Mercury: 115 days 52 min. 42 sec. 12 thirds

When we have reduced these circuits to the degrees of a circle and multiplied by the ratio of 365 to the number of days and minutes, we shall have as the annual movements [of parallax]:

Saturn: 347° 32′ 2″   54‴ 12⁗
Jupiter: 329° 25′ 8″   15‴ 6⁗
Mars: 168° 28′ 29″ 13‴ 12⁗
Venus: 225°   1′ 48″ 54‴ 30⁗
Mercury: 3(360°) + 53° 56′ 46″ 54‴ 40⁗

[135ᵃ] The three-hundred-sixty-fifth part of these is the daily movement:

Saturn: 57′ 7″ 44‴
Jupiter: 54′ 9″ 3‴ 49⁗
Mars: 27′ 41″ 40‴ 8⁗
Venus: 36′ 49″ 28‴ 35⁗
Mercury: 3°   6′ 24″ 7‴ 43⁗

according as they are set out in the following tables, like the mean movement of
the sun and moon.

But we thought it unnecessary to set down their proper movements in this
way. For the proper movements are determined by the subtraction of the movements of parallax from the mean movement of the sun, as the proper movement
of the planet and the mean movement of parallax compose the mean movement
of the sun. For the proper annual movements in relation to the sphere of the
fixed stars are as follows for the upper planets:

Saturn: 12° 12′ 46″ 12‴ 52⁗
Jupiter: 30° 19′ 40″ 51‴ 58⁗
Mars: 191° 16′ 19″ 53‴ 52⁗

But in the case of Venus and Mercury, since their proper movements are not
apparent to us[1], the movement of the sun itself is used by us instead; and it
furnishes a way of investigating and demonstrating their apparent movements,
in the following tables.

[1]The proper movements of Venus and Mercury are not apparent to us in that their positions
are never viewed without parallax.

SATURN'S MOVEMENT OF PARALLAX IN YEARS AND PERIODS OF SIXTY YEARS

Egyptian Years	60°	°	Movement '	"	'''	Egyptian Years	60°	°	Movement '	"	'''
1	5	47	32	3	9	31	5	33	33	37	59
2	5	35	4	6	19	32	5	11	5	41	9
3	5	22	36	9	29	33	5	8	37	44	19
4	5	10	8	12	38	34	4	56	9	47	28
5	4	57	40	15	48	35	4	43	41	50	38
6	4	45	12	18	58	36	4	31	13	53	48
7	4	32	44	22	7	37	4	18	45	56	57
8	4	20	16	25	17	38	4	6	18	0	7
9	4	7	48	28	27	39	3	53	50	3	17
10	3	55	20	31	36	40	3	41	22	6	26
11	3	42	52	34	46	41	3	18	54	9	36
12	3	30	24	37	56	42	3	16	26	12	46
13	3	17	56	41	5	43	3	3	58	15	55
14	3	5	28	44	15	44	2	51	30	19	5
15	2	53	0	47	25	45	2	39	2	22	15
16	2	40	32	50	34	46	2	26	34	25	24
17	2	28	4	53	44	47	2	14	6	28	34
18	2	15	36	56	54	48	2	1	38	31	44
19	2	3	9	0	3	49	1	49	10	34	53
20	1	50	41	3	13	50	1	36	42	38	3
21	1	38	13	6	23	51	1	24	14	41	13
22	1	25	45	9	32	52	1	11	46	44	22
23	1	13	17	12	42	53	0	59	18	47	32
24	1	0	49	15	52	54	0	46	50	50	42
25	0	48	21	19	1	55	0	34	22	43	51
26	0	35	53	22	11	56	0	21	54	57	1
27	0	23	25	25	21	57	0	9	27	0	11
28	0	10	57	28	30	58	5	56	59	3	20
29	5	58	29	31	40	59	5	44	31	6	30
30	5	46	1	34	50	60	5	32	3	9	40

SATURN'S MOVEMENT OF PARALLAX IN PERIODS OF SIXTY DAYS

Days	60°	°	Movement '	"	'''	Days	60°	°	Movement '	"	'''
1	0	0	57	7	44	31	0	29	30	59	46
2	0	1	54	15	28	32	0	30	28	7	30
3	0	2	51	23	12	33	0	31	25	15	14
4	0	3	48	30	56	34	0	32	22	22	58
5	0	4	45	38	40	35	0	33	19	30	42
6	0	5	42	46	24	36	0	34	16	38	26
7	0	6	39	54	8	37	0	35	13	46	1
8	0	7	37	1	52	38	0	36	10	53	55
9	0	8	34	9	36	39	0	37	8	1	39
10	0	9	31	17	20	40	0	38	5	9	23
11	0	10	28	25	4	41	0	39	2	17	7
12	0	11	25	32	49	42	0	39	59	24	51
13	0	12	22	40	33	43	0	40	56	32	35
14	0	13	13	48	17	44	0	41	53	40	19
15	0	14	16	56	1	45	0	42	50	48	3
16	0	15	14	3	45	46	0	43	47	55	47
17	0	16	11	11	29	47	0	44	45	3	31
18	0	17	8	19	13	48	0	45	42	11	16
19	0	18	5	26	57	49	0	46	39	19	0
20	0	19	2	34	41	50	0	47	36	26	44
21	0	19	59	42	25	51	0	48	33	34	28
22	0	20	56	50	9	52	0	49	30	42	12
23	0	21	53	57	53	53	0	50	27	49	56
24	0	22	51	5	38	54	0	51	24	57	40
25	0	23	48	13	22	55	0	52	22	5	24
26	0	24	45	21	6	56	0	53	19	13	8
27	0	25	42	28	50	57	0	54	16	20	52
28	0	26	39	36	34	58	0	55	13	28	36
29	0	27	36	44	18	59	0	56	10	36	20
30	0	28	33	52	2	60	0	57	7	44	5

JUPITER'S MOVEMENT OF PARALLAX IN YEARS AND PERIODS OF SIXTY YEARS

Egyptian Years	60°	°	'	"	'''	Egyptian Years	60°	°	'	"	'''
1	5	29	25	8	15	31	2	11	59	15	48
2	4	58	50	16	30	32	1	41	24	24	3
3	4	28	15	24	45	33	1	10	49	32	18
4	3	57	40	33	0	34	0	40	14	40	33
5	3	27	5	41	15	35	0	9	39	48	48
6	2	56	30	49	30	36	5	39	4	57	8
7	2	25	55	57	45	37	5	8	30	5	18
8	1	55	21	6	0	38	4	37	55	13	33
9	1	24	46	14	15	39	4	7	20	21	48
10	0	54	11	22	31	40	3	36	45	30	4
11	0	23	36	30	46	41	3	6	10	38	19
12	5	53	1	39	1	42	2	35	35	46	34
13	5	22	25	47	16	43	2	5	0	54	49
14	4	51	51	55	31	44	1	34	26	3	4
15	4	21	17	3	46	45	1	3	51	11	19
16	3	50	42	12	1	46	0	33	16	19	34
17	3	20	7	20	16	47	0	2	41	27	49
18	2	49	32	28	31	48	5	32	6	36	4
19	2	18	57	35	46	49	5	1	31	44	19
20	1	48	22	45	2	50	4	30	56	52	34
21	1	17	47	58	17	51	4	0	22	0	50
22	0	47	13	1	32	52	3	29	47	9	5
23	0	16	38	9	47	53	2	59	12	17	20
24	5	45	3	18	2	54	2	28	37	25	33
25	5	15	28	26	17	55	1	58	2	33	50
26	4	44	53	34	32	56	1	27	27	42	5
27	4	14	18	42	47	57	0	56	52	50	20
28	3	43	43	51	2	58	0	26	17	58	35
29	3	13	8	59	17	59	5	55	43	6	50
30	2	42	34	7	33	60	5	25	8	15	6

JUPITER'S MOVEMENT OF PARALLAX IN PERIODS OF SIXTY DAYS

Days	60°	°	'	"	'''	Days	60°	°	'	"	'''
1	0	0	54	9	3	31	0	27	58	40	58
2	0	1	49	18	7	32	0	28	52	50	2
3	0	2	42	27	11	33	0	29	46	59	5
4	0	3	36	36	15	34	0	30	41	8	9
5	0	4	30	45	19	35	0	31	35	17	13
6	0	5	24	54	22	36	0	32	29	26	17
7	0	6	19	3	26	37	0	33	23	35	21
8	0	7	13	12	30	38	0	34	17	44	25
9	0	8	7	21	34	39	0	35	11	53	29
10	0	9	1	30	38	40	0	36	6	2	32
11	0	9	55	39	41	41	0	37	0	11	36
12	0	10	49	48	45	42	0	37	54	20	40
13	0	11	43	57	49	43	0	38	48	29	44
14	0	12	38	6	53	44	0	39	42	38	47
15	0	13	32	15	57	45	0	40	36	47	51
16	0	14	26	25	1	46	0	41	30	56	55
17	0	15	20	34	4	47	0	42	25	5	59
18	0	16	14	43	8	48	0	43	19	15	3
19	0	17	8	52	12	49	0	44	13	24	6
20	0	18	3	1	16	50	0	45	7	33	10
21	0	18	57	10	20	51	0	46	1	42	14
22	0	19	51	19	23	52	0	46	55	51	18
23	0	20	45	28	27	53	0	47	50	0	22
24	0	21	39	37	31	54	0	48	44	9	26
25	0	22	33	46	35	55	0	49	38	18	29
26	0	23	27	55	39	56	0	50	32	27	33
27	0	24	22	4	43	57	0	51	26	36	37
28	0	25	16	13	46	58	0	52	20	45	41
29	0	26	10	22	50	59	0	53	14	54	45
30	0	27	4	31	54	60	0	54	9	3	49

Mars' Movement of Parallax in Years and Periods of Sixty Years

Egyptian Years	60°	°	′	″	‴	Egyptian Years	60°	°	′	″	‴
1	2	48	28	30	36	31	3	2	43	48	38
2	5	36	57	1	12	32	5	51	12	19	14
3	2	25	25	31	48	33	2	39	40	49	50
4	5	13	54	2	24	34	5	28	9	20	26
5	2	2	22	33	0	35	2	16	37	51	2
6	4	50	51	3	36	36	5	5	6	21	38
7	1	39	19	34	12	37	1	53	34	52	14
8	4	27	48	4	48	38	4	42	3	22	50
9	1	16	16	35	24	39	1	30	31	53	26
10	4	4	45	6	0	40	4	19	0	24	2
11	0	53	13	36	36	41	1	7	28	54	38
12	3	41	42	7	12	42	3	55	57	25	14
13	0	30	10	37	46	43	0	44	25	55	50
14	3	18	39	8	24	44	3	32	54	26	26
15	0	7	7	39	1	45	0	21	22	57	3
16	2	55	36	9	37	46	3	9	51	27	39
17	5	44	4	40	13	47	5	58	19	58	15
18	2	32	33	10	49	48	2	46	48	28	51
19	5	21	1	41	25	49	5	35	16	59	27
20	2	9	30	12	1	50	2	23	45	30	3
21	4	57	58	42	37	51	5	12	14	0	39
22	1	46	27	13	13	52	2	0	42	31	15
23	4	34	55	43	49	53	4	49	11	1	51
24	1	23	24	14	25	54	1	37	39	32	27
25	4	11	52	45	1	55	4	26	8	3	3
26	1	0	21	15	37	56	1	14	36	33	39
27	3	48	49	46	13	57	4	3	5	4	15
28	0	37	18	16	49	58	0	51	33	34	51
29	3	25	46	47	25	59	3	40	2	5	27
30	0	14	15	18	2	60	0	28	30	36	4

Mars' Movement of Parallax in Periods of Sixty Days

Days	60°	°	′	″	‴	Days	60°	°	′	″	‴
1	0	0	27	41	40	31	0	14	18	31	51
2	0	0	55	23	20	32	0	14	46	13	31
3	0	1	23	5	1	33	0	15	14	55	12
4	0	1	50	46	41	34	0	15	41	36	52
5	0	2	18	28	21	35	0	16	9	18	32
6	0	2	46	10	2	36	0	16	37	0	13
7	0	3	13	51	42	37	0	17	4	41	53
8	0	3	41	33	22	38	0	17	32	23	33
9	0	4	9	15	3	39	0	18	0	5	14
10	0	4	36	35	43	40	0	18	27	46	54
11	0	5	4	38	24	41	0	18	55	28	35
12	0	5	32	20	4	42	0	19	23	10	15
13	0	6	0	1	44	43	0	19	50	51	55
14	0	6	27	43	25	44	0	20	18	33	36
15	0	6	55	25	5	45	0	20	46	15	16
16	0	7	23	6	45	46	0	21	13	56	56
17	0	7	50	48	26	47	0	21	41	38	37
18	0	8	18	30	6	48	0	22	9	20	17
19	0	8	46	11	47	49	0	22	37	1	57
20	0	9	13	53	27	50	0	23	4	43	38
21	0	9	41	35	7	51	0	23	32	25	18
22	0	10	9	16	48	52	0	24	0	6	59
23	0	10	36	58	28	53	0	24	27	48	39
24	0	11	4	40	8	54	0	24	55	30	19
25	0	11	32	21	48	55	0	25	23	12	0
26	0	12	0	3	29	56	0	25	50	53	40
27	0	12	27	45	9	57	0	26	18	35	20
28	0	12	59	25	50	58	0	26	46	17	1
29	0	13	23	8	30	59	0	27	13	58	41
30	0	13	50	50	11	60	0	27	41	40	22

Venus' Movement of Parallax in Years and Periods of Sixty Years

Egyptian Years	60°	°	'	"	'''	Egyptian Years	60°	°	'	"	'''
1	3	45	1	45	3	31	2	15	54	16	53
2	1	30	3	30	7	32	0	0	56	1	57
3	5	15	5	15	11	33	3	45	57	47	1
4	3	0	7	0	14	34	1	30	59	32	4
5	0	45	8	45	18	35	5	16	1	17	8
6	4	30	10	30	22	36	3	1	3	2	12
7	2	15	12	15	25	37	0	46	4	47	15
8	0	0	14	0	29	38	4	31	6	32	19
9	3	45	15	45	33	39	2	16	8	17	23
10	1	30	17	30	36	40	0	1	10	2	26
11	5	15	19	15	40	41	3	46	11	47	30
12	3	0	21	0	44	42	1	31	13	32	34
13	0	45	22	45	47	43	5	16	15	17	37
14	4	30	24	30	51	44	3	1	17	2	41
15	2	15	26	15	55	45	0	46	18	47	45
16	0	0	28	0	58	46	4	31	20	32	48
17	3	45	29	46	2	47	2	16	22	17	52
18	1	30	31	31	6	48	0	1	24	2	56
19	5	15	33	16	9	49	3	46	25	47	59
20	3	0	35	1	13	50	1	31	27	33	3
21	0	45	36	46	17	51	5	16	29	18	7
22	4	30	38	31	20	52	3	1	31	3	10
23	2	15	40	16	24	53	0	46	32	48	14
24	0	0	42	1	28	54	4	31	34	33	18
25	3	45	43	46	31	55	2	16	36	18	21
26	1	30	45	31	35	56	0	1	38	3	25
27	5	15	47	16	39	57	3	46	39	48	29
28	3	0	49	1	42	58	1	31	41	33	32
29	0	45	50	46	46	59	5	16	43	18	36
30	4	20	52	31	50	60	3	1	45	3	40

Venus' Movement of Parallax in Periods of Sixty Days

Days	60°	°	'	"	'''	Days	60°	°	'	"	'''
1	0	0	36	59	28	31	0	19	6	43	46
2	0	1	13	58	57	32	0	19	43	43	14
3	0	1	50	58	25	33	0	20	20	42	43
4	0	2	27	57	54	34	0	20	57	42	11
5	0	3	4	57	22	35	0	21	34	41	40
6	0	3	41	56	51	36	0	22	11	41	9
7	0	4	18	56	20	37	0	22	48	40	37
8	0	4	55	55	48	38	0	23	25	40	6
9	0	5	32	55	17	39	0	24	2	39	34
10	0	6	9	54	45	40	0	24	39	39	3
11	0	6	46	54	14	41	0	25	16	38	31
12	0	7	23	53	43	42	0	25	53	38	0
13	0	8	0	53	11	43	0	26	30	37	29
14	0	8	37	52	40	44	0	27	7	36	57
15	0	9	14	52	8	45	0	27	44	36	26
16	0	9	51	51	37	46	0	28	21	35	54
17	0	10	28	51	5	47	0	28	58	35	23
18	0	11	5	50	34	48	0	29	35	34	52
19	0	11	42	50	2	49	0	30	12	34	20
20	0	12	19	49	31	50	0	30	49	33	49
21	0	12	56	48	59	51	0	31	26	33	17
22	0	13	33	48	28	52	0	32	3	32	46
23	0	14	0	47	57	53	0	32	40	32	14
24	0	14	47	47	26	54	0	33	17	31	43
25	0	15	24	46	54	55	0	33	54	31	12
26	0	16	1	46	23	56	0	34	31	30	40
27	0	16	38	45	51	57	0	35	8	30	9
28	0	17	15	45	20	58	0	35	45	29	37
29	0	17	52	44	48	59	0	36	22	29	6
30	0	18	29	44	17	60	0	36	59	28	35

MERCURY'S MOVEMENT OF PARALLAX IN YEARS AND PERIODS OF SIXTY YEARS

Egyptian Years	60°	°	′	″	‴	Egyptian Years	60°	°	′	″	‴
1	0	53	57	23	6	31	3	52	38	56	21
2	1	47	54	46	13	32	4	46	36	19	28
3	2	41	52	9	19	33	5	40	33	42	34
4	3	35	49	32	26	34	0	34	31	5	41
5	4	29	46	55	32	35	1	28	28	28	47
6	5	23	44	18	39	36	2	22	25	51	54
7	0	17	41	41	45	37	3	16	23	15	0
8	1	11	39	4	52	38	4	10	20	38	7
9	2	5	36	27	58	39	5	4	18	1	13
10	2	59	33	51	5	40	5	58	15	24	20
11	3	53	31	14	11	41	0	52	12	47	26
12	4	47	28	37	18	42	1	46	10	10	33
13	5	41	26	0	24	43	2	40	7	33	39
14	0	35	23	23	31	44	3	34	4	56	46
15	1	29	20	46	37	45	4	28	2	19	52
16	2	23	18	9	44	46	5	21	59	42	59
17	3	17	15	32	50	47	0	15	57	6	5
18	4	11	12	55	57	48	1	9	54	29	12
19	5	5	10	19	3	49	2	3	51	52	18
20	5	59	7	42	10	50	2	57	49	15	25
21	0	53	5	5	16	51	3	51	46	38	31
22	1	47	2	28	23	52	4	45	44	1	38
23	2	40	59	51	29	53	5	39	41	24	44
24	3	34	57	14	36	54	0	33	38	47	51
25	4	28	54	37	42	55	1	27	36	10	57
26	5	22	52	0	49	56	2	21	33	34	4
27	0	16	49	23	55	57	3	15	30	57	10
28	1	10	46	47	2	58	4	9	28	20	17
29	2	4	44	10	8	59	5	3	25	43	23
30	2	58	41	33	15	60	5	57	23	6	30

MERCURY'S MOVEMENT OF PARALLAX IN PERIODS OF SIXTY DAYS

Days	60°	°	′	″	‴	Days	60°	°	′	″	‴
1	0	3	6	24	13	31	1	36	18	31	3
2	0	6	12	48	27	32	1	39	24	55	17
3	0	9	19	12	41	33	1	42	31	19	31
4	0	12	25	36	54	34	1	45	37	43	44
5	0	15	32	1	8	35	1	48	44	7	58
6	0	18	38	25	22	36	1	51	50	32	12
7	0	21	44	49	35	37	1	54	56	56	25
8	0	24	51	13	49	38	1	58	3	20	39
9	0	27	57	38	3	39	2	1	9	44	53
10	0	31	4	2	16	40	2	4	16	9	6
11	0	34	10	26	30	41	2	7	22	33	20
12	0	37	16	50	44	42	2	10	28	57	34
13	0	40	23	14	57	43	2	13	35	21	47
14	0	43	29	39	11	44	2	16	41	46	1
15	0	46	36	3	25	45	2	19	48	10	15
16	0	49	42	27	38	46	2	22	54	34	28
17	0	52	48	51	52	47	2	26	0	58	42
18	0	55	55	16	6	48	2	29	7	22	56
19	0	59	1	40	19	49	2	32	13	47	9
20	1	2	8	4	33	50	2	35	20	11	23
21	1	5	14	28	47	51	2	38	26	35	37
22	1	8	20	53	0	52	2	41	32	59	50
23	1	11	27	17	14	53	2	44	39	24	4
24	1	14	33	41	28	54	2	47	45	48	18
25	1	17	40	5	41	55	2	50	52	12	31
26	1	20	46	29	55	56	2	53	58	36	45
27	1	23	52	54	9	57	2	57	5	0	59
28	1	26	59	18	22	58	3	0	11	25	12
29	1	30	5	42	36	59	3	3	17	49	26
30	1	33	12	6	50	60	3	6	24	13	40

2. Demonstration of the Regular and Apparent Movements of These Planets According to the Theory of the Ancients

[140ᵇ] Accordingly this is the way the mean movements are. Now let us turn to the apparent irregularity. The ancient mathematicians who kept the earth immobile imagined in the case of Saturn, Jupiter, Mars, and Venus eccentric circles bearing epicycles, and another further eccentric circle, with respect to which the epicycle and the planet in the epicycle should move regularly.

In this way let AB be an eccentric circle, and let its centre be at C. Let ABC be its diameter, whereon D is the centre of the Earth, so that A is the apogee and B the perigee. Let DC be bisected at E, and with E as centre let FG another eccentric circle to the first be described. Let H be anywhere on this eccentric circle, and with H as centre let the epicycle IK be described. Through its centre let there be drawn the straight line $IHKC$ and similarly $LHME$. Now let it be understood that on account of the latitudes of the planet the eccentric circles are inclined to the plane of the ecliptic and similarly the epicycle to the plane of the eccentric circle; but here they are represented as if in one plane for the sake of ease of demonstration. Accordingly the ancients say that this whole plane together with points E and C moves around D—the centre of the ecliptic—in the movement of the sphere of the fixed stars: by this they mean that these points have unchanging positions in the sphere of the fixed stars. And they say that the epicycle moves eastward in circle FHG but in accordance with line IHC, and in relation to this line the planet revolves regularly in epicycle IK. But it is clear that the regularity of the epicycle should occur in relation to E the centre of its deferent[1], and the revolution of the planet in relation to line LME. Accordingly they concede that in this case the regularity of the circular movement can occur with respect to a foreign and not the proper centre; similarly and more so in the case of Mercury. But I think I have already made a sufficient refutation of that in the case of the moon. These and similar things furnished us with an occasion for working out the mobility of the Earth and some other ways by which regularity and the principles of this art might be preserved, and the ratio of apparent irregularity rendered more constant.

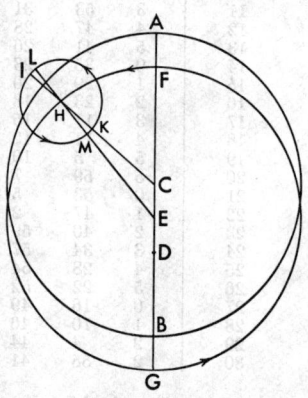

3. General Demonstration of Apparent Irregularity on Account of the Movement of the Earth

[141ᵃ] Accordingly there are two reasons why the regular movement of a planet should appear irregular: on account of the movement of the Earth and on account of its proper movement. We shall make both of them clear generally and separately by ocular demonstration, whereby they can be better distinguished from one another; and we shall begin with the movement which mixes itself with all of them on account of the movement of the Earth: and first

[1]The deferent of an epicycle is the circle on the circumference of which the centre of the epicycle moves.

in the case of Venus and Mercury, which are comprehended by the [orbital] circle of the Earth.

Therefore let AB be the circle eccentric to the sun, which the centre of the Earth describes during its annual circuit in the way we explained above; and let C be its centre. But now let us put down that the planet has no other irregularity except this one; and that will be the case if we make DE, the orbital circle of Venus or Mercury, homocentric with AB; and DE should be inclined to AB on account of its latitude. But for the sake of ease of demonstration they can be thought of as if in the same plane. Let the Earth be assumed at point A; and from A let there be drawn the lines of sight AFL and AGM touching the circle of the planet at points F and G; and let ACB the diameter common to both circles be drawn.

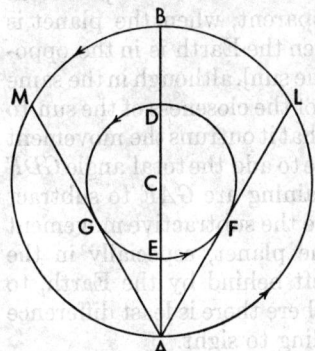

Now let the movement of both the Earth and the planet be in the same direction, *i.e.*, eastward, but with greater velocity in the case of the planet than in that of the Earth. Therefore C and line ACB will appear to the eye borne along at A to move in accordance with the mean movement of the sun; but the planet in circle DFG as in an epicycle will traverse arc FDG eastward in greater time than it will the remaining arc GEF westward; and in the upper arc it will add the total angle FAG to the mean movement of the sun, and in the lower arc will subtract the same. Accordingly where the subtractive movement of the planet, especially around E the perigee, is greater than the additive [movement] of C, it will seem to A to retrograde in proportion to the excelling [movement]—as happens in these planets, when line CE has a greater ratio to line AE than the movement at A has to the movement of the planet, according to the demonstrations of Apollonius of Perga, as will be said later. But where the additive movement is equal to the subtractive, [141^{b}] the planet will seem to come to a stop on account of the mutual equilibrium; all this agrees with the appearances.

Accordingly if there were no other irregularity in the movement of the planet, as Apollonius opined, this would be sufficient. But the greatest angular elongations from the mean movement of the sun, which these planets have in the morning and evening and which are understood by angles FAE and GAE, are not everywhere equal, neither the one to the other, nor are the sums of the two equal; for the apparent reason that the route of these planets is not along circles homocentric with the terrestrial circle but along certain others, by which they effect the second irregularity.

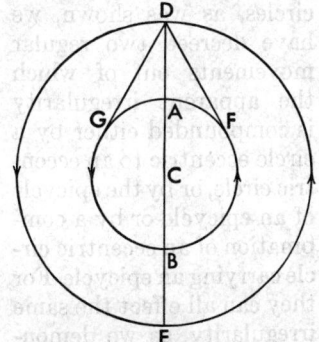

The same thing is also demonstrated in the case of the three upper planets, Saturn, Jupiter, and Mars, which circle around the Earth. For let the former circle of the Earth be drawn again, and let DE be as an exterior homocentric circle in the

same plane: let the position of the planet be taken anywhere, at point
D; and from D let there be drawn $DACBE$ the common diameter and DF and
DG straight lines touching the orbital circle of the Earth at points F and G.
It is manifest that from point A only will the true position of the planet in
DE the line of mean movement of the sun be apparent, when the planet is
opposite the sun and is nearest to the Earth. For when the Earth is in the opposite position at B, the opposition [of the planet and the sun], although in the same
straight line, will not be at all apparent on account of the closeness of the sun to
C. But as the movement of the Earth is speedier, so that it outruns the movement
of the planet, it will seem along FBG the arc of apogee to add the total angle GDF
to the movement of the planet and along the remaining arc GAF to subtract
the same, according as arc GAF is smaller. But where the subtractive movement
of the Earth excels the additive movement of the planet, especially in the
neighbourhood of A, the planet will seem to be left behind by the Earth, to
move westward and to come to a stop at the place where there is least difference
between the movements which are contrary according to sight.

And so it is once more manifest that all these apparent movements—which
the ancients were looking into by means of the epicycles of the individual planets
—occur on account of the movement of the Earth. But since in spite of the
opinion of Apollonius and the ancients the movement of the planet is not found
regular, as the irregular revolution of the Earth with respect to the planet produces that; accordingly the planets are not carried in a homocentric circle but
in some other which we shall demonstrate straightway.

4. Why the Proper Movements of the Planets Appear Irregular

[142ᵃ] But since their proper movements in longitude follow approximately
the same mode except for
Mercury, which is seen to
differ from them, we shall
treat of those four planets
together, but another place
has been given over to
Mercury. Accordingly as
the ancients placed one
movement in two eccentric
circles, as was shown, we
have decreed two regular
movements out of which
the apparent irregularity
is compounded either by a
circle eccentric to an eccentric circle, or by the epicycle
of an epicycle or by a combination of an eccentric circle carrying an epicycle. For
they can all effect the same
irregularity, as we demonstrated above in the case of
the sun and the moon.

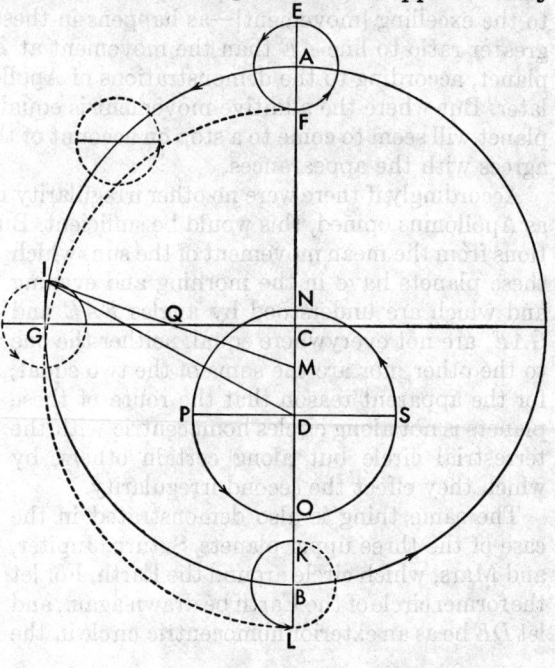

Accordingly let AB be an eccentric circle around centre C. Let ACB be the diameter drawn through the highest and lowest apsis of the planet and containing the mean position of the sun. On ACB let D be the centre of the orbital circle of the Earth; and with the highest apsis A as centre and the third part of CD as radius, let epicycle EF be described. Let F be its perigee, and let the planet be placed there. Now let the movement of the epicycle along eccentric circle AB take place eastward; and let the movement of the planet in the upper arc [of the epicycle] take place similarly eastward [142^b] but in the remaining arc westward; and let the revolutions of the epicycle and the planet be proportionately equal to one another.

On that account when the epicycle is at the highest apsis of the eccentric circle and the planet on the contrary is at the perigee of the epicycle, the relation between their movements is reversed[1] with respect to one another, since both the planet and the epicycle have traversed their semicircle. But in both mean quadrants each will have its mean apsis, and then only will the diameter[2] of the epicycle be parallel to line AB; and at the midpoints [between the mean quadrants and the perigee or apogee] the diameter will be perpendicular to AB: the rest of the time always moving towards AB or moving away. All that is easily understood as following from the movements.

Hence it will also be demonstrated that by this composite movement the planet does not describe a perfect circle in accordance with the theory of the ancient mathematicians but a curve differing imperceptibly from one.

For let the same epicycle KL be drawn again, and let B be its centre. Let AG the quadrant of a circle be assumed, and let HI be an epicycle around G. Let CD be cut into three equal parts, and let

$$CM = \tfrac{1}{3}CD = GI.$$

And let GC and IM, which cut one another at Q, be joined.

Accordingly since, by hypothesis

and
$$\text{arc } AG = \text{arc } HI$$

then
$$\text{angle } ACG = 90°;$$

And
$$\text{angle } HGI = 90°.$$

$$\text{angle } IQG = \text{angle } MQC,$$

because they are vertical angles. Therefore triangles GIQ and QCM are equiangular; and they have correspondingly equal sides, since by hypothesis

And
$$\text{base } GI = \text{base } CM.$$

therefore
$$QI > QC = QM > QG;$$

but
$$IQM > GQC,$$

$$FM = ML = AC = CG.$$

Therefore the circle which is described around centre M through points F and L and is hence equal to circle AB will cut line IM. The same demonstra-

---

[1] That is to say, during the hemicycle of movement wherein the epicycle is passing from the lowest to the highest apsis of the eccentric circle and the planet is passing from the apogee to the perigee of the epicycle, the movement on the epicycle adds to the movement on the eccentric circle; but during the hemicycle wherein the epicycle is passing from the highest to the lowest apsis, the movement on the epicycle subtracts from the movement on the eccentric circle.

[2] In this passage Copernicus is speaking as if the planet were borne around the epicycle by the revolving diameter, although he usually speaks as if the diameter of the epicycle pointed perpetually at the centre of the homocentric circle.

tion will hold in the opposite quadrant. Accordingly by the regular movements of the epicycle in the eccentric circle the planet in the epicycle will not describe a perfect circle but a quasi-circle—as was to be demonstrated.[1]

Now around centre D let NO the annual orbital circle of the Earth be described; let IDR be extended; and let PDS be drawn parallel to CG. Accordingly IDR will be the straight line of the true movement of the planet; GC, the straight line of the mean and regular movement. And R will be the true apogee of the Earth with respect to the planet; and S, the mean apogee. Accordingly angle RDS or IDP is the difference between the regular and the apparent movement of both, namely between angle ACG and angle CDI.

But in place of eccentric circle AB we may take an equal homocentric circle around D as the deferent of the epicycle, whose radius is equal to DC and which is the deferent of the other epicycle, whose semi-diameter is half MD.[2] Now let the first epicycle be moved [143ᵃ] eastward, but the second in the opposite direction; and lastly let the planet on it [i.e., on the second epicycle] be deflected by the twofold movement. The same things will happen as before and no differently from in the moon, or by some other of the aforesaid modes.

But here we have chosen the eccentric circle bearing the epicycle, because by remaining always between the sun and C centre D is meantime found to have changed, as was shown in the case of solar appearances. But as the remaining appearances do not accord proportionately with this change there must be some other irregularity in those planetary movements: this irregularity, although very slight, is perceptible in the case of Mars and Venus, as will be seen in the right place.

Accordingly we shall soon demonstrate from observations that these hypotheses are sufficient for the appearances; and we shall do that first in the case of Saturn, Jupiter, and Mars: in them the position of the apogee and the distance CD are very difficult to find and of the greatest importance, since the rest is easily demonstrable by means of the apogee and the distance CD. Now in this case we shall use the method we used concerning the moon, namely a comparison of three ancient solar oppositions with the same number of modern ones, which the Greeks call their "acronychial gleams" and we the "deeps of the night," namely when the planet opposite the sun falls upon the straight line of the mean movement of the sun, where it throws off all that irregularity which the movement of the Earth brings to it. Such positions are determined by observations with an astrolabe and by computation of the oppositions of the sun, until it is clear that the planet has arrived at a point opposite the sun.

5. DEMONSTRATIONS OF THE MOVEMENT OF SATURN

Accordingly we shall begin with Saturn by taking three oppositions once observed by Ptolemy. The first of them occurred in the 11th year of Hadrian on

---

[1]As has been pointed out, if in the foregoing diagram we consider a point X so situated on semi-diameter CA that CX is equal to GI (and consequently DM is equal to MX), then since the planet on reaching point I has expended one quarter of its periodic time and has traversed one quarter of a full revolution about point X, evidently point X is analogous to the centre of a Ptolemaic equant, point M (the centre of the quasi-circle) to the centre of the Ptolemaic deferent, and point D (the centre of the sun for Copernicus) to the centre of the Earth.

[2]As in the accompanying diagram:

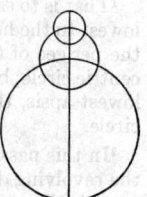

the 7th day of the month Pachom at the first hour of night; in the year of Our Lord 127 on the 7th day before the Kalends of April, 17 equal hours after midnight in relation to the Cracow meridian, which we find an hour distant from Alexandria. Now the position of the planet in relation to the sphere of the fixed stars, to which as to the starting-point of the regular movement we are referring all these things, was found to be at approximately 174°40′, since [143ᵇ] the sun by its simple movement was then opposite at 354°40′ from the horn of Aries, the starting-point assumed.

The second opposition was in the 17th year of Hadrian on the 18th day of the month Epiphi by the Egyptian calendar; but by the Roman, in the year of Our Lord 133 on the 3rd day before the Nones of June, 11 equatorial hours after midnight: he found the planet at 243°3′, while by its mean movement the sun was at 63°3′, 15 hours after midnight.

He recorded the third as occurring in the 20th year of Hadrian on the 24th day of the month Mesori by the Egyptian calendar; which was in the year of Our Lord 136 on the 8th day before the Ides of July, 11 hours after midnight (similarly according to the Cracow meridian) at 277°37′, while by its mean movement the sun was at 97°37′.

Accordingly in the first interval there are 6 years 70 days 55 minutes [of a day], during which the planet is moved 62°23′ in relation to sight, and the mean movement of the Earth with respect to the planet, i.e., the movement of parallax, is 352°44′. Accordingly the 7°16′ in which the circle is deficient belong to the mean movement of the planet, so that it is 75°39′.

In the second interval there are 3 Egyptian years 35 days 50 minutes; the apparent movement of the planet is 34°34′, [the movement] of parallax 356°43′; and the remaining 3°17′ of a circle are added to the apparent movement of the planet, so that the mean movement is 37°51′.

After this survey let *ABC* the eccentric circle of the planet be described. Let

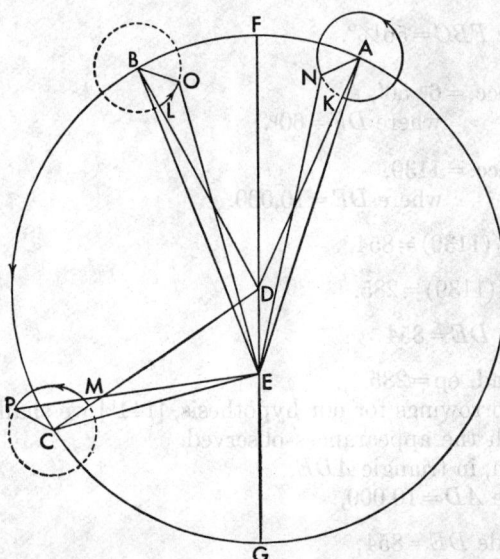

D be its centre, and *FDG* its diameter, whereon *E* is the centre of the great orbital circle of the Earth. Now let *A* be the centre of the epicycle at the first opposition to the sun; *B*, at the second; and *C*, at the third; and around them let the same epicycle be described with a radis equal to one-third of *DE*. Let the centres *A*, *B*, and *C* be joined to *D* and *E* by straight lines, which will cut the circumference of the epicycle at points *K*, *L*, and *M*. And let there be taken arc *KN* similar to *AF*, arc *LO* similar to *BF*, and *MP* similar to *FBC*; and let *EN*, *EO*, and *EP* be joined. Therefore by computation arc $AB = 75°39'$

and

arc $BC = 37°51'$;

and of the angles of apparent movement,

angle $NEO = 68°23'$

and

angle $OEP = 34°34'$.

Our problem is to examine the positions of highest and lowest apsis, *i.e.*, of F and G, together with the distance DE between the centres, without which there is no way of discerning the regular and the apparent [144ᵃ] movement.

But here too we run into as great a difficulty as in this part of Ptolemy, since, if the given angle NEO comprehended the given arc AB, and [angle] OEP [arc] BC, the entrance to demonstrating what we are looking for would be already opened. But the known arc AB subtends the unknown angle AEB, and similarly the unknown angle BEC is subtended by the known arc BC; for it was necessary for both of them to be known. But AEN, BEO, and CEP, the differences between the angles, cannot be perceived, unless arcs AF, FB, and FBC are first set up as similar to those on the epicycle; accordingly these things are mutually dependent so as to be simultaneously known or unknown. Therefore those who were destitute of the means of demonstration relied upon detours and the *a posteriori* method, as the straightforward and *a priori* approach was not open. So Ptolemy in this investigation expended his energies in a prolix argument and a great multitude of calculations, which I judge boring and supererogatory to review, especially as in our calculations, which follow, we shall copy the same method approximately.

Finally in going over his calculations again he found that

arc $AF = 57°1'$,
arc $BF = 18°37'$,

and

arc $FBC = 56\frac{1}{2}°$.

But

ecc. $= 6^p\ 50'$,
where $DF = 60^p$.

But

ecc. $= 1139$,
where $DF = 10,000$.

Now

$\frac{3}{4}(1139) \doteq 854$,

and

$\frac{1}{4}(1139) \doteq 285$.

Hence

$DE = 854$

and

rad. ep $= 285$.

Making these assumptions and borrowings for our hypothesis, [144ᵇ] we shall show that these things agree with the appearances observed.

Now at the first solar opposition, in triangle ADE,

side $AD = 10,000$,

and

side $DE = 854$;

and

angle $ADE = 180° -$ angle ADF.

Hence, by means of what we have shown concerning plane triangles,
$$\text{side } AE = 10,489,$$
and
$$\text{angle } DEA = 53°6',$$
and
$$\text{angle } DAE = 3°55',$$
$$\text{where 4 rt. angles} = 360°.$$
But
$$\text{angle } KAN = \text{angle } ADF = 57°1'.$$
Therefore by addition
$$\text{angle } NAE = 60°56'.$$
Accordingly in triangle NAE two sides are given:
$$\text{side } AE = 10,489,$$
$$\text{side } NA = 285$$
$$\text{where } AD = 10,000,$$
and
$$\text{angle } NAE \text{ is given.}$$
Hence
$$\text{angle } AEN = 1°22';$$
and, by subtraction,
$$\text{angle } NED = 51°44',$$
$$\text{where 4 rt. angles} = 360°.$$
Similarly at the second solar opposition. For in triangle BDE
$$\text{side } DE = 854,$$
$$\text{where } BD = 10,000;$$
and
$$\text{angle } BDE = 180° - BDF = 161°22'.$$
So triangle BDE too has its sides and angles given:
$$\text{side } BE = 10,812,$$
$$\text{where } BD = 10,000,$$
and
$$\text{angle } DBE = 1°27',$$
and
$$\text{angle } BED = 17°11'.$$
But
$$\text{angle } OBL = \text{angle } BDF = 18°36'.$$
Therefore, by addition
$$\text{angle } EBO = 20°3'.$$
Accordingly in triangle EBO two sides are given together with angle EBO:
$$BE = 10,812$$
and
$$BO = 285.$$
By what we have shown concerning plane triangles
$$\text{angle } BEO = 32'.$$
Hence
$$\text{angle } BED = 16°39'.$$
Moreover, in the third solar opposition, in triangle CDE, as before,
$$\text{side } CD \text{ is given}$$
and
$$\text{side } DE \text{ is given;}$$
and
$$\text{angle } CDE = 180° - 56°29'.$$

By the fourth rule for plane triangles
$$\text{base } CE = 10,512,$$
$$\text{where } CD = 10,000;$$
and
$$\text{angle } DCE = 3°53'$$
and, by subtraction,
$$\text{angle } CED = 52°36'.$$
Therefore, by addition,
$$\text{angle } ECP = 60°22',$$
$$\text{where 4 rt. angles} = 360°.$$
So also in triangle ECP two sides are given together with angle ECP; further-more,
$$\text{angle } CEP = 1°22',$$
whence, by subtraction,
$$\text{angle } PED = 51°14'.$$
Hence, of the total angles of apparent movement,
$$\text{angle } OEN = 68°23',$$
and
$$\text{angle } OEP = 34°35',$$
which agree with the observations. And the position of the highest apsis of
of the eccentric circle
$$F = 226°20'$$
from the head of Aries. And as the then existing precession of [145ª] the spring
equinox was 6°40',
$$226°20' + 6°40' = 23° \text{ of Scorpio,}$$
in accordance with Ptolemy's conclusion. For the apparent position of the
planet at this third solar opposition, as was reported above, was 227°37'.
And as the angle of apparent movement,
$$\text{angle } PED = 51°14'.$$
Hence
$$227°37' - 51°14' = 226°23',$$
which is the position of the
highest apsis of the eccentric
circle.

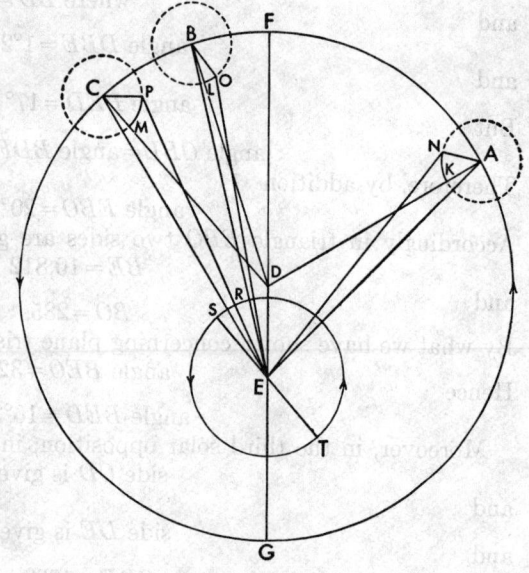

Now let there be described
RST the annual orbital circle
of the Earth, which will cut
line PE at point R; and let the
diameter SET be drawn parallel to the line of mean movement of the planet.
Accordingly, as
angle SED = angle CDF,
angle SER will be the difference and the additosubtraction
between the apparent and
mean movement, $i.e.$, between
angles CDF and PED, and
angle $SER = 5°16'$.

And there is the same difference between the mean and the true movements of parallax. Now

$$\text{arc } RT = 180° - \text{arc } SER = 174°44',$$

which is the regular movement of parallax from starting-point T, *i.e.*, from the mean conjunction of the sun and the planet, to this third solar opposition or true opposition of the Earth and the planet.

Accordingly at the time of this observation, namely in the 20th year of the reign of Hadrian, but in the 136th year of Our Lord on the 8th day before the Ides of July, 11 hours after midnight, we have the movement of anomaly of Saturn from the highest apsis of its eccentric circle as $56\frac{1}{2}°$, and the mean movement of parallax as $174°44'$, as was timely to demonstrate on account of what follows.

6. On Three Other Solar Oppositions of Saturn Recently Observed

[145[b]] Now since the computation of the movement of Saturn handed down by Ptolemy has no small discrepancy with our times, and since it cannot be understood right away in what quarter the error lies, we are forced to make new observations, out of which we have again taken three solar oppositions. The first opposition was in the year of Our Lord 1514, on the 3rd day before the Nones of May $1\frac{1}{5}$ hours before midnight, at which time Saturn was discovered at $205°24'$.

The second was in the year of Our Lord 1520 on the third day before the Ides of July at midday, and the planet was at $273°25'$.

The third was in the year of Our Lord 1527 on the 6th day before the Ides of October $6\frac{2}{5}$ hours after midnight; and Saturn appeared at $7'$ from the horn of Aries.

Accordingly between the first and second solar oppositions there are 6 Egyptian years 70 days 33 minutes [of a day], during which time the apparent movement of Saturn is $68°1'$.

From the second to the third there are 7 Egyptian years 89 days 46 minutes, and the apparent movement of the planet is $86°42'$; and the mean movement during the first interval is $75°39'$; and during the second, $88°29'$. Accordingly in investigating the highest apsis and the eccentricity, we must at first abide by the rule of Ptolemy, just as if the planet moved in a simple eccentric circle; and although that is not sufficient, nevertheless we shall be led fairly near and shall arrive at the truth more easily.

Accordingly, let ABC be the circle in which the planet is moved regularly: and let the first opposition be at A, the second at B, and the third at C. Let the centre of the orbital circle of the Earth be taken within it as D. Let AD, BD, and CD be joined, and let any one of them be extended in a straight line to the opposite part of the circumference—say CDE—and let AE and BE be joined.

Accordingly, since

$$\text{angle } BDC = 86°42',$$
$$\text{where 2 rt. angles} = 180°;$$
$$\text{angle } BDE = [146^a]\ 93°18';$$

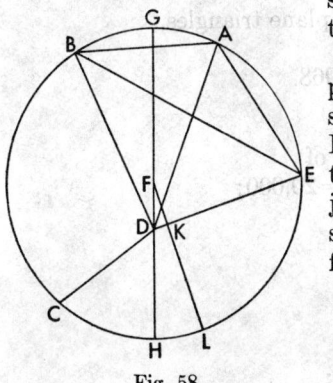

Fig. 58

but   angle $BDE = 186°36'$,

$\qquad$ where 2 rt. angles $= 360°$.

And, as intercepting arc BC,

$\qquad$ angle $BED = 88°29'$,

and

$\qquad$ angle $DBE = 84°55'$.

Accordingly, as the angles of triangle BDE are given, the sides are given by the table:

$$BE = 19,953$$

and

$$DE = 13,501$$

$\qquad$ where diameter of circle

$\qquad$ circumscribing triangle $= 20,000$.

Similarly in triangle ADE, since

$\qquad$ angle $ADC = 154°43'$,

$\qquad$ where 2 rt. angles $= 180°$;

$\qquad$ angle $ADE = 180° -$ angle $ADC = 25°17'$;

but

$\qquad$ angle $ADE = 50°34'$,

$\qquad$ where 2 rt. angles $= 360°$.

And, as intercepting arc ABC,

$\qquad$ angle $AED = 164°8'$,

and

$\qquad$ angle $DAE = 145°18'$:

hence the sides are established:

$$DE = 19,090$$

and

$$AE = 8,542,$$

$\qquad$ where diameter of circle

$\qquad$ circumscribing triangle $ADE = 20,000$.

But

$$AE = 6,043$$

$\qquad$ where $DE = 13,501$ and

$\qquad$ $BE = 19,953$.

Hence too, in triangle ABE, these two sides BE and EA have been given; and, as intercepting arc AB,

$\qquad$ angle $AEB = 75°39'$.

Accordingly by what we have shown concerning plane triangles,

$$AB = 15,647$$

$\qquad$ where $BE = 19,968$.

But according as

$\qquad$ ch. $AB = 12,266$,

$\qquad$ where diameter of

$\qquad$ eccentric circle $= 20,000$;

$\qquad$ $EB = 15,664$

and

$$DE = 10,599.$$

Accordingly, in proportion to chord BE,

$\qquad$ arc $BAE = 103°7'$.

Hence, by addition,

$\qquad$ arc $EABC = 191°36'$;

and
$$\text{arc } CE = 360° - \text{arc } EABC = 168°24';$$
and hence
$$\text{ch. } CDE = 19,898.$$
And
$$CD = CDE - DE = 9,299.$$

And now it is manifest that, if CDE were the diameter of the eccentric circle, the positions of highest and lowest apsis would fall upon it, and the distance between the centres would be evident; but because segment $EABC$ is greater, the centre will be in it. Let F be the centre, and let the diameter $GFDG$ be extended through F and D, and let FKL be drawn at right angles to CDE.

Now it is manifest that
$$\text{rect. } CD, DE = \text{rect. } GD, DH.$$
But
$$\text{rect. } GD, DH + \text{sq. } FD = \text{sq. } (\tfrac{1}{2}GDH) = \text{sq. } FDH.$$
Accordingly
$$\text{sq. } FDH - \text{rect. } CD, DE = \text{sq. } FD.$$
Therefore
$$FD = 1,200$$
$$\text{where radius } GF = 10,000;$$
but
$$FD = 7^\mathrm{p}12'$$
$$\text{where radius} = 60^\mathrm{p},$$
[146$^\mathrm{b}$] which differs little from Ptolemy.

But since
$$CDK = \tfrac{1}{2}CDE = 9,949$$
and
$$CD = 9,299,$$
therefore
$$DK = CDK - CD = 650,$$
$$\text{where } GF = 10,000$$
$$\text{and } FD = 1,200.$$
But
$$DK = 5,411$$
$$\text{where } FD = 10,000.$$
And since
$$DK = \tfrac{1}{2} \text{ ch. } 2 \, DFK,$$
$$\text{angle } DFK = 32°45',$$
$$\text{where 4 rt. angles} = 360°;$$
and as standing at the centre of the circle it intercepts a similar chord and arc HL on the circumference.

But
$$\text{arc } CHL = \tfrac{1}{2}CLE = 84°13';$$
therefore
$$\text{arc } CH = CHL - HL = 51°28',$$
which is the distance from the third opposition to the perigee.
Now
$$180° - 51°28' = CBG = 128°32'$$
from the highest apsis to the third opposition. And since
$$\text{arc } CB = 88°29',$$
$$\text{arc } BG = CBG - CB = 40°3',$$

from the highest apsis to the second solar opposition. Then, as

$$\text{arc } BGA = 75°39',$$
$$\text{arc } GA = BGA - BG = 35°36'$$

from the first opposition to the apogee G.

Now let ABC be a circle with diameter $FDEG$, centre D, apogee F, perigee G. Let

$$\text{arc } AF = 35°36',$$
$$\text{arc } FB = 40°3',$$

and

$$\text{arc } FBC = 128°32'.$$

Now let DE be taken as three
quarters of what has already
been shown to be the distance
between the centres, *i.e.*, let

$$DE = 900;$$

and

quarter distance $= 300$
    where radius $= 10,000$.
And with that quarter distance
as radius, let the epicycle be described around centres A, B,
and C—and let the figure be
completed according to the hypothesis set before us. But if
with this lay-out we wish to
elicit the observed positions of
Saturn [147ᵃ] by the method

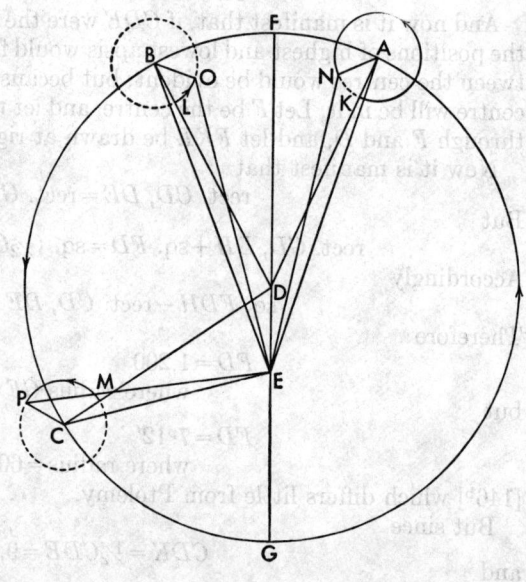

handed down above and soon to be repeated, we shall find some discrepancy.

And—to speak briefly, so as not to burden the reader with many words or seem to have laboured more in indicating by-ways than in pointing out the high road—these things will, by means of what we have shown concerning triangles, necessarily lead us to the conclusion that

$$\text{angle } NEO = 67°35'$$

and

$$\text{angle } OEP = 87°12'.$$

But angle OEP is ½° greater than the apparent angle, and the angle NEO is 26′ smaller. And we find that they square with one another only if we move the apogee forward a little, and set up

$$\text{arc } AF = 38°50',$$
$$\text{arc } FB = 36°49',$$
$$\text{arc } FBC = 125°18',$$
$$DE = 854,$$

which is the distance between the centres, and

$$\text{rad. ep.} = 285,$$
$$\text{where } FD = 10,000;$$

and that agrees approximately with Ptolemy, as set out above. For it is clear from this that these magnitudes agree with the three apparent solar oppositions observed.

Since at the first opposition, in triangle ADE,

$$side\ DE = 854,$$
$$where\ AD = 10,000,$$

and

$$angle\ ADE = 141°10',$$
$$where\ angle\ ADE + angle\ ADF = 2\ rt.\ angles;$$

hence it is shown that

$$side\ AE = 10,679,$$
$$where\ radius\ FD = 10,000,$$
$$angle\ DAE = 2°52',$$

and

$$angle\ DEA = 35°58'.$$

Similarly in triangle AEN, since

$$angle\ KAN = angle\ ADF;$$
$$angle\ EAN = 41°42',$$

and

$$side\ AN = 285,$$
$$where\ AE = 10,679.$$

Hence

$$angle\ AEN = 1°3'.$$

But

$$angle\ DEA = 35°58';$$

accordingly, by subtraction,

$$angle\ DEN = 34°55'.$$

In the second solar opposition triangle DEB has two sides given:

$$DE = 854,$$
$$where\ DB = 10,000$$

and

$$angle\ BDE = 153°11'.$$

Accordingly

$$BE = 10,697,$$
$$angle\ DBE = 2°45',$$

and

$$angle\ BED = 34°4'.$$

But

$$angle\ LBO = angle\ BDF;$$

therefore, as at the centre,

$$angle\ EBO = 39°34'.$$

Now this angle is comprehended by the given sides:

$$BO = 285$$

and

$$BE = 10,697;$$

hence

$$angle\ BEO = 59'.$$

And

$$angle\ OED = angle\ BED - angle\ BEO = 33°5'.$$

But in the first solar opposition it has already been shown that

$$angle\ DEN = 34°55'.$$

Therefore by addition

$$angle\ OEN = 68°,$$

by which the distance of the first solar opposition from the second becomes apparent; and it harmonizes with the observations.

The same thing will be shown at the third opposition.
In triangle CDE

$$\text{angle } CDE = 54°42',$$
$$\text{side } CD = 10,000,$$

and

$$\text{side } DE = 854;$$

[147ᵇ] hence

$$\text{side } EC = 9,532,$$
$$\text{angle } CED = 121°5',$$

and

$$\text{angle } DCE = 4°13';$$

therefore by addition

$$\text{angle } PCE = 129°31'.$$

So again in triangle EPC

$$\text{side } CE = 9,532$$

and

$$\text{side } PC = 285,$$

and

hence

$$\text{angle } PCE = 129°31':$$

$$\text{angle } PEC = 1°18'.$$

And

$$\text{angle } PED = \text{angle } CED - \text{angle } PEO = 119°47'$$

from the highest apsis of the eccentric circle to the position of the planet at the third opposition.

Now it was shown that there were 33°5′ to the second solar opposition: accordingly between the second and third solar oppositions of Saturn there remain 86°42′, which agree with the observations. Now the position of Saturn was found by observation at that time to be at 7′ from the assumed starting-point of the first star of Aries, and it was shown that there were 60°13′ from it to the lowest apsis of the eccentric circle: accordingly the lowest apsis is approximately 60⅓°, and the position of the highest apsis is diametrically opposite at 240⅓°.

Now let RST the great orbital circle of the Earth be set around its centre E, and let its diameter SET be parallel to CD the line of mean movement; and let

$$\text{angle } FDC = \text{angle } DES.$$

Therefore the Earth and our point of sight will be on line PE, namely at point R. Now

$$\text{angle } PES = 5°31',$$

and angle PES or arc RS is the difference between FDC the angle of regular movement and DEP the angle of apparent movement.
Now

$$\text{arc } RT = 180° - 5°31' = 174°29'$$

which is the distance of the planet from the apogee of the orbital circle, *i.e.*, from T, as if from the mean position of the sun.

And so we have demonstrated that in the year of Our Lord 1527 on the sixth day before the Ides of October at 6⅖ hours after midnight, the move-

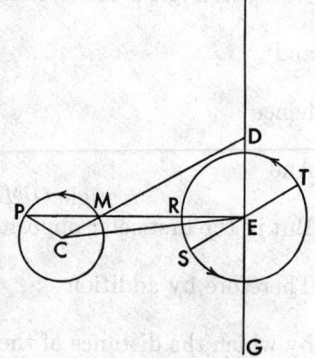

ment of anomaly of Saturn from the highest apsis of the eccentric circle was 125°18′, the movement of parallax was 174°29′, and the position of the highest apsis was at 240°21′ from the first star of Aries in the sphere of the fixed stars.

7. On the Examination of the Movement of Saturn

[148ᵃ] Now it was shown that Saturn at the time of the last of the three observations of Ptolemy was by its movement of parallax at 174°44′, and the position of the highest apsis of the eccentric circle was at 226°23′, from the head of the constellation of Aries. Accordingly it is clear that in the midtime between the two observations Saturn has completed 1344 revolutions minus ¼° of regular parallaxes.

Now from the 20th year of Hadrian on the 24th day of the Egyptian month Mesori one hour before midday to the year of Our Lord 1527 on the 6th day before the Ides of October at 6 hours [after midnight, the time] of this observation, there are 1392 Egyptian years 75 days 48 minutes [of a day].

Hence if we wish to get the movement itself from the table, we shall similarly find 359°45′, the movement beyond the 1343 revolutions of parallax. Accordingly what was set down concerning the mean movements of Saturn is correct. Moreover during that time the simple movement of the sun is 82°30′. If 359°45′ are subtracted from 82°30′, the remainder is the 82°45′ of the mean movement of Saturn, which are already being added up in its 47th revolution, in harmony with the computation. Meanwhile too the position of the highest apsis of the eccentric circle has been moved forward to 13°58′ in the sphere of the fixed stars. Ptolemy believed it to be fixed in the same way, but now it appears to move approximately 1° per 100 years.

8. On Determining the Positions of Saturn

Now from the beginning of the years of Our Lord to the 20th of Hadrian on the 24th day of the month Mesori at 1 hour before midday, the time of Ptolemy's observation, there are 135 Egyptian years 222 days 27 minutes [of a day], during which time Saturn's movement of parallax was 328°55′. The subtraction of 328°55′ from 174°44′ leaves 205°49′ [148ᵇ] as the locus of distance of the mean position of the sun from the mean [position] of Saturn, and as its movement of parallax at midnight before the Kalends of January.

From the first Olympiad to this locus 775 Egyptian years 12½ days comprehend a movement of 70°55′ besides the whole revolutions. The subtraction of 70°55′ from 205°49′ leaves 134°54′ for the beginning of the Olympiads at noon on the 1st day of the month Hekatombaion.

Then after 451 years 247 days there are 13°7′ besides the whole revolutions: the addition of 13°7′ to 134°54′ puts the locus [of the years] of Alexander the Great at 148°1′ on noon of the 1st day of the month Thoth by the Egyptian calendar; and there are 278 years 118½ days to [years of] Caesar; the movement is 247°20′, and it sets up the locus at 35°21′ on midnight before the Kalends of January.

9. On the Parallaxes of Saturn, Which Arise from the Annual Orbital Circle of the Earth, and How Great the Distance of Saturn Is [from the Earth]

In this way it has been demonstrated that the regular movements of Saturn in longitude are at one with the apparent. For the other apparent movements which occur in the case of Saturn are, as we said, parallaxes arising from the annual orbital circle of the Earth, since, as the magnitude of the Earth in relation to the distance of the moon causes parallaxes, so too its orbital circle, in which it revolves annually, should in the case of the five wandering stars cause [parallaxes] which are far more evident in proportion to the magnitude of the orbital circle. Now such parallaxes cannot be determined, unless the altitude of the planet—which, however, it is possible to apprehend through any one observation of a parallax—becomes known first.

We have such [an observation] in the case of Saturn in the year of Our Lord 1514 on the sixth day before the Kalends of May 5 equatorial hours after the preceding midnight. For Saturn was seen to be in a straight line with the stars in the forehead of Scorpio, namely with the second and third stars, which have the same longitude and are at 209° of the sphere of the fixed stars. Accordingly the position of Saturn is made evident through them. Now there are 1514 Egyptian years 61 days 13 minutes [of a day] from the beginning of the years of Our Lord to this time; and according to [149ᵃ] calculation the mean position of the sun was at 315°41', the anomaly of parallax of Saturn was at 116°31', and for that reason the mean position of Saturn was 199°10' and that of the highest apsis of the eccentric circle was at approximately 240⅓°.

Now in accordance with our problem, let ABC be the eccentric circle: let D be its centre, and on the diameter BDC let B be the apogee, C the perigee, and E the centre of the orbital circle of the Earth. Let AD and AE be joined, and with A as centre and ⅓ DE as radius let the epicycle be drawn. On the epicycle let F be the position of the planet; and let

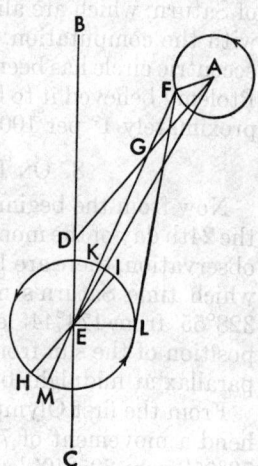

angle DAF = angle ADB.

And through E the centre of the orbital circle of the Earth let HI be drawn, as if in the same plane with circle ABC, and as a diameter, parallel to AD, so as to have it understood that with respect to the planet the apogee of the orbital circle is at H and the perigee at I. Now on the orbital circle let

arc HL = 116°31'

in accordance with the computation of the anomaly of parallax; let FL and EL be joined, and let $FKEM$ produced cut both arcs of the orbital circle.

Accordingly since by hypothesis

angle ADB = angle DAF = 41°10',

and

angle ADE = 130° − ADB = 138°50';

and

DE = 854

whence in triangle ADE

where AD = 10,000:

side AE = 10,667,

angle DEA = 38°9',

and

angle EAD = 3°1':

therefore by addition

angle EAF = 44°12'.

So again in triangle FAE

$$\text{side } FA = 285$$
$$\text{where } AE = 10,667,$$
$$\text{side } FKE = 10,465,$$

and

$$\text{angle } AEF = 1°5':$$

accordingly it is manifest that

$$\text{angle } AEF + \text{angle } DAE = 4°6',$$

which is the total difference or additosubtraction between the mean and the true position of the planet. Wherefore if the position of the Earth had been at K or M, the position of Saturn would have been apparent as if from centre E and would have been seen to be at 203°16′ from the constellation of Aries. But with the Earth at L, Saturn is seen to be at 209°. The difference [149b] of 5°44′ goes to the parallax in accord with angle KFL. But by calculation of the regular movement

$$\text{arc } HL = 116°31',$$

and

$$\text{arc } ML = \text{arc } HL - \text{add. } HM = 112°25'.$$

And by subtraction[1]

$$\text{arc } LIK = 67°35':$$

hence

$$\text{angle } KEL = 67°35'.$$

Wherefore in triangle FEL the angles are given, and the ratio of the sides is given too: Hence

$$EL = 1,090$$
$$\text{where } EF = 10,465,$$
$$\text{and } AD = BD = 10,000;$$

but

$$EL = 6^{\text{p}}32',$$
$$\text{where } BD = 60^{\text{p}},$$
$$\text{by usage of the ancients;}$$

and there is very little difference between that and what Ptolemy gave.

Accordingly

$$BDE = 10,854,$$

and, as the remainder of the diameter

$$CE = 9,146.$$

But since the epicycle when at B always subtracts 285 from the altitude of the planet, but adds the same amount, i.e., its radius, when at C; on that account the greatest distance of Saturn from centre E will be 10,569, and the least 9,431, where $BD = 10,000$. By this ratio the altitude of the apogee of Saturn is $9^{\text{p}}42'$, where the radius of the orbital circle of the Earth $= 1^{\text{p}}$; and the altitude of the perigee is $8^{\text{p}}39'$: hence it is quite evident by the mode set forth above in the case of the small parallaxes of the moon that the parallaxes of Saturn can be greater. And when Saturn is at the apogee,

$$\text{greatest parallax} = 5°45';$$

and when at the perigee,

$$\text{greatest parallax} = 6°39';$$

and they differ from one another by 44′—measuring the angles by the lines coming from the planet and tangent to the orbital circle of the Earth. In this way the particular differences in the movement of Saturn have been found, and we shall afterwards set them out simultaneously and in conjunction with those of the five planets.

[1]Arc $MLIK = 180°$.

10. Demonstrations of the Movement of Jupiter

Having solved the problems concerning Saturn, we shall use the same method and order of demonstration in the case of the movement of Jupiter too, and first we shall repeat three positions reported and demonstrated by Ptolemy, and by the foreshown transformation of circles we shall reconstitute them as the same or as very little different.

The first of the solar oppositions was in the 17th year of Hadrian on the 1st day of the month Epiphi by the Egyptian calendar 1 hour before the following midnight [150ᵃ] at 23°11′ of Scorpio, as he says, but after deducting the precession of the equinoxes, at 226°33′.

He recorded the second as occurring on the 21st year of Hadrian on the 13th day of the month Phaophi by the Egyptian calendar 2 hours before the following midnight, at 7°54′ of Pisces; but with respect to the sphere of the fixed stars it was 331°16′.

The third was during the 1st year of Antoninus in the month Athyr during the night following the 20th day of the month 5 hours after midnight, at 7°45′ in the sphere of the fixed stars.

Accordingly from the first opposition to the second there were 3 Egyptian years 106 days 23 hours, and the apparent movement of the planet was 104°43′. From the second to the third opposition there was 1 year 37 days 7 hours, and the apparent movement of the planet was 36°29′. During the first interval of time the mean movement was 99°55′; during the second it was 33°26′.

Now he found that the arc of the eccentric circle from the highest apsis to the first opposition was 77°15′; and next, 2°50′ from the second opposition to the lowest apsis; and from that to the third opposition, 30°36′. Now the eccentricity of the whole circle was 5½ᵖ whereof the radius is 60ᵖ; but it is 917, whereof the radius would be 10,000; and all that corresponds approximately to the observations.

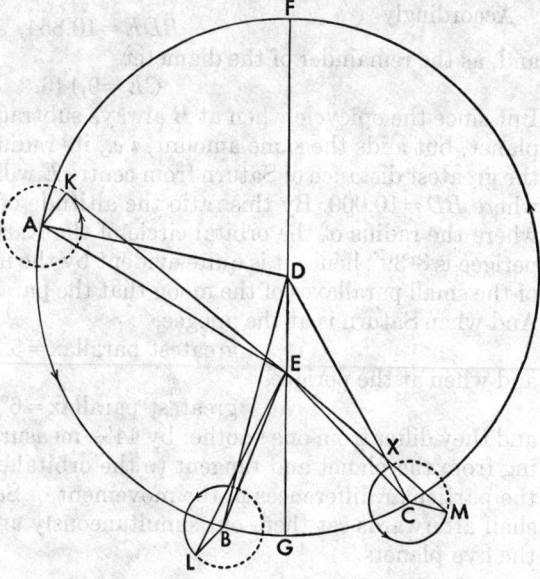

Now let *ABC* be the circle; and from the first opposition to the second let

arc *AB* = 99°55′;

and let

arc *BC* = 33°26′.

Through the centre *D* let diameter *FDG* be drawn, so that from the highest apsis *F*

FA = 77°15′,

and

FAB = 177°10′,

GC = 30°36′.

Now let *E* be taken as the centre of the orbital circle of the Earth. Let the distance between the centres be equal to three-quarters 917, *i.e.*, let

DE = 687;

let
$$\text{rad. ep.} = 229,$$
which is one-quarter distance, and let the epicycle be described at points A, B, and C. Let AD, BD, CD, AE, BE, and CE be joined; and in the epicycles let AK, BL, and BM be joined in such a way that
$$\text{angle } DAK = \text{angle } ADF,$$
$$\text{angle } DBL = \text{angle } FDB,$$
and
$$\text{angle } DCM = \text{angle } FDC.$$
Finally let K, L, and M be joined to E by straight lines.

Accordingly, since in triangle ADE
$$\text{angle } ADE = 102°45',$$
because angle ADF is given; and
$$\text{side } DE = 687,$$
$$\text{where } AD = 10,000;$$
$$\text{side } AE = 10,174,$$
$$\text{angle } EAD = 3°48',$$
and
$$\text{angle } DEA = 73°27';$$
and by addition
$$\text{angle } EAK = 81°3'.$$
Accordingly in [150ᵇ] triangle AEK two sides have been given:
$$EA = 10,174$$
and
$$AK = 229,$$
and
$$\text{angle } EAK = 81°3';$$
it will be clear that
$$\text{angle } AEK = 1°17'.$$
Hence, by subtraction,
$$\text{angle } KEO = 72°10'.$$
Something similar will be shown in triangle BED. For the sides BD and DE always remain equal to the corresponding sides in the first triangle; but
$$\text{angle } BDE = 2°50'.$$
For that reason
$$\text{base } BE = 9,314,$$
$$\text{where } DB = 10,000;$$
and
$$\text{angle } DBE = 12'.$$
So once more, in triangle ELB two sides are given; and
$$\text{angle } EBL = 177°22';$$
moreover
$$\text{angle } LEB = 4'.$$
But
$$\text{angle } FEL = \text{angle } FDB - 16' = 176°54'.$$
And as
$$\text{angle } KED = 72°10';$$
$$\text{angle } KEL = \text{angle } FEL - \text{angle } KED = 104°44',$$
which is the angle of apparent movement between the first and the second termini observed; and there is approximate agreement.

Similarly at the third opposition, in triangle CDE two sides CD and DE have been given, and
$$\text{angle } CDE = 30°36';$$
$$\text{base } EC = 9,410$$
and
$$\text{angle } DCE = 2°8'.$$

Whence in triangle ECM

$$\text{angle } ECM = 147°49';$$

hence

$$\text{angle } CEM = 39';$$

and because the exterior angle is equal to the sum of the interior and opposite angles

$$\text{angle } DXE = \text{angle } ECX + \text{angle } CEX = 2°47'$$

and

$$\text{angle } FDC - \text{angle } DEM = 2°47'.$$

Hence

$$\text{angle } GEM = 180° - \text{angle } DEM = 33°23';$$

and, by addition,

$$\text{angle } LEM = [151^a] \ 36°29',$$

which is the distance from the second opposition to the third; and that agrees with the observations. But since this third solar opposition was found to be at 7°45' [in the sphere of the fixed stars] and 33°23' to the east of the lowest apsis; the remainder of the semicircle gives us the position of the highest apsis as 154°22' in the sphere of the fixed stars.

Now around E let there be drawn RST the annual orbital circle of the Earth with diameter SET parallel to line DC. Now it has been made clear that

$$\text{angle } GDC = \text{angle } GER = 30°36';$$

and

$$\text{angle } DXE = \text{angle } RES = \text{arc } RS = 2'47',$$

the distance of the planet from the mean perigee of the orbital circle. Hence by addition

$$\text{arc } TSR = 182°47',$$

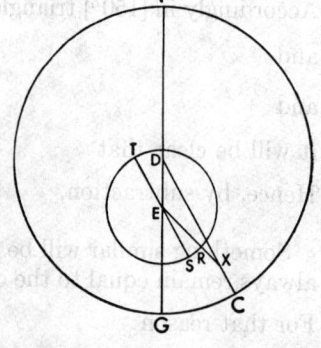

which is the distance from the highest apsis of the orbital circle.

And by this we have confirmation of the fact that at the time of the third opposition of Jupiter during the first year of Antoninus on the 20th day of the month Athyr by the Egyptian calendar 5 hours after the following midnight the planet Jupiter by its anomaly of parallax was at 182°47'. Its regular position in longitude was at 4°58', and the position of the highest apsis of the eccentric circle was at 154°22'. All these things are in perfect agreement with our hypothesis of the mobility of the Earth and absolute regularity [of movement].

11. ON THREE OTHER OPPOSITIONS OF JUPITER RECENTLY OBSERVED

Having recorded three positions of the planet Jupiter and evaluated them in this way, we shall set up three others in their place, which we observed with greatest care at the solar oppositions of Jupiter.

The first was in the year of Our Lord 1520 on the day before the Kalends of May 11 hours after the preceding midnight, at 220°18' of the sphere of the fixed stars.

The second was in the year of Our Lord 1526 on the fourth day before the Kalends of December 3 hours after midnight, at 48°34'.

But the third opposition was in the year of Our Lord 1529 on the Kalends of February 18 hours after midnight, at 113°44'.

From the first [151ᵇ] to the second there are 6 years 212 days 40 minutes [of a day], during which time the apparent movement of Jupiter was 208°6′. From the second to the third opposition there are 2 Egyptian years 66 days 39 minutes [of a day], and the apparent movement of the planet is 65°10′. But the regular movement of the planet during the first interval is 199°40′, and during the second 66°10′.

With this as a paradigm let eccentric circle *ABC* be described, in which the

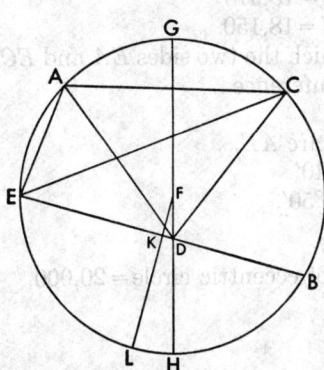

planet is assumed to move simply and regularly. And let the three positions observed be designated in the order of the letters *A*, *B*, and *C* in such a way that

$$\text{arc } AB = 199°40′$$

and

$$\text{arc } BC = 66°10′,$$

on that account

$$\text{arc } AC = 360° - (AB + BC) = 94°10′.$$

Moreover let *D* be taken as the centre of the annual orbit of the Earth. Let *AD*, *BD* and *CD* be joined; and let any of them, say *DB*, be extended in a straight line *BDE* to both arcs of the circle; and let *AC*, *AE* and *CE* be joined.

Accordingly, since

$$\text{angle } BDC = 65°10′,$$

where 4 rt. angles at centre = 360°;
and that is the angle of apparent movement, and since

$$\text{angle } CDE = 180° - 65°10′ = 114°50′,$$

but

$$\text{angle } CDE = 229°40′,$$

where 2 rt. angles at circumference = 360°;
and since, as standing on arc *BC* of circumference,

$$\text{angle } CED = 66°10′,$$

and accordingly

$$\text{angle } DCE = 64°10′;$$

therefore, as triangle *CDE* has its angles given, it has its sides given too:

$$CE = 18,150$$

and

$$ED = 10,918$$

where diameter of circle circumscribing triangle = 20,000.

Similarly, in triangle *ADE*, since

$$\text{angle } ADB = 151°54′,$$

which is the remainder of the circle after the subtraction of the given distance between the first opposition and the second; accordingly

$$\text{angle } ADE = 180° - 151°54′ = 28°6′,$$

as at the centre, but as on the circumference

$$\text{angle } ADE = 56°12′;$$

and, as on arc *BCA* of the circumference

$$\text{angle } AED = 160°20′;$$

and

$$\text{angle } EAD = 143°28′.$$

Hence

and

side $AE = 9,420$

side $ED = 18,992$

where diameter of circle circumscribing triangle $ADE = 20,000$.

But

$AE = 5,415$

where $ED = 10,918$

and $CE = 18,150$

Again therefore we shall have triangle EAC, of which the two sides EA and EC are given; and, as standing on arc AC of the circumference

angle $AEC = 94°10'$.

[152ª] Hence it will be shown that, as standing on arc AE,

angle $ACE = 30°40'$,

angle $ACE + $ arc $AC = 124°50'$,

and

$CE = $ ch. $EAC = 17,727$

where diameter of eccentric circle $= 20,000$.

And by the ratio given before,

and

$DE = 10,665$,

It follows that

arc $BCAE = 191°$.

and

arc $EB = 360° - 191° = 169°$,

and by subtraction

$BDE = $ ch. $EB = 19,908$

$BD = 9,243$.

Accordingly, since $BCAE$ is the greater segment, it will contain F the centre of the circle. Now let the diameter $GFDH$ be drawn. It is manifest that

rect. $ED, DB = $ rect. GD, DH,

which is therefore also given. But

Now

rect. $GD, DH + $ sq. $FD = $ sq. FDH.

Therefore

sq. $FDH - $ rect. $GD, DH = $ sq. FD.

$FD = 1,193$,

where $FG = 10,000$,

but

$FD = 7^\text{p}9'$,

where $FG = 60^\text{p}$.

Now let BE be bisected at K, and let FKL be extended; accordingly FKL will be at rt. angles to BE. And since

and

$BDK = \frac{1}{2} BE = 9,954$

$DB = 9,243$,

then, by subtraction,

$DK = 711$.

Accordingly in triangle DFK, which has its sides given,

angle $DFK = 36°35'$,

and similarly

arc $HL = 36°35'$.

But

$$\text{arc } LHB = 84\tfrac{1}{2}°;$$

and, by subtraction,

$$\text{arc } BH = 47°55',$$

which is the distance of the second position from the perigee.
And

$$\text{arc } BCG = 180° - 47°55' = 132°5',$$

which is the distance of the apogee from the second position.
And

$$\text{arc } BCG - \text{arc } BC = 132°5' - 66°10' = 65°55',$$

which is the distance from the third position to the apogee G.
Now

$$99°10' - 65°55' = 28°15',$$

which is the distance from the apogee to the first position of the epicycle. That harmonizes too little with the appearances, as the planet does not run through the proposed eccentric circle: hence this method of demonstration which is based upon an uncertain principle cannot give us any certainty. One sign of this among others is that Ptolemy in the case of Saturn recorded a too great distance between the centres and in the case of Jupiter a too small distance; but the same thing seemed a great enough distance to us, so that evidently upon the assumption of different arcs of circles for the same planet [152^b] that which is sought does not come about in the same way. Not otherwise was it possible to compound the apparent and the regular movements at the three proposed termini and then at all the termini, unless we kept the total egression of eccentricity of the centres which was recorded by Ptolemy as $5^p30'$, whereof the radius of the eccentric circle is 60^p, but which is 917 parts, whereof the radius is 10,000. And let the arc from the highest apsis to the first opposition be $45°2'$; from the lowest apsis to the second opposition $64°42'$; and from the third opposition to the highest apsis $49°8'$.

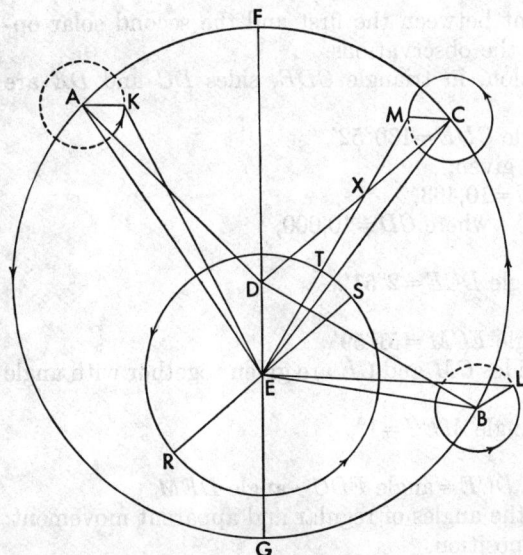

For let the above figure of the eccentric circle carrying an epicycle be repeated, inasmuch as it fits this example. So by our hypothesis

$$DE = 687,$$

which is three-quarters of the total distance between the centres. And

radius of epicycle $= 229$,

where $FD = 10,000$,

which is the remaining quarter of the distance. Accordingly, since

angle $ADF = 45°2'$,

triangle ADE will have the two sides AD and DE given, together with angle ADE: hence it is shown that

side $AE = 10,496$,

where $AD = 10,000$;

and
$$\text{angle } DAE = 2°39'.$$
And since
$$\text{angle } DAK = \text{angle } ADF,$$
by addition
$$\text{angle } EAK = 47°41'.$$
Also in triangle AEK the two sides AK and AE are given. Hence
$$\text{angle } AEK = 57'.$$
Now
$$\text{angle } KED = \text{angle } ADF - (\text{angle } AEK + \text{angle } DAE) = 41°26',$$
as the angle of apparent movement at the first solar opposition.

[153^a] In triangle BDE a similar thing will be shown. Since the two sides BD and DE are given, and
$$\text{angle } BDE = 64°42';$$
$$\text{side } BE = 9,725$$
$$\text{where } BD = 10,000$$
and
$$\text{angle } BDE = 3°40'.$$
Furthermore, in triangle BEL the two sides BE and BL are also given, and
$$\text{angle } EBL = 118°58':$$
$$\text{angle } BEL = 1°10';$$
and hence
$$\text{angle } DEL = 110°28'.$$
But it has already been made clear that
$$\text{angle } AED = 41°26',$$
therefore, by addition,
$$\text{angle } KEL = 151°54'.$$
Hence
$$360° - 151°54' = 208°6',$$
the angle of apparent movement between the first and the second solar oppositions; and that agrees with the observations.

Finally, at the third opposition, in triangle CDE, sides DC and DE are given in the same way; and
$$\text{angle } CDE = 130°52'.$$
On account of angle FDC being given,
$$\text{side } CE = 10,463,$$
$$\text{where } CD = 10,000,$$
and
$$\text{angle } DCE = 2°51'.$$
Therefore, by addition,
$$\text{angle } ECM = 51°59'.$$
Now in triangle ECM the two sides CM and CE are given together with angle MCE:
$$\text{angle } MEC = 1°,$$
and
$$\text{angle } MEC + \text{angle } DCE = \text{angle } FDC - \text{angle } DEM,$$
and angles FDC and DEM are the angles of regular and apparent movement. And hence, at the third solar opposition,
$$\text{angle } DEM = 45°17'.$$

But it has already been shown that
$$\text{angle } DEL = 90°28';$$
accordingly
$$\text{angle } LEM = 65°10',$$
which is the distance between the second and the third solar oppositions observed; and that agrees with the observations. But since the third position of Jupiter was viewed at 113°44' of the sphere of the fixed stars, it shows that the position of the highest Jovial apsis is at approximately 159°.

But if around centre E we now describe RST the orbital circle of the Earth, of which the diameter RES is parallel to DC, then it will be manifest that at the third opposition of Jupiter
$$\text{angle } FDX = \text{angle } DES = 49°8',$$
and that the apogee of the regular movement in parallax is at R.

But now that the Earth has passed through 180° plus arc ST, it is in conjunction with Jupiter at its solar opposition; and
$$\text{arc } ST = 3°51',$$
according as angle SET has been shown to be of the same magnitude.

And so it is clear from this that in the year of Our Lord, 1529, on the Kalends of February 19 hours after midnight, [153^b] the regular movement of anomaly of parallax of Jupiter was at 183°51', but by its proper movement Jupiter was at 109°52'; and the apogee of the eccentric circle is approximately 159° from the horn of the constellation of the Ram, as was to be investigated.

12. CONFIRMATION OF THE REGULAR MOVEMENT OF JUPITER

But it has already been seen above that at the last of the three solar oppositions observed by Ptolemy the planet Jupiter by its proper movement was at 4°58' with an anomaly of parallax of 182°47'. Hence it is clear that during the time between the two observations the movement of parallax of Jupiter was 1°5' besides the full revolutions and its proper movement was approximately 104°54'. The time, however, which flowed between the 1st year of Antoninus on the 20th day of the month Athyr by the Egyptian calendar at 5 hours after the following midnight and the year of Our Lord 1529 on the Kalends of February 18 hours after the preceding midnight was 1392 Egyptian years 99 days 37 minutes of a day, to which time there similarly corresponds according to the above calculation 1°5' besides the whole revolutions, by which the regular revolutions of the Earth has anticipated Jupiter 1267 times; and so the number is seen to harmonize with the observations and is held as certain and exact.

And it is also manifest that during this time the highest and lowest apsides of the eccentric circle moved 4½° to the east. The equal distribution [of the movement] yields approximately 1° per 300 years.

13. POSITIONS TO BE ASSIGNED TO THE MOVEMENT OF JUPITER

But the time from the last of the three observations, in the 1st year of Antoninus on the 20th day of the month Athyr at 4 hours after the following midnight, going back to the beginning of the years of Our Lord, amounts to 136 Egyptian years 314 days 10 minutes [of a day], during which time the mean movement of [154^a] parallax was 84°31'. The subtraction of 84°31' from 182°47' leaves 98°16' for the movement up to midnight on the Kalends of January at the beginning of the years of Our Lord.

Backward to the first Olympiad there were 775 Egyptian years 12½ days, during which time a movement of 70°58' was reckoned besides the whole revolutions. The subtraction of 70°58' from 98°16' leaves 27°18' as the position for the Olympiad.

Coming down from there for 451 years 247 days, there are 110°52', which together with the movement for the first Olympiad amount to 138°10' for the position of the years of Alexander at noon of the 1st day of the month Thoth by the Egyptian calendar. And so for any others.

14. On Investigating the Parallaxes of Jupiter and Its Altitude in Relation to the Orbital Circle of Terrestrial Revolution

In order to investigate the remaining apparent movements of parallax in the case of Jupiter, we carefully observed its position in the year of Our Lord 1520 on the 12th day before the Kalends of March 6 hours before noon, and we perceived through the instrument that Jupiter was 4°31' to the west of the first bright star in the forehead of Scorpio; and since the position of the fixed star was at 209°40', it is clear that the position of Jupiter was at 205°9' in the sphere of the fixed stars.

Accordingly from the beginning of the years of Christ to the time of this observation there were 1520 equal years 62 days 15 minutes [of a day], during which time the mean movement of the sun is calculated to have been 309°16', and the anomaly of parallax 111°15', whereby the mean position of the planet Jupiter is put at 198°1'. And since at this our time the position of the highest apsis of the eccentric circle was found to be at 159°, the anomaly of the eccentric circle of Jupiter was 39°1'.

Following this example, let eccentric circle ABC be described with centre D and diameter ADC. Let A be the apogee, and C the perigee; and for that reason let E the centre of the annual orbital circle of the Earth be on DC. Now let

arc $AB = 39°1'$;

and with B as centre let the epicycle be described with BF as radius equal to one third of distance DE. Let

angle DBF = angle [154^b] ADB;

and let the straight lines BD, BE, and FE be joined. Accordingly since in triangle BDE two sides are given:

DE = 687,

where $BD = 10,000$;

and since these two sides comprehend the given angle BDE, and

angle $BDE = 140°59'$:

it will be shown that

base $BE = 10,543$

and

angle DBE = angle ADB − angle $BED = 2°21'$,

which is the difference between angle BED and angle ADB. Therefore, by addition,

angle $EBF = 41°22'$.

Accordingly in triangle EBF angle EBF is given together with the two sides comprehending it:

$EB = 10,543$

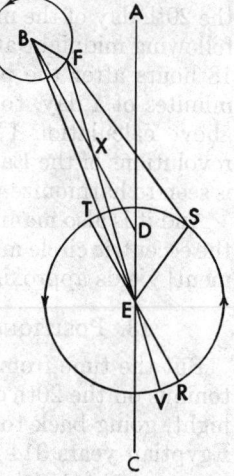

and
$$BF = \frac{1}{3}\, DE = 229,$$
where $BD = 10{,}000$.

It follows from this that
$$\text{side } FE = 10{,}373$$
and
$$\text{angle } BEF = 50'.$$

Now as lines BD and FE cut one another in point X,
$$\text{angle } DXE = \text{angle } BDA - \text{angle } FED$$
and angles FED and BDA are the angles of mean and true movement; and
$$\text{angle } DXE = \text{angle } DBE + \text{angle } BEF = 3°11'.$$

Now
$$\text{angle } FED = 39°1' - 3°11' = 35°50'$$
from the highest apsis of the eccentric circle to the planet.
But the position of the highest apsis was at $159°$; and
$$159° + 35°50' = 194°50',$$
which was the true position of Jupiter with respect to centre E, but the apparent position was at $205°9'$. Accordingly, the difference of $10°19'$ is due to the parallax.

Now let RST the orbital circle of the Earth be described around centre E; and let its diameter RET be parallel to DB, so that R is the apogee of parallax. Moreover, in accordance with the measure of the mean anomaly of parallax, let
$$\text{arc } RS = 111°15';$$
and let FEV be extended in a straight line to both arcs of the orbital circle of the Earth. The true apogee of the planet will be at V; angle REV is equal to the difference between regular and apparent movement; and
$$\text{angle } REV = \text{angle } DXE.$$

Hence, by addition,
$$\text{arc } VRS = 114°26',$$
and by subtraction
$$\text{angle } FES = 65°34'.$$

[155ᵃ] But since
$$\text{angle } EFS = 10°19';$$
$$\text{angle } FSE = 104°7'.$$

Hence, as in triangle EFS the angles are given, the ratio of the sides will be given too:
$$FE : ES = 9{,}698 : 1{,}791.$$

Accordingly
$$FE = 10{,}373$$
and
$$ES = 1{,}916,$$
where $BD = 10{,}000$.

For Ptolemy however
$$ES = 11^{\text{p}}30',$$
where radius of eccentric circle $= 60^{\text{p}}$;
and that is approximately the same ratio as
$$1{,}916 : 10{,}000;$$

and therein we do not seem to differ from Ptolemy at all.
Accordingly

$$\text{dmtr. } ADC : \text{dmtr. } RET = 5^{\text{p}}13' : 1^{\text{p}}.$$

Similarly

$$AD : ES = AD : RE = 5^{\text{p}}13'9'' : 1^{\text{p}}$$

thus

$$DE = 21'9''$$

and

$$BF = 7'10''.$$

Accordingly, when Jupiter is at apogee,

$(ADF—BF)$: radius of orbital circle of Earth $= 5^{\text{p}}27'29'' : 1^{\text{p}}$.

And when Jupiter is at perigee;

$(EC+BF)$: radius of orbital circle of Earth $= 4^{\text{p}}58'49'' : 1^{\text{p}}$;

and when in the mean positions, as is proportional. Hence it is gathered that Jupiter at apogee has a greatest parallax of 10°35′, and at perigee 11°35′: there is a difference of 1° between them. So the regular movements of Jupiter have been demonstrated to be at one with the apparent.

15. On the Planet Mars

We must now inspect the revolutions of Mars by taking three ancient solar oppositions, with which we shall connect the mobility of the Earth in antiquity. Accordingly of those oppositions which Ptolemy recorded, the first was in the 15th year of Hadrian on the 26th day of Tybi the 5th month by the Egyptian calendar 1 equatorial hour after the midnight following. And he says that it was at 21° of Gemini, but in relation to the sphere of the fixed stars was at 84°20′.

He noted the second opposition [155^{b}] as occurring in the 19th year of Hadrian on the 6th day of Pharmuthi the 8th month by the Egyptian calendar 3 hours before the following midnight at 28°50′ of Leo but at 142°10′ in the sphere of the fixed stars.

The third was in the 2nd year of Antoninus on the 12th day of Epiphi the 11th month by the Egyptian calendar 2 equatorial hours before the following midnight at 2°34′ of Sagittarius but at 235°54′ of the sphere of the fixed stars.

Accordingly, between the first and second oppositions there are 4 Egyptian years 69 days 20 hours or 50 minutes of a day, and the apparent movement of the planet was 67°50′ besides the whole revolutions. From the second opposition to the third there were 4 years 96 days and 1 hour, and the apparent movement of the star was 93°44′. Now during the first interval the mean movement was 81°44′ besides the complete revolutions; during the second interval it was 95°28′. Then he found that the total distance between the centres was 12^{p}, whereof the radius of the eccentric circle was 60^{p}; but it was 2,000 whereof the radius was 10,000. And the mean movement from the first opposition to the highest apsis was 41°33′; and then it was 40°11′ from the highest apsis to the second opposition; and from the third opposition to the lowest apsis it was 44°21′: But by our hypothesis of regular movements there will be three-quarters of that distance, i.e., 1,500 between the centres of the eccentric circle and the orbital circle of the Earth, and the remaining quarter of 500 will be the radius of the epicycle.

Now thus let eccentric circle ABC be described with centre D, and with FDG

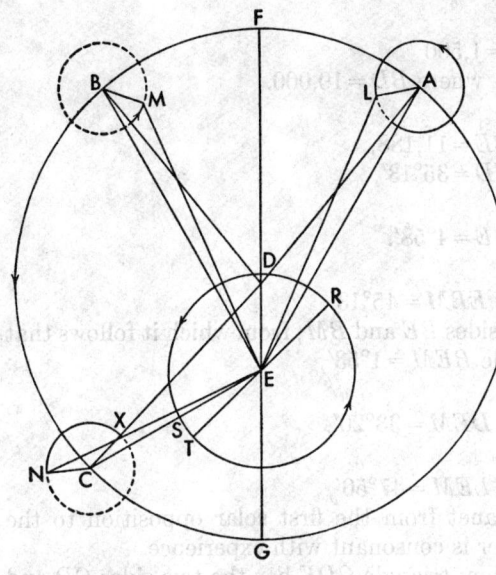

as the diameter through both apsides; and let E the centre of the orbital circle of annual revolution be on the diameter. Let A, B, and C be the points of solar opposition, in that order; and let

arc $AF = 41°34'$,
arc $FB = 40°11'$,

and

arc $CG = 44°21'$.

At the separate points A, B, and C let the epicycle be described with one-third of distance DE as radius. And let AD, BD, CD, AE, BE, and CE be joined. On the epicycle let AL, BM, and CN be joined, but in such a way that

angle DAL = angle ADF,
angle DBM = angle BDF,

and

angle DCN = angle CDF.

Accordingly, since in triangle ADE

angle $ADE = 138°26'$,

because angle FDA was given and also the two sides, *viz.*,

$DE = 1,500$

where $AD = 10,000$;

it follows from this that

side $AE = 11,172$,

and

angle $DAE = 5°7'$.

[156ᵃ] Hence, by addition,

angle $EAL = 46°41'$.

So also in triangle EAL angle EAL is given, together with the two sides:

$AE = 11,172$

and

$AL = 500$,

where $AD = 10,000$.

Moreover,

angle $AEL = 1°56'$;

and

angle AEL + angle $DAE = 7°3'$,

which is the total difference between angles ADF and LED; and hence

angle $DEL = 34\frac{1}{2}°$.

Similarly at the second opposition: in triangle BDE

angle $BDE = 139°49'$

and

side $DE = 1,500$
where $BD = 10,000$.

Hence

side $BE = 11,188$,
angle $BED = 35°13'$,

and

angle $DBE = 4°58'$.

Therefore

angle $EBM = 45°13'$

and is comprehended by the given sides BE and BM, from which it follows that
angle $BEM = 1°53'$,

and by subtraction

angle $DEM = 33°20'$.

Accordingly

angle $LEM = 47°50'$,

whereby the movement of the planet from the first solar opposition to the second is apparent; and the number is consonant with experience.

Again at the third solar opposition: triangle CDE has the two sides CD and DE given, which comprehend angle CDE. And
angle $CDE = 44°21'$;

hence

base $CE = 8,988$,
where $CD = 10,000$
and $DE = 1,500$;

and

angle $CED = 135°39'$,

and

angle $DCE = 6°42'$.

This again in triangle CEN

angle $ECN = 142°21'$

and is comprehended by the known sides EC and CN: hence too
angle $CEN = 1°52'$.

[156ᵇ] Therefore by subtraction

angle $NED = 127°5'$

at the third solar opposition. But it has already been shown that
angle $DEM = 33°20'$.

Hence by subtraction

angle $MEN = 93°45'$,

and is the angle of apparent movement between the second and the third solar oppositions, wherein the calculation agrees sufficiently with the observations. But at this last observed opposition of Mars the planet was seen at 235°54', being 127°5' distant from the apogee of the eccentric circle, as was shown: therefore the position of the apogee of the eccentric circle of Mars was at 108°50' in the sphere of the fixed stars.

Now let RST the annual orbital circle of the Earth be described around centre E with diameter RET parallel to DC, so that R is the apogee of parallax and T the perigee. Accordingly the planet was seen on EX at 235°54′, in longitude, and it was shown that

$$\text{angle } DXE = 8°34′,$$

the difference between the regular and the apparent movement; and on that account

$$\text{mean movement} = 244\frac{1}{2}°;$$

but, at the centre,

$$\text{angle } SET = \text{angle } DXE = 8°34′.$$

Accordingly

$$\text{arc } RS = \text{arc } RT - \text{arc } ST = 180° - 8°34′ = 171°26′,$$

the mean movement of parallax of the planet. Furthermore among other things we have demonstrated by this hypothesis of the mobility of the Earth that in the 2nd year of Antoninus on the 12th day of the month Epiphi by the Egyptian calendar 10 equal hours after midday the planet Mars by its mean movement in longitude was at 244½°, and the anomaly of parallax was at 171°26′.

16. On Three Other Solar Oppositions of Mars Which Have Been Observed Recently

We have compared these three of Ptolemy's observations of Mars with three other observations, which we did not take carelessly. The first was in the year of Our Lord 1512 on the Nones of June, 1 hour after midnight, and the position of Mars was found to be at 235°33′, according as the sun was opposite [157ᵃ] at 55°33′ from the first star of Aries in the sphere of the fixed stars as a starting-point.

The second was in the year of Our Lord 1518 on the day before the Ides of December 8 hours after midday; and the planet was apparent at 63°2′.

The third was in the year of Our Lord 1523 on the 8th day before the Kalends of March 8 hours before noon, at 183°20′.

Accordingly from the first to the second opposition there were 6 Egyptian years 191 days 45 minutes [of a day]; from the second to the third 4 years 72 days 23 minutes.

During the first interval of time the apparent movement was 187°29′, and the regular movement was 168°7′. During the second interval of time the apparent movement was 80°18′, and the regular was 83°.

Now let the eccentric circle of Mars be repeated again, except that here

$$\text{arc } AB = 168°7′$$

and

$$\text{arc } BC = 83°.$$

Accordingly, by the same method which we employed in the case of Saturn and Jupiter—let us pass over in silence the multitude, complication, and boredom of the calculations—we finally find that the apogee of Mars is on arc BC. For it is manifest that the apogee cannot be in arc AB because there the apparent movement is 19°22′ greater than the mean. Again the apogee cannot be in arc CA, because even if BC the arc preceding CA is the lesser, nevertheless arc BC exceeds the apparent movement by a greater difference than arc CA does. But it was shown above that in the eccentric circle the lesser and decreased movement takes place around the apogee. Accordingly the apogee will be held correctly to be in arc BC.

Let the apogee be F; and let FDG be the diameter of the circle. And let the centre of the orbital circle of the Earth be on the diameter. Accordingly, we find that

arc $FCA = 125°29'$,

arc $BF = 66°18'$,

and

arc $FC = 16°36'$;

but

$DE = 1,460$,

where radius $DE = 10,000$, which is the distance between the centres; and

semi-diameter of epicycle $= 500$:

whence the apparent and regular movements are shown to be consonant with one another and to agree with experiments.

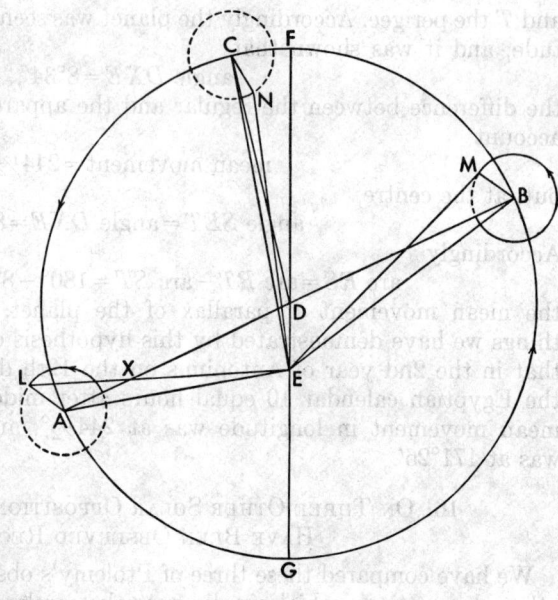

Therefore let the figure be filled out, as before. For it will be shown that, since in triangle ADE two sides AD and DE are known and

angle $ADE = 54°31'$

from the first opposition of Mars to the perigee;

angle $DAE = 7°24'$,

and by subtraction

angle $AED = 118°5'$;

and

side $AE = 9,229$.

Now by hypothesis

angle $DAL =$ angle FDA.

Accordingly by addition

angle $EAL = 132°53'$.

So too in triangle EAL the two sides EA and AL comprehending the given angle at A are themselves given: [157b] accordingly

angle $AEL = 2°12'$,

and

angle $LED = 115°53'$.

Similarly it will be shown in the case of the second opposition that, since in triangle BDE the two given sides DB and BE comprehend angle BDE, and

angle $BDE = 113°35'$,

then by what we have shown concerning plane triangles

angle $DBE = 7°11'$,

angle $DEB = 59°13'$,

and

$$\text{base } BE = 10{,}668,$$
$$\text{where } DB = 10{,}000$$
$$\text{and } BM = 500.$$

And by addition

$$\text{angle } EBM = 73°36'.$$

So too in triangle EBM, since the sides comprehending the given angle are given, it will be shown that

$$\text{angle } BEM = 2°36';$$

and by subtraction

$$\text{angle } DEM = 56°38'.$$

Then

$$\text{angle } MEG = 180° - \text{angle } DEM = 123°22'.$$

But it has already been shown that

$$\text{angle } LED = 115°53';$$

hence

$$\text{angle } LEG = 64°7';$$

and

$$\text{angle } LEG + \text{angle } GEM = 187°29',$$
$$\text{where 4 rt. angles} = 360°.$$

And that agrees with the apparent distance from the first opposition to the second.

A similar thing can be seen at the third opposition. For it has been shown that

$$\text{angle } DCE = 2°6',$$

and

$$\text{side EC} = 11{,}407,$$
$$\text{where } CD = 10{,}000.$$

Accordingly, as

$$\text{angle } ECN = 18°42',$$

and as sides CE and CN of triangle ECN have already been given, it will be clear [158a] that

$$\text{angle } CEN = 50'.$$

And

$$\text{angle } CEN + \text{angle } DCE = 2°56',$$

which is the difference by which angle DEN of apparent movement is exceeded by angle FDC of regular movement. Therefore

$$\text{angle } DEN = 13°40',$$

which agrees approximately with the apparent movement observed between the second and the third oppositions.

Accordingly, since the planet Mars, as we told you, was apparent in this position at 133°20' from the head of the constellation of Aries; and it has been shown that

$$\text{angle } FEN = 13°40';$$

it is manifest upon calculation backward that the position of the apogee of the eccentric circle at this last observation was at 119°40' in the sphere of the fixed stars.

At the time of Antoninus, Ptolemy found it at 108°50', and so during the time between then and now it has moved $10\,{}^{10}\!/_{12}°$ eastward. Moreover we have found a lesser distance between the centres, *i.e.*, 40, whereof the radius of the eccentric circle is given as 10,000—not because either Ptolemy or ourselves made a slip, but manifestly because the centre of this orbital circle of the Earth has approached the centre of the orbital circle of Mars, while the sun has remained immobile. For these things correspond approximately to one another, as will be shown below clearer than day.

Now let the annual orbital circle of the Earth be described around the centre E; and let its diameter SER be parallel to CD on account of the equality of revolutions. Let R be the regular apogee with respect to the planet, S the perigee, and T the Earth. Now let ET be extended; the line of sight of the planet will thus cut CD at point X. Now the line of sight along ETX, as was said at the last opposition, is at $133°20'$ of longitude.

Moreover, it has been shown that

angle $DXE = 2°56'$,

for angle DXE is the difference by which angle XDF of mean movement exceeds angle XED of apparent movement. But angle SET is equal to its alternate angle DXE, and is the additosubtraction arising from the parallax. Now

$$180° - 2°56' = 177°4',$$

which is the regular movement of the anomaly of parallax from R the apogee of the regular movement—and hence we have shown here that in the year of Our Lord 1523 on the 8th day before the Kalends of March, 7 equatorial hours before noon, the planet Mars by its mean movement in longitude was at $136°16'$; and its regular anomaly of parallax was at $177°4'$, and the highest apsis of the eccentric circle was at $119°40'$, as was to be shown.

17. CONFIRMATION OF THE MOVEMENT OF MARS

[158^b] Now it was made clear above that in the last of Ptolemy's three observations Mars by its mean movement was at $244\frac{1}{2}°$, and its anomaly of parallax was at $171°26'$. Accordingly during the year between there was a movement of $5°38'$ besides the complete revolutions. Now for the 2nd year of Antoninus on the 12th day of Epiphi the 11 month by the Egyptian calendar 9 hours after midday, *i.e.*, 3 equatorial hours before the following midnight, with respect to the Cracow meridian, to the year of Our Lord 1523 on the 8th day before the Kalends of March 7 hours before noon, there were 1384 Egyptian years 251 days 19 minutes [of a day]. During that time there were by the above calculation $5°38'$ and 648 complete revolutions of anomaly of parallax. Now the regular movement of the sun was held to be $257\frac{1}{2}°$. The subtraction from $257\frac{1}{2}°$ of the $5°38'$ of the movement of parallax leaves $251°52'$ as the mean movement of Mars in longitude. And all that agrees approximately with what was set down just now.

18. DETERMINATION OF THE POSITION OF MARS

Now from the beginning of the years of Our Lord to the 2nd year of Antoninus on the 12th day of the month Epiphi by the Egyptian calendar at 3 hours before midnight there were 138 Egyptian years 180 days 52 minutes [of a day], and during that time the movement of parallax was 293°4'. And when 293°4' is subtracted from the 171°26' of Ptolemy's last observation—a complete revolution being borrowed—there remain 238°22' at the [beginning of] the first year of Our Lord on midnight of the Kalends of January.

From the first Olympiad to this time there were 775 Egyptian years 12½ days, during which the movement of parallax was 254°1'. When 254°1' has similarly been subtracted from 238°22' and a revolution borrowed, its [159ª] position at the first Olympiad remains as 344°21'.

Similarly by calculating the movements according to the other intervals of time we shall have its position at the beginning of the years of Alexander as 120°39' and at the beginning of the years of Caesar as 211°25'.

19. How Great the Orbital Circle of Mars Is in Terms of the Parts of Which the Annual Orbital Circle of the Earth Is the Unit

Moreover we took observations of the conjunction of Mars with the first bright star of the Chelae—called the southern Claw—which occurred in 1512 on the Kalends of January. For on the morning of that day 6 equatorial hours before noon we saw Mars ¼° distant from the fixed star but deflected towards the solstitial rising, by which it was signified that Mars was already in longitude ⅛° to the east of the star but ⅕° distant in northern latitude. Now it was established that the position of the star was 191°20' with a northern latitude of 40'. So it was clear that the position of Mars was at 191°28' with a northern latitude of 51'. But at this time the anomaly of parallax by calculation was 98°28'; the mean position of the sun was at 262°, and the mean position of Mars at 163°32', and the anomaly of the eccentric circle was 43°52'.

With that before us let the eccentric circle ABC be described. Let D be its centre, ADC its diameter, A the apogee, C the perigee, and let

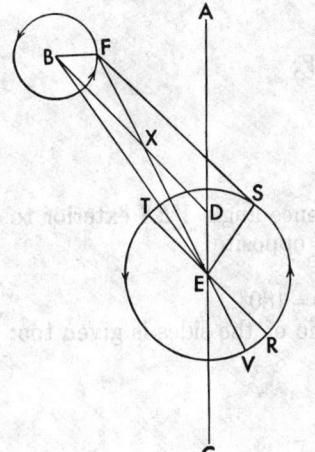

$$\text{ecc. } DE = 1,460,$$
where $AD = 10,000$.

Now let
$$\text{arc } AB = 43°52'.$$
Now with B as centre and radius BF of 500, whereof AD is 10,000, let the epicycle be described. Let
$$\text{angle } DBF = \text{angle } ADB;$$
and let BD, BE, BF, and FE be joined. Moreover, let RST the great orbital circle of the Earth be described around centre E with its diameter RET parallel to BD; and on the diameter let R be the apogee of the planet's regular movement of parallax, and T the perigee. Now let the Earth be at S; and in accordance with the regular anomaly of parallax as computed, let
$$\text{arc } RS = 98°28'.$$
Let FE be extended in the straight line FEV, which will cut BD at point X and the convex arc of the orbital circle of the Earth at V, where the true apogee of parallax is.

Accordingly, in triangle BDE [159^b] two sides are given:
$$DE = 1,460,$$
where $BD = 10,000$;
and they comprehend angle BDE. And
$$\text{angle } ADB = 43°52';$$
now
$$\text{angle } BDE = 180° - 43°52' = 136°8'.$$
Hence it will be shown that
$$\text{base } BE = 11,097$$
and
$$\text{angle } DBE = 5°13'.$$
But by hypothesis
$$\text{angle } DBF = \text{angle } ABD;$$
by addition
$$\text{angle } EBF = 49°5',$$
and is comprehended by the given sides EB and BF. On that account
$$\text{angle } BEF = 2°$$
and
$$\text{side } FE = 10,776,$$
where $DB = 10,000$.
Accordingly
$$\text{angle } DXE = 7°13',$$
because
$$\text{angle } DXE = \text{angle } XBE + \text{angle } XEB,$$
the interior and opposite angles. Angle DXE is the subtractive additosubtraction, the difference by which angle ADB exceeds angle XED, and by which the mean position of Mars exceeds the true. Now the mean position is reckoned as $163°32'$; therefore the true position is to the west at $156°19'$. But its position appears to be at $191°28'$ to those viewing it from S. Therefore its parallax, or commutation, is $35°9'$ eastward. Therefore it is clear that
$$\text{angle } EFS = 35°9'.$$
Now as RT is parallel to BD,
$$\text{angle } DXE = \text{angle } REV,$$
and similarly
$$\text{arc } RV = 7°13'.$$
Thus, by addition,
$$\text{arc } VRS = 105°41',$$
which is the corrected anomaly of parallax, and hence angle VES exterior to triangle FES is given. Hence, as being interior and opposite
$$\text{angle } FSE = 70°32',$$
where 2 rt. angles $= 180°$.
But as the angles of the triangle are given, the ratio of the sides is given too: therefore
$$FE = 9,428$$
and
$$ES = 5,727$$
where diameter of circle
circumscribing triangle $= 10,000$.
Accordingly
$$[160^a] \quad ES = 6,580,$$

where $EF = 10,776$

and $BD = 10,000$;

and that is approximately the same as Ptolemy's findings. But by addition

$$ADE = 11,460,$$

and by subtraction

$$EC = 8,540.$$

And at the lowest apsis of the eccentric circle the epicycle adds the 500 which it subtracts at A the highest apsis, so that the remainder at the highest apsis is 10,960, and the sum at the lowest apsis is 9,040. Accordingly, in so far as the radius of the orbital circle of the Earth is 1^p, Mars will have a greatest distance of $1^p39'57''$ at its apogee, a least distance of $1^p22'26''$, and a mean distance of $1^p31'11''$. So too in the case of Mars the movements, magnitudes, and distances have been explicated in a fixed ratio by means of the movement of the Earth.

20. On the Planet Venus

Now that we have set out the movements of the three higher planets Saturn, Jupiter, and Mars which circle around the Earth, it is time to speak of the planets which the Earth circles around. And first of Venus, which admits an easier and clearer demonstration of its movement than does Mercury, if only the necessary observations of some positions are not wanting; since if its greatest distances, i.e., at morning and at evening, in either direction from the mean position of the sun are found equal to one another, then we have as certain that the highest or lowest apsis of the eccentric circle of Venus is at the midpoint between these two positions of the sun. The apsides are distinguished from one another by the fact that such equal [angular] elongations are smaller when they take place around the apogee and greater when they take place around the perigee. Finally at its other positions we perceive through the differences by which the angular elongations exceed one another how far distant the orb of Venus is from the highest or lowest apsis and also what its eccentricity is, according as these things have been passed on to us by Ptolemy with great clarity, so that there is no need to repeat them separately, except in so far as things from Ptolemy's observations are applicable to our hypothesis of terrestrial mobility.

He took as his first observation one made by the mathematician Theo of Alexandria in the 16th year of Hadrian, he tells us, on the 21st day of the month Pharmuthi, at the first hour of the following night; and that was in the year of Our Lord 132 on the evening of the 8th day before the Ides of March. And Venus was seen at its greatest evening distance of $47\frac{1}{4}°$ from the mean position of the sun, [160^b] while the mean position of the sun was by calculation at $337°41'$ in the sphere of the fixed stars. With this observation he compared one of his own which he said he made in the 4th year of Antoninus on the 12th day of the month Thoth at daybreak, i.e., in the year of Our Lord 142 on the early morning of the third day before the Kalends of August. He says that at this time the greatest morning elongation of Venus was equal to the previous elongation and was $47°$ $15'$ from the mean position of the sun, which was at $119°$ in the sphere of the fixed stars and which on the previous date had been at $337°41'$. Now it is manifest that midway between these mean positions are the apsides diametrically opposite one another at $48\frac{1}{3}°$ and $228\frac{1}{3}°$. When the $6\frac{2}{3}°$ of the precession of the equinoxes has been added to both of them, they will fall upon $25°$ of Taurus and of Scorpio according to Ptolemy, and the diametrically opposite highest and lowest apsides of Venus must be at those positions.

Once more for the further confirmation of the thing, he assumed another observation made by Theo in the 4th year of Hadrian at morning twilight on the 20th day of the month Athyr, which was in the year of Our Lord 119 on the morning of the fourth day before the Ides of October, at which time Venus was again found at a great distance of 47°32′ from the mean position of the sun at 181°13′. With that he connected his own observation made in the 21st year of Hadrian, which was the year of Our Lord 136, on the 9th day of the month Mechyr by the Egyptian calendar but by the Roman calendar the 8th day before the Kalends of January, at the first hour of the following night, and the evening distance was found to be 47°32′ from the mean position of the sun at 265°25′. But in the preceding observation made by Theo the mean position of the sun was at 191°13′. Again the apsides fall midway between these positions, at 48°20′ and at 228°20′ approximately, where the apogee and the perigee must be. And they are distant from the equinoxes at 25° of Taurus and at 25° of Scorpio, and Ptolemy separated them by two other observations as follows.

The first observation was made by Theo in the 13th year of Hadrian on the 3rd day of the month Epiphi, but in the year of Our Lord 129 at early morning on the 12th day before the Kalends of January, and he found the farthest morning elongation of Venus to be 44°48′, while the sun by its mean movement was at $48^{10}/_{12}°$, and Venus was apparent at 4° of the sphere of the fixed stars. Ptolemy himself made the other observation in the 21st year of Hadrian on the 2nd day of the month [161ª] Tybi by the Egyptian calendar, which was by the Roman calendar the year of Our Lord 136 on the 5th day before the Kalends of January at the 1st hour of the following night, while the sun by its mean movement was at 228°54′, from which Venus had a greatest evening elongation of 47°16′ and was itself apparent at $276\frac{1}{6}°$. Hence the apsides are distinguished from one another, that is to say, the highest is put at $48\frac{1}{3}°$, where the shorter wanderings of Venus are, and the lowest at $228\frac{1}{3}°$, where the greater wanderings are—as was to be demonstrated.

21. What the Ratio of the Diameters of the Orbital Circle of the Earth and of Venus Is

Furthermore from these last two observations the ratio of the diameters of the orbital circles of the Earth and Venus will be apparent. For let AB the orbital circle of the Earth be described around centre C. Let ACB be its diameter through both apsides; and on ACB let D be taken as the centre of the orbital circle of Venus which is eccentric to circle AB. Now let A be the position of the apogee; and when the Earth is there, the centre of the orbital circle of Venus is at its greatest distance, while AB is the line of mean movement of the sun—$48\frac{1}{3}°$ at A and $228\frac{1}{3}°$ at B. Now let the straight lines AE and BF be drawn touching the orbital circle of Venus at points E and F, and let DE and DF be joined. Accordingly, since as at the centre

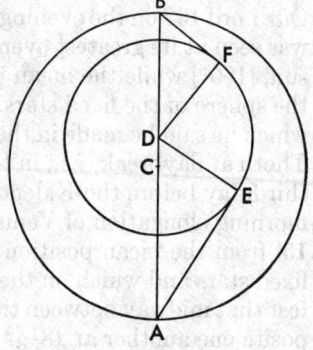

$$\text{angle } DAE = 44\tfrac{4}{5}°,$$

and

$$\text{angle } AED = 90°,$$

then triangle DAE will have its angles given and hence its sides:
$$DE = \tfrac{1}{2} \text{ ch. } 2\, DAE = 7,046,$$
$$\text{where } AD = 10,000.$$

In the same way in the right triangle BDF
$$\text{angle } DBF = 47\tfrac{1}{3}°,$$

and

$$\text{ch. } DF = 7,346,$$
$$\text{where } BD = 10,000.$$

Accordingly

$$BD = 9,582,$$
$$\text{where } DF = DE = 7,046.$$

Hence by addition

$$ACB = 19,582$$

and

$$AC = \tfrac{1}{2}ACB = 9,791;$$

and by subtraction

$$CD = 209.$$

Accordingly, in so far as

$$[161^b] \; AC = 1^p,$$
$$DE = 43\tfrac{1}{6}',$$

and

$$CD \doteq 1\tfrac{1}{4}';$$

and

$$DE = DF \doteq 7,193$$

and

$$CD \doteq 213,$$
$$\text{where } AC = 10,000.$$

And that was to be demonstrated.

22. On the Twofold Movement of Venus

But by the argument from two of Ptolemy's observations, Venus does not have a simple regular movement around D. He made the first observation in the 18th year of Hadrian on the 2nd day of the month Pharmuthi by the Egyptian calendar, but by the Roman calendar it was the year of Our Lord 134 at early morning on the 12th day before the Kalends of March. For at that time the sun by its mean movement was at $318\tfrac{10}{12}°$; and Venus, which was apparent in the morning at $275\tfrac{1}{4}°$ of the ecliptic, had reached a farthest limit of elongation of $43°35'$.

He made the second in the 3rd year of Antoninus on the 4th day of the month Pharmuthi by the Egyptian calendar, which by the Roman calendar was in the year of Our Lord 140 on the evening of the 12th day before the Kalends of March. And at that time the mean position of the sun was at $318\tfrac{10}{12}°$; and Venus was at a greatest evening elongation of $48\tfrac{1}{3}°$ and was visible at $7\tfrac{10}{12}°$ in longitude.

With that set out, let point G be taken as the position of the Earth in the

same terrestrial orbital circle, so
that arc AG is a quadrant of a
circle—the quadrant which
measures how far the sun diametrically opposite at both observations according to its mean
movement was seen to be west
of the apogee of the eccentric
circle of Venus. Let GC be
joined, and let DK be drawn
parallel to GC. Let GE and GF
be drawn touching the orbital
circle of Venus; and let DE, DF,
and DG be joined. Accordingly, since,

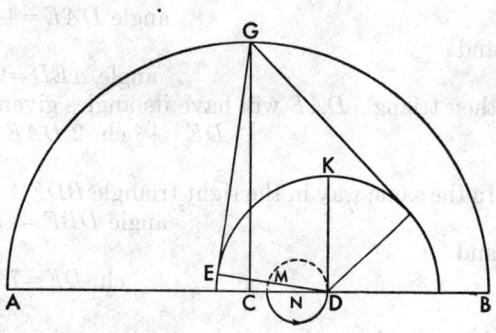

$$\text{angle } EGC = 43°35',$$
which was the morning elongation at the time of the first observation, and since
$$\text{angle } CGF = 48\tfrac{1}{3}°,$$
which was the evening elongation at the time of the second observation;
$$\text{angle } EGF = \text{angle } EGC + \text{angle } CGF = 91\tfrac{11}{12}°;$$
and accordingly
$$\text{angle } DGF = \tfrac{1}{2}EGF = 45°47\tfrac{1}{2}';$$
and by subtraction
$$\text{angle } CGD = 2°23'.$$

But

$$\text{angle } DCG = 90°.$$
Accordingly, as the angles of triangle CGD are given, the ratios of the sides
are given too; and

$$CD = 416,$$
$$\text{where } CG = 10,000.$$
Now it has already been shown that the distance between the centres was 208;
and now the distance has become approximately twice as great. Accordingly, if
CD is bisected at point M, similarly
$$[162^a] \quad DM = 208,$$
the total variation in this approach and withdrawal. Again if DM is bisected at
N, it will be seen to be the mean and regular point in this movement.

Hence, as in the case of the three higher planets, the movement of Venus happens to be compounded of two regular movements, either by reason of the
epicycle of an eccentric circle, as above, or by any other of the aforesaid modes.
This planet however is somewhat different from the others in the order and commensurability of its movements; and, as I opine, there will be an easier and more
convenient demonstration by means of the eccentric circle of an eccentric circle.
In this way let us take N as centre and DN as radius and describe a small circle,
on which [the centre of] the orbital circle of Venus is borne and moved around
according to the law that whenever the Earth falls upon diameter ACB, on
which the highest and lowest apsides of the eccentric circle are, the centre of
orbital circle of the planet will always be at least distance, i.e., at point M; and
when the Earth is at its mean apsis, i.e., at G, the centre of the orbital circle of

the planet will reach point D and the greatest distance CD. Hence you are given to understand that at the time when the Earth has made one orbital circuit, the centre of the orbital circle of the planet has made two revolutions around centre N in the same direction as the Earth, $i.e.$, eastward. For according to such an hypothesis in the case of Venus, all the regular and apparent movements agree with the observations, as will be shown later. Now all this which has so far been demonstrated concerning Venus is found to be consonant with our times, except that the eccentricity has decreased approximately one sixth, so that what before was 416 is now 350, as many observations teach us.

23. On the Examination of the Movement of Venus

In this connection I have taken two positions observed very accurately, the first by Timochares in the 13th year of Ptolemy Philadelphus the 52nd year after the death of Alexander in the early morning [162^{b}] of the 18th day of Mesori the eight month by the Egyptian calendar; and it was recorded that Venus was seen to have occupied the position of the fixed star which is westernmost of the four stars in the left wing of Virgo and is sixth in the description of the sign; its longitude $151\frac{1}{2}°$, its northern latitude $1\frac{1}{6}°$; and it is of third magnitude. Accordingly the position of Venus was made manifest in this way; and the mean position of the sun was by calculation at $194°23'$.

With this as an example, let the figure be drawn with point A still at $48°20'$:

arc $AE = 146°3'$,
and by subtraction
arc $BE = 33°57'$.
Angle $CEG = 42°53'$,
which is the angular distance of the planet from the mean position of the sun. Accordingly, since
line $CD = 312$,
where $CE = 10,000$,
and
angle $BCE = 33°57'$;
in triangle CDE
angle $CED = 1°1'$,
and
base $DE = 9,743$.
But
angle $CDF = 2BCE = 67°54'$;
and
angle $BDF = 180° - 67°54' = 112°6'$.

And, as the exterior angle of triangle CDE,
angle $BDE = 33°57'$.

Hence it is clear that
angle $EDF = 144°4'$,

and

$$DF = 104,$$
$$\text{where } DE = 9{,}743.$$

So in triangle DEF

$$\text{angle } DEF = 20',$$

and by addition

$$\text{angle } CEF = 1°21',$$

and

$$\text{side } EF = 9{,}831.$$

But it has already been shown that

$$\text{angle } CEG = 42°53';$$

accordingly, by subtraction,

$$\text{angle } FEG = 41°32';$$

and, as radius of the orbital circle,

$$FG = 7{,}193,$$
$$\text{where } EF = 9{,}831$$

Accordingly, since in triangle EFG angle FEG and the ratios of the sides are given, the remaining angles are given too. And

$$[163^a]\ \text{angle } EFG = 72°5'.$$
$$\text{Arc } KLG = 180° + \text{angle } EFG = 252°5',$$

measured from the highest apsis of the orbital circle. And so we have shown that in the 13th year of Ptolemy Philadelphus on the 18th day of the month Mesori the anomaly of parallax of Venus was 252°5'.

We ourselves made observations of a second position of Venus in the year of Our Lord 1529 on the 4th day before the Ides of March, 1 hour after sunset and at the beginning of the 8th hour after midday. We saw the moon begin to occult Venus at the midpoint of the dark part between the horns, and the occultation lasted till the end of the hour or a little later, until the planet was seen to emerge towards the west on the other side at the midpoint of the gibbosity of the horns. Accordingly it is clear that at the middle of the hour or thereabouts, the centres of the moon and Venus were in conjunction, and we had a full view at Frauenburg. Venus was still in her evening increase [of elongation] and this side of the point of tangency of the orbital circle with a line from the Earth. Accordingly from the birth of Christ there have been 1529 Egyptian years 87 days 7½ hours by apparent time but by equal time 7 hours 34 minutes, and the mean position of the sun considered simply had reached 332°11'; and the precession of the equinoxes was 27°24'. The regular movement of the moon was 33°57' away from the sun, the regular movement of anomaly was 205°1', and the movement in latitude was 71°59'. Hence it is reckoned that the true position of the moon was at 10°, but measured from the equinox it was at 7°24' of Taurus with a northern latitude of 1°13'. But since the 15° of Libra were rising, on that account the lunar parallax in longitude was 48°32', and so the apparent position [of the moon] was at 6°26' of Taurus; but its longitude in the sphere of the fixed stars was 9°11' with a northern latitude of 41'; and the apparent position of Venus was at an evening distance of 37°1' from the mean position of the sun, and the distance of the Earth from the highest apsis of Venus was 76°9' to the west.

Now let the figure be drawn again according to the previous mode of con-

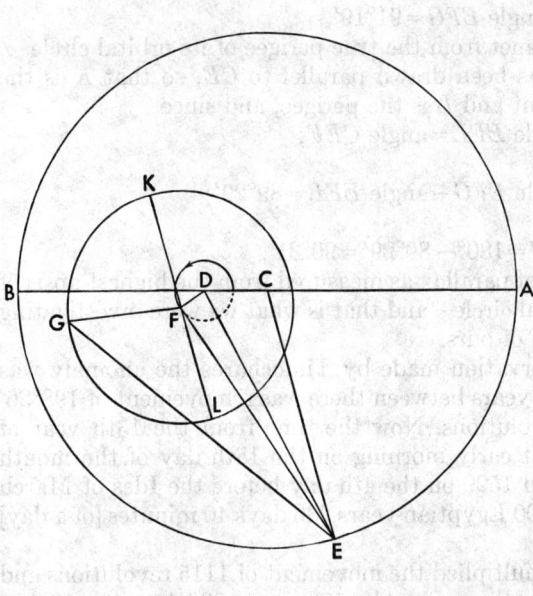

struction, except that
> angle $ECA = 76°9'$,

and
> angle $CDF = 2ECA =$
> $152°18'$;

and
> ecc. $CD = 246$,

as it is found today; and
> $DF = 104$,
> where $CE = 10,000$.

Therefore in triangle CDE, by subtraction
> angle $DCE = 103°51'$

and is comprehended by the given sides. From that it will be shown that
> angle $CED = 1°15'$,

and
> base $DE = 10,056$,

and
> angle [163b] $CDE =$
> $74°54'$.

But
> angle $CDF = 2ACE = 152°18'$.

And
> angle $EDF =$ angle $CDF -$ angle $CDE = 77°24'$.

So again in triangle DEF two sides are given;
> $DF = 104$,
> where $DE = 10,056$;

and they comprehend the given angle EDF. Moreover,
> angle $DEF = 35'$,

and
> base $EF = 10,034$.

Hence by addition
> angle $CEF = 1°50'$.

Furthermore,
> angle $CEG = 37°1'$,

which measures the apparent distance of the planet from the mean position of the sun.

Now
> angle $FEG =$ angle $CEG -$ angle $CEF = 35°11'$.

Similarly in triangle EFG two sides are given:
> $EF = 10,034$,
> where $FG = 7,193$

and the angle at E is given: hence too the remaining angles are calculable:
> angle $EGF = 53\frac{1}{2}°$

and
$$\text{angle } EFG = 91°19',$$
which is the distance of the planet from the true perigee of its orbital circle.

But since diameter KFL has been drawn parallel to CE, so that K is the apogee of the regular movement and L is the perigee, and since
$$\text{angle } EFL = \text{angle } CEF;$$
then
$$\text{angle } LFG = \text{angle } EFG - \text{angle } EFL = 89°29';$$
and
$$\text{arc } KG = 180° - 89°29' = 90°31',$$
which is the planet's anomaly of parallax as measured from the highest apsis of regular movement of the orbital circle—and that is what we were investigating at the time of this observation of ours.

But at the time of the observation made by Timochares the anomaly was 252°5'; accordingly during the years between there was a movement of 198°26' besides the 1115 complete revolutions. Now the time from the 13th year of Ptolemy [164ᵃ] Philadelphus at early morning on the 18th day of the month Mesori to the year of Our Lord 1529 on the 4th day before the Ides of March 7½ hours after midday was 1800 Egyptian years 236 days 40 minutes [of a day] approximately.

Accordingly when we have multiplied the movement of 1115 revolutions and 198°26' by 365 days, and divided the product by 1800 years 226 days 40 minutes, we shall have an annual movement of 225°1'45"3'''40''''.

Once more the distribution of this through 365 days leaves a daily movement of 36'59"28''', which were added to the table which we set out above.

24. On the Positions of the Anomaly of Venus

Now from the first Olympiad to the 13th year of Ptolemy Philadelphus at early morning of the 18th day of the month Mesori there are 503 Egyptian years 228 days 40 minutes [of a day], during which time the movement was reckoned to be 290°39'. But if 290°39' is subtracted from 252°5' and 360° is borrowed, the remainder will be 321°26', the position of the movement at the beginning of the first Olympiad.

The remaining positions are in proportion to the movement and time so often spoken of: 81°52' at the beginning of the years of Alexander; 70°26' at the beginning of the years of Caesar; and 126°45' at the beginning of the years of Our Lord.

25. On Mercury

It has been shown how Venus is bound up with the movement of the Earth and in what ratio of circles the regularity of its movement is concealed. Mercury remains, and without fail will also submit to the principle assumed, although it has more complicated wanderings than Venus or any of the aforesaid planets. It has been established experimentally by ancient observations that in the sign of Libra, Mercury has its least angular elongations from the sun and has *greater* elongations in the opposite sign, as is right. But Mercury does not have its *greatest* elongations in this position but in some other positions higher and beyond, as in Gemini and Aquarius, particularly at the time of Antoninus according to Ptolemy; and that occurs in the case of no other planet. When the ancient mathematicians, who supposed the reason for this [164ᵇ] to be the immobility of the Earth and the movement of Mercury in its great epicycle along an eccentric circle, had noticed that one simple eccentric circle could not account satisfactorily for these appearances, not only did they grant that the movement on the eccentric circle was not around its own centre but around a foreign centre, but they were also compelled to admit that this same eccentric circle carrying the epicycle moved along another small circle, as they admitted the moon's eccentric circle did. And so there were three centres, namely that of the eccentric circle carrying the epicycle, that of the small circle, and that of the circle which the moderns call the equant. They passed over the first two circles and acknowledged that the epicycle did not move regularly except around the centre of the equant, which was the most foreign to the true centre, to its ratio, and to both the centres already extant. But they judged that the appearances of this planet could be saved by no other scheme, as Ptolemy declares at great length in his *Composition.*

But in order that this last planet may be freed from the liability to injury and disparagement and that the regularity of its movement in relation to the mobility of the Earth may be no less clear than in the case of the other preceding planets; we shall assign to it too a circle eccentric to an eccentric circle instead of the epicycle which the ancients assumed, but in a way different from that of Venus. And nevertheless an epicycle does move on the eccentric circle, but the planet is not borne on its circumference but up and down along its diameter: that can take place through regular circular movements, as was set forth above in connection with the precession of the equinoxes. And it is not surprising, since Proclus in his commentary on the *Elements* of Euclid admits that a straight line can be described by many movements, by all of which movements its appearance will be demonstrable.

But in order that the hypothesis may be grasped more perfectly, let *AB* be

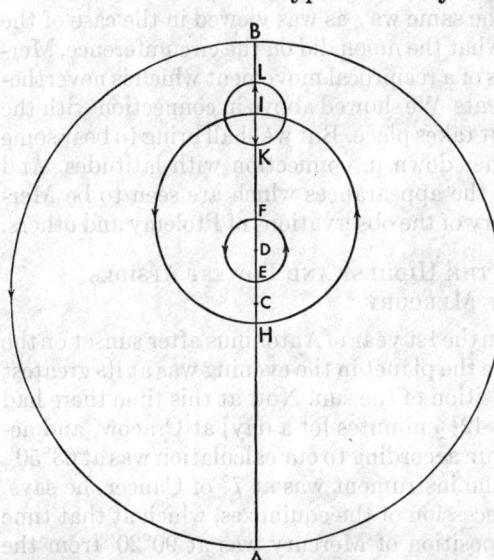

the great orbital circle of the Earth with centre *C* and diameter *ACB*. And on *ACB* between points *B* and *C* let *D* be taken as a centre and with one-third *CD* as radius let the small circle *EF* be described, so that *F* is its greatest distance from *C*, and *E* its least. Let *HI* the orbital circle of Mercury be described around centre *F*; and then with *I* the highest apsis as centre let the epicycle which the planet traverses be added. Let *HI* be the orbital circle which is eccentric to an eccentric circle and carries the epicycle. When the figure has been drawn in this way, all those things will fall in order on the straight line *AHCEDFKILB.*

Meanwhile let the planet be set up at K, *i.e.*, at the least distance KF from centre F. [165ª] Now with that point established as the starting-point of the revolutions of Mercury, let it be understood that the centre F makes two revolutions for every one of the Earth, and in the same direction too, *i.e.*, eastward; similarly too the planet on LK, but along the diameter, up and down with respect to the centre of circle HI.

For it follows from this that whenever the Earth is at A or B, the centre of the orbital circle of Mercury is at F, which is the position farthest away from C; but whenever the Earth is at the middle quadrants, the centre is at E which is the position nearest [to C], and this in a manner contrary to that of Venus. Moreover, according to this law Mercury traversing the diameter of epicycle KL is nearest to the centre of the orbital circle carrying the epicycle, *i.e.*, is at K, when the Earth falls upon the diameter AB; and when the Earth is at its mean positions, the planet will be at L the most distant position. In this way there take place the two twin revolutions of the centre of the orbital circle on the circumference of the small circle EF and of the planet along the diameter LK which are equal to one another and commensurable with the annual movement of the Earth.

But meanwhile let the epicycle or line FI be moved by its own proper movement along orbital circle HI, and let its centre move regularly, completing one revolution simply and with respect to the sphere of the fixed stars in approximately 88 days. But by that movement, whereby it outruns the movement of the Earth and which we call the movement of parallax, it has with respect to the Earth one revolution in 116 days, as can be derived more exactly [165 ᵇ] from the table of mean movements. Hence it follows that Mercury by its own proper movement does not always describe the same circumference of a circle, but in proportion to its distance from the centre of its orbital circle it describes a circumference of greatly varying magnitude, least at point K, greatest at L, and middling around I, in practically the same way as was viewed in the case of the lunar epicycle on an epicycle. But what the moon did on the circumference, Mercury does on the diameter by means of a reciprocal movement which is nevertheless compounded of regular movements. We showed above in connection with the precession of the equinoxes how that takes place. But we shall bring to bear some other things concerning this, farther down in connection with latitudes. And this hypothesis is sufficient for all the appearances which are seen to be Mercury's, as is manifest from the history of the observations of Ptolemy and others.

26. On the Positions of the Highest and Lowest Apsides of Mercury

For Ptolemy observed Mercury in the 1st year of Antoninus after sunset on the 20th day of the month Epiphi, while the planet in the evening was at its greatest angular distance from the mean position of the sun. Now at this time there had been 137 Christian years 188 days 42½ minutes [of a day] at Cracow, and accordingly the mean position of the sun according to our calculation was at 63°50′, and the planet observed through the instrument was at 7° of Cancer, he says. But after the subtraction of the precession of the equinoxes, which at that time was 6°40′, it was shown that the position of Mercury was at 90°20′ from the beginning of Aries in the sphere of the fixed stars, and its greatest angular elongation from the mean position of the sun was 26½°.

He made a second observation in the 4th year of Antoninus on the early morning of the 19th day of the month Phamenoth when 140 years 67 days 12 minutes [of a day] approximately had passed since the beginning of the years of Christ, and the mean position of the sun was at 303°19'. Now Mercury was apparent through the instrument at 13½° of Capricorn, but it was at approximately 276°49' from the fixed beginning of Aries, and accordingly the greatest morning distance was similarly 26½°. Accordingly since the limits of elongation on either side of the mean position of the sun are equal, it is necessary that the apsides of Mercury be either way at the midpoint between these positions, *i.e.*, between 226°49' and 90°20'. And they are 3°34' and 183°34' diametrically opposite, where the highest and the lowest apsides [166ᵃ] of Mercury must be.

As in the case of Venus, the apsides are distinguished through two observations. He made the first in the 19th year of Hadrian on the early morning of the 15th day of the month Athyr, while the mean position of the sun was at 182°38'. The greatest morning distance of Mercury from the sun was 19°3', since the apparent position of Mercury was at 163°35'. And in the same 19th year of Hadrian, which was the year of Our Lord 135, at dusk of the 19th day of the month Pachon by the Egyptian calendar, Mercury was found by the aid of the instrument at 27°43' in the sphere of the fixed stars, while the sun by its mean movement was at 4°28'. Again it was shown that the greatest evening distance of the planet was 23°15'—which is greater than the previous distance—whence it was clear enough that the apogee of Mercury at that time could be only at approximately 183½°—as was to be taken note of.

27. How Great the Eccentricity of Mercury Is and What the Commensurability of Its Circles Is

Moreover through this the distance between the centres and the magnitudes of the orbital circles are demonstrated simultaneously. For let AB be the straight line passing through A the highest and B the lowest apsis of Mercury, and also the diameter of the great circle, whose centre is D. And with D taken as centre let the orbital circle of the planet be described. Therefore let lines AE and BF be drawn touching the orbital circle, and let DE and DF be joined.

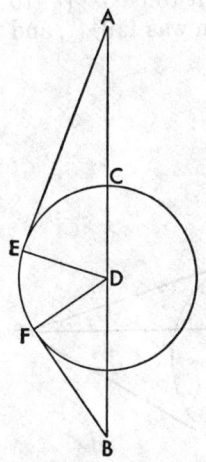

Accordingly, since at the first of the two preceding observations the greatest morning distance of the planet was seen to be 19°3',

$$\text{angle } CAE = 19°3'.$$

But at the second observation the greatest evening distance was seen to be 23¼°. Accordingly, as both of the right triangles AED and BFD have their angles given, [166ᵇ] the ratios of their sides will be given too, so that, as radius of the orbital circle,

$$ED = 32,639,$$
$$\text{where } AD = 100,000.$$

But

$$FD = 39,474,$$
$$\text{where } BD = 100,000.$$

But according as
$$FD = ED$$
as radius of the orbital circle,
$$FD = 32,639,$$
$$\text{where } AD = 100,000;$$
and by subtraction
$$DB = 82,685$$
Hence
$$AC = \tfrac{1}{2}AB = 91,342;$$
and by subtraction
$$CD = 8,658,$$
which is the distance between the centres. And the radius of the orbital circle of Mercury will be 21′26″, where $AC = 1^\mathrm{p} = 60′$;
and
$$CD = 5′4″;$$
and
$$DF = 35,733$$
and
$$CD = 9,479,$$
$$\text{where } AC = 100,000$$
as was to be demonstrated.

But these magnitudes also do not stay everywhere the same; but are quite different from those found in connection with the mean apsides, as the apparent morning and evening longitudes observed at those positions and recorded by Theo and Ptolemy teach us. For Theo observed the evening limit of Mercury in the 14th year of Hadrian on the 18th day of the month Mesori after sunset; and at 129 years 216 days 45 minutes [of a day] after the birth of Christ, while the mean position of the sun was $93\tfrac{1}{2}°$, *i.e.*, approximately at the mean apsis of Mercury. Now the planet was seen through the instrument to be $31\tfrac{0}{12}°$ to the west of Basiliscus in Leo; and on that account its position was $119\tfrac{3}{4}°$, and its greatest evening distance was $26\tfrac{1}{4}°$.

Ptolemy reported that the second limit was observed by him in the 2nd year of Antoninus on the 21st day of the month Mesori at early morning, at which time there had been 138 Christian years 219 days 12 minutes, and the mean position of the sun was similarly $93°39′$; [167a] and the greatest morning distance of Mercury from that was found to be $20\tfrac{1}{4}°$. For Mercury was visible at $73\tfrac{2}{5}°$ in the sphere of the fixed stars.

Therefore let $ACDB$ which is the diameter of the great orbital circle [of the Earth] and which passes through the apsides of Mercury, be again drawn, as before; and at point C let CE the line of mean movement of the sun be erected at right angles. Let point F be taken between C and D; and let the orbital circle of Mercury be described around F. Let the straight lines EH and EG touch this small circle; and let FG, FH, and EF be joined.

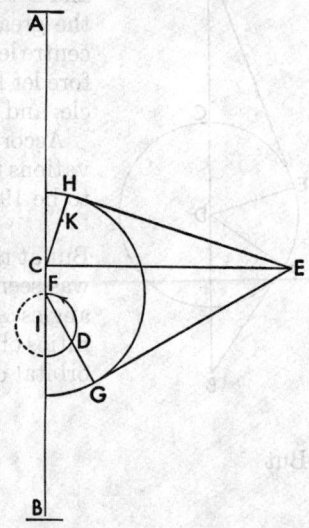

Now once more our problem is to find point F, and what ratio radius FG has to AC. For since

$$\text{angle } CEG = 26\tfrac{1}{4}°,$$

and

$$\text{angle } CEH = 20\tfrac{1}{4}°;$$

accordingly by addition

$$\text{angle } HEG = 46\tfrac{1}{2}°.$$

And

$$\text{angle } HEF = \tfrac{1}{2}HEG = 23\tfrac{1}{4}°.$$

And so by subtraction

$$\text{angle } CEF = 3°.$$

For that reason the sides of the right triangle CEF are given:

$$CF = 524$$

and

$$FE = 10,014,$$
$$\text{where } CE = AC = 10,000.$$

But it has been shown already that

$$CD = 948,$$

while the Earth is at the highest or lowest apsis of the planet. Hence DF will be the excess [of CD over CF] and the diameter of the small circle which the centre of the orbital circle of Mercury describes.

$$DF = 424,$$

and

$$\text{radius } IF = 212.$$

Hence by addition

$$CFI = 736.$$

Similarly, as in triangle HEF

$$\text{angle } H = 90°,$$

and

$$\text{angle } HEF = 23\tfrac{1}{4}°:$$

hence

$$FH = 3,947,$$
$$\text{where } EF = 10,000.$$

But

$$FH = 3,953,$$
$$\text{where } EF = 10,014$$
$$\text{and } CE = 10,000.$$

Now it has been shown above that

$$FK = 3,573.$$

Therefore by subtraction

$$HK = 380,$$

which is the greatest difference in the planet's distance from F the centre of its orbital circle; and this greatest difference is found when the planet is between its highest or lowest apsis and its mean apsis. On account of this varying distance from F the centre of its orbital circle, the planet describes unequal circles in proportion to the varying distances—the least distance being 3,573, the greatest 3,953, and the mean 3,763—as was to be demonstrated.

28. Why the Angular Digressions of Mercury at Around 60° from the Perigee Appear Greater Than Those at the Perigee

Hence too it will seem less surprising that Mercury has greater angular digressions at a distance of 60° from the perigee than when at the perigee, since they are also greater than the ones which we have already demonstrated; consequently it was held by the ancients that in one revolution [167ᵇ] of the Earth, Mercury's orb was twice very near to the Earth.

For let the construction be made such that

$$\text{angle } BCE = 60°.$$

On that account

$$\text{angle } BIF = 120°.$$

For F is put down as making two revolutions for one of E the Earth. Therefore let EF and EI be joined. Accordingly, since it has been shown that

$$CI = 736,$$
$$\text{where } EC = 10,000,$$

and

$$\text{angle } ECI = 60°;$$

hence in triangle ECI

$$\text{base } EI = 9,655;$$

and

$$\text{angle } CEI \eqsim 3°47',$$

which is the difference between angle ACE and angle CIE. But

$$\text{angle } ACE = 120°.$$

Accordingly

$$\text{angle } CIE = 116°13'.$$

But also

$$\text{angle } FIB = 120°,$$

since by construction

$$\text{angle } FIB = 2\ ECI;$$

and

$$\text{angle } CIF = 180° - 120° = 60°;$$

[and

$$\text{angle } BIE = 63°47']$$

hence by subtraction

$$\text{angle } EIF = 56°13'.$$

But it was shown that

$$IF = 212,$$
$$\text{where } EI = 9,655;$$

and EI and IF comprehend the given angle EIF. Hence it is inferred that

$$\text{angle } FEI = 1°4';$$

and by subtraction

$$\text{angle } CEF = 2°44',$$

which is the difference between the centre of the orbital circle of the planet and the mean position of the sun; and

$$\text{side } EF = 9,540.$$

Now let GH the orbital circle of Mercury be described around centre F; and from E let EG be drawn touching the orbital circle, and let FG and FH be joined.

We must first examine how great the radius FG or FH is under these circumstances; and we shall do that as follows

For let a small circle be taken, whose

$$\text{diameter} = 380,$$
$$\text{where } AC = 10,000.$$

And let it be understood that the planet on straight line FG or FH approaches and recedes from centre F along that diameter or along a line equal to it, as we set forth above in connection with the precession of the equinoxes. And in accordance with our hypothesis, wherein angle BCE intercepts 60° of the circumference, let

$$\text{arc } KM = 120°;$$

and let MN be drawn at right angles to KL. And since

$$MN = \tfrac{1}{2} \text{ ch. } 2ML = \tfrac{1}{2} \text{ ch. } 2\, KM,$$

then

$$LN = 95,$$

which is one quarter of the diameter—as is shown by [168ª] Euclid's *Elements*, XIII, 12 and V, 15. Accordingly,

$$KN = \tfrac{3}{4}\, KL = 285.$$

Line KN and the least distance of the planet added together make the distance sought for this position, *i.e.*,

$$FG = FH = 3,858,$$
$$\text{where } AC = 10,000$$
$$\text{and } EF = 9,540.$$

Wherefore two sides of right triangle FEG or FEH have been given: so angle FEG or FEH will also be given. For

$$FG = FH = 4,044,$$
$$\text{where } EF = 10,000;$$

and

$$FG = FH = \text{ch. } 23°52',$$

so that by addition

$$\text{angle } GEH = 47°44'.$$

But at the lowest apsis only $46\tfrac{1}{2}°$ is seen, and at the mean apsis similarly $46\tfrac{1}{2}°$. Accordingly the elongation here becomes $1°14'$ greater, not because the orbital circle of the planet is nearer to the Earth than it was at the perigee, but because the planet is here describing a greater circle than there. All these things are consonant with both present and past observations, and follow from the regular movements.

29. Examination of the Mean Movements of Mercury

For it is found by the ancient observations that in the 21st year of Ptolemy Philadelphus in the morning twilight of the 19th day of the month Thoth by the Egyptian calendar, Mercury was apparent on the straight line passing through the first and second of the stars in the forehead of Scorpio and was two lunar diameters distant to the east but was separated from the first star by one lunar diameter to the north. Now it is known that the position of the first star is

$209\frac{2}{3}°$ in longitude and $1\frac{1}{3}°$ in northern latitude; and the position of the second is 209° in longitude and $1\frac{5}{6}°$ in southern latitude. From that it was concluded that the position of Mercury was $110\frac{2}{3}°$ in longitude and approximately $1\frac{5}{6}°$ in northern latitude. Now there were 59 years 17 days 45 minutes [of a day] since the death of Alexander; and the mean position of the sun according to our calculation was 228°8′; and the morning distance of the star was 17°28′ and was still increasing, as was noted during the four following days. Hence it was certain that the planet had not yet arrived at the farthest morning limit or at the point of tangency of its orbital circle, but was still moving in the lower part of the circumference nearer to the Earth. But since the highest apsis was at 183°20′, there were 44°48′ to the mean position of the sun.

[168ᵇ] Therefore again let ACB be the diameter of the great orbital circle, as above; and from centre C let CE the line of mean movement of the sun be drawn, in such fashion that

$$\text{angle } ACE = 44°48′.$$

And let there be described around centre I the small circle on which the centre F of the eccentric circle is borne. And since by hypothesis

$$\text{angle } BIF = 2 \text{ angle } ACE,$$

let

$$\text{angle } BIF = 89°36′.$$

And let EF and EI be joined.

Accordingly, in triangle ECI two sides have been given:

$$CI = 736\frac{1}{2},$$
$$\text{where } CE = 10,000.$$

And sides CI and CE comprehend the given angle ECI. And

$$\text{angle } ECI = 180° - \text{angle } ACE = 135°12′; \text{ side } EI = 10,534;$$

and

$$\text{angle } CEI = 2°49′,$$

which is the excess of angle ACE over angle EIC. Therefore too

$$\text{angle } CIE = 41°59′.$$

But

$$\text{angle } CIF = 180° - \text{angle } BIF = 90°24′.$$

Therefore by addition

$$\text{angle } EIF = 132°23′;$$

and angle EIF is comprehended by the given sides EI and IF of triangle EFI, and

$$\text{side } EI = 10,534$$

and

$$\text{side } IF = 211\frac{1}{2},$$
$$\text{where } AC = 10,000.$$

Hence

$$\text{angle } FEI = 50′;$$

and
$$\text{side } EF = 10,678$$
And by subtraction
$$\text{angle } CEF = 1°59'.$$
Now let the small circle LM be taken; and let
$$\text{diameter } LM = 380,$$
$$\text{where } AC = 10,000.$$
And in accordance with the hypothesis let
$$\text{arc } LN = 89°36'.$$
Let chord LN also be drawn; and let NR be drawn perpendicular to LM. Accordingly, since
$$\text{sq. } LN = \text{rect. } LM, LR;$$
that ratio being given,
$$\text{side } LR = 189,$$
$$\text{where diameter } LM = 380.$$
That straight line, *i.e.*, LR, measures the distance of the planet from F the centre of its orbital circle at the time when line EC has completed angle ACE. Accordingly, by the addition of this [169ª] line to the least distance
$$189 + 3,573 = 3,672,$$
which is the distance at this position.

Accordingly, with the centre F and radius 3,762, let a circle be described; and let EG be drawn cutting the convex circumference at point G, in such a way that
$$\text{angle } CEG = 17°28',$$
which is the apparent angular elongation of the planet from the mean position of the sun. Let FG be joined; and let FK be drawn parallel to CE. Now
$$\text{angle } FEG = \text{angle } CEG - \text{angle } CEF = 15°29'.$$
Hence in triangle EFG two sides have been given;
$$EF = 10,678,$$
and
$$FG = 3,762,$$
and
$$\text{angle } FEG = 15°29':$$
whence it will be clear that
$$\text{angle } EFG = 33°46'.$$
Now, since
$$\text{angle } EFK = \text{angle } CEF,$$
$$\text{angle } KFG = \text{angle } EFG - \text{angle } RFK = 31°48';$$
and
$$\text{arc } KG = 31°48',$$
which is the distance of the planet from K the mean perigee of its orbital circle.
$$\text{Arc } KG + 180° = 211°48',$$
which was the mean movement of the anomaly of parallax at the time of this observation—as was to be shown.

30. On Three Modern Observations of the Movements of Mercury

The ancients have directed us to this method of examining the movement of this planet, but they were favoured by a clearer atmosphere at a place, where the Nile—so they say—does not give out vapours as the Vistula does among us. For nature has denied that convenience to us who inhabit a colder region, where fair weather is rarer; and furthermore on account of the great obliquity of the sphere it is less frequently possible to see Mercury, as its rising does not fall within our vision at its greatest distance from the sun when it is in Aries or Pisces, and its setting in Virgo and Libra is not visible; and it is not apparent in Cancer or Gemini at evening or early morning, and never at night, except when the sun has receded through the greater part of Leo. On this account the planet has made us take many detours and undergo much labour in order to examine its wanderings. On this account we have borrowed three positions from those which have been carefully observed at Nuremburg.

The first observation was taken by Bernhard Walther, a pupil of Regiomontanus, in the year of Our Lord 1491 on the 9th of September, the fifth day before the Ides, 5 equal hours after midnight, by means of an astrolabe brought into relation with the Hyades. And he saw Mercury at $13\frac{1}{2}°$ [169^b] of Virgo with a northern latitude of $1\frac{5}{6}°$; and at that time the planet was at the beginning of its morning occultation, while during the preceding days its morning [elongation] had decreased continuously. Accordingly there were 1491 Egyptian years 258 days $12\frac{1}{2}$ minutes [of a day] since the beginning of the years of Our Lord; the simple mean position of the sun was at 149°48' from the spring equinox but in 26°47' of Virgo, wherein the position of Mercury was approximately $13\frac{1}{2}°$.

The second was taken by Johann Schöner in the year of Our Lord 1504 on the 5th day before the Ides of January $6\frac{1}{2}$ hours after midnight, when 10° of Scorpio was in the middle of the heavens over Nuremburg; and the planet was apparent at $3\frac{1}{3}°$ of Capricorn with a northern latitude of 45'. Now by our calculation the mean position of the sun away from the spring equinox was at 27°7' of Capricorn and a morning Mercury was 23°42' to the west of that.

The third observation was taken by this same Johann Schöner in the same year 1504 on the 15th day before the Kalends of April, at which time he found Mercury at $26\frac{1}{10}°$ of Aries with a northern latitude of approximately 3°, while 25° of Cancer was in the middle of the heavens over Nuremburg—as seen through an astrolabe brought into relation with the Hyades, at $12\frac{1}{2}$ hours after midday, at which time the mean position of the sun away from the spring equinox was at 5°39' of Aries, and an evening Mercury was 21°17' away from the sun.

Accordingly from the first position to the second, there are 12 Egyptian years 125 days 3 minutes [of a day] 45 seconds, during which time the simple movement of the sun was 120°14', and Mercury's movement of anomaly of parallax was 316°1'. During the second interval there were 69 days 31 minutes 45 seconds the simple mean position of the sun was 68°32', and Mercury's mean anomaly of parallax was 216°.

Accordingly we wish to examine the movements of Mercury during our time by means of these three observations, and I think we must grant that the commensurability of the circles has remained from Ptolemy's time to now, since in the case of the other planets the good authorities who preceded us are not found to have been mistaken here. If we have the position of the apsis of the eccentric circle together with these observations, nothing further should be desired in the case of the apparent movement of this planet. Now we have taken the position of the highest apsis as $211\frac{1}{2}°$, i.e., at $28\frac{1}{2}°$ of Scorpio; for it was not possible to take it as less without prejudice to the observations. And so we shall have the anomaly of the eccentric circle—I mean [170ᵃ] the distance of the mean movement of the sun from the apogee—as 298°15′ at the first terminus, as 58°29′ at the second, and as 127°1′ at the third.

Therefore let the figure be constructed as before, except that

$$\text{angle } ACE = 61°45',$$

which measures the westward distance of the line of mean movement of the sun from the apogee at the time of the first observation; and then the rest according to the hypothesis. And since

$$IC = 736\tfrac{1}{2},$$

where $AC = 10,000$;

and angle ECI in triangle ECI is also given; then

$$\text{angle } CEI = 3°35',$$

and

$$\text{side } IE = 10,369,$$

where $EC = 10,000$;

and

$$IF = 211\tfrac{1}{2}.$$

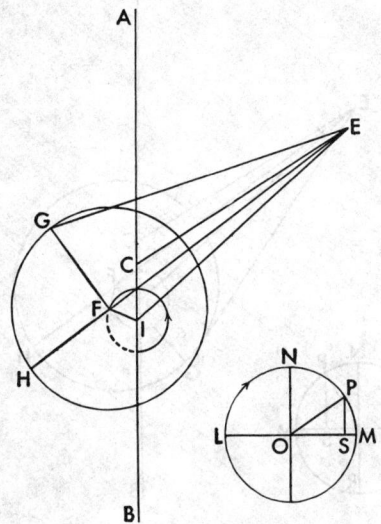

So in triangle EFI also there are two sides having a given ratio; and since by construction

$$\text{angle } BIF = 2 \text{ angle } ACE;$$
$$\text{angle } BIF = 123\tfrac{1}{2}°,$$

and

$$\text{angle } CIF = 180° - 123\tfrac{1}{2}° = 56\tfrac{1}{2}°.$$

Therefore by addition

$$\text{angle } EIF = 114°40'.$$

Accordingly

$$\text{angle } IEF = 1°5',$$

and

$$\text{side } EF = 10,371.$$

Hence

$$\text{angle } CEF = 2\tfrac{1}{2}°.$$

But in order that we may know how greatly the orbital circle, whose centre is F, is increased by the movement of approach and withdrawal from the apogee or perigee, let a small circle be drawn and quadrisected by the diameters LM, NR at centre O. And let

$$\text{angle } POM = 2 \text{ angle } ACE = 123\tfrac{1}{2}°;$$

and from point P let PS be drawn perpendicular to LM. Accordingly by the ratio given,

$$OP : OS = LO : OS = 10,000 : 8,349 = 190 : 105.$$

Whence

$$LS = 295,$$

where [170ᵇ] $AC = 10,000$;

and LS measures the farther removal of the planet from centre F.

As the least distance is 3,573,

$$LS + 3,573 = 3,868,$$

which is the present distance.

And with 3,868 as radius and F as centre, let circle HG be drawn. Let EG be joined; and let EF be extended in the straight line EFH. Accordingly, it has been shown that

angle $CEF = 2\frac{1}{2}°$,

and by observation

angle $GEC = 13\frac{1}{4}°$,

which is the morning distance of the planet from the mean sun.

Therefore by addition

angle $FEG = 15\frac{3}{4}°$.

But in triangle EFG

$EF : EG = 10,371 : 3,868$;

and angle EFG is also given; that shows us that

angle $EGF = 49°8'$.

Hence

angle $GFH = 64°53'$,

as it is the exterior angle; and

$360° -$ angle $GFH = 295°7'$,

which is the true anomaly of parallax. And

$295°7' +$ angle $CEF = 297°37'$,

the mean and regular anomaly of parallax—which is what we were looking for. And

$$297°37' + 316°1' = 253°38',$$

which is the regular anomaly of parallax at the second observation—and we shall show that this number is certain and is consonant with the observations.

For let us make

angle $ACE = 58°29'$

in accordance with the second movement of anomaly of the eccentric circle. Then also in triangle CEI two sides are given:

$IC = 736$,

where $EC = 10,000$;

and IC and EC comprehend angle ECI, and

angle $ECI = 121°31'$;

accordingly

side $EI = 10,404$

and

angle $CEI = 3°28'$.

Similarly, since in triangle EIF

angle $EIF = 118°3'$,

and

side $IF = 211\frac{1}{2}°$,

where $IE = 10,404$:

side $EF = 10,505$,

and

angle $IEF = 61'$.

And so by subtraction

angle $FEC = 2°27'$,

which is the additive additosubtraction of the eccentric circle; and the addition of angle FEC to the mean movement of parallax makes the true movement to be 256°5'.

Now also in the epicycle of approach [171ª] and withdrawal let us take
$$\text{angle } LOP = 2 \text{ angle } ACE = 116°58'.$$
Then too, as in right triangle OPS
$$OP : OS = 1,000 : 455;$$
$$OS = 85,$$
$$\text{where } OP = OL = 190.$$

And by addition
$$LOS = 276.$$
The addition of LOS to the least distance of 3,573 makes 3,849.

With 3,849 as radius let circle HG be described around centre F, so that the apogee of parallax is at point H from which the planet has the westward distance of 103°55' of arc HG, which measures the difference between a full revolution and the 256°5' of the movement of corrected parallax. And on that account
$$\text{angle } EFG = 180° - 103°55' = 76°5'.$$
So again in triangle EFG two sides are given:
$$FG = 3,849,$$
$$\text{where } EF = 10,505.$$

On that account
$$\text{angle } FEG = 21°19';$$
and
$$\text{angle } CEG = \text{angle } FEG + \text{angle } CEF = 23°46'.$$
That is the apparent distance between C the centre of the great orbital circle and G the planet; and it differs very little from the observation.

All this will be further confirmed by the third example, wherein we have set down that
$$\text{angle } ACE = 127°1',$$
or
$$\text{angle } BCE = 180° - 127°1' = 52°59'.$$
Hence it is shown that
$$\text{angle } CEI = 3°31',$$
and
$$\text{side } IE = 9,575,$$
$$\text{where } EC = 10,000.$$

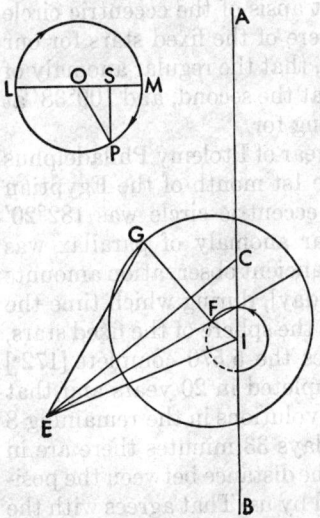

And since by construction
$$\text{angle } EIF = 49°28',$$
and the sides comprehending angle EIF are given:
$$FI = 211\tfrac{1}{2},$$
$$\text{where } EI = 9,575;$$
$$\text{side } EF = 9,440,$$
and
$$\text{angle } IEF = 59'.$$
Angle $FEC = $ angle $IEC - 59' = 2°32'$,
which is the subtractive additosubtraction of the anomaly of the eccentric circle. When the 2°32' has been added to the mean anomaly of parallax,

which we reckoned as 109°38' after adding the 216° of the second [movement of anomaly], the sum will be the 112°10' of the true anomaly of parallax.

Now in the epicycle let
$$\text{angle } LOP = 2 \text{ angle } ECI = 105°58';$$
here too by the ratio $PO : OS$,

so that by addition
$$OS = 52,$$
$$LOS = 242.$$
Now the least distance is 3,573; and
$$3,573 + 242 = 3,815,$$
which is the corrected distance.

With 3,815 as radius and F as centre, let the circle be described, in which the highest apsis of parallax is H, which is on the straight line made by extending line EFH. And in proportion to the true anomaly of parallax [171b] let
$$\text{arc } HG = 112°10';$$
and let GF be joined. Therefore
$$\text{angle } GFE = 180° - 112°10' = 67°50',$$
which is comprehended by the given sides:
$$GF = 3,815$$
and

$$EF = 9,440.$$

Hence

$$\text{angle } FEG = 23°50'.$$
Now angle CEF is the additosubtraction; and
$$\text{angle } CEG = \text{angle } FEG - \text{angle } CEF = 21°18',$$
which is the apparent angular distance between the evening planet and the centre of the great orbital circle. And that is approximately the distance found by observation.

Therefore these three positions which are in agreement with observations testify indubitably that the position of the highest apsis of the eccentric circle is the one which we assumed at 211½° in the sphere of the fixed stars for our time; and that what follows is also certain, namely, that the regular anomaly of parallax was 297°37' at the first position, 253°38' at the second, and 109°38' at the third position; and that is what we were looking for.

But at the ancient observation made in the 21st year of Ptolemy Philadelphus in the early morning of the 19th day of Thoth, the 1st month of the Egyptian calendar the position of the highest apsis of the eccentric circle was 182°20' according to Ptolemy, and the position of regular anomaly of parallax was 211°47'. Now the time between this latest and that ancient observation amounts to 1768 Egyptian years 200 days 33 minutes [of a day], during which time the highest apsis of the eccentric circle moved 28°10' in the sphere of the fixed stars, and the movement of parallax was 257°51' besides the 5,570 complete [172a] revolutions—as approximately 63 periods are completed in 20 years and that amounts to 5,544 periods in 1,760 years and 26 revolutions in the remaining 8 years 200 days. Similarly in the 1,768 years 200 days 33 minutes there are in addition to the 5,570 revolutions 257°51', which is the distance between the position observed in ancient times and the one observed by us. That agrees with the numbers which we set out in the tables. Now when we have compared the 28°10' with the time during which the apogee of the eccentric circle has moved, it will be seen to have moved 1° per 63 years, if only the movement were regular.

31. On Determining the Former Positions of Mercury

Accordingly there have been 1504 Egyptian years 87 days 48 minutes [of a day] from the beginning of the years of Our Lord to the hour of the last observation, during which time Mercury's movement of anomaly of parallax was 63°14′—not counting the complete revolutions. When 63°14′ has been subtracted from 109°38′, it will leave 46°24′ as the position of the movement of anomaly at the beginning of the years of Our Lord.

Again between that time and the beginning of the first Olympiad there are 775 Egyptian years 12½ days, during which the movement was calculated to be 95°3′ besides the whole revolutions.

If 95°3′ is subtracted from the position at the beginning of the years of our Lord and one revolution is borrowed, 311°21′ will be left as the position at the time of the first Olympiad.

Moreover between this and the death of Alexander there are 451 years 247 days, and by computation the position is 213°3′.

32. On Another Explanation of Approach and Withdrawal

But before we leave Mercury, let us survey another method no less credible than the former, by which that approach and withdrawal can take place and can be understood.

For let *GHKP* be a circle quadrisected at centre *F*, and around centre *F* let

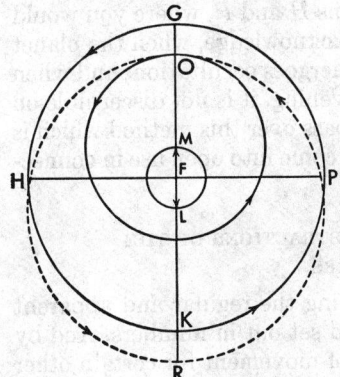

LM a small homocentric circle be inscribed. And again, with *L* as centre and radius *LFO* equal to *FG* or *FH*, let another circle *OR* be described.

Now let it be postulated that this whole configuration of circles [172^b] together with its sections *GFR* and *HFP* moves eastward around centre *F* in a daily movement of approximately 2°7′—namely, a movement as great as that whereby the movement of parallax of the planet exceeds the movement of the Earth in the ecliptic—away from the apogee of the eccentric circle of the planet; and the planet meanwhile furnishes the remaining movement away from *G* along *OR* the proper circle of parallax; and this movement is approximately equal to the terrestrial movement. Let it also be assumed that in this same annual revolution the centre of *OR*, the orbital circle which carries the planet, is borne by a movement of libration along a diameter *LFM* which is twice as great as the one which we laid down at first; and let it move back and forth, as was said above.

With this as the set-up, we have placed the Earth by its mean movement in a position corresponding to the apogee of the eccentric circle of the planet; and at that time the centre of the orbital circle carrying the planet, at *L*; and the planet itself, at point *O*. The planet then being at its least distance from *F* will describe by its whole movement its least circle, whose radius is *FO*. Consequently, when the Earth is in the neighbourhood of the mean apsis, the planet falling upon point *H* at its greatest distance from *F* will describe its greatest arcs, namely in proportion to the circle having F as centre. For at that time OR the deferent coincides with circle GH on account of the unity of centre at F. Hence as the Earth advances in the direction of the perigee and the centre of the orbital circle OR towards M the other extreme, the orbital circle itself is placed beyond GK, and the planet at R again is at its least distance from F, and the same things occur as in the beginning. For here the three revolutions—namely, that of the Earth through the apogee of the eccentric orbital circle of Mercury, the libration of the centre along diameter LM, and the movement of the planet in the same direction away from line FG—are equal to one another, and only the movement of the sections GH and KP away from the apsis of the eccentric circle is different from those revolutions, as we said.

And so in the case of this planet nature has sported a wonderful variety, but one which she has confirmed by a perpetual, certain, and unchanging order. And we should note here that the planet does not traverse the middle spaces of quadrants GH and KP without any irregularity in longitude, provided that the diversity of the centres, which comes into play, necessarily makes some additosubtraction; but the instability of that centre prevents that. For if, for example, the centre abided at L and the planet proceeded from O, then it would admit greatest irregularity at H in proportion [173ᵃ] to the eccentricity FL. But it follows from the assumptions that the planet proceeding from O begins and promises to cause the irregularity which is due to FL the distance between the centres; but as the mobile centre approaches the midpoint F, more and more is taken away from the promised irregularity, and it is made void to such an extent that it wholly vanishes at the mean sections H and P, where you would expect it to be greatest. And nevertheless, as we acknowledge, when the planet is made small beneath the rays of the sun[1], it undergoes occultation; and when the planet is rising or setting in the morning or evening, it is not discernible on the curves of the circle. And we are unwilling to pass over this method which is no less rationable than the former, and which will come into open use in connection with the movements in latitude.

33. On the Tables of the Additosubtractions of the Five Wandering Stars

These things have been demonstrated concerning the regular and apparent movements of Mercury and the other planets and set out in numbers. And by their example the way to calculating differences of movement for certain other positions will be clear. And for this use we have made ready separate tables for each planet: six columns, thirty rows, ascending by triads of 3°, as is usual. The first two columns will contain the common numbers—both of the anomaly of the eccentric circle and of the parallax. The third, the sums of the additosubtractions of the eccentric circle—I mean the total differences occurring between the regular and irregular movements of the orbital circles. The fourth, the proportional minutes—and they go up to 60′—by which the parallaxes are increased or diminished on account of the greater or lesser distance of the Earth. The fifth, the additosubtractions which are the parallaxes occurring at the highest apsis of the eccentric circle and which arise from the great orbital circle. The sixth and last, their excesses over the parallaxes which take place at the lowest apsis of the eccentric circle. And the tables are as follows:

[1] *i.e.*, when the planet is in conjunction with the sun.

ADDITIONS-AND-SUBTRACTIONS OF SATURN

Common Numbers		Addito-subtractions of the eccentric circle		Proportional Minutes	Parallaxes of the orbital circle of the Earth		Excesses over the parallax of the lowest apsis	
Deg.	Deg.	Deg.	Min.	Min.	Deg.	Min.	Deg.	Min.
3	357	0	20	0	0	17	0	2
6	354	0	40	0	0	34	0	4
9	351	0	58	0	0	51	0	6
12	348	1	17	0	1	3	0	8
15	345	1	36	1	1	23	0	10
18	342	1	55	1	1	40	0	12
21	339	2	13	1	1	56	0	14
24	336	2	31	2	2	11	0	16
27	333	2	49	2	2	26	0	18
30	330	3	6	3	2	42	0	19
33	327	3	33	3	2	56	0	21
36	324	3	39	4	3	10	0	23
39	321	3	55	4	3	25	0	24
42	318	4	10	5	3	38	0	26
45	315	4	25	6	3	52	0	27
48	312	4	39	7	4	5	0	29
51	309	4	52	8	4	17	0	31
54	306	5	5	9	4	28	0	33
57	303	5	17	10	4	38	0	34
60	300	5	29	11	4	49	0	35
63	297	5	41	12	4	59	0	36
66	294	5	50	13	5	8	0	37
69	291	5	59	14	5	17	0	38
72	288	6	7	16	5	24	0	38
75	285	6	14	17	5	31	0	39
78	282	6	19	18	5	37	0	39
81	279	6	23	19	5	42	0	40
84	276	6	27	21	5	46	0	41
87	273	6	29	22	5	50	0	42
90	270	6	31	23	5	52	0	42
93	267	6	31	25	5	52	0	43
96	264	6	30	27	5	53	0	44
99	261	6	28	29	5	53	0	45
102	258	6	26	31	5	51	0	46
105	255	6	22	32	5	48	0	46
108	252	6	17	34	5	45	0	45
111	249	6	12	35	5	40	0	45
114	246	6	6	36	5	36	0	44
117	243	5	58	38	5	29	0	43
120	240	5	49	39	5	22	0	42
123	237	5	40	41	5	13	0	41
126	234	5	28	42	5	3	0	40
129	231	5	16	44	4	52	0	39
132	228	5	3	46	4	41	0	37
135	225	4	48	47	4	29	0	35
138	222	4	33	48	4	15	0	34
141	219	4	17	50	4	1	0	32
144	216	4	0	51	3	46	0	30
147	213	3	42	52	3	30	0	28
150	210	3	24	53	3	13	0	26
153	207	3	6	54	2	56	0	24
156	204	2	46	55	2	38	0	22
159	201	2	27	56	2	21	0	19
162	198	2	7	57	2	2	0	17
165	195	1	46	58	1	42	0	14
168	192	1	25	59	1	22	0	12
171	189	1	4	59	1	2	0	9
174	186	0	43	60	0	42	0	7
177	183	0	22	60	0	21	0	4
180	180	0	0	60	0	0	0	0

Additions-and-Subtractions of Jupiter

Common Numbers		Addito-subtractions of the eccentric circle		Proportional Minutes		Parallaxes of the orbital circle of the Earth		Excesses over the parallax of the lowest apsis	
Deg.	Deg.	Deg.	Min.	Min.	Sec.	Deg.	Min.	Deg.	Min.
3	357	0	16	0	3	0	28	0	2
6	354	0	31	0	12	0	56	0	4
9	351	0	47	0	18	1	25	0	6
12	348	1	2	0	30	1	53	0	8
15	345	1	18	0	45	2	19	0	10
18	342	1	33	1	3	2	46	0	13
21	339	1	48	1	23	3	13	0	15
24	336	2	2	1	48	3	40	0	17
27	333	2	17	2	18	4	6	0	19
30	330	2	31	2	50	4	32	0	21
33	327	2	44	3	26	4	57	0	23
36	324	2	58	4	10	5	22	0	25
39	321	3	11	5	40	5	47	0	27
42	318	3	23	6	43	6	11	0	29
45	315	3	35	7	48	6	34	0	31
48	312	3	47	8	50	6	56	0	34
51	309	3	58	9	53	7	18	0	36
54	306	4	8	10	57	7	39	0	38
57	303	4	17	12	0	7	58	0	40
60	300	4	26	13	10	8	17	0	42
63	297	4	35	14	20	8	35	0	44
66	294	4	42	15	30	8	52	0	46
69	291	4	50	16	50	9	8	0	48
72	288	4	56	18	10	9	22	0	50
75	285	5	1	19	17	9	35	0	52
78	282	5	5	20	40	9	47	0	54
81	279	5	9	22	20	9	59	0	55
84	276	5	12	23	50	10	8	0	56
87	273	5	14	25	23	10	17	0	57
90	270	5	15	26	57	10	24	0	58
93	267	5	15	28	33	10	25	0	59
96	264	5	15	30	12	10	33	1	0
99	261	5	14	31	43	10	34	1	1
102	258	5	12	33	17	10	34	1	1
105	255	5	10	34	50	10	33	1	2
108	252	5	6	36	21	10	29	1	3
111	249	5	1	37	47	10	23	1	3
114	246	4	55	39	0	10	15	1	3
117	243	4	49	40	25	10	5	1	3
120	240	4	41	41	50	9	54	1	2
123	237	4	32	43	18	9	41	1	1
126	234	4	23	44	46	9	25	1	0
129	231	4	13	46	11	9	8	0	59
132	228	4	2	47	37	8	56	0	58
135	225	3	50	49	2	8	27	0	57
138	222	3	38	50	22	8	5	0	55
141	219	3	25	51	46	7	39	0	53
144	216	3	13	53	6	7	12	0	50
147	213	2	59	54	10	6	43	0	47
150	210	2	45	55	15	6	13	0	43
153	207	2	30	56	12	5	41	0	39
156	204	2	15	57	0	5	7	0	35
159	201	1	59	57	37	4	32	0	31
162	198	1	43	58	6	3	56	0	27
165	195	1	27	58	34	3	18	0	23
168	192	1	11	59	3	2	40	0	19
171	189	0	53	59	36	2	0	0	15
174	186	0	35	59	58	1	20	0	11
177	183	0	17	60	0	0	40	0	6
180	180	0	0	60	0	0	0	0	0

ADDITIONS-AND-SUBTRACTIONS OF MARS

Common Numbers		Additio-subtractions of the eccentric circle		Proportional Minutes		Parallaxes of the orbital circle of the Earth		Excesses over the parallax of the lowest apsis	
Deg.	Deg.	Deg.	Min.	Min.	Sec.	Deg.	Min.	Deg.	Min.
3	357	0	32	0	0	1	8	0	8
6	354	1	5	0	2	2	16	0	17
9	351	1	37	0	7	3	24	0	25
12	348	2	8	0	15	4	31	0	33
15	345	2	39	0	28	5	38	0	41
18	342	3	10	0	42	6	45	0	50
21	339	3	41	0	57	7	52	0	59
24	336	4	11	1	13	8	58	1	8
27	333	4	41	1	34	10	5	1	16
30	330	5	10	2	1	11	11	1	25
33	327	5	38	2	31	12	16	1	34
36	324	6	6	3	2	13	22	1	43
39	321	6	32	3	32	14	26	1	52
42	318	6	58	4	3	15	31	2	2
45	315	7	23	4	37	16	35	2	11
48	312	7	47	5	16	17	39	2	20
51	309	8	10	6	2	18	42	2	30
54	306	8	32	6	50	19	45	2	40
57	303	8	53	7	39	20	47	2	50
60	300	9	12	8	30	21	49	3	0
63	297	9	30	9	27	22	50	3	11
66	294	9	47	10	25	23	48	3	22
69	291	10	3	11	28	24	47	3	34
72	288	10	19	12	33	25	44	3	46
75	285	10	32	13	38	26	40	3	59
78	282	10	42	14	46	27	35	4	11
81	279	10	50	16	4	28	29	4	24
84	276	10	56	17	24	29	21	4	36
87	273	11	1	18	45	30	12	4	50
90	270	11	5	20	8	31	0	5	5
93	267	11	7	21	32	31	45	5	20
96	264	11	8	22	58	32	30	5	35
99	261	11	7	24	32	33	13	5	51
102	258	11	5	26	7	33	53	6	7
105	255	11	1	27	43	34	30	6	25
108	252	10	56	29	21	35	3	6	45
111	249	10	45	31	2	35	34	7	4
114	246	10	33	32	46	35	59	7	25
117	243	10	11	34	41	36	21	7	46
120	240	10	7	36	16	36	37	8	11
123	237	9	51	38	1	36	49	8	34
126	234	9	33	39	46	36	54	8	59
129	231	9	13	41	30	36	53	9	24
132	228	8	50	43	12	36	45	9	49
135	225	8	27	44	50	36	25	10	17
138	222	8	2	46	26	35	59	10	47
141	219	7	36	48	1	35	25	11	15
144	216	7	7	49	35	34	30	11	45
147	213	6	37	51	2	33	24	12	12
150	210	6	7	52	22	32	3	12	35
153	207	5	34	53	38	30	26	12	54
156	204	5	0	54	50	28	5	13	28
159	201	4	25	56	0	26	8	13	7
162	198	3	49	57	6	23	28	12	47
165	195	3	12	57	54	20	21	12	12
168	192	2	35	58	22	16	51	10	59
171	189	1	57	58	50	13	1	9	1
174	186	1	18	59	11	8	51	6	40
177	183	0	39	59	44	4	32	3	28
180	180	0	0	60	0	0	0	0	0

ADDITIONS-AND-SUBTRACTIONS OF VENUS

Common Numbers		Addito-subtractions of the eccentric circle		Proportional Minutes		Parallaxes of the orbital circle of the Earth		Excesses over the parallax of the lowest apsis	
Deg.	Deg.	Deg.	Min.	Min.	Sec.	Deg.	Min.	Deg.	Min.
3	357	0	6	0	0	1	15	0	1
6	354	0	13	0	0	2	30	0	2
9	351	0	19	0	10	3	45	0	3
12	348	0	25	0	39	4	59	0	5
15	345	0	31	0	58	6	13	0	6
18	342	0	36	1	20	7	28	0	7
21	339	0	42	1	39	8	42	0	9
24	336	0	48	2	23	9	56	0	11
27	333	0	53	2	59	11	10	0	12
30	330	0	59	3	38	12	24	0	13
33	327	1	4	4	18	13	37	0	14
36	324	1	10	5	3	14	50	0	16
39	321	1	15	5	45	16	3	0	17
42	318	1	20	6	32	17	16	0	18
45	315	1	25	7	22	18	28	0	20
48	312	1	29	8	18	19	40	0	21
51	309	1	33	9	31	20	52	0	22
54	306	1	36	10	48	22	3	0	24
57	303	1	40	12	8	23	14	0	26
60	300	1	43	13	32	24	24	0	27
63	297	1	46	15	8	25	34	0	28
66	294	1	49	16	35	26	43	0	30
69	291	1	52	18	0	27	52	0	32
72	288	1	54	19	33	28	57	0	34
75	285	1	56	21	8	30	4	0	36
78	282	1	58	22	32	31	9	0	38
81	279	1	59	24	7	32	13	0	41
84	276	2	0	25	30	33	17	0	43
87	273	2	0	27	5	34	20	0	45
90	270	2	0	28	28	35	21	0	47
93	267	2	0	29	58	36	20	0	50
96	264	2	0	31	28	37	17	0	53
99	261	1	59	32	57	38	13	0	55
102	258	1	58	34	26	39	7	0	58
105	255	1	57	35	55	40	0	1	0
108	252	1	55	37	23	40	49	1	4
111	249	1	53	38	52	41	36	1	8
114	246	1	51	40	19	42	18	1	11
117	243	1	48	41	45	42	59	1	14
120	240	1	45	43	10	43	35	1	18
123	237	1	42	44	37	44	7	1	22
126	234	1	39	46	6	44	32	1	26
129	231	1	35	47	36	44	49	1	50
132	228	1	31	49	6	45	4	1	36
135	225	1	27	50	12	45	10	1	41
138	222	1	22	51	17	45	5	1	47
141	219	1	17	52	33	44	51	1	53
144	216	1	12	53	48	44	22	2	0
147	213	1	7	54	28	43	36	2	6
150	210	1	1	55	0	42	34	2	13
153	207	0	55	55	57	41	12	2	19
156	204	0	49	56	47	39	20	2	34
159	201	0	43	57	33	36	58	2	27
162	198	0	37	58	16	33	58	2	27
165	195	0	31	58	59	30	14	2	27
168	192	0	25	59	39	25	42	2	16
171	189	0	19	59	48	20	20	1	56
174	186	0	13	59	54	14	7	1	26
177	183	0	7	59	58	7	16	0	46
180	180	0	0	60	0	0	16	0	0

ADDITIONS-AND-SUBTRACTIONS OF MERCURY

Common Numbers		Additosubtractions of the eccentric circle		Proportional Minutes		Parallaxes of the orbital circle of the Earth		Excesses over the parallax of the lowest apsis	
Deg.	Deg.	Deg.	Min.	Min.	Sec.	Deg.	Min.	Deg.	Min.
3	357	0	8	0	3	0	44	0	8
6	354	0	17	0	12	1	28	0	15
9	351	0	26	0	24	2	12	0	23
12	348	0	34	0	50	2	56	0	31
15	345	0	43	1	43	3	41	0	38
18	342	0	51	2	42	4	25	0	45
21	339	0	59	3	51	5	8	0	53
24	336	1	8	5	10	5	51	1	1
27	333	1	16	6	41	6	34	1	8
30	330	1	24	8	29	7	15	1	16
33	327	1	32	10	35	7	57	1	24
36	324	1	39	12	50	8	38	1	32
39	321	1	46	15	7	9	18	1	40
42	318	1	53	17	26	9	59	1	47
45	315	2	0	19	47	10	38	1	55
48	312	2	6	22	8	11	17	2	2
51	309	2	12	24	31	11	54	2	10
54	306	2	18	26	17	12	31	2	18
57	303	2	24	29	17	13	7	2	26
60	300	2	29	31	39	13	41	2	34
63	297	2	34	33	59	14	14	2	42
66	294	2	38	36	12	14	46	2	51
69	291	2	43	38	29	15	17	2	59
72	288	2	47	40	45	15	46	3	8
75	285	2	50	42	58	16	14	3	16
78	282	2	53	45	6	16	40	3	24
81	279	2	56	46	59	17	4	3	32
84	276	2	58	48	50	17	27	3	40
87	273	2	59	50	36	17	48	3	48
90	270	3	0	52	2	18	6	3	56
93	267	3	0	53	43	18	23	4	3
96	264	3	1	55	4	18	37	4	11
99	261	3	0	56	14	18	48	4	19
102	258	2	59	57	14	18	56	4	27
105	255	2	58	58	1	19	2	4	34
108	252	2	56	58	40	19	3	4	42
111	249	2	55	59	14	19	3	4	49
114	246	2	53	59	40	18	59	4	54
117	243	2	49	59	57	18	53	4	58
120	240	2	44	60	0	18	42	5	2
123	237	2	39	59	49	18	27	5	4
126	234	2	34	59	35	18	8	5	6
129	231	2	28	59	19	17	44	5	9
132	228	2	22	58	59	17	17	5	9
135	225	2	16	58	32	16	44	5	6
138	222	2	10	57	56	16	7	5	3
141	219	2	3	56	41	15	25	4	59
144	216	1	55	55	27	14	38	4	52
147	213	1	47	54	55	13	47	4	41
150	210	1	38	54	25	12	52	4	26
153	207	1	29	53	54	11	51	4	10
156	204	1	19	53	23	10	44	3	53
159	201	1	10	52	54	9	34	3	33
162	198	1	0	52	33	8	20	3	10
165	195	0	51	52	18	7	4	2	43
168	192	0	41	52	8	5	43	2	14
171	189	0	31	52	3	4	19	1	43
174	186	0	21	52	2	2	54	1	9
177	183	0	10	52	2	1	27	0	35
180	180	0	0	52	2	0	0	0	0

34. How the Positions in Longitude of the Five Planets Are Calculated

[178[b]] Therefore by means of the tables drawn up in this way by us we shall calculate without any difficulty the positions in longitude of the five wandering stars. There is approximately the same method of computation in all of them, though the three outer planets differ slightly from Venus and Mercury in this respect.

Therefore let us speak of Saturn, Jupiter, and Mars first. In their case the calculation is such that the mean movements—that is, the simple movement of the sun and the movement of parallax of the planet—are sought for any given time by the method described above. Next, the position of the highest apsis of the eccentric circle is subtracted from the simple position of the sun, and the movement of parallax is subtracted from the remainder; the first remainder is the anomaly of the eccentric circle of the planet. We shall look it up among the common numbers in one of the first two columns of the table, and correspondingly in the third column we shall take the additosubtraction of the eccentric circle, and the proportional minutes in the following column. We shall add this additosubtraction to the movement of anomaly of parallax and subtract it from the anomaly of the eccentric circle, if the number whereby we entered [the table] was found in the first column; and conversely we shall subtract it from the anomaly of the eccentric circle—if the number was found in the second column. The sum or remainder will be the corrected anomaly of parallax or the corrected anomaly of the eccentric circle—the proportional minutes being reserved for a use we shall speak of soon. Then we shall look up this corrected anomaly [of parallax] in the first two columns of common numbers; and from the corresponding place in the fifth column we shall take the additosubtraction arising from the movement of parallax, together with its excess found in the last column; and of that excess we shall take the proportional part in accordance with the number of proportional minutes; and we shall always add this proportional part to the additosubtraction. The sum will be the true parallax of the planet; and is to be subtracted from the corrected anomaly of parallax, if the [corrected anomaly] is less than a semicircle, or added, if greater than a semicircle. For in this way we shall have the true and apparent distance of the planet westward from the mean position of the sun; and when we have subtracted that distance from the mean position of the sun, the remainder will be the sought position of the planet [179[a]] in the sphere of the fixed stars, and the addition of the precession of the equinoxes will determine the position of the planet in relation to the spring equinox.

In the case of Venus and Mercury we shall use the distance from the highest apsis to the mean position of the sun as the anomaly of the eccentric circle; and by means of this anomaly we shall correct the movement of parallax and the anomaly of the eccentric circle, as was said already. But if the additosubtraction of the eccentric circle and the corrected parallax are of the same quality or species [i.e., are both additive or both subtractive], they are simultaneously added to or subtracted from the mean position of the sun. But if they are of different species, the lesser is subtracted from the greater; and by means of the remainder there will take place that which we have just mentioned, according to the additive or subtractive property of the greater number; and the final result will be the position which we are looking for.

35. ON THE STATIONS AND RETROGRADATIONS OF THE FIVE WANDERING STARS

Moreover, the knowledge of where and when the stations, retrogradations, and returns take place and how great they are seems also to pertain to the account of movement in longitude. The mathematicians, especially Apollonius of Perga, have dealt a good deal with them; but they have done so under the assumption of only one irregular movement, namely, that whereby the planets are moved with respect to the sun and which we have called the parallax due to the great orbital circle of the Earth.

For if the circles of the planets—whereon all the planets are borne with unequal periods of revolution but in the same direction, *i.e.*, towards the east—are homocentric with the great orbital circle of the Earth, and some planet on its own orbital circle and within the great orbital circle, such as Venus or Mercury, has greater velocity than the movement of the Earth has; *and if a straight line drawn from the Earth cuts the orbital circle of the planet in such a way that half the segment comprised within the orbital circle has the same ratio to the line which extends from our point of vision the Earth to the lower and convex arc of the intersected orbital circle, as does the movement of the Earth to the velocity of the planet then, if a point is made at the extremity of this line drawn to the arc which is at the perigee of the circle of the planet, the point will separate the retrogradation from the progression, so that when the planet is at that position, it will have the appearance of stopping.*

Similarly in the case of the three outer planets which have a movement slower than the velocity [179^b] of the Earth, *if a straight line drawn through our point of vision cuts the great orbital circle in such a way that half the segment comprised within the orbital circle has the same ratio to the line which extends from the planet to our point of vision located on the nearer and convex surface of the orbital circle, as does the movement of the planet to the velocity of the Earth; then the planet when in that position will present to our vision the appearance of stopping.*

But if half the segment comprised within the circle, as was said, has a greater ratio to the remaining external segment than the velocity of the Earth has to the velocity of Venus or Mercury, or than the movement of any of the three upper planets has to the velocity of the Earth; then the planet will progress eastward; but if the ratio is less, then it will retrograde westward.

In order to demonstrate all this, Apollonius took a certain lemma, which was in accord with the hypothesis of the immobility of the Earth but which none the less squares with our principle of terrestrial mobility and which for that reason we too shall employ. And we can enunciate it in this form: *if the greater side of a triangle is so cut that one of the segments is not less than the adjoining side, then this segment will have a greater ratio to the remaining segment than the angles on the side cut, taken in reverse order, will have to one another.*

For let BC be the greater side of triangle ABC; and if on side BC

$$CD < AC,$$

then I say that

$$CD : BD > \text{angle } ABC : \text{angle } BCA.$$

Now it is demonstrated as follows. Let the parallelogram $ADCE$ be completed; and BA and CE extended will meet at point E. Accordingly since

$$AE < AC,$$

the circle described with centre A and radius AE will
pass through C or beyond it. Now let GEC be the circle,
and let it pass through C. Since

$$\text{trgl. } AEF > \text{sect. } AEG,$$

while

$$\text{trgl. } AEC < \text{sect. } AEC;$$

then

$$\text{trgl. } AEF : \text{trgl. } AEC > \text{sect. } AEG : \text{sect. } AEC.$$

But

$$\text{trgl. } AEF : \text{trgl. } AEC = \text{base } FE : \text{base } EC.$$

Therefore

$$FE : EC > \text{angle } FAE : \text{angle } EAG.$$

But

$$FE : EC = CD : DB.$$

And

$$\text{angle } FAE = \text{angle } ABC;$$

and

$$\text{angle } EAC = \text{angle } BCA.$$

Accordingly

$$[180^a] \quad CD : DB > \text{angle } ABC : \text{angle } ACB.$$

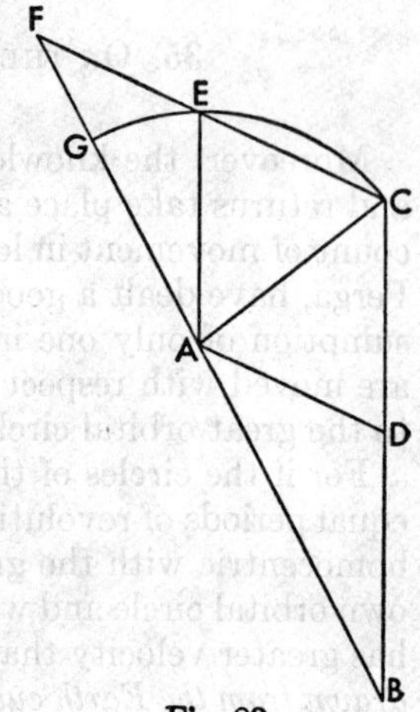

Now it is manifest that the ratio will be much greater if it is not assumed that

$$CD = AC = AE$$

but that

$$CD > AE.$$

Fig. 83

Now let ABC be the circle of Venus or Mercury around centre D; and let the
Earth E outside the circle be movable around the same centre D. From E our
point of vision let the straight line $ECDA$ be drawn through the centre of the
circle; and let A be the position farthest from the Earth, and C the nearest. And
let DC be put down as having a greater ratio to CE than the movement of the
point of vision has to the velocity of the planet. Accordingly it is possible to
find a line EFB such that half BF has the same ratio to FE that the movement
of the point of vision has to the movement of the planet. For let line EFB be
moved away from centre D and be decreased along FB and increased along EF,
until we meet with what is demanded.

I say that *when the planet is set up at point F, it will present to us the appearance
of stopping; and that whatever size of the arc we take on either side of F, we shall find
the planet progressing, if the arc is taken in the direction of the apogee, and retrograding, if in the direction of the perigee.*

For first let the arc FG be taken in the direction of the apogee: let EGK be
extended, and let BG, DG, and DF be joined. Accordingly since in triangle BGE
segment BF of the greater side BE is greater than BG, then

$$BF : EF > \text{angle } FEG : \text{angle } GBF.$$

Furthermore,

$$\tfrac{1}{2}BF : FE > \text{angle } FEG : 2 \text{ angle } GBF,$$

i.e.,

$$\tfrac{1}{2}BF : FE > \text{angle } FEG : \text{angle } GDF.$$

But

$$\tfrac{1}{2}BF : FE = \text{movement of Earth} : \text{movement of planet}.$$

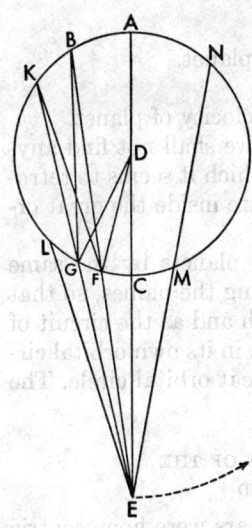

Therefore

angle *FEG* : angle *GDF* < velocity of
Earth : velocity of planet.

Now let

angle *FEL* : angle *FDG* = movement of
Earth : movement of planet.

Therefore

angle *FEL* > angle *FEG*.

Accordingly, during the time in which the planet traverses arc *GF* of the orbital circle, our line of sight [180^b] will be thought to have traversed during that time the contrary space between line *EF* and line *EL*. It is manifest that in the same time in which to our sight arc *GF* transports the planet westward in accordance with the smaller angle *FEG*, the passage of the Earth drags it back eastward in accordance with the greater angle *FEL*, so that the planet will go on increasing its angular distance eastward by angle *GEL* and will not seem to have come to a stop yet.

Now it is manifest that the opposite of this can be shown by the same means. If in the same diagram we put down that

½*GK* : *GE* = movement of Earth : velocity of planet;

and if we take arc *GF* in the direction of the perigee and away from straight line *EK*, and join *KF* and make triangle *KEF*, where

GE > EF;

then

KG : *GE* < angle *FEG* : angle *FKG*.

Thus too

½*KG* : *GE* < angle *FEG* : 2 angle *FKG*,

i.e.,

½*KG* : *GE* < angle *FEG* : angle *GDF*,

conversely to what was shown before. And it is inferred by the same means that

angle *GDF* : angle *FEG* < velocity of planet : velocity of line of sight.

Accordingly, when angle *GDF* has been made greater, so that the angles have the same ratio, then the planet will complete a greater movement westwards than progression demands.

Hence it is also manifest that if we make

arc *FC* = arc *CM*

the second station will be at point *M*; and if line *EMN* is drawn,

½*MN* : *ME* = ½*BF* : *FE* = velocity of Earth : velocity of planet;

and accordingly points *M* and *F* will designate the two stations and will determine the whole arc *FCM* as retrogressive and the remainder of the circle as progressive.

Moreover, it follows that at certain distances

DC : *CE* > velocity of Earth : velocity of planet;

and it will not be possible to draw another straight line in the ratio [which the velocity of the Earth has to the velocity of the planet]; and the planet will not seem to stop or to retrograde. For since it was assumed that in triangle *DEG*

DC < *EG*;

angle *CEG* : angle *CDG* < *DC* : *CE* ·

but
$$DC : CE > \text{velocity of Earth : velocity of planet.}$$
Therefore also

angle CEG : angle $CDG <$ velocity of Earth : velocity of planet.
Where that occurs, the planet will progress; [181ª] and we shall not find anywhere in the orbital circle of the planet an arc through which it seems to retrograde. All this concerning Venus and Mercury, which are inside the great orbital circle [of the Earth].

We can demonstrate this concerning the three outer planets by the same
method and with the same diagrams—merely by reversing the names, so that
we put down ABC as the great orbital circle of the Earth and as the circuit of
our point of vision and the planet at E, whose movement in its own orbital circle is less than the speed of our point of vision in the great orbital circle. The
rest of the demonstration will proceed as before.

36. How the Times, Positions, and Arcs of the Retrogradations are Determined

Now if the orbital circles which bear the wandering stars were homocentric
with the great orbital circle, it would be easy to establish that which the demonstrations promise, as the ratio of the velocity of the planet to the velocity of
the point of vision would always be the same. But the orbital circles are eccentric, and hence their movements appear as irregular. For that reason it will be
necessary for us to assume irregular and corrected movements everywhere as the
differences of velocity and to employ them in the demonstrations, and not the
simple and regular movements, except when the planet happens to be at its
mean longitudes, the only place where it seems to be carried in its orbital circle
with a mean movement.

Now we shall show this in the case of Mars, so that the retrogradations of the
other planets may become clearer by means of this ex-
ample. For let ABC be the great orbital circle, on which
our point of vision revolves; and let the planet be at
point E. From the planet let the straight line $ECDA$ be
drawn through the centre of the orbital circle; and let
EFB also be drawn. Half of chord BF—i.e., chord
GF—will have the ratio to line EF which the varying
velocity of the planet has to the velocity of the line of
sight, whereby it exceeds the planet. Our problem is to
find arc FC of half the retrogradation, or ABF, so as to
know at what distance from its farthest position from
A the planet becomes stationary and what the angle
comprehended by FEC is. For by means of this we shall
foretell the time and position of such an affection of
the planet.

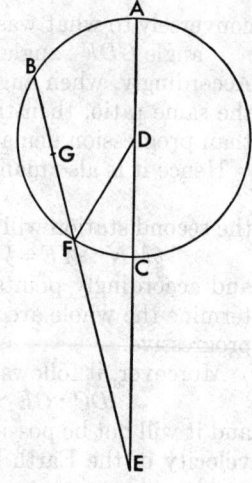

Now let the planet be placed at the mean apsis of the
eccentric circle, where the movements of longitude and
of anomaly differ very little from the regular movements. Therefore in the case of the planet Mars, since
its mean movement [that is half of the line BF] [181ᵇ]
is 1ᵖ8°7″, the motion of parallax, which is the relation of our vision to the mean

movement of the star, consists of one part and is the straight line EF. Hence
$$EB = 3^\text{p}16'14''$$
and likewise
$$\text{rect. } BE, EF = 3^\text{p}16'14''.$$
Now we have shown that
$$DA = 6,580,$$
$$\text{where } DE = 10,000,$$
and DA is the radius of the orbital circle.
But
$$DA = 39^\text{p}29',$$
$$= \text{where } DE = 60^\text{p};$$
and
$$AE : EC = 99^\text{p}29' : 20^\text{p}31'.$$
And
$$\text{rect. } AE, EC = \text{rect. } BE, EF = 2,041^\text{p}4'.$$
Accordingly by reduction
$$2,041^\text{p}4' \div 3^\text{p}16'14'' = 624^\text{p}4',$$
and similarly
$$\text{side } EF = 24^\text{p}58'52'',$$
$$\text{where } DE = 60^\text{p}.$$
But
$$EF = 4,163$$
$$\text{where } DE = 10,000$$
$$\text{and } DF = 6,580.$$
Accordingly, as the sides of triangle DEF are given,
$$\text{angle } DEF = 27°15',$$
which is the angular retrogradation of the planet, and
$$\text{angle } CDF = 16°50',$$
which is the angular anomaly of parallax. Accordingly, since the planet, when first stationary, appeared on line EF; and the planet, when opposite the sun, on line EC; if the planet is not moved eastward, the 16°15' of arc CF will comprehend the 27°25' of angle AEF found to be the retrogradation; but according to the ratio set forth of the velocity of the planet to the velocity of our line of sight, 16°5' corresponds to the section of the anomaly of parallax and approximately 19°6'39'' corresponds [to the section of the anomaly] of longitude of the planet. Now
$$27°15' - 19°6'39'' = 8°8',$$
which is the distance from the other station to the solar opposition—and there are approximately 36½ days during which the anomaly in longitude is 19°6'39'' —and hence the total retrogradation is 16°16' in 73 days. These things which have been demonstrated for the mean longitudes of the eccentric circle can be similarly demonstrated for other positions—the planet being credited with an always varying velocity, according as its position demands, as we said.

Hence in Saturn, Jupiter, and Mars the same way of demonstration is open, provided we take the point of sight instead of the planet and the planet instead of the point of sight. Now the reverse of what occurs in the orbital circles which the Earth encloses occurs in the orbital circles which enclose the Earth; and let that be enough, so that we won't have to repeat the same old song. Nevertheless, since the variable movement of the planet with respect to the point of sight and to the ambiguity of the stationary points—of which the theorem of Apollonius does not relieve us—give no little difficulty; I do not know whether it would not be better to investigate the stations simply and in connection with the nearest position, by the method whereby we investigate by means of the known numbers of their movements the conjunction of the planet, when opposite the sun, with the line of mean movement of the sun, or the conjunctions of any of the planets. And we shall leave that to your pleasure.

BOOK SIX

[182ª] WE have indicated to the best of our ability what power and effect the assumption of the revolution of the Earth has in the case of the apparent movement in longitude of the wandering stars and in what a sure and necessary order it places all the appearances. It remains for us to occupy ourselves with the movements of the planets by which they digress in latitude and to show how in this case too the selfsame mobility of the Earth exercises its command and prescribes laws for them here also. Moreover this is a necessary part of the science, as the digressions of these planets cause no little variation in the rising and setting, apparitions and occultations, and the other appearances of which there has been a general exposition above. And their true positions are said to be known only when their longitude together with their latitude in relation to the ecliptic has been established. Accordingly by means of the assumption of the mobility of the Earth we shall do with perhaps greater compactness and more becomingly what the ancient mathematicians thought to have demonstrated by means of the immobility of the Earth.

1. General Exposition of the Digression in Latitude of the Five Wandering Stars

The ancients found in all the planets two digressions in latitude answering to their twofold irregularity in longitude—one digression taking place by reason of the eccentricity of the orbital circles, and the other in accordance with the epicycles. In place of the epicycles, as has been often repeated, we have taken the single great orbital circle of the Earth—not that the orbital circle has some inclination with respect to the plane of the ecliptic fixed once and forever, since they are the same, but that the orbital circles of the planets are inclined to this plane [182ᵇ] with a variable obliquity, and this variability is regulated according to the movement and revolutions of the great orbital circle of the Earth.

But since the three higher planets, Saturn, Jupiter, and Mars, move longitudinally under different laws from those under which the remaining two do, so also they differ not a little in their latitudinal movement. Accordingly, the ancients first examined where and how great their farthest northern limits in latitude were. Ptolemy found the limits in the case of Saturn and Jupiter around the beginning of Libra, but in the case of Mars around the end of Cancer near the apogee of the eccentric circle. But in our time we found this northern limit in the case of Saturn at 7° of Scorpio, in the case of Jupiter at 27° of Libra, in the case of Mars at 27° of Leo, according as the apogees have been changing around down to our time; for the inclinations and the cardinal points of latitude follow upon the movement of those orbital circles. At corrected or apparent distances of 90° between these limits, they seem to be making no digression in latitude, wherever the Earth happens to be at that time. Therefore, when they are at these mean longitudes, they are understood to be at the common section

813

of their orbital circles with the ecliptic, just as the moon was at the ecliptic sections. Ptolemy calls these points the nodes: the ascending node, after which the planet enters upon northern latitudes; and the descending node, after which the planet crosses over into southern latitudes—not that the great orbital circle of the Earth, which always remains the same in the plane of the ecliptic, gives them any latitude; but every digression in latitude is measured from the nodes and varies greatly in positions different from the nodes. And according as the Earth approaches other positions, where the planets are seen to be opposite the sun and *acronycti*, the planets always move with a greater digression than in any other position of the Earth: in the northern semicircle to the north, and in the southern to the south, and with greater variation than the approach or withdrawal of the Earth demands. By that happening, it is known that the inclination of their orbital circles is not fixed, but that it changes in a certain movement of libration commensurable with the revolutions of the great circle of the Earth, as will be said a little farther on.

Now Venus and Mercury seem to digress somewhat differently but under a fixed law which has been observed to hold at the mean, highest, and lowest apsides. For at the mean longitudes, namely when the line of the mean movement of the sun is at a quadrant's distance from their highest or lowest apsis, and the planets as evening or morning stars are themselves at a distance of a quadrant of their orbital circle from the same line of mean movement of the sun; [183ª] the ancients found that the planets had not digressed from the ecliptic, and hence the ancients understood them to be at that time the common section of their separate orbital circles and the ecliptic. This section passes through their apogees and perigees; and accordingly when they are higher or lower than the Earth, they then make manifest digressions—the greatest digressions at their greatest distances from the Earth, *i.e.*, at the evening apparition or at the morning occultation, when Venus is farthest north, and Mercury farthest south. And conversely at a position nearer to the Earth, when they undergo occultation in the evening or emerge in the morning, Venus is to the south, and Mercury to the north. Vice versa, when the Earth is at the position opposite to this and at the other mean apsis namely, when the anomaly of the eccentric circle is 270°— Venus is apparent at its greater southern distance from the Earth, and Mercury is to the north, and at a nearer position of the Earth Venus is to the north, and Mercury to the south. At the solstice of the Earth at the apogee of these planets, Ptolemy found that the latitude of Venus the morning star was northern, and of Venus the evening star, southern; and inversely in the case of Mercury: southern when the morning star, and northern when the evening star. These relations are similarly reversed at the opposite position of the perigee, so that Venus Lucifer is seen in the south, and Venus Vesperugo in the north; but Mercury as morning star in the north, and Mercury as evening star in the south. And the ancients found that at both these positions the northern digression of Venus was always greater than the southern, and that the southern digression of Mercury was greater than the northern.

Taking this as an occasion, the ancients reasoned out a twofold latitude for this position, and a threefold latitude universally. They called the first latitude, which occurs at the mean longitudes, the inclination; the second, which occurs at the highest and lowest apsides, the obliquation; and the third one, which occurs in conjunction with the second, the deviation: it is always northern in the case of Venus and southern in the case of Mercury. Between these four limits the latitudes are mixed with one another, and alternately increase and decrease and yield mutually; and we shall give the right causes for all that.

2. Hypotheses of the Circles on Which the Planets Are Moved in Latitude

Accordingly in the case of these five planets we must assume that their orbital circles are inclined to the plane of the ecliptic—the common section being through the diameter of the ecliptic—by a variable but regular inclination, [183^b] since in Saturn, Jupiter, and Mars the angle of section receives a certain libration around that section as around an axis, like the libration which we demonstrated in the case of the precession of the equinoxes, but simple and commensurable with the movement of parallax. The angle of section is increased and decreased by this libration within a fixed period, so that, whenever the Earth is nearest to the planet, *i.e.*, to the planet in opposition to the sun, the greatest inclination of the orbital circle of the planet occurs; at the contrary position the least inclination; at the mean position, the mean inclination: consequently, when the planet is at its farthest limit of northern or southern latitude, its latitude appears much greater at the nearness of the Earth than at its greatest distance from the Earth. And although this irregularity can be caused only by the unequal distances of the Earth, in accordance with which things nearer seem greater than things farther away; nevertheless there is a rather great difference between the excess and the deficiency of these planetary latitudes: and that cannot take place unless the orbital circles too have a movement of libration with respect to their obliquity. But, as we said before, in the case of things which are undergoing a libration, we must take a certain mean between the extremes.

In order that this may be clearer, let *ABCD* be the Earth's great orbital circle in the plane of the ecliptic with centre *E*; and let *FGKL* the orbital circle of the

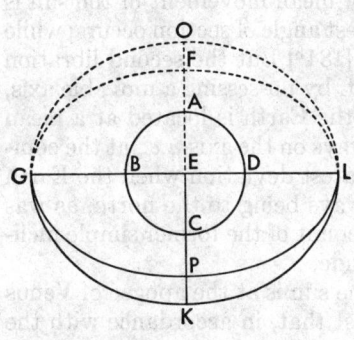

planet be inclined to *ABCD* in a mean and permanent declination whereof *F* is the northern limit in latitude, *K* the southern, *G* the descending node of section, and *BED* the common section, which is extended in the straight lines *GB* and *DL*. And those four termini do not change, except along with the movement of the apsides. Let it be understood however that the movement of the planet in longitude takes place not on the plane of circle *FG* but on *OP*, another circle which is inclined to and homocentric with *FG*. These two circles cut one another in that same [184^a] straight line *GBDL*. Therefore, while the planet is being borne on orbital circle *OP*, it meanwhile falls upon plane *FK* by the movement of libration, goes beyond plane *FK* in either direction, and on that account makes the latitude appear variable.

For first let the planet be at point *O* at its greatest northern latitude and at its position nearest to the Earth in *A*; then the latitude of the planet will increase in proportion to *OGF* the angle of greatest inclination of orbital circle *OGP*. This movement [of libration] is a movement of approach and withdrawal, because by hypothesis it is commensurable with the movement of parallax: if then the Earth is at B, point O will coincide with F, and the latitude of the planet will appear less in the same position than before; and it will be much less if the Earth is at point C. For O will cross over to the farthest and most diverse part of its libration, and will leave only as much latitude as is in excess over the subtractive libration of the northern latitude, namely over the angle equal to OGF. Hence the latitude of the planet around F in the north will increase throughout the remaining semicircle CDA, until the Earth returns to the first point A, from which it set out. There will be the same way of progress for the meridian planet set up around point K—the movement of the Earth starting from C. But if the planet, in opposition to the sun or hidden by it, is at one of the nodes G or L, even though at that time the orbital circles FK and OP have their greatest inclination to one another, on that account no planetary latitude is perceptible, namely because the planet is at the common section of the orbital circles. From that, I judge, it is easily understood how the northern latitude of the planet decreases from F to G; and the southern latitude increases from G to K, but vanishes totally at L and becomes northern. And this is the way with those three higher planets.

Venus and Mercury differ from them no little in their latitudes, as in longitude, because they have the common sections of the orbital circles located through the apogee and perigee. Now their greatest inclinations at the mean apsides become changeable by a movement of libration, as in the case of the higher planets; but they undergo furthermore a libration dissimilar to the first. Nevertheless both librations are commensurable with the revolutions of the Earth, but not in the same way. For the first libration has the following property; when there has been one revolution of the Earth with respect to the apsides of the planets, there have been two revolutions of the movement of libration having as an immobile axis the section through the apogee and the perigee, which we spoke of; so that whenever the line of mean movement of the sun is at the perigee or apogee of the planets, the greatest angle of section occurs; while the least angle occurs at the mean longitudes. [184$^\mathrm{b}$] But the second libration supervening upon this one differs from it in that, by possessing a movable axis, it has the following effect: namely, that when the Earth is located at a mean longitude, the planet of Venus or Mercury is always on the axis, *i.e.*, at the common section of this libration, but shows its greatest deviation when the Earth is in line with its apogee or perigee—Venus always being to the north, as was said, and Mercury to the south; although on account of the former simple inclination they should at this time be lacking latitude.

For example, when the mean movement of the sun is at the apogee of Venus and Venus is in the same position, it is manifest that, in accordance with the simple inclination and the first libration, Venus, being at the common section of its orbital circle with the plane of the ecliptic, would at that time have had no latitude; but the second libration, which has its section or axis along the transverse diameter of the eccentric orbital circle and cuts at right angles the diameter passing through the highest and lowest apsis, adds its greatest deviation to the planet. But if at this time Venus is in one of the other quadrants and around the mean apsides of its orbital circle, then the axis of this libration will coincide with the line of mean movement of the sun, and Venus itself will add to the northern obliquity the greatest deviation, which it subtracts from the southern obliquity and leaves smaller. In this way the libration of deviation is made commensurate with the movement of the Earth.

In order that these things may be grasped more easily, let *ABCD* be drawn

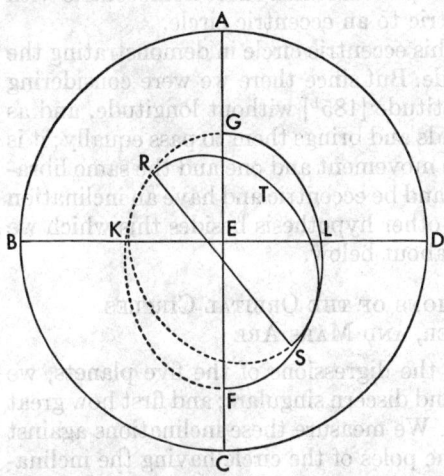

again as the great orbital circle. Let *FGK* be the orbital circle of Venus or Mercury: it is eccentric to circle *ABC* and inclined to it in accordance with the equal inclination *FGK*. Let *FG* be the common section of these two circles through *F* the apogee of the orbital circle and *G* the perigee. First for the sake of an easier demonstration let us put down *GKF* the inclination of the eccentric orbital circle as simple and fixed, or, if you prefer, as midway between the greatest and the least inclination, except that the common section *FG* [185ª] changes according to the movement of the perigee and apogee. When the Earth is on this common section, *i.e.*, at *A* or *C*, and the planet is on the same line, it is manifest that at that time the planet would have no latitude, since all latitude is sideways in the semicircles *GKF* and *FLG*, whereon the planet effects its northern or southern approaches, as has been said, in proportion to the inclination of circle *FKG* to the plane of the ecliptic. Now some call this digression of the planet the obliquation; others, the reflexion. But when the Earth is at *B* or *D*, *i.e.*, at the mean apsides of the planet, there will be the same latitudes *FKG* and *GFL* above and below; and they call them the declinations. And so these latitudes differ nominally rather than really from the former latitudes, and even the names are interchanged at the middle positions. But since the angle of inclination of these circles is found to be greater in the obliquation than in the declination, the ancients understood this as taking place through a certain libration, curving itself around section *FG* as an axis, as was said above. Accordingly since the angle of section is known in both cases, it will be easy to understand from the difference between them how great the libration from least to greatest inclination is.

Now let there be understood another circle, the circle of deviation, which is inclined to circle *GKFL* and homocentric in the case of Venus but eccentric to the eccentric circle in the case of Mercury, as will be said later: And let *RS* be their common section as axis of libration, an axis movable in a circle, in such fashion that when the Earth is at *A* or *B*, the planet is at the farthest limit of deviation, wherever that is, as at point *T*; and as far as the Earth has advanced from *A*, so far away from *T* let the planet be understood to have moved, while the inclination of the circle of deviation decreases, so that when the Earth has measured the quadrant *AB*, the planet should be understood as having arrived at the node of this latitude, *i.e.*, at *R*. But as at this time the planes coincide at the mean movement of libration and are tending in different directions, the remaining semicircle of the deviation, which before was southerly, becomes northern; and as Venus passes into this semicircle, Venus avoids the south and seeks the north again, never to seek the south by this libration, just as Mercury, by crossing in the opposite direction, stays in the south; and Mercury also differs from Venus in that its libration takes place not in a circle homocentric with an eccentric circle but in a circle eccentric to an eccentric circle.

We employed an epicycle instead of this eccentric circle in demonstrating the irregularity in the movement in longitude. But since there we were considering longitude without latitude, and here latitude [185ᵇ] without longitude, and as one and the same revolution comprehends and brings them to pass equally; it is clear enough that it is one and the same movement and one and the same libration which can cause both irregularities and be eccentric and have an inclination at the same time; and that there is no other hypothesis besides this which we have just spoken of and will say more about below.

3. How Great the Inclinations of the Orbital Circles of Saturn, Jupiter, and Mars Are

After setting out our hypothesis for the digressions of the five planets, we must descend to the things themselves and discern singulars; and first how great the inclinations of the single circles are. We measure these inclinations against the great circle which passes through the poles of the circle having the inclination and is at right angles to the ecliptic; the transits in latitude are observed in relation to this great circle. For when we have apprehended these [inclinations], the way of learning the latitudes of each planet will be disclosed. Beginning once more with the three higher planets, we find that according to Ptolemy the digression of Saturn in opposition to the sun at the farthest limits of southern latitude was 3°5′, the digression of Jupiter 2°7′, that of Mars 7°; but in opposite positions, namely when they were in conjunction with the sun, the digression of Saturn was 2°2′, that of Jupiter 1°5′, and that of Mars only 5′, so that it almost touched the ecliptic—according as it is possible to mark the latitudes from the observations which he took in the neighbourhood of their occultations and apparitions.

Let that be kept before us; and in the plane which is at right angles to the ecliptic and through its centre, let AB be the common section [of the plane] with the ecliptic, and CD the common section [of the plane] with any of the three eccentric circles through the greatest northern and southern limits. Moreover,

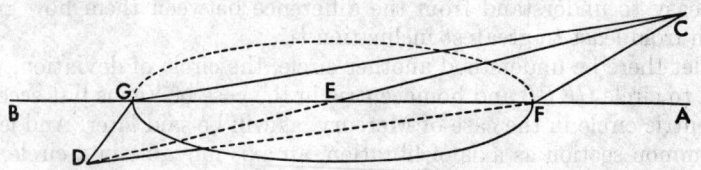

let E be the centre of the ecliptic, and FEG the diameter of the great orbital circle of the Earth. Now let D be the southern latitude and C the northern; and let CF, CG, DF, and DG be joined.

But the ratios of EG the great orbital circle of the Earth to ED the eccentric circle of the planet at any of their given positions have already been demonstrated above in the cases of the single [planets]. But the positions of greatest latitudes have been given by the observations. Therefore, since angle BGD, the angle of greatest southern latitude and an exterior angle of triangle EGD, has been given, the interior and opposite angle GED, the angle of greatest southern inclination of the eccentric circle to the plane of the ecliptic, will also be given by what has been shown concerning plane triangles.

Similarly we shall demonstrate the least inclination by means of the least southern latitude, namely by means of angle [186ᵃ] EFD. Since in triangle EFD the ratio of side EF to side ED is given together with angle EFD, we shall have GED given, the exterior angle and angle of least southern inclination: hence from the difference between both declinations we shall have the total libration of the eccentric circle in relation to the ecliptic. Moreover against these angles of inclination we shall measure the opposite northern latitudes, that is to say, angles AFC and EGC; and if they agree with the observations, it will be a sign that we have not erred at all.

Now as our example we shall take Mars, which has a greater digression in latitude than any of the others. Ptolemy marked the greatest southern latitude as being approximately $7°$ in the case of the perigee of Mars, and the greatest northern latitude as $4°20'$ at the apogee. But as we have assumed that

$$\text{angle } BGD = 6°50',$$

we shall find that correspondingly

$$\text{angle } AFC \doteqdot 4°30'.$$

For since

$$EG : ED = 1^\mathrm{p} : 1^\mathrm{p}22'26''$$

and since

$$\text{angle } BCD = 6°50';$$
$$\text{angle } DEG \doteqdot 1°51',$$

which is the angle of greatest southern inclination.
And since

$$EF : CE = 1^\mathrm{p} : 1^\mathrm{p}39'57'',$$

and

$$\text{angle } CEF = \text{angle } DEG = 1°51';$$

it follows that, as angle CFA is the exterior angle which we spoke of,

$$\text{angle } CFA = 4\tfrac{1}{2}°,$$

when the planet is in opposition to the sun.

Similarly, in the opposite position where it is in conjunction with the sun, if we assume that

$$\text{angle } DFE = 5',$$

then, since sides DE and EF and angle EFD are given,

$$\text{angle } EDF = 4',$$

and, as exterior angle,

$$\text{angle } DEG \doteqdot 9',$$

which is the angle of least inclination. And that will show us that

$$\text{angle } CGE = 6',$$

which is the angle of northern latitude. Therefore, by the subtraction of the least inclination from the greatest,

$$1°5' - 9' = 1°42',$$

which is the libration of this inclination, and

$$\tfrac{1}{2}(1°42') \doteqdot 50\tfrac{1}{2}'.$$

In the case of the other two, Jupiter and Saturn, there is a similar method for discovering the angles of the inclinations together with the latitudes; for the greatest inclination of Jupiter is 1°42′, and the least 1°18′; [186ᵇ] so that its total libration does not comprehend more than 24′. Now the greatest inclination of Saturn is 2°44′, and the least 2°16′; and the libration between them is 19′. Hence by means of the least angles of inclination, which occur at the opposite position, when the planets are hidden beneath the sun, their digressions in latitude away from the ecliptic will be exhibited: that of Saturn as 2°3′ and that of Jupiter as 1°6′—as were to be shown and reserved for the tables to be drawn up below[1]

4. ON THE EXPOSITION OF THE OTHER LATITUDES IN PARTICULAR AND IN GENERAL

Now that these things have been shown, the latitudes of these three planets will be made clear in general and in particular. For as before, let AB the line through the farthest limits of digression be the common section of the plane perpendicular to the ecliptic. And let the northern limit be at A; and let CD,

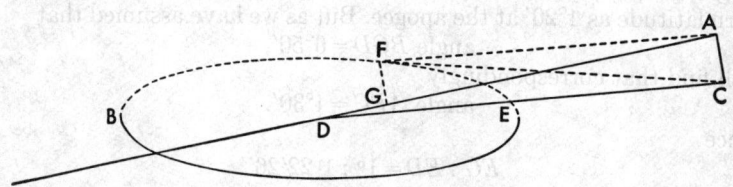

which cuts AB in point D, be the perpendicular common section of the orbital circle of the planet. And with D as centre let EF the great orbital circle of the Earth be described. From the opposition, which is at E, let any known arc, such as EF, be measured, and from F and from C, the position of the planet, let the perpendiculars CA and FG be drawn to AB; and let FA and FC be joined.

We are first looking to see how great ADC the angle of inclination of the eccentric circle is, with this set-up. Now it has been shown that the inclination was greatest when the Earth was at point E. Moreover it has been made clear that the total libration is commensurate with the revolution of the Earth on circle EF in relation to the diameter BE, as the nature of libration demands. Therefore on account of arc EF being given, the ratio of ED to EG will be given; and that is the ratio of the total libration to which angle ADC has just now decreased. For that reason angle ADC is given in this case. Accordingly triangle ADC has all its angles given together with its sides. But since by the foregoing, CD has a given ratio to ED, the ratio of CD to the remainder DG is given. Accordingly the ratios of CD and AD to GD are given. And hence the remainder AG is given. Hence too FG is given; for

$$FG = \tfrac{1}{2} \text{ ch. 2 } EF.$$

Therefore as two sides of the right triangle AGF have been given, side AF is given, and the ratio of AF to AC. Finally as two sides of right triangle ACF [187ᵃ] have been given, angle AFC will be given; and that is the angle of apparent latitude, which we were looking for.

[1]p. 835.

Once more we shall take Mars as our example of this. Let its limit of greatest southern latitude be around A, which is approximately at its lowest apsis. Now let the position of the planet be at C, where—as has been demonstrated—the angle of inclination was greatest, *i.e.*, 1°50′, when the Earth was at point E. Now let us put the Earth at point F and the movement of parallax at 45° in accordance with arc EF: therefore

$$\text{line } FG = 7,071,$$
$$\text{where } ED = 10,000,$$

and

$$GE = 10,000 - 7,071 = 2,929,$$

which is the remainder of the radius. Now it has been shown that

$$\tfrac{1}{2} \text{ libration of angle } ADC = 50\tfrac{1}{2}';$$

and half of the libration has the following ratio of increase and decrease in this case,

$$DE : GE = 50\tfrac{1}{2}' : 15'.$$

Now at present

$$\text{angle } ADC = 1°50' - 15' = 1°35',$$

which is the angle of inclination. On that account triangle ADC will have its sides and angles given; and since it has been shown above that

$$CD = 9,040,$$
$$\text{where } ED = 6,580;$$
$$FG = 4,653,$$
$$AD = 9,036,$$

and by subtraction

$$AEG = 4,383,$$

and

$$AC = 249\tfrac{1}{2}.$$

Accordingly, in right triangle AFG, since

$$\text{perpendicular } AG = 4,383$$

and

$$\text{base } FG = 4,653$$
$$\text{side } AF = 6,392.$$

Thus finally in triangle ACF, whereof

$$\text{angle } CAF = 90°$$

and sides AC and AF are given,

$$\text{angle } ACF = 2°15',$$

which is the angle of apparent latitude in relation to the Earth placed at F. We shall apply similar reasoning in the case of Saturn and Jupiter.

5. On the Latitudes of Venus and Mercury

Venus and Mercury remain, and their transits in latitude will be demonstrated, as I said, by means of three simultaneous and complicated latitudinal divagations. [187ᵇ] In order that they may be discerned separately, we shall begin with the one which the ancients call declination, as if from a simpler handling of it. And it happens to the declination alone to be sometimes separate from the others; and that occurs around the mean longitudes and around the nodes in accordance with the exact movements in longitude when the Earth has moved through a quadrant of a circle from the apogee or perigee of the planet. For when the Earth is very near, a northern or southern latitude of 6°22′ is found

in the case of Venus, and 4°5′ in the case of Mercury; but at the greatest distance
from the Earth, 1°2′ in the case of Venus; and in the case of Mercury, 1°45′.
Thereby the angles of inclination at this position are made manifest by means
of the tables of additosubtractions which have been drawn up; and for Venus
in that position at its greatest distance from the Earth the latitude is 1°2′, and
at its least distance 6°22′, and on either side [of the mean latitude] the arc of
the circle [through the poles of the orbital circle and perpendicular to the plane
of the ecliptic] is approximately 2½°; but in the case of Mercury the 1°45′ at
its greatest distance and the 4°5′ at its least demand 6¼° as the [total] arc of
its circle: consequently the angle of inclination of the circles of Venus is 2°30′,
and that of Mercury is 6¼°, whereof four right angles are equal to 360°. By
means of these [angles] the particular latitudes of declination can be unfolded,
as we shall demonstrate, and first in the case of Venus.

For in the plane of the ecliptic and through the centre of the perpendicular
plane, let *ABC* be the common section [of the two planes] and *DBE* the common
section [of the perpendicular plane] with the plane of the orbital circle of Venus.

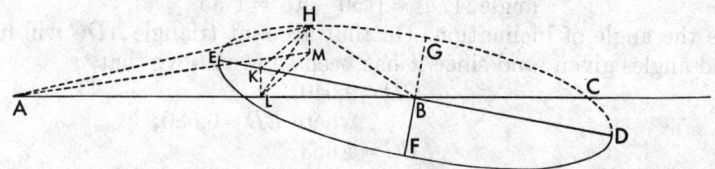

And let *A* be the centre of the Earth, *B* the centre of the orbital circle of the
planet, and *ABE* the angle of inclination of the orbital circle to the ecliptic.
Let circle *DFEG* be described around *B*, and let diameter *FBG* be drawn perpendicular to diameter *DE*. Now let it be understood that the plane of the circle
is so related to the assumed perpendicular plane that lines in the plane of the
circle which are drawn at right angles to *DE* are parallel to one another and to
the plane of the ecliptic; and in the plane of the circle line *FBG* alone has been
drawn.

Now our problem is to find out, by means of the given straight lines *AB* and
BC together with angle *ABE* the given angle of inclinations, how far distant in
latitude the planet is, when, for example, [188ᵃ] it is 45° distant from *E* the point
nearest to the Earth; and, following Ptolemy, we have chosen this position so
that it may become apparent whether the inclination of the orbital circle adds
any difference in longitude to Venus or Mercury. For such differences should be
most visible around the positions midway between the limits *D*, *F*, *E*, and *G*,
because the planet when situated at these four limits has the same longitude as
it would have without declination, as is manifest of itself.

Therefore, as was said, let us assume that
$$\text{arc } EH = 45°;$$
and let *HK* be drawn perpendicular to *BE*, and *KL* and *HM* perpendicular to
the plane of the ecliptic; and let *HB*, *LM*, *AM*, and *AH* be joined. We shall
have the right parallelogram *LKHM*, as *HK* is parallel to the plane of the ecliptic. For angle *LAM* comprehends the additosubtraction in longitude; and angle
HAM comprehends the transit in latitude, since *HM* also falls perpendicular
upon the same plane of the ecliptic. Accordingly, since

angle $HBE = 45°$;
$$HK = \tfrac{1}{2} \text{ ch. } 2 HE = 7,071,$$
where $EB = 10,000$.

Similarly in triangle KBL

angle $BKL = 2\tfrac{1}{2}°$

and

angle $BLK = 90°$,

and

side $BK = 7,071$,
where $BE = 10,000$;

hence

side $KL = 308$

and

side $BL = 7,064$.

But since, by what was shown above,
$$AB : BE = 10,000 : 7,193;$$

then

$$HK = 5,086,$$

and

$$HM = KL = 221,$$

and

$$BL = 5,081;$$

hence, by subtraction,
$$LA = 4,919.$$

Moreover, as in triangle ALM side AL is given, and
$$LM = HK,$$

and

angle $ALM = 90°$;

then

side $AM = 7,075$

and

angle $MAL = 45°57'$,

which is the additosubtraction or great parallax of Venus according to calculation. Similarly, as in triangle MAH

side $AM = 7,075$

and

side $MH = KL$;
angle $MAH = 1°47'$, .

which is the angular declination in latitude.

And if it is not boring to examine what difference in the longitude of Venus is caused by this inclination, let us take triangle ALH, as we understand side LH to be the diagonal of parallelogram $LKHM$. For
$$LH = 5,091,$$
where $AL = 4,919$

and

angle $ALH = 90°$:

hence

side $AH = 7,079$.

Accordingly, as the ratio of the sides is given,

$$\text{angle } HAL = 45°59'.$$

But it has been shown that

$$\text{angle } MAL = 45°57';$$

therefore there is a difference of only $2'$, as was to be shown.

Again, in the case of Mercury, [188^b] with a similar scheme of declination we shall demonstrate the latitudes with the help of a diagram similar to the foregoing: wherein

$$\text{arc } EH = 45°,$$

so that again

$$HK = KB = 7,071,$$
$$\text{where side } AB = 10,000.$$

Accordingly, as can be gathered from the differences in longitude which have already been demonstrated, in this case

$$BK = KH = 2,975,$$
$$\text{where radius } BH = 3,953$$
$$\text{and} \qquad AB = 9,964.$$

And since it has been shown that

$$\text{angle of inclination } ABE = 6°15',$$
$$\text{where 4 rt. angles} = 360°;$$

accordingly, as the angles of right triangle BKL are given,

$$\text{base } KL = 304$$

and

$$\text{perpendicular } BL = 2,778.$$

And so by subtraction

$$AL = 7,186.$$

But also

$$LM = HK = 2,795;$$

accordingly, as in triangle ALM

$$\text{angle } L = 90°$$

and sides AL and LM have been given;

$$\text{side } AM = 7,710$$

and

$$\text{angle } LAM = 21°16',$$

which is the additosubtraction calculated.

Similarly, since in triangle AMH side AM has been given,

$$\text{side } MH = KL$$

and

$$\text{angle } M = 90°,$$

which is comprehended by sides AM and MH;

$$\text{angle } MAH = 2°16',$$

which is the latitude sought for. But if we wish to inquire how much is due to the true and the apparent additosubtraction, let us take LH the diagonal of the parallelogram: we deduce from the sides [of the parallelogram] that

$$LH = 2,811.$$

And

$$AL = 7,186.$$

Hence

$$\text{angle } LAH = 21°23',$$

which is the additosubtraction of apparent movement and has an excess of approximately 7′ over the previously reckoned difference, [angle *LAM*], as was to be shown.

6. On the Second Transit in Latitude of Venus and Mercury According to the Obliquation of Their Orbital Circles in the Apogee and the Perigee

That is enough on the transit in latitude of these planets, which occurs around the mean longitudes of their orbital circles: we have said that these latitudes are called the declinations. Now we must speak of those latitudes which occur at the perigee and apogee and to which the third digression, the deviation, is conjoined—not as the latitudes occur in the three higher planets, but as follows, in order that the third digression may be more easily separated and discerned by reason. For Ptolemy observed that these latitudes appeared greatest at the time when the planets were on the straight lines from the centre of the Earth which touch the orbital circles; and that occurs, [189ᵃ] as we said, at their greatest morning and evening distances from the sun. He found that the northern latitudes of Venus were ⅓° greater than the southern, but that the southern latitudes of Mercury were approximately ½° greater than the northern. But, wishing to reduce the difficulty and labour of calculations, he took in accordance with a certain mean ratio 2½° in different directions of latitude; the latitude themselves subtend these degrees in the circle perpendicular to the ecliptic and around the Earth, against which circle the latitudes are measured—especially as he did not think the error would on that account be very great, as we shall soon show. But if we take only 2½° as the equal digression on each side of the ecliptic and exclude the deviation for the time being, until we have determined the latitudes of the obliquations, our demonstrations will be simpler and easier. Accordingly we must first show that this latitudinal digression is greatest around the point of tangency of the eccentric circle, where the additosubtractions in longitude are also greatest.

For let there be drawn the common section of the plane of the ecliptic and the plane of the eccentric circle of Venus or Mercury—the common section through

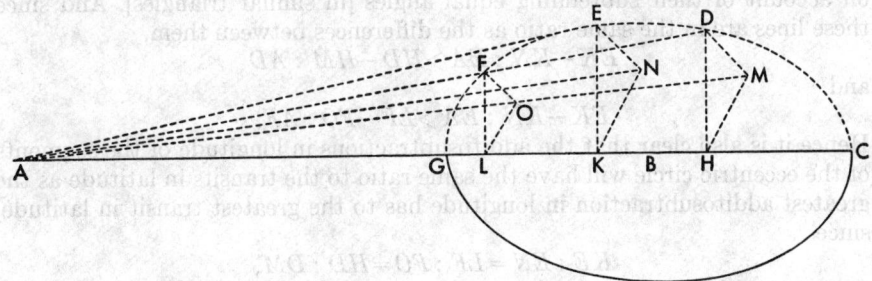

the apogee and the perigee; and on it let *A* be taken as the position of the Earth and *B* as the centre of eccentric circle *CDEFG* which is inclined to the ecliptic, so that straight lines drawn anywhere at right angles to *CG* comprehend angles equal to the obliquation; and let *AE* be drawn tangent to the circle, and *AD* as cutting it somewhere. Moreover, from points *D*, *E*, and *F* let *DH*, *EK*, and *FL* be drawn perpendicular to line *CG*, and *DM*, *EN*, and *FO* perpendicular to the underlying plane of the ecliptic; and let MH, NK, and OL be joined, and also AN and AOM; for AOM is a straight line, since its three points are each in two planes—namely, in the plane of the ecliptic and in the plane ADM perpendicular to the plane of the ecliptic.

Accordingly since in the present obliquation the angles HAM and KAN comprehend the additosubtractions of these planets; and the angles DAM and EAN are the digressions in latitude: [189^b] I say, first, that angle EAN, the angle situated at the point of tangency, where the additosubtraction in longitude is also approximately greatest, is the greatest of all the angles of latitude.

For since angle EAK is greater than any of the others,

$$KE : EA > HD : DA$$

and

$$KE : EA > LF : FA.$$

But

$$EK : EN = HD : DM = LF : FO.$$

For, as we said,

$$\text{angle } EKN = \text{angle } HDM = \text{angle } LFO;$$

and

$$\text{angle } M = \text{angle } N = \text{angle } O = 90°.$$

Therefore

$$NE : EA > MD : DA$$

and

$$NE : EA > DF : FA;$$

and again

$$\text{angle } DMA = \text{angle } ENA = \text{angle } OFA = 90°.$$

Accordingly

$$\text{angle } EAN > \text{angle } DAM,$$

and angle EAN is greater than each of the other angles constructed in this way. Whence it is manifest that among the differences occurring between the additosubtractions and arising from the obliquation in longitude, the difference which is determined at point E in the greatest transit is the greatest. For

$$HD : HM = KE : KN = LF : FO,$$

on account of their subtending equal angles [in similar triangles]. And since these lines are in the same ratio as the differences between them,

$$EK - KN : EA > HD - HM : AD$$

and

$$EK - KN : EA > LF - FO : AF.$$

Hence it is also clear that the additosubtractions in longitude of the segments of the eccentric circle will have the same ratio to the transits in latitude as the greatest additosubtraction in longitude has to the greatest transit in latitude, since

$$KE : EN = LF : FO = HD : DM,$$

—as was set before us to be demonstrated.

7. How Great the Angles of Obliquation of Venus and Mercury Are

Having first noted all that, let us see how great an angle is comprehended by the obliquation of the planes of either planet; and let us repeat what was said before: each planet has 5° between its greatest and least distance [in latitude], so that for the most part they become more northern or southern at contrary times and in accordance with their position on the orbital circle, for when the transit or manifest difference of Venus makes a digression greater or less than 5° through the apogee or perigee of the eccentric circle, the transit of Mercury however is more or less at ½°.

[190ª] Accordingly as before, let ABC be the common section of the ecliptic

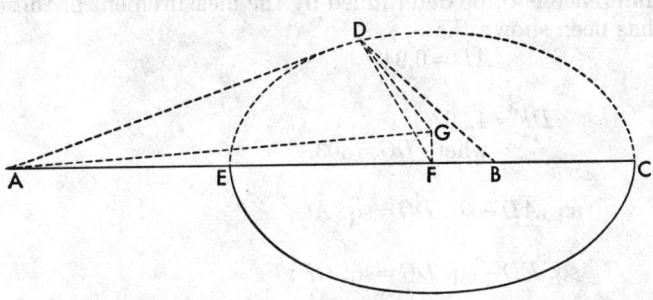

and the eccentric circle; and let the orbital circle of the planet be described around centre B oblique to the plane of the ecliptic in the way set forth. Now from the centre of the Earth let straight line AD be drawn touching the orbital circle at point D; and from D let DF be drawn perpendicular to CBE and DG perpendicular to the underlying plane of the ecliptic; and let BD, FG, and AG be joined. Moreover, let it be assumed that

angle $DAG = 2\frac{1}{2}°$,

where 4 rt. angles $= 360°$,

which is half the difference in latitude set forth for each planet.

Our problem is to find how great the angle of obliquation between the planes is, *i.e.*, to find angle DFG.

Accordingly, since in the case of the planet Venus it has been shown that

the greater distance, at the apogee $= 10,208$,

where radius $= 7,193$,

and

the lesser, at the perigee $= 9,792$,

and

the mean distance $= 10,000$,

which Ptolemy decided to assume in this demonstration, as he wished to avoid labour and difficulty and to make an epitome; for where the extremes do not cause any great difference, it is better to use the mean. Accordingly,

$AB : BD = 10,000 : 7,193$,

and

angle $ADB = 90°$.

Therefore

side $AD = 6,947$.

Again, since

angle $DAG = 2\frac{1}{2}°$

and

angle $AGD = 90°$;

accordingly, the angles of triangle AGD are given, and

side $DG = 303$,

where $AD = 6,947$.

Thus also, two sides DF and DG have been given, and
$$\text{angle } DGF = 90°;$$
hence
$$\text{angle } DFG = 3°29';$$
which is the angle of inclination or obliquation. But since the excess of angle DAF over angle FAG comprehends the difference made by the parallax in longitude, hence that difference is to be determined by the measurement of those magnitudes. For it has been shown that
$$AD = 6,947$$
and
$$DF = 4,997,$$
$$\text{where } DG = 303.$$
Now
$$\text{sq. } AD - \text{sq. } DG = \text{sq. } AG,$$
and
$$\text{sq. } FD - \text{sq. } DG = \text{sq. } GF;$$
therefore
$$AG = 6,940$$
and
$$FG = 4,988.$$
But
$$FG = 7,187,$$
$$\text{where } AG = 10,000,$$
and
$$\text{angle } FAG = 45°57';$$
and
$$DF = 7,193,$$
$$\text{where } AD = 10,000,$$
and
$$\text{angle } DAF = 46°.$$
Therefore at the greatest obliquation the additosubtraction of the parallax is deficient by approximately $3'$. [190$^\text{b}$] Now it was made clear that at the mean apsis the angle of inclination of the orbital circles was $2\frac{1}{2}°$; but here it has increased by approximately $1°$, which the first movement of libration—of which we have spoken—has added to it.

There is a similar demonstration in the case of Mercury. For the greatest distance of the orbital circle from the Earth is 10,948, where the radius of the orbital circle is 3,573; the least is 9,052; and the mean between these is 10,000. Moreover
$$AB : BD = 10,000 : 3,573.$$
Therefore
$$\text{side } AD = 9,340;$$
and since
$$BD : BF = AB : AD;$$
therefore
$$DF = 3,337.$$
And since
$$\text{angle } DAG = 2\frac{1}{2}°,$$

which is the angle of latitude;
$$DG = 407,$$
$$\text{where } DF = 3,337.$$
And so in triangle DFG the ratio of these two sides is given,
and
$$\text{angle } G = 90°;$$
hence
$$\text{angle } DFG = 7°.$$
And that is the angle of inclination or obliquation between the orbital circle of Mercury and the plane of the ecliptic. But it has been shown that around the mean longitudes or quadrants the angle of inclination was 6°15′. Therefore 45′ have now been added to it by the movement of libration.

There is a similar argument in picking out the additosubtractions and their differences, after it has been shown that
$$DG = 407,$$
$$\text{where } AD = 9,340$$
$$\text{and } DF = 3,337.$$
Accordingly,
$$\text{sq. } AD - \text{sq. } DG = \text{sq. } AG,$$
and
$$\text{sq. } DF - \text{sq. } DG = \text{sq. } FG.$$
Therefore
$$AG = 9,331$$
and
$$FG = 3,314;$$
hence it is inferred that
$$\text{angle } GAF = 20°48′,$$
which is the additosubtraction, and
$$\text{angle } DAF = 20°56′,$$
which is approximately 8′ greater than the angle proportionate to the obliquation. It still remains for us to see if such angles of obliquation and the latitudes in accordance with the greatest and least distance of the orbital circle are found to be in conformity with those gathered from observation.

Wherefore once more with the same diagram; and first at the greatest distance of the orbital circle of Venus, let
$$AB : BD = 10,208 : 7,193.$$
And since
$$\text{angle } ADB = 90°;$$
$$DF = 5,102.$$
[191ᵃ] But it has been found that
$$\text{angle } DFG = 3°29′,$$
which is the angle of obliquation; hence
$$\text{side } DG = 309,$$
$$\text{where } AD = 7,238.$$
Accordingly,
$$DG = 427,$$
$$\text{where } AD = 10,000;$$
whence it is concluded that at the greatest distance from the Earth
$$\text{angle } DAG = 2°27′.$$

But at the least distance

$$AB = 9,792,$$

where radius of orbital circle $= 7,193$.

And

$$AD = 6,644,$$

which is perpendicular to the radius; and similarly, since

$$BD : DF = AB : AD,$$
$$DF = 4,883.$$

But

angle $DFG = 3°28'$;

therefore

$$DG = 297,$$

where $AD = 6,644$.

And as the sides of the triangle have been given,

angle $DAG = 2°34'$.

But neither 3' nor 4' is large enough to be measured by means of an astrolabe; therefore that which was considered to be the greatest latitude of obliquation of the planet Venus is correct.

Again, let the greatest distance of the orbital circle of Mercury be taken, *i.e.*, let

$$AB : AD = 10,948 : 3,573;$$

consequently, by demonstrations similar to the foregoing, we still infer that

$$AD = 9,452$$

and

$$DF = 3,085.$$

But here too we have it recorded that

angle $DFG = 7°$,

which is the angle of obliquation; hence

$$DG = 376,$$

where $DF = 3,085$

and $DA = 9,452$.

Accordingly, as the sides of right triangle DAG are given,

angle $DAG = 2°17'$,

which is the greatest digression in latitude. But at the least distance

$$AB : BD = 9,052 : 3,573;$$

therefore

$$AD = 8,317$$

and

$$DF = 3,283.$$

Now since by reason of this same [obliquation]

$$DF : DG = 3,283 : 400,$$

where $AD = 8,317$;

whence

angle $DAG = 2°45'$.

Accordingly there is a difference of at least 13' between the $2\frac{1}{2}°$ of the digression in latitude according to the mean ratio and the digression at the apogee; and at the most a difference of 15' between the mean digression and that at the perigee. And in making our calculations according to the mean ratio we shall use $\frac{1}{4}°$ as the difference; for it is not sensibly diverse from the observed differences.

Having demonstrated these things and also that the greatest additosub-tractions in longitude have the same ratio to the greatest transit in latitude as the additosubtractions in the remaining sections of the orbital circle have to the particular transits in latitude, we shall have at hand the numbers of all the latitudes, which occur on account of the obliquation of the orbital circle of Venus and Mercury. But we have calculated only those latitudes which occur midway between the apogee and the perigee, as we said; and it was shown that the greatest of these latitudes is $2\frac{1}{2}°$, and the greatest [191^b] additosubtraction in the case of Venus is 46° and that in the case of Mercury about 22°. And in the tables of irregular movements we have already placed the additosubtrac-tions opposite the particular sections of the orbital circles. Accordingly in the case of each of the two planets we shall take from the $2\frac{1}{2}°$ a part proportionate to the excess of the greatest additosubtraction over each of the lesser additosub-tractions; we shall inscribe it in the table to be drawn up below with all its num-bers; and in this way we shall have unfolded all the particular latitudes of the obliquations which occur when the Earth is at their highest apsis and at their lowest—just as we set forth the latitudes of the declinations in the case of the mean quadrants and mean longitudes. The latitudes which occur between these four limits can be unfolded by the subtle art of mathematics with the help of the proposed hypothesis of circles but not without labour. Now Ptolemy—who is compendious wherever he can be so—seeing that each of these aspects of lati-tude as a whole and in all its parts increased and decreased proportionally, like the latitude of the moon, accordingly took twelve parts of it, since their greatest latitude is 5° and that number is a twelfth part of 60, and made proportional minutes out of them, to be used not only in the case of these two planets but also in that of the three higher planets, as will be made clear below.

8. On the Third Aspect of the Latitude of Venus and Mercury, Which They Call the Deviation

Now that these things have been set forth, it still remains to say something about the third movement in latitude, which is the deviation. The ancients, who held the Earth down at the centre of the world, believed that the deviation took place by reason of the inclination of an eccentric circle which has an epicycle and which revolves around the centre of the Earth—the deviation occurring most greatly when the epicycle is at the apogee or perigee and being always $\frac{1}{6}°$ to the north in the case of Venus and $\frac{3}{4}°$ to the south in the case of Mercury, as we said before. It is not however sufficiently clear whether they meant the in-clination of the orbital circles to be equal and always the same: for their num-bers indicate that, when they order a sixth part of the proportional minutes to be taken as the deviation of Venus, and three parts out of four as that of Mer-cury. That does not hold, unless the angle of inclination always remains [192^a] the same, as is demanded by the ratio of the minutes, which they take as their base. But if the angle remains the same, it is impossible to understand how the latitude of the planets suddenly springs back from the common section into the same latitude which it had just left, unless you say that takes place in the manner of refraction of light, as in optics. But here we are dealing with move-ment, which is not instantaneous but is by its own nature measured by time. Accordingly we must acknowledge that a libration such as we have expounded is present in those [circles] and makes the parts of the circle move over in different directions: And that necessarily follows, as the numbers differ $\frac{1}{5}°$ in the case of Mercury. That should seem less surprising, if in accordance with our hypothesis this latitude is variable and not wholly simple but does not produce any apparent error, as is to be seen in the case of all differences, as follows:

For in the plane perpendicular to the ecliptic let [*ABC*] be the common section [of the two planes], and in the common section let *A* be the centre of the Earth and *B* the centre of the circle *CDF* at greatest or least distance from the

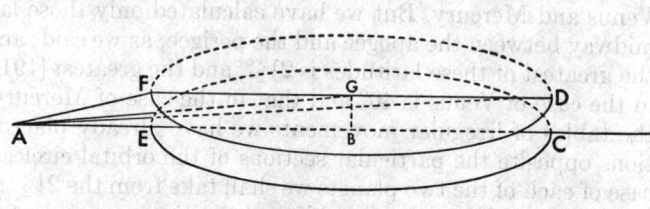

Earth and as it were through the poles of the inclined orbital circle. And when the centre of the orbital circle is at the apogee or the perigee, *i.e.*, on line *AB*, the planet, wherever it is, is at its greatest deviation, in accordance with the circle parallel to the orbital circle; and *DF* is the diameter parallel to *CBE*, the diameter of the orbital circle. And *DF* and *CBE* are put down as the common sections of the planes perpendicular to plane *CDF*. Now let *DF* be bisected at *G*, which will be the centre of the parallel circle; and let *BG*, *AG*, *AD*, and *AF* be joined. Let us put down that

$$\text{angle } BAG = 10',$$

as in the greatest deviation of Venus. Accordingly, in triangle *ABG*

$$\text{angle } B = 90°;$$

and we have the following ratio for the sides:

$$AB : BG = 10,000 : 29.$$

But

$$\text{line } ABC = 17,193;$$

and by subtraction

$$AE = 2,807;$$

and

$$\frac{1}{2} \text{ ch. } 2 \, CD = \frac{1}{2} \text{ ch. } 2 \, EF = BG.$$

Accordingly

$$\text{angle } CAD = 6'$$

and

$$\text{angle } EAF = 15'.$$

Now

$$\text{angle } BAG - \text{angle } CAD = 4',$$

while

$$\text{angle } EAF - \text{angle } BAG = 5';$$

and those differences can be neglected on account of their smallness. Accordingly, when the Earth is situated at its apogee or perigee, the apparent deviation of Venus will be slightly more or less than 10', [192[b]] in whatever part of its orbital circle the planet is.

But in the case of Mercury when

$$\text{angle } BAG = 45',$$

and

$$AB : BG = 10,000 : 131,$$

and
$$ABC = 13,573,$$

and by subtraction
$$AE = 6,827;$$

then
$$\text{angle } CAD = 33'$$

and
$$\text{angle } EAF = 70'.$$

Accordingly, angle CAD has a deficiency of 12', and angle EAF has an excess of 25'. But these differences are practically obliterated beneath the rays of the sun before Mercury emerges into our sight, wherefore the ancients considered only its apparent and as it were simple deviation. But if anyone wishes to examine with least labour the precise ratio of their passages when hidden beneath the sun, we shall show how that takes place, as follows. We shall take Mercury as our example, because it makes a more considerable deviation than Venus.

For let AB be the straight line in the common section of the orbital circle of

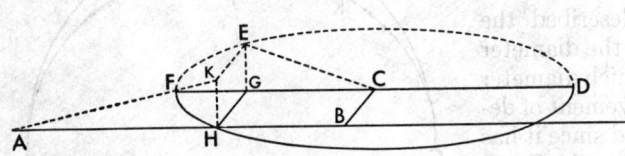

the planet and the ecliptic, while the Earth — which is at A—is at the apogee or the perigee of the planet's orbital circle. Now let us put down that
$$AB = 10,000$$
indifferently, as if the mean between greatest and least distance, as we did in the case of the obliquation. Now around centre C let there be described circle DEF, which is parallel to the eccentric orbital circle at a distance CB; and the planet on this parallel circle be understood as being at this time at its greatest deviation. Let DCF be the diameter of this circle, which is also necessarily parallel to AB; and DCF and AB are in the same plane perpendicular to the orbital circle of the planet. Therefore, for example, let
$$\text{arc } EF = 45°,$$
in relation to which we shall examine the deviation of the planet. And let EG be drawn perpendicular to CF, and EK and GH perpendicular to the underlying plane of the orbital circle. Let the right parallelogram be completed by joining HK; and let AE, AK, and EC also be joined.

Now in the greatest deviation of Mercury
$$BC = 131,$$
$$\text{where } AB = 10,000.$$

And
$$CE = 3,573;$$
and the angles of the right triangle EGC are given; hence
$$\text{side } EG = KH = 2526.$$

And since
$$BH = EG = CG,$$
$$AH = BA - BH = 7,474.$$

Accordingly, since in triangle AHK

$$\text{angle } H = 90°$$

and the sides of comprehending angle H are given;

$$\text{side } AK = 7,889.$$

But

$$\text{side } KE = CB = GH = 131.$$

Accordingly, since in triangle [193ᵃ] AKE the two sides AK and KE comprehending the right angle K have been given, angle KAE is given, which answers to the deviation we were seeking for the postulated arc EF and differs very little from the angle observed. We shall do similarly in the case of Venus and the other planets; and we shall inscribe our findings in the subjoined table.

Having made this exposition, we shall work out proportional minutes for the deviations between these limits. For let ABC be the eccentric orbital circle of Venus or Mercury; and let A and C be the nodes of this movement in latitude, and B the limit of greatest deviation. And with B as centre let there be described the small circle DFG, with the diameter DBF across it, along which diameter the libration of the movement of deviation takes place. And since it has been laid down that when the Earth is at the apogee or the perigee of the eccentric orbital circle of the planet,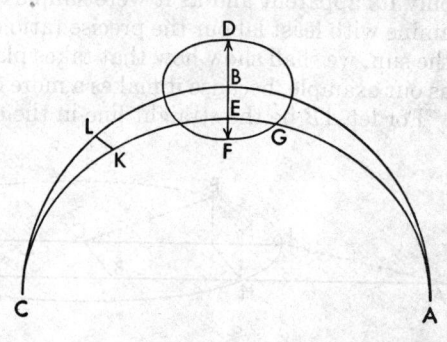
the planet itself is at its greatest deviation, namely in point F, where at this time the circle carrying the planet touches the small circle. Now let the Earth be somewhere removed from the apogee or perigee of the eccentric circle of the planet; and in accordance with this movement let a similar arc FG be taken on the small circle. Let circle AGC be described, which bears the planet and will cut the small circle, and the diameter DF at point E; and let the planet be taken as being on this circle at point K in accordance with arc EK which is by hypothesis similar to arc FG; and let KL be drawn perpendicular to circle ABC.

Our problem is to find by means of FG, EK, and BE the magnitude of KL, i.e., the distance of the planet from circle ABC. For since by means of arc FG arc EG will be given as a straight line hardly different from a circular or convex line, and EF will similarly be given in terms of the parts, whereof BF and the remainder BE will be given; for

$$BF : BE = \text{ch. } 2\,CE : \text{ch. } 2\,CK = BE : KL.$$

Accordingly if we put down BF and the radius of circle CE in terms of the same number, sixty, we shall have from them the number which picks out BE. When that number has been multiplied by itself and the product divided by sixty, we shall have KL, the minutes proportional to arc EK; and we shall inscribe them similarly in the fifth and last column of the table which follows:

LATITUDES OF SATURN, JUPITER, AND MARS

| Common Numbers | | SATURN | | | | JUPITER | | | | MARS | | | | Proportional Minutes | |
| Northern | Southern | Northern | Southern | Northern | Southern | |
Deg.	Deg.	Deg.	Min.	Deg.	Min.	Deg.	Min.	Deg.	Min.	Deg.	Min.	Deg.	Min.	Deg.	Min.
3	357	2	3	2	2	1	6	1	5	0	6	0	5	59	48
6	354	2	4	2	2	1	7	1	5	0	7	0	5	59	36
9	351	2	4	2	3	1	7	1	5	0	9	0	6	59	6
12	348	2	5	2	3	1	8	1	6	0	9	0	6	58	36
15	345	2	5	2	3	1	8	1	6	0	10	0	8	57	48
18	342	2	6	2	3	1	8	1	6	0	11	0	8	57	0
21	339	2	6	2	4	1	9	1	7	0	12	0	9	56	48
24	336	2	7	2	4	1	9	1	7	0	13	0	9	54	36
27	333	2	8	2	5	1	10	1	8	0	14	0	10	53	18
30	330	2	8	2	5	1	10	1	8	0	14	0	11	52	0
33	327	2	9	2	6	1	11	1	9	0	15	0	11	50	12
36	324	2	10	2	7	1	11	1	9	0	16	0	12	48	24
39	321	2	10	2	7	1	12	1	10	0	17	0	12	46	24
42	318	2	11	2	8	1	12	1	10	0	18	0	13	44	24
45	315	2	11	2	9	1	13	1	11	0	19	0	15	42	12
48	312	2	12	2	10	1	13	1	11	0	20	0	16	40	0
51	309	2	13	2	11	1	14	1	12	0	22	0	18	37	36
54	306	2	14	2	12	1	14	1	13	0	23	0	20	35	12
57	303	2	15	2	13	1	15	1	14	0	25	0	22	32	36
60	300	2	16	2	15	1	16	1	15	0	27	0	24	30	0
63	297	2	17	2	16	1	17	1	17	0	29	0	25	27	12
66	294	2	18	2	18	1	18	1	18	0	31	0	27	24	24
69	291	2	20	2	19	1	19	1	19	0	33	0	29	21	24
72	288	2	21	2	21	1	21	1	21	0	35	0	31	18	24
75	285	2	22	2	22	1	22	1	22	0	37	0	34	15	24
78	282	2	24	2	24	1	24	1	24	0	40	0	37	12	24
81	279	2	25	2	26	1	25	1	25	0	42	0	39	9	24
84	276	2	27	2	27	1	27	1	27	0	45	0	42	6	24
87	273	2	28	2	28	1	28	1	28	0	48	0	45	3	12
90	270	2	30	2	30	1	30	1	30	0	51	0	49	0	0
93	267	2	31	2	31	1	31	1	31	0	55	0	52	3	12
96	264	2	33	2	33	1	33	1	33	0	59	0	56	6	24
99	261	2	34	2	34	1	34	1	34	1	2	1	0	9	9
102	258	2	36	2	36	1	36	1	36	1	6	1	4	12	12
105	255	2	37	2	37	1	37	1	37	1	11	1	8	15	15
108	252	2	39	2	39	1	39	1	39	1	15	1	12	18	18
111	249	2	40	2	40	1	40	1	40	1	19	1	17	21	21
114	246	2	42	2	42	1	42	1	42	1	25	1	22	24	24
117	243	2	43	2	43	1	43	1	43	1	31	1	28	27	12
120	240	2	45	2	45	1	44	1	44	1	36	1	34	30	0
123	237	2	46	2	46	1	46	1	46	1	41	1	40	32	37
126	234	2	47	2	48	1	47	1	47	1	47	1	47	35	12
129	231	2	49	2	49	1	49	1	49	1	54	1	55	37	36
132	228	2	50	2	51	1	50	1	51	2	2	2	5	40	6
135	225	2	52	2	53	1	53	1	53	2	10	2	15	42	12
138	222	2	53	2	54	1	52	1	54	2	19	2	26	44	24
141	219	2	54	2	55	1	53	1	55	2	29	2	38	47	24
144	216	2	55	2	56	1	55	1	57	2	37	2	48	48	24
147	213	2	56	2	57	1	56	1	58	2	47	3	4	50	12
150	210	2	57	2	58	1	58	1	59	2	51	3	20	52	0
153	207	2	58	2	59	1	59	2	1	3	12	3	32	53	18
156	204	2	59	3	0	2	0	2	2	3	23	3	52	54	36
159	201	2	59	3	1	2	1	2	3	3	34	4	13	55	48
162	198	3	0	3	2	2	2	2	4	3	46	4	36	57	0
165	195	3	0	3	2	2	2	2	5	3	57	5	0	57	48
168	192	3	1	3	3	2	3	2	5	4	9	5	23	58	36
171	189	3	1	3	3	2	3	2	6	4	17	5	48	59	6
174	186	3	2	3	4	2	4	2	6	4	23	6	15	59	36
177	183	3	2	3	4	2	4	2	7	4	27	6	35	59	48
180	180	3	2	3	5	2	4	2	7	4	30	6	50	60	0

LATITUDES OF VENUS AND MERCURY

Common Numbers		VENUS				MERCURY				Deviation of Venus		Deviation of Mercury		Proportional Minutes of the Deviation	
		Declination		Obliquation		Declination		Obliquation							
Deg.	Deg.	Deg.	Min.	Deg.	Min.	Deg.	Min.	Deg.	Min.	Deg.	Min.	Deg.	Min.	Min.	Min.
3	357	1	2	0	4	0	7	1	45	0	5	0	33	59	36
6	354	1	2	0	8	0	7	1	45	0	11	0	33	59	12
9	351	1	1	0	12	0	7	1	45	0	16	0	33	58	25
12	348	1	1	0	16	0	7	1	44	0	22	0	33	57	14
15	345	1	0	0	21	0	7	1	44	0	27	0	33	55	41
18	342	1	0	0	25	0	7	1	43	0	33	0	33	54	9
21	339	0	59	0	29	0	7	1	42	0	38	0	33	52	12
24	336	0	59	0	33	0	7	1	40	0	44	0	34	49	43
27	333	0	58	0	37	0	7	1	38	0	49	0	34	47	21
30	330	0	57	0	41	0	8	1	36	0	55	0	34	45	4
33	327	0	56	0	45	0	8	1	34	1	0	0	34	42	0
36	324	0	55	0	49	0	8	1	30	1	6	0	34	39	15
39	321	0	53	0	53	0	8	1	27	1	11	0	35	35	53
42	318	0	51	0	57	0	8	1	23	1	16	0	35	32	51
45	315	0	49	1	1	0	8	1	19	1	21	0	35	29	41
48	312	0	46	1	5	0	8	1	15	1	26	0	36	23	40
51	309	0	44	1	9	0	8	1	11	1	31	0	36	26	34
54	306	0	41	1	13	0	8	1	8	1	35	0	36	30	39
57	303	0	38	1	17	0	8	1	4	1	40	0	37	17	40
60	300	0	35	1	20	0	8	0	59	1	44	0	38	15	0
63	297	0	32	1	24	0	8	0	54	1	48	0	38	12	20
66	294	0	29	1	28	0	9	0	49	1	52	0	39	9	55
69	291	0	26	1	32	0	9	0	44	1	56	0	39	7	38
72	288	0	23	1	35	0	9	0	38	2	0	0	40	5	39
75	285	0	20	1	38	0	9	0	32	2	3	0	41	3	57
78	282	0	16	1	42	0	9	0	26	2	7	0	42	2	34
81	279	0	12	1	46	0	9	0	21	2	10	0	42	1	28
84	276	0	8	1	50	0	10	0	16	2	14	0	43	0	40
87	273	0	4	1	54	0	10	0	8	2	17	0	44	0	10
90	270	0	0	1	57	0	10	0	0	2	20	0	45	0	0
93	267	0	5	2	0	0	10	0	8	2	23	0	45	0	10
96	264	0	10	2	3	0	10	0	15	2	25	0	46	0	40
99	261	0	15	2	6	0	10	0	23	2	27	0	47	1	28
102	258	0	20	2	9	0	11	0	31	2	28	0	48	2	34
105	255	0	26	2	12	0	11	0	40	2	29	0	48	3	57
108	252	0	32	2	15	0	11	0	48	2	29	0	49	5	39
111	249	0	38	2	17	0	11	0	57	2	30	0	50	7	38
114	246	0	44	2	20	0	11	1	6	2	30	0	51	9	55
117	243	0	50	2	22	0	11	1	16	2	30	0	51	12	20
120	240	0	59	2	24	0	12	1	25	2	29	0	52	15	0
123	237	1	8	2	26	0	12	1	35	2	28	0	53	17	40
126	234	1	18	2	27	0	12	1	45	2	26	0	54	20	39
129	231	1	28	2	29	0	12	1	55	2	23	0	55	23	34
132	228	1	38	2	30	0	12	2	6	2	20	0	56	26	40
135	225	1	48	2	30	0	13	2	16	2	16	0	57	29	41
138	222	1	59	2	30	0	13	2	27	2	11	0	57	32	51
141	219	2	11	2	29	0	13	2	37	2	6	0	58	35	53
144	216	2	25	2	28	0	13	2	47	2	0	0	59	39	25
147	213	2	43	2	26	0	13	2	57	1	53	1	0	42	0
150	210	3	3	2	22	0	13	3	7	1	46	1	1	45	4
153	207	3	23	2	18	0	13	3	17	1	38	1	2	47	21
156	204	3	44	2	12	0	14	3	26	1	29	1	3	49	43
159	201	4	5	2	4	0	14	3	34	1	20	1	4	52	12
162	198	4	26	1	55	0	14	3	42	1	10	1	5	54	9
165	195	4	49	1	42	0	14	3	48	0	59	1	6	55	41
168	192	5	13	1	27	0	14	3	54	0	48	1	7	57	14
171	189	5	36	1	9	0	14	3	58	0	36	1	7	58	25
174	186	5	52	0	48	0	14	4	2	0	24	1	8	59	12
177	183	6	7	0	25	0	14	4	4	0	12	1	9	59	36
180	180	6	22	0	0	0	14	4	5	0	0	1	10	60	0

9. On the Calculation of the Latitudes of the Five Wandering Stars

[195^b] Now this is the method of calculating the latitudes of the five wandering stars by means of these tables. For in the case of Saturn, Jupiter, and Mars we shall take the discrete, or corrected, anomaly of the eccentric circle among the common numbers: in the case of Mars, the anomaly as is; in that of Jupiter, after the subtraction of 20°; and in that of Saturn, after the addition of 50°. Accordingly we shall note the numbers which occur in the region of the 60's, in the proportional minutes placed in the last column. Similarly by means of the corrected anomaly of parallax we shall determine the proper number of each planet, corresponding to the latitude: the first and northern latitude, if the proportional minutes are in the first half of the column—which happens when the anomaly of the eccentric circle is less than 90° or more than 270°; the second and southern latitude, if the proportional minutes are in the second half of the column, i.e., if the anomaly of the eccentric circle, whereby the table was entered upon, was more than 90° or less than 270°. Accordingly if we adjust one of these latitudes to its 60's, the result will be the distance north or south of the ecliptic in accordance with the denomination of the circles assumed.

But in the case of Venus and Mercury the three latitudes of declination, obliquation, and deviation, which are marked down separately, are to be taken first by means of the corrected anomaly of parallax, except that in the case of Mercury one tenth of the obliquation is to be subtracted, if the anomaly of the eccentric circle and its number are found in the first column of the table, or merely added, if in the second column of the table; and the remainder or sum is to be kept.

And we must discern whether their denominations are northern or southern, since if the corrected anomaly of parallax is in the apogeal semicircle, i.e., is less than 90° or more than 270° and the anomaly of the eccentric circle is also less than a semicircle; or again, if the anomaly of parallax is in the perigeal arc, i.e., is more than 90° and less than 270° and the anomaly of the eccentric circle is greater than a semicircle; the declination of Venus will be northern and that of Mercury southern. But if the anomaly of parallax is in the perigeal arc and the anomaly of the eccentric circle is less than a semicircle; [196^a] or if the anomaly of parallax is in the apogeal arc and the anomaly of the eccentric circle is more than a semicircle; conversely the declination of Venus will be southern and that of Mercury northern. But in the case of the obliquation, if the anomaly of parallax is less than a semicircle and the anomaly of the eccentric circle is apogeal; or if the anomaly of parallax is greater than a semicircle and the anomaly of the eccentric circle is perigeal; the obliquation of Venus will be to the north and that of Mercury to the south; and vice versa. But the deviations of Venus always remain northern and those of Mercury southern.

Then, corresponding to the corrected anomaly of the eccentric circle, the proportional minutes should be taken which are common to all the five planets, although they are ascribed to the three higher planets. These are assigned to the obliquation and lastly to the deviation. After this, when we have added 90° to the same anomaly of the eccentric circle, we shall once more take the sum and find the common proportional minutes which correspond to it and assign them to the latitude of declination. Having placed these things in this order, we shall adjust each of the three particular latitudes set forth to their proportional minutes; and the result will be the corrected latitude for the position and time, so that at last we may have the sum of the three latitudes of the two planets. If all the latitudes are of one denomination, they are added together; but if not, only the two are added which have the same denomination; and according as the sum is greater or less than the third latitude, which is different from them, there will be a subtraction; and the remainder will be the predominant latitude sought for.

Johannes Kepler

EPITOME OF COPERNICAN
ASTRONOMY

BIOGRAPHICAL NOTE

JOHANNES KEPLER, 1571-1630

KEPLER was born December 27, 1571, at Weil in the Duchy of Wurttemberg. He came from a noble but poverty-stricken family, and, as he later noted, was himself a premature and sickly son such as the planets had foretold. His father was a soldier of fortune and frequently away from home until he acquired a tavern in 1577. Kepler, in the periods when he was not working in the tavern, attended a German elementary school at Leonberg, but domestic bankruptcy after three years led to his being withdrawn and sent to labor in the fields.

Kepler's intellectual gifts were considered to indicate that he had a theological vocation, and in 1584 he was sent as a charity student to the Protestant seminary at Adelberg. Two years later he transferred to the college at Maulbronn. A brilliant examination for the bachelor's degree in 1588 enabled Kepler to go to the University of Tübingen, where he prepared for the master's degree in philosophy. As a part of the regular course of studies, he learned astronomy with Mästlin, who introduced him to the work of Copernicus. He wrote a paper on the reconciliation of the Copernican view with Sacred Scripture, but his principal desire was to enter the ministry. It was with considerable reluctance that he was finally persuaded in 1594 to accept the first post offered to him, the chair of astronomy at the Lutheran school of Graz.

While filling his office as astronomer at Graz, Kepler began to speculate on the order and distances of the planets. On July 19, 1595, he carefully noted down his "discovery" that "God in creating the universe and regulating the order of the cosmos had in view the five regular bodies of geometry as known since the days of Pythagoras and Plato." He embodied his theory on these relations in his first published work on astronomy, entitled the *Precursor of Cosmographic Dissertations or the Cosmographic Mystery*, which appeared late in 1596. The book brought its author much fame and a friendly correspondence with the two most eminent astronomers of the time, Tycho Brahe and Galileo.

In 1598 the Catholic archduke of Styria issued an edict of banishment against Protestant preachers and professors, and Kepler fled to the Hungarian border. Although reinstated in his post by the favor of the Jesuits, Kepler gladly accepted an offer from Tycho Brahe in 1600 to serve as his assistant at the observatory near Prague. A year later, upon the death of Tycho, Kepler was appointed his successor as imperial mathematician.

In his new post Kepler inherited the records of Tycho's observations. Utilizing these records and the results of his own observations at the Prague observatory, Kepler published a series of works which soon gained him a European reputation. To satisfy the astrological proclivities of the emperor, he first wrote a treatise *On the More Certain Foundations of Astrology* (1602). His prognostications were highly successful; commenting on this fact, he remarked that "Nature, which has conferred upon every animal the means of subsistence, has given astrology as an adjunct and ally to astronomy." A preliminary study of optics resulted in the publication of his *Optical Part of Astronomy* (1604), which, as completed by the *Dioptrics* (1611), contained important discoveries in the theory of vision. But Kepler's great work during these years was the elaboration of a new theory of the planets. Inspired by Gilbert's book on the magnet and his own investigations of the orbit of Mars, which he had been studying since his first meeting with Tycho, Kepler published in 1609 his *New Aetiological Astronomy or Celestial Physics together with Commentaries on the Movements of the Planet Mars*, in which he enunciated the laws of elliptical orbits and of equal areas.

Meanwhile in his personal life Kepler was harassed upon every side. His salary was continually in arrears; his wife "fell a prey to despondent melancholy, . . . became seriously ill with Hungarian fever, epilepsy, and fits," and finally died; his three children succumbed to smallpox; and Prague itself became a battlefield. After "the terrible year of 1611," Kepler, while still retaining the position of court astronomer, gratefully accepted the offer to become mathematician to Upper Austria. He moved to Linz, re-married in 1613, and resumed his astronomical investigations; but his personal fortunes showed little improvement.

The twelve years of Kepler's residence at Linz saw the publication of many of his most important astronomical works. The *Harmonies of the World* appeared in 1619. Its dedication to James I of England was acknowledged with an invitation to that country, but Kepler, despite his distraught circumstances, refused to leave, as two years previously he had declined the chair of mathematics at Bologna. For some time he had been working upon the project of comprehending the whole scheme of the heavens in one great treatise to be called *Hipparchus*. The difficulties presented by the lunar theory finally compelled him to abandon his intention, and he recast a portion of his materials in the form of a dialogue intended for the general public, which was published as the *Epitome of Astronomy* (1618-21). In addition to these works and many essays dealing with chronology, Kepler devoted years to preparing for publication the astronomical tables compiled from his own observations and those of Tycho. In spite of financial difficulties and civil and religious conflict, they finally appeared in 1627 under the title of the *Rudolphine Tables*.

By this time Kepler's claims upon the insolvent imperial treasury amounted to twelve thousand florins. In 1628, under an arrangement with the emperor, the debt was transferred to Duke Wallenstein of Friedland, and Kepler moved with his family to Sagan in Silesia. Wallenstein's promises were only partially fulfilled, and in 1630 Kepler went to Ratisbon to present his case to the Diet. Shortly after his arrival he was taken ill with a fever and died on November 15. He was buried at Ratisbon. The epitaph, of his own composition, reads: "I had measured the heavens; now I measure earth's shadows. Mind came from the heavens, Body's shadow has fallen."

CONTENTS

*For the information of the reader, the trans-
lator here appends a table of contents of the
first and untranslated part of the work:*

BOOK FOUR

Herein the natural and archetypal causes of Celestial Physics *that is, of all the magnitudes, movements, and proportions in the heavens are explained and thus the Principles of the Doctrine on the Schemata are demonstrated.*

This book is designed to serve as a supplement to Aristotle's On the Heavens.

TO THE READER

It has been ten years since I published my *Commentaries on the Movements of the Planet Mars.* As only a few copies of the book were printed, and as it had so to speak hidden the teaching about celestial causes in thickets of calculations and the rest of the astronomical apparatus, and since the more delicate readers were frightened away by the price of the book too; it seemed to my friends that I should be doing right and fulfilling my responsibilities, if I should write an epitome, wherein a summary of both the physical and astronomical teaching concerning the heavens would be set forth in plain and simple speech and with the boredom of the demonstrations alleviated. I did that before many years had passed. But meanwhile various delays came between the book and publication: the little book itself was not up to date in spots, and, unless I am mistaken, it was also incomplete in the form in which it was given, and even the plan of publication began to totter. For in the "doctrine concerning the sphere"—published before three years were up—I seemed to certain people to be more diffuse in arguing about the diurnal movement or repose of the earth than befitted the form of an epitome. Accordingly I reflected that if the readers had not digested that part, which was however absent from no epitome of astronomy, all the more strange to them would be this Fourth Book, which airs so many new and unthought-of things concerning the whole nature of the heavens—so that you might doubt whether you were doing a part of physics or astronomy, unless you recognized that speculative astronomy is one whole part of physics.

On the other hand, I considered that this was a matter for the sake of my amplifying which and impressing it upon the public, *i.e.*, for the sake of my writing this little book, many men of letters had become my friends: that these speculations could not be omitted, unless I spent my devotion in giving attention to the darkness of a doctrine of schemata which was robbed of its proper principles. At least, necessity—how I wish she were sometimes less importunate!—cut short this disputation: for necessity makes that which cannot be done otherwise seem to be undertaken as if by design. The press

845

groaned and the work on the doctrine of schemata was being struck off, when its lawful godfather, whom I mentioned in the foreword to the Spherical Doctrine, attained his former state, and was sleeping, or perhaps giving up the ghost, and as the liberality of this most eminent patron was paying for the parts of this book, it became necessary for me suddenly to set out and to break off the work. At that same time the printers had reached the end of the Fourth Book and the Frankfort market-day was at hand. I decided that it would be best if the Fourth Book, the subject-matter of which includes both physics and astronomy, were also published separately; whence, according to the choice of the astronomer buying, it could be passed over, or inserted into the rest of the epitome. Kind reader, you have the reasons for this publication, and I hope you will find them satisfactory.

But as regards this branch of philosophizing: it will not be out of keeping with the job at hand if I here set down in advance some things from the recent letter which I wrote to a man who is intimate with a great Prince and is himself also a great man. In this letter a comparison was undertaken between this book—or the related work *On the Harmonies*, published in the previous year—and Aristotle's books *On the Heavens* and *Metaphysics*; and this philosophy [*i.e.*, modern astronomy] was cleared of the worn-out charges of being esoteric and seeking after novelty.

Accordingly, these are the excerpts from the aforesaid letter which have to do with the present undertaking:

It seems to me I have nothing to worry about in the case of Aristotle: His Most Serene Highness is a Platonist in philosophy and a Christian in religion: His Most Serene Highness cannot dislike whatever is the more convincing, whether it be that the world was first made at a fixed beginning in time as was my work *On thë Harmonies*, or will be destroyed at some time, or is merely liable to destruction, like the alterations of the ether and the celestial atmosphere; nor will he ever prefer the Master Aristotle to the truth of which Aristotle was ignorant.

But if His Most Serene Highness has a high opinion of Aristotle, wheresoever he reveals the mysteries of philosophy, if he makes any serious remark or any praiseworthy attempt; for indeed he is the man who in *On the Heavens* (Book II, Chapter 5) asks: "For what reason are there many movements?" So I ask: "What are the reasons for the number of the planets?" He asks in the following chapter: "For what reason are the heavens borne from east to west rather than from west to east?" So I ask: "Why is any planet moved with so much speed, no more, no less?" In Chapter 9 he asks: "Do the stars give forth sounds which are modulated [*contemperatos*] harmonically?" and answers no: I split up his judgment, for I grant that no sounds are given forth but I affirm and demonstrate that the movements are modulated according to harmonic proportions. In Chapter 10 he asks "about the order of the spheres, the intervals, and the ratio of the movements to the orbital circles"; but he merely asks and fails in the attempt. Not only do I answer these questions with most luminous demonstrations by means of the five regular solids, but also I add the number of the planets, which has been deduced from the Archetype, so that it may be clear that the world is created. In Chapter 12 he asks: "Why in the descent from the upper to the lower planets are not the movements of the single planets found to be more manifold?" and he pronounces a judgment most elegantly tempered by the modesty of confession and the wisdom of assertion. "Let us try," he says, "to say only that which appears as true; for we judge that the readiness" even to put forward what is probable "is worthy of being characterized as modesty rather than presumption, if anyone, in things concerning which there are very great difficulties, is content—in order to satisfy his thirst for philosophy—with even slight discussions such as these." But I myself, led on by this same praiseworthy thirst for philosophy, first wiped away from the eyes of astronomy those mists of the multiplicity of movements in the single planets: then I gave a demonstration of the following: that the movement of the planet is not uniform throughout its whole circuit—as Aristotle argued in Chapters 6 and 7; but that in reality the movement is increased and decreased at places in its period which are fixed and are opposite to one another; and I explained the efficient or intsrumental causes of this increase as the lessening of the interval between the planet and the sun, from which as from a source that movement arises. Then, as in each and every planet there is a very fast movement and a very slow movement and in a fixed proportion, I did not merely raise the question as to the reason for this proportion in the single planets separately and in all the planets in relation to one another; and why Saturn and Jupiter have middling eccentricities, Mars a great eccentricity, the Sun and Venus slight eccentricities, and Mercury a very great eccentricity; but I also brought forward a solution of this very great difficulty, and not a trifling discussion but one wholly legitimate; and I took my solution from the Archetype of the harmonic cosmos: whence it is established that this cosmos cannot be better than it is and that it is impossible that the world should not have been created at a fixed beginning in time.

This attempt of mine ought not to have been checked by shyness, but should have been brought forth into the light with strength of mind, namely, with the highest confidence in the visible works of God—if one has leisure for knowledge of them—or at the exhortation of Aristotle himself, who judged that in these questions you should not suppress or be silent about probabilities any more than about fully explored certainties. Then he is that same Aristotle who, in the *Metaphysics*, Book XII, Chapter 8, in which place he built up the most sublime part of his philosophy, the part concerning the gods and the number of them; who, I say, sends his students to the astronomers and who defers to the astronomers in respect to their authority and the weight of their testimony; indeed he would never have scorned Tycho Brahe or even myself, if that fatal necessity of the generations had made us contemporaries. For he orders his students "to read through both," that is to say, Eudoxus and Callippus, for the one had corrected the errors of the other; and today that would be to read both Ptolemy and Tycho: "but to follow" not, he says, the more ancient, but "the more accurate." And so, if Aristotle is dear to that most just Prince, I call Aristotle to witness that he has suffered no injury, if the astronomer, using the arguments which modern times have put forward concerning the heavens, has indicated that creatures arose in the heavens and will disappear once more—in opposition to the opinion of him who alleges experience, but experience not sufficiently long.

As regards the academies, they are established in order to regulate the studies of the pupils and are concerned not to have the program of teaching change very often: in such places, because it is a question of the progress of the stu-

dents, it frequently happens that the things which have to be chosen are not
those which are most true but those which are most easy. And by that division
in things which makes different people form different judgements, it so happens
that certain people are in error contrary to their own opinion. It seems to me
that the truth concerning the mutable nature of the heavens can be taught
conveniently; but someone else judges that students and teachers equally
are thrown into confusion by this doctrine. But it is not without its use in explaining even those parts of the philosophy of Aristotle which are clearly false,
as Book VIII of the *Physics* concerning celestial movement and Book II of
On the Heavens concerning the eternity of the heavens—so that a comparison
could be made between the philosophy of the gentiles and the truth of Christian
dogma. Accordingly, if certain subtleties which are difficult to grasp should
not be laid before beginners, or if they should not be preferred to the accepted
and necessary teachings, it does not follow that therefore those things should
neither be written nor read privately. You can count few academies in which
it is a part of the program to explain the *Metaphysics* of Aristotle: yet Aristotle
wrote the *Metaphysics* too, a very useful work in the judgement of the professors on all the faculties. Therefore, in order that no one should consider
His Most Serene Highness blameworthy, if he observes the rules of the academies, and if he believes that the honour of the academics—even if they have
sinned greatly in judgement—should be defended against presumptuous critics,
against untimely quarrellers: so in turn I do not let myself be easily persuaded
that this most wise Prince will seek to have all people remain publicly and
privately inside the boundaries of academic philosophy; and to have no one
labour privately in bringing forward these things, that is to say, in the manifestation of the works of God.

But His Most Supreme Highness will not pick a fight concerning the heavens;
for he knows that the philosophers speak of the visible heavens; and Christ of
the invisible heavens, or, as the schools say, of the empyrean, or, as the simple
Christians take it, of the blessed seats, which no corruption will ever touch:
since not Tycho, not I, but Christ Himself pronounces concerning this visible
world: "Heaven and Earth shall pass away," and the Psalmist, "they shall
grow old like a garment"; and Peter, "They shall be destroyed root and all,
and be consumed by burning in the fire." And that will occur in order that the
alterations in the heavens should not destroy their eternity, if there should
be such an eternity, just as the terrestrial alterations, which are perrennial
and return in a circle, destroy the Earth's eternity which was equally believed
by Aristotle. But this kind of argument against Aristotle will perhaps seem
too contentious. Therefore let us use his own testimony instead; for he is not
everywhere consistent: in the *Metaphysics* he attributes movement to the
celestial bodies for its own sake and teaches "that they are moved in order
that they may be moved"; but in *On the Heavens*, being admonished by the
things themselves, he attributes something or other like the terrestrial, something multiplex and turbulent to the stars or rather to their movers, who by
means of these mechanisms and movements seek another end outside of the
movement itself, and one mover attains this end with more difficulty than
another: in this way, as a matter of fact, he adduces the fewness of movements
in the moon as witness of the inferior condition of the moon and its closer
kinship to the Earth. For he means to say that the celestial bodies which can-

not wholly attain the highest end by their own nature do not employ many motions; and that it would have been wholly useless for the Earth to have a movement to attain that end, but that the Earth is absolutely at rest there; that the moon progresses somewhere and stretches out towards that end; the higher bodies attain the end, but by many movements; and the highest heaven, by the one simple movement. And so he compares the actions, the πράξεις of the moon—that is the word he uses—to the uniform life of plants, but the πράξεις of the higher bodies, to the more varied life of animals. Yet he makes all those bodies to be in need of these actions because they have their end and their blessedness outside of themselves. Accordingly, in the epilogue to the Fifth Book of the *Harmonies,* I wish for Aristotle as my reader and critic; as it is not right that I should wish to take up any more of the time of His Most Serene Highness, the highest judgement of the Prince. I am sure of one thing at least, that if he would direct the cultivated power of his mind toward those things which Aristotle wrote and toward my epilogue, everything would be agreed between us, and he would by his own judgement harmonize the discord which now, as you predict, he might feel between us.

In order to counter the envious charge of novelty-hunting, it would be first in my program, even though His Most Serene Highness can easily see all things for himself, to warn him fully of the distinction between the love—or thirst, to use the Aristotelian word—for the knowledge of natural things and the lust for contradicting and holding the opposite opinion. All philosophers, whether Greek or Latin, and all the poets too, recognize a divine ravishment in investigating the works of God: and not merely in investigating them privately but even in teaching them publicly: and it can be inferred that the false charge of esoteric novelty-hunting cannot cling to this ravishment.

> There is God in us, and our warmth comes from His movements: This Spirit has descended from the heavenly seats.

There is no need of this declamation before you, or before His Most Supreme Highness: only I must make some further mention of the boundary posts. For the boundary posts of investigation should not be set up in the narrow minds of a few men. "The world is a petty thing, unless everyone finds the whole world in that which he is seeking," as Seneca says. But the boundary posts of true speculation are the same as those of the fabric of the world; but the Christian religion has put up some fences around false speculation which is on the wrong track, in order that error may not rush headlong but may become in other respects harmless in itself. Antiquity teaches us by examples how vainly man sets up boundary posts where God has not set them up: how severely all the astronomers were blamed by the first Christians. Did not Eusebius write of an astronomer that he preferred to desert Christianity—I suppose because he was excommunicated—rather than his profession? Who today would opine that Eusebius is to be imitated? Did not those who taught that there were antipodes seem to Tertullian and to Augustine to be overwise? And, indeed, there was a Virgil Bishop of Salisbury who was removed from his office because he dared to assert this same fact. How many times were the Roman philosophers exiled from the city? And at that, under the ancient manners, wherewith the Roman State was established. Yet today we set up academies everywhere: we order that philosophy be taught, that astronomy be taught, that the antipodes be taught.

But I even in private free myself from the blame of seeking after novelty by suitable proofs: let my doctrines say whether there is love of truth in me or love of glory: for most of the ones I hold have been taken from other writers: I build my whole astronomy upon Copernicus' hypotheses concerning the world, upon the observations of Tycho Brahe, and lastly upon the Englishman, William Gilbert's philosophy of magnetism. If I rejoiced in novelty, I could have devised something like the Fracastorian or Patrician systems. Just as one who rejoices in occupations but rarely in companions, never of himself descends to dice or to a game of chess; similarly for me there is so much importance in the true doctrine of others or even in correcting the doctrines which are not in every respect well established, that my mind is never at leisure for the game of inventing new doctrines that are contrary to the true. Whatever I profess outwardly, that I believe inwardly: nothing is a worse cross for me than—I do not say, to speak what is contrary to my thought—to be unable to utter my inmost sentiments. I know that many innovators are produced by the same affect; but they are easily argued out of the error which seduces them. No one shows that I have committed an error. But because certain people cannot grasp the subtleties of things, they lay the charge of novelty-hunting upon me.

I now descend to the work itself, the *Harmonies:* I do not doubt that he who condemns the itch to devise new things and the presumption to profess new and grandiose things will find in the epilogue to the Fifth Book[1] that which he will mark critically. For here the sun-spots and little flames are brought forward as evidence of there being exhalations from the sun which are analogous to exhalations from the Earth: here things corresponding to the generation of animals are established as occurring in the planets—here the confines of the mysteries of Christian religion are touched: we knock at the doors of the science of the Magi, of theurgy, of the idolatry of the Persians, and of those who worship the sun as god—as the interjection of frequent warnings does not dissimulate.

Accordingly, if what has been said so far concerning these esoteric things is not satisfactory: at any rate let this be impressed upon His Most Serene Highness: that this chapter contributes nothing in its own right except conjectures; and although it adds a good deal to the form of the work: because—as the opening of the chapter has it—reason itself leads "from the Muses to Apollo": nevertheless, since the other parts of the work are established by means of their proper demonstrations, the chapter, or epilogue, can be considered as cut off from the rest. For even without the epilogue, the following thesis is upheld by incontrovertible demonstrations: *that in the farthest movements of any two planets, the universe was stamped with the adornment of harmonic proportions; and, accordingly, in order that this adornment might be brought into concord with the movements, the eccentricities which fell to the lot of each planet had to be brought into concord.* The most wise Prince will easily reckon how great an addition this makes in illustrating the glory of the fabric of the world, and of God the Architect.

But if, however, even this inquiry is accused of being esoteric: I indeed confess that the head of astronomy is struck off. And since astronomy is studied either for its own sake as a philosophy or for the sake of making astronomical

[1]*See Harmonies of the World*, pp. 1080–1085.

predictions; then, if I am to cast my ballot in the question of future contingencies, His Most Serene Highness repudiates any secondary end for this exact and subtle investigation of physical causes which does not offer itself for the uses of daily life: therefore the taking away from me of the primary end slays this whole subtle astronomy and plainly makes it useless.

Nevertheless, in order that I may arm myself against this eventuality also: I will grant that this work of mine, the *Harmonies*, is nothing except as it were a certain picture of the edifice of astronomy; and though it may be erased at the pleasure of him who spits upon it, nevertheless the house called astronomy stands by itself: and I know that astronomy is not condemned by His Most Serene Highness but is held of great value on account of its certitude in predicting movements: perhaps, therefore, he will judge its architect—who is almost the only renovator after the Master Tycho and who thought it worth while to devote his life to this work—to be not unworthy of his favour.

These extracts from the letter, most of which have to do with the investigation of very hidden causes which is to be viewed in this little book, should be spoken and understood. And now it is time for the reader to pass on to the little book.

FIRST BOOK ON THE DOCTRINE OF THE SCHEMATA

On the Position, Order, and Movement of the Parts of the World; or, on the System of the World

[433] *What is the subject of the doctrine of the schemata?*

The proper movements of the planets; we call them the secondary movements; and the planets, the secondary movables.

Why do you call them the proper movements of the planets?

1. Because the apparent daily movement—with which the doctrine on the sphere is concerned—and which is common to both the planets and the fixed stars, and so to the whole world, is seen to travel from the east to the west; but the far slower single movements of the single planets travel in the opposite direction from west to east; and therefore it is certain that these movements cannot depend upon that common movement of the world—which we have discussed so far—but should be assigned to the planets themselves, and thus they are generically proper to the planets.

2. But even if in these proper movements of the single [434] planets from west to east there is also present something common, not diurnal but annual, which is extrinsic and betrays that its cause lies in eyesight alone, outside the truth of the thing; and which meanwhile makes the planet in its proper movement have the appearance of retrograding, that is, from east to west, nevertheless because this common movement is so woven into the single periods of the single planets, and so variously transformed, that at first glance you cannot discern what is common to all the planets and what is proper to each: accordingly this whole composite movement of each planet, as it meets the eyes, is said to be proper to each planet specifically; especially since this movement which is common to many does not have its origin in that first

common movement of the whole world, but in the proper movement of each planet.

How many parts are there to the doctrine of the schemata?

Above (in Book I, page 15), the whole doctrine was divided into its three proper parts: the first, concerning the principles wherewith Copernicus demonstrates the secondary movements—the material of Book IV; the second, concerning the machinery whereby these movements are laid before the eyes, *viz.*, concerning the eccentric and similar circles—the material of Book V; and the third, concerning the apparent movements of the single planets and the common accidents of the planets taken together—the material of Book VI; and the fourth part, which is common to the doctrines on the sphere and on the schemata, concerns the apparent movement of the eighth sphere—the material of Book VII.

What are the hypotheses or principles wherewith Copernican astronomy saves the appearances in the proper movements of the planets?

They are principally: (1) that the sun is located at the centre of the sphere of the fixed stars—or approximately at the centre—and is immovable in place; (2) that the single planets move really around the sun in their single systems, which are compounded of many perfect circles [435] revolved in an absolutely uniform movement; (3) that the Earth is one of the planets, so that by its mean annual movement around the sun it describes its orbital circle between the orbital circles of Mars and of Venus; (4) that the ratio of its orbital circle to the diameter of the sphere of the fixed stars is imperceptible to sense and therefore, as it were, exceeds measurements; (5) that the sphere of the moon is arranged around the Earth as its centre, so that the annual movement around the sun—and so the movement from place to place—is common to the whole sphere of the moon and to the Earth.

Do you judge that these principles should be held to in this Epitome?

Since astronomy has two ends, to save the appearances and to contemplate the true form of the edifice of the world—of which I have treated in Book I, folia 4 and 5—there is no need of all these principles in order to attain the first end: but some can be changed and others can be omitted; however, the second principle must necessarily be corrected: and even though most of these principles are necessary for the second end, nevertheless they are not yet sufficient.

Which of these principles can be changed or omitted and the appearances still be saved?

Tycho Brahe demonstrates the appearances with the first and third principles changed: for he, like the ancients, places the Earth immobile, at the centre of the world; but the sun—which even for him is the centre of the orbital circles of the five planets—and the system of all the spheres he makes to go around the Earth in the common annual movement, while at the same time in this common system any planet completes its proper movements. Moreover, he omits the fourth principle altogether and exhibits the sphere of the fixed stars as not much greater than the sphere of Saturn.

[436] *What in turn do you substitute for the second principle and what else do you add to the true form of the dwelling of the world or to what belongs to the nature of the heavens?*

Even though the true movements are to be left singly to the single planets, nevertheless these movements do not move by themselves nor by the revolutions of spheres—for there are no solid spheres—but the sun in the centre of the world, revolving around the centre of its body and around its axis, by this revolution becomes the cause of the single planets going around.

Further, even though the planets are really eccentric to the centre of the sun: nevertheless there are no other smaller circles called epicycles, which by their revolution vary the intervals between the planet and the sun; but the bodies themselves of the planets, by an inborn force [*vi insite*], furnish the occasion for this variation.

What, then, will the material of Book IV be?

Book IV will contain celestial physics itself, or the form and proportions of the fabric of the world and the true causes of the movements. This will be the primary function of the astronomer—as we said in Book I, folium 5, namely, the demonstration of his hypotheses.

Review the principal parts of Book IV.

There will be three principal parts of Book IV.

The first is on the bodies themselves; the second, on the movements of those bodies; the third, on the real accidents of the movements.

For the first part will teach the conformation of the whole universe, its division into parts or principal regions; the place of the sun at its centre; the number, magnitude, and order or position of the planetary spheres; and lastly, the ratios of all the bodies of the world to one another.

The second part will teach the revolution of the sun around its axis, and its effect in making the planets revolve; the causes of the proportionality of the movements among themselves, *i.e.*, of the periodic [437] times; the immobility of the centre of the sun and the annual movement of the centre of the Earth around the sun; the revolution of the Earth around its axis and its effect in making the moon revolve; the additional help in moving the moon given by the light of the sun; and what the causes of the proportions between the day, month, and year are.

The third part will disclose the causes of the threefold irregularity of the altitude, longitude, and latitude in the single planets—and how these irregularities are doubled in the moon by the force of the illumination from the sun.

PART I

1. On the Principal Parts of the World

[438] *What do you judge to be the lay-out of the principal parts of the world?*

The Philosophy of Copernicus reckons up the principal parts of the world by dividing the figure of the world into regions. For in the sphere, which is the image of God the Creator and the Archetype of the world—as was proved in Book I—there are three regions, symbols of the three persons of the Holy

Trinity—the centre, a symbol of the Father; the surface, of the Son; and the intermediate space, of the Holy Ghost. So, too, just as many principal parts of the world have been made—the different parts in the different regions of the sphere: the sun in the centre, the sphere of the fixed stars on the surface, and lastly the planetary system in the region intermediate between the sun and the fixed stars.

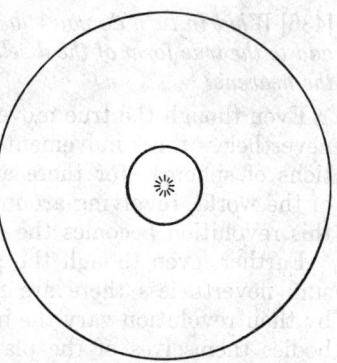

I thought the principal parts of the world are reckoned to be the heavens and the earth?

Of course, our uncultivated eyesight from the Earth cannot show us any other more notable parts—as was said in Book I, folia 8, 9, 10—since we tread upon the one with our feet and are roofed over by the other, and since both parts seem to be commingled and cemented together in the common limbo of the horizon—like a globe in which stars, clouds, birds, man, and the various kinds of terrestrial animals are enclosed.

But we are practised in the discipline which discloses the causes of things, shakes off the deceptions of eyesight, and carries the mind higher and farther, outside of the boundaries of eyesight. Hence it should not be surprising to anyone that eyesight should learn from reason, that the pupil should learn something new from his master which he did not know before—namely, that the Earth, considered alone and by itself, should not be reckoned among the primary parts of the great world but should be added to one of the primary parts, *i.e.*, to the planetary region, the movable world, and that the Earth has the proportionality of a beginning in that part; and that the sun in turn should be separated from the number of stars and set up as one of the principal parts of the whole universe. But I am speaking now of the Earth in so far as it is a part of the edifice of the world, and not of the dignity of the governing creatures which inhabit it.

By what properties do you distinguish these members of the great world from one another?

The perfection of the world consists in light, heat, movement, and the harmony of movements. These are analogous to the faculties of the soul: light, to the sensitive; heat, to the vital and the natural; movement, to the animal; harmony, to the rational. And indeed the adornment [*ornatus*] of the world consists in light; its life and growth, in heat; and, so to speak, its action, in movement; and its contemplation—wherein Aristotle places blessedness—in harmonies. Now since three things necessarily come together for every affection, namely, the cause *a qua*, the subject *in quo*, and the form *sub qua*—therefore, in respect to all the aforesaid affections of the world, the sun exercises the function of the efficient cause; the region of the fixed stars that of the thing forming, containing, and terminating; and the intermediate space, that of the subject—in accordance with the nature of each affection. Accordingly, in all these ways the sun is the principal body of the whole world.

For as regards light: since the sun is very beautiful with light and is as if the

eye of the world, like a source of light or very brilliant torch, the sun illum-
inates, paints, and adorns the bodies of the rest of the world; the intermediate
space is not itself light-giving, but light-filled and transparent and the channel
through which light is conducted from its source, and there exist in this region
the globes and the creatures upon which the light of the sun is poured and
which make use of this light. The sphere of the fixed stars plays the role of the
river-bed in which this river of light runs, and is as it were an opaque and
illuminated wall, reflecting and doubling the light of the sun: you have very
properly likened it to a lantern, which shuts out the winds.

Thus in animals the cerebrum, the seat of the sensitive faculty imparts
to the whole animal all its senses, and by the act of common sense causes the
presence of all those senses as if arousing them and ordering them to keep watch.
And in another way, in this simile, the sun is the image of common sense;
the globes in the intermediate space of [440] the sense-organs; and the sphere
of the fixed stars of the sensible objects.

As regards heat: the sun is the fireplace [*focus*] of the world; the globes in
the intermediate space warm themselves at this fireplace, and the sphere of
the fixed stars keeps the heat from flowing out, like a wall of the world, or a
skin or garment—to use the metaphor of the Psalm of David. The sun is fire,
as the Pythagoreans said, or a red-hot stone or mass, as Democritus said—and
the sphere of the fixed stars is ice, or a crystalline sphere, comparatively speaking. But if there is a certain vegetative faculty not only in terrestrial creatures
but also in the whole ether throughout the universal amplitude of the world—
and both the manifest energy of the sun in warming and physical considerations
concerning the origin of comets lead us to draw this inference—it is believable
that this faculty is rooted in the sun as in the heart of the world, and that
thence by the oarage of light and heat it spreads out into this most wide space
of the world—in the way that in animals the seat of heat and of the vital
faculty is in the heart and the seat of the vegetative faculty in the liver, whence
these faculties by the intermingling of the spirits spread out into the remaining
members of the body. The sphere of the fixed stars, situated diametrically
opposite on every side, helps this vegetative faculty by concentrating heat,
as they say; as it were a kind of skin of the world.

As regards movement: the sun is the first cause of the movement of the
planets and the first mover of the universe, even by reason of its own body.
In the intermediate space the movables, *i.e.*, the globes of the planets, are
laid out. The region of the fixed stars supplies the movables with a place and a
base upon which the movables are, as it were, supported; and movement is
understood as taking place relative to its absolute immobility. So in animals
the cerebellum is the seat of the motor faculty, and the body and its members
are that which is moved. The Earth is the base of an animal body; the body,
the base of the arm or head, and the arm, the base of the finger. And the
movement of each part takes place upon this base as upon something immovable.

Finally, as regards the harmony of the movements: the sun occupies that
place in which alone the movements of the planets [441] give the appearance
of magnitudes harmonically proportioned [*contemperatarum*]. The planets
themselves, moving in the intermediate space, exhibit the subject or terms,
wherein the harmonies are found; the sphere of the fixed stars, or the circle
of the zodiac, exhibits the measures whereby the magnitude of the apparent

movements is known. So too in man there is the intellect, which abstracts universals and forms numbers and proportions, as things which are not outside of intellect; but individuals [*individua*], received inwardly through the senses are the foundation of universals; and indivisible [*individuae*] and discrete unities, of numbers; and real terms of proportions. Finally, memory, divided as it were into compartments of quantities and times, like the sphere of the fixed stars, is the storehouse and repository of sensations. And further, there is never judgment of sensations except in the cerebrum; and the effect of joy never arises from a sense-perception except in the heart.

Accordingly, the aforesaid vegetating corresponds to the nutritive faculty of animals and plants; heating corresponds to the vital faculty; movement, to the animal faculty; light, to the sensitive; and harmony, to the rational. Wherefore most rightly is the sun held to be the heart of the world and the seat of reason and life, and the principal one among three primary members of the world; and these praises are true in the philosophic sense, since the poets honour the sun as the king of the stars, but the Sidonians, Chaldees, and Persians—by an idiom of language observed in German too—as the queen of the heavens, and the Platonists, as the king of intellectual fire.

These three members of the world do not seem to correspond with sufficient neatness to the three regions of a sphere: for the centre is a point, but the sun is a body; and the outer surface is understood to be continuous, yet the region of fixed stars does not shine as a totality, but is everywhere sown with shining points discrete from one another; and finally, the intermediate part in a sphere fills the whole expanse, but in the world the space between the sun [442] and the fixed stars is not seen to be set in motion as a whole.

As a matter of fact, the question indicates the neatest answer concerning the three parts of the world. For since a point could not be clothed or expressed except by some body—and thus the body which is in the centre would fail of the indivisibility of the centre—it was proper that the sphere of the fixed stars should fail of the continuity of a spherical surface, and should burst open in the very minute points of the innumerable fixed stars; and that finally the middle space should not be wholly occupied by movement and the other affections, nor be completely transparent, but slightly more dense, since it could not be altogether empty but had to be filled by some body.

Are there solid spheres [orbes] *whereon the planets are carried? And are there empty spaces between the spheres?*

Tycho Brahe disproved the solidity of the spheres by three reasons: the first from the movement of comets; the second from the fact that light is not refracted; the third from the ratio of the spheres.

For if spheres were solid, the comets would not be seen to cross from one sphere into another, for they would be prevented by the solidity; but they cross from one sphere into another, as Brahe shows.

From light thus: since the spheres are eccentric, and since the Earth and its surface—where the eye is—are not situated at the center of each sphere; therefore if the spheres were solid, that is to say far more dense than that very limpid ether, then the rays of the stars would be refracted before they reached our air, as optics teaches; and so the planet would appear irregularly and in places far different from those which could be predicted by the astronomer.

The third reason comes from the principles of Brahe himself; for they bear witness, as do the Copernican, that Mars is sometimes nearer the Earth than the sun is. But Brahe could not believe this interchange to be possible [443] if the spheres were solid, since the sphere of Mars would have to intersect the sphere of the sun.

Then what is there in the planetary regions besides the planets?

Nothing except the ether which is common to the spheres and to the intervals: it is very limpid and yields to the movable bodies no less readily than it yields to the lights of the sun and stars, so that the lights can come down to us.

If it is ether, then it will be a material body having density. Therefore will not its matter resist the movable bodies somewhat?

On the contrary, the ether is more rarefied than our air, since it is very pure, being spread over a space which is practically immense.

How do you prove this?

In optics, by refractions. For our air, which is contiguous to the ether, causes a refraction of approximately 30'. But water contiguous to air causes a refraction of approximately 48°, whence the ratio of the density of water to air, and of air to ether is somehow established by taking the cubes of the numbers. For 30' is contained approximately 100 times in 48°; and in squares, that is 10,000 times, and in cubes 1,000,000 times. Therefore air is that many times more rarefied than water, and ether than air.

Nevertheless the matter of the ether is not absolutely null: are the stars therefore still impeded by it?

We can without any inconvenience grant such a small impediment of movement and such a small resistance of the ether to the movable bodies, just as even before this it must be granted that they offer some resistance on account of the proper matter of their bodies, as will be made clear below. And what if no resistance should be granted to the ether, [444] since it is fairly credible that the ether which surrounds the movable globe the most closely accompanies the globe on account of the very great limpidity [of the ether]?

2. ON THE PLACE OF THE SUN AT THE CENTRE OF THE WORLD

By what arguments do you affirm that the sun is situated at the centre of the world?

The very ancient Pythagoreans and the Italian philosophers supply us with some of those arguments in Aristotle (*On the Heavens*, Book, II, Chapter 13); and these arguments are drawn from the dignity of the sun and that of the place, and from the sun's office of vivification and illumination in the world.

State the first argument from dignity.

This is the reasoning of the Pythagoreans according to Aristotle: the more worthy place is due to the most worthy and most precious body. Now the sun— for which they used the word "fire," as sects purposely hiding their teachings— is worthier than the Earth and is the most worthy and most precious body in the whole world, as was shown a little before. But the surface and centre, or midpoint, are the two extremities of a sphere. Therefore one of these places is due

to the sun. But not the surface; for that which is the principal body in the whole
world should watch over all the bodies; but the centre is suited for this function,
and so they used to call it the Watchtower of Jupiter. And so it is not proper
that the Earth should be in the middle. For this place belongs to the sun, while
the Earth is borne around the centre of its yearly movement.

What answer does Aristotle make to this argument?

1. He says that they assume something which is not granted, namely, that
the centre [445] of magnitude, *i.e.*, of the sphere, and the centre of the things,
i.e., of the body of the world, and so of nature, *i.e.*, of informing or vivifying, are
the same. But just as in animals the centre of vivification and the centre of the
body are not the same—for the heart is inside but is not equally distant from
the surface—we should think in the same way about the heavens, and we should
not fear for the safety of the whole universe or place a guard at the centre;
rather, we should ask what sort of body the heart of the world of the centre or
vivification is and in what place in the world it is situated.

2. He tries to show the dissimilarity between the midpart of the nature and
the midpart of place. For the midpart of nature, or the most worthy and precious body, has the proportionality of a beginning. But in the midpart of place is
the last, in quantity considered metaphysically, rather than the first or the beginning. For that which is the midpart of quantity, *i.e.*, is the farthest in, is bounded or circumscribed. But the limits are that which bounds or circumscribes. Now
that which goes around on the outside, and limits and encloses, is of greater excellence and worth than that which is on the inside and is bounded: for matter is
among those things which are bounded, limited, and contained; but form, or the
essence of any creature, is of the number of those things which limit, circumscribe, and comprehend. He thinks that he has proved in this way that not so
much the midpart of the world as the extremity belongs to the sun, or as he
understood it, to the fire of the Pythagoreans.

How do you rebut this refutation of Aristotle's?

1. Even if it be true that not in all creatures and least in animals is the principal part of the whole creature at the centre of the whole mass: however, since
we are arguing about the world, nothing is more probable than this. For the
figure of the world is spherical, and that of an animal is not. For animals need
organs extending outside themselves, with which they stand upon the ground,
and upon which they may move, and with which they may take within themselves the food, drink, [446] forms of things, and sounds received from outside.
The world on the contrary, is alone, having nothing outside, resting on itself
immobile as a whole; and it alone is all things. And so there is no reason why the
heart of the world should be elsewhere than in the centre in order that what it
is, *viz.*, the heart, might be equally distant from all the farthest parts of the
world, that is to say, by an interval everywhere equal.

2. Furthermore, as regards his telling us to ask what sort of body the principal part of the whole universe is: he is confused by that riddle of the Pythagoreans and believes that they claim that this element is principal. He is not
wrong however in telling us to do that. And accordingly we, following the advice
of Aristotle, have picked out the sun; and neither the Pythagoreans in their mys-
tical sense nor Aristotle himself are against us. And when we ask in what place

in the world the sun is situated, Copernicus, as being skilled in the knowledge of the heavens, shows us that the sun is in the midpart. The others who exhibit its place as elsewhere are not forced to do this by astronomical arguments but by certain others of a metaphysical character drawn from the consideration of the Earth and its place. Both we and they set a value upon these arguments; and they themselves too by means of these arguments do not show but seek the place of the sun. So if when seeking the place of the sun in the world, we find that it is the centre of the world; we are doing just as Aristotle; and his refutation does not apply to us.

3. As regards the fact that Aristotle, directly contradicting the Pythagoreans ascribes vileness to the centre, he does that contrary to the nature of figures and contrary to their geometrical or metaphysical consideration.

For above in Book I, the centre was absolutely not last in the sphere, but wholly its most regular beginning of generation in the mind, and it manifests the likeness of the Holy Trinity, in shadowing forth God the Father, who is the First Person.

4. Finally it can be seen by anyone that he who judges as a physicist of those things which are geometrical does not do rightly, unless what he questions concerning matter and form [447] had been taken over by analogy from a consideration of geometrical figures. For indeed, in solid quantities the inward corporeality, everywhere spread out equally and not by itself partaking of any figure, is a true image of matter in physical things; but the outward figure of the corporeality, composed of fixed surfaces which bound the solidity, represent the

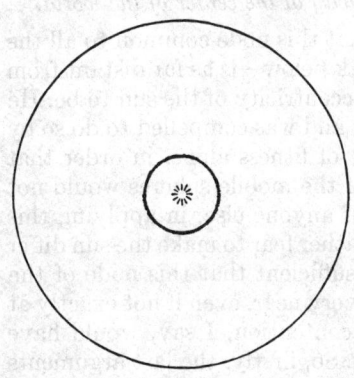

form in physical things. And so this comparison is permitted to him simply; but it appears from that that he plays equivocally with "midpart" [*medium*]. For though the Pythagoreans spoke of the inmost point of the sphere [as the midpart or centre]; he understood the whole space within the surface as comprehended by the word "midpart." Accordingly we must grant him the victory as regards the space, but it is a useless victory; for the Pythagoreans and Copernicus win as regards the midpart of all this space. For even if the midpart as a space does not deserve the name of limit; nevertheless as centre it does deserve this name. And in this respect [448] it must be added to the forms and boundaries: since above (in Book I) the centre was the origin of generation of the sphere, metaphysically considered.

Prove by means of the office of the sun that the centre is due to it.

That has already been partly done in rebutting the Aristotelian refutation. For (1) if the whole world, which is spherical, is equally in need of the light of the sun and its heat, then it would be best for the sun to be at the midpart, whence light and heat may be distributed to all the regions of the world. And that takes place more uniformly and rightly, with the sun resting at the centre than with the sun moving around the centre. For if the sun approached certain regions for the sake of warming them, it would draw away from the opposite regions and would cause alternations while it itself remained perfectly simple. And it is surprising that some people use jokingly the similitude of light at the centre of the lamp, as it is a very apt similitude, least fitted to satirize this opinion but suited rather to painting the power of this argument.

(2) But a special argument is woven together concerning light, which presupposes fitness, not necessity. Imagine the sphere of the fixed stars as a concave mirror: you know that the eye placed at the centre of such a mirror gazes upon itself everywhere: and if there is a light at the centre, it is everywhere reflected at right angles from the concave surface and the reflected rays come together again at the centre. And in fact that can occur at no other point in the concave mirror except at the centre. Therefore, since the sun is the source of light and eye of the world, the centre is due to it in order that the sun—as the Father in the divine symbolizing—may contemplate itself in the whole concave surface—which is the symbol of God the Son—and take pleasure in the image of itself, and illuminate itself by shining and inflame itself by warming. These melodious little verses apply to the sun:

> *Thou who dost gaze at thy face*
> *and dost everywhere leap back*
> *from the navel of the upper air*
> *O gushing up of the gleams flowing*
> *through the glass emptiness, Sun,*
> *who dost again swallow thy reflections.*

Nevertheless Copernicus did not place the sun exactly at the center of the world?

It was the intention of Copernicus to show that this node common to all the planetary systems—of which node we shall speak below—is as far distant from the centre of the sun as the ancients made the eccentricity of the sun to be. He established this node as the centre of the world, and was compelled to do so by no astronomical demonstration but on account of fitness alone, in order that this node and, as it were, the common centre of the mobile spheres would not differ from the very centre of the world. But if anyone else, in applying this same fitness, wished to contend that we should rather fear to make the sun differ from the centre of the world, and that it was sufficient that this node of the region of the moving planets should be situated very near, even if not exactly at the centre—anyone who wished to make this contention, I say, would have raised no disturbance in Copernican astronomy. So, firstly, the last arguments concerning the place of the sun at the centre are nevertheless unaffected by this opinion of Copernicus concerning the distance of this node from the sun. But secondly we must not agree to the opinion of Copernicus that this node is distant from the centre of the sun. For the common node of the region of the mobile planets is in the sun, as will be proved below; and so by some probable arguments either the one or the other point is set down at the centre of the sphere of the fixed stars, and by the same arguments the other point is brought to the same place, even with the approval of Copernicus.

3. On the Order of the Movable Spheres

How are the planets divided among themselves?

Into the primary and the secondary. The primary planets are those whose bodies are borne around the sun, as will be shown below; the secondary planets are those whose own circles are arranged not around the sun but around one of the primary planets and who also share in the movement of the primary planet around the sun. Saturn is believed to have two such secondary planets and to draw them around with itself: they come into sight now and then with the help of a telescope. Jupiter has four such planets around itself: D, E, F, H. The Earth (B) has one (C) called the moon. It is not yet clear in the case of Mars, Venus, and Mercury whether they too have such a companion or satellite.

Then how many planets are to be considered in the doctrine on schemata?

No more than seven: the six so-called primary planets: (1) Saturn, (2) Jupiter, (3) Mars, (4) the Earth—the sun to eyesight, (5) Venus, (6) Mercury,

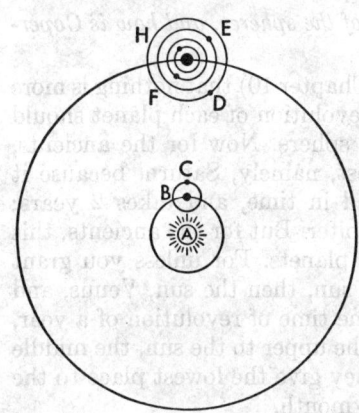

and (7) only one of the secondary planets, the moon, because it alone revolves around our home, the Earth; the other secondary planets do not concern us who inhabit the Earth, [451] and we cannot behold them without excellent telescopes.

In what order are the planets laid out: are they in the same heaven or in different heavens?

Eyesight places them all in that farthest and highest sphere of the fixed stars and opines that they move among the fixed stars. But reason persuades men of all times and of all sects that the case is different. For if the centres of all the planets were in the same sphere and since we see that to sight they are fairly often in conjunction with one another: accordingly one planet would impede the other, and their movements could not be regular and perpetual.

But the reasoning of Copernicus and ancient Aristarchus, which relies upon observations, proves that the regions of the single planets are separated by very great intervals from one another and from the fixed stars.

What is the difference here between the reasoning of Copernicus and that of the ancients?

1. The reasoning of the ancients is merely probable, but the demonstration of Copernicus, arising from his principles, brings necessity.

2. They teach only that there is not more than one planet in any one sphere: Copernicus further adds how great a distance any planet must necessarily be above another.

3. Now the ancients built up one heaven upon another, like layers in a wall, or, to use a closer analogy, like onion skins: the inner supports the outer; for they thought that all intervals had to be filled by spheres and that the higher sphere must be set down as being only as great as the lower sphere of a known magnitude allows; and that is only a material conformation. Copernicus, having measured by his observation the intervals between the single spheres, showed that there is such a great distance between two planetary spheres, that it is unbelievable that it should be filled with spheres. And so this lay-out

of his urges the speculative mind to spurn matter and the contiguity of spheres and to look towards the investigation of the formal lay-out or archetype, with reference to which the intervals were made.

4. The ancients, with their material structure, were forced to make the planetary or mobile world many parts greater than Copernicus was forced to do with his formal lay-out. But Copernicus, on the contrary, made the region of the mobile planets not very large, while he made the motionless sphere of the fixed stars immense. The ancients do not make it much greater than the sphere of Saturn.

5. The ancients do not explain and confirm as they desire the reason for their lay-out; Copernicus establishes his lay-out excellently by reasons.

What do you mean by the reasons for the lay-out of the spheres, and how is Copernicus outstanding in this respect?

Aristotle teaches in *On the Heavens* (Book II, Chapter 10) that nothing is more consonant with reason than that the times of revolution of each planet should correspond to the altitude or amplitude of its sphere. Now for the ancients, the highest planet was the same as the slowest, namely, Saturn, because it takes 30 years. Jupiter follows it in place and in time, and takes 2 years; Mars, which takes less than 2 years, follows Jupiter. But for the ancients, this proportionality was changed in the remaining planets. For unless you grant to the Earth an annual movement around the sun, then the sun, Venus, and Mercury—three distinct planets—have the same time of revolution of a year, nevertheless they give them different spheres: the upper to the sun, the middle to Venus, and the third to Mercury. Finally they give the lowest place to the moon, as it takes the shortest time, namely a month.

But Copernicus, postulating that the Earth moves around the sun, keeps the same proportion of movement and time in all the planets. For him the sun

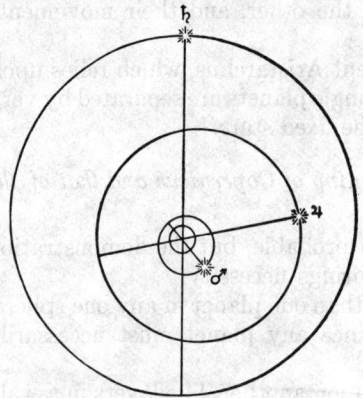

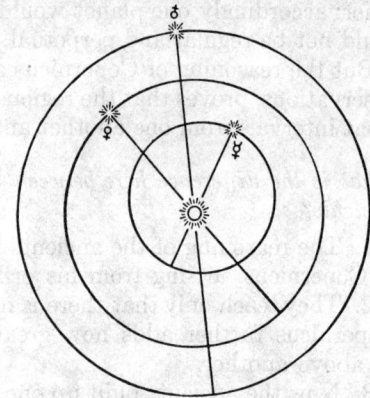

Schema of Saturn, Jupiter, Mars, and the Earth

[454] Schema of the Earth, Venus, and Mercury, with orbit of the Earth enlarged

is at the centre of the world and is thus the farthest in; it is without the revolution of the centre, that is to say, it is motionless with respect to the centre and the axis. But a few years after this, the body [453] of the sun was perceived to move around its motionless axis more quickly than the space of one month. Mercury, the nearest, circles around the sun in the smallest sphere and completes its revolution in 3 months; around this sphere moves Venus in a larger sphere and in a longer period of time, *viz.*, 7½ months. Around the heaven of Venus moves the Earth with its satellite the moon—for the moon is a secondary planet, whose proportionality is not counted among the primary planets—and it revolves in a period of 12 months. After, follow Mars, Jupiter, and Saturn, as with the ancients, each with its satellite. After Saturn, comes the sphere of the fixed stars—and it is distant by such an immense interval that it is absolutely at rest.

What measure does Copernicus use in measuring the intervals of the single planets?

We must use a measure so proportioned that the other spheres can be compared, a measure very closely related to us and thus somehow known to us: such is the amplitude of the sphere whereon the centre of the Earth and the little sphere of the moon revolve—or its semidiameter, the distance of the Earth from the sun. This distance, like a measuring rod, is suitable for the business. For the Earth is our home; and from it we measure the distances of the heavens; and it occupies the middle position among the planets and for many reasons— on which below—it obtains the proportionality of a beginning among them. [455] But the sun, by the evidence and judgment of our sight, is the principal planet. But by the vote of reason cast above, the sun is the heart of the region of moving planets proposed for measurement. And so our measuring rod has two very signal termini, the Earth and the sun.

How great therefore are the intervals between the single spheres?

The Copernican demonstrations show that the distance of Saturn is a little less than ten times the Earth's from the sun; that of Jupiter, five times; that of Mars, one and one-half times; that of Venus, three-quarters; and that of Mercury, approximately one-third.

And so the diameter of the sphere of Saturn is less than twice the length of its neighbour Jupiter's; the diameter of Jupiter is three times that of the lower planet Mars; the diameter of Mars is one and one-half times that of the terrestrial sphere placed around the sun; the diameter of the Earth's sphere is more than one and one-third that of Venus; and that of Venus is approximately five-thirds or eight-fifths that of Mercury. However, it should be noted that the ratios of the distances are different in other parts of the orbits, especially in the case of Mars and Mercury.

What is the cause of the planetary intervals upon which the times of the periods follow?

The archetypal cause of the intervals is the same as that of the number of the primary planets, being six.

I implore you, you do not hope to be able to give the reasons for the number of the planets, do you?

This worry has been resolved, with the help of God, not badly. Geometrical reasons are co-eternal with God—and in them there is first the difference between the curved and the straight line. Above (in Book I) it was said that the curved somehow bears a likeness to God; the straight line represents creatures. And first in the adornment of the world, the farthest region of the fixed stars has been made spherical, in that geometrical likeness of God, because as a corporeal God—worshipped by the gentiles under the name of Jupiter—it had to contain all the remaining things in itself. Accordingly, rectilinear [456] magnitudes pertained to the inmost contents of the farthest sphere; and the first and most beautiful magnitudes to the primary contents. But among rectilinear magnitudes the first, the most perfect, the most beautiful, and most simple are those which are called the five regular solids. [457] More than 2,000 years ago Pythagoreans said that these five were the figures of the world, as they believed that the four elements and the heavens—the fifth essence—were conformed to the archetype for these five figures.

But the truer reason for these figures including one another mutually is in order that these five figures may conform to the intervals of the spheres. Therefore, if there are five spherical intervals, it is necessary that there be six spheres: just as with four linear intervals, there must necessarily be five digits.

What are these five regular figures?

The cube, tetrahedron, dodecahedron, icosahedron, and octahedron.

How are these figures divided, and into what classes?

The cube, tetrahedron, and dodecahedron are primary; the octahedron and the icosahedron are secondary.

Why do you make the former primary and the latter secondary?

The three former figures have a prior origin, and the most simple angle (*i.e.*, trilinear), and their own proper planes. The two latter have their origin in the primary figures, and a more composite angle made from many lines, and borrowed planes.

What is the order of the primary figures?

They are said to be primary merely with respect to the secondary; but even among themselves they have this order of priority: cube, tetrahedron, dodecahedron. For in those figures there appears the first of all metaphysical oppositions, that between the same and the other, or the different. Sameness is seen in the cube, and difference in the remaining two figures; and between these figures there is also the first geometrical contrariety, namely, the contrariety between the greater-than and less-than. For the cube is [458] the thing itself [*res ipsa*], the tetrahedron is less than the cube, and the dodecahedron is greater than the cube; or, the cube is the first solid figure gener-

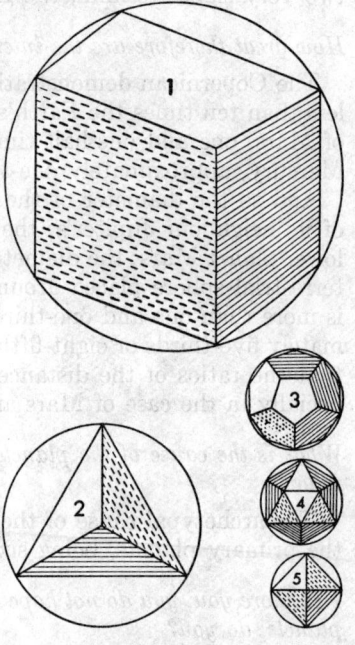

ated, the tetrahedron is the first of the solid figures cut out of the cube, and the dodecahedron is the first of the composite figures made by adding to, and covering over, the cube. This same idea is dominant in their planes: the tetragon, the triangle, and the pentagon. For the tetragon is generated first of all by drawing the most simple and regular lines, as was said in Book i; and it is broken up into two triangles; but the pentagon is composed of three suitable triangles.

Explain the generation, primacy, and form of the cube.

Rectilinear magnitudes have an origin visible to the mind; the spherical, as was said above, brings a certain character of eternity or of eternal generation. For with a sphere postulated, the point at its centre is postulated, and so are the infinite points on its surface. Therefore, line arises from the flowing of point to point; surface arises from the sideways flowing of the line; and body, from the sideways flowing of the surface. If the flowing of the point is straight and also the shortest, there arises a straight line bounded by two points. If the flowing of the straight line is such that all its points flow equally, a parallelogram arises bounded by four lines; and if the parallelogram flows in the same way, the parallelepiped arises, bounded by six planes. Again, if the flowing of the line is equal to the flowing straight line, and the line along which the flowing takes place makes any angle with the flowing line except a right angle, there arises the plane called the rhomboid, whose sides are equal. But if the line makes a right angle, it is a square which arises. And if the square also flows, there arises the cube, the six planes of which are all squares and are thus equal to one another. Now the shortest is prior to the crooked; and the equal and similar is prior to the unequal and dissimilar, and the straight, or right, to the oblique. Therefore, in this way among the lines generated, the straight line is prior—for the circle is posterior to the plane, and the plane to the straight line; and among surfaces the square is prior. Thus among magnitudes, that which exists perfectly [459] (*i.e.,* with three dimensions), that is to say, the cube, is shown to be first among bodies.

Explain the primacy of the tetrahedron among the segments, and the mode of section of the cube, and its form.

By subtracting from the bodies, so that something lesser exists, the other solid

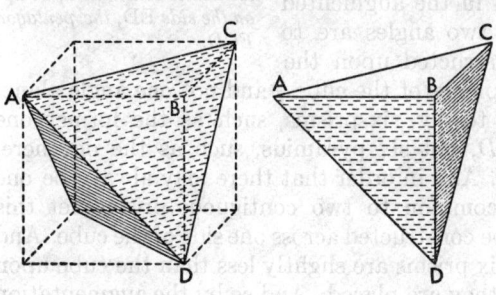

figures usually come to be. We must judge that the first of them is the solid figure which exists if the first figure generated (*viz.,* the cube) is cut most simply and most equally. But the section—among the sections which designate a new plane figure—is not equal or more simple than when you cut through four angles of the cube completely. For you are cutting out the same number of equilateral tetrahedrons—and the single tetrahedrons A, C, and D have a solid right angle B above the triangular base. There remains as it were the bowels of the cube, namely, the fifth tetrahedron, similar to itself in all respects, and bounded by four equilateral triangles. But if you make the section of the cube of which I have spoken in Book i, there will not be five but six irregular tetrahedrons. So the tetrahedron is the first figure coming from the decreasing of the bodies. But it is a third part of the body of the cube cut, and any angle cut away, such as *BACD*, is the sixth part of the same whole.

[460] *Explain the origin of the dodecahedron by addition, and give the reasons for its posteriority among the three primary bodies, and its priority among the bodies generated by addition.*

As in subtracting from the cube, four planes are constructed in place of the four angles of the cube which have been cut off; four angles remain to the tetrahedron, but the angles are decreased and are still of the same species (*i.e.*, trilinear), so too, if we wish to construct the first of the increased bodies, or of those which are greater than the cube, in place of the planes of the cube we construct angles, but we transmit the angles of the cube as clothed and increased, though they also remain trilinear; or, what leads to the same thing, upon the twelve sides of the cube the same numbers of planes are to be built, just as, in the former case, upon the six sides of the tetrahedron the same number of squares were built. For as the cube roofs over the tetrahedron, so this increased solid figure which we are investigating roofs over the cube.

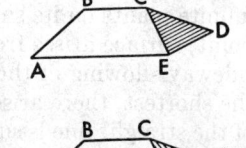

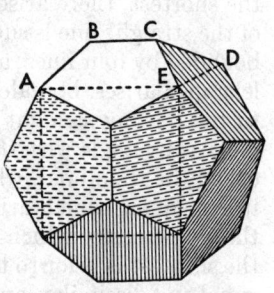

[461] But if instead of the single planes of the cube we set up single angles—if we set up six quadrilinear angles, because the six planes of the cube are quadrilaterals—the eight trilinear angles of the cube remain. Therefore the figure would be mixed. Therefore in order that the trilinear angle may remain in the augmented figure, two angles are to be constructed upon the single planes of the cube—and not one angle alone;

Here AE, ED, *and the remaining dotted lines are the sides of the roofed-over cube.* AED *is the plane of the cube; and the two angles* B *and* C *come to be instead of it; and* A *and* E *the angles of the cube remain. But upon the side of the cube* AE, *the pentagon* ABCE *is constructed, as upon the side* ED, *the pentagon* ECD.

that is to say, six prisms, such as the former one *BCAED*, not six pyramids, such as the one here, *BADC*. And in order that there may always be one plane common to two contiguous prisms, let this plane be constructed across one side of the cube. And these six prisms are slightly less than the cube upon which they are placed. And so by the augmentation twelve angles are made—and by the addition of the eight angles of the cube, the sum of the angles is twenty.

How do you infer the form of the plane of the dodecahedron?

The angles of the figure, as was said already, should be twenty; and each single angle is bounded by three lines, any one of which adjoins two angles; and so there are twenty times three or sixty points. But two points determine one line. Therefore there are thirty lines or sides to the figure, and there are potentially sixty with respect to the planes of the figure. For any [462] side of the figure adjoins two planes. But the division of the sixty lines or plane sides by the twelve planes—which are necessary for this solid figure—gives a quotient of five. Therefore the planes are quinquelateral. So among the augmented figures the dodecahedron, having pentagonal planes, is again first.

What is the origin of the secondary figures and why are there only two?

Three other figures correspond to the cube, the tetrahedron, and the dodecahedron; but one of them coincides with its primary figure. And these second- ary figures are generated by subtracting from the three primary figures, but by subtraction of a different kind, where a line is not left in the place of the plane, but an angle, *i.e.*, in the place of the surface of the primary figure, there is—not a line of the secondary figure, but—a point; while the number of lines remains. But at the same time—as before—a plane of the secondary figure is generated in place of the angle of the primary figure. And the plane is triangular, because the angle of the primary figure is trilinear, and by joining together the centres of three planes of the primary figure a solid angle is constructed. So these figures are generated secondly as if the bowels of the first figures.

For whatever appears outwardly falls away from the cube, and there remain of the cube only six centres, as it were the navels of six planes. And there are six angles to the new figure. And [463] because the cube has eight angles, the figure gets eight plane equilateral triangles in their place. Hence it is called an octahedron; and it is the sixth part of its cube.

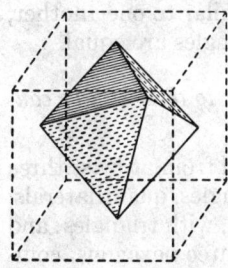

As regards the tetrahedron: in place of its plane triangles four angles are constructed; and in place of its four angles four triangles are constructed; and a figure arises which is the same as its primary figure. And so it is not judged to be new. However, it is the twenty-seventh part of the tetrahedron in which it is inscribed.

As regards the dodecahedron: [464] in place of the twelve bases it gives the twelve angles of the new figure; and in place of its twenty angles it gives twenty triangular bases: whence the figure is called an icosahedron. And it is slightly less than half the size of its original dodecahedron.

One of the primary figures was produced by subtracting from the cube; and one by adding to the cube. And now the secondary figures are generated by subtracting from these two primary figures. Is nothing produced by adding to the secondary figures?

To this second subtraction there also corresponds a second addition to those three primary figures—an angle arising in place of the plane, and a plane in place of the angle. But the figures are the same as those produced by former subtraction. For just as formerly the octahedron was inscribed in the cube, and the icosahedron in the dodecahedron: so now in turn the cube is made to be inscribed in the octahedron, and the dodecahedron in the icosahedron. Accordingly, when all these operations have been performed, the first five figures are found.

Why do you call them the most simple figures?

Because each of them is bounded by planes of one species alone, *viz.*, triangles or quadrilaterals or pentagons, and by solid angles of one species alone—the three primary figures by the trilinear angle, the octahedron by the quadrilinear angle, and the icosahedron by the quinquelinear angle. The other figures vary [465] either with respect to the angle or with respect to the plane. For there are some which have one genus of planes, as the rhombus in this diagram, but no one genus of solid angles. For the dodecahedral rhombus has six quadrilinear angles and [467] eight trilinear angles; and the thirty-sided rhombus has twelve quinquelinear angles and twenty trilinear angles. There are other figures which mingle diverse planes having uniform solid angles, as the thirteen species of the Archimedean solids.

Why do you call those five figures the most beautiful and the most perfect?

Because they imitate the sphere—which is an image of God—as much as a rectilinear figure possibly can, arranging all their angles in the same sphere. And they can all be inscribed in a sphere. And as the sphere is everywhere similar to itself, so in this case the planes of any one figure are all similar to one another, and can be inscribed in one and the same circle; and the angles are equal.

Is there not some other method by which more figures similar to these can be constructed?

None at all. For a solid angle of any figure is constructed from at least three planes. Accordingly, equilateral triangles can join with triangles, quadrilaterals, and pentagons in order to form a solid angle; quadrilaterals, with triangles; and pentagons, similarly with triangles. But six triangles, or three hexagons, complete a surface, and cannot form a solid angle. But magnitudes larger than these, as three heptagons, or three of any other figure, exceed the sum of four right angles which are laid around the same point in a plane. See the scholium to the last proposition in Book XIII of Euclid and Book II of my *Harmonies*.

Then how are the number of the primary spheres and the intervals of the planetary orbits taken from these figures?

Any solid figure is understood to have two spheres, one circumscribed around it and the other touching the centres of its planes; whence the first view of the solid figure [468] as it were invites some architect to circumscribe and to inscribe spheres. So whatever the ratio of the outer sphere to the inner sphere is, that has been made to be the ratio of the sphere of the upper planet to the nearest lower sphere, between which spheres there is the aforesaid interval.

What are the ratios of the spheres in the single figures?

Let the semidiameter of the circumscribed sphere be 100,000. The ratio of the semidiameter of the inscribed sphere is as follows:

In the cube	57,735	The square is equal to one-third of the square on the radius of the circumscribed sphere.
In the tetrahedron	33,333	One-third of the radius of the circumscribed sphere.
In the dodecahedron	79,465	An irrational part, the square on which is between
In the icosahedron	79,465	two-thirds and three-fifths of the square on the radius of the circumscribed sphere: namely, by the subtraction of the square on the apotome from eleven-fifteenths of the square on the radius.
In the octahedron	57,735	The square is equal to one-third of the square on the radius of the circumscribed sphere.

But the octahedron has at the middle section of itself a square formed by the four lines bounding it in the middle, and if a circle is inscribed in this square, its radius will be 70,711, the square on which is equal to half the square on the radius of the circumscribed circle.

Show now what the place of the sphere of the Earth is among these figures.

The five bodies were distributed into two classes above: into those generated first, and those generated second. The former had a trilinear angle, and the latter a plurilinear. For as Adam was the first-born, and Eve was not his daughter but a part of him—and they are both called the first-made, [469] but Cain and Abel and their sisters are their offspring; so the cube is in the first place, wherefrom have arisen, differently and more simply, the tetrahedron— as it were a rib of the cube—and the dodecahedron, but in such a way that all three remain among the primary figures. The octahedron and the icosahedron, with their triangular planes, are as it were the offspring born of the cube and dodecahedron as fathers and from the tetrahedron as mother; and each of them bears a likeness to its parent.

So the three first figures of the same class had to enclose the circuit of the centre of the Earth and the two figures generated second, as the other class, should be enclosed by the sphere in which the Earth revolves, and so this sphere had to be made a boundary common to both orders, because the Earth, the home of the image of God, was going to be chief among the moving globes. For in this way the nature of being inscribed is kept in the second class and that of circumscribing in the first class. For it is more natural and more fitting that the octahedron should be inscribed in the cube, and the icosahedron in the dodecahedron, than the cube in the octahedron, and the dodecahedron in the icosahedron.

And so in this way the circuit of the centre of the Earth was placed in the middle between the planets; for three planets had to be placed outside, on account of the three primary figures; and two had to be placed inside its circuit— on account of the two figures of the second class—to which the sun is added as a third in the inmost embrace of the centre of the mobile spheres. And so Saturn, Jupiter, and Mars were made the higher planets, and Venus, Mercury, and the sun, the lower. But the moon, which has a private movement around the Earth during the same common circuit of the Earth, is among the secondary planets, as was said above.

What is the order among the three outer figures and what place among the planets does each hold?

The cube is the first of the figures, and therefore it was placed between the two farthest spheres, those of Saturn and Jupiter. In the generation of the figures the tetrahedron follows: therefore, it got [470] the place between Jupiter and Mars. The dodecahedron was the last of the three: therefore, the last place was assigned to it between the orbital regions of Mars and of the Earth.

How do you place the two inner figures?

Although the octahedron has the nature of the cube, of which it is the first parts, and the icosahedron that of the dodecahedron, of which it is the last parts; nevertheless the next place after the dodecahedron did not belong to the octahedron, for two reasons. For, first, the two classes of figures are somehow opposed to one another: therefore it was fitting that the beginning of the placing should be at the opposite termini. But since the first place of the outer figures was judged to be the place which tended the more outward; consequently the first place of the inner figures was judged to be the place which tended the more to the interior towards the centre. Secondly, it was more becoming to the nature of the similar figures; the dodecahedron and the icosahedron, and better suited to their being inscribed within one another, that they should succeed one another very closely, with the circuit or sphere of the Earth coming in between, at which as at a common boundary both classes of figures stop.

Therefore it was caused that the icosahedron should be placed between the orbits of the Earth and of Venus, but the octahedron between the inmost orbits, those of Venus and Mercury. But the sun does not have a sphere in which its centre is carried around; and therefore it is outside the number of the primary moving bodies, but it has in itself the source of the movement outside, the fixed stars have stillness in themselves, and they furnish a place for the moving bodies and contain them.

Is there found between these spheres which you have given to each figure the ratio of the figures?

There is found so much the same ratio that, although there is some very small deficiency, nevertheless no interval between two planets approaches nearer to the ratios of the spheres of another figure [471] than those intervals which have been ascribed with the best of reasons to the two planets.

For you see that as Saturn's sphere had less than twice the diameter of the sphere of Jupiter, and Venus' similarly had less than twice the diameter of Mercury's, namely, five-thirds or eight-fifths; so also in the cube and in the octahedron 100,000 is less than twice 57,775. For if you take three-fifths of 100,000 you will have 60,000; but if you take five-eighths, then 62,500 will be the result. Again, as the sphere of Mars had a very small ratio to the sphere which carries the centre of the Earth, and one nearly equal to the ratio of the sphere of the Earth to that of Venus; so too you will see between the spheres of the dodecahedron and of the icosahedron a very small ratio, namely, that of 100,000 to 79,465. You see, thirdly, that, just as the sphere of Jupiter has a very great ratio to the sphere of Mars, namely triple; so too, in the case of the tetrahedron the diameter of the circumscribed sphere is three times the diameter of the inscribed sphere.

If the intervals approach so nearly to the ratios of the figures, why then does some discrepancy remain?

1. Because the archetype of the movable world is constituted not only of the five regular [solid] figures—by which the chariots of the planets and the number of the courses were determined—but also of the harmonic proportions with which the courses themselves were attuned, as it were, to the idea of celestial music or of a harmonic concord of six voices. Now since this musical ornamentation demanded a difference of movement in any given planet—a difference between the slowest and the fastest movement; and this difference is made by the variation of the interval between the planet and the sun; and since the magnitude or ratio of this variation was required to be different in different planets; hence it was necessary that some very small amount should be taken away from the intervals which are exhibited by the figures as uniform and without variation, and that it should be left to the freedom of the composer to represent the harmonies of movement.

[472] 2. And nevertheless that which the regular solids have of their very own was not neglected in this very small discrepancy. For just as the ratio of the spheres of the tetrahedron is perfect, *i.e.*, rational simply, that of the cube and the octahedron, half-perfect, *i.e.*, rational in square but irrational in length, but that of the dodecahedron and of the icosahedron are wholly imperfect, *i.e.*, absolutely irrational; so also the ratio of the tetrahedral planets imitates the figure almost exactly, *i.e.*, in approximately the extremities of the intervals. But the ratios of the cubic and octahedral planets are less exactly like the figures, because the extreme intervals recede from the figures while the intermediate intervals square with them. But the whole intervals of the dodecahedral and icosahedral planets abandon the ratios of their figures, although they approach no others more nearly. Now see how the longest interval of Mars is almost exactly a third part of the least interval of Jupiter, as in the tetrahedron the [diameter of the] inside sphere is one-third [of the diameter] of the outer sphere: so that in this way if the angles of the tetrahedron are placed in the inmost sphere of Jupiter, the tetrahedral planes somehow touch the farthest sphere of Mars. See again how if the angles of the cube are placed in the sphere of Saturn and the angles of the octahedron in the inmost sphere of Venus, the planes of the figures sink into the regions [*i.e.*, spheres] of Jupiter and Mercury, and do not pass above the total regions but enter in approximately as far as the middle. Finally, see how, if the angles of the dodecahedron are placed in the inmost sphere of Mars and the angles of the icosahedron in the inmost sphere of the Earth, the planes of the figures by no means reach to the inscribed regions of the Earth and of Venus, but that nevertheless no planetary intervals approach more nearly to the least ratios of these figures. Concerning these things, see my *Harmonies* (Book v, Proposition XLIX and *passim*), where the causes not only of the exact magnitude of the ratios between two spheres but also of the opposite intervals of any single planet are dug up.

[473] *No other conclusion concerning the interposition of the figures can be drawn from the periodic times, can it?*

All ratios of time in this case are greater than the ratios of their orbits and also greater than the ratios of their figures, as will be unfolded in the second part of this book. Nevertheless the property of the figures can be recognized without difficulty even among the time ratios. For as there are three ratios among the figures—the greatest ratio which is alone, and the middle and the least, which are both found in two cases—the greatest ratio is found in the tetrahedron alone, the middle ratio in the cube and the octahedron, and the least ratio in the dodecahedron and the icosahedron; so the greatest and the solitary ratio of times is found between Jupiter and Mars, approximately that of 6 to 1, nearly 12 years to less than 2 years, an argument for the interposition of the tetrahedron. But between Saturn and Jupiter and between Venus and Mercury the ratio of times is less and in both cases approximately the same, an argument for the interposition of the cognate bodies, in the first case the cube and in the second case the octahedron, which have approximately the same ratios between their spheres. For as the 30 years of Saturn are to the 12 years of Jupiter, so approximately are the 225 days of Venus to the 88 days of Mercury. And finally there is the least ratio of times between Mars and the Earth and between the Earth and Venus, and again it is practically the same in both cases, an argument for the interposition, in the first case of the dodecahedron, and in the second case of the icosahedron, which are bodies cognate and having the same ratio. For as the 687 days of Mars are to the 365¼ days of the Earth, so the 365¼ days are to 194 days, since instead of these Venus has 225 days, a little more, and makes the least time ratio of all. The causes of such a small discrepancy are unfolded in my *Harmonies* (Book v).

You do not have any other evidence, do you, except that from the two classes of figures that the globe [474] of the Earth has the principal proportionality in location?

Indeed it is not by chance that the mean interval between the Earth, the middle planet, and the sun is found to be almost exactly a mean proportional between the shortest interval of Mars, the lowest of the higher planets, and the longest interval of Venus, the highest of the lower planets. For, as was said above, the space between Mars and Venus was left for the Earth—left undetermined by the inscribing of figures and open and free, so that in dividing it by the sphere of the Earth, either this ratio or some other, if the other were better, could be expressed. Therefore the mean in the classes of the figures, and the middle wall between the higher and the lower planets had to be a mean geometrically too.

Then what determined this interval which the inscribings did not determine?

Even if there is a certain augmented figure, the aculeate or wedge-shaped dodecahedron, which is taken as determining this interval as accurately as the interval between Jupiter and Mars is determined by the tetrahedron, and the relationship of that imperfect figure with its cognates, the dodecahedron and the icosahedron, is seen not to lack its proper ratio; nevertheless the figures alone do not determine these intervals or any others exactly, but this job was left to the ornament of harmonic movements, which demands a certain amount of freedom in determining these intervals exactly.

4. ON THE RATIOS OF THE PRINCIPAL BODIES OF THE WORLD
TO ONE ANOTHER

Where do you judge that the beginning should be made in investigating the ratios of bodies?

From the Earth (1) as the home of the speculative creature, [475] and (2) of the same image of God the Creator; (3) for we read in the holy *Book of Moses* that in the beginning God created the Heaven and the Earth; (4) moreover, the sphere of the Earth is the middle figure between the planets, and their common boundary and even a geometrical mean proportional between the territories of the higher and the lower planets; (5) finally, the very structure of these ratios cries in a loud voice that God the Creator in fitting the bodies and intervals to the solar body, as to a measure prior to their generation, made His beginning at the Earth.

What do you judge to be the reason for the magnitude of the solar body?

The following things argue that the solar globe is the first of all the bodies of the world in the order of creation, at least in the archetypal order; if not also in the temporal: (1) Moses makes light the work of the first day, and instead of light we can understand the solar body. (2) Above by many votes, the solar body obtained the principate among natural things; why not also in quantity and in time, in which it was created?

Furthermore, the first body, because first, does not acquire any ratio to the bodies following; but rather the bodies following acquire a ratio to it as first. Wherefore there is no archetypal cause of the magnitude of the sun: nor could there have been a different globe twice as great as it is now, because the rest of the universe and the whole world and man in it would have had to be twice as great as they now are.

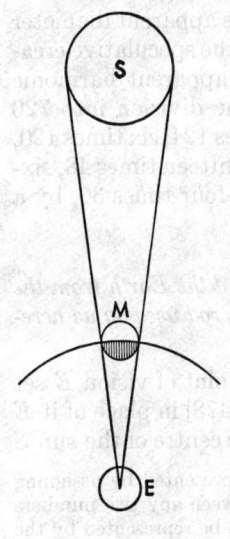

Then by what means was the magnitude of the Earth adjusted to the solar globe?

By means of vision of the sun. For the Earth was going to be the home of the speculative creature, and for his sake the universe and world have been made. But now speculation has its origin in the vision of the stars: [476] wherefore too the magnitude of the things to be contemplated had to have its origin in the magnitude of the things to be seen. But the first visible is light or the sun, as it is (1) the work of the first day and (2) the most excellent of all visible things, the principal, the primary, and that which was going to be the cause of the visibility of all the rest. So it follows that the beginning [*principium*] in proportioning the bodies of the world was taken from the vision of the sun from the Earth; just as in the case of the upper planets the regions of the world were separated by the mean proportionality of the orbit of the Earth.

How great does the diameter of the sun appear to be on the Earth?

It is established by the very old observations of Aristarchus and by the most recent of our time, that, if the Earth is at its greatest distance from the sun, and with the point of vision E as centre a circle is described, then exactly one-seven-hundred-twentieth of that circle, *i.e.*, $\frac{1}{2}°$, is occupied and so to speak defined by the diameter of the sun; or, what is the same thing, the angle E, comprehended by the lines touching each rim of S the sun, is one-seven-hundred twentieth of four right angles.

What do you think is the reason for this number?

We must seek the archetypal cause of the first thing among the first causes. But there is no geometrical cause for the division of a circle into 720 parts [477] in a figure lacking that number of sides. For this figure is derived by bisection from a figure having 45 sides; and there is no [geometrical] demonstration of that figure, as is proved in the *Harmonies*, Book I. It follows that this sectioning of the circle is taken from the composition of figures and so from harmonic ratios. And it seems to bring about the necessity that the circle of the zodiac, wherein all the planets had to practise their harmonic movements in reality and the sun in appearance—that this circle, I say, should be divided into parts of a harmonic numbering by the appearance of the first body. But the least number which offers itself in determining all the parts of the monochord and in setting up the twofold scale of the octave [*systema diapason duplex*], *i.e.*, in the minor and the major mode—I say that this number is 720, as was shown in the *Harmonies*, Book III, Chapter 6[1].

Wherefore, since the movements of all the planets, as I show in Book v of the *Harmonies*, had to be adjusted to this twofold scale; it was fitting that the first body, which was the leader of the dance to this music, by its apparent diameter on the Earth, should, in the eyes of the Earth-dweller—*i.e.*, the speculative creature—divide that circle as an index and measure of the apparent harmonic movements, by the division of the monochord, *i.e.*, by the division into 720 parts, which is twice 360, thrice 240, four times 180, five times 124, six times 120, eight times 90, nine times 80, ten times 72, twelve times 60, fifteen times 48, sixteen times 45, eighteen times 40, twenty times 36, twenty-four times 30, by a multiplex form of division into aliquot parts.

Then what follows in respect to the interval between the sun and the Earth from the assumption of this hypothesis? or, what is the magnitude of this rod used by us heretofore as a measure of the planetary spheres?

If S the diameter of the sun had to occupy $\frac{1}{2}°$ with the point of vision E set up on the Earth; it is necessary that the point of vision, or [478] in place of it E the centre of the terrestrial globe, should be distant from the centre of the sun S

---

[1]In Kepler's musical system, if the intervals in the octave are represented by assigning whole numbers to the eight tones in such fashion that the ratio between any two numbers will express the analogous musical interval, then the minor scale will be represented by the following sequence, in least numbers:

$$72 : 81 : 90 : 96 : 108 : 120 : 128 : 144$$

Similarly, the major scale, as follows:

$$360 : 405 : 432 : 480 : 540 : 576 : 640 : 720$$

Now if the two scales are combined, "the twofold scale of the octave, *i.e.*, in the minor and the major mode" thus produced will be represented by the following sequence, in least whole numbers:

$$360 : 405 : 432 : 450 : 480 : 540 : 576 : 600 : 640 : 720$$

to the extent of a little more than 229 semidiameters of the round body of the sun S, as we are taught in geometry.

I have the interval; tell me also the magnitude of the terrestrial globe and give reasons.

These things are not yet sufficient to determine the magnitude of the Earth; but it is the work of one axiom added to another. Without doubt, because the Earth was going to be the home of the measuring creature; and the Earth by its body had to become the measure of the bodies of the world, and by its semidiameter the measure of the intervals, as the line is the measure of lines. But since the measuring of bodies is different from the measuring of lines, and since the ratio between the terrestrial body and the solar body is first, as is the ratio between the diameter of the Earth and the interval between the Earth and the sun; nothing is more in agreement with a right and fitting and ordered proportioning than that the equality of both ratios should be postulated—so that as many times as the terrestrial body E is contained in the solar body S, so many times also is the semidiameter of the Earth E contained in SE, the interval between the centres of the sun and the Earth; so that in this way, as the terrestrial body E is to the solar body S, so the semidiameter of the Earth E is to SE, the distance between the centres.

How is the magnitude of the semidiameter of the Earth got from these two axioms?

Let the semidiameter of the sun S be put down as 100,000 parts, so that the interval SE between the centres of the sun and the Earth will be 22,918,166 such parts. The cube of 100,000, *i.e.*, 1,000,000,000,000,000 is to be divided by the interval 22,918,166; and the [square] root of the quotient—which is the continued sine 0°15'0" is to be taken, and it will be 6,606. That will be the magnitude [479] of the semidiameter of the Earth. For as 6,606—the semidiameter of the Earth—is contained 3,469⅓ times in 22,918,166—the interval between the sun and the Earth—so too the cube of 6,606—the semidiameter of the Earth—is contained the same number of times, *i.e.*, 3,469⅓ in the cube of 100,000, the semidiameter of the sun. But it is known from geometry that the ratio of cubes to one another is the same as the ratio of the globes inscribed in the same cubes. So the semidiameter of the sun S will contain the semidiameter of the Earth E a little more than fifteen times; but the body of the sun S will contain the body of the Earth E approximately 3,469 times.

You say that its magnitude is approximately three times what the ancients assigned to the longest distance of the sun from the Earth, for they set a lesser distance, only 1200 times the semidiameter of the Earth: and you say twenty times the [former] ratio of bodies, because they made the sun only 166 times greater than the Earth: do not you respect their astronomical observations?

Not at all. For the ancients made the sun as near as a parallax of 3' should have made it to be. Whence Tycho Brahe reasoned that when Mars is nearer to the Earth than the sun is, Mars should be observed to have a parallax much greater than 3'. But I have observed that the parallax of Mars is not at all perceptible to sense. Therefore the distance of Mars, even when most near, is greater than 1200 semidiameters; and the distance of the sun is greater too.

[480] The diameters of Mars and Venus can be observed through the ancient

instruments and through the Belgian telescope of modern times; and they are found to be of a very few minutes. Therefore, if the sun is as near as the ancients say it is; then these planets—each in its own ratio—will become as near as Tycho Brahe said, out of Copernicus. If Mars is so near; it will be even smaller in its visible diameter. Therefore Mars will be smaller than the Earth, namely, the higher planet will be smaller than the lower; so that there will be no proportion [analogia] between the magnitude of the bodies and their order—and that is not in agreement with the adornment of the world.

The greater the distance of the sun is set down to be, the smaller the parallax of the sun becomes. And the smaller the parallax of the sun, the greater the parallax of the moon from the sun; if the simple parallax of the moon is taken from its own principles, and that is of great service in correcting the doctrine of eclipses. Therefore such a great magnitude for the interval of the sun is confirmed rather than refuted by astronomical observations.

And it accords with the prayer of physics that the solar body, which gives movement to all the other planets, should be much greater than all the mobile bodies fused together into one.

The determination of what body follows most closely upon the determination of the Earth?

Of the moon, a secondary planet: (1) because this star has been assigned to the Earth as its private property, so that the moon might help with the growth of earthly creatures and be observed by the speculative creature on the Earth, and that the observation of the stars might begin with it. (2) Because the reasons for the ratio to be established are practically the same.

Tell the foundations of the ratio between the moon and the Earth, by reason of the body and by reason of the interval.

1. Again, the visible diameter of the moon at its greatest distance from the Earth had to occupy $\frac{1}{720}$ of the circle, both on account of the number itself, as before, and also on account of the eclipses of the sun, a spectacle ordained by the Creator in order that the speculative creature should thereby be taught concerning the rationale of the course of the stars. And teaching would be done most rightly if the semidiameters of the sun and moon were to appear equal at the greatest distance of each: so that in this way the moon could cover the sun exactly, during this relationship of both stars, if it occurred. And so M the moon and S the sun make the same angle at E the Earth.

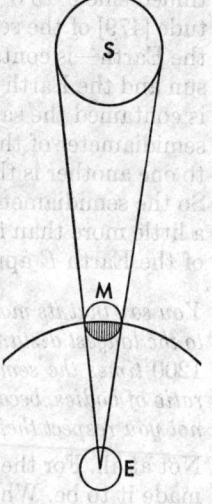

2. Moreover, it was fitting that the ratio between the terrestrial body and the lunar body should be to the ratio between the distance of the moon and the semidiameter of the Earth as in the former case the ratio between the solar body and the terrestrial body was to the ratio between the solar interval and the semidiameter of the Earth: namely, the proportion holding between the pair of ratios should in both cases be the same. For the moon, a secondary and terrestrial planet, made in order to

obscure the sun, should have followed the example of the ratios of the sphere of the sun or the Earth.

What follows from this?

Two things follow from postulating the two axioms. And either one of these two things by itself, by a wonderful concord of probabilities, even if it did not follow from the foregoing, [482] could be employed in place of an axiom, since they are very worthy of belief by themselves. The first is as follows: that since the proportion of ratios on the part of the sun is one of equality, *i.e.*, as many times as the body of the Earth E is contained in the greater body of the sun S, so many times is the semidiameter of the Earth E contained in SE the distance or semidiameter of the sphere of the Earth or sun. But that proportion is not more probable than the following: that the body of the Earth E will contain the lunar body M, which is narrower and smaller, as many times as the semidiameter of the Earth E is contained in the distance or semidiameter of the lunar orbit EM, and the former proportion is no more probable than this latter. This very proportion, employed as an axiom, has its own dignity; hence, because the Earth is the home of the measuring creature, therefore the Earth by its own body measures even the smaller lunar body, just as previously it measured the solar body which is greater than it: and by its semidiameter it measures the semidiameter of the lunar sphere. But both proportions are in the ratio of equality, because M the lunar sphere is alone placed around E the Earth, just as the Earth's sphere is placed around the sun; and so the measurement of the lunar sphere and the lunar body, prior to the other planetary bodies, is no less proper to the Earth than previously the measuring of the solar body and the solar sphere was. But in its own proper measuring, it is right for the ratio of equality to hold, as first and principal, if nothing prevents it.

The second thing which follows from the premises by a long circle of demonstration—see it in my *Hipparchus*—is as follows: that by this reasoning the semidiameter of the moon's orbit or the distance EM is a mean proportional between the distance ES, or semidiameter of the Earth's sphere, and the semidiameter of the terrestrial body: so that as the semidiameter of the Earth E is to EM the semidiameter of the moon's sphere, so EM is to ES the semidiameter of the Earth's sphere or the sun's. Here again there is an equality of both ratios which is itself probable, because what the Earth's sphere placed around the sun is to the sun is what the moon's sphere placed around the Earth is to the moon.

[483] *Do observations agree with this interval between the moon and the Earth?*

Down to the last hair: for Brahe found that in its quadratures the distance of the perigeal moon from the Earth was slightly less than 54 semidiameters of the Earth; but the distance of the apogeal moon in the same quadratures is more than 59, slightly less than 60. And from these beginnings it is inferred that the first distance is 54, the second 59.

How is the magnitude of the semidiameter of the moon to be inferred from the axioms and conclusions employed as axioms, which have been posited?

1. If the semidiameter of the moon M is set down as 100,000 parts, so that the interval EM between the centres of the moon and the Earth is 22,918,166

such parts: the cube of 100,000, *i.e.*, 1,000,000,000,000,000, is to be multiplied by 22,918,166; and the fourth root of the product is to be taken: the fourth root will be 389,085, showing the magnitude of the semidiameter of the Earth in terms of the same parts. For just as 389,085 the semidiameter of the Earth is contained in 22,918,166, the distance to the moon, a little less than 59 times, so too the cube of 389,085 will contain the cube of 100,000 slightly less than 59 times, and so the globe of the Earth will contain the globe of the moon slightly less than 59 times. Thus the semidiameter of the terrestrial body *E* will contain the semidiameter of the lunar body *M* less than four times.

2. Differently and more simply, from a later conclusion: the square root of 3,469⅓, *viz.*, of the distance to the sun, is taken, and it is slightly less than 59; and *EM* the distance of the moon is 59 whereof the semidiameter of the Earth is 1. But if 1 the semidiameter of the Earth is divided by 59, and the cube root of the quotient is taken, the result will be the semidiameter of the lunar body in terms of the same dimensions.

Then what is the ratio of the diameters of the sun and moon inferred to be?

The same as the ratio of the solar sphere to the lunar sphere, or that of the [484] lunar [sphere] to the terrestrial body, *viz.*, the ratio holding between slightly less than 59 to 1. And so the solar body contains the lunar body more than 200,000 times.

What are the ratios of the planetary globes to one another?

Nothing is more in concord with nature than that the order of magnitudes should be the same as the order of spheres, so that among the six primary planets, Mercury should have the least body, because it is inmost, and should obtain the most narrow sphere; that next to Mercury should be Venus, which is larger, but still smaller than the Earth, because moving around in a sphere narrower than the Earth's but nevertheless wider than Mercury's; that the larger globe of Mars should be next to the Earth, because its sphere is outside and more spacious, but the lowest of the higher spheres; then the larger globe of Jupiter, in the middle among the higher planets; and finally Saturn's globe, the largest of the moving bodies, because it is the highest.

Now since bodies have three dimensions, along the diameters, across the surfaces, or in the space contained by the surfaces—or the corporeality—the ratio of the surfaces is the ratio of the squares of the diameters, and the ratio of the bodies is the ratio of the cubes of the diameters; it is consonant that one of the three ratios of the globes should have been made equal to the ratio of the intervals. For example, since Saturn is approximately 10 times farther away from the sun than the Earth, either the diameter of Saturn will be 10 times the diameter of the Earth, the surface 100 times the surface of the Earth and the body 1,000 times the body of the Earth: or the surface of Saturn will be 10 times the surface of the Earth, so that the ratio of the bodies will become the ratio of the ⅔ power of the intervals, and thus Saturn will be 30 times larger than the Earth, just as it is 30 times slower; while the ratio of the diameters will be merely the ratio of the square roots of the intervals, *viz.*, Saturn's diameter will be a little more than thrice the Earth's: or the bodies themselves have the ratio of the intervals, so that Saturn will be only ten times greater than the Earth, just as it is ten times farther away [from the sun], while in the surfaces the ratio of the ³⁄₂ power of the intervals will be kept, and in the diameters the ratio of the cube roots of the intervals. And so the diameter of Saturn's body will be slightly greater than twice the diameter of the terrestrial body.

Of these three modes, the first is refuted beyond controversy both by the archetypal reasons and also by the observations of the diameters made with the help of the Belgian telescope; up to now I have approved of the second mode, and Remus Quietanus of the third. On my side the better reasons, the archetypal, seemed to stand; on Remus' side the observations stand; but in such a delicate question I was afraid that the observations were not certain enough not to be taken exception to.

Nevertheless I yield the place to Remus and his observations. For Jupiter, opposite the sun and in the perigee of its eccentric circle, was frequently seen by me to occupy approximately 50″; Remus observes Saturn to occupy 30″; Mars, opposite the sun and its perigee in the Aquarius, appears greater than Jupiter, but not much greater. As a matter of fact, if a body equal to the Earth were seen at as great an interval as we assign to the sun, *viz.*, 3,469 semidiameters of the earth, it would appear to have a diameter of 2′. But now at the perigeal distance of Mars, the same body which is equal to the Earth will be perceived to occupy more than 5′ and thus to be equal to six Jupiters. Therefore, the greater the diameter of the globe of Mars is than the diameter of the Earth, the larger will it be in appearance. Therefore, we ought not to make this diameter of the globe of Mars more than one-sixth greater than the diameter of the Earth, as takes place in the third mode.

But this argument will make war perhaps not unsuccessfully with the help of the archetypal reasons: for just as previously we made the ratio of the bodies of the sun and Earth, and of the Earth and moon, the same as the ratio between the semidiameter of the Earth and the semidiameters of the spheres, so now the ratio of the planetary bodies is set down the same as the ratio between the semidiameters of the spheres. So Saturn in its bodily bulk will be slightly less than ten times greater than the Earth; Jupiter will be more than five times; Mars, one and one-half times; but Venus slightly less than three-quarters of the terrestrial body; and Mercury slightly greater than one-third of the same.

[486] *Just as the body of the Earth, so should not all the planetary bodies be attuned to the solar body by the same laws as the Earth?*

By no means. For if we were to follow this, the planetary bodies would be great in an order contrary to the order of the spheres, *viz.*, Mercury would be greatest; and Saturn smallest with a diameter less than one-third the diameter of the Earth. That, however, is repugnant both to the aforesaid reasons and to observations of their diameters. For Saturn opposite the sun, when it is nine times farther away from the sun than the Earth, occupies approximately 30″; therefore if it were near to the sun, it would occupy 4½′, since the Earth at an interval of that size would occupy 2′. And so the diameter of Saturn is more than twice as great as the diameter of the Earth.

And this is to say, as I said at the very beginning of this section, that it is very clear from the things themselves that the beginning of setting up the ratios must be made at the Earth. For observations of the moon and the eclipses bear witness to the equality of the two ratios, one of which is between the lunar body and the terrestrial body, and the other between the semidiameter of the Earth and the lunar sphere: we can by no means resist the certitude of the observations. Now it was very probable that the Earth too should be attuned to the sun by the same laws: and when we had set down that, we already had observations agreeing with it distantly: because the observations do not bear out the sun's having a nearness of 1,200 semidiameters of the Earth, but require twice or thrice that distance; and this attunement absolutely demands thrice that distance. Therefore the Earth is certainly the measure both of the solar and lunar bodies and of the solar and lunar spheres. But thus the body of Saturn or any other planetary body can by no means become the measure of both things: once more we bring forward as witnesses of this the certain observations of the diameters. Therefore the Earth alone is the real measure; but the nature of dimensions demands that the beginning of the conformation be taken from the measure.

What should we hold concerning the rarity and density of these six globes?

First, it is not consonant that all the planets should have the same density of matter. For where any multitude of bodies is necessary, there too a variety of conditions is required in order to make distinction, in order that they may be truly many. But the principal condition of bodies as bodies is the internal disposition of the parts. For inequality of bulks somehow happens to the bodies themselves on account of the surfaces bounding the bulks, and the internal part of one body does not differ from the part of another body in this circumscription of bulk. But the principal argument for the dissimilarity of matter is drawn from the consideration of the periodic times: for that consideration will not advance, if we make the globes have the same density, as we shall hear below.

Second, it is consonant that whatever body is nearer to the sun is also denser. For the sun itself is the most dense of all bodies in the world, and its immense and manifold force, which could not exist without a proportionate subject, bears witness to this thing: and the very places which are near the centre wear a certain form [gerunt ideam] of narrowness, such as exists in the condensation of much matter into a narrow place.

Third, nevertheless rarity should not be measured out in proportion to the greatness of the bodies, and density in proportion to the smallness. For example, by the above, both the distance and the amplitude of the globe of Saturn are to the distance and amplitude of the globe of Jupiter as 10 is to 5, approximately. I say that the density of matter of the globe of Saturn must not be put in the same ratio to the density of the globe of Jupiter as the ratio between 5 and 10.

For, if anyone followed this, he would sin against another law of variety by introducing not an unequal amount [copiam] of matter but the same amount throughout all the planets. For when 10 the bulk [488] of Saturn has been multiplied by 5 the density, the product will be 50 the amount of matter, which is as great as the product obtained by multiplying 5 the bulk of Jupiter by 1 its density. But it seems to be preferable and more elegant that the bulks of globes of different density should not be equal to one another, and that the density of globes of unequal bulks should not be the same, and that the amount of matter should not be distributed in equal portions throughout all the globes, which differ in bulk and in the density of their matter. Rather, all these things should vary, so that in whatever order the moving globes succeed one another after the centre, in the same order—order, I say, not ratio—let us measure out not only the spaces between the bodies and the rarity of the bodies but also the amount of matter: thus if Saturn has 50 as its amount of matter, Jupiter should be left with less than 50 but more than 25 the half of that—say 36. For thus the bodies will be as 50 is to 25, the amount of matter as 50 is to 36, the rarity as 50 is to 36, or as 36 is to 25, or the contrary density as 25 is to 36 or as 36 is to 50.

Furthermore, although formerly I upheld the equality of the amount of matter, I have been compelled to assign the ratio of the periodic times to the greatness of the bodies; so that just as Saturn has 30 years and Jupiter 12 years, so too the amplitude of the globe of Saturn to the globe of Jupiter is as 30 is to 12. But the observations of the diameters, made by myself and by Remus, refute this ratio as being too great.

Fourthly, the following things persuade us that the ratio of the amount of matter should be set down as precisely the ratio of the square roots of the bulks or amplitudes—and thus the ratio of the ½th powers of the diameters of the globes and the ratio of the ¾th powers of the surfaces. For first, it happens that the ratio of the amount of matter and the ratio of the density are both the ratio of the square roots of the intervals from the sun, and that thus the amount of matter and the density participate equally but inversely in that ratio: hence the amount of matter is greater, hence the density of the same great body is less: and that is the best mean [mediatio] of all. For example, Saturn will be twice as high as Jupiter, one and one-half times as heavy, and one and one-half times rarer, or Jupiter is one and one-half times denser. And in comparing the ratios of one planet: Saturn will be twice as high as heavy and twice as ample as rare.

Moreover, this same ratio of the square roots of the intervals is established by the following geometrical propriety: as above, between the intervals of two planets from the sun—for example, let the intervals be 1 and 64 for the sake of easier reckoning—let there be set down two mean proportionals 4 and 16, that is to say, in order to form the two remaining dimensions of the bodies, so that the bodies of the mobile globes would be to one another as 1 is to 64; but the surfaces of the globes as 1 is to 16 or as 4 is to 64, and finally their diameters as 1 is to 4 or as 4 is to 16 or as 16 is to 64. So now between 1 and 64 the intervals of the same two planets from the sun, let there be set down one mean proportional 8; that is to say: in order to form physically the matter within the bodies, for the matter is one thing only; so again let the intervals between the globes be as 1 is to 64, but let the amount of matter and the rarity too be in a lesser ratio, as 1 is to 8 or as 8 is to 64; or inversely the density, as 8 is to 1, or as 64 is to 8. For in this proportion it makes no difference in what manner it is that the corporeality is condensed or rarefied, whether it is merely in length or also in breadth, or finally in all three dimensions. For the ratio introduced prescribes an amount of the thing to be condensed; and different modes of condensation may be found, with the amount always remaining the same.

Therefore if by means of these principles we compute the densities of the planetary bodies and always seek a mean proportional between two planetary intervals from the sun, or, more precisely, between the diameters of two spheres or orbits, and if we finally compare all the numbers to some common round number and reduce them to round numbers: the result will be the numbers which follow in the table; and I have found that the terrestrial matters which I have placed next to them agree fairly closely with them in their ratio—as you can see in my book which I wrote in the year 1616 in the German language concerning weights and measures:

[490]	Saturn	324	The hardest precious stones
	Jupiter	438	The loadstone
	Mars	810	Iron
	Earth	1000	Silver
	Venus	1175	Lead
	Mercury	1605	Quicksilver

So that we may reserve gold—whose density in this proportion is 1,800 or 1,900—for the sun.

Finally what do you set down as the ratio of greatness holding between those three principal regions of the world, between the space wherein is the sun, the space or region of the mobile bodies, and the space of the whole world or the region bounded by the sphere of the fixed stars?

Even if the reasons of Copernicus do not extend to determining by observation the altitude of the sphere of the fixed stars: so that the altitude seems to be like infinity: for in comparison with this distance the total interval between the sun and the Earth, which by the judgement of the ancients embraces 1,200, and by our reasons 3,469, semidiameters of the globe of the Earth, is imperceptible: nevertheless reason, making a stand upon the traces found, discloses a footpath for arriving even at this ratio.

But in the beginning we must glance at the example of the terrestrial and the solar and the lunar spheres, because the ratios of the whole world are derived from the Earth's own proper ratios. And the region described by these three bodies and their courses is as it were a small world. For what the sun is in the Copernican region of the fixed stars—that is, what the Earth is in the sphere or region of the sun—in appearance, at any rate, and for Tycho also is the truth of the thing. And just as the sun is at the centre of the sphere of the fixed stars, unmoving in an unmoving home; so too with respect to the movement of the moon, the Earth is motionless at the centre of the, so to speak, motionless sphere of the sun. For just as the region of the moving bodies is arranged around the sun, so also the sphere of the moon is drawn around the Earth: in the former case the sphere of the fixed stars is the boundary for the planets; here the sun itself is the boundary for the moon, and she returns to this boundary at the end of a month when all her phases are completed.

Therefore it is consonant that, just as by necessary reasons the sphere of the moon was made a mean proportional between the apparent sphere of the sun and the terrestrial body at its centre; so too the region of the moving bodies, or the outmost circle of Saturn, becomes a mean proportional between the outmost sphere of the fixed stars and the solar body at the centre of the world.

Again the same thing is accomplished, even without reference to the small world, by the consideration of the great world itself. For since in one respect the movable bodies strive after the immobility of the encircling body, which supplies the place, while they struggle against the movement, so that they are not moved with such great speed as the mover strives after; in another respect they receive movement from the mover to a certain degree, so that movement from the mover and rest from the body supplying the place are somehow mixed together in the movable bodies. Therefore if it is permissible to state a physical thing in mathematical words, the movable bodies can very aptly be called a mean proportional between the body which is the source of movement, and the immovable body which supplies the place.

But since this thing is true [verum] physically and spatially—for the source is inside, the thing supplying the place is outside, and the movable bodies are in the middle—therefore nothing is more probable [verisimilius] than that even geometrically the semidiameter of the region of the movable bodies should be the mean proportional between the semidiameter of the solar body and the semidiameter of the sphere of the fixed stars, so that just as the solar globe is to the spherical system of all the planets, so this system is to the spherical body of the whole world, which is bounded by the region of the fixed stars. See the diagram on page 854.

How do we know the ratio of the diameter of the solar body to the diameter of the region of the movable bodies?

With the aid of mathematical instruments, from the angle which the solar body occupies in our vision. For since [492] this angle is approximately ½°, it follows that the sun has a distance of 229 of its semidiameters from our vision. But our point of vision is on the Earth; and the diameter of the sphere of the Earth, placed around the sun, is slightly greater than ⅒ of the diameter of the sphere of Saturn. Therefore the outmost sphere of the movable bodies, *i.e.*, Saturn's, contains approximately ten times as many diameters of the sun [as the terrestrial sphere does], *i.e.*, about 2,000. In the diagram on page 854 this [outmost sphere of Saturn] is the middle circle.

How great does the sphere of the fixed stars turn out to be by this reasoning?

As the diameter of Saturn's sphere, the outmost sphere of the movable bodies, contains the diameter of the solar body about 2,000 times, so too the diameter of the sphere of the fixed stars would contain the diameter of Saturn's sphere about 2,000 times. And so the diameter of the sphere of the fixed stars will contain about 4,000,000 diameters of the solar body, and—according to the ratio between the solar and terrestrial bodies believed by the ancients—more than five times as many diameters of the Earth, *i.e.*, 20,000,000; and by our reasoning, three times that, *i.e.*, 60,000,000.

But is not this amplitude of the sphere of the fixed stars unbelievable, for you make it to be 2,000 times greater than the sphere of Saturn, although among the ancients this sphere stood just above Saturn?

But much more unbelievable is the rapidity—for the ancients—of the sphere of the fixed stars and Saturn. And since it is necessary for one of these two opinions to stand, it is more probable that the sphere of the fixed stars should be 2,000 or 1,000 times wider than the ancients said than that it should be 24,000 times faster than Copernicus said. For in the former case there is no movement present in a subject which is very spacious and as it were infinite; but in the later case an as it were infinite movement is placed in the small sphere of Saturn. In itself such a great amplitude is not repugnant to Brahe's observations, nor is it discordant with reason that bodies which are at rest should be distant from the movable bodies by such an immense interval.

[493] *How do you know that such a great amplitude is not repugnant to Braahe's observations?*

He observed the greatest altitude of the pole star—which at that time was at 7° of the Ram—in the year 1586 at the midnight after the autumn equinox; and it was 58°51'. He observed the greatest altitude [of the same star] on the winter solstice on December 26 at about the sixth hour of the evening, and he found it again at 58°51'. And so there was no difference; even though during the month of September the horizon cut the sphere of the fixed stars lower down—by approximately the whole semidiameter of the sphere in which the Earth is borne— than on December 26, because on the first date the sun was apparent in the Libra; and on the second date, in the Capricornus. The same thing occurred when the least altitude was observed on the midnight after the spring equinox and after the winter solstice at 6 o'clock in the morning; for in both cases the altitude was found to be 52°59½', although during the month of March the horizon cut the sphere of the fixed stars higher up—by approximately the whole semidiameter of the sphere wherein the Earth is borne—than in December. Therefore the diameter of the sphere wherein the Earth is borne is not perceptible through Brahe's instruments.

And so since the diameter [of the terrestrial sphere] does not make a difference of 1' in the sphere of the fixed stars, therefore it is not $\frac{1}{3500}$th part of the semidiameter of the sphere of the fixed stars. Therefore the semidiameter of Saturn's sphere—which is approximately 10 times the semidiameter of the terrestrial sphere—is not equal to $\frac{1}{350}$th part or $\frac{1}{400}$th part of the semidiameter of the sphere of the fixed stars. But it is much less possible to decide whether therefore it is $\frac{1}{2000}$th part, *i.e.*, where the aforesaid altitudes of the polar star differ by $\frac{1}{5}'$ or 12'', since the diameter of the pole star seems to be equal to at least 1', and since we cannot believe in the diligence of observers to the extent of $\frac{1}{5}'$.

According to Brahe, Saturn has a distance of 12,300 semidiameters of the Earth from the centre of the Earth. Therefore its diurnal circle, when it is on the equator, contains 77,314 semidiameters of the Earth, *i.e.*, 66,420,000 German miles; and their division into 24 hours make the portion of one hour to be 2,767,500; and the sum of 240 miles—for according to Copernicus that was the space traversed by Saturn in one hour—are 1/12,500th part of that.

But according to Ptolemy, by Copernicus' corrections, the ratio of the spheres would be as follows:

The moon is 64⅙ semidiameters distant from the Earth.
505⅚ for the body of the moon and Mercury's

65	lowest point in sphere of Mercury	28½ : 91½
209	highest point	
1	for the body of Mercury and Venus'	

210	lowest point in sphere of Venus	1⅔ : 19⅚
1,407	highest point	
7	for the body of Venus and the sun's	

1,414	lowest point of solar sphere		Although
1,537	highest point	$57\frac{1}{2} : 62\frac{1}{2}$	Copernicus
6	for the solar body		has 1094 : 1190
2	for the body of Mars		

1,545	lowest point in sphere of Mars	$14\frac{1}{2} : 105\frac{1}{2}$
11,241	highest point	
2	for the body of Mars	
5	for the body of Jupiter	

11,248	lowest point of sphere of Jupiter	$45\frac{3}{4} : 74\frac{1}{4}$
18,253	highest point	
5	for the body of Jupiter	
5	for the body of Saturn	

18,263	lowest point of sphere of Saturn	$49\frac{4}{5} : 70\frac{1}{5}$
25,737	highest point	
5	for the body of Saturn	

25,742 This is twice as wide as [495] what Brahe has; and the 240 miles, the hourly movement of Saturn in Copernicus, is smaller than 1/24,000th part of Saturn's hourly movement in Ptolemy.

What do you think are the ratios of density of the solar body, the ether which permeates the whole universe, and the sphere of the fixed stars which encloses all things from the outside?

Since these three bodies are analogous to the centre, the surface of the sphere and the interval, three symbols of the three persons of the Holy Trinity; it is believable that there is only as much matter in one as there is in either one of the two remaining: in such fashion that a third part of the matter of the whole universe should be packed together into the body of the sun, although in comparison with the amplitude of the world the body of the sun is very narrow; that likewise a third part of the matter should be spread out thin throughout the immense expanse of the world; that the sun should in this fashion possess within its own body as much matter as outside of itself the sun is fated to illuminate with the mighty power of light and to penetrate with its rays; and that finally, a third part of the matter should have been rolled out in the form of a spherical surface and thrown around the world on the outside as a wall. And in order that we may shadow forth the proportion to some extent of a known thing which is similar, even if we cannot equal the proportion, let us imagine that the solar body is all gold, the sphere of the fixed stars of water, or glass, or crystal, and the inside space full of air. Whence we are able to understand to a certain extent what divine Moses signified by the Firmament—"raquia," which properly means expansion, *viz.*, the blowing in of the ether—and what by the super-celestial waters. For similarly boys have a game which is an image of creation, when they make bubbles out of soap and water by blowing air into them. The difference is that God holds up the drop—so to speak—of water on the inside [496] at the centre. In the case of the boys, the drop of water, on account of its weight, does not remain at the centre, and is not separated from the surface by the blowing but sticks at the bottom of the bubble.

How great do you set down the thickness to be, or the distance between the inner and the outer surface of the sphere of the fixed stars?

Since we have given it as much matter as is in the total expanse of the world which it embraces; with the exception of the matter which is in the very narrow globe of the sun, but since by no means must the matter of the sphere of the fixed stars be set down as having the same desnsity as the matter in the region of the mobile bodies but a density which is a mean proportional between the density of the ether and the density of matter in the solar body; therefore the sphere of the fixed stars should have an extension which is a mean proportional between the extension [497] of the solar body and the extension of the celestial ether. But, as above, the ratio of the diameter of the sun to the diameter of the ether was as 1 is to 4,000,000. Therefore the ratio of the extensions is the ratio of the cubes, *i.e.*, 1 to 64,000,000,000,000,000,000. But the mean proportional between these numbers is 8,000,000,000. Therefore, that number of spaces equal to the body of the sun will be equal to the space between the concave and convex surfaces of the sphere of the fixed stars. And so the whole world, when its three members have been added together, is represented by the number 64,000,008,000,000,001. And its cube root, 4,000,000$\frac{1}{6,000}$, shows that this sphere, having a thickness of $\frac{1}{6,000}$th part of the semidiameter of the solar body and thrown up around the celestial ether, embraces in its body 8,000,000,000 spaces equal to the solar body. Therefore this skin, or tunic of the world, or crystalline supercelestial sphere, is of such great subtlety, on account of the amplitude of its expansion, that if you made it coagulate into one spherical mass, it would have a semidiameter 2,000 times greater than the semidiameter of the solar body, since at present it is not more thick than $\frac{6}{1,000}$ of the semidiameter of the solar body, or a little more than 2,000 German miles.

How great will the sun appear to be if you imagine an eye placed on one of the fixed stars?

The 4,000,000th part of the semidiameter of the [sphere of the] fixed stars subtends about $\frac{1}{20}''$. Therefore the solar body appears to have a diameter of $\frac{1}{600}'$, and it measures the great circle 1,296,000 times; or the apparent diameter of the sun from among the fixed stars is $\frac{1}{18,000}$th part of its apparent diameter viewed from the earth.

How great in turn do the fixed stars appear from the Earth?

Skilled observers deny that any magnitude as it were [498] of a round body can be uncovered by looking through a telescope; or rather, if a more perfect instrument is used, the fixed stars can be represented as mere points, from which shining rays, like hairs, go forth and are spread out.

Does it seem therefore that any one of the fixed stars is such a body as the sun is, and that the sun in turn is seen from the fixed stars to be of so great and of such an appearance as any one of the fixed stars?

I do not think so: for these observations do not prevent the sun from having a body of greater bulk than the fixed stars. Moreover, the view of the sun from such a great interval would be brighter than that of whatever fixed stars. For if, for example, you pierce through a wall with only a pin, so that the sun can shine through the hole, a greater brightness is poured through from the beams than all the fixed stars shining together in a cloudless sky would give. And the eye is not injured by any of the fixed stars; but it cannot bear to look towards the sun even from a distance.

PART II

ON THE MOVEMENT OF THE BODIES OF THE WORLD

1. HOW MANY AND OF WHAT SORT ARE THE MOVEMENTS?

[499] *What was the opinion of Copernicus concerning the movement of bodies? For him, what was in motion and what was at rest?*

There are two species of local movement: for either the whole thing turns, while remaining in its place, but with its parts succeeding one another. This movement can be called δίνητις—lathe-movement, or cone-movement—from the resemblance; or rotation from a rotating pole. Or else the whole thing is borne from place to place circularly. The Greeks call this movement φορά, the Latins *circuitus*, or *circumlatio*, or *ambitus*. But they call both movements generally revolution.

Accordingly Copernicus lays down that the sun is situated at the centre of the world and is motionless as a whole, *viz.*, with respect to its centre and axis. Only a few years ago, however, we grasped by sense that the sun turns with respect to the parts of its body, *i.e.*, around its centre and axis—as reasons had led me to assert for a long time—and with such great speed that one rotation is completed in the space of 25 or 26 days.

Now according as each of the primary bodies is nearer the sun, so it is borne around the sun in a shorter period, under the same common circle of the zodiac, and all in the same direction in which the parts of the solar body precede them [500]—Mercury in the space of three months, Venus in seven and one-half months, the Earth with the lunar heaven in twelve months, Mars in twenty-two and one-half months or less than two years, Jupiter in twelve years, Saturn in thirty years. But for Copernicus the sphere of the fixed stars is utterly immobile.

The Earth meanwhile revolves around its own axis too, and the moon around the Earth—still in the same direction (if you look towards the outer parts of the world) as all the primary bodies.

Now for Copernicus all these movements are direct and continuous, and there are absolutely no stations or retrogradations in the truth of the matter.

By what arguments is it proved that the sphere of the fixed stars does not move?

It was shown in Book I that the sphere of the fixed stars does not rotate around its centre and axis. For we attribute wholly to the Earth whatever appearance of this meets the eyes. Let the other arguments be sought there, in folium 104 *et seqq.* Let us repeat two things alone as proper to this place, one as regards the speed. For if the outmost sphere contains at least 4,000,000 diameters of the sun in its diameter; the circumference will be more than 12,-566,370 solar diameters in length. And if all that revolves in 24 hours, then in one hour 523,600 diameters will revolve; in one minute 8,727; in one second—which is approximately equal to the heart-beat of man—145 diameters of the sun, which is not less than 13,000 German miles; and so during the space of time during which the artery once dilates and again contracts, with a twin pulse-beat, around 7,500,000 (German) miles of the greatest circle would be revolved—and Saturn, in an orbit 2,000 times narrower, would still traverse approximately 4,000 miles.

The second argument destroys completely every movement of the sphere of the fixed stars. For it is not apparent for whose good, since nothing is outside of it, it changes its position and appearances by being moved to what place or from what place, and since it obtains by rest [501] whatever it could acquire by any movement. For the movements of all bodies are understood from its rest; and unless it gives them a place, as it can do perfectly by being at rest, nothing can be moved.

How is the ratio of the periodic times, which you have assigned to the mobile bodies, related to the aforesaid ratio of the spheres wherein those bodies are borne?

The ratio of the times is not equal to the ratio of the spheres, but greater than it, and in the primary planets exactly the ratio of the ⅔th powers. That is to say, if you take the cube roots of the 30 years of Saturn and the 12 years of Jupiter and square them, the true ratio of the spheres of Saturn and Jupiter will exist in these squares. This is the case even if you compare spheres which are not next to one another. For example, Saturn takes 30 years; the Earth takes one year. The cube root of 30 is approximately 3.11. But the cube root of 1 is 1. The squares of these roots are 9.672 and 1. Therefore the sphere of Saturn is to the sphere of the Earth as 9,672 is to 1,000. And a more accurate number will be produced, if you take the times more accurately.

What is gathered from this?

Not all the planets are borne with the same speed, as Aristotle wished, otherwise their times would be as their spheres, and as their diameters; but according as each planet is higher and farther away from the sun, so it traverses less space in one hour by its mean movement: Saturn—according to the magnitude of the solar sphere believed in by the ancients—traverses 240 German miles (in one hour), Jupiter 320 German miles, Mars 600, the centre of the Earth 740, Venus 800, and Mercury 1,200. And if this is to be according to the solar interval proved by me in the above, the number of miles must everywhere be tripled.

2. CONCERNING THE CAUSES OF THE MOVEMENT OF THE PLANETS

[502] *State the opinion of the ancient astronomers as to how the planets move.*

The ancients, Eudoxus and Callippus, and their follower Ptolemy did not advance beyond circles, wherewith they were accustomed to demonstrate the phenomena—not worrying as to how the planets completed these circles: for in Book XIII of the *Almagest*, Chapter 2, Ptolemy writes as follows:

"But let no one judge that these interweavings of circles which we postulate are difficult, on the ground that he sees that for men the manual imitation of these interweavings is quite intricate. For it is not right for our human things to be compared on a basis of equality with the immortal gods, and for us to seek the evidence for very lofty things from examples of very unlike things.

"For is anything more unlike anything than those things which are always in the same state are unlike those things which never stay like themselves, and than those things which can everywhere be impeded by all things are unlike those things which can be impeded not even by themselves? Indeed we must try hard to fit the most simple hypotheses to the celestial movements, in so far as that is possible; but if that is not successful, whatever sort of hypotheses can be used. For if only all things which appear in the heavens are given as a consequence of these hypotheses, then there is no reason for being surprised that interweavings of this sort can occur in the movements of the celestial bodies. For these [interwoven circles] do not have a nature which may impede their movement, but only a nature which has grown fitted to give way and to offer a place for the natural motions of each planet, even if the motions happen to be contrary to one another: so much so that all the circles, speaking absolutely, can interpenetrate all circles with no more difficulty than the movements can be perceived. And these movements occur with ease not only around the single circles, but also around the whole spheres, and around the axes of curved and closed surfaces. For even if the various interweavings of circles, on account of the different movements, and the engrafting of one circle in another are very difficult in the customary representations which are constructed by the human hand, and do not succeed so easily that the movements themselves are not at all impeded: nevertheless we see in the heavens that such a manifold concourse of movements by no means stands in the way of the single movements taking place. Indeed, we should not judge what is simple in celestial bodies by the examples of things which seem to us to be simple, since not even here does the same thing seem to be equally simple in all lands. For it will easily happen that he who wishes to judge celestial things in this way will not recognize as simple any of those movements which take place in the heavens, not even the invariable constancy of the first movement: because it is not only difficult but utterly impossible to find among men this thing (namely, something which stays in the same state perpetually). Therefore we must not form our judgement upon terrestrial things, but upon the natures of the things which are in the heavens and upon the unchanging steadfastness of their movements. So it comes about that in this way all the movements are seen to be simple, and much more simple than those movements which seem to us to be simple. For we are unable to suspect them of any labor or any difficulty in their revolutions."[1] So Ptolemy.

What do you find lacking in this opinion of Ptolemy's?

Even if it is true for many reasons that we should not judge of the ease of celestial movements from the difficulty of the movements of the elements, nevertheless it does not follow that with respect to the celestial movements no terrestrial cases are akin; and Ptolemy seems to draw out this excuse to such lengths that he undermines the whole possibility [*universalem rationem*] of astronomy; and so the excuse satisfies neither the astronomers nor the philosophers, and cannot be tolerated in a Christian discipline.

For as regards astronomy, he brings all hypotheses under suspicion of falsity so long as he argues so strongly for the diversity of celestial and terrestrial things, so that even reason is put down as erring in its judgment [504] of what is geometrically simple. For if that which to our reasoning concerning the heavens seems to be composite, because our reason compounds circles, is simple in the heavens themselves, therefore in the heavens circles are not compounded with one another in order to fashion one movement. Therefore the astronomer is making a false supposition, and, as is extremely astonishing, is eliciting the truth from things which are absolutely false. But that is to destroy the honor of astronomy, which Aristotle upholds in his books of

[1] I have, for obvious reasons, translated Kepler's Latin rather than Ptolemy's Greek. C. G. Wallis.

Metaphysics, believing that "the astronomers should be listened to on the form, lay-out, and movements of the celestial bodies." But in truth Ptolemy reveals himself as regards what he desires: for he says to construct hypotheses which are as simple as possible, if that can be done. And so if anyone constructs simpler hypotheses than he—understanding simplicity geometrically— he on the contrary will not defend his composite hypotheses by this excuse but will say to prefer the hypotheses which seem simpler to us men of the earth, even if we employ terrestrial examples.

As regards philosophy: the philosophers will deny that it is sufficient that the matter of the celestial body should be liquid and permeable by the globes and so should not resist the motions of the globes through it. For they ask what this thing is which leads the globe around, especially if it is established that the matter of the globes resists the movers. They ask by what force the mover moves the body from place to place, as there is no immobile field remaining underneath, and since a round body does not possess the services of feet or wings, by the motion of which animals transport their bodies through the ether, or birds through the air by pressing upon and springing up from the air-current. They ask by what light of the mind, by what means the mover perceives or forms the centres of the circles and the encircling orbits. Finally, neither theology nor the nature of things can bear that Ptolemy, who is steeped in pagan superstition, should make the stars to be visible gods—namely, by inferring immortal life from their eternal motion—and should attribute more to them than belongs to God Himself the Founder—that is to say, that geometrical reasons which are really composite, and the understanding whereof [505] God wished man His image to have in common with Him, should be simple in the stars.

State Aristotle's opinion as to how the planets move in a circle.

Aristotle, believing that the heavens were joined together by solid spheres— though of an equivocal matter—and the later philosophers, whom the Arabs seem to have followed, and after them Peurbach the writer on the schemata— they, I say, at first believed astronomy as regards the number of circles necessary in order to demonstrate the appearances: so Aristotle believed Eudoxus and Callippus concerning the twenty-five spheres. He attributed to the spheres the same number of motor intelligences, who were to revolve in their mind the time of the period and the region of the world into which the motion was to proceed. But since it was probable that all the spheres should look to the same beginning, Aristotle judged that twenty-four other spheres should be placed between these twenty-five spheres, and he called them ἀνελίττοντες, or counter-turners: namely, in order that each lower sphere should be freed by the interposition of the counter-turner from the carrying off which it was going to suffer from the higher sphere on account of the contiguity of the surfaces. The counter-turners move in an equal time and in a direction opposite to that of the higher sphere, and by that resistance give an appearance of rest, wherein as in an immobile place the lower sphere is stayed and completes its own proper period. And so the mover of each sphere was appointed to give to his own sphere and to all the lower spheres which it embraced a most regular movement within the higher sphere which was placed in contiguity to this sphere. But since that philosopher had decided that movement was eternal, he appointed movers which were also eternal and immaterial, because material things could not have an infinite power. Therefore it followed that the movers were separate and immobile beginnings. But since this eternal duration of the celestial essence seemed to him to be the goodness and perfection of the whole world, as being opposed to destruction, which was something evil; he also gave to these beginnings the highest perfection and the understanding of this perfection, and from understanding the good the will [506] to pursue it, lest [the intelligence] should not do well that which is good; in this way he introduced to us separate minds and finally gods, as the administrators of the everlasting movement of the heavens— just as Ptolemy did. As a matter of fact Scaliger, who professed Christianity, and other followers of Aristotle dispute as to whether this movement of the spheres is voluntary and as to whether the beginning of will in the movers is understanding and desire. And indeed, if the world were eternal as Aristotle contended, at any rate the fixed region in which the planet revolves would bear witness concerning the understanding. For we Christians cannot deny that the highest wisdom has presided over the instituting of the movements whereby the planet is made to run into its own region and is dispatched into its own spaces as if from the barriers; but Aristotle assigned this office to the movers themselves, as being eternal.

Furthermore, motor souls were added, tightly bound to the spheres and informing them, in order that they might assist the intelligences somewhat; or because it seemed necessary for the first mover and the movable to unite in some third thing; or because the power of movement was finite with respect to the space to be traversed and the movement was not of an infinite speed but was described in a time measured out according to space: and that argued that the ratio of the motor power to the movable body and to the spaces was fixed and measured.

And so by this solidity of the spheres and by the constant strength of the motor power absolutely all the movements or celestial appearances were so taken care of, that—given the beginning of movement—then indeed every variation in the movements would arise from the lay-out and plurality of the spheres without any labour or worry on the part of the intelligence; and the spheres moved around poles which were at rest—in approximately the way in which in Book I the terrestrial body was said to rotate around its axis and its poles. And by that movement every sphere—and certain people make them wholly of adamant, so that they by no means yield to any body—carried around its planet, which was bound to the sphere at a fixed place; and one sphere supported another [507] as was said above: and there was no fear that the globes or spheres would fall, bound to one another in this way.

How do you feel about this philosophy?

Again, I do not raise as an objection to it so much the authority of the Christian discipline as the absurdity of the teaching which fashions gods whose functions are among the works of nature and which meanwhile ascribes to them from eternity such things as are necessarily started by one first beginning of all things at the commencement of time. And since this reasoning cannot do without its theology, the whole thing is overthrown by the denial of gods.

Further, solid spheres cannot be granted, as was proved above. But once more, this philosophy rests upon solid spheres, and it is overthrown by undermining them. For Aristotle will readily grant that a body cannot be transported by its soul from place to place, if the sphere lacks the organ which reaches out through the whole circuit to be traversed, and if there is no immobile body upon which the sphere may rest.

Moreover, even if we grant solid spheres, nevertheless there are vast intervals between the spheres. Either these intervals will be filled by useless spheres which contribute nothing to the state of movement; or else, if there are not solid spheres throughout these intervals, then the spheres will not touch one another or carry one another.

Finally this theory abandons itself, in seeing to it that one sphere rests upon another, but forgetting the lowest sphere. For if we are to grant that spheres are supported by spheres and that they are contiguous to one another, then what supports the lowest sphere of the moon or by what columns is it supported upon the Earth, which, as they suppose, is at rest? Since nowhere on the surface of the Earth is any solidity met with: the winds, clouds, and birds freely and easily come and go everywhere. Why doesn't the great weight of the heavens sink down upon us, especially when the denser parts of the spheres [508] approach our zenith? Or if the heavens have no weight, what need do we have of spheres for carrying the planetary globes?

If there are no solid spheres, then there will seem to be all the more need of intelligences in order to regulate the movements of the heavens, although the intelligences are not gods. For they can be angels or some other rational creature, can they not?

There is no need of these intelligences, as will be proved; and it is not possible for the planetary globe to be carried around by an intelligence alone. For in the first place, mind is destitute of the animal power sufficient to cause movement, and it does not possess any motor force in its assent alone, and it cannot be heard or perceived by the irrational globe; and even if mind were perceived, the material globe would have no faculty of obeying or of moving itself. But before this, it has already been said that no animal force is sufficient for transporting the body from place to place, unless there are organs and some body which is at rest and on which the movement can take place. Therefore the question falls back to the above.

But on the contrary the natural powers which are implanted in the planetary bodies can enable the planet to be transported from place to place.

But let it be posited as sufficient for movement that the intelligence should will movement into this or that region: then the discovery of the figure whereon the line of movement is ordered will be irrational. For we are convinced by the astronomical observations which have been taken correctly that the route of a planet is approximately circular and as a matter of fact eccentric—that is, the centre [of the circle] is not at the centre of the world or of some body; and furthermore that during the succession of ages the planet crosses from place to place. Now as many arguments can be drawn up against the discovery of such an orbit as there are parts of it alreayd described.

For firstly, the orbit of the planet is not a perfect circle. But if mind caused the orbit, it would lay out the orbit in a perfect circle, [509] which has beauty and perfection to the mind. On the contrary, the elliptic figure of the route of the planet and the laws of the movements whereby such a figure is caused smell of the nature of the balance or of material necessity rather than of the conception and determination of the mind, as will be shown below.

Finally, in order that we may grant that a different idea from that of a circle shines in the mind of the mover: it is asked by what means the mind can apply this or that [idea] to the regions of the world. Now the circle is described around some one fixed centre, but the ellipse, which is the figure of the planetary orbits, is described around two centres.

Then what seat will you give to mind, so that it may measure out a circle or an elliptic orbit on the liquid plains of the ether? You do not place the mind at the centre, do you? For then you are placing it in the ether, which is not different from all the remaining space of the world, because the orbit of the planet is eccentric to the solar body. But this is exceedingly absurd, since elsewhere the beginning of individuation of souls is assigned to the matter and to the body, to which the soul is added, and this matter differs in place and time and in many other marks from the remaining matter of the world. Surely no other position belongs to the soul and to the mind than that which comes through its body, which the soul informs. And by what force will mind be moved from place to place in a small circle around the centre of the world, so that it may be at the centres of the planetary orbits in the succession of ages, if the mind is without a body and is no more able to be moved than to be given a position in space? By what means will mind view its position or its distance from the centre of the world?

But let it be granted that the mind has a view from its seat at the centre: then how will it cause the planet, which is very distant, to trace its orbit around this centre? If the mind had the planet tied by a rope, perhaps the planet would fly around, being tied to the centre. Perhaps the mind, looking out from the centre, could perceive—especially if it were endowed with bodily eyes— whether the planet were moving in a circle, if the planet were always viewed making an equal angle; but if it should go outside of its circle, in what way would the mind lead it back, if it did not see the orbit by itself? [510] But how does the mind understand the orbit, which is not stamped on the body as its special property? For here there is no question of the intellectual idea of a circle, wherein there is no distinction of great and small, but of the real route of the planet, which has a fixed magnitude in addition to the idea.

But if you place the motor mind outside of the centre of its orbit, its condition will be worse. For either it will be in the body which is at the centre of the world; and thus all the minds will be in the same body, and the above difficulties with respect to keeping the planet in its orbit and with respect to the discovery of the orbit will remain. Or else the mind will be in the globe of the planet: then in both cases it is asked by what means the mind knows where the centre is, around which the orbit of the planet should be organized; and how great the distance of the mind and its globe from that point is. For Avicenna rightly judged that if the mover of the planet is a mind, it has need of knowledge of the centre and of its distance from the centre. For the circle is defined and perfected by the same things, the centre and the equal curvature around it, viz., the distance of the circumference from the centre; and so, however much you exalt the motor mind, nevertheless the circle is nothing else to God except what has already been said. And this same thing should be understood proportionally concerning the figure of the ellipse.

Why do you say that a celestial body, which is unchanging with respect to its matter, cannot be moved by assent alone? For if the celestial bodies are neither heavy nor light, but most suited for circular movement, then do they resist the motor mind?

Even if a celestial globe is not heavy in the way in which a stone on the earth is said to be heavy, and is not light in the way in which among us fire is said to be light: nevertheless by reason of its matter it has a natural ἀδυναμία or powerlessness of crossing from place to place, and it has a natural inertia or rest whereby it rests [511] in every place where it is placed alone. And hence in order that it may be moved out of its position and its rest, it has need of some power which should be stronger than its matter and its naked body, and which should overcome its natural inertia. For such a faculty is above the capacity of nature and is a sprout of form, or a sign of life.

Whence do you prove that the matter of the celestial bodies resists its movers, and is overcome by them, as in a balance the weights are overcome by the motor faculty?

This is proved in the first place from the periodic times of the rotation of the single globes around their axes, as the terrestrial time of one day and the solar time of approximately twenty-five days. For if there were no inertia in the matter of the celestial globe—and this inertia is as it were a weight in the globe—there would be no need of a virtue [*virtute*] in order to move the globe; and if the least virtue for moving the globe were postulated, then there would be no reason why the globe should not revolve in an instant. But the revolutions of the globes take place in a fixed time, which is longer for one planet and shorter for another: hence it is apparent that the inertia of matter is not to the motor virtue in the ratio in which nothing is to something. Therefore the inertia is not nil, and thus there is some resistance of celestial matter.

Secondly, this same thing is proved by the revolution of the globes around the sun—considering them generally. For one mover by one revolution of its own globe moves six globes, as we shall hear below. Wherefore if the globes did not have a natural resistance of a fixed proportion, there would be no reason why they should not follow exactly the whirling movement of their mover, and thus they would revolve with it in one and the same time. Now indeed all the globes go in the same direction as the mover with its whirling movement, nevertheless no globe fully attains the speed of its mover, and one follows another more slowly. Therefore they mingle the inertia of matter with the speed of the mover in a fixed proportion.

The ratio of the periodic times seems to be the work of a mind and not of material necessity.

The most accurately harmonic attunement of the extreme movements—the slowest and the fastest movement in any given planet—is the work of the highest and most adored creator Mind or Wisdom. But if the lengths of the periodic times were the work of a mind, they would have something of beauty, like the rational ratios, duplicate, triplicate, and so on. But the ratios of the periodic times are irrational [*ineffabiles, irrationales vulgo*] and thus partake of infinity, wherein there is no beauty for the mind, as there is no definiteness [*finitio*].

Secondly, these times cannot be the work of a mind—I am not speaking of the Creator but of the nature of the mover; because the unequal delays in different parts of the circle add up to the times of one period. But the unequal delays arise from material necessity, as will be said below, and as if by reason of the balance [*ex ratione staterae*].

Therefore by what force do you suspend your material globes and the Earth in especial, so that each remains within the boundaries of its region, though it is destitute of the bonds of the solid spheres?

Since it is certain that there are no solid spheres, it is necessary that we should take refuge in this inertia of matter, whereby any globe, placed in any place on the world beyond the motor virtues, naturally rests in that place, because matter, as such, has no faculty of transporting its body from place to place.

Then what is it which makes the planets move around the sun, each planet within the boundaries of its own region, if there are not any solid spheres, and if the globes themselves cannot be fastened to anything else and made to stick there, and if without solid [513] spheres they cannot be moved from place to place by any soul?

Even if things are very far removed from us and which are without a real exemplification are difficult to explain and give rise to quite uncertain judgements, as Ptolemy truly warns; nevertheless if we follow probability [*verisimilitudinem*] and take care not to postulate anything which is contrary to us, it will of necessity be clear that no mind is to be introduced which should turn the planets by the dictation of reason and so to speak by a nod, and that no soul is to be put in charge of this revolution, in order that it should impress something into the globes by the balanced contest of the forces, as takes place in the revolution around the axis; but that there is one only solar body, which is situated at the centre of the whole universe, and to which this movement of the primary planets around the body of the sun can be ascribed.

3. On the Revolution of the Solar Body Around its Axis and its Effect in the Movement of the Planets

By what reasons are you led to make the sun the moving cause or the source of movement for the planets?

1. Because it is apparent that in so far as any planet is more distant from the sun than the rest, it moves the more slowly—so that the ratio of the periodic times is the ratio of the ³⁄₂th powers of the distances from the sun. Therefore we reason from this that the sun is the source of movement.

2. Below we shall hear the same thing come into use in the case of the single planets—so that the closer any one planet approaches the sun during any time, it is borne with an increase of velocity in exactly the ratio of the square.

3. [514] Nor is the dignity or the fitness of the solar body opposed to this, because it is very beautiful and of a perfect roundness and is very great and is the source of light and heat, whence all life flows out into the vegetables: to such an extent that heat and light can be judged to be as it were certain instruments fitted to the sun for causing movement in the planets.

4. But in especial, all the estimates of probability are fulfilled by the sun's rotation in its own space around its immobile axis, in the same direction in which all the planets proceed: and in a shorter period than Mercury, the nearest to the sun and fastest of all the planets.

For as regards the fact that it is disclosed by the telescope in our time and can be seen every day that the solar body is covered with spots, which cross the disk of the sun or its lower hemisphere within 12 or 13 or 14 days, slowly at the beginning and at the end, but rapidly in the middle, which argues that they are stuck to the surface of the sun and turn with it; I proved in my *Commentaries on Mars*, Chapter 34, by reasons drawn from the very movement of the planets, long before it was established by the sun-spots, that this movement necessarily had to take place.

What do you think should be held concerning the solar body and the force whereby it turns around its axis?

It was said in the first Book that this body—or any other which revolves around its own axis—was not merely moved in a gyre by the Creator's omnipotence at the commencement of things, but it also seems to continue this movement by the reinforcement of a motor soul. For even if, by means of some other rationale there unfolded, the movement could be continued, nevertheless the dailiness and yearliness of this movement, in which the total life of the world consists, is more rightly obtained by the reinforcement of a soul.

Do you have any other arguments besides movement which make it likely that a soul is present in the solar body?

1. A strong argument is drawn from the matter of the solar body and its [515] illumination, which seems to be a quality in the solar body, sprung from the very mighty informing by a soul—namely, a soul whose matter, it is consonant, as was said above, is the most dense matter among the bodies of the world: therefore it is right to believe that very great forces are present in that soul, which dominates and sets on fire the enduring matter.

2. Moreover, I think a soul must be postulated rather than an inanimate form, because it is apparent from the rising of sun-spots and their dispersion and from the unequal illumination of different parts in different times that there is not one continuous and perpetually uniform energy [*energiam*] in all the parts of the solar body, but that it admits movement and variation and interchanges, and that such things take place in the solar globe as take place in the terrestrial globe, *mutatis mutandis*, so that from its inmost bowels hither and yon things which look like clouds are breathed out—which are perhaps black soot—and when their matter has been consumed, the light of the parts which before were covered by those spots becomes more bright. And since these interchanges are perennial, they smell of the guardianship of a soul rather than a simple form.

3. Moreover, light in itself [*per se*] is something akin to the soul: no less than this same thing was proven of heat in Book I. For on the earth nothing is set on fire [*inflammatur*], that is to say, is made luminous, which was not engendered by some soul in a body: as a trunk from the soul of the shoot, alcohol from the soul growing in the vine, sparks from iron and stones, which are things cooked up in the bowels of the Earth by the soul of the Earth. But that light is something akin to our flames is clear from the fact that light concentrated by concave or convex lenses sets on fire in such fashion that there are flames and coals. And so it is consonant that the solar body, wherein the light is present as in its source, is endowed with a soul which is the originator, the preserver, and the continuator.

4. And the function of the sun in the world seems to persuade us of nothing else except that just as it has to illuminate all things, so it is possessed [516] of light in its body; and as it has to make all things warm, it is possessed of heat; as it has to make all things live, of a bodily life; and as it has to move all things, it itself is the beginning of the movement; and so it has a soul in itself.

You don't, do you, further add mind or intelligence to the sould of the sun, in order for it to regulate this movement of the sun around the axis?

There is absolutely no need of mind for the functions of movement. For the region in which the sun revolves exists from the first commencement of things. But the constancy of the revolution and of the periodic time, as was explained above, depends upon the ratio of the constant power of the mover to the obstinancy [*contumaciam*] of the matter. But the directing of the solar axis perpetually towards the same region is stillness rather than the work of mind, since from the first commencement of things none of this movement has been impressed upon the axis. But also the mean circle between the extremes of the axis, the poles, necessarily follows the direction of the axis; and it, regulated by the same perpetually fixed points, abides as the axis abides. Finally, the laying hold of the planetary bodies, which the rotation of the sun makes to revolve, is a bodily virtue, not animal, not mental.

And let these things be said with respect to movement. However, with respect to the inferences concerning intelligence, to which the consideration of the celestial harmonies leads, see the last chapter in Book v of my *Harmonies*.

Then does the sun by the rotation of its body make the planets revolve? And how can this be, since the sun is without hands with which it may lay hold of the planet, which is such a great distance away, and by rotating may make the planet revolve with itself?

Instead of hands there is the virtue of its body, which is emitted in straight lines throughout the whole amplitude of the world, and which—[517] because it is a form of the body—rotates along with the solar body like a very rapid vortex; moving through the total amplitude of the circuit—whatever magnitude it reaches to—with equal speed; and the sun revolves in the narrowest space at the centre.

Could you make the thing clearer by some example?

Indeed there comes to our assistance the attraction between the loadstone and the iron pointer, which has been magnetized by the loadstone and which gets magnetic force by rubbing. Turn the loadstone in the neighbourhood of the pointer; the pointer will turn at the same time. Although the laying hold is of a different kind, nevertheless you see that not even here is there any bodily contact.

The example is certain, but obscure; explain what that virtue is and of what genus of things.

Just as there are two bodies, the mover and the moved, so there are also two powers, by which the movement is administered; one is passive and verges more towards matter, namely the likeness of the planetary body to the solar body, with respect to the bodily form; and there is one part of the planetary body which is friendly to the sun, and the opposite part is unfriendly. The other power [*potentia*] is active and smells more of form—that is to say, the solar body has the force (*vim*) to attract the planet with respect to its friendly part and to repulse it with respect to its unfriendly part, and finally to keep it, if it were placed thus, so that it does not direct either its "friendly" or its "unfriendly" part against the sun.

How can it be that the whole planetary body is like or akin to the solar body, but one part of the planet is friendly to the sun and the other part is unfriendly to the sun?

Doubtless, too, since the loadstone attracts the loadstone, the bodies are akin; but the attraction takes place with respect to one part alone; and the repulsion, [518] with respect to the opposite part. Therefore friendliness and the unfriendless are named from the effect of rushing together or of flying apart, not from the unlikeness of the bodies.

Whence comes this diversity of the opposite parts of the same body?

In loadstones the diversity comes from the situation of the parts in the whole. For if you break the loadstone AB at CD, then wheresoever the pieces are transposed to, parts A and CD of the two pieces are mutually repellent.[1] In the whole loadstone these parts formerly looked towards the same region of the world. But if the pieces are put next to one another, so that the former relative situation of the parts occurs, as CAD, BCD, then the pieces attract[2] one another.

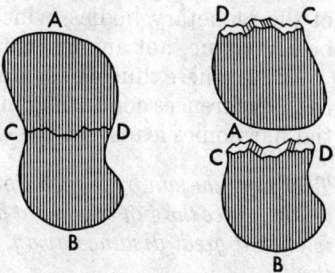

In the heavens the thing is arranged somewhat differently. For the sun possesses this active and energetic faculty of attracting or repulsing or retaining the planet, not as a loadstone does, in one region, but in all the parts of its body. And so it is believable that the centre of the solar body corresponds to one extremity or region of a loadstone, but the whole surface to the other region of the loadstone. Therefore in the bodies of the planets, that part or extremity which at the first commencement of things and at the first placing of the planet [519] looked towards the sun is akin to the centre of the sun and is attracted by the sun; but the part which stretched out away from the sun towards the fixed stars came to possess the nature of the surface of the sun; and if it is turned towards the sun, the sun repulses the planet.

In order that I may better understand the effect of the whirling-movement of the sun, say what you judge would have been the case if the sun did not have a whirling-movement.

Just as a loadstone does not stop attracting a loadstone which has its friendly part turned towards it, until it brings the second loadstone into bodily contact and unites it completely to itself; and if the unfriendly part is turned towards it, either it turns the second loadstone around and in the same way attracts the loadstone which has been turned around; or else, if it cannot turn the loadstone

[1]*Reading* repellunt *for* attrahunt.
[2]*Reading* attrahunt *for* repellunt.

around, it repels it, and in this case the [first] loadstone does not leave any place to the second within the sphere of its virtue, if only it is not hindered. So we must consider in the case of the sun, that if it did not turn around its axis, none of the primary planets would revolve around the sun; but a part of the planets would voyage towards the sun perpetually, until they were united to it by contact; and the part which turn their behind towards the sun would be repulsed towards the fixed stars; but the planets which show their side to the sun would stick to their place and be utterly immobile, while the attractive virtue of the sun struggles with the repulsive.

Then what takes place now by the sun's rotating around its axis?

Indubitably by the turning of the solar body the virtue too is turned, just as by the turning of a loadstone the attractive force of one part is transferred to different regions of the world. And since by means of that virtue of its body the sun has laid hold of the planet, either attracting it or repelling it, or hesitating between the two, it makes the planet also revolve with it and together with the planet perhaps all the surrounding ether. Indeed, it retains them by attraction and repulsion; and by retention it makes them revolve.

If this were the case, would not all the planets make their periodic returns at the same time as the sun?

Yes, if only this were the case. But it has been said before this, that besides this motor force of the sun there is also a natural inertia in the planets themselves with respect to movement: hence by reason of their matter they are inclined to remain in their own place. So the motor power of the sun [*potentia vectoria*] and the powerlessness or material inertia of the planet are at war with one another. Each has its share of victory: the motor power moves the planet from its seat; the material inertia removes its own, *i.e.*, the planetary, body somewhat from those bonds by which it was laid hold of by the sun, so that it is laid hold of first by one part and then by another part of this circle of virtue

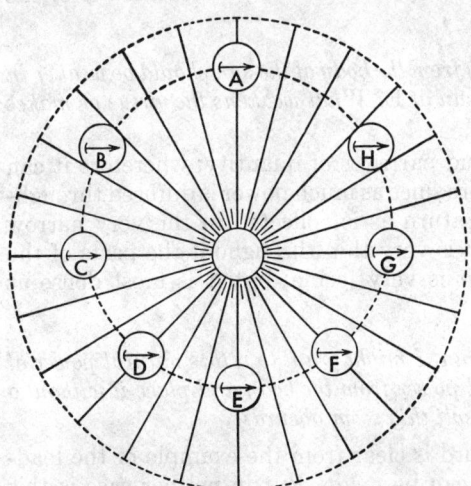

[*circularis virtutis*] and as it were circumference of the sun—that is, by the part which comes next after the part from which the planet has just loosed itself.

In the diagram, the form [*species*] of the rotated solar body is understood by the outer circle designated by dots; [521] and such a circle is understood to be drawn through any position whatsoever of the planet *A*, *B*, *C*, *D*, *E*, *F*, *G*, or *H*. Let the sun, and with the sun its form, turn from right to left: first, let the planet *A* be laid hold of by that part of the form of the sun which is designated by the ray *A*; let the ray *A* be moved through a fixed interval of time as far as the place of the ray D; and let it draw the planet, which however resists and tries to loose itself. Thus, as in the same interval of time the planet is propelled from A to B, so the first ray leaves the planet behind it by the space BD. But in turn, the ray H has succeeded it and lays hold of the planet in B. For as far as A was moved forward to D, so far has H proceeded to B.

But if all things are effected by natural powers which are set at work and at war to move the inertia of matter, how can the planets preserve their periodic times, so that the periodic times are always exactly equal?

More easily than by the assistance of mind. For as the ratio of the total motor virtue to the matter of the globe to be moved is invariable, it follows that the periodic times are perpetually equal.

But why does one planet free itself from this grasp more completely than another, so that Saturn moves only 240 miles in one hour while Mercury moves 1200 miles according to Copernicus?

1. Because the virtue flowing from the solar body has the same degrees of weakness in different intervals which the intervals themselves have, or the amplitude of the spheres described with these intervals: that is the mightiest cause.

2. Moreover there is something of a cause in the inertia of the planetary globes or in the greater or less resistance, whereby the ratio only half corresponds; but more of this somewhat later on.

The body of the planet is always the same but it is repelled by the sun and attracted to it, as you wish; therefore it passes through different degrees of motor virtue: therefore the ratio of the power to the planetary body does not remain constant.

Not absolutely, if we consider the parts of one revolution; and so the same planet becomes faster in one part of its revolution, as above in E, than in another part A, as will be said below. But in spite of this the general total motor virtue [*collecta universa virtus vectoria*] throughout all those degrees through which the planet passes during one revolution always and at every restitution is of the same magnitude.

How is it possible that the virtue flowing from the body of the sun should be weaker in the greater interval at A *than near the sun at* E*? What weakens the virtue or makes it feeble?*

Because that virtue is corporeal and partakes of quantity: wherefore it can be dispersed and thinned out. Therefore since as much power is diffused throughout the very wide orbital circle of Saturn as is collected in the very narrow orbital circle of Mercury: therefore it is very thin throughout the parts of the orbital circle of Saturn, and hence it is very feeble; but it is most dense at Mercury and hence is very strong.

If it were a question of the body of the sun, I might grant to it this natural power of moving: but you draw out this material power from the body and place it without a subject in the very spacious ether. Doesn't this seem absurd?

[523] That it should not seem absurd is clear from the example of the loadstone, to which this same objection can be made. But in neither case is this force without a proportional subject. For in this way at the very source the sub-

ject of the natural faculty is the body of the sun, or the threads stretching out from the centre to its circumference; thus even in this very emanation, I think a rational distinction should be made between the immaterial form [*speciem*] of the solar body, which flows as far as the planets and beyond, and its force or energy which actually lays hold of the planet and moves it—so that the form is the subject of the force, though it is not a body but an immaterial form of a body.

Could you give an example of this thing?

There is a true example in the light and heat of the sun. There is no doubt but that just as the whole sun is luminous, so it is all on fire, and that on account of the density of its matter it should indeed be compared to a glowing mass of gold, or to anything else which may be denser. Now from that light [*ex luce illa*] of the sun there emanates and comes down to us a form which is not corporeal, not material, which we call the illumination [*lumen*] or rays of the sun and which however is subject to dimensions and accidents. For it flows on straight lines and may be condensed or rarefied, and many indeed be cut by a mirror and by glass, namely, by reflection and refraction, as we are taught in Optics. Moreover, this form of the sun's light [*lucis*] bears its heat with it; and in proportion to the greatness or smallness of the strength whereby it falls upon bodies which can be illuminated, it warms them to a greater or to a lesser extent.

Therefore just as that form (*species*) or illumination (*lumen*)—which form we know with certainty to flow down from the light (*luce*) of the sun—is the subject of the heat-giving faculty, which has similarly been extended from the sun, through a form; so too the solar body's immaterial form, come down as far as the planets, has as its companion the form of that energetic virtue (*speciem illius virtutis energeticae*) in the solar body; and this form strives to unite like things to itself and to repel unlike.

There is a more clear example in this same light: when it passes through coloured glass or coloured weavings or has been communicated to coloured surfaces, [524] it itself is coloured. Hence, it cannot be denied that, although the light is an immaterial form of the light which flowed into the coloured body, it becomes the subject of that colour and as it were even the outward-going vehicle of it.

What if this very light and not some other form from the body of the sun were the subject of the prehensive faculty whereby the sun lays hold of the planetary bodies?

Not absolutely; for it seems rather that we should take it that an immaterial form flows off from its body, in which form the prehensive force and the light inhere, but in the light the colour and heat—each of them drawn from its own source.

State the reasons for this distinction between the immaterial forms from one and the same solar globe.

1. The matter of the solar body must be something distinct from the light in it. For the movement of rays of light in a straight line takes place in an instant; but the turning of the solar body takes place in time. But if we were to postulate that the bare form of the light is the subject and vehicle of the prehensive virtue, then one and alone the light of the sun could lay claim to being

the whole essence of its body. For the same thing which is found in the form from the thing is found in the thing as in its origin [*orginaliter*].

2. Dimensionality applies to emanated light doubtless not wholly by reason of the inward essence of the light, but by reason of something different from the light itself, namely, because the light is in a body of some certain magnitude and because the forms emanate together as much from body as from light.

3. The form of light emanates from the surface of the luminous body, or if really from the depths of a pellucid body, still as if from the surface. And so the light is considered as a surface, [525] and it has the same properties which other surfaces have with respect to movement and impact; but the body which is beneath the illuminated surface suffers nothing, because nothing has come down from the inward corporeality of the source of light: now the force laying hold of a body must necessarily come down from a body, so that there may be a moving cause which is proportional to its movable object. And so it is subject to bodily dimensions and moves bodies: not only with respect to the surface but also winding its way into their very matter.

4. Hence, too, no matter on the surface of the object resists the light in such a way that the surface is not illuminated instantaneously; but what resists the light, *i.e.*, something opaque, resists it perpetually and is never overcome, as long as it remains opaque. But the virtue which lays hold does not overcome every whit: for the resistance of matter in the planetary body stands up against it and restricts it: hence the planet does not follow exactly the forward movement of the prehensive force, but is left behind and abandoned by it and in that mutual struggle there is place for time.

5. There is the same reason for the further difference that light is bounded and stopped by the surfaces of opaque bodies, so that it goes on no farther into other bodies lying in the same straight line. But this force which moves the planet by laying hold of it is not stopped by its surface, but goes into the body which it lays hold of, and moreover goes on through the body into the body of a farther planet, if it so happens that two planets are on a straight line with the sun: consequently the movement is not disturbed at all by the interposition of bodies. But if movement arose from the illumination of light, this would be absurd; for as often as the higher planet was eclipsed by the lower, so often and so long would its movement cease until the lower planet by its speed should remove itself from the line [with the sun].

6. Finally, that the planetary movement is not necessarily from the naked light of the sun is shown by the examples of other things where movement similar to the celestial movements takes place without light, as can be seen in the case of the loadstone; and this will be shown below by the example of the moon, which is moved by the earth, a body which is luminous to the least extent. And even if at that time the illumination of the earth and the moon has a share [526] and even if it co-operates in many ways in moving the moon, nevertheless it does not do that *per se*, but merely strengthens the motor form from the earth (*specimen motricem telluris*), as will be said in the proper place.

What is the likeness between the form of light and the form of this prehensive virtue?

There is a very close likeness in the genesis and conditions of both forms: the descent of each from the luminous body takes place instantaneously; each remains of average greatness and smallness without loss, is not taxed; nothing perishes in the journey from its source, nothing is scattered between the source and the illuminable or movable thing.

Therefore each is an immaterial outflow, not like the outflow of odours, which are conjoined to a decrease of the substance; not like the outflow of heat from a raging furnace, or anything similar, by which the spaces in between are filled. For this form is not anywhere except in the opposite and withstanding body; the form of the light on its opaque surface, but the form from the motor virtue in the total corporeality: but in the intermediate space between the sun and the surface, the form is not but has been. But if they were to meet the concave spherical surface of an opaque body, both solar forms would be scattered in that concavity together with all that abundance with which they have emanated from the body of the sun: in this way as much of the form would be in a wide and farther-away sphere of this sort as is in the narrow and nearer sphere. And since the ratio of convex spheres is the ratio of the squares of their diameters: therefore the form will be made weaker in unequal spheres in the ratio of the square of its distance. And again because circles have the same simple ratio as their diameters: therefore in longitude the form is weaker in the same ratio of its distance from its source.

Where are the arguments for this comparison gotten from?

These properties of light have been demonstrated in optics. [527] The same things are proved by analogy concerning the motor power of the sun, keeping the difference between the works of illumination and movement and between the objects of each. And these same things are found to be consonant with astronomical experiments.

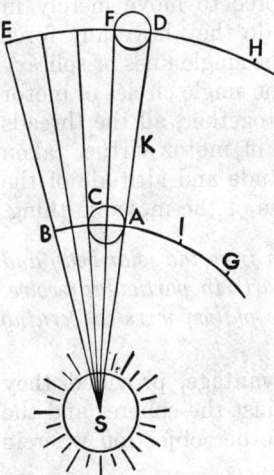

For since one and the same planet, as will be said below, in parts of the eccentric circle which are really equal but are at unequal distances from the sun, makes unequal delays and does that in this very ratio of the distances therefore it follows that the motor virtue is attenuated in longitude in the same ratio wherein the light is attenuated in longitude, namely in the ratio of the amplitude of the circles which have those distances or semidiameters. In this diagram, let the sun be *S*, the same planet *CA* as nearer and *FD* as farther away. And let *DH* and *AI* be equal parts of the eccentric circle—that is to say, at opposite positions on the eccentric circle. Let *DH* be the farther away, and *AI* the nearer. Accordingly as *SD* is to *SA*, so the delay of the planet in *DH* is to the delay of the planet in *AI*. From this it also follows that as *SD* is to *SA*, so inversely is the density of *CA*, the light which is at a lower distance, to the density of *FD*, the light which is farther away.

[528] *But if the light is attenuated in the ratio of the squares of the intervals,* i.e., *in the ratio of the surfaces; why therefore does not the motor virtue too become weaker in the ratio of the squares rather than in the simple?*

Because the motor virtue has as subject a form from the solar body, not according as it is merely body but according as it is set in motion in a revolution around its immobile axis and poles.

Therefore even if the form from the solar body is attenuated in longitude and in latitude no less than the light is; nevertheless this attenuation contributes towards the weakening of the motor virtue only by reason of the longitude: for the local movement which the sun gives to the planets takes place only in lon-- gitude, wherein even the parts of the solar body are mobile, not also in latitude towards the poles of the body with respect to which the sun is immobile.

But nevertheless the movable bodies have latitude no less than longitude. Wherefore they are borne by this virtue so that they each have their latitude as well as longitude. Therefore why is not this motor virtue weakened in latitude, and that in the ratio of the squares of the intervals?

Indeed the planetary bodies have not only these two dimensions but also the third dimension of thickness or altitude; and they occupy this virtue clearly in three ways: and exactly for that reason the prehensive, vehicular, and motor virtue of one planet is not one circle lacking latitude, but is con- stituted of an infinite number as it were of circles parallel in latitude and in altitude. But it does not accordingly follow that the attenuation of this virtue should be in the ratio of the squares or cubes of the intervals or semidiameters. For just as elsewhere in geometry equimultiples have the same ratio: so also here in physics, as one least physical line—as a part of the planetary body—is to the thinness of one circle of virtue, in the simple ratio of the intervals; so is an infinity of least physical lines—as all the parts of the planetary body laid out in latitude as well as in altitude—to the same number of circles of the motor virtue, which all together and singly have force to move merely in longitude; but neither singly nor taken all together do they have any force to move in latitude or in altitude. Therefore, just as the single lines or solitary threads of two planetary bodies would be moved by the single circles of motor virtue in the simple ratio of the intervals; so, taken together, all the threads of the planetary globe are moved by all the circles of motor virtue, taken together, in the same simple proportion: for the latitude and altitude of the motor virtue is not of its essence but of the accidents of the movable thing.

Nevertheless are not these statements concerning the form from the solar body and from the solar virtue, which makes the planets and the Earth in particular revolve, more difficult to believe than the former statements of the philospohers concerning intelligences, motor souls, and solid spheres?

Their being more difficult to believe is no disadvantage, provided they are easy to comprehend; and the objection made against the spheres and the intelligences cannot be made against them—or any other objection wherein the charge of impossibility is made.

For in the first place, wherever they exceed belief there is none the less a true example in the loadstone. Then, if anyone should doubt whether the faculties of a loadstone, *i.e.*, terrestrial faculties, are present in the heavens, or whether the Earth, a heavy body, could be transported from place to place by an immaterial form from the sun; let him regard the moon, which is so much akin to the Earth: he sees it revolve without any solid sphere underlying it. [530] But that bodily forms which pass one another back and forth are strong enough to cause movement is shown by this same moon, which moves the seas on the Earth by the form given out. So we are not lacking in examples. And the mode by which we perceive in mind what sort of form it is does not disturb us: alone the unbelievable strength [*fortitudo*] of this form keeps us in doubt. And indeed we can rightly answer here with Ptolemy that it is never proper to appraise the virtues of divine works according to our weakness, or their greatness according to our smallness.

Now the appraisal of mode and figures belongs to mind; but in this appraisal there should be no judgment of greatness or smallness, *i.e.*, of indefinite quantities.

4. On the Causes of the Ratio of the Periodic Times

In the beginning of this consideration of movement you said that the periodic times of the planets are found to be quite exactly in the ratio of the ³⁄₂th powers of their orbits or circles. I ask what the cause of this thing is.

Four causes come together in establishing the length of the periodic time. The first is the length of the route; the second is the weight or the amount [*copia*] of matter to be transported; the third is the strength of the motor virtue; the fourth is the bulk [*moles*] or space in which the matter to be transported is unrolled. For as is the case in a mill, where the wheel is turned by the force of the stream, so that, the wider and longer the wings, planks, or oars which you fasten to the wheel, the greater the force of the stream pouring through the width and depth which you will divert into the machine; so too

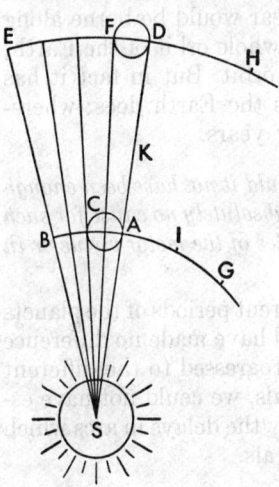

that is the case in this celestial vortex of the solar form moving rapidly in a gyro—and this form causes the movement. [531] Consequently the more space the body—*A* or *D* in this case—occupies, the more widely and deeply it occupies the motor virtue, as in this case *BCA* understood according to its width; and the more swiftly, other things being equal, is it borne forward; and the more quickly does it complete its periodic journey.

But the circular journeys of the planets are in the simple ratio of the intervals. For as *SA* is to *SD*, so too is the whole circle *BA* to the whole circle *ED*. But the weight, or the amount of matter in the different planets, is in the ratio of the ½th powers of the intervals, as was proved above, so that always the higher planet has more matter and is moved the more slowly and piles up the more time in its period, since even before now by reason of its journey it would have wanted more time. For with *SK* taken as a mean proportional between *SA* and *SD* the intervals of the two planets; as *SK* is to the greater distance *SD*, so the amount of matter in the planet *A* is to the amount in the planet *D*. But the third and fourth causes balance one another in the comparison of the different planets. But the simple ratio of the intervals plus the ratio of the ½th powers constitute the ratio of the ³⁄₂th powers of the same. Therefore the periodic times are in the ratio

of the ⅔th powers of the intervals. Consequently if *SD*, *SK*, *SA*, and *SL*
are continued [mean] proportionals, then *SL* will be to *SD* [532] as the time
period of planet *A* is to the time period of planet *D*.

*Prove, in comparing two planets, that the weakening of the motor virtue is exactly
balanced by the amplitude wherewith the movable planetary bodies occupy the
virtue.*

The bulks or expanses of the bodies are in the simple and direct ratio of the
intervals, as was demonstrated above. That is, as *SA* is to *SD*, so is the bulk
of the planetary body at *A* to the bulk of the other planet at *D*. But too the
motor virtue is dense and strong, in the simple ratio of the intervals but inversely; for as the same interval *SA* is to *SD*, so the strength of the form *CA*
is to the strength of the form *FD*. Therefore the virtue is in turn occupied
in the same ratio in which it is weakened; for example, Saturn is borne by a
power ten times feebler than the virtue by which the Earth is; but conversely,
it occupies with its body ten times more of the virtue of its region than the
Earth with its body occupies of the virtue of its region. And let the total
virtue which Saturn occupies by its bulk be divided into ten parts which are
equal in expanse (*spatio*) to the total virtue which the Earth occupies. Any
one of these parts or expanses of virtue has only one tenth of the strength
which that one part which is occupied by the Earth has, wherefore those ten
parts added together into one are equal in power [*potestate*] to that one part
by which the Earth is borne. And so if in the amplitude of the more rarefied
globe of Saturn there were not more matter than in the narrowness of the
denser terrestrial body, the globe of Saturn in one year would be borne along
as great a distance of its orbit as is the length of the whole orbit of the Earth;
and thus in ten years it would complete its proper orbit. But in fact it has
approximately thrice as much matter and weight as the Earth does; wherefore it requires thrice as long a time, namely thirty years.

[533] *What need was there to teach of this balancing? Would it not have been enough
for establishing a demonstration to set down that there is absolutely no cause for such
an irregular movement as this either in the different grades of the motor virtue or in
the different amplitudes of the planetary globes?*

Now for the demonstration that the ratio of the different periods of the planets
is the ratio of the ⅔th power of the intervals, it would have made no difference
whether this or that were set down. But if we had progressed to the different
delays of one and the same planet at different intervals, we could not have established from the same genus of things the reason why the delays in arcs which
are exactly equal should follow the ratio of the intervals.

*Then what is the reason why the farther distant from the sun any equal arc of the
eccentric circle is, the longer delays does the planet make in that arc, and in the ratio
of the intervals?*

The reason is indeed the weakening of the motor virtue: just as light is *SD*
the longer interval from the sun is diffused more thinly along the length *FD*
than is the diffusion of the same in the shorter interval *SA*. And so what of the
virtue was at that time occupied by the body of the planet, as *FD*, is more weak
than what of the denser virtue is occupied by the same *CA* which is nearer.

For here the three remaining causes are missing. For the arc or route is assumed in both cases to be of the same length, as *DH*, *AI*: the density of the body remains the same, and the magnitude of the figure likewise; because *FD* and *CA* are in this case one and the same planet. The strength of the virtue alone is left. But more on this in the following.

[534] *In this case we seem to meet a greater difficulty than above. For when the planet is nearer to the sun, it occupies not only longer arcs of the circles of the motor virtue but also denser arcs: wherefore should it not extend its delays in the ratio of the squares rather than in the simple ratio of the intervals?*

Now the same thing is said as above, and the same answer is made. For even if Saturn at that time did not come down into the sphere of the Earth: nevertheless we were comparing the expanse of power occupied by Saturn not merely with that which the Earth would have occupied in the sphere of Saturn but also with that which the Earth would occupy in its own sphere. Therefore, as before, the fact that the circles are denser (*confertiores*) is to be assigned to the form from the body; and this form is something distinct from the inhering motor virtue, which extends in longitude alone and gets no advantage from the condensation of its subject in latitude—unless a thin line without width (*latitudine carens*) has no natural force in length (*in longum*): where the width (*latitudo*) of such a line is judged not by the density but by the expanse, namely on account of the width of the bodies to be moved, as I taught above.

5. On the Annual Movement of the Earth

Accordingly this philosophy of Copernicus makes the Earth one of the planets and sets it revolving among the stars: I ask what, besides what has been said, is required for the easier perception of the teaching and the arguments.

Since the annual movement of the Earth becomes necessary, because it has been postulated that the centre of the sun is at rest at the centre of the world, and since this movement is caused [535] by the revolution of the sun in that space and clearly removes the truth of the stopping and retrogradation of the planets and explains it as a mere deception of sight: we must distinguish carefully the following questions: (1) Whether the sun sticks to the centre of the world. (2) Whether all the five spheres of the planets and the middle sphere of the Earth are drawn up around the sun, so that the sun is in the embrace of all. (3) Whether the sun occupies the very centre of the whole planetary system, or whether it stands outside of that. (4) Whether this centre of the system and the sun in it revolve in an annual movement, or whether the Earth has an annual movement through the sections opposite to those in which the sun is thought to be moving at any time.

You have proved above that (1) the sun is at the centre of the sphere of the fixed stars. Now prove also that (2) it is within the embrace of the planetary spheres.

That the sun is at the centre of the planetary revolutions is proved first from an accident of this movement, namely, the appearance of stoppings and retrogradings, which are deceptions of sight, or even because the planets seem to be faster when progressing than they really are.

For to begin with the lower planets, now for a long time during the many ages which followed Ptolemy—let us say nothing at present of ancient Aristarchus—it was perceived by the authors Martianus Capella, Campanus, and others, that it is not possible for the sun, Venus, and Mercury to have the same period of time, namely, a year, unless they have the same sphere and unless the sun is at the centre of the two spheres of Venus and Mercury and these planets revolve around the sun: for that reason, when these planets seem to retrograde, they are not really retrograding but are advancing in the same direction in the sphere of the fixed stars but are going around the sun. And that is more consonant with the nature of celestial things.

[536] A few years ago Galileo confirmed this argument by a very clear demonstration: by means of a telescope he disclosed the illumination of Venus. When Venus is progressing and is in the neighbourhood of the sun, it has a round figure; when retrograding, a horn-shaped figure. For from this it is proven with the utmost certainty that its illumination comes from the sun, that when Venus appears round and progresses straight ahead, it is above the sun; but that when it is horn-shaped and retrograding, it is below the sun, and that it thus revolves around the sun. Let the demonstration of this thing by reason of light be joined to the demonstrations of the illuminations of the moon. In the case of Mercury, Marius brings forward similar things by the aid of the telescope: the feebleness of its light was recognized as the planet came down to the Earth: and that is a sign that the form (*speciem*) of the illumination is changed and the light has become weaker in the horn, so that it moves the eye less when near than when far away. And that would be absurd without this weakening in the horn; because elsewhere things which are nearer appear greater than if they had drawn away farther. [537] Now as regards the three upper planets, Aristarchus, Copernicus, and Tycho Brahe demonstrate that if we set them in order around the sun and put the sun as, so to speak, the common centre of the five planets, so that the movement of the sun, whether true or apparent, affects all the spheres of the five planets, we are freed—as before in the case of Venus and Mercury, from two eccentric circles, so now in the upper planets—(1) from three epicycles; (2) from the blind unbelievable harmony of their real movement with the movement of the sun; (3) and just as above in the case of Venus and Mercury, they have no real stations and retrogradations with respect to the sun, around which they revolve; (4) thus also very many complications in the latitudinal movement are removed from the doctrine of the schemata; (5) and finally the reasons are disclosed for the difference which makes the five planets become stationary and retrograding, but never the sun and the moon; and (6) why Saturn, the highest of the upper planets, has the least arc of retrogradation; Jupiter, the middle one, the middle arc; and Mars, the nearest one, the greatest arc. All these things will be explained below in Book VI. But the ancient astronomers were totally ignorant of the reasons for these appearances.

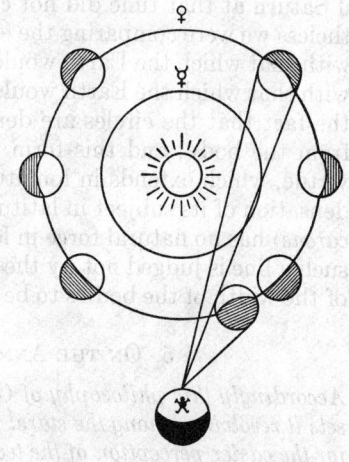

3. But even the secondary planets bear some witness to this thing. For Marius found that in the world of Jupiter the restitutions of the jovial satellites around Jupiter is never regular with respect to the lines which we cast out from the centre of the Earth to Jupiter; but that they are regular, if they are compared with the lines drawn through Jupiter from the centre of the sun. And that argues strongly that the orbit of Jupiter is arranged around the sun and that the distance of the sun from the centre of the orbit of Jupiter is sure and somehow fixed; but that throughout the year the Earth varies its distances from this centre.

How many sects of astronomers are there with respect to this theory, from which the second argument is drawn?

Three: the first, commonly known by the name of the ancients, [538] nevertheless has Ptolemy as its coryphaeus; the second and third are ascribed to the moderns. Though the second, named after Copernicus, is the oldest, Tycho Brahe is the founder of the third.

Accordingly Ptolemy treats the single wandering stars only separately, and he ascribes the apparent causes of all the movements, retrogradations, and stations, to their separate spheres. None the less in the case of each planet he sets down one unchanging sphere which completes its period with respect to the movement of the sun: but Ptolemy does not explain from what causes that comes about—unless the Latin writers, hypnotized by their complete ignorance of the rays, attribute some obscure force to the constant rays of the sun.

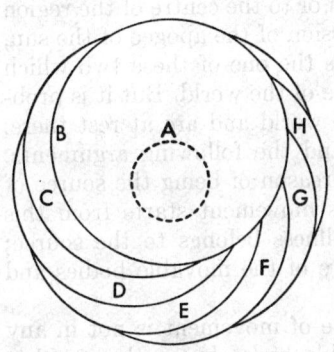

The remaining two founders compare the planets with one another; and the things which are found to be common to their movements are deduced from the same common cause. But this common cause, which makes the planets seem stationary and retrograding in some fixed configuration of the planet and the sun, is still attributed by Brahe to the real movement of all the planetary spheres; but it is completely removed by Copernicus from the spheres of the planets. For Brahe teaches that all the five spheres of the primary planets are bound together at some common point, which is not far distant from the centre of each sphere—as if here all the spheres were described in the common circular table *B*—and that this, so to speak, common node or knot really revolves with the sun during the year, and that very near to this node the sun—in the small circle made with dots—makes all the spheres revolve along with itself; and so to speak dislocates them from their own regions in the world—in the manner wherein bolters, grasping a sieve by one part of its rim, turn it with their hands and shake it; hence, for example, the position of the whole planetary system during the month of June is along circle *B*, during August along *C*, during October along *D*, during December along *E*, during February along *F*, during March along *G*, whence once more along *B*: meanwhile the planet, which has not been disturbed at all by this dislocation of its sphere, [539] completes its own circle on the sphere around its, as it were, fixed centre. But as regards the time of one year, Copernicus leaves the centres of the spheres absolutely fixed and also the centre of the sun fixed in the neighbourhood of the aforesaid centres. But he ascribes to the Earth, and thus to our eyesight, an annual movement around the sun: hence, since our eyesight thinks that itself is at rest, the sun seems to move with an annual movement and all the five planets seem now to stop, now to go in the opposite direction, now to advance forward very fast.

So by what arguments do you prove (3) *that that common node or common node or centre of all the primary systems is not* [merely] *very near to the sun but is in the body of the sun at its centre?*

In the teaching of astronomy the following arguments for this thing are drawn:

1. From the movement of altitude and longitude of the planets. [540] Observations duly taken bear witness that the longest line in the schema of each and any primary planet, which exactly bisects the orbital circle into two semicircles equal in the magnitude and speed of their parts, passes through the centre of the sun. Therefore all the five lines of altitude always meet at the centre of the sun. See the diagram on page 862.

2. From the movement of latitude of the planets. For we learn from the same class of things, that is, from observations, that the orbit of each and any primary planet is cut by the ecliptic at the positions opposite the centre of the sun, not opposite any other neighbouring point.

3. But if the centre of the sun and the centre of the region of the movable bodies were different, then the very slow movement in the small circle would have to be ascribed either to the centre of the sun or to the centre of the region of the movable bodies, on account of the progression of the apogee of the sun, as will be taught in Books VI and VII. And thus the one of these two which moves could not either be or remain at the centre of the world. But it is probable that both of them are at the centre of the world and are at rest there: the sun does so on account of the preceding and the following arguments. But the node of the movable bodies does so by reason of being the source of movement, and we have already said that this movement starts from this common centre of the movable bodies. But stillness belongs to the source; and on account of stillness, a place at the centre of the movable bodies and at the centre of the whole world.

4. The seat to be assigned to this same source of movement is not in any mathematical point, very near to the most noble body, but rather in that most noble body, for three reasons: first, in order for us to avoid the absurdity that the source of movement—which is necessarily set down as being at that common node of all the spheres, as will be proved below—should be very near to the heart of the world, but nevertheless should not be at the very heart of the world, namely the sun; secondly, because the motor force cannot reside in a mathematical point but requires a body, namely the heart of the world, the sun; thirdly, because the motor force absolutely demands for itself the centre of the world, where the sun itself is: just as stillness belongs to the surface of the world, so movement belongs to the inside.

5. [541] But in especial, the following thing must be taken out of the reach of Brahe's judgement and be demonstrated; that the centre of the region of

the movable bodies does not differ from the centre of the sun. For if Brahe admits this, he will be forced to assign some movement to the sun; and he will be forced to admit that besides the centre of the sun, there is another, different centre for the movable bodies; and by this movement it comes about that the sun now precedes this centre, now follows it, now stands above, now stands below; and nevertheless both always have the same period of time.

(6) As a matter of fact, something absurd and surprising would happen to Brahe. For the sun would be moved by an eccentric movement, having its apsis today in the Cancer. But the centre of the movable bodies would have the apsis of its eccentric movement in the opposite sign of the Capricornus. But what would be the reason for this thing?

(7) These two last arguments furnish an argument against Copernicus also inasmuch as he places that common node of the planets very near to the sun, but not in the sun itself. For the movements of all the remaining primary planets agree in the fact that the points around which their movements appear regular are different in position from the common centre of the region of the movable bodies: the Earth alone would keep this point as the measure of its movement, if the sun were not in the centre of the region of the movable bodies. But what would be the cause of this difference?

(8) Finally the reason why Copernicus and Brahe make these two centres different is not sufficient nor astronomical enough. For they were led to that by the fact that they wished in the forms of their hypotheses to express their every-way equipollence to the Ptolemaic form. But it was not necessary that they should step exactly in Ptolemy's foot-prints. For indeed Ptolemy did not build up all the parts of his hypothesis from observations, but he based many things upon the preconceived and false opinion that it is necessary to presuppose that the movements of the planets are regular throughout the whole circle—and that is demonstrated by observations to be false. Let anyone who wishes fully to understand these astronomical arguments which are placed here under one aspect—let him go to my *Commentaries on the Movements of the Planet Mars.*

[542] *Finally by what arguments do you prove* (4) *that the centre of the sun, which is at the midpoint of the planetary spheres and bears their whole system—does not revolve in some annual movement, as Brahe wishes, but in accordance with Copernicus sticks immobile in one place, while the centre of the Earth revolves in an annual movement?*

Even though the other necessarily follows from the demonstration of the one, nevertheless certain arguments pertain more closely to the sun and certain to the Earth; and certain others equally to both.

First on this side was the same argument whereby we just now claimed for the sun the midpoint of the spheres: namely, that the superfluous multitude of spheres and movements has been removed. For as it is much more probable that there should be some one system of spheres of the sun and that it should be common to the centre of the sun and to that node of the five spheres, according to Tycho Brahe, than that we should believe according to Ptolemy that in any one of the five planets, over and above the spheres which have to do with their proper movements, there is present one whole system of spheres exactly like the sixth system of the sun; so also it is now much more probable that the centre of one Earth should revolve in an annual movement and the sun be at rest, according to Copernicus, than that, according to Brahe, this node of the five systems together with the spheres and planets themselves and the sun as a sixth should have the same annual movement besides the other movements which are proper to each. For even though Brahe removed from the true systems of the planets those five superfluous schemata of Ptolemy, which are like those of the sun, and reduced them to that common node of the systems, hid them, and melted them down into one; nevertheless he left in the world the very thing which was effected by those schemata: that any planet, over and above that movement which must really be granted to it, should be moved by the movement of the sun and should mix both into that one movement. And since there are no solid spheres, [543] from this mixing there are caused in the expanse of the world very involved spirals. See the diagram of this involution in my *Commentaries on Mars*, folium 3.

Copernicus on the contrary by means of this one simple movement of the centre of the Earth stripped the five planets completely of this extrinsic movement of the sun, and made the centres of the six primary planets—that is, the Earth and the remaining five—each describe singly a simple and always similar orbit, or line very close to a circle, in the expanse of the world.

The second argument is from the movement in latitude. If epicycles revolve around an Earth at rest, either according to Ptolemy or according to Brahe; it will be necessary for those epicycles, especially those of the lower planets, in different ways to seek the sides as well as the head and feet, that is, to have a twofold libration. But with the Earth in motion, all the orbital circles have a constant inclination to the ecliptic. See Book VI, Part III where the latitudes of the lower planets supply us with a very clear argument for the movement of the Earth.

Thirdly, just as above, in the doctrine on the sphere, the diurnal revolution of the Earth being granted, the immense sphere of the fixed stars was freed from a diurnal movement of incalculable speed; so now, an annual movement being granted to this same Earth after the model of the other planets, we have ended that very slow movement of the fixed stars, which is called by Copernicus the precession of the equinoxes. See Book VII as regards these things. For it is much more believable to attribute them to the axis of the Earth, a very small body, than to such a great bulk.

Fourthly, the consideration of the ratios of the spheres wars on this side. For it is by no means probable that the centre of a great sphere should revolve in a small sphere. For the proper spheres of the three upper planets are much greater than the sphere of the sun—Saturn's approximately ten times greater; Jupiter's five times; Mars' one and one half times. Therefore these five spheres are not carried around or dislocated from their position; but their centres remain approximately fixed, and, as a consequence, instead of this movement common to them and to the sun, the Earth revolves.

[544] The fifth argument, which is related to the preceding one, is the same as that whereby Brahe tried to disprove the solidity of the spheres. For if Brahe's reasoning holds, as the orbit of Mars is one and one half times the orbit of the sun, so the body of

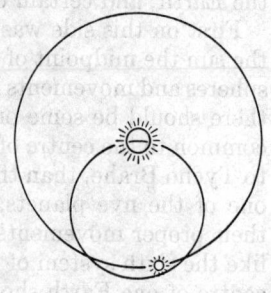

Mars at fixed times returns to that point in the world's expanse where the sun was at other times. And it is quite unbelievable that the regions which the primary planets pass through should be so jumbled together; since in Copernicus they are not only distinct, but are kept separate by very large intervals of emptiness.

I make the sixth argument similar to the fourth: from the magnitude of the movable bodies. For it is more believable that the body around which the smaller bodies revolve should be great. For just as Saturn, Jupiter, Mars, Venus, and Mercury are all smaller bodies than the solar body around which they revolve; so the moon is smaller than the Earth around which the moon revolves; so the four satellites of Jupiter are smaller than the body of Jupiter itself, around which they revolve. But if the sun moves, the sun which is the greatest, and the three higher planets which are all greater than the Earth, will revolve around the Earth which is smaller. Therefore it is more believable [545] that the Earth, a small body, should revolve around the great body of the sun.

The seventh reason is drawn from the reasons for the intervals, which were unfolded above in the first part of this book. These reasons are disturbed and maimed, unless we grant to the Earth too its own sphere, which Copernicus gives to it between the spheres of Mars and of Venus. For even if the interval between Saturn and Jupiter could be deduced from the cube, that of Jupiter and Mars from the tetrahedron, and that of Venus and Mercury from the octahedron, even in Brahe's ordering: yet there would still remain between Mars and Venus a single interval. But there remain two figures in the number of figures of the world. And the interval between Mars and Venus, which is in a greater ratio than double would not square with one of these figures, the dodecahedron or the icosahedron; nor could it be deduced from two figures, not even by the interposition of some sphere between them.

Eighthly, the same things are to be said concerning the harmony of the celestial movements, which are made up of the same numbers and proportions as our musical scale. And if you consider the excellence of the work or the pleasantness of contemplation, or finally the unavoidable force of the persuasion, this harmony can truly be called the soul and life of all astronomy. But this harmony is at last complete only if the Earth in its own place and rank among the planets strikes its own string and as it were sings its own note through a variation of a semitone: otherwise there would be no manifesting of its semitone, and that again is the soul of the song. As a matter of fact, if the semitone of the Earth is gone, there is destroyed from among the celestial movements the manifesting of the genera of song, i.e., the major and the minor modes, the most pleasant, most subtle, and most wonderful thing in this whole discussion. But concerning this in the *Harmonies*.[1]

Ninthly, if we consider the force of Brahe's ordering and if we image for ourselves some matter of the five dislocatable spheres, which matter together with the region of the movable bodies is dislocated by the annual movement; then in this matter, in this, I say, celestial sphere which extends throughout all the planetary regions, the Earth even when at rest [546] will describe such an orbit around the sun as Copernicus assigned to it between the spheres of Mars and Venus—the sun and the centre of the region of the movable bodies being at rest.

[1]See pp. 1009 ff.

And so by an absurd and unfitting reason a joke leads us from a distance to the same beauty—namely, that the Earth should progress along one circle or sphere, while being at rest. It is more believable that the sixth orbit of the Earth is described by the real movement of the very Earth, just as the remaining five orbits are described by the same number of movements.

The tenth argument, taken from the periodic time, is as follows: the apparent movement of the sun has 365 days, which is the mean measure between Venus' period of 225 days and Mars' period of 687 days. Therefore does not the nature of things shout out loud that the circuit in which those 365 days are taken up has the mean position between the circuits of Mars and of Venus around the sun: and thus this is not the circuit of the sun around the Earth—for none of the primary planets has its orbit arranged around the Earth, as Brahe admits— but the circuit of the Earth around the resting sun, just as the other primary planets, namely Mars and Venus, complete their own periods by running around the sun?

The eleventh argument is taken from the motor causes—by the supposition of Brahe's opinion, though it is not admitted by all. For because there are no solid spheres, therefore the motor faculties can be placed nowhere except in the movable bodies. But thus the condition of the motor souls will become mighty hard, and harder that of the intelligences, while the motor souls are ordered to transport the body, in which they are, from place to place by a twofold movement, without the resistance of anything, but the intelligences are ordered to look to very many things—so that they may carry the planet in its own rank by two in all respects distinct and mixed-together movements. For at least at one and the same moment they are forced to look to the beginnings, centre, periods, and figures of either movement. But if the sun is at rest and the earth is moved, each planet has only one movement, and that movement can be effected by bodily magnetic powers. For there is barely need of the animal faculty for the one revolution of the solar body, but there is absolutely no need anywhere for the supervision of mind. See my *Commentaries on Mars passim.*

The twelfth is from the source of movement. For it has just been demonstrated in many ways, and it will be confirmed below, that every movement of the primary planets, and in part even the secondary planets, arises from the sun. But it is right to believe that the first cause of movement is immobile. Therefore the sun sticks immobile to its own place—and as a consequence the Earth moves in an annual movement, in place of the sun.

The thirteenth is from motor instruments. For if we let the sun and the Earth revolve around their own axes, then the forms from these bodies (*horum corporum species*) become the subjects of the motor powers by which the six planets are moved by the sun, and the moon by the Earth. But if the sun revolves in an annual movement while the Earth is at rest, then no form from a body, which form should introduce movement, is at hand for moving the sun. And if the Earth does not revolve around its axis once a day, it does not have anything whereby it may move the moon. But this argument urges the daily movement more strongly [than the annual].

The fourteenth argument is from the movement in longitude. If the sun moves, carrying around with it the system of all the spheres, something novel occurs in the case of the sun. For some body will move itself, or else it surely will be moved by some special outside mover, since the other primary bodies are moved by one common sun, and thus by something other than themselves. But if the Earth moves in a circle and is also moved by the sun, like the other primary bodies, nothing novel happens. And so it is probable that the Earth is moved, for a probable cause of its movement appears; and it is probable that the sun remains fixed.

The fifteenth argument is from the movement in altitude. It has already been said in part, and it will be demonstrated below more fully, that all the planets have a movement of libration in a straight line, which proceeds towards the sun and by means of this libration obey the laws of their speed and slowness in any position on the eccentric circle. And thus it is certain that the sun is the cause of this variation in all five planets. But it has been demonstrated in the *Commentaries on Mars* that the same thing takes place on the Earth, if it moves, [548] namely that the Earth too has a libration along its diameter in the direction of the sun. But if it is put down that the sun is moving, then on the contrary the Earth becomes the cause of the sun's slowness and speed and thus of its revolution too. But indeed let the bodies of the sun and the Eearth themselves be viewed, and let the judgement be made as to whether it is more probable that the sun, which is the source of movement of the five planets and is many times greater than the Earth, should be moved by the Earth, or whether on the contrary the Earth, one among the primary planets, should be moved by the common source of movement of the remaining planets. See the *Commentaries on Mars*.

The sixteenth probability is as follows. Now in Book I it was maintained by many arguments and by the refutations of their contraries that the Earth has a diural rotation around its axis, and among those arguments not the weakest were as follows: If the Earth is put down as having a diurnal movement, the final and instrumental cause of the obliquity of the ecliptic can be taken from this same Earth; and, with the Earth at rest, neither of these [causes] can be explained, nor can they be sought from the sphere of the fixed stars, wherein the zodiac is, without a glance at this petty little body which is called Earth. Therefore the transportation of the centre of the Earth can no longer be absurd. But the probability is sufficient, if the remaining arguments demand the thing itself. For this is not to be offered as a necessary argument: because even though the sun rotates around its own axis, nevertheless it is immovable in place, as a whole.

The seventeenth reason: If the Earth revolves in an annual movement, not only do we find a more probable cause for the precession of the equinoxes than if we assign this variation to the sun, the first body; but also by this same means we give a reason for the irregular progression of the planetary nodes, and by the inclination of the axis of the diurnal movement of the Earth we explain the causes of the change in the obliquity of the ecliptic, just as in the case of some irregularity in the precession of the equinoxes—which irregularity we disapproved by the third argument. But one must necessarily be profoundly ignorant of the causes of so many of these phenomena, if the Earth does not revolve in an annual movement.

[549] Let the eighteenth argument come from the end of movement, by which it is proved that movement belongs to the Earth as the home of the speculative creature. For it was not fitting that man, who was going to be the dweller in this world and its contemplator, should reside in one place of it as in a closed cubicle: in that way he would never have arrived at the measurement and con-

templation of the so distant stars, unless he had been furnished with more than human gifts; or rather since he was furnished with the eyes which he now has and with the faculties of his mind, it was his office to move around in this very spacious edifice by means of the transportation of the Earth his home and to get to know the different stations, according as they are measurers—*i.e.*, to take a promenade— so that he could all the more correctly view and measure the single parts of his house. Now you understand that—in order that the first part of this Book IV might be fitted properly together—its writer needed to have the Earth a ship and its annual voyage around the sun. But if the Earth moves, the sun is necessarily at rest.

6. On the Diurnal Revolution of the Terrestrial Body Around its Axis and its Effect in Moving the Moon, and on the Mutual Proportions of the Year, Month, and Day

Because, in addition to the annual revolution around the sun, the diurnal rotation too is assigned to the Earth, which is one of the primary planets: I ask, you do not believe, do you, that all the primary planets turn in this way around their axes?

That is very probable, firstly in the case of Venus, as being seen to exhibit one spot after another—taking as a sign its sparkling, which is of a different form from the sparkling of the fixed stars; [550] again in the case of Jupiter, as bearing four satellites; and Saturn, which bears two just as the Earth bears one, the aforesaid moon: concerning which satellites below.

By what principles is this rotation of bodies around their axes brought to pass?

In Book I, which concerns the Earth, and in this Book IV, which concerns the sun, it has been said that these bodies are turned by an inborn animal principle or something similar. But that this principle is not alone in rotating the Earth but is assisted by the sun is gathered from two pieces of evidence: first, because the number of daily revolutions of the Earth in a year, which is 365¼, exceeds the proximate archetype, which is 360. For it is fitting that, unless the internal motor force of the Earth were nourished by the perpetual presence of the sun, the Earth would have moved along somewhat more slowly around its axis; and thus in the same space of a year it would have made fewer revolutions, namely only 360. With this postulated, it follows that the 5¼ remaining and as it were supernumerary revolutions are added to those 360 on account of some assistance from the sun. The other piece of evidence names this circumstance: that that part of the difference of time which the preceding Books I and III, folia 108 and 286, spoke of, and which Tycho Brahe is seen to have brought to light by clear experiments with eclipses, and which I reduced to physical form, is relevant here. For because this additosubtractive difference of time puts the summer revolution of the Earth as slightly slower than the winter: that indeed could not come from an inborn principle in the Earth, as such principles are wont to be perpetually uniform; but it must come from the intervals between the sun and the Earth, which in our hemisphere are longer in the summer than in the winter.

Perhaps every force causing this whirling movement is in the sun alone, none in any principle of movement inborn separately in the earth?

This is repugnant to both of the aforesaid reasons. For (1) if [551] the number 365¼ were not composed of the two effects of two distinct causes, there would be no reason why it is not one of the archetypal numbers, that is, one of the round numbers rather than one of the disjointed and ignoble fractions. (2) If the true physical additosubtractive difference of time is postulated: then, if the sun caused everything, the whole diurnal revolutions of the Earth would be proportional to the intervals between the sun and the Earth. But the magnitude of this additosubtractive difference of time demands that not the whole revolutions but merely some small parts of the revolutions should be proportional to those variable intervals.

You reckon the internal virtue of the Earth at 360 revolutions in one year; what reason for this number do you have to show from the archetype?

Because the sun had to cover the 720th part of its circle or apparent course at its farthest distance from the Earth; I believe that such great strength has been united to this virtue of the whirling movement, that the sun in any revolution of the Earth could appear to have progressed through two such small parts of its circle—according to the number of the two parts of the revolution, of which one part is called day, and the other is called night—to the view from any one place on the surface of the Earth. Consequently if two spaces of the ecliptic are stamped by the positions of the sun on two successive noons, there would be intercepted an empty or unstamped space equal to either of them; and as day is to night, so would the space filled by the sun be to the empty space— the diurnal space around the centre of the sun to the nocturnal space.

For in all these things, the nature of man, the observer creature and future dweller on the Earth, was taken up among the archetypal causes—as being one who was going to reckon the magnitude of the solar body and contemplate the differences of day and night.

[552] *But if this had been sought, it seems that it would also have been obtained. But you yourself admit that those ratios have been disturbed, since on account of those further increments from the sun the 360 days have become 365¼ and thus the diurnal journeys have become shorter.*

1. It cannot be said that this was sought simply, but merely in the adjustment of the principle of internal movement in the Earth: and in that manner it was obtained. 2. But even if in this secondary movement the concourse of causes disturbs the number instituted; still this disturbance was not so great but that during the months of November and January this magnitude is obtained: because then the magnitude of the diurnal movement of the sun is 1° or twice 30′. And long before, even if there were no such disturbance, the magnitude of the diurnal movement of the sun would have been such only twice during the year, on account of the necessary irregularity of the apparent movement of the sun.

How does the sun strengthen the motor virtue of the Earth by increasing the speed of the diurnal revolution of the Earth?

It is very probable that this takes place by the mediation of the light of the sun [*mediante solis lumine*], which the sun pours upon the Earth, through the illumination of the Earth's hemisphere. For because the physical additosubtractive difference [*aequatio*] of time demands unequal daily revolutions of the Earth, according as its distances from the sun vary; certainly at a short interval the illumination is strong as coming from a denser light; and weaker at a long distance, as from a thinner and thus lesser light; and that occurs—as regards the one dimension of longitude, into which the movement proceeds—in the very ratio of the distances. And so the amount of light which there is at any given time is fitted, by means of the distances, for distributing this acceleration throughout the year.

[553] *What are the effects of the daily revolution of the Earth, and, in general, of the revolutions of the primary bodies around their axes?*

Two: the first, which is proper to the Earth, is that for us who dwell on the Earth, all the stars in the heavens, both the fixed and the wandering, and so also the sun and the moon are seen every day to rise in the east and set in the west; although with respect to this diurnal movement they remain fixed in their places. I have treated of this deceptive appearance in the first three books on the doctrine of the sphere. The other effect, which is physical and most true and is common to all the primary bodies, and hence to the sun, is that the primary planets, by means of the form departed from their body set in revolution, move their secondary planets—as the Earth, the moon—and cause the secondary planets to move in the same direction but more slowly, and as if left behind.

By what arguments is it made probable that the primary planets share their own movements around themselves with the secondary planets, and especially the Earth with the moon?

The moon and Earth give the first evidence. For, just as above, from the fact that the planets, on drawing near to the sun, are borne more speedily, we reasoned that the sun by means of the form from its body, *i.e.*, its form set in rotation, moves the planets around itself in the same direction; so also, because we find that (1) in so far as the moon draws nearer to the Earth—but not to the sun—so much the more speedily does it move around the Earth, and (2) in the same direction in which the Earth revolves around its axis; it is with the greatest probability that we derive that movement of the moon from the whirling of the Earth; and that is all the more probable, because (3) there is also the correspondence that, just as the rotation of the sun around its axis is shorter than the shortest period of Mercury, so too the Earth rotates approximately thirty times, before the moon has one restitution. For if the moon revolved more quickly than the Earth, its movement could not wholly come [554] from the rotation of the Earth. (4) But belief in this thing is confirmed by the comparison of the four satellites of Jupiter and Jupiter with the six planets and the sun. For even if in the case of the body of Jupiter we do not have the evidence as to whether it rotates around its axis, which we do have in the case of the terrestrial body and the solar body in particular, that is to say, evidence from sense-perception. But sense-perception testifies that exactly as it is with the six planets around the sun, so too is the case with the four satellites of Jupiter: in such fashion that the farther any satellite can digress from Jupiter, the slowlier does it make its return around the body of Jupiter. And that indeed does not occur in the same ratio but in a greater, that is, in the ratio of the $\frac{3}{2}$th power of the distance of each planet from Jupiter: and that is exactly the same as the ratio which we found above among the six planets. For Marius in his *World of Jupiter* reports that the distances of the four Jovial satellites from Jupiter are as follows: 3, 5, 8, 13 (or 14 according to Galileo); just as if their small spheres were separated by the three rhomboidal solids. (I) The rhomboidal dodecahedron between the inmost spheres, whose intervals are 3 and 5. (II) The rhomboidal triacontahedron (folium 464) between the middle spheres, whose intervals are

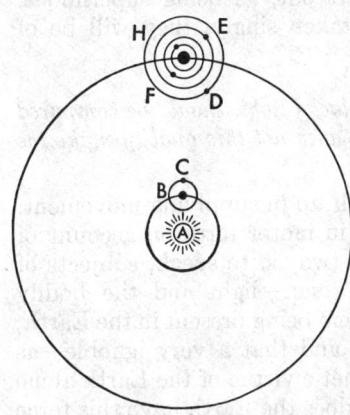

5 and 8, and (III) the cube, which is not truly rhomboidal, but is a beginning of the rhomboidal solids, between the extremes, which have the intervals 8 and 13 (or 14). Now the same Marius reports the periodic times as follows: 1 day 18½ hours; 3 days 13⅓ hours; 7 days 2 hours; 16 days 18 hours; everywhere the ratio is greater than double, and is accordingly greater than the ratio of the intervals 3, 5, 8, 13, or 14, but smaller than that of the squares, which constitute the ratios of the 2nd powers of the intervals, [555] namely 9, 25, 64, 169 or 196; just as also the ⅔th powers are greater than the 1st powers, but smaller than the 2nd powers.

Therefore since the agreement of the Jovial satellites with the six primary planets is so exact, not only did we rightly infer above from this that the body of Jupiter turns around its axis like the sun, so that the proportion holds for all its members; but here already, over and above that, we are confirming not improperly the general statement that this rotation of the primary bodies around their axes is the cause of the circuit of the secondary bodies around the primary bodies. That (5) is so much the more probable because we see that, just as the sun is greater than all the planets which it moves, so too the Earth is much greater than its moon, and Jupiter than its satellites, and for that reason, like the sun, fit for moving them. The remaining probabilities have to do with the moon again. For (6) that the bodies of the moon and earth are akin is taught us by the telescope, which reveals signs in the moon of mountains and of seas, such as they are in our globe of the Earth. Even Aristotle, elsewhere a very sharp defender of the fifth essence of the heavens, recognized this kinship, and, according to Averroes, he said that the moon seemed to be a certain ethereal Earth. I am silent as to Plutarch and the other philosophers in Macrobius.

Accordingly, just as the kinship of their bodies makes the loadstone attract loadstone or iron; so also in the case of the moon it is not unbelievable that she should be moved by the terrestrial body which is akin, although neither in that case nor in this case is there any contact between the bodies. And furthermore (7) why is it surprising that the moon should be moved by the Earth, since we see that in turn the moon also, by its passing above the vertices of places, causes the ebb and flow of the ocean on the Earth? Is not this a clear enough evidence of the sharing of movements by these two bodies? Finally (8) the same thing is confirmed by the remaining part of the proportion: the sun and Earth wheel around their axes, as experience makes us certain—in the case of the sun, of itself [per se], in the case of the moon, only in Copernicus—namely in order that by this rotation they may give movement to the planets placed around them—the sun to the six primary planets, and the Earth to the moon: that the moon in turn does not wheel around the axis [556] of its own body is argued by the spots. But why is this so? If not because no further planet is seen to go around the moon. Accordingly the moon has no planet to which it gives movement by the rotation of its body. Accordingly, in the moon, the rotation was left out, as being superfluous.

If these eight arguments are not of use as taken singly, they will be of service as taken together.

But does it not seem absurd that the Earth, which lacks light, should be compared as an equal with the sun, the source of light? For does not this quality make the motor force of the sun more probable?

Even if the light [*lumen*] of the sun works itself up in supplying movement, nevertheless the body of the sun is not potent in motor force on account of the light alone. For there is nothing to prevent two, so to speak, subjects of motor virtue from being found together in the sun—light and the bodily affection of magnetism—and only the latter of them being present in the Earth; just because the Earth moves only one planet and that a very ignoble—as one of the secondary planets. Nor does the magnetic virtue of the Earth alone move it without any assistance, as we hear; nor does the Earth have this force wholly *from* itself, though the force is *in* the Earth; but, the Earth seems to have partly drawn off this force as by a certain canal by the continuation of the line from the sun into itself and especially in the illumination of its body, and it seems to have turned aside this force into a new source, namely into its own body—as was said a little while before, and will be said more clearly below.

The rotation of the Earth keeps to the equatorial circle; but the movement of the moon, to the zodiac, which has a great declination from the equator. Therefore it is not probable, is it, that the movement of the moon comes from the rotation of the Earth?

This does not bother us any more in the case of the moon than in that of the other planets. For even if they have a declination towards certain regions of their own [557] and, so to speak, hold the rudder in their hands and turn at their judgement and sail sideways or towards the banks of the river, none the less they are seized by the force of the common whirlpool of motion flowing out from the sun; and so they have the movement of the common river to thank even for the distinct movement of their own, just as the moon has the direct movement of the Earth along the equator to thank for its own oblique movement through the zodiac.

Why therefore does the moon keep its whole route along the zodiac rather than along the equator?

Because in addition to the proper circuit of the moon around the terrestrial globe—concerning which up to now—the whole heaven of the moon is also moved in the movement shared with the centre of the earth along the zodiac around the sun, like the other planets. And it comes about from the composition [of these movements] that with respect to the centre of the sun the moon always holds to a direct course eastward not only at the time when the sun and the Earth, with their distances from the moon overlapping, hurry the full moon into the same region, but also at the time when the sun impels the dark or void moon forward, while the Earth—with respect to the centre of the sun—impels it backward. For this impulse from the Earth is still much less than that from the sun: wherefore it diminishes the movement's bearing eastward, but does not wholly absorb it, much less turn it in the contrary direction. See the diagram of this composite movement of the moon in the *Commentaries of Mars*, folium 149.

Therefore since that flow of the solar form advancing along the zodiac is greater, and is other than the terrestrial form, which, proceeding along the equator, is less; and moreover since when the moon and sun are in conjunction, by reason of the speed and the region of rising and setting, in the space of the world more is in obedience to the sun than to the Earth: I believe that hence it comes about that by reasons of the latitudinal regions too, the moon is more obedient to the solar form as the stronger—as its whole heaven around the sun, so also its body around the Earth—and is compelled to advance along the zodiac [558] or to regulate according to zodiac its own orbit around the Earth.

From this does not anomaly arise in the lunar movement, if the moon at the tropic points advances according to the lead of the terrestrial form, because the zodiac and the equator are parallel at those points, but at the equinoctial points it crosses obliquely this form from the terrestrial body?

Again, in order to solve this objection, I make the same answer as in the case of the latitudes. Namely, that the form from the terrestrial body is very strong in its midpart under the equator, but is weaker to the sides of the equator; because even at the source, namely in the terrestrial globe, the circles parallel to the equator, as being smaller, are set in motion more slowly than the equator, the great circle. Accordingly a balancing takes place: so that where the moon experiences a strong motor form, there it does not comply with the whole form but goes off crosswise—and where it complies with the whole form and is utterly obedient to it, there the moon experiences it weak. Notwithstanding, I do not proclaim anything concerning the balancing in all its respects, since lunar observations still disagree in very small amounts from any given calculations, and since it is uncertain to what that discrepancy should be referred.

How too can the moon be borne around the sun in an annual movement, but the four satellites around Jupiter in a common duodecennial movement, so that meanwhile neither does the moon abandon or let go of the Earth nor the four Jovial satellites Jupiter, if the moon is not bound by a solid sphere to the Earth, and they to Jupiter?

Now the secondary planets are borne around the sun by the same virtue of the solar form, whereby also their primary planets, the Earth and Jupiter, are borne; but they would revolve more speedily than their primary planets, inasmuch as they are readier for movement by reason of their density, bulk, or weight, if they were not held back [559] and laid hold of by the Earth and Jupiter by means of a magnetic force similar to that with which the sun too is endowed. But this prehensive force, as was said above concerning the planets too, is determined by the contrary virtues of the approach and withdrawal of the moon from the Earth; for as the Earth revolves around its axis, by this laying hold it makes the moon revolve but meanwhile changes the region of its own body with respect to which approach and withdrawal takes place. See the diagram on page 899. Imagine the friendly region (*plagam amicam*) of the lunar globe to be turned towards the Earth and not to be changed about with the contrary region. Imagine also that the Earth does not rotate around its axis, but is nevertheless borne around the sun: in this case the moon will run the same course as the Earth, and meanwhile it will be attracted by the Earth, until it comes into contact with it. In turn imagine the same thing concerning the unfriendly region: in this case the moon will flee the Earth until it gets outside of the sphere of magnetic virtue of the Earth: then it will wholly give itself up to seizure by the sun alone, and thus will wander completely away from the Earth.

You have said that the middle circle of the Earth is slightly less than sixty times narrower than the sphere of the moon. But this same circle of the Earth is only thirty times faster than the moon because the moon returns in 29½ days. Therefore the circle of the Earth is slower than the centre of the moon around the Earth in the ratio of two to one. How then does a body, which proceeds more slowly, give to the moon a movement twice as great and twice as fast as its own movement?

This objection does not apply uniquely to lunar movement, but generally to all the planets; and there is nothing absurd in it. For the solar and terrestrial bodies do not move [things] by contact, but by the spreading out or unfolding of their forms into every orbit of the movable body. Now in so far as the form from the terrestrial body flows out through space, it turns with the Earth, its source, in the same time of 24 hours, since nevertheless in that place where it lays hold of the moon, it is of the same amplitude as the sphere of the moon. [560] Therefore that form, sixty times wider than the Earth, passes through the total orbit of the moon thirty times in one month, although within the same interval the moon, following after the form from the Earth, has only one periodic return. And so it remains probable that the movement of that form from the terrestrial body moves the moon; but in such a way nevertheless that the inertia of the lunar body overcomes diurnally about 29 parts of the expanse of virtue and is overcome with respect to not more than the thirtieth.

Why do you set down that the sun concurs with the motor form of the Earth even in that movement whereby the moon revolves around the Earth?

1. Because Tycho Brahe found that the mean movement of the moon—that is, without the anomaly which exists in all planets on account of the eccentricity of the orbit—[561] still has an anomaly or is irregular. For the moon is always speedier in the syzygies, as here in CD and GH, and slower in the quadratures EF and IK than the ratio of eccentricity accounts for—whether in either case it is in the apogee or in the perigee or in any other position on its eccentric circle; and—if we are to insist firmly upon Tycho's hypothesis for the said variation—the moon is exactly as much faster in the syzygies as it is slower in the quadratures.

But the form itself from the Earth—the form set in rotation and to be understood by the circle $DFHK$—is of uniform speed all around, as much

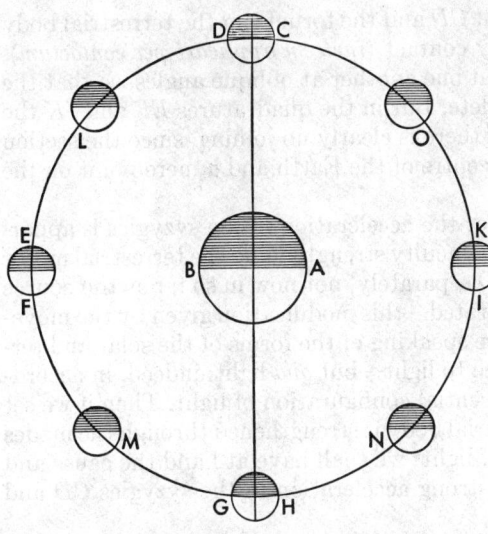

in those parts which are turning at the syzygies D and H as in those parts which are turning at the quadratures F and K—that is to say, for one and the same interval between the moon and the Earth. Accordingly other causes of movement which may be adjusted to the phases of the moon must be added to this motor form. But the phases of the moon are caused by the sun. Therefore the sun assists the movement of the moon around the Earth.

2. Belief in this concurrence of the sun is strengthened by the fact that before this, on pages 917 and 918, the same sun was summoned in order to aid the speed of the Earth in revolving, by the illumination of the [terrestrial globe] —here represented by the middle circle AB. For from this, as in the example of the Earth, we first understood that even in the light of the sun there is present a power of quickening movement. Then from the same thing we weave a necessary argument even for the moon. For if, according as $DFHK$ the form from the terrestrial body AB is set in whirling motion, it moves the moon; but the sun accelerates this whirling motion: therefore the sun will accelerate the moon too by means of the Earth and the acceleration of its form.

Then this illumination is not disposed in one way when the moon is turning in the quadratures F *and* K, *and in another way when the moon is turning in the syzygies* D *and* H?

By no means. For in both cases the halves of the globes are illuminated, both of the Earth AB, which gives movement, and of the moon CD or GH, to which movement is given. Rather, it has already been said that the speed of the Earth from this illumination [562] is equal at both times.

Whence then does this disparity of effect come to this accessory cause, so that it accelerates the movement of the moon very much in the syzygies D *and* H *but not at all in the quadratures* F *and* K? *And what on the contrary slows the movement of the moon in the quadratures* F *and* K?

No part of celestial physics was more difficult to explain than this. And in order to straighten things out, where possible, we must make use of the diagram on this page.

Accordingly you remember that all the circles which bound the illumination of the lunar globe, as CD and GH, were parts of the same number of spherical surfaces, into which the light coming from the sun as from a centre is spread out; while the circle $DFHK$ represents the form of the terrestrial body AB at the center of its position, and this form moves the moon. You see that in the syzygies D and H the form from the light CD and the form from the terrestrial body $OCDL$ are joined to one another by contact (*invicem applicari per contactum*), and that at L, M, N, and O they cut one another at oblique angles, so that the joining (*applicatio*) is more incomplete. But in the quadratures EF and IK the cutting is at right angles; therefore there is clearly no joining, since the section of the moon stretches towards the centre of the Earth and a mere point on the circle NIO corresponds to it.

Therefore, since no other cause for the acceleration in the syzygies is apparent, we shall have to set down that a faculty strengthening the terrestrial motor form ODL is present in the light CD separately, not now in so far as the source of the light, *i.e.*, the solar body, is rotated—this modification given by the movement was valid above, since we were speaking of the forms of the solar and terrestrial bodies without any reference to light—but *qua* light: indeed, in accordance with the true and somehow essential configuration of light. Then if we set down that this form from the terrestrial body is strengthened through the modes of its joining to the circles (*orbes*) of light; we shall have at hand the cause and the measure of there being a very strong acceleration in the syzygies CD and GH, but none in the quadratures.

[563] But since by $DFHK$ is represented not merely the form of the terrestrial body as agent or mover, but also the very orbit of the moon as of the patient or thing moved—although at that time the Earth must not be placed at the centre of the circle but near by—we must conceive further either that at the syzygies CD and GH the lunar body is better disposed towards movement according to the diffusion or the surface of the light than in EF and IK, where the moon cuts the circles of diffusion crosswise, or that the road of the moon in D and H is made as it were slippery, but rough in F and K—as on a table with grooves running crosswise in the wood. And that is not very absurd. For since the power of strengthening the movement is present in the light, as it was laid down; surely where one dimension of the light stretches, it is likely that the passage is easy.

Furthermore, as regards the effect, the same thing is said by him who says that the moon is accelerated in D and H and slowed up in F and K and in both cases in the simple ratio which these joinings (*applicationes*) produce, and by him who says that the moon is very greatly accelerated in D and H and none at all in F and K, but in the ratio of the squares of that which results from the joinings posited here.

Unless anyone prefers to ascribe this twofold efficacy of the light to the two dimensions of the surface of the light; so that, although any immaterial forms of bodies are diffused no less than light is diffused both in longitude and in latitude; nevertheless those forms up to now have been effectual only with reference to longitude; but this [light] is effectual with reference both to longitude and latitude: on account of the fact that the form moves as moved; but it is moved only in longitude; while light strengthens as light, *i.e.*, according as it possesses its own density, both in longitude and in latitude.

Why do you attribute the force to strengthen the motor cause to the light separately and outside of its reference to the rotation of its source?

Because in so far as the form from the rotating source moves [the moon], it always moves it eastward in the direction $CIDL$; and in the beginning of this section we already finished with its effect [564] in moving the moon. But this force from the light is potent in accelerating the moon even westward in the direction *MNH*, with reference to the centre of the sun, at that time namely when the moon appears to us to be void of light or in conjunction with the sun. Therefore the light does not by itself bring movement and direction together (*conciliat motui plagam*), but by means of the acceleration of the form *MHN*.

If this force is present in light, greater force will be present in the denser light around GH, *as being in the neighbourhood of the sun; a lesser in the more scattered light, around the full moon in* CD, *since it is farther away from the sun by a thirtieth part of the distance: therefore the new moon will be speedier than the full, other things being equal.*

The more perfect joining balances the weakness of the light *CD*, as *CD* is of a more regular concavity than *GH*. Therefore since the strengthening takes place through the joining of the forms: in the full moon the more scattered light, joined more perfectly, accomplishes as much as in the new moon the denser light, joined more imperfectly, does. Now the intervals between the moon and the sun which measure out density to the light and which measure out the curvature to the circles *DC* and *GH* are the same: wherefore the density is perfectly balanced in longitude by the curves *CD* and *GH*. But the effect of the light on one side is balanced by the diversity of the joining on the other. For even though *CD* and *GH* are equally curved; nevertheless in the first case the convex *OCDL* winds into the concave *CD*; in the second case the convex *MGHN* is turned towards *GH* the form from light, which is convex towards the Earth.

If that addition of 133° to the 12 restitutions (synodos) *in the sidereal year comes from the acceleration of the lunar movement in the syzygies, the magnitude of the acceleration must correspond too.*

Indeed in Tycho Brahe the movement [565] of the moon in the syzygies is accelerated only 1′26″ per 1°, and is slowed 1′26″ per 1° in the quadratures; wherefore if the slowing is effaced by the twofold acceleration, the greatest acceleration of the syzygies will be 2′52″. Wherefore if the sines squared of all the 90° bring their small portions into one sum, we shall have as the aggregate 2°9′; therefore in the sidereal year 106°22′ but not 132°45′.

But in the first place the magnitude of the greatest variation is not very certain in Tycho, who exhibits it as 40½′ at 45°; and so, if the variation is set down as 51′, we equal the aforesaid sum—3′34″40‴ being taken as the acceleration of 1°, or in Tycho's formulation 1′47″20‴, and an equal slowing up at 90° or in the quadratures; and thus in one quadrant the sum of 2°41′ is added up, and that sum will acquire great probability below, when we deal with the causes of the irregularities. Then if in particular we keep Tycho's small magnitude, at 45°; the preceding and the subsequent magnitudes, distributed in another formulation than Tycho's, could give the desired sum; or else there are hidden from us very minute causes, which take away something from the 133° in the treatment of the variation.

Then in what proportion do you think the monthly movement of the moon around the Earth should be distributed among those two causes, namely the form of the terrestrial body and the circle of illumination of the bodies?

We see that while the Earth revolves around its axis approximately 29½ times, in the meantime the moon returns around the Earth once, namely from sun to sun. So it happens that in one year or 365 days 6 hours 9 minutes 26 seconds the moon returns twelve times and adds on more than one third of the thirteenth revolution, that is, 132°¼′. Therefore it is likely that the density of matter in the lunar body is so proportioned to the archetypal degree [566] of strength in the form from the terrestrial body, that unless illumination aided the daily revolution of the Earth and also by means of this [revolution] aided the progress of the moon, the moon itself by reason of the simple motor virtue of the Earth would return slightly more slowly, that is to say, exactly twelve times. With this laid down, it follows that those remaining and as it were supernumerary 132¼° of the incomplete thirteenth revolution must be attributed to the other motor cause, namely the illumination.

Then you evaluate the density of the lunar body as proportioned to twelve lunar revolutions in one year: what will you say is the archetypal cause of this number?

The cause seems to be composite of geometrical beauty and of the office of this planet in the world: as follows: For the moon is a secondary planet assigned to the Earth, and it keeps to its own private course around the Earth. But 360 revolutions were allotted to the Earth, while the centre of the Earth makes one return around the sun. Then, just as among the upper planets, the sphere of the moon had to be a mean proportional between the body of the Earth and the sphere wherein the centre of the Earth really revolves, but the sun apparently; so also the revolutions of the moon had to be more than one but fewer than 360. And indeed the mean proportional between 1 and 361 is 19; but because the number 361 is not 360 and because 19 does not have any beauty either geometrical or harmonical; then the two numbers nearest to 19, which when multiplied together, give 360 and are the most beautiful geometrically and harmonically, should be chosen. Now the nearest numbers which give 360 are 18 and 20, because the first is smaller by unity alone, and the second greater than 19 by unity alone. But there is no demonstration of a figure of 18 sides. The numbers following nearest are 15 and 24, which also give 360. Now there are geometrical demonstrations of them, but rather worthless ones; nor do they give any outstanding ratio, [567] but only the ratio between 5 and 8; nor are they the most excellent and first of all in harmonics. But the numbers 12 and 30—for there are no others nearer which give 360—excel in all ways: both geometrically, as being generated from the first figures inscribed in the circle, and harmonically, because all harmonies are represented by these two divisions of the string. Then of the numbers which, when multiplied together, give 360, there are none more beautiful.

Furthermore, a number [not] less than 12 and not greater than 30 was due to the revolutions of the moon; because the sphere of the moon exhibits an image of the sphere of the sun, it was fitting too that, just as the year, which is the periodic time of the sun, is divided into 360, a great multitude, so also the month, which is the periodic time of the moon, should be allotted parts or days greater in number than all the months in the year; and that the multitude should increase with the progress, if in the first place the year, the long time, were divided into 12 months, the big parts, and thence the month, the short time, into 30 days, the little parts; for multitude is becoming to small things.

And it would not have been of the same beauty, if there had been thirty months in the year, and each month had been of twelve days.

How do you make it probable that the increase in the annual revolutions of the Earth above the number 360 and this addition to the annual movement of the moon beyond the twelve monthly revolutions of the moon come from the same cause?

The very reasons of this philosophy bear witness to this thing; so that, because the daily rotation of the terrestrial globe moves the moon, the greater in number and speedier the rotations are, they move the moon with greater speed, and make it return more often. And especially so does the comparison of the number of days in the solar year—365 days 6 hours and a little more—with the archetypal number 360 and with the number of days in the lunar year—354 days and a little less than 9 hours.

[568] For since 360 days in the year—making the moon revolve 12 times—should have come from the archetype, but they have become 365 by the intervention of the other cause; accordingly all the revolutions have become faster in the ratio of 360 to 365, and in that ratio stronger with respect to moving the moon. But at the same time they have become greater in number, *i.e.*, 365. Therefore the faculty of the 360 archetypal revolutions should be evaluated at the number 360. But the faculty of these actual 365 revolutions should be evaluated not at the number 365, because these revolutions are faster, but at the number which is a third proportional, namely 370°36′50″—if we attend to the minutiae. But if the faculty stamped with the number 360 would have moved the moon so that it would have completed 12 returns with respect to the sun and would have ended the last of those returns at its initial position beneath the fixed stars: therefore, in the same proportion, the faculty evaluated at the number 371[1] will make the moon outrun the sun 12 times and go 127°10′ beyond its initial position: and because, after the 360 days which were in the archetype have been completed, the sun is still 5°10′ distant from its initial position beneath the fixed stars, and because the circle, which in the archetype had been divided among the 12 positions of the full moons, has been narrowed by that interval, accordingly the addition of these 5°10′ to those 127°10′ makes 132°20′. See how near this reasoning comes to the truth in the astronomical tables; for they give the excess of the moon in the sidereal year as 132°45′, only 25′ more.

We will also infer the same thing from the days of the lunar year, as follows: The motor faculty of the 360 revolutions of the Earth would have given the moon its twelfth return with respect to the sun and to its initial position; therefore the faculty of revolutions fewer in number but so much the stronger will accomplish just as much. Accordingly as 365 revolutions is to 360, so the faculty of the 360 archetypal days is to the faculty of the 354 actual days and 19 hours, 33 minutes. Therefore so many terrestrial revolutions, now become more intense, would have given the moon its twelfth return with respect to the sun, if only the intervals between two syzygies had not been contracted by the increase in the number of the revolutions. But because, with the insertion of the supernumerary days in the year, the 360th day as [569] archetypal breaks up the measure of contraction of the zodiac, from which 5°6′41″ are due proportionally to the length of the lunar year; accordingly the moon too is relieved [*sublevatur*] of the same number of degrees; so that even when those degrees have not been

---

[1]To be precise: in the actual computation Kepler uses the number 370°36′50″.

traversed in the expanse of the world, nevertheless the moon makes its twelfth return with respect to the sun. Now those degrees are equivalent to 10 hours 4 minutes. And when 10 hours 4 minutes have been subtracted from 19 hours 33 minutes which were found, 9 hours 29 minutes remain in addition to the 354 days. Instead of these 9 hours 29 minutes the astronomical tables give 8 hours 49 minutes, so that less than an hour is missing. And that small difference can be assigned to other minute circumstances. Meanwhile it has been proved exactly enough in both ways that this straying from the whole and beautiful numbers is due to the concurrence of the causes of the lunar movement. And the reason is clear why 360 is approximately a mean proportional between the lengths of the lunar year and the solar sidereal year.

PART III

ON THE REAL AND TRUE IRREGULARITY OF THE PLANETS AND ITS CAUSES

From what do the planets have that name which signifies wanderers *in this language?*

From the manifold variety of their proper movements. For if you follow the judgment of the eyes, that variety has no law, no determined circle, no definite time, if a comparison is made with the fixed stars.

In how many ways do the planets seem to wander?

In three ways: (1) In the longitude of the sphere of the fixed stars, which we said extends along the ecliptic. (2) In latitude [570] or to the two sides of the ecliptic, towards its poles. (3) In altitude, *i.e.*, in the straight line stretching from the centre of vision into the depth of the ether. Nevertheless this variety is not uncovered by the eyes alone; but reasoning from the diverse apparent magnitude of the bodies and the arcs assents to it.

What must be held concerning these wanderings of the planets? Do they really wander in so many various ways, or is sight merely deceived?

Even though that movement is not wholly such as meets the eyes, it is present in the planetary bodies themselves; but much deception of sight winds its way in here. Nevertheless when these deceptions have been removed by the mind, some irregularity of movements still remains and is really present in all the planets.

Then what is that true movement of the planets through their surroundings?

It is constant with respect to the whole periods; and proceeds around the sun, the centre of the world, always eastward towards the signs which follow. It never sticks in one place, as though stationary, and much less does it ever retrograde. But nevertheless it is of irregular speed in its parts; and it makes the planet in one fixed part of its circuit digress rather far from the sun, and in the opposite part come very near to the sun: and so the farther it digresses, the slower it is; and the nearer it approaches, the faster it is. Finally, in one part of the circle it departs from the ecliptic to the north, and in the other, to the south. And so the planet is left with a real irregularity and one which is threefold, too: in longitude, in latitude and in altitude. The astronomers prove that by suitable evidence—concerning which in Book VI.

1. THE CAUSES OF THE TRUE IRREGULARITIES

[571] *State what the ancients thought about the causes of this irregularity.*

The ancients wished it to be the office of the astronomer to bring forward such causes of this apparent irregularity as would bear witness that the true movement of the planet or spheres is most regular, most equal, and most constant, and also of the most simple figure, that is, exactly circular. And they judged that you should not listen to him who laid down that there was actually any irregularity at all in the real movements of these bodies.

Do you judge that this axiom should be kept?

I make a threefold answer: I. That the movements of the planets are regular, that is, ordered and described according to a fixed and immutable law is beyond controversy. For if this were not the case, astronomy would not exist, nor could the celestial movements be predicted. II. Therefore it follows that there is some conformity between the whole periods. For that law, of which I have spoken, is one and everlasting; the circuits or traversings of the celestial course are numberless. But if they all have the same law and rule, then all the circuits are similar to one another and equal in the passage of time.

III. But it has not yet been granted that the movement is really regular even in the diverse parts of any given circuit. (1) For astronomy bears witness that, if with our mind we remove all deceptions of sight from that confused appearance of the planetary motion, the planet is left with such a circuit that in its different parts, which are really equal, the speed of the planet is irregular—just as there is apparent inequality in the angles at the sun which are equal with respect to time. And Ptolemy himself, by setting up different centres in accordance with the rule of movement of eccentrics and epicycles, makes those circles of his to move more swiftly at one time, and more slowly at another. (2) [572] Finally, astronomy, if handled with the right subtlety, bears witness in this case that the routes or single circuits of the planets are not arranged exactly in a perfect circle but are ellipses.

But by what arguments did the ancients establish their opinion which is the opposite of yours?

By four arguments in especial: (1) From the nature of movable bodies. (2) From the nature of the motor virtue. (3) From the nature of the place in which the movement occurs. (4) From the perfection of the circle.

Will you state their argument from the nature of bodies?

They reasoned that those bodies are not composed of the elements, and so neither generation or corruption nor alteration has any rights over them. The experience of all the ages bears witness to this: for the bodies are always viewed as the same and are not found to have changed at all in mass or in number or in form. But the movements of the bodies made up of elements are for this very reason various and inconstant, because the elements are variously mixed in the constitution of the bodies and are at war with one another within the mixed bodies. Therefore in the celestial bodies, where there is no such mixture and no war of the elements as in mixed bodies, there is also no place for turbulence, none for irregularity.

What answer do you judge should be made to this argument?

If the argument is speaking of disordered turbulence of movements, there is none such in the heavens: there are no celestial disturbances as in thunder-storms,

Flame and drops of water at war with one another

because the composition of the bodies of the world is of a very different family. But if the argument is in opposition to every regular irregularity also; [573] then not every irregularity, certainly not that regular intensification and re-mission of movements, comes from the war of the elements mixed together in the moved bodies, nor from the bodies being mutable. For some irregularity arises just because they are bodies, bodies which are moved and which give movement too, and because they are made up of their own matter, their own magnitude, and their own figure both inwardly and outwardly, and in ac-cordance with their magnitudes and figures they are endowed with their natural power too. And in accordance with their natural power they are less movable at a distance than at near-by, where the faculties of mover and moved are in agreement rather than at war. Thus by one part of its body the load-stone attracts iron, and by the other repels iron; not in either case on account of any mixture of elements, but on account of the inward rectilinear con-figuration, in accordance with which the loadstone has an inborn virtue. Thus the same loadstone attracts more strongly iron when near-by than when farther away—not that when the loadstone is nearer, it has more of fire or Earth, but because its virtue is weakened with its distance. Nevertheless the celestial bodies—*i.e.*, the bodies of the world—remain everlasting and im-mutable as regards their total masses [*moles*]. For the changes which come about on their surfaces can bring on nothing sufficient to disturb [*nullum momentum ad turbandos*] the movements of the total masses [*molium*]. And upon this everlastingness of the whole globes and upon the fact that in the world there is nothing disordered which impedes their movements, there depend this regularity of the circlings, and the everlasting similarity, and the constant regularity, with respect to the whole cycles, of the irregularity in the single parts.

Will you review the second argument of the ancients taken from the mover cause?

They said, the motor virtues of the celestial bodies are of the most simple substance; they are minds divine and most pure, which do unceasingly what they do; they are everlastingly similar; they employ a most equal struggle of forces, and they are never tired, because they feel no labour. [574] And so there is no reason why they should move their globes differently at different times. And accordingly even the figures of the movements, on account of the very nature of the minds, are most perfect circles.

What do you oppose to this?

Even though the motor virtue is neither some god nor a mind, nevertheless we must grant what the argument intends—chiefly too in the case of that motor cause which a truer philosophy brings in, namely in the case of the natural power of the bodies, because wherever and in so far as such a power is alone, it moves [a body] most regularly and in a perfect circle, and does that by the sole necessity of effort and by the everlasting simplicity of its essence. That is the case in the rotation of the solar body and in that of the Earth too in especial; for this rotation comes from one sole motor cause: whether it be a quality of the body or a sprout of the soul born with the body. For the axis with its two opposite poles stays fixed; but the body revolves around the axis most regularly and in a circle. This would be the case still, if any planetary globe were always at the same distance from the sun. For it would be carried by the sun with utmost regularity in a perfect circle, by means of the immaterial form released from the solar body set in a very regular movement of rotation. And by reason of this same very regular movement even that form from the body revolves in the amplitude of the expanse of the world, like a swift whirlpool.

But although so far we have granted the argument of the ancients, nevertheless regularity of movements in every respect does not yet follow from this. For not only do the motor virtue and the movable body come together in the movements, but also the inward rectilinear configuration of the movable body; and in proportion to its diversity of posture in relation to the sun, this configuration is affected in diverse ways in the movement: in one region it is repelled, in another it is attracted towards the inside. The axis of the magnetic movable body comes in, and so does being at rest in the parallel posture; and from that inward repose and from that revolution coming from outside there results that change of posture [575] of the parts of the planet in relation to the sun. Finally there advenes the interval between the sun and the planet, and this interval varies with the attraction and repulsion. But when the interval has been changed and the planet comes into a denser or more rarefied virtue, then its movement too necessarily suffers intensification or remission, and the figure of its route becomes elliptical. So with reference to the concourse of so many required things, the virtue moving the planet cannot be called simple, because it moves by means of different degrees of its form.

What was the ancients' argument from place?

They considered that the region of the elements was around the centre of the world; the heavens at the surface. Therefore to the bodies made up of elements belongs rectilinear movement, which has a beginning and an end and which, disbursed according to the contrary principles of heaviness and lightness, brings any of those bodies back into its own place; and hence in proportion to different nearnesses to the natural place, or mark, there are different speeds, and finally pure rest. But the celestial bodies move everlastingly in the circular expanse of the world: and that argues that they are neither heavy nor light, and that they are not moved for the sake of rest or for the sake of occupying a place—for they are always circling in their place—but that accordingly they are moved only in order to be moved; and so their movement must be regular, and the form of their movement must be other than rectilinear, namely suited to an eternity of movement, that is, returning into itself.

What answer do you make to this third argument?

Not every irregularity of movements comes from heaviness and lightness, the properties of the elements; but some comes from the change of the distance too, as is clear in the case of the lever and the balance; and this cause produces intensification [576] and remission of movements, as has been explained so far. We must however remark that there is nevertheless some kinship between the principles of heaviness and lightness in the elements and the natural inertia of the planetary globe with respect to movement, but no irregularity of movement is explained by this kinship.

But as regards the figure of the movement, the argument concludes nothing more than we can grant, namely that the movement bends back into itself. And not only the circular but also the elliptical are of such a kind; and so the assumptions are not denied. For in truth bodies which revolve around their axes are moved only in order that by their everlasting motion they may obey some necessity of their own globe—some bodies indeed in order that they may carry the planets around themselves in everlasting circles.

State the fourth argument of the ancients which was taken from the circular figure.

They philosophized that of all movements which return into themselves the circular is the most simple and the most perfect and that something of straightness is mixed in with all the others, such as the oval and similar figures: accordingly this circular movement is most akin to the very simple nature of the bodies, to the motors, which are divine minds—for its beauty and perfection is somehow of the mind—and finally to the heavens, which have a spherical figure.

How must this be refuted?

To this I make answer as follows: Firstly, if the celestial movements were the work of mind, as the ancients believed, then the conclusion that the routes of the planets are perfectly circular would be plausible. For then the form of movement conceived by the mind would be to the virtue a rule and mark to which the movement would be referred. But the celestial movements are not the work of mind but of nature, that is, of the natural power of the bodies, or else a work of the soul acting uniformly in accordance with those bodily powers; [577] and that is not proved by anything more validly than by the observation of the astronomers, who, after rightfully removing the deceptions of sight, find that the elliptical figure of revolution is left in the real and very true movement of the planet; and the ellipse bears witness to the natural bodily power and to the emanation and magnitude of its form.

Then, even if we grant them their intelligences, nevertheless they do not yet obtain what they want, namely the complete perfection of the circle. For if it were a question only of the beauty of the circle, the circle would very rightly be decided upon by mind and would be suitable for any bodies whatsoever and especially the celestial, as bodies are partakers of magnitude, and the circle is the most beautiful magnitude. But because in addition to mind there was then need of natural and animal faculties also for the sake of movement; those faculties followed their own bent [*ingenium*], nor did they do everything from the dictate of mind, which they did not perceive, but they did many things from material necessity. So it is not surprising if those faculties, which are mingled together, could not attain perfection completely. The ancients themselves admit that the routes of the planets are eccentric, which seems to be a much greater deformity than the ellipse. And nevertheless they could not guard against this deformity by means of the province of those minds of theirs.

Now I have often reminded you that while I deny that the celestial movements are the work of mind; I am not at that moment speaking of the Creator's Mind, which all things indeed befit, whether circular or elliptical, whether administered and represented by minds or compelled by material necessity from the beginnings once laid down.

2. On the Causes of Irregularity in Longitude

[578] *Then what causes do you bring forward as to why, although all the routes of the primary planets are arranged around the sun, nevertheless the angles—in which as if from the centre of the sun, the different parts of the route of one planet are viewed— are not completed by the planet in proportional times?*

Two causes concur, the one optical, the other physical, and each of almost equal effect. The first cause is that the route of the planet is not described around the sun at an equal distance everywhere; but one part of it is near the sun, and the opposite part is so much the farther away from the sun. But of equal things, the near are viewed at a greater angle, and the far away, at a smaller; and of those which are viewed at an equal angle, the near are smaller, and the far away are greater.

The other cause is that the planet is really slower at its greater distance from the sun, and faster at its lesser.

Therefore if the two causes are made into one, it is quite clear that of two arcs which are equal to sight, the greater time belongs to the arc which is greater in itself, and a much greater time on account of the real slowness of the planet in that farther arc.

But could not one cause suffice, so that, because generally the orbit of the planet draws as far away from the sun on one side as it draws near on the other, we might make such a great distance that all this apparent irregularity might be explained merely by this unequal distance of the parts of the orbit?

Observations do not allow us to make the inequality of the distances as great as the inequality [579] of the time wherein the planet makes equal angles at the sun; but they bear witness that the inequality of the distances is sufficient to explain merely half of this irregularity: therefore the remainder comes from the real acceleration and slowing up of the planet.

What are the laws and the instances of this speed and slowness?

There is a genuine instance in the lever. For there, when the arms are in equilibrium, the ratio of the weights hanging from each arm is the inverse of the ratio of the arms. For a greater weight hung from the shorter arm makes a moment equal to the moment of the lesser weight which is hung from the longer arm. And so, as the short arm is to the long, so the weight on the longer arm is to the weight on the shorter arm. And if in our mind we remove the other arm, and if instead of the weight on it we conceive at the fulcrum an equal power to lift up the remaining arm with its weight; then it is apparent that this power at the fulcrum does not have so much might over a weight which is distant as it does over the same weight when near. So too astronomy bears witness concerning the planet that the sun does not have as much power to move it and to make it revolve when the planet is farther away from the sun in a straight line, as it does when the interval is decreased. And, in brief, if on the orbit of the planet you take arcs which are equally distant, the ratio between the distances of each arc from the sun is the same as the ratio of the times which the planet spends in those arcs. Thus let the centre of the sun or world be represented by the fulcrum of the lever, and its motor power by one arm and the weight on it—and we have already given the order to dissemble the arm and the weight, and mentally to reduce them to the fulcrum; but let the planet be represented by the weight on the remaining arm, and the interval between the sun and the planet, by the arm for that weight.

[580] Let AC be the lever, D and B the weights hanging from C and A, FE the fulcrum, and FEC and FEA right angles. As CE is to EA, so is the weight B on EA to the weight D on EC. Remove mentally EA, and let the power formed through EA by the weight B be the power of the fulcrum E; accordingly this power of the fulcrum E will keep the weight D, hung from C, in horizontal equilibrium, that is, so that FEC will be a right angle. But if 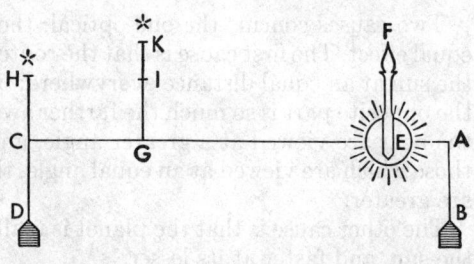 this same weight, pulled away from C, approaches as near as G, then the same power of E will have more might over this weight, and will lift it up above the line EC.

Now let E be not the fulcrum but the sun, and let D be the planet; and EC and EG the different distances of the planet from the sun. Accordingly observations bear witness that as EC is to EG, so is GK, the forward movement of the planet when nearer at G, to GI or CH, the forward movement of the planet when farther away at C.

Then do you attribute weight to the planet?

It was said in the above that we must consider that instead of weight there is that natural and material resistance or inertia with respect to leaving a place once occupied; and that this inertia snatches the planet as it were out of the hands of the rotating sun, so that the planet does not yield absolutely to that force which lays hold of it.

[581] *What is the reason why the sun does not lay hold of the planet with equal strength from far away and from near-by?*

The weakening of the form from the solar body is greater in a longer outflow than in a shorter; and although this weakening occurs in the ratio of the squares of the intervals, *i.e.*, both in longitude and in latitude, nevertheless it works only in the simple ratio: the reasons have been stated above.

3. The Causes of the Irregularity in Altitude

But what pushes the planet out into more distant spaces and leads it back towards the sun?

The same which lays hold of the planet, the sun, namely, by means of the virtue of the form which has flowed out from its body throughout all the spaces of the world. For repulsion and attraction are as it were certain elements of this laying hold. For repulsion and attraction take place according to the lines of virtue going out from the centre of the sun; and since these lines revolve along with the sun, it is necessary for the planet too which is repelled and attracted to follow these lines in proportion to their strength in relation to the resistance of the planetary body. So the contrary movements of repulsion and attraction somehow compose this laying hold.

Do you attribute to the simple body of the sun and to its immaterial form the operations of attraction and repulsion which are contrary and so not simple?

The natural action or ἐνέργεια of moving [582] the planetary body for the sake of assimilation or of bringing it back to its primal posture is one [in number]; but it seems to be diverse on account of the diversity of the object. For only in one region is the planetary body in concord with the solar body; in the other region it is discordant. But it belongs to the same simple work to embrace like things and to spit out unlike things. This opinion is strengthened by the case of magnets; for though they are not celestial bodies, nevertheless they do not have that biform virtue from the composition of elements but from a simple bodily form.

Therefore the planetary body itself will be composed of contrary parts?

No, indeed. For it follows only that the planetary globe has an inward configuration of straight lines or threads, like magnetic threads, which happen to be terminated in contrary regions; and in one of these regions, not on account of the body itself but on account of its posture in relation to the sun, there reigns friendship [*familiaritas*] with the sun; and in the other region, discord.

But isn't it unbelievable that the celestial bodies should be certain huge magnets?

Then read the philosophy of magnetism of the Englishman William Gilbert; for in that book, although the author did not believe that the Earth moved among the stars, nevertheless he attributes a magnetic nature to it, by very many arguments, and he teaches that its magnetic threads or filaments extend in straight lines from south to north. Therefore it is by no means absurd or incredible that any one of the primary planets should be what one of the primary planets, namely the Earth, is.

[583] *Granted that the planet has an inward rectilinear magnetic configuration: then what is it that makes the planet turn one region of its body after another towards the sun? It does not turn its threads about, does it?*

By no means: rather we should ask what it is which keeps the planetary body from removing its own magnetic axis from the posture which it has once taken with respect to the parts of the world, although nevertheless its body, like the terrestrial body, revolves around its axis and at the same time is moved out of its place and is transported in a circle around the sun. For out of this direction of the magnet towards the same region of the world during the whole circuit and out of the transportation of the body from place to place around the sun there is compounded, as out of two elements, the following effect: that the planetary globe changes the posture of its regions with respect to the sun. See the diagram on page 939.

What examples are there of this change?

Again there is a familiar example in the magnetic compass, namely where the iron needle has been magnetized. For into whatever place it may be transported, the compass needle always looks towards the north. And so if, carrying the compass, you march around some castle, then at one time the head and at another time the tail of the needle looks towards the castle, [584] because in every part of its circuit the head always looks towards the north.

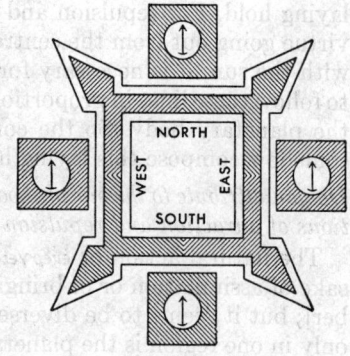

There was another astronomical example above in the third book, when we said that while the Earth revolves around the sun, the axis of terrestrial rotation remains in the same everlasting parallel posture—folium 248.

Then what causes do you assign for the pointing of the magnetic threads of the planetary body towards the same region of the world throughout the whole circuit of the planet?

The same as were indicated in Book I, folium 116[1], by which the axis of terrestrial rotation is made steadfast. For firstly the parallel posture of the threads manifests a certain sameness, which is rest rather than motion. The cause of that does not seem to be any natural power which is positive or active, but rather one which is privative of all movement. And so that natural inertia of matter with respect to movement seems to have an inward rectilinear configuration and to be extended in accordance with these threads or to be rendered stronger and more unconquerable by the condensation of parts in a straight line.

But if this is not probable: then let there be [two] distinct ἀδυναμίαι or powerlessnesses; the first belongs to all matter considered to be without inward configuration: and it enables the planet not to depart from its own place, unless it be drawn forth from the outside, namely by the sun. The second belongs to the planetary body according as it has a configuration of straight

---

[1]There are three possible causes. (1) Since the form of the turning is joined to the globe and is directed towards a definite region and not towards all indiscriminately, it follows with geometric necessity that the axis of this turning is directed constantly towards the lateral regions as long as the middle circle of the turning does not stray from its own region. (2) There is a private cause of motion, namely the natural inertia of the matter of the globe, due to the dragging of the axis, which necessitates force to turn it aside from its position; since, however, no power of motion is brought to bear against it, it remains at rest in its position. (3) There is an internal, positive, natural power in the rectilinear threads, which are parallel to the axis, to maintain them in their original position. For the power of movement nests in these threads of the entire globe; they are distributed circularly around the axis with equal strength on all sides and by means of them this power turns the body. Thus therefore in turn the axis, maintaining itself in its proper direction through a natural constancy fixes also the region of the turning, with the result that because of the inclination of the axis, the circle of the movement is also necessarily inclined.

threads on the inside, and by reason of it these threads are kept safe so that they are not deflected by the revolution of the body or moved out of their posture. Finally the philosophizers are free to determine whether what I have just spoken of is merely an ἀδυναμία or a δύναμις

You define this ἀδυναμία or δύναμις merely by the preservation of the posture. But what if something else were absent, and that δύναμις looked towards some other fixed parts of the starry heavens?

In Book I, page 116, when it was a question of the axis of terrestrial rotation which is similarly immovable, an answer was given as to why such a thing should not be thought of: namely because there is no reason why the axis should point towards some empty point in the heavens rather than towards some star, and why in this direction rather than in that; and because these planetary threads, no less than the axis of terrestrial rotation above, are found in the succession of ages to swerve slightly and thus to desert their original stars of reference [*fixas pristinas*] and to slope towards other succeeding stars, as can be judged in general. For that movement is so very slow that within the 1400 years from Ptolemy to us this cannot be safely enough affirmed of all the planets.

Perhaps those axes of rotation of the bodies play the roles of the threads which you bring in here instead of librations

The axis of the daily rotation of the earth—of which I have spoken in the doctrine of spheres—forever points in longitude towards the beginnings of the Crab and of the Goat. For this axis prolonged in both directions marks out the poles of the world, as in Book II, page 150. But the arc drawn from the pole of the world perpendicular to the ecliptic passes also through the poles of the ecliptic: therefore it is the colure of the solstices and marks out the beginnings of the said signs.

But the threads by which the Earth is repelled from the sun or attracted pass from sign to sign. The aphelion [586] of the Earth was formerly in the Archer, but now it is at 6° of the Goat. Therefore the axis of rotation of the Earth and the thread which changes the interval are different.

Then it seems that the Earth nevertheless should be at its greatest distance in the beginning of the Goat. For if the whole body of the Earth rotates around that axis, the thread will be rotated too, in so far as it differs in posture from the axis, and it will describe as it were two cones with their vertices meeting at the centre of the Earth, and only at one moment of the day will it look towards its proper place: during the rest of the day it will revolve around the beginning of the Goat pointed out by the axis of the Earth. And thus it will pile up all its own force at this axis, and by a certain as it were spiral line will draw the Earth away from the sun and always towards the region pointed at by the axis.

Certainly in this way, by the tight connection of the thread with the axis of daily movement, what is spoken of would take place, and the apsis of the Earth would never depart from the beginning of the Goat. Or else we are therefore compelled to admit that the globe is inside an outer crust: in such fashion that the crust rotates during the daily movement, while the globe having the threads does not rotate; and the ordinary magnetic virtue belongs to the outward crust, because it always shows the poles of daily rotation but not the apsis of the sun or Earth.

Whence let some physicist come to the help of J. C. Scaliger, who argues about the rising of rivers and the ebb and flow of the sea; and let the physicist see if these separated bowels of the Earth can aid him in his labour. Even though the moon and the soul of the Earth are sufficient for me.

If the planetary globes have an inward rectilinear magnetic configuration, why do you not rather ascribe to them themselves the reason for their fleeing from the sun and approaching the sun, in proportion to the diversity [587] of the regions of their body, as was done in the Commentaries on Mars?

1. Because astronomy bears witness that this drawing away from the sun and drawing near to it takes place in a line so to speak extended towards the sun, in so far as the intermingled revolution does not vary the line. But the magnetic threads are rarely stretched out towards the sun.

2. Because two very diverse things would be attributed to those magnetic threads. For first, they would point towards the same region of the world—which is something like rest; then they would move their body in place, now away from the sun, now towards the sun. But by means of repulsion and attraction this [movement of approach and withdrawal] is united more simply with the laying hold and making bodies revolve, which the sun furnishes.

3. Furthermore, it is more probable that the form of the solar body and its virtue continue as far as to the planets than that their form and virtue continue as far as to the sun, so that, when repelling it, they flee, and when attracting it, they seek. For the sun is a huge body; while a planetary body is quite small. The light and heat of the sun manifestly descend to us; the sun makes the planets revolve. Accordingly before this, things were clear concerning other virtues of the sun. But we do not have such and so evident testimony concerning the prolongation of planetary virtue as far as to the sun.

4. It will be shown below that the threads of the body suffer some slight deflection on account of the sun. Therefore it is probable that the libration of the whole body also comes to it from the sun rather than that it is inborn; that is, it is a passion from another, not an action or movement from the planet itself.

But would you set down that this virtue is at least shared between the sun and the planets and that the force of repulsion and attraction passes back and forth from one to the other, just as it is shared between two magnets?

No: rather this is the fifth reason why this repulsion and attraction is not attributed to the planets themselves: in order that there be no mutual attraction and repulsion according to [588] the very institute of the Creator, who does nothing in vain. Therefore, if the virtue of the planet extended as far as to the sun, then the planets, in the direct ratio of the bodies, would move the sun out of the position which it occupies at the centre of the world, or at least the sun ought to stagger, attracted now in this direction, now in that, according as many planets having a like faculty assail the sun from one side.

You seem not to avoid the following inconveniences: for the sun, leaning against the form and virtue of its body as against a pole and pushing the planets, pushes itself out proportionally, and drawing the planet as it were with its claws, it similarly draws itself to the planet?

We have avoided this in every way by denying mutual attraction and repulsion. For firstly, neither the shape [*forma*] nor lay out [*dispositio*] of the bodies will be directed towards this, if such a virtue of the planet [589] does not extend to the sun. Then something such does not actually follow—as though short of the Creator's design—from material necessity alone. For the bulk is so great, the density of matter in the solar body is so great, and its force of attraction and repulsion is so great; and in turn the weakness of the planet and the weakness of its resistance are so great; that the sun is in no danger of losing its position. Thus when a ship sticks fast in the sands and cannot be torn away and moved from its place except by two hundred horses, nevertheless one hundred horses, though they are half of the required virtue, do not move forward half of the lone thing, because there is no mean half-way between the moved and the not-moved, since they are contradictory.

State a convincing hypothesis as to how any planet completes its circuits and is meanwhile attracted and repelled.

Let us begin with that moment when the magnetic threads offer their sides to the sun, so that both extremeties of the threads are equally distant from the sun; and this takes place, by the foregoing diagram, at *A* the greatest distance of all: at this time the sun is neither repelling the planet nor attracting it; but, as if hesitating between both, it nevertheless lays hold of the planet; and by means of the rotation of its body and the flowing out of its form, the sun makes to move forward from *A* to *B* the planet which it has laid hold of, and the sun overcomes its resistance and in turn is overcome by the planet, so that the sun lets it fall, so to speak out of its hands, *i.e.*, out of the preceding rays *A* of its form and virtue, and takes it up again with the following rays *H*, and does so in the fixed ratio of the virtue of the form in that interval. In this way the planet is moved forward, while in the meantime the magnetic threads, by the force of direction, look towards the same region of the world, in such fashion that the region friendly to the sun is gradually turned towards the sun, and the discordant bends away from the sun: at that time therefore the globe begins to be attracted—only a little, if there is little difference between the distances of the extremities from the sun: by this attraction the planet will go, from the wide circle begun at *A*, gradually inward to *B* and will betake itself towards the sun, as if into a narrower circle and a stronger, because denser, virtue [590] of laying hold: hence it frees itself less easily from the virtue and so is moved on more speedily. This attraction, which is very slow at the start very near to *A*, is very rapid at the time when the sun has the whole friendly hemisphere of the planet within its view, but the whole discordant hemisphere is

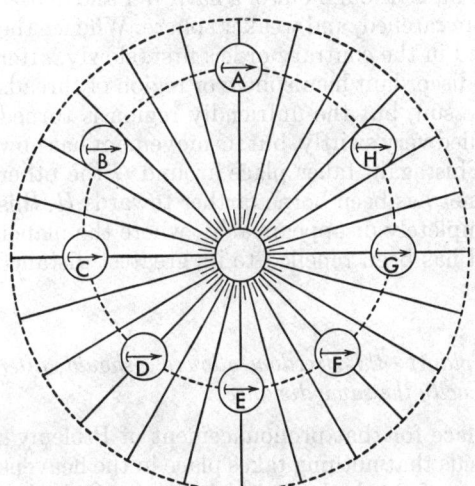

hidden behind the planetary body, *i.e.*, when the magnetic threads point in a straight line towards the sun; and that takes place around C, a quarter of the whole circular ambit. Thence around D once more this attraction towards the sun becomes more lax; but the velocity of the progress along the circle continues to increase, because the interval between the planet and the sun is still decreasing on account of the attraction. This relaxing of the attraction amounts to almost nothing in the beginning after C; soon, it is felt more and more, the more the unfriendly part of the planet thrusts itself out and offers itself to the view of the sun, towards D, until half of the circuit has been traversed and once more both hemispheres of the revolving globe regard the sun equally. For at that time all attraction stops, and the planet is very near to the sun, and so is very speedy, because it is struggling with a very dense and a very strong virtue of laying hold and frees itself hardly at all from that encompassing virtue.

But immediately the globe is borne beyond this place E on its orbit towards E, because already the discordant hemisphere is nearer the sun than the friendly hemisphere and is advancing more and more towards the sun. The planet too begins to be pushed away from the sun, as though out of a narrower and denser sphere of solar form into a wider, more rarefied, and weaker sphere. Whence the decreases in its movement follow, and in the contrary order: first, slowly, after E towards F; then, where the whole discordant hemisphere or region of threads points in a straight line towards the sun, but the unfriendly region is turned away from the sun: the planet is repelled very swiftly, but its movement has now once more slackened to middling. This again takes place around G the other quarter of the circuit. When the planet has been borne farther towards H, this repulsion again slackens, until it completely disappears at A, where the planet has returned to its primal place and has been repelled to its greatest distance from the sun.

[591] *But it is unbelievable that the planet—this freedom allowed—should, after completing its return, be restored to exactly the same distance.*

Doubtless this is at last a good place for that pronouncement of Ptolemy's written out above, where he reminds us that nothing takes place in the heavens which hinders the natural movements of any body or which makes the bodies stray as it were from their foot-paths. And so, if such laws of movement have been instituted by nature that the planet return unto itself most exactly, then this will most certainly take place, although without the shackles of spheres, in the free ether. But the laws were made as we described them. For the halves of the circuit are equal to one another—the one in which the planet is attracted and the other in which it is repelled. Equal times are taken by both halves. Moreover, the virtue of the sun is the same and everlasting—both as attracting and as repulsing. And it has the same ratio to the planetary inertia, which is always the same, because in an everlasting body. Accordingly it does as much by attraction in one half, as it does by repulsion in the other. Why then should we be doubtful concerning the restitution of the planetary body to the original distance within one period of time?

Also in these terrestrial and violent movements, are not the movable bodies separated from that which was the cause of movement, as in scorpions, ballistae, catapults, bombardae, and slings? And weapons hurled fly through the free air, and nevertheless they reach their appointed place. And, for a wonder, there are some sclopetarii and slingers with a sureness of aim that cannot be imitated. If in this case the form of that movement—which movement was in the thrower at the movement of throw and was directed towards a fixed region—the form impressed into the movable body for a short time and vanishing has such power that, as long as the movable is carried by a form which has not yet become completely feeble, it does not cease to strive for its appointed region: by how much firmer defences will the certitude of the celestial returns be protected, which are governed [592] by the inward and plainly united and hence everlasting threads of the movable thing—since in the first case the air disturbs the movement by its impact and encounter; and in the second case the density of the ether to be passed through is clearly nil in effect or else has a very slight effect.

Why are not the librations of the different planets in the same ratio to their mean distances, that is, why is the eccentricity of Mercury greatest, next, that of Mars, and then those of Saturn, Jupiter, and the Earth, while that of Venus is least?

The instrumental cause is the different strength of the threads, whether that is produced by nature or by posture. But the final cause is the same as that of the eccentricities themselves, namely in order that by reason of these eccentricities the movements of the planets should become very fast and very slow in such measure as would suffice for the harmonies to be exhibited through them. Book v of my *Harmonies* has to do with this.

There remains one difficulty with respect to the direction of the threads towards the same region of the world. For since you said that one region of the threads has friendship with the sun, and the other is in discord with the sun, so that in conformity with the former or the latter region the sun either attracts or repels the body of the planet, it seems that the sun has the power over the planet to do what is less, namely to move these threads out of their parallel posture and to turn them towards itself, before the planet is transported into a position from which the threads can look towards the sun.

There is nothing absurd in something like this taking place, so that the sun struggles with the direction of the threads, just as it struggles with the inertia [593] of the body with respect to movement in place—provided we keep in mind that the sun accomplishes less with respect to deflecting the threads than in moving the whole body in place, just as it also accomplishes less in respect to attracting the planet. And this tempering pertains to the Creator's plan, lest the planets should come into contact with the sun, if they were not transported into the opposite half of the circuit in a shorter time than the whole interval of time which could be spent in the direct attraction of the thread.

Therefore, since the circling of the planet around the sun forestalls the deflection of the threads, hence, although in one quadrant of the circuit the threads deflect somewhat towards the sun in their friendly region, and away from the sun in their discordant region; nevertheless, because the planet is transported into the other quadrant before the deflection of the threads becomes total, it follows equally that there is a change in the posture of the contrary regions, which are turned towards the sun, just as if the threads were not deflected; therefore in the remaining quadrant the sun by the same force gives a counter-deflection in the other direction to the planetary threads, which lie in the contrary position and turn their unfriendly region towards the sun. And so by the earlier contrary deflection the sun again restores the planetary threads to their parallel posture. In Book v this deflection and counter-deflection become the principal means of calculation.

Could you cite a common example of this direction and mixed sloping of the threads?

There is an example in the magnetic needle. For although it looks towards the north if it is free, nevertheless it is somewhat deflected from the north if a magnet approaches obliquely: for then it bows somewhat towards the magnet.

What things are required for the perfect restitution of the threads to the parallel posture?

That the sun expends as much of its forces in deflecting—say, through the quadrant *PIN*, attracting *H* the solipetal region of thread downward from line *IS* towards itself—as it expends in restoring, as through the quadrant *NER*, drawing back *G* the same region of thread upwards towards line *SY*, which is nearer to itself. But this can take place only if, with *PR* as the line of the apsides and *PN* and *NR* as full quarters of the orbit, *NQ* the thread of the planet, situated at *N*, the limit of the quadrants, points precisely towards the sun *A*. For even though, in the upper quadrant *PN*, the sun *A* administers this deflection *SIH, BNQ*, at long distances *AP, AI*, etc., and so with a feebler virtue, but in the lower quadrant *NR* at the short distances *AS, AR* and so with a stronger virtue; yet in turn the planet delays longer in the upper quadrant *PN* and undergoes those feeble forces of deflection for a longer time; while in the lower quadrant *NR* the planet makes a shorter delay and has a shorter time in which to undergo the strong forces which counteract the deflection. And there is perfect counterbalancing. For the same perfect counterbalancing can also cause that at *N*, one and the same limit of the quadrants, the distance *AN*—in the rightly drawn orbit— should be equal to the semidiameter *BP*—as will be made clear in Book v.

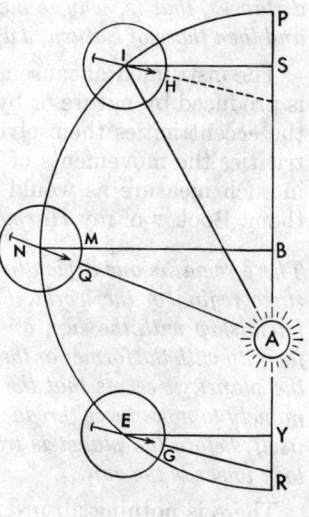

But what if the planet were to direct the thread NQ *towards the sun not precisely after traversing* PN *the upper quadrant of the orbit but at some later time?*

Here the burden of proof is on the opposition. For where the thread points towards the sun is the limit of the quadrants, which are measured from the apsides. For *IH*, the deflection of the thread with respect to the perpendicular *IS*, is always increasing, as long as the thread *H* seeks the sun. But the increment of libration increases with it—the effect with the cause.

[595] Therefore if, in this work of attraction of the planet towards the sun, more than a quadrant of the orbit is traversed with reference to the fixed stars; then more than a quadrant will have to be traversed by the planet in re-

storing the right angle between the thread and the sun at R and in the effect [of the restoration], or the remaining part of the libration, whereby the planet is brought from the nearness NA to the nearness RA, by the same degrees of increments which are now decreasing in the contrary order.

Therefore, when the quadrants are added together, their excess over the semi-circle shows the magnitude of the change in direction of the threads under the fixed stars in half of one period, or the magnitude of the transportation east-ward of B the centre of the orbit and PR the line of the apsides. Therefore if this magnitude is subtracted from that which is more than half of the orbit as estimated with respect to the fixed stars, there will remain not more than half of the elliptic orbit as reckoned from the apsis P.

Then do the apsides abide, or are they transported from one place to another under the fixed stars?

In the case of Jupiter the comparison of observations made by the ancients with those of today bears witness that the apsides stand approximately under the same fixed stars, or retrograde very little. But in the case of all the remaining planets, the apsides are found to have left their original seats, by a movement in the direction eastward—as in the case of the apogee of the moon—but in the case of the planets by extremely slow movements, though the apogee of the moon progresses quite perceptibly.

What is the reason why in the case of the primary planets, the threads are found so perfectly restored—after the whole periodic returns have been completed—that the progress of the apsides is imperceptible?

Because it is the same sun which gives a libration to the planetary body and

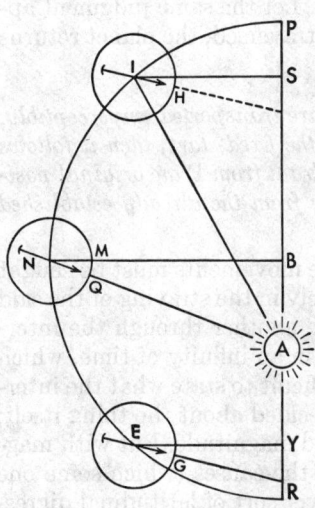

which deflects and restores its threads; and because in both acts it is the same threads by which as by instruments the planet is given a libration and is deflected: then there is no cause why the forces for both acts should not be measured out through equal times. For just as the planet, which points its thread NQ directly [596] at the sun, would at some fixed time be joined even in contact with the sun, if it did not leave the line NA; so too the same planet, placed at the same N and, by a fiction, directing its thread at right angles to the line NA, would be turned around together with its thread in a fully equal time, so that in the end it would direct the thread NQ towards the sun. But just as to the libration there is added a third work, namely the moving of the planet out of its posture AN, so that the thread NQ no longer points towards the sun and hence is not attracted with the same strength towards the sun—and in this way it is seen too that full

contact does not take place by a movement along NA, but is forestalled by the transportation from N to R, and the planet gets no nearer than RA; so too this same transportation of the planet from N to R anticipates this deflection of the thread, so that the thread will point at the sun long before it could have been rotated a whole quadrant by the sun; and so, instead of the quadrant of rotation, no more than arc QM is needed. But the angles of the past deflections, or the virtue expended in them, are measured by the sines—as will be made clear by examples of natural things in Book v. Wherefore as PB the total mean distance—or in the ellipse, NA—is to BA the magnitude of half the libration—the work of one quadrant; and this magnitude is the same as the eccentricity—so also NQ the semidiameter of the planetary globe, which is employed as the whole sine, will be to the sine of MNQ the angle of greatest deflection; and MNQ will be the angle of greatest deflection at the time when, by the transportation of the planet, a quadrant from P the place of greatest distance PA has been exactly completed.

But with the assumption of this proportion, it is demonstrated that the thread NQ points towards the sun A at the time when PN is a quadrant under the fixed stars, precisely. For let AN be equal to PB, [597] as in the ellipse; and let B be the centre of the eccentric circle, and ABN a right angle, because its measure NR is a quadrant. Now from Q the solipetal limit drop the perpendicular QM upon BN. Two right triangles ABN and QMN are formed. And because it is assumed that $NQ : QM : : NA : AB$, then $N, Q,$ and A will be in one straight line, or Q will point towards the sun.

But it has already been demonstrated above that if, when PN a quadrant under the fixed stars has been completed, the thread Q of the planet points towards the sun, so that BNQ is its angle of deflection; then it follows that in NR the other quadrant under the fixed stars the thread NQ is restored and BNQ the angle of deflection is annulled. Hence when the planet stands at R, the thread is once more parallel to BN, as it was at P. And this restitution of threads is complete after the semicircle has been traversed. Let the same judgment apply to the other semicircle; for when that has been traversed, the planet returns to the same position under the fixed stars.

But since experience bears witness that the apsides are transported imperceptibly, and do not remain under the same positions among the fixed stars; then it follows that NQ *looks towards the sun at not precisely a quadrant from* P *the original position of the apsis. What is the cause of this straying from the already established ratio of regularity?*

It seems that the imperceptible slowness of these movements must be sought for in material necessity—if anything else is—namely in the straying of the said movements, the libration and deflection, from one another through the intervention of a third movement. For it diffuses itself in an infinity of time, which has no beauty, as being indeterminate. But it is difficult to state what the intervening cause is: because all astronomers are not decided about the thing itself; nor, for most of them, does the thing have any fixed magnitude. But with magnitude removed, we lack any means of examining the causes (which some one might have searched into by conjecture) of whatever sort of latitudinal digression the planets may have away from the ecliptic. For the digression does not take place without the deflection of the threads NQ to AN the ray of the sun— a deflection as great as the digression of each planet. [598] It is consonant with such a greater or lesser deflection that the work of the threads should be somewhat weakened—and that variously, in proportion to the varying relation of the digressions to the apsides. In Saturn, Mars, Venus, and Mercury the mean longitudes[1] have some latitude, but none in Jupiter; and the apsides of Saturn, Mars, Venus, and Mercury progress in that proportion, while those of Jupiter stand still. Therefore since in other respects the force to deflect the thread of the planetary body becomes greatest at the apsides P and R, where the thread is presented to the sun at right angles, it is believable that this force becomes slightly weaker on account of the latitude. And the reason the force does not suffer the same loss from the libration too is that there the libration is almost nil in itself. In turn, the force of deflection at N is almost nil, while the libration is greatest: therefore the force of deflection suffers loss from libration here but not there, in proportion to the latitude. And it can happen that the deflection of the thread can be slowed up in this way; and with that given, what has already been unfolded takes place; the thread looks towards the sun more slowly, namely beyond the boundaries of the quadrant. But it has been demonstrated before that at that time the apsides are transported eastwards. Then, this can be the cause of the said phenomenon—a cause linked to physical or geometrical necessities, in accordance with the principles previously laid down.

2. But in the meantime I would not rigidly deny that this effect can be a part of the design, so that it is not a consequence of necessity, or a mere consequence: because we are still ignorant of the magnitude of it. Then there will be room to speak about the final cause: to the final cause belongs the mutual tempering of the forces of libration, of the deflection of the threads, and of the revolution, in some fixed proportion: in order that, because the librations were prepared in order to set up the harmonies of the movements, any given harmony should not be born always in some one configuration of two planets, but in the succession of the ages would pass through absolutely all the configurations, and in order that thus all the harmonies of movements—which Book v of the *Harmonies* is about—should be mingled with all the harmonic configurations—which is the matter of Book iv of the *Harmonies*.

NOTE BY KEPLER: Pages 942-44. A new and hasty correction has perverted the original and well-meditated text: 1. There is a *petitio principi*. 2. It is not in my design that on page 942, fourth line from bottom, there should have been a case of necessity: the direct variation of the libration with the deflection. 3. In the same place, the cause is not a cause. 4. One thing was proposed on page 942, and something else was demonstrated on page 944: on page 942 it was a question of the fixed stars: and on page 944, of the apsides.

The true cause of the almost perfect restitution is of physical necessity. For either the threads remain parallel, or else in one half they are deflected downward away from the apsis, as NQ, and in the other half, upward, since in both directions the counterbalancing is perfect, as was said on page 942; moreover thus the threads are parallel to one another at both apsides; therefore the restitution is perfect.

Therefore on page 944 something false and contradictory is proposed: the straying of the libration from the deflection. Instead, the cause was to be given which is suggested on pages 941-42. For in the upper quadrant PN the sun gives a slightly smaller deflection, in the lower quadrant NR, a slightly greater counter-deflection; if at any rate the fixed stars have their termini at the quadrants. Accordingly since the solipetal terminus G is at R, the point of the fixed stars, and is already above SY, and is therefore still nearer the sun; therefore the planet is still sailing on: wherefore R the perigeal apsis will be beyond R in the fixed stars. If the latitude of the planet is

[1]For *apsides* reading *longitudines mediae*. See note by Kepler below.

the cause of this thing, it will have to be explained in another way than on page 945, where instead of apsides read mean longitudes, because in Jupiter P is not the node but the limit. Nor is it sufficient to look to Jupiter and to say the reason the apsis is standing still is that the apsis is at the limit. But it is necessary to explain this too: why the progress of the apsides in the case of the other planets of very unequal periods is approximately equal under the fixed stars.

4. ON THE MOVEMENT IN LATITUDE

[599] *Under what laws do the planets digress in latitude away from the ecliptic?*

Again, under a very simple law: that the plane which they circumscribe with the centre of their body be exactly even in any period and that it be inclined to the plane of the ecliptic in a constant and invariable inclination—except in the case of the moon.

If level planes are inclined to one another, they meet and cut one another in one straight line. I ask what that common line is, from which the orbit of the planet is inclined to the plane of the ecliptic.

In all the planets, this line passes through the centre of the sun; and the line of each planet extends to its own proper places on the ecliptic, which are opposite to one another from the centre of the sun.

How is this established?

Because, since the planet at two different points on its return, as at C and D, is seen to be under the ecliptic without any lati-tude; these two positions on the orbit are found by calculation to be in the same straight line CAD with the sun A; so that if ACM was at 17° of the Bull, the interval of time until the planet was seen again on ecliptic, togeth-er with the hypothesis of the eccentric circle, ex-hibits the line ADO of the other position on the eccentric circle at 17° of the Scorpion, that is, op-posite 17° of the Bull.

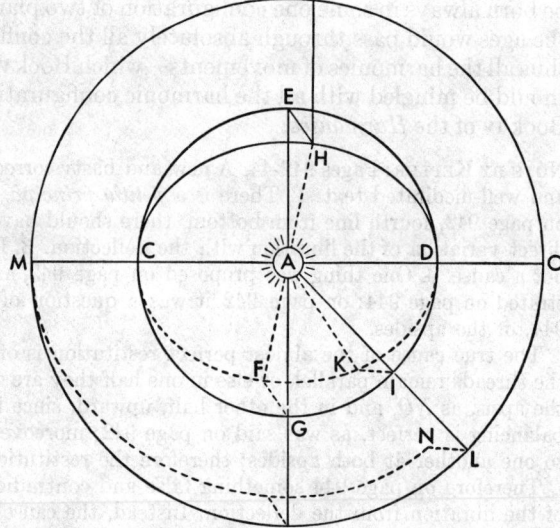

What is gathered from this?

The same as above, on page 910. For since the planes of all six eccentric circles meet at the one common centre of the sun; then all cannot meet at once anywhere except at this centre of the sun, because the line of section is not common to all, but [600] proper to each planet. But different lines cannot meet at more than one point.

Accordingly because the sun is the node common to all the systems: therefore either nature moves the planets by bodily virtues, or else mind, by rational commands. For the planets the sun is a fixed mark, which all their revolutions regard.

What causes do you assign for the movement in latitude?

In the case of the planets the sun is not the cause—unless the remote cause—for this deviation from the plane of the ecliptic; nor is there any need for the planet's intelligence in this work, nor for the above disproved substructure of solid spheres, upon which as upon chariots the planets travel along their orbit; and there is much less need of the spheres here than in the case of the librations into opposite altitudes or in the case of the movement in longitude. But some certain formation of the planetary bodies is alone sufficient to twist their orbits away from the ecliptic and to twist them back again.

Why is not the sun ranked as a cause, since it has already been said that the lines of section go through the solar body itself?

[601] Because one and the same sun, by means of one and the same form of its body, which form revolves in a uniform and very direct current along the mean circle between the poles of rotation of the sun, cannot carry different planets through other different paths, unless the planets add from out of themselves the causes of this differing digression in latitude.

Of what sort do you hint that this formation of the planetary bodies is?

It can be either essential, that is, belonging to the inward rectilinear magnetic thread, or else accidental, namely, the rotation of the planetary globe around its axis performed in such a way that the threads or axis of rotation retain their parallel posture during the whole circuit of the body and have such a direction that, when the planet is on the ecliptic, it touches the orbit and deflects at one terminus somewhat towards the north, and at the other towards the south.

Do you have a common example of this deflection?

The oars of ships supply some sort of example. For if the ship is being driven forward by winds, but an oar is tied obliquely to the stern, then the ship against which the line of wind is bearing is turned gradually to the side.

The oar, pole, or rudder always directs the ship towards one single region. How therefore do the planets now depart to the sides of the ecliptic and now return from there to the ecliptic?

If the rudder of the ship is turned, the ship too deflects to the other side. Even though the planets keep their threads straight, in a parallel posture, and unturned, nevertheless the planets are transported to the opposite parts of their circuit, wherein the threads, [602] by reason of their original posture, have the opposite inclination to their orbit; wherefore too the planets in the other semicircle are driven towards the opposite regions.

In order that I may better understand this movement, state what surface one such thread or axis produces during the revolution of the planet around the sun?

Let us lay down that when the planet is on the ecliptic, as here at C and E, then *AB* the thread of latitude does not have any inclination with respect to the sun—though this can take place differently but with the same effect, if the posture is equivalent—but has such an inclination with respect to the plane of the ecliptic, that *EA* or *CA* the half [of the thread] is to be understood to be sunken below the paper—which represents the plane of the ecliptic—but the remaining half *EB* or *CB* stands out above the paper, and the angle of inclination is as great as the latitude is accustomed to be at the limits—*F* the limit above the paper and *D* the limit below. Moreover, let the movement of the solar form, as if of a river or wind, be from *E* towards *F*, *C*, and *D*.

[603] Then since this movement at *E* is going to advance contrary to the sunken half of the thread *AE*, but at *C* is similarly going to advance contrary to *BC* the half which stands out and which is opposite *AE*. Furthermore, at *E* the movement pushes the planet up above the paper, in the direction whither *B* the front terminus tends; but at *C* it pushes the planet downward below the paper in the direction whither *A* the terminus in front of that position tends. In a rudder the opposite takes place, because the rudder is pushed by the force of the river, not driven by an inborn aptitude. But since meanwhile the thread *AB* remains in a posture parallel to itself throughout its whole circuit;

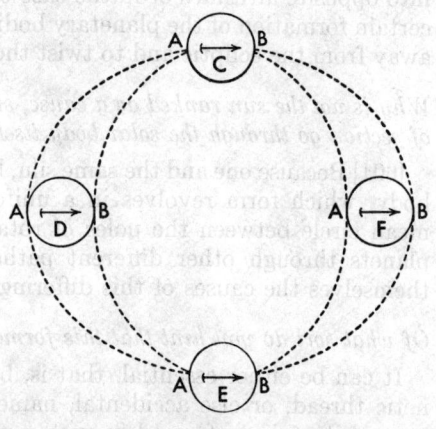

hence, when the planet is most northern at *F* or most sunken in the south at *D*; neither terminus *A* nor terminus *B* is in front, but the thread *AB*, which stretches out as it were into the depth of this river, *i.e.*, towards the sun, and which receives the attack on the right side, furnishes no cause for further removal into any region: wherefore a changing around takes place at these points, so that, although before point *F* the terminus *B* had been in front, now after point *F* the terminus *A* is in front; and so the planet begins to approach the ecliptic once more, at first with imperceptible progress.

From this it is now clear what sort of figure is engendered. For because the thread *AB* is moved from *E* towards that very region towards which the front terminus *B* tends; then the surface which is produced by *AB* is at point *E* diminished to a mere line, which nevertheless gradually becomes a surface, and, having arisen from the point *E*, acquires at *F* its greatest latitude, equal to the length of the thread *AB*: thence once more the surface is diminished as far as *C*, the segment of the circuit which is opposite *E*, the first-mentioned segment: there again the surface disappears into a line. The same things are to be understood of the opposite semicircle *CDE*. But the thread borne thus to *F* and *D* at an inclination and always following its own lead will produce a perfect plane, *i.e.*, in so far as it keeps its posture parallel; and if this plane is continued, it will pass through the centre of the sun because the thread *AB* looks towards the sun—at *F* with the terminus *A*; but at *D*, with the terminus *B*.

But with this continuation of the plane removed, if that which is produced by the thread [604] is alone considered: it will be such a form as two little crescents exhibit between the two ellipses, *BCAE* the outer ellipse, and *EACB* the inner, which touch one another at *C* and *E*, so that the same line *CE* is the major diameter of the smaller ellipse *EACB*, but the transverse diameter of the greater ellipse *CBAE*.

Moreover, the centre of the planetary body will revolve in a perfect plane, which in this figure was made circular, namely *CDEF*, although the plane itself also, as is clear from what was said above, bends away from the perfection of a circle to an ellipse with its lopped-off sides.

The oar or rudder of a ship stretches out from the ship straight into the waves or wind: but these threads lie concealed within the round body of the planet: therefore it is not the same force which is in rudders.

It is not necessary that all things should correspond in an analogy. But in place of the oars there is the other much more suitable force in the threads. And just as, above, the threads have a natural inertia contrary to the deflection of themselves, or rather a power to keep their posture parallel during the transportation of the body; so now also there is present in the threads of latitude, in addition to the similar force to keep their posture parallel, a natural power of agility too, or of following exactly the same line and of directing along that line the movement produced in the planet, in so far as the movement tends towards the same region as the other extremity of the thread.

Compare this form of movement in latitude with the ancient astronomy in an everyday example.

Here we entrust the planet to the river, with an oblique rudder, by means of which the planet, while floating down, may cross from one bank to the opposite. But the ancient astronomy built a solid bridge—the solid spheres—above this river—the width of the zodiac—and transports the lifeless planet [605] along the bridge as if in a chariot. But if the whole contrivance is examined carefully, it appears that this bridge has no props by which it is supported, nor does it rest upon the Earth, which they believed to be the foundation of the heavens.

Nevertheless is not this theory of the movement in latitude more difficult than if someone imagines solid spheres?

But, reader, you ought to remember that we are here busy with the physical theory of causes, on account of which any hypothesis is applied in order that we may know what of truth exists in such an hypothesis or astronomical fiction. But below, in Books v and vi, for the sake of understanding, we shall not reject the whole circles and their inclinations to the ecliptic; because they are equivalent to these attractions of threads to the sides of the ecliptic.

If that earlier libration of the planet in altitude and this digression in latitude had the same boundary-posts on the ecliptic and were effected by the same threads, the causes which you assign would be probable.

Indeed, what prevents one and the same globe from having twofold rectilinear threads stretching out over the whole body, so that from some it receives a libration in altitude, and by the others is rowed backward and forward? Thus on the surface of rivers a threefold movement of the parts is discerned—each movement proceeding in its own direction: the first is the flow of water, the second that of the waves, which that flow casts crosswise to the banks in a continuous series, the third comes from the wind. For if a contrary wind blows obliquely, it roughens the surface of the waters, and starts another series of smaller waves moving in their own direction, and these waves advance on top of the earlier waves, which are not troubled. Thus above in Book I [606] I mentioned the nature [*substantia*] of the belly, which represents a triple-woven tunic and contains three kinds of threads, distinct as to their regions, the seats of the three faculties of attraction, retention, and expulsion: although the weaving belongs to not one but three tunics.

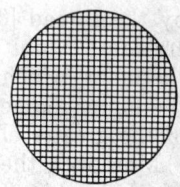

Do not the farthest digressions of the planets always occur at the same positions on the zodiac, or do even these digressions change their positions?

Observation of the progression of the limits is more difficult still than that of the apsides: nevertheless they are seen to be going back gradually westward in the sphere of the fixed stars and more slowly than the apsides are progressing; there is a case of both in the movements of the moon.

If the limits retrograde and the apsides progress, will the threads productive of latitude remain inwoven with the threads of longitude, both of which you have given to the same globe?

This retrogradation clears our way to the inward substance of the globes, into which narrows we have already been compelled to go, in the comparison of the daily revolution of the Earth with its threads of libration. Accordingly here too we can seek within the outer crust a separate globe—like the yolk within the white of egg—supplied with its own threads, and able to revolve according to the same laws, and with the strength of its forces different from that of the outer crust, if need be; so that both of them [the crust and the globe] can be deflected by the same outside cause, with different measures of speed, if there is need of this.

For thus in the case of the belly which I have already brought in, there are three tunics: the outmost, the inmost, and the middle; and one of them can be passive, if the others are injured, or be active, while the others are at rest; although they are unlike this thing, in that they are not separated from one another.

The ancient astronomy places solid and plainly adamantine spheres on top of other spheres, where no body is visible to us and the whole region is as transparent as if it were empty. [607] Therefore it will not take offence if we construct something similar in the globes, which are visible and palpable bodies.

Cannot this already mentioned axis of revolution of the outer crust of the planetary bodies perform this office of deflecting the movement of the planets latitudinally?

This cause rests upon very great probability, as will have to be said in Books VI and VII in the explanation of the schemata of the sun and the eighth sphere. Nevertheless nothing certain can be affirmed of all [the planets]: because even though we said it was believable that the remaining primary planets rotate around the axes of their bodies, nevertheless the regions towards which these axes tend or incline are unknown to us. Wherefore we have an example in the Earth alone. And the moon, a secondary planet does not rotate, although none the less it completes its latitudes.

How can it be effected that the limits of digressions retrograde westward?

In Book VII part of this appearance will be explained as accidental, not as physical or real. But what remains of this movement and is real is caused by the deflection [*nutu*] westward of the threads of latitude: so that they remain in one and the same plane precisely, during their whole circuit, but the threads themselves—*i.e.*, the globe itself—are deflected backward over the centre of their body secretly in accordance with these threads.

From what causes does this counter-deflection arise?

Up to now the probability of most of the causes brought forward was clear. But in this last train of astronomical matters, the causes have ill success; and both understanding and belief in those things which one is able to devise have to work hard. Let us however speak of as much as we can find out. [608] We have said that the nature of the threads of latitude consists in an aptitude to move forward into the region of their own parallel direction. We have said moreover that while the planet is being transported from C or E, the position which it has on the ecliptic, into D or F, the position of farthest digression north or south, in the meantime those threads remain parallel, and for that reason it comes about that, since there at C and E the threads touched the orbit, now here at D and F they are sunken in the depth towards the sun, whither that movement to which they are deflected does not tend; rather at that time, the motor river from the sun, so to speak, meets the crosswise threads AB at right angles, more speedily below—that is, at A in the position F and at B in the position D—than above and on the outside. Therefore if the threads are deflected towards the movement, it is surprising if this deflection, which with its lower side seeks the region of the movement, takes something away from the paralleleity and does so at both limits? So the retrogradation of the limits follows, since no counterbalancing exists. For A is pushed out, at F, along the road EAC; and B is pushed out, at D, along the same road CBE: so in both cases B will be deflected below the paper.

But if this cause is not admitted, then let the motor soul be summoned to twist together, by its laws, an inside kernel within the outer crust, according to the design of the Workman that by the interweaving of the orbits with one another and their frequent plurification and condensation the solidity of the sphere might be somewhat penetrated by the planet in the succession of ages.

Why is the regression of the limits slower than the progression of the apsides?

Although there is doubt concerning Mercury, there is also some doubt concerning Jupiter: nevertheless let us follow probability on account of the clear example of the moon, and let us say that the cause is as follows: because a disturbance, if there is any, coming from one and the same outside cause is necessarily more perceptible in a great movement than in a small. Now the transposition of the apsides arises from a great movement, which is the deflection and counter-deflection of the threads in any semicircle, [609] and is as great as the optical additosubtractive difference [*aequatio*], and it would become greater and altogether total if it were not anticipated by the revolution of the planetary globe. But the transposition of limits takes place through a small movement, the digression of a few degrees in latitude, and is not greater than this measure of it, so that this digression can give rise to nothing else whereby the transposition of the limits may be hindered. Wherefore the same rays of the sun which introduce movements in both cases, by the laws already explained, have more manifest effects there [in the transposition of the apsides] than here [in the transposition of the limits]. In addition there is the fact that in the first case rays of the sun act in relation to a greater diversity than in the second, other things being equal. For in the first case the obliquity of the rays of the sun with respect to the threads—and this obliquity tends to the side—or the angle of latitude, whereby the work [of the threads] is weakened, was perceptible. In this second case the diversity between the parts of the planetary globe, and hence between the termini of the threads of latitude—the terminus nearest the sun and that farthest away from the sun—to which diversity we assign the movement of the limits, is mighty small. Accordingly by right this second work is less than that.

5. ON THE TWOFOLD IRREGULARITIES OF THE MOON AND THEIR CAUSES

These things which up to now have been argued concerning the causes by which the true movements of the primary planets are made irregular are not also to be understood concerning the moon, a secondary planet, are they?

1. On the whole, the moon imitates the same general form of movement, around the Earth, as that which the planets keep to around the sun; and so too we ought to set down the same causes within the lunar body, that is, threads of magnetism, their rectilinear tract, and the contrary regions of that tract—one region friendly to the Earth and the opposite region unfriendly—and finally the approximate parallel-eity to itself of this tract throughout the whole circuit of the moon. [610] According-ly, when the moon has been transported into the opposite position, there is a changing around of the regions; and in

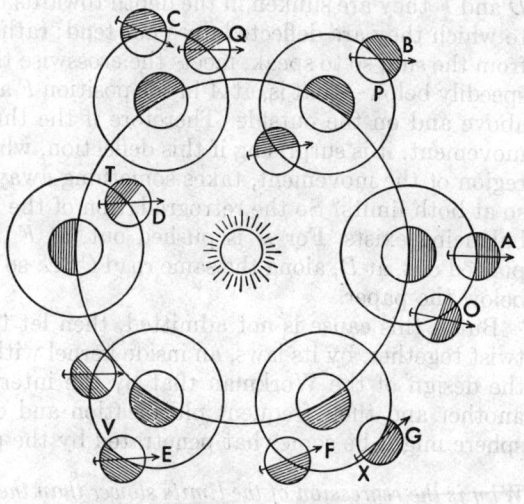

conformity with the friendly region the moon is attracted by the form of the terrestrial body; and in conformity with the unfriendly region it is repelled. And its movement in longitude too is increased or decreased in that proportion; and similarly we must conceive of other threads in its body, by means of which threads the moon's digressions from the ecliptic are produced.

In this diagram are represented some positions of the Earth going around the sun, together with the surrounding lunar heaven; and in the heaven of the moon some positions of the moon going around the Earth. But the image of the magnetized needle signifies the magnetic threads in the lunar globe, by reason of which the moon becomes eccentric to the Earth. For the points A, B, C, D, E, F, and G signify the region friendly to the Earth, and they lie at the second mean longitude, and so at A and G the moon is situated at the mean position between the perigee and the apogee; [611] at B, Q, and D it is a little before the apogee; at C, a little after the apogee; and at E and F, a little before the perigee.

2. But since this movement of the Earth, as was explained above, is derived from two sources, as it were—namely, from the daily rotation of the Earth, and from the rotation of the sun around its own axis—and this sun is the midpart of the great sphere common to the Earth and the lunar heaven; so it will be reasonable that the true and real movement of the moon around the Earth—and in so far as that revolution around the sun, which is shared by both and is accidental to the whole lunar heaven, is removed from it mentally—has two sources, as it were, and suffers all those affects as twofold which the movements of the primary planets have as simple. And this is perfectly consonant with the experience and skill of artists, and with the words arising from this twofoldness. For not merely in the [pages] above, according as there was a solitary mean movement in some one of planets, was there a mean movement and a semi-monthly variation of this mean movement in the case of the moon; but also here [hoc loco], where it is a question of the periodic irregularity of this move-ment, and this irregularity is not semimonthly like the variation but monthly or rather semiannual: we find in the moon a twofold intensification and remis-sion of mean movement at the contrary moments of the period, instead of the simple intensification and remission found in any one of the primary planets—and finally instead of the simple digression of the primary planets in latitude also a twofold digression.

What cause does the magnitude of the moon's eccentricity have?

In the *Harmonies* I demonstrate that the variety of lunar movements de-termines precisely the perfect fourth, which seems to have an affinity with the quadratures and syzygies of the moon. Therefore in order that this interval might be represented by a composite movement, the eccentricity was made to be as great as it is.

[612] *What diversity is found between those irregularities common to the moon and the planets and these irregularities proper to the moon?*

1. Just as, in the above, the movement of the moon around the Earth had two elements, as it were, one from the rotation of the Earth around its axis, the other from the joining [ex applicatione] of the solar light with this motor form from the Earth—whereof the first was free of the phases of the moon, and the other was bound up with the phases; so now also, of the two irregularities, that earlier one is found to be an accident of the earlier element or the mean move-ment and to have its own proper termini, which we shall call the apogee; and the first type of digression in latitude has its own termini, distinct from the termini of the apogee, and they are called limits and nodes. But the later ir-regularity, which arises from a later element, or else is an accident of the ac-celeration in the syzygies, and is called by Ptolemy the nodding [annutus] of the

epicycle, has termini in common with the lunar month and phases—as does the second type [*forma*] of digression in latitude.

2. That earlier irregularity both of longitude and latitude is always constant throughout all its periods, that is, it is forever of the same magnitude: but each of the later irregularities become greatest in one month only of any half year, smaller in the remaining months, and in certain months, which divide the year into two parts, almost nil, namely, where the opposite affects, of this second acceleration and retardation and likewise of the northern and southern latitude, begin to pass into the contrary halves of the lunations.

3. And so those earlier irregularities have their magnitude and the laws of their distribution from their own proper causes; but the second irregularities take their magnitudes and affects from the presence of the first irregularities in any one semicircle of lunation; they have laws of distribution alone separate, and adjusted to the cycles of lunations, but none the less similar to the earlier [laws].

4. The following fact is also related: that in the moon we find the movement of the apsides eastwards, and the movement of the limits [613] westwards, much faster than in the primary planets, not merely in the ratio of the faster periodic return of the moon, but quite perceptibly; and moreover the retrogression of the limits is more than twice as slow as the progression of the apsides.

The moon is not seen alternately to turn now this part of its body, now the opposite, to the Earth. For we always view the same spots on the face of the moon. Wherefore the causes of the approach and withdrawal of the moon from the Earth cannot be sought from this.

1. It is not necessary that at two opposite times of a period the lunar magnetic threads should point in a straight line towards the Earth; it is sufficient if at those moments they at least be deflected towards the Earth in their alternate regions, and if the posture of the threads remain parallel throughout the whole circuit of the moon. For it can come about in this way too that now one region of threads deflects more to the Earth, and now the opposite region. But if this deflection is small, our eyesight is not so sharp that in the disc of the moon it can observe very precisely whether on the rims of the lunar globe, which look towards the poles of the ecliptic, some minute particles present themselves to view, which are not seen at any other time. For those parts of the globe are shelving and of a very tenuous appearance, and the illumination frequently fails, now on this rim, now on that, on account of the inconstancy of the lunar countenance.

2. For a long time we left it as uncertain, whether there is a globe within the globe, like the kernel within the shell, having a different rotation from that—as the case of the Earth and also the movement in latitude suggested. And so such an inner globe could direct towards the Earth regions which are alternately reversed—notwithstanding that the outer crust always turns the same spots towards the Earth. For between these and similar things, it is uncertain exactly what the manner of this motion is: it is alone very certain that, whatever the manner is, it has been fitted to physical and magnetic causes, [614] *i.e.*, corporeal and thus geometrical; and I have put forward examples of such causes in both cases here.

Then does not this second irregularity of longitude really come from some second eccentricity or digression of the moon from the Earth, just as the first irregularity has its cause in the change of the interval?

No: the observation of the parallaxes of the moon, together with a consideration of the eclipses, opposes this; and the ratios of the distance of the bodies from the first body militate against it—the ratios put forward in the first part of this book. But it can be argued that there is absolutely no change of interval bound up with the phases; because, though different experimenters make different corrections in the case of this hypothesis, the magnitude of this change is always made smaller and smaller. Ptolemy set it down as very large; Regiomontanus reduced it; Copernicus halved it and transposed it from the figure [*ex forma*] of an eccentric circle into the figure of the second epicycle; again, Tycho Brahe got hold of it and claimed a part for the equant circle, for which he together with Copernicus was accustomed to substitute an epicycle of twofold movement. I have changed around the intervals at the syzygies with those at the quadratures, and have transposed the cycles from the month to the year; relying upon these discoveries made in latter times, I at least found that absolutely no change of intervals occurred through the cycles of the phases.

Then from what comes this second acceleration and retardation, which are bound up with the phases?

From the varying relation of the eccentric circle of the moon to the phases. For while the moon goes around the Earth, its mover, according to the simple and forever uniform law of eccentricity, just as any one of the primary planets goes around the sun; it comes about by accident that at different times the moon has different distances from its movement's other mover, which accelerates the moon in the syzygies. For if its longer interval from the Earth occurs at the syzygies, where its greatest acceleration takes place; then the terrestrial form, unrolled in a wider sphere, is weakened at one of the syzygies— weakened not merely in its own native and archetypal vigour, but also in the reception of strengthening from the sun. In turn, if this longer interval between the moon and the Earth is found at the quadratures, where there is no acceleration; then there is no loss in the reception of nil vigour, and no gain with the short interval at the perigee.

In the diagram on page 952 are depicted in the globes of the Earth and moon, the circles of illumination which divide the light part from the dark. But since the apogee of the moon, through the whole year and thus through all the positions of the lunar heaven, remains at the same point, *i.e.*, the threads *WF* remain approximately parallel to themselves throughout the whole circuit, but the Earth together with the lunar heaven crosses from point to point hence the threads are joined in different ways at different times to the circles of illumination—which spread out in accordance with a circle homocentric with the sun and exhibiting the density of the light in longitude—as you may see in the arcs *DT, EV, FW, GX, AO,* and *BP.* Accordingly the same thing takes place also at the apogee and perigee of the moon, as they always point towards the places 90° distant from the place or region of point *A, B, Q,* etc.

But what if the longer interval stretches towards the sun? Will not the movement be weakened in that way? And yet the moon is passing through a denser light.

Indeed, this is what we remarked about above. For the light of the sun does not move [the moon] by itself but by means of the form of the terrestrial body, to which it transmits the laws and modes of its own work. Accordingly just as above light did not give the direction of movement, but the form of the terrestrial body gave a direction, somewhere plainly contrary to the direction in which the sun moves around its axis; so now also the motor form from the Earth is strengthened in proportion to its own native strength, weakly where it is weak, namely at its farther distance from the Earth its source; strongly where it is strong, at its shorter distance from the Earth—whatever the variation in the distance of the moon from the sun may be, [616] as above, in the case of the causes of the variation, we spoke of the counterbalancings of this.

What is the measure [modus] of this monthly additosubtractive difference, when it is very great, and what is the cause of its measure?

Tycho Brahe makes it equal to the physical part of the analyzed periodic additosubtractive difference [*aequationis periodicae solutae*], according to my formulation, because since the total periodic difference is approximately 5° I claim half of that for the physical cause, the customary amount for all the planets—that is, 2°30′: accordingly Brahe exhibits the synodic difference to be that much—as if the motor form from the terrestrial body became precisely twice as strong at the near distance, and twice as weak at the far, through this strengthening by the light, and that is the time when it is without this strengthening. And if it is asked why that ratio holds, it seems that it can have no cause [617] except this relation of equality, as the most simple and therefore the most beautiful ratio.

But Ptolemy exhibits its measure as slightly greater, and just as much as above, from the addition of 132° 45′ to 12 synods, we inferred the variation of one quadrant to be, namely 2°41′. But if this measure and magnitude is to be kept at both distances, then it seems that the cause must be transferred from design to geometrical necessity, namely, because the increase of the interval, *i.e.*, the eccentricity, utterly exhausts that which the acceleration by the light at that syzygy had given; but in turn at the other syzygy the subtraction of the eccentricity from the interval adds as much to the speed as was also produced by the acceleration given by the light.

So in a month, which is with-

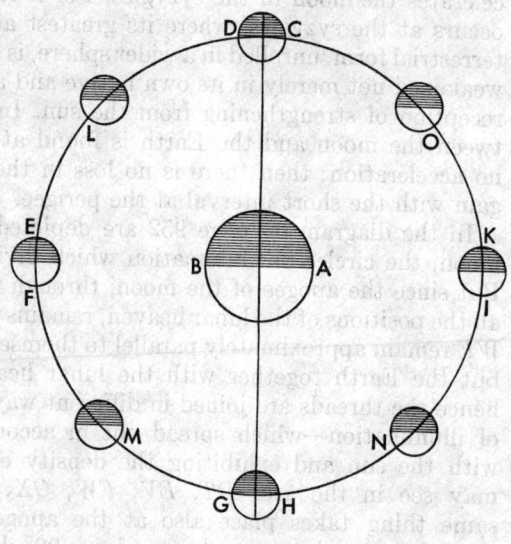

out the synodic additosubtractive difference, namely when in this diagram the apogee is at *EF* and the perigee at *IK*, the parts of acceleration given by the light are equal at both syzygies, because the intervals between the moon and Earth at both syzygies, as *AC* and *AH*, are equal during that month; in the succeeding months, as inequality of intervals arises gradually at the syzygies— for example, if *L* were the apogee and *N* the perigee, then the distance *AC* would certainly be greater than *AH*—there also arises some monthly additosubtractive difference, which always becomes greatest during that whole month at *EF* and *IK;* finally in that month wherein the synodic additosubtractive difference is complete—for example, if the apogee is at *CD*—there is no acceleration at the syzygy *CD*, but at the other syzygy *GH* the acceleration is twice as great as in the month just spoken of; at that time at the quadratures *F* and *K* the additosubtractive difference is the greatest of all those which can occur during the total year. But at *G* very near to the perigee, there are four parts to the very small additosubtractive difference, (1) the optical, as in the planets, (2) the physical, as in the planets, (3) the variation due to light, (4) the intensification of the same on account of the distance being diminished. The ratio of these four parts to one another is of geometrical necessity. But the sum composed thus of all four was so attuned by design that *GH* the perigeal movement of the moon at the syzygy would be to *CD* the movement of the moon at the quadrature as 4 is to 3; and that the harmony would be the perfect fourth.

[618] For that reason it comes about that although these two, (1) the measure of acceleration at the syzygies and (2) the measure of eccentricity, are bound to one another by no necessity; nevertheless the eccentricity exactly destroys the acceleration at the apogeal syzygy and doubles it at the perigeal syzygy. I say that at present, while I have been unable to investigate it.

What probable cause do you assign to the so great speed of the apsides and limits of the moon, if the apsides and limits of the primary planets are incomparably slower?

Indeed the effect of the composition of motor virtues in the moon is made clear. For just as in the above pages we said that the simple force of the Earth was attuned to harmonic numbers—at any rate in the rotation of the terrestrial body around its axis, to 360 perfect days, but in the revolution of the moon around the Earth, to exactly the 12 months in one year, or in one periodic return of the centre of the Earth around the sun; so now too let us say that in the deflection and restitution of the threads of the moon—those by which the libration and those by which digressions in latitude are produced—their simple forces are attuned to the great length of the periodic time of the moon in the same proportion as was kept in the other planets. But just as in the above, on account of additional aid from the sun, both in making the terrestrial globe rotate and in making the moon revolve, the archetypal numbers were disturbed in their final effect, so that instead of 360 days there were 365¼, and instead of 12 lunations in the year, approximately 12⅓; so now too on account of this increase in the same acceleration of the moon from the illumination of the sun, the moon comes to the mean latitudes of its circuit before the threads are deflected in the right measure; and so the thread looks towards the sun from a deeper place (*loco profundiori*) than a quarter [of the distance] from apsis [to apsis]. And I inculcated above that the transportation of the apsides took place when that occurred. But it is quite right that this transposition of the apsides should be perceptible, because that increase [619] is perceptible, namely approximately 11°; none the less this transposition is smaller, *i.e.*, slightly more than 3° in a month: (1) because those degrees [of increase] are for the most part added on at the syzygies, but the threads are most deflected and counter-deflected at the mean longitudes without reference to the syzygies; in such a way that the effects of degrees equal in number are very distant from one another; and it is probable that something still remains hidden at that node, and that by our ignorance of it the movements of the moon have not yet been worked out to the minute, not even in Tycho's calculation. (2) Because the deflection of the threads is anticipated not merely in place and time but also in magnitude for that very reason. For if the moon had advanced more slowly, or if the deflection of the threads were as great in the accelerated moon as it would have been in the slow moon, the apsides would be transported even farther. But it comes about by the acceleration of the moon that the thread points towards the sun before it reaches the just measure of deflection originally assigned to it. And by the mixture of these things it comes about that a certain mean, $3\frac{1}{4}°$ between the nothing or something imperceptible—which would be the case without the acceleration of the moon—and the 11°—which the acceleration causes—overflows into the movement of the apsides. The same things are to be said concerning the impulsion or deflection of the threads of latitude; for it ought to have been imperceptible, as in the primary planets—if the moon, like the primary planets was going to advance according to a simple force. But because the acceleratory force which is added to the moon is evaluated at approximately 11° of longitude in efficacy; and if this force fell upon these threads of latitude during the whole cycle, it would deflect them, as not fortified against itself, the whole 11°; but since it gets possession of them only at the limits where they are in opposition to it, it gives them however a deflection of $1\frac{1}{2}°$ in one period. And the precession of the limits follows upon this deflection.

But although from the observation of so many ages exact determinations have been made of the magnitudes and ratio of these two movements of the apsides and the limits; there still remains room for talent. For he who brings forward such causes of these things that from the causes the magnitude itself follows, will drive his chariot to the goal. And philosophers ought all the more [620] to strive, because, over and above so many other experiments, in this question too the moon is our mistress in acquiring knowledge of the celestial bodies, and by its own example it throws light upon the nature of all the planets.

How is it that besides its accustomed periodic latitudes the moon also makes synodic digressions to the north and to the south?

Just as that force of light which strengthens the terrestrial form, the mover of the moon, borrows the region of movement and the proportions of the work itself from that very form which it strengthens; moreover just as, in the case of longitude, that force passes over into the inborn character [*ingenium*] of the orbit according to the measure of the mutual joining; so we must set down that that force does the same thing in the case of latitude. It facilitated the movement in longitude, because it extends in longitude; therefore it will facilitate the movement in latitude, because it has the other dimension of latitude also, *i.e.*, because light is a surface partaking of density, as we have often recounted from optics. Accordingly at the syzygies, where the thread of latitude is tangent to the orbit and has been deflected in proportion to the latitude of the terrestrial form, the latitude of light joining itself to the terrestrial form facilitates the digressions, so that they take place at an angle greater than that which the thread makes with the plane of the ecliptic; and in that way the moon arrives in the quadratures at farther limits to the north and to the south than those which the thread showed at the syzygies. Conversely, during the other quarter of the year the thread of latitude, which is tangent to the orbit in the quadratures, does not fit itself to the dimension of the form of light in latitude, but points approximately towards the sun, just as the orbit itself of the moon does. Therefore just as in that place the movement in longitude is not at all facilitated by the light, but is made more difficult as it were; so the same thing overflows into the digression in latitude, so that it does not become greater than the angle by which the thread of latitude is deflected towards the ecliptic; and thus the moon does not arrive in the syzygies at limits farther than those which the thread showed in the quadratures. But what happens to the moon turning at the limits, or with what face the light of the sun beholds the moon, namely, when [621] the thread of latitude points towards the Earth, has nothing to do with latitude.

Since you reduce everything to the bodily threads of the globes and to the immaterial forms from the rotating bodies of the sun and Earth, and lastly to the light of the sun as a strengthening cause, you leave nothing to the animal faculties: hence you seem to be philosophizing just as if someone were to contend that its triple threads were sufficient to the belly for its operation and that there is no need of the animal faculty?

Rather, I admit a soul in the body of the sun as the overseer of the rotation of the sun and as the superintendent of the movement of the whole world. Nor in Book I did I deny absolutely that the planetary bodies had single souls as overseers of the rotation of their bodies. But just as it was not necessary to introduce a special soul into the threads of the belly; for it is sufficient for one common soul from the heart or liver to advance, through its own form or through heat, into the belly and to employ the faculties of its threads; so too in the world that form—of light, or heat, and thus too, if you will—from the soul of the sun, flowing out together with light and heat and penetrating even where light and heat are shut out, *i.e.*, into the inner threads of bodies, seems to be sufficient; hence, just as the soul in the body has no power without the organ of the belly, so too the soul of the world has no power without these laws and without the geometrical lay-out of bodies.

Therefore let the status of the controversy be noted: for it is certainly one thing to reduce every cause [*rationem*] of dispensing celestial movement—although involving contradictions, and hence impossible—simply to the hidden forces of some soul, after rejecting all bodily organs and all the means which the human mind can devise—and that is the sanctuary [622] of all ignorance, the death of all philosophy, but is nevertheless the common practice of most of those who write or speak about astronomy, and in the above was noted in part even in Ptolemy himself. It is something else first to discern within the bodies everything suited for movement, so that the possibility of movements may be apparent—even with common examples—and afterwards finally to pour in a motor soul on top of all those things, as upon the human body compacted of all muscles and nerves. For if the soul can perform its functions anywhere by bodily organs, it will have no need in them for design and discourse, acts proper to an intellectual soul—just as, on the contrary, if it performed everything by design and discourse, it would not want those bodily organs.

In brief, the philosophers have commented upon the intelligences, which draw forth the celestial movements out of themselves as out of a commentary, which employ consent, will, love, self-understanding, and lastly command; the soul or motor souls of mine are of a lower family and bring in only an impetus—as if a certain matter of movement—by a uniform contention of forces, without the work of mind. But they find the laws, or figure, of their movements in their own bodies, which have been conformed to Mind—not their own but the Creator's—in the very beginning of the world and attuned to effecting such movements.

END OF BOOK FOUR, THE FIRST BOOK ON THE DOCTRINE OF THE
SCHEMATA OR OF CELESTIAL PHYSICS

BOOK FIVE

LETTER OF DEDICATION

[631] To the Very Reverend, Most Illustrious, Most Highborn, Most Noble, Vigorous, etc. Lords, To the Orders of the Archduchy of Austria-on-the-Anisana, To My Most Gracious Lords:

Four years after the publication of the first part of *Copernican Astronomy*, which contains the doctrine of the sphere unfolded in three books, one year after the publication of Book IV, wherein I have handed on the celestial physics, or the principles of the doctrine of the schemata of the planetary movements; there at last follows some time the speculative part—so called from the schemata, that is, the manual instruments wherein as in mirrors [*speculis*] the movements of the single planets are represented.

[632] If I regard the circumstances of the time, this publication, alas! arrives in town late, after a very destructive war has arisen and the assemblages of students for whom these things are written have either been dispersed by the confusions of war or thinned out and wasted away by the expectation of war; after Austria, hitherto my nurse and benefactor, has struck against a very hard reef and seems to be called away from the guardianship of these beauties to serious care for her own safety; and after I too, forced by the hatefulness of a private enemy to leave my home at Linz, have been moving around for nearly a year away from home.

If the causes of such great delays have to be mentioned, I shall not allege the supineness of my publisher—which has lasted from the publication of the doctrine of the sphere up to now—or the inconveniences of present war or the fears of threatening war: the fact that this publication has been prevented till now calls for thanks, not blame. Then what cause shall I mention, whereby I may preserve my reputation and wash away the charge of negligence? "While our womanly manners are at work," says Comicus, "while they dress their hair, a year passes by." But if the manners of astronomy are known to anyone, he will be able to say that he has never known a slower or more painstaking woman. [633] For unless this time had been interposed, wherein my designs might reach their maturity, there was danger that that finicalness, now that the whole world was squeamish, would demand new outlays and new adornments. For the computation of the *Ephemerides* and the publication of the books of the *Harmonies*—the works of the intermediate time—gave me many warnings that although most of the things which have to do with the six planets had been drawn up or at least indicated twelve years ago in my *Commentaries on Mars:* and although, taken over from that and put together into the form of a textbook, they had remained in my writing desk for seven years now, awaiting the work of the printer and engraver;

nevertheless as often as I reread them, what with additions or elucidations or transpositions of the text, the necessity of making a new copy was imposed upon me. To such an extent that not a trace of the first draft was left in what was shown to the printer. Now as regards the moon, the last of the planets: when I first gave my attention to the publication of this *Epitome*, I had no special concern about the moon, because Tycho Brahe's hypotheses about the moon already existed, and they could [634] in general be found to be equivalent to those hypotheses too by which the manifold movements of this planet were reduced to my physical causes. Moreover those hypotheses existed as shadowed forth in the *Commentaries on Mars*, and as worked out further in my *Hipparchus*. But they were of such sort as to suppose two circles in the moon, eccentric in each case—a thing quite inimical to physical speculations, and hence intolerable. The computation of the *Ephemerides* rested upon those bases: and from the foreword to it, it is apparent that the form of the calculation has been changed again and again, because its agreement with appearance fluctuates and vacillates everywhere.

Finally the great felicity of my speculations freed astronomy from this cross in the month of April 1620, when, after the physical causes had been considered more carefully, it appeared that the second eccentric circle of the moon was superfluous, so that there was no further need for imagining it with reference to the movements in longitude. And it was already time to put the finishing touch upon the fourth book of the *Epitome*, which is about the principles of the doctrine of the schemata. That done, I transferred my attention to the publication of it, in the midst of the Bavarian armies and the frequent sicknesses and deaths both of soldiers [635] and of civilians. However, in the year 1621 the *Ephemeris* was at once computed, and—after the fashion of my other *Ephemerides*—the foreword was made to signify publicly my rejoicing over the conquering of the second eccentric circle of the moon. But, forestalled by the necessity of my journey, I could not yet publish this *Ephemeris*.

Now as regards this last part of the *Epitome*, comprehended in three books; although after the publication of Book IV, I am away from home and spend no little time in journeys and in the law-courts, nevertheless I have been allowed to be at leisure the greater part of the time, and I have devoted all that time to the care of this publication. When I came to Tübingen at the end of the year 1620, in order to expound to Maestlin a new rationale of lunar hypotheses, I began to write down questions about the other planets and the moon too in accordance with the physical hypothesis finally discovered.

As soon as I returned to my family at Ratisbon, I reread the questions and gave them over to be copied. In the meantime I turned to the last part of Book VI, up to now postponed, because I hoped of its being easy, and it seemed that it could be put together between proof-readings; but [636] I found it laborious, not so much for the difficulty as for the multitude and variety of questions and the worry over the method. A short time I spent at a monastery passed in drawing up the ancient epochs and in computing the eclipses. At once, as soon as I returned to Tübingen, I saw that the fourth part of Book VI, on the moon, would have to be reshaped and work repeated, because the definitions conceived verbally did not yet accurately represent the force of my hypothesis.

During the last months May and June, Stuttgart gave the last little book, which was also included in the last part of my cares up to now: because the astronomers have too little evidence concerning the movements of the eighth sphere; but most of the things which could be said concerning this matter had been conceived by me in the *Commentaries on Mars*, in Book III of the *Epitome*, long published, and on other pages. Nevertheless many things arose on the occasion of my conversation with Maestlin, my old leader in taking the route of Copernican astronomy, and many things through the reading of books which I had hitherto been unable to get hold of in Austria. And if publication had not been postponed till now, these things would necessarily have to have been passed over.

[637] Meanwhile, with the shore of this voyage in sight, *i.e.*, the end of this work, and after being refreshed by money sent secretly to Linz, then by the argument of the faith and kindness of your Very Reverend Doctor of Divinity, Antony, President at Krembsmunster, and finally with a truce intervening in the law-courts—my great grief—I gave June over to the journey to Frankfort, and to looking after the printing. And here once more, while the work is being undertaken, while the pages, diagrams, and forms are being prepared, a month passes by. And this sidereal lady, who heretofore bore witness to her fretfulness by her countenance and her noddings, now ratifies and exercises her fretfulness, after finally coming to the press, by quarrels and abusive language, only not by hands and weapons.

Therefore, Very Reverend, Illustrious, Highborn Lords, let her stand before you to plead my cause, which can be got hold of for me from the daily delayings of this publication. Come to an understanding with her. If you have become experienced in listening to her sarcasm, you will not easily demand scrupulous accounts of time from him who proves that the case is with him as with her, especially if he can show the value of the time and the work.

But after I myself too, whom I believe to care for those arts, *i.e.*, the proclaiming of the divine works, [638] and who has followed the footprints of divine providence in an indefatigable search—after I recall to mind what utility the little book will have drained from this delay in time; I am not so frightened by your adversities, Masters—which have meanwhile risen up against you and the wretched province or else seem to make further threats—as not to perform my task, fulfill the promise made to you in the dedication of the little book on the sphere, and pay my debt, because I have hitherto been living off your subsidy. For I hope that there is so much divine mercy left in the store-house that He will that this horrible tempest be calmed, the clouds dispersed, and the sun at last shine again upon the penitent, and that some place be left even in Austria for these peaceful arts, the labour over which He does not stop caring for, and that there be gathered together in Austria once again some number of those who learn from these arts the praises of God their Creator. I hope that this little book will be of service to those people. For it contains the first adumbration, so to speak, of the Rudolphine tables, and the approximate numbers. If these numbers are assumed as true, the lovers of this discipline may exercise themselves with them until the Rudolphine tables themselves come out, furnished with everything accurately corrected, fixed for calculation, and ready for use. Furthermore, [639] if outsiders get any utility from my books, as there are very many people not only in Germany but also in the surrounding kingdoms and provinces who seek these books at Frankfort; it is right for them to learn from this dedication of mine that, for whatever value this book has, they ought to give thanks also to your liberality, Masters, wherewith uninterruptedly you have fostered me throughout these very difficult times. With that learnt, according as each is most disposed towards the arts of mathematics, most devoted to God, and most assiduous in gratitude, the crown of the virtues; so let him very frequently join his prayers with mine to the most merciful God: that, with the tumults of war calmed, the devastation restored, and hatred extinguished, golden peace returning may smile upon the Empire of the Most Powerful Divine Ferdinand II, Emperor of Rome, Our August Lord, and that God may revivify all the provinces of His Majesty, and especially Austria-on-the-Anisana, with the fruitful showers of His grace. And that finally to you, Very Reverend, Illustrious, Highborn, Noble, Vigorous Masters, God may bring and make permanent for many years safety, health, riches, and dignities, for His own glory, for the preservation of the Church, for the adornment of the most glorious Emperor, and finally for the necessary cultivation of those arts [640] wherein the divine name is held in honour. Farewell, Masters, and hold within your liking your little client, who is absent in body for a short while, but quite present in spirit for all acts of obedience. At Frankfort on the Kalends of July 1621.

Reverend and Illustrious Lords, Farewell,

your most devoted Mathematician,

JOHANNES KEPLER

SECOND BOOK ON THE DOCTRINE OF THE SCHEMATA

PART I. ON THE ECCENTRIC CIRCLES, OR SCHEMATA OF THE PLANETS

[641] *If you set up no solid spheres in the heavens and if all the movements of the planets are regulated by natural faculties, which are implanted in the bodies of the planets: then I ask what will the theory [ratio] of astronomy be? For it seems that the theory cannot do without the imagining of circles and spheres.*

It can easily do without the useless furniture of fictitious circles and spheres. But there is such great need of imagining the true figures, in which the routes of the planets are arranged, that we are impoverishing Astronomy and that the big job to be worked on by the true astronomer is to demonstrate from observations what figures the planetary orbits possess; and to devise such hypotheses, or physical principles, [642] as can be used to demonstrate the figures which are in accord with the deductions made from observations. Therefore when once the figure of the planetary orbit has been established, then will come the second and more popular exercise of the astronomer: to formulate, and to give the rules of, an astronomical calculus in accordance with this true figure, or even to make use of the figure as expressed in material instruments not otherwise than the solid spheres of the ancients were used, and through these figures to lay the movements of the planets before the eyes.

Therefore what is the subject-matter of the Fifth Book, the second book on the doctrine of the schemata, and how do you keep its subject-matter separate from that of the preceding Fourth and the following Sixth?

So far, in the Fourth Book, the physical principles of movements—among other things—have been demonstrated by reasons and by experiments. Out of these physical principles the Fifth Book will form the figures of the planetary orbits and will explain the powers [*potestates*] of those figures; and there the inmost sanctuaries of geometry will have to be searched. The Sixth will teach the use of these figures in the schemata of the single planets and put them into operation. So the Fourth contains the theory; the Fifth, the instrument; and the Sixth the practice; the Fourth was physical, the Fifth is geometrical, and the Sixth will be properly astronomical.

How many parts does Book V have?

Two: in the first part the eccentric circle and its plane are connected up with physical causes: in the second, there are given definitions of the astronomical terms which occur universally among all the planets in the case of the eccentric circle; and the method of calculation is explained in so far as it relates to this part.

Then what sort of figure of the planetary orbit is formed according to the physical principles of Book IV?

If the body of the planet did not have magnetic threads, [643] so that in accordance with one of the regions of magnetic threads it is drawn to the north, and in accordance with the other region towards the south—in accordance with one region it is attracted towards the sun, and in accordance with the other is repelled; then the sun in the rotation of its body around its axis, carrying around the immaterial form of its own body throughout the widest spaces of the world, would carry around with itself the planet held fast by that form, and (1) if the planet at the start had been situated under the ecliptic, its whole route would be arranged along the plane of the ecliptic; (2) and so the planet would always return to that very point where the start was made; (3) the body of the sun and the planetary orbit would have the same centre; (4) the figure of the orbit would be a perfect circle; (5) the planet in all equal portions of this circle would be moved with equal speed.

But because we have laid down that in the body of any planet there are present twofold threads:therefore by the mingling of the faculties of the planet's body and the sun's motor power, (1) the planet describes an orbit oblique to the ecliptic; and because the threads of latitude remain in approximately a parallel posture during the whole circuit but not wholly so, and hence they are deflected gradually after many revolutions: therefore (2) the plane contained by the orbit of the planet is approximately a perfect plane but not wholly so; and hence, when one revolution has been completed, the centre of the planetary globe does not return exactly to its starting-point, but it entwines a new circle with the first circle traversed and described—after the fashion of the circles of the natural days—of which I have spoken in Book III, page 291—or after the fashion of the thread which the silk-worm drops, throwing the thread around itself and building a little house by the inweaving of many entwined circles. For this reason the longest digressions in latitude are not found in all ages in the same parts of the zodiac. And because the threads of libration make the planet to be drawn away from the sun to one side but then to be driven away from that region; accordingly the planet (3) describes its orbit around the sun but not as around its own centres, that is to say, it describes an orbit eccentric to the sun: [644] and for this reason the orbit is not (4) a perfect circle, but one slightly narrower and more pressed in on the sides, like the figure of an ellipse. (5) For the same cause and because the form of the solar body, which form gives movement to the planet, is slighter and weaker in the larger circle, it is not possible for the planet to be moved with the same speed in all the parts of its orbit; but the planet is slow at a long distance from the sun and fast at a short distance. Finally because too the threads of libration are moved out of their parallel posture by very many successive revolutions, so too the positions on the zodiac where the planets are highest and slowest do not always remain but gradually move eastward.

Have you not described an intricate figure for the route of the planet and one that cannot readily be laid before the eyes especially in a plane?

Even if this is true, it is nevertheless not new to astronomy or something found only in Copernicus; and there is no need for all things to be represented in the same plane; but those interweavings, which have arisen from the very slow movement of the boundary-posts of latitude and altitude, can be disentangled with the same dexterity which the ancient astronomers employed and with less apparatus.

How did the ancients disentangle the movements of latitude and of altitude?

They devised for the latitudes one circle or sphere which is the carrier or deferent of the nodes, the outermost circle of the whole schema of the planet—and for the altitudes two spheres of unequal thickness, which they named the altitudes of the deferents [*deferentium auges*].

Why do you judge that those spheres or circles should not be used?

Because they were made for laying physical explanations of movement before the imagination rather than astronomical. And so by their use [645] those false physical opinions concerning the solidity of the circles or spheres were established; and in turn the true judgments were obscured concerning the causes of their irregularities and of their very slow transportation—these causes were demonstrated in Book IV.

Therefore what do you substitute for these three circles or spheres in laying your astronomical explanations before the imagination?

It is sufficient if we draw two straight lines from the centre of the sun, one through the intersection of the planet's orbit with the ecliptic, the other through the centre of the planet's orbit—both lines, on either side and everywhere under the fixed stars—and if we teach that the movement of the first line is under the ecliptic towards the westward signs and that the movement of the second line is eastward under the circle, in the sphere of the fixed stars, which is in the same plane as the orbit of the planet—both movements most regular, the first movement from the mean equinoctial point and the second movement from the line of intersections [of the planet's orbit with the ecliptic]. Unless something should here be taken from Book VII on the ground that even the ecliptic is dislocated and does not always run through the same fixed stars.

When this separation has been made, what remains for our imagination concerning the figure of the route of the planet?

The orbit remains as a perfect ellipse in a true and most regular plane inclined to the plane of the ecliptic at constant angles, by which plane of the ecliptic this orbit is cut in the line drawn through the centre of the solar body—as was stated on page 946, Book IV. The planet moves in this orbit with unequal speed through its parts and returns to the intersections, and so to the equinoctial points—not to say to the fixed stars and to the line through the centres, by absolutely equal measures of periodic times, so far as they are considered in themselves.

Does not this imaging trespass upon the physical causes and measures of the movements of one period?

Not very far, provided we keep in mind that those things which are abstracted by means of the said two lines from the real inweaving and interconnection of many orbits [646] are not furnished physically by those two lines but by the inclination of the real threads of the planet's body.

By what right do you make this also a part of Copernican astronomy, since that author abided by the opinion of the ancients concerning perfect circles?

I admit that this formulation of the hypotheses is not Copernican. But because the part concerning the eccentric circle is subordinate to the general hypothesis which employs the annual movement of the Earth and the stillness of the sun: therefore the name comes from the more important part of the hypothesis. Moreover, this small part of the hypothesis is bound up with necessary arguments arising from the repose of the sun and the movement of the Earth, the doctrines of Copernicus; and so this part has a good title for being referred to Copernicus.

What is the method of procedure whereby it will be demonstrated by the physical causes established in Book IV that such a figure of the orbit arises and what speed the planet has through the parts of its orbit?

We must start with the approach and withdrawal of the planet from the sun; and first, we must determine the geometrical measure of the strength of the forces exerted in giving the planet a movement of libration in any posture of the threads. And secondly, we must prepare a compendious geometrical measure of the effect of the attraction or repulsion, which is heaped up through any whole arc of the orbit by all the increments of the forces. Thirdly, we must demonstrate that the elliptical figure of the orbit arises from such a libration completed during the revolution. Fourthly, we must show that the plane of the ellipse exhibits the measures of the time and of the delays which the planet makes in any arc of its elliptical orbit. Fifthly, we must teach the equivalence of the plane of a circle and the plane of an ellipse with respect to this measuring of time. Finally, we shall have to demonstrate that when the revolution of the threads of latitude has been thus procured, as [647] was laid down in Book IV, the regularity of the orbital plane is established. By these demonstrations the studious astonomer— for the popular astronomer has no need of Book IV or of this first part of Book V —will have his curiosity satisfied concerning this part of the calculus of movements. The other part of Book V will teach how to construct this calculus; and Book VI, how to bring it into use by the application of this elliptical orbit and its plane to the great circle or sphere.

1. Concerning the Increment of Libration

Begin with the first and say on what principles the measure (modus) *of increment of the libration in every position of the planet is formed or determined.*

Two causes, one active and one passive, come together for the formation of this increment. The active cause is the quantity (*modulus*) of the forces of libration in themselves, that is to say, how great the quantity (*modulus*) is found to be in any equal arc of the eccentric orbit. The passive is the varying lay-out of the planetary body with respect to the sun; for not every lay-out receives or admits that whole quantity (*modulus*) of forces, but any lay-out receives its own proper portion [of the forces].

So what measures the quantity of the forces for giving the planet a movement of libration?

These three do: first, the distance of the arc of the orbit from the sun; secondly, the magnitude of this arc; and thirdly, the time which the planet takes to turn through this arc.

What does this distance of the arc—and of the planet in the arc—from the sun have to do with the forces of libration?

The ratio of the distances is the inverse of the ratio of the tenuity of the solar form. This same form carries the planet around and gives it a movement of libration, now attracting it and now repulsing it, as was said in Book IV, page 903. And so the farther the arc is distant from the sun, the weaker at any moment of time is the libration of the planet moving in the arc. For this reason alone, the sun would expend unequal forces in different arcs of the eccentric circle which are equal to one another.

[648] *What effect does the magnitude of the arc of the planet have?*

Because in a long arc much force is expended, and in a short arc little force: therefore if equal arcs are assumed, so much and so far should the forces be equal.

What does the time, taken separately, have to do with the increase of forces, and what do all three causes, taken together?

Since—Book IV, pages 903-06—it has been shown that the farther the planet is distant from the sun, the longer does it delay in the equal arcs of the orbit; and so much the longer does it feel the motor force of the sun, the greater the magnitude of that arc: but since it has already been said that the farther any one of the equal arcs of the orbit is distant from the sun, so much the feebler is the movement of libration which the planet undergoes: wherefore the more feeble the libration is in one moment of time, in any of the equal arcs of the orbit, so much the longer does the planet revolve and undergo a libration in that arc. Therefore since the feebleness of the forces is balanced by the stretch of time wherein the planet experiences those forces in itself—and this occurs in the same ratio on both sides, namely, in the ratio of the distances from the sun: hence there is the final effect that in the equal arcs of the eccentric circle the quantity (*modulus*) of the forces of libration is disbursed by the sun and is absolutely equal with respect to the sun as an agent. See diagrams on pages 903 and 934.

Now therefore state the measure of the portion of the quantity of the solar forces which the planet admits into itself in any posture with respect to the sun.

We must consider the angle which the rays [*radii*] of the sun make with the magnetic threads of the planetary globe. For the sine of the angle complementary to this measures this portion of forces admitted. For since the efficient causes of the libration are the ray of the sun and the magnetic threads of the planet's body, two physical lines; it is right to seek the measure of the strength of the libration from the angle between these lines and from its sine.

[649] For example, let *A* be the sun; and *I*, *E*, the centre of the planetary

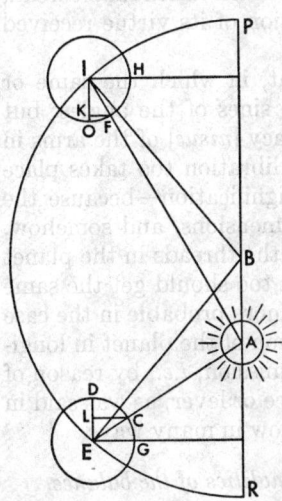

body; *RP* the line drawn through *A* the sun and through *B* the centre of the orbit; *EG* and *IH* the magnetic threads will be practically perpendicular to *RP*—at least if the counterbalancing of the semicircles is considered—and *H* and *F* are the solipetal termini. For it was laid down in Book IV page 935 that during the revolution of the body the magnetic threads stay practically parallel to themselves and at points *P* and *R* provide no occasion of attraction or repulsion, because there the positions of both the solipetal and the solifugal termini are equally distant from the sun at *A*. But in the intermediate positions, where the solipetal or the solifugal termini regard the sun directly, the strength of the libration is greatest of all. *AE* and *AI* are the rays of the sun. Let lines *ED* and *IO* be drawn parallel to line *RP*, and let perpendiculars be dropped upon them from points *F* and *C*, wherein the rays of the sun cut the middle circles of the planetary globe; and let the perpendiculars be *CL* and *FK*. Here the angles made by the rays of the sun with the threads are *AEG* and *AIH*; the complementary angles are *CED* and *FIO*, or the arcs *CD* and *FO*, and *CL* and *FK* are the sines of these angles, according as *IH* or *EG* is the total sine of 100,000. Therefore it is established that as *EG* and *IH* are to *LC* and *KF*, so the total quantity of the forces from the sun which are present at *I* or *E* is to the portion which the planet admits at the postures of the threads *EG* and *IH*.

Why do you take the sine as the measure, rather than the complement of the angle or arc?

Because, although any magnetic thread is present in a spherical body, nevertheless it is not a circle, but is a physical straight line; because it works most strongly towards undergoing attraction or is very strongly disposed towards admitting the forces of the solar ray into itself, when it points towards the sun in a straight line: or else—what is the same thing—when it is perpendicular to the plane of illumination of the circle, which bounds the part of the globe which is turned towards the sun; but when [650] it is inclined obliquely to that plane, it is equivalent, as to a shorter line, to the perpendicular drawn from its terminus to that plane. Thus the solar ray, considered with respect to the work of heating, heats most strongly when it strikes a surface at right angles; but when at oblique angles, it warms less, in the measure that the line drawn from the sun perpendicularly to the same plane continued is shorter than the oblique ray.

The following explanation will be more elegant: If you consider that the whole globe is made up simply of threads, whereof the longest threads are those in the great circle of the globe; and the shorter, those in the latitudinal circles. In this way not only will *EG*, like *IH*, be a thread; but also the aforementioned sines *LC* and *KF*, which are marked out by the solar ray *AE* and *AI* at the termini *C* and *F:* those sines are latitudinal threads. Therefore the smaller *CL* and *FK* are than *GE* and *HI*, so much the less of the forces from the solar ray does any one thread of the whole body admit into itself, on account of the solar ray falling obliquely upon itself. Thus the solar ray, by marking out the latitudinal thread, marks out the sine, which is the measure of the portion of its virtue received into the threads.

Furthermore, every artificial or natural movement, in which the same or analogous principles concur, is measured out by the sines of the angles; but principally and most clearly, the movement or tendency [*nisus*] of the arms in the balance and in the lever. Accordingly since this libration too takes place between movements which are natural in a wider signification—because the libration power of the solar form is a partaker of dimensions, and somehow, though without matter, corporeal; but the lay-out of the threads in the planet again is corporeal; it is not absurd that this libration too should get the same laws as the balance and the lever. And that is all the more probable in the case of the libration towards the sun, because the progression of the planet in longitude along its orbit, by reason of intensification or remission, *i.e.*, by reason of speed and slowness, obeys the laws of the same balance or lever, as was said in Book IV, page 887 and 906, and will be made clear below in many ways.

[651] *Compare this speed of libration with the proportionalities of the balance.*

The line from the sun into the threads is like the haft of the balance, the threads like the arms of the balance; and the regions of the threads like the tray; and the weights in the trays are, in the case of the planet, the attraction towards the sun, or repulsion from the same; and both are of the same family of things. For as the sun attracts the planet, so the Earth attracts bodies, and on account of this attraction, bodies are said to be heavy. But the sun attracts the planet with respect to one region and repels it with respect to the other, and does this with varying intensity; while the Earth attracts weights without any distinction being made as to posture. Accordingly that which in the balance is inequality of weights, in the planet becomes the diversity of posture of the threads with respect to the sun: for here the planet exhibits both weights on the balance as the same weight. And just as in the balance, the heavier weight comes down towards the Earth, and the lighter moves up away from the Earth; so in this case the whole globe of the planet suffers the affect (*affectionem*) of the prevailing region. Hence if the friendly region is more attracted by the sun [than the unfriendly region is repelled], the whole planet approaches the sun; but if the unfriendly region is more repelled, the whole globe of the planet is repelled by the sun. Therefore too the measure, in accordance with which the weights of the balance are at war with one another, will be dominant in the disbursing of this attraction and repulsion. But in the balance the victory of the weights is evaluated [652] at the sine of the complement of the angle between the haft or handle (*manubrium*) and the arm of the lighter weight, as will be proved. Wherefore too in the libration of the planetary body towards the sun, the passion of the region of thread nearer the sun will overcome the passion of the opposite region in the ratio of the sine of the complement of the angle between the solar ray and the thread. But the effect of victory, in the movement of the planets, is the strength of the libration belonging to each position. Accordingly this strength, or the increment born of that [strength] of libration, will similarly be evaluated at the sine of the complement of the angle with the threads.

Let AD be the handle or haft; and let AB and AC, the arms in the same straight line BC, be each equal to AD. Let H be the lighter weight hanging from B: and I, the heavier weight, hanging from C. Accordingly the weights, which by their power (*potestate*) are at points B and C, have an altitude as great as BC the length of the arms; and the weights contend for this altitude, which is DE. For if the greater weight completely overcame the other, the arm BA would coincide with the handle DA; and the greater weight C would be in the place of altitude E, and would lift the lesser up to D the very top; but because the heavier weight does not overcome the lighter completely, therefore the perpendicular BF drawn from the end of arm B to the handle DA shows that the weight B is lifted through FA, a part of the altitude, and that the weight C goes down the same amount, namely through AG. Accordingly

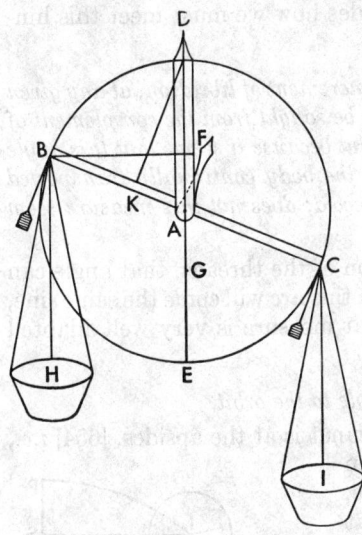

$$DF : FE :: \text{weight } H : \text{weight } I.$$
$$FE : FG :: \text{weight } I : \text{weight } I - \text{weight } H.$$
$$DE : FG :: DA : FA :: \text{weights } I \ \& \ H : \text{weight } I - \text{weight } H.$$

But if BA is set down as the total sine, FA will be the sine of angle FBA, which is the complement of angle FAB.

In the same way if EA is the ray from the sun, BC the magnetic thread of the planetary body, H or B the lesser strength of repulsion, and I or C the greater strength of attraction—because C has approached nearer to the sun than B—then, if BA exhibits the strongest attraction and with no angle BAD, AF will represent the attraction at the existing angle BAF or GAC.

Apply these things to the proportionality of the lever too.

The proportionality [ratio] of the lever is the same, with only the following difference: [653] in the balance the fulcrum A is at the midpoint between B and C the extremities of the arms, and thence the unequal weights make BC not remain parallel to the horizon: but in the lever the line of weights remains parallel to the horizon, while the fulcrum divides the length of the arms not at the midpoint but nearer the heavier weight, so that the arms have the inverse ratio of the weights.

For example, if DA the handle of the balance is equal to the arms BA and AC, a lever will be formed, and the weights hanging from B and C will be suspended at equilibrium with respect to the horizon—as follows: DK the perpendicular drawn from D to BC will be the handle; and BK and KC will be the arms; and as formerly DF was to FE, so now BK is to KC. Then as BK the shorter arm is to KC the longer arm, so the lesser weight H to be suspended from C is to the greater weight I to be suspended from B.

The reader must be warned that mechanical experimentation is difficult: because the weight and thickness of the arms themselves cannot be guarded against mechanically. Now they ought to constitute geometrically a pure line without weight and width. It may be seen in Archimedes how we must meet this hindrance in part.

I grasp that the measure of the strength, or of the increment of libration, at any given posture of the threads of the planetary body must be sought from the complement of the angle made by the thread with the solar ray; but because it seems that this angle is discovered with difficulty, in that not only is the body continually transported from place to place, but also its threads are deflected; does not this measure seem uncertain and therefore unsuited for use?

On the contrary, on account of this deflection of the threads, that angle can be converted to the arc of the orbit, so that from this arc will come the same sine, *i.e.*, the same measure, and for this reason that measure is very well adapted to use.

Teach and demonstrate this converting of the angle to the orbit.

You remember that at the start when the planet is at the apsides, [654] *i.e.*, at the beginning of the orbit, the angle between the ray of the sun and the thread is a right angle. Again in Book IV, page 941, it was shown that thread NQ of this figure points towards A the sun, or is one with NA the ray from the sun—the angle here being null—when PN a quadrant of the orbit from apsis P has been traversed: hence the arc of the orbit from the apsis measures the complement of this angle. Therefore it remains to be demonstrated, that even the intermediate angles made by the thread and the sun, as HIA, between a right angle and no angle, have as their complements the middle arcs of the orbit, as PI, between no arc and a quadrant, so that the two together make 90°.

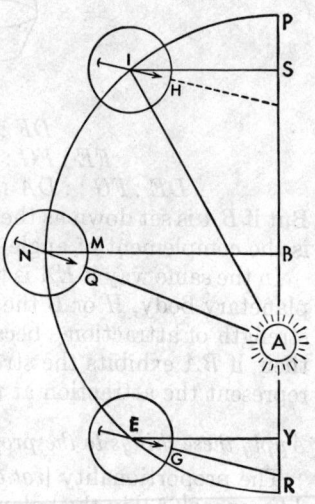

It is demonstrated as follows: On page 944, it was said that $IS : NB :: $ angle $HIS : $ angle QNB. That [ratio] is used for the sake of discerning IS and NB, although, by the force of physical speculation, that [ratio] is true of the sines of angles IAP and NAP. But now

$$\sin AIB : \sin ANB :: \sin IAP : \sin NAP.$$

For

$$BI : BA :: \sin BAI : \sin BIA.$$

And

$$BI : BA :: BN : BA :: \sin BAN : \sin BNA.$$

Therefore

sin *BAI* : sin *BAN* : : sin *IAP* : sin *NAP* : : sin *AIB* : sin *ANB*.

Therefore if the foregoing terms are compared with one another, angle *HIS* will be found equal to angle *AIB*, and angle *QNB* to angle *ANB*; and, if equals are subtracted [from equals], angle *SIB* will be equal to angle *HIA*—just as, by proportion, angle *BNB* will be equal to angle *ANA*. But the measure of angle *SIB* is arc *IN*, because the measure of angle *SBI* is arc *PI*. Therefore too the measure of angle *HIA* will be arc *IN*, the complement of arc *PI*. Therefore, given *PI* the arc of the orbit, *SI* the sine of the arc, *i.e.*, the measure of the increment of libration, is also given immediately.

2. On the Sum of the Libration Gone Through With

I comprehend the measure of the increment, or of the strength of libration, at any given moment. But I should like to know the measure of the part of the libration gone through with from the beginning up to that moment.

That measure is got from the versed sine of the same orbital arc so far traversed. For as the whole major diameter of the ellipse is to the total libration, or—what amounts to the same—as the semidiameter of the orbit is to the eccentricity, so also the versed sine of each arc on the orbit starting from the apsis is to the part of the libration which is gone through with in the meantime, while the planet is traversing that arc.

By what means is this demonstrated?

By means of that very measure of the increments of libration which has just now been confirmed by its own demonstration.

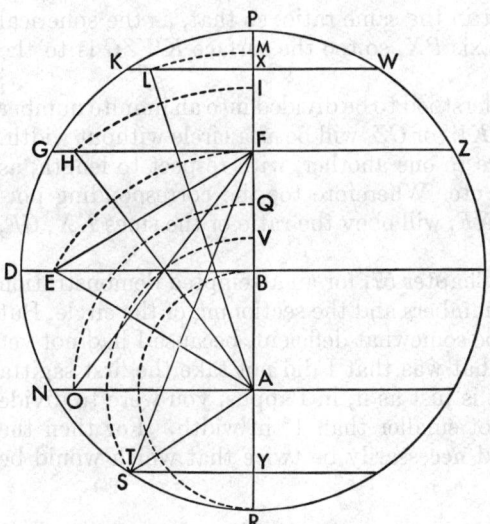

For let *PD* be a perfect circle whose centre is *B*. Let *A* be the sun, and *PBAR* the line of the apsides: and let *P* and *R* be the highest and lowest apsides. Let *AB* be the eccentricity; and let its double, *PB*, be the total libration. Now let the circle be divided into equal least parts—starting at *P*. And let the parts be *PK*, *KG*, *GD*, *DN*, *NS* and *SR*. And from these divisions let the perpendiculars *KX*, *GF*, *DB*, *NA*, and *SY* be drawn to *PR*.

Therefore, by the foregoing, as the sine *KX* is to sines *GF*, *DB*, *NA*, *SY*, and *RR*—a point instead of a line—so the increments of libration corresponding to arcs *PK*, *KG*, etc. are to one another—that is, as *PM* is to *MI*, *IF*, *FQ*, *QV*, and *VB*. And that is true provided it is understood that the division is continued to infinity, when *KX* and *RR* are understood to be equal. Therefore since points *P*, *M*, *I*, *F*, *Q*, *V*, and *B* are put down as separating the said increments of libration; let them be transposed to the different distances of the planet from the sun A: that is to say, with A as centre and with intervals AM, AI, AF, AQ, and AV let the arcs ML, IH, FE, QO, and VT be described in such fashion that a planetary orbit [656] which is an ellipse may be understood to drop from P to R through the points L, H, E, O, and T. The distances of the planet from the sun will be AP, AL, AH, AE, AO, AT, and AR. But the versed sines of the said arcs PK, PG, etc. will be PX, PF, PB, PA, PY, and PR. I say that as the whole diameter PR, the sagitta of arc PDR, is to PB the total libration, so the sagittae of the single arcs are to the single increments of libration, namely so is PX to PM, so PF to PI, so PB to PF, so PA to PQ, so PY to PV.

For it has been put down that PM and PI the parts of the libration are in the ratio of the sines KX, GF, etc. But now also the parts PX, PF, etc. of the total sagitta PR are in the same ratio of the sines KX, GF, etc.—and in the same state of infinite division, where—no less than before—the point R plays the role of line RR.

Therefore, by alternation, the parts of the libration correspond in the same ratio to the parts of the sagitta—and as a consequence, any total portion of the libration from the beginning P corresponds to its total sagitta in the same ratio.

[657] *Whence do we know that the parts* PX *and* XF *of the diameter* PR, *considered as the sagittae are in the ratio of the sines* KX *and* GF *which determine them?*

Pappus made a demonstration, *Mathematical Collections*, Book v, Prop. 36. If a sphere—to be understood by PGZ—is cut by any number whatsoever of parallel planes, as KW, GZ, etc., then the surface of the sphere and the axis of the sections, as PR, are always cut in the same ratio: so that, as the spherical surface KPW is to portion of the axis PX, so too the surface $KWZG$ is to the portion XF, and so for the rest.

But if the spherical surface is understood to be divided into an infinite number of equal zones, then any zone, say KW or GZ, will be as a circle without width. But the circles KXW and GFZ are to one another, with respect to length, as their semidiameters KX, and GF, etc. Wherefore too the corresponding portions of the axis PR, namely PX, XF, will obey the ratio of the sines KX, GF, by which they are determined.

See the *Commentaries on Mars*, Chapter 57, for an attempted demonstration of the same theorem by means of numbers and the sectioning of the circle. But in that place this ratio seemed to be somewhat deficient, because I had not yet read Pappus. But the reason for that was that I did not take the first sagitta from a small enough arc, and that is just as if, in Pappus, you were to divide the spherical surface into parts not smaller than 1° in width. For then the width of the narrowest zone would necessarily be twice that which would be true.

Although PK, KG, *and the remaining arcs taken from the circle are equal, yet it does not seem that* PL, LH, *etc., the arcs of the true orbit are equal, but are greater towards* E. *Does not this destroy the certitude of the demonstration?*

Not at all. For the fact that the arcs are greater towards E [658] must be attributed to these very librations, as will be apparent below. But the same thing cannot be either the only cause or a concurrent cause of itself: so that I may pass over the disturbance, because, even if any is to be admitted, it would clearly be imperceptible.

3. On the Figure of the Orbit

I see that the measure of the libration is found in the versed sines of the arcs of the orbit starting from the apsis—by the principles and causes of movement which have been assumed. It is left for you to prove that by this form of libration an elliptic orbit is constituted, concerning which you have said the observations bear witness.

That the planetary orbit *PLHEOTR* and the opposite half becomes an ellipse is demonstrated from the properties of this figure which are identical with the properties which the libration so far described exhibits.

What are the identical properties of the ellipse?

1. It is clear, from the *Conics* of Apollonius of Perga, that the ellipse [659] around which a circle is circumscribed, with the longer diameter of the ellipse as the common diameter, cuts all the ordinates to that diameter in the same ratio of the segments.

For example, if the lines *KX*, *GF*, *DB*, *NA*, and *SY* are ordinates applied to

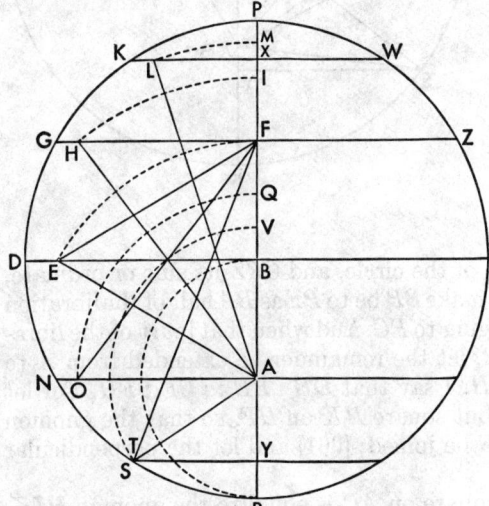

PR, and if the curved line *PLHEOTR* is an ellipse, then necessarily *DB* : *BE* : : *GF* : *FH* : : *KX* : *XL* : : *NA* : *AO* : : *SY* : *YT*.

2. The ellipse has two points, from which it is described as from centres; I am accustomed to call these two points the "foci." Accordingly if the lines drawn from the two foci to any point on the ellipse, or even the lines drawn from one focus to the points opposite the centre of the ellipse, are added together, they are always equal to the longer diameter. Hence when they are drawn to those points on the ellipse which are in the shorter diameter lying midway between the vertices, each of them is equal to the semidiameter of the circle.

For example, if *A* is the focus, *B* the centre of the circle, *AB* and *BF* equal, *F* will be the other focus. And the sum of *AH* and *HF* will be equal to the diameter *PR*. So will the sum of *AL* and *LF*, and the sum of *AO* and *OF*. Wherefore, since *BE* is the shorter semidiameter, and *E* is the point on it, *AE* and *EF* will be equal, and each of them will be equal to the semidiameter *BP* or *BR*, or *BD*.

This is applied to the planets, as follows: we have said that observations bear witness that the planets are at a distance of the semidiameter of the eccentric circle from the sun—one focus of this ellipse—at a time when they have traversed exactly a quadrant of the orbit from apsis *P*.

Demonstrate that these properties of an ellipse are exhibited in the planetary orbit which arises from these librations.

Then, in accordance with the laws so far given, let there be described a new figure, namely, with centre *B,* the circle *PDR,* to which the ellipse should be tangent. Let *PR* be the longer diameter of the ellipse, and on *PR* let *A* be a focus, or the place of the sun. Now let *DT* be drawn through *B* perpendicular to *PR;* the shorter diameter will be on *DT.* And because *BA* the eccentricity is half of the libration, therefore half the libration has been completed at the completion of the quadrant. Therefore the planet falling upon line *DB* will be less distant from the sun [660] than at *P,* and the difference will be equal to *BA.* Therefore it will have a distance equal to the magnitude *PB.* Wherefore let an interval equal to *BP* be extended from *A* to *DB,* and let its terminus be *E.* Therefore the orbit of the planet will cut *DB* at *E.*

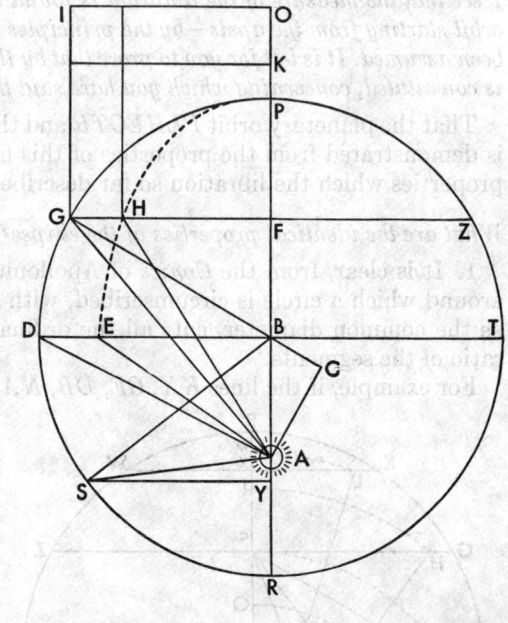

Again let there be taken *PG* an arc of the circle, and *GFZ* its sine or ordinate, and *PF* the versed sine. Accordingly make *BP* be to *PF* as *BA* half of the libration is to the part [of the libration] belonging to *PG.* And when that [part of the libration] has been subtracted from *AP,* let the remainder be extended from *A* to *GF,* and let its terminus fall upon *H.* I say that *DB : BE : : GF : FH.* For let square *GIOF* be described on *GF,* but square *HK* on *HF,* so that the gnomon *HIK* is made. Then let *GA* and *GB* be joined; [661] and let the perpendicular *AC* be drawn to *GB* continued.

I say in the first place that the square on *AC* is equal to the gnomon *HIK.* For

$$BP : PF : : BA : AP - AH.$$

Wherefore too

$$PB : BF : : BA : AH - BP.$$

But too

$$PB : BF : : GB : BF : : AB : BC$$

because the right triangles *GFB* and *ACB* have their **vertical angles *GBF* and *ABC* equal. Therefore

$$BC = AH - BP.$$

But too

$$CG - BP = CG - BG = BC.$$

Wherefore

$$GC = HA.$$

But

$$\text{sq. } GC + \text{sq. } AC = \text{sq. } GA.$$

But on the other hand

$$\text{sq. } AF + \text{sq. } FG = \text{sq. } GA.$$

Therefore

$$\text{sq. } GF + \text{sq. } FA = \text{sq. } GC + \text{sq. } CA.$$

Therefore

$$(\text{sq. } GC + \text{sq. } CA) - \text{sq. } GC = \text{sq. } CA.$$

But

$$\text{sq. } AH = \text{sq. } GC$$

and

$$\text{sq. } AH = \text{sq. } AF + \text{sq. } FH.$$

Therefore

$$(\text{sq. } GF + \text{sq. } FA) - \text{sq. } AH = \text{gnom. } HIK.$$

From this the remainder of the proposed demonstration is easily woven together.

For as one sine GF is to its perpendicular AC, so all the other sines are to their own perpendiculars from A. Therefore as GO the square on the sine is to the square on AC, i.e., to the gnomon HIK, so the squares of all the sines are to their gnomons. Wherefore also, if the gnomons are subtracted, as GO the square of one sine GF is to HK the square on FH—which has been determined by HA the distance of the planet from the sun—so the square on any sine is to the square of its minor determined by its distance. But if the squares are proportional to one another, the sides themselves are proportional to one another. Therefore as GF is to FH, the portion terminated by AH; so any sine, such as DB, is to BE, the portion terminated by AE. And this proportionality [ratio] is true of the ellipse.

The other property of the ellipse is clear of itself.

For in accordance with the rule of the laws of libration, that is, because half of the libration, equal to BA, should be completed in PE [662] a quadrant of the orbit, we extend AE—which is equal to BP the remainder [of the libration] —from A to DB. For, because A is one focus, if the line extended from B along BP is set down equal to BA, the other focus will be marked out: its distance from E will be equal to AE, and the sum of the two focal distances will be equal to the diameter—and that is the case in an ellipse.

What is the ratio of DE, *the width of the crescent cut off by the ellipse from the circle, to the eccentricity* BA?

The eccentricity BA is a mean proportional between DE and ET. In the same way too, every perpendicular, such as AC, is a mean proportional between GH and HZ, the remainder of the chord.

For the rectangle GH, HZ is equal to the gnomon HIK. But this gnomon is equal to the square on AC. Therefore too the rectangle GH, HZ is equal to

the same square on *AC*. Therefore *GH*, *AC*, and *HZ* are in
continued proportion.

What shall I hold concerning the
length of this elliptical orbit and
of its parts?

If the figures of the circle and
the ellipse are cut by an infinite
number of ordinates, *GF*, *DB*
etc., the first portions ending in
P will be—*GP* will be to *PH*—
as *GF* is to *FH*; but the last portions ending in *D* and *E*—*GD*
will be to *HE*—will be equal to
one another: so the ratio of *DB*
to *BE*, which started at *P*, is
gradually obliterated, and at *D*
and *E* vanishes into the mere
ratio of equality. But the total
arcs, which started at *P*, have to
one another a ratio compounded
of all the ratios of all the least

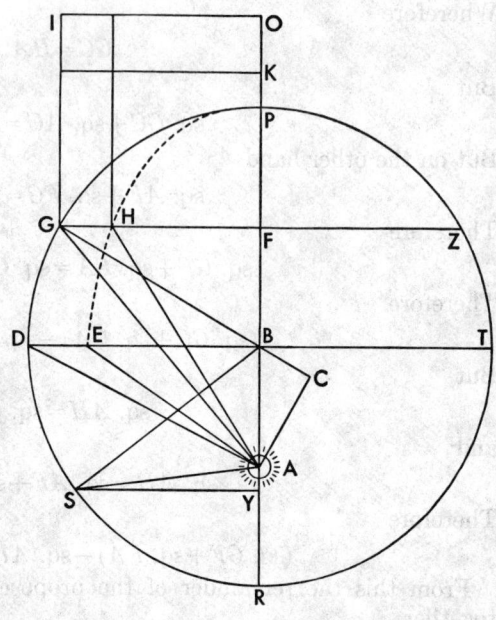

particles; and so they never lay aside completely the full ratio *DB* to *BE*. For
the quadrant *DP* is to the quadrant *PE*, and also the total circular line is to
the total elliptical line, as *DB* is to the arithmetic mean between *DB* and *BE*,
which is slightly longer than the mean proportional.

Because use will also be made of the plane of the ellipse, I ask in what ratio will
the plane of the ellipse be to the plane of the circle; and hence the plane of any seg-
ment of the semicircle to the plane of the segment—of the semiellipse—made by the
same ordinate?

Apollonius demonstrates in his *Conics* that the ratio of the longer diameter
to the shorter holds everywhere. Hence if *DB* and *GF* are ordinates, as *DB* is to
BE, so is the area of the semicircle *PDR* to the area of the semiellipse *PER*; and
as *GF* is to *FH*, *i.e.*, as *DB* is to *BE*, so *GPF* a segment of the semicircle is to
HPF a segment of the semiellipse; and so too *GRF* a greater segment of the
semicircle is to *HRF* a greater segment of the semiellipse.

[664] Now let the semicircle be cut by the straight line *GA*, but the semiellipse
by the straight line *HA*; there will be the triangles *HAF* and *GAF* having the
same altitude *FA*. Wherefore
base *GF* : base *FH* : : area *GAF* : area *FAH*.

But
GF : *FH* : : area *GPF* : area *FPH*.

Wherefore
GF : *FH* : : *DB* : *BE* : : comp. area *PGA* : comp. area *PHA*.

Finally I should like to know what ratio the lines from the centre of the figure to
the circumference of the ellipse have to the semidiameter of the circle?

A very small ratio indeed, as *BE* is less than the semidiameter *BD* by *DE*
the total width of the crescent. But all the remaining lines, such as *BH*, have

a lesser difference between themselves and the semidiameter BG than at any given place, the width of the crescent, such as GH, is.

For in the triangle GHB, the sum of the two sides GH and BH must exceed the third side GB. Therefore the ratio of the defect at E to the defect at H is greater than the ratio of DE to GH. But this last is the ratio of the sine DB to sine GF. Therefore the ratio of the defect at E to the defect at H is greater than that of sine DB to sine GF.

Conversely, the ratio of the squares on GF and HF is as GF^2 is to HF^2. But

$$\text{sq. } GF + \text{sq. } BF : \text{sq. } HF + \text{sq. } BF < GF^2 : FH^2.$$

Wherefore

$$\text{side } GB : \text{side } BH < GF : FH.$$

Therefore the greater BF is, the more the ratio $GB : BH$ is diminished, so as not to equal the ratio $GF : FH$. And conversely, the more PF increases, the more the ratio $GB : BH$ increases, approaching the ratio $GF : FH$. But PF increases slowly from P, but quickly near DB. Therefore if GH everywhere stayed of the same magnitude, it would vary the defect HB slowly around P, quickly around D. But GH does not remain the same, but increases quickly around P, slowly around D—that is, it increases with its sines GF and DB. Again therefore the defect HB increases quickly around P, but slowly around E. Therefore

$$\text{defect } EB : \text{defect } HB < \text{sag. } PB : \text{sag. } PF.$$

But

$$\text{arc } DP : \text{arc } PG > \sin DB : \sin GF$$
$$< \text{sag. } BP : \text{sag. } FP.$$

Therefore the ratio of the defect, of lines BH, [665] approaches the ratio of the degrees PG. However, towards D it verges upon the ratio of sine DB to sine GF. But towards P it verges upon the ratio of sagitta BP to sagitta FP.

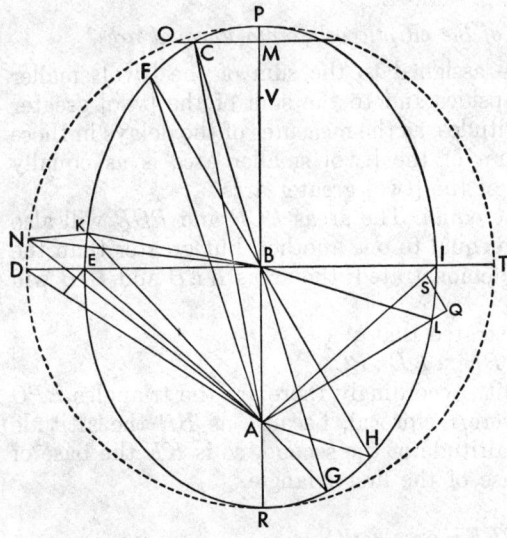

4. On the Measure of Time, or of the Delay made by the Planet in any Arc of its Orbit

How is the plane of the segment of an ellipse fitted for measuring the delay of the planet in the arc of that segment?

Not otherwise than if by the division of the circle into equal parts unequal arcs of the ellipse are constituted—small arcs around the apsides, and greater around the mean longitudes—as follows:

With centre B and distance BP, let the circle $PDRT$ be described. Let PBR be its diam-

eter, and on *PBR*, as on the line of the apsides, let *A* be the sun, [666] the
source of movement, towards *R*; *AB* the eccentricity, and *BV* equal to *AB*,
towards *P*; so that *P* and *R* are the apsides.

Now with the points *A* and *V* as the foci, let the ellipse *PERI* be described,
which is tangent to the circle at *P* and *R*, and which represents the orbit
of the planet. And let *EI* be the shorter diameter, and *DT* the diameter of the
circle, which are at right angles to *PR*.

Now let the semicircle *PDR* be divided into small equal parts, and let
P, O, N, D, R, and *T* be the points between the divisions; and from these
points let there be drawn to *PR* the line of apsides the perpendiculars, such
as *OM* and *NK*, cutting the ellipse at points *C* and *K*. Therefore if the points
C, K, E, and *I* of the sections are joined with *A* the sun, I say that the delay
of the planet in arc *PC* is measured by the area *PCA*, the delay in the arc
PCK is measured by the area *PCKA*, the delay in *PE* is measured by the
area *PEA*, and finally the delay in *PER*, half of the orbit from apsis *P* to
apsis *R*, is measured by the area *PERP*, which is half of the total area of the
ellipse *PERIP*.

[667] *Show in what ratio, by means of this sectioning, the mean parts of the planetary orbit are made greater than the parts around the apsides.*

In the ratio of the longer semidiameter to the shorter.

For in the circle let there be the equal parts *PO* and *ND*—*PO* at the apsis
P, and *ND* at the mean longitude *D*. Therefore, since on the sectioned ellipse
the arcs *PC* and *KE* correspond to them, it has already been said above that
KE is equal to *ND*—the most minute division being supposed—then *KE*
will also be equal to *PO*. Moreover, it was said that as *OM* is to *MC*, *i.e.*, as
DB is to *BE*, or the longer semidiameter *PB* to the shorter semidiameter
BE, so *PO* the arc of the circle is to *PC* the arc of the ellipse; therefore as
PB is to *BE*, so also will *KE* the arc of the ellipse at the mean longitude be to
PC the arc at the apsis.

What follows from this sectioning of the elliptic orbit into unequal arcs?

It follows that equal areas are assigned to the sum of the [two] smaller
orbital arcs taken around both apsides and to the sum of the [two] greater
arcs taken around both mean longitudes, as the measures of the delays in those
arcs—though nevertheless the sum of the [two] smaller arcs is as equally
distant from the sun as the sum of the [two] greater arcs.

For as above let *PC* and *RG* be equal. The areas *PCB* and *RGB* will also
be equal. Again let *KE* and *LI* be equal to one another, but greater than the
former arcs, as has already been demonstrated: the areas *KEB* and *LIB* will
also be equal.

But it has already been demonstrated that

$$PB : BE :: KE : PC$$

in the given sectioning of the orbit. Accordingly there are the triangles *BPC*
and *BEK*—rectilinear or as it were reciprocal, because as *BP* the altitude
of the first triangle is to *BE* the altitude of the second, so is *KE* the base of
the second triangle to *PC* the base of the first triangle.
Wherefore

$$\text{area } BEK = \text{area } BPC.$$

Therefore

$$\text{area } BEK + \text{area } BIL = \text{area } BPC + \text{area } BRG.$$

But

$$\text{area } BPC + \text{area } BRG = \text{area } APC + \text{area } ARG,$$

because

$$[668] \quad \text{alt. } BP + \text{alt. } PR = \text{alt. } AP + \text{alt. } AR.$$

And

$$\text{area } BEK + \text{area } BIL = \text{area } AEK + \text{area } AIL,$$

because on base EK or on the line touching it at E, the triangles BEK and AEK have the same altitude BE and the same base EK, and on base IL or on the line touching it at I the triangles BIL and AIL have the same altitude BI and the same base IL. Therefore the areas EAK and IAL are assigned to the long arcs KE and LI; and areas APC and ARG, which are equal to them [in sum], are assigned to the shorter arcs PC and RG, since nevertheless the sum of the distances EA and AI from the sun is equal to the sum of the distances PA and AR, as was demonstrated before.

If equal areas are assigned to unequal arcs equally distant from the sun, while the times or delays of unequal arcs equally distant from the sun ought also to be unequal—by the axiom employed above—then how do equal areas measure unequal delays?

Although in this way the pairs of arcs are really unequal to one another, nevertheless they are equivalent [*aequipollent*] to equal arcs in partaking of periodic time.

For it has been said in the above that, if the orbit of the planet is divided into the most minute equal parts, the delays of the planet in them increase in the ratio of the distances between them and the sun. But this is to be understood not of all equal parts as such, but principally of those which are opposite the sun in a straight line, as PC and RG, where there are the right angles APC and ARG. But in the case of the other parts which face the sun obliquely, this is to be understood only of that which in any of those parts belongs to the movement around the sun. For since the orbit of the planet is eccentric, therefore in order to form it two elements of movement are mingled together—as has been demonstrated already: one element comes from the revolution around the sun by reason of one solar virtue; the other comes from the libration towards the sun by reason of another solar virtue distinct from the first. For example, in arc IL the termini I and L are at unequal distances from A the source of movement; therefore let AL continued to Q as AQ be a mean proportional between AL and AI. And if with centre A and distance [669] AQ the arc QS is described cutting the longer line AI in S, arc QS is of the first element of the composite movement; but the difference between AL and AI, or the sum of LQ and SI, is of the second element of the movement, which must be separated out in mind. For none of the periodic time is due to it, since it [the second element] has already in the above received its own portion under other laws, when it was a question of the libration. But this second element of movement can be separated out in no other way than by this sectioning of the orbit into unequal parts, which we gave above. For the quantity whereby the sum of the arcs KE and LI exceeds the sum of the arcs PC and RG comes wholly from the second element of the movement; and with that excess separated out, there remains of the first element something which is equal to the sum of the arcs PC and RG, which I demonstrate as follows.

For by the above demonstrations, AE and AI are equal to BP and BR. Let arcs [of circles] be described through points E and I, and let the first arc cut away and subtract as much from the area AEK towards K, as the second arc adds to area AIL above L: Hence in this fashion the triangles—or rather sectors—get these new right bases instead of the oblique bases KE and LI: Wherefore if the area equal

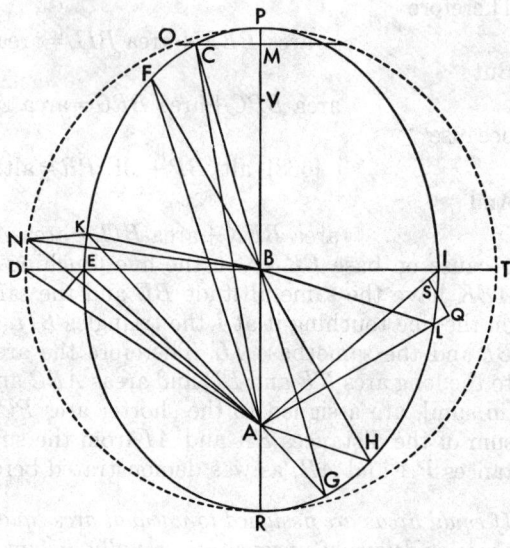

to the sum of PCB and RGB is applied to AE and AI, the bases or arcs described through E and I are equal to the bases described through P and R. But it was previously demonstrated that

$$\text{area } KEA + \text{area } LIA = \text{area } PCB + \text{area } RGB.$$

Therefore the sum of the oblique bases KE and LI which has to do with the revolution around the sun is equal to the sum of the arcs PC and RG, where almost no libration with respect to the sun is mixed in with it, because AP and AC are imperceptibly different, like AR and AG.

The same things will also be demonstrated of the other small parts of the orbit: for example, if CF is taken and CB and FB are continued to G and H, and if GH, corresponding to CF, is joined, and the four points are connected with A the source of movement. For it was demonstrated in the above that

$$CA + AG = PA + AR = PR$$

and

$$FA + AH = PA + AR = PR.$$

Wherefore too, as previously,

$$\text{area } ACF + \text{area } AGH = \text{area } BCF + \text{area } BGH,$$

and hence

$$\text{area } ACF + \text{area } AGH = \text{area } APC + \text{area } ARG,$$

although by the proportionality of sectioning set up, CF [670] will be slightly longer than PC, and GH longer than RG. For the sum of the new arcs described with centre A and distances AC and AG and cutting AF and AH will be equal to the arcs PC and RG; because the greater the circle of the first arc than the circle of the second arc, the smaller an angle CAF does the first arc measure, and the greater an angle GAH does the second arc measure, so that thus

$$\text{angle } CAF + \text{angle } GAH = \text{angle } PAC + \text{angle } RAG.$$

Therefore, since the regularity of the first element in the planetary movement, namely the regularity of the progression around the sun, consists in the equality of the angles around the sun, *i.e.*, in the equality of the sum of two angles; and since the area of the ellipse is equally distributed among the arcs which subtend these angles, that is, two areas are always equal to two other areas: therefore rightly—up to now and in so far as we are dealing with pairs of arcs—is the area set up as the measure of time; because the delays of time ought to be equal not to equal arcs as such but to their equal progressions around the sun, at the same distance from the sun.

Then in this way let the area of the ellipse be rightly distributed between the pairs of opposite arcs; now demonstrate that the single triangles are separately the most exact measures of the single delays?

The demonstration is easy by means of the foregoing.

For since by our axiom the delay of the planet in arc PC is to the delay in the equal arc RG, as AP the distance of arc PC from the source of motion is to AR the distance of arc RG; but since also the area of triangle PCA is to the area of triangle RGA—which has its base RG equal to PC the base of the first triangle—as PA the altitude of triangle PCA is to RA the altitude of triangle RGA: Wherefore the delay of the planet in arc PC is to the delay in the equal arc RG as the area of triangle PCA is to the area of triangle RGA.

In the same way it will be demonstrated that the delay of the planet in CF —which is equal in power (*potestate*) to CP—is to the delay of the same in GH, as the area ACF is to the area AGH—where the sum of each pair of areas is equal to the sum of the [two] prior areas, and so on in order. Therefore the total area of the ellipse—which has been cut up at A into triangles—[671] is distributed among the arcs in the same proportion wherein the total periodic time has been distributed among them. Therefore the single triangles are proportionally the most exact measures of their single arcs.

A demonstration of this full equivalence is given in my *Commentaries on Mars*, Chapter 59, page 291. On that page at the line *Apsis longiorem*, one word, *erit*, has brought in great obscurity; and if you change it to *computaretur*, everything will be clearer. Although I confess that the thing is given rather obscurely there, and most of the trouble comes from the fact that there the distances are not considered as triangles, but as numbers and lines.

5. On the Equivalence of the Circular Plane and the Plane of the Ellipse in Measuring the Delays in the Arcs

Does it not seem to be a hard, unaccustomed, not to say complicated, job for the calculator to be reduced to using the plane of the ellipse in computing the time?

On the contrary, in the opinion of all the job becomes easier by the employment of the elliptical plane instead of the circular; so much so that the ancient calculus is by no means to be compared to this new one for ease.

Demonstrate the equivalence of the planes with respect to measuring time.

Then let there be repeated the figure exhibited on page 978 where we demonstrated the generation of the plane of the ellipse.

And because it has already been demonstrated that as half of the periodic time—wherein the planet traverses *PER* half of the orbit—is to the time which the planet spends in *PH* or in *PE*, precisely so is the area *PER* to the area *PHA* or *PEA*. But it was also demonstrated above that

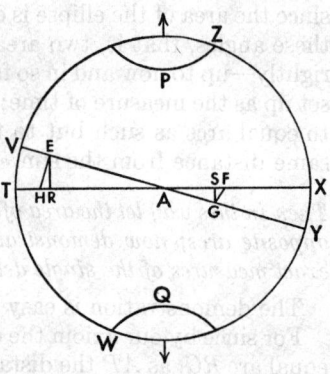

PDR : PER :: PGA : PHA :: PDA : PEA.

For they all have the same ratio as [672] *DB* to *BE*. And thus too, by alternation, as the area *PER* is to *PHA* or to *PEA*, so the area *PDR* is to *PGA* or to *PDA*. Therefore as half the periodic time of arc *PER* is to the time of arc *PH* or *PE*, so the area *PDR* is to *PGA* or *PDA*. Wherefore in these segments of the semicircular plane there is found a very exact measure of the delays which the planet makes in any given arc of the ellipse.

Now also show the convenience of this measuring.

Let the segment *PGA* be taken, and let a straight line be drawn from *G* to the centre *B*. Therefore the ratio of the sector *GBP* to the whole plane of the circle is given by the given magnitude of the arc *PG*—so that there is no need of computation. For the total periodic time and the total plane of the circle are divided into 360°—astronomical fashion. Therefore *GBA* the other part of the segment is left. But the computation of it is easy. For as *DB* the total sine is to *GF* the sine of the given arc *PG*, so is area *DBA* to area *GBA*. Therefore once the area of the great triangle *DBA* has been determined, that is, by the multiplication of half the eccentricity by the total sine and by the conversion of the result into astronomical terms, it will ever afterwards be useful.

Does not the circular plane have some other further use?

In the schema of the moon there is a special use of it in demonstrating one of its irregularities, which the moon possesses uniquely, in contrast to all the other planets. But because this Fifth Book is given over only to those properties which are common to all the planets; therefore what remains of the geometrical apparatus for carrying out the demonstration of this special use is rightly postponed to Book VI Part IV, *i.e.*, to the schema of the moon.

In what way does the old Ptolemaic astronomy measure the delays of the planet in any arc of its eccentric circle, or what does it have instead of the circular plane?

For this it uses a special circle, which has the name of "equant," [673] of which the centre would in our figures be the other focus—in the last diagram, *F*, in the next to the last, *V*; because the other focus is as far distant, towards *P* the highest apsis, from *B* the centre of the eccentric circle, as *A* the sun, towards *R* the lowest apsis, is distant from the same centre of the eccentric circle. For if a line is drawn from *V* the centre of the equant through the body of the planet, the arc of the equant intercepted between this line and *VP* the line of the apsides is set down as the measure of the time which the planet spends in the arc of its orbit.

This hypothesis seems to be more convenient for manual representations by means of the instruments called schemata: why do you not keep it, since you have already twice employed substitute quantities in place of the true?

1. Because the equant never says the truth perfectly, unless we wish to give its centre an irregular movement of libration. And in that way we should, draw away from simplicity of hypotheses, and set up an astronomy which is more complicated and laborious in practice than the astronomy of these two books, the fourth and fifth, in the explanation of causes. And with these causes once perceived, and not even believed in but merely laid down, practice afterwards becomes easy in the second part of Book v and in Book vi.

2. Because in Ptolemy the proportionality (*ratio*) of this equant is one thing in the higher planets, something else in the two lower planets, something else in the moon, and now it would be something else again in the sun. But for us the plane of the eccentric circle serves the same use in the same way in all the planets.

3. Because the equant circle is very distant from the true causes of the movements. And the plane of the [eccentric] circle represents these causes very closely, because it is of the same family as the plane of the ellipse.

Let it be understood that the same things are spoken against other equivalences, which the wonderful force of human ingenuity is accustomed to bring forward: for example, by means of a single libration of the centre of the eccentric circle in the shorter diameter of our ellipse—although the libration needs the contrary motions of two equal circles—[674] David Fabricius both saves the movements inward of the planet away from the sides (*a lateribus*) of our immovable eccentric circle and at the same time gives the apsis a movement of libration—so that now, by means of numbering continued from the apsis, which has the libration, to the planetary body, the eccentric circle itself furnishes us with a measure of time. For neither absolute regularity of movements nor perfect precision is obtained, nor is there a curtailment of labour. And the causes of the movements are hidden and denied.

But I absolutely reject the Copernican machinery, which makes two epicycles having the ratio of one to two in their movements revolve on a concentric circle. For observations bear witness that at the mean positions between the apsides the planet moves inward towards the sides. But this Copernican hypothesis by a contrary proportionality [*ratione*] makes it wander outward.[1] These small parts of the Copernican hypotheses must be completely corrected. But his general hypothesis of the annual movement of the Earth must be saved, whence the name of this teaching comes.

6. On the Regularity of the Digressions in Latitude

The calculus of latitude is not certain, is it, if there are no solid spheres, even though special threads in the planetary body take their place?

If we lay down those things which were laid down in Book iv, page 948, and

[1]See *Revolutions of the Heavenly Spheres*, Book v, Chapter iv.

which are absolutely possible and concordant, then it is absolutely necessary for the perfect plane of an ellipse to arise.

For in this diagram let *TZX* be a circle through the poles of the ellipse. Either let *A* be the sun, if *TZX* is a plane; or, if *TAX* is a hemisphere, let *A* first be the position, on the concave surface, of the lower intersection of the ellipse *TX* and *EG* the orbit of the planet, —so that the poles of the orbit are at *Z* and *W*. Let the threads of latitude point along *GA* [*dirigantur secundum* GA]; and let them have the faculty of deflecting the movement *XAT*, given by the sun, through the angle *GAX;* and during the whole circuit let the threads remain

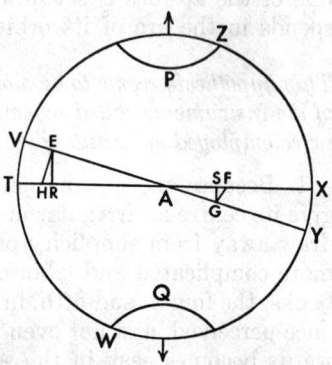

parallel. [675] It is clear that while the planet is turning at *A* the lower section, the threads stretched along *GA* will direct the planet according to the total angle, and the planet will come in a perfect plane as far as *G*, by ascending up to the plane drawn through the poles. And because now the thread at *G* points towards the sun *A* and not crosswise over the ecliptic; accordingly here the planet will not digress any farther, but *G* will be the limit: thence, gradually raised up above the plane *ZXW*, the planet will direct its thread along the line drawn from intersection *A* through the sun *A*, until the planet comes to *A*, now the upper intersection on the convex surface. Therefore just as at *A* there is the greatest angle of inclination of the thread with the ecliptic *TX*, and the angle decreases rapidly; but at *G* and *E* there is no angle of inclination of the thread with the plane [*longitudinem*] of the ecliptic, and this smallness of inclination lasts a long time; so too if out of the circuit *EAG* there is made a perfect plane, its parts at *A* have their greatest inclination with the ecliptic *TX*, and the inclination decreases quickly. But around *G* and *E* the rim of the plane —which is understood to stretch downward into the depth of the sphere or upward—extends for a long time approximately parallel to the plane of the ecliptic. Therefore if instead of the operation of the thread we employ the product itself, that is, *EAG*, as a perfect plane, the calculus will be absolutely consonant with the principles.

CONCLUSION OF THE FIRST PART OF BOOK V

Then let what has been written so far be done for geometers endowed with a keen mind, who do not think it right to admit into their calculus that which has not been confirmed by a very accurate demonstration and deduced from the natural principles of the movements.

PART TWO

ON THE ASTRONOMICAL TERMS ARISING FROM CALCULATIONS AND THE ECCENTRIC ORBIT

[676] *How is the orbit of any planet called?*

It is called by the ancient name of "eccentric," *sc.* circle. For even if the orbits

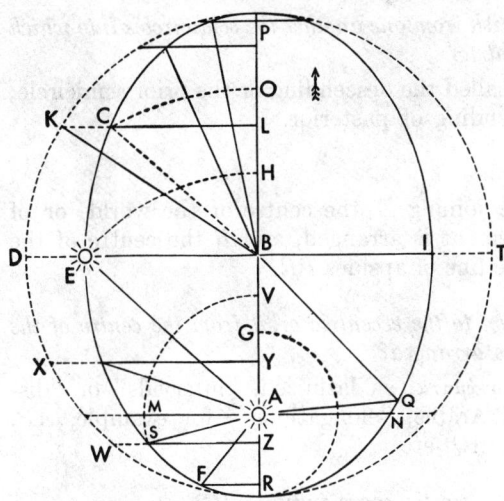

are elliptical, as *PERI* here, and have as it were two centres, *A* and *L*, which, in physical language, we call the "hearths" or "foci," and the sun itself, as centre of the world, is situated at one of those foci; nevertheless also the point midway between the foci, as *B*, is with peculiar [677] rightness called the "centre" by writers on conics. And furthermore, for the sake of measurement, a perfect circle *PDR* having its centre *B* distinct from *A* the centre of the world is circumscribed around the figure.

In astronomy, what name does PR *the longer diameter of the ellipse have?*

It is called the "line of apsides," because, since it is drawn through *A* the centre of the world and *B* the centre of the orbit, its sections with the orbit designate *P* the highest apsis and *R* the lowest.

Why are they called the highest apsis and the lowest, and what other name do they have?

The word "apsis" is taken from wheels; for the apsides are points on the eccentric, *P* the farthest away from *A* the sun and *R* the nearest to it. But in geometry the explanation of the meaning is clearer. For the word "apsis" is derived from "being tangent"; and indeed in points *P* and *R* the director circle is tangent to the elliptic orbit. The Latin translations of Arabian books express the Greek words "apsis," "apsides" by the words "aux," "auges"—as if the Arabs had changed the Greek Psi to Xi. However some one who boasts a knowledge of the Arabic language asserted to me that the word "augh" signifies altitude.

Book vi will call those points the "aphelion" and the "perihelion," in the case of the primary planets; and in the case of the moon, the "apogee" and the "perigee."

What necessity compels us to suppose, instead of the circular route of the planet believed in by the ancients, an elliptical route, i.e., one falling away from the circle, and to set up in it a longer diameter and on that longer diameter the sun?

Both of them are demonstrated from the observations and by means of a very sure demonstration in the *Commentaries on the Movements of the Planet Mars*, and they are employed in Book iv on page 862 in the diagrams and on pages 910 and 932 and 933, and also in the first part of Book v. Therefore, unless we made these hypotheses, we should never represent the observations.

[678] *By what names do we distinguish from one another the semicircles into which the line of apsides divides the eccentric?*

The one half, *PER* or *PDR*, is called the descending or the prior semicircle; the other, *RIP* or *RTP*, the ascending or posterior.

What is eccentricity?

In Greek, ἐκκεντρότης is the line joining *A* the centre of the world, or of the body around which the movement is arranged, and *B* the centre of the eccentric—namely *AB*, part of the line of apsides *PR*.

What is the name of the lines drawn to the eccentric orbit from the centre of the body around which the movement is arranged?

In Greek, they are called ἀποστήματα; as latinized, "intervals" or "distances"; in translations from the Arabic, "elongations"—for example, *AP*, *AC*, *AE*, *AM*, *AS*, *AF*, *AR*, *AN*, *AQ*, etc.

[679] *Which among these elongations are the more important?*

AP, the longer elongation, in Arabic, or the aphelial or apogeal distance; *AR*, the shorter elongation or perihelial distance or perigeal distance, in the case of the moon; and the mean elongation, which is the arithmetic mean between the longer and shorter elongation: the one which is in the descending semicircle, namely *AE*, is called the first mean elongation, and the one in the ascending semicircle, such as *AI*, the second.

What else does "mean elongation" signify?

By metonymy, it is used for those points on the orbit which are at a mean distance from the sun, such as *E* and *I*, namely those points which are at a distance of a quadrant or 90° before or after the apsides. And sometimes it is also used for the point in the zodiac which is 90° distant before or after the position in the zodiac on which the extension of the line of apsides falls.

Here we must note emphatically that it is not the extension of line *AE* of the same name which falls upon this degree of the ecliptic called the mean elongation, but rather line *BE* from the centre, or its parallel, *AM*—as being lines which make right angles with *PR* the lines of apsides.

What is the name for the difference between the mean elongation or distance and any other whatsoever?

This difference is called the "libration" of the planet, because the total libration, as in the movement of the trays of the balance, is slow in the beginning, when the planet is at its greatest distance from the sun, and in the end, when the planet is nearest the sun; it is fast in the middle.

In the diagram, since *AP* is the longest distance, and *AR* the shortest, then let *AR* be transposed to line *AP* and extended from *A* to *G*, so that the total libration can be laid before the eyes in a single line *AP* which is as it were at rest; the total libration will be *PG*, twice the eccentricity *BA*. Accordingly this libration is slow around *P* and *G*, [680] namely when the planet is either in *P* or in *R*, fast around *H*, when the planet or line *AH* has been transferred to line *AE* or *AI*.

You have said that a circle is circumscribed around the orbit for the sake of measurement. State in how many ways this circle conduces towards the measurement of that orbit.

Four ways: (1) This circle designates and divides the arcs of the elliptic orbit. For example, arc *PC* receives its name and specification from arc *PK*.

(2) The circle gives the measures of the librations of the planet and thus determines the lengths of the intervals between the planet and the sun. For example, *AC* or *AO* is determined by arc *PK* or its complement *KD*, because arc *PK* gives the magnitude of the libration *HO* which must be added to the semidiameter *AH*.

(3) The circle exhibits also the measure of the time which the planet spends in any arc of its elliptic orbit. For example, we learn through arc *PK* how long the planet moves in arc *PC*.

(4) When those things have been found, we can also investigate the angle at the sun subtended by the arc of the orbit. For example, if arc *PK* is not known, if line *AC* is unknown, angle *CAP* cannot be found.

1. Concerning Designation

In what way does the circle designate and divide the arcs of the ellipse, and by what means, and wherefore?

Since the circumference of an ellipse cannot be divided geometrically into equal parts, nor can parts into which it has been divided be designated from their number: therefore, in place of the ellipse, the circle is divided into equal parts—starting from the apsides, and from the points of division perpendiculars cutting the ellipse are drawn to the line of apsides. Therefore the arc of the circle between the aphelion and any perpendicular whatsoever supplies the name for the arc of the ellipse intercepted between the same limits and applies its number of degrees and minutes to that arc.

[681] Let arc *PK* be 50°0′, and *KL* cutting the ellipse in *C* perpendicular to *PR*. Therefore too *PC* the arc of the ellipse is said to be 50°0′.

But the name is untrue, since the arc of the ellipse is not so great—neither with reference to the circle nor with reference to the total elliptic orbit.

This causes no trouble, for there is no question of anything at present except the name; and the name is not the name of the apparent measure, but of the geometrical determination and division. And there is no need to know the true length of the arc of the ellipse as if measured with a yardstick, provided we may afterwards learn how great an angle is made at the centre of the sun by the arc of the ellipse so determined and how long the planet delays in that arc. As a matter of fact, in the first part of Book v, I demonstrate that this arc of the ellipse is as great, if not in length, at least in power.

How are these perpendiculars called which cut the ellipse?

In the circle, they are called the sines of the arcs of the circle which begin at the aphelion; in the ellipse, they are generically called ordinates, *viz.*, to the axis. For example, here *KL* is the sine of arc *KP*. *CL* is the ordinate.

But specifically, that which is drawn through the centre of the figure—as *EBI*—is called the shorter diameter or minor axis of the figure. We can employ the Greek term "diacentre." Finally, the perpendicular, such as *MAN*, which passes through the centre of the sun is without a name, although it is among the principal ones. Let it be called by the new name "dihelion."

Now what is the function of those two perpendiculars, the diacentre and the dihelion?

They divide the orbit into upper and lower parts: the diacentre, into parts which are equal but unequal in respect to time and apparent movement; the dihelion, into parts which are [682] unequal both in time and in length but which none the less appear equal as it were from the sun.

For example, *EPI* which is constituted by *EBI* is 180°, but it appears to be less than 180° by angle *EAI*. But the greater segment *MPN* cut off by line *MAN* and *MRN* the lesser segment both appear equal in magnitude to 180°.

2. CONCERNING LIBRATION

Tell how to measure and compute the librations and how to determine the intervals.

Let *PK* be an arc of the eccentric less than 90°, for example, 46°18′51″; therefore *KD* its complement will be 43°41′9″, and *BL* its sine, 69.070; and let eccentricity *AB* or half libration *PH* be 9.265, whereof *BP* is 100.000. Therefore
$$9.265 \times 69.070 = 6.399,$$
if the last five decimals are ignored; and hence the libration *OH* will be 6.399, which is to be added to *BP* or *AH* in the upper semicircle; and *AO* or its equal *AC*, namely the distance of the planet from the sun will be 106.399 (whereof the semidiameter is 100.000) which goes with arc *PK* or *PC*.

But if the arc of the eccentric is 313°41′9″, the excess over and above three quadrants or 270° will also be 43°41′9″, which gives the same sine as a multiplicand. Hence when the libration of 6.399 is produced, that same number is to be added to the upper semicircle which is an ascending semicircle.

But if the semidiameter *BP* receives a different mensuration, for example, 152.342, we shall multiply *BP* by the 1.06399 of *AC*, and (if the last five decimal places are ignored) *AC* will be 162.090 at this distance.

By means of Napier's invention, this whole operation is finished most expeditiously in a single addition. For the logarithm of the sine of arc *KD* is added to the logarithms of 9.265 the eccentricity and of 152.343 the mensuration proposed; and the sum produced as a logarithm will give a libration of 9.748 to be added to the distance 152.342.

[683] So next, if arc *PW* is greater than 90°, viz., 133°39′7″; *DW* its excess over and above 90° is 43°39′7″; and its sine or logarithm, together with the two aforesaid beginnings, will give a libration of 9.777 to be subtracted from 152.342, as in the semicircle below the diacentre: hence the corresponding interval *AS* will be 142.565.

The same thing will hold, if the arc of the eccentric is 226°20′53″. For its complement with respect to 270° will be 43°39′7″—as great in the ascending semicircle as was *DW* in the descending semicircle.

Review the principal moments in the libration.

1. When the planet begins to move away from the apsis, then simultaneously the libration commences—that is, the planet, which had just before finished its ascent away from the sun, begins to descend towards the sun.

2. When the planet is 60° away from the apsis, then the libration is equal to half the eccentricity.

3. When the planet has traversed 90° of the orbit from the apsis, then half of the libration has been completed, so that the planet is at a distance from the sun of a semidiameter of the eccentric. For example, if *PD* is 90°, then *AE* equals *BD*.

4. When the planet has traversed 120° from the apsis, three quarters of the libration have been completed.

5. When the planet is at the lowest apsis, then it is nearest to the sun and has completed the total libration. The order through the ascending semicircle is the reverse.

6. If the planet has traversed equal arcs on the eccentric, on one occasion from the aphelion, on the other occasion from the perihelion, then the sum of those two distances from the sun is equal to the diameter. For example, if a straight line is drawn from *B* to *Q*, then the sum of *CA* and *AQ* is equal to *RP*.

3. CONCERNING THE DELAY OF THE PLANET IN ANY ARC

What does the word "anomaly" mean?

Although, properly speaking, anomaly—irregularity—is an affect of the movement of the planet, nevertheless astronomers employ this [684] word for the very movement in which the irregularity is present. And since the following three measurable things come together in the movement: the space to be traversed, the temporal delay in the space, and the apparent magnitude of the space; the word "anomaly" is to be applied to all three. And again, with reference to time, the use of the word is twofold. For, *primo*, Ptolemy employs it for the total time which the planet spends while its total irregularity returns to its starting point, and he counts as many anomalies as there are periodic returns such as these.

Secundo, parts of this total time are commonly called anomalies, according as Ptolemy said a movement was a complete part of the *full* anomaly.

Then how many anomalies are there as parts of a whole?

Three anomalies are denominated in any position of the planet whatsoever: (1) mean anomaly; (2) anomaly of the eccentric; and (3) the corrected anomaly.

What is the mean anomaly?

It is the interval of time which the planet spends in any arc of its orbit—beginning at the apsis: this interval is reduced to degrees and minutes, whereof the total anomaly is equivalent to 360° by mathematical or astronomical enumeration.

Why is it called mean?

Not from being, as it were, a mean proportional between its related anomalies, as will be remarked a little later; but it is called mean in imitation of the ancient astronomy which usually speaks of the mean anomaly instead of the mean—*i.e.*, uniform—movement of anomaly, because the time thus reduced to mathematical terms indicates, by means of the number of degrees and minutes, how great an arc of its circle the planet would have been going to traverse, if during that whole time which we call the mean anomaly it had moved in a uniform movement which was a mean between the slowest and the fastest movement.

How should the mean anomaly be determined or measured in these diagrams, according to the ancient astronomy?

If the distance *BL* equal to the eccentricity *AB* is marked off in the line of apsides *BP*, as was said in Part I of Book V; the mean anomaly, according to the ancient astronomy, would be the arc of the equant circle described around *L*—the arc which progresses eastwards and is intercepted by two lines drawn from *L*, the one through apsis *P* and the other through the planetary body *C*. Or it would be the angle between those lines at *L*, or the difference between that angle and 360°. For example, in this case if *C* were the planet, then angle *PLC* could be used instead of the mean anomaly approximately.

Define the line of mean movement and the mean position of the planet, according to this ancient hypothesis of the equant.

It would be the line drawn from the centre of the sun to the sphere of the fixed stars parallel to the line which has been drawn from the centre of the equant, or from the other focus of the ellipse, through the planetary body. And either one of these lines in the sphere of the fixed stars would indicate the mean position of the planet. In the diagram, if *C* were the planet and *AM* were parallel to *LC*, then *AM* would be the line of its mean movement.

If therefore in this new formulation of astronomy, no equant circle is expressed, then in terms of what other magnitude will the mean anomaly be computed or measured?

In terms of the area comprehended between the arc of the circle which designates and determines the proposed arc of the orbit and between the two straight lines which connect the extremities of the arc with the centre of the sun. For example, if the proposed position of the planet is *C*, then if a line be drawn from *C* perpendicular to *PR* which will cut circle *PD* in *K*, and if *PA* and *KA* are joined, area *PKA* is the measure of the mean anomaly, whereof the area of the whole circle is equivalent to 360°.

[686] *Tell how to compute the mean anomaly or the amount of time which the planet spends in the proposed arc.*

Again, let eccentricity *AB* be 9.265, whereof the semidiameter *BP* is 100.000. First of all, we must take the area of the greatest triangle which has a right angle at *B* and an altitude *BD*. The multiplication of this area by half *AB* will give a product of 4632.50000. The value of this area *DAB* is to be expressed by the number of seconds, whereof the total area of the circle *PDT* is 360° or 21,600′ or 1,296,000″. Therefore, since if *BP* is 100.000, the area of the circle by calculation is 314,159.26536, area *DAB* is 19,110″.

Now let arc *PC* be given by arc *PK* which designates it; and let it be 46° 18′51″. Therefore the sine of *PK*, namely *KL* the altitude of triangle *BKA*, multiplied by the value of the greatest triangle—and the last five decimals cut off from the product—will give triangle *AKB* a value of 3819″, which is 3°50′19″. But sector *KBP* is equal in value to the number of degrees which have been given in arc *PK*, namely 46°18′51″. Therefore by the addition of the areas, *PKA* is 50°9′10,″ and the mean anomaly is of that magnitude.

In this way, the area of the additosubtractive triangle (*trianguli aequatorii*) is to be added, as long as the sector or arc is smaller than a semicircle; but if the arc is greater than a semicircle, the area is to be subtracted.

State the rule for the relation between these triangles.

Any two triangles equally distant from the vertices, the one from the highest apsis, and the other from the lowest apsis, are of equal magnitude. For example, if arcs *PK* and *RW* are equal, areas *BKA* and *BWA* will also be equal.

What is the anomaly of the eccentric?

It is the arc of the eccentric circle measured eastwards and intercepted between the line of apsides and the perpendicular drawn to that line through the planetary or through any proposed [687] point on the orbit. For example, with *C* as the proposed point on the orbit or with the planet revolving at that point, if through *C* perpendicular to *PAR* line *KCL* is drawn cutting the circle in *K*, arc *PK* will be the anomaly of the eccentric.

In what sense is anomaly of the eccentric used?

Here too the phrase "of movement" is understood [between "anomaly" and "of the eccentric"]. For although, according to the figure, in arc *PK* of the circle no irregularity or anomaly is apparent: nevertheless the movement of the planet in orbit *PC* is truly anomalous or irregular in three respects: first, by reason of its elliptic figure which bends with unequal curvature according to the difference of its parts and is unequally distant from the centre of the figure; second, by reason of its speed, which is not the same in all parts of its orbit; thirdly, by reason of its apparent movement as seen from the sun, because equal parts of the orbit subtend unequal angles at the sun. Therefore since the arc *PK* concurs in all those determinations, as has been said: wherefore with the same right wherewith the ancient astronomy introduced the equant circle and by means of that computed the mean anomaly, we ourselves circumscribe an eccentric circle *PK* around the real orbit *PC* and by means of that compute the anomaly of the eccentric, employing something uniform in measuring that which is not uniform.

And indeed in the ancient astronomy the equant circle seduced the physicists into imagining that either the circle or at any rate the movement was real: but here no one can be seduced, since it is apparent to the eyes that *PC* the true orbit of the planet coincides with this artificial circle *PK* only in the two points *P* and *R*, the apsides, and throughout the remaining tract it betakes itself, within the embrace of the eccentric, towards the centre of the figure.

What is the corrected anomaly?

It is the arc of the great circle in the plane of the ecliptic which is marked out by the continuation of the plane of the planetary orbit: this arc is measured eastwards from the position of the apsis to the very position of the planet or the apparent position of any other point on the orbit. Or—which amounts to the same thing—it is the angle which any arc of the true planetary orbit subtends or which is formed by the two aforesaid lines at the centre of the sun, or the difference between that angle and 360°.

For example, if the planet is in *C*, the corrected anomaly is angle *PAC*. And if the planet is at *Q*, then the corrected anomaly is made up of the two right angles *PAM* and *MAR* and also angle *RAQ*. But if with centre *A* a circle of any magnitude whatsoever be described, and thus even a circle in the sphere of the fixed stars, the arc of this circle measured eastwards from AP as far as AC or continued to AG will also be called the corrected anomaly.

Why is it called "corrected" [coaequata]?

Practitioners used to call it the corrected movement of anomaly or simply the corrected anomaly, not as if the irregular movement assumed had been corrected in such a way as to become a regular [aequalis] movement, but with a plainly contrary meaning: Now since in the beginning a time or portion of the periodic time is laid down, and since this time, as reduced to astronomical terms, indicates how great an arc of its circle the planet would have been going to traverse within this interval of time, if it had been moving with a uniform movement: so it is the office of the astronomer to show how much of the really irregular apparent movement of the planet corresponds to this time and this fictitious uniform movement. Therefore "corrected movement" means the same thing as movement to which an additosubtraction has been applied and which has been converted to an apparent movement, namely by putting on the irregularity which the appearances introduce into it: on account of this irregularity the total period is called the anomaly.

Therefore since you have distinguished these three anomalies and formulated them by means of a fictitious eccentric circle circumscribed around the orbit: I ask whether the true orbit of the planet could not be put to the same use.

Although there is no need, nevertheless that is possible on account of their equipollence. For, as has been said in Book v, Part i, the area PCA measures the time and hence the mean anomaly; and anyone who wishes to can understand the anomaly of the eccentric circle also by arc PC. But angle PAC has even before this been called the corrected anomaly.

How are these three related anomalies distinguished in magnitude?

The number of degrees and minutes of the anomaly of the eccentric is always a mean between the others. But before a semicircle has been completed, the so-called mean anomaly is always the greatest of the three, and the corrected, the least; but after the semicircle, the so-called mean is the least in magnitude and the corrected the greatest.

4. CONCERNING THE ANGLE AT THE SUN

Tell how to compute the corrected anomaly or the angle at the sun.

There are various modes; but the most compendious is the one which [690] employs the interval between the planet and the sun. For we need that for other uses too.

Now there are three cases of this mode. For either the planet is above the diacentre, or below the dihelion, or between the diacentre and the dihelion.

1. Therefore first let the planet be above the diacentre DBT, viz., in C; and let PK the anomaly of the eccentric be $47°42'20''$, and let LB the sine of its complement KD be 67.277, so that the libration of the planet will be 6.233. By the addition of 6.233 to BP let AC the interval between the planet and the sun be exactly 106.233 in terms whereof BP is 100.000. Accordingly let this same LB the sine of the complement be added to the 9.265 of eccentricity BA, in such

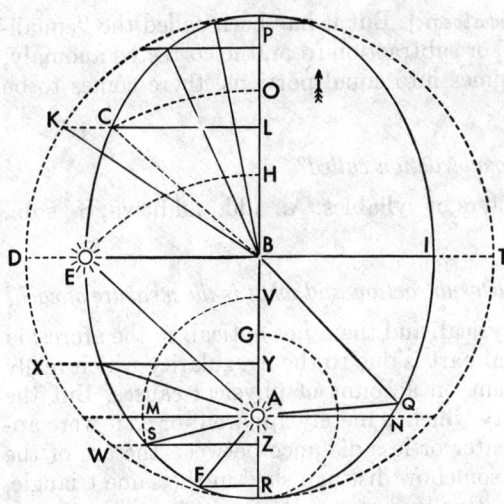

fashion that LA the other side of right triangle CAL is 76.542. Accordingly if LA is divided by CA and five ciphers are added, the quotient of 72.051 as a sine shows the arc to be 46°5′48″, which is equal to angle LCA, whereof the complement, which is 43°54′12″, is the required angle LAC or PAC.

If you subtract the logarithm of half the divisor from the logarithm of half the dividend, the logarithm of the same sine or arc remains.

2. Secondly, let the planet be below the dihelion MAN, viz., in S; and let PW be the anomaly of the eccentric and DW its excess over and above 90°. Accordingly in the same way as above, the libration found by means of BZ the sine of that arc is to be subtracted from the radius, so that the exact interval AS may be manifest. So too the eccentricity BA is now to be subtracted from sine BZ, so that AZ the other side of the right triangle remains. Then once more, if the number of side AZ—to which five ciphers have been added—is divided by side AS, the quotient will be the sine of angle ASZ, to which angle MAS is equal, which is the excess of the required angle PAS over and above angle PAM which is right or 90°.

3. Thirdly, let the planet be between DBT and MAN. Accordingly let PX be the anomaly of the eccentric and DX its excess over and above 90°, and BY the sine whereby the subtractive libration is computed, since the sine lies below B. But since the sine is less than eccentricity BA, it is to be subtracted from this eccentricity, so that YA remains. Accordingly we must operate on YA and on the exact interval, as in the first case.

[691] *What do you call the eccentric position of the planet?*

That point in the zodiac on which there falls the straight line drawn from the centre of the sun through the planetary body.

What is the "equalization" [aequatio] or "additosubtraction"[prosthaphaeresis], and what is the reason for the name?

It is the difference between the number of degrees and minutes of the mean anomaly and the degrees and minutes of the corrected anomaly. Or, according to the old astronomical formulation, it is the angle at the centre of the sun and its measure, the arc of the great circle in the sphere of the fixed stars intercepted between the lines of the mean and of the apparent movement of the planet. Now since in one semicircle this angle is to be subtracted [from the mean movement] and in the other semicircle it is to be added to the mean movement, so that the movement may be corrected: hence it has been called by the compound name "additosubtraction" [προσθαφαίρεσις]. But it has been called the "equalization" because by its addition to, or subtraction from, the corrected anomaly, which divides unequal arcs and times into equal portions, there comes to be the mean and uniform anomaly.

By what epithet or title is the additosubtraction called?

By two words or their index letters or syllables: A., add., additive; S., sub., subtractive.

How many parts are there to the additosubtraction and what is the measure of each?

There are two parts, the one physical, and the other optical, to the aforesaid additosubtraction. For the physical part is due to the irregularity which really accedes to the planetary movement on account of physical causes. But the optical part is due to an irregularity which is merely apparent or as it were apparent, *i.e.*, on account of the greater or less distance between the arc of the orbit and the sun. Both parts are somehow distinguished in the same triangle, which is hence called additosubtractive [*aequatorium*].

For if A and B the termini of the eccentricity are joined to [692] the planetary body C, the physical part of the additosubtraction finds its measure in area BAC —or by equipollence, in area BAK; while the optical part of the additosubtraction would be equal to angle BCA, if that were computed: angle BKA, which is easier to compute, is always slightly less than angle BCA.

What use is there for this additosubtraction?

In this formulation of astronomy made new, there is no necessary or very great need of the total additosubtraction composed of both elements. For the anomalies are not determined through this additosubtraction; but on the contrary through the comparison of the corrected anomaly—which we first compute—with the mean anomaly, we elicit the additosubtraction, if at any time we wish to use it.

But three distinct anomalies are laid down in the tables. For, first, the anomaly of the eccentric is placed on the left, according to the order of the whole degrees, from 1° to 180°; and that is done [693] because the anomaly of the eccentric being given becomes the starting-point for computing the others, and also the distance or interval between the planet and the sun. Secondly, there is found under the same head and as corresponding to this anomaly of the eccentric, the physical part of the additosubtraction or the value of the area of the additosubtractive triangle in degrees and minutes and seconds: and from this inclusion of the anomaly of the eccentric together with the physical part of the additosubtraction beneath the same head, we understand that the sum of the two constitutes the corresponding mean anomaly. Thirdly, to the right of this and in a separate column is placed the corrected anomaly corresponding to the arc. If anyone now wishes to learn the composite additosubtraction, let him subtract the corrected anomaly from the mean anomaly found next to it or from the sum of the anomaly of the eccentric and the physical part of the additosubtraction; and the remainder will be the required additosubtraction, which in the descending semicircle is called subtractive, and in the ascending, additive.

Nevertheless state how these parts of the additosubtraction are related, if they are compared with one another.

The smaller the eccentricity, the nearer they approach to equality: in the upper semicircle however, above the diacentre, the optical part is slightly smaller than the physical part; but in the lower semicircle, below the diacentre, it is slightly greater.

For example, in the accompanying diagram, let A be the sun and PAR the

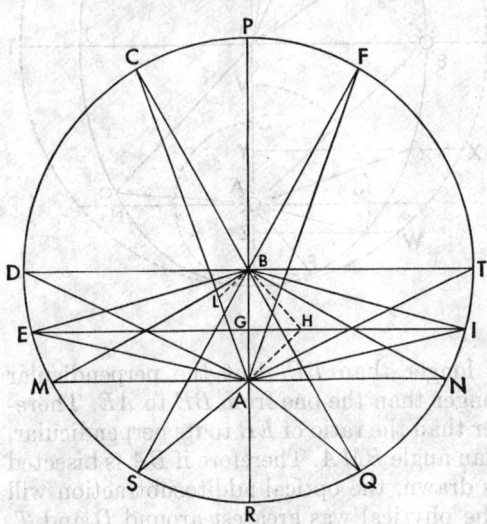

line of apsides, and DBT and MAN are at right angles to PAR; and DPT the upper semi-circle, or so to speak, and DRT the lower semicircle. In the upper semicircle let the additosub-tractive triangles be BCA and BFA, and BSA and BQA in the lower. Therefore since the areas of the triangles are the measure of the physical part of the ad-ditosubtraction, while the angles at C, F, S, and Q are the meas-ure of the optical part: then surely the upper areas are greater parts, while the lower areas are lesser parts, of the area of 360° of the total circle than those angles of theirs are of four right angles or 360°. For the cen-tres C and S and CB and SB as the lengths of the semidiameters, let there be described the arc BL ending at CA and the arc BH ending at SA continued: these arcs measure angles C and S. But areas CBL and SBH are equivalent to these same arcs. Therefore if these areas were the optical [694] parts of the ad-ditosubtractions, the two parts of one additosubtraction would be equal. But not CBL but the greater area CBA is the measure of the optical part; and thus, in the lower semicircle, not SBH but the smaller area SBA in the lower. There-fore in the upper semicircle the physical part exceeds, and the optical part in the lower.

Where is the composite additosubtraction greatest?

Of the parts, the prior one, the physical, is greatest at D and T, the extremi-ties of the diacentre, because the altitude of no triangle can be greater than BD or BT, which is the semidiameter in the circle and even in the ellipse, the longest of the ordinates. The posterior part, the optical, would be greatest, if the orbit were circular, at M and N the extremities of the dihelion: for there the line drawn from centre B perpendicular to the straight line MA would be the longest, but that line is the sine of angle BMA the optical part, whereof BM is the sine of the total additosubtraction. For upon EA, a higher line, there falls from B a shorter perpendicular than BA.

But because the orbit of the planet is elliptical, accordingly the optical part of the additosubtraction is [695] greatest between M and D, and thus between N and T. For, first, angle BMA is greater than angle ADB, because both are right triangles upon the same base, but altitude DB is greater than altitude MA, namely the shorter diameter is greater than any other ordinate whatsoever. Second, if points B and I are marked at the centres of arcs DM and TN or thereabouts, angles AEB and AIB will again be greater than AMB and ANB. For, of all the lines drawn from centre B to the orbit, BD is the shortest; and the farther away the other lines are, the longer they

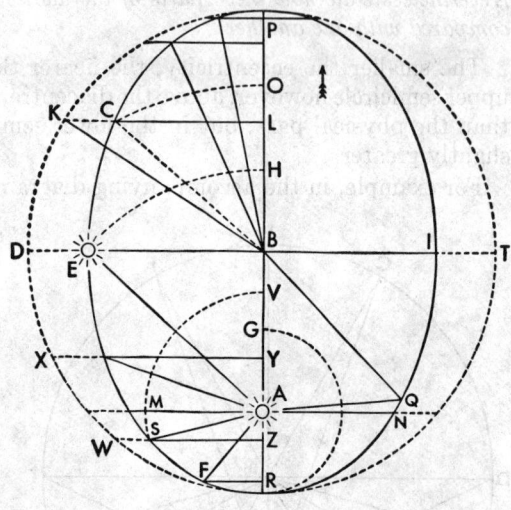

are. Therefore BM is perceptibly longer than BE. But the perpendicular from B to AM is not perceptibly longer than the one from BE to AE. Therefore the ratio of MB to BA is greater than the ratio of EB to its perpendicular. And so angle BEA is also greater than angle BMA. Therefore if BA is bisected at G, and the perpendicular EGI is drawn, the optical additosubtraction will be greatest around E and I. But the physical was greatest around D and T. Therefore the composite additosubtraction is greatest at the mean position between D and E and between T and I.

You have taught us how to compute the mean anomaly and the corrected anomaly from the assumption of anomaly of the eccentric: but practice more frequently requires us, given the mean anomaly, as from the time given, to find the others: teach this too.

Here there is no direct way; but he who wishes to compute this without tables must apply the rule of suppositions, namely by supposing that the anomaly of the eccentric—PK, in the accompanying diagram—is of this or of that magnitude, and upon that assumption, compute his mean anomaly PKA. For if PKA turns out to be as great as it was given to be, then the supposition as to PK the anomaly of the eccentric will be right. But if it does not turn out as great, then the supposition is to be corrected in view of the result, and the work done over again.

Could you by way of example teach a convenient method, lest through unfamiliarity one err too much in mistaken suppositions?

Then let the foregoing example be used again, and let the said mean anomaly [696] or area PKA be $50°9'10''$. It is manifest that, if the area of triangle KBA were known, the remaining area KBP would have the same number of degrees as its arc PK; and hence, if the value of KBA is subtracted from PKA, the remainder will be PK the anomaly of the eccentric. Therefore since PKA

is greater than *PKB*, the sine of arc *PX* will be smaller than the sine of 50°
9'10", and therefore smaller than 76.775. In our first supposition, let this sine
be 70.000 for the sake of ease in multiplication.

Accordingly if this sine is multiplied by the value of triangle *DBA*—which
was 11,910" in the preceding example—and the last five decimal places are
cut off, the product *BKA* will be 8,337" or 2°18'57". Add these 2°18'57" to the
arc of sine 70.000, which is 44°25'. The area *PKA* will be 46°44'. This is too
small, for it is deficient in 3°25', since it ought to be 50°9', the quantity given.

Accordingly, in the second supposition, let a greater sine be supposed, by
the addition of the deficiency of 3°25' to the 44°25' of the arc previously supposed, so that *PC* will be about 47°50'; its sine is approximately 74.000, which
I choose for the sake of ease in calculation again. The multiplication of 74.000
by 11,910" makes *PKA* to be 7'56" greater, namely 2°26'53". Add this to the
PK of the second supposition, namely to the 47°44'6" of *PKB*. Arc *PKA* will
be 50°10'59"; and there will be an excess of 1'49" over the required 50°9'10".

And so we understand that this very small excess is to be subtracted from
the third supposition of *PK*, and the remainder will be the required anomaly
of the eccentric or *PK* will be equal to 47°42'17". It is possible to prove this.
For the sine of this arc is 73.969, and the multiplication of that by 11,910"
gives 2°26'50" for *KBA*. And the addition of that to 47°42'17" gives 50°9'7",
which is imperceptibly different from the requisite 50°9'10".

5. On the Digression of the Planets Away from the Ecliptic

What is understood by the name "orbit"?

Properly speaking, it is that line which the planet describes around the sun

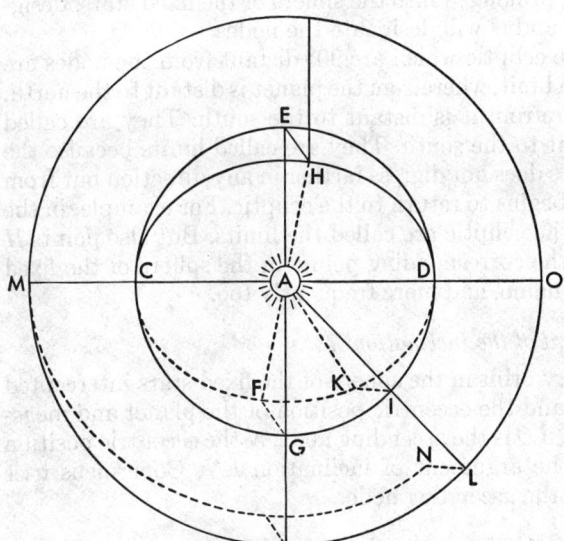

by means of the centre of
its body. For example, in
the diagram, if *ECGD* is a
part of the plane of the
ecliptic, *HCFD* will be the
orbit.

But in a secondary sense,
it is understood to be the
[697] great circle wherein
the plane of the orbit continued cuts the sphere of
the fixed stars. For example, here it is section *MN*
which has been made by
plane *CAK* continued.

*What do you call the "in-
clination of the planet" or
"of any point in its orbit,"
and what is the "circle of
inclination"?*

Properly speaking, plan-
ets or points do not have an inclination, but lines or planes do. But because
those planes are circumscribed around the orbits of the planets, and because

the lines of movement of the planets are understood as having been described in those planes: in common usage these words have been transferred to the planets themselves, for the sake of brevity in speaking.

Therefore since that which below, in Book vi, will be called latitude, participates in that adventitious or optical irregularity—which is the second thing we will investigate—wherefore, in order that things which are distinct may also be distinguished by their names, let the real digression of the planet from the ecliptic be called, not latitude, but inclination. Now it is defined as being the arc of the great circle, in the sphere of the fixed stars, described around the sun, [698] perpendicular to the ecliptic and called the circle of inclination, which arc is intercepted between the ecliptic and the eccentric position of the planet. Or, it is the angle at the sun which this arc measures.

In the diagram, if A is the sun, $FKDHC$ the orbit, and MLO the ecliptic, the inclination of point K will be angle KAI or NAL or its arc NL described around the sun A.

What do you call "nodes," and what, "limits"?

The nodes are the two points on the ecliptic wherein it is cut by the plane of the orbit continued. In Greek, σύνδεσμοι, because in them different routes, the apparent route of the sun and that of the planet, are knotted together. The one is "the ascending node," where the planet leaves the southern hemisphere and turns northward; the other "the descending node," which transfers the planet to the south—the words "ascending" and "descending" having been accommodated to our hemisphere, as that in which the first founders of astronomy lived. For example, if the plane of the orbit and the plane of the ecliptic coincide in line CAD, which, on being prolonged into the sphere of the fixed stars, designates the ecliptic section, M and O will designate the nodes.

[699] But the points on the ecliptic which are 90° distant from the nodes are called the limits: the northern limit, wherefrom the planet is distant to the north, and the southern limit, wherefrom it is distant to the south. They are called limits, wherefrom it is distant to the south. They are called limits because the planet arriving at those points does not digress farther in any direction but from that place turns around and begins to return to the ecliptic. For example, in the diagram points E and G on the ecliptic are called the limits. But also points H and F on the real orbit and the corresponding points in the sphere of the fixed stars, are called by the same name, and more frequently too.

What do you call "the argument of the inclination"?

It is the arc of the planetary orbit in the sphere of the fixed stars intercepted between the ascending node and the eccentric position of the planet and measured eastwards. For example, if O is the ascending node, N the eccentric position of the planet, OMN will be the argument of inclination LN. Copernicus uses the northern limit instead of the ascending node.

The greatest inclination of the limit for any given planet is not the same throughout all the ages, is it?

According to the physical principles employed in Book iv, of itself it is unchangeable. But on account of the dislocation of the ecliptic—concerning which I shall speak in Book vii—it can change *per accidens*.

How is the inclination of the planet computed?

No differently from the way in which the declination of a point on the ecliptic was computed in Book III. If the sine of the greatest inclination is multipled by the sine of the argument of the inclination, and the last five decimal places are cut off from the product, the sine of the inclination will be given. See the method followed on folium 245 *et seqq.* If instead of the sines of the arcs you employ their logarithms, the multiplication will be converted to simple addition.

What is the eccentric position of the planet on the ecliptic?

That point on the ecliptic wherein it is cut by the circle of inclination drawn through the eccentric position [700] in the simple sense. For example, if the eccentric position—in the simple sense—of the planet at K is N and NL is the circle of inclination, and angles NLM and NLO are right, L will be the eccentric position of the planet on the ecliptic. It is not called the ecliptic position simply, because it also involves the second irregularity, the matter of Book VI; but the word "eccentric" is added in order for us to understand that it is a question of that position which is determined on the ecliptic by the eccentric alone, without the introduction of the great sphere, whereof I shall speak in Book VI.

What is the eccentric longitude of the planet held to be?

The arc of the ecliptic measured eastwards from the beginning of the Ram to the circle of inclination of the planet or its eccentric position on the ecliptic. It is called the eccentric longitude, not because it is measured on the eccentric but because the eccentric causes it.

What is meant by "the reduction to the ecliptic"?

The small arc which is equal to the difference between the argument of the inclination and the eccentric longitude—that is, the difference between the two arcs, one on the orbit and the other on the ecliptic, beginning at the common node and ending at the circle of inclination. For example, in this case it is the difference between MN and ML.

How is it computed?

Not otherwise than on page 255, Book III, the difference between the right ascension and the corresponding arc on the ecliptic is computed. For if the sine of the complement of the greatest inclination is multiplied by the tangent of the argument of the inclination, and the last five decimal places are cut away from the product, the tangent of the argument of the reduction will be given.

Or else: the antilogarithm of the greatest inclination is added to the mesologarithm of the argument, and thus the sum will be the mesologarithm of the argument of the reduction.

A compendious and more useful method, even for the ascension, is as follows. The greatest reduction around 45° from the node, if multiplied by the sine of twice any arc, and the last five decimals cut off, constitute the required reduction for the arc taken simply.

[701] *How is this reduction to be employed, and in relation to what?*

When the planet is progressing from the nodes to the limits, the reduction is to be subtracted from the argument of the inclination; it is to be added, when the planet is progressing from the limits to the nodes; then the result, if added to the ascending node, constitutes the eccentric longitude of the position of the planet.

What do you call "the foreshortening"?

It is the particle of the distance of the planet from the centre of the sun which corresponds to the sagitta of the inclination of the planet in the same ratio in which the total interval corresponds to the total sine.

Let *A* be the sun, and *P* and *Q* the poles of the ecliptic. Let *TAX* represent the plane of the ecliptic and *EAG* the plane of the orbit. Let the planet now be at *E* or *G* and with *A* as centre and intervals *AE*, *AG* let the arcs *EH* and *GF* be drawn; and from *E* and *G* let the perpendiculars *ER* and *GS* be dropped upon *TX*. *HR* and *SF* will be the foreshortenings.

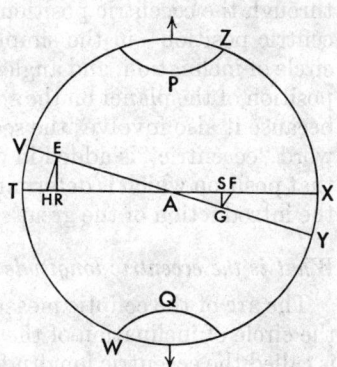

What is the foreshortened distance?

It is the straight line in the plane of the ecliptic between the centre of the sun and the perpendicular from the centre of the planetary body. In the diagram, if the planet is at *E* or *G*, then *AR* or *AS* is the foreshortened distance.

How is the foreshortened distance computed?

The assumed distance, expressed in the numbers of the measurement proper to each planet, is multipled by the sine of the complement of the inclination of the assumed distance, and the last five decimal places are removed from the product. Or, the logarithm [702] of the distance is added to the antilogarithms of the proper inclination, and the sum is the logarithm which is the index of the foreshortened distance.

Where is the distance foreshortened the most?

Around the limits, and more around the limit which is nearer the aphelion. For example, if *V* and *Y* are the limits, and thus *Z* and *W* are the poles of the orbit, and *V* is nearer the aphelion than *Y*, then *HR* will be longer than *FS* and will be the longest of all.

6. On the Movement of the Apsides and Nodes

How do you define the movement of the apsis among the primary planets?

It is the arc of the orbit in the sphere of the fixed stars intercepted between that point on the orbit which is at the same distance from the moving node as a fixed point on the ecliptic—*viz.*, the beginning of the Ram, or even the first star of the Ram—and the position of the highest apsis, and measured eastwards.

What kind of movement is this movement of the apsides?

It is set down as being uniform, (1) on account of its unbelievable slowness whereby the astronomers are impeded to such an extent that they cannot precisely investigate this movement in its single parts; (2) because we have an instance of regularity in one planet, where the period of the apsis of this physical movement, which we touched upon in Book IV, page 945, as resting upon mere conjectures, cannot be prejudicial to this regularity at all, although in virtue of them it seems that this movement can be made irregular. But more about this in Book VI, in connection with the single planets.

What is to be understood by the movement of the nodes in the primary planets, or what is the longitude of the node?

The movement of the node is the arc on the ecliptic measured westwards [703] from a fixed point on it—namely, either from the beginning of the Ram or from the position of the first star of the Ram—to the position of the ascending node. But if the measurement is made eastwards, then this arc too can be called the longitude of the node.

What kind of movement is this movement of the nodes?

Although it is reasonable that even the movement of this point is uniform of itself, nevertheless it seems that some irregularity is present in it *per accidens*, on account of the dislocation of the ecliptic, with which Book VII is concerned.

What figures do the movement of the nodes and limits describe?

The nodes proceed along the great circle of the ecliptic, while the limits of the orbit, in so far as their inclination is assumed to remain unchangeable, proceed in circles parallel to the ecliptic or to that circle with reference to which their inclination is unchangeable.

In order to aid the understanding, their movements can be represented by a

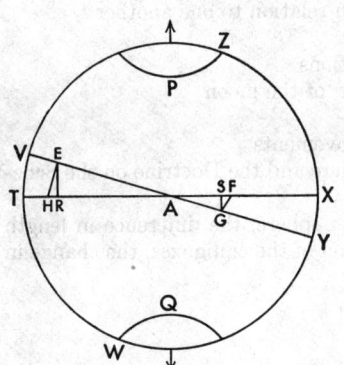

not absurd picture [of the movements] of the poles, provided we remember that, physically speaking, there is no need of the poles. For example, in the accompanying diagram, let the orbit be *VY*—by the continuation of the plane to the sphere of the fixed stars—and let its poles *Z* and *W* move in small circles around *P* and *Q* the poles of the ecliptic *TX*. Therefore in what direction away from *P* pole *Z* moves at any time, the limit *V* moves in this same direction away from point *T* on the ecliptic, and so does the limit *Y* away from point *X* on the ecliptic; and the circuit of *Z* in the small circle, which is parallel to *TX* in the same direction is followed by the limit *V* in northern parallel which is as much greater [than the small circle] as it is nearer to *TX*; and similarly *Y*, in the southern parallel. For the following six points will always be found in the great circle of inclination: *Z* and *W* the poles of the orbit, *P* and *Q* the poles of the ecliptic, and *V* and *Y* the limits of the orbit.

Accordingly, up to now we have been concerned with the definitions of the terms having to do with the planetary orbit and the eccentric circle circumscribed around it. Since they are common to all the five planets, they have been put ahead in Book v. However, we shall teach their employment, with respect to the single planets, in Book vi, which follows[1].

THE END OF BOOK FIVE, THE SECOND BOOK ON THE DOCTRINE OF THE SCHEMATA OR OF CELESTIAL PHYSICS

Johannes Kepler

THE HARMONIES OF
THE WORLD

CONTENTS

BOOK FIVE

BOOK FIVE

Concerning the very perfect harmony of the celestial movements, and the genesis of eccentricities and the semidiameters, and the periodic times from the same.

After the model of the most correct astronomical doctrine of today, and the hypothesis not only of Copernicus but also of Tycho Brahe, whereof either hypotheses are today publicly accepted as most true, and the Ptolemaic as outmoded.

I commence a sacred discourse, a most true hymn to God the Founder, and I judge it to be piety, not to sacrifice many hecatombs of bulls to Him and to burn incense of innumerable perfumes and cassia, but first to learn myself, and afterwards to teach others too, how great He is in wisdom, how great in power, and of what sort in goodness. For to wish to adorn in every way possible the things that should receive adornment and to envy no thing its goods—this I put down as the sign of the greatest goodness, and in this respect I praise Him as good that in the heights of His wisdom He finds everything whereby each thing may be adorned to the utmost and that He can do by his unconquerable power all that he has decreed.

GALEN, on the Use of Parts. BOOK III

PROEM

[268] As regards that which I prophesied two and twenty years ago (especially that the five regular solids are found between the celestial spheres), as regards that of which I was firmly persuaded in my own mind before I had seen Ptolemy's *Harmonies*, as regards that which I promised my friends in the title of this fifth book before I was sure of the thing itself, that which, sixteen years ago, in a published statement, I insisted must be investigated, for the sake of which I spent the best part of my life in astronomical speculations, visited Tycho Brahe, [269] and took up residence at Prague: finally, as God the Best and Greatest, Who had inspired my mind and aroused my great desire, prolonged my life and strength of mind and furnished the other means through the liberality of the two Emperors and the nobles of this province of Austria-on-the-Anisana: after I had discharged my astronomical duties as much as sufficed, finally, I say, I brought it to light and found it to be truer than I had even hoped, and I discovered among the celestial movements the full nature of harmony, in its due measure, together with all its parts unfolded in Book III—not in that mode wherein I had conceived it in my mind (this is not last in my joy) but in a very different mode which is also very excellent and very perfect. There took place in this intervening time, wherein the very laborious reconstruction of the movements held me in suspense, an extraordinary augmentation of my desire and incentive for the job, a reading of the *Harmonies* of Ptolemy, which had

been sent to me in manuscript by John George Herward, Chancellor of Bavaria, a very distinguished man and of a nature to advance philosophy and every type of learning. There, beyond my expectations and with the greatest wonder, I found approximately the whole third book given over to the same consideration of celestial harmony, fifteen hundred years ago. But indeed astronomy was far from being of age as yet; and Ptolemy, in an unfortunate attempt, could make others subject to despair, as being one who, like Scipio in Cicero, seemed to have recited a pleasant Pythagorean dream rather than to have aided philosophy. But both the crudeness of the ancient philosophy and this exact agreement in our meditations, down to the last hair, over an interval of fifteen centuries, greatly strengthened me in getting on with the job. For what need is there of many men? The very nature of things, in order to reveal herself to mankind, was at work in the different interpreters of different ages, and was the finger of God—to use the Hebrew expression; and here, in the minds of two men, who had wholly given themselves up to the contemplation of nature, there was the same conception as to the configuration of the world, although neither had been the other's guide in taking this route. But now since the first light eight months ago, since broad day three months ago, and since the sun of my wonderful speculation has shone fully a very few days ago: nothing holds me back. I am free to give myself up to the sacred madness, I am free to taunt mortals with the frank confession that I am stealing the golden vessels of the Egyptians, in order to build of them a temple for my God, far from the territory of Egypt. If you pardon me, I shall rejoice; if you are enraged, I shall bear up. The die is cast, and I am writing the book—whether to be read by my contemporaries or by posterity matters not. Let it await its reader for a hundred years, if God Himself has been ready for His contemplator for six thousand years.

The chapters of this book are as follows:
1. Concerning the five regular solid figures.
2. On the kinship between them and the harmonic ratios.
3. Summary of astronomical doctrine necessary for speculation into the celestial harmonies.
4. In what things pertaining to the planetary movements the simple consonances have been expressed and that all those consonances which are present in song are found in the heavens.
5. That the clefs of the musical scale, or pitches of the system, and the genera of consonances, the major and the minor, are expressed in certain movements.
6. That the single musical Tones or Modes are somehow expressed by the single planets.
7. That the counterpoints or universal harmonies of all the planets can exist and be different from one another.
8. That four kinds of voice are expressed in the planets: soprano, contralto, tenor, and bass.
[270] 9. Demonstration that in order to secure this harmonic arrangement, those very planetary eccentricities which any planet has as its own, and no others, had to be set up.
      10. Epilogue concerning the sun, by way of very fertile conjectures.

Before taking up these questions, it is my wish to impress upon my readers the very exhortation of Timaeus, a pagan philosopher, who was going to speak on the same things: it should be learned by Christians with the greatest admiration, and shame too, if they do not imitate him: 'Αλλ' ὦ Σώκρατες, τοῦτο γε δὴ πντες, ὅσοι καὶ κατὰ βραχὺ σωφροσύνης μετέχουσιν, ἐπὶ πασῇ ὁρμῇ καὶ σμίκρου καὶ μεγάλου πράγματος θεὸν ἀεί που καλοῦσιν. ἡμᾶς δὲ τοὺς περὶ τοῦ πάντος λόγους ποιεῖσθαι πῃ μέλλοντας . . . , εἰ μὴ πανταπασι παραλλάττομεν, ἀνάγκη θεούς τε καὶ θεὰς ἐπικαλουμενους εὔχεσθαι πάντα, κατὰ νοῦν ἐκείνοις μέν μάλιστα, ἐπομένως δὲ ἡμῖν εἰπεῖν. For truly, Socrates, since all who have the least particle of intelligence always invoke God whenever they enter upon any business, whether light or arduous; so too, unless we have clearly strayed away from all sound reason, we who intend to have a discussion concerning the universe must of necessity make our sacred wishes and pray to the Gods and Goddesses with one mind that we may say such things as will please and be acceptable to them in especial and, secondly, to you too.

1. Concerning the Five Regular Solid Figures

[271] It has been said in the second book how the regular plane figures are fitted together to form solids; there we spoke of the five regular solids, among others, on account of the plane figures. Nevertheless their number, five, was there demonstrated; and it was added why they were designated by the Platonists as the figures of the world, and to what element any solid was compared on account of what property. But now, in the anteroom of this book, I must speak again concerning these figures, on their own account, not on account of the planes, as much as suffices for the celestial harmonies; the reader will find the rest in the *Epitome of Astronomy*, Volume II, Book IV.

Accordingly, from the *Mysterium Cosmographicum*, let me here briefly inculcate the order of the five solids in the world, whereof three are primary and two secondary. For the *cube* (1) is the outmost and the most spacious, because firstborn and having the nature [*rationem*] of a *whole*, in the very form of its generation. There follows the *tetrahedron* (2), as if made a *part*, by cutting up the cube; nevertheless it is primary too, with a solid trilinear angle, like the cube. Within the tetrahedron is the *dodecahedron* (3), the last of primary figures, namely, like a solid composed of parts of a cube and similar parts of a tetrahedron, *i.e.*, of irregular tetrahedrons, wherewith the cube inside is roofed over. Next in order is the *icosahedron* (4) on account of its similarity, the last of the secondary figures and having a plurilinear solid angle. The *octahedron* (5) is inmost, which is similar to the cube and the first of the secondary figures and to which as inscriptile the first place is due, just as the first outside place is due to the cube as circumscriptile.

[272] However, there are as it were two noteworthy weddings of these figures, made from different classes: the males, the cube and the dodecahedron, among the primary; the females, the octahedron and the icosahedron, among the secondary, to which is added one as it were bachelor or hermaphrodite, the tetrahedron, because it is inscribed in itself, just as those female solids are inscribed in the males and are as it were subject to them, and have the signs of the feminine sex, opposite the masculine, namely, angles opposite planes. Moreover, just as the tetrahedron is the element, bowels, and as it were rib of the male

cube, so the feminine octahedron is the element and part of the tetrahedron in another way; and thus the tetrahedron mediates in this marriage.

The main difference in these wedlocks or family relationships consists in the following: the ratio of the cube is *rational*. For the tetrahedron is one third of the body of the cube, and the octahedron half of the tetrahedron, one sixth of the cube; while the ratio of the dodecahedron's wedding is *irrational [ineffabilis]* but *divine*.

The union of these two words commands the reader to be careful as to their significance. For the word *ineffabilis* here does not of itself denote any nobility, as elsewhere in theology and divine things, but denotes an inferior condition. For in geometry, as was said in the first book, there are many irrationals, which do not on that account participate in a divine proportion too. But you must look in the first book for what the divine ratio, or rather the divine section, is. For in other proportions there are four terms present; and three, in a continued proportion; but the divine requires a single relation of terms outside of that of the proportion itself, namely in such fashion that the two lesser terms, as parts make up the greater term, as a whole. Therefore, as much as is taken away from this wedding of the dodecahedron on account of its employing an irrational proportion, is added to it conversely, because its irrationality approaches the divine. This wedding also comprehends the solid star too, the generation whereof arises from the continuation of five planes of the dodecahedron till they all meet in a single point. See its generation in Book II.

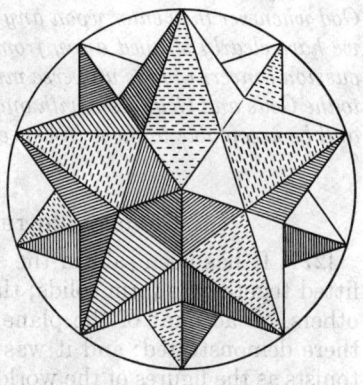

Lastly, we must note the ratio of the spheres circumscribed around them to those inscribed in them: in the case of the tetrahedron it is rational, 100,000 : 33,333 or 3 : 1; in the wedding of the cube it is irrational, but the radius of the inscribed sphere is rational in square, and is itself the square root of one third the square on the radius [of the circumscribed sphere], namely 100,000 : 57,735; in the wedding of the dodecahedron, clearly irrational, 100,000 : 79,465; in the case of the star, 100,000 : 52,573, half the side of the icosahedron or half the distance between two rays.

2. ON THE KINSHIP BETWEEN THE HARMONIC RATIOS AND THE FIVE REGULAR FIGURES

[273] This kinship [*cognatio*] is various and manifold; but there are four degrees of kinship. For either the sign of kinship is taken from the outward form alone which the figures have, or else ratios which are the same as the harmonic arise in the construction of the side, or result from the figures already constructed, taken simply or together; or, lastly, they are either equal to or approximate the ratios of the spheres of the figure.

In the first degree, the ratios, where the character or greater term is 3, have kinship with the triangular plane of the tetrahedron, octahedron, and icosahedron; but where the greater term is 4, with the square plane of the cube; where 5, with the pentagonal plane of the dodecahedron. This similitude on the part of the plane can also be extended to the smaller term of the ratio, so that wherever the number 3 is found as one term of the continued doubles, that ratio is held to be akin to the three figures first named: for example, 1 : 3 and 2 : 3 and 4 : 3 and 8 : 3, et cetera; but where the number is 5, that ratio is abolutely assigned to the wedding of the dodecahedron: for example, 2 : 5 and 4 : 5 and 8 : 5, and thus 3 : 5 and 3 : 10 and 6 : 5 and 12 : 5 and 24 : 5. The kinship will be less probable if the sum of the terms expresses this similitude, as in 2 : 3 the sum of the terms is equal to 5, as if to say that 2 : 3 is akin to the dodecahedron. The kinship on account of the outward form of the solid angle is similar: the solid angle is trilinear among the primary figures, quadrilinear in the octahedron, and quinquelinear in the icosahedron. And so if one term of the ratio participates in the number 3, the ratio will be connected with the primary bodies; but if in the number 4, with the octahedron; and finally, if in the number 5, with the icosahedron. But in the feminine solids this kinship is more apparent, because the characteristic figure latent within follows upon the form of the angle: the tetragon in the octahedron, the pentagon in the icosahedron; and so 3 : 5 would go to the sectioned icosahedron for both reasons.

The second degree of kinship, which is genetic, is to be conceived as follows: First, some harmonic ratios of numbers are akin to one wedding or family, namely, perfect ratios to the single family of the cube; conversely, there is the ratio which is never fully expressed in numbers and cannot be demonstrated by numbers in any other way, except by a long series of numbers gradually approaching it: this ratio is called *divine*, when it is perfect, and it rules in various ways throughout the dodecahedral wedding. Accordingly, the following consonances begin to shadow forth that ratio: 1 : 2 and 2 : 3 and 2 : 3 and 5 : 8. For it exists most imperfectly in 1 : 2, more perfectly in 5 : 8, and still more perfectly if we add 5 and 8 to make 13 and take 8 as the numerator, if this ratio has not stopped being harmonic.

Further, in constructing the side of the figure, the diameter of the globe must be cut; and the octahedron demands its bisection, the cube and the tetrahedron its trisection, the dodecahedral wedding its quinquesection. Accordingly, the ratios between the figures are distributed according to the numbers which express those ratios. But the square on the diameter is cut too, or the square on the side of the figure is formed from a fixed part of the diameter. And then the squares on the sides are compared with the square on the diameter, and they constitute the following ratios: in the cube 1 : 3, in the tetrahedron 2 : 3, in the octahedron 1 : 2. Wherefore, if the two ratios are put together, the cubic and the tetrahedral will give 1 : 2; the cubic and the octahedral, 2 : 3; the octahedral and the tetrahedral, 3 : 4. The sides in the dodecahedral wedding are irrational.

Thirdly, the harmonic ratios follow in various ways upon the already constructed figures. For either the number of the sides of the plane is compared with the number of lines in the total figure; [274] and the following ratios arise: in the cube, 4 : 12 or 1 : 3; in the tetrahedron 3 : 6 or 1 : 2; in the octahedron 3 : 12 or 1 : 4; in the dodecahedron 5 : 30 or 1 : 6; in the icosahedron 3 : 30 or 1 : 10. Or else the number of sides of the plane is compared with the number of planes; then the cube gives 4 : 6 or 2 : 3, the tetrahedron 3 : 4, the octahedron 3 : 8, the dodecahedron 5 : 12, the icosahedron 3 : 20. Or else the number of sides or angles of the plane is compared with the number of solid angles, and the cube gives 4 : 8 or 1 : 2, the tetrahedron 3 : 4, the octahedron 3 : 6 or 1 : 2, the dodecahedron with its consort 5 : 20 or 3 : 12 (*i.e.*, 1 : 4). Or else the number of planes is compared with the number of solid angles, and the cubic wedding gives 6 : 8 or 3 : 4, the tetrahedron the ratio of equality, the dodecahedral wedding 12 : 20 or 3 : 5. Or else the number of all the sides is compared with the number of the solid angles, and the cube gives 8 : 12 or 2 : 3, the tetrahedron 4 : 6 or 2 : 3, and the octahedron 6 : 12 or 1 : 2, the dodecahedron 20 : 30 or 2 : 3, the icosahedron 12 : 30 or 2 : 5.

Moreover, the bodies too are compared with one another, if the tetrahedron is stowed away in the cube, the octahedron in the tetrahedron and cube, by geometrical inscription. The tetrahedron is one third of the cube, the octahedron half of the tetrahedron, one sixth of the cube, just as the octahedron, which is inscribed in the globe, is one sixth of the cube which circumscribes the globe. The ratios of the remaining bodies are irrational.

The fourth species or degree of kinship is more proper to this work: the ratio of the spheres inscribed in the figures to the spheres circumscribing them is sought, and what harmonic ratios approximate them is calculated. For only in the tetrahedron is the diameter of the inscribed sphere rational, namely, one third of the circumscribed sphere. But in the cubic wedding the ratio, which is single there, is as lines which are rational only in square. For the diameter of the inscribed sphere is to the diameter of the circumscribed sphere as the square root of the ratio 1 : 3. And if you compare the ratios with one another, the ratio of the tetrahedral spheres is the square of the ratio of the cubic spheres. In the dodecahedral wedding there is again a single ratio, but an irrational one, slightly greater than 4 : 5. Therefore the ratio of the spheres of the cube and octahedron is approximated by the following consonances: 1 : 2, as proximately greater, and 3 : 5, as proximately smaller. But the ratio of the dodecahedral spheres is approximated by the consonances 4 : 5 and 5 : 6, as proximately smaller, and 3 : 4 and 5 : 8, as proximately greater.

But if for certain reasons 1 : 2 and 1 : 3 are arrogated to the cube, the ratio of the spheres of the cube will be to the ratio of the spheres of the tetrahedron as the consonances 1 : 2 and 1 : 3, which have been ascribed to the cube, are to 1 : 4 and 1 : 9, which are to be assigned to the tetrahedron, if this proportion is to be used. For these ratios, too, are as the squares of those consonances. And because 1 : 9 is not harmonic, 1 : 8 the proximate ratio takes its place in the tetrahedron. But by this proportion approximately 4 : 5 and 3 : 4 will go with the dodecahedral wedding. For as the ratio of the spheres of the cube is approximately the cube of the ratio of the dodecahedral, so too the cubic consonances 1 : 2 and 2 : 3 are approximately the cubes of the consonances 4 : 5 and 3 : 4. For 4 : 5 cubed is 64 : 125, and 1 : 2 is 64 : 128. So 3 : 4 cubed is 27 : 64, and 1 : 3 is 27 : 81.

3. A Summary of Astronomical Doctrine Necessary for Speculation into the Celestial Harmonies

First of all, my readers should know that the ancient astronomical hypotheses of Ptolemy, in the fashion in which they have been unfolded in the *Theoricae* of Peurbach and by the other writers of epitomes, are to be completely removed from this discussion and cast out of [275] the mind. For they do not convey the true lay out of the bodies of the world and the polity of the movements.

Although I cannot do otherwise than to put solely Copernicus' opinion concerning the world in the place of those hypotheses and, if that were possible, to persuade everyone of it; but because the thing is still new among the mass of the intelligentsia [*apud vulgus studiosorum*], and the doctrine that the Earth is one of the planets and moves among the stars around a motionless sun sounds very absurd to the ears of most of them: therefore those who are shocked by the unfamiliarity of this opinion should know that these harmonical speculations are possible even with the hypotheses of Tycho Brahe—because that author holds, in common with Copernicus, everything else which pertains to the lay out of the bodies and the tempering of the movements, and transfers solely the Copernican annual movement of the Earth to the whole system of planetary spheres and to the sun, which occupies the centre of that system, in the opinion of both authors. For after this transference of movement it is nevertheless true that in Brahe the Earth occupies at any time the same place that Copernicus gives it, if not in the very vast and measureless region of the fixed stars, at least in the system of the planetary world. And accordingly, just as he who draws a circle on paper makes the writing-foot of the compass revolve, while he who fastens the paper or tablet to a turning lathe draws the same circle on the revolving tablet with the foot of the compass or stylus motionless; so too, in the case of Copernicus the Earth, by the real movement of its body, measures out a circle revolving midway between the circle of Mars on the outside and that of Venus on the inside; but in the case of Tycho Brahe the whole planetary system (wherein among the rest the circles of Mars and Venus are found) revolves like a tablet on a lathe and applies to the motionless Earth, or to the stylus on the lathe, the midspace between the circles of Mars and Venus; and it comes about from this movement of the system that the Earth within it, although remaining motionless, marks out the same circle around the sun and midway between Mars and Venus, which in Copernicus it marks out by the real movement of its body while the system is at rest. Therefore, since harmonic speculation considers the eccentric movements of the planets, as if seen from the sun, you may easily understand that if any observer were stationed on a sun as much in motion as you please, nevertheless for him the Earth, although at rest (as a concession to Brahe), would seem to describe the annual circle midway between the planets and in an intermediate length of time. Wherefore, if there is any man of such feeble wit that he cannot grasp the movement of the earth among the stars, nevertheless he can take pleasure in the most excellent spectacle of this most divine construction, if he applies to their image in the sun whatever he hears concerning the daily movements of the Earth in its eccentric—such an image as Tycho Brahe exhibits, with the Earth at rest.

And nevertheless the followers of the true Samian philosophy have no just cause to be jealous of sharing this delightful speculation with such persons, because their joy will be in many ways more perfect, as due to the consummate perfection of speculation, if they have accepted the immobility of the sun and the movement of the earth.

Firstly [1], therefore, let my readers grasp that today it is absolutely certain among all astronomers that all the planets revolve around the sun, with the exception of the moon, which alone has the Earth as its centre: the magnitude of the moon's sphere or orbit is not great enough for it to be delineated in this diagram in a just ratio to the rest. Therefore, to the other five planets, a sixth, the Earth, is added, which traces a sixth circle around the sun, whether by its own proper movement with the sun at rest, or motionless itself and with the whole planetary system revolving.

Secondly [II]: It is also certain that all the planets are eccentric, *i.e.*, they change their distances from the sun, in such fashion that in one part of their circle they become farthest away from the sun, [276] and in the opposite part they come nearest to the sun. In the accompanying diagram three circles apiece have been drawn for the single planets: none of them indicate the eccentric route of the planet itself; but the mean circle, such as *BE* in the case of Mars, is equal to the eccentric orbit, with respect to its longer diameter. But the orbit itself, such as *AD*, touches *AF*, the upper of the three, in one place *A*, and the lower circle *CD*, in the opposite place *D*. The circle *GH* made with dots and described through the centre of the sun indicates the route of the sun according to Tycho Brahe. And if the sun moves on this route, then absolutely all the points in this whole planetary system here depicted advance upon an equal route, each upon his own. And with one point of it (namely, the centre of the sun) stationed at one point of its circle, as here at the lowest, absolutely each and every point of the system will be stationed at the lowest part of

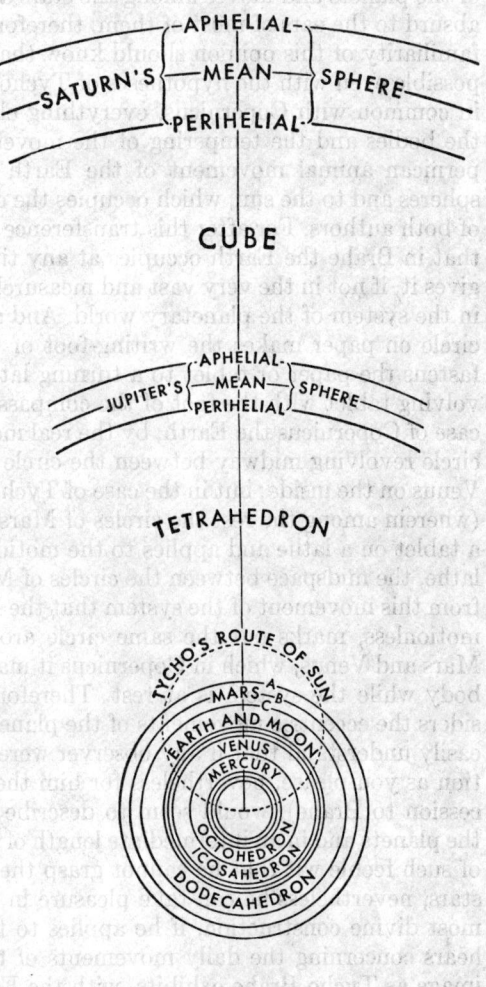

its circle. However, on account of the smallness of the space the three circles of Venus unite in one, contrary to my intention.

Thirdly [III]: Let the reader recall from my *Mysterium Cosmographicum*, which I published twenty-two years ago, that the number of the planets or circular routes around the sun was taken by the very wise Founder from the five regular solids, concerning which Euclid, so many ages ago, wrote his book which is called the *Elements* in that it is built up out of a series of propositions. But it has been made clear in the second book of this work that there cannot be more regular bodies, *i.e.*, that regular plane figures cannot fit together in a solid more than five times.

Fourthly [IV]: As regards the ratio of the planetary orbits, the ratio between two neighbouring planetary orbits is always of such a magnitude that it is easily apparent that each and every one of them approaches the single ratio of the spheres of one of the five regular solids, namely, that of the sphere circumscribing to the sphere inscribed in the figure. Nevertheless it is not wholly equal, as I once dared to promise concerning the final perfection of astronomy. For, after completing the demonstration of the intervals from Brahe's observations, I discovered the following: if the angles of the cube [277] are applied to the inmost circle of Saturn, the centres of the planes are approximately tangent to the middle circle of Jupiter; and if the angles of the tetrahedron are placed against the inmost circle of Jupiter, the centres of the planes of the tetrahedron are approximately tangent to the outmost circle of Mars; thus if the angles of the octahedron are placed against any circle of Venus (for the total interval between the three has been very much reduced), the centres of the planes of the octahedron penetrate and descend deeply within the outmost circle of Mercury, but nonetheless do not reach as far as the middle circle of Mercury; and finally, closest of all to the ratios of the dodecahedral and icosahedral spheres—which ratios are equal to one another—are the ratios or intervals between the circles of Mars and the Earth, and the Earth and Venus; and those intervals are similarly equal, if we compute from the inmost circle of Mars to the middle circle of the Earth, but from the middle circle of the Earth to the middle circle of Venus. For the middle distance of the Earth is a mean proportional between the least distance of Mars and the middle distance of Venus. However, these two ratios between the planetary circles are still greater than the ratios of those two pairs of spheres in the figures, in such fashion that the centres of the dodecahedral planes are not tangent to the outmost circle of the Earth, and the centres of the icosahedral planes are not tangent to the outmost circle of Venus; nor, however, can this gap be filled by the semidiameter of the lunar sphere, by adding it, on the upper side, to the greatest distance of the Earth and subtracting it, on the lower, from the least distance of the same. But I find a certain other ratio of figures—namely, if I take the augmented dodecahedron, to which I have given the name of echinus, (as being fashioned from twelve quinquangular stars and thereby very close to the five regular solids), if I take it, I say, and place its twelve points in the inmost circle of Mars, then the sides of the pentagons, which are the bases of the single rays or points, touch the middle circle of Venus. In short: the cube and the octahedron, which are consorts, do not penetrate their planetary spheres at all; the dodecahedron and the icosahedron, which are consorts, do not wholly reach to theirs, the tetrahedron exactly touches both: in the first case there is falling short; in the second, excess; and in the third, equality, with respect to the planetary intervals.

Wherefore it is clear that the very ratios of the planetary intervals from the sun have not been taken from the regular solids alone. For the Creator, who is the very source of geometry and, as Plato wrote, "practices eternal geometry," does not stray from his own archetype. And indeed that very thing could be inferred from the fact that all the planets change their intervals throughout fixed periods of time, in such fashion that each has two marked intervals from the sun, a greatest and a least; and a fourfold comparison of the intervals from the sun is possible between two planets: the comparison can be made between either the greatest, or the least, or the contrary intervals most remote from one another, or the contrary intervals nearest together. In this way the comparisons made two by two between neighbouring planets are twenty in number, although on the contrary there are only five regular solids. But it is consonant that if the Creator had any concern for the ratio of the spheres in general, He would also have had concern for the ratio which exists between the varying intervals of the single planets specifically and that the concern is the same in both cases and the one is bound up with the other. If we ponder that, we will comprehend that for setting up the diameters and eccentricities conjointly, there is need of more principles, outside of the five regular solids.

Fifthly [v]: To arrive at the movements between which the consonances have been set up, once more I impress upon the reader that in the *Commentaries on Mars* I have demonstrated from the sure observations of Brahe that daily arcs, which are equal in one and the same eccentric circle, are not traversed with equal speed; but that these differing *delays in equal parts of the eccentric observe the ratio of their distances from the sun,* the source of movement; and conversely, that if equal times are assumed, namely, one natural day in both cases, the corresponding *true diurnal arcs* [278] *of one eccentric orbit have to one another the ratio which is the inverse of the ratio of the two distances from the sun.* Moreover, I demonstrated at the same time that *the planetary orbit is elliptical and the sun, the source of movement, is at one of the foci of this ellipse; and so, when the planet has completed a quarter of its total circuit from its aphelion, then it is exactly at its mean distance from the sun, midway between its greatest distance at the aphelion and its least at the perihelion.* But from these two axioms it results *that the diurnal mean movement of the planet in its eccentric is the same as the true diurnal arc of its eccentric at those moments wherein the planet is at the end of the quadrant of the eccentric measured from the aphelion, although that true quadrant appears still smaller than the just quadrant.* Furthermore, it follows *that the sum of any two true diurnal eccentric arcs, one of which is at the same distnace from the aphelion that the other is from the perihelion, is equal to the sum of the two mean diurnal arcs.* And as a consequence, *since the ratio of circles is the same as that of the diameters, the ratio of one mean diurnal arc to the sum of all the mean and equal arcs in the total circuit is the same as the ratio of the mean diurnal arc to the sum of all the true eccentric arcs, which are the same in number but unequal to one another.* And those things should first be known concerning the true diurnal arcs of the eccentric and the true movements, so that by means of them we may understand the movements which would be apparent if we were to suppose an eye at the sun.

Sixthly [vi]: But as regards the arcs which are apparent, as it were, from the sun, it is known even from the ancient astronomy that, among true movements which are equal to one another, that movement which is farther distant from the centre of the world (as being at the aphelion) will appear smaller to a beholder at that centre, but the movement which is nearer (as being at the perihelion) will similarly appear greater. Therefore, since moreover the true diurnal arcs at the near distance are still greater, on account of the faster movement, and still smaller at the distant aphelion, on account of the slowness of the movement, I demonstrated in the *Commentaries on Mars* that *the ratio of the apparent diurnal arcs of one eccentric circle is fairly exactly the inverse ratio of the squares of their distances from the sun.* For example, if the planet one day when it is at a distance from the sun of 10 parts, in any measure whatsoever, but on the opposite day, when it is at the perihelion, of 9 similar parts: it is certain that from the sun its apparent progress at the aphelion will be to its apparent progress at the perihelion, as 81 : 100.

But that is true with these provisos: First, that the eccentric arcs should not be great, lest they partake of distinct distances which are very different—*i.e.*, lest the distances of their termini from the apsides cause a perceptible variation; second, that the eccentricity should not be very great, for the greater its eccentricity (*viz.*, the greater the arc becomes) the more the angle of its apparent movement increases beyond the measure of its approach to the sun, by Theorem 8 of Euclid's *Optics*; none the less in small arcs even a great distance is of no moment, as I have remarked in my *Optics*, Chapter 11. But there is another reason why I make that admonition. For the eccentric arcs around the mean anomalies are viewed obliquely from the centre of the sun. This obliquity subtracts from the magnitude of the apparent movement, since conversely the arcs around the apsides are presented directly to an eye stationed as it were at the sun. Therefore, when the eccentricity is very great, then the eccentricity takes away perceptibly from the ratio of the movements; if without any diminution we apply the mean diurnal movement to the mean distance, as if at the mean distance, it would appear to have the same magnitude which it does have—as will be apparent below in the case of Mercury. All these things are treated at greater length in Book v of the *Epitome of Copernican Astronomy*; but they have been mentioned here too because they have to do with the very terms of the celestial consonances, considered in themselves singly and separately.

Seventhly [VII]: If by chance anyone runs into those diurnal movements which are apparent [279] to those gazing not as it were from the sun but from the Earth, with which movements Book VI of the *Epitome of Copernican Astronomy* deals, he should know that their rationale is plainly not considered in this business. Nor should it be, since the Earth is not the source of the planetary movements, nor can it be, since with respect to deception of sight they degenerate not only into mere quiet or apparent stations but even into retrogradation, in which way a whole infinity of ratios is assigned to all the planets, simultaneously and equally. Therefore, in order that we may hold for certain what sort of ratios of their own are constituted by the single real eccentric orbits (although these too are still apparent, as it were to one looking from the sun, the source of movement), first we must remove from those movements of their own this image of the adventitious annual movement common to all five, whether it arises from the movement of the Earth itself, according to Copernicus, or from the annual movement of the total system, according to Tycho Brahe, and the winnowed movements proper to each planet are to be presented to sight.

Eighthly [VIII]: So far we have dealt with the different delays or arcs of one and the same planet. Now we must also deal with the comparison of the movements of two planets. Here take note of the definitions of the terms which will be necessary for us. We give the name of *nearest apsides* of two planets to the perihelion of the upper and the aphelion of the lower, notwithstanding that they tend not towards the same region of the world but towards distinct and perhaps contrary regions. By *extreme movements* understand the slowest and the fastest of the whole planetary circuit; by *converging or converse extreme movements*, those which are at the nearest apsides of two planets—namely, at the perihelion of the upper planet and the aphelion of the lower; by *diverging or diverse*, those at the opposite apsides—namely, the aphelion of the upper and the perihelion of the lower. Therefore again, a certain part of my *Mysterium Cosmographicum*, which was suspended twenty-two years ago, because it was not yet clear, is to be completed and herein inserted. For after finding the true intervals of the spheres by the observations of Tycho Brahe and continuous labour and much time, at last, at last the right ratio of the periodic times to the spheres

though it was late, looked to the unskilled man,

yet looked to him, and, after much time, came,

and, if you want the exact time, was conceived mentally on the 8th of March in this year One Thousand Six Hundred and Eighteen but unfelicitously submitted to calculation and rejected as false, finally, summoned back on the 15th of May, with a fresh assault undertaken, outfought the darkness of my mind by the great proof afforded by my labor of seventeen years on Brahe's observations and meditation upon it uniting in one concord, in such fashion that I first believed I was dreaming and was presupposing the object of my search among the principles. But it is absolutely certain and exact that *the ratio which exists between the periodic times of any two planets is precisely the ratio of the $\frac{3}{2}$th power of the mean distances*, i.e., *of the spheres themselves*; provided, however, that the arithmetic mean between both diameters of the elliptic orbit be slightly less than the longer diameter. And so if any one take the period, say, of the Earth, which is one year, and the period of Saturn, which is thirty years, and extract the cube roots of this ratio and then square the ensuing ratio by squaring the cube roots, he will have as his numerical products the most just ratio of the distances of the Earth and Saturn from the sun.[1] For the cube root of 1 is 1, and the square of it is 1; and the cube root of 30 is greater than 3, and therefore the square of it is greater than 9. And Saturn, at its mean distance from the sun, is slightly higher [280] than nine times the mean distance of the Earth from the sun. Further on, in Chapter 9, the use of this theorem will be necessary for the demonstration of the eccentricities.

Ninthly [IX]: If now you wish to measure with the same yardstick, so to speak, the true daily journeys of each planet through the ether, two ratios are to be compounded—the ratio of the true (not the apparent) diurnal arcs of the eccentric, and the ratio of the mean intervals of each planet from the sun (because that is the same as the ratio of the amplitude of the spheres), i.e., *the true diurnal arc of each planet is to be multiplied by the semidiameter of its sphere*: the products will be numbers fitted for investigating whether or not those journeys are in harmonic ratios.

Tenthly [X]: In order that you may truly know how great any one of these diurnal journeys appears to be to an eye stationed as it were at the sun, although this same thing can be got immediately from the astronomy, nevertheless it will also be manifest if you multiply the ratio of the journeys by the inverse ratio not of the mean, but of the true intervals which exist at any position on

---

[1]For in the *Commentaries on Mars*, chapter 48, page 232, I have proved that this Arithmetic mean is either the diameter of the circle which is equal in length to the elliptic orbit, or else is very slightly less.

the eccentrics: *multiply the journey of the upper by the interval of the lower planet from the sun, and conversely multiply the journey of the lower by the interval of the upper from the sun.*

Eleventhly [XI]: And in the same way, if the apparent movements are given, at the aphelion of the one and at the perihelion of the other, or conversely or alternately, the ratios of the distances of the aphelion of the one to the perihelion of the other may be elicited. But where the mean movements must be known first, *viz.*, the inverse ratio of the periodic times, wherefrom the ratio of the spheres is elicited by Article VIII above: then *if the mean proportional between the apparent movement of either one of its mean movement be taken, this mean proportional is to the semidiameter of its sphere* (which is already known) *as the mean movement is to the distance or interval sought.* Let the periodic times of two planets be 27 and 8. Therefore the ratio of the mean diurnal movement of the one to the other is 8 : 27. Therefore the semidiameters of their spheres will be as 9 to 4. For the cube root of 27 is 3, that of 8 is 2, and the squares of these roots, 3 and 2, are 9 and 4. Now let the apparent aphelial movement of the one be 2 and the perihelial movement of the other $33\frac{1}{3}$. The mean proportionals between the mean movements 8 and 27 and these apparent ones will be 4 and 30. Therefore if the mean proportional 4 gives the mean distance of 9 to the planet, then the mean movement of 8 gives an aphelial distance 18, which corresponds to the apparent movement 2; and if the other mean proportional 30 gives the other planet a mean distance of 4, then its mean movement of 27 will give it a perihelial interval of $3\frac{3}{5}$. I say, therefore, that the aphelial distance of the former is to the perihelial distance of the latter as 18 to $3\frac{3}{5}$. Hence it is clear that if the consonances between the extreme movements of two planets are found and the periodic times are established for both, the extreme and the mean distances are necessarily given, wherefore also the eccentricities.

Twelfthly [XII]: It is also possible, from the different extreme movements of one and the same planet, to find the *mean movement.* The mean movement is not exactly the arithmetic mean between the extreme movements, nor exactly the geometric mean, but it is as much less than the geometric mean as the geometric mean is less than the [arithmetic] mean between both means. Let the two extreme movements be 8 and 10: the mean movement will be less than 9, and also less than the square root of 80 by half the difference between 9 and the square root of 80. In this way, if the aphelial movement is 20 and the perihelial 24, the mean movement will be less than 22, even less than the square root of 480 by half the difference between that root and 22. There is use for this theorem in what follows.

[281] Thirteenthly [XIII]: From the foregoing the following proposition is demonstrated, which is going to be very necessary for us: Just as the ratio of the mean movements of two planets is the inverse ratio of the $\frac{3}{2}$th powers of the spheres, so the ratio of two apparent converging extreme movements always falls short of the ratio of the $\frac{3}{2}$th powers of the intervals corresponding to those extreme movements; and in what ratio the product of the two ratios of the corresponding intervals to the two mean intervals or to the semidiameters of the two spheres falls short of the ratio of the square roots of the spheres, in that ratio does the ratio of the two extreme converging movements exceed the ratio of the corresponding intervals; but if that compound ratio were to exceed the

ratio of the square roots of the spheres, then the ratio of the converging movements would be less than the ratio of their intervals.[1]

Let the ratio of the spheres be $DH : AE$; let the ratio of the mean movements be $HI : EM$, the $\frac{3}{2}$th power of the inverse of the former. Let the least interval of the sphere of the first be CG; and the greatest interval of the sphere of the second be BF; and first let $DH : CG$ comp. $BF : AE$ be smaller than the $\frac{1}{2}$th power of $DH : AE$. And let GH be the apparent perihelial movement of the upper planet, and FL the aphelial of the lower, so that they are converging extreme movements.

I say that
$$GK : FL = BF : CG$$
$$BF^{\frac{3}{2}} : CG^{\frac{3}{2}}.$$

For
$$HI : GK = CG^2 : DH^2;$$
and
$$FL : EM = AE^2 : BF^2.$$

Hence
$$HI : GK \text{ comp. } FL : EM = CG^2 : DH^2 \text{ comp. } AE^2 : BF^2.$$

But
$$CG : DH \text{ comp. } AE : BF < AE^{\frac{1}{2}} : DH^{\frac{1}{2}}$$

by a fixed ratio of defect, as was assumed. Therefore too
$$HI : GK \text{ comp. } FL : EM \quad AE^{\frac{3}{2}} : DH^{\frac{3}{2}}$$
$$AE : DH$$

by a ratio of defect which is the square of the former. But by number VIII
$$HI : EM = AE^{\frac{3}{2}} : DH^{\frac{3}{2}}.$$

Therefore let the ratio which is smaller by the total square of the ratio of defect be divided into the ratio of the $\frac{3}{2}$th powers; that is,
$$HI : EM \text{ comp. } GK : HI \text{ comp. } EM : FL \quad AE^{\frac{1}{2}} : DH^{\frac{1}{2}}$$

by the excess squared. But
$$HI : EM \text{ comp. } GK : HI \text{ comp. } EM : FL = GK : FL.$$

Therefore
$$GK : FL \quad AE^{\frac{1}{2}} : DH^{\frac{1}{2}}$$

by the excess squared. But
$$AE : DH = AE : BF \text{ comp. } BF : CG \text{ comp. } CG : DH.$$

And
$$CG : DH \text{ comp. } AE : BF \quad AE^{\frac{1}{2}} : DH^{\frac{1}{2}}$$

by the simple defect. Therefore
$$BF : CG \quad AE^{\frac{1}{2}} : DH^{\frac{1}{2}}$$

by the simple excess. But
$$GK : FL \quad AE^{\frac{1}{2}} : DH^{\frac{1}{2}}$$

but by the excess squared. But the excess squared is greater than the simple excess. Therefore the ratio of the movements GK to FL is greater than the ratio of the corresponding intervals BF to CG.

---

[1]Kepler always measures the magnitude of a ratio from the greater term to the smaller, rather than from the antecedent to the consequent, as we do today. For example, as Kepler speaks, 2 : 3 is the same as 3 : 2, and 3 : 4 is greater than 7 : 8.—C. G. Wallis.

In fully the same way, it is demonstrated even contrariwise that if the planets approach one another in G and F beyond the mean distances in H and E, in such fashion that the ratio of the mean distances $DH : AE$ becomes less than $DH^{\frac{1}{2}} : AE^{\frac{1}{2}}$, then the ratio of the movements $GK : FL$ becomes less than the ratio of the corresponding intervals $BF : CG$. For you need to do nothing more than to change the words *greater* to *less*, $>$ to $<$, *excess* to *defect*, and conversely.

In suitable numbers, because the square root of $\frac{4}{9}$ is $\frac{2}{3}$; and $\frac{5}{8}$ is even greater than $\frac{2}{3}$ by the ratio of excess $^{15}\!/_{16}$; and the square of the ratio $8 : 9$ [282] is the ratio $1600 : 2025$, *i.e.*, $64 : 81$; and the square of the ratio $4 : 5$ is the ratio $3456 : 5400$, *i.e.*, $16 : 25$; and finally the $\frac{3}{2}$th power of the ratio $4 : 9$ is the ratio $1600 : 5400$, *i.e.*, $8 : 27$: therefore too the ratio $2025 : 3456$, *i.e.*, $75 : 128$, is even greater than $5 : 8$, *i.e.*, $75 : 120$, by the same ratio of excess (*i.e.*, $120 : 128$), $15 : 16$; whence $2025 : 3456$, the ratio of the converging movements, exceeds $5 : 8$, the inverse ratio of the corresponding intervals, by as much as $5 : 8$ exceeds $2 : 3$, the square root of the ratio of the spheres. Or, what amounts to the same thing, the ratio of the two converging intervals is a mean between the ratio of the square roots of the spheres and the inverse ratio of the corresponding movements.

Moreover, from this you may understand that the ratio of the diverging movements is much greater than the ratio of the $\frac{3}{2}$th powers of the spheres, since the ratio of the $\frac{3}{2}$th powers is compounded with the squares of the ratio of the aphelial interval to the mean interval, and that of the mean to the perihelial.

4. In What Things Having to do with the Planetary Movements Have the Harmonic Consonances been Expressed by the Creator, and in What Way?

Accordingly, if the image of the retrogradation and stations is taken away and the proper movements of the planets in their real eccentric orbits are winnowed out, the following distinct things still remain in the planets: 1) The distances from the sun. 2) The periodic times. 3) The diurnal eccentric arcs. 4) The diurnal delays in those arcs. 5) The angles at the sun, and the diurnal arcs apparent to those as it were gazing from the sun. And again, all of these things, with the exception of the periodic times, are variable in the total circuit, most variable at the mean longitudes, but least at the extremes, when, turning away from one extreme longitude, they begin to return to the opposite. Hence when the planet is lowest and nearest to the sun and thereby delays the least in one degree of its eccentric, and conversely in one day traverses the greatest diurnal arc of its eccentric and appears fastest from the sun: then its movement remains for some time in this strength without preceptible variation, until, after passing the perihelion, the planet gradually begins to depart farther from the sun in a straight line; at that same time it delays longer in the degrees of its eccentric circle; or, if you consider the movement of one day, on the following day it goes forward less and appears even more slow from the sun until it has drawn close to the highest apsis and made its distance from the sun very great: for then longest of all does it delay in one degree of its eccentric; or on the contrary in one day it traverses its least arc and makes a much smaller apparent movement and the least of its total circuit.

Finally, all these things may be considered either as they exist in any one planet at different times or as they exist in different planets: whence, by the assumption of an infinite amount of time, all the affects of the circuit of one planet can concur in the same moment of time with all the affects of the circuit of another planet and be compared, and then the total eccentrics, as compared with one another, have the same ratio as their semidiameters or mean intervals; but the arcs of two eccentrics, which are similar or designated by the same number [of degrees], nevertheless have their true lengths unequal in the ratio of their eccentrics. For example, one degree in the sphere of Saturn is approximately twice as long as one degree in the sphere of Jupiter. And conversely, the diurnal arcs of the eccentrics, as expressed in astronomical terms, do not exhibit the ratio of the true journeys which the globes complete in one day [283] through the ether, because the single units in the wider circle of the upper planet denote a quarter part of the journey, but in the narrower circle of the lower planet a smaller part.

Therefore let us take the second of the things which we have posited, namely, the periodic times of the planets, which comprehend the sums made up of all the delays—long, middling, short—in all the degrees of the total circuit. And we found that from antiquity down to us, the planets complete their periodic returns around the sun, as follows in the table:

| | Days | Minutes of a day | Therefore the mean diurnal movements | | |
			Min.	Sec.	Thirds
Saturn	10,759	12	2	0	27
Jupiter	4,332	37	4	59	8
Mars	686	59	31	26	31
Earth with Moon	365	15	59	8	11
Venus	224	42	96	7	39
Mercury	87	58	245	32	25

Accordingly, in these periodic times there are no harmonic ratios, as is easily apparent, if the greater periods are continuously halved, and the smaller are continuously doubled, so that, by neglecting the intervals of an octave, we can investigate the intervals which exist within one octave.

	Saturn	Jupiter	Mars	Earth	Venus	Mercury	
	10,759^{D}12'						
	5,379^{D}36'	4,332^{D}37'				87^{D}58'	
Halves	2,689^{D}48'	2,166^{D}19'			224^{D}42'	175^{D}56'	Doubles
	1,344^{D}54'	1,083^{D}10'	686^{D}59'	365^{D}15'	449^{D}24'	351^{D}52'	
	672^{D}27'	541^{D}35'					

All the last numbers, as you see, are counter to harmonic ratios and seem, as it were, irrational. For let 687, the number of days of Mars, receive as its measure 120, which is the number of the division of the chord: according to this measure Saturn will have 117 for one sixteenth of its period, Jupiter less than 95 for one eighth of its period, the earth less than 64, Venus more than 78 for twice its period, Mercury more than 61 for four times its period. These numbers do not make any harmonic ratio with 120, but their neighbouring numbers—60, 75, 80, and 96—do. And so, whereof Saturn has 120, Jupiter has approximately 97, the Earth more than 65, Venus more than 80, and Mercury less than 63. And whereof Jupiter has 120, the Earth has less than 81, Venus less than 100, Mercury less than 78. Likewise, whereof Venus has 120, the Earth has less than 98, Mercury more than 94. Finally, whereof the Earth has 120, Mercury has less than 116. But if the free choice of ratios had been effective here, consonances which are altogether perfect but not augmented or diminished would have been taken. Accordingly we find that God the Creator did not wish to introduce harmonic ratios between the sums of the delays added together to form the periodic times.

[284] And although it is a very probable conjecture (as relying on geometrical demonstrations and the doctrine concerning the causes of the planetary movements given in the *Commentaries on Mars*) that the bulks of the planetary bodies are in the ratio of the periodic times, so that the globe of Saturn is about thirty times greater than the globe of the Earth, Jupiter twelve times, Mars less than two, the Earth one and a half times greater than the globe of Venus and four times greater than the globe of Mercury: not therefore will even these ratios of bodies be harmonic.

But since God has established nothing without geometrical beauty, which was not bound by some other prior law of necessity, we easily infer that the periodic times have got their due lengths, and thereby the mobile bodies too have got their bulks, from something which is prior in the archetype, in order to express which thing these bulks and periods have been fashioned to this measure, as they seem disproportionate. But I have said that the periods are added up from the longest, the middling, and the slowest delays: accordingly geometrical fitnesses must be found either in these delays or in anything which may be prior to them in the mind of the Artisan. But the ratios of the delays are bound up with the ratios of the diurnal arcs, because the arcs have the inverse ratio of the delays. Again, we have said that the ratios of the delays and intervals of any one planet are the same. Then, as regards the single planets, there will be one and the same consideration of the following three: the arcs, the delays in equal arcs, and the distance of the arcs from the sun or the intervals. And because all these things are variable in the planets, there can be no doubt but that, if these things were allotted any geometrical beauty, then, by the sure design of the highest Artisan, they would have been received that at their extremes, at the aphelial and perihelial intervals, not at the mean intervals lying in between. For, given the ratios of the extreme intervals, there is no need of a plan to fit the intermediate ratios to a definite number. For they follow of themselves, by the necessity of planetary movement, from one extreme through all the intermediates to the other extreme.

Therefore the intervals are as follows, according to the very accurate observations of Tycho Brahe, by the method given in the *Commentaries on Mars* and investigated in very persevering study for seventeen years.

Intervals Compared with Harmonic Ratios[1]

Of Two Planets		Of Single Planets
Converging *Diverging*		

Of Two Planets		Of Single Planets
	Saturn's aphelion 10,052. a.	More than a minor whole tone $\dfrac{10,000}{9,000}$
$\dfrac{a}{d}=\dfrac{2}{1}$, $\dfrac{b}{c}=\dfrac{5}{3}$	perihelion 8,968. b.	Less than a major whole tone $\dfrac{10,000}{8,935}$
	Jupiter's aphelion 5,451. c.	No concordant ratio but approximately 11 : 10, a discordant or diminished 6 : 5.
$\dfrac{c}{f}=\dfrac{4}{1}$, $\dfrac{d}{e}=\dfrac{3}{1}$	perihelion 4,949. d.	
	Mar's aphelion 1,665. e.	Here 1662 : 1385 would be the consonance 6 : 5, and 1665 : 1332 would be 5 : 4
$\dfrac{e}{h}=\dfrac{5}{3}$, $\dfrac{f}{g}=\dfrac{17}{20}$	perihelion 1,382. f.	
	Earth's aphelion 1,018. g.	Here 1025 : 984 would be the diesis 24 : 25. Therefore it does not have the diesis.
$\dfrac{g}{k}=\dfrac{2}{1\frac{1}{2}}$ viz. $\dfrac{1000}{710}, \dfrac{h}{i}=\dfrac{27}{20}$	perihelion 982. h.	
	Venus' aphelion 729. i.	Less than a sesquicomma.
$\dfrac{i}{m}=\dfrac{12}{5}$, $\dfrac{k}{i}=\dfrac{243}{160}$	perihelion 719. k.	More than one third of a diesis.
	Mercury's aphelion 470. l.	243 : 160, greater than a perfect fifth but less than a harmonic 8 : 5
	perihelion 307. m.	

[285] Therefore the extreme intervals of no one planet come near consonances except those of Mars and Mercury.

But if you compare the extreme intervals of different planets with one another, some harmonic light begins to shine. For the extreme diverging intervals of Saturn and Jupiter make slightly more than the octave; and the con-

---

[1]GENERAL NOTE: Throughout this text Kepler's *concinna* and *inconcinna* are translated as "concordant" and "discordant." *Concinna* is usually used by Kepler of all intervals whose ratios occur within the "natural system" or the just intonation of the scale. *Inconcinna* refers to all ratios that lie outside of this system of tuning. "Consonant" (*consonans*) and "dissonant" (*dissonans*) refer to qualities which can be applied to intervals within the musical system, in other words to "concords." "Harmony" (*harmonia*) is used sometimes in the sense of "concordance" and sometimes in the sense of "consonance."

Genus durum and *genus molle* are translated either as "major mode" and "minor mode," or as "major scale" and "minor scale," or as "major kind" and "minor kind" (of consonances). The use of *modus*, to refer to the ecclesiastical modes, occurs only in Chapter 6.

As our present musical terms do not apply strictly to the music of the sixteenth and seventeenth centuries, a brief explanation of terms here may be useful. This material is taken from Kepler's *Harmonies of the World*, Book III.

An octave system in the minor scale (*Systema octavae in cantu molli*)

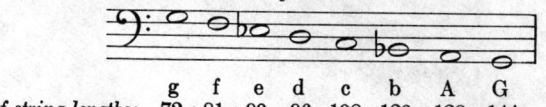

         g   f   e   d   c   b   A   G
Ratios of string lengths: 72 : 81 : 90 : 96 : 108 : 120 : 128 : 144

verging, a mean between the major and minor sixths. So the diverging extremes of Jupiter and Mars embrace approximately the double octave; and the converging, approximately the fifth and the octave. But the diverging extremes of the Earth and Mars embrace somewhat more than the major sixth; the converging, an augmented fourth. In the next couple, the Earth and Venus, there is again the same augmented fourth between the converging extremes; but we lack any harmonic ratio between the diverging extremes: for it is less than the semi-octave (so to speak) *i.e.*, less than the square root of the ratio 2 : 1. Finally, between the diverging extremes of Venus and Mercury there is a ratio slightly

In the major scale (*In cantu duro*)

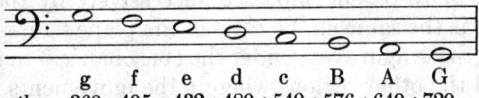

g   f   e   d   c   B   A   G

Ratios of string lengths: 360 : 405 : 432 : 480 : 540 : 576 : 640 : 720

As in all music, these scales can be repeated at one or more octaves above. The ratios would then all be halved, *i.e.*,

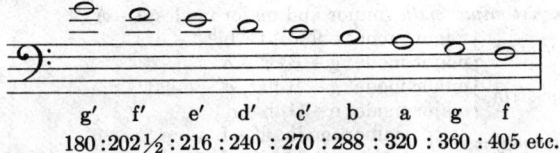

g'   f'   e'   d'   c'   b   a   g   f

180 : 202½ : 216 : 240 : 270 : 288 : 320 : 360 : 405 etc.

Various intervals which Kepler considers are:

80 : 81   *comma* (of Didymus), difference between major and minor whole tones ($\frac{8}{9} \div \frac{9}{10}$)

24 : 25   *diesis* [difference between e – e flat or B – b flat or between a semitone and a minor whole tone ($\frac{15}{16} \div \frac{9}{10}$)]

128 : 135   *lemma* [difference between a semitone and a major whole tone ($\frac{15}{16} \div \frac{8}{9}$)]

243 : 256   *Plato's lemma* (not found in this system but in the Pythagorean tuning)

15 : 16   *semitone* { minor mode between e flat – d, b flat – A
{ major mode between e – d, B – A

9 : 10   *minor whole tone* { minor mode f – e flat, c – b flat
{ major mode e – d, B – A

8 : 9   *major whole tone* { minor mode: g – f, d – c, A – G
{ major mode: g – f, d – c, A – G

27 : 32   *sub-minor third* (major and minor modes: f – d, c – A)

5 : 6   *minor third* { minor mode: e – flat – c, b flat – G
{ major mode: g – e, d – B

4 : 5   *major third* { minor mode: g – e – flat, d – b – flat
{ major mode: e – c, B – G

64 : 81   *ditone* (Pythagorean third) (major and minor modes: a – f)

243 : 320   *lesser imperfect fourth* (inversion of "greater imperfect fifth") see below

3 : 4   *perfect fourth* { minor mode: g – d, f – c, e flat – b flat, d – A, c – G
{ major mode: g – d, f – c, e – B,   , d – A, c – G

20 : 27   *greater imperfect fourth* { minor mode: b' flat – f
{ major mode: a – e

32 : 45   *augmented fourth* { minor mode: a – e flat
{ major mode: b – f

45 : 64   *diminished fifth* { minor mode: e – flat – A
{ major mode: f – B

27 : 40   *lesser imperfect fifth* { minor mode: f – b flat
{ major mode: e – A

2 : 3   *perfect fifth* { minor mode: g – c, d – G
{ major mode: g – c, d – G

less than the octave compounded with the minor third; between the converging there is a slightly augmented fifth.

Accordingly, although one interval was somewhat removed from harmonic ratios, this success was an invitation to advance further. Now my reasonings were as follows: First, in so far as these intervals are lengths without movement, they are not fittingly examined for harmonic ratios, because movement is more properly the subject of consonances, by reason of speed and slowness. Second, inasmuch as these same intervals are the diameters of the spheres, it is believable that the ratio of the five regular solids applied proportionally is more dominant in them, because the ratio of the geometrical solid bodies to the celestial spheres (which are everywhere either encompassed by celestial matter, as the ancients hold, or to be encompassed successively by the accumulation of many revolutions) is the same as the ratio of the plane figures which may be inscribed in a circle (these figures engender the consonances) to the celestial circles of movements and the other regions wherein the movements take place. Therefore, if we are looking for consonances, we should look for them not in these

---

160 : 243   *greater imperfect fifth* (compound of ditone and minor third $^{64}/_{81} \times ^{5}/_{6}$)

81 : 128   *imperfect minor sixth* (minor and major modes: f – A)

5 : 8   *minor sixth* $\begin{cases}\text{minor mode: e flat – G, } b^{1b+} - d \\ \text{major mode: g – B, c' – e}\end{cases}$

3 : 5   *major sixth* $\begin{cases}\text{minor mode: g – B flat, c' – e flat} \\ \text{major mode: e – G, b – d}\end{cases}$

64 : 27   *greater major sixth* $\begin{cases}\text{minor mode: d' – f, a – c} \\ \text{major mode: d' – f, a – c}\end{cases}$

1 : 2   *octave* (g – G, a – A, b – B, b flat – b flat)

All these are simple intervals. When one or more octaves are added to any simple intervals the resultant interval is a "compound" interval.

1 : 3 equals $\frac{1}{2} \times \frac{2}{3}$—an octave and a perfect fifth

3 : 32 equals $(\frac{1}{2})^3 \times \frac{3}{4}$—three octaves and a perfect fourth

1 : 20 equals $(\frac{1}{2})^4 \times ^{1}\frac{9}{20}$—four octaves and a major third

Concords: All intervals from diesis downward on above list.

Consonances: Minor and major thirds and sixths, perfect fourth, fifth, and octave.

"Adulterine" consonances: sub-minor third, ditone, lesser imperfect fourth and fifth, greater imperfect fourth and fifth, imperfect minor sixth, greater major sixth.

Dissonances: All other intervals.

Throughout this work Kepler, after the fashion of the theorists of his time, uses the ratios of string lengths rather than the ratios of vibrations as is usually done today. String lengths are, of course, inversely proportionate to the vibrations. That is, string lengths 4 : 5 are expressed in vibrations as 5:4. This accounts for the descending order of the scale, which follows the increasing numerical order. It is an interesting fact that Kepler's minor and major scales are inversions of each other and hence, when expressed in ratios of vibrations, are in the opposite order from those in ratios of string lengths:

Notes resulting from ratios of vibrations

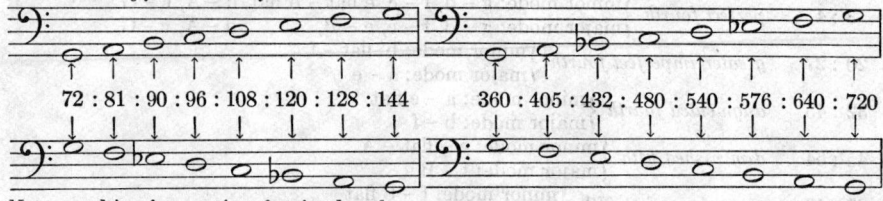

72 : 81 : 90 : 96 : 108 : 120 : 128 : 144   360 : 405 : 432 : 480 : 540 : 576 : 640 : 720

Notes resulting from ratios of string lengths

An arbitrary pitch G is chosen to situate these ratios. This g or "gamma" was usually the lowest tone of the sixteenth-century musical gamut.   ELLIOTT CARTER, JR.

intervals in so far as they are the semidiameters of spheres but in them in so far as they are the measures of the movements, *i.e.*, in the movements themselves, rather. Absolutely no other than the mean intervals can be taken as the semidiameters of the spheres; but we are here dealing with the extreme intervals. Accordingly, we are not dealing with the intervals in respect to their spheres but in respect to their movements.

Accordingly, although for these reasons I had passed on to the comparison of the extreme movements, at first the ratios of the movements remained the same in magnitude as those which were previously the ratios of the intervals, only inverted. Wherefore too, certain ratios, which are discordant and foreign to harmonies, as before, have been found between the movements. But once again I judged that this happened to me deservedly, because I compared with one another eccentric arcs which are not expressed and numbered by a measure of the same magnitude but are numbered in degrees and minutes which are of diverse magnitude in diverse planets, nor do they from our place give the appearance of being as great as the number of each says, except only at the centre of the eccentric of each planet, which centre rests upon no body; and hence it is also unbelievable that there is any sense or natural instinct in that place in the world which is capable of perceiving this; or, rather, it was impossible, if I was comparing the eccentric arcs of different planets with respect to their appearance at their centres, which are different for different planets. But if diverse apparent magnitudes are compared with one another, they ought to be apparent in one place in the world in such a way that that which possesses the faculty of comparing them may be present in that place from which they are all apparent. Accordingly, I judged that the appearance of these eccentric arcs should be removed from the mind or else should be formed differently. But if I removed the appearance and applied my mind to the diurnal journeys of the planets, I saw that I had to employ the rule which I gave in Article IX of the preceding chapter. [286] Accordingly if the diurnal arcs of the eccentric are multiplied by the mean intervals of the spheres, the following journeys are produced:

	Diurnal movements	Mean intervals	Diurnal journeys
Saturn at aphelion	1′53″	9510	1065
at perihelion	2′7″		1208
Jupiter at aphelion	4′44″	5200	1477
at perihelion	5′15″		1638
Mars at aphelion	28′44″	1524	2627
at perihelion	34′34″		3161
Earth at aphelion	58′6″	1000	3486
at perihelion	60′13″		3613
Venus at aphelion	95′29″	724	4149
at perihelion	96′50″		4207
Mercury at aphelion	201′0″	388	4680
at perihelion	307′3″		7148

Thus Saturn traverses barely one seventh of the journey of Mercury; and hence, as Aristotle judged consonant with reason in Book II of *On the Heavens*, the planet which is nearer the sun always traverses a greater space than the planet which is farther away—as cannot hold in the ancient astronomy.

And indeed, if we weigh the thing fairly carefully, it will appear to be not very probable that the most wise Creator should have established harmonies between the planetary journeys in especial. For if the ratios of the journeys are harmonic, all the other affects which the planets have will be necessitated and bound up with the journeys, so that there is no room elsewhere for establishing harmonies. But whose good will it be to have harmonies between the journeys, or who will perceive these harmonies? For there are two things which disclose to us harmonies in natural things: either light or sound: light apprehended through the eyes or hidden senses proportioned to the eyes, and sound through the ears. The mind seizes upon these forms and, whether by instinct (on which Book IV speaks profusely) or by astronomical or harmonic ratiocination, discerns the concordant from the discordant. Now there are no sounds in the heavens, nor is the movement so turbulent that any noise is made by the rubbing against the ether. Light remains. If light has to teach these things about the planetary journeys, it will teach either the eyes or a sensorium analogous to the eyes and situated in a definite place; and it seems that sense-perception must be present there in order that light of itself may immediately teach. Therefore there will be sense-perception in the total world, namely in order that the movements of all the planets may be presented to sense-perceptions at the same time. For that former route—from observations through the longest detours of geometry and arithmetic, through the ratios of the spheres and the other things which must be learned first, down to the journeys which have been exhibited—is too long for any natural instinct, for the sake of moving which it seems reasonable that the harmonies have been introduced.

Therefore with everything reduced to one view, I concluded rightly [287] that the true journeys of the planets through the ether should be dismissed, and that we should turn our eyes to the apparent diurnal arcs, according as they are all apparent from one definite and marked place in the world—namely, from the solar body itself, the source of movement of all the planets; and we must see, not how far away from the sun any one of the planets is, nor how much space it traverses in one day (for that is something for ratiocination and astronomy, not for instinct), but how great an angle the diurnal movement of each planet subtends in the solar body, or how great an arc it seems to traverse in one common circle described around the sun, such as the ecliptic ,in order that these appearances, which were conveyed to the solar body by virtue of light, may be able to flow, together with the light, in a straight line into creatures, which are partakers of this instinct, as in Book IV we said the figure of the heavens flowed into the foetus by virtue of the rays.

Therefore, if you remove from the proper planetary movement the parallaxes of the annual orbit, which gives them the mere appearances of stations and retrogradations, Tycho's astronomy teaches that the diurnal movements of the planets in their orbits (which are apparent as it were to spectator at the sun) are as shown in the table on the opposite page.

Note that the great eccentricity of Mercury makes the ratio of the movements differ somewhat from the ratio of the square of the distances. For if you make the square of the ratio of 100, the mean distance, to 121, the aphelial distance, be the ratio of the aphelial movement to the mean movement of 245′32″, then an aphelial movement of 167 will be produced; and if the square of the ratio of 100 to 79, the perihelial distance, be the ratio of the perihelial to the same mean movement, then the perihelial movement will become 393; and both cases are

Harmonies Between Two Planets	Apparent Diurnal Movements		Harmonies Between the Movements of Single Planets
Diverging Converging			
	Saturn at aphelion	1′46″ a.	$1 : 48″ : 2′15″ = 4 : 5,$
	at perihelion	2′15″ b.	major third
$\dfrac{a}{d}=\dfrac{1}{3}, \quad \dfrac{b}{c}=\dfrac{1}{2}$			
	Jupiter at aphelion	4′30″ c.	$4′35″ : 5′30″ = 5 : 6,$
	at perihelion	5′30″ d.	minor third
$\dfrac{c}{f}=\dfrac{1}{8}, \quad \dfrac{d}{e}=\dfrac{5}{24}$			
	Mars at aphelion	26′14″ e.	$25′21″ : 38′1″ = 2 : 3,$
	at perihelion	38′1″ f.	the fifth
$\dfrac{e}{h}=\dfrac{5}{12}, \quad \dfrac{f}{g}=\dfrac{2}{3}$			
	Earth at aphelion	57′3″ g.	$57′28″ : 61′18″ = 15 : 16,$
	at perihelion	61′18″ h.	semitone
$\dfrac{g}{k}=\dfrac{3}{5}, \quad \dfrac{h}{i}=\dfrac{5}{8}$			
	Venus at aphelion	94′50″ i.	$94′50″ : 98′47″ = 24 : 25,$
	at perihelion	97′37″ k.	diesis
$\dfrac{i}{m}=\dfrac{1}{4}, \quad \dfrac{k}{l}=\dfrac{3}{5}$			
	Mercury at aphelion	164′0″ l.	$164′0″ : 394′0″ = 5 : 12,$
	at perihelion	384′0″ m.	octave and minor third

greater than I have here laid down, because the mean movement at the mean anomaly, viewed very obliquely, does not appear as great, *viz.*, not as great as 245′32″, but about 5′ less. Therefore, too, lesser aphelial and perihelial movements will be elicited. But the aphelial [appears] lesser and the perihelial greater, on account of theorem 8, Euclid's *Optics*, as I remarked in the preceding Chapter, Article vi.

Accordingly, I could mentally presume, even from the ratios of the diurnal eccentric arcs given above, that there were harmonies and concordant intervals between these extreme apparent movements of the single planets, since I saw that everywhere there the square roots of harmonic ratios were dominant, but knew that the ratio of the apparent movements was the square of the ratio of the eccentric movements. But it is possible by experience itself, or without any ratiocination to prove what is affirmed, as you see [288] in the preceding table. The ratios of the apparent movements of the single planets approach very close to harmonies, in such fashion that Saturn and Jupiter embrace slightly more than the major and minor thirds, Saturn with a ratio of excess of 53 : 54, and Jupiter with one of 54 : 55 or less, namely approximately a sesquicomma; the Earth, slightly more (namely 137 : 138, or barely a semicomma) than a semitone; Mars somewhat less (namely 29 : 30, which approaches 34 : 35 or 35 : 36) than a fifth; Mercury exceeds the octave by a minor third rather than a whole tone, *viz.*, it is about 38 : 39 (which is about two commas, *viz.*, 34 : 35 or 35 : 36) less than a whole tone. Venus alone falls short of any of the concords the diesis; for its ratio is between two and three commas, and it exceeds two thirds of a diesis, and is about 34 : 35 or 35 : 36, a diesis diminished by a comma.

The moon, too, comes into this consideration. For we find that its hourly apogeal movement in the quadratures, *viz.*, the slowest of all its movements, to be 26'26''; its perigeal movement in the syzygies, *viz.*, the fastest of all, 35'12'', in which way the perfect fourth is formed very precisely. For one third of 26'26'' is 8'49'', the quadruple of which is 35'16''. And note that the consonance of the perfect fourth is found nowhere else between the apparent movements; note also the analogy between the fourth in consonances and the quarter in the phases. And so the above things are found in the movements of the single planets.

But in the extreme movements of two planets compared with one another, the radiant sun of celestial harmonies immediately shines at first glance, whether you compare the diverging extreme movements or the converging. For the ratio between the diverging movements of Saturn and Jupiter is exactly the duple or octave; that between the diverging, slightly more than triple or the octave and the fifth. For one third of 5'30'' is 1'50'', although Saturn has 1'46'' instead of that. Accordingly, the planetary movements will differ from a consonance by a diesis more or less, *viz.*, 26 : 27 or 27 : 28; and with less than one second acceding at Saturn's aphelion, the excess will be 34 : 35, as great as the ratio of the extreme movements of Venus. The diverging and converging movements of Jupiter and Mars are under the sway of the triple octave and the double octave and a third, but not perfectly. For one eighth of 38'1'' is 4'45'', although Jupiter has 4'30''; and between these numbers there is still a difference of 18 : 19, which is a mean between the semitone of 15 : 16 and the diesis of 24 : 25, namely, approximately a perfect lemma of 128 : 135.[1] Thus one fifth of 26'14'' is 5'15'', although Jupiter has 5'30''; accordingly in this case the quintuple ratio is diminished in the ratio of 21 : 22, the augment in the case of the other ratio, *viz.*, approximately a diesis of 24 : 25.

The consonance 5 : 24 comes nearer, which compounds a minor instead of a major third with the double octave. For one fifth of 5'30'' is 1'6'', which if multiplied by 24 makes 26'24'', does not differ by more than a semicomma. Mars and the Earth have been allotted the least ratio, exactly the sesquialteral or perfect fifth: for one third of 57'3'' is 19'1'', the double of which is 38'2'', which is Mars' very number, *viz.*, 38'11''. They have also been allotted the greater ratio of 5 : 12, the octave and minor third, but more imperfectly. For one twelfth of 61'18'' is 5'6½'', which if multiplied by 5 gives 25'33'', although instead of that Mars has 26'14''. Accordingly, there is a deficiency of a diminished diesis approximately, *viz.*, 35 : 36. But the Earth and Venus together have been allotted 3 : 5 as their greatest consonance and 5 : 8 as their least, the major and minor sixths, but again not perfectly. For one fifth of 97'37'', which if multiplied by 3 gives 58'33'', which is greater than the movement of the Earth in the ratio 34 : 35, which is approximately 35 : 36: by so much do the planetary ratios differ from the harmonic. Thus one eighth of 94'50'' is 11'51'' +, five times which is 59'16'', which is approximately equal to the mean movement of the Earth. Wherefore here the planetary ratio is less than the harmonic [289] in the ratio of 29 : 30 or 30 : 31, which is again approximately 35 : 36, the diminished diesis; and thereby this least ratio of these planets approaches the consonance of the perfect fifth. For one third of 94'50'' is 31'37'', the double of which is 63'14'', of which the 61'18'' of the perihelial movement of the Earth falls short in the ratio

[1] *cf.* Footnote to *Intervals Compared with Harmonic Ratios*, p. 1026.

of 31 : 32, so that the planetary ratio is exactly a mean between the neighbouring harmonic ratios. Finally, Venus and Mercury have been allotted the double octave as their greatest ratio and the major sixth as their least, but not absolutely perfectly. For one fourth of 384' is 96'0", although Venus has 94'50". Therefore the quadruple adds approximately one comma. Thus one fifth of 164' is 32'48", which if multiplied by 3 gives 98'24", although Venus has 97'37". Therefore the planetary ratio is diminished by about tow thirds of a comma, *i.e.*, 126 : 127.

Accordingly the above consonances have been ascribed to the planets; nor is there any ratio from among the principal comparisons (*viz.*, of the converging and diverging extreme movements) which does not approach so nearly to some consonance that, if strings were tuned in that ratio, the ears would not easily discern their imperfection—with the exception of that one excess between Jupiter and Mars.

Moreover, it follows that we shall not stray far away from consonances if we compare the movements of the same field. For if Saturn's 4 : 5 comp. 53 : 54 are compounded with the intermediate 1 : 2, the product is 2 : 5 comp. 53 : 54, which exists between the aphelial movements of Saturn and Jupiter. Compound with that Jupiter's 5 : 6 comp. 54 : 55, and the product is 5 : 12 comp 54 : 55, which exist between the perihelial movements of Saturn and Jupiter. Thus compound Jupiter's 5 : 6 comp. 54 : 55 with the intermediate ensuing ratio of 5 : 24 comp. 158 : 157, the product will be 1 : 6 comp. 36 : 35 between the aphelial movements. Compound the same 5 : 24 comp. 158 : 157 with Mars' 2 : 3 comp. 30 : 29, and the product will be 5 : 36 comp. 25 : 24 approximately, *i.e.*, 125 : 864 or about 1 : 7, between the perihelial movements. This ratio is still alone discordant. With 2 : 3 the third ratio among the intermediates, compound Mars' 2 : 3 less 29 : 30; the result will be 4 : 9 comp. 30 : 29, *i.e.*, 40 : 87, another discord between the aphelial movements. If instead of Mars' you compound the Earth's 15 : 16 comp. 137 : 138, you will make 5 : 8 comp. 137 : 138 between the perihelial movements. And if with the fourth of the intermediates, 5 : 8 comp. 31 : 30, or 2 : 3 comp. 31 : 32, you compound the Earth's 15 : 16 comp. 137 : 138, the product will be approximately 3 : 5 between the aphelial movements of the Earth and Venus. For one fifth of 94'50" is 18'58", the triple of which is 56'54", although the Earth has 57'3". If you compound Venus' 34 : 35 with the same ratio, the result will be 5 : 8 between the perihelial movements. For one eighth of 97'37" is 12'12"+ which if multiplied by 5 gives 61'1", although the Earth has 61'18". Finally, if with the last of the intermediate ratios, 3 : 5 comp. 126 : 127 you compound Venus' 34 : 35, the result is 3 : 5 comp. 24 : 25, and the interval, compounded of both, between the aphelial movements, is dissonant. But if you compound Mercury's 5 : 12 comp. 38 : 39, the double octave or 1 : 4 will be diminished by approximately a whole diesis, in proportion to the perihelial movements.

Accordingly, perfect consonances are found: between the converging movements of Saturn and Jupiter, the octave; between the converging movements of Jupiter and Mars, the octave and minor third approximately; between the converging movements of Mars and the Earth, the fifth; between their perihelial, the minor sixth; between the extreme converging movements of Venus and Mercury, the major sixth; between the diverging or even between the perihelial, the double octave: whence without any loss to an astronomy which has been built, most subtly of all, upon Brahe's observations, it seems that the residual very slight discrepancy can be discounted, especially in the movements of Venus and Mercury.

But you will note that where there is no perfect major consonance, as between Jupiter and Mars, there alone have I found the placing of the solid figure to be approximately perfect, since the perihelial distance of Jupiter is approximately three times the aphelial distance of Mars, in such fashion that this pair of planets strives after the perfect consonance in the intervals which it does not have in the movements.

[290] You will note, furthermore, that the major planetary ratio of Saturn and Jupiter exceeds the harmonic, *viz.*, the triple, by approximately the same quantity as belongs to Venus; and the common major ratio of the converging and diverging movements of Mars and the Earth are diminished by approximately the same. You will note thirdly that, roughly speaking, in the upper planets the consonances are established between the converging movements, but in the lower planets, between movements in the same field. And note fourthly that between the aphelial movements of Saturn and the Earth there are approximately five octaves; for one thirty-second of 57′3″ is 1′47″, although the aphelial movement of Saturn is 1′46″.

Furthermore, a great distinction exists between the consonances of the single planets which have been unfolded and the consonances of the planets in pairs. For the former cannot exist at the same moment of time, while the latter absolutely can; because the same planet, moving at its aphelion, cannot be at the same time at the opposite perihelion too, but of two planets one can be at its aphelion and the other at its perihelion at the same moment of time. And so the ratio of plain-song or monody, which we call choral music and which alone was known to the ancients,[1] to polyphony—called "figured song,"[2] the invention of the latest generations—is the same as the ratio of the consonances which the single planets designate to the consonances of the planets taken together. And so, further on, in Chapters 5 and 6, the single planets will be compared to the choral music of the ancients and its properties will be exhibited in the planetary movements. But in the following chapters, the planets taken together and the figured modern music will be shown to do similar things.

5. In the Ratios of the Planetary Movements which are Apparent as it were to Spectators at the Sun, have been Expressed the Pitches of the System, or Notes of the Musical Scale, and the Modes of Song [Genera Cantus], the Major and the Minor[3]

Therefore by now I have proved by means of numbers gotten on one side from astronomy and on the other side from harmonics that, taken in every which way, harmonic ratios hold between these twelve termini or movements of the six planets revolving around the sun or that they approximate such ratios within an imperceptible part of least concord. But just as in Book III in the first chapter, we first built up the single harmonic consonances separately, and then

---

[1]The choral music of the Greeks was monolinear, everyone singing the same melody together.—E. C., Jr.

[2]In plain-song all the time values of the notes were approximately equal, while in "figured song" time values of different lengths were indicated by the notes, which gave composers an opportunity both to regulate the way different contrapuntal parts joined together and to produce many expressive effects. Practically all melodies since this time are in "figured song" style.—E. C., Jr.

[3]See note to *Intervals Compared with Harmonic Ratios*, p. 1026.

we joined together all the consonances—as many as there were—in one common system or musical scale, or, rather, in one octave of them which embraces the rest in power, and by means of them we separated the others into their degrees or pitches [*loca*] and we did this in such a way that there would be a scale; so now also, after the discovery of the consonances [*harmoniis*] which God Himself has embodied in the world, we must consequently see whether those single consonances stand so separate that they have no kinship with the rest, or whether all are in concord with one another. Notwithstanding it is easy to conclude, without any further inquiry, that those consonances were fitted together by the highest prudence in such fashion that they move one another about within one frame, so to speak, and do not jolt one another out of it; since indeed we see that in such a manifold comparison of the same terms there is no place where consonances do not occur. For unless in one scale all the consonances were fitted to all, it could easily have come about (and it has come about wherever necessity thus urges it) that many dissonances should exist. For example, if someone had set up a major sixth between the first and the second term, and likewise a major third between the second and the third term, without taking the first into account, then he would admit a dissonance and the discordant interval 12 : 25 be-between the first and third.

But come now, let us see whether that which we have already inferred by reasoning is really found in this way. [291] But let me premise some cautions, that we may be the less impeded in our progress. First, for the present, we must conceal those augments or diminutions which are less than a semitone; for we shall see later on what causes they have. Second, by continuous doubling or contrary halving of the movements, we shall bring everything within the range of one octave, on account of the sameness of consonance in all the octaves.

Accordingly the numbers wherein all the pitches or clefs [*loca seu claves*] of the octave system are expressed have been set out in a table in Book III, Chapter 7[1],

¹The table is as follows:

Concordant Intervals	Lengths of Strings	In familiar notes
	1080	High g
Semitone		
	1152	f ♯
Lemma		
	1215	f
Semitone		
	1296	e
Diesis		
	1350	e ♭
Semitone		
	1440	d
Semitone		
	1536	c ♯
Lemma		
	1620	c
Semitone		
	1728	b
Diesis		
	1800	b ♭
Semitone		
	1920	A
Semitone		
	2048	G ♯
Lemma		
	2160	Low G

i.e., understand these numbers of the length of two strings. As a consequence, the speeds of the movements will be in the inverse ratios.

Now let the planetary movements be compared in terms of parts continuously halved. Therefore

Movement of Mercury at perihelion,	7th subduple, or $\frac{1}{128}$,	3′0″
at aphelion,	6th subduple, or $\frac{1}{64}$,	2′34″
Movement of Venus at perihelion,	5th subduple, or $\frac{1}{32}$,	3′3″
at aphelion,	5th subduple, or $\frac{1}{32}$,	2′58″
Movement of Earth at perihelion,	5th subduple, or $\frac{1}{32}$,	1′55″
at aphelion,	5th subduple, or $\frac{1}{32}$,	1′47″
Movement of Mars at perihelion,	4th subduple, or $\frac{1}{16}$,	2′23″
at aphelion,	3rd subduple, or $\frac{1}{8}$,	3′17″
Movement of Jupiter at perihelion,	subduple, or $\frac{1}{2}$,	2′45″
at aphelion,	subduple, or $\frac{1}{2}$,	2′15″
Movement of Saturn at perihelion,		2′15″
at aphelion,		1′46″

Now the aphelial movement of Saturn at its slowest—*i.e.*, the slowest movement—marks *G*, the lowest pitch in the system with the number 1′46″. Therefore the aphelial movement of the Earth will mark the same pitch, but five octaves higher, because its number is 1′47″, and who wants to quarrel about one second in the aphelial movement of Saturn? But let us take it into account, nevertheless; the difference will not be greater than 106 : 107, which is less than a comma. If you add 27″, one quarter of this 1′47″, the sum will be 2′14″, although the perihelial movement of Saturn has 2′15″; similarly the aphelial movement of Jupiter, but one octave higher. Accordingly, these two movements mark the note *b*, or else are very slightly higher. Take 36″, one third of 1′47″, and add it to the whole; you will get as a sum 2′23″ for the note *c*; and here's the perihelion of Mars of the same magnitude but four octaves higher. To this same 1′47″ add also 54″, half of it, and the sum will be 2′41″ for the note *d*; and here the perihelion of Jupiter is at hand, but one octave higher, for it occupies the nearest number, *viz.*, 2′45″. If you add two thirds, *viz.*, 1′11″, the sum will be 2′58″; and here's the aphelion of Venus at 2′58″. Accordingly, it will mark the pitch or the note *e*, but five octaves higher. And the perihelial movement of Mercury, which is 3′0″, does not exceed it by much but is seven octaves higher. Finally, divide the double of 1′47″, *viz.*, 3′34″, into nine parts and subtract one part of 24″ from the whole; 3′10″ will be left for the note *f*, which the 3′17″ of the aphelial movement of Mars marks approximately but three octaves higher; and this number is slightly greater than the just number and approaches the note *f* sharp. For if one sixteenth of 3′34″, *viz.*, 13½″, is subtracted from 3′34″, then 3′20½″ is left, to which 3′17″ is very near. And indeed in music *f* sharp is often employed in place of *f*, as we can see everywhere.

Accordingly all the notes of the major scale [*cantus duri*] (except the note *a* which was not marked by harmonic division, in Book III, Chapter 2) are marked by all the extreme movements of the planets, except the perihelial movements of Venus and the Earth [292] and the aphelial movement of Mercury, whose number, 2′34″, approaches the note *c* sharp. For subtract from the 2′41″ of *d* one sixteenth or 10″, and 2′30″ remains for the note *c* sharp. Thus only the perihelial movement of Venus and the Earth are missing from this scale, as you may see in the table.

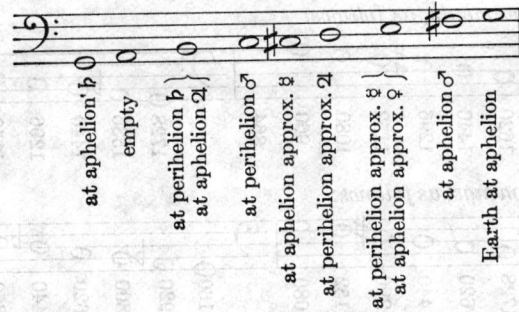

On the other hand, if the beginning of the scale is made at 2′15″, the aphelial movement of Saturn, and we must express the note G in those degrees: then for the note A is 2′32″, which closely approaches the aphelial movement of Mercury; for the note b flat, 2′42″, which is approximately the perihelial movement of Jupiter, by the equipollence of octaves; for the note c, 3′0″, approximately the perihelial movement of Mercury and Venus; for the note d, 3′23″ and the aphelial movement of Mars is not much graver, viz., 3′17″, so that here the number is about as much less than its note as previously the same number was greater than its note; for the note e flat, 3′36″, which the aphelial movement of the Earth approximates; for the note e, 3′50″, and the perihelial movement of the Earth is 3′49″; but the aphelial movement of Jupiter again occupies g. In this way, all the notes except f are expressed within one octave of the minor scale by most of the aphelial and perihelial movements of the planets, especially by those which were previously omitted, as you see in the table.

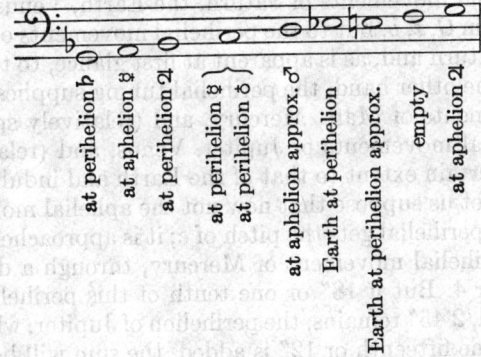

Previously, however, f sharp was marked and a omitted; now a is marked, f sharp is omitted; for the harmonic division in Chapter 2 also omitted the note f.

Accordingly, the musical scale or system of one octave with all its pitches, by means of which natural song[1] is transposed in music, has been expressed in the heavens by a twofold way and in two as it were modes of song. There is this sole difference: in our harmonic sectionings both ways start together from one and the same terminus G; but here, in the planetary movements, that which was previously b now becomes G in the minor mode.

[1] Natural song: music in the basic major or minor system without accidentals. E. C., Jr.

In the celestial movements, as follows:

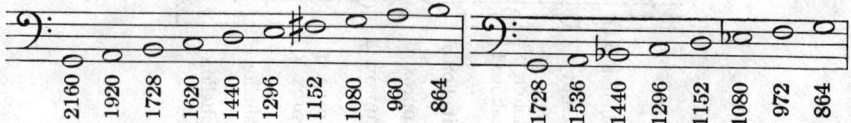

By harmonic sectionings, as follows:

For as in music 2160 : 1800, or 6 : 5, so in that system which the heavens express, 1728 : 1440, namely, also 6 : 5; and so for most of the remaining, 2160 : 1800, 1620, 1440, 1350, 1080 as 1728 : 1440, 1296, 1152, 1080, 864.

Accordingly you won't wonder any more that a very excellent order of sounds or pitches in a musical system or scale has been set up by men, since you see that they are doing nothing else in this business except to play the apes of God the Creator and to act out, as it were, a certain drama of the ordination of the celestial movements.

But there still remains another way whereby we may understand the twofold musical scale in the heavens, where one and the same system but a twofold tuning [*tensio*] is embraced, one at the aphelial movement of Venus, the other at the perihelial, because the variety of movements of this planet is of the least magnitude, as being such as is comprehended within the magnitude of the diesis, the least concord. And the aphelial tuning [*tensio*], as above, has been given to the aphelial movements of Saturn, the Earth, Venus, and (relatively speaking) Jupiter, in *G, e, b,* but to the perihelial movements of Mars and (relatively speaking) Saturn and, as is apparent at first glance, to those of Mercury, in *c, e,* and *b.* On the other hand, the perihelial tuning supplies a pitch even for the aphelial movements of Mars, Mercury, and (relatively speaking) Jupiter, but to the perihelial movements of Jupiter, Venus, and (relatively speaking) Saturn, and to a certain extent to that of the Earth and indubitably to that of Mercury too. For let us suppose that now not the aphelial movement of Venus but the 3′3″ of the perihelial gets the pitch of *e;* it is approached very closely by the 3′0″ of the perihelial movement of Mercury, through a double octave, at the end of Chapter 4. But if 18″ or one tenth of this perihelial movement of Venus is subtracted, 2′45″ remains, the perihelion of Jupiter, which occupies the pitch of *d;* and if one fifteenth or 12″ is added, the sum will be 3′15″, approximately the perihelion of Mars which occupies the pitch of *f;* and thus in *b,* the perihelial movement of Saturn and the aphelial movement of Jupiter have approximately the same tuning. But one eighth, or 23″, if multiplied by 5, gives 1′55″, which is the perihelial movement of the Earth; and, although it does not square with the foregoing in the same scale, as it does not give the interval 5 : 8 below *e* nor 24 : 25 above *G,* nevertheless if now the perihelial movement of Venus and so too the aphelial movement of Mercury, outside of the order, occupy the pitch *e*-flat instead of *e,* then there the perihelial movement of the Earth will occupy the pitch of *G,* and the aphelial movement of Mercury is in concord, because 1′1″, or one third of 3′3″, if multiplied by 5, gives 5′5″, half of which, or

2′32″, approximates the aphelion of Mercury, which in this extraordinary adjustment will occupy the pitch of *c*. Therefore, all these movements are of the same tuning with respect to one another; but the perihelial movement of Venus together with the three (or five) prior movements, *viz.*, in the same harmonic mode, divides the scale differently from the aphelial movement of the same in its tuning, *viz.*, in the major mode [*denere duro*]. Moreover, the perihelial movement of Venus, together with the two posterior movements, divides the same scale differently, *viz.*, not into concords but merely into a different order of concords, namely one which belongs to the minor mode [*generis mollis*].

But it is sufficient to have laid before the eyes in this chapter what is the case casually, but it will be disclosed in Chapter 9 by the most lucid demonstrations why each and every one of these things was made in this fashion and what the causes were not merely of harmony but even of the very least discord.

6. In the Extreme Planetary Movements the Musical Modes or Tones Have Somehow Been Expressed

[294] This follows from the aforesaid and there is no need of many words; for the single planets somehow mark the pitches of the system with their perihelial movement, in so far as it has been appointed to the single planets to traverse a certain fixed interval in the musical scale comprehended by the definite notes of it or the pitches of the system, and beginning at that note or pitch of each planet which in the preceding chapter fell to the aphelial movement of that planet: *G* to Saturn and the Earth, *b* to Jupiter, which can be transposed higher to *G*, *f*-sharp to Mars, *e* to Venus, *a* to Mercury in the higher octave. See the single movements in the familiar terms of notes. They do not form articulately the intermediate positions, which you here see filled by notes, as they do the extremes, because they struggle from one extreme to the opposite not by leaps and intervals but by a continuum of tunings and actually traverse all the means (which are potentially infinite)—which cannot be expressed by me in any other way than by a continuous series of intermediate notes. Venus remains approximately in unison and does not equal even the least of the concordant intervals in the difference of its tension.

[In Modern notation:

—E. C. Jr.]

But the signature of two accidentals (flats) in a common staff and the formation of the skeletal outline of the octave by the inclusion of a definite concordant interval are a certain first beginning of the distinction of Tones or Modes [*modorum*]. Therefore the musical Modes have been distributed among the planets. But I know that for the formation and determination of distinct Modes many things are requisite, which belong to human song, as containing (a) distinct [order of] intervals; and so I have used the word *somehow*.

But the harmonist will be free to choose his opinion as to which Mode each planet expresses as its own, since the extremes have been assigned to it here. From among the familiar Modes, I should give to Saturn the Seventh or Eighth, because if you place its key-note at G, the perihelial movement ascends to b; to Jupiter, the First or Second Mode, because its aphelial movement has been fitted to G and its perihelial movement arrives at b flat; to Mars, the Fifth or Sixth Mode, not only because Mars comprehends approximately the perfect fifth, which interval is common to all the Modes, but principally because when it is reduced with the others to a common system, it attains c with its perihelial movement and touches f with its aphelial, which is the key-note of the Fifth or Sixth Mode or Tone; I should give the Third or Fourth Mode to the Earth, because its movement revolves within a semitone, while the first interval of those Modes is a semitone; but to Mercury will belong indifferently all the Modes or Tones on account of the greatness of its range; to Venus, clearly none on account of the smallness of its range; but on account of the common system the Third and Fourth Mode, because with reference to the other planets it occupies e. (The Earth sings MI, FA, MI so that you may infer even from the syllables that in this our domicile MIsery and FAmine obtain.)[1]

7. The Universal Consonances of All Six Planets, Like Common Four-Part Counterpoint, Can Exist

[295] But now, Urania, there is need for louder sound while I climb along the harmonic scale of the celestial movements to higher things where the true archetype of the fabric of the world is kept hidden. Follow after, ye modern musicians, and judge the thing according to your arts, which were unknown to antiquity. Nature, which is never not lavish of herself, after a lying-in of two thousand years, has finally brought you forth in these last generations, the first true images of the universe. By means of your concords of various voices, and through your ears, she has whispered to the human mind, the favorite daughter of God the Creator, how she exists in the innermost bosom.

(Shall I have committed a crime if I ask the single composers of this generation for some artistic motet instead of this epigraph? The Royal Psalter and the other Holy Books can supply a text suited for this. But alas for you! No more than six are in concord in the heavens. For the moon sings here monody separately, like a dog sitting on the Earth. Compose the melody; I, in order that the book may progress, promise that I will watch carefully over the six parts. To him who more properly expresses the celestial music described in this work, Clio will give a garland, and Urania will betroth Venus his bride.)

It has been unfolded above what harmonic ratios two neighbouring planets would embrace in their extreme movements. But it happens very rarely that two, especially the slowest, arrive at their extreme intervals at the same time; For example, the apsides of Saturn and Jupiter are about 81° apart. According-

[1]See note on hexachordal system.

ly, while this distance between them measures out the whole zodiac by definite twenty-year leaps[1], eight hundred years pass by, and nonetheless the leap which concludes the eighth century, does not carry precisely to the very apsides; and if it digresses much further, another eight hundred years must be awaited, that a more fortunate leap than that one may be sought; and the whole route must be repeated as many times as the measure of digression is contained in the length of one leap. Moreover, the other single pairs of planets have periods like that, although not so long. But meanwhile there occur also other consonances of two planets, between movements whereof not both are extremes but one or both are intermediate; and those consonances exist as it were in different tunings [*tensionibus*]. For, because Saturn tends from *G* to *b*, and slightly further, and Jupiter from *b* to *d* and further; therefore between Jupiter and Saturn there can exist the following consonances, over and above the octave: the major and minor third and the perfect fourth, either one of the thirds through the tuning which maintains the amplitude of the remaining one, but the perfect fourth through the amplitude of a major whole tone. For there will be a perfect fourth not merely from *G* of Saturn to *cc* of Jupiter but also from *A* of Saturn to *dd* of Jupiter and through all the intermediates between the *G* and *A* of Saturn and the *cc* and *dd* of Jupiter. But the octave and the perfect fifth exist solely at the points of the apsides. But Mars, which got a greater interval as its own, received it in order that it should also make an octave with the upper planets through some amplitude of tuning. Mercury received an interval great enough for it to set up almost all the consonances with all the planets within one of its periods, which is not longer than the space of three months. On the other hand, the Earth, and Venus much more so, on account of the smallness of their intervals, limit the consonances, which they form not merely with the others but with one another in especial, to visible fewness. But if three planets are to concord in one harmony, many periodic returns are to be awaited; nevertheless there are many consonances, so that they may so much the more easily take place, while each nearest consonance follows after its neighbour, and very often threefold consonances are seen to exist between Mars, the Earth, and Mercury. But the consonances of four planets now begin to be scattered throughout centuries, and those of five planets throughout thousands of years.

But that all six should be in concord [296] has been fenced about by the longest intervals of time; and I do not know whether it is absolutely impossible for this to occur twice by precise evolving or whether that points to a certain beginning of time, from which every age of the world has flowed.

But if only one sextuple harmony can occur, or only one notable one among many, indubitably that could be taken as a sign of the Creation. Therefore we must ask, in exactly how many forms are the movements of all six planets reduced to one common harmony? The method of inquiry is as follows: let us begin with the Earth and Venus, because these two planets do not make more than two consonances and (wherein the cause of this thing is comprehended) by means of very short intensifications of the movements.

Therefore let us set up two, as it were, skeletal outlines of harmonies, each skeletal outline determined by the two extreme numbers wherewith the limits

---

[1]That is to say, since Saturn and Jupiter have one revolution with respect to one another every twenty years, they are 81° apart once every twenty years, while the end-positions of this 81° interval traverse the ecliptic in leaps, so to speak, and coincide with the apsides approximately once in eight hundred years. C. G. W.

of the tunings are designated, and let us search out what fits in with them from the variety of movements granted to each planet.

Harmonies of all the Planets, or Universal Harmonies in the Major Mode

In order that b may be in concord		At gravest Tuning	At most acute Tuning	[Modern notation
☿	e^7	380'20''		5 x 8va
	b^6	285'15''	292'48''	
	g^6	228'12''	234'16''	
♀	e^6	190'10''	195'14''	4 x 8va
	e^5	95'5''	97'37''	
☾	g^4	57'3''	58'34''	2 x 8va
	b^3	35'39''	36'36''	
♂	g^3	28'32''	29'17''	8va
♃	b		4'34''	
♄	B	2'14''		
	G	1'47''	1'49''	

E. C., Jr.]

In order that c may be in concord		At Gravest tuning	At most acute tuning	[Modern notation
☿	e^7	380'20''		5 x 8va
	c^7	204'16''	312'21''	
	g^6	228'12''	234'16''	
♀	e^6	190'10''	195'14''	4 x 8va
	e^5	95'5''	97'37''	
☾	g^4	57'3''	58'34''	2 x 8va
	c^4	38'2''	39'3''	
♂	g^3	28'32''	29'17''	8va
♃	c^1	4'45''	4'53''	
♄	G	1'47''	1'49''	

E. C., Jr.]

Saturn joins in this universal consonance with its aphelial movement, the Earth with its aphelial, Venus approximately with its aphelial; at highest tuning, Venus joins with its perihelial; at mean tuning, Saturn joins with its perihelial, Jupiter with its aphelial, Mercury with its perihelial. So Saturn can join in with two movements, Mars with two, Mercury with four. But with the rest remaining, the perihelial movement of Saturn and the aphelial of Jupiter are not allowed. But in their place, Mars joins in with perihelial movement.

The remaining planets join in with single movements, Mars alone with two, and Mercury with four.

[297] Accordingly, the second skeletal outline will be that wherein the other possible consonance, 5 : 8, exists between the Earth and Venus. Here one eighth of the 94′50″ of the diurnal aphelial movement of Venus or 11′51″ +, if multiplied by 5, equals the 59′16″ of the movement of the Earth; and similar parts of the 97′37″ of the perihelial movement of Venus are equal to the 61′1″ of the movement of the Earth. Accordingly, the other planets are in concord in the following diurnal movements:

Harmonies of all the Planets, or Universal Harmonies in the Minor Mode

In order that ♭ may be in concord		At gravest tuning	At most acute tuning	[Modern notation:
☿	e♭⁷	379′20″		5 x 8va
	b♭⁷	284′32″	295′56″	
	g⁶	237′4″	244′4″	
♀	e♭⁶	189′40″	195′14″	4 x 8va
	e♭⁵	94′50″	97′37″	
♁	g⁴	59′16″	61′1″	2 x 8va
	b♭⁴	35′35″	36′37″	
♂	g³	29′38″	30′31″	8va
♃	b♭¹		4′35″	
♄	b♭	2′13″		
	G	3′51″	1′55″	

E. C., Jr.]

Here again, in the mean tuning Saturn joins in with its perihelial movement, Jupiter with its aphelial, Mercury with its perihelial. But at highest tuning approximately the perihelial movement of the Earth joins in.

In order that c may be in concord	At gravest tuning	At most acute tuning	[Modern notation:
☿ eb7	379'20"		5 x 8va
☿ c7	316'5"	325'26"	
g6	237'4"	244'4"	
♀ eb6	189'40"	195'14"	4 x 8va
♀ c6		162'43"	
eb5	94'50"	97'37"	
g4	59'16"	61'1"	2 x 8va
♂ g3	29'38"	30'31"	8va
♃ c1	4'56"	5'5"	
♄ G	3'51"	1'55"	

E. C., Jr.]

An here, with the aphelial movement of Jupiter and the perihelial movement of Saturn removed, the aphelial movement of Mercury is practically admitted besides the perihelial. The rest remain.

Therefore astronomical experience bears witness that the universal consonances of all the movements can take place, and in the two modes [generum], the major and minor, and in both genera of form, or (if I may say so) in respect to two pitches and in any one of the four cases, with a certain latitude of tuning and also with a certain variety in the particular consonances of Saturn, Mars, and Mercury, of each with the rest; and that is not afforded by the intermediate movements alone, but by all the extreme movements too, except the aphelial movement of Mars and the perihelial movement of Jupiter; because since the former occupies f sharp; and the latter, d Venus, which occupies perpetually the intermediate e flat or e, does not allow those neighbouring dissonances in the universal consonance, as she would do if she had space to go beyond e or e flat. This difficulty is caused by the wedding of the Earth and Venus, or the male and the female. These two planets divide the kinds [genera] of consonances into the major and masculine and the minor and feminine, according as the one spouse has gratified the other—namely, either the Earth is in its aphelion, as if preserving [298] its marital dignity and performing works worthy of a man, with

Venus removed and pushed away to her perihelion as to her distaff; or else the Earth has kindly allowed her to ascend into aphelion or the Earth itself has descended into its perihelion towards Venus and as it were, into her embrace, for the sake of pleasure, and has laid aside for a while its shield and arms and all the works befitting a man; for at that time the consonance is minor.

But if we command this contradictory Venus to keep quiet, *i.e.*, if we consider what the consonances not of all but merely of the five remaining planets can be, excluding the movement of Venus, the Earth still wanders around its *g* string and does not ascend a semitone above it. Accordingly $b\flat$, b, c, d, $e\flat$, and e can be in concord with g, whereupon, as you see, Jupiter, marking the d string with its perihelial movement, is brought in. Accordingly, the difficulty about Mars' aphelial movement remains. For the aphelial movement of the Earth, which occupies g, does not allow it on f sharp; but the perihelial movement, as was said above in Chapter v, is in discord with the aphelial movement of Mars by about half a diesis.

Harmonies of the Five Planets, with Venus Left Out

Major mode (Genus durum)		At gravest tuning	At most acute tuning	[Modern notation:
	d⁷	342′18″	351′24″	
♄	b⁶	285′15″	292′48″	
	g⁶	228′12″	234′16″	
♀ in	d⁶	171′9″	175′42″	
discord				
	e⁵	95′5″	97′37″	
♂	g⁴	57′3″	58′34″	
	b³	35′39″	36′36″	
	g³	28′31″	29′17″	
♃	d¹	5′21″	5′30″	
	b¹		4′35″	
♭ B		2′13″		
G		1′47″		

E. C., JR.]

Here at the most grave tuning, Saturn and the Earth join in with their aphelial movements; at the mean tuning, Saturn with its perihelial and Jupiter with its aphelial; at the most acute, Jupiter with its perihelial.

Minor mode (Genus molle)		At gravest tuning	At most acute tuning	[Modern notation:
☿	d⁷	342′18″	351′24″	
	b⁶	273′50″	280′57″	5 x 8va
	g⁶	228′12″	234′16″	
♀ in discord	d⁶	171′9″	175′42″	4 x 8va
	e⁵	95′5″	97′37″	
♂	g⁴	57′3″	58′34″	2 x 8va
	b³	34′14″	35′8″	
	g³	28′31″	29′17″	8va
♃	d¹	5′21″	5′30″	
♄	B	2′8″	2′12″	
	G	1′47″	1′50″	

E. C., Jr.]

Here the aphelial movement of Jupiter is not allowed, but at the most acute tuning Saturn practically joins in with its perihelial movement.

But there can also exist the following harmony of the four planets, Saturn, Jupiter, Mars, and Mercury, wherein too the aphelial movement of Mars is present, but it is without latitude of tuning.

In order that b may be in concord

₲	d⁷		335′50″
	b⁶		279′52″
	f#⁶		209′52″
	d⁶		167′55″
♂	b³		34′59″
	f#³		26′14″
♃	d¹		5′15″
♭	B		2′11″

[Modern notation:

5 x 8va
4 x 8va
2 x 8va
8va

E. C., JR.]

In order that a may be in concord

₲	d⁷	
	a⁶	
	f#⁶	
	d⁶	
♂	a³	
	f#³	
♃	d¹	
♭	A	

[Modern notation:

5 x 8va
4 x 8va
2 x 8va
8va

E. C., JR.]

Accordingly the movements of the heavens are nothing except a certain ever-lasting polyphony (intelligible, not audible) with dissonant tunings, like certain syncopations or cadences (wherewith men imitate these natural dissonances), which tends towards fixed and prescribed clauses—the single clauses having six terms (like voices)— and which marks out and distinguishes the immensity of time with those notes. Hence it is no longer a surprise that man, the ape of his Creator, should finally have discovered the art of singing polyphonically [*per concentum*], which was unknown to the ancients, namely in order that he might play the everlastingness of all created time in some short part of an hour by means of an artistic concord of many voices and that he might to some extent taste the satisfaction of God the Workman with His own works, in that very sweet sense of delight elicited from this music which imitates God.

NOTE: The comparison Kepler draws between the celestial harmonies and the polyphonic music of his time may be clarified by a simple example for four voices from—Palestrina, *O Crux:*

X   Consonant
    harmonies
Y   Dissonant
    syncopations
Z   Resolutions of
    dissonances

Cadence

As will be observed each of the four voices (as it would also be with the six to which Kepler refers) moves from one consonant chord to another while following a graceful melodic line. Sometimes bits of scales or passing tones are added to give a voice more melodic freedom expressiveness. For the same reason a voice may remain on the same note while the other voices change to a new chord. When this becomes a dissonance (called a syncopation) in the new chord it usually resolves by moving one step downward to a tone that is consonant with the other voices. As in this example each section or "caluse" ends with a cadence.

E. C., JR.

8. In the Celestial Harmonies Which Planet Sings Soprano, Which Alto, Which Tenor, and Which Bass?

Although these words are applied to human voices, while voices or sounds do not exist in the heavens, on account of the very great tranquillity of movements, and not even the subjects in which we find the consonances are comprehended under the true genus of movement, since we were considering the movements solely as apparent from the sun, and finally, although there is no such cause in the heavens, as in human singing, for requiring a definite number of voices in order to make consonance (for first there was the number of the six planets revolving around the sun, from the number of the five intervals taken from the regular figures, and then afterwards—in the order of nature, not of time—the congruence of the movements was settled): I do not know why but nevertheless this wonderful congruence with human song has such a strong effect upon me that I am compelled to pursue this part of the comparison, also, even without any solid natural cause. For those same properties which in Book III, [300] Chapter 16, custom ascribed to the bass and nature gave legal grounds for so doing are somehow possessed by Saturn and Jupiter in the heavens; and we find those of the tenor in Mars, those of the alto are present in the Earth and Venus, and those of the soprano are possessed by Mercury, if not with equality of intervals, at least proportionately. For howsoever in the following chapter the eccentricities of each planet are deduced from their proper causes and through those eccentricities the intervals proper to the movements of each, none the less there comes from that the following wonderful result (I do not know whether it is occasioned by the procurement and mere tempering of necessities): (1) as the bass is opposed to the alto, so there are two planets which have the nature of the alto, two that of the bass, just as in any Mode of song there is one [bass and one alto] on either side, while there are single representatives of the other single voices. (2) As the alto is practically supreme in a very narrow range [in angustiis] on account of necessary and natural causes unfolded in Book III, so the almost innermost planets, the Earth and Venus, have the narrowest intervals of movements, the Earth not much more than a semitone, Venus not even a diesis. (3) And as the tenor is free, but none the less progresses with moderation, so Mars alone—with the single exception of Mercury—can make the greatest interval, namely a perfect fifth. (4) And as the bass makes harmonic leaps, so Saturn and Jupiter have intervals which are harmonic, and in relation to one another pass from the octave to the octave and perfect fifth. (5) And as the soprano is the freest, more than all the rest, and likewise the swiftest, so Mercury can traverse more than an octave in the shortest period. But this is altogether per accidens; now let us hear the reasons for the eccentricities.

9. The Genesis of the Eccentricities in the Single Planets from the Procurement of the Consonances between their Movements

Accordingly, since we see that the universal harmonies of all six planets cannot take place by chance, especially in the case of the extreme movements, all of which we see concur in the universal harmonies—except two, which concur in harmonies closest to the universal—and since much less can it happen by chance that all the pitches of the system of the octave (as set up in Book III) by means of harmonic divisions are designated by the extreme planetary movements, but least of all that the very subtle business of the distinction of the celestial consonances into two modes, the major and minor, should be the outcome of chance, without the special attention of the Artisan: accordingly it follows that the Creator, the source of all wisdom, the everlasting approver of order, the eternal and superexistent geyser of geometry and harmony, it follows, I say, that He, the Artisan of the celestial movements Himself, should have conjoined to the five regular solids the harmonic ratios arising from the regular plane figures, and out of both classes should have formed one most perfect archetype of the heavens: in order that in this archetype, as through the five regular solids the shapes of the spheres shine through on which the six planets are carried, so too through the consonances, which are generated from the plane figures, and deduced from them in Book III, the measures of the eccentricities in the single planets might be determined so as to proportion the movements of the planetary bodies; and in order that there should be one tempering together of the ratios and the consonances, and that the greater ratios of the spheres should yield somewhat to the lesser ratios of the eccentricities necessary for procuring the consonances, and conversely those in especial of the harmonic ratios which had a greater kinship with each solid figure should be adjusted to the planets— in so far as that could be effected by means of consonances. And in order that, finally, in that way both the ratios of the spheres and the eccentricities of the single planets might be born of the archetype simultaneously, while from the amplitude of the spheres and the bulk of the bodies the periodic times of the single planets might result.

[301] While I struggle to bring forth this process into the light of human intellect by means of the elementary form customary with geometers, may the Author of the heavens be favourable, the Father of intellects, the Bestower of mortal senses, Himself immortal and superblessed, and may He prevent the darkness of our mind from bringing forth in this work anything unworthy of His Majesty, and may He effect that we, the imitators of God by the help of the Holy Ghost, should rival the perfection of His works in sanctity of life, for which He choose His church throughout the Earth and, by the blood of His Son, cleansed it from sins, and that we should keep at a distance all the discords of enmity, all contentions, rivalries, anger, quarrels, dissensions, sects, envy, provocations, and irritations arising through mocking speech and the other works of the flesh; and that along with myself, all who possess the spirit of Christ will not only desire but will also strive by deeds to express and make sure their calling, by spurning all crooked morals of all kinds which have been veiled and painted over with the cloak of zeal or of the love of truth or of singular erudition or modesty over against contentious teachers, or with any other showy garment. Holy Father, keep us safe in the concord of our love for one another, that we may be one, just as Thou art one with They Son, Our Lord, and with the Holy Ghost, and just as through the sweetest bonds of harmonies Thou hast made all Thy works one; and that from the bringing of Thy people into concord the body of Thy Church may be built up in the Earth, as Thou didst erect the heavens themselves out of harmonies.

PRIOR REASONS

I. AXIOM. *It is reasonable that, wherever in general it could have been done, all possible harmonies were due to have been set up between the extreme movements of the planets taken singly and by twos, in order that that variety should adorn the world.*

II. AXIOM *The five intervals between the six spheres to some extent were due to correspond to the ratio of the geometrical spheres which inscribe and circumscribe the five regular solids, and in the same order which is natural to the figures.*

Concerning this, see Chapter 1 and the *Mysterium Cosmographicum* and the *Epitome of Copernican Astronomy.*

III. PROPOSITION. *The intervals between the Earth and Mars, and between the Earth and Venus, were due to be least, in proportion to their spheres, and thereby approximately equal; middling and approximately equal between Saturn and Jupiter, and between Venus and Mercury; but greatest between Jupiter and Mars.*

For by Axiom II, the planets corresponding in position to the figures which make the least ratio of geometrical spheres ought likewise to make the least ratio; but those which correspond to the figures of middling ratio ought to make the greatest; and those which correspond to the figures of greatest ratio, the greatest. But the order holding between the figures of the dodechahedron and the icosahedron is the same as that between the pairs of planets, Mars and the Earth, and the Earth and Venus, and the order of the cube and octahedron is the same as that of the pair Saturn and Jupiter and that of the pair Venus and Mercury; and, finally, the order of the tetrahedron is the same as that of the pair Jupiter and Mars (see Chapter 3). Therefore, the least ratio will hold between the planetary spheres first mentioned, while that between Saturn and Jupiter is approximately equal to that between Venus and Mercury; and, finally, the greatest between the spheres of Jupiter and Mars.

IV. AXIOM. *All the planets ought to have their eccentricities diverse, no less than a movement in latitude, and in proportion to those eccentricities also their distances from the sun, the source of movement, diverse.*

As the essence of movement consists not in *being* but in *becoming*, so too the form or figure of the region which any planet traverses in its movement does not become solid immediately from the start but in the succession of time acquires at last not only length but also breadth and depth (its perfect ternary of dimensions); and, gradually, thus, by the interweaving and piling up of many circuits, the form of a concave sphere comes to be represented—just as out of the silk-worm's thread, by the interweaving and heaping together of many circles, the cocoon is built.

V. PROPOSITION. *Two diverse consonances were to have been attributed to each pair of neighbouring planets.*

For, by Axiom IV, any planet has a longest and a shortest distance from the sun, wherefore, by Chapter 3, it will have both a slowest movement and a fastest. Therefore, there are two primary comparisons of the extreme movements, one of the diverging movements in the two planets, and the other of the converging. Now it is necessary that they be diverse from one another, because the ratio of the diverging movements will be greater, that of the converging, lesser. But, moreover, diverse consonances had to exist by way of diverse pairs of planets, so that this variety should make for the adornment of the world—by Axiom I—and also because the ratios of the intervals between two planets are diverse, by Proposition III. But to each definite ratio of the spheres there correspond harmonic ratios, in quantitative kinship, as has been demonstrated in Chapter 5 of this book.

VI. PROPOSITION. *The two least consonances, 4 : 5 and 5 : 6, do not have a place between two planets.*

For

$$5 : 4 = 1,000 : 800$$

and

$$6 : 5 = 1,000 : 833.$$

But the spheres circumscribed around the dodecahedron and icosahedron have a greater ratio to the inscribed spheres than 1,000 : 795, etc., and these two ratios indicate the intervals between the nearest planetary spheres, or the least distances. For in the other regular solids the spheres are farther distant from one another. But now the ratio of the movements is even greater than the ratios of the intervals, unless the ratio of the eccentricities to the spheres is vast —by Article XIII of Chapter 3. Therefore the least ratio of the movements is greater than 4 : 5 and 5 : 6. Accordingly, these consonances, being hindered by the regular solids, receive no place among the planets.

VII. PROPOSITION. *The consonance of the perfect fourth can have no place between the converging movements of two planets, unless the ratios of the extreme movements proper to them are, if compounded, more than a perfect fifth.*

For let 3 : 4 be the ratio between the converging movements. And first, let there be no eccentricity, no ratio of movements proper to the single planets, but both the converging and the mean movements the same; then it follows that the corresponding intervals, which by this hypothesis will be the semidiameters of the spheres, constitute the ⅔d power of this ratio, *viz.*, 4480 : 5424 (by Chapter 3). But this ratio is already less than the ratio of the spheres of any regular figure; and so the whole inner sphere would be cut by the regular planes of the figure inscribed in any outer sphere. But this is contrary to Axiom II.

Secondly, let there be some composition of the ratios between the extreme movements, and let the ratio of the converging movements be 3 : 4 or 75 : 100, but let the ratio of the corresponding intervals be 1,000 : 795, since no regular figure has a lesser ratio of spheres. And because the inverse ratio of the movements exceeds this ratio of the intervals by the excess 750 : 795, then if this excess is divided into the ratio 1,000 : 795, according to the doctrine of Chapter 3, the result will be 9434 : 7950, the square root of the ratio of the spheres. Therefore the square of this ratio, *viz.*, 8901 : 6320, *i.e.*, 10,000 : 7,100 is the ratio of the spheres. Divide this by 1000 : 795, the ratio of the converging intervals, the result will be 7100 : 7950, about a major whole tone. The compound of the two ratios which the mean movements have to the converging movements on either side must be at least so great, in order that the perfect fourth may be possible between the converging movements. Accordingly, the compound ratio of the diverging extreme intervals to the converging extreme intervals is about the square root of this ratio, *i.e.*, two tones, and again the converging intervals are the square of this, *i.e.*, more than a perfect fifth. Accordingly, if the compound of the proper movements of two neighbouring planets is less than a perfect fifth, a perfect fourth will not be possible between their converging movements.

VIII. PROPOSITION. *The consonances 1 : 2 and 1 : 3, i.e., the octave and the octave plus a fifth were due to Saturn and Jupiter.*

For they are the first and highest of the planets and have obtained the first figure, the cube, by Chapter 1 of this book; and these consonances are first in the order of nature and are chief in the two families of figures, the bisectorial or tetragonal and the triangular, by what has been said in Book I. But that which is chief, the octave 1 : 2, is approximately greater than the ratio of the spheres of the cube, [303] which is 1 : $\sqrt{3}$; wherefore it is fitted to become the lesser ratio of the movements of the planets on the cube, by Chapter 3, Article XIII; and, as a consequence, 1 : 3 serves as the greater ratio.

But this is also the same as what follows: for if some consonance is to some ratio of the spheres of the figures, as the ratio of the movements apparent from the sun is to the ratio of the mean intervals, such a consonance will duly be attributed to the movements. But it is natural that the ratio of the diverging movements should be much greater than the ratio of the $\frac{3}{2}$th powers of the spheres, according to the end of Chapter 3, *i.e.*, it approaches the square of the ratio of the spheres; and moreover 1 : 3 is the square of the ratio of the spheres of the cube, which we call the ratio of 1 : $\sqrt{3}$. Therefore, the ratio of the diverging movements of Saturn and Jupiter is 1 : 3. (See above, Chapter 2, for many other kinships of these ratios with the cube.)

IX. PROPOSITION. *The private ratios of the extreme movements of Saturn and Jupiter compounded were due to be approximately 2 : 3, a perfect fifth.*

This follows from the preceding; if the perihelial movement of Jupiter is triple the aphelial movement of Saturn, and conversely the aphelial movement of Jupiter is double the perihelial of Saturn, then 1 : 2 and 1 : 3 compounded inversely give 2 : 3.

X. AXIOM. *When choice is free in other respects, the private ratio of movements, which is prior in nature or of a more excellent mode or even which is greater, is due to the higher planet.*

XI. PROPOSITION. *The ratio of the aphelial movement of Saturn to the perihelial was due to be 4 : 5, a major third, but that of Jupiter's movements 5 : 6, a minor third.*

For as compounded together they are equivalent to 2 : 3; but 2 : 3 can be divided harmonically no other way than into 4 : 5 and 5 : 6. Accordingly God the composer of harmonies divided harmonically the consonance 2 : 3, (by Axiom I) and the harmonic part of it which is greater and of the more excellent major mode, as masculine, He gave to Saturn the greater and higher planet, and the lesser ratio 5 : 6 to the lower one, Jupiter (by Axiom x).

XII. PROPOSITION. *The great consonance of 1 : 4, the double octave, was due to Venus and Mercury.*

For as the cube is the first of the primary figures, so the octahedron is the first of the secondary figures, by Chapter 1 of this book. And as the cube considered geometrically is outer and the octahedron is inner, *i.e.*, the latter can be inscribed in the former, so also in the world Saturn and Jupiter are the beginning of the upper and outer planets, or from the outside; and Mercury and Venus are the beginning of the inner planets, or from the inside, and the octahedron has been placed between their circuits: (see Chapter 3). Therefore, from among the consonances, one which is primary and cognate to the octahedron is due to Venus and Mercury. Furthermore, from among the consonances, after 1 : 2 and

1 : 3, there follows in natural order 1 : 4; and that is cognate to 1 : 2, the consonance of the cube, because it has arisen from the same cut of figures, *viz.*, the tetragonal, and is commensurable with it, *viz.*, the double of it; while the octahedron is also akin to, and commensurable with the cube. Moreover, 1 : 4 is cognate to the octahedron for a special reason, on account of the number four being in that ratio, while a quadrangular figure lies concealed in the octahedron and the ratio of its spheres is said to be 1 : $\sqrt{2}$.

Accordingly the consonance 1 : 4 is a continued power of this ratio, in the ratio of the squares, *i.e.*, the 4th power of 1 : $\sqrt{2}$ (see Chapter 2). Therefore, 1 : 4 was due to Venus and Mercury. And because in the cube 1 : 2 has been made the smaller consonance of the two, since the outermost position is over against it, in the octahedron there will be 1 : 4, the greater consonance of the two, as the innermost position is over against it. But too, this is the reason why 1 : 4 has here been given as the greater consonance, not as the smaller.[1] For since the ratio of the spheres of the octahedron is the ratio of 1 : $\sqrt{3}$, then if it is postulated that the inscription of the octahedron among the planets is perfect (although it is not perfect, but penetrates Mercury's sphere to some extent— which is of advantage to us): accordingly, the ratio of the converging movements must be less than the $\frac{3}{2}$th powers of 1 : $\sqrt{3}$; but indeed 1 : 3 is plainly the square of the ratio 1 : $\sqrt{3}$ and is thus greater than the exact ratio; all the more then will 1 : 4 be greater than the exact ratio, as greater than 1 : 3. Therefore, not even the square root of 1 : 4 is allowed between the converging movements. Accordingly, 1 : 4 cannot be less than the octahedric; so it will be greater.

Further: 1 : 4 is akin to the octahedric square, where the ratio of the inscribed and circumscribed circles is 1 : $\sqrt{2}$, just as 1 : 3 is akin to the cube, where the ratio of the spheres is 1 : $\sqrt{3}$. For as 1 : 3 is a power of 1 : $\sqrt{3}$, *viz.*, its square, [304] so too here 1 : 4 is a power of 1 : $\sqrt{2}$, *viz.*, twice its square, *i.e.*, its quadruple power. Wherefore, if 1 : 3 was due to have been the greater consonance of the cube (by Proposition VII), accordingly 1 : 4 ought to become the greater consonance of its octahedron.

XIII. PROPOSITION. *The greater consonance of approximately 1 : 8, the triple octave, and the smaller consonance of 5 : 24, the minor third and double octave, were due to the extreme movements of Jupiter and Mars.*

For the cube has obtained 1 : 2 and 1 : 3, while the ratio of the spheres of the tetrahedron, which is situated between Jupiter and Mars, called the triple ratio, is the square of the ratio of the spheres of the cube, which is called the ratio of 1 : $\sqrt{3}$. Therefore, it was proper that ratios of movements which are the squares of the cubic ratios should be applied to the tetrahedron. But of the ratios 1 : 2 and 1 : 3 the following ratios are the squares: 1 : 4 and 1 : 9. But 1 : 9 is not harmonic, and 1 : 4 has already been used up in the octahedron. Accordingly, consonances neighbouring upon these ratios were to have been taken, by Axiom I. But the lesser ratio 1 : 8 and the greater 1 : 10 are the nearest. Choice between these ratios is determined by kinship with the tetrahedron, which has nothing in common with the pentagon, since 1 : 10 is of a pentagonal cut, but the tetrahedron has greater kinship with 1 : 8 for many reasons (see Chapter 2).

Further, the following also makes for 1 : 8: just as 1 : 3 is the greater consonance of the cube and 1 : 4 the greater consonance of the octahedron, because

---

[1]*Smaller* (lesser) and *greater* consonances are equivalent to our modern "more closely spaced" and "more widely spaced" consonances. E. C., Jr.

they are powers of the ratios between the spheres of the figures, so too 1 : 8 was due to be the greater consonance of the tetrahedron, because as its body is double that of the octahedron inscribed in it, as has been said in Chapter 1, so too the term 8 in the tetrahedral ratio is double the term 4 in the tetrahedral ratio.

Further, just as 1 : 2 the smaller consonance of the cube, is one octave, and 1 : 4, the greater consonance of the octahedron, is two octaves, so already 1 : 8, the greater consonance of the tetrahedron, was due to be three octaves. Moreover, more octaves were due to the tetrahedron than to the cube and octahedron, because, since the smaller tetrahedral consonance is necessarily greater than all the lesser consonances in the other figures (for the ratio of the tetrahedral spheres is greater than all the spheres of figures): too the greater tetrahedral consonance was due to exceed the greater consonances of the others in number of octaves. Finally, the triple of octave intervals has kinship with the triangular form of the tetrahedron, and has a certain perfection, as follows: every three is perfect; since even the octuple, the term [of the triple octave], is the first cubic number of perfect quantity, namely of three dimensions.

A greater consonance neighbouring upon 1 : 4 or 6 : 24 is 5 : 24, while a lesser is 6 : 20 or 3 : 10. But again 3 : 10 is of the pentagonal cut, which has nothing in common with the tetrahedron. But on account of the numbers 3 and 4 (from which the numbers 12, 24 arise) 5 : 24 has kinship with the tetrahedron. For we are here neglecting the other lesser terms, *viz.*, 5 and 3, because their lightest degree of kinship is with figures, as it is possible to see in Chapter 2. Moreover, the ratio of the spheres of the tetrahedron is triple; but the ratio of the converging intervals too ought to be approximately so great, by Axiom II. By Chapter 3, the ratio of the converging movements approaches the inverse ratio of the $\frac{3}{2}$th powers of the intervals, but the $\frac{3}{2}$th power of 3 : 1 is approximately 1000 : 193. Accordingly, whereof the aphelial movement of Mars is 1000, the [perihelial] of Jupiter will be slightly greater than 193 but much less than 333, which is one third of 1,000. Accordingly, not the consonance 10 : 3, *i.e.*, 1,000 : 333, but the consonance 24 : 5, *i.e.*, 1,000 : 208, takes place between the converging movements of Jupiter and Mars.

XIV. PROPOSITION. *The private ratio of the extreme movements of Mars was due to be greater than 3 : 4, the perfect fourth, and approximately 18 : 25.*

For let there be the exact consonances 5 : 24 and 1 : 8 or 3 : 24, which are commonly attributed to Jupiter and Mars (Proposition XIII). Compound inversely 5 : 24, the lesser with 3 : 24, the greater; 3 : 5 results as the compound of both ratios. But the proper ratio of Jupiter alone has been found to be 5 : 6, in Proposition XI, above. Then compound this inversely with the composition 3 : 5, *i.e.*, compound 30 : 25 and 18 : 30; there results as the proper ratio of Mars 18 : 25, which is greater than 18 : 24 or 3 : 4. But it will become still greater, if, on account of the ensuing reasons, the common greater consonance 1 : 8 is increased.

XV. PROPOSITION. *The consonances 2 : 3, the fifth; 5 : 8, the minor sixth; and 3 : 5, the major sixth were to have been distributed among the converging movements of Mars and the Earth, the Earth and Venus, Venus and Mercury, and in that order.*

For the dodecahedron and the icosahedron, the figures interspaced between Mars, the Earth, and Venus have the least ratio between their circumscribed and inscribed spheres. [305] Therefore from among possible consonances the least are due to them, as being cognate for this reason, and in order that Axiom II may have place. But the least consonances of all, *viz.*, 5 : 6 and 4 : 5, are not possible, by Proposition IV. Therefore, the nearest consonances greater than they, *viz.*, 3 : 4 or 2 : 3 or 5 : 8 or 3 : 5 are due to the said figures.

Again, the figure placed between Venus and Mercury, *viz.*, the octahedron, has the same ratio of its spheres as the cube. But by Proposition VII, the cube received the ocatve as the lesser consonance existing between the converging movements. Therefore, by proportionality, so great a consonance, *viz.*, 1 : 2, would be due to the octahedron as the lesser consonance, if no diversity intervened. But the following diversity intervenes: if compounded together, the private ratios of the single movements of the cubic planets, *viz.*, Saturn and Jupiter, did not amount to more than 2 : 3; while, if compounded, the ratios of the single movements of the octahedral planets, *viz.*, Venus and Mercury will amount to more than 2 : 3, as is apparent easily, as follows: For, as the proportion between the cube and octahedron would require if it were alone, let the lesser octahedral ratio be greater than the ratios here given, and thereby clearly as great as was the cubic ratio, *viz.*, 1 : 2; but the greater consonance was 1 : 4, by Proposition XII. Therefore if the lesser consonance 1: 2 is divided into the one we have just laid down, 1 : 2, still remains as the compound of the proper movements of Venus and Mercury; but 1 : 2 is greater than 2 : 3 the compound of the proper movements of Saturn and Jupiter; and indeed a greater eccentricity follows upon this greater compound, by Chapter 3, but a lesser ratio of the converging movements follows upon the greater eccentricity, by the same Chapter 3. Wherefore by the addition of a greater eccentricity to the proportion between the cube and the octahedron it comes about that a lesser ratio than 1 : 2 is also required between the converging movements of Venus and Mercury. Moreover, it was in keeping with Axiom I that, with the consonance of the octave given to the planets of the cube, another consonance which is very near (and by the earlier demonstration less than 1 : 2) should be joined to the planets of the octahedron. But 3 : 5 is proximately less than 1 : 2, and as the greatest of the three it was due to the figure having the greatest ratio of its spheres, *viz.*, the octahedron. Accordingly, the lesser ratios, 5 : 8 and 2 : 3 or 3 : 4, were left for the icosahedron and dodecahedron, the figures having a lesser ratio of their spheres.

But these remaining ratios have been distributed between the two remaining planets, as follows. For as, from among the figures, though of equal ratios between their spheres, the cube has received the consonance 1 : 2, while the octahedron the lesser consonance 3 : 5, in that the compound ratio of the private movements of Venus and Mercury exceeded the compound ratio of the private movements of Saturn and Jupiter; so also although the dodecahedron has the same ratio of its spheres as the icosahedron, a lesser ratio was due to it than to the icosahedron, but very close on account of a similar reason, *viz.*, because this figure is between the Earth and Mars, which had a great eccentricity in the foregoing. But Venus and Mercury, as we shall hear in the following, have the least eccentricities. But since the octahedron has 3 : 5, the icosahedron, whose species are in a lesser ratio, has the next slightly lesser, *viz.*, 5 : 8; accordingly, either 2 : 3, which remains, or 3 : 4 was left for the dodecahedron, but more likely 2 :3, as being nearer to the icosahedral 5 :8; since they are similar figures.

But 3 : 4 indeed was not possible. For although, in the foregoing, the private ratio of the extreme movements of Mars was great enough, yet the Earth—as has already been said and will be made clear in what follows—contributed its own ratio, which was too small for the compound ratio of both to exceed the perfect fifth. Accordingly, Proposition VII, 3 : 4 could not have place. And all the more so, because—as will follow in Proposition XVII—the ratio of the converging intervals was due to be greater than 1,000 : 795.

XVI. PROPOSITION. *The private ratios of movements of Venus and Mercury, if compounded together, were due to make approximately 5 : 12.*

For divide the lesser harmonic ratio attributed in Proposition XV to this pair jointly into the greater of them, 1 : 4 or 3 : 12, by Proposition XII; there results 5 : 12, the compound ratio of the private movements of both. And so the private ratio of the extreme movements of Mercury alone is less than 5 : 12, the magnitude of the private movement of Venus. Understand this of these first reasons. For below, by the second reasons, through the addition of some variation to the joint consonances of both, it results that only the private ratio of Mercury is perfectly 5 : 12.

XVII. PROPOSITION. *The consonance between the diverging movements of Venus and the Earth could not be less than 5 : 12.*

For in the private ratio of its movements Mars alone has received more than the perfect fourth and more than 18 : 25, by Proposition XIV. But their lesser consonance is the perfect fifth, [306] by Proposition XV. Accordingly, the ratio compounded of these two parts is 12 : 25. But its own private ratio is due to the Earth, by Axiom IV. Therefore, since the consonance of the diverging movements is made up out of the said three elements, it will be greater than 12 : 25. But the nearest consonance greater than 12 : 25, *i.e.*, 60 : 125, is 5 : 12, *viz.*, 60 : 144. Wherefore, if there is need of a consonance for this greater ratio of the two planets, by Axiom I, it cannot be less than 60 : 144 or 5 : 12.

Therefore up to now all the remaining pairs of planets have received their two consonances by necessary reasons; the pair of the Earth and Venus alone has as yet been allotted only one consonance, 5 : 8, by the axioms so far employed. Therefore, we must now take a new start and inquire into its remaining consonance, *viz.*, the greater, or the consonance of the diverging movements.

POSTERIOR REASONS

XVIII. AXIOM. *The universal consonances of movements were to be constituted by a tempering of the six movements, especially in the case of the extreme movements.*

This is proved by Axiom I.

XIX. AXIOM. *The universal consonances had to come out the same within a certain latitude of movements, namely, in order that they should occur the more frequently.*

For if they had been limited to indivisible points of the movements, it could have happened that they would never occur, or very rarely.

XX. AXIOM. *As the most natural division of the kinds* [generum] *of consonances is into major and minor, as has been proved in Book 3, so the universal consonances of both kinds had to be procured between the extreme movements of the planets.*

XXI. AXIOM. *Diverse species of both kinds of consonances had to be instituted, so that the beauty of the world might well be composed out of all possible forms of variety—and by means of the extreme movements, at least by means of some extreme movements.*

By Axiom I.

XXII. PROPOSITION. *The extreme movements of the planets had to designate pitches or strings* [chordas] *of the octave system, or notes* [claves] *of the musical scale.*

For the genesis and comparison of consonances beginning from one common term has generated the musical scale, or the division of the octave into its pitches or tones [sonos], as has been proved in Book 3. Accordingly, since varied consonances between the extremes of movements are required, by Axioms I, XX, and XXI, wherefore the real division of some celestial system or harmonic scale by the extremes of movements is required.

XXIII. PROPOSITION. *It was necessary for there to be one pair of planets, between the movements of which no consonances could exist except the major sixth 3 : 5 and the minor sixth 5 : 8.*

For since the division into kinds of consonances was necessary, by Axiom XX, and by means of the extreme movements at the apsides, by XXII, because solely the extremes, *viz.*, the slowest and the fastest, need the determination of a manager and orderer, the intermediate tensions come of themselves, without any special care, with the passage of the planet from the slowest movement to the fastest: accordingly, this ordering could not take place otherwise than by having the diesis or 24 : 25 designated by the extremes of the two planetary movements, in that the kinds of consonances are distinguished by the diesis, as was unfolded in Book 3.

But the diesis is the difference either between two thirds, 4 : 5 and 5 : 6, or between two sixths, 3 : 5 and 5 : 8, or between those ratios increased by one or more octave intervals. But the two thirds, 4 : 5 and 5 : 6, did not have place between two planets, by Proposition VI, and neither the thirds nor the sixths increased by the interval of an octave have been found, except 5 : 12 in the pair of Mars and the Earth, and still not otherwise than along with the related 2 : 3, and so the intermediate ratios 5 : 8 and 3 : 5 and 1 : 2 were alike admitted. Therefore, it remains that the two sixths, 3 : 5 and 5 : 8, were to be given to one pair of planets. But too the sixths alone were to be granted to the variation of their movements, in such fashion that they would neither expand their terms to the proximately greater interval of one octave, 1 : 2, [307] nor contract them to the narrows of the proximately lesser interval of the fifth, 2 : 3. For, although it is true that the same two planets, which make a perfect fifth with their extreme converging movements, can also make sixths and thus traverse the diesis too, still this would not smell of the singular providence of the Orderer of movements. For the diesis, the least interval— which is potentially latent in all the major intervals comprehended by the extreme movements—is itself at that time traversed by the intermediate movements varied by continuous tension, but it is not determined by their extremes, since the part is always less than the whole, *viz.*, the diesis than the greater interval 3 : 4 which exists between 2 : 3 and 1 : 2 and which whole would be here assumed to be determined by the extreme movements.

XXIV. PROPOSITION. *The two planets which shift the kind* [genus] *of harmony, which is the difference between the private ratios of the extreme movements, ought to make a diesis, and the private ratio of one ought to be greater than a diesis, and they ought to make one of the sixths with their aphelial movements and the other with their perihelial.*

For, since the extremes of the movements make two consonances differing by a single diesis, that can take place in three ways. For either the movement of one planet will remain constant and the movement of the other will vary by a diesis, or both will vary by half a diesis and make 3 : 5, a major sixth, when the upper is at its aphelion and the lower in its perihelion, and when they move out of those intervals and advance towards one another, the upper into its perihelion and the lower into its aphelion, they make 5 : 8, a minor sixth; or, finally, one varies its movement from aphelion to perihelion more than the other does, and there is an excess of one diesis, and thus there is a major sixth between the two aphelia, and a minor sixth between the two perihelia. But the first way is not legitimate, for one of these planets would be without eccentricity, contrary to Axiom IV. The second way was less beautiful and less expedient; less beautiful, because less harmonic, for the private ratios of the movements of the two planets would have been out of tune [*inconcinnae*], for whatever is less than a diesis is out of tune; moreover it occasions one single planet to labour under this ill-concordant small difference—except that indeed it could not take place, because in this way the extreme movements would have wandered from the pitches of the system or the notes [*clavibus*] of the musical scale, contrary to Proposition XXII. Moreover, it would have been less expedient, because the sixths would have occurred only at those moments in which the planets would have been at the contrary apsides; there would have been no latitude within which these sixths and the universal consonances related to them could have occurred; accordingly, these universal consonances would have been very rare, with all the [*harmonic*] positions of the planets reduced to the narrow limits of definite and single points on their orbits, contrary to Axiom XIX. Accordingly, the third way remains: that both of the planets should vary their own private movements, but one more than the other, by one full diesis at the least.

XXV. PROPOSITION. *The higher of the planets which shift the kind of harmony ought to have the ratio of its privte movements less than a minor whole tone 9 : 10; while the lower, less than a semitone 15 : 16.*

For they will make 3 : 5 either with their aphelial movements or with their perihelial, by the foregoing proposition. Not with their perihelial, for then the ratio of their aphelial movements would be 5 : 8. Accordingly, the lower planet would have its private ratio one diesis more than the upper would, by the same foregoing proposition. But that is contrary to Axiom X. Accordingly, they make 3 : 5 with their aphelial movements, and with their perihelial 5 : 8, which is 24 : 25 less than the other. But if the aphelial movements make 3 : 5, a major sixth, therefore, the aphelial movement of the upper together with the perihelial of the lower will make more than a major sixth; for the lower planet will compound directly its full private ratio.

In the same way, if the perihelial movements make 5 : 8, a minor sixth, the perihelial movement of the upper and the aphelial movement of the lower will make less than a minor sixth; for the lower planet will compound inversely its full private ratio. But if the private ratio of the lower equalled the semitone 15 : 16, then too a perfect fifth could occur over and above the sixths, because the minor sixth, diminished by a semitone, because the perfect fifth; but this is contrary to Proposition xxiii. Accordingly, the lower planet has less than a semitone in its own interval. And because the private ratio of the upper is one diesis greater than the private ratio of the lower, but the diesis compounded with the semitone makes 9 : 10 the minor whole tone.

XXVI. PROPOSITION. *On the planets which shift the kind of harmony, the upper was due to have either a diesis squared, 576 : 625, i.e., approximately 12 : 13, as* [308] *the interval made by its extreme movements, or the semitone 15 : 16, or something intermediate differing by the comma 80 : 81 either from the former or the latter; while the lower planet, either the simple diesis 24 : 25, or the difference between a semitone and a diesis, which is 125 : 128, i.e., approximately 42 : 43; or, finally and similarly, something intermediate differing either from the former or from the latter by the comma 80 : 81, viz., the upper planet ought to make the diesis squared diminished by a comma, and the lower, the simple diesis diminished by a comma.*

For, by Proposition xxv, the private ratio of the upper ought to be greater than a diesis, but by the preceding proposition less than the [minor] whole tone 9 : 10. But indeed the upper planet ought to exceed the lower by one diesis, by Proposition xxiv. And harmonic beauty persuades us that, even if the private ratios of these planets cannot be harmonic, on account of their smallness, they should at least be from among the concordant [*ex concinnis*] if that is possible, by Axiom i. But there are only two concords less than 9 : 10, the [minor] whole tone, *viz.*, the semitone and the diesis; but they differ from one another not by the diesis but by some smaller interval, 125 : 128. Accordingly, the upper cannot have the semitone; nor the lower, the diesis; but either the upper will have the semitone 15 : 16, and the lower, 125 : 128, *i.e.*, 42 : 43; or else the lower will have the diesis 24 : 25, but the upper the diesis squared, approximately 12 : 13. But since the laws of both planets are equal, therefore, if the nature of the concordant had to be violated in their private ratios, it had to be violated equally in both, so that the difference between their private intervals could remain an exact diesis, which is necessary for distinguishing the kinds of consonances, by Proposition xxiv. But the nature of the concordant was then violated equally in both, if the interval whereby the private ratio of the upper planet fell short of the diesis squared and exceeded the semitone is the same interval whereby the private ratio of the lower planet fell short of a simple diesis and exceeded the interval 125 : 128.

Furthermore, this excess or defect was due to be the comma 80 : 81, because, once more, no other interval was designated by the harmonic ratios, and in order that the comma might be expressed among the celestial movements as it is expressed in harmonics, namely, by the mere excess and defect of the intervals in respect to one another. For in harmonics the comma distinguishes between major and minor whole tones and does not appear in any other way.

It remains for us to inquire which ones of the intervals set forth are preferable —whether the diesis, the simple diesis for the lower planet and the diesis squared for the upper, or the semitone for the upper and 125 : 128 for the lower. And the dieses win by the following arguments: For although the semitone has been variously expressed in the musical scale, yet its allied ratio 125 : 128 has not been expressed. On the other hand, the diesis has been expressed variously and the diesis squared somehow, *viz.*, in the resolution of whole tones into dieses, semitones, and lemmas; for then, as has been said in Book III, Chapter 8, two dieses proximately succeed one another in two pitches. The other argument is that in the distinction into kinds, the laws of the diesis are proper but not at all those of the semitone. Accordingly, there had to be greater consideration of the diesis than of the semitone. It is inferred from everything that the private ratio of the upper planet ought to be 2916 : 3125 or approximately 14 : 15, and that of the lower, 243 : 250 or approximately 35 : 36.

It is asked whether the Highest Creative Wisdom has been occupied in making these tenuous little reckonings. I answer that it is possible that many reasons are hidden from me, but if the nature of harmony has not allowed weightier reasons—since we are dealing with ratios which descend below the magnitude of all concords—it is not absurd that God has followed even those reasons, wherever they appear tenuous, since He has ordained nothing without cause. It would be far more absurd to assert that God has taken at random these magnitudes below the limits prescribed for them, the minor whole tone; and it is not sufficient to say: He took them of that magnitude because He chose to do so. For in geometrical things, which are subject to free choice, God chose nothing without a geometrical cause of some sort, as is apparent in the edges of leaves, in the scales of fishes, in the skins of beasts and their spots and the order of the spots, and similar things.

XXVII. PROPOSITION. *The ratio of movements of the Earth and Venus ought to have been greater than a major sixth between the aphelial movements; less than a minor sixth between the perihelial movements.*

By Axiom xx it was necessary to distinguish the kinds of consonances. But by Proposition XXIII that could not be done except through the sixths. Accordingly, since by Proposition xv the Earth and Venus, planets next to one another and icosahedral, had received the minor sixth, 5 : 8, it was necessary for the other sixth, 3 : 5, to be assigned to them, but not between the converging or diverging extremes, but between the extremes of the same field, one sixth [309] between the aphelial, and the other between the perihelial, by Proposition XXIV. Furthermore, the consonance 3 : 5 is cognate to the icosahedron, since both are of the pentagonal cut. See Chapter 2.

Behold the reason why exact consonances are found between the aphelial and perihelial movements of these two planets, but not between the converging, as in the case of the upper planets.

XXVIII. PROPOSITION. *The private ratio of movements fitting the Earth was approximately 14 : 15, Venus, approximately 35 :36.*

For these two planets had to distinguish the kinds of consonances, by the preceding proposition; therefore, by Proposition XXVI, the Earth as the higher was due to receive the interval 2916 : 3125, *i.e.*, approximately 14 : 15, but Venus as the lower the interval 243 : 250, *i.e.*, approximately 35 : 36.

Behold the reason why these two planets have such small eccentricities and, in proportion to them, small intervals or private ratios of the extreme movements, although nevertheless the next higher planet, Mars, and the next lower, Mercury, have marked eccentricities and the greatest of all. And astronomy confirms the truth of this; for in Chapter 4 the Earth clearly had 14 : 15, but Venus 34 : 35, which astronomical certitude can barely discern from 35 : 36 in this planet.

XXIX. PROPOSITION. *The greater consonance of the movements of Mars and the*

Earth, viz., *that of the diverging movements, could not be from among the consonances greater than 5 : 12.*

Above, in Proposition XVII, it was not any one of the lesser ratios; but now it is not any one of the greater ratios either. For the other common or lesser consonance of these two planets is 2 : 3, when the private ratio of Mars, which by Proposition XIV exceeds 18 : 25, makes more than 12 : 25, *i.e.*, 60 : 125. Accordingly, compound the private ratio of the Earth 14 : 15, *i.e.*, 56 : 60, by the preceding proposition. The compound ratio is greater than 56 : 125, which is approximately 4 : 9, *viz.*, slightly greater than an octave and a major whole tone. But the next greater consonance than the octave and whole tone is 5 : 12, the octave and minor third.

Note that I do not say that this ratio is neither greater nor smaller than 5 : 12; but I say that if it is necessary for it to be harmonic, no other consonance will belong to it.

XXX. PROPOSITION. *The private ratio of movements of Mercury was due to be greater than all the other private ratios.*

For by Proposition XVI the private movements of Venus and Mercury compounded together were due to make about 5 : 12. But the private ratio of Venus, taken separately, is only 243 : 250, *i.e.*, 1458 : 1500. But if it is compounded inversely with 5 : 12, *i.e.*, 625 : 1500, Mercury singly is left with 625 : 1458, which is greater than an octave and a major whole tone; although the private ratio of Mars, which is the greatest of all those among the remaining planets, is less than 2 : 3, *i.e.*, the perfect fifth.

And thereby the private ratios of Venus and Mercury, the lowest planets, if compounded together, are approximately equal to the compounded private ratios of the four higher planets, because, as will now be apparent immediately, the compounded private ratios of Saturn and Jupiter exceed 2 : 3; those of Mars fall somewhat short of 2 : 3: all compounded, 4 : 9, *i.e.*, 60 : 135. Compound the Earth's 14 : 15, *i.e.*, 56 : 60, the result will be 56 : 135, which is slightly greater than 5 : 12, which just now was the compound of the private ratios of Venus and Mercury. But this has not been sought for nor taken from any separate and singular archetype of beauty but comes of itself, by the necessity of the causes bound together by the consonances hitherto established.

XXXI. PROPOSITION. *The aphelial movement of the Earth had to harmonize with the aphelial movement of Saturn, through some certain number of octaves.*

For, by Proposition XVIII, it was necessary for there to be universal consonances, wherefore also there had to be a consonance of Saturn with the Earth and Venus. But if one of the extreme movements of Saturn had harmonized with neither of the Earth's and Venus', this would have been less harmonic than if both of its extreme movements had harmonized with these planets, by Axiom I. Therefore both of Saturn's extreme movements had to harmonize, the aphelial with one of these two planets, the perihelial with the other, since nothing would hinder, as was the case with the first planet. Accordingly these consonances will be either identisonant[1] [*identisonae*] or diversisonant [*diversisonae*], *i.e.*, either of continued double proportion or of some other. But both of them cannot be of some other proportion, for between the terms 3 : 5 (which determine the greater consonance between the aphelial movements of the Earth and Venus, by Proposition XXVII) two harmonic means cannot be set up; for the sixth cannot be

[1]"Identisonant consonances" are such as 3 : 5, 3 : 10, 3 : 20, etc.

divided into three intervals (see Book III). Accordingly, Saturn could not, [310] by means of both its movements, make an octave with the harmonic means between 3 and 5; but in order that its movements should harmonize with the 3 of the earth and the 5 of Venus, it is necessary that one of those terms should harmonize identically, or through a certain number of octaves, with the others, *viz.*, with one of the said planets. But since the identisonant consonances are more excellent, they had to be established between the more excellent extreme movements, *viz.*, between the aphelial, because too they have the position of a principle on account of the altitude of the planets and because the Earth and Venus claim as their private ratio somehow and as a prerogative the consonance 3 : 5, with which as their greater consonance we are now dealing. For although, by Proposition XXII, this consonance belongs to the perihelial movement of Venus and some intermediate movement of the Earth, yet the start is made at the extreme movements and the intermediate movements come after the beginnings.

Now, since on one side we have the aphelial movement of Saturn at its greatest altitude, on the other side the aphelial movement of the Earth rather than Venus is to be joined with it, because of these two planets which distinguish the kinds of harmony, the Earth, again, has the greater altitude. There is also another nearer cause: the posterior reasons—with which we are now dealing—take away from the prior reasons but ony with respect to minima, and in harmonics that is with respect to all intervals less than concords. But by the prior reasons the aphelial movement not of Venus but of the Earth, will approximate the consonance of some number of octaves to be established with the aphelial movement of Saturn. For compound together, first, 4 : 5 the private ratio of Saturn's movements, *i.e.*, from the aphelion to the perihelial of Saturn (Proposition XI), secondly, the 1 : 2 of the converging movements of Saturn and Jupiter, *i.e.*, from the perihelion of Saturn to the aphelion of Jupiter (by Proposition VIII), thirdly, the 1 : 8 of the diverging movements of Jupiter and Mars, *i.e.*, from the aphelion of Jupiter to the perihelion of Mars (by Proposition XIV), fourthly, the 2 : 3 of the converging movements of Mars and the Earth, *i.e.*, from the perihelion of Mars to the aphelion of the Earth (by Proposition XV): you will find between the aphelion of Saturn and the perihelion of the Earth the compound ratio 1 : 30, which falls short of 1 : 32, or five octaves, by only 30 : 32, *i.e.*, 15 : 16 or a semitone. And so, if a semitone, divided into particles smaller than the least concord, is compounded with these four elements there will be a perfect consonance of five octaves between the aphelial movements of Saturn and the Earth, which have been set forth. But in order for the same aphelial movement of Saturn to make some number of octaves with the aphelial movement of Venus, it would have been necessary to snatch approximately a whole perfect fourth from the prior reasons; for if you compound 3 : 5, which exists between the aphelial movements of the Earth and Venus, with the ratio 1: 30 compounded of the four prior elements, then as it were from the prior reasons, 1 : 50 is found between the aphelial movements of Saturn and Venus: This interval differs from 1 : 32, or five octaves, by 32 : 50, *i.e.*, 16 : 25, which is a perfect fifth and a diesis; and from six octaves, or 1 : 64, it differs by 50 : 64, *i.e.*, 25 : 32, or a perfect fourth minus a diesis. Accordingly, an indentisonant consonance was due to be established, not between the aphelial movements of Venus and Saturn but between those of Venus and the

Earth, so that Saturn might keep a diversisonant consonance with Venus.

XXXII. PROPOSITION. *In the universal consonances of planets of the minor scale the exact aphelial movement of Saturn could not harmonize precisely with the other planets.*

For the Earth by its aphelial movement does not concur in the universal consonance of the minor scale, because the aphelial movements of the Earth and Venus make the interval 3 : 5, which is of the major scale (by Proposition XVII). But by its aphelial movement Saturn makes an identisonant consonance with the aphelial movement of the Earth (by Proposition XXXI). Therefore, neither does Saturn concur by its aphelial movement. Nevertheless, in place of the aphelial movement there follows some faster movement of Saturn, very near to the aphelial, and also in the minor scale—as was apparent in Chapter 7.

XXXIII. PROPOSITION. *The major kind of consonances and musical scale is akin to the aphelial movements; the minor to the perihelial.*

For although a major consonance (*dura harmonia*] is set up not only between the aphelial movement of the Earth and the aphelial movement of Venus but also between the lower aphelial movements and the lower movements of Venus as far as its perihelion; and, conversely, there is a minor consonance not merely between the perihelial movement of Venus and the perihelial of the Earth but also between the higher movements of Venus as far as the aphelion and the higher movements of the Earth (by Propositions XX and XXIV). Accordingly, the major scale is designated properly only in the aphelial movements, the minor, only in the perihelial.

XXXIV. PROPOSITION. *The major scale is more akin to the upper of the two planets, the minor, to the lower.*

[311] For, because the major scale is proper to the aphelial movements, the minor, to the perihelial (by the preceding proposition), while the aphelial are slower and graver than the perihelial; accordingly, the major scale is proper to the slower movements, the minor to the faster. But the upper of the two planets is more akin to the slow movements, the lower, to the fast, because slowness of the private movement always follows upon altitude in the world. Therefore, of two planets which adjust themselves to both modes, the upper is more akin to the major mode of the scale, the lower, to the minor. Further, the major scale employs the major intervals 4 : 5 and 3 : 5, and the minor, the minor ones, 5 : 6 and 5 : 8. But, moreover, the upper planet has both a greater sphere and slower, *i.e.*, greater movements and a lengthier circuit; but those things which agree greatly on both sides are rather closely united.

XXXV. PROPOSITION. *Saturn and the Earth embrace the major scale more closely Jupiter and Venus, the minor.*

For, first, the Earth, as compared with Venus and as designating both scales along with Venus, is the upper. Accordingly, by the preceding proposition, the Earth embraces the major scale chiefly; Venus, the minor. But with its aphelial movement Saturn harmonizes with the Earth's aphelial movement, through an octave (by Proposition XXXI): wherefore too (by Proposition XXXIII) Saturn embraces the major scale. Secondly, by the same proposition, Saturn by means of its aphelial movement nurtures more the major scale and (by Proposition XXXII) spits out the minor scale. Accordingly, it is more closely related to the major scale than to the minor, because the scales are properly designated by the extreme movements.

Now as regards Jupiter, in comparison with Saturn it is lower; therefore as the major scale is due to Saturn, so the minor is due to Jupiter, by the preceding proposition.

XXXVI. PROPOSITION. *The perihelial movement of Jupiter had to concord with the perihelial movement of Venus in one scale but not also in the same consonance; and all the less so, with the perihelial movement of the Earth.*

For, because the minor scale chiefly was due to Jupiter, by the preceding proposition, while the perihelial movements are more akin to the minor scale (by Proposition XXX), accordingly, by its perihelial movement Jupiter had to designate the key of the minor scale, *viz.*, its definite pitch or key-note [*phthongum*]. But too the perihelial movements of Venus and the Earth designate the same scale (by Proposition XXVIII); therefore the perihelial movement of Jupiter was to be associated with their perihelial movements in the same tuning, but it could not constitute a consonance with the perihelial movements of Venus. For, because (by Proposition VIII) it had to make about 1 : 3 with the aphelial movement of Saturn, *i.e.*, the note [*clavem*] d of that system, wherein the aphelial movement of Saturn strikes the note G, but the aphelial movement of Venus the note e: accordingly, it approached the note e within an interval of least consonance. For the least consonance is 5 : 6, but the interval between d and e is much smaller, *viz.*, 9 : 10, a whole tone. And although in the perihelial tension [*tensione*] Venus is raised from the d of the aphelial tension yet this elevation is less than a diesis, (by Proposition XXVIII). But the diesis (and hence any smaller interval) if compounded with a minor whole tone does not yet equal 5 : 6 the interval of least consonance. Accordingly, the perihelial movement of Jupiter could not observe 1 : 3 or thereabouts with the aphelial movement of Saturn and at the same time harmonize with Venus. Nor with the Earth. For if the perihelial movement of Jupiter had been adjusted to the key of the perihelial movement of Venus in the same tension in such fashion that below the quantity of least concord it should preserve with the aphelial movement of Saturn the interval 1 : 3, *viz.*, by differing from the perihelial movement of Venus by a minor whole tone, 9 : 10 or 36 : 40 (besides some octaves) towards the low. Now the perihelial movement of the Earth differs from the same perihelial movement of Venus by 5 : 8, *i.e.*, by 25 : 40. And so the perihelial movements of the Earth and Jupiter differ by 25 : 36, over and above some number of octaves. But that is not harmonic, because it is the square of 5 : 6, or a perfect fifth diminished by one diesis.

XXXVII. PROPOSITION. *It was necessary for an interval equal to the interval of Venus to accede to the 2 : 3 of the compounded private consonances of Saturn and Jupiter and to 1 : 3 the great consonance common to them.*

For with its aphelial movement Venus assists in the proper designation of the major scale; with its perihelial, that of the minor scale, by Propositions XXVII and XXXIII. But by its aphelial movement Saturn had to be in concord also with the major scale and thus with the aphelial movement of Venus, by Proposition XXXV, but Jupiter's perihelial with the perihelial of Venus, by the preceding proposition. Accordingly, as great as Venus makes its interval from aphelial to perihelial to be, so great an interval must also accede to that movement of Jupiter which makes 1 : 3 with the aphelial movement of Saturn—to the very perihelial movement of Jupiter. But the consonance of the converging movements of Jupiter and Saturn is precisely 1 : 2, by Proposition VIII. Accordingly, if the interval 1 : 2 is divided into the interval [312] greater than 1 : 3, there results, as the compound of the private ratios of both, something which is proportionately greater than 2 : 3.

Above, in Proposition xxvi, the private ratio of the movements of Venus was 243 : 250 or approximately 35 : 36; but in Chapter 4, between the aphelial movement of Saturn and the perihelial movement of Jupiter there was found a slightly greater excess beyond 1 : 3, *viz.*, between 26 : 27 and 27 : 28. But the quantity here prescribed is absolutely equalled, by the addition of a single second to the aphelial movement of Saturn, and I do not know whether astronomy can discern that difference.

XXXVIII. PROPOSITION. *The increment 243 : 250 to 2 : 3, the compound of the private ratios of Saturn and Jupiter, which was up to now being established by the prior reasons, was to be distributed among the planets in such fashion that of it the comma 80 : 81 should accede to Saturn and the remainder, 19,683 : 20,000 or approximately 62 : 63, to Jupiter.*

It follows from Axiom xix that this was to have been distributed between both planets so that each could with some latitude concur in the universal consonances of the scale akin to itself. But the interval 243 : 250 is smaller than all concords: accordingly no harmonic rules remain whereby it may be divided into two concordant parts, with the single exception of those of which there was need in the division of 24 : 25, the diesis, above in Proposition xxvi; namely, in order that it may be divided into the comma 80 : 81 (which is a primary one of those intervals which are subordinate to the concordant) and into the remainder 19,683 : 20,000, which is slightly greater than a comma, *viz.*, approximately 62 : 63. But not two but one comma had to be taken away, lest the parts should become too unequal, since the private ratios of Saturn and Jupiter are approximately equal (according to Axiom x extended even to concords and parts smaller than those) and also because the comma is determined by the intervals of the major whole tone and minor whole tone, not so two commas. Furthermore, to Saturn the higher and mightier planet was due not that part which was greater, although Saturn had the greater private consonance 4 : 5, but that one which is prior and more beautiful, *i.e.*, more harmonic. For in Axiom x the consideration of priority and harmonic perfection comes first, and the consideration of quantity comes last, because there is no beauty in quantity of itself. Thus the movements of Saturn become 64 : 81, an adulterine[1] major third, as we have called them in Book iii, Chapter 12, but those of Jupiter, 6,561 : 8,000.

I do not know whether it should be numbered among the causes of the addition of a comma to Saturn that the extreme intervals of Saturn can constitute the ratio 8 : 9, the major whole tone, or whether that resulted without further ado from the preceding causes of the movements. Accordingly, you here have, in place of a corollary, the reason why, above in Chapter 4, the intervals of Saturn were found to embrace approximately a major whole tone.

XXXIX. PROPOSITION. *Saturn could not harmonize with its exact perihelial movement in the universal consonances of the planets of the major scale, nor Jupiter with its exact aphelial movement.*

For since the aphelial movement of Saturn had to harmonize exactly with the aphelial movements of the Earth and Venus (by Proposition xxxi), that movement of Saturn which is 4 : 5 or one major third faster than its aphelial will also

---

[1]See footnote to *Intervals Compared with Harmonic Ratios*, 1026.

harmonize with them. For the aphelial movements of the Earth and Venus make a major sixth, which, by the demonstrations of Book III, is divisible into a perfect fourth and a major third, therefore the movement of Saturn, which is still faster than this movement already harmonized but none the less below the magnitude of a concordant interval, will not exactly harmonize. But such a movement is Saturn's perihelial movement itself, because it differs from its aphelial movement by more than the interval 4 : 5, *viz.*, one comma or 80 : 81 more (which is less than the least concord), by Proposition XXXVIII. Accordingly the perihelial movement of Saturn does not exactly harmonize. But neither does the aphelial movement of Jupiter do so precisely. For while it does not harmonize precisely with the perihelial movement of Saturn, it harmonizes at a distance of a perfect octave (by Proposition VIII), wherefore, according to what has been said in Book III, it cannot precisely harmonize.

XL. PROPOSITION. *It was necessary to add the lemma of Plato to 1 : 8, or the triple octave, the joint consonance of the diverging movements of Jupiter and Mars established by the prior reasons.*

For because, by Proposition XXXI, there had to be 1 : 32, *i.e.*, 12 : 384, between the aphelial movements of Saturn and the Earth, but there had to be 3 : 2, *i.e.*, 384 : 256, from the aphelion of the Earth to the perihelion of Mars [313] (by Proposition XV), and from the aphelion of Saturn to its perihelion, 4 : 5 or 12 : 15 with its increment (by Proposition XXXVIII); finally, from the perihelion of Saturn to the aphelion of Jupiter 1 : 2 or 15 : 30 (by Proposition VIII); accordingly, there remains 30 : 256 from the aphelion of Jupiter to the perihelion of Mars, by the subtraction of the increment of Saturn. But 30 : 256 exceeds 32 : 256 by the interval 30 : 32, *i.e.*, 15 : 16 or 240 : 256, which is a semitone. Accordingly, if the increment of Saturn, which (by Proposition XXXVIII) had to be 80 : 81, *i.e.*, 240 : 243, is compounded inversely with 240 : 243, the result is 243 : 256; but that is the lemma of Plato,[1] *viz.*, approximately 19 : 20, see Book III. Accordingly, Plato's lemma had to be compounded with the 1 : 8.

And so the great ratio of Jupiter and Mars, *viz.*, of the diverging movements, ought to be 243 : 2,048, which is somehow a mean between 243 : 2,187 and 243 : 1,944, *i.e.*, between 1 : 9 and 1 : 8, whereof proportionality required the first, above; and a nearer harmonic concord, the second.

XLI. PROPOSITION. *The private ratio of the movements of Mars has necessarily been made the square of the harmonic ratio 5 : 6, viz., 25 : 36.*

For, because the ratio of the diverging movements of Jupiter and Mars had to be 243 : 2,048, *i.e.*, 729 : 6,144, by the preceding proposition, but that of the converging movements 5 : 24, *i.e.*, 1,280 : 6,144 (by Proposition XIII), therefore the compound of the private ratios of both was necessarily 729 : 1,280 or 72,900 : 128,000. But the private ratio of Jupiter alone had to be 6,561 : 8,000, *i.e.*, 104,976 : 128,000 (by Proposition XXVIII). Therefore, if the compound ratio of both is divided by this, the private ratio of Mars will be left as 72,900 : 104,976, *i.e.*, 25 : 36, the square root of which is 5 : 6.

In another fashion, as follows: There is 1 : 32 or 120 : 3,840 from the aphelial movement of Saturn to the aphelial movement of the Earth, but from that same movement to the perihelial of Jupiter there is 1 : 3 or 120 : 360, with its increment. But from this to the aphelial movement of Mars is 5 : 24 or 360 : 1,728. Accordingly, from the aphelial movement of Mars to the aphelial move-

[1] *Timaeus*, 36.

ment of the Earth, there remains 1,728 : 3,840 minus the increment of the ratio of the diverging movements of Saturn and Jupiter. But from the same aphelial movement of the Earth to the perihelial of Mars there is 3 : 2, *i.e.*, 3,840 : 2,500. Therefore between the aphelial and perihelial movements of Mars there remains the ratio 1,728 : 2,560, *i.e.*, 27 : 40 or 81 : 120, minus the said increment. But 81 : 120 is a comma less than 80 : 120 or 2 : 3. Therefore, if a comma is taken away from 2 : 3, and the said increment (which by Proposition xxxviii is equal to the private ratio of Venus) is taken away too, the private ratio of Mars is left. But the private ratio of Venus is the diesis diminished by a comma, by Proposition xxvi. But the comma and the diesis diminished by a comma make a full diesis or 24 : 25. Therefore if you divide 2 : 3, *i.e.*, 24 : 36 by the diesis 24 : 25, Mars' private ratio of 25 : 36 is left, as before, the square root of which, or 5 : 6, goes to the intervals, by Chapter 3.

Behold again the reason why—above, in Chapter 4—the extreme intervals of Mars have been found to embrace the harmonic ratio 5 : 6.

XLII. Proposition. *The great ratio of Mars and the Earth, or the common ratio of the diverging movements, has been necessarily made to be 54 : 125, smaller than the consonance 5 : 12 established by the prior reasons.*

For the private ratio of Mars had to be a perfect fifth, from which a diesis has been taken away, by the preceding proposition. But the common or minor ratio of the converging movements of Mars and the Earth had to be a perfect fifth or 2 : 3, by Proposition xv. Finally, the private ratio of the Earth is the diesis squared, from which a comma is taken away, by Propositions xxvi and xxviii. But out of these elements is compounded the major ratio or that of the diverging movements of Mars and the Earth—and it is two perfect fifths (or 4 : 9, *i.e.*, 108 : 243) plus a diesis diminished by a comma, *i.e.*, plus 243 : 250; namely, it is 108 : 250 or 54 : 125, *i.e.*, 608 : 1,500. But this is smaller than 625 : 1,500, *i.e.*, than 5 : 12, in the ratio 602 : 625, which is approximately 36 : 37, smaller than 625 : 1,500, *i.e.*, than 5 : 12, in the ratio 602 : 625, which is approximately 36 : 37, smaller than the least concord.

XLIII. Proposition. *The aphelial movement of Mars could not harmonize in some universal consonance; nevertheless it was necessary for it to be in concord to some extent in the scale of the minor mode.*

For, because the perihelial movement of Jupiter has the pitch *d* of acute tuning in the minor mode, and the consonance 5 : 24 ought to have existed between that and the aphelial movement of Mars, therefore, the aphelial movement of Mars occupies the adulterine pitch of the same acute tuning. I say *adulterine* for, although in Book iii, Chapter 12, the adulterine consonances were reviewed and deduced from the composition of systems, certain ones which exist in the simple natural system were omitted. [314] And so, after the line which ends 81 : 120, the reader may add: if you divide into it 4 : 5 or 32 : 40, there remains 27 : 32, the subminor sixth,[1] which exists between *d* and *f* or *c* and *e*[2] or *a* and *c* of even the simple octave. And in the ensuing table, the following should be in the first line; for 5 : 6 there is 27 : 32, which is deficient.

From that it is clear that in the natural system the true note [*clavem*] *f*, as regulated by my principles, constitutes a deficient or adulterine minor sixth with the note *d*. Accordingly since between the perihelial movement of Jupiter set

[1]Here "sixth" (*sexta*) should probably be "third" (*tertia*). E. C., Jr.
[2]*C* and *e* do not produce a subminor third in the "natural system." E. C., Jr.

up in the true note *d* and the aphelial movement of Mars there is a perfect minor sixth over and above the double octave, but not the diminished (by Proposition XIII), it follows that with its aphelial movement Mars designates the pitch which is one comma higher than the true note *f*; and so it will concord not absolutely but merely to a certain extent in this scale. But it does not enter into either the pure or the adulterine universal harmony. For the perihelial movement of Venus occupies the pitch of *e* in this tuning [*tensionem*]. But there is dissonance between *e* and *f*, on account of their nearness. Therefore, Mars is in discord with the perihelial movement of one of the planets, *viz.*, Venus. But too it is in discord with the other movements of Venus; they are diminished by a comma less than a diesis: wherefore, since there is a semitone and a comma between the perihelial movement of Venus and the aphelial movement of Mercury, accordingly, between the aphelion of Venus and the aphelion of Mars there will be a semitone and a diesis (neglecting the octaves), *i.e.*, a minor whole tone, which is still a dissonant interval. Now the aphelial movement of Mars concords to that extent in the scale of the minor mode, but not in that of the major. For since the aphelial movement of Venus concords with the *e* of the major mode, while the aphelial movement of Mars (neglecting the octaves) has been made a minor whole tone higher than *e*, then necessarily the aphelial movement of Mars in this tuning would fall midway between *f* and *f* sharp and would make with *g* (which in this tuning would be occupied by the aphelial movement of the Earth) the plainly discordant interval 25 : 27, *viz.*, a major whole tone diminished by a diesis.

In the same way, it will be proved that the aphelial movement of Mars is also in discord with the movements of the Earth. For because it makes a semitone and comma with the perihelial movement of Venus, *i.e.*, 14 : 15 (by what has been said), but the perihelial movements of the Earth and Venus make a minor sixth 5 : 8 or 15 : 24 (by Proposition XXVII). Accordingly, the aphelial movement of Mars together with the perihelial movement of the Earth (the octaves added to it) will make 14 : 24 or 7 : 12, a discordant interval and one not harmonic, like 7 : 6. For any interval between 5 : 6 and 8 : 9 is dissonant and discordant, as 6 : 7 in this case. But no other movement of the Earth can harmonize with the aphelial movement of Mars. For it was said above that it makes the discordant interval 25 : 27 with the Earth (neglecting the octaves); but all from 6 : 7 or 24 : 28 to 25 : 27 are smaller than the least harmonic interval.

XLIV. COROLLARY. *Accordingly it is clear from the above Proposition XLIII concerning Jupiter and Mars, and from Proposition XXXIX concerning Saturn and Jupiter, and from Proposition XXXVI concerning Jupiter and the Earth, and from Proposition XXXII concerning Saturn, why—in Chapter 5, above—it was found that all the extreme movements of the planets had not been adjusted perfectly to one natural system or musical scale, and that all those which had been adjusted to a system of the same tuning did not distinguish the pitches [loca] of that system in a natural way or effect a purely natural succession of concordant intervals. For the reasons are prior whereby the single planets came into possession of their single consonances; those whereby all the planets, of the universal consonances; and finally, those whereby the universal consonances of the two modes, the major and the minor: when all those have been posited, an omniform adjustment to one natural system is prevented. But if those causes had not necessarily come first, there is no doubt that either one system and one tuning of it would have embraced the extreme movements*

of all the planets; or, if there was need of two systems for the two modes of song, the
major and minor, the very order of the natural scale would have been expressed not
merely in one mode, the major, but also in the remaining minor mode. Accordingly,
here in Chapter 5, you have the promised causes of the discords through least inter-
vals and intervals smaller than all concords.

XLV. PROPOSITION. *It was necessary for an interval equal to the interval of*
Venus to be added to the common major consonance of Venus and Mercury, the
double octave, and also the private consonance of Mercury, which were established
above in Propositions XII and XIII by the prior reasons, [315] in order that the
private ratio of Mercury should be a perfect 5 : 12 and that thus Mercury should
with both its movements harmonize with the single perihelial movement of Venus.

For, because the aphelial movement of Saturn, the highest and outmost
planet, circumscribed around its regular solid, had to harmonize with the aphelial movement of the Earth, the highest movement of the Earth, which divides the classes of figures; it follows by the laws of opposites that the perihelial
movement of Mercury as the innermost planet, inscribed in its figure, the lowest
and nearest to the sun, should harmonize with the perihelial movement of the
Earth, with the lowest movement of the Earth, the common boundary: the former in order to designate the major mode of consonances, the latter the minor
mode, by Propositions XXXIII and XXXIV. But the perihelial movement of Venus
had to harmonize with the perihelial movement of the Earth in the consonance
5 : 3, by Proposition XXVII; therefore too the perihelial movement of Mercury
had to be tempered with the perihelial of Venus in one scale. But by Proposition
XII the consonance of the diverging movements of Venus and Mercury was determined by the prior reasons to be 1 : 4; therefore, now by these posterior reasons it was to be adjusted by the accession of the total interval of Venus. Accordingly, not from further on, from the aphelion, but from the perihelion of Venus
to the perihelion of Mercury there is a perfect double octave. But the consonance 3 : 5 of the converging movements is perfect, by Proposition XV. Accordingly if 1 : 4 is divided by 3 : 5, there remains to Mercury singly the private
ratio 5 : 12, perfect too, but not further (by Proposition XVI, through the prior
reasons) diminished by the private ratio of Venus.

Another reason. Just as only Saturn and Jupiter are touched nowhere on the
outside by the dodecahedron and icosahedron wedded together, so only Mercury is untouched on the inside by these same solids, since they touch Mars on
the inside, the Earth on both sides, and Venus on the outside. Accordingly, just
as something equal to the private ratio of Venus has been added distributively
to the private ratios of movements of Saturn and Jupiter, which are supported
by the cube and tetrahedron; so now something as great was due to accede to
the private ratio of solitary Mercury, which is comprehended by the associated
figures of the cube and tetrahedron; because, as the octahedron, a single figure
among the secondary figures, does the job of two among the primary, the cube
and tetrahedron (concerning which see Chapter 1), so too among the lower
planets there is one Mercury in place of two of the upper planets, *viz.*, Saturn
and Jupiter.

Thirdly, just as the aphelial movement of the highest planet Saturn had to
harmonize, in some number of octaves, *i.e.*, in the continued double ratio, 1 : 32,
with the aphelial movement of the higher and nearer of the two planets which
shift the mode of consonance (by Proposition XXXI); so, *vice versa*, the perihelial

movement of the lowest planet Mercury, again through some number of octaves, *i.e.*, in the continued double ratio, 1 : 4, had to harmonize with the perihelial movement of the lower and similarly nearer of the two planets which shift the mode of consonance.

Fourthly, of the three upper planets, Saturn, Jupiter, and Mars, the single but extreme movements concord with the universal consonances; accordingly both extreme movements of the single lower planet, *viz.*, Mercury, had to concord with the same; for the middle planets, the Earth and Venus, had to shift the mode of consonances, by Propositions XXXIII and XXXIV.

Finally, in the three pairs of the upper planets perfect consonances have been found between the converging movements, but adjusted [*fermentatae*] consonances between the diverging movements and private ratios of the single planets; accordingly, in the two pairs of the lower planets, conversely, perfect consonances had to be found not between the converging movements chiefly, nor between the diverging, but between the movements of the same field. And because two perfect consonances were due to the Earth and Venus, therefore two perfect consonances were due to Venus and Mercury also. And the Earth and Venus had to receive as perfect a consonance between their aphelial movements as between their perihelial, because they had to shift the mode of their consonance; but Venus and Mercury, as not shifting the mode of their consonance, did not also require perfect consonances between both pairs, the aphelial movements and the perihelial; but there came in place of the perfect consonance of the aphelial movements, as being already adjusted the perfect consonance of the converging movements, so that just as Venus, the higher of the lower planets, has the least private ratio of all the private ratios of movements (by Proposition XXVI), and Mercury, the lower of the lower, has received the greatest ratio of all the private ratios of movements (by Proposition XXX), so too the private ratio of Venus should be the most imperfect of all the private ratios or the farthest removed from consonances, while the private ratio of Mercury should be most perfect of all the private ratios, *i.e.*, an absolute consonance without adjustment, and that finally the relations should be everywhere opposite.

For He Who is before the ages and on into the ages thus adorned the great things of His wisdom: nothing excessive, nothing defective, no room for any censure. How lovely are his works! All things, in twos, one [316] *against one, none lacking its opposite. He has strengthened the goods—adornment and propriety—of each and every one and established them in the best reasons, and who will be satiated seeing their glory?*

XLVI. AXIOM. *If the interspacing of the solid figures between the planetary spheres is free and unhindered by the necessities of antecedent causes, then it ought to follow to perfection the proportionality of geometrical inscriptions and circumscriptions, and thereby the conditions of the ratio of the inscribed to the circumscribed spheres.*

For nothing is more reasonable than that physical inscription should exactly represent the geometrical, as the work, its pattern.

XLVII. PROPOSITION. *If the inscription of the regular solids among the planets was free, the tetrahedron was due to touch with its angles precisely the perihelial sphere of Jupiter above it, and with centres of its planes precisely the aphelial sphere of Mars below it. But the cube and the octahedron, each placing its angles in the perihelial sphere of the planet above, were due to penetrate the sphere of the inside planet with the centres of their planes, in such fashion that those centres should turn within the aphelial and perihelial spheres: on the other hand, the dodecahedron and icosahedron, grazing with their angles the perihelial spheres of their planets on the outside, were due not quite to touch with the centres of their planes the aphelial spheres of their inner planets. Finally, the dodecahedral echinus, placing its angles in the perihelial sphere of Mars, was due to come very close to the aphelial sphere of Venus with the midpoints of its converted sides which interdistinguish two solid rays.*

For the tetrahedron is the middle one of the primary figures, both in genesis and in situation in the world; accordingly, it was due to remove equally both regions, that of Jupiter and that of Mars. And because the cube was above it and outside it, and the dodecahedron was below it and within it, therefore it was natural that their inscription should strive for the contrariety wherein the tetrahedron held a mean, and that the one of them should make an excessive inscription, and the other a defective, *viz.*, the one should somewhat penetrate the inner sphere, the other not touch it. And because the octahedron is cognate to the cube and has an equal ratio of spheres, but the icosahedron to the dodecahedron, accordingly, whatever the cube has of perfection of inscription, the same was due to the octahedron also, and whatever the dodecahedron, the same to the icosahedron too. And the situation of the octahedron's similar to the situation of the cube, but that of the icosahedron to the situation of the dodecahedron, because as the cube occupies the one limit to the outside, so the octahedron occupies the remaining limit to the inside of the world, but the dodecahedron and icosahedron are midway: accordingly even a similar inscription was proper, in the case of the dodecahedron, one penetrating the sphere of the inner planet, in that of the icosahedron, one falling short of it.

But the echinus, which represents the icosahedron with the apexes of its angles and the dodecahedron with the bases, was due to fill, embrace, or dispose both regions, that between Mars and the Earth with the dodecahedron as well as that between the Earth and Venus with the icosahedron. But the preceding axiom makes clear which of the opposites was due to which association. For the tetrahedron, which has a rational inscribed sphere, has been allotted the middle position among the primary figures and is surrounded on both sides by figures of incommensurable spheres, whereof the outer is the cube, the inner the dodecahedron, by Chapter 1 of this book. But this geometrical quality, *viz.*, the rationality of the inscribed sphere, represents in nature the perfect inscription of the planetary sphere. Accordingly, the cube and its allied figure have their inscribed spheres rational only in square, *i.e.*, in power alone; accordingly, they ought to represent a semiperfect inscription, where, even if not the extremity of the planetary sphere, yet at least something on the inside and rightfully a mean between the aphelial and perihelial spheres—if that is possible through other reasons—is touched by the centres of the planes of the figures. On the other hand, the dodecahedron and its allied figure have their inscribed spheres clearly irrational both in the length of the radius and in the square; accordingly, they ought to represent a clearly imperfect inscription and one touching absolutely nothing of the planetary sphere, *i.e.*, falling short and not reaching as far as the aphelial sphere of the planet with the centres of its planes.

Although the echinus is cognate to the dodecahedron and its allied figure, nevertheless it has a property similar to the tetrahedron. For the radius of the sphere inscribed in its inverted sides is indeed incommensurable with the radius of the circumscribed sphere, but it is, however, commensurable with the length of the distance between two neighbouring angles. And so the perfection of the commensurability of rays is approximately as great as in the tetrahedron; but elsewhere the imperfection is as great as in the [317] dodecahedron and its allied figure. Accordingly it is reasonable too that the physical inscription belonging to it should be neither absolutely tetrahedral nor absolutely dodecahedral but of an intermediate kind; in order that (because the tetrahedron was due to touch the extremity of the sphere with its planes, and the dodecahedron, to fall short of it by a definite interval) this wedge-shaped figure with the inverted sides should stand between the icosahedral space and the extremity of the inscribed sphere and should nearly touch this extremity—if nevertheless this figure was to be admitted into association with the remaining five, and if its laws could be allowed, with the laws of the others remaining. Nay, why do I say "could be allowed"? For they could not do without them. For if an inscription, which was loose and did not come into contact fitted the dodecahedron, what else could confine that indefinite looseness within the limits of a fixed magnitude, except this subsidiary figure cognate to the dodecahedron and icosahedron, and which comes almost into contact with its inscribed sphere and does not fall short (if indeed it does fall short) any more than the tetrahedron exceeds and penetrates —with which magnitude we shall deal in the following.

This reason for the association of the echinus with the two cognate figures (*viz.*, in order that the ratio of the spheres of Mars and Venus, which they had left indefinite, should be made determinate) is rendered very probable by the fact that 1,000, the semidiameter of the sphere of the Earth, is found to be practically a mean proportional between the perihelial sphere of Mars and the aphelial sphere of Venus; as if the interval, which the echinus assigns to the cognate figures, has been divided between them as proportionally as possible. XLVIII. PROPOSITION. *The inscription of the regular solid figures between the planetary spheres was not the work of pure freedom; for with respect to very small magnitudes it was hindered by the consonances established between the extreme movements.*

For, by Axioms I and II, the ratio of the spheres of each figure was not due to be expressed immediately by itself, but by means of it the consonances most akin to the ratios of the spheres were first to be sought and adjusted to the extreme movements.

Then, in order that, by Axioms XVIII and XX, the universal consonances of the two modes could exist, it was necessary for the greater consonances of the single pairs to be readjusted somewhat, by means of the posterior reasons. Accordingly, in order that those things might stand, and be maintained by their own reasons, intervals were required which are somewhat discordant with those which arise from the perfect inscription of figures between the spheres, by the laws of movements unfolded in Chapter 3. In order that it be proved and made manifest how much is taken away from the single planets by the consonances established by their proper reasons; come, let us build up, out of them, the intervals of the planets from the sun, by a new form of calculation not previously tried by anyone.

Now there will be three heads to this inquiry: First, from the two extreme movements of each planet the similar extreme intervals between it and the sun will be investigated, and by means of them the radius of the sphere in those dimensions, of the extreme intervals, which are proper to each planet. Secondly, by means of the same extreme movements, in the same dimensions for all, the mean movements and their ratio will be investigated. Thirdly, by means of the ratio of the mean movements already disclosed, the ratio of the spheres or mean intervals and also one ratio of the extreme intervals, will be investigated; and the ratio of the mean intervals will be compared with the ratios of the figures.

As regards the first: we must repeat, from Chapter 3, Article VI, that the ratio of the extreme movements is the inverse square of the ratio of the corresponding intervals from the sun. Accordingly, since the ratio of the squares is the square of the ratio of its sides, therefore, the numbers, whereby the extreme movements of the single planets are expressed, will be considered as squares and the extraction of their roots will give the extreme intervals, whereof it is easy to take the arithmetic mean as the semidiameter of the sphere and the eccentricity. Accordingly the consonances so far established have prescribed:

[318]Planets Props.	Ratios of movements	The roots either prolonged or of their multiples	Therefore the semidiameter of the sphere	Eccentricity	In dimensions whereof the semidiameter of the sphere is 100,000
Saturn by XXXVIII	64 : 81	80 : 90	85	5	5,882
Jupiter by XXXVIII	6,561 : 8,000	81,000 : 89,444	85,222	4,222	4,954
Mars by XLI	25 : 36	50 : 60	55	5	9,091
Earth by XXVIII	2,916 : 3,125	93,531 : 96,825	95,178	1,647	1,730
Venus by XXVIII	243 : 250	9,859 : 10,000	99,295	705	710
Mercury by XLV	5 : 12	63,250 : 98,000	80,625	17,375	21,551

For the second of the things proposed, we again have need of Chapter 3, Article XII, where it was shown that the number which expresses the movement which is as a mean in the ratio of the extremes is less than their arithmetic mean, also less than the geometric mean by half the difference between the geometric and arithmetic means. And because we are investigating all the mean movements in the same dimensions, therefore let all the ratios hitherto established between different twos and also all the private ratios of the single planets be set out in the measure of the least common divisible. Then let the means be sought: the arithmetic, by taking half the difference between the extreme movements of each planet, the geometric, by the multiplication of one extreme into the other and extracting the square root of the product; then by subtracting half the difference of the means from the geometric mean, let the number of the mean movement be constituted in the private dimensions of each planet, which can easily, by the rule of ratios, be converted into the common dimensions.

[319] Therefore, from the prescribed consonances, the ratio of the mean diurnal movements has been found, viz., the ratio between the numbers of the degrees and minutes of each planet. It is easy to explore how closely that approaches to astronomy.

Harmonic ratios of two	Numbers of the extreme movements		Private ratios of the single planets	Continued means of the single planets		Halves of the difference	Number of the mean movement in dimensions	
				Arithmetic	Geometric		Private	Common
[1	♄	139,968	64					
				72.50	72.00	.25	71.75	156,917
[1	♄	177,147	81					
2	♃	354,294	6,561					
				7,280.5	7,244.9	17.8	7,227.1	390,263
5	♃	432,000	8,000					
[24	♂	2,073,600	25					
				30.50	30.00	.25	29.75	2,467,584
[2	♂	2,985,984	36					
32 3	♁	4,478,976	2,916					
				3,020.500	3,018.692	.904	3,017.788	4,635,322
[5	♁	4,800,000	3,125					
5 [8	♀	7,464,960	243					
				246.500	246.475	.0125	246.4625	7,571,328
[1 [3	♀	7,680,000	250					
[5	☿	12,800,000	5					
				8.500	7.746	.377	7.369	18,864,680
4	☿	30,720,000	12					

The third head of things proposed requires Chapter 3, Article VIII. For when the ratio of the mean diurnal movements of the single planets has been found, it is possible to find the ratio of the spheres too. For the ratio of the mean movements is the ⅔th power of the inverse ratio of the spheres. But, too, the ratio of the cube numbers is the ⅔th power of the ratio of the squares of those same square roots, given in the table of Clavius, which he subjoined to his *Practical Geometry*. Wherefore, if the numbers of our mean movements (curtailed, if need be, of an equal number of ciphers) are sought among the cube numbers of that table, they will indicate on the left, under the heading of the squares, the numbers of the ratio of the spheres; then the eccentricities ascribed above to the single planets in the private ratio of the semidiameters of each may easily be converted by the rule of ratios into dimensions common to all, so that, by their addition to the semidiameters of the spheres and subtraction from them, the extreme intervals of the single planets from the sun may be established. Now we shall give to the semidiameter of the terrestrial sphere the round number 100,000, as is the practice in astronomy, and with the following design: because this number or its square or its cube is always made up of mere ciphers; and so too we shall raise the mean movement of the Earth to the number 10,000,000,-000 and by the rule of ratios make the number of the mean movement of any planet be to the number of the mean movement of the Earth, as 10,000,000,000 is to the new measurement. And so the business can be carried on with only five cube roots, by comparing those single cube roots with the one number of the Earth.

In the original dimensions	Numbers of the mean movements In the new dimensions found in inverse order among the cubes	Numbers of the ratio of the spheres found among the squares	Semi-diameters as above	Eccentricities in dimensions Private as above	Common	Extreme intervals resulting Aphelion	Perihelion
♄ 156,917	29,539,960	9,556	85	5	562	10,118	8,994
♃ 390,263	11,877,400	5,206	85,222	4,222	258	5,464	4,948
♂ 2,467,584	1,878,483	1,523	55	5	138	1,661	1,384
♁ 4,635,322	1,000,000	1,000	95,178	1,647	17	1,017	983
♀ 7,571,328	612,220	721	99,295	705	5	726	716
☿ 18,864,680	245,714	392	80,625	17,375	85	476	308

Accordingly, it is apparent in the last column what the numbers turn out to be whereby the converging intervals of two planets are expressed. All of them approach very near to those intervals, which I found from Brahe's observations. In Mercury alone is there some small difference. For astronomy is seen to give the following intervals to it: 470, 388, 306, all shorter. It seems that the reason for the dissonance may be referred either to the fewness of the observations or to the magnitude of the eccentricity. (See Chapter 3). But I hurry on to the end of the calculation.

For now it is easy to compare the ratio of the spheres of the figures with the ratio of the converging intervals.

[320] For if the semidiameter of the sphere circumscribed around the figure

which is commonly 100,000	becomes:	Then the semidiameter of the sphere or circle inscribed in:	instead of:	becomes:	Although by the consonances the interval is:	
In the cube	8,994	♄ [Saturn]	57,735	5,194	Mean	♃ 5,206
In the tetrahedron	4,948	♃ [Jupiter]	33,333	1,649	Aphelial	♂ 1,661
In the dodecahedron	1,384	♂ [Mars]	79,465	1,100	Aphelial	♁ 1,018
In the icosahedron	983	♁ [Earth]	79,465	781	Aphelial	♀ 726
In the echinus	1,384	♂ [Mars]	52,573	728	Aphelial	♀ 726
In the octahedron	716	♀ [Venus	57,735	413	Mean	☿ 392
In the square in the octahedron	716	♀ [Venus]	70,711	506	Aphelial	☿ 476
	or 476	☿ [Mercury]	70,711	336	Perihelial	☿ 308

That is to say, the planes of the cube extend down slightly below the middle circle of Jupiter; the octahedral planes, not quite to the middle circle of Mercury; the tetrahedral, slightly below the highest circle of Mars; the sides of the echinus, not quite to the highest circle of Venus; but the planes of the dodecahedron fall far short of the aphelial circle of the Earth; the planes of the icosa-dron also fall short of the aphelial circle of Venus, and approximately propor-tionally; finally, the square in the octahedron is quite inept, and not unjustly, for what are plane figures doing among solids? Accordingly, you see that if the planetary intervals are deduced from the harmonic ratios of movements hither-to demonstrated, it is necessary that they turn out as great as these allow, but not as great as the laws of free inscription prescribed in Proposition XLV would require: because this κόσμος γεωμέτρικος [geometrical adornment] of perfect in-scription was not fully in accordance with that other κόσμον ἁρμόνικον ἐνδεχόμενον [possible harmonic adornment]—to use the words of Galen, taken from the epigraph to this Book v. So much was to be demonstrated by the calculation of numbers, for the elucidation of the prescribed proposition.

I do not hide that if I increase the consonance of the diverging movements of Venus and Mercury by the private ratio of the movements of Venus, and, as a consequence, diminish the private ratio of Mercury by the same, then by this process I produce the following intervals between Mercury and the sun: 469, 388,307, which are very precisely represented by astronomy. But, in the first place, I cannot defend that diminishing by harmonic reasons. For the aphelial movement of Mercury will not square with that musical scale, nor in the planets which are opposite in the world is the planetary principle [ratio] of opposition of all conditions kept. Finally, the mean diurnal movement of Mercury becomes too great, and thereby the periodic time, which is the most certain fact in all astronomy, is shortened too much. And so I stay within the harmonic polity here employed and confirmed throughout the whole of Chapter 9. But none the less with this example I call you all forth, as many of you as have happened to read this book and are steeped in the mathematical disciplines and the knowl-edge of highest philosophy: work hard and either pluck up one of the conso-nances applied everywhere, interchange it with some other, and test whether or not you will come so near to the astronomy posited in Chapter 4, or else try by reasons whether or not you can build with the celestial movements something better and more expedient and destroy in part or in whole the layout applied by me. But let whatever pertains to the glory of Our Lord and Founder be equally permissible to you by way of this book, and up to this very hour I myself have taken the liberty of everywhere changing those things which I was able to discover on earlier days and which were the conceptions of a sluggish care or hurrying ardour.

[321] XLIX. ENVOI. *It was good that in the genesis of the intervals the solid figures should yield to the harmonic ratios, and the major consonances of two planets to the universal consonances of all, in so far as this was necessary.*

With good fortune we have arrived at 49, the square of 7; so that this may come as a kind of Sabbath, since the six solid eights of discourse concerning the construction of the heavens has gone before. Moreover, I have rightly made an *envoi* which could be placed first among the axioms: because God also, enjoying the works of His creation, "saw all things which He had made, and behold! they were very good."

There are two branches to the *envoi*: First, there is a demonstration concern-ing consonances in general, as follows: For where there is choice among different things which are not of equal weight, there the more excellent are to be put first and the more vile are to be detracted from, in so far as that is necessary, as the very word ὁ κόδμος, which signifies *adornment*, seems to argue. But inasmuch as life is more excellent than the body, the form than the material, by so much does harmonic adornment excel the geometrical.

For as life perfects the bodies of animate things, because they have been born for the exercise of life—as follows from the archetype of the world, which is the divine essence—so movement measures the regions assigned to the planets, each that of its own planet: because that region was assigned to the planet in order that it should move. But the five regular solids, by their very name, pertain to the intervals of the regions and to the number of them and the bodies; but the consonances to the movements. Again, as matter is diffuse and indefinite of itself, the form definite, unified, and determinant of the material, so too there are an infinite number of geometric ratios, but few consonances. For although among the geometrical ratios there are definite degrees of determinations, formation, and restriction, and no more than three can exist from the ascription of spheres to the regular solids; but nevertheless an accident common to all the rest follows upon even these geometrical ratios: an infinite possible section of magnitudes is presupposed, which those ratios whose terms are mutually incommensurable somehow involve in actuality too. But the harmonic ratios are all rational, the terms of all are commensurable and are taken from a definite and finite species of plane figures. But infinity of section represents the material, while commensurability or rationality of terms represents the form. Accordingly, as material desires the form, as the rough-hewn stone, of a just magnitude indeed, the form of a human body, so the geometric ratios of figures desire the consonances—not in order to fashion and form those consonances, but because this material squares better with this form, this quantity of stone with this statue, even this ratio of regular solids with this consonance—therefore in order so that they are fashioned and formed more fully, the material by its form, the stone by the chisel into the form of an animate being; but the ratio of the spheres of the figure by its own, *i.e.*, the near and fitting, consonance.

The things which have been said up to now will become clearer from the history of my discoveries. Since I had fallen into this speculation twenty-four years ago, I first inquired whether the single planetary spheres are equal distances apart from one another (for the spheres are apart in Copernicus, and do not touch one another), that is to say, I recognized nothing more beautiful than the ratio of equality. But this ratio is without head or tail: for this material equality furnished no definite number of mobile bodies, no definite magnitude for the intervals. Accordingly, I meditated upon the similarity of the intervals to the spheres, *i.e.*, upon the proportionality. But the same complaint followed. For although to be sure, intervals which were altogether unequal were produced between the spheres, yet they were not unequally equal, as Copernicus wishes, and neither the magnitude of the ratio nor the number of the spheres was given. I passed on to the regular plane figures: [322] intervals were formed from them by the ascription of circles. I came to the five regular solids: here both the number of the bodies and approximately the true magnitude of the intervals was disclosed, in such fashion that I summoned to the perfection of astronomy the discrepancies remaining over and above. Astronomy was perfect these twenty years; and behold! there was still a discrepancy between the intervals and the regular solids, and the reasons for the distribution of unequal eccentricities among the planets were not disclosed. That is to say, in this house the world, I was asking not only why stones of a more elegant form but also what form would fit the stones, in my ignorance that the Sculptor had fashioned them in the very articulate image of an animated body. So, gradually, especially during these last three years, I came to the consonances and abandoned the regular solids in respect to minima, both because the consonances stood on the side of the form which the finishing touch would give, and the regular solids, on that of the material—which in the world is the number of bodies and the rough-hewn amplitude of the intervals—and also because the consonances gave the eccentricities, which the regular solids did not even promise—that is to say, the consonances made the nose, eyes, and remaining limbs a part of the statue, for which the regular solids had prescribed merely the outward magnitude of the rough-hewn mass.

Wherefore, just as neither the bodies of animate beings are made nor blocks of stone are usually made after the pure rule of some geometrical figure, but something is taken away from the outward spherical figure, however elegant it may be (although the just magnitude of the bulk remains), so that the body may be able to get the organs necessary for life, and the stone the image of the animate being; so too as the ratio which the regular solids had been going to prescribe for the planetary spheres is inferior and looks only towards the body and material, it has to yield to the consonances, in so far as that was necessary in order for the consonances to be able to stand closely by and adorn the movement of the globes.

The other branch of the *envoi*, which concerns universal consonances, has a proof closely related to the first. (As a matter of fact, it was in part assumed above, in xviii, among the Axioms.) For the finishing touch of perfection, as it were, is due rather to that which perfects the world more; and conversely that thing which occupies a second position is to be detracted from, if either is to be detracted from. But the universal harmony of all perfects the world more than the single twin consonances of different neighbouring twos. For harmony is a certain ratio of unity; accordingly the planets are more united, if they all are in concord together in one harmony, than if each two concord separately in two consonances. Wherefore, in the conflict of both, either one of the two single consonances of two planets was due to yield, so that the universal harmonies of all could stand. But the greater consonances, those of the diverging movements, were due to yield rather than the lesser, those of the converging movements. For if the divergent movements diverge, then they look not towards the planets of the given pair but towards other neighbouring planets, and if the converging movements converge, then the movements of one planet are converging toward the movement of the other, conversely: for example, in the pair Jupiter and Mars the aphelial movement of Jupiter verges toward Saturn, the perihelial of Mars towards the Earth: but the perihelial movement of Jupiter verges toward Mars, the aphelial of Mars toward Jupiter. Accordingly the consonance of the converging movements is more proper to Jupiter and Mars; the consonance of the diverging movements is somehow more foreign to Jupiter and Mars. But the ratio of union which brings together neighbouring planets by twos and twos is less disturbed if the consonance which is more foreign and more removed from them should be adjusted than if the private ratio should be, *viz.*, the one which exists between the more neighbouring movements of neighbouring planets. None the less this adjustment was not very great. For the proportionality has been found in which may stand the universal consonances of all the planets may exist (and these in two distinct modes), and in which (with a certain latitude of tuning merely equal to a comma) may also be embraced the single consonances of two neighbouring planets; the consonances of the converging movements in four pairs, perfect, of the aphelial movements in one pair, of the perihelial movements in two pairs, likewise perfect; the consonances of the diverging movements in four pairs, these, however, within the difference of one diesis (the very small interval by which the human voice [323] in figured song nearly always errs; the single consonance of Jupiter and Mars, this between the diesis and the semitone. Accordingly it is apparent that this mutual yielding is everywhere very good.

Accordingly let this do for our *envoi* concerning the work of God the Creator. It now remains that at last, with my eyes and hands removed from the tablet of demonstrations and lifted up towards the heavens, I should pray, devout and supplicating, to the Father of lights: *O Thou Who dost by the light of nature promote in us the desire for the light of grace, that by its means Thou mayest transport us into the light of glory, I give thanks to Thee, O Lord Creator, Who hast delighted me with Thy makings and in the works of Thy hands have I exulted. Behold! now, I have completed the work of my profession, having employed as much power of mind as Thou didst give to me; to the men who are going to read those demonstrations I have made manifest the glory of Thy works, as much of its infinity as the narrows of my intellect could apprehend. My mind has been given over to philosophizing most correctly: if there is anything unworthy of Thy designs brought forth by me—a worm born and nourished in a wallowing place of sins—breathe into me also that which Thou dost wish men to know, that I may make the correction: If I have been allured into rashness by the wonderful beauty of Thy works, or if I have loved my own glory among men, while I am advancing in the work destined for Thy glory, be gentle and merciful and pardon me; and finally deign graciously to effect that these demonstrations give way to Thy glory and the salvation of souls and nowhere be an obstacle to that.*

10. Epilogue Concerning the Sun, by way of Conjecture[1]

From the celestial music to the hearer, from the Muses to Apollo the leader of the Dance, from the six planets revolving and making consonances to the Sun at the centre of all the circuits, immovable in place but rotating into itself. For although the harmony is most absolute between the extreme planetary movements, not with respect to the true speeds through the ether but with respect to the angles which are formed by joining with the centre of the sun the termini of the diurnal arcs of the planetary orbits; while the harmony does not adorn the termini, *i.e.*, the single movements, in so far as they are considered in themselves but only in so far as by being taken together and compared with one another, they become the object of some mind; and although no object is ordained in vain, without the existence of some thing which may be moved by it, while those angles seem to presuppose some action similar to our eyesight or at least to that sense-perception whereby, in Book IV, the sublunary nature perceived the angles of rays formed by the planets on the Earth: still it is not easy for dwellers on the Earth to conjecture what sort of sight is present in the sun, what eyes there are, or what other instinct there is for perceiving those angles

[1]See Kepler's commentary on this epilogue in the *Epitome*, page 850-51.

even without eyes and for evaluating the harmonies of the movements entering into the antechamber of the mind by whatever doorway, and finally what mind there is in the sun. None the less, however those things may be, this composition of the six primary spheres around the sun, cherishing it with their perpetual revolutions and as it were adoring it (just as, separately, four moons accompany the globe of Jupiter, two Saturn, but a single moon by its circuit encompasses, cherishes, fosters the Earth and us its inhabitants, and ministers to us) and this special business of the harmonies, which is a most clear footprint of the highest providence over solar affairs, now being added to that consideration, [324] wrings from me the following confession: not only does light go out from the sun into the whole world, as from the focus or eye of the world, as life and heat from the heart, as every movement from the King and mover, but conversely also by royal law these returns, so to speak, of every lovely harmony are collected in the sun from every province in the world, nay, the forms of movements by twos flow together and are bound into one harmony by the work of some mind, and are as it were coined money from silver and gold bullion; finally, the curia, palace, and praetorium or throne-room of the whole realm of nature are in the sun, whatsoever chancellors, palatines, prefects the Creator has given to nature: for them, whether created immediately from the beginning or to be transported hither at some time, has He made ready those seats. For even this terrestrial adornment, with respect to its principal part, for quite a long while lacked the contemplators and enjoyers, for whom however it had been appointed; and those seats were empty. Accordingly the reflection struck my mind, what did the ancient Pythagoreans in Aristotle mean, who used to call the centre of the world (which they referred to as the "fire" but understood by that the sun) "the watchtower of Jupiter," Διος φυλακήν; what, likewise, was the ancient interpreter pondering in his mind when he rendered the verse of the Psalm as: "He has placed His tabernacle in the sun."

But also I have recently fallen upon the hymn of Proclus the Platonic philosopher (of whom there has been much mention in the preceding books), which was composed to the Sun and filled full with venerable mysteries, if you excise that one κλῦθ (hear me) from it; although the ancient interpreter already cited has explained this to some extent, viz., in invoking the sun, he understands Him Who has placed His tabernacle in the sun. For Proclus lived at a time in which it was a crime, for which the rulers of the world and the people itself inflicted all punishments, to profess Jesus of Nazareth, God Our Savior, and to contemn the gods of the pagan poets (under Constantine, Maxentius, and Julian the Apostate). Accordingly Proclus, who from his Platonic philosophy indeed, by the natural light of the mind, had caught a distant glimpse of the Son of God, that true light which lighteth every man coming into this world, and who already knew that divinity must never be sought with a superstitious mob in sensible things, nevertheless perferred to seem to look for God in the sun rather than in Christ a sensible man, in order that at the same time he might both deceive the pagans by honoring verbally the Titan of the poets and devote himself to his philosophy, by drawing away both the pagans and the Christians from sensible beings, the pagans from the visible sun, the Christians from the Son of Mary, because, trusting too much to the natural light of reason, he spit out the mystery of the Incarnation; and finally that at the same time he might take over from them and adopt into his own philosophy whatever the Christians

had which was most divine and especially consonant with Platonic philosophy.[1]
And so the accusation of the teaching of the Gospel concerning Christ is laid
against this hymn of Proclus, in its own matters: let that Titan keep as his
private possessions χρῦσα ἡνία [golden reins] and ταμιεῖυν φαοῦς, μεσσατίην, αἰθερος
ἕδρην, κοδμοῦ κραδιαῖον ἐριφεγγέᾳ κυκλὸν [a treasury of light, a seat at the midpart
of the ether, a radiant circle at the heart of the world], which visible aspect
Copernicus too bestows upon him; let him even keep his παλιννοστοὺς διφρείς
[cyclical chariot-drivings], although according to the ancient Pythagoreans he
does not possess them but in their place τὸ κέντρον, Διὸς φυλακήν [the centre, the
watchtower of Zeus]—which doctrine, misshapen by the forgetfulness of ages,
as by a flood, was not recognized by their follower Proclus; let him also keep
his γενεθλὴν Βλαστησασαν [offspring born] of himself, and whatever else is of
nature; in turn, let the philosophy of Proclus yield to Christian doctrines, [325]
let the sensible sun yield to the Son of Mary, the Son of God, Whom Proclus
addresses under the name of the Titan, ζωαρκεὸς, ὦ ἄνα, πηγῆς αὐτὸς ἔχων κλῆδα
[O lord, who dost hold the key of the life-supporting spring], and that πάντα τεῆς
ἔπλησας ἐλερσινοοῖο προνοίης [thou didst fulfill all things with thy mind-awakening
foresight], and that immense power over the μοιράων [fates], and things which
were read of in no philosophy before the promulgation of the Gospel[2], the
demons dreading him as their threatening scourge, the demons lying in ambush
for souls, ὄφρα ὑφιτενοῦς λαθοῖντο πατρὸς περιφέγγεος αὐλῆς [in order that they
might escape the notice of the light-filled hall of the lofty father]; and who
except the Word of the Father is that εἰκὼν παγγενετάο θεοῦ, οὖ φάεντος ἀπ' ἀρρήτου
γενετῆρος παύσατο στοιχείων ὀρυμάγδος ἐπ' ἀλληλοῖσιν ἰόντων [image of the all-beget-
ting father, upon whose manifestation from an ineffable mother the sin of the elements changing into one another ceased], according to the following: *The Earth
was unwrought and a chaotic mass, and darkness was upon the face of the abyss,
and God divided the light from the darkness, the waters from the waters, the sea from
the dry land;* and: *all things were made by the very Word.* Who except Jesus of
Nazareth the Son of God, ψυχῶν ἀναγωγεύς [the shepherd of souls], to whom ἱκεσιὴ
πολυδάκρυος [the prayer of a tearful suppliant] is to be offered, in order that He
cleanse us from sins and wash us of the filth ῆης γενέθλῆς [of generation]—as if
Proclus acknowledged the fomes of original sin—and guard us from punish-
ment and evil, πρηυνὼν θόον ὄμμα δικῆς [by making mild the quick eye of justice],
namely, the wrath of the Father? And the other things we read of, which
are as it were taken from the hymn of Zacharias (or, accordingly, was that
hymn a part of the *Metroace?*) Αχλυύ ἀποσκεδάσας ὀλεσίμβροτού ἰολοχεύτόυ
[dispersing the poisonous, man-destroying mist], *viz.*, in order that He may
give to souls living in darkness and the shadows of death the φάος ἀγνὸν
[holy light] and ὄλβόν ἀστυφελικτόν ἀπ' ἐυσεβίνέρατείης [unshaken happiness from

---

[1]It was the judgment of the ancients concerning his book *Metroace* that in it he set forth,
not without divine rapture, his universal doctrine concerning God; and by the frequent tears
of the author apparent in it all suspicion was removed from the hearers. None the less this
same man wrote against the Christians eighteen epichiremata, to which John Philoponus opposed himself, reproaching Proclus with ignorance of Greek thought, which none the less he
had undertaken to defend. That is to say, Proclus concealed those things which did not make
for his own philosophy.

[2]Nevertheless in Suidas some similar things are attributed to ancient Orpheus, nearly
equal to Moses, as if his pupil; see too the hymns of Orpheus, on which Proclus wrote commentaries.

lovely piety]; for that is to serve God in holiness and justice all our days.

Accordingly, let us separate out these and similar things and restore them to the doctrine of the Catholic Church to which they belong. But let us see what the principal reason is why there has been mention made of the hymn. For this same sun which ὕψοθεν ἁρμνίης ῥῦμα πλοῦσιον ἐξοτεύει [sluices the rich flow of harmony from on high]—so too Orpheus κόσμου τὸν ἐναρμόνιον δρόμον ἕλκων [making move the harmonious course of the world]—the same, concerning whose stock Phoebus about to rise κιθάρῃ ὑπὸ θέσκελα μελπῶν εὐνάξει μεγὰ κῦμα βαρυφλσισβοῖο γενεθλής [sings marvellous things on his lyre and lulls to sleep the heavy-sounding surge of generation] and in whose dance Paean is the partner, πλήσας ἁρμονίης παναπήμονος εὔρεα κόσμν [striking the wide sweep of innocent harmony]—him, I say, does Proclus at once salute in the first verse of the hymn as πῦρος νοεροῦ βασιλέα [king of intellectual fire]. By that commencement, at the same time, he indicates what the Pythagoreans understood by the word of fire (so that it is surprising that the pupil should disagree with the masters in the position of the centre) and at the same time he transfers his whole hymn from the body of the sun and its quality and light, which are sensibles, to the intelligibles, and he has assigned to that πῦρ νοερὸς [intellectual fire] of his—perhaps the artisan fire of the Stoics—to that created God of Plato, that chief or self-ruling mind, a royal throne in the solar body, confounding into one the creature and Him through Whom all things have been created. But we Christians, who have been taught to make better distinctions, know that this eternal and uncreated "Word," Which was "with God" and Which is contained by no abode, although He is within all things, excluded by none, although He is outside of all things, took up into unity of person flesh out of the womb of the most glorious Virgin Mary, and, when the ministry of His flesh was finished, occupied as His royal abode the heavens, wherein by a certain excellence over and above the other parts of the world, *viz.*, through His glory and majesty, His celestial Father too is recognized to dwell, and has also promised to His faithful, mansions in that house of His Father: as for the remainder concerning that abode, we believe it superfluous to inquire into it too curiously or to forbid the senses or natural reasons to investigate that which the eye has not seen nor the ear heard and into which the heart of man has not ascended; but we duly subordinate the created mind—of whatsoever excellence it may be—to its Creator, and we introduce neither God-intelligences with Aristotle and the pagan philosophers nor armies of innumerable planetary spirits with the Magi, nor do we propose that they are either to be adored or summoned to intercourse with us by theurgic superstitions, for we have a careful fear of that; but we freely inquire by natural reasons what sort of thing each mind is, especially if in the heart of the world [326] there is any mind bound rather closely to the nature of things and performing the function of the soul of the world—or if also some intelligent creatures, of a nature different from human perchance do inhabit or will inhabit the globe thus animated (see my book *on the New Star*, Chapter 24, "On the Soul of the World and Some of Its Functions"). But if it is permissible, using the thread of analogy as a guide, to traverse the labyrinths of the mysteries of nature, not ineptly, I think, will someone have argued as follows: The relation of the six spheres to their common centre, thereby the centre of the whole world, is also the same as that of διανοία [discussive intellection] to νοῦς [intuitive intellection], according as these faculties are distinguished by Aristotle, Plato, Proclus, and the rest; and the relation of the single planets' revolutions in place around the sun to the ἀμετάθεδον [unvarying] rotation of the sun in the central space of the whole system (concerning which the sun-spots are evidence; this has been demonstrated in the *Commentaries on the Movement of Mars*) is the same as the relation of τὸ διανοητικὸν to τὸ νοερὸν, that of the manifold discourses of ratiocination to the most simple intellection of the mind. For as the sun rotating into itself moves all the planets by means of the form emitted from itself, so too—as the philosophers teach—mind, by understanding itself and in itself all things, stirs up ratiocinations, and by dispersing and unrolling its simplicity into them, makes everything to be understood. And the movements of the planets around the sun at their centre and the discourses of ratiocinations are so interwoven and bound together that, unless the Earth, our domicile, measured out the annual circle, midway between the other spheres—changing from place to place, from station to station—never would human ratiocination have worked its way to the true intervals of the planets and to the other things dependent from them, never would it have constituted astronomy. (See the *Optical Part of Astronomy*, Chapter 9.)

On the other hand, in a beautiful correspondence, simplicity of intellection follows upon the stillness of the sun at the centre of the world, in that hitherto we have always worked under the assumption that those solar harmonies of movements are defined neither by the diversity of regions nor by the amplitude of the expanses of the world. As a matter of fact, if any mind observes from the sun those harmonies, that mind is without the assistance afforded by the movement and diverse stations of his abode, by means of which it may string together ratiocinations and discourse necessary for measuring out the planetary intervals. Accordingly, it compares the diurnal movements of each planet, not as they are in their own orbits but as they pass through the angles at the centre of the sun. And so if it has knowledge of the magnitude of the spheres, this knowledge must be present in it *a priori*, without any toil of ratiocination: but to what extent that is true of human minds and of sublunary nature has been made clear above, from Plato and Proclus.

Under these circumstances, it will not have been surprising if anyone who has been thoroughly warmed by taking a fairly liberal draft from that bowl of Pythagoras which Proclus gives to drink from in the very first verse of the hymn, and who has been made drowsy by the very sweet harmony of the dance of the planets begins to dream (by telling a story he may imitate Plato's Atlantis and, by dreaming, Cicero's Scipio): throughout the remaining globes, which follow after from place to place, there have been disseminated discursive or ratiocinative faculties, whereof that one ought assuredly to be judged the most excellent and absolute which is in the middle position among those globes, *viz.*, in man's earth, while there dwells in the sun simple intellect, πῦρ νοερὸν, or νοῦς, the source, whatsoever it may be, of every harmony.

For if it was Tycho Brahe's opinion concerning that bare wilderness of globes that it does not exist fruitlessly in the world but is filled with inhabitants: with how much greater probability shall we make a conjecture as to God's works and designs even for the other globes, from that variety which we discern in this globe of the Earth. For He Who created the species which should inhabit the waters, beneath which however there is no room for the air [327] which living things draw in; Who sent birds supported on wings into the wilderness of the air; Who gave white bears and white wolves to the snowy regions of the North, and as food for the bears the whale, and for the wolves, birds' eggs; Who gave lions to the deserts of burning Libya and camels to the wide-spread plains of Syria, and to the lions an endurance of hunger, and to the camels an endurance of thirst: did He use up every art in the globe of the Earth so that He was unable, every goodness so that he did not wish, to adorn the other globes too with their fitting creatures, as either the long or short revolutions, or the nearness or removal of the sun, or the variety of eccentricities or the shine or darkness of the bodies, or the properties of the figures wherewith any region is supported persuaded?

Behold, as the generations of animals in this terrestrial globe have an image of the male in the dodecahedron, of the female in the icosahedron—whereof the dodecahedron rests on the terrestrial sphere from the outside and the icosahedron from the inside: what will we suppose the remaining globes to have, from the remaining figures? For whose good do four moons encircle Jupiter, two Saturn, as does this our moon this our domicile? But in the same way we shall ratiocinate concerning the globe of the sun also, and we shall as it were incorporate conjectures drawn from the harmonies, *et cetera*—which are weighty of themselves—with other conjectures which are more on the side of the bodily, more suited for the apprehension of the vulgar. Is that globe empty and the others full, if everything else is in due correspondence? If as the Earth breathes forth clouds, so the sun black smoke? If as the Earth is moistened and grows under showers, so the sun shines with those combusted spots, while clear flamelets sparkle in its all fiery body. For whose use is all this equipment, if the globe is empty? Indeed, do not the senses themselves cry out that fiery bodies dwell here which are receptive of simple intellects, and that truly the sun is, if not the king, at least the queen πυρὸς νοεροῦ [of intellectual fire]?

Purposely I break off the dream and the very vast speculation, merely crying out with the royal Psalmist: *Great is our Lord and great His virtue and of His wisdom there is no number: praise Him, ye heavens, praise Him, ye sun, moon, and planets, use every sense for perceiving, every tongue for declaring your Creator. Praise Him, ye celestial harmonies, praise Him, ye judges of the harmonies uncovered* (and you before all, old happy Mastlin, for you used to animate these cares with words of hope): *and thou my soul, praise the Lord thy Creator, as long as I shall be: for out of Him and through Him and in Him are all things, καὶ τὰ αἰσθητὰ καὶ τὰ νοερὰ [both the sensible and the intelligible]; for both whose whereof we are utterly ignorant and those which we know are the least part of them; because there is still more beyond. To Him be praise, honour, and glory, world without end. Amen.*

THE END

This work was completed on the 17th or 27th day of May, 1618; but Book v was reread (while the type was being set) on the 9th or 19th of February, 1619. At Linz, the capital of Austria—above the Enns.

things draw in; Who sent them supported on wings into the wilderness of the air; Who gave white bears and white wolves to the snowy regions of the North, and as food for the bears the whales, and for the wolves, birds' eggs; Who gave lions to the deserts of burning Libya, and camels to the wide-spread plains of Syria, and to the lions an endurance of hunger, and to the camels an endurance of thirst; did He use up every art in the production of the Earth, so that He was unable, every goodness so that He had not the mind to adorn the other globes too with their fitting creatures, as either the long or short revolutions, or the nearness or removal of the sun, or the variety of eccentricities or the spottedness or purity of the bodies, or the properties of the figures wherewith any region is supported, persuaded?

Behold, as the generations of animals in this terrestrial globe have an image of the male in the dodecahedron of the fabric in the feet, &c.

THE END

This work was completed on the 17th or 27th day of May, 1618; but Book V was reset (while the type was being set) on the 9th or 19th of February, 1619. At Linz, the capital of Austria.—Above the lines.